WHERE TO STAY ENGLAND 98

KV-576-239

CONTENTS

Key to Symbols

Inside back cover

Front cover:
The Falcon Hotel, Stratford-Upon-Avon.
Back cover: (from top)
Gilpin Lodge,
Windermere, Cumbria.
Ye Olde Salutation Inn,
Weobley, Herefordshire.
Middlethorpe Hall, York, North
Yorkshire.

WELCOME TO THE GUIDE

If you're looking for accommodation look no further than **Where to Stay**. It offers a selection of establishments throughout England. You'll also find ideas about what to do while you're away, plus a wealth of useful information and maps. Have a great trip!

Sure signs of where to stay

Many different types of accommodation are described in this guide, though they all have one thing in common. Each entry has been inspected (or applied for inspection) under the ETB's official National Quality Grading and Classification Scheme.

The Scheme is your assurance of facilities and service: Crowns show you the range of facilities provided to guests; Quality Gradings indicate the overall standard of welcome, service and accommodation.

To find out more, turn to page 4.

Easy to use

Whether you know exactly in which town you want to stay or have only an idea of the area you wish to visit, it couldn't be easier to find accommodation to suit you in *Where to Stay*.

Turn to the Information section beginning on page 523 for lots of useful information and advice on making a booking, as well as events and location maps. It's all there to make finding your accommodation easy and put your mind at rest - and make sure you've nothing to think about but planning what to visit when you arrive!

For this reason, we've included a comprehensive town index and full colour location maps to help you locate your accommodation easily. We've also listed establishment entries in alphabetical order by location, region by region. In fact, you'll find all the information you need is listed in an easy-to-follow format.

A SIGN OF
OF QUALITY

The English Tourist Board's National Quality Grading and Classification Scheme will help you find the accommodation that really suits you. Whatever the size of the establishment, the Scheme provides you with the kind of detailed, reliable information you need about facilities, comfort and service.

Classification of facilities

An establishment's assessment under the Scheme will usually consist of two parts: the first, using the Crown symbol, classifies the range of services and facilities provided for guests; the second, from De Luxe to Approved, indicates the overall quality standard of these services and facilities.

The range of services and facilities provided is classified under one of six bands: from **Listed** (clean and comfortable accommodation, but limited range of services and facilities) to **Five Crown** (providing a full range of services and facilities). Please note that a higher number of Crowns does not necessarily imply that the quality on offer is superior to that available at an establishment with fewer Crowns.

Quality grading

A separate quality grading indicates the overall standard of services and facilities. Graded establishments are awarded one of the following quality gradings:

DE LUXE
(excellent overall standard)

HIGHLY COMMENDED
(very good overall standard)

COMMENDED
(good overall standard)

APPROVED
(acceptable overall standard)

Before awarding a quality grading, Tourist Board inspectors check in as a guest, only identifying themselves after paying the bill. They assess the warmth of the welcome and level of care and service they receive, as well as the standard and state of the decor, furnishings and fittings. Their overall assessment takes the nature and size of the

establishments into account; you will therefore find that all types of accommodation have been able to achieve a Highly Commended or De Luxe quality grading.

If no quality grade appears alongside the Crown classification, it means that the proprietor has applied for but was still awaiting inspection at the time of going to press.

Range of facilities

Listed and then **One to Five Crown** tell you the range of facilities provided. The more Crowns, the wider the range. Below is an indication of some of the facilities you can expect under each classification.

Listed Clean and comfortable accommodation, but limited range of facilities and services.

👑 There will be additional facilities, including washbasin and chair in your bedroom, and you will have the use of a telephone.

👑👑 There will be a colour TV in your bedroom or in a lounge and you can enjoy morning tea/coffee in your room. At least some of the bedrooms will have private bath (or shower) and WC.

👑👑👑 At least half of the bedrooms will have private bath (or shower) en-suite. You will also be able to order a hot evening meal.

👑👑👑👑 Your bedroom will have a colour TV, radio and telephone; 90% of bedrooms will have private bath and/or shower and WC en-suite. There will be lounge service until midnight and evening meals can be ordered up to 2030 hours.

👑👑👑👑👑 Every bedroom will have private bath, fixed shower and WC en-suite. The restaurant will be open for breakfast, lunch and dinner (or you can take meals in your room from breakfast until midnight) and you will benefit from an all-night lounge service. A night porter will also be on duty.

Lodge accommodation

The Lodge classification covers purpose-built bedroom accommodation that you will find along major roads and motorways. The range of facilities is indicated by **One** to **Three Moon** symbols. A separate quality grading indicates the overall standard of these facilities.

🌙 Your bedroom will have at least a washbasin and radio or colour TV. Tea/coffee may be from a vending machine in a public area.

🌙🌙 Your room will have colour TV, tea/coffee-making facilities and en-suite bath or shower with WC.

🌙🌙🌙 You will find colour TV and radio, tea/coffee-making facilities and comfortable seating in your bedroom and there will be a bath, shower and WC en-suite. The reception will be staffed throughout the night.

Accessible Scheme

If you have difficulty walking or are a wheelchair user, it is important to be able to identify those establishments that will be able to cater for your requirements. If you book accommodation displaying an Accessible symbol, there's no longer any guesswork involved. Establishments can be awarded one of these categories of accessibility:

Category 1 accessible to all wheelchair users including those travelling independently

Category 2 accessible to a wheelchair user with assistance

Category 3 accessible to a wheelchair user able to walk short distances and up at least three steps.

See page 10 for a full list of establishments in this guide who have an Accessible symbol.

ƒINDING
YOUR IDEAL
ACCOMMODATION

Whatever your requirements, your preferences or your price range, Where to Stay will lead you straight to a selection of fine accommodation in England. From prices, quality and facilities on offer, you can see what's available at a glance.

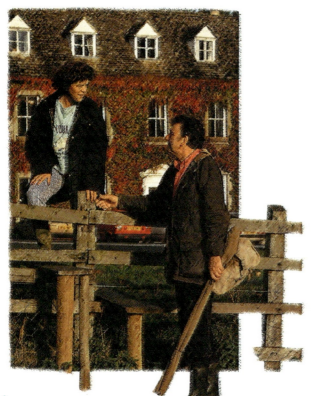

Regional sections

The guide is divided into ten regional sections. See the map on page 12. Each section contains an alphabetical listing of the region's cities, towns and villages with their accommodation establishments.

At the beginning of each section is a brief description of the area and a selection of interesting places to visit which may persuade you to stay a little longer - an illustrative map shows where they can be found.

Town index and location maps

The town index on page 551 and the colour location maps at the back of the guide show all the places featuring accommodation in this guide.

If the place you plan to visit is included in the town index, turn to the page number given for accommodation.

If, however, it is not included in the town index - or you just have a general idea of the area in which you wish to stay - use the colour location maps. You will find accommodation in all the places printed in black. Then simply refer back to the town index for the relevant page.

Service and facilities

Each accommodation listing contains detailed information to help you decide if it is right for you. This information has been provided by the proprietors themselves, and our aim has been to ensure that it is as objective and factual as possible.

Below the establishment name you will find the Crown classification, Listed or One to Five Crown, which indicates the range of services and facilities provided. The quality grading, De Luxe, Highly Commended, Commended or Approved tells you the overall standard of services and facilities. Detailed information on classification and gradings can be found on page 524.

At-a-glance symbols at the end of each entry give you additional information on services and facilities - a key to symbols can be found on the back cover flap. Keep this open to refer to as you read.

Accessibility

If you are a wheelchair user or have difficulty walking, look for the Accessible symbol. You will find a full list of entries participating in the National Accessible Scheme on page 10.

Check for changes

Please remember that changes may occur after the guide is printed. When you have found a suitable place to stay we advise you to contact the establishment to check availability, and also to confirm prices and any specific facilities which may be important to you. The coupons at the back of the guide will help you with your enquiries.

Then make your booking and, if you have time, confirm it in writing.

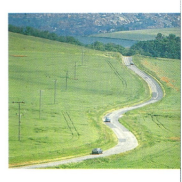

Further information

You may find it useful to read the information pages at the back of this guide (see page 523), particularly the section on cancellations.

Town Name ▶

Map reference ▶

Town description ▶

Establishment name ▶
National Crown classification ▶
and quality grading

Address, telephone and ▶
fax numbers

Establishment description ▶

National wheelchair access ▶
category

Accommodation, ▶
price guide and facilities

At-a-glance symbols - see ▶
flap on back cover

KNUTSFORD
Cheshire
Map Ref 4 A2

Derives its name from Canute, King of the Danes, said to have forded the local stream. Ancient and colourful May Day celebrations. Nearby is the Georgian mansion of Tatton Park. Tourist Information Centre
☎ (01565) 632611 or 632210

Picklings Lodge
♛ ♛ ♛ COMMENDED

Longtown Road, Pickmere, Nr Knutsford, WA16 0YZ
☎ (01565) 989
17th C former lodge with extensive landscaped gardens, private woodland and lake. In the heart of the Cheshire countryside yet only 5 minutes from the M6 motorway. Home-grown produce.
Wheelchair access category 2 ♿
Bedrooms: 2 single, 1 double
Bathrooms: 5 private
Bed & breakfast

per night:	£min	£max
Single	27.00	35.00
Double	54.00	70.00

Half board per person:	£min	£max
Daily	37.00	45.00

Lunch available
Evening meal 1800 (last orders 2130)
Parking for 18
Cards accepted: Access, Visa
🏄 📞 🛏 🍳 ⊡ ⚡ 🛒 🍴 🛏 🏛

A LOOK AT SOME
OF THE BEST

The award of a DE LUXE quality grade recognises an establishment's excellent overall standard of things such as a warm welcome, general atmosphere and ambience, efficiency of service, as well as the quality of facilities and standard of fittings.

The inspector's overall assessment takes the nature and size of an establishment into account; you will therefore find all types of accommodation can achieve a DE LUXE quality grading.

These pages feature those establishments in *Where to Stay* that have achieved the highest quality grade of DE LUXE. Use the Town Index at the back of the guide to find page numbers for their fully detailed entries.

Severn Lodge, Ironbridge, Shropshire

Ashdown Park Hotel, Wych Cross, East Sussex

Blagdon Manor Country Hotel, Ashwater, Devon

Broadview Gardens, Crewkerne, Somerset

Buckland Manor, Buckland, Gloucestershire

Chewton Glen Hotel, Health & Country Club, New Milton, Hampshire

De Vere Grand Harbour, Southampton, Hampshire

Devonshire Arms Country House Hotel, Bolton Abbey, North Yorkshire

Gidleigh Park, Chagford, Devon

Gilpin Lodge Country House Hotel and Restaurant, Windermere, Cumbria

Hall House, Hertford, Hertfordshire

Holly Lodge, Bath, Bath & North East Somerset

Horsted Place Sporting Estate & Hotel, Uckfield, East Sussex

Hotel Riviera, Sidmouth, Devon

Lainston House, Winchester, Hampshire

The Swan Hotel, Bibury, Gloucestershire

8

Chewton Glen Hotel, Health & Country Club, New Milton, Hampshire

Linthwaite House Hotel, Windermere, Cumbria
Malt House, Diss, Norfolk
Meadowland, Bath, Bath & North East Somerset
Middlethorpe Hall, York, North Yorkshire
The Old Parsonage, Royal Tunbridge Wells, Kent
The Old Rectory, Broadway, Hereford & Worcester
Old Vicarage Hotel, Bridgnorth, Shropshire
Pickett Howe, Buttermere, Cumbria

Horsted Place Sporting Estate & Hotel, Uckfield, East Sussex

Hotel Riviera, Sidmouth, Devon

Severn Lodge, Ironbridge, Shropshire
Stock Hill Country House Hotel, Gillingham, Dorset
Swallow Hotel, Birmingham, West Midlands
The Swan Hotel, Bibury, Gloucestershire
Swinside Lodge, Keswick, Cumbria
Tavern House, Tetbury, Gloucestershire

*N*ATIONAL ACCESSIBLE SCHEME

Throughout Britain, the Tourist Boards are inspecting all types of places to stay, on holiday or business, that provide accessible accommodation for wheelchair users and others who may have difficulty walking.

The Tourist Boards recognise three categories of accessibility:

 Category 1
Accessible to all wheelchair users including those travelling independently.

 Category 2
Accessible to a wheelchair user with assistance.

 Category 3
Accessible to a wheelchair user able to walk short distances and up at least three steps.

If you have additional needs or special requirements of any kind, we strongly recommend that you make sure these can be met by your chosen establishment before you confirm your booking.

The criteria the Tourist Boards have adopted do not necessarily conform to British Standards or to Building Regulations. They reflect what the Boards understand to be acceptable to meet the practical needs of wheelchair users.

The following establishments listed in this *Where to Stay* guide had been inspected and given an access category at the time of going to press. Use the Town Index at the back of the guide to find page numbers for their full entries.

 Category 1

CHESHUNT, HERTFORDSHIRE
- Cheshunt Marriott Hotel
CROOKHAM, NORTHUMBERLAND
- The Coach House
DURHAM
- Royal County Hotel
HULL, EAST RIDING OF YORKSHIRE
- Kingstown Hotel
OXFORD, OXFORDSHIRE
- Westwood Country Hotel
SANDRINGHAM, NORFOLK
- Park House
SELSEY, WEST SUSSEX
- St Andrews Lodge
SOUTHAMPTON, HAMPSHIRE
- Botley Park Hotel, Golf & Country Club
THEDDINGWORTH, LEICESTERSHIRE
- Hothorpe Hall
WELLS, SOMERSET
- Burcott Mill
WILMSLOW, CHESHIRE
- Dean Bank Hotel
WINDERMERE, CUMBRIA
- Burnside Hotel
YORK, NORTH YORKSHIRE
- Swallow Hotel

CAMBRIDGE, CAMBRIDGESHIRE
- Holiday Inn (Cambridge)
CASTLE DONINGTON, LEICESTERSHIRE
- Donington Park Farmhouse Hotel
GARBOLDISHAM, NORFOLK
- Ingleneuk Lodge
GREAT YARMOUTH, NORFOLK
- Horse & Groom Motel
HULL, EAST RIDING OF YORKSHIRE
- Quality Royal Hotel
IREBY, CUMBRIA
- Woodlands Country House
LANCASTER, LANCASHIRE
- Lancaster House Hotel
LONDON, GREATER LONDON
- The Bonnington in Bloomsbury
MANCHESTER, GREATER MANCHESTER
- Novotel Manchester West
NEWTON AYCLIFFE, DURHAM
- Redworth Hall
NORWICH, NORFOLK
- Beeches Hotel & Victorian Gardens
- Hotel Norwich
SALISBURY, WILTSHIRE
- Grasmere House
SHAP, CUMBRIA
- Shap Wells Hotel
ST IVES, CORNWALL
- Chy-an-Dour Hotel
YORK, NORTH YORKSHIRE
- Novotel York

 Category 2

BRIDGNORTH, SHROPSHIRE
- Old Vicarage Hotel
BRIDGWATER, SOMERSET
- Friarn Court Hotel

 Category 3

ALDERLEY EDGE, CHESHIRE
- The Alderley Edge Hotel
AMBLESIDE, CUMBRIA
- Borrans Park Hotel

- Kirkstone Foot Country House
- Rowanfield Country Guesthouse

BASSENTHWAITE LAKE, CUMBRIA
- Pheasant Inn

BIRMINGHAM, WEST MIDLANDS
- Swallow Hotel

BOLTON ABBEY, NORTH YORKSHIRE
- Devonshire Arms Country House

BRADFORD, WEST YORKSHIRE
- Novotel Bradford

BRIGHTON & HOVE, EAST SUSSEX
- Brighton Oak Hotel

BRISTOL,
- Swallow Royal Hotel

CHELTENHAM, GLOUCESTERSHIRE
- The Prestbury House Hotel and Restaurant

CHESTER, CHESHIRE
- Dene Hotel
- Green Bough Hotel and Restaurant

CHESTERFIELD, DERBYSHIRE
- Abbeydale Hotel

CHIPPING, LANCASHIRE
- Gibbon Bridge Hotel

CIRENCESTER, GLOUCESTERSHIRE
- King's Head Hotel

CRESSBROOK, DERBYSHIRE
- Cressbrook Hall

CROMER, NORFOLK
- Cliftonville Hotel

EASTBOURNE, EAST SUSSEX
- Congress Hotel

ELLERBY, NORTH YORKSHIRE
- Ellerby Hotel

EXETER, DEVON
- St Andrews Hotel

FAREHAM, HAMPSHIRE
- Avenue House Hotel

FINEDON, NORTHAMPTONSHIRE
- Tudor Gate Hotel

FROME, SOMERSET
- Fourwinds Guest House

GRANGE-OVER-SANDS, CUMBRIA
- Netherwood Hotel

GRANTHAM, LINCOLNSHIRE
- Kings Hotel

GREAT YARMOUTH, NORFOLK
- Burlington Palm Court Hotel

GRIMSBY, NORTH EAST LINCOLNSHIRE
- Millfields

HARROGATE, NORTH YORKSHIRE
- The Boar's Head Hotel
- St George Swallow Hotel

HELMSLEY, NORTH YORKSHIRE
- Pheasant Hotel

HEMEL HEMPSTEAD, HERTFORDSHIRE
- The Bobsleigh Inn

IPSWICH, SUFFOLK
- Novotel Ipswich

KESWICK, CUMBRIA
- Derwentwater Hotel

KIDDERMINSTER, HEREFORD & WORCESTER
- The Granary Hotel and Restaurant

LANGHO, LANCASHIRE
- Mytton Fold Hotel & Golf Complex

LEYBURN, NORTH YORKSHIRE
- Golden Lion Hotel and Restaurant

LINCOLN, LINCOLNSHIRE
- Damon's Motel

LONDON, GREATER LONDON
- Westland Hotel

LOWER WHITLEY, CHESHIRE
- Tall Trees Lodge

LUDLOW, SHROPSHIRE
- The Feathers at Ludlow

LYMINGTON, HAMPSHIRE
- Our Bench

LYTHAM ST ANNES, LANCASHIRE
- Chadwick Hotel

MARGATE, KENT
- Lonsdale Court Hotel

MARKFIELD, LEICESTERSHIRE
- Field Head Hotel

MILDENHALL, SUFFOLK
- Smoke House

MORPETH, NORTHUMBERLAND
- Linden Hall Hotel

NEWMARKET, SUFFOLK
- Heath Court Hotel

NORWICH, NORFOLK
- Elm Farm Chalet Hotel
- Old Rectory

NOTTINGHAM, NOTTINGHAMSHIRE
- The Nottingham Gateway Hotel

RAVENSTONEDALE, CUMBRIA
- The Black Swan Hotel

REDCAR, TEES VALLEY
- Falcon Hotel

ROTHERHAM, SOUTH YORKSHIRE
- Best Western Elton Hotel

ROYAL TUNBRIDGE WELLS, KENT
- The Spa Hotel

SANDBACH, CHESHIRE
- Saxon Cross Hotel

SKEGNESS, LINCOLNSHIRE
- Saxby Hotel

SKIPTON, NORTH YORKSHIRE
- Hanover International Hotel & Club

SOUTH NORMANTON, DERBYSHIRE
- Swallow Hotel

SOUTHPORT, MERSEYSIDE
- Scarisbrick Hotel

STAMFORD, LINCOLNSHIRE
- Garden House Hotel

STRATFORD-UPON-AVON, WARWICKSHIRE
- East Bank House
- Grosvenor Hotel

SWANAGE, DORSET
- The Pines Hotel

TENTERDEN, KENT
- Little Silver Country Hotel

TORQUAY, DEVON
- Frognel Hall

WARRINGTON, CHESHIRE
- The Park Royal International Hotel

WESTON-SUPER-MARE, NORTH SOMERSET
- Moorlands

WHITLEY BAY, TYNE & WEAR
- Malborough Hotel
- York House Hotel

WINDERMERE, CUMBRIA
- The Burn How Garden House Hotel & Motel
- Linthwaite House Hotel

YORK, NORTH YORKSHIRE
- Heworth Court Hotel
- Savages Hotel

The National Accessible Scheme forms part of the Tourism for All Campaign that is being promoted by all National and Regional Tourist Boards. Additional help and guidance on finding suitable holiday accommodation for those with special needs can be obtained from:

Holiday Care Service
2nd Floor, Imperial Buildings,
Victoria Road,
Horley, Surrey RH6 7PZ
Tel: (01293) 774535
Fax: (01293) 784647
Minicom: (01293) 776943

MAP AND KEY TO REGIONAL SECTIONS

This Where to Stay *guide is divided into* 10 *regional sections as shown on the map below. To identify each regional section and its page number, please refer to the key opposite. The index lists the counties of England and indicates under which regional section you will find them.*

3 Northumbria

2 Cumbria

5 Yorkshire

4 North West

6 Heart of England

7 East of England

9 South of England

London **1**

10 South East England

8 West Country

Colour location maps showing all the cities, towns and villages with accommodation listed in this guide, and an index to the place names, can be found at the back of the guide.

As you are probably aware, the boundaries and names of a number of counties in England were recently changed as the result of local government reorganisation. The main county changes have been reflected in *Where to Stay*, particularly in the county index opposite, the regional section maps, in the colour location maps at the back and in the town descriptions.**

If you want to find out more about what there is to see and do in a particular area, contact the appropriate Regional Tourist Board. Details are given both at the beginning and end of each regional section.

KEY TO MAP

COUNTY INDEX

** This is how you will find the following county changes have been reflected in *Where to Stay*:

Avon is replaced by Bath & North East Somerset, City of Bristol, North Somerset and South Gloucestershire

Cleveland is replaced by Tees Valley

Humberside is replaced by East Riding of Yorkshire and North Lincolnshire

Although there have been changes to the unitary authority boundaries in the following areas, you will see that the familiar regional names have been retained for: Greater Manchester, Merseyside, South Yorkshire, Tyne & Wear, West Midlands and West Yorkshire

*U*SE YOUR *i*'s

When it comes to your next England break, the first stage of your journey could be closer than you think. You've probably got a Tourist Information Centre nearby which is there to serve the local community - as well as visitors.

So make us your first stop. We'll be happy to help you, wherever you're heading.

Many Tourist Information Centres can provide you with maps and guides, helping you plan well in advance. And sometimes it's even possible for us to book your accommodation, too.

A visit to your nearest Information Centre can pay off in other ways as well. We can point you in the right direction when it comes to finding out about all the special events which are happening in the local region.

In fact, we can give you details of places to visit within easy reach... and perhaps tempt you to plan a day trip or weekend away.

Across the country, there are more than 550 Tourist Information Centres so you're never far away. You'll find the address of your nearest Tourist Information Centre in your local Phone Book, or call Freepages on 0800 192 192.

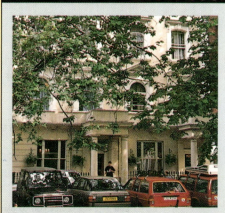

15

RASOOL COURT HOTEL

19-21 Penywern Road, Earl's Court, London, SW5 9TT
Tel: (0171) 373 8900 Fax: (0171) 244 6835
Email: younis@rasool.demon.co.uk

57-bedroom hotel located just near the Earl's Court Tube Station.

Very convenient for the West End
and Heathrow Airport.
All rooms with colour TV
and direct-dial telephone.

Prices:
Singles from £29
Doubles from £40
Triple from £54
(including taxes and
continental breakfast).

WHERE TO STAY IN ENGLAND

Published by: English Tourist Board,
Thames Tower, Black's Road,
Hammersmith, London W6 9EL.
ISBN 0 86143 204 5
Managing Editor: Jane Collinson
Technical Manager: Marita Sen
Compilation & Production: Guide
Associates, Croydon
Design and illustrations: Jackson Lowe
Marketing, Lewes, East Sussex
Colour Photography: Mike Williams
(front cover)
Cartography: Colin Earl
Typesetting: Reed Technologies and
Information Services, London and
Jackson Lowe Marketing, Lewes
Printing and Binding: Bemrose Security
Printing, Derby
Advertisement Sales: Madison Bell Ltd,
3 St. Peter's Street, Islington Green,
London N1 8JD. (0171) 359 7737.
© English Tourist Board (except
where stated)

The English Tourist Board
The Board is a statutory body
created by the Development of
Tourism Act 1969 to develop and
market England's tourism. Its main
objectives are to provide a welcome
for people visiting England; to
encourage people living in England to
take their holidays there; and to
encourage the provision and
improvement of tourist amenities and
facilities in England. The Board has a
statutory duty to advise the
Government on tourism matters
relating to England and, with
Government approval and support,
administers the national classification
and grading schemes for tourist
accommodation in England.

*L*ONDON

Welcome to a voyage of discovery. In a truly great city like London, contrasts, interest and enjoyment are endless. There's the glitter of theatre land, West End shopping, the historic Tower of London and St. Katharine's Dock. Excellent shopping, restaurants, museums and galleries, plus a host of year-round events add to the list of things to do.

For a feel of the open air stroll on Hampstead Heath, or in one of the great parks. Try surprising Little Venice, with its pretty canals, colourful boats and towpath walk past the rich and famous, or perhaps one of London's many lively street markets.

London has so many distinctly different areas, each with its own special atmosphere to fit your mood and interests.

Greater London, comprising the
32 London Boroughs

FOR MORE INFORMATION CONTACT:
London Tourist Board
6th floor, Glen House, Stag Place, London SW1E 5LT

Where to Go in London – see pages 18-20
Where to Stay in London – see pages 25-47

17

LONDON

Where to Go and What to See

You will find hundreds of interesting places to visit during your stay in London, just some of which are listed in these pages. Contact any Tourist Information Centre in the region for more ideas on days out in London.

■ Bank of England Museum
Bartholomew Lane,
London EC2R 8AH
Tel: (0171) 601 5545/5491
Museum illustrating the history of the Bank since 1694. Displays include gold bars, banknotes, modern dealing desk and interactive video systems.

■ British Library Exhibition Galleries
Great Russell Street,
London WC1B 3DG
Tel: (0171) 412 7000
Manuscript Saloon, Grenville Library and King's Library - displaying the Magna Carta, Gutenberg Bible, Shakespeare and illuminated manuscripts.

■ British Museum
Great Russell Street,
London WC1B 3DG
Tel: (0171) 636 1555
One of the great museums of the world, showing the works of man from all over the world from prehistoric times to the present day.

■ Cabinet War Rooms
Clive Steps,
King Charles Street,
London SW1A 2AQ
Tel: (0171) 903 6961
The underground headquarters used by Winston Churchill and the British Government during World War II. Includes Cabinet Room, Transatlantic Telephone Room and Map Room.

■ Chislehurst Caves
Old Hill,
Chislehurst,
Kent BR7 5NB
Tel: (0181) 467 3264
Over 20 miles of caves, parts of which date from 6000 BC. Features include the Druid's Altar, Roman well, haunted pool and World War II exhibition.

■ Design Museum
Shad Thames,
London SE1 2YD
Tel: (0171) 403 6933
A study collection showing the development of design in mass production. Review of new products, graphics gallery and temporary exhibitions.

■ Hampton Court Palace
Hampton Court,
Surrey KT8 9AU
Tel: (0181) 781 9500
Oldest Tudor palace in England with many attractions including Tudor kitchens, tennis courts, maze, state apartments and King's apartment.

HMS Belfast
Morgan's Lane, Tooley Street,
London SE1 2JH
Tel: (0171) 407 6434
*World War II cruiser weighing
11,500 tonnes, now a floating naval
museum with seven decks to explore.
Many naval exhibits also on show.*

Imperial War Museum
Lambeth Road,
London SE1 6HZ
Tel: (0171) 416 5000
*The story of 20thC war from
Flanders to Bosnia. Features include
the Blitz Experience, Operation
Jericho and the Trench Experience.*

Kensington Palace State Apartments
Kensington Gardens,
London W8 4PX
Tel: (0171) 937 9561
*Furniture and ceiling paintings from
Stuart-Hanoverian periods, rooms
from the Victorian era and works of
art from the Royal Collection. Also
Royal Ceremonial Dress Collection.*

London Aquarium
County Hall,
Riverside Building,
London SE1 7PB
Tel: (0171) 967 8000
*Visitors are submerged into a
stunning display of hundreds of
varieties of fish and sealife from
around the world.*

London Brass Rubbing Centre
St Martin-in-the-Fields Church,
Trafalgar Square,
London WC2N 4JJ
Tel: (0171) 930 9306
*Knights, unicorns and kings are
traditional brass rubbings for visitors
to buy or make themselves. Also
unusual Celtic designs and historical
gifts.*

London Dungeon
28-34 Tooley Street,
London SE1 2SZ
Tel: (0171) 403 0606
*The world's first medieval horror
museum. Now featuring two major
shows, 'The Jack the Ripper
Experience' and 'The Theatre of the
Guillotine'.*

London Planetarium
Marylebone Road,
London NW1 5LR
Tel: (0171) 935 6861
*Completely refurbished, visitors can
now experience a virtual reality trip
through space and wander through
interactive Space Zones before the
show.*

London Toy and Model Museum
21-23 Craven Hill, Bayswater,
London W2 3EN
Tel: (0171) 706 800
*Over 20 themed galleries housing
toys from trains to dolls and
working models. Ride-on carousel
and steam train in the garden.*

London Zoo
Regent's Park,
London NW1 4RY
Tel: (0171) 722 3333
*One of the world's most famous
zoos with over 8,000 animals
including rhinos, venomous snakes,
penguins and piranhas. Programme
of events, Moonlight World and
Children's Zoo.*

Madame Tussaud's
Marylebone Road,
London NW1 5LR
Tel: (0171) 935 6861
*World-famous collection of wax
figures in themed settings which
include The Garden Party, 200
Years, Superstars, The Grand Hall,
The Chamber of Horrors and The
Spirit of London.*

Museum of Mankind
6 Burlington Gardens,
London W1X 2EX
Tel: (0171) 437 2224
*Ethnography department of the
British Museum housing collections
from Africa, Australia, the Pacific
Islands, North and South America.*

National Gallery
Trafalgar Square,
London WC2N 5DN
Tel: (0171) 747 2885
*Gallery displaying Western painting
from 1260-1920. Includes work by
Botticelli, Leonardo da Vinci,
Rembrandt, Gainsborough, Turner,
Renoir, Cezanne and Van Gogh.*

■ National Portrait Gallery
St. Martin's Place
London WC2H 0HE
Tel: (0171) 306 0055
Permanent collection of portraits of famous men and women from the Middle Ages to the present day.

■ National Maritime Museum
Romney Road, Greenwich,
London SE10 9NF
Tel: (0181) 858 4422/
(0181) 312 6565
Britain's maritime heritage illustrated through artefacts, models, paintings, navigation instruments, archives and photographs. Regular exhibitions and a children's gallery.

■ Natural History Museum
Cromwell Road,
London SW7 5BD
Tel: (0171) 938 9123
Home of the wonders of the natural world, one of the most popular museums in the world and one of London's finest landmarks.

■ Old Royal Observatory
Greenwich Park,
London SE10 9NF
Tel: (0181) 858 4422/
(0181) 312 6565
Museum of time and space and site of the Greenwich Meridian.

Working telescopes and planetarium, timeball, Wren's Octagon Room and intricate clocks and computer simulations.

■ Rock Circus
London Pavilion, Piccadilly Circus,
London W1V 9LA
Tel: (0171) 734 7203/8025
Amazing combination of stereo sound through personal headsets, audio-animatronic (moving) and Madame Tussaud's wax figures of over 50 rock stars.

■ Royal Mews
Buckingham Palace,
London SW1A 1AA
Tel: (0171) 839 1377/
(0171) 799 2331
See the Queen's carriage horses, carriages and harness used on State occasions including the Coronation Coach built 1761.

■ Science Museum
Exhibition Road,
London SW7 2DD
Tel: (0171) 938 8000/8080
Over 200,000 exhibits covering almost every imaginable sector of science, technology, industry and medicine.

■ Thames Barrier Visitors' Centre
Unity Way, London SE18 5NJ
Tel: (0181) 305 4188
Exhibition with 10-minute video, a working scale model and a multimedia show. Also riverside walkways, children's play area and buffet.

■ Theatre Museum
Russell Street,
London WC2E 7PA
Tel: (0171) 836 7891
Five galleries illustrating the history of performance in the United Kingdom. The collection includes displays on theatre, ballet, dance, musical stage, rock and pop music.

■ Tower Bridge Experience
Tower Bridge, London SE1 2UP
Tel: (0171) 403 3761
Exhibition explaining the history of the bridge and how it operates. Original steam-powered engines on view. Panoramic views from fully-glazed walkways. Gift shop.

■ Tower of London
Tower Hill,
London EC3N 4AB
Tel: (0171) 709 0765
Home of the 'Beefeaters' and ravens, the building spans 900 years of British history. On display are the nation's Crown Jewels, regalia and armoury robes.

FIND OUT MORE

A free information pack about holidays and attractions in London is available on written request from:
London Tourist Board and Convention Bureau,
6th floor, Glen House,
Stag Place, London SW1E 5LT.

tOURIST INFORMATION

Tourist and leisure information can be obtained from Tourist Information Centres throughout England. Details of centres and other information services in Greater London are given below. The symbol ⊨ means that an accommodation booking service is provided.

Tourist Information Centres

Points of arrival
Victoria Station, Forecourt, SW1 ⊨
Easter-October, daily 0800-1900. November-Easter, reduced opening hours.
Liverpool Street Underground Station, EC2 ⊨
Monday-Friday 0800-1800. Saturday-Sunday 0845-17.30.
Heathrow Terminals 1, 2, 3 Underground Station Concourse (Heathrow Airport) ⊨
Daily 0800-1800.
Heathrow Terminal 3 Arrivals Concourse ⊨
0600-2300.
Waterloo International Arrivals Hall ⊨
0830-2230.
The above information centres provide a London and Britain tourist information service, offer a hotel accommodation booking service, stock free and saleable publications on Britain and London and sell theatre tickets, tourist tickets for bus and underground and tickets for sightseeing tours.

Inner London
British Travel Centre ⊨
12 Regent Street, Piccadilly Circus, SW1Y 4PQ
Monday-Friday 0900-1830.
Saturday-Sunday 1000-1600

(0900-1700 Saturdays May-September).
Canary Wharf Tourist Information Centre
Ground Floor, Cabot Place West, London E14
Tel: (0171) 512 9800
Monday-Friday 0900-1800.
Saturday, Sunday & Bank Holiday Monday 1000-1700.
Greenwich Tourist Information Centre ⊨
46 Greenwich Church Street, SE10 9BL.
Tel: (0181) 858 6376
April-September, daily 1015-1645. October-March, reduced opening hours.
Hackney Museum and Tourist Information Centre
Central Hall, Mare Street, E8
Tel: (0181) 985 9055
Tuesday-Friday 1000-1700.
Closed 1230-1330.
Saturday 1330-1700.
Islington Tourist Information Centre ⊨
44 Duncan Street, N1 8BW
Tel: (0171) 278 8787
Monday 1400-1600.
Tuesday-Saturday 1000-1700.
Closed Saturday 1330-1430.
Lewisham Tourist Information Centre
Lewisham Library, 199-201 Lewisham High Street, SE13 6LG
Tel: (0181) 297 8317
Monday 1000-1700.
Tuesday-Friday 0900-1700

Southwark Tourist Information Centre ⊨
Unit 4, Lower Level, Cotton's Centre, Middle Yard
SE1 2QJ
Tel: (0171) 403 8299
Monday-Friday 1000-1700.
Saturday-Sunday 1100-1700.
(Reduced winter opening).
Tower Hamlets Tourist Information Centre
107a Commercial Street, E1 6BG
Tel: (0181) 375 2549
Monday-Friday 0930-1630.

Outer London
Bexley Tourist Information Centre
Central Library, Townley Road, Bexleyheath DA6 7HJ
Tel: (0181) 303 9052
Monday, Tuesday, Thursday 0930-2000. Wednesday & Friday 0930-1730. Saturday 0930-1700.
Also at Hall Place Visitor Centre
Bourne Road, Bexley
Tel: (01322) 558676
June-September, daily 1130-1630.
Croydon Tourist Information Centre ⊨
Katharine Street, Croydon CR9 1ET
Tel: (0181) 253 1009
Monday-Wednesday & Friday 0900-1800. Thursday 0930-1800.
Saturday 0900-1700.

**Foots Cray Tourist
Information Centre** 🛏
Tesco Store Car Park,
Edgington Way, Sidcup
DA14 5AH
Summer only, Monday-Saturday
0900-1700. Sunday 1000-1600.

**Harrow Tourist
Information Centre**
Civic Centre, Station Road,
Harrow HA1 2XF
Tel: (0181) 424 1103
Monday-Friday 0900-1700.

**Hillingdon Tourist
Information Centre**
Central Library, 14 High Street,
Uxbridge UB8 1HD
Tel: (01895) 250706
Monday, Tuesday & Thursday
0930-2000. Friday & Wednesday
0930-1730. Saturday 0930-1600.

**Hounslow Tourist
Information Centre**
24 The Treaty Centre, Hounslow
High Street, Hounslow TW3 1ES
Tel: (0181) 572 8279
Monday, Wednesday, Friday
& Saturday 0930-1730.
Tuesday, Thursday 0930-2000.

**Kingston Tourist Information
Centre**
The Market House,
The Market Place,
Kingston upon Thames KT1 1JS.
Tel: (0181) 547 5592
Monday-Friday 1000-1700.
Saturday 0900-1600.

**Redbridge Tourist
Information Centre**
Town Hall, High Road, Ilford,
Essex IG1 1DD
Tel: (0181) 478 3020
Monday-Friday 0830-1700.

**Richmond Tourist
Information Centre** 🛏
Old Town Hall, Whittaker
Avenue, Richmond upon Thames
TW9 1TP
Tel: (0181) 940 9125
Monday-Friday 1000-1800.
Saturday 1000-1700. May-
October, also Sunday 1015-1615.

**Twickenham Tourist
Information Centre**
The Atrium, Civic Centre, York
Street, Twickenham TW1 3BZ
Tel: (0181) 891 7272
Monday-Thursday 0900-1715.
Friday 0900-1700.

Visitorcall

The London Tourist Board and
Convention Bureau's 'Phone
Guide to London' operates 24
hours a day. To access a full
range of information call 0839
123456. To access specific lines
dial 0839 123 followed by:

What's on this week - 400
What's on next 3 months - 401
Sunday in London - 407
Rock and pop concerts - 422
Popular attractions - 480
Where to take children - 424
Museums - 429
Palaces (including Buckingham
Palace) - 481
Current exhibitions - 403
Changing the Guard - 411
Popular West End shows - 416
London dining - 485
Calls cost 49p per minute at all
times (as at April 97).
To order a Visitorcall card
please call (0171) 971 0026.
Information for callers using
push-button telephones: (0171)
971 0027.

Artsline

London's information and advice
service for disabled people on
arts and entertainment.
Call (0171) 388 2227.

Hotel Accommodation Service

The London Tourist Board and
Convention Bureau helps visitors
to find and book accommodation
at a wide range of prices in hotels
and guesthouses, including budget
accommodation, throughout the
Greater London area.

Reservations are made with
hotels which are members of
LTB, denoted in this guide with
the symbol 𝐌 by their name.
Reservations can be made by
credit card holders via the
telephone accommodation
reservations service on (0171)
932 2020 by simply giving the
reservation clerk your card
details (Mastercard, Visa or
Switch) and room requirements.
LTB takes an administrative
booking fee. The service
operates Monday-Friday 0930-
1730.

Reservations on arrival are
handled at the Tourist
Information Centres operated by
LTB at Victoria Station,
Heathrow Underground,
Liverpool Street Station,
Waterloo International and
Heathrow Terminal 3. Go to any
of them on the day when you
need accommodation. A
communication charge and a
refundable deposit are payable
when making a reservation.

Which part of London?

The majority of tourist
accommodation is situated in the
central parts of London and is
therefore very convenient for
most of the city's attractions and
night life.

However, there are many hotels
in outer London which provide
other advantages, such as easier
parking. In the 'Where to Stay'
pages which follow, you will find
accommodation listed under
INNER LONDON (covering the
E1 to W14 London Postal Area)
and OUTER LONDON
(covering the remainder of
Greater London). Colour maps 6
and 7 at the back of the guide
show place names and London
Postal Area codes and will help
you to locate accommodation in
your chosen area of London.

LONDON INDEX

If you are looking for accommodation in a particular establishment in London and you know its name, this index will give you the page number of the full entry in the guide.

ENQUIRY COUPONS

To help you obtain further information about advertisers and accommodation featured in this guide you will find enquiry coupons at the back. Send these directly to the establishments in which you are interested. Remember to complete both sides of the coupon.

AT-A-GLANCE SYMBOLS

Symbols at the end of each accommodation entry
give useful information about services
and facilities. A key to symbols can be found
inside the back cover flap.

Keep this open for easy reference.

WHERE TO STAY (LONDON)

Accommodation entries in this section are listed under **Inner London** (covering the postcode areas E1 to W14) and **Outer London** (covering the remainder of Greater London) - please refer to the colour location maps 6 and 7 at the back of this guide. If you want to look up a particular establishment, use the index on the previous pages which will give you the page number.

At-a-glance symbols at the end of each accommodation entry give useful information about services and facilities. A key to symbols can be found inside the back cover flap. Keep this open for easy reference.

INNER LONDON

Colour maps 6 & 7 at the back of the guide show place names and London Postal Area Codes and will help you locate accommodation in your chosen area of London

LONDON E7

Forest View Hotel ᴧᴧ

😋 😋 APPROVED

227 Romford Road, Forest Gate, London E7 9HL
☎ (0181) 534 4844
Fax (0181) 534 8959
Catering for business and tourist clientele, this hotel has en-suite rooms with tea/coffee making, direct-dial telephone and TV. Full English breakfast. Warm and friendly atmosphere, competitive rates.
Bedrooms: 8 single, 5 double, 2 twin, 2 triple, 3 family rooms
Bathrooms: 3 en-suite, 4 private, 3 public

Bed & breakfast

per night:	£min	£max
Single	38.00	38.00
Double	55.00	66.00

Half board per person:

	£min	£max
Daily	45.00	50.00
Weekly	315.00	350.00

Evening meal 1830 (last orders 2100)
Parking for 15
Cards accepted: Amex, Mastercard, Visa, Switch/Delta

Grangewood Lodge Hotel ᴧᴧ

Listed

104 Clova Road, Forest Gate, London E7 9AF
☎ (0181) 534 0637 & 503 0941
Fax (0181) 217 0392
Comfortable budget accommodation in a quiet road. Pleasant garden. Easy access to central London, Docklands and M11. 12 minutes to Liverpool Street station.
Bedrooms: 10 single, 1 double, 5 twin, 2 triple
Bathrooms: 3 public, 1 private shower

Bed & breakfast

per night:	£min	£max
Single	18.00	20.00
Double	28.00	34.00

Parking for 2
Cards accepted: Mastercard, Visa

LONDON E10

Sleeping Beauty Motel ᴧᴧ

🅠 APPROVED

543 Lea Bridge Road, Leyton, London E10 7EB
☎ (0181) 556 8080
Fax (0181) 556 8080

All rooms en-suite with bath and shower, satellite TV, direct-dial telephone, hairdryer, hospitality tray,
trouser press, mini fridge, safe. Ironing facilities, 24-hour reception, lift, free car park, bar.
Bedrooms: 16 double, 61 twin, 4 triple
Bathrooms: 80 en-suite

Bed & breakfast

per night:	£min	£max
Single	40.00	50.00
Double	45.00	60.00

Parking for 74
Cards accepted: Amex, Diners, Mastercard, Visa, Switch/Delta

LONDON N1

Kandara Guest House ᴧᴧ

Listed APPROVED

68 Ockendon Road, London N1 3NW
☎ (0171) 226 5721 & 226 3379
Small family-run guesthouse near the Angel, Islington. Free street parking and good public transport to West End and City.
Bedrooms: 4 single, 2 double, 2 twin, 2 triple
Bathrooms: 3 public

Bed & breakfast

per night:	£min	£max
Single	27.00	30.00
Double	38.00	40.00

Cards accepted: Mastercard, Visa

A key to symbols can be found inside the back cover flap.

LONDON N4

Costello Palace Hotel ⋔

Listed APPROVED

374 Seven Sisters Road, Finsbury
Park, London N4 2PG
☎ (0181) 802 6551
Fax (0181) 802 9461

Fully refurbished, family-run, attractive
hotel. Conveniently situated for all
amenities. All rooms en-suite with Sky
TV, telephone. Full English breakfast.
Free car park.
Bedrooms: 3 single, 17 double,
20 twin, 4 triple
Bathrooms: 44 en-suite, 1 public

Bed & breakfast

per night:	£min	£max
Single	38.00	45.00
Double	55.00	60.00

Parking for 35
Cards accepted: Diners, Mastercard,
Visa, Switch/Delta

Kent Hall Hotel

Listed

414 Seven Sisters Road, London
N4 2LX
☎ (0181) 802 0800 & 802 5100
Fax (0181) 802 9070
Close to Manor House underground,
10 minutes from central London. Ideal
for groups and school parties.
Bedrooms: 3 single, 11 twin,
11 triple
Bathrooms: 10 en-suite, 15 private
showers

Bed & breakfast

per night:	£min	£max
Single	25.00	35.00
Double	45.00	50.00

Parking for 4

New Pembury Hotel ⋔

APPROVED

328 Seven Sisters Road, Finsbury
Park, London N4 2AP
☎ (0181) 800 5310
Fax (0181) 809 6362

Please mention this guide
when making your booking.

Recently renovated, welcoming hotel.
Modern rooms, all en-suite, with
tea/coffee facilities, direct-dial
telephone and Sky TV. Friendly
bar/cafe. Easy access to West End and
central London. Competitive prices.
Bedrooms: 22 single, 15 double,
16 twin, 5 triple, 1 family room
Bathrooms: 59 en-suite, 4 public

Bed & breakfast

per night:	£min	£max
Single	40.00	45.00
Double	60.00	65.00

Lunch available
Evening meal 1800 (last orders
2200)
Parking for 15
Cards accepted: Amex, Mastercard,
Visa, Switch/Delta

Spring Park Hotel

400 Seven Sisters Road, London
N4 2LX
☎ (0181) 800 6030
Fax (0181) 802 5652
Overlooking Finsbury Park, next to
Manor House underground station for
Piccadilly line direct to the West End
and Heathrow Airport.
Bedrooms: 10 single, 19 double,
20 twin, 1 triple
Bathrooms: 36 en-suite, 7 public

Bed & breakfast

per night:	£min	£max
Single	29.00	45.00
Double	40.00	62.00

Half board per

person:	£min	£max
Daily	38.50	54.50
Weekly	250.00	300.00

Lunch available
Evening meal 1800 (last orders
0000)
Parking for 70
Cards accepted: Amex, Mastercard,
Visa, Switch/Delta

LONDON N7

Five Kings Guest House ⋔

APPROVED

59 Anson Road, Tufnell Park,
London N7 0AR
☎ (0171) 607 3996 & 607 6466
Privately-run guesthouse in a quiet

residential area. 15 minutes to central
London. Unrestricted parking in road.
Bedrooms: 6 single, 3 double, 3 twin,
2 triple, 2 family rooms
Bathrooms: 9 en-suite, 3 public,
2 private showers

Bed & breakfast

per night:	£min	£max
Single	20.00	28.00
Double	30.00	38.00

Cards accepted: Mastercard, Visa

LONDON N8

White Lodge Hotel ⋔

APPROVED

1 Church Lane, Hornsey, London
N8 7BU
☎ (0181) 348 9765
Fax (0181) 340 7851
Small, friendly, family hotel offering
personal service. Easy access to all
transport, for sightseeing and business
trips.
Bedrooms: 7 single, 3 double, 3 twin,
3 family rooms
Bathrooms: 8 en-suite, 3 public

Bed & breakfast

per night:	£min	£max
Single	26.00	28.00
Double	36.00	44.00

Evening meal 1800 (last orders
1900)
Cards accepted: Mastercard, Visa

LONDON N10

Raglan Hall Hotel

COMMENDED

8-12 Queens Avenue, Muswell Hill,
London N10 3NR
☎ (0181) 883 9836
Fax (0181) 883 5002
Email: raglanhall@aol.com
CR Best Western
Located in a quiet tree-lined avenue of
north London. Lovely secluded garden
and patio. Modern English food.
Friendly relaxed atmosphere.
Bedrooms: 8 single, 20 double,
10 twin, 8 triple
Bathrooms: 46 en-suite

Bed & breakfast

per night:	£min	£max
Single	96.95	101.95
Double	108.90	112.90

Half board per

person:	£min	£max
Daily	113.45	118.45
Weekly	794.15	829.15

Evening meal 1900 (last orders
2145)
Parking for 8

Cards accepted: Amex, Diners,
Mastercard, Visa, Switch/Delta

☎🖐🛆🕭📞🖵📶🎱⌣🗞📺
◐🖵🛄🍴110🏃❄🌼ⁿ🚲🛇SP🖼T◉

Parkland Walk Guest House

Listed COMMENDED

12 Hornsey Rise Gardens, London
N19 3PR
☎ (0171) 263 3228 & 0973 382982
Fax (0171) 263 3965
Email: parklandwalk
@monomark.demon.co.uk.
*Friendly Victorian family house in
residential area, Highgate/Crouch End.
Near many restaurants and convenient
for central London. Non-smokers only.
Past British Tourist Authority award
winner - Best Small Hotel in London
competition.*
Bedrooms: 3 single, 1 double, 1 twin,
1 family room
Bathrooms: 3 en-suite, 1 private,
1 public

Bed & breakfast

per night:	£min	£max
Single	26.00	45.00
Double	45.00	60.00

Cards accepted: Amex

☎🕭📞🖵📶🎱🛆🛄🗞📺🖵🛆
🍴8❄🌼🌾🚲

The White House 𝒜𝒜

🖐🖐🖐 COMMENDED

Albany Street, Regent's Park,
London NW1 3UP
☎ (0171) 387 1200
Fax (0171) 388 0091
ℂℝ Utell International
*Near Regent's Park, the zoo and
Madame Tussaud's. A few minutes
from Euston Station and about 10
minutes' walk from Oxford Circus.
There are 3 underground stations
within walking distance.*
Bedrooms: 53 single, 216 double,
239 twin, 53 triple
Suites available
Bathrooms: 561 en-suite

Bed & breakfast

per night:	£min	£max
Single	155.00	181.00
Double	174.00	205.00

Lunch available
Evening meal 1830 (last orders
2230)
Parking for 7
Cards accepted: Amex, Diners,
Mastercard, Visa, Switch/Delta

☎🕭📞🖵📶🎱🛄⌣🗞📺◐🖵
🛆🍴130🍽🌼🌾🛇SP🖼T

Dillons Hotel 𝒜𝒜

21 Belsize Park, Hampstead, London
NW3 4DU
☎ (0171) 794 3360
Fax (0171) 586 1104
*Small private guesthouse, close to
central London, with excellent transport
facilities nearby.*
Bedrooms: 3 single, 2 double, 5 twin,
1 triple, 2 family rooms
Bathrooms: 7 private, 3 public

Bed & breakfast

per night:	£min	£max
Single	26.00	34.00
Double	37.00	45.00

Cards accepted: Amex, Mastercard,
Visa, Switch/Delta

☎🛄🗞📺🖵🛆🌾🚲SP🖼

The Langorf Hotel 𝒜𝒜

🖐🖐 COMMENDED

20 Frognal, Hampstead, London
NW3 6AG
☎ (0171) 794 4483
Fax (0171) 435 9055
*Three minutes' walk from Finchley
Road underground, this elegant
Edwardian residence in Hampstead
boasts attractive bedrooms with full
facilities. BTA Spencer Trophy
runner-up.*
Bedrooms: 1 single, 18 double,
8 twin, 4 triple
Bathrooms: 31 en-suite

Bed & breakfast

per night:	£min	£max
Single	67.00	79.00
Double	85.00	99.00

Lunch available
Evening meal 1800 (last orders
2300)
Cards accepted: Amex, Diners,
Mastercard, Visa

☎🖐🕭📞🖵📶🎱🛄⌣📺◐🖵📄🖵
🛆🌾🚲SP🖼T

Rilux House

🖐🖐

1 Lodge Road, London NW4 4DD
☎ (0181) 203 0933
Fax (0181) 203 6446
*High standard, all private facilities,
kitchenette and garden. Quiet. Close to
underground, buses, M1, 20 minutes
West End. Convenient for Wembley,
easy route to Heathrow, direct trains to
Gatwick and Luton airports. Close to
Middlesex University.*
Bedrooms: 1 twin
Bathrooms: 1 en-suite

Bed & breakfast

per night:	£min	£max
Single	30.00	35.00
Double	50.00	60.00

Half board per

person:	£min	£max
Daily	38.00	42.00

Parking for 1

☎🖐🛆🕭📞🖵📶🎱🛄🛆⌣🗞📺🖵
🛆❄🌾🚲ⁿ🛇SP T

Cavendish Guest House

🖐 APPROVED

24 Cavendish Road, London
NW6 7XP
☎ (0181) 451 3249
*In a quiet residential street, 5 minutes'
walk from Kilburn underground station,
15 minutes' travelling time to the West
End. Easy access to Wembley Stadium,
Heathrow, Gatwick. 10 minutes from
M1.*
Bedrooms: 4 single, 1 double, 1 twin,
2 triple
Bathrooms: 2 en-suite, 2 public

Bed & breakfast

per night:	£min	£max
Single	26.00	28.00
Double	40.00	46.00

Parking for 4

☎🕭📞🖵📶🎱🛄🖵🛆🌾🚲

Charlotte Guest House &
Restaurant 𝒜𝒜

Listed

221 West End Lane, West
Hampstead, London NW6 1XJ
☎ (0171) 794 6476
Fax (0171) 431 3584
*Rooms with private facilities.
Restaurant and coffee lounge. French
and German spoken. Guests staying at
least 7 nights each receive a free
London Travel Card for the period of
their stay. Next door to rail station and
200 metres to Underground. Access to
West End or City in 10 to 15 minutes.*
Bedrooms: 12 single, 12 double,
12 twin
Bathrooms: 18 en-suite, 6 public

Bed & breakfast

per night:	£min	£max
Single	25.00	35.00
Double	35.00	45.00

Half board per

person:	£min	£max
Daily	30.00	45.00
Weekly	210.00	335.00

Lunch available
Evening meal 1800 (last orders
2200)
Cards accepted: Amex

☎🖐🛆🖵📶🎱🛄⌣🗞📺🖵🛆🌾🚲SP T

LONDON NW6

Continued

Dawson House Hotel ⋀

72 Canfield Gardens, London
NW6 3ED
☎ (0171) 624 0079 & 624 6525
Fax (0171) 372 3469

A truly charming Victorian house, lovingly restored and tastefully decorated, set within its own gardens. The hotel typifies the great Victorian town houses of the past, yet offers every modern amenity, ensuring that guests enjoy a relaxing and memorable stay.
Bedrooms: 6 single, 5 double, 1 twin, 2 triple, 1 family room
Suites available
Bathrooms: 15 en-suite, 2 public
Bed & breakfast

per night:	£min	£max
Single	35.00	35.00
Double	52.00	52.00

Cards accepted: Mastercard, Visa, Switch/Delta

🐕♿&📞📧💻👁🗝UL✂📺◑ ▥ 🖼♨✳🚗 OAP ↘ SP T

LONDON NW10

J and T Guest House

Listed COMMENDED

98 Park Avenue North, Willesden
Green, London NW10 1JY
☎ (0181) 452 4085
Fax (0181) 450 2503
Small guesthouse in north west London close to underground. Easy access to Wembley Stadium complex. 5 minutes from M1.
Bedrooms: 1 single, 1 double, 3 twin, 1 triple
Bathrooms: 6 en-suite
Bed & breakfast

per night:	£min	£max
Single	30.00	35.00
Double	42.00	54.00

Parking for 2
Cards accepted: Mastercard, Visa, Switch/Delta

🐕♿&📞📧💻👁🗝UL ▥ 🖼✳🚗 T

You are advised to confirm
your booking in writing.

LONDON SE1

Novotel London Waterloo ⋀

👑👑👑 COMMENDED

113 Lambeth Road, London SE1 7LS
☎ (0171) 793 1010
Fax (0171) 793 0202
CR Novotel

Three minutes from Waterloo Station by car. Conveniently located opposite Houses of Parliament and Big Ben. Good transport links. Air conditioned rooms with mini-bar, hair dryers.
Bedrooms: 187 double
Suites available
Bathrooms: 187 en-suite
Bed & breakfast

per night:	£min	£max
Single	109.00	115.00
Double	129.00	136.00

Lunch available
Evening meal 1900 (last orders 0000)
Parking for 46
Cards accepted: Amex, Diners, Mastercard, Visa, Switch/Delta

🐕&📞📧💻👁🗝🖐S✂📺◑▥ ⊜ ▤🍴40🥤🍽♨🚗↘SP T

LONDON SE3

Bardon Lodge Hotel

👑👑👑 COMMENDED

15-17 Stratheden Road, Blackheath,
London SE3 7TH
☎ (0181) 853 4051
Fax (0181) 858 7357
CR The Independents/Minotel
Within walking distance of Greenwich Park, the Observatory and Blackheath village. One minute's drive from the A2 and three quarters of a mile from the Millennium site.
Bedrooms: 13 single, 11 double, 3 twin, 1 triple, 3 family rooms
Bathrooms: 27 en-suite, 2 public, 4 private showers
Bed & breakfast

per night:	£min	£max
Single	60.00	75.00
Double	80.00	100.00

Evening meal 1900 (last orders 2130)
Parking for 32
Cards accepted: Amex, Diners, Mastercard, Visa, Switch/Delta

🐕♿&📞📧💻👁🗝🖐S🖼📺◑▥◐ ▤🍴40♨↘SP T

Clarendon Hotel ⋀

👑👑👑 APPROVED

8-16 Montpelier Row, Blackheath,
London SE3 0RW
☎ (0181) 318 4321
Fax (0181) 318 4378
Facing the heath and 22 minutes by train from central London. 10 minutes' walk from Greenwich, 5 minutes' walk from Greenwich Royal Park.
Bedrooms: 44 single, 54 double, 69 twin, 24 triple, 2 family rooms
Suites available
Bathrooms: 160 en-suite, 4 private, 14 public
Bed & breakfast

per night:	£min	£max
Single	47.50	80.00
Double	65.00	130.00

Half board per person:	£min	£max
Daily	59.45	91.95

Lunch available
Evening meal 1830 (last orders 2145)
Parking for 80
Cards accepted: Amex, Diners, Mastercard, Visa, Switch/Delta

🐕♿&📞💻👁🗝🖐S✂🖼📺◑ ▥📖♨▤🍴200✳↘SP🏠 T ®

LONDON SE9

Meadow Croft Lodge ⋀

👑 COMMENDED

96-98 Southwood Road, New
Eltham, London SE9 3QS
☎ (0181) 859 1488
Fax (0181) 859 1488
Between A2 and A20, near New Eltham station with easy access to London. Warm and friendly atmosphere. TV in rooms. British Tourist Authority London B&B award 1990.
Bedrooms: 4 single, 3 double, 9 twin, 1 family room
Bathrooms: 1 private, 4 public, 9 private showers
Bed & breakfast

per night:	£min	£max
Single	20.00	27.00
Double	38.50	44.00

Parking for 9
Cards accepted: Amex, Mastercard, Visa

🐕♿💻👁🗝UL✂🖼📺▥🖼♨✳🍴

Weston House

👑 APPROVED

8 Eltham Green, Eltham, London
SE9 5LB
☎ (0181) 850 5191
Fax (0181) 850 0030
Recently refurbished, friendly, comfortable hotel in Greenwich conservation area close to National

Maritime Museum. 20 minutes from central London, convenient for A2, M20 and A205.
Bedrooms: 3 single, 2 double, 3 twin, 1 triple, 1 family room
Bathrooms: 4 en-suite, 1 public, 4 private showers

Bed & breakfast

per night:	£min	£max
Single	30.00	30.00
Double	40.00	45.00

Parking for 6
Cards accepted: Mastercard, Visa, Switch/Delta

LONDON SE22

Bedknobs 🏔

Listed COMMENDED

58 Glengarry Road, East Dulwich, London SE22 8QD
☎ (0181) 299 2004
Fax (0181) 693 5611
Carefully restored Victorian family-run house offering many home comforts, excellent service and a warm welcome. Past winner of BTA London B&B Award.
Bedrooms: 1 double, 2 twin
Bathrooms: 2 public

Bed & breakfast

per night:	£min	£max
Single	25.00	40.00
Double	45.00	60.00

Cards accepted: Mastercard, Visa, Switch/Delta

LONDON SE27

The White House

Listed APPROVED

242 Norwood Road, West Norwood, London SE27 9AW
☎ (0181) 670 3607 & 761 8892
Fax (0181) 670 6440
Listed Georgian house with forecourt parking, on main road. Buses and trains to the city and 15 minutes by train to

Wimbledon. Close to Crystal Palace National Sports Centre.
Bedrooms: 2 single, 1 family room
Bathrooms: 3 en-suite, 1 public

Bed & breakfast

per night:	£min	£max
Single	16.00	20.00
Double	26.00	30.00

Parking for 3

LONDON SW1

Airways Hotel, NationLodge Ltd 🏔

Listed APPROVED

29-31 St George's Drive, Victoria, London SW1V 4DG
☎ (0171) 834 0205
Fax (0171) 932 0007

Within walking distance of Buckingham Palace and Westminster Abbey. Convenient for Harrods and theatreland. Friendly personal service. Full English breakfast.
Bedrooms: 8 single, 9 double, 11 twin, 5 triple, 5 family rooms
Bathrooms: 38 en-suite, 1 public

Bed & breakfast

per night:	£min	£max
Single	40.00	55.00
Double	45.00	69.00

Cards accepted: Amex, Diners, Mastercard, Visa, Switch/Delta

Please check prices and other details at the time of booking.

Blair Victoria 🏔

Listed APPROVED

78-82 Warwick Way, London SW1V 1RZ
☎ (0171) 828 8603 & (0468) 660 098
Fax (0171) 976 6536
Close to Victoria station, behind a period facade, the hotel offers comfort, service and interior-decorated accommodation.
Bedrooms: 9 single, 10 double, 9 twin, 4 triple, 1 family room
Bathrooms: 33 en-suite

Bed & breakfast

per night:	£min	£max
Single	54.00	59.00
Double	69.00	80.00

Cards accepted: Amex, Diners, Mastercard, Visa

Carlton Hotel 🏔

Listed APPROVED

90 Belgrave Road, Victoria, London SW1V 2BJ
☎ (0171) 976 6634 & 932 0913
Fax (0171) 821 8020
Small, friendly bed and breakfast near Victoria station and within walking distance of famous landmarks such as Buckingham Palace, Trafalgar Square and Piccadilly Circus.
Bedrooms: 4 single, 5 double, 2 twin, 6 triple
Bathrooms: 11 en-suite, 1 public, 1 private shower

Bed & breakfast

per night:	£min	£max
Single	35.00	39.00
Double	45.00	49.00

Cards accepted: Amex, Mastercard, Visa, Switch/Delta

LONDON SW1

Continued

Caswell Hotel **M**

Listed APPROVED

25 Gloucester Street, London
SW1V 2DB
☎ (0171) 834 6345
Pleasant, family-run hotel, near Victoria coach and rail stations, yet in a quiet location.
Bedrooms: 1 single, 6 double, 6 twin, 3 triple, 2 family rooms
Bathrooms: 7 en-suite, 5 public

Bed & breakfast per night:	£min	£max
Single	30.00	55.00
Double	42.00	70.00

Cards accepted: Mastercard, Visa, Switch/Delta

Dolphin Square Hotel **M**

≋≋≋≋ COMMENDED

Dolphin Square, London SW1V 3LX
☎ (0171) 834 3800
Fax (0171) 798 8735
Email: dolphin-square-hotel
@Compuserve.com
Ⓒ Grand Heritage

An all-suite hotel/apartment complex, with private gardens, in central London. Extensive leisure facilities include own sports and health club with swimming pool, gym and squash.
Bedrooms: 19 single, 95 double, 35 twin, 2 triple
Bathrooms: 151 en-suite

Bed & breakfast per night:	£min	£max
Single	100.00	120.00
Double	140.00	200.00

Half board per person:	£min	£max
Daily	115.00	160.00
Weekly	805.00	1120.00

Lunch available
Evening meal 1800 (last orders 2230)
Parking for 200
Cards accepted: Amex, Diners, Mastercard, Visa, Switch/Delta

Dover Hotel **M**

Listed APPROVED

44 Belgrave Road, London
SW1V 1RG
☎ (0171) 821 9085
Fax (0171) 834 6425
Small friendly bed and breakfast hotel with easy access to all major attractions and 3 minutes from Victoria rail and coach stations.
Bedrooms: 4 single, 9 double, 7 twin, 9 triple, 4 family rooms
Bathrooms: 29 en-suite, 1 public, 4 private showers

Bed & breakfast per night:	£min	£max
Single	40.00	50.00
Double	50.00	65.00

Cards accepted: Amex, Diners, Mastercard, Visa, Switch/Delta

Elizabeth Hotel **M**

≋ COMMENDED

37 Eccleston Square, Victoria,
London SW1V 1PB
☎ (0171) 828 6812

Friendly, quiet hotel overlooking magnificent gardens of stately residential square (circa 1835), close to Belgravia yet within 5 minutes' walk of Victoria. Free colour brochure.
Bedrooms: 6 single, 5 double, 4 twin, 16 triple, 7 family rooms
Bathrooms: 35 en-suite, 2 public

Bed & breakfast per night:	£min	£max
Single	40.00	55.00
Double	62.00	80.00

Ad See display advertisement on page 29

Knightsbridge Green Hotel **M**

≋≋ HIGHLY COMMENDED

159 Knightsbridge, London
SW1X 7PD
☎ (0171) 584 6274
Fax (0171) 225 1635
Email: theKGHotel@aol.com
Small family-owned and run hotel close to Harrods, offering spacious accommodation at competitive rates.
Bedrooms: 7 single, 3 double, 5 twin, 12 triple
Suites available
Bathrooms: 27 en-suite

Bed & breakfast per night:	£min	£max
Single	90.00	100.00
Double	130.00	

Half board per person:	£min	£max
Daily	99.50	164.50
Weekly	696.50	1151.50

Cards accepted: Amex, Diners, Mastercard, Visa

Luna-Simone Hotel **M**

Listed APPROVED

47 Belgrave Road, London
SW1V 2BB
☎ (0171) 834 5897
Fax (0171) 828 2474
Friendly, good value, bed and breakfast hotel. Within easy walking distance of Victoria rail, underground and coach stations. Opposite bus stop.
Bedrooms: 3 single, 11 double, 11 twin, 10 triple
Bathrooms: 19 en-suite, 4 public, 5 private showers

Bed & breakfast per night:	£min	£max
Single	25.00	30.00
Double	40.00	65.00

Cards accepted: Mastercard, Visa

Melbourne House **M**

Listed COMMENDED

79 Belgrave Road, London
SW1V 2BG
☎ (0171) 828 3516
Fax (0171) 828 7120
Family-run bed and breakfast. All rooms en-suite with tea and coffee facilities, colour TV. Good value. Book early.
Bedrooms: 2 single, 5 double, 5 twin, 1 triple, 1 family room
Suites available
Bathrooms: 14 en-suite

Bed & breakfast per night:	£min	£max
Single	40.00	45.00
Double	55.00	68.00

Cards accepted: Mastercard, Visa

Melita House Hotel ⚑

Listed APPROVED

35 Charlwood Street, London
SW1V 2DU
☎ (0171) 828 0471 & 834 1387
Fax (0171) 932 0988
Email: melita@compuserve.com
Family-run, budget B & B (full English breakfast), close to Victoria station. Warm, friendly and with extensive facilities.
Bedrooms: 6 single, 5 double, 5 twin, 1 triple, 2 family rooms
Bathrooms: 11 en-suite, 2 private, 1 public, 4 private showers

Bed & breakfast per night:

	£min	£max
Single	30.00	42.00
Double	45.00	52.00

Cards accepted: Amex, Mastercard, Visa, Switch/Delta

Vegas Hotel ⚑

Listed APPROVED

104 Warwick Way, London
SW1V 1SD
☎ (0171) 834 0082
Fax (0171) 834 5623
Close to Victoria coach and underground stations and 15 minutes from Buckingham Palace. Satellite colour TV, telephone, radio, alarm clock in all rooms.
Bedrooms: 1 single, 3 double, 9 twin
Bathrooms: 11 en-suite, 1 public, 2 private showers

Bed & breakfast per night:

	£min	£max
Single	40.00	49.50
Double	49.50	69.00

Cards accepted: Amex, Diners, Mastercard, Visa, Switch/Delta

Windermere Hotel ⚑

COMMENDED

142-144 Warwick Way, Victoria, London SW1V 4JE
☎ (0171) 834 5163 & 834 5480
Fax (0171) 630 8831
Email: 100773.1171
@compuserve.com
BTA Trophy winner. Small, friendly hotel with well-equipped bedrooms and a cosy lounge. English breakfast and dinner are served in the elegant licensed restaurant.
Bedrooms: 3 single, 11 double, 5 twin, 1 triple, 3 family rooms
Bathrooms: 19 en-suite, 2 public

Bed & breakfast per night:

	£min	£max
Single	49.00	67.00
Double	59.00	92.00

Half board per person:

	£min	£max
Daily	40.00	56.50

Evening meal 1800 (last orders 2130)
Cards accepted: Amex, Mastercard, Visa, Switch/Delta

Blair House Hotel ⚑

APPROVED

34 Draycott Place, London
SW3 2SA
☎ (0171) 581 2323 & 225 0771
Fax (0171) 823 7752
Homely hotel in a quiet, elegant street, close to Harrods and museums.
Bedrooms: 1 single, 4 double, 6 twin
Bathrooms: 11 en-suite, 1 public

Bed & breakfast per night:

	£min	£max
Single	70.00	85.00
Double	90.00	115.00

Cards accepted: Amex, Diners, Mastercard, Visa, Switch/Delta

Windmill on the Common ⚑

HIGHLY COMMENDED

Southside, Clapham Common, London SW4 9DE
☎ (0181) 673 4578
Fax (0181) 675 1486
Well-appointed bedrooms overlooking Clapham Common. A la carte/table d'hote restaurant and traditional busy Youngs pub serving good bar food. Easy access into central London (underground station 5 minutes' walk from hotel).
Bedrooms: 20 double, 9 twin
Bathrooms: 29 en-suite

Bed & breakfast per night:

	£min	£max
Single	70.00	90.00
Double	80.00	115.00

Lunch available
Evening meal 1900 (last orders 2200)
Parking for 30
Cards accepted: Amex, Diners, Mastercard, Visa, Switch/Delta

For ideas on places to visit refer to the introduction at the beginning of this section.

Amsterdam Hotel ⚑

Listed COMMENDED

7 Trebovir Road, London SW5 9LS
☎ (0171) 370 5084
Fax (0171) 244 7608
Inter Europe
Comfortable, attractively furnished rooms all with private bathroom, colour TV and direct-dial telephone.
Bedrooms: 6 single, 6 double, 4 twin, 2 triple, 2 family rooms
Bathrooms: 20 en-suite, 1 public

Bed & breakfast per night:

	£min	£max
Single	65.00	84.00
Double	80.00	95.00

Cards accepted: Amex, Diners, Mastercard, Visa

Beaver Hotel ⚑

APPROVED

57-59 Philbeach Gardens, London SW5 9ED
☎ (0171) 373 4553
Fax (0171) 373 4555
In a quiet, tree-lined crescent of late Victorian terraced houses, close to Earl's Court Exhibition Centre and 10 minutes from the West End.
Bedrooms: 17 single, 6 double, 10 twin, 4 triple
Bathrooms: 24 en-suite, 5 public

Bed & breakfast per night:

	£min	£max
Single	30.00	50.00
Double		70.00

Parking for 23
Cards accepted: Amex, Diners, Mastercard, Visa

Hogarth Hotel

COMMENDED

33 Hogarth Road, Kensington, London SW5 0QQ
☎ (0171) 370 6831
Fax (0171) 373 6179
Best Western
Modern hotel near Earl's Court within walking distance of Olympia and Earl's Court Exhibition Centres. All en-suite designer bedrooms are well-equipped and have benefited from a recent refurbishment.
Bedrooms: 7 single, 27 double, 50 twin, 1 triple
Bathrooms: 85 en-suite

Bed & breakfast per night:

	£min	£max
Single	93.50	103.50
Double	117.00	137.00

Continued ▶

LONDON SW5
Continued

Half board per person:

	£min	£max
Daily	115.00	125.00

Lunch available
Evening meal 1800 (last orders 2130)
Parking for 18
Cards accepted: Amex, Diners, Mastercard, Visa, Switch/Delta

🐕🚭📞🖃🖵⬇🖊🅂✂⬤⬆🛏🖫 ⏢50 ⬧ SP T

Lord Jim Hotel ⋀
Listed

23-25 Penywern Road, London
SW5 9TT
☎ (0171) 370 6071 & 0956 238277
Fax (0171) 373 8919
Budget-priced, well-serviced bed and breakfast, ideally situated for Earl's Court and Olympia exhibition halls. Convenient for museums, city, and Heathrow and Gatwick airports (via Victoria).
Bedrooms: 8 single, 6 double, 5 twin, 9 triple, 7 family rooms
Bathrooms: 11 en-suite, 6 public, 3 private showers

Bed & breakfast per night:

	£min	£max
Single	20.00	48.00
Double	30.00	52.00

Cards accepted: Amex, Diners, Mastercard, Visa

🐕🚭📞🖃🖵⬇ UL 🏋 TV ◑ ⬆ 🛏 🖂 ✻🐾⬧ SP T

Merlyn Court Hotel ⋀
👁️👁️

2 Barkston Gardens, London
SW5 0EN
☎ (0171) 370 1640
Fax (0171) 370 4986

Well-established, family-run, good value hotel in quiet Edwardian square, close to Earl's Court and Olympia. Direct underground link to Heathrow, the West End and rail stations. Car park nearby.
Bedrooms: 4 single, 4 double, 4 twin, 2 triple, 3 family rooms
Bathrooms: 11 en-suite, 6 public, 1 private shower

Bed & breakfast per night:

	£min	£max
Single	28.00	50.00
Double	45.00	60.00

Cards accepted: Mastercard, Visa, Switch/Delta

🐕🚭📞🖃🖵⬇ UL ✂ 🏋 TV 🖂 🖂 OAP ⬧ SP T

Mowbray Court Hotel ⋀
Listed **APPROVED**

28-32 Penywern Road, Earl's Court,
London SW5 9SU
☎ (0171) 370 2316 & 370 3690
Fax (0171) 370 5693
Tourist class hotel near Earl's Court Exhibition Centre.
Bedrooms: 30 single, 15 double, 15 twin, 20 triple, 8 family rooms
Bathrooms: 72 en-suite, 8 public

Bed & breakfast per night:

	£min	£max
Single	40.00	52.00
Double	52.00	62.00

Cards accepted: Amex, Diners, Mastercard, Visa, Switch/Delta

🐕🚭📞🖃🖵⬇✂🏋 TV ◑ ⬆ 🛏 🖂🐾⬧ SP T

ENQUIRY COUPONS

To help you obtain further information about advertisers featured in this guide you will find enquiry coupons at the back. Send these directly to the establishments in which you are interested. Remember to complete both sides of the coupon.

Rasool Court Hotel ♙

`Listed` `APPROVED`

19-21 Penywern Road, Earl's Court,
London SW5 9TT
☎ (0171) 373 8900 & 373 4893
Fax (0171) 244 6835
Email: younis@rasool.demon.co.uk
*Located near Earl's Court underground
station. Few minutes' tube journey to
the West End and direct route to
Heathrow Airport. All rooms have
colour TV and direct-dial telephone.*
Bedrooms: 27 single, 15 double,
7 twin, 8 triple
Bathrooms: 20 en-suite, 4 public,
25 private showers
Bed & breakfast

per night:	£min	£max
Single	29.00	35.00
Double	40.00	46.00

Cards accepted: Amex, Diners,
Mastercard, Visa, Switch/Delta
🛏🕔⑤📞🖵🗐UL🎱⊘◐⬆🔟🛬✗
`Ad` See display advertisement on
page 14

Swallow International Hotel ♙

`👑👑👑👑` `COMMENDED`

Cromwell Road, London SW5 0TH
☎ (0171) 973 1000
Fax (0171) 244 8194
ⓒ Swallow
*Bright modern hotel offering an
exclusive leisure club. Near Earl's Court
and Olympia Exhibition Halls,
fashionable Knightsbridge and
Kensington's parks and museums.
Short break packages available.*
Bedrooms: 28 single, 131 double,
226 twin, 36 triple
Suites available
Bathrooms: 421 en-suite
Bed & breakfast

per night:	£min	£max
Single	138.00	
Double	166.00	

Lunch available
Evening meal 1800 (last orders
2345)
Parking for 70
Cards accepted: Amex, Diners,
Mastercard, Visa
🛏🕔🍴📞🖵🌂🔌🕯⑤✂◐⬆💻
⑧🖊🏧220🍴✗🏌🚭SP🔟

Swiss House Hotel ♙

`Listed` `COMMENDED`

171 Old Brompton Road, London
SW5 0AN
☎ (0171) 373 2769 & 373 9383
Fax (0171) 373 4983
Email: recep@swiss-hh.demon.co.uk

*High quality budget priced hotel,
conveniently situated near London
museums, shopping/exhibition centres.
Gloucester Road underground station is
within easy walking distance. Winner of
BTA award for best value B&B in
London.*
Bedrooms: 5 single, 5 double, 2 twin,
4 triple
Bathrooms: 15 en-suite, 1 public,
1 private shower
Bed & breakfast

per night:	£min	£max
Single	42.00	59.00
Double	75.00	75.00

Cards accepted: Amex, Diners,
Mastercard, Visa, Switch/Delta
🛏🕔⑤📞🖵🗐UL🎱✂◐🔟🛬⬆💻
🖊🌂🚗🟦`DAP`🚭SP🔟

Windsor House ♙

`Listed` `APPROVED`

12 Penywern Road, London
SW5 9ST
☎ (0171) 373 9087
Fax (0171) 385 2417

*Budget-priced bed and breakfast
establishment in Earl's Court. Easily
reached from airports and motorway.
The West End is minutes away by
underground. NCP parking.*
Bedrooms: 2 single, 4 double, 4 twin,
1 triple, 7 family rooms
Bathrooms: 10 en-suite, 6 public,
7 private showers
Bed & breakfast

per night:	£min	£max
Single	26.00	40.00
Double	34.00	50.00

🛏🕔📞🖵UL⑤🎱◐💻🖊🌂`DAP`
🚭SP🔟
`Ad` See display advertisement on
page 32

York House Hotel ♙

`👑` `APPROVED`

27-28 Philbeach Gardens, London
SW5 9EA
☎ (0171) 373 7519 & 373 7579
Fax (0171) 370 4641
*Conveniently located close to Earl's
Court and Olympia exhibition centres
and the West End. Underground direct
to Heathrow Airport.*
Bedrooms: 16 single, 3 double,
3 twin, 2 triple, 3 family rooms
Bathrooms: 1 en-suite, 6 public
Bed & breakfast

per night:	£min	£max
Single	29.00	
Double	47.00	

Cards accepted: Amex, Diners,
Mastercard, Visa
🛏🕔🍴📞🖵🔟❄✗SP🔟

LONDON SW7

Abcone Hotel ♙

`👑👑` `APPROVED`

10 Ashburn Gardens, London
SW7 4DG
☎ (0171) 460 3400
Fax (0171) 460 3444
Email: aliuk@compuserve.com.
*Close to Gloucester Road underground
and convenient for High Street
Kensington, Knightsbridge, Olympia,
Earl's Court, museums and Hyde Park.*
Bedrooms: 17 single, 15 double,
3 twin
Bathrooms: 28 en-suite, 4 public
Bed & breakfast

per night:	£min	£max
Single	40.00	79.00
Double	50.00	95.00

Half board per person:	£min	£max
Daily	35.00	89.00

Evening meal 1900 (last orders
2230)
Cards accepted: Amex, Diners,
Mastercard, Visa, Switch/Delta
🛏🕔1⑤📞🖵🗐⬆❗⑤🎱◐⬆💻
🖊✗🌂🚭SP🏨🔟

Five Sumner Place Hotel ♙

`Listed` `HIGHLY COMMENDED`

5 Sumner Place, South Kensington,
London SW7 3EE
☎ (0171) 584 7586
Fax (0171) 823 9962
Email: no.5@dial.pipex.com
*Recent winner of Best Small Hotel in
London Award. Situated in South
Kensington, the most fashionable area.
This family-owned and run hotel offers
first-class service and personal
attention.*
Bedrooms: 3 single, 5 double, 5 twin
Bathrooms: 13 en-suite, 1 public

Continued ▶

LONDON SW7

Continued

Bed & breakfast

per night:	£min	£max
Single	81.00	95.00
Double	105.00	135.00

Cards accepted: Amex, Mastercard, Visa

Hotel Number Sixteen ♏

HIGHLY COMMENDED

16 Sumner Place, London SW7 3EG
☎ (0171) 589 5232
Fax (0171) 584 8615
With atmosphere of a comfortable town house in very attractive street. Secluded award-winning gardens. Winner of the Spencer Trophy.
Bedrooms: 9 single, 23 double, 4 triple
Bathrooms: 32 en-suite, 2 private, 1 public, 1 private shower

Bed & breakfast

per night:	£min	£max
Single	80.00	115.00
Double	150.00	180.00

Cards accepted: Amex, Diners, Mastercard, Visa, Switch/Delta

LONDON SW11

Barclay Court Private Hotel ♏

APPROVED

12-14 Hafer Road, London SW11 1HF
☎ (0171) 228 5272
Fax (0171) 924 5431
Family-run establishment on main A3. Direct rail connection to Gatwick Airport and Victoria station from nearby Clapham Junction.
Bedrooms: 6 single, 3 double, 3 twin, 2 triple
Bathrooms: 1 en-suite, 3 public, 9 private showers

Bed & breakfast

per night:	£min	£max
Single	30.00	36.00
Double	40.00	48.00

Cards accepted: Amex, Mastercard, Visa

LONDON SW19

Compton Guest House

Listed

65 Compton Road, Wimbledon, London SW19 7QA
☎ (0181) 947 4488 & 879 3245
Fax (0181) 947 4488
Family-run guesthouse in pleasant, peaceful area, 5 minutes from Wimbledon station (British Rail and District Line). Easy access to the West End, central London, M1, M2, M3, M4 and M25. Quality rooms, with excellent service. About 12 minutes' walk to Wimbledon tennis courts.
Bedrooms: 2 single, 1 double, 2 twin, 1 triple, 2 family rooms
Bathrooms: 2 public

Bed & breakfast

per night:	£min	£max
Single	35.00	40.00
Double	48.00	66.00

Parking for 2

LONDON W1

The Berners Hotel ♏

HIGHLY COMMENDED

10 Berners Street, London W1A 3BE
☎ (0171) 636 1629
Fax (0171) 580 3972
Email: berners@berners.co.uk

Edwardian building restored to its original beauty and elegance, a few minutes' walk from Oxford Circus and Soho.
Bedrooms: 37 single, 135 double, 45 twin
Suites available
Bathrooms: 217 en-suite

Bed & breakfast

per night:	£min	£max
Single	165.00	315.00
Double	210.00	330.00

Lunch available
Evening meal 1730 (last orders 2230)
Cards accepted: Amex, Diners, Mastercard, Visa

Brown's Hotel ♏

HIGHLY COMMENDED

Albemarle Street and Dover Street, London W1X 4BP
☎ (0171) 493 6020
Fax (0171) 493 9381
Email: brownshotel
@UKbusiness.com
Ⓒⓡ Forte/Utell International

Situated in Mayfair, close to Bond Street, Royal Academy, Sotheby's, Brown's offers the perfect location to enjoy the best of British hospitality.
Bedrooms: 21 single, 51 double, 30 twin, 12 triple, 3 family rooms
Suites available
Bathrooms: 117 en-suite

Bed & breakfast

per night:	£min	£max
Single	240.00	
Double	268.00	

Lunch available
Evening meal 1800 (last orders 2200)
Cards accepted: Amex, Diners, Mastercard, Visa, Switch/Delta

The Edward Lear Hotel ♏

APPROVED

30 Seymour Street, Marble Arch, London W1H 5WD
☎ (0171) 402 5401
Fax (0171) 706 3766
Family-run Georgian town residence, once the home of Edward Lear, famous poet and painter, with informal but efficient atmosphere. In a central location, 1 minute from Oxford Street and Marble Arch.
Bedrooms: 13 single, 4 double, 10 twin, 2 triple, 2 family rooms
Bathrooms: 3 en-suite, 1 private, 6 public, 7 private showers

Bed & breakfast

per night:	£min	£max
Single	39.50	72.00
Double	60.00	85.00

Cards accepted: Diners, Mastercard, Visa, Switch/Delta

The Leonard ♏

HIGHLY COMMENDED

15 Seymour Street, London
W1H 5AA
☎ (0171) 935 2010
Fax (0171) 935 6700
⊙ Grand Heritage
*Four 18th C town houses, elegantly
restored. Accommodation is mainly
suites, all with air conditioning and hi-fi
systems. 24-hour room service and
friendly staff.*
Bedrooms: 22 double, 1 triple,
3 family rooms
Suites available
Bathrooms: 26 en-suite

Bed & breakfast

per night:	£min	£max
Single	205.00	275.00
Double	205.00	275.00

Lunch available
Cards accepted: Amex, Diners,
Mastercard, Visa, Switch/Delta

🐎🛅📞🖃🖵💆🗑🗝🏸📺◐
🖩🖥⊛🏧🛗50🕏♂️🍴🚐 SP ♠️
T

Lincoln House Hotel ♏

COMMENDED

33 Gloucester Place, London
W1H 3PD
☎ (0171) 486 7630
Fax (0171) 486 0166
*Georgian hotel of distinctive character.
En-suite rooms with all modern
comforts. Superb location, competitively
priced, in the heart of London's West
End.*
Bedrooms: 6 single, 8 double, 4 twin,
3 triple, 1 family room
Bathrooms: 20 en-suite, 2 private,
2 public

Bed & breakfast

per night:	£min	£max
Single	59.00	69.00
Double	75.00	89.00

Cards accepted: Amex, Diners,
Mastercard, Visa, Switch/Delta

🐎🛅📞🖵💆🗑🗝🏸📺◐🚐🍴
🚐 SP ♠️ T

Marble Arch Inn ♏

Listed APPROVED

49-50 Upper Berkeley Street,
Marble Arch, London W1H 7PN
☎ (0171) 723 7888
Fax (0171) 723 6060
*Friendly hotel at Marble Arch, within
minutes of Hyde Park and Oxford
Street and within easy reach of other
major attractions.*
Bedrooms: 2 single, 8 double, 9 twin,
6 triple, 4 family rooms
Bathrooms: 25 en-suite, 2 public,
4 private showers

Bed & breakfast

per night:	£min	£max
Single	40.00	50.00
Double	50.00	65.00

Cards accepted: Amex, Diners,
Mastercard, Visa, Switch/Delta

🐎🛅📞🖃🖵💆🗑🗝UL🗝📺◐🖩
🖩🖥 DAP 🗝 SP T ⊛

The Park Lane Hotel ♏

HIGHLY COMMENDED

Piccadilly, London W1Y 8BX
☎ (0171) 499 6321
Fax (0171) 499 1965
*On Piccadilly overlooking Green Park
towards Buckingham Palace, offering
good service and modern facilities.*
Bedrooms: 50 single, 100 double,
100 twin, 20 triple, 40 family rooms
Suites available
Bathrooms: 310 en-suite

Bed & breakfast

per night:	£min	£max
Single	222.63	769.98
Double	266.98	786.98

Lunch available
Evening meal 1900 (last orders
2300)
Parking for 150
Cards accepted: Amex, Diners,
Mastercard, Visa, Switch/Delta

🐎📞🖃🖵🍴🗑S🗝🗝◐🖩🖥⊛
🏧🛗500🕏♂️ DAP 🗝 SP ♠️ T

Hotel La Place ♏

COMMENDED

17 Nottingham Place, London
W1M 3FF
☎ (0171) 486 2323
Fax (0171) 486 4335

*Small, friendly and safe (especially for
single women) townhouse hotel with a
bar (open 24 hours) and a restaurant.*
Bedrooms: 7 single, 6 double, 3 twin,
2 triple, 3 family rooms
Suites available
Bathrooms: 21 en-suite

Bed & breakfast

per night:	£min	£max
Single	79.00	150.00
Double	95.00	160.00

Lunch available
Evening meal 1800 (last orders
2030)
Cards accepted: Amex, Diners,
Mastercard, Visa, Switch/Delta

🐎🛅📞🖃🖵💆🗑🍴S🗝🗝📺◐
🖩🖥🏧🛗8🕏🍴🚐 DAP 🗝 SP ♠️ T

Abbey Court Hotel ♏

Listed

174 Sussex Gardens, London
W2 1TP
☎ (0171) 402 0704
Fax (0171) 262 2055
*Central London hotel, reasonable prices.
Within walking distance of Lancaster
Gate, Paddington station and Hyde
Park. Easy access to tourist attractions
and shopping. Car parking at modest
charge.*
Bedrooms: 14 single, 24 double,
7 twin, 10 triple, 2 family rooms
Bathrooms: 57 en-suite

Bed & breakfast

per night:	£min	£max
Single	29.00	39.00
Double	39.00	58.00

Parking for 20
Cards accepted: Amex, Mastercard,
Visa, Switch/Delta

🐎🛅📞🖃🖵UL🗝🗝📺◐🖩🖥🚐
♠️ DAP 🗝 SP T

Ad See display advertisement on
page 36

Albro House Hotel ♏

APPROVED

155 Sussex Gardens, London
W2 2RY
☎ (0171) 724 2931 & 706 8153
Fax (0171) 262 2278
*Ideally located in pleasant area near
public transport. Nice rooms, all
en-suite. English breakfast. Languages
spoken. Friendly and safe. Some
parking available.*
Bedrooms: 2 single, 6 double, 5 twin,
4 triple, 3 family rooms
Suites available
Bathrooms: 17 en-suite, 1 public

Bed & breakfast

per night:	£min	£max
Single	38.00	52.00
Double	48.00	68.00

Parking for 1
Cards accepted: Amex, Diners,
Mastercard, Visa

🐎🛅📞🖵💆🗑UL🗝🗝📺🖩🖥🚐♠️
🚐 DAP 🗝 SP T

Please check prices and other
details at the time of booking.

Establishments should be
open throughout the year,
unless otherwise stated.

ACCOMMODATION

Allandale Hotel **M**

Listed **APPROVED**

3 Devonshire Terrace, Lancaster Gate, London W2 3DN
☎ (0171) 723 8311 & 723 7807
Fax (0181) 905 4891

Small, select family hotel will impress you with its careful service. Full English breakfast. All bedrooms have private shower and toilet, colour TV and central heating. Close to Hyde Park, West End, Lancaster Gate/Paddington stations.
Bedrooms: 2 single, 8 double, 5 twin, 2 triple, 3 family rooms
Bathrooms: 18 en-suite, 1 public
Bed & breakfast

per night:	£min	£max
Single	38.00	42.00
Double	47.00	55.00

Cards accepted: Amex, Diners, Mastercard, Visa, Switch/Delta

Ashley Hotel

Listed **APPROVED**

15 Norfolk Square, London W2 1RU
☎ (0171) 723 3375
Fax (0171) 723 0173
Very popular town house hotel in quiet garden square. Quality rooms with private showers and toilets, TV, tea-making facilities. Owned and managed by the same Welsh family for 30 years.
Bedrooms: 18 single, 16 double, 6 twin, 8 triple, 5 family rooms
Bathrooms: 41 en-suite, 7 public
Bed & breakfast

per night:	£min	£max
Single	31.00	43.00
Double	63.00	66.00

Cards accepted: Mastercard, Visa, Switch/Delta

Beverley House Hotel **M**

COMMENDED

142 Sussex Gardens, London W2 1UB
☎ (0171) 723 3380
Fax (0171) 262 0324
Refurbished bed and breakfast hotel, serving traditional English breakfast and offering high standards at low prices. Close to Paddington station, Hyde Park and museums.

Bedrooms: 6 single, 5 double, 6 twin, 6 triple
Bathrooms: 23 en-suite
Bed & breakfast

per night:	£min	£max
Single	40.00	55.00
Double	49.00	73.00

Evening meal 1800 (last orders 2200)
Parking for 2
Cards accepted: Amex, Diners, Mastercard, Visa

Duke of Leinster **M**

Listed

34 Queen's Gardens, London W2 3AA
☎ (0171) 258 0079 & 258 1839
Fax (0171) 262 0741
Centrally located near Hyde Park, 10 minutes' walk from Queensway underground. Former residence of the Duke of Leinster. Minimum prices shown are winter rates.
Bedrooms: 4 single, 21 double, 9 twin, 8 triple
Bathrooms: 42 en-suite
Bed & breakfast

per night:	£min	£max
Single	49.00	54.00
Double	69.00	74.00

Cards accepted: Amex, Diners, Mastercard, Visa

Dylan Hotel **M**

Listed

14 Devonshire Terrace, Lancaster Gate, London W2 3DW
☎ (0171) 723 3280
Fax (0171) 402 2443
Small hotel in central location, 4 minutes from Paddington and Lancaster Gate underground stations. Marble Arch, Hyde Park and Oxford Street close by. Not just a hotel, a home from home.
Bedrooms: 4 single, 4 double, 7 twin, 3 triple
Bathrooms: 7 private, 3 public, 4 private showers
Bed & breakfast

per night:	£min	£max
Single	30.00	42.00
Double	50.00	65.00

Cards accepted: Amex, Diners, Mastercard, Visa, Switch/Delta

Garden Court Hotel **M**

30-31 Kensington Gardens Square, London W2 4BG
☎ (0171) 229 2553
Fax (0171) 727 2749
Friendly, family-run town house hotel established in 1954, in a quiet Victorian garden square in central London. Convenient for all transport. All rooms have TV, telephone and hairdryers.
Bedrooms: 13 single, 7 double, 6 twin, 6 triple, 2 family rooms
Bathrooms: 16 en-suite, 5 public, 1 private shower
Bed & breakfast

per night:	£min	£max
Single	34.00	48.00
Double	50.00	75.00

Cards accepted: Mastercard, Visa

Hyde Park Rooms Hotel **M**

Listed

137 Sussex Gardens, Hyde Park, London W2 2RX
☎ (0171) 723 0225 & 723 0965
Small centrally located private hotel with personal service. Clean, comfortable and friendly. Within walking distance of Hyde Park and Kensington Gardens. Car parking available.
Bedrooms: 5 single, 6 double, 2 twin, 1 triple
Bathrooms: 7 en-suite, 2 private, 2 public
Bed & breakfast

per night:	£min	£max
Single	26.00	38.00
Double	38.00	50.00

Parking for 3
Cards accepted: Amex, Diners, Mastercard, Visa, Switch/Delta

Kensington Gardens Hotel

HIGHLY COMMENDED

9 Kensington Gardens Square, London W2 4BH
☎ (0171) 221 7790
Fax (0171) 792 8612
Beautifully refurbished Victorian building, centrally situated close to Bayswater and Queensway underground stations. Easy access to airports and British Rail stations.
Bedrooms: 8 single, 5 double, 2 twin, 2 triple
Bathrooms: 9 en-suite, 4 private, 4 private showers

Continued ▶

LONDON W2

Continued

Bed & breakfast
per night:

	£min	£max
Single	45.00	50.00
Double	70.00	75.00

Lunch available
Evening meal 1900 (last orders
2300)
Cards accepted: Amex, Diners,
Mastercard, Visa, Switch/Delta

🐴👶📞💷🖵♿🖎🚭🅂✂🏴🅣🄫⬚🖩
🛄🛪🕸 SP 🅣

London Guards Hotel ⋀

👑 COMMENDED

36-37 Lancaster Gate, London
W2 3NA
☎ (0171) 402 1101
Fax (0171) 262 2551
*Air conditioned and completely
refurbished hotel, opened in May 1997,
in a quiet residential area of Lancaster
Gate. Bar and coffee shop facilities.*
Bedrooms: 2 single, 13 double,
11 twin, 9 triple, 4 family rooms
Bathrooms: 39 en-suite
Bed & breakfast
per night:

	£min	£max
Single	95.00	105.00
Double	105.00	135.00

Lunch available
Evening meal 1900 (last orders
2100)
Cards accepted: Amex, Diners,
Mastercard, Visa, Switch/Delta

🐴👶📞💷🖵♿🖎🚭✂🏴🄍⬚🖩Ⓔ
🛄🛪🕸 SP 🅣

Nayland Hotel ⋀

👑 COMMENDED

132-134 Sussex Gardens, London
W2 1UB
☎ (0171) 723 4615
Fax (0171) 402 3292
*Centrally located, close to many
amenities and within walking distance
of Hyde Park and Oxford Street.
Quality you can afford.*
Bedrooms: 11 single, 8 double,
17 twin, 5 triple
Bathrooms: 41 en-suite
Bed & breakfast
per night:

	£min	£max
Single	46.00	62.00
Double	52.00	78.00

Evening meal 1800 (last orders
2100)
Parking for 5
Cards accepted: Amex, Diners,
Mastercard, Visa

🐴👶📞💷🖵♿🖎🚭🏴🅣🄍⬚🖩🛄
🛪🕸🏟🅣

Oxford Hotel ⋀

Listed

13-14 Craven Terrace, Paddington,
London W2 3QD
☎ (0171) 402 6860 & 0800 318798
Fax (0171) 706 4318
*Refurbished budget hotel, all rooms
with en-suite shower/toilet. Close to bus
routes and underground. Family rooms
available. All have microwave and
fridge.*
Bedrooms: 1 double, 8 twin, 9 family
rooms
Bathrooms: 18 en-suite, 1 public
Bed & breakfast
per night:

	£min	£max
Single	60.00	60.00
Double	65.00	65.00

Cards accepted: Amex, Diners,
Mastercard, Visa

🐴👶12👶📞💷♿🖎🚭Ⓤ🅛✂🏴🅣⬚🖩
🛄🛺 DAP 🕸 SP 🅣

Parkwood Hotel ⋀

👑 APPROVED

4 Stanhope Place, London W2 2HB
☎ (0171) 402 2241
Fax (0171) 402 1574
*Smart town house only 1 minute's walk
away from Oxford Street and Speakers'
Corner, Hyde Park.*
Bedrooms: 5 single, 2 double, 7 twin,
4 triple
Bathrooms: 12 en-suite, 2 public
Bed & breakfast
per night:

	£min	£max
Single	45.00	55.00
Double	59.00	65.00

Cards accepted: Mastercard, Visa

🐴👶📞💷🖵♿🖎🚭Ⓤ🅛✂🏴🅣⬚🖩
🛄🛺 DAP 🕸 SP

Prince William Hotel ⋀

Listed APPROVED

42-44 Gloucester Terrace, London
W2 3DA
☎ (0171) 724 7414
Fax (0171) 706 2411
*Central location in Paddington, close to
Hyde Park and Oxford Street. Clean,
comfortable accommodation, residents'
lounge, restaurant and bar. Secretarial
and fax services.*
Bedrooms: 23 single, 7 double,
11 twin, 2 triple
Bathrooms: 34 private, 2 public,
6 private showers
Bed & breakfast
per night:

	£min	£max
Single	39.00	55.00
Double	55.00	75.00

Evening meal 1730 (last orders
2230)
Cards accepted: Amex, Diners,
Mastercard, Visa, Switch/Delta

🐴👶📞💷🖵♿🖎🚭🅂🏴🅣⬚🖩🛄
DAP SP 🏟🅣

Rose Court Hotel ⋀

👑👑👑 APPROVED

1-3 Talbot Square, London W2 1TR
☎ (0171) 723 5128 & 723 8671
Fax (0171) 723 1855
*Privately-run Victorian town house in a
quiet garden square. Close to
Paddington and the West End.*
Bedrooms: 7 single, 11 double,
16 twin, 5 triple, 3 family rooms
Bathrooms: 41 en-suite, 1 public
Bed & breakfast
per night:

	£min	£max
Single	40.00	56.00
Double	48.00	70.00

Half board per
person:

	£min	£max
Daily	50.00	64.00
Weekly	325.00	380.00

Lunch available
Evening meal 1800 (last orders
2100)
Cards accepted: Amex, Diners,
Mastercard, Visa, Switch/Delta

🐴👶📞💷♿🖎🚭✂🏴🅣🄍⬚🖩🛄🛪
DAP SP 🅣

Royal Park Hotel ⋀

👑👑👑 APPROVED

2-5 Westbourne Terrace, London
W2 3UL
☎ (0171) 402 6187
Fax (0171) 224 9426
*Modernised hotel built in 1854.
Comfortable and well-placed for bus
and underground to the West End. Free
car parking available.*
Bedrooms: 8 single, 10 double,
35 twin, 8 triple, 2 family rooms
Bathrooms: 63 en-suite
Bed & breakfast
per night:

	£min	£max
Single	60.00	61.00
Double	78.00	80.00

Evening meal 1800 (last orders
2200)
Parking for 15
Cards accepted: Amex, Mastercard,
Visa, Switch/Delta

🐴👶👶📞💷🖵♿🖎🚭🅂🏴🅣🄍⬚🖩
🛄🛺 SP 🏟🅣

Please check prices and other
details at the time of booking.

Establishments should be
open throughout the year,
unless otherwise stated.

Ruddimans Hotel ♨

Listed APPROVED

160-162 Sussex Gardens, London
W2 1UD
☎ (0171) 723 1026 & 723 6715
Fax (0171) 262 2983
*Comfortable hotel close to West End
and London's attractions, offering
generous English breakfast and good
service at reasonable prices. Car park.*
Bedrooms: 8 single, 13 double,
6 twin, 11 triple, 3 family rooms
Bathrooms: 33 en-suite, 2 public

Bed & breakfast

per night:	£min	£max
Single	26.00	36.00
Double	42.00	50.00

Parking for 4
Cards accepted: Amex, Mastercard,
Visa, Switch/Delta

St David's and Norfolk Court Hotel ♨

Listed APPROVED

16 Norfolk Square, Hyde Park,
London W2 1RS
☎ (0171) 723 3856 & 723 4963
Fax (0171) 402 9061
*Small, friendly hotel in front of a quiet
garden square. Central location,
economical prices. Reckons to serve the
"best English breakfast" in London.*
Bedrooms: 14 single, 18 double,
14 twin, 12 triple
Bathrooms: 2 private, 16 public,
4 private showers

Bed & breakfast

per night:	£min	£max
Single	30.00	40.00
Double	46.00	56.00

Cards accepted: Amex, Diners,
Mastercard, Visa

Sass House Hotel ♨

Listed APPROVED

10-11 Craven Terrace, London
W2 3QD
☎ (0171) 262 2325
Fax (0171) 262 0889
*Budget accommodation, convenient for
central London, Hyde Park and West
End. Paddington and Lancaster Gate
underground stations nearby. Easy
access to tourist attractions.*
Bedrooms: 8 double, 7 twin, 8 triple
Bathrooms: 23 en-suite, 1 public

Bed & breakfast

per night:	£min	£max
Single	26.00	36.00
Double	35.00	54.00

Cards accepted: Amex, Mastercard,
Visa, Switch/Delta

Ad See display advertisement on
page 36

Springfield Hotel

Listed APPROVED

154 Sussex Gardens, London
W2 1UD
☎ (0171) 723 9898
Fax (0171) 723 0874
*Small hotel close to Hyde Park and
Marble Arch.*
Bedrooms: 2 single, 6 double, 6 twin,
6 triple
Bathrooms: 20 en-suite, 3 public

Bed & breakfast

per night:	£min	£max
Single	40.00	45.00
Double	50.00	55.00

Parking for 2
Cards accepted: Amex, Diners,
Mastercard, Visa, Switch/Delta

Westland Hotel ♨

👑👑👑👑 APPROVED

154 Bayswater Road, London
W2 4HP
☎ (0171) 229 9191
Fax (0171) 727 1054
CR The Independents
*Small, friendly hotel. Well located for
West End shopping, touring or relaxing
in a beautiful park. Your
home-from-home.*
Wheelchair access category 3♿
Bedrooms: 2 single, 6 double,
19 twin, 3 triple, 1 family room
Bathrooms: 31 en-suite

Bed & breakfast

per night:	£min	£max
Single	80.00	
Double	95.00	105.00

Half board per person:

	£min	£max
Daily	58.00	63.00

Lunch available
Evening meal 1830 (last orders
2230)
Parking for 9
Cards accepted: Amex, Diners,
Mastercard, Visa, Switch/Delta

Westpoint Hotel ♨

Listed

170-172 Sussex Gardens, London
W2 1TP
☎ (0171) 402 0281
Fax (0171) 224 9114
*Inexpensive accommodation in central
London. Close to Paddington and
Lancaster Gate underground stations.
Easy access to tourist attractions,
shopping and Hyde Park.*
Bedrooms: 12 single, 15 double,
16 twin, 14 triple, 6 family rooms
Bathrooms: 31 en-suite, 10 public,
9 private showers

Bed & breakfast

per night:	£min	£max
Single	28.00	38.00
Double	38.00	56.00

Parking for 15
Cards accepted: Amex, Mastercard,
Visa, Switch/Delta

Ad See display advertisement on
page 36

LONDON W3

Acton Grange Guest House ♨

Listed

317 Uxbridge Road, Acton, London
W3 9QU
☎ (0181) 992 0586
*Family-run, small, friendly
establishment. Ten minutes from
Heathrow Airport; excellent transport
facilities (central London 25 minutes).*
Bedrooms: 1 single, 3 double, 1 twin,
1 triple
Bathrooms: 2 public

Bed & breakfast

per night:	£min	£max
Single	22.00	22.00
Double	42.00	44.00

Parking for 2

Acton Park Hotel ♨

👑👑👑

116 The Vale, Acton, London
W3 7JT
☎ (0181) 743 9417
Fax (0181) 743 9417
*Small, friendly, family-run hotel, just off
the North Circular Road. Between
Heathrow and the West End,
overlooking parkland. Ample parking.*
Bedrooms: 7 single, 4 double, 8 twin,
2 triple
Bathrooms: 21 en-suite

Bed & breakfast

per night:	£min	£max
Single	47.00	50.00
Double	57.00	61.00

Lunch available
Evening meal 1800 (last orders
2200)
Parking for 15
Cards accepted: Amex, Diners,
Mastercard, Visa, Switch/Delta

LONDON W4

Chiswick Hotel ⋈

⚜⚜ COMMENDED

73 High Road, London W4 2LS
☎ (0181) 994 1712
Fax (0181) 742 2585

Large, tastefully converted Victorian hotel. Self-contained apartments available. Relaxed atmosphere. Close to Heathrow Airport and central London.
Bedrooms: 28 single, 11 double, 7 twin, 4 triple, 3 family rooms
Bathrooms: 53 en-suite, 2 public

Bed & breakfast per night:

	£min	£max
Single	70.00	75.00
Double	95.00	100.00

Evening meal 1800 (last orders 2100)
Parking for 20
Cards accepted: Amex, Diners, Mastercard, Visa, Switch/Delta

🛏🕭📞📠🖥📺⚓🚭🛈💲🕭📺◐🖥
🛎🍴✿🗡 SP T

LONDON W5

Abbey Lodge Hotel

⚜⚜ APPROVED

51 Grange Park, Ealing, London W5 3PR
☎ (0181) 567 7914
Fax (0181) 579 5350
All rooms en-suite and with remote-control colour TV. Complimentary hot drinks 24 hours a day. Very close to 3 underground lines.
Bedrooms: 10 single, 2 double, 1 twin, 2 triple, 1 family room
Bathrooms: 16 en-suite

Bed & breakfast per night:

	£min	£max
Single	35.00	40.00
Double	47.00	52.00

Cards accepted: Diners, Mastercard, Visa, Switch/Delta

🛏🕭📠 UL 🗡📺🖥🛎✿ DAP SP T

Creffield Lodge ⋈

Listed APPROVED

2-4 Creffield Road, Ealing, London W5 3HN
☎ (0181) 993 2284
Fax (0181) 992 7082
Victorian property on 3 floors, located in residential road, adjacent to and with use of all the facilities of the 150-bedroom Jarvis Carnarvon Hotel.

Bedrooms: 12 single, 7 double, 4 twin, 1 triple
Bathrooms: 13 en-suite, 4 public

Bed & breakfast per night:

	£min	£max
Single	40.00	65.00
Double	85.00	90.00

Lunch available
Evening meal 1830 (last orders 2130)
Parking for 20
Cards accepted: Amex, Diners, Mastercard, Visa, Switch/Delta

🛏🕭📞📠🖥⚓🚭🖥🗡 SP T

Grange Lodge Hotel

⚜⚜ APPROVED

48-50 Grange Road, Ealing, London W5 5BX
☎ (0181) 567 1049
Fax (0181) 579 5350
Quiet, comfortable hotel within a few hundred yards of the underground station. Midway between central London and Heathrow.
Bedrooms: 8 single, 2 double, 2 twin, 2 triple
Bathrooms: 9 en-suite, 2 public

Bed & breakfast per night:

	£min	£max
Single	35.00	40.00
Double	47.00	52.00

Parking for 8
Cards accepted: Diners, Mastercard, Visa, Switch/Delta

🛏🕭🖥 S 🗡📺🖥🛎✿ DAP SP T

LONDON W6

Dalmacia Hotel ⋈

Listed APPROVED

71 Shepherd's Bush Road, Hammersmith, London W6 7LS
☎ (0171) 603 2887 & 602 5701
Fax (0171) 602 9226

Family-run bed and breakfast within easy reach of the West End. All rooms en-suite with satellite TV, hairdryer, tea/coffee facilities and direct-dial telephone.
Bedrooms: 3 single, 6 double, 4 twin, 3 triple
Bathrooms: 16 en-suite

Bed & breakfast per night:

	£min	£max
Single	32.00	38.00
Double	52.00	60.00

Evening meal 1830 (last orders 2100)
Parking for 4

Cards accepted: Amex, Diners, Mastercard, Visa, Switch/Delta

🛏🕭📞📠🖥⚓🚭 UL 🛈 S 🗡🍴◐
🖥🛎✿🗡 DAP SP T

LONDON W7

Wellmeadow Lodge Hotel ⋈

⚜⚜ HIGHLY COMMENDED

24 Wellmeadow Road, London W7 2AL
☎ (0181) 567 7294
Fax (0181) 566 3468
Ⓡ Logis of GB

Charming establishment combining the highest hotel standards with the atmosphere of a private home. En-suite facilities, delicious breakfasts second to none with home-made items.
Bedrooms: 3 single, 4 double, 3 twin
Bathrooms: 10 en-suite

Bed & breakfast per night:

	£min	£max
Single	60.00	110.00
Double	80.00	120.00

Half board per person:

	£min	£max
Daily	77.00	130.00
Weekly	539.00	910.00

Lunch available
Evening meal 1800 (last orders 1900)
Cards accepted: Amex, Mastercard, Visa, Switch/Delta

🛏🕭📞📠🖥⚓🚭 UL 🖥 S 🗡🖥🛎
🍴✿🗡🐾🗡 SP

LONDON W8

Hotel Atlas-Apollo ⋈

⚜⚜ COMMENDED

18-30 Lexham Gardens, London W8 5JE
☎ (0171) 835 1155
Fax (0171) 370 4853
Ⓡ The Independents/Utell International

Friendly, long established hotel, situated close to Earl's Court and Olympia exhibition centres and the shopping areas of Knightsbridge and Kensington High Street.

Bedrooms: 26 single, 7 double,
44 twin, 14 triple
Bathrooms: 91 en-suite

Bed & breakfast

per night:	£min	£max
Single	60.00	65.00
Double	70.00	75.00

Cards accepted: Amex, Diners,
Mastercard, Visa, Switch/Delta

London Lodge Hotel 👐

136 Lexham Gardens, London
W8 6JE
☎ (0171) 244 8444
Fax (0171) 373 6661
*Attractive hotel ideally situated in a
quiet residential street in the heart of
Kensington. Perfectly placed for
business, shopping and seeing London.
Special weekday/weekend packages
available.*
Bedrooms: 7 single, 8 double,
12 twin, 1 triple
Bathrooms: 28 en-suite

Bed & breakfast

per night:	£min	£max
Single	75.00	119.00
Double	85.00	139.00

Half board per

person:	£min	£max
Daily	93.00	137.00
Weekly	582.00	959.00

Lunch available
Evening meal 1800 (last orders
2230)
Cards accepted: Amex, Diners,
Mastercard, Visa, Switch/Delta

Vicarage Private Hotel

COMMENDED

10 Vicarage Gate, Kensington,
London W8 4AG
☎ (0171) 229 4030
Fax (0171) 792 5989
Email: mandy&jim
@vichotel.demon.co.uk
*Delightful, family-run Victorian
townhouse hotel, situated in a quiet
garden square, offering a generous
freshly-cooked English breakfast and a
"home-from-home" atmosphere. Ideally
located for tourist attractions and
transport facilities.*
Bedrooms: 7 single, 2 double, 5 twin,
1 triple, 3 family rooms
Bathrooms: 5 public

> You are advised to confirm
> your booking in writing.

Bed & breakfast

per night:	£min	£max
Single	40.00	
Double	64.00	

LONDON W11

London Kensington Hilton 👐

COMMENDED

179-199 Holland Park Avenue,
London W11 4UL
☎ (0171) 603 3355
Fax (0171) 602 9397
Utell International
*Modern hotel with easy access to
shops, exhibition centres and Heathrow
Airport by Airbus A2 service.*
Bedrooms: 193 single, 136 double,
274 twin
Suite available
Bathrooms: 603 en-suite

Bed & breakfast

per night:	£min	£max
Single	140.00	160.00
Double	160.00	180.00

Lunch available
Evening meal 1730 (last orders
2230)
Parking for 100
Cards accepted: Amex, Diners,
Mastercard, Visa, Switch/Delta

LONDON WC1

Academy Hotel 👐

COMMENDED

17-25 Gower Street, London
WC1E 6HG
☎ (0171) 631 4115
Fax (0171) 636 3442
Consort
*"One of London's Top 10 most stylish
hotels" - LA Times '96. Georgian hotel
of immense charm and character.
Restaurant/bar/library and patio
garden.*
Bedrooms: 8 single, 24 double,
4 twin
Suites available
Bathrooms: 36 en-suite, 2 public

Bed & breakfast

per night:	£min	£max
Single	103.00	118.00
Double	135.00	150.00

Half board per

person:	£min	£max
Daily	78.00	85.00

Lunch available
Evening meal 1800 (last orders
2300)

Cards accepted: Amex, Diners,
Mastercard, Visa, Switch/Delta

Albany Hotel

Listed APPROVED

34 Tavistock Place, London
WC1H 9RE
☎ (0171) 837 9139 & 833 0459
Fax (0171) 8330459
*Small, friendly hotel in central London,
open all year round.*
Bedrooms: 3 single, 3 double, 4 twin,
1 triple
Bathrooms: 4 public

Bed & breakfast

per night:	£min	£max
Single	34.00	36.00
Double	45.00	48.00

Lunch available
Evening meal 1830 (last orders
2130)
Cards accepted: Amex, Diners,
Mastercard, Visa

Arran House Hotel 👐

77 Gower Street, London
WC1E 6HJ
☎ (0171) 636 2186 & 637 1140
Fax (0171) 436 5328
*Small, comfortable, family-run bed and
breakfast hotel in central London,
convenient for theatres, shopping and
public transport.*
Bedrooms: 6 single, 6 double, 4 twin,
10 triple, 2 family rooms
Bathrooms: 5 en-suite, 5 private,
5 public, 4 private showers

Bed & breakfast

per night:	£min	£max
Single	35.00	46.00
Double	47.00	65.00

Parking for 2
Cards accepted: Mastercard, Visa,
Switch/Delta

The Bonnington in Bloomsbury 👐

COMMENDED

92 Southampton Row, London
WC1B 4BH
☎ (0171) 242 2828
Fax (0171) 831 9170
Logis of GB
*Between the City and West End. Close
to mainline stations and on the
underground to Heathrow Airport.*

Continued ▶

LONDON WC1
Continued

Wheelchair access category 2 &
Bedrooms: 109 single, 44 double,
45 twin, 17 triple
Bathrooms: 215 en-suite

Bed & breakfast

per night:	£min	£max
Single	68.00	99.50
Double	105.00	126.00

Lunch available
Evening meal 1730 (last orders
2230)
Cards accepted: Amex, Diners,
Mastercard, Visa, Switch/Delta

🏇🕴📞💻🖵💷⚲🖂🛏🍴120 ⚲ SP 🎭 ⚙

Crescent Hotel ⋈
`Listed`

49-50 Cartwright Gardens, London
WC1H 9EL
☎ (0171) 387 1515
Fax (0171) 383 2054

*Recently refurbished, comfortable,
family-run hotel in a quiet Georgian
crescent, with private gardens and
tennis courts. All rooms have colour TV
and tea/coffee tray, most are en-suite.*
Bedrooms: 9 single, 2 double, 2 twin,
9 triple, 2 family rooms
Bathrooms: 15 en-suite, 4 public,
3 private showers

Bed & breakfast

per night:	£min	£max
Single	38.00	55.00
Double	68.00	72.00

Cards accepted: Mastercard, Visa,
Switch/Delta

🏇🕴📞💻🖵💷 UL TV 🛏 🔍❄✈ 🚐 SP 🎭

Garth Hotel ⋈
`Listed`

69 Gower Street, London
WC1E 6HJ
☎ (0171) 636 5761
Fax (0171) 637 4854
*Centrally situated family-run bed and
breakfast accommodation, convenient
for shops, theatres and travel. TV in
rooms. Tea/coffee-making facilities.
Some rooms en-suite.*
Bedrooms: 3 single, 4 double, 5 twin,
3 triple, 2 family rooms
Bathrooms: 1 en-suite, 3 public,
10 private showers

Bed & breakfast

per night:	£min	£max
Single	32.00	40.00
Double	45.00	58.00

Cards accepted: Amex, Mastercard,
Visa, Switch/Delta

🏇🕴📞💻💷 UL 🖂🛏🚿🛏🍴30 ❄ DAP ⚲
SP 🎭 T

George Hotel ⋈
☎ APPROVED

58-60 Cartwright Gardens, London
WC1H 9EL
☎ (0171) 387 8777
Fax (0171) 387 8666
*Central London hotel in a quiet square.
Comfortable, bright rooms with satellite
TV, direct-dial telephone, tea/coffee.
Gardens and tennis courts available for
guest use.*
Bedrooms: 15 single, 4 double,
4 twin, 10 triple, 7 family rooms
Bathrooms: 4 en-suite, 12 public,
4 private showers

Bed & breakfast

per night:	£min	£max
Single	39.50	45.00
Double	49.50	59.50

Cards accepted: Mastercard, Visa,
Switch/Delta

🏇🕴📞💻🖵💷♦⚲ UL ✂🖂 TV 🛏 💷
🚿🔍❄✈ DAP ⚲ SP 🎭 T

Gower House Hotel ⋈
`Listed` APPROVED

57 Gower Street, London
WC1E 6HJ
☎ (0171) 636 4685
Fax (0171) 636 4685
*Friendly bed and breakfast hotel, close
to Goodge Street underground station
and within easy walking distance of
British Museum, shops, theatres and
restaurants.*
Bedrooms: 4 single, 2 double, 6 twin,
3 triple, 1 family room
Bathrooms: 3 private, 3 public

Bed & breakfast

per night:	£min	£max
Single	35.00	37.00
Double	45.00	47.00

Cards accepted: Mastercard, Visa

🏇🕴📞💻♦⚲✂ TV 🛏 💷🚿🛏❄✈ T

St Athan's Hotel ⋈
`Listed` APPROVED

20 Tavistock Place, Russell Square,
London WC1H 9RE
☎ (0171) 837 9140 & 837 9627
Fax (0171) 833 8352
*Simple, small but clean family-run hotel
offering bed and breakfast.*
Bedrooms: 16 single, 15 double,
15 twin, 4 triple, 5 family rooms
Bathrooms: 15 en-suite, 12 public

Bed & breakfast

per night:	£min	£max
Single	30.00	38.00
Double	40.00	48.00

Lunch available
Cards accepted: Amex, Diners,
Mastercard, Visa

🏇🕴 UL 🖂 TV 🛏 💷🚿🛏 DAP ⚲ SP T

Thanet Hotel
`Listed` COMMENDED

8 Bedford Place, London WC1B 5JA
☎ (0171) 580 3377 & 636 2869
Fax (0171) 323 6676
*Comfortable, family-run hotel, with
colour TV, tea and coffee and
direct-dial telephones. All en-suite
rooms. Next to British Museum, close
to London's famous Theatreland. Full
English breakfast.*
Bedrooms: 4 single, 5 double, 4 twin,
3 family rooms
Bathrooms: 16 en-suite

Bed & breakfast

per night:	£min	£max
Single	54.00	57.00
Double	71.00	74.00

Cards accepted: Amex, Diners,
Mastercard, Visa, Switch/Delta

🏇🕴📞💻🖵♦⚲ UL S 🛏 💷🚿🖂✈
🚐 ⚲ SP 🎭

LONDON WC2

Royal Adelphi Hotel ⋈
👑👑👑

21 Villiers Street, London
WC2N 6ND
☎ (0171) 930 8764
Fax (0171) 930 8735
*Centrally located and ideal for
theatreland, near Embankment and
Charing Cross underground. All rooms
with colour TV, hairdryer, tea/coffee
facilities. Most rooms have private
bathrooms.*
Bedrooms: 20 single, 12 double,
13 twin, 2 triple
Bathrooms: 34 en-suite, 4 public

Bed & breakfast

per night:	£min	£max
Single	45.00	60.00
Double	60.00	80.00

Lunch available
Evening meal 1800 (last orders
2300)
Cards accepted: Amex, Diners,
Mastercard, Visa, Switch/Delta

🏇🕴📞💻🖵💷♦⚲🎧🍴 TV 🛏 💷
🍴20 SP T

Establishments should be
open throughout the year,
unless otherwise stated.

OUTER LONDON

Colour maps 6 & 7 at the back of the guide show place names and London Postal Area Codes and will help you locate accommodation in your chosen area of London

BARNET

West Lodge Park
HIGHLY COMMENDED

Cockfosters Road, Hadley Wood, Barnet, Hertfordshire EN4 0PY
☎ (0181) 440 8311
Fax (0181) 449 3698
White-painted William IV country house set in 35 acres of grounds in rolling countryside. Fine restaurant and very comfortable bedrooms with lots of cossetting extras. Leisure club nearby.
Bedrooms: 13 single, 23 double, 7 twin
Bathrooms: 43 en-suite

Bed & breakfast per night:

	£min	£max
Single	84.50	119.50
Double	125.00	175.00

Half board per person:

	£min	£max
Daily	80.00	87.50

Lunch available
Evening meal 1930 (last orders 2145)
Parking for 200
Cards accepted: Amex, Mastercard, Visa, Switch/Delta

BEXLEY

Tourist Information Centre ☎ (0181) 303 9052

Buxted Lodge
APPROVED

40 Parkhurst Road, Bexley, Kent DA5 1AS
☎ (01322) 554010 & 0831 794031
Victorian lodge retaining many original features. 30 minutes to central London by British Rail.
Bedrooms: 2 single, 3 double, 2 twin, 2 triple
Bathrooms: 3 en-suite, 4 public, 5 private showers

Bed & breakfast per night:

	£min	£max
Single	25.00	30.00
Double	40.00	50.00

Half board per person:

	£min	£max
Daily	35.00	40.00
Weekly	245.00	280.00

Evening meal 1830 (last orders 2000)

Parking for 14
Cards accepted: Mastercard, Visa, Switch/Delta

BEXLEYHEATH

Swallow Hotel
HIGHLY COMMENDED

1 Broadway, Bexleyheath, Kent DA6 7JZ
☎ (0181) 298 1000
Fax (0181) 298 1234
Email: info@swallowhotel.com
Swallow
Easy access to London and just minutes from junction 2 of the M25. Spacious, double-size bedrooms with marble-finish bathrooms, leisure club with extensive facilities including fitness room with the latest computerised equipment. Short break packages available.
Bedrooms: 54 single, 35 double, 35 twin, 10 triple, 8 family rooms
Suites available
Bathrooms: 142 en-suite

Bed & breakfast per night:

	£min	£max
Single	70.00	105.00
Double	90.00	125.00

Lunch available
Evening meal 1830 (last orders 2215)
Parking for 86
Cards accepted: Amex, Diners, Mastercard, Visa, Switch/Delta

BROMLEY

Glendevon House Hotel
APPROVED

80 Southborough Road, Bickley, Bromley BR1 2EN
☎ (0181) 467 2183
Small hotel with private car park. Convenient for central London. Caters for tourists and business people.
Bedrooms: 5 single, 3 double, 1 twin, 1 triple
Bathrooms: 4 en-suite, 1 public, 1 private shower

Bed & breakfast per night:

	£min	£max
Single	26.50	37.00
Double	43.50	45.00

Parking for 6
Cards accepted: Mastercard, Visa

Please check prices and other details at the time of booking.

CROYDON

Tourist Information Centre ☎ (0181) 253 1009

Alpha Guest House
APPROVED

99 Brigstock Road, Thornton Heath, Surrey CR7 7JL
☎ (0181) 684 4811 & 665 0032
Fax (0181) 405 0302
Modern, family-run residence in ideal location near Croydon (20 minutes from Victoria Station). Tea and coffee-making facilities, satellite TV, free parking and varied breakfasts.
Bedrooms: 5 single, 1 double, 4 twin, 1 triple
Bathrooms: 6 en-suite, 2 public

Bed & breakfast per night:

	£min	£max
Single	22.00	28.00
Double	35.00	40.00

Parking for 5
Cards accepted: Visa, Switch/Delta

Croydon Hotel

112 Lower Addiscombe Road, Croydon CR0 6AD
☎ (0181) 656 7233
Fax (0181) 655 0211
Close to central Croydon (route A222) and 10 minutes' walk from East Croydon station. Opposite shops and restaurants. Frequent direct trains to Victoria and Gatwick Airport.
Bedrooms: 1 single, 2 double, 3 twin, 2 triple
Bathrooms: 6 en-suite, 1 public

Bed & breakfast per night:

	£min	£max
Single	24.00	35.00
Double	40.00	48.00

Parking for 4
Cards accepted: Mastercard, Visa

Hayesthorpe Hotel

48-52 St Augustine's Avenue, Croydon CR2 6JJ
☎ (0181) 688 8120
Fax (0181) 680 1099
Quiet, family-style hotel located in South Croydon, just off the London Brighton Road.
Bedrooms: 10 single, 5 double, 7 twin, 3 triple
Bathrooms: 25 en-suite

Continued ▶

CROYDON

Continued

Bed & breakfast

per night:	£min	£max
Single	40.00	55.00
Double	50.00	65.00

Evening meal 1900 (last orders 2100)
Parking for 6
Cards accepted: Amex, Diners, Mastercard, Visa, Switch/Delta

Kirkdale Hotel

22 St Peter's Road, Croydon
CRO 1HD
☎ (0181) 688 5898
Fax (0181) 680 6001
Character Victorian house decorated to a high standard. Close to Croydon's shopping and business areas, theatre, restaurants and station. Easy travel to London, Gatwick and Brighton.
Bedrooms: 8 single, 9 double, 2 twin
Bathrooms: 19 en-suite
Bed & breakfast

per night:	£min	£max
Single	30.00	52.00
Double	45.00	59.00

Parking for 12
Cards accepted: Amex, Mastercard, Visa, Switch/Delta

Markington Hotel

9 Haling Park Road, South Croydon, Surrey CR2 6NG
☎ (0181) 681 6494
Fax (0181) 688 6530
Friendly, comfortable private hotel with fully equipped rooms, all en-suite. Free car parking. Bar, restaurant. Close to public transport.
Bedrooms: 10 single, 6 double, 2 twin, 2 triple
Bathrooms: 20 en-suite, 2 public
Bed & breakfast

per night:	£min	£max
Single	35.00	52.00
Double	45.00	58.00

Evening meal 1830 (last orders 2030)
Parking for 17
Cards accepted: Amex, Mastercard, Visa, Switch/Delta

Selsdon Park

HIGHLY COMMENDED
Sanderstead, South Croydon, Surrey CR2 8YA
☎ (0181) 657 8811
Fax (0181) 651 6171
Ⓡ Grand Heritage/Principal

Country house hotel, 10 minutes from the M25, 30 minutes from London and Gatwick, set in 200 acres of parkland. Special weekend rates.
Bedrooms: 40 single, 50 double, 80 twin
Suite available
Bathrooms: 170 en-suite
Bed & breakfast

per night:	£min	£max
Single	107.00	
Double	165.00	

Lunch available
Evening meal 1930 (last orders 2200)
Parking for 265
Cards accepted: Amex, Diners, Mastercard, Visa, Switch/Delta

ENFIELD

Royal Chace Hotel

COMMENDED
162 The Ridgeway, Enfield, Middlesex EN2 8AR
☎ (0181) 366 6500
Fax (0181) 367 7191
Email: royal.chace@dial.pipex.com
Pleasant hotel of character, set in Green Belt, with access to London and M25. Ideal for businessmen and tourists. Special weekend rates available.
Bedrooms: 70 double, 19 twin, 3 family rooms
Bathrooms: 92 en-suite
Bed & breakfast

per night:	£min	£max
Single	84.50	
Double	99.50	

Lunch available
Evening meal 1900 (last orders 2145)
Parking for 300
Cards accepted: Amex, Diners, Mastercard, Visa, Switch/Delta

HAMPTON COURT

Mitre Hotel

COMMENDED
Hampton Court Road, Hampton Court, East Molesey, Surrey KT8 9BN
☎ (0181) 979 9988
Fax (0181) 979 9777

Historic 17th C building overlooking Hampton Court Palace and River Thames. Elegantly decorated, spacious en-suite rooms, including a four-poster.
Bedrooms: 15 double, 20 twin, 1 triple
Suite available
Bathrooms: 36 en-suite
Bed & breakfast

per night:	£min	£max
Single	75.00	135.00
Double	90.00	180.00

Half board per person:

	£min	£max
Daily	65.00	110.00

Lunch available
Evening meal 1900 (last orders 2130)
Parking for 15
Cards accepted: Amex, Diners, Mastercard, Visa, Switch/Delta

HARROW

Tourist Information Centre ☎ (0181) 424 1100 or 424 1102

Crescent Hotel

COMMENDED
58-62 Welldon Crescent, Harrow, Middlesex HA1 1QR
☎ (0181) 863 5491 & 863 5163 &
Freephone 0800 0264003
Fax (0181) 427 5965
Email: jivraj@crsnhtl.demon.co.uk.
Ⓡ The Independents

Modern, friendly hotel with full facilities in the heart of Harrow. Five minutes to underground, easy access to Wembley, West End, Heathrow and major

*motorways. Website:
http://www.crsnthtl.demon.co.uk.*
Bedrooms: 9 single, 3 double, 6 twin,
2 family rooms
Bathrooms: 12 en-suite, 3 public
**Bed & breakfast
per night:**

	£min	£max
Single	35.00	45.00
Double	50.00	60.00

**Half board per
person:**

	£min	£max
Daily	53.00	63.00
Weekly	371.00	441.00

Lunch available
Evening meal 1900 (last orders
2030)
Parking for 7
Cards accepted: Amex, Diners,
Mastercard, Visa, Switch/Delta

🖧🕯📞📧🖵💧🎣🇸🏛📺🌙💻🖨
🍴25❋ DAP 🚫 SP Ⓣ

Hindes Hotel ⋀⋀

👑👑👑

8 Hindes Road, Harrow, Middlesex
HA1 1SJ
☎ (0181) 427 7468
Fax (0181) 424 0673
*Homely owner-run bed and breakfast
hotel near the M1. West End 15
minutes by underground. Convenient
for Wembley Stadium complex.*
Bedrooms: 4 single, 4 double, 6 twin
Bathrooms: 7 en-suite, 2 public
**Bed & breakfast
per night:**

	£min	£max
Single	31.00	39.00
Double	44.00	52.00

Parking for 20
Cards accepted: Amex, Diners,
Mastercard, Visa, Switch/Delta

🖧🕯📧🖵💧UL🇮🇸🏛📺🌙💻🖨🍴
❋🚐🚫Ⓣ

Lindal Hotel

👑👑👑 COMMENDED

2 Hindes Road, Harrow, Middlesex
HA1 1SJ
☎ (0181) 863 3164
Fax (0181) 427 5435
*In busy town centre. Easy reach
motorways, central London, Wembley
complex and Heathrow. 8 minutes'
walk to tube stations.*
Bedrooms: 7 single, 4 double, 5 twin,
2 triple, 1 family room
Bathrooms: 19 en-suite
**Bed & breakfast
per night:**

	£min	£max
Single	39.95	45.00
Double	50.00	58.00

**Half board per
person:**

	£min	£max
Daily		56.00

Lunch available

Evening meal 1900 (last orders
2045)
Parking for 17
Cards accepted: Mastercard, Visa

🖧🕯📧🖵🇸🏛🌙💻🖨⊖
🍴30🚐 DAP SP Ⓣ ⊚

The Quality Harrow Hotel ⋀⋀

👑👑👑👑 COMMENDED

12-22 Pinner Road, Harrow,
Middlesex HA1 4HZ
☎ (0181) 427 3435
Fax (0181) 861 1370
Ⓒ Logis of GB
*Friendly, family-run hotel near Wembley
and convenient for central London.
New air-conditioned restaurant and
function suite. Non-smoking
conservatory. Easy access motorways
and Heathrow. Free parking.*
Bedrooms: 17 single, 19 double,
14 twin, 2 family rooms
Bathrooms: 52 en-suite
**Bed & breakfast
per night:**

	£min	£max
Single	74.00	89.00
Double	94.00	105.00

Lunch available
Evening meal 1800 (last orders
2130)
Parking for 58
Cards accepted: Amex, Diners,
Mastercard, Visa, Switch/Delta

🖧🕯📞📧🖵💧🎣🇸🏛📺
⊟💻🖨🍴200∪🅿❋

HAYES

Shepiston Lodge

Listed APPROVED

31 Shepiston Lane, Hayes, Middlesex
UB3 1LJ
☎ (0181) 573 0266 & 569 2536
Fax (0181) 569 2536
*Homely guesthouse, 10 minutes from
Heathrow Airport. Close M4, M25 and
convenient for London. Rooms with
colour TV, tea/coffee facilities. Parking
facility for holiday periods. Bar and
evening meals.*
Bedrooms: 3 single, 1 double, 6 twin,
3 triple
Bathrooms: 3 public, 7 private
showers
**Bed & breakfast
per night:**

	£min	£max
Single	28.50	31.50
Double	40.50	44.50

Evening meal 1800 (last orders
2100)
Parking for 13
Cards accepted: Amex, Diners,
Mastercard, Visa, Switch/Delta

🖧🕯📧💧🎣🇸🏛📺💻🖨❋✂ DAP
🚫Ⓣ

HEATHROW AIRPORT

See under Hayes, Hounslow

HOUNSLOW

*Tourist Information Centre ☎ (0181) 572
8279*

Ashdowne House

👑

9 Pownall Gardens, Hounslow,
Middlesex TW3 1YW
☎ (0181) 572 0008
Fax (0181) 570 1939
*Very comfortable Victorian house with
elegant rooms, all en-suite and non
smoking. Conveniently situated for
travel to Heathrow and central London.*
Bedrooms: 2 single, 2 double, 2 twin
Bathrooms: 6 en-suite
**Bed & breakfast
per night:**

	£min	£max
Single	46.00	
Double	60.00	66.00

Parking for 4
Cards accepted: Mastercard, Visa

🖧🕯🚲📧🖵💧🎣UL🇸🏛✂💻🖨🐾
🚐

KINGSTON UPON THAMES

*Tourist Information Centre ☎ (0181) 547
5592*

Hotel Antoinette of Kingston ⋀⋀

👑👑👑 APPROVED

Beaufort Road, Kingston upon
Thames, Surrey KT1 2TQ
☎ (0181) 546 1044
Fax (0181) 547 2595
Ⓒ Minotel
*Tourist hotel located 20 minutes by
train from London. Ideal base for
visiting Hampton Court, Kew, Windsor,
Chessington World of Adventures and
Thorpe Park.*
Bedrooms: 24 single, 8 double,
34 twin, 24 triple, 9 family rooms
Bathrooms: 99 en-suite
**Bed & breakfast
per night:**

	£min	£max
Single	44.00	55.00
Double	58.00	65.00

Evening meal 1830 (last orders
2115)
Parking for 100
Cards accepted: Amex, Mastercard,
Visa, Switch/Delta

🖧🕯🚲📞🖵💧🇸✂🏛📺🌙⊟💻
🖨🍴120🔍❋ SP Ⓣ

KINGSTON UPON THAMES

Continued

Chase Lodge Hotel

 COMMENDED

10 Park Road, Hampton Wick,
Kingston upon Thames, Surrey
KT1 4AS
☎ (0181) 943 1862
Fax (0181) 943 9363

Small hotel in quiet conservation area.
Close to Hampton Court, River Thames
and 23 minutes to the centre of
London. Excellent restaurant open to
non-residents.
Bedrooms: 2 single, 7 double, 3 twin
Bathrooms: 12 en-suite

Bed & breakfast

per night:	£min	£max
Single	48.00	80.00
Double	62.00	135.00

Half board per person:

	£min	£max
Daily	45.00	94.00
Weekly	301.00	644.00

Lunch available
Evening meal (last orders 2200)
Cards accepted: Amex, Diners,
Mastercard, Visa, Switch/Delta

🛏🖐🖥📞🍴🖵💷🍷🎱🗝✕📺◐
🖧🛆🍽🏊50 ∪🏃❀ DAP ✕ SP T

ORPINGTON

The Mary Rose Hotel ⋀

⚜⚜⚜ APPROVED

40-50 High Street, St Mary Cray,
Orpington, Kent BR5 3NJ
☎ (01689) 871917 & 875369
Fax (01689) 839445
CR The Independents
16th C listed inn. Land traversed by
River Cray. 30 minutes from Hever and
Leeds Castles, Chartwell, Greenwich. 25
minutes from central London,
convenient for M25 and British Rail.
Bedrooms: 4 single, 12 double,
6 twin, 5 triple, 7 family rooms
Bathrooms: 20 en-suite, 10 private,
2 public

Bed & breakfast

per night:	£min	£max
Single	22.50	34.50
Double	49.50	75.00

Lunch available
Evening meal 1900 (last orders
2115)
Parking for 50

Cards accepted: Amex, Diners,
Mastercard, Visa, Switch/Delta

🛏🖐🖖📞🖵🍴💷🍷🗝 S 🐾📺🛆🍽🏊250
∪🏃🚗 DAP ✕ SP 🏤 T

RICHMOND

Tourist Information Centre ☎ (0181) 940
9125

Quinns Hotel ⋀

⚜⚜ APPROVED

48 Sheen Road, Richmond, Surrey
TW9 1AW
☎ (0181) 940 5444
Fax (0181) 940 1828
Ideally located for business or pleasure,
within easy reach of central London,
airports and local places of interest.
Bedrooms: 8 single, 16 double,
10 twin, 3 triple, 1 family room
Bathrooms: 18 en-suite, 6 public

Bed & breakfast

per night:	£min	£max
Single	35.00	65.00
Double	50.00	80.00

Parking for 14
Cards accepted: Amex, Diners,
Mastercard, Visa, Switch/Delta

🛏🖐🖖📞🖵🍴🗝 UL 🍷🗝📺◐🖧🛆🍽✕
SP T

Richmond Park Hotel

Listed APPROVED

3 Petersham Road, Richmond,
Surrey TW10 6UH
☎ (0181) 948 4666
Fax (0181) 940 7376
Privately-owned hotel in the heart of
Richmond. All rooms en-suite with
direct-dial telephone, colour TV, radio
and tea/coffee-making facilities.
Bedrooms: 6 single, 14 double,
2 twin
Bathrooms: 22 en-suite

Bed & breakfast

per night:	£min	£max
Single		55.00
Double		69.00

Cards accepted: Amex, Mastercard,
Visa, Switch/Delta

🛏📞🖵🍴🗝🍷🗝✕🍽🛆∪🚗 SP

Riverside Hotel

⚜⚜⚜

23 Petersham Road, Richmond,
Surrey TW10 6UH
☎ (0181) 940 1339
Elegant Victorian house overlooking the
Thames, close to Richmond Bridge.
En-suite rooms, colour TVs, tea and
coffee facilities.
Bedrooms: 4 single, 5 double, 3 twin,
1 triple
Bathrooms: 12 en-suite, 1 private
shower

Bed & breakfast

per night:	£min	£max
Single	36.00	50.00
Double	65.00	70.00

Parking for 5
Cards accepted: Amex, Mastercard,
Visa

🛏📞🖵🍷 UL 🍴🗝📺🛆🍽🍷🚗 SP
T

RUISLIP

Barn Hotel

⚜⚜⚜⚜ COMMENDED

Sherley's Farm, West End Road,
Ruislip, Middlesex HA4 6JB
☎ (01895) 636 057
Fax (01895) 638 379
17th C hotel set in 2 acres of
landscaped rose gardens and lawns.
Minutes from central London and
Heathrow. Adjacent to underground.
Own free car park.
Bedrooms: 25 single, 21 double,
11 twin
Bathrooms: 57 en-suite

Bed & breakfast

per night:	£min	£max
Single	50.00	79.00
Double	60.00	90.00

Half board per person:

	£min	£max
Daily	67.75	95.65
Weekly	585.85	

Lunch available
Evening meal 1900 (last orders
2130)
Parking for 50
Cards accepted: Amex, Diners,
Mastercard, Visa, Switch/Delta

🛏🖐🖖📞🖵🍴🗝🍷🍷 S 🐾📺
◐🖧🛆🍽🏊110🏃❀✕✕ SP 🏤 T

SUTTON

Ashling Tara Hotel

⚜⚜⚜ COMMENDED

50 Rosehill, Sutton, Surrey SM1 3EU
☎ (0181) 641 6142
Fax (0181) 644 7872
House hotel opposite open parkland.
Short walk to Sutton town centre. All
rooms en-suite, lounge/bar and
restaurant. On-site parking. Convenient
M25, Heathrow/Gatwick Airports.
Underground station 1 mile from hotel.
Bedrooms: 5 single, 4 double, 4 twin,
2 family rooms
Bathrooms: 14 en-suite, 1 private
shower

Bed & breakfast

per night:	£min	£max
Single	60.00	70.00
Double	78.00	90.00

Half board per person:	£min	£max
Daily	75.00	80.00
Weekly	485.00	500.00

Evening meal 1900 (last orders 2100)
Parking for 32
Cards accepted: Amex, Mastercard, Visa

🐎🛗📞🖾☐🛝🖉🗝🍴🗲🎢📺🖿📠🍴40✳🛩🐾 SP T

WEMBLEY

Adelphi Hotel ♨

👑👑 APPROVED

4 Forty Lane, Wembley, Middlesex
HA9 9EB
☎ (0181) 904 5629
Fax (0181) 908 5314
*Close to Wembley Stadium and
Wembley Park underground, 15
minutes from West End. Attractive
decor. TV lounge, tea/coffee in rooms.*
Bedrooms: 4 single, 4 double, 3 twin
Bathrooms: 7 en-suite, 2 public

**Bed & breakfast
per night:**

	£min	£max
Single	30.00	39.00
Double	40.00	49.00

Evening meal 2000 (last orders 2100)
Parking for 12
Cards accepted: Amex, Mastercard, Visa

🐎🛗☐🛝🗝UL🎢📺◑🖿📠✳🛩
DAP 🐾 SP

Arena Hotel ♨

👑👑 APPROVED

6 Forty Lane, Wembley, Middlesex
HA9 9EB
☎ (0181) 908 0670 & 908 2850
Fax (0181) 908 2007
*Spacious en-suite accommodation with
TV and satellite link in every room.
Recent refurbishment, only 1800 yards
from Wembley Stadium complex. Easy
access by all transport routes. Parking.*
Bedrooms: 2 single, 2 double, 3 twin,
3 triple, 3 family rooms
Bathrooms: 13 en-suite, 1 public

**Bed & breakfast
per night:**

	£min	£max
Single	35.00	39.00
Double	45.00	49.00

**Half board per
person:**

	£min	£max
Daily	35.00	39.00
Weekly	210.00	280.00

Evening meal 2000 (last orders 2100)
Parking for 15
Cards accepted: Amex, Diners, Mastercard, Visa, Switch/Delta

🐎🛗☐🛝UL🎢📺◑🖿📠✳ DAP 🐾
SP T

The Brookside Hotel

👑👑 APPROVED

32 Brook Avenue, Wembley,
Middlesex HA9 8PH
☎ (0181) 904 3333 & 908 5725
Fax (0181) 908 3333
*20 minutes from central London, a
stone's throw from Wembley Stadium
and Conference Centre. Overlooks
Wembley Park station.*

Bedrooms: 3 single, 3 double, 1 twin,
2 triple, 2 family rooms
Suites available
Bathrooms: 10 en-suite, 2 public

**Bed & breakfast
per night:**

	£min	£max
Single	28.00	38.00
Double	58.00	65.00

Parking for 8
Cards accepted: Amex, Diners, Mastercard, Visa, Switch/Delta

🐎🛗📞🖾☐🛝🗝UL🎢📺◑🖿
📠✳🛩🐾 SP T

Elm Hotel ♨

👑👑 APPROVED

1-7 Elm Road, Wembley, Middlesex
HA9 7JA
☎ (0181) 902 1764
Fax (0181) 903 8365
Ⓡ The Independents
*Ten minutes' walk (1200 yards) from
Wembley Stadium and Conference
Centre. 150 yards from Wembley
Central underground and mainline
station.*
Bedrooms: 5 single, 8 double, 8 twin,
3 triple, 2 family rooms
Suites available
Bathrooms: 26 en-suite

**Bed & breakfast
per night:**

	£min	£max
Single	35.00	45.00
Double	47.00	57.00

Parking for 7
Cards accepted: Mastercard, Visa, Switch/Delta

🐎🛗🖾📞☐🛝🖉S🎢◑🖿📠🍴30

AT-A-GLANCE SYMBOLS

Symbols at the end of each accommodation entry

give useful information about services

and facilities. A key to symbols can be found

inside the back cover flap.

Keep this open for easy reference.

USE YOUR *i*'s

There are more than 550
Tourist Information Centres
throughout England offering friendly
help with accommodation and
holiday ideas as well as
suggestions of places to visit
and things to do. There may well be
a centre in your home town which
can help you before you set out.
You'll find addresses in the
local Phone Book or simply
call Freepages 0800 192 192.

ENQUIRY COUPONS

To help you obtain further information
about advertisers and accommodation featured in
this guide you will find enquiry coupons at the back.
Send these directly to the establishments
in which you are interested.
Remember to complete both sides of the coupon.

CHECK THE MAPS

The colour maps at the back of this guide show
all the cities, towns and villages for which you will
find accommodation entries.

Refer to the town index to find the page
on which it is listed.

CUMBRIA

Cumbria's glorious lakeland is surely the jewel in the crown of England's scenic heritage. Its vistas of shining water, majestic mountains and forests inspire artists, writers and all lovers of beauty.

The area is a paradise for walkers and climbers, while the less energetic can marvel at the views from the comfort of a steam train or one of the picturesque lake steamers.

Beyond the lakes are villages and working farms, as well as museums devoted to topics ranging from the worlds of Wordsworth and Beatrix Potter, to Roman life and the region's shipbuilding past. Today, Cumbria's coastal fringe of long, sandy beaches is a favourite with families.

The county of Cumbria

FOR MORE INFORMATION CONTACT:
Cumbria Tourist Board
Ashleigh, Holly Road, Windermere,
Cumbria LA23 2AQ
Tel: (015394) 44444 **Fax:** (015394) 44041

Where to Go in Cumbria – see pages 50-53
Where to Stay in Cumbria – see pages 54-92

CUMBRIA

Where to Go and What to See

You will find hundreds of interesting places to visit during your stay in Cumbria, just some of which are listed in these pages. The number against each name will help you locate it on the map (page 53). Contact any Tourist Information Centre in the region for more ideas on days out in Cumbria.

5 **South Tynedale Railway**
Railway Station, Alston,
Cumbria CA9 3JB
Tel: (01434) 381696
A 2ft gauge railway along part of the route of the former Alston to Haltwhistle branch line through South Tynedale. Preserved British and overseas steam and diesel engines.

1 **Birdoswald Roman Fort**
Gilsland, Carlisle,
Cumbria CA6 7DD
Tel: (016977) 47602/47604
Remains of a Roman fort on one of the best parts of Hadrian's Wall with excellent views of the Irthing Gorge. The visitor centre brings to life the story of Birdoswald.

2 **Linton Tweeds**
Shaddon Mills,
Shaddon Gate,
Carlisle,
Cumbria CA2 5TZ
Tel: (01228) 27569
Shows the history of weaving in Carlisle up to Linton's day. Hands-on weaving and other activities for visitors.

3 **Tullie House Museum and Art Gallery**
Castle Street, Carlisle,
Cumbria CA3 8TP
Tel: (01228) 34781
Major tourist complex featuring a museum, art gallery, education facility, lecture theatre, shops, herb garden, restaurant and terrace bars.

4 **Four Seasons Farm Experience**
Sceugh Mire,
Southwaite, Carlisle,
Cumbria CA4 0LS
Tel: (016974) 73753
An open farm where you can meet the animals, bottle feed the lambs in spring and make your own bread and butter.

6 **Hutton-in-the-Forest**
Skelton, Penrith,
Cumbria CA11 9TH
Tel: (017684) 84449
A 13thC pele tower with later additions. Tapestries, armour, furniture, paintings, china. Formal gardens, ornamental lake, dovecote, woods with specimen trees and nature walk.

7 **Senhouse Roman Museum**
The Battery,
Sea Brows, Maryport,
Cumbria CA15 6JD
Tel: (01900) 816168
Once the headquarters of Hadrian's Coastal Defence system. UK's largest group of Roman altar stones and inscriptions. Roman military equipment, stunning sculpture.

8 Jennings Brothers plc

The Castle Brewery,
Cockermouth,
Cumbria CA13 9NE
Tel: (01900) 823214
Guided tours of Jennings - a traditional brewery producing distinctive local beers. Gift and souvenir shop.

9 Lakeland Sheep and Wool Centre

Egremont Road, Cockermouth,
Cumbria CA13 OQX
Tel: (01900) 822673
An all weather attraction with live sheep shows and working dog demonstrations. Includes large screen and other tourism exhibitions on the area, a wool shop and cafe/restaurant.

10 Whinlatter Forest Park and Visitor Centre

Braithwaite, Keswick,
Cumbria CA12 5TW
Tel: (017687) 78469
Forestry interpretative exhibition with audiovisual presentations. Working model of forest operations. Lecture theatre, walks, trails, orienteering, shop and cafe.

11 Threlkeld Quarry and Mining Museum

Threlkeld, Keswick,
Cumbria CA12 4TT
Tel: (017687) 79747
Unique collection of mining and quarrying artefacts, memorabilia and minerals including earth-moving machines, quarry and mining tubs.

12 The Beacon

West Strand, Whitehaven,
Cumbria CA28 7LY
Tel: (01946) 592302
Discover the industrial, maritime and social history of Whitehaven and surrounding area. Includes meteorology office weather gallery with satellite linked equipment.

13 Sellafield Visitor Centre

Sellafield, Seascale,
Cumbria CA20 1PG
Tel: (019467) 27027
Exhibition of nuclear power and the nuclear industry.

14 Dove Cottage and Wordsworth Museum

Town End,
Grasmere, Ambleside,
Cumbria LA22 9SH
Tel: (015394) 35544/35003
Wordsworth's home from 1799-1808. Poet's possessions, museum with manuscripts, farmhouse reconstruction, paintings and drawings. Special events throughout the year.

15 Rydal Mount

Ambleside,
Cumbria LA22 9LU
Tel: (015394) 33002
William Wordsworth's home for 37 years. Family portraits, furniture, first editions and personal possessions. Garden landscaped by the poet, 9thC Norse mound, magnificent views.

16 Muncaster Castle, Gardens and Owl Centre

Ravenglass,
Cumbria CA18 1RQ
Tel: (01229) 717614/717203
A 14thC pele tower with 15thC and 19thC additions. Gardens contain an exceptional collection of rhododendrons and azaleas. Extensive collection of owls.

17 Ravenglass and Eskdale Railway

Ravenglass,
Cumbria CA18 1SW
Tel: (01229) 717171
England's oldest narrow-gauge railway runs for 7 miles through glorious scenery to the foot of England's highest hills. Most trains are steam hauled.

18 Steam Yacht Gondola

Pier Cottage, Coniston,
Cumbria LA21 8AJ
Tel: (015394) 41288
Victorian steam-powered vessel, now National Trust owned, cruises Coniston Water. Completely renovated with wonderful saloon.

19 Amazonia
Glebe Road,
Bowness-on-Windermere,
Windermere,
Cumbria LA23 3HE
Tel: (015394) 48002
Large display of exotic reptiles and insects from around the world including pythons, crocodiles and tarantula spiders! Visitors are able to handle certain animals.

20 The World of Beatrix Potter
The Old Laundry, Crag Brow,
Bowness-on-Windermere,
Windermere,
Cumbria LA23 3BX
Tel: (015394) 88444
The life and works of Beatrix Potter presented on a 9-screen video wall. Film on her life, and 3-dimensional recreations of some of the scenes from her popular tales.

21 Sizergh Castle
Kendal,
Cumbria LA8 8AE
Tel: (015395) 60070
Strickland family home for 750 years, now National Trust owned. 14thC pele tower, 15thC great hall, 16thC wings. Stuart connections. Rock garden, rose garden, daffodils.

22 Ullswater Navigation and Transit Co
13 Maude Street, Kendal,
Cumbria LA9 4QD
Tel: (01539) 721626/
(017684) 82229
One or two hour cruises on beautiful Ullswater, or combine a walk with a return boat ride.

23 Graythwaite Hall Gardens
Newby Bridge, Ulverston,
Cumbria LA12 8BA
Tel: (015395) 31248
Rhododendrons, azaleas and flowering shrubs. Laid out by T Mawson 1888-1890.

24 Lakeland Wildlife Oasis
Hale, Milnthorpe,
Cumbria LA7 7BW
Tel: (015395) 63027
A wildlife exhibition where living animals and 'hands-on' displays illustrate evolution in the animal kingdom. Gift shop.

25 Lakeside and Haverthwaite Railway
Haverthwaite Station,
Ulverston,
Cumbria LA12 8AL
Tel: (015395) 31594
Standard gauge steam railway operating a daily seasonal service through the beautiful Leven valley. Steam and diesel locomotives on display.

26 Holker Hall and Gardens
Cark in Cartmel,
Cumbria LA11 7PL
Tel: (015395) 58328
Victorian new wing, formal and woodland garden, deer park, motor museum, adventure playground and gift shop. Exhibitions include Timeless Toys and Teddies.

27 South Lakes Wild Animal Park
Crossgates,
Dalton-in-Furness,
Cumbria LA15 8JR
Tel: (01229) 466086
Wild animal park in over 14 acres with more than 120 species from around the world. Large water fowl ponds, cafe, miniature railway.

28 The Dock Museum
North Road,
Barrow-in-Furness,
Cumbria LA14 2PW
Tel: (01229) 870871
Presents the story of steel shipbuilding for which Barrow is famous. Interactive displays, nautical adventure playground.

SCOTLAND

NORTHUMBERLAND

0 — 20 Miles
0 — 30 Kms

Longtown
Gilsland **1**

Brampton

Carlisle **2** **3**

Southwaite **4**

Alston **5**

Skelton **6**

Maryport **7**

Bassenthwaite

Broughton
8 **9**
Cockermouth

Workington

Braithwaite
10
Keswick

11 Threlkeld

CUMBRIA

Penrith

Pooley Bridge

Appleby-in-Westmorland

DURHAM

Whitehaven **12**

Cleator Moor

Egremont

Grasmere **14**

Ambleside **15**

Brough

Kirkby Stephen

Seascale **13**

Windermere

Coniston

18

19 **20** Bowness-on-Windermere

16 **17**
Ravenglass

21 **22** Kendal

Newby Bridge **23**

Sedbergh

24 Milnthorpe

Millom

Grange-over-Sands

Kirkby Lonsdale

NORTH YORKSHIRE

Ulverston

25
26
Cark in Cartmel

27
Dalton-in-Furness

Barrow-in-Furness **28**

LANCS

FIND OUT MORE

Further information about holidays and attractions in Cumbria is available from: **Cumbria Tourist Board,** Ashleigh, Holly Road, Windermere, Cumbria LA23 2AQ. Tel: (015394) 44444

These publications are available from the Cumbria Tourist Board:

■ **Cumbria The Lake District Touring Map** - including tourist information and touring caravan and camping parks £3.95.
■ **Days Out in Cumbria** - Over 200 ideas for a great day out £1.25.

■ **Short Walks** - Good for Families - route descriptions, maps and information for 14 walks in lesser known areas of Cumbria 95p.
■ **Wordsworth's Lake District** - folded map showing major Wordsworthian sites plus biographical details 60p. Japanese language version £1. Laminated poster £1.

WHERE TO STAY (CUMBRIA)

Accommodation entries in this region are listed in alphabetical order of place name, and then in alphabetical order of establishment.

Map references refer to the colour location maps at the back of this guide. The first number indicates the map to use; the letter and number which follow refer to the grid reference on the map.

At-a-glance symbols at the end of each accommodation entry give useful information about services and facilities. A key to symbols can be found inside the back cover flap.

Keep this open for easy reference.

AMBLESIDE

Cumbria
Map ref 5A3

Market town situated at the head of Lake Windermere and surrounded by fells. The historic town centre is now a conservation area and the country around Ambleside is rich in historic and literary associations. Good centre for touring, walking and climbing.
Tourist Information Centre
☎ (015394) 32582

The Anchorage
👑👑 COMMENDED
Rydal Road, Ambleside LA22 9AY
☎ (015394) 32046
Modern detached guesthouse offering a good standard of accommodation and own private car park. 300 metres from town centre and amenities.
Bedrooms: 4 double, 1 twin
Bathrooms: 4 en-suite, 1 public
Bed & breakfast

per night:	£min	£max
Double	36.00	48.00

Parking for 7
Open February–November

Borrans Park Hotel ᴍ
👑👑👑 HIGHLY COMMENDED
Borrans Road, Ambleside LA22 0EN
☎ (015394) 33454
Fax (015394) 33003
Peacefully situated between the village and lake. Enjoy candlelit dinners, 120 fine wines, and four-poster bedrooms with private spa baths.

Wheelchair access category 3 ♿
Bedrooms: 9 double, 1 twin, 2 triple
Bathrooms: 12 en-suite
Bed & breakfast

per night:	£min	£max
Single	30.00	50.00
Double	60.00	80.00

Half board per person:

	£min	£max
Daily	47.50	67.50
Weekly	255.00	330.00

Evening meal 1900 (last orders 1800)
Parking for 20
Cards accepted: Mastercard, Visa, Switch/Delta

The Churchill Hotel ᴍ
👑👑 COMMENDED
Lake Road, Ambleside LA22 OBH
☎ (015394) 33192
Fax (015394) 34900
In the centre of Ambleside, heart of English Lakeland, only minutes away from the many attractions of the Lakes. We aim to make you feel welcome and relaxed.
Bedrooms: 2 single, 9 double, 2 triple
Bathrooms: 13 en-suite
Bed & breakfast

per night:	£min	£max
Single	18.50	30.00
Double	35.00	60.00

Lunch available
Evening meal 1900 (last orders 2100)
Parking for 12
Cards accepted: Mastercard, Visa, Switch/Delta

Claremont House ᴍ
👑👑 APPROVED
Compston Road, Ambleside LA22 9DJ
☎ (015394) 33448
Fax (015394) 33448
All rooms have colour TV and tea/coffee makers, most are en-suite. Family-run, friendly atmosphere.
Bedrooms: 2 single, 3 double, 1 triple
Bathrooms: 4 en-suite, 1 public
Bed & breakfast

per night:	£min	£max
Single	14.00	20.00
Double	30.00	40.00

Cards accepted: Amex, Mastercard, Visa, Switch/Delta

The Dower House
👑👑 COMMENDED
Wray Castle, Ambleside LA22 0JA
☎ (015394) 33211
The house overlooks Lake Windermere, 3 miles from Ambleside. Through the main gates of Wray Castle and up the drive.
Bedrooms: 2 double, 1 twin
Bathrooms: 2 en-suite, 1 private, 2 public
Bed & breakfast

per night:	£min	£max
Single	22.00	22.00
Double	44.00	45.00

Half board per person:

	£min	£max
Daily	33.00	34.00
Weekly	231.00	232.00

Evening meal 1900 (last orders 1930)
Parking for 14

🎠 5 ⬥ 🖢 UL 🅂 ♨ TV 🛏 ❀ ✕ 🚲 🖙
SP

Easedale Guest House

🏵🏵 COMMENDED

Compston Road, Ambleside
LA22 9DJ
☎ (015394) 32112
Charming Victorian house with private car park. Overlooking Loughrigg Fell and tennis courts. Friendly and comfortable, serving generous breakfasts. Advice given for walking and sightseeing. No smoking, please.
Bedrooms: 7 double
Bathrooms: 4 en-suite, 1 private, 1 public
Bed & breakfast
per night:

	£min	£max
Double	32.00	50.00

Parking for 7

🎠 ▢ ⬥ UL 🖢 🅂 ✕ TV 🛏 🛏 ✕ 🚲 🖙

Elder Grove Hotel M

🏵🏵 COMMENDED

Lake Road, Ambleside LA22 0DB
☎ (015394) 32504
Fax (015394) 32504
Delightful small hotel, owned and

managed by the Haywood family, offering comfortable en-suite bedrooms; delicious food and wines. Heating. Parking.
Bedrooms: 2 single, 7 double, 2 twin, 1 triple
Bathrooms: 12 en-suite
Bed & breakfast
per night:

	£min	£max
Single	25.00	28.00
Double	50.00	56.00

Half board per
person:

	£min	£max
Daily	42.00	45.00
Weekly	280.00	294.00

Evening meal 1915 (last orders 2015)
Parking for 14
Open February–November
Cards accepted: Amex, Mastercard, Visa, Switch/Delta

🎠 5 🛏 🖢 ╲ 📧 ▢ ⬥ 🖢 🅂 ✕ 🎱
TV 🛏 🛏 🚲 SP T

Fisherbeck Hotel M

🏵🏵🏵 COMMENDED

Lake Road, Ambleside LA22 0DH
☎ (015394) 33215
Fax (015394) 33600

Noted for hospitality, service and comfort, with some refurbished superior rooms. Fine food, sheltered garden, car parking, fell views. Special breaks available. Leisure club facilities. Fishing.
Bedrooms: 1 single, 14 double, 2 twin, 3 triple
Bathrooms: 17 private, 2 public
Bed & breakfast
per night:

	£min	£max
Single	29.00	40.00
Double	58.00	80.00

Half board per
person:

	£min	£max
Daily	45.00	56.00
Weekly	301.00	378.00

Lunch available
Evening meal 1900 (last orders 2030)
Parking for 20
Cards accepted: Mastercard, Visa

🎠 🛏 ╲ 📧 ▢ ⬥ 🖢 🅂 ♨ TV 🛏 🛏 🍴
🏊 ❀ ✕ SP

AMBLESIDE
Continued

Ghyll Head Hotel ⚠
🏅🏅🏅 APPROVED

Waterhead, Ambleside LA22 0HD
☎ (015394) 32360 & 0500 200148
(Freephone)
Family hotel in a good position overlooking Lake Windermere and ideal for touring the Lake District.
Bedrooms: 3 single, 3 double, 1 twin, 7 triple, 1 family room
Bathrooms: 13 en-suite, 1 public

Bed & breakfast

per night:	£min	£max
Single	24.50	27.50
Double	49.00	55.00

Half board per person:

	£min	£max
Daily	35.00	38.00
Weekly	235.00	255.00

Evening meal 1830 (last orders 1930)
Parking for 12

Kirkstone Foot Country House Hotel ⚠
🏅🏅🏅 HIGHLY COMMENDED

Kirkstone Pass Road, Ambleside
LA22 9EH
☎ (015394) 32232
Fax (015394) 32232

Secluded 17th C manor house and renowned restaurant, set in its own grounds, with adjoining self-contained apartments and cottages.
Wheelchair access category 3↑
Bedrooms: 9 double, 3 twin, 1 triple
Bathrooms: 13 en-suite

Bed & breakfast

per night:	£min	£max
Single	35.00	45.00
Double	70.00	90.00

Half board per person:

	£min	£max
Daily	50.00	70.00
Weekly	350.00	400.00

Evening meal 1930 (last orders 2030)
Parking for 30
Open February–December

Cards accepted: Amex, Diners, Mastercard, Visa, Switch/Delta

Langdale Hotel and Country Club ⚠
🏅🏅🏅 HIGHLY COMMENDED

Great Langdale, Ambleside
LA22 9JD
☎ (015394) 37302
Fax (015394) 37694
En-suite hotel, winner of 1986 Civic Trust environmental award, in 35 acres of wooded grounds. Indoor country club, large pool, spa-bath, sports facilities, restaurants and bars. Minimum stay 2 nights.
Bedrooms: 41 double, 24 twin
Bathrooms: 65 en-suite

Bed & breakfast

per night:	£min	£max
Double	70.00	90.00

Half board per person:

	£min	£max
Daily	85.00	110.00

Lunch available
Evening meal 1900 (last orders 2200)
Parking for 120
Cards accepted: Amex, Diners, Mastercard, Visa, Switch/Delta

Ad See display advertisement on page 55

Lattendales ⚠
🏅🏅 COMMENDED

Compston Road, Ambleside
LA22 9DJ
☎ (015394) 32368
Traditional Lakeland home in the heart of Ambleside. A central base for walking or touring, offering comfortable accommodation and local produce.
Bedrooms: 2 single, 2 double, 2 twin
Bathrooms: 4 en-suite, 1 public

Bed & breakfast

per night:	£min	£max
Single	15.00	17.50
Double	32.00	42.00

Half board per person:

	£min	£max
Daily	28.00	32.00
Weekly	180.00	210.00

Evening meal 1830 (last orders 1700)

Laurel Villa ⚠
🏅🏅🏅 HIGHLY COMMENDED

Lake Road, Ambleside LA22 0DB
☎ (015394) 33240
Detached Victorian house, visited by Beatrix Potter. En-suite bedrooms overlooking the fells. Within easy reach of Lake Windermere and the village. Private car park.
Bedrooms: 7 double, 1 twin
Bathrooms: 8 en-suite

Bed & breakfast

per night:	£min	£max
Single	50.00	50.00
Double	60.00	80.00

Half board per person:

	£min	£max
Daily	50.00	100.00

Evening meal 1900 (last orders 1700)
Parking for 10
Cards accepted: Amex, Mastercard, Visa

Lyndhurst Hotel ⚠
🏅🏅 COMMENDED

Wansfell Road, Ambleside
LA22 0EG
☎ (015394) 32421
Small, attractive Lakeland hotel with private car park. Quietly situated for town and lake. Pretty rooms, delicious food - a delightful experience.
Bedrooms: 5 double, 1 twin
Bathrooms: 6 en-suite

Bed & breakfast

per night:	£min	£max
Single	25.00	30.00
Double	39.00	50.00

Half board per person:

	£min	£max
Daily	33.00	39.00
Weekly	225.00	250.00

Evening meal 1830 (last orders 1830)
Parking for 9

The Old Vicarage ⚠
🏅🏅 COMMENDED

Vicarage Road, Ambleside
LA22 9DH
☎ (015394) 33364
Fax (015394) 34734

Quietly situated in own grounds in

heart of village. Car park, quality en-suite accommodation, friendly service. Family-run. Pets welcome.
Bedrooms: 7 double, 1 twin, 1 triple, 1 family room
Bathrooms: 10 en-suite
Bed & breakfast

per night:	£min	£max
Double	46.00	

Parking for 12
Cards accepted: Mastercard, Visa, Switch/Delta

Queens Hotel M

COMMENDED

Market Place, Ambleside LA22 9BU
☎ (015394) 32206
Fax (015394) 32721
In the heart of the Lakes and convenient for walking, climbing and other leisure activities. 2 fully licensed bars, choice of restaurant or bar meals.
Bedrooms: 4 single, 14 double, 3 twin, 2 triple, 3 family rooms
Bathrooms: 26 en-suite
Bed & breakfast

per night:	£min	£max
Single	25.00	35.00
Double	50.00	70.00

Half board per

person:	£min	£max
Daily	38.00	48.00
Weekly	244.00	300.00

Lunch available
Evening meal 1900 (last orders 2130)
Parking for 12
Cards accepted: Amex, Diners, Mastercard, Visa, Switch/Delta

Rothay Garth Hotel M

COMMENDED

Rothay Road, Ambleside LA22 0EE
☎ (015394) 32217
Fax (015394) 34400
Distinctive Victorian country house with elegant Loughrigg restaurant overlooking lovely gardens and nearby mountains. Close to village centre and Lake Windermere. All-season breaks.
Bedrooms: 2 single, 9 double, 2 twin, 2 triple, 1 family room
Suite available
Bathrooms: 14 en-suite, 1 public
Bed & breakfast

per night:	£min	£max
Single	36.00	49.00
Double	72.00	98.00

Half board per

person:	£min	£max
Daily	53.00	67.00
Weekly	323.00	381.00

Lunch available
Evening meal 1900 (last orders 2100)
Parking for 17
Cards accepted: Amex, Diners, Mastercard, Visa, Switch/Delta

Rothay Manor Hotel M

HIGHLY COMMENDED

Rothay Bridge, Ambleside LA22 0EH
☎ (015394) 33605
Fax (015394) 33607

Elegant Regency country house hotel with a well-known restaurant. Balcony rooms overlook the garden. Suites for families and disabled guests. Free use of nearby leisure club.
Bedrooms: 2 single, 5 double, 3 twin, 5 triple, 3 family rooms
Suites available
Bathrooms: 18 en-suite
Bed & breakfast

per night:	£min	£max
Single	79.00	
Double	122.00	137.00

Half board per

person:	£min	£max
Daily	79.00	115.00

Lunch available
Evening meal 1945 (last orders 2100)
Parking for 50
Open February–December
Cards accepted: Amex, Diners, Mastercard, Visa

Rowanfield Country Guesthouse M

HIGHLY COMMENDED

Kirkstone Road, Ambleside LA22 9ET
☎ (015394) 33686
Fax (015394) 31569

Idyllic setting, panoramic lake and mountain views. Laura Ashley style decor. Scrumptious food created by

proprietor/chef. Superior room available at supplement.
Wheelchair access category 3
Bedrooms: 5 double, 1 twin, 1 triple
Bathrooms: 7 en-suite
Bed & breakfast

per night:	£min	£max
Double	54.00	60.00

Half board per

person:	£min	£max
Daily	44.00	47.00
Weekly	267.00	286.00

Evening meal 1900 (last orders 1900)
Parking for 8
Open March–December
Cards accepted: Mastercard, Visa, Switch/Delta

The Rysdale Hotel M

COMMENDED

Rothay Road, Ambleside LA22 0EE
☎ (015394) 32140 & 33999
Family-run hotel with magnificent views over park and fells. Good food, licensed bar. Friendly, personal service. Ideal walking base. No smoking.
Bedrooms: 4 single, 4 double, 1 triple
Bathrooms: 6 en-suite, 2 public
Bed & breakfast

per night:	£min	£max
Single	16.00	25.00
Double	34.00	50.00

Parking for 2
Cards accepted: Mastercard, Visa

The Salutation Hotel M

HIGHLY COMMENDED

Lake Road, Ambleside LA22 9BX
☎ (015394) 32244
Fax (015394) 34157
Consort
Traditional hotel overlooking central Ambleside, with comfortable rooms and leisure facilities available. Warm and friendly welcome assured.
Bedrooms: 3 single, 21 double, 8 twin, 4 triple
Bathrooms: 36 en-suite
Bed & breakfast

per night:	£min	£max
Single	34.00	47.00
Double	68.00	94.00

Half board per

person:	£min	£max
Daily	47.00	60.00
Weekly	292.00	360.00

Lunch available

Continued ▶

AMBLESIDE
Continued

Evening meal 1900 (last orders 2100)
Parking for 40
Cards accepted: Amex, Mastercard, Visa, Switch/Delta

Smallwood House Hotel ♏
COMMENDED

Compston Road, Ambleside
LA22 9DJ
☎ (015394) 32330
Family-run hotel in central position, offering warm and friendly service, good home cooking and value-for-money quality and standards.
Bedrooms: 6 double, 3 twin, 2 triple, 2 family rooms
Bathrooms: 12 en-suite, 2 public

Bed & breakfast
per night:	£min	£max
Single	25.00	29.00
Double	35.00	46.00

Half board per
person:	£min	£max
Daily	35.00	40.00
Weekly	225.00	245.00

Lunch available
Evening meal 1800 (last orders 2000)
Parking for 11
Cards accepted: Mastercard, Visa

Thorneyfield Guest House ♏
COMMENDED

Compston Road, Ambleside
LA22 9DJ
☎ (015394) 32464
Fax (015394) 32464
Email: doano
@thorneyfield.demon.co.uk.
Cosy family-run guesthouse in the town centre with friendly and helpful service. Close to the park, miniature golf, tennis and lake. Large family rooms available.
Bedrooms: 3 double, 1 triple, 2 family rooms
Bathrooms: 5 en-suite, 1 private

Bed & breakfast
per night:	£min	£max
Single	14.00	16.00
Double	28.00	40.00

Parking for 12
Cards accepted: Mastercard, Visa, Switch/Delta

Wateredge Hotel ♏
HIGHLY COMMENDED

Waterhead Bay, Ambleside
LA22 0EP
☎ (015394) 32332
Fax (015394) 31878

Delightfully situated on shores of Windermere, the family-run Wateredge offers quiet relaxation, elegant comfort, excellent cuisine, beautiful lake views and, above all, personal unobtrusive service.
Bedrooms: 3 single, 11 double, 8 twin
Bathrooms: 22 en-suite

Bed & breakfast
per night:	£min	£max
Single	45.00	64.00
Double	70.00	148.00

Half board per
person:	£min	£max
Daily	55.00	94.00
Weekly	375.00	630.00

Lunch available
Evening meal 1900 (last orders 2030)
Parking for 25
Open February–December
Cards accepted: Amex, Mastercard, Visa, Switch/Delta

Waterhead Hotel ♏
COMMENDED

Lake Road, Ambleside LA22 0ER
☎ (015394) 32566
Fax (015394) 31255
Ⓒ Best Western
On the edge of Lake Windermere, an ideal central base for touring the lovely English Lakes.
Bedrooms: 4 single, 12 double, 11 twin, 1 triple
Bathrooms: 28 en-suite

Bed & breakfast
per night:	£min	£max
Single	40.00	40.00
Double	80.00	112.00

Half board per
person:	£min	£max
Daily	50.50	65.50
Weekly	303.00	393.00

Lunch available
Evening meal 1900 (last orders 2100)

Parking for 50
Cards accepted: Amex, Diners, Mastercard, Visa, Switch/Delta

APPLEBY-IN-WESTMORLAND
Cumbria
Map ref 5B3

Former county town of Westmorland, at the foot of the Pennines in the Eden Valley. The castle was rebuilt in the 17th C, except for its Norman keep, ditches and ramparts. It now houses a Rare Breeds Survival Trust Centre. Good centre for exploring the Eden Valley.
Tourist Information Centre
☎ (017683) 51177

Appleby Manor Country House Hotel ♏
HIGHLY COMMENDED

Roman Road,
Appleby-in-Westmorland CA16 6JB
☎ (017683) 51571
Fax (017683) 52888
Email: 100043.1561
@compuserve.com
Ⓒ Best Western
Award-winning country house hotel with fine timber features, in wooded grounds overlooking Appleby Castle. Panoramic views of the Pennines and the Lakeland fells. Indoor leisure club.
Bedrooms: 14 double, 8 twin, 1 triple, 7 family rooms
Suite available
Bathrooms: 30 en-suite

Bed & breakfast
per night:	£min	£max
Single	69.00	79.00
Double	98.00	118.00

Half board per
person:	£min	£max
Daily	54.50	74.50
Weekly	327.00	447.00

Lunch available
Evening meal 1900 (last orders 2100)
Parking for 51
Cards accepted: Amex, Diners, Mastercard, Visa, Switch/Delta

COLOUR MAPS
Colour maps at the back of this guide pinpoint all places in which you will find accommodation listed.

Bongate House ⚔

⚜ ⚜ ⚜ COMMENDED

Appleby-in-Westmorland
CA16 6UE
☎ (017683) 51245
Family-run Georgian guesthouse on the outskirts of a small market town. Large garden. Relaxed friendly atmosphere, good home cooking.
Bedrooms: 1 single, 3 double, 2 twin, 1 triple, 1 family room
Bathrooms: 5 en-suite, 1 public

Bed & breakfast

per night:	£min	£max
Single	17.50	17.50
Double	35.00	40.00

Half board per

person:	£min	£max
Daily	26.50	29.00
Weekly	170.00	190.00

Evening meal 1900 (last orders 1800)
Parking for 10

🐴7🛏♿🛁[S]✗🏵▥ 🚗∪♪🅿❀ SP 🏠T

BARROW-IN-FURNESS

Cumbria
Map ref 5A3

On the Furness Peninsula in Morecambe Bay, an industrial and commercial centre with sandy beaches and nature reserves on Walney Island. Ruins of 12th C Cistercian Furness Abbey. The Dock Museum tells the story of the area and Forum 28 houses a modern theatre and arts centre.
Tourist Information Centre ☎ (01229) 870156

Abbey House Hotel ⚔

⚜ ⚜ ⚜ ⚜ COMMENDED

Abbey Road, Barrow-in-Furness
LA13 0PA
☎ (01229) 838282
Fax (01229) 820403
Friendly country house hotel, in idyllic location for that romantic weekend and an excellent base for touring the Lake District.
Bedrooms: 3 single, 14 double, 5 twin, 6 triple
Bathrooms: 28 en-suite, 1 public

Bed & breakfast

per night:	£min	£max
Single	44.95	69.95
Double	64.95	89.95

Lunch available
Evening meal 1900 (last orders 2130)
Parking for 60
Cards accepted: Amex, Diners, Mastercard, Visa, Switch/Delta

🐴♿🛡🍴📞🖵♿🛁[S]✗🎱❍
✉▥ 🚗🎔🍽100∪♪❀🅽 SP 🏠T

Arlington House Hotel and Restaurant ⚔

⚜ ⚜ ⚜ HIGHLY COMMENDED

200-202 Abbey Road,
Barrow-in-Furness LA14 5LD
☎ (01229) 831976
Fax (01229) 870990
Relaxed hotel with an elegant restaurant. In the town, yet not far away from the Lakes and sea.
Bedrooms: 2 double, 6 twin
Bathrooms: 8 en-suite

Bed & breakfast

per night:	£min	£max
Single	52.00	57.00
Double	70.00	77.00

Evening meal 1930 (last orders 2045)
Parking for 20
Cards accepted: Mastercard, Visa

🐴📞🖵♿🔌[S]▥🚗🎔🛡 ⤢
🅿❀🍽🚗 SP

BASSENTHWAITE

Cumbria
Map ref 5A2

Standing in an idyllic setting, nestled at the foot of Skiddaw and Ullock Pike, this village is just a mile from Bassenthwaite Lake, the one true "lake" in the Lake District. The area is visited by many varieties of migrating birds.

Ravenstone Hotel ⚔

⚜ ⚜ ⚜ HIGHLY COMMENDED

Bassenthwaite, Keswick CA12 4QG
☎ (017687) 76240
Fax (017687) 76240
Charming dower house offering comfort and relaxation in beautiful surroundings. Elegant lounge and bar with log fires. Games room with full-size snooker table.
Bedrooms: 2 single, 10 double, 5 twin, 2 triple, 1 family room
Bathrooms: 20 en-suite

Bed & breakfast

per night:	£min	£max
Single	30.00	32.00
Double	60.00	64.00

Half board per

person:	£min	£max
Daily	42.00	44.00
Weekly	280.00	294.00

Evening meal 1900 (last orders 1930)
Parking for 20
Open February–October

🐴🚪🖵♿🛡[S]▥▥🚗🎔❀🍽🚗🅽
SP

BASSENTHWAITE LAKE

Cumbria
Map ref 5A2

The northernmost and only true "lake" in the Lake District. Visited annually by many species of migratory birds.

Link House ⚔

⚜ ⚜ ⚜ COMMENDED

Bassenthwaite Lake, Cockermouth
CA13 9YD
☎ (017687) 76291
Fax (017687) 76670
Licensed country house at Bassenthwaite Lake. Superb views. Traditional home cooking, log fire, conservatory bar, nearby leisure club facilities.
Bedrooms: 3 single, 3 double, 2 twin, 1 triple
Bathrooms: 8 en-suite, 1 private, 1 public

Bed & breakfast

per night:	£min	£max
Single	18.00	27.00
Double	52.00	54.00

Half board per

person:	£min	£max
Daily	31.00	40.00
Weekly		250.00

Evening meal 1900 (last orders 1900)
Parking for 8
Open February–November
Cards accepted: Mastercard, Visa, Switch/Delta

🐴7♿🖵♿🔌[S]▥▥🚗❀🍽🚗
🅽 SP T

Ouse Bridge Hotel ⚔

⚜ ⚜ ⚜ COMMENDED

Dubwath, Bassenthwaite Lake,
Cockermouth CA13 9YD
☎ (017687) 76322
Small family-run hotel quietly situated overlooking Bassenthwaite Lake and Skiddaw. Only 8 miles from Keswick. Home cooking. Country location.
Bedrooms: 2 single, 4 double, 2 twin, 2 triple
Bathrooms: 8 en-suite, 2 public

Bed & breakfast

per night:	£min	£max
Single	24.00	31.00
Double	38.00	52.00

Half board per

person:	£min	£max
Daily	26.00	33.00
Weekly	195.00	210.00

Evening meal 1900 (last orders 1930)
Parking for 22

Continued ▶

BASSENTHWAITE LAKE
Continued

Open February–December
Cards accepted: Amex, Mastercard,
Visa, Switch/Delta

🛇5🖵♿🍴♨🕭🎯(TV)▥💻✕🚬 SP
T

Pheasant Inn 𝗠
🌸 HIGHLY COMMENDED

Bassenthwaite Lake, Cockermouth
CA13 9YE
☎ (017687) 76234
Fax (017687) 76002
*Peacefully situated just off the A66 at
the northern end of Bassenthwaite
Lake. A 16th C farmhouse with all the
charm and character of that age.*
Wheelchair access category 3♿
Bedrooms: 5 single, 8 double, 7 twin
Bathrooms: 20 en-suite

Bed & breakfast

per night:	£min	£max
Single	68.00	70.00
Double	110.00	120.00

Lunch available
Evening meal 1900 (last orders
2030)
Parking for 80
Cards accepted: Mastercard, Visa

🛇🍴🎯♿🕭✕▥💻📷❀🚬 SP 🏠

BORROWDALE
Cumbria
Map ref 5A3

Stretching south of Derwentwater
to Seathwaite in the heart of the
Lake District, the valley is walled by
high fellsides. It can justly claim to
be the most scenically impressive
valley in the Lake District. Excellent
centre for walking and climbing.

Derwent House 𝗠
🌸 COMMENDED

Grange-in-Borrowdale, Borrowdale,
Keswick CA12 5UY
☎ (017687) 77658
Fax (017687) 77217

*Victorian, family-run guesthouse in
lovely Borrowdale. Comfortable rooms
enjoy beautiful views of surrounding
fells. No smoking in bedrooms and
dining rooms, please.*

Bedrooms: 1 single, 5 double, 3 twin,
1 triple
Bathrooms: 6 en-suite, 1 public

Bed & breakfast

per night:	£min	£max
Single	25.00	30.00
Double	40.00	52.00

Half board per

person:	£min	£max
Daily	35.00	40.00
Weekly	238.00	259.00

Evening meal 1900 (last orders
1900)
Parking for 15
Open February–December

🛇🍴🖵♿♨(S)✕♪▥💻📷U❀
✕🚬 DAP SP T

Hazel Bank 𝗠
🌸🌸 HIGHLY COMMENDED

Rosthwaite, Borrowdale, Keswick
CA12 5XB
☎ (017687) 77248
Fax (017678) 77373
*Comfortable and well-appointed
country house in the beautiful, peaceful
Borrowdale Valley. Ideal base for
walking or touring. Non-smokers only,
please.*
Bedrooms: 1 single, 2 double, 3 twin
Bathrooms: 6 en-suite

Half board per

person:	£min	£max
Daily		46.00
Weekly		287.00

Evening meal 1900 (last orders
1900)
Parking for 12
Open April–October
Cards accepted: Mastercard, Visa,
Switch/Delta

🛇6♿🍴🖵♿♨🕭✕♪▥💻📷❀
🚬 SP 🏠

Leathes Head Hotel and
Restaurant 𝗠
🌸🌸🌸 HIGHLY COMMENDED

Borrowdale, Keswick CA12 5UY
☎ (017687) 77247
Fax (017687) 77363
Email: 100755,2245
@compuserve.UK

*Edwardian country house with a warm
welcome and magnificent views in the
heart of Borrowdale. Menus change
daily, with emphasis on fresh local
produce.*

Bedrooms: 2 single, 4 double, 2 twin,
2 triple, 1 family room
Bathrooms: 11 en-suite

Bed & breakfast

per night:	£min	£max
Single	39.00	49.00
Double	70.00	80.00

Half board per

person:	£min	£max
Daily	49.50	59.50
Weekly	275.00	350.00

Evening meal 1900 (last orders
2030)
Parking for 25
Open February–December
Cards accepted: Mastercard, Visa,
Switch/Delta

🛇🍴♿📞🍴🖵♿🕭🎯♨(S)✕♪▥(TV)▥
💻🏠30U♪✕🚬❀ DAP 🚬 SP T

Mary Mount 𝗠
🌸🌸 COMMENDED

Borrowdale, Keswick CA12 5UU
☎ (017687) 77223
*Set in 4.5 acres of gardens and
woodlands on the shores of
Derwentwater, 2.5 miles from Keswick.
Views across lake to Catbells and
Maiden Moor. Families and pets
welcome.*
Bedrooms: 1 single, 5 double, 5 twin,
2 triple, 1 family room
Bathrooms: 14 en-suite

Bed & breakfast

per night:	£min	£max
Single	25.00	29.00
Double	50.00	58.00

Lunch available
Evening meal 1830 (last orders
2045)
Parking for 40
Open February–December
Cards accepted: Mastercard, Visa

🛇♿📞🍴🖵♿♨(S)♪▥💻📷❀🚬✕
SP

Seatoller House 𝗠
Listed COMMENDED

Seatoller, Borrowdale, Keswick
CA12 5XN
☎ (017687) 77218
Fax (017687) 77218
*This 300-year-old house has
accommodated visitors to Borrowdale
for well over a century. It continues to
be known for its homely, friendly and
informal atmosphere, good food and
fine location.*
Bedrooms: 1 double, 3 twin, 5 triple
Bathrooms: 3 en-suite, 6 private

Bed & breakfast

per night:	£min	£max
Single	29.00	
Double	56.00	

Half board per person:	£min	£max
Daily	38.00	
Weekly	225.00	

Evening meal 1900 (last orders 1800)
Parking for 15
Open March–November
🏇5♿👜Ⓢ✕🅿️🏧▯📠❀🐾🎏

Stakis Keswick Lodore Hotel ⚊

👑👑👑👑 HIGHLY COMMENDED

Borrowdale, Keswick CA12 5UX
☎ (017687) 77285
Fax (017687) 77343
Largely refurbished hotel with excellent sports and family facilities. Fantastic views of lake and fells beyond. Beautiful grounds and gardens for a relaxing holiday. Half board overnight price based on minimum 2-night stay.
Bedrooms: 10 single, 20 double, 44 twin, 1 triple
Suites available
Bathrooms: 75 en-suite, 1 public

Bed & breakfast per night:	£min	£max
Single	35.00	63.00
Double	70.00	126.00

Half board per person:	£min	£max
Daily	39.50	76.00
Weekly	276.50	479.00

Lunch available
Evening meal 1930 (last orders 2130)
Parking for 123
Cards accepted: Amex, Diners, Mastercard, Visa, Switch/Delta
🏇🚗📞📧▯🖥🅂✕🅼⊙▯
🏧🚲🏊80🐬🎿♣✎🕿🎿🎣⚓⛵
🎿❀DAP🏂SP🎏Ⓣ

BRAITHWAITE

Cumbria
Map ref 5A3

Braithwaite nestles at the foot of the Whinlatter Pass and has a magnificent backdrop of the mountains forming the Coledale Horseshoe.

Coledale Inn ⚊

👑👑👑 COMMENDED

Braithwaite, Keswick CA12 5TN
☎ (017687) 78272
Victorian country house hotel and Georgian inn, in a peaceful hillside position away from traffic, with superb mountain views. Families and pets welcome.
Bedrooms: 1 single, 6 double, 1 twin, 3 triple, 1 family room
Bathrooms: 12 en-suite

Bed & breakfast per night:	£min	£max
Single	20.00	24.00
Double	50.00	58.00

Lunch available
Evening meal 1830 (last orders 2100)
Parking for 15
Cards accepted: Mastercard, Visa
🏇♿📧▯♦Ⓢ✕🅼▯🍽🛏❀
🎏🏂SP🎏

BRAMPTON

Cumbria
Map ref 5B2

Excellent centre for exploring Hadrian's Wall. Wednesday is market day around the Moot Hall in this delightful sandstone-built town. Wall plaque marks the site of Bonnie Prince Charlie and his Jacobite army headquarters whilst they laid siege to Carlisle Castle in 1745.

Sands House Hotel ⚊

👑 COMMENDED

The Sands, Brampton CA8 1UG
☎ (016977) 3085
Fax (016977) 3297

17th C coaching inn. Fully licensed, famous restaurant. En-suite rooms with colour TV, tea-maker and telephone. On A69, close to Hadrian's Wall and Lanercost Priory.
Bedrooms: 4 double, 4 twin, 2 triple
Bathrooms: 10 en-suite, 1 public

Bed & breakfast per night:	£min	£max
Single	34.00	36.00
Double	49.00	52.00

Lunch available
Evening meal 1800 (last orders 2200)
Parking for 50
Cards accepted: Diners, Mastercard, Visa, Switch/Delta
🏇♿📞📧▯♦Ⓢ🅼▯🍽50
♣🏂DAP🏂SPⓉ

BROUGHTON-IN-FURNESS

Cumbria
Map ref 5A3

Old market village whose historic charter to hold fairs is still proclaimed every year on the first day of August in the market square. Good centre for touring the pretty Duddon Valley.

Eccle Riggs Manor Hotel Hotel and Leisure Park Ltd ⚊

👑👑 COMMENDED

Foxfield Road, Broughton-in-Furness LA20 6BN
☎ (01229) 716398 & 716780
Fax (01229) 716958
Ⓜ Minotel
Victorian mansion set in 60 acres with panoramic views of the Coniston hills. Own golf-course and swimming pool.
Bedrooms: 5 double, 1 twin, 3 triple, 3 family rooms
Bathrooms: 12 en-suite

Bed & breakfast per night:	£min	£max
Single	39.50	46.50
Double	62.00	75.00

Half board per person:	£min	£max
Daily	54.50	61.50
Weekly	381.15	442.65

Lunch available
Evening meal 1900 (last orders 2100)
Parking for 80
Cards accepted: Mastercard, Visa, Switch/Delta
🏇🚗📞📧▯♦🖥Ⓢ🅼▯🍽
🍽120🐬🎿♣✎❀🏂SP🎏Ⓣ◎

The Garner Guest House ⚊

👑👑 COMMENDED

Church Street, Broughton-in-Furness LA20 6HJ
☎ (01229) 716462
Comfortable Victorian family house of character, with a sunny walled garden. On the outskirts of this old market town.
Bedrooms: 1 double, 1 twin
Bathrooms: 2 en-suite

Bed & breakfast per night:	£min	£max
Single	23.00	
Double	42.00	

🏇5▯♦ⓊⓁ🅂🖥TV▯🚗❀🏊

For further information on accommodation establishments use the coupons at the back of this guide.

A key to symbols can be found inside the back cover flap.

BUTTERMERE

Cumbria
Map ref 5A3

Small village surrounded by high mountains, between Buttermere Lake and Crummock Water. An ideal centre for walking and climbing the nearby peaks and for touring.

Bridge Hotel ♠

HIGHLY COMMENDED

Buttermere, Cockermouth
CA13 9UZ
☎ (017687) 70252
Fax (017687) 70252

Historic Lakeland hotel with modern comforts and facilities, in an Area of Outstanding Natural Beauty. Superb walking country. Dogs welcome.
Bedrooms: 2 single, 8 double, 12 twin
Bathrooms: 21 en-suite, 1 private

Bed & breakfast per night:	£min	£max
Single	38.00	43.00
Double	76.00	86.00

Half board per person:	£min	£max
Daily	54.00	62.00
Weekly		360.00

Lunch available
Evening meal 1900 (last orders 2030)
Parking for 60
Cards accepted: Mastercard, Visa, Switch/Delta

Pickett Howe ♠

DE LUXE

Buttermere Valley, Cockermouth
CA13 9UY
☎ (01900) 85444
Fax (01900) 85209

Winner of 2 national awards (1994,1997) for excellence in service and cuisine. Luxuriously appointed and peacefully situated 17th C farmhouse,

renowned for creative cooking, relaxing atmosphere and jacuzzis!
Bedrooms: 3 double, 1 twin
Bathrooms: 4 en-suite

Bed & breakfast per night:	£min	£max
Double	74.00	76.00

Half board per person:	£min	£max
Daily	59.00	61.00
Weekly	420.00	420.00

Evening meal from 1915
Parking for 6
Open April–November
Cards accepted: Mastercard, Visa

CARLISLE

Cumbria
Map ref 5A2

Cumbria's only city is rich in history. Attractions include the small red sandstone cathedral and 900-year-old castle with magnificent view from the keep. Award-winning Tullie House Museum and Art Gallery brings 2,000 years of Border history dramatically to life. Excellent centre for shopping.
Tourist Information Centre ☎ *(01228) 512444*

Avondale

HIGHLY COMMENDED

3 St Aidan's Road, Carlisle CA1 1LT
☎ (01228) 23012
Michael and Angela Hayes welcome you to their attractive Edwardian house. Comfortable, spacious rooms. Quiet situation. Private parking. Close to centre.
Bedrooms: 1 double, 2 twin
Bathrooms: 1 en-suite, 1 public

Bed & breakfast per night:	£min	£max
Double	40.00	40.00

Evening meal 1830 (last orders 1200)
Parking for 3

Calreena Guest House ♠

APPROVED

123 Warwick Road, Carlisle
CA1 1JZ
☎ (01228) 25020 & (0410) 577171
Comfortable, friendly guesthouse. Central heating, home cooking. Colour TV and tea-making facilities in all rooms. 2 minutes from city centre, railway and bus stations and from M6, junction 43.

Bedrooms: 1 single, 1 double, 1 twin, 1 triple
Bathrooms: 2 public

Bed & breakfast per night:	£min	£max
Single	15.00	15.00
Double	26.00	26.00

Half board per person:	£min	£max
Daily	20.00	20.00
Weekly	120.00	120.00

Evening meal 1700 (last orders 1500)
Cards accepted: Mastercard, Visa

Cartref

Listed COMMENDED

44 Victoria Place, Carlisle CA1 1EX
☎ (01228) 22077
Family-run guesthouse central to shopping, bus/rail stations and restaurants. Personal service. Colour TV and tea/coffee in all rooms.
Bedrooms: 4 single, 1 double, 2 twin, 4 triple
Bathrooms: 4 public

Bed & breakfast per night:	£min	£max
Single	17.00	19.00
Double	32.00	34.00

Half board per person:	£min	£max
Daily	23.00	25.00
Weekly	160.00	175.00

Lunch available
Evening meal 1700 (last orders 1900)
Cards accepted: Mastercard, Visa

Corner House Hotel and Bar ♠

APPROVED

4 Grey Street, Off London Road, Carlisle CA1 2JP
☎ (01228) 33239
Fax (01228) 46628
Refurbished family-run hotel and bar. Short/long stay. All rooms en-suite. Four poster/family rooms available. Sky TV in lounge, games room, pool/darts. Easy access city attractions, bus, trains, golf, racing. M6 junctions 42/43.
Bedrooms: 3 single, 4 double, 2 twin, 1 triple
Bathrooms: 10 en-suite, 1 public

Bed & breakfast per night:	£min	£max
Single	25.00	30.00
Double	40.00	45.00

Half board per person:	£min	£max
Daily	33.00	38.00
Weekly	196.00	224.00

Lunch available
Evening meal 1730 (last orders 2030)
Cards accepted: Mastercard, Visa, Switch/Delta
☎ [S] [TV] [OAP] [SP] [T]

Cornerways Guest House

[COMMENDED]

107 Warwick Road, Carlisle CA1 1EA
☎ (01228) 21733
Five minutes to rail and bus stations and city centre. M6 exit 43. Colour TV, central heating in all bedrooms. Tea and coffee facilities. Lounge, pool table, payphone.
Bedrooms: 3 single, 1 double, 4 twin, 1 triple, 1 family room
Bathrooms: 1 en-suite, 2 public

Bed & breakfast per night:	£min	£max
Single	14.00	16.00
Double	26.00	32.00

Half board per person:	£min	£max
Daily	19.00	21.00
Weekly	130.00	130.00

Evening meal 1600 (last orders 1900)
Parking for 6
[UL]

County Hotel

[COMMENDED]

9 Botchergate, Carlisle CA1 1QP
☎ (01228) 31316
Fax (01228) 401805
Email: cohot@enterprise.net.uk
Built in 1853 and extensively refurbished with every modern convenience. City centre location, adjacent to railway station. Parking on premises.
Bedrooms: 27 single, 16 double, 27 twin, 10 triple, 4 family rooms
Bathrooms: 84 en-suite

Bed & breakfast per night:	£min	£max
Single	50.00	75.00
Double	70.00	80.00

Half board per person:	£min	£max
Daily	50.00	50.00

Lunch available
Evening meal 1900 (last orders 2145)
Parking for 100
Cards accepted: Amex, Diners, Mastercard, Visa, Switch/Delta
☎ [S] [TV] 150 [OAP] [SP] [T]

Crosby Lodge Country House Hotel

[HIGHLY COMMENDED]

High Crosby, Crosby-on-Eden, Carlisle CA6 4QZ
☎ (01228) 573 618
Fax (01228) 573428

18th C country mansion overlooking parkland and the river. Chef/proprietor provides a renowned English and continental menu complemented by outstanding wine list.
Bedrooms: 1 single, 4 double, 3 twin, 3 triple
Bathrooms: 11 en-suite

Bed & breakfast per night:	£min	£max
Single	75.00	80.00
Double	95.00	125.00

Half board per person:	£min	£max
Daily	74.50	90.50

Lunch available
Evening meal 1930 (last orders 2100)
Parking for 40
Open February–December
Cards accepted: Amex, Mastercard, Visa, Switch/Delta
☎ [S] 20 [SP]

Hazeldene Guest House

[COMMENDED]

Orton Grange, Wigton Road, Carlisle CA5 6LA
☎ (01228) 711953
Detached property with garden area, access to swimming pool and children's play area. 2 miles west of Carlisle on bus route. Comfortable accommodation. Residential licence.
Bedrooms: 2 single, 2 double
Bathrooms: 2 en-suite, 1 public

Bed & breakfast per night:	£min	£max
Single	16.00	18.00
Double	32.00	36.00

Half board per person:	£min	£max
Daily	22.00	24.00
Weekly	130.00	150.00

Lunch available
Evening meal 1700 (last orders 2000)
Parking for 6
[S] [TV] [SP]

Langleigh House

[COMMENDED]

6 Howard Place, Carlisle CA1 1HR
☎ (01228) 30440
Beautifully restored late Victorian house, 5 minutes' walk from city centre. Friendly atmosphere. All rooms en-suite. Private car park.
Bedrooms: 1 single, 1 double, 1 twin, 1 triple
Bathrooms: 4 en-suite

Bed & breakfast per night:	£min	£max
Single	25.00	25.00
Double	36.00	36.00

Parking for 10
[UL]

Royal Hotel

[APPROVED]

9 Lowther Street, Carlisle CA3 8ES
☎ (01228) 22103
Fax (01228) 23904
Family-run hotel. All bedrooms have colour TV. Breakfast, bar lunches and evening meals served.
Bedrooms: 8 single, 4 double, 8 twin, 3 triple
Bathrooms: 16 en-suite, 3 public

Bed & breakfast per night:	£min	£max
Single	21.00	30.00
Double	35.00	46.00

Lunch available
Evening meal 1830 (last orders 2030)
Cards accepted: Mastercard, Visa
☎ [S] [TV] [OAP] [SP]

Swallow Hilltop Hotel

[COMMENDED]

London Road, Carlisle CA1 2PQ
☎ (01228) 529255
Fax (01228) 25238
[CR] Swallow
Comfortable, modern hotel with leisure facilities. Ideal touring base for the Borders, Lakes, Hadrian's Wall and the Solway Coast. Special cabaret weekends. Short break packages available. Half board price is based on a minimum 2-night stay.
Bedrooms: 2 single, 46 double, 42 twin, 2 family rooms
Bathrooms: 92 en-suite

Bed & breakfast per night:	£min	£max
Single	80.00	85.00
Double	99.00	105.00

Continued ▶

CARLISLE

Continued

Half board per person:	£min	£max
Daily	85.00	130.00

Lunch available
Evening meal 1900 (last orders 2200)
Parking for 350
Cards accepted: Amex, Diners, Mastercard, Visa, Switch/Delta
[S] [TV] 500 [OAP] [SP] [T]

Vallum House Garden Hotel

COMMENDED

Burgh Road, Carlisle CA2 7NB
☎ (01228) 21860

In a select residential area on the west side of the city, en route to the Solway coast. Close to Stoneyholm Golf Course and Edward I monument. Bar meals available lunchtime and evening plus a la carte.

Bedrooms: 6 single, 2 twin, 1 triple
Bathrooms: 5 en-suite, 2 public

Bed & breakfast per night:	£min	£max
Single	28.00	35.00
Double	45.00	50.00

Lunch available
Evening meal 1800 (last orders 2100)
Parking for 50
Cards accepted: Mastercard, Visa
[S] [TV] 25 [SP] [T]

Warwick Lodge

HIGHLY COMMENDED

112 Warwick Road, Carlisle CA1 1LF
☎ (01228) 23796

A well-restored and appointed town house built in the 1880s. Within walking distance of the city centre and historic sites.

Bedrooms: 2 triple
Bathrooms: 2 en-suite

Bed & breakfast per night:	£min	£max
Single	23.00	25.00
Double	32.00	36.00

Parking for 3
[UL] [SP]

For ideas on places to visit refer to the introduction at the beginning of this section.

CARTMEL

Cumbria
Map ref 5A3

Picturesque conserved village based on a 12th C priory with a well-preserved church and gatehouse. Just half a mile outside the Lake District National Park, this is a peaceful base for walking and touring, with historic houses and beautiful scenery.

Aynsome Manor Hotel

HIGHLY COMMENDED

Cartmel, Grange-over-Sands LA11 6HH
☎ (015395) 36653
Fax (015395) 36016

Lovely old manor house, nestling in the vale of Cartmel. Good food, attentive service and log fire comfort. Lunches served on Sundays. No smoking in restaurant.

Bedrooms: 6 double, 4 twin, 2 triple
Bathrooms: 12 en-suite, 1 public

Half board per person:	£min	£max
Daily	46.00	62.00
Weekly	296.00	350.00

Evening meal 1900 (last orders 2030)
Parking for 20
Open February–December
Cards accepted: Amex, Mastercard, Visa, Switch/Delta
[S] [SP] [T]

All accommodation in this guide has been graded, or is awaiting a grading, by a trained Tourist Board inspector.

The symbols in each entry give information about services and facilities. A key to these symbols appears at the back of this guide.

The Cavendish at Cartmel

Listed COMMENDED

Cavendish Street, Cartmel, Grange-over-Sands LA11 6QA
☎ (015395) 36240 & 0860 700334
Fax (015395) 36620
[CR] Wayfarer

Cartmel's oldest hostelry, voted best pub 1996 by Good Pub Guide for its award-winning beers. Very popular with locals and visitors.

Bedrooms: 8 double, 2 twin
Bathrooms: 10 en-suite

Bed & breakfast per night:	£min	£max
Single	30.00	35.00
Double	60.00	70.00

Half board per person:	£min	£max
Daily	41.50	51.50
Weekly	290.50	360.50

Lunch available
Evening meal 1800 (last orders 2130)
Parking for 20
Cards accepted: Mastercard, Visa, Switch/Delta
[S] [SP] [T]

CLEATOR

Cumbria
Map ref 5A3

6 miles from the Georgian port of Whitehaven and with easy access to the western fells. Features a grotto similar to that in Lourdes, France.

Grove Court

COMMENDED

Cleator Gate, Cleator CA23 3DT
☎ (01946) 810503
Fax (01946) 815412

Family-run hotel with reputation for food. Convenient for Lake District and Solway coast. Popular meeting place for meals.

Bedrooms: 5 double, 4 twin, 1 family room
Suite available
Bathrooms: 10 en-suite

Bed & breakfast per night:	£min	£max
Single	47.50	50.00
Double	60.00	75.00

Lunch available
Evening meal 1900 (last orders 2200)
Parking for 100
Cards accepted: Amex, Diners, Mastercard, Visa
[S] [TV] 50 [SP]

COCKERMOUTH

Cumbria
Map ref 5A2

Ancient market town at confluence of Rivers Cocker and Derwent. Birthplace of William Wordsworth in 1770. The house where he was born is at the end of the town's broad, tree-lined main street and is now owned by the National Trust. Good touring base for the Lakes. *Tourist Information Centre ☎ (01900) 822634*

Rose Cottage ♨
ᵕᵕ COMMENDED

Lorton Road, Cockermouth
CA13 9DX
☎ (01900) 822189

In a pleasant position, this guesthouse is within easy reach of the Lakes and the coast.
Bedrooms: 1 single, 3 double, 1 twin, 2 triple
Bathrooms: 3 en-suite, 2 public

Bed & breakfast per night:

	£min	£max
Single	22.00	30.00
Double	35.00	45.00

Half board per person:

	£min	£max
Daily	28.00	40.00
Weekly	175.00	225.00

Evening meal 1900 (last orders 2030)
Parking for 12
Cards accepted: Amex, Mastercard, Visa

🛌🛋🖥📺♨🔌💷🍴🚫📺📼 ♨🐕 SP T

Trout Hotel ♨
ᵕᵕᵕᵕ HIGHLY COMMENDED

Crown Street, Cockermouth
CA13 0EJ
☎ (01900) 823591
Fax (01900) 827514
Attractive black and white listed building, dating from c 1670, on banks of River Derwent adjacent to own award-winning gardens. 12 miles west of Keswick off A66.
Bedrooms: 4 single, 20 double, 8 twin, 2 triple
Bathrooms: 34 en-suite

Bed & breakfast per night:

	£min	£max
Single	59.95	105.00
Double	79.95	140.00

Half board per person:

	£min	£max
Daily	99.75	149.95

Lunch available
Evening meal 1900 (last orders 2130)
Parking for 50
Cards accepted: Amex, Mastercard, Visa, Switch/Delta

🛌🐕🛋📞🖥📺♨🍷🔌💷🍴📺🍺🖥 ♨🏠150🔌🏊♻🚫 SP ♨ T

CONISTON

Cumbria
Map ref 5A3

The 803m fell Coniston Old Man dominates the skyline to the east of this village at the northern end of Coniston Water. Arthur Ransome set his "Swallows and Amazons" stories here. Coniston's most famous resident was John Ruskin, whose home, Brantwood, is open to the public. Good centre for walking.

Crown Hotel ♨
ᵕᵕ APPROVED

Coniston LA21 8EA
☎ (015394) 41243
Fax (015394) 41804
At the foot of Coniston Old Man, 10 minutes' walk to the lake where Donald Campbell attempted to break the world water speed record.
Bedrooms: 4 double, 1 twin, 3 triple
Bathrooms: 1 private, 2 public

Bed & breakfast per night:

	£min	£max
Single	20.00	35.00
Double	35.00	48.00

Half board per person:

	£min	£max
Daily	30.00	50.00
Weekly	160.00	260.00

Lunch available
Evening meal 1900 (last orders 2100)
Parking for 30
Cards accepted: Amex, Diners, Mastercard, Visa, Switch/Delta

🛌🖥♨🔌💷🖥 🚗🍴 ♨🔱🚫✈ SP T ◉

Half board prices are given per person, but in some cases these may be based on double/twin occupancy.

Old Rectory Hotel ♨
ᵕᵕᵕ HIGHLY COMMENDED

Torver, Coniston LA21 8AY
☎ (015394) 41353
Fax (015394) 41156

Tastefully converted rectory offering delightful accommodation, set in 3 acres with pastoral views. Imaginative cooking in conservatory dining room. Superb local walks.
Bedrooms: 1 single, 4 double, 2 twin, 1 triple
Bathrooms: 8 en-suite

Bed & breakfast per night:

	£min	£max
Single	19.50	30.00
Double	39.00	60.00

Half board per person:

	£min	£max
Daily	29.50	42.50
Weekly	196.00	282.00

Evening meal 1930 (last orders 1930)
Parking for 10
Cards accepted: Mastercard, Visa

🛌🐕🖥📺♨🔌💷🍴🖥🚗🚶 ♨🚗🚫 SP T ◉

Shepherds Villa ♨
ᵕᵕ APPROVED

Tilberthwaite Avenue, Coniston
LA21 8EE
☎ (015394) 41337
Friendly, comfortable, family-run guesthouse. Spacious accommodation in a quiet spot on the edge of the village. A warm welcome to everyone.
Bedrooms: 4 double, 1 twin, 3 triple, 2 family rooms
Bathrooms: 4 en-suite, 1 private, 2 public

Bed & breakfast per night:

	£min	£max
Single	17.00	21.00
Double	34.00	42.00

Lunch available
Parking for 10
Cards accepted: Mastercard, Visa, Switch/Delta

🛌5🖥♨🔌💷🍴📺📺🖥🚗♨ ✈🚫 SP T

Establishments should be open throughout the year, unless otherwise stated.

CONISTON

Continued

Sun Hotel Coniston

👑👑👑 COMMENDED

Coniston LA21 8HQ
☎ (015394) 41248

Country house hotel and 16th C inn, in spectacular mountain setting on the fringe of the village and at the foot of Coniston Old Man.
Bedrooms: 1 single, 7 double, 3 twin
Bathrooms: 9 en-suite, 2 private
Bed & breakfast per night:

	£min	£max
Single	25.00	35.00
Double	50.00	70.00

Half board per person:

	£min	£max
Daily	42.00	48.00
Weekly	264.60	302.40

Lunch available
Evening meal 1900 (last orders 2045)
Parking for 20
Cards accepted: Diners, Mastercard, Visa

Wheelgate Country House Hotel

👑👑👑 HIGHLY COMMENDED

Little Arrow, Torver, Coniston LA21 8AU
☎ (015394) 41418
Delightful 17th C country house with attractive bedrooms, oak-beamed lounge and dining room. Complimentary leisure facilities. Perfect Lakeland retreat.
Bedrooms: 2 single, 7 double
Bathrooms: 9 en-suite
Bed & breakfast per night:

	£min	£max
Single	25.00	30.00
Double	50.00	60.00

Evening meal 1930 (last orders 1930)
Parking for 9
Open March–November
Cards accepted: Amex, Mastercard, Visa

CROSTHWAITE

Cumbria
Map ref 5A3

Small village in the picturesque Lyth Valley off the A5074. St Kentigern's church is home to a memorial of the poet Robert Southey. The valley itself is famous for its Damson plums.

Crosthwaite House

👑👑 HIGHLY COMMENDED

Crosthwaite, Kendal LA8 8BP
☎ (015395) 68264
Mid-18th C building with unspoilt views of the Lyth and Winster valleys, 5 miles from Bowness and Kendal. Family atmosphere and home cooking. Self-catering cottages also available.
Bedrooms: 1 single, 3 double, 2 twin
Bathrooms: 6 en-suite
Bed & breakfast per night:

	£min	£max
Single	20.00	22.00
Double	40.00	44.00

Half board per person:

	£min	£max
Daily	32.00	34.00
Weekly	220.00	230.00

Evening meal 1900 (last orders 1900)
Parking for 10
Open March–November
Cards accepted: Amex

DENT

Cumbria
Map ref 5B3

Very picturesque village with narrow cobbled streets, lying within the boundaries of the Yorkshire Dales National Park.

George and Dragon Hotel

👑👑 COMMENDED

Main Street, Dent, Sedbergh LA10 5QL
☎ (01539) 625256
Excellent centre for exploring the Yorkshire Dales National Park. Owned by, and serves beer from, Dent's own small brewery.
Bedrooms: 4 double, 3 twin, 2 triple
Bathrooms: 3 en-suite, 2 public
Bed & breakfast per night:

	£min	£max
Single	25.00	33.00
Double	40.00	50.00

Half board per person:

	£min	£max
Daily	29.00	34.00
Weekly	185.00	210.00

Lunch available
Evening meal 1900 (last orders 2200)
Parking for 14
Cards accepted: Mastercard, Visa

EGREMONT

Cumbria
Map ref 5A3

Old market town with a wide tree-lined street. One of its attractions is the 12th C Norman castle built of red sandstone.
Tourist Information Centre ☎ *(01946) 820693*

Old Vicarage Guest House

👑 COMMENDED

Thornhill, Egremont CA22 2NX
☎ (01946) 841577
Imposing 19th C vicarage of character in attractive grounds. Within easy reach of sea and mountains.
Bedrooms: 3 triple
Bathrooms: 2 public
Bed & breakfast per night:

	£min	£max
Single	14.00	15.50
Double	28.00	31.00

Parking for 6

ENDMOOR

Cumbria
Map ref 5B3

Village on the A65 between Kendal and Kirkby Lonsdale, convenient for touring South Lakes and for the M6.

Summerlands Tower

👑👑 HIGHLY COMMENDED

Endmoor, Kendal LA8 0ED
☎ (015395) 61081
Fine Victorian country guesthouse offering spacious and tastefully decorated accommodation, surrounded by 3 acres of mature gardens and woodlands. 3 miles from M6 junction 36.
Bedrooms: 1 double, 1 twin
Bathrooms: 1 en-suite, 1 private
Bed & breakfast per night:

	£min	£max
Single	27.00	32.00
Double	44.00	54.00

Parking for 6

ENNERDALE

Cumbria
Map ref 5A3

The most western valley of the Lake District. The small village of Ennerdale Bridge is an ideal centre for walking and rock climbing and lies just one mile west of Ennerdale Water. Pillar and Pillar Rock, famous for its rock climbs, towers over the lake.

Shepherd's Arms Hotel

COMMENDED

Ennerdale Bridge, Ennerdale, Cleator CA23 3AR
☎ (01946) 861249
Fax (01946) 861249
Small hotel with an informal and relaxed atmosphere, situated in the centre of Ennerdale Bridge. Bar and restaurant, open fires. Popular with walkers.
Bedrooms: 1 single, 3 double, 4 twin
Bathrooms: 6 en-suite, 2 private

Bed & breakfast per night:

	£min	£max
Single	26.00	28.00
Double	48.00	52.00

Half board per person:

	£min	£max
Daily	38.00	40.00
Weekly	230.00	260.00

Lunch available
Evening meal 1930 (last orders 2030)
Parking for 8

ESKDALE

Cumbria
Map ref 5A3

Several minor roads lead to the west end of this beautiful valley, or it can be approached via the east over the Hardknott Pass, the Lake District's steepest pass. Scafell Pike and Bow Fell lie to the north and a miniature railway links the Eskdale Valley with Ravenglass on the coast.

Woolpack Inn

APPROVED

Boot, Eskdale CA19 1TH
☎ (01946) 723230
Fax (01946) 723230
Comfortable hotel serving real ale and home-cooked food, set in beautiful scenery at the head of the Eskdale Valley.
Bedrooms: 3 double, 4 twin, 1 family room
Bathrooms: 1 public, 4 private showers

Bed & breakfast per night:

	£min	£max
Single	19.50	27.00
Double	39.00	54.00

Lunch available
Evening meal 1800 (last orders 2100)
Parking for 40
Cards accepted: Mastercard, Visa

GRANGE-OVER-SANDS

Cumbria
Map ref 5A3

Set on the beautiful Cartmel Peninsula, this tranquil resort, known as Lakeland's Riviera, overlooks Morecambe Bay. Pleasant seafront walks and beautiful gardens. The bay attracts many species of wading birds.

Clare House

COMMENDED

Park Road, Grange-over-Sands LA11 7HQ
☎ (015395) 33026 & 34253

Charming hotel with well-appointed bedrooms and pleasant lounges, set in grounds with magnificent bay views. Delightful meals prepared from the best ingredients.
Bedrooms: 3 single, 2 double, 11 twin, 1 triple
Bathrooms: 16 en-suite, 1 public

Bed & breakfast per night:

	£min	£max
Single	30.00	33.00
Double	60.00	66.00

Half board per person:

	£min	£max
Daily	44.00	47.00
Weekly	270.00	295.00

Lunch available
Evening meal 1845 (last orders 1915)
Parking for 16
Open April–October

The Cumbria Grand Hotel

COMMENDED

Lindale Road, Grange-over-Sands LA11 6EN
☎ (015395) 32331
Fax (015395) 34534
In 25 acres of grounds overlooking

Morecambe Bay, with easy access to the M6 and the Lake District. Tennis court, trim trail, snooker room.
Bedrooms: 17 single, 26 double, 80 twin, 6 triple
Bathrooms: 126 en-suite, 3 private

Bed & breakfast per night:

	£min	£max
Single	42.00	50.00
Double	65.00	78.00

Half board per person:

	£min	£max
Daily	42.00	60.00
Weekly	220.00	270.00

Lunch available
Evening meal 1830 (last orders 2030)
Parking for 120
Cards accepted: Amex, Diners, Mastercard, Visa, Switch/Delta

Grange Hotel

Station Square, Grange-over-Sands LA11 6EJ
☎ (015395) 33666
Fax (015395) 35064
 Consort

Victorian hotel with panoramic views over Morecambe Bay. Renowned for its service, food and leisure facilities.
Bedrooms: 4 single, 15 double, 16 twin, 6 triple
Bathrooms: 41 en-suite

Bed & breakfast per night:

	£min	£max
Single	45.00	54.00
Double	78.00	88.00

Lunch available
Evening meal 1900 (last orders 2100)
Parking for 50
Cards accepted: Amex, Diners, Mastercard, Visa, Switch/Delta

Hampsfell House Hotel

COMMENDED

Hampsfell Road, Grange-over-Sands LA11 6BG
☎ (015395) 32567
Peaceful country setting in own grounds. Fresh and imaginatively prepared food. Extensive wine list. Ample safe parking.

Continued ▶

GRANGE-OVER-SANDS

Continued

Bedrooms: 4 double, 4 twin, 1 triple
Bathrooms: 9 en-suite, 1 public

Bed & breakfast per night:	£min	£max
Single	25.00	30.00
Double	50.00	58.00

Half board per person:	£min	£max
Daily	35.00	45.00
Weekly	240.00	260.00

Lunch available
Evening meal 1830 (last orders 2030)
Parking for 20
Cards accepted: Mastercard, Visa
🐴 🛏 📺 ☕ ✋ 🔒 [S] 🚭 [R] [TV] ▥ ⛟ ✿ 🚌 [SP] 🏠 [T]

Mayfields

[COMMENDED]

3 Mayfield Terrace, Kents Bank Road, Grange-over-Sands LA11 7DW
☎ (015395) 34730
Victorian terraced town house, tastefully furnished and equipped to a high standard. In a pleasant position on fringe of town close to promenade and open countryside.
Bedrooms: 1 single, 1 double, 1 twin
Bathrooms: 2 en-suite, 1 private shower

Bed & breakfast per night:	£min	£max
Single	18.00	18.00
Double	38.00	40.00

Half board per person:	£min	£max
Daily	30.00	32.00
Weekly	188.00	200.00

Lunch available
Evening meal from 1830
Parking for 3
🐴 📺 ☕ ✋ [UL] 🔒 [S] 🚭 [R] [TV] ▥ ⛟ ✿ 🐕 🚌 [SP] ◎

Methven Hotel

[COMMENDED]

Kents Bank Road, Grange-over-Sands LA11 7DU
☎ (015395) 32031
Pleasantly proportioned Victorian building with half an acre of garden and superb panoramic views across Morecambe Bay. Ideal for a quiet and peaceful holiday.
Bedrooms: 4 double, 4 twin, 2 triple
Bathrooms: 10 en-suite, 1 public

Bed & breakfast per night:	£min	£max
Single	30.00	35.00
Double	50.00	60.00

Half board per person:	£min	£max
Daily	35.50	38.00
Weekly	238.00	255.50

Lunch available
Evening meal 1830 (last orders 2030)
Parking for 10
🐴 🛏 📺 ☕ 🔒 [S] 🚭 [R] ▥ ⛟ ✿ 🚌 ✈ [SP] 🏠

Netherwood Hotel

[COMMENDED]

Grange-over-Sands LA11 6ET
☎ (015395) 32552
Fax (015395) 34121
Built in 1893 and a building of high architectural and historic interest.
Wheelchair access category 3
Bedrooms: 4 single, 16 double, 4 twin, 2 triple, 3 family rooms
Bathrooms: 29 en-suite, 2 public

Bed & breakfast per night:	£min	£max
Single	45.00	55.00
Double	90.00	110.00

Half board per person:	£min	£max
Daily	61.00	71.00
Weekly	420.00	483.00

Lunch available
Evening meal 1900 (last orders 2030)
Parking for 160
Cards accepted: Mastercard, Visa, Switch/Delta
🐴 ☎ 📠 📺 ☕ 🔒 [S] 🚭 ◐ [I] ▥ ⛟ 🏛150 ✋ ✿ ✈ [SP] 🏠 [T]

GRASMERE

Cumbria
Map ref 5A3

Described by William Wordsworth as "the loveliest spot that man hath ever found", this village, famous for its gingerbread, is in a beautiful setting overlooked by Helm Grag. Wordsworth lived at Dove Cottage. The cottage and museum are open to the public.

Ash Cottage Guest House

[COMMENDED]

Red Lion Square, Grasmere, Ambleside LA22 9SP
☎ (015394) 35224
Detached guesthouse with its own award-winning garden, in the centre of Grasmere village. English home cooking our speciality.
Bedrooms: 1 single, 3 double, 3 twin, 1 triple
Bathrooms: 8 en-suite

Bed & breakfast per night:	£min	£max
Double	21.00	28.50

Half board per person:	£min	£max
Daily	32.00	39.00

Evening meal 1900 (last orders 1900)
Parking for 10
🐴7 🛏 ☎ 📺 ☕ ✋ 🔒 [S] 🚭 [R] ▥ ⛟ ✿ 🐕 🚌 ✈ [SP]

Bridge House Hotel

[COMMENDED]

Stock Lane, Grasmere, Ambleside LA22 9SN
☎ (015394) 35425
Fax (015394) 35523
Comfortable hotel in 2 acres of peaceful woodland gardens beside the River Rothay in village centre. King-sized rooms, king-sized beds. Imaginative cuisine. Ample parking (yes, really!) relaxation guaranteed.
Bedrooms: 9 double, 9 twin
Bathrooms: 18 en-suite

Bed & breakfast per night:	£min	£max
Single	36.00	39.00
Double	72.00	78.00

Half board per person:	£min	£max
Daily	46.00	49.00
Weekly	274.00	289.00

Evening meal 1900 (last orders 1930)
Parking for 25
Open February–November and Christmas
Cards accepted: Mastercard, Visa, Switch/Delta
🐴 🛏 📠 ☎ 📺 ☕ ✋ 🔒 [S] [R] ▥ ⛟ ✿ 🐕 🚌 ✈ [SP]

The Grasmere Hotel

[HIGHLY COMMENDED]

Grasmere, Ambleside LA22 9TA
☎ (015394) 35277
Fax (015394) 35277

In the midst of beautiful mountain scenery with the restaurant overlooking a large garden, the river and surrounding hills.
Bedrooms: 1 single, 9 double, 2 twin
Bathrooms: 12 en-suite

Bed & breakfast

per night:	£min	£max
Single	25.00	40.00
Double	50.00	80.00

Half board per

person:	£min	£max
Daily	35.00	55.00
Weekly	245.00	385.00

Evening meal 1930 (last orders 2030)
Parking for 16
Open February–December
Cards accepted: Amex, Mastercard, Visa, Switch/Delta

How Foot Lodge

COMMENDED
Town End, Grasmere LA22 9SQ
☎ (015394) 35366

Lovely Victorian guesthouse owned by the Wordsworth Trust, in own grounds overlooking Grasmere Lake and close to Dove Cottage.
Bedrooms: 4 double, 2 twin
Bathrooms: 6 en-suite

Bed & breakfast

per night:	£min	£max
Single	30.00	40.00
Double	50.00	58.00

Parking for 6
Open February–December
Cards accepted: Mastercard, Visa

Lake View Country House

COMMENDED
Lake View Drive, Grasmere, Ambleside LA22 9TD
☎ (015394) 35384
In private grounds overlooking the lake and with private access. Located in the village but off the main road.
Bedrooms: 1 single, 3 double, 1 twin
Bathrooms: 3 en-suite, 1 public

Bed & breakfast

per night:	£min	£max
Single	24.50	28.50
Double	49.00	57.00

Half board per

person:	£min	£max
Daily	34.00	38.00
Weekly	228.00	256.00

Evening meal 1830 (last orders 1500)
Parking for 10
Open February–November

Moss Grove Hotel

COMMENDED
Grasmere, Ambleside LA22 9SW
☎ (015394) 35251
Fax (015394) 35691
Email: martinw@globalnet.co.uk
Minotel

Elegant Lakeland hotel. Some four-poster bedrooms with south-facing balconies. Cosy bar, conservatory, sauna and use of adjacent indoor swimming pool.
Bedrooms: 2 single, 7 double, 3 twin, 1 triple, 1 family room
Bathrooms: 13 en-suite, 2 public

Bed & breakfast

per night:	£min	£max
Single	26.00	45.00
Double	52.00	90.00

Half board per

person:	£min	£max
Daily	34.00	90.00
Weekly	272.00	370.00

Lunch available
Evening meal 1930 (last orders 2030)
Parking for 16
Open February–November
Cards accepted: Mastercard, Visa, Switch/Delta

Oak Bank Hotel

HIGHLY COMMENDED
Broadgate, Grasmere, Ambleside LA22 9TA
☎ (015394) 35217
Fax (015395) 35685
A gem rarely to be found. Family-run since 1981. A small hotel of superior accommodation and award-winning cordon bleu cuisine.
Bedrooms: 1 single, 9 double, 4 twin, 1 family room
Bathrooms: 15 en-suite

Bed & breakfast

per night:	£min	£max
Single	27.50	47.50
Double	55.00	95.00

Half board per

person:	£min	£max
Daily	31.00	60.50
Weekly	217.00	388.00

Evening meal 1900 (last orders 2300)
Parking for 15
Open February–December
Cards accepted: Mastercard, Visa, Switch/Delta

Raise View Guest House

COMMENDED
White Bridge, Grasmere, Ambleside LA22 9RQ
☎ (015394) 35215 & 0378 146313
Fax (015394) 35126
Email: John@raisevw.demon.
Situated at the northern edge of Grasmere, with uninterrupted views of Easedale and easy access to many fine walks. Log fires and a homely atmosphere.
http://www.raisevw.demon.co.uk
Bedrooms: 4 double, 2 twin
Bathrooms: 6 en-suite

Bed & breakfast

per night:	£min	£max
Double	46.00	52.00

Parking for 6
Open February–November

Red Lion

COMMENDED
Red Lion Square, Grasmere, Ambleside LA22 9SS
☎ (015394) 35456
Fax (015394) 35579
Best Western
200-year-old coaching inn refurbished to highest standards, including our own leisure facilities. Good food and friendly staff.
Bedrooms: 3 single, 15 double, 12 twin, 4 family rooms
Bathrooms: 34 en-suite

Bed & breakfast

per night:	£min	£max
Single	38.00	51.00
Double	76.00	102.00

Half board per

person:	£min	£max
Daily	51.00	64.00
Weekly	312.00	384.00

Lunch available
Evening meal 1900 (last orders 2100)
Parking for 38
Cards accepted: Amex, Diners, Mastercard, Visa, Switch/Delta

GRASMERE
Continued

The Swan ⋔
⬢⬢⬢⬢ HIGHLY COMMENDED
Grasmere, Ambleside LA22 9RF
☎ (015394) 35551
Fax (015394) 35741
Ⓒ Forte
A homely hotel at the foot of Dunmail Raise on the Windermere to Keswick road.
Bedrooms: 2 single, 20 double, 14 twin
Bathrooms: 36 en-suite
Bed & breakfast per night:

	£min	£max
Single	45.00	75.00
Double	80.00	140.00

Half board per person:

	£min	£max
Daily	55.00	85.00
Weekly	315.00	455.00

Lunch available
Evening meal 1900 (last orders 2100)
Parking for 40
Cards accepted: Amex, Diners, Mastercard, Visa, Switch/Delta
🐎🛠️📞🖥️🛏️🍷🔌✂️🅿️🛗🖨️🍴
🍽️ 35 ⛴️❄️🚗🚫 SP 🏤 T

HAWKSHEAD
Cumbria
Map ref 5A3

Lying near Esthwaite Water, this village has great charm and character. Its small squares are linked by flagged or cobbled alleys and the main square is dominated by the market house, or Shambles, where the butchers had their stalls in days gone by.

Belmount Country House
⬢ APPROVED
Outgate, Ambleside LA22 ONJ
☎ (015394) 36535
Fine, family-run Georgian house standing in 3 acres. Superb views. Warm welcome.
Bedrooms: 3 double, 2 twin, 3 triple, 2 family rooms
Bathrooms: 3 public
Bed & breakfast per night:

	£min	£max
Single	22.50	
Double	35.00	

Half board per person:

	£min	£max
Daily	26.00	
Weekly	182.00	

Evening meal 1900 (last orders 1600)
Parking for 12
🐎🪆🛗 S ✂️ 🅿️ TV 🛏️ 🚗❄️🚗🚫 SP

Greenbank House Hotel ⋔
⬢ APPROVED
Hawkshead, Ambleside LA22 0NS
☎ (015394) 36497
Well-appointed family-run country house hotel in this picturesque village. Central for all activities. Good home cooking.
Bedrooms: 4 single, 7 double, 1 twin
Bathrooms: 6 en-suite, 3 public
Bed & breakfast per night:

	£min	£max
Single	21.00	25.00
Double	42.00	50.00

Evening meal 1830 (last orders 1600)
Parking for 12
🐎🪆🛗 S ✂️ 🅿️ TV 🛏️ 🚗❄️🚗🚫 SP

Grizedale Lodge Hotel and Restaurant in the Forest ⋔
⬢⬢⬢ COMMENDED
Grizedale, Hawkshead, Ambleside LA22 OQL
☎ (015394) 36532
Fax (015394) 36572
Comfortable former shooting lodge with sun-terrace and log fires. In magnificent Grizedale Forest, midway between Coniston and Windermere. Close to forest walks and sculpture trails.
Bedrooms: 6 double, 2 twin, 1 triple
Bathrooms: 9 en-suite
Bed & breakfast per night:

	£min	£max
Single	28.00	37.50
Double	55.00	65.00

Half board per person:

	£min	£max
Daily	48.50	61.00
Weekly	290.00	325.00

Lunch available
Evening meal 1900 (last orders 2000)
Parking for 25
Open February–December
Cards accepted: Amex, Mastercard, Visa, Switch/Delta
🐎🪆🛗 S ✂️ 🅿️ 🛏️ 🚗❄️🚗🚫 SP T

Queens Head Hotel ⋔
⬢⬢⬢ COMMENDED
Main Street, Hawkshead, Ambleside LA22 0NS
☎ (015394) 36271
Fax (015394) 36722
Located between Lakes Windermere and Coniston. The home of Beatrix Potter, Wordsworth's grammar school and Ann Tyson's cottage. Fishing and bowling green facilities available.
Bedrooms: 10 double, 1 twin, 2 triple
Bathrooms: 11 en-suite, 2 private, 2 public
Bed & breakfast per night:

	£min	£max
Single	35.00	45.00
Double	56.50	73.50

Half board per person:

	£min	£max
Weekly	212.00	245.25

Lunch available
Evening meal 1815 (last orders 2130)
Cards accepted: Mastercard, Visa, Switch/Delta
🐎🛠️📞🖥️🛏️🍷🔌✂️ S ✂️ 🛏️ 🚗 U ▶️ 🚗🚫 SP 🏤 T

Red Lion Inn ⋔
⬢⬢ APPROVED
The Square, Hawkshead, Ambleside LA22 0NS
☎ (015394) 36213
Fax (015394) 36747
14th C coaching inn in the centre of Hawkshead, a uniquely beautiful village in England's most beautiful corner.
Bedrooms: 9 double, 2 twin, 1 triple
Bathrooms: 12 en-suite
Bed & breakfast per night:

	£min	£max
Single	29.00	40.00
Double	58.00	70.00

Half board per person:

	£min	£max
Daily	47.00	50.00
Weekly	295.00	350.00

Lunch available
Evening meal 1900 (last orders 2130)
Parking for 12
Cards accepted: Amex, Diners, Mastercard, Visa, Switch/Delta
🐎📞🖥️🍷🔌✂️ S ✂️ 🛏️ 🚗🍴▶️❄️🚫 SP 🏤 T

Silverholme ⋔
⬢⬢⬢ COMMENDED
Graythwaite LA12 8AZ
☎ (015395) 31332

Set in its own grounds, overlooking Lake Windermere and with lake access, this small mansion house provides a quiet, comfortable, relaxed atmosphere. Home cooking.

Bedrooms: 2 double, 1 triple
Bathrooms: 3 en-suite

Bed & breakfast

per night:	£min	£max
Single	22.00	23.00
Double	44.00	46.00

Half board per person:

	£min	£max
Daily	35.00	36.00
Weekly	222.00	227.00

Lunch available
Evening meal 1800 (last orders 1800)
Parking for 7

🛇🚪🛏🕯♿🖐Ⓢ✂🅟📺▥ 🍽☕❀🚐🆖SP♿T

HELTON

Cumbria
Map ref 5B3

"A place on the side of a hill", Helton nestles in a quiet, undisturbed corner of the Lakes yet has easy access to Penrith and junction 40 of the M6.

Beckfoot Country House 🄼

👑👑👑 COMMENDED

Helton, Penrith CA10 2QB
☎ (01931) 713241
Fax (01931) 713391
Email: malcolmwh@aol.com
Ⓖ Logis of GB
Nestling in the Lakeland Fells of the Lowther Valley near Haweswater. Ideal walking base. M6 exit 39 (south) and 40 (north).
Bedrooms: 1 single, 2 double, 2 twin, 1 triple
Bathrooms: 6 en-suite

Bed & breakfast

per night:	£min	£max
Single	26.00	32.00
Double	52.00	64.00

Half board per person:

	£min	£max
Daily	42.00	48.00
Weekly	250.00	288.00

Evening meal 1900 (last orders 1930)
Parking for 12
Open March–November
Cards accepted: Amex, Mastercard, Visa

🛇🚪🖐Ⓢ✂🅟📺▥☕🍽12 ❀🚐SP♿⊚

Half board prices are given per person, but in some cases these may be based on double/twin occupancy.

HEVERSHAM

Cumbria
Map ref 5B3

This attractive village is set on a hill, and has a grammar school founded in 1613.

The Blue Bell at Heversham 🄼

👑👑👑 HIGHLY COMMENDED

Princes Way, Heversham, Milnthorpe LA7 7EE
☎ (015395) 62018
Fax (015395) 62455

Country hotel in a rural haven, an ideal touring centre. Adjacent to A6 south of Kendal. Readily accessible from junctions 35 or 36 of M6.
Bedrooms: 1 single, 14 double, 6 twin, 1 triple
Bathrooms: 22 en-suite

Bed & breakfast

per night:	£min	£max
Single	39.50	49.50
Double	64.00	95.00

Half board per person:

	£min	£max
Daily	59.00	69.00
Weekly	413.00	483.00

Lunch available
Evening meal 1900 (last orders 2130)
Parking for 100
Cards accepted: Amex, Diners, Mastercard, Visa, Switch/Delta

🛇🍽🕯🚪🛏♿🖐🍷Ⓢ✂🅟📺① ▥🍽☕🍴80 🕯♿U✦🆖SP♿T⊚

IREBY

Cumbria
Map ref 5A2

A picturesque village which was once a thriving market town. About 500 ft above sea level, it lies just outside the Lake District National Park. Good views of Skiddaw and the surrounding fells.

Woodlands Country House 🄼

👑👑👑 HIGHLY COMMENDED

Ireby CA5 1EX
☎ (016973) 71791
Fax (016973) 71482
In traditional Cumbrian village, 4 miles north of Bassenthwaite. Victorian former vicarage, in its own grounds,

---

overlooking open fells. Pets, walkers and wheelchair users welcome. Warm welcome assured.
Wheelchair access category 2♿
Bedrooms: 3 double, 2 twin, 2 triple
Bathrooms: 7 en-suite

Bed & breakfast

per night:	£min	£max
Double	55.00	60.00

Half board per person:

	£min	£max
Daily	40.00	43.00
Weekly	225.00	250.00

Evening meal 1900 (last orders 1600)
Parking for 12
Open March–October and Christmas
Cards accepted: Amex, Mastercard, Visa, Switch/Delta

🛇🛏♿🚪🖐🍷Ⓢ✂🅟📺▥☕🍽▶ ❀🚐🆖SP♿T⊚

KENDAL

Cumbria
Map ref 5B3

The "Auld Grey Town" lies in the valley of the River Kent with a backcloth of limestone fells. Situated just outside the Lake District National Park, it is a good centre for touring the Lakes and surrounding country. Ruined castle, reputed birthplace of Catherine Parr.
Tourist Information Centre ☎ *(01539) 725758*

Brantholme

Listed COMMENDED

7 Sedbergh Road, Kendal LA9 6AD
☎ (01539) 722340
Family-run guesthouse in own grounds. All rooms with private facilities. Good meals from fresh local produce.
Bedrooms: 3 twin
Bathrooms: 2 en-suite, 1 private

Bed & breakfast

per night:	£min	£max
Single	19.00	25.00
Double	38.00	40.00

Half board per person:

	£min	£max
Daily	25.00	31.00
Weekly	161.00	210.00

Evening meal 1830 (last orders 1730)
Parking for 6
Open March–November

🛇🆖Ⓢ✂📺▥❀🍴🚐SP♿

KENDAL
Continued

Fairways Guest House
⚜⚜ COMMENDED

102 Windermere Road, Kendal
LA9 5EZ
☎ (01539) 725564
On the main Kendal-Windermere road. Victorian guesthouse with en-suite facilities. TV, tea and coffee in all rooms. Four-poster bedrooms. Private parking.
Bedrooms: 3 double
Bathrooms: 3 en-suite, 1 public

Bed & breakfast per night:

	£min	£max
Single	17.00	20.00
Double	34.00	38.00

Parking for 4

Garden House M
⚜⚜ HIGHLY COMMENDED

Fowling Lane, Kendal LA9 6PH
☎ (01539) 731131
Fax (01539) 740064
Elegant country house offering personal service. Ideal touring base for Lakes and dales. Ample parking. 2-day breaks available. All rooms with private facilities.
Bedrooms: 2 single, 4 double, 3 twin, 1 triple, 1 family room
Bathrooms: 11 en-suite

Bed & breakfast per night:

	£min	£max
Single	49.50	52.50
Double	70.00	79.00

Half board per person:

	£min	£max
Daily	53.00	65.00
Weekly	350.00	380.00

Lunch available
Evening meal 1900 (last orders 2130)
Parking for 15
Cards accepted: Amex, Diners, Mastercard, Visa, Switch/Delta

Heaves Hotel M
⚜⚜ APPROVED

Kendal LA8 8EF
☎ (015395) 60269 & 60396
Fax (015395) 60269

Georgian mansion in 10 acres, 4 miles from M6, junction 36, and Kendal. Billiard room, library. Family owned and run.
Bedrooms: 4 single, 4 double, 5 twin, 1 triple, 1 family room
Bathrooms: 10 en-suite, 1 private, 2 public

Bed & breakfast per night:

	£min	£max
Single	20.00	30.00
Double	40.00	62.00

Half board per person:

	£min	£max
Daily	32.50	42.50
Weekly	213.50	478.10

Lunch available
Evening meal 1900 (last orders 2000)
Parking for 24
Cards accepted: Amex, Diners, Mastercard, Visa, Switch/Delta

Hillside Guest House
⚜⚜ COMMENDED

4 Beast Banks, Kendal LA9 4JW
☎ (01539) 722836
Small elegant Victorian guesthouse near the shops and town facilities, convenient for the Lakes, Yorkshire Dales and Morecambe Bay.
Bedrooms: 2 single, 3 double, 1 twin
Bathrooms: 4 en-suite, 2 public

Bed & breakfast per night:

	£min	£max
Single	16.00	20.00
Double	32.00	38.00

Parking for 2
Open March–November

Lakeland Natural M
⚜⚜⚜ COMMENDED

Low Slack, Queens Road, Kendal
LA9 4PH
☎ (01539) 733011
Fax (01539) 733011
Vegetarian, non-smoking guesthouse with all rooms en-suite. Magnificent views overlooking Kendal, extensive gardens and adjoining woods, ideal for walkers. Special weekly rates available.
Bedrooms: 1 double, 1 twin, 1 triple, 1 family room
Bathrooms: 4 en-suite

Bed & breakfast per night:

	£min	£max
Single	23.00	27.00
Double	46.00	54.00

Half board per person:

	£min	£max
Daily	36.50	40.50

Evening meal 1900 (last orders 1900)
Parking for 7
Cards accepted: Mastercard, Visa

Newlands M
⚜⚜ COMMENDED

37 Milnthorpe Road, Kendal
LA9 5QG
☎ (01539) 725340
Open door to a friendly Victorian guesthouse. Town centre, shops, museums within walking distance. Ideally situated for the Lakes and Yorkshire Dales.
Bedrooms: 1 single, 2 double, 2 triple
Bathrooms: 2 en-suite, 1 public

Bed & breakfast per night:

	£min	£max
Single	16.00	19.00
Double	32.00	38.00

Half board per person:

	£min	£max
Daily	23.50	26.50
Weekly	145.00	165.00

Evening meal from 1830
Parking for 5

RoadChef Lodge M
⚜⚜⚜ COMMENDED

Killington Lake Motorway Service Area, M6 Southbound, Kendal
LA8 0NW
☎ (015396) 21666 & 20739
Fax (015396) 21660
GR RoadChef
RoadChef Lodges offer high specification rooms at affordable prices, in popular locations suited to both the business and private traveller. Prices are per room and do not include breakfast.
Bedrooms: 14 double, 20 twin, 2 family rooms
Bathrooms: 36 en-suite

Bed & breakfast per night:

	£min	£max
Double	43.50	

Lunch available
Parking for 100
Cards accepted: Amex, Diners, Mastercard, Visa, Switch/Delta

The National Grading and Classification Scheme is explained at the back of this guide.

Union Tavern

159 Stricklandgate, Kendal LA9 4RF
☎ (01539) 724004
Newly refurbished family hotel on main Windermere A5284 road, close to market town centre. Evening restaurant, live entertainment at weekends.
Bedrooms: 2 double, 4 twin
Bathrooms: 3 en-suite, 1 public

Bed & breakfast

per night:	£min	£max
Single		18.00
Double	30.00	40.00

Lunch available
Evening meal 1800 (last orders 2000)
Parking for 6

KESWICK

Cumbria
Map ref 5A3

Beautifully positioned town beside Derwentwater and below the mountains of Skiddaw and Blencathra. Excellent base for walking, climbing, watersports and touring. Motor-launches operate on Derwentwater and motor boats, rowing boats and canoes can be hired.
Tourist Information Centre
☎ *(017687) 72645*

Acorn House Hotel ⚋

Ambleside Road, Keswick
CA12 4DL
☎ (017687) 72553
Fax (017687) 75332

Elegant Georgian house set in colourful garden. All bedrooms tastefully furnished, some four-poster beds. Cleanliness guaranteed. Close to town centre. Good off-street parking.
Bedrooms: 6 double, 1 twin, 3 triple
Bathrooms: 9 en-suite, 1 private

Bed & breakfast

per night:	£min	£max
Single	27.50	40.00
Double	50.00	60.00

Parking for 10
Open February–November
Cards accepted: Mastercard, Visa

The Anchorage ⚋

14 Ambleside Road, Keswick
CA12 4DL
☎ (017687) 72813
Comfortable house, serving good home cooking, with owners who make every effort to please.
Bedrooms: 1 single, 3 double, 2 triple
Bathrooms: 6 en-suite, 1 public

Bed & breakfast

per night:	£min	£max
Single	18.00	21.00
Double	36.00	42.00

Half board per

person:	£min	£max
Daily	28.00	31.00
Weekly	190.00	210.00

Evening meal 1830 (last orders 1500)
Parking for 7

Applethwaite Country House Hotel ⚋

Applethwaite, Keswick CA12 4PL
☎ (017687) 72413
Fax (017687) 75706

Characterful Victorian Lakeland-stone residence in idyllic, peaceful setting 1.5 miles from Keswick. Superb elevated position, stunning panoramic views. Relaxed informal atmosphere. Delicious home cooking, vegetarians welcome.
Bedrooms: 1 single, 7 double, 2 twin, 2 triple
Bathrooms: 12 en-suite, 1 public

Bed & breakfast

per night:	£min	£max
Single	29.00	33.00
Double	58.00	66.00

Half board per

person:	£min	£max
Daily	42.00	46.50
Weekly	265.00	295.00

Evening meal 1900 (last orders 1850)
Parking for 10
Open February–November
Cards accepted: Mastercard, Visa

Berkeley Guest House ⚋

The Heads, Keswick CA12 5ER
☎ (017687) 74222
On a quiet road overlooking Borrowdale Valley, with splendid views from each comfortable room. Close to the town centre and lake.
Bedrooms: 1 single, 3 double, 1 triple
Bathrooms: 2 en-suite, 1 public

Bed & breakfast

per night:	£min	£max
Double	29.00	44.00

Open February–November

Bonshaw Guest House

Listed COMMENDED

20 Eskin Street, Keswick CA12 4DG
☎ (017687) 73084

Small, friendly, comfortable guesthouse, providing good home cooking. Convenient for town centre and all amenities. En-suite rooms available. Non-smokers only, please.

Bedrooms: 3 single, 2 double, 1 twin, 1 triple
Bathrooms: 2 en-suite, 1 public

Bed & breakfast per night:

	£min	£max
Single	15.00	20.00
Double	30.00	40.00

Half board per person:

	£min	£max
Daily	25.00	30.00
Weekly	175.00	210.00

Evening meal 1830 (last orders 1600)
Parking for 6
Cards accepted: Amex, Mastercard, Visa

Brierholme Guest House

COMMENDED

21 Bank Street, Keswick CA12 5JZ
☎ (017687) 72938

Select guesthouse in town centre. High quality accommodation, all rooms having mountain views, tea-making facilities and colour TV. Private parking.

Bedrooms: 6 double
Bathrooms: 4 en-suite, 1 private, 1 private shower

Bed & breakfast per night:

	£min	£max
Double	36.00	46.00

Half board per person:

	£min	£max
Daily	28.00	33.00

Evening meal (last orders 1500)
Parking for 6

Please mention this guide when making your booking.

The symbol after an establishment name indicates that it is a Regional Tourist Board member.

The Cartwheel

COMMENDED

5 Blencathra Street, Keswick CA12 4HW
☎ (017687) 73182

Family-run guesthouse in a quiet area yet close to town and park and only a short walk to the lake.

Bedrooms: 1 single, 3 double, 2 twin
Bathrooms: 4 en-suite, 1 public

Bed & breakfast per night:

	£min	£max
Single	15.00	18.00
Double	30.00	36.00

Half board per person:

	£min	£max
Daily	23.00	26.00
Weekly	146.00	164.00

Evening meal 1830 (last orders 1900)
Cards accepted: Mastercard, Visa, Switch/Delta

Castle Inn Hotel

COMMENDED

Bassenthwaite, Keswick CA12 4RG
☎ (017687) 76401
Fax (017687) 76604
Email: partners @castlinn.demon.co.uk
Best Western

Hotel with extensive leisure facilities, including a large indoor swimming pool. Two good restaurants. Free children's accommodation. Friendliest welcome. Superb views.

Bedrooms: 2 single, 24 double, 15 twin, 2 triple, 5 family rooms
Suite available
Bathrooms: 48 en-suite

Bed & breakfast per night:

	£min	£max
Single	59.00	65.00
Double	98.00	130.00

Half board per person:

	£min	£max
Daily	59.00	65.00
Weekly	354.00	390.00

Lunch available
Evening meal 1830 (last orders 2130)
Parking for 100
Cards accepted: Amex, Diners, Mastercard, Visa, Switch/Delta

Chaucer House Hotel

COMMENDED

Derwentwater Place, Ambleside Road, Keswick CA12 4DR
☎ (017687) 72318 & 73223
Fax (017687) 75551
Minotel

Beautiful Victorian house. Quiet family-run hotel overlooked by Skiddaw, Grisedale and Derwentwater. Delicious, home-cooked meals including bread, jams and chutney.

Bedrooms: 7 single, 13 double, 11 twin, 3 triple, 1 family room
Bathrooms: 32 en-suite, 4 public, 3 private showers

Bed & breakfast per night:

	£min	£max
Single	29.00	38.00
Double	58.00	83.50

Half board per person:

	£min	£max
Daily	41.00	54.50
Weekly	255.00	337.00

Lunch available
Evening meal 1830 (last orders 2030)
Parking for 26
Open February–November
Cards accepted: Amex, Mastercard, Visa

Cherry Trees

COMMENDED

16 Eskin Street, Keswick CA12 4DQ
☎ (017687) 71048

Attractive en-suite rooms, substantial home-cooked meals. Non-smokers only, please. 5 minutes' walk from town centre, 10 minutes to lake.

Bedrooms: 1 single, 2 double, 1 twin, 1 triple
Bathrooms: 4 en-suite, 1 private

Bed & breakfast per night:

	£min	£max
Single	19.00	19.00
Double	38.00	44.00

Half board per person:

	£min	£max
Daily	29.00	32.00

Evening meal 1800 (last orders 1900)
Open February–October and Christmas

Clarence House ⚠

☗☗☗ COMMENDED

14 Eskin Street, Keswick CA12 4DQ
☎ (017687) 73186
High quality accommodation, all en-suite. Four-poster and ground floor rooms. 5 minutes' walk from lake, parks and shops. Non-smoking.
Bedrooms: 1 single, 4 double, 3 twin, 1 triple
Bathrooms: 8 en-suite, 1 private

Bed & breakfast

per night:	£min	£max
Double	38.00	46.00

Half board per

person:	£min	£max
Daily	30.00	34.00
Weekly	200.00	214.00

Evening meal from 1830
🛏4🍳🖥☐📞🛈🍴🖾 🖵🏇
SP

Craglands ⚠

☗☗☗ HIGHLY COMMENDED

Penrith Road, Keswick CA12 4LJ
☎ (017687) 74406
Well-appointed Victorian house in a quiet position on the outskirts of Keswick. Superb views, friendly atmosphere and good food using fresh local produce.
Bedrooms: 1 single, 3 double, 1 twin
Bathrooms: 5 en-suite

Bed & breakfast

per night:	£min	£max
Single	30.00	30.00
Double	46.00	50.00

Half board per

person:	£min	£max
Daily	43.00	45.00
Weekly	250.00	270.00

Evening meal 1900 (last orders 2000)
Parking for 5
🛏8🖥☐📞🛈🆄🛈S🍴🖾🖵
🌼🛠🏇🔌SP

Dalegarth House Country Hotel ⚠

☗☗☗ COMMENDED

Portinscale, Keswick CA12 5RQ
☎ (017687) 72817
Fax (017687) 72817
Edwardian house 1 mile from Keswick, with views of Skiddaw and Derwentwater. Licensed bar, 2 lounges and 6-course evening meal. Non-smokers only, please.
Bedrooms: 1 single, 5 double, 3 twin, 1 triple
Bathrooms: 10 en-suite

Bed & breakfast

per night:	£min	£max
Single	27.00	29.00
Double	54.00	58.00

Half board per

person:	£min	£max
Daily	40.00	43.00
Weekly	255.00	265.00

Evening meal 1900 (last orders 1730)
Parking for 12
Cards accepted: Mastercard, Visa
🛏5🍳🖥☐📞🛈S🍴🖾TV🖾 🖵
🌼🐾🏇🔌SP

Derwentwater Hotel ⚠

☗☗☗☗ HIGHLY COMMENDED

Portinscale, Keswick CA12 5RE
☎ (017687) 72538
Fax (017687) 71002
Email: derwentwater.hotel.
@dailpipex.com
🆖 The Independents

Award-winning hotel with unrivalled lake shore location in 16 acres of conservation grounds. Panoramic lake views from our Victorian conservatory. Premier rooms and suites available. Half-board available for stays of 2 nights or more.
Wheelchair access category 3♿
Bedrooms: 7 single, 20 double, 20 twin, 2 triple
Suites available
Bathrooms: 49 en-suite

Bed & breakfast

per night:	£min	£max
Single	69.00	89.00
Double	110.00	165.00

Half board per

person:	£min	£max
Daily	58.00	89.00
Weekly	295.00	450.00

Evening meal 1900 (last orders 2130)
Parking for 140
Cards accepted: Amex, Diners, Mastercard, Visa, Switch/Delta
🛏🍳🖥📞🖥☐📞🛈🆄🛈S🍴🖾🔘
🖪🖾🖵🍷🆄🎵▶🌼🔌SPⓣ
Ad See display advertisement on page 73

The Grange Country House Hotel ⚠

☗☗☗☗ HIGHLY COMMENDED

Manor Brow, Ambleside Road, Keswick CA12 4BA
☎ (017687) 72500
A building of charm, fully restored and refurbished, with many antiques. Quiet, overlooking Keswick with panoramic
mountain views. Log fires, freshly prepared food and attractive bedrooms.
Bedrooms: 7 double, 3 twin
Bathrooms: 10 en-suite, 1 public

Bed & breakfast

per night:	£min	£max
Double	64.00	74.00

Half board per

person:	£min	£max
Daily	46.50	53.50
Weekly	325.00	339.00

Evening meal 1900 (last orders 2030)
Parking for 13
Open March–November
Cards accepted: Mastercard, Visa
🛏7🍳📞🖥☐📞🛈🆁🛈S🍴🖾🖾
🖪🆄♿🌼🏇SP🏵

Greystones ⚠

☗☗☗ HIGHLY COMMENDED

Ambleside Road, Keswick CA12 4DP
☎ (017687) 73108
Traditional Lakeland house with excellent fell views. Quiet location, a few minutes' walk from town centre and the lake. Tastefully furnished rooms.
Bedrooms: 1 single, 5 double, 2 twin
Bathrooms: 7 en-suite, 1 private

Bed & breakfast

per night:	£min	£max
Single	23.50	25.00
Double	47.00	50.00

Half board per

person:	£min	£max
Daily	37.50	39.00

Evening meal 1900 (last orders 1400)
Parking for 9
Open February–November
Cards accepted: Mastercard, Visa
🛏10🖥☐📞🛈🆁🛈🍴🖾🖾🖵🏇🏵
Ⓣ

Hazeldene Hotel ⚠

☗☗☗ APPROVED

The Heads, Keswick CA12 5ER
☎ (017687) 72106
Fax (017687) 75435
Beautiful and central with open views of Skiddaw and Borrowdale and Newlands Valleys. Midway between town centre and Lake Derwentwater.
Bedrooms: 5 single, 9 double, 4 twin, 4 triple
Bathrooms: 17 en-suite, 3 private, 2 public

Bed & breakfast

per night:	£min	£max
Single	24.00	30.00
Double	48.00	60.00

Continued ▶

KESWICK
Continued

Half board per person:

	£min	£max
Daily	38.00	44.00
Weekly	256.00	296.00

Evening meal from 1830
Parking for 18
Open February–November
Cards accepted: Mastercard, Visa

Highfield Hotel ⚕
👑👑👑 COMMENDED
The Heads, Keswick CA12 5ER
☎ (017687) 72508

Friendly, family-run hotel quietly situated between town and lake. Superb views, cheerful, relaxed atmosphere. Large private car park.
Bedrooms: 2 single, 8 double, 5 twin, 2 triple
Bathrooms: 17 en-suite, 1 public

Bed & breakfast per night:

	£min	£max
Single	28.00	30.00
Double	48.00	60.00

Half board per person:

	£min	£max
Daily	36.00	45.00
Weekly	240.00	300.00

Evening meal 1830 (last orders 1800)
Parking for 19
Cards accepted: Mastercard, Visa, Switch/Delta

Hunters Way Guest House ⚕
👑 COMMENDED
4 Eskin Street, Keswick CA12 4DH
☎ (017687) 72324 & 0374 818366
Spacious, attractive guesthouse, 5 minutes' walk from town centre and beautiful countryside. Imaginative menu with home cooking - vegetarians welcome. Non-smoking.
Bedrooms: 2 single, 3 double, 1 twin
Bathrooms: 4 en-suite, 1 private, 1 public

Bed & breakfast per night:

	£min	£max
Single	17.00	18.00
Double	38.00	40.00

Half board per person:

	£min	£max
Daily	29.50	30.50
Weekly	192.50	192.50

Evening meal from 1830
Open February–November

King's Arms Hotel ⚕
👑👑👑 COMMENDED
Main Street, Keswick CA12 5BL
☎ (017687) 72083

Charming 18th C coaching inn with oak-beamed bar/lounge and refurbished air-conditioned restaurant. Traditional English home cooking. Bedrooms of high quality, all en-suite with colour TV, tea/coffee makers. Free use of nearby leisure club.
Bedrooms: 9 double, 4 twin
Bathrooms: 13 en-suite

Bed & breakfast per night:

	£min	£max
Single	38.00	49.00
Double	53.00	69.00

Half board per person:

	£min	£max
Daily	36.50	40.00
Weekly	238.00	255.00

Lunch available
Evening meal 1800 (last orders 2200)
Cards accepted: Mastercard, Visa, Switch/Delta

Ladstock Country House Hotel ⚕
👑👑👑 COMMENDED
Thornthwaite, Keswick CA12 5RZ
☎ (017687) 78210
Fax (017687) 78088
CR Consort

18th C country house hotel 3 miles from Keswick, set in own grounds. Panoramic views. Rooms with four-poster beds. 3-day breaks. Weddings and conferences.

Bedrooms: 11 double, 6 twin, 1 triple, 1 family room
Bathrooms: 19 en-suite, 2 public

Bed & breakfast per night:

	£min	£max
Single	36.00	46.00
Double	54.00	76.00

Half board per person:

	£min	£max
Daily	50.00	60.00
Weekly	300.00	360.00

Lunch available
Evening meal 1900 (last orders 2030)
Parking for 100
Cards accepted: Mastercard, Visa

Latrigg House ⚕
👑👑 APPROVED
St Herbert Street, Keswick CA12 4DF
☎ (017687) 73068
Homely guesthouse offering a warm and friendly welcome and good food, in a quiet area of town with views of Skiddaw.
Bedrooms: 1 single, 2 double, 2 twin, 1 family room
Bathrooms: 3 en-suite, 1 public

Bed & breakfast per night:

	£min	£max
Single	14.00	18.50
Double	28.00	37.00

Half board per person:

	£min	£max
Daily	23.00	28.50
Weekly	160.00	182.00

Evening meal 1900 (last orders 2000)
Parking for 1
Cards accepted: Mastercard, Visa, Switch/Delta

Linnett Hill Hotel ⚕
👑👑👑 COMMENDED
4 Penrith Road, Keswick CA12 4HF
☎ (017687) 73109
Charming 1812 hotel overlooking Skiddaw and Latrigg Hills. Opposite parks, gardens and river. Fresh home-cooked food, including a la carte menus with quality wines. Secure car park. Non-smoking establishment.
Bedrooms: 1 single, 7 double, 2 twin
Bathrooms: 10 en-suite

Bed & breakfast per night:

	£min	£max
Single	25.00	40.00
Double	46.00	48.00

Half board per person:	£min	£max
Daily	38.50	42.00
Weekly	248.50	259.00

Evening meal 1900 (last orders 1830)
Parking for 12
Cards accepted: Mastercard, Visa

Littletown Farm ⋀⋀

ᗑᗑ COMMENDED

Newlands, Keswick CA12 5TU
☎ (017687) 78353

150-acre mixed farm. In the beautiful, unspoilt Newlands Valley. En-suite bedrooms. Comfortable residents' lounge, dining room and cosy bar. Traditional 4-course dinner 6 nights a week.
Bedrooms: 1 single, 4 double, 2 twin, 1 triple, 1 family room
Bathrooms: 6 en-suite, 1 public

Bed & breakfast per night:	£min	£max
Single	24.00	30.00
Double	48.00	56.00

Half board per person:	£min	£max
Daily	36.00	40.00
Weekly	220.00	250.00

Evening meal from 1900
Parking for 10
Open March–December
Cards accepted: Mastercard, Visa

Lyzzick Hall Hotel ⋀⋀

ᗑᗑᗑᗑ HIGHLY COMMENDED

Underskiddaw, Keswick CA12 4PY
☎ (017687) 72277
Fax (017687) 72278
Peaceful country house hotel in its own grounds, with panoramic views, good food and a friendly, relaxed atmosphere. Heated indoor swimming pool, sauna and spa.
Bedrooms: 3 single, 12 double, 7 twin, 3 family rooms
Bathrooms: 25 en-suite, 1 public

Bed & breakfast per night:	£min	£max
Single	39.00	43.00
Double	78.00	86.00

Half board per person:	£min	£max
Daily	49.00	53.00
Weekly	330.00	350.00

Lunch available
Evening meal 1900 (last orders 2130)
Parking for 30
Open February–December
Cards accepted: Amex, Diners, Mastercard, Visa, Switch/Delta

Maple Bank ⋀⋀

ᗑᗑᗑ COMMENDED

Braithwaite, Keswick CA12 5RY
☎ (017687) 78229 & 78066
Email: maplebank@msn.com
Friendly country guesthouse with magnificent views of Skiddaw and surrounding countryside. Delicious home cooking. Open four seasons, including Christmas and New Year.
Bedrooms: 6 double, 1 twin
Bathrooms: 7 en-suite

Bed & breakfast per night:	£min	£max
Double	46.00	48.00

Half board per person:	£min	£max
Daily	34.00	36.00
Weekly	219.00	226.00

Evening meal 1830 (last orders 1600)
Parking for 10
Cards accepted: Mastercard, Visa

Priorholme Hotel ⋀⋀

ᗑᗑ COMMENDED

Borrowdale Road, Keswick CA12 5DD
☎ (017687) 72745
This Georgian hotel with charm and character has a 200-year-old bar and is on a quiet road 3 minutes' walk from the town, the lake and the theatre.
Bedrooms: 2 single, 5 double, 1 twin
Bathrooms: 6 en-suite, 1 public

Bed & breakfast per night:	£min	£max
Single	18.00	26.00
Double		52.00

Half board per person:	£min	£max
Daily	33.00	41.00
Weekly	217.00	273.00

Evening meal 1900 (last orders 1930)
Parking for 7

Open February–December
Cards accepted: Mastercard, Visa, Switch/Delta

Ravensworth Hotel ⋀⋀

ᗑᗑᗑ HIGHLY COMMENDED

29 Station Street, Keswick CA12 5HH
☎ (017687) 72476
Non-smoking family-run licensed hotel, decorated to a high standard of comfort, situated close to Keswick's amenities. An ideal Lake District base.
Bedrooms: 7 double, 1 twin
Bathrooms: 7 en-suite, 1 private

Bed & breakfast per night:	£min	£max
Double	32.00	50.00

Parking for 5
Open February–November and Christmas
Cards accepted: Mastercard, Visa

Rickerby Grange ⋀⋀

ᗑᗑᗑ COMMENDED

Portinscale, Keswick CA12 5RH
☎ (017687) 72344

Detached country hotel in its own gardens, in a quiet village on the outskirts of Keswick. Provides imaginative cooking, a cosy bar and quiet lounge. Ground floor bedrooms available.
Bedrooms: 2 single, 7 double, 1 twin, 3 triple
Bathrooms: 11 en-suite, 1 private, 1 public

Bed & breakfast per night:	£min	£max
Single	27.00	27.00
Double	54.00	54.00

Half board per person:	£min	£max
Daily	39.00	39.00
Weekly	250.00	250.00

Evening meal 1900 (last orders 1800)
Parking for 14
Open February–November

KESWICK
Continued

Royal Oak Hotel ⚕

👑👑👑 COMMENDED

Rosthwaite, Borrowdale, Keswick
CA12 5XB
☎ (017687) 77214
*Small, family-run, traditional Lakeland
hotel 6 miles south of Keswick. Cosy
atmosphere, home cooking and friendly
service.*
Bedrooms: 2 single, 4 double, 2 twin,
3 triple, 1 family room
Bathrooms: 8 en-suite, 3 public

Half board per person:	£min	£max
Daily	25.00	40.00
Weekly	179.00	242.00

Evening meal 1900 (last orders
1900)
Parking for 12
Cards accepted: Mastercard, Visa

🐎🖪♿🛎Ⓢℙ🅃🚽🛏❄🚲ＳＰ⊕

Skiddaw Hotel ⚕

👑👑👑👑 HIGHLY COMMENDED

Market Square, Keswick CA12 5BN
☎ (017687) 72071
Fax (017687) 74850

*Family-owned town centre hotel,
offering true hospitality and excellent
cuisine. In-house saunas, free midweek
golf, free use of nearby exclusive leisure
club.*
Bedrooms: 7 single, 14 double,
11 twin, 8 triple
Bathrooms: 40 en-suite

Bed & breakfast per night:	£min	£max
Single	36.00	38.00
Double	66.00	70.00

Half board per person:	£min	£max
Daily	43.00	45.00

Lunch available
Evening meal 1800 (last orders
2200)
Parking for 21
Cards accepted: Amex, Mastercard,
Visa, Switch/Delta

🐎🚗📞📭🖥♿🛎Ⓢ✂🛏🚽🛏
🖪🍴70🔊ＵＰ🐾ＳＰ🅃

Swan Hotel and Country Inn ⚕

👑👑👑 APPROVED

Thornthwaite, Keswick CA12 5SQ
☎ (01768) 78256

*Set amidst magnificent Lakeland
scenery, in a quiet, elevated position
overlooking Skiddaw and the Derwent
Valley.*
Bedrooms: 5 double, 4 twin, 2 triple,
1 family room
Bathrooms: 12 en-suite, 2 public

Bed & breakfast per night:	£min	£max
Single	20.00	
Double	25.00	

Half board per person:	£min	£max
Daily	40.00	
Weekly	270.00	

Lunch available
Evening meal (last orders 2200)
Parking for 30
Open February–December
Cards accepted: Mastercard, Visa

🐎🖪📭🖥♿🛎Ⓢ✂🛏🚽🛏🖪❄🐾ＳＰ🎠🅃

Swinside Lodge ⚕

👑👑 DE LUXE

Newlands, Keswick CA12 5UE
☎ (017687) 72948
Fax (017687) 72948
*Quietly situated informal country hotel
offering the highest standards of
comfort, service and hospitality. Noted
for enjoyable food which demonstrates
a serious and dedicated approach to
the cooking.*
Bedrooms: 5 double, 2 twin
Bathrooms: 7 en-suite

Bed & breakfast per night:	£min	£max
Single	47.00	60.00
Double	78.00	105.00

Half board per person:	£min	£max
Daily	64.00	80.00

Evening meal 1930 (last orders
2000)
Parking for 12
Open February–November and
Christmas

🐎10📭🖥♿🚷ＵＬ♿✂🛏🖪🖪❄
🍴🚲🐾ＳＰ🅃

Thwaite Howe Hotel ⚕

👑👑 HIGHLY COMMENDED 🦟

Thornthwaite, Keswick CA12 5SA
☎ (017687) 78281
Fax (017687) 78529
*Traditional country house hotel in a
tranquil position with magnificent views.
Award-winning food and fine wines.*
Bedrooms: 5 double, 3 twin
Bathrooms: 8 en-suite

Half board per person:	£min	£max
Daily	41.00	47.00

Evening meal 1900 (last orders
1900)
Parking for 12
Open March–October
Cards accepted: Mastercard, Visa,
Switch/Delta

🐎12📞📭🖥♿🛎Ⓢ✂🛏🖪🖪
ＵＰ❄🚲ＳＰ

KIRKBY LONSDALE

Cumbria
Map ref 5B3

Charming old town of narrow
streets and Georgian buildings, set
in the superb scenery of the Lune
Valley. The Devil's Bridge over the
River Lune is probably 13th C.
Tourist Information Centre
☎ *(015242) 71437*

The Copper Kettle

Listed APPROVED

3-5 Market Street, Kirkby Lonsdale,
Carnforth, Lancashire LA6 2AU
☎ (015242) 71714
*Part of an old manor house, built in
1610, on the border between the
Yorkshire Dales and the Lakes.*
Bedrooms: 2 double, 1 twin, 1 triple
Bathrooms: 1 en-suite, 3 public

Bed & breakfast per night:	£min	£max
Single	23.00	23.00
Double	32.00	38.00

Half board per person:	£min	£max
Daily	26.00	32.00
Weekly	180.00	225.00

Lunch available
Evening meal 1800 (last orders
2100)
Cards accepted: Amex, Diners,
Mastercard, Visa, Switch/Delta

🐎🖥♿🛎Ⓢ✂🛏🖪🐾🐾ＳＰ🎠

For further information on
accommodation establishments
use the coupons at the
back of this guide.

Pheasant Inn ⚘

👑👑👑 COMMENDED

Casterton, Kirkby Lonsdale,
Carnforth, Lancashire LA6 2RX
☎ (015242) 71230
Fax (015242) 71230
*Old world country inn specialising in
food and service, ideal for touring the
Lakes, dales and coast. Situated amidst
the peaceful Lunesdale Fells.*
Bedrooms: 2 single, 6 double, 2 twin
Bathrooms: 10 en-suite
Bed & breakfast

per night:	£min	£max
Single		37.50
Double		64.00

Lunch available
Evening meal 1830 (last orders
2100)
Parking for 40
Cards accepted: Diners, Mastercard,
Visa, Switch/Delta

🐎🏕🛴🚲📞🏠🖥🚭Ⓢ🔆📺🖩
🎒🍽20Ↄ🅿✿🚐🏵 SP 🏤

Whoop Hall Inn ⚘

👑👑👑 COMMENDED

Burrow with Burrow, Kirkby
Lonsdale (A65), Carnforth,
Lancashire LA6 2HP
☎ (01524) 271284
Fax (01524) 272154
ⒸⓇ Minotel/The Independents
*17th C coaching inn offering super
food and local specialities. Between
Lakes and dales, 6 miles from M6,
junction 36. Ideal for business or
pleasure.*
Bedrooms: 3 single, 13 double,
3 twin, 3 triple, 1 family room
Bathrooms: 23 en-suite
Bed & breakfast

per night:	£min	£max
Single	50.00	57.50
Double	68.00	80.00

Lunch available
Evening meal 1800 (last orders
2200)
Parking for 120
Cards accepted: Amex, Diners,
Mastercard, Visa, Switch/Delta

🐎🏕🛴🚲📞🏠🖥🚭Ⓢ🔆◐
🖩🎒🍽100 🚴📶Ↄ🅿✿ OAP 🏵 SP T

> You are advised to confirm
> your booking in writing.

> Establishments should be
> open throughout the year,
> unless otherwise stated.

The two Langdale valleys (Great
Langdale and Little Langdale) lie in
the heart of beautiful mountain
scenery. The craggy Langdale Pikes
are almost 2500 ft high. An ideal
walking and climbing area and base
for touring.

Eltermere Country House Hotel ⚘

👑👑👑 COMMENDED

Elterwater, Ambleside LA22 9HY
☎ (015394) 37207

*Friendly country house hotel in a quiet
rural setting in the heart of the
Langdale Valley. Personally run by the
owners.*
Bedrooms: 3 single, 9 double, 6 twin
Bathrooms: 15 en-suite, 3 public
Bed & breakfast

per night:	£min	£max
Single	27.00	39.50
Double	54.00	79.00

Half board per person:	£min	£max
Daily	36.00	53.50
Weekly	225.00	332.00

Evening meal 1900 (last orders
2000)
Parking for 20

🐎🏕🏠🚲📞🏠🚭Ⓢ🔆🖩◐🎒🍽🌸
🍴🚐🏵 SP T

Three Shires Inn ⚘

👑👑👑 COMMENDED

Little Langdale, Ambleside
LA22 9NZ
☎ (015394) 37215
Fax (015394) 37127
*Traditional Lakeland inn near foot of
Wrynose Pass in beautiful Little
Langdale Valley. An ideal area for
walkers and touring.*
Bedrooms: 5 double, 5 twin
Bathrooms: 10 en-suite, 2 public
Bed & breakfast

per night:	£min	£max
Single	27.00	40.00
Double	54.00	80.00

Half board per person:	£min	£max
Daily	36.00	54.00
Weekly	290.00	330.00

Lunch available

Evening meal 1900 (last orders
2000)
Parking for 22
Open February–December

🐎👤🚲📶🏠Ⓢ🔆🚭📺🖩🎒🍽🌸🍴
🚐🏵 SP 🏤

Village divided by A65 between
Kirkby Lonsdale and Kendal.
Appears in the Domesday Book.
Boasts many fine farmhouses dating
back to the 17th C and a disused
mill that has stood on Lupton Beck
for 700 years.

The Plough Hotel ⚘

👑👑👑 COMMENDED

Cow Brow, Lupton LA6 1PJ
☎ (015395) 67227
Fax (015395) 67848
*Tastefully refurbished country inn
renowned for the warmth of its
welcome. Superb food, real ales and
well-appointed rooms.*
Bedrooms: 8 double, 2 twin, 1 triple,
2 family rooms
Suite available
Bathrooms: 13 en-suite
Bed & breakfast

per night:	£min	£max
Single	35.00	35.00
Double	56.00	70.00

Lunch available
Evening meal 1800 (last orders
2115)
Parking for 80
Cards accepted: Mastercard, Visa,
Switch/Delta

🐎🏠📞👤🏠Ⓢ🚭🖩🎒🍽150📞Ↄ
🍴🌸🚐🏵 SP T

Set in an unspoilt valley, this hamlet
has a simple, white church with a
3-decker pulpit and box pews.

Near Howe Farm Hotel ⚘

👑👑 COMMENDED

Mungrisdale, Penrith CA11 0SH
☎ (017687) 79678
*Farmhouse in quiet surroundings 1 mile
from Mungrisdale, half a mile from the
A66 and within easy reach of all the
Lakes.*
Bedrooms: 3 double, 1 twin, 2 triple,
1 family room
Bathrooms: 4 en-suite, 1 public
Continued ▶

MUNGRISDALE
Continued

Bed & breakfast per night:

	£min	£max
Single	22.00	22.00
Double	34.00	44.00

Half board per person:

	£min	£max
Daily	27.00	32.00
Weekly	189.00	224.00

Evening meal 1700 (last orders 1700)
Parking for 10

NEWBY BRIDGE
Cumbria
Map ref 5A3

At the southern end of Windermere on the River Leven, this village has an unusual stone bridge with arches of unequal size. The Lakeside and Haverthwaite Railway has a stop here, and steamer cruises on Lake Windermere leave from nearby Lakeside.

Swan Hotel M
HIGHLY COMMENDED

Newby Bridge, Ulverston LA12 8NB
☎ (015395) 31681
Fax (015395) 31917
Logis of GB
Privately-owned hotel enjoying a beautiful site at the foot of Lake Windermere. We offer facilities appreciated by both holiday and business visitors.
Bedrooms: 7 single, 13 double, 10 twin, 6 triple
Suite available
Bathrooms: 36 en-suite

Bed & breakfast per night:

	£min	£max
Single	60.00	90.00
Double	96.00	140.00

Half board per person:

	£min	£max
Daily	48.00	102.00

Lunch available
Evening meal 1900 (last orders 2130)
Parking for 106
Cards accepted: Amex, Mastercard, Visa, Switch/Delta

Whitewater Hotel M
COMMENDED

The Lakeland Village, Backbarrow, Newby Bridge, Ulverston LA12 8PX
☎ (015395) 31133
Fax (015395) 31881
Minotel
Old mill built of Lakeland stone, converted into a hotel with all facilities, including a leisure centre in the grounds.
Bedrooms: 4 single, 14 double, 7 twin, 10 triple
Bathrooms: 35 en-suite

Bed & breakfast per night:

	£min	£max
Single	65.00	75.00
Double	95.00	110.00

Lunch available
Evening meal 1915 (last orders 2100)
Parking for 50
Cards accepted: Amex, Diners, Mastercard, Visa, Switch/Delta

ORTON
Cumbria
Map ref 5B3

Small, attractive village with the background of Orton Scar, it has some old buildings and a spacious green. George Whitehead, the itinerant Quaker preacher, was born here in 1636.

Mountain Lodge Hotel M

Orton, Penrith CA10 3SB
☎ (015396) 24351
Fax (015396) 24354
Nestling above Lune Gorge on the outskirts of the Lake District, with easy access from M6. Outstanding, friendly service with excellent food and large en-suite bedrooms.
Bedrooms: 20 double, 24 twin, 9 family rooms
Suites available
Bathrooms: 53 en-suite

Bed & breakfast per night:

	£min	£max
Single	50.00	53.50
Double	60.00	67.00

Half board per person:

	£min	£max
Daily	45.00	69.50

Lunch available
Evening meal 1900 (last orders 2100)
Parking for 10

Cards accepted: Amex, Diners, Mastercard, Visa, Switch/Delta

PENRITH
Cumbria
Map ref 5B2

Ancient and historic market town, the northern gateway to the Lake District. Penrith Castle was built as a defence against the Scots. Its ruins, open to the public, stand in the public park. High above the town is the Penrith Beacon, made famous by William Wordsworth.
Tourist Information Centre ☎ (01768) 867466

Beacon Bank Hotel M
HIGHLY COMMENDED

Beacon Edge, Penrith CA11 7BD
☎ (01768) 862633
Fax (01768) 899055
Victorian house of character, set in peaceful landscaped gardens. Residential licence, good food and service, spacious, comfortable, high standard accommodation. Five minutes from M6 junction 40. A no smoking hotel.
Bedrooms: 2 single, 5 double, 1 twin
Bathrooms: 8 en-suite

Bed & breakfast per night:

	£min	£max
Single	29.00	40.00
Double	40.00	60.00

Half board per person:

	£min	£max
Daily	35.00	45.00

Evening meal 1900 (last orders 1900)
Parking for 10

Brantwood Country Hotel M
COMMENDED

Stainton, Penrith CA11 0EP
☎ (01768) 862748
Fax (01768) 890164

Family-owned and run. Standing in secluded gardens in rural location, 1.5 miles from M6 junction 40 and 3 miles from Ullswater.
Bedrooms: 2 single, 7 double, 2 triple
Bathrooms: 11 en-suite, 1 public

Bed & breakfast

per night:	£min	£max
Single	38.50	50.00
Double	57.00	71.00

Half board per

person:	£min	£max
Daily	45.00	65.00

Lunch available
Evening meal 1830 (last orders 2100)
Parking for 40
Cards accepted: Amex, Mastercard, Visa, Switch/Delta

🛍️♿️🚗📞🖂🖵♿️🛎️⓵S🔏ﭏ♨️🖥️⬛ 🛏️🍽️60✿🐾🐕DAP🌸SP🎣T

Edenhall Hotel
👑👑👑 COMMENDED

Edenhall, Penrith CA11 8SX
☎ (01768) 881454
Fax (01768) 881454
In the Eden Valley. Peaceful country house hotel with good food and wines. Plenty of country walks for the energetic.
Bedrooms: 6 single, 9 double, 11 twin, 2 triple, 1 family room
Bathrooms: 24 en-suite

Bed & breakfast

per night:	£min	£max
Single	50.00	65.00
Double	75.00	130.00

Half board per

person:	£min	£max
Daily	65.00	80.00

Lunch available
Evening meal 1900 (last orders 2100)
Parking for 78
Cards accepted: Mastercard, Visa

🛍️♿️🚗📞🖂🖵♿️🛎️ﭏ🖥️TV⬛🛏️🍽️50 🏊✿🌸SP

George Hotel
👑👑👑 COMMENDED

Penrith CA11 7SU
☎ (01768) 862696
Fax (01768) 868223
CR Logis of GB
Historic coaching inn with beamed ceilings and open fires. Centrally positioned. Local reputation for hospitality, food and wine. Ideal touring base for Lakes, Pennines and Eden Valley.
Bedrooms: 11 single, 10 double, 9 twin
Bathrooms: 30 en-suite, 1 public

Bed & breakfast

per night:	£min	£max
Single	42.75	45.75
Double	58.00	75.00

Half board per

person:	£min	£max
Daily	56.75	49.75

Lunch available

Evening meal 1900 (last orders 2100)
Parking for 30
Cards accepted: Mastercard, Visa, Switch/Delta

🛍️♿️📞🖂🖵♿️🛎️⓵S🔏♨️🖥️⬛🛏️140 SP 🎣T

Norcroft Guesthouse
👑👑 COMMENDED

Graham Street, Penrith CA11 9LQ
☎ (01768) 862365
Fax (01768) 862365
Spacious Victorian house with large comfortable rooms. In a quiet residential area near the town centre.
Bedrooms: 1 single, 2 double, 2 twin, 1 triple, 2 family rooms
Bathrooms: 7 en-suite, 1 public

Bed & breakfast

per night:	£min	£max
Single	17.00	28.00
Double	32.00	42.00

Half board per

person:	£min	£max
Daily	27.00	36.50
Weekly	174.00	195.00

Evening meal 1900 (last orders 1630)
Parking for 7

🛍️♿️🖵♿️🛎️ﭏ🖥️TV⬛🛏️🐾🐕 DAP🌸SP

Woodland House Hotel Ⓜ
👑👑👑 COMMENDED

Wordsworth Street, Penrith CA11 7QY
☎ (01768) 864177
Fax (01768) 890152
Email: idaviesa@cix.compulink.co.uk.
Elegant and spacious red sandstone house with library of books and maps for walkers, nature lovers and sightseers. Ideal base for exploring Eden Valley, Lakes, Pennines. A no-smoking hotel.
Bedrooms: 3 single, 2 double, 2 twin, 1 triple
Bathrooms: 7 en-suite, 1 private

Bed & breakfast

per night:	£min	£max
Single	23.00	28.00
Double		45.00

Half board per

person:	£min	£max
Daily	33.00	38.00

Evening meal 1845 (last orders 1430)
Parking for 6

🛍️🖵♿️🛎️⓵S🔏♨️🖥️TV⬛🛏️🐾🐕 🌸SP

Surrounded by fells, the Howgills to the south-west and Wild Boar Fell to the south-east, this village has a fine church with an unusual interior where sections of the congregation sit facing one another.

The Black Swan Hotel Ⓜ
👑👑👑 COMMENDED

Ravenstonedale, Kirkby Stephen CA17 4NG
☎ (015396) 23204
Fax (015396) 23604
Delightful family-run hotel, set amidst beautiful countryside in a picturesque village. Renowned for food, comfort and hospitality. Private fishing. 5 minutes from M6 junction 38.
Wheelchair access category 3♿
Bedrooms: 1 single, 9 double, 5 twin
Bathrooms: 14 en-suite, 1 private, 1 public

Bed & breakfast

per night:	£min	£max
Single	40.00	45.00
Double	70.00	80.00

Half board per

person:	£min	£max
Daily	53.00	58.00
Weekly	320.00	393.00

Lunch available
Evening meal 1800 (last orders 2100)
Parking for 30
Cards accepted: Amex, Diners, Mastercard, Visa

🛍️♿️📞🖂🖵♿️🛎️⓵S🔏🖥️TV⬛ 🛏️🍽️14🔍♨️🏊♨️✿🐕🌸SP

On the extensive sands of the Kent Estuary between Milnthorpe and Arnside. Magnificent views across the bay. Immediately behind the village lie the remains of the dismantled railway and station and behind this the old quarry face dominates the landscape.

Kingfisher House and Restaurant
👑👑 COMMENDED

Sandside, Milnthorpe LA7 7HW
☎ (015395) 63909
Overlooking Kent Estuary and Lakeland
Continued ▶

SANDSIDE
Continued

hills, perfect for bird-watching, golf, rambling. All food home-cooked using fresh produce.
Bedrooms: 1 single, 1 double, 1 twin, 1 family room
Bathrooms: 4 en-suite

Bed & breakfast

per night:	£min	£max
Single	25.00	
Double	40.00	

Half board per person:

	£min	£max
Daily	33.50	

Lunch available
Evening meal 1630 (last orders 2030)
Parking for 22
Cards accepted: Mastercard, Visa

SAWREY
Cumbria
Map ref 5A3

Far Sawrey and Near Sawrey lie near Esthwaite Water.

Buckle Yeat Guest House ⋀
👑👑 COMMENDED
Sawrey, Ambleside LA22 0LF
☎ (015394) 36446 & 36538
Fax (015394) 36446
Old cottage guesthouse with log fires. Centrally situated for touring Lakeland, walking, bird-watching. Central heating throughout.
Bedrooms: 1 single, 4 double, 2 twin
Bathrooms: 6 en-suite, 1 private

Bed & breakfast

per night:	£min	£max
Single	22.50	25.00
Double	45.00	50.00

Parking for 9
Cards accepted: Amex, Mastercard, Visa, Switch/Delta

Ees Wyke Country House ⋀
👑👑👑 HIGHLY COMMENDED
Sawrey, Ambleside LA22 0JZ
☎ (015394) 36393
Fax (015394) 36393

Charming Georgian country house

overlooking the peaceful and beautiful Esthwaite Water. Fine views of the lake, mountains and fells.
Bedrooms: 5 double, 3 twin
Bathrooms: 6 en-suite, 2 private, 1 public

Bed & breakfast

per night:	£min	£max
Single	42.00	54.00
Double	84.00	88.00

Half board per person:

	£min	£max
Daily	54.00	56.00
Weekly		372.00

Evening meal 1900 (last orders 1930)
Parking for 10
Open March–December
Cards accepted: Amex

Sawrey Hotel ⋀
👑👑 COMMENDED
Far Sawrey, Ambleside LA22 0LQ
☎ (015394) 43425
Fax (015394) 43425

Country inn on the quieter side of Windermere, 1 mile from the car ferry on B5285 to Hawkshead. The bar is in the old stables and has log fires.
Bedrooms: 3 single, 9 double, 5 twin, 3 triple
Bathrooms: 18 en-suite, 1 public

Bed & breakfast

per night:	£min	£max
Single	24.00	29.00
Double	48.00	58.00

Half board per person:

	£min	£max
Daily	33.00	39.00
Weekly	210.00	236.00

Lunch available
Evening meal 1900 (last orders 2045)
Parking for 30
Cards accepted: Mastercard, Visa, Switch/Delta

All accommodation in this guide has been graded, or is awaiting a grading, by a trained Tourist Board inspector.

Sawrey House Country Hotel ⋀
👑👑👑 HIGHLY COMMENDED
Near Sawrey, Ambleside LA22 0LF
☎ (015394) 36387
Fax (015394) 36010
Warm, friendly atmosphere. Quality bedrooms, many with lake views, good food, log fire. Hotel overlooks Esthwaite Waters, magnificent views.
Bedrooms: 1 single, 6 double, 2 twin, 2 triple
Bathrooms: 11 en-suite

Bed & breakfast

per night:	£min	£max
Single	35.00	40.00
Double	55.00	100.00

Half board per person:

	£min	£max
Daily	40.00	65.00
Weekly	340.00	420.00

Evening meal 1930 (last orders 2030)
Parking for 20
Open February–December
Cards accepted: Mastercard, Visa

Tower Bank Arms ⋀
Listed COMMENDED
Near Sawrey, Ambleside LA22 0LF
☎ (015394) 36334
Fax (015394) 36334
Next door to Hill Top, the former home of Beatrix Potter. It features in the tale of Jemima Puddleduck.
Bedrooms: 2 double, 1 twin
Bathrooms: 3 en-suite

Bed & breakfast

per night:	£min	£max
Single		35.00
Double		48.00

Lunch available
Evening meal 1830 (last orders 2100)
Parking for 8
Cards accepted: Amex, Mastercard, Visa, Switch/Delta

West Vale Country Guest House ⋀
👑👑👑 HIGHLY COMMENDED
Far Sawrey, Hawkshead, Ambleside LA22 0LQ
☎ (015394) 42817
A warm welcome awaits you at this peaceful family-run guesthouse, with home cooking, log fire and fine views.
Bedrooms: 5 double, 1 twin, 2 triple
Bathrooms: 6 en-suite, 2 private, 1 public

Bed & breakfast per night:	£min	£max
Single	23.00	23.00
Double	46.00	46.00

Half board per person:	£min	£max
Daily	34.00	34.00
Weekly	224.00	224.00

Lunch available
Evening meal 1900 (last orders 1600)
Parking for 8
Open March–October
7 [S] [TV]

SHAP

Cumbria
Map ref 5B3

Village lying nearly 1000 ft above sea-level, amongst impressive moorland scenery. Shap Abbey, open to the public, is hidden in a valley nearby. Most of the ruins date from the early 13th C, but the tower is 16th C. The famous Shap granite and limestone quarries are nearby.

Shap Wells Hotel

♛♛♛♛ COMMENDED

Shap, Penrith CA10 3QU
☎ (01931) 716628
Fax (01931) 716377
[CR] The Independents

In a secluded valley in the Shap Fells. Ideal for exploring the Lakes, dales and Border country. Daily half board price is based on minimum 2-night stay.

Wheelchair access category 2
Bedrooms: 12 single, 39 double, 37 twin, 7 triple, 4 family rooms
Suites available
Bathrooms: 99 en-suite, 2 public

Bed & breakfast per night:	£min	£max
Single	50.00	55.00
Double	75.00	80.00

Half board per person:	£min	£max
Daily	38.00	55.00
Weekly	203.00	560.00

Lunch available
Evening meal 1900 (last orders 2030)
Parking for 200
Open February–December
Cards accepted: Amex, Diners, Mastercard, Visa, Switch/Delta
[G] [S] [TV]
200 [SP] [T]

You are advised to confirm your booking in writing.

TROUTBECK

Cumbria
Map ref 5A2

On the Penrith to Keswick road, Troutbeck was the site of a series of Roman camps. The village now hosts a busy weekly sheep market.

Lane Head Farm Guest House

♛♛ COMMENDED

Troutbeck, Penrith CA11 0SY
☎ (017687) 79220

Charming 17th C former farmhouse in quiet location, 4 miles from Ullswater lake. Good home cooking, table licence. Log fire, some en-suite and four-poster rooms.

Bedrooms: 1 single, 5 double, 2 twin, 1 family room
Bathrooms: 5 en-suite, 1 public

Bed & breakfast per night:	£min	£max
Single	18.00	25.00
Double	36.00	50.00

Half board per person:	£min	£max
Daily	27.00	34.00
Weekly	189.00	238.00

Evening meal 1700 (last orders 1900)
Parking for 10
Open April–December
[G] [S] [TV]
[SP]

TROUTBECK

Cumbria
Map ref 5A3

Most of the houses in this picturesque village are 17th C, some retain their spinning galleries and oak-mullioned windows. At the south end of the village is Townend, owned by the National Trust and open to the public, an excellently preserved example of a yeoman farmer's or statesman's house.

High Green Lodge

♛ COMMENDED

High Green, Troutbeck, Windermere LA23 1PN
☎ (015394) 33005

Here all mornings are magical - sun, swans, Swallows and Amazons. Cosy en-suite/king-size rooms in peaceful lodge with fantastic views down valley/Lake Garbon Pass. Four-posters. Walkers'/motorists' paradise. Fabulous breakfast, gourmet food at pubs nearby.

Bedrooms: 2 double, 1 twin
Bathrooms: 3 en-suite

Bed & breakfast per night:	£min	£max
Single		35.00
Double	45.00	70.00

Parking for 10
[G] [UL] [S] [SP]

Mortal Man Hotel

♛♛♛ COMMENDED

Troutbeck, Windermere LA23 1PL
☎ (015394) 33193
Fax (015394) 31261

Ideal centre for walking, touring or for a very quiet and restful holiday. Beautiful location with homely charm.

Bedrooms: 2 single, 4 double, 6 twin
Bathrooms: 12 en-suite

Half board per person:	£min	£max
Daily	50.00	60.00
Weekly	310.00	370.00

Lunch available
Evening meal 1930 (last orders 2000)
Parking for 30
Open February–November
5 [S]
[SP] [T]

ULLSWATER

Cumbria
Map ref 5A3

This beautiful lake, which is over 7 miles long, runs from Glenridding to Pooley Bridge. Lofty peaks ranging around the lake make an impressive background. A steamer service operates along the lake between Pooley Bridge, Howtown and Glenridding in the summer.

Glenridding Hotel

♛♛♛♛ HIGHLY COMMENDED

Glenridding, Penrith CA11 0PB
☎ (017684) 82228
Fax (017684) 82555
[CR] Best Western

Old established family hotel, adjacent to the lake and surrounded by mountains. We offer value breaks, log fires, real ales and good food. 2 restaurants, pub. Children and pets welcome.

Bedrooms: 5 single, 20 double, 11 twin, 4 family rooms
Bathrooms: 40 en-suite

Bed & breakfast per night:	£min	£max
Single	66.00	
Double	90.00	

Half board per person:	£min	£max
Daily	59.50	
Weekly	357.00	

Continued ▶

ULLSWATER
Continued

Lunch available
Evening meal 1900 (last orders 2030)
Parking for 30
Cards accepted: Amex, Diners, Mastercard, Visa, Switch/Delta

Moss Crag ⋀
COMMENDED

Glenridding, Penrith CA11 0PA
☎ (017684) 82500
Traditional Westmorland stone-built house by Glenridding Beck and Dodd. Only 5 minutes' walk to Ullswater Lake where one can sail, fish, canoe or windsurf.
Bedrooms: 5 double, 1 twin
Bathrooms: 4 private, 1 public

Bed & breakfast per night:

	£min	£max
Single	25.00	30.00
Double	35.00	50.00

Half board per person:

	£min	£max
Daily	31.00	38.50
Weekly	204.75	255.00

Lunch available
Evening meal 1930 (last orders 1930)
Parking for 9
Open January–November

Patterdale Hotel ⋀
COMMENDED

Patterdale, Lake Ullswater, Penrith CA11 0NN
☎ (017684) 82231
Fax (017684) 82440
Family-run hotel, within the same family for 65 years. All rooms with private facilities, colour TV and telephone. Lift to all floors.
Bedrooms: 13 single, 16 double, 24 twin, 2 family rooms
Bathrooms: 55 en-suite, 5 public

Bed & breakfast per night:

	£min	£max
Single	30.00	
Double	60.00	

Half board per person:

	£min	£max
Daily	45.00	
Weekly	280.00	

Lunch available
Evening meal 1900 (last orders 2000)
Parking for 100

Open March–December
Cards accepted: Mastercard, Visa, Switch/Delta

Ullswater House ⋀
COMMENDED

Pooley Bridge, Penrith CA10 2NN
☎ (017684) 86259
Centrally situated in Pooley Bridge. The well appointed rooms are quiet, and each has a fridge containing alcoholic and soft drinks.
Bedrooms: 2 double, 1 twin
Bathrooms: 3 en-suite

Bed & breakfast per night:

	£min	£max
Single	20.00	30.00
Double	40.00	40.00

Half board per person:

	£min	£max
Daily	30.00	30.00
Weekly	200.00	200.00

Evening meal 1900 (last orders 1900)
Parking for 4

ULVERSTON
Cumbria
Map ref 5A3

Market town lying between green fells and the sea. There is a replica of the Eddystone lighthouse on the Hoad which is a monument to Sir John Barrow, founder of the Royal Geographical Society. Birthplace of Stan Laurel, of Laurel and Hardy.
Tourist Information Centre ☎ (01229) 587120

Trinity House Hotel ⋀
HIGHLY COMMENDED

Prince's Street, Ulverston LA12 7NB
☎ (01229) 587639 & (080222) 6273
Fax (01229) 588552
Email: hotel@trinityhouse.furness.co.uk.
Georgian former rectory, elegant licensed restaurant with local food. En-suite bedrooms are spacious and stylishly decorated.
Bedrooms: 5 double, 2 twin
Bathrooms: 7 en-suite

Bed & breakfast per night:

	£min	£max
Single	45.00	45.00
Double	50.00	65.00

Half board per person:

	£min	£max
Daily	37.00	57.00
Weekly	240.00	290.00

Lunch available

Evening meal 1900 (last orders 2100)
Parking for 8
Cards accepted: Amex, Mastercard, Visa, Switch/Delta

WHITEHAVEN
Cumbria
Map ref 5A3

Historic Georgian port on the west coast. The town was developed in the 17th C and many fine buildings have been preserved. The Beacon Heritage Centre includes a Meteorological Office Weather Gallery. Start or finishing point of Coast to Coast, Whitehaven to Sunderland, cycleway.
Tourist Information Centre ☎ (01946) 695678

Corkickle Guest House ⋀
1 Corkickle, Whitehaven CA28 8AA
☎ (01946) 692073 & 0850 172828
Fax (01946) 692073
Small Georgian guesthouse offering high standards of comfort. Conveniently situated for business or leisure visitors. Residential licence.
Bedrooms: 2 single, 2 double, 2 twin
Bathrooms: 4 en-suite, 1 private, 1 public, 1 private shower

Bed & breakfast per night:

	£min	£max
Single	24.50	30.00
Double	44.00	44.00

Half board per person:

	£min	£max
Daily	36.50	42.00

Evening meal from 1900
Parking for 2

All accommodation in this guide has been graded, or is awaiting a grading, by a trained Tourist Board inspector.

ACCESSIBILITY

Look for the symbols which indicate accessibility for wheelchair users. These are described in detail at the front of this guide.

WINDERMERE

Cumbria
Map ref 5A3

Once a tiny hamlet before the introduction of the railway in 1847, now adjoins Bowness which is on the lakeside. Centre for sailing and boating. A good way to see the lake is a trip on a passenger steamer. Steamboat Museum has a fine collection of old boats.
Tourist Information Centre
☎ *(015394) 46499*

Applegarth Hotel ℳ

🏵 COMMENDED
College Road, Windermere
LA23 1BU
☎ (015394) 43206

Elegant Victorian mansion house with individually designed bedrooms and four-poster suites. Lovely fell views from most rooms. Cosy restaurant and bar. Please pre-book dinner to avoid disappointment. Complimentary use of local country club.
Bedrooms: 4 single, 11 double, 2 triple, 1 family room
Bathrooms: 18 en-suite
Bed & breakfast
per night:

	£min	£max
Single	23.00	35.00
Double	44.00	80.00

Half board per
person:

	£min	£max
Daily	36.00	56.00
Weekly	238.00	280.00

Evening meal 1900 (last orders 1930)
Parking for 25
Open February–November and Christmas
Cards accepted: Amex, Mastercard, Visa

🛏🏠📞🖃⬜✆🎵⊠📺🖳🛋❊⌖
SP 🏮 T

Ashleigh Guest House ℳ

🏵 COMMENDED
11 College Road, Windermere
LA23 1BU
☎ (015394) 42292 & (0468) 358111
Beautiful, comfortable Victorian home in quiet, central location with stunning mountain views. All rooms en-suite, old pine furniture. Breakfast choice. Non-smoking.

Bedrooms: 1 single, 3 double, 1 triple
Bathrooms: 5 en-suite
Bed & breakfast
per night:

	£min	£max
Single	15.00	26.00
Double	30.00	50.00

Parking for 1

🛏5♿🖃⬜✆🎵UL⬜S⌖✂🛋📺
🖳❊⌖✈🚍⊠ SP ◉

Belsfield House ℳ

🏵 COMMENDED
4 Belsfield Terrace, Kendal Road, Bowness-on-Windermere, Windermere LA23 3EQ
☎ (015394) 45823
Family-run guesthouse in the heart of Bowness, 2 minutes' walk from the lake front.
Bedrooms: 2 single, 3 double, 4 triple
Bathrooms: 9 en-suite
Bed & breakfast
per night:

	£min	£max
Single	21.00	27.00
Double	38.00	50.00

Parking for 9

🛏🏠♿⬜UL⬜S🖳🖳🛋🛋✂ SP

Boston House ℳ

🏵 COMMENDED
4 The Terrace, Windermere
LA23 1AJ
☎ (015394) 43654
Fax (015394) 43654

Charmingly peaceful Victorian listed building within 5 minutes' walk of trains and town centre. Delicious food, panoramic views and/or four-poster beds, private parking.
Bedrooms: 3 double, 1 twin, 1 family room
Bathrooms: 5 en-suite, 2 public
Bed & breakfast
per night:

	£min	£max
Double	39.00	54.00

Half board per
person:

	£min	£max
Daily	29.00	39.00
Weekly	195.00	245.00

Evening meal 1900 (last orders 1900)
Parking for 6
Open January–November
Cards accepted: Mastercard, Visa

🛏🏠🖃⬜✆🎵⊠S🖳📺🖳🛋
🚍 SP 🏮

Bowfell Cottage ℳ

🏵 APPROVED
Middle Entrance Drive, Storrs Park, Bowness-on-Windermere, Windermere LA23 3JY
☎ (015394) 44835
Cottage in a delightful setting, about 1 mile south of Bowness just off the A5074, offering traditional Lakeland hospitality.
Bedrooms: 1 double, 1 twin, 1 triple
Bathrooms: 1 public
Bed & breakfast
per night:

	£min	£max
Single	18.00	18.00
Double	34.00	36.00

Half board per
person:

	£min	£max
Daily	27.00	28.00
Weekly	170.00	175.00

Evening meal 1800 (last orders 2000)
Parking for 6

🛏🖃⬜✆UL⬜S🖳📺🖳🛋🔌🚶♿
❊🚍 DAP ⊠ SP T

Brooklands ℳ

🏵 COMMENDED
Ferry View,
Bowness-on-Windermere, Windermere LA23 3JB
☎ (015394) 42344
Comfortable guesthouse in rural setting on the outskirts of Bowness village, with fine lake and mountain views. Close to Lake Windermere marina and shops. Golf nearby. Car parking.
Bedrooms: 1 single, 1 double, 1 twin, 3 triple
Bathrooms: 5 en-suite, 1 private
Bed & breakfast
per night:

	£min	£max
Single	16.00	21.00
Double	32.00	42.00

Parking for 6

🛏⬜✆UL🖳📺🖳🛋🔌🚍 SP

The Burn How Garden House Hotel and Motel ℳ

🏵🏵🏵 HIGHLY COMMENDED
Back Belsfield Road, Windermere
LA23 3HH
☎ (015394) 46226
Fax (015394) 47000
Ⓒ Best Western

Unique combination of Victorian houses and private chalets in secluded
Continued ▶

WINDERMERE
Continued

gardens in the heart of a picturesque village. Full facilities. Four-poster beds available.
Wheelchair access category 3♿
Bedrooms: 2 single, 8 double, 8 twin, 8 triple
Bathrooms: 25 en-suite, 1 private

Bed & breakfast

per night:	£min	£max
Single	57.00	61.00
Double	76.00	92.00

Half board per

person:	£min	£max
Daily	55.00	64.00
Weekly	250.00	390.00

Lunch available
Evening meal 1900 (last orders 2030)
Parking for 30
Open February–December
Cards accepted: Amex, Diners, Mastercard, Visa, Switch/Delta

🛁👤🚗📞🖥🖵♿🅿️🛏Ⓢ⤢🏊🚭🍴 ▥ 🍷🌳❄️✕🚲🐾 SP T ⊛

Burnside Hotel ⋀
👑👑👑👑 HIGHLY COMMENDED

Kendal Road,
Bowness-on-Windermere,
Windermere LA23 3EP
☎ (015394) 42211 & 44530
Fax (015394) 43824
🆁 Inter Europe
Set in extensive gardens with superb views over Lake Windermere, 300 yards from the steamboat pier and village centre. Full leisure centre.
Wheelchair access category 1♿
Bedrooms: 1 single, 30 double, 11 twin, 11 triple, 4 family rooms
Suites available
Bathrooms: 57 en-suite

Bed & breakfast

per night:	£min	£max
Single	50.00	75.00
Double	70.00	117.00

Half board per

person:	£min	£max
Daily	53.00	84.00
Weekly	357.00	434.00

Lunch available
Evening meal 1830 (last orders 2145)
Parking for 80
Cards accepted: Amex, Diners, Mastercard, Visa, Switch/Delta

🛁👤🚗📞🖥🖵♿🅿️🛏Ⓢ⤢🏊🍷
🌞▥🍴🎿100🐾✕♣🏊🔥↺🚶❄️
DAP 🚭 SP T ⊛

Cedar Manor Hotel ⋀
👑👑👑👑 HIGHLY COMMENDED

Ambleside Road, Windermere
LA23 1AX
☎ (015394) 43192
Fax (015394) 45970
Traditional Lakeland house with interesting architectural features. Elegantly furnished and in a country garden setting. Some rooms have lake views.
Bedrooms: 9 double, 3 twin
Bathrooms: 12 en-suite

Bed & breakfast

per night:	£min	£max
Single	32.50	53.00
Double	65.00	86.00

Half board per

person:	£min	£max
Daily	43.00	67.00
Weekly	217.00	357.00

Lunch available
Evening meal 1930 (last orders 2030)
Parking for 16
Cards accepted: Mastercard, Visa

🛁👤🚗📞🖵♿🅿️🛏Ⓢ⤢🏊💧
▥🍷🚶🎿🐾🚭 SP 🏠 T

Cranleigh Hotel ⋀
👑👑👑 COMMENDED

Kendal Road,
Bowness-on-Windermere,
Windermere LA23 3EW
☎ (015394) 43293
Comfortable, quiet hotel, 2 minutes' walk from lake and village centre. Free use of private leisure club. Garden, private parking, bar.
Bedrooms: 9 double, 2 twin, 2 triple, 2 family rooms
Bathrooms: 14 en-suite, 1 private

Bed & breakfast

per night:	£min	£max
Single	30.00	40.00
Double	40.00	64.00

Half board per

person:	£min	£max
Daily	30.50	42.50
Weekly	183.00	255.00

Lunch available
Evening meal 1900 (last orders 2100)
Parking for 15
Cards accepted: Mastercard, Visa

🛁👤🚗📞🖵♿🅿️🛏Ⓢ⤢🏊 TV ▥ 🍷🚗
❄️✕ SP T

Damson Dene Hotel ⋀
👑👑👑 COMMENDED

Crosthwaite, Kendal LA8 8JE
☎ (015395) 68676
Fax (015395) 68227
Experience the unique atmosphere of this hotel, set in the tranquil Lyth Valley

---

near Windermere. Leisure centre open all year, roaring log fires in winter.
Bedrooms: 5 single, 17 double, 10 twin, 2 family rooms
Bathrooms: 34 en-suite

Bed & breakfast

per night:	£min	£max
Single	30.00	42.00
Double	60.00	84.00

Half board per

person:	£min	£max
Daily	42.00	54.00
Weekly	252.00	324.00

Lunch available
Evening meal 1900 (last orders 2100)
Parking for 102
Cards accepted: Mastercard, Visa, Switch/Delta

🛁👤🚗📞🖥🖵♿🅿️🛏Ⓢ⤢🏊 TV
▥🍷🎿100🌞✕♣🏊🔥↺🚶❄️ DAP
🚭 SP T ⊛

Elim House ⋀
Listed COMMENDED

Biskey Howe Road,
Bowness-on-Windermere,
Windermere LA23 2JP
☎ (015394) 42021
Family-run, warm, friendly accommodation with lake and shops close by. Offers breakfast, en-suite rooms with TV and tea/coffee facilities. Private car park.
Bedrooms: 8 double
Bathrooms: 6 en-suite, 1 public

Bed & breakfast

per night:	£min	£max
Single	18.00	25.00
Double	40.00	50.00

Parking for 8

🛁10🚗🖵♿ UL 🛏▥🚗✕🚲🚭 SP

Fairfield Country House Hotel ⋀
👑👑👑 COMMENDED

Brantfell Road,
Bowness-on-Windermere,
Windermere LA23 3AE
☎ (015394) 46565
Fax (015394) 46565
Email: ray&barb
@fairfield.dial.lakesnet.co.uk.
Small, friendly 200-year-old country house with half an acre of peaceful secluded gardens. 2 minutes' walk from Lake Windermere and village. Private car park, leisure facilities.
Bedrooms: 1 single, 5 double, 1 twin, 1 triple, 1 family room
Bathrooms: 8 en-suite, 1 private, 1 public

Bed & breakfast

per night:	£min	£max
Single	23.00	30.00
Double	46.00	60.00

Half board per person:	£min	£max
Daily	42.50	49.50
Weekly	291.50	321.50

Evening meal 1900 (last orders 1900)
Parking for 14
Cards accepted: Mastercard, Visa

🛏🔥🏨📧📺🚲♿🍽🅂🔌📺📺
Ⓔ🏠⋃♪🎵🌸✈🚠🚭 SP

Fayrer Garden House Hotel ⋀⋀

👑👑👑 HIGHLY COMMENDED

Lyth Valley Road,
Bowness-on-Windermere,
Windermere LA23 3JP
☎ (015394) 88195
Fax (015394) 45986
Ⓒ🅡 Logis of GB

Beautiful, well-appointed country house in splendid grounds overlooking Lake Windermere. Noted for food. Four posters, jacuzzis, free leisure facilities. Special breaks.
Bedrooms: 1 single, 14 double, 3 triple
Bathrooms: 18 en-suite

Bed & breakfast per night:	£min	£max
Single	30.00	55.00
Double	55.00	140.00

Half board per person:	£min	£max
Daily	45.00	89.00

Lunch available
Evening meal 1915 (last orders 2030)
Parking for 20
Cards accepted: Amex, Mastercard, Visa, Switch/Delta

🛏🔥🏨📞📧📺♿🍽🔌📺📺🔌🛋
👣25🔍⋃♪🌸🚠🚭 SP 🅣Ⓔ

Firgarth ⋀⋀

👑👑 APPROVED

Ambleside Road, Windermere
LA23 1EU
☎ (015394) 46974
Elegant Victorian house offering good breakfast, friendly atmosphere, private parking, close to lake viewpoint. Ideally situated for touring all areas of Lakeland. Tours arranged. Full en-suite facilities. Colour TV and tea-makers.
Bedrooms: 1 single, 4 double, 2 triple, 1 family room
Bathrooms: 8 en-suite

Bed & breakfast per night:	£min	£max
Single	16.50	21.50
Double	33.00	40.00

Parking for 8
Cards accepted: Amex, Diners, Mastercard, Visa, Switch/Delta

🛏4📧🖥Ⓤ♿🍽🔌📺🛋🛋🚶💆 DAP
🚭 SP

Gilpin Lodge Country House Hotel and Restaurant ⋀⋀

👑👑👑👑 DE LUXE

Crook Road, Windermere
LA23 3NE
☎ (015394) 88818
Fax (015394) 88058

Elegant and friendly hotel in rural setting, 2 miles from Windermere. Sumptuous bedrooms, renowned cuisine, gardens. Country club nearby. Telephone 0800 269460 (toll free in UK).
Bedrooms: 11 double, 3 twin
Bathrooms: 14 en-suite

Bed & breakfast per night:	£min	£max
Single	75.00	100.00
Double	90.00	140.00

Half board per person:	£min	£max
Daily	65.00	90.00
Weekly	390.00	570.00

Lunch available
Evening meal 1900 (last orders 2045)
Parking for 40
Cards accepted: Amex, Diners, Mastercard, Visa, Switch/Delta

🛏7🏨📞📧📺♿🍽🅂🔌📺🛋
🛋👣25⋃♪🌸✈🚠🚭 SP 🅣

Glenville Hotel ⋀⋀

👑👑👑 COMMENDED

Lake Road, Windermere LA23 2EQ
☎ (015394) 43371

Standing in its own grounds, midway between Windermere and Bowness and perfectly positioned for access to all amenities. The lake is an easy 10-minute walk. Car park.

Bedrooms: 1 single, 4 double, 3 triple
Bathrooms: 7 en-suite, 1 private, 1 public

Bed & breakfast per night:	£min	£max
Single	20.00	30.00
Double	37.00	48.00

Half board per person:	£min	£max
Daily	30.50	36.00
Weekly	213.50	252.00

Evening meal 1800 (last orders 1900)
Parking for 12
Open February–December
Cards accepted: Mastercard, Visa

🛏🔥📧♿🍽🅂🍽📺📺🛋🛋🌸✈
🚭 SP 🅣

Hideaway Hotel ⋀⋀

👑👑👑 COMMENDED

Phoenix Way, Windermere
LA23 1DB
☎ (015394) 43070
Fax (015394) 48664

Friendly, small hotel away from the main road, with a pleasant garden, well-trained chefs, open fires and well-equipped, comfortable bedrooms.
Bedrooms: 2 single, 7 double, 3 twin, 3 triple
Bathrooms: 15 en-suite

Bed & breakfast per night:	£min	£max
Single	30.00	42.00
Double	60.00	120.00

Half board per person:	£min	£max
Daily	38.00	62.00
Weekly	210.00	365.00

Evening meal 1930 (last orders 2000)
Parking for 16
Open February–December
Cards accepted: Amex, Mastercard, Visa

🛏🔥🏨📞📧📺♿🍽🅂🔌📺🛋🛋
⋃🌸🚠🚭 SP

Holly Lodge ⋀⋀

👑👑 COMMENDED

6 College Road, Windermere
LA23 1BX
☎ (015394) 43873
Fax (015394) 43873
Traditional Lakeland stone guesthouse,
Continued ▶

WINDERMERE
Continued

built in 1854. In a quiet area off the main road, close to the village centre, buses, railway station and all amenities.
Bedrooms: 1 single, 5 double, 2 twin, 3 triple
Bathrooms: 6 en-suite, 2 public
Bed & breakfast

per night:	£min	£max
Single	18.00	21.00
Double	36.00	42.00

Half board per

person:	£min	£max
Daily	29.00	32.00

Evening meal from 1830
Parking for 7

Holly Park House ⋀
⚜⚜⚜ COMMENDED
1 Park Road, Windermere
LA23 2AW
☎ (015394) 42107

Elegant stone-built Victorian guesthouse with nicely furnished spacious rooms. Quiet area, convenient for village shops and coach/rail services.
Bedrooms: 2 double, 4 triple
Bathrooms: 6 en-suite
Bed & breakfast

per night:	£min	£max
Single	26.00	30.00
Double	36.00	44.00

Evening meal 1830 (last orders 1930)
Parking for 4
Cards accepted: Amex, Mastercard, Visa

Knoll Hotel ⋀
⚜⚜⚜ COMMENDED
Lake Road, Windermere LA23 2JF
☎ (015394) 43756
Fax (015394) 88496
Email: knoll.hotel@ccs.prestel.co.uk
In quiet grounds, with magnificent views overlooking Lake Windermere and the mountains. Free use of Parklands leisure club.
Bedrooms: 4 single, 4 double, 1 twin, 3 triple
Bathrooms: 9 en-suite, 1 public

Bed & breakfast

per night:	£min	£max
Single	25.00	36.00
Double	66.00	72.00

Half board per

person:	£min	£max
Daily	40.00	50.00
Weekly		315.00

Evening meal 1900 (last orders 1930)
Parking for 15
Cards accepted: Mastercard, Visa

Langdale Chase Hotel ⋀
⚜⚜⚜ HIGHLY COMMENDED
Windermere LA23 1LW
☎ (015394) 32201
Fax (015394) 32604

Country house hotel in landscaped gardens on the edge of Lake Windermere. Excellent views of mountains and lake. Great dining experience.
Bedrooms: 1 single, 12 double, 17 twin
Bathrooms: 30 en-suite
Bed & breakfast

per night:	£min	£max
Single	47.00	65.00
Double	85.00	130.00

Half board per

person:	£min	£max
Daily	55.00	100.00

Lunch available
Evening meal 1900 (last orders 2045)
Parking for 50
Cards accepted: Amex, Diners, Mastercard, Visa, Switch/Delta

Langdale View Guest House ⋀
⚜ COMMENDED
114 Craig Walk, Off Helm Road, Bowness-on-Windermere, Windermere LA23 3AX
☎ (015394) 44076
Quiet guesthouse with home cooking. En-suite rooms, some with views. Non-smoking. Friendly atmosphere. Will collect from station.
Bedrooms: 1 single, 3 double, 1 twin
Bathrooms: 4 en-suite, 1 private

Bed & breakfast

per night:	£min	£max
Single	17.00	23.00
Double	34.00	46.00

Half board per

person:	£min	£max
Daily	27.00	33.00
Weekly	175.00	220.00

Evening meal 1800 (last orders 1600)
Parking for 6

Lindeth Fell Country House Hotel ⋀
⚜⚜⚜⚜ HIGHLY COMMENDED
Windermere LA23 3JP
☎ (015394) 43286 & 44287
Fax (015394) 47455

Beautifully situated in magnificent private grounds on the hills above Lake Windermere, Lindeth Fell offers brilliant views, modern English cooking and elegant surroundings. All bedrooms have full facilities, many have lake views.
Bedrooms: 2 single, 5 double, 5 twin, 2 triple
Bathrooms: 14 en-suite
Bed & breakfast

per night:	£min	£max
Single	50.00	65.00
Double	100.00	120.00

Half board per

person:	£min	£max
Daily	60.00	75.00
Weekly	399.00	470.00

Lunch available
Evening meal 1930 (last orders 2030)
Parking for 20
Cards accepted: Mastercard, Visa

Lindeth Howe Country House Hotel ⋀
⚜⚜⚜ HIGHLY COMMENDED
Longtail Hill, Bowness-on-Windermere, Windermere LA23 3JF
☎ (015394) 45759
Fax (015394) 46368
Email: lindeth.howe.@dialin.net

19th C country house hidden in 6 acres of beautiful, secluded gardens overlooking Lake Windermere. Cosy bar and log fires on chilly evenings. All rooms have satellite colour TV, direct-dial telephone and baby listening, some have spa bath. Sauna, sunbeds. Free membership of local leisure club.
Bedrooms: 9 double, 2 twin, 3 triple
Bathrooms: 14 en-suite

Bed & breakfast

per night:	£min	£max
Single	48.50	
Double	68.00	108.00

Half board per person:

	£min	£max
Daily	51.50	71.50

Evening meal 1900 (last orders 2030)
Parking for 30
Open February–December
Cards accepted: Mastercard, Visa, Switch/Delta

🐴🦽🏠📞🖲️🖥️👶♨️🔓§✂️🛏️🖥️▪️ 🍴🛥️🛶🎵🎯🍽️🚲🏵️ SP 🎡 T

Lindisfarne

👑👑 COMMENDED

Sunny Bank Road, Windermere
LA23 2EN
☎ (015394) 46295
Traditional detached Lakeland house. Situated in quiet area, close to lake, shops and scenic walks. Varied breakfast. Friendly and flexible hosts.
Bedrooms: 2 double, 1 twin, 1 family room
Bathrooms: 2 en-suite, 1 private, 1 public

Bed & breakfast

per night:	£min	£max
Single	15.00	20.00
Double	28.00	37.00

Half board per person:

	£min	£max
Daily	25.00	30.00
Weekly	150.00	170.00

Evening meal 1800 (last orders 2000)
Parking for 4

🐴🖲️🖥️👶♨️ UL 🔓§🛏️🖥️▪️🚲❄️🚐 🏵️ SP T

Map references apply to the colour maps at the back of this guide.

Linthwaite House Hotel ⋀

👑👑👑👑👑 DE LUXE

Crook Road,
Bowness-on-Windermere,
Windermere LA23 3JA
☎ (015394) 88600
Fax (015394) 88601
Email: admin@linhotel.u-net.com
Ⓒ Grand Heritage
Peaceful location in 14 acres of gardens, 1 mile south of village and with panoramic views over the lake. English Tourist Board's Hotel of the Year, 1994.
Wheelchair access category 3♿
Bedrooms: 1 single, 13 double, 4 twin
Suite available
Bathrooms: 18 en-suite

Bed & breakfast

per night:	£min	£max
Single	90.00	100.00
Double	130.00	220.00

Half board per person:

	£min	£max
Daily	69.00	140.00
Weekly	434.70	882.00

Lunch available
Evening meal 1915 (last orders 2045)
Parking for 30
Cards accepted: Amex, Mastercard, Visa, Switch/Delta

🐴7🦽🏠📞🖲️🖥️👶♨️🔓§✂️🛏️🖥️ ▪️🚲40🛶🎵🎯🍽️🚲🏵️ SP 🎡 T ◎

Low Wood Hotel ⋀

👑👑👑👑 COMMENDED

Windermere LA23 1LP
☎ (015394) 33338
Fax (015394) 34072
Ⓒ Best Western

Almost a mile of lake frontage. Boat launching, water ski tuition and superb lake and mountain views. Also leisure centre, indoor heated swimming pool, bubble beds, sauna room, health and beauty centre, gymnasium, conference centre, syndicate rooms, video and computer link-up.
Bedrooms: 19 single, 39 double, 38 twin, 2 triple, 1 family room
Bathrooms: 99 en-suite

Bed & breakfast

per night:	£min	£max
Single	55.00	58.00
Double	110.00	140.00

Half board per person:

	£min	£max
Daily	65.00	83.00
Weekly	390.00	498.00

Lunch available
Evening meal 1900 (last orders 2130)
Parking for 200
Cards accepted: Amex, Diners, Mastercard, Visa, Switch/Delta

🐴🦽🏠📞🖲️🖥️👶♨️🔓§✂️🛏️◎ 📖 ▪️🚲🍴340🚲🎯🍽️🚲❄️🎵🎶🏃 ❄️🚶 SP 🎡 T

Mountain Ash Hotel ⋀

👑👑👑 COMMENDED

Ambleside Road, Windermere
LA23 1AT
☎ (015394) 43715
Fax (015394) 88480
Lakeland-stone hotel refurbished to provide comfortable accommodation, including four-poster beds and spa baths. Cocktail bar, conservatory and locally renowned traditional cuisine.
Bedrooms: 3 single, 19 double
Bathrooms: 22 en-suite

Bed & breakfast

per night:	£min	£max
Double	50.00	110.00

Half board per person:

	£min	£max
Daily	39.50	70.00

Lunch available
Evening meal 1900 (last orders 2100)
Parking for 30
Cards accepted: Mastercard, Visa, Switch/Delta

🐴🦽🏠📞🖲️🖥️👶♨️§🛏️🖥️▪️ 🛶❄️🚐 OAP 🚶 SP

Oakbank House ⋀

👑👑 COMMENDED

Helm Road,
Bowness-on-Windermere,
Windermere LA23 3BU
☎ (015394) 43386

Panoramic views of Lake Windermere, 1 minute from shops and restaurants. Spacious, comfortable, tastefully furnished rooms, all en-suite. Friendly family-run hotel.
Bedrooms: 3 double, 2 twin, 6 triple
Bathrooms: 10 en-suite, 1 private

Continued ▶

WINDERMERE
Continued

Bed & breakfast per night:

	£min	£max
Single	25.00	32.00
Double	46.00	60.00

Parking for 10
Cards accepted: Mastercard, Visa, Switch/Delta

🐎🖐🚗📞🖥️🅿️📶🛎️📺🖥️💻🍴❄️🌸 SP T

Oldfield House ⚊
☗☗ COMMENDED

Oldfield Road, Windermere
LA23 2BY
☎ (015394) 88445
Fax (015394) 43250

Friendly, informal atmosphere within a traditionally-built Lakeland residence. Quiet central location, free use of swimming and leisure club.
Bedrooms: 2 single, 4 double, 1 triple, 1 family room
Bathrooms: 8 en-suite, 1 public
Bed & breakfast per night:

	£min	£max
Single	20.00	32.50
Double	38.00	60.00

Parking for 7
Open February–December
Cards accepted: Amex, Mastercard, Visa, Switch/Delta

🐎🖐🚗📞🖥️📺🖥️🅿️🛎️🔒✂️🖥️💻🌸✈️🚗 SP T

Osborne Guest House
☗☗ COMMENDED

3 High Street, Windermere
LA23 1AF
☎ (015394) 46452
Traditional Lakeland house, central for all transport, tours and walks. Clean, comfortable accommodation. Full breakfast. Developed by present owners since 1982.
Bedrooms: 2 double, 2 triple
Bathrooms: 3 en-suite, 1 private
Bed & breakfast per night:

	£min	£max
Single	15.00	20.00
Double	30.00	39.00

Cards accepted: Mastercard, Visa

🐎🚗📞🖥️📺💻✂️🖥️📺💻🖥️✈️🚗
DAP 🚭 SP T

The Poplars ⚊
☗☗ COMMENDED

Lake Road, Windermere LA23 2EQ
☎ (015394) 42325 & 46690
Fax (015394) 42325
Small family-run guesthouse on the main lake road, offering en-suite accommodation coupled with fine cuisine and homely atmosphere. Golf and fishing can be arranged.
Bedrooms: 1 single, 3 double, 2 twin, 1 triple
Bathrooms: 6 en-suite, 1 private, 1 public
Bed & breakfast per night:

	£min	£max
Single	20.00	22.50
Double	40.00	45.00

Half board per person:

	£min	£max
Daily	32.00	34.50
Weekly	210.00	224.00

Evening meal 1800 (last orders 1800)
Parking for 7
Open February–December

🐎🖐3🚗📞🖥️🛎️🅿️📺💻🖥️🚗♪🍴🚗
SP T

Quarry Garth Country House Hotel and Restaurant ⚊
☗☗☗ HIGHLY COMMENDED

Troutbeck Bridge, Windermere
LA23 1LF
☎ (015394) 88282 & 443761
Fax (015394) 46584
CR Logis of GB

This gracious and mellow Edwardian country house is set in 8 acres of lakeland gardens near Lake Windermere. Residents are captivated by excellent cuisine, antique furniture, original paintings, collectors' items, open fires, four-poster beds, candlelight and a relaxed family-style welcome.
Bedrooms: 1 single, 9 double, 1 twin, 1 triple
Bathrooms: 11 en-suite, 1 private, 1 public
Bed & breakfast per night:

	£min	£max
Single	45.00	60.00
Double	90.00	110.00

Half board per person:

	£min	£max
Daily	65.00	75.00
Weekly	399.00	472.50

Lunch available

Evening meal 1830 (last orders 2115)
Parking for 40
Cards accepted: Amex, Mastercard, Visa, Switch/Delta

🐎🚗📞🖥️🛎️📶🅿️✂️🖥️💻🚗🍴20 ♻
❄️🚗🚭 SP ®

Ravensworth Hotel ⚊
☗☗☗☗ COMMENDED

Ambleside Road, Windermere
LA23 1BA
☎ (015394) 43747
Fax (015394) 43250
Close to the village centre, lake and fells. English and continental cooking. Variety of accommodation including four-poster beds.
Bedrooms: 2 single, 9 double, 2 twin, 1 triple
Bathrooms: 14 en-suite
Bed & breakfast per night:

	£min	£max
Single	27.50	29.50
Double	49.00	73.00

Half board per person:

	£min	£max
Daily	40.50	49.50
Weekly	255.00	275.00

Evening meal 1900 (last orders 2030)
Parking for 16
Cards accepted: Mastercard, Visa

🐎🖐🚗📞🖥️📶🖥️💻🛎️🔒✂️🖥️💻🚗
🍴📶♻️♪🏃🌸🚗🚭 SP T

Rocklea ⚊
☗☗ COMMENDED

Brookside, Lake Road, Windermere
LA23 2BX
☎ (015394) 45326
Charming, family-run, traditional Lakeland-stone guesthouse in a quiet central location. Very comfortable with a warm, friendly atmosphere. Parking.
Bedrooms: 1 single, 4 double, 2 twin
Bathrooms: 5 en-suite, 1 public
Bed & breakfast per night:

	£min	£max
Single	17.00	23.00
Double	32.00	46.00

Parking for 6
Cards accepted: Mastercard, Visa

🐎3🖥️🛎️🖥️💻🚗🚗

Rosemount Private Hotel ⚏

Lake Road, Windermere LA23 2EQ
☎ (015394) 43739
Fax (015394) 43739

Impressive and well situated
guesthouse, tastefully decorated and
furnished. Warm welcome and
excellent breakfast, all at unbeatable
prices. Non-smokers only, please.
Bedrooms: 2 single, 5 double, 1 twin
Bathrooms: 5 en-suite, 3 private

Bed & breakfast

per night:	£min	£max
Single	18.50	26.00
Double	37.00	52.00

Parking for 8
Open February–November
Cards accepted: Mastercard, Visa

⚏8🛆⛔📺♿🛎Ⓢ✗🅿🖭🖥⚏►✕ DAP
SP T

Royal Hotel ⚏

👑👑

Queens Square,
Bowness-on-Windermere,
Windermere LA23 3DB
☎ (015394) 43045
Fax (015394) 44990
Hotel with a difference. Exciting new
themed rooms, McGinty's Irish fun pub
and the Circuit sports bar. Free
unlimited use of superb leisure club.
Bedrooms: 6 single, 14 double,
3 twin, 6 triple
Bathrooms: 29 en-suite

Bed & breakfast

per night:	£min	£max
Single	25.95	29.95
Double	51.90	59.90

Parking for 21
Cards accepted: Amex, Diners,
Mastercard, Visa, Switch/Delta

⚏🛆📞⛔🖥♿Ⓢ✗🖭🖥📍↻⭐
🐾🏠

St John's Lodge ⚏

👑👑👑 COMMENDED

Lake Road, Windermere LA23 2EQ
☎ (015394) 43078
Small private hotel midway between
Windermere and the lake, managed by
the chef/proprietor and convenient for
all amenities and services. Facilities of
local sports and leisure club available
to guests.
Bedrooms: 1 single, 9 double, 2 twin,
2 triple
Bathrooms: 12 en-suite, 2 private

Bed & breakfast

per night:	£min	£max
Single	20.00	28.00
Double	38.00	52.00

Half board per

person:	£min	£max
Daily	32.50	38.50
Weekly	210.00	250.00

Evening meal 1900 (last orders
1800)
Parking for 11
Open February–October
Cards accepted: Mastercard, Visa

⚏5🛆⛔🖥♿🛎Ⓢ✗🅿Ⓞ🖭⚏
🚌 DAP SP T

South View ⚏

👑👑 APPROVED

Cross Street, Windermere
LA23 1AE
☎ (015394) 42951
Unique in Windermere village - the
only guesthouse with own heated
indoor swimming pool open all year.
Excellent breakfast. Quiet yet central.
Bedrooms: 1 single, 3 double, 1 twin,
1 family room
Bathrooms: 5 en-suite, 1 private,
1 public

Bed & breakfast

per night:	£min	£max
Single	19.00	26.00
Double	38.00	52.00

Evening meal 1830 (last orders
1600)
Parking for 6
Cards accepted: Amex, Mastercard,
Visa

⚏📬🖥♿🗇UL♿Ⓢ✗🅿🖭♿⚏
✕🔍⚙✖🚌 SP 🏠 T

Virginia Cottage ⚏

👑👑 COMMENDED

1 and 2 Crown Villas, Kendal Road,
Bowness-on-Windermere,
Windermere LA23 3EJ
☎ (015394) 44891
Charming 19th C cottage, 1 minute
from the lake, shops, restaurants and
entertainment. Wide range of rooms,
friendly atmosphere, family run.
Bedrooms: 1 single, 7 double,
3 triple
Bathrooms: 3 en-suite, 3 private,
3 public, 2 private showers

Bed & breakfast

per night:	£min	£max
Single	18.00	20.00
Double	33.00	54.00

Parking for 9

⚏🛆🖥♿🗇UL♿Ⓢ🅿🖭⚏🚌 SP T

Westlake ⚏

👑👑 COMMENDED

Lake Road, Windermere LA23 2EQ
☎ (015394) 43020 & 0850 779886
Family-run, private hotel between
Windermere and the lake. All rooms
en-suite, with colour TV and
tea-making facilities. Private parking.
Bedrooms: 1 single, 3 double, 1 twin,
2 triple
Bathrooms: 7 en-suite

Bed & breakfast

per night:	£min	£max
Single	19.00	30.00
Double	38.00	50.00

Evening meal 1830 (last orders
1530)
Parking for 8
Cards accepted: Mastercard, Visa

⚏5🛆⛔🖥♿🛎Ⓢ✗🅿📺🖭⚏
✕🚌 SP T

White Lodge Hotel ⚏

👑👑👑 COMMENDED

Lake Road, Windermere LA23 2JJ
☎ (015394) 43624
Fax (015394) 47000
Victorian family-owned hotel with good
home cooking, only a short walk from
Bowness Bay. All bedrooms have
private bathroom, colour TV and
tea-making facilities, some with lake
views and four-posters.
Bedrooms: 3 single, 6 double, 2 twin,
1 triple
Bathrooms: 12 en-suite

Bed & breakfast

per night:	£min	£max
Single	24.00	31.00
Double	48.00	60.00

Half board per

person:	£min	£max
Daily	34.00	42.00
Weekly	240.00	265.00

Lunch available
Evening meal 1900 (last orders
2000)
Parking for 20
Open March–November
Cards accepted: Mastercard, Visa

⚏🛆⛔🖥♿🛎Ⓢ✗🅿📺🖭⚏►
⚙✖ SP 🏠 T ◎

Wild Boar Hotel ⚏

👑👑👑 COMMENDED

Crook, Kendal LA23 3NF
☎ (015394) 45225
Fax (015394) 42498
CR Best Western
17th C former inn, renowned for its
food. In Gilpin Valley, on B5284, 3 miles
from the lake and half-a-mile from
golf-course.

Continued ►

WINDERMERE
Continued

Bedrooms: 1 single, 16 double, 17 twin, 2 triple
Bathrooms: 36 en-suite
Bed & breakfast

per night:	£min	£max
Single	55.50	
Double	111.00	

Half board per

person:	£min	£max
Daily	65.50	
Weekly	393.00	

Lunch available
Evening meal 1900 (last orders 2100)
Parking for 80
Cards accepted: Amex, Diners, Mastercard, Visa, Switch/Delta

The Willowsmere Hotel ♏
COMMENDED

Ambleside Road, Windermere LA23 1ES
☎ (015394) 43575 & 44962
Fax (015394) 43575
Offers a comfortable and friendly atmosphere. Run by the fifth generation of local hoteliers. Varied food using fresh local produce.
Bedrooms: 2 single, 4 double, 1 twin, 6 triple
Bathrooms: 13 en-suite
Bed & breakfast

per night:	£min	£max
Single	26.00	29.00
Double	52.00	58.00

Half board per

person:	£min	£max
Daily	36.00	42.50
Weekly	252.00	266.00

Lunch available
Evening meal 1900 (last orders 1900)
Parking for 40
Open February–November
Cards accepted: Amex, Diners, Mastercard, Visa, Switch/Delta

Woodlands ♏
HIGHLY COMMENDED

New Road, Windermere LA23 2EE
☎ (015394) 43915 & (0468) 596142
Fax (015394) 48558
Family-run hotel in a convenient location. Renowned for its high standard of cleanliness and comfort. Ample car parking.

Bedrooms: 2 single, 10 double, 1 twin, 1 family room
Bathrooms: 14 en-suite
Bed & breakfast

per night:	£min	£max
Single	22.00	40.00
Double	44.00	80.00

Half board per

person:	£min	£max
Daily	35.50	53.50
Weekly	248.50	

Evening meal from 1900
Parking for 14
Cards accepted: Mastercard, Visa, Switch/Delta

WITHERSLACK
Cumbria
Map ref 5A3

Tranquil village on the east bank of the River Winster, at the south end of the Lyth Valley, famed for its damsons. Good base for touring.

The Old Vicarage Country House Hotel ♏
HIGHLY COMMENDED

Church Road, Witherslack, Grange-over-Sands LA11 6RS
☎ (015395) 52381
Fax (015395) 52373
Email: hotel@old-vic.demon.co.uk

Near the Lakes, far from the crowds. Enjoy award-winning food and wine in a beautiful family-owned historic house.
Bedrooms: 9 double, 4 twin, 1 triple
Bathrooms: 14 en-suite
Bed & breakfast

per night:	£min	£max
Single	59.00	79.00
Double	98.00	138.00

Half board per

person:	£min	£max
Daily	55.00	85.00
Weekly	385.00	525.00

Evening meal 2000 (last orders 2030)
Parking for 25
Cards accepted: Amex, Mastercard, Visa, Switch/Delta

WORKINGTON
Cumbria
Map ref 5A2

A deep-water port on the west Cumbrian coast. There are the ruins of the 14th C Workington Hall, where Mary Queen of Scots stayed in 1568.

Hunday Manor Hotel ♏
HIGHLY COMMENDED

Hunday, Workington CA14 4JF
☎ (01900) 61798
Fax (01900) 601202
Manor house set in 4 acres of woodland and gardens overlooking the Solway and Scottish coastline.
Bedrooms: 5 single, 4 double, 4 twin
Bathrooms: 13 en-suite
Bed & breakfast

per night:	£min	£max
Single	40.00	50.00
Double	50.00	65.00

Half board per

person:	£min	£max
Daily	54.95	64.95
Weekly	350.00	384.65

Lunch available
Evening meal 1900 (last orders 2130)
Parking for 50
Cards accepted: Amex, Mastercard, Visa, Switch/Delta

Morven Guest House
APPROVED

Siddick Road, Siddick, Workington CA14 1LE
☎ (01900) 602118 & 602002
Fax (01900) 602118
Detached house north-west of town. Ideal base for western Lakes and coast. Start of coast to coast cycleway. Car park, cycle storage.
Bedrooms: 2 single, 1 double, 3 twin
Bathrooms: 5 en-suite, 1 private
Bed & breakfast

per night:	£min	£max
Single	25.00	32.00
Double	40.00	46.00

Half board per

person:	£min	£max
Daily	36.00	42.00

Lunch available
Evening meal 1800 (last orders 1600)
Parking for 20

NORTHUMBRIA

Northumbria is an area of breathtaking contrasts. Here you can discover magnificent forests, the seals of the Farne Islands, seaside resorts and charming villages dotted along golden beaches. Or simply take in the stunning scenery of the Durham Dales, the Pennines and Hadrian's Wall.

Experience the region's industrial, religious and cultural past: Durham's handsome Norman cathedral and castle, ancient Lindisfarne Abbey, or a working mine. Travel Stockton's railway heritage trail or entertain the family with a trip to massive Metroland.

Revel in sophisticated, big-city pleasures too, with exciting attractions, shopping and great night life!

The counties of Durham, Northumberland, Tees Valley and Tyne & Wear

FOR MORE INFORMATION CONTACT:
Northumbria Tourist Board
Aykley Heads, Durham DH1 5UX
Tel: (0191) 375 3000 **Fax:** (0191) 386 0899
Internet http://www.ntb.org.uk

Where to Go in Northumbria – see pages 94-97
Where to Stay in Northumbria – see pages 98-117

NORTHUMBRIA

Where to Go and What to See

You will find hundreds of interesting places to visit during your stay in Northumbria, just some of which are listed in these pages. The number against each name will help you locate it on the map (page 97). Contact any Tourist Information Centre in the region for more ideas on days out in Northumbria.

1 Lindisfarne Castle
Holy Island
Berwick-upon-Tweed TD15 2SH
Tel: (01289) 389244
Fort converted into a private home in 1903 for Edward Hudson by the architect Sir Edwin Lutyens.

2 Farne Islands
Seahouses off
Northumberland Coast,
Northumberland
Tel: (01665) 720651
Bird reserve holding around 55,000 pairs of breeding birds of 21 species. Also home to a large colony of grey seals.

3 Bamburgh Castle
Bamburgh,
Northumberland NE69 7DF
Tel: (01668) 214515
Magnificent coastal castle completely restored in 1900. Collections of china, porcelain, furniture, paintings, arms and armour.

4 Alnwick Castle
Alnwick,
Northumberland NE66 1NQ
Tel: (01665) 510777
Largest inhabited castle in England after Windsor Castle. Home of the Percys, Dukes of Northumberland since 1309.

5 Kielder Water
Leaplish Waterside Park,
Kielder,
Hexham,
Northumberland NE48 1BX
Tel: (01434) 250312
Largest man-made lake in Western Europe. Water sports, fishing, log cabins, cycle hire, crazy golf, restaurant, sauna, solarium and pool.

6 Whitehouse Farm Centre
North White House Farm,
Stannington, Morpeth,
Northumberland NE61 6AW
Tel: (01670) 789998/789571
A great day out in the country. Learn how a farm works and see guinea pigs, rabbits, chicks, ducks and exotic animals.

7 Belsay Hall, Castle and Gardens
Belsay,
Newcastle upon Tyne NE20 0DX
Tel: (01661) 881636
House of the Middleton family for 600 years in 30 acres of landscaped gardens and winter garden. 14thC castle, ruined 17thC manor house and neo-classical hall.

8 Sea Life Centre
Grand Parade,
Long Sands,
Tynemouth,
North Shields,
Tyne and Wear NE30 4JF
Tel: (0191) 257 6100/258 1031
*More than 30 hi-tech displays
provide encounters with dozens of
sea creatures. Journey beneath the
North Sea and discover thousands
of amazing creatures.*

9 South Shields Museum
Ocean Road,
South Shields,
Tyne and Wear NE33 2AU
Tel: (0191) 456 8740
*Visit the fascinating reconstruction
of William Black Street where
famous novelist Catherine Cookson
grew up. Discover how the area's
natural environment and history
were shaped.*

10 Souter Point Lighthouse
Coast Road,
Whitburn,
South Shields,
Tyne and Wear SR6 7NH
Tel: (0191) 529 3161
*The lighthouse and associated
buildings were constructed in 1871
and contained the most advanced
lighthouse technology of its day. See
the engine room, battery room and
light tower.*

11 Castle Keep
Saint Nicholas Street,
Castle Garth,
Newcastle upon Tyne NE1 1RQ
Tel: (0191) 232 7938
*Built 1168-1178. One of the finest
surviving examples of a Norman
keep in the country. Panoramic
views of the city from the roof.
Small museum within keep.*

12 Laing Art Gallery
Higham Place,
Newcastle upon Tyne NE1 8AG
Tel: (0191) 232 7734/6989
*Paintings and watercolours,
including works by Northumbrian
born artist John Martin. Award-
winning interactive displays 'Art on
Tyneside' and 'Children's Gallery'.
Cafe and shop.*

13 Newcastle Discovery Museum
Blandford House,
Blandford Square,
Newcastle upon Tyne NE1 4JA
Tel: (0191) 232 6789.
*A wide variety of experiences for all
the family to enjoy. Visit the Science
Factory, Great City, Fashion Works,
maritime history and Pioneers
Gallery.*

14 Hadrian's Wall
Hexham,
Northumberland NE46 4EP
Tel: (01434) 681379
*Fort built for 500 cavalrymen.
Remains include five gateways,
barrack blocks, commandant's
house and headquarters. Finest
Roman military bath-house in
Britain.*

15 Cherryburn: Thomas Bewick Birthplace Museum
Cherryburn,
Station Bank,
Mickley ,
Stocksfield,
Northumberland NE43 7DB
Tel: (01661) 843276
*Birthplace cottage (1700) and
farmyard. Printing house using
original printing blocks. Introductory
exhibition of the life, work and
countryside from 1753 to 1828.*

16 Metroland
MetroCentre,
Gateshead,
Tyne and Wear NE11 9YZ
Tel: (0191) 493 2048
*Europe's only indoor theme park
within a large shopping complex.
Roller coaster, dodgems, swinging
chairs, pirate ship plus live
entertainment daily.*

17 The Wildfowl and Wetlands Trust
District 15,
Washington,
Tyne and Wear NE38 8LE
Tel: (0191) 416 5454/416 5801
Collection of 1,250 wildfowl of 108 varieties. Viewing gallery, picnic areas, hides and winter wild bird feeding station. Flamingos, wild grey heron. Food available.

18 Beamish
The North of England
Open Air Museum,
Beamish,
County Durham DH9 ORG
Tel: (01207) 231811
Visit a town, colliery village, farm and railway station recreated to show life in the North of England early this century. Pockerley Manor illustrates life in the early 1800s.

19 Durham Castle
Palace Green,
Durham DH1 3RW
Tel: (0191) 374 3863/3800
Castle founded in 1072, Norman chapel dating from 1080. Kitchens and great hall dated 1499 and 1284 respectively. Fine example of motte and bailey castle.

20 Durham Cathedral
The College,
Durham DH1 3EH
Tel: (0191) 386 4266
Widely considered to be the finest example of Norman church architecture in England. Has the tombs of St Cuthbert and The Venerable Bede.

22 High Force Waterfall
Forest-in-Teesdale,
Middleton-in-Teesdale,
County Durham DL12
Tel: (01833) 640209
High Force is the most majestic of the waterfalls on the River Tees. The falls are only a short walk from a bus stop, car park and picnic area.

23 Otter Trust
North Pennines Reserve,
Vale House Farm,
Bowes,
Barnard Castle,
County Durham DL12 9RH
Tel: (01833) 628457
A branch of the famous Otter Trust. See Asian and British otters, red and fallow deer and several rare breeds of farm animals in this 230-acre wildlife reserve.

24 Killhope Leadmining Centre
Cowshill, St John's Chapel,
Bishop Auckland,
County Durham DL13 1AR
Tel: (01388) 537505
Britain's most complete lead mining site. Includes crushing mill with 34ft water wheel, reconstruction of Victorian machinery and miners' accommodation.

25 Hartlepool Historic Quay
Maritime Avenue, Hartlepool,
Cleveland TS24 0XZ
Tel: (01429) 860006/860077
An exciting reconstruction of a seaport of the 1800s with buildings and lively quayside authentically reconstructed.

26 Saltburn Smugglers Heritage Centre
Ship Inn, Saltburn-by-the-Sea,
Cleveland TS12 1HF
Tel: (01287) 625252/622422
Experience the authentic sights, sounds and smells of Saltburn's smuggling heritage. Listen to tales of John Andrew, 'King of the Smugglers'.

27 Gisborough Priory
Church Street, Guisborough,
Cleveland TS14 6HG
Tel: (01287) 633801/
(01642) 444000
Remains of a priory founded by Robert de Brus in 1119AD in the grounds of Gisborough Hall. Main arch and window of east wall virtually intact.

28 Preston Hall Museum
Yarm Road,
Stockton-on-Tees,
Cleveland TS18 3RH
Tel: (01642) 781184/791424
A Georgian country house set in a park which is a museum of Victoriana. Return to a bygone age, stroll along a high street and explore 100 acres of parkland overlooking the Tees.

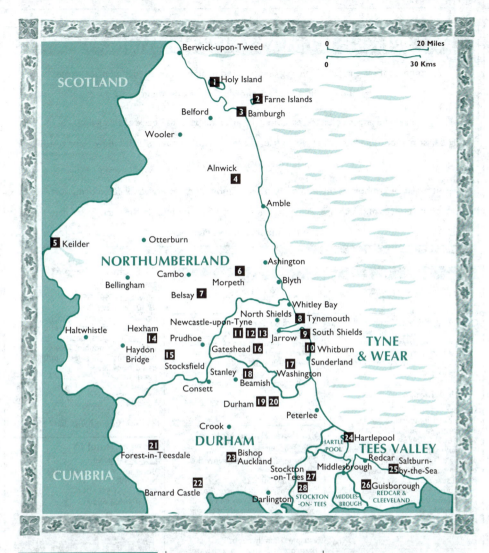

SCOTLAND

Berwick-upon-Tweed

1 Holy Island

2 Farne Islands

Belford **3** Bamburgh

Wooler

Alnwick
4

Amble

5 Keilder

● Otterburn

NORTHUMBERLAND

Cambo ● **6**

Bellingham

Belsay **7**

Morpeth

Ashington ●

● Blyth

Whitley Bay

North Shields **8** Tynemouth

Newcastle-upon-Tyne

11 12 13 Jarrow **9** South Shields

Haltwhistle

Hexham ●

Prudhoe **14**

Haydon
Bridge

Gateshead **16**

10 Whitburn

Sunderland

TYNE
& WEAR

15

Stocksfield

Stanley ●

Consett

Beamish **18**

17 Washington

Durham **19 20**

Peterlee

Crook ●

21

Forest-in-Teesdale

DURHAM

HARTLE
POOL

24 Hartlepool

TEES VALLEY

Bishop **23**
Auckland

Redcar Saltburn-
25 by-the-Sea

CUMBRIA

22

Barnard Castle

Stockton
-on-Tees **27**

Darlington

Middlesbrough

STOCKTON
-ON-TEES

MIDDLES
BROUGH

26 Guisborough

REDCAR &
CLEEVELAND

28

FIND OUT MORE

Further information about holidays and attractions in Northumbria is available from: **Northumbria Tourist Board,** Aykley Heads, Durham DH1 5UX. Tel: (0191) 375 3000 Internet - http://www.ntb.org.uk

The following publications are available free from the Northumbria Tourist Board:

■ **Northumbria 1998** - information on the region, including hotels, self-catering and caravan and camping parks

■ **North of England Bed & Breakfast Map** - value for money bed and breakfast accommodation in Northumbria and Cumbria

■ **Going Places** - information on what to do, where to go, what to see and where to eat throughout the region

■ **Educational Opportunities** - guide to group accommodation and attractions

■ **Selected North Country Inns** - accommodation in traditional Inns in Northumbria and Cumbria

■ **Stay on a Farm** - farm holidays in Northumbria

■ **Freedom** - caravan/camping guide to the North of England

WHERE TO STAY (NORTHUMBRIA)

Accommodation entries in this region are listed in alphabetical order of place name, and then in alphabetical order of establishment.

Map references refer to the colour location maps at the back of this guide. The first number indicates the map to use; the letter and number which follow refer to the grid reference on the map.

At-a-glance symbols at the end of each accommodation entry give useful information about services and facilities. A key to symbols can be found inside the back cover flap. Keep this open for easy reference.

ALNMOUTH

Northumberland
Map ref 5C1

Quiet village with pleasant old buildings, at the mouth of the River Aln where extensive dunes and sands stretch along Alnmouth Bay. 18th C granaries, some converted to dwellings, still stand.

Saddle Hotel ⋈

⚜⚜⚜ APPROVED

24-25 Northumberland Street, Alnmouth, Alnwick NE66 2RA
☎ (01665) 830476
Personally supervised by owners and offering a high standard of accommodation. Fourteen awards for food in seven years.
Bedrooms: 4 double, 4 twin, 1 triple
Bathrooms: 9 en-suite
Bed & breakfast

per night:	£min	£max
Single	30.00	35.00
Double	50.00	60.00

Half board per person:

	£min	£max
Daily	35.00	45.00

Lunch available
Evening meal 1830 (last orders 2100)
Cards accepted: Mastercard, Visa, Switch/Delta

A key to symbols can be found inside the back cover flap.

ALNWICK

Northumberland
Map ref 5C1

Ancient and historic market town, entered through the Hotspur Tower, an original gate in the town walls. The medieval castle, the second biggest in England and still the seat of the Dukes of Northumberland, was restored from ruin in the 18th C.
Tourist Information Centre ☎ (01665) 510665

Bondgate House Hotel ⋈

⚜⚜⚜ COMMENDED

20 Bondgate Without, Alnwick NE66 1PN
☎ (01665) 602025
Small family-run hotel near the medieval town gateway and interesting local shops. Well-placed for touring. Most rooms are en-suite.
Bedrooms: 1 single, 2 double, 2 twin, 2 triple, 1 family room
Bathrooms: 5 en-suite, 2 private, 1 public, 1 private shower
Bed & breakfast per night:

	£min	£max
Single	24.00	26.00
Double	41.00	43.00

Half board per person:

	£min	£max
Daily	35.00	

Evening meal 1830 (last orders 1630)
Parking for 8
Cards accepted: Mastercard, Visa, Switch/Delta

21 Boulmer Village ⋈

COMMENDED

Alnwick NE66 3BS
☎ (01665) 577262
Traditional fisherman's cottage overlooking the North Sea in a working fishing village. Easy access.
Bedrooms: 1 double, 1 twin
Bathrooms: 2 en-suite, 1 public
Bed & breakfast per night:

	£min	£max
Single	20.00	25.00
Double	36.00	40.00

Parking for 15

Hotspur Hotel ⋈

⚜⚜⚜ APPROVED

Bondgate Without, Alnwick NE66 1PR
☎ (01665) 510101
Fax (01665) 605033

Originally a coaching inn, centrally located, offering a warm welcome and friendly hospitality. Tastefully furnished bedrooms, all en-suite. High standard of food, fine ales.
Bedrooms: 2 single, 9 double, 11 twin, 1 family room
Bathrooms: 20 en-suite, 1 public
Bed & breakfast per night:

	£min	£max
Single	30.00	35.00
Double	60.00	70.00

Half board per person:	£min	£max
Daily	42.50	47.50
Weekly	245.00	262.50

Lunch available
Evening meal 1900 (last orders 2100)
Parking for 20
Cards accepted: Amex, Diners, Mastercard, Visa

🛎🔌🛏🖥♨🖾🚿📺🛗♿ 🍴15 ♦▶✕🗴 SP 🏠

White Swan Hotel ⩗
♛♛♛ COMMENDED
Bondgate Within, Alnwick
NE66 1TD
☎ (01665) 602109
Fax (01665) 510400
Ⓡ MacDonald
Former coaching inn, partly traditional, with a log fire in the cosy reception area/lounge. Groups welcome.
Bedrooms: 4 single, 14 double, 36 twin, 1 triple, 3 family rooms
Bathrooms: 58 en-suite

Bed & breakfast per night:	£min	£max
Single	65.00	80.00
Double	74.00	94.00

Half board per person:	£min	£max
Daily	37.50	99.50
Weekly	262.50	696.50

Lunch available
Evening meal 1900 (last orders 2130)
Parking for 30
Cards accepted: Amex, Mastercard, Visa, Switch/Delta

🛎🍴🔌🛏🖥♨🖾🚿🕭 Ⓢ🚿♿🕭 ⊙🛗
🛗🍴150▶❄🖾 OAP 🗴 SP 🏠 T

BAMBURGH

Northumberland
Map ref 5C1

Village with a spectacular red sandstone castle standing 150 ft above the sea. On the village green the magnificent Norman church stands opposite a museum containing mementoes of the heroine Grace Darling.

Mizen Head Hotel ⩗
♛♛♛ COMMENDED
Lucker Road, Bamburgh NE69 7BS
☎ (01668) 214254
Privately-owned, fully licensed hotel in own grounds, with accent on good food and service. Convenient for beaches, castle and golf. 2 minutes' walk from village centre.
Bedrooms: 2 single, 5 double, 4 twin, 4 family rooms
Bathrooms: 11 en-suite, 2 public

Bed & breakfast per night:	£min	£max
Single	22.50	45.00
Double	45.00	79.00

Half board per person:	£min	£max
Daily	34.00	58.00
Weekly	231.00	325.00

Lunch available
Evening meal 1830 (last orders 2000)
Parking for 30
Cards accepted: Mastercard, Visa

🛎🖾🔌🛏♨🕭🖾 Ⓢ♿📺🛗 ♿🍴30
❄🗴 SP T

Waren House Hotel ⩗
♛♛♛ HIGHLY COMMENDED
Waren Mill, Belford NE70 7EE
☎ (01668) 214581
Fax (01668) 214484
Traditional, beautifully restored, award-winning country house in 6 acres overlooking Holy Island. Quality accommodation and food, 250+ bin wine list. Adults only.
Bedrooms: 6 double, 3 twin
Suites available
Bathrooms: 9 en-suite

Bed & breakfast per night:	£min	£max
Single	55.00	80.00
Double	110.00	185.00

Half board per person:	£min	£max
Daily	73.45	105.00
Weekly	360.00	450.00

Evening meal 1900 (last orders 2030)
Parking for 26

Cards accepted: Amex, Diners, Mastercard, Visa, Switch/Delta

🛏🔌🖾🛏♨🕭 Ⓢ🖾♿🕭🖾 ♿
🍴24 ♦∪▶❄🐾 OAP 🗴 SP 🏠 T ®

BARNARD CASTLE

Durham
Map ref 5B3

High over the Tees, a thriving market town with a busy market square. Bernard Baliol's 12th C castle (now ruins) stands nearby. The Bowes Museum, housed in a grand 19th C French chateau, holds fine paintings and furniture. Nearby are some magnificent buildings.
Tourist Information Centre ☎ (01833) 690909 or 630272

Montalbo Hotel
♛♛♛ COMMENDED
Montalbo Road, Barnard Castle, County Durham DL12 8BP
☎ (01833) 637342
Fax (01833) 637342
Small, family-run hotel offering attractive and comfortable bedrooms at reasonable prices. Excellent choice of food served every evening.
Bedrooms: 2 single, 2 double, 2 twin, 1 triple
Bathrooms: 7 en-suite, 1 public

Bed & breakfast per night:	£min	£max
Single	25.00	35.00
Double	38.00	45.00

Half board per person:	£min	£max
Daily	31.00	47.00

Lunch available
Evening meal 1900 (last orders 2100)
Parking for 4
Cards accepted: Mastercard, Visa, Switch/Delta

🛎🖾🔌🛏♨🕭 Ⓢ🖾♿🕭🖾 ♿🐾🗴 SP

BARNARD CASTLE

Continued

The Morritt Arms Hotel ⋒

🛡🛡🛡 COMMENDED

Greta Bridge, Rokeby, Barnard
Castle, County Durham DL12 9SE
☎ (01833) 627232
Fax (01833) 627392
ℭℜ Consort

*Hidden gem, twixt Yorkshire and
Durham Dales. Charming 17th C inn.
Private gardens, good food, log fires,
cosy lounges, real ale. Excellent walking.
Half board prices are based on a
minimum 2-night stay.*
Bedrooms: 3 single, 11 double,
4 twin
Bathrooms: 18 en-suite

Bed & breakfast

per night:	£min	£max
Single	49.50	59.50
Double	69.50	89.50

Half board per

person:	£min	£max
Daily	59.00	69.00

Lunch available
Evening meal 1900 (last orders
2130)
Parking for 100
Cards accepted: Amex, Diners,
Mastercard, Visa, Switch/Delta

BARRASFORD

Northumberland
Map ref 5B2

Lovely village on the North Tyne
River, overlooked by the restored
14th C Haughton Castle on the
opposite bank.

Barrasford Arms ⋒

🛡🛡 APPROVED

Barrasford, Hexham NE48 4AA
☎ (01434) 681237
*Small country hotel in this lovely
hamlet, only 8 miles from Hexham and
4 miles to the Roman Wall. An ideal
centre for touring Northumberland.*
Bedrooms: 1 double, 3 twin, 1 triple
Bathrooms: 4 en-suite, 1 public

Bed & breakfast

per night:	£min	£max
Single	20.00	26.00
Double	32.00	36.00

Evening meal 1930 (last orders
2115)
Parking for 46
Cards accepted: Mastercard, Visa

BELFORD

Northumberland
Map ref 5B1

Small market town on the old
coaching road, close to the coast,
the Scottish border and the
north-east flank of the Cheviots.
Built mostly in stone and very
peaceful now that the A1 has
by-passed the town, Belford makes
an ideal centre for excursions to the
moors and coast.

Purdy Lodge ⋒

🛡🛡 COMMENDED

Adderstone Services, Belford
NE70 7JU
☎ (01668) 213000
Fax (01668) 213111
ℭℜ The Independents/Minotel

*Situated 40 miles north of Newcastle,
75 miles south of Edinburgh on the A1.
Comfortable accommodation. 5.5 miles
away from breathtaking Bamburgh
coast. Prices shown below are per room
per night for single, double or family,
excluding breakfast.*
Bedrooms: 3 double, 10 twin,
6 triple, 1 family room
Bathrooms: 20 en-suite

Bed & breakfast

per night:	£min	£max
Single	39.50	39.50
Double	39.50	39.50

Lunch available
Evening meal 1830 (last orders
2130)
Parking for 60
Cards accepted: Amex, Diners,
Mastercard, Visa, Switch/Delta

BELLINGHAM

Northumberland
Map ref 5B2

Set in the beautiful valley of the
North Tyne close to the Kielder
Forest, Kielder Water and lonely
moorland below the Cheviots. The
church has an ancient stone wagon
roof fortified in the 18th C with
buttresses.
*Tourist Information Centre ☎ (01434)
220616*

Riverdale Hall Hotel ⋒

🛡🛡🛡 COMMENDED

Bellingham, Hexham NE48 2JT
☎ (01434) 220254
Fax (01434) 220457
ℭℜ The Independents

*Spacious country hall in large grounds.
Indoor swimming pool, sauna, fishing,
cricket field and golf opposite.
Award-winning hotel restaurant. The
Cocker family's 20th year.*
Bedrooms: 3 single, 4 double, 9 twin,
4 triple
Bathrooms: 20 en-suite, 2 public

Bed & breakfast

per night:	£min	£max
Single	40.00	48.00
Double	67.00	84.00

Half board per

person:	£min	£max
Daily	53.00	67.00
Weekly	275.00	355.00

Lunch available
Evening meal 1830 (last orders
2200)
Parking for 60
Cards accepted: Amex, Diners,
Mastercard, Visa, Switch/Delta

The map references refer
to the colour maps towards
the end of the guide.
The first figure is the
map number; the letter and
figure which follow indicate
the grid reference
on the map.

BERWICK-UPON-TWEED

Northumberland
Map ref 5B1

Guarding the mouth of the Tweed, England's northernmost town with the best 16th C city walls in Europe. The handsome Guildhall and barracks date from the 18th C. Three bridges cross to Tweedmouth, the oldest built in 1634.
Tourist Information Centre ☎ (01289) 330733

Queens Head Hotel ⚠

👑👑 APPROVED
Sandgate, Berwick-upon-Tweed TD15 1EP
☎ (01289) 307852
Fax (01289) 307852
Near the town centre, opposite the swimming baths and adjacent to the historic town walls.
Bedrooms: 1 single, 1 double, 2 twin, 2 triple
Bathrooms: 6 en-suite, 1 public
Bed & breakfast per night:

	£min	£max
Single	30.00	35.00
Double	50.00	55.00

Half board per person:

	£min	£max
Daily	40.00	50.00
Weekly	250.00	

Lunch available
Evening meal 1830 (last orders 2100)
Cards accepted: Amex, Mastercard, Visa, Switch/Delta

ACCESSIBILITY

Look for the ♿ symbols which indicate accessibility for wheelchair users. These are described in detail at the front of this guide.

Information on accommodation listed in this guide has been supplied by the proprietors. As changes may occur you are advised to check details at the time of booking.

BISHOP AUCKLAND

Durham
Map ref 5C2

Busy market town on the bank of the River Wear. The Bishop's Palace, a castellated Norman manor house altered in the 18th C, stands in beautiful gardens. Entered from the market square by a handsome 18th C gatehouse, the park is a peaceful retreat of trees and streams.
Tourist Information Centre ☎ (01388) 604922 or 602610

Greenhead Country House Hotel ⚠

👑👑 HIGHLY COMMENDED
Fir Tree, Crook, County Durham DL15 8BL
☎ (01388) 763143
Fax (01388) 763143

Perfectly situated at the foot of Weardale, north-west of Bishop Auckland. Surrounded by open fields and woodland yet only 15 minutes from Durham City. Its tranquillity is enhanced as only private resident guests are catered for - no public bars or discos.
Bedrooms: 1 single, 3 double, 2 twin
Bathrooms: 6 en-suite
Bed & breakfast per night:

	£min	£max
Single	40.00	40.00
Double	50.00	60.00

Evening meal 1800 (last orders 1700)
Parking for 15
Cards accepted: Mastercard, Visa

Park Head Hotel ⚠

👑👑 COMMENDED
New Coundon, Bishop Auckland, County Durham DL14 8QB
☎ (01388) 661727
Attractive family-run hotel with en-suite bedrooms, half a mile north of Bishop Auckland and 6 miles south of Durham. Food served in restaurant, carvery and bar.
Bedrooms: 8 single, 8 double, 13 twin, 4 triple
Suites available
Bathrooms: 33 en-suite

Bed & breakfast per night:

	£min	£max
Single	48.00	58.00
Double	55.00	72.00

Half board per person:

	£min	£max
Daily	34.00	46.00
Weekly	240.00	280.00

Lunch available
Evening meal 1900 (last orders 2200)
Parking for 108
Cards accepted: Amex, Mastercard, Visa, Switch/Delta

BLANCHLAND

Northumberland
Map ref 5B2

Beautiful medieval village rebuilt in the 18th C with stone from its ruined abbey, for lead miners working on the surrounding wild moors. The village is approached over a stone bridge across the Derwent or, from the north, through the ancient gatehouse.

Lord Crewe Arms Hotel ⚠

👑👑👑 HIGHLY COMMENDED
Blanchland, Consett, County Durham DH8 9SP
☎ (01434) 675251
Fax (01434) 675337
Originally Blanchland Abbey (built in 13th C), now a hotel, reputedly with a delightful ghost. Set in the Derwent Valley and surrounded by Northumberland moors.
Bedrooms: 12 double, 6 twin, 2 triple
Bathrooms: 20 en-suite
Bed & breakfast per night:

	£min	£max
Single	80.00	
Double	110.00	

Evening meal 1900 (last orders 2115)
Cards accepted: Amex, Diners, Mastercard, Visa, Switch/Delta

The symbols in each entry give information about services and facilities. A key to these symbols appears at the back of this guide.

BROTTON

Tees Valley
Map ref 5C3

Hunley Hall Golf Club ⚑

ⴲⴲⴲ COMMENDED

Brotton, Saltburn-by-the-Sea, North Yorkshire TS12 2QQ
☎ (01287) 676216
Fax (01287) 678250
Situated on the Captain Cook trail between Middlesbrough and Whitby, with unrivalled coastal views.
Bedrooms: 5 twin, 1 triple
Bathrooms: 6 en-suite

Bed & breakfast

per night:	£min	£max
Single	35.00	35.00
Double	50.00	50.00

Half board per

person:	£min	£max
Daily	39.00	49.00
Weekly	259.00	329.00

Lunch available
Evening meal 1830 (last orders 2130)
Parking for 88
Cards accepted: Mastercard, Visa, Switch/Delta

🛇🕊️🖤❏♿🕴️🛎️S🌂🏛️🖾⬛U🅿️✕ 🚐🛇SP◉

CONSETT

Durham
Map ref 5B2

Former steel town on the edge of rolling moors. Modern development includes the shopping centre and a handsome Roman Catholic church, designed by a local architect. To the west, the Derwent Reservoir provides water sports and pleasant walks.

Bee Cottage Farm ⚑

ⴲⴲ HIGHLY COMMENDED

Castleside, Consett, County Durham DH8 9HW
☎ (01207) 508224

46-acre livestock farm. 1.5 miles west of the A68, between Castleside and Tow Law. Unspoilt views. Ideally located for Beamish Museum and Durham. No smoking. Tea-room open 1-6 pm.

Bedrooms: 1 single, 3 double, 2 twin, 1 triple, 2 family rooms
Suites available
Bathrooms: 1 en-suite, 2 private, 5 public

Bed & breakfast

per night:	£min	£max
Single	25.00	
Double	44.00	

Half board per

person:	£min	£max
Daily	38.50	

Lunch available
Evening meal 1930 (last orders 2000)
Parking for 20

CORBRIDGE

Northumberland
Map ref 5B2

Small town on the River Tyne. Close by are extensive remains of the Roman military town Corstopitum, with a museum housing important discoveries from excavations. The town itself is attractive with shady trees, a 17th C bridge and interesting old buildings, notably a 14th C vicarage.

Fox & Hounds Hotel ⚑

ⴲⴲ COMMENDED

Stagshaw Bank, Corbridge NE45 5QW
☎ (01434) 633024
Fax (01434) 633024

400-year-old coaching inn with a 70-seat conservatory restaurant. Owners operate and live on premises.
Bedrooms: 1 single, 3 double, 3 twin, 1 triple
Bathrooms: 8 en-suite

Bed & breakfast

per night:	£min	£max
Single	30.00	30.00
Double	40.00	40.00

Lunch available
Evening meal 1800 (last orders 2100)
Parking for 50

🛇🕊️🖤❏♿🕴️🛎️S🖾🏛️⬛🅿️⚫🌸✕ 🛇🏧T

Lion of Corbridge Hotel

ⴲⴲ COMMENDED

Bridge End, Corbridge NE45 5AX
☎ (01434) 632504
Fax (01434) 632571
ℂℝ The Independents
Family-run hotel on a bank of the River Tyne with emphasis on comfort and good food. Room on ground floor especially equipped for disabled. Special 2-3 day breaks available (room, breakfast and dinner £160.00 to £190.00 respectively).
Bedrooms: 8 double, 6 twin
Bathrooms: 14 en-suite

Bed & breakfast

per night:	£min	£max
Single	45.00	
Double	64.00	

Lunch available
Evening meal 1830 (last orders 2130)
Parking for 60
Cards accepted: Amex, Diners, Mastercard, Visa, Switch/Delta

🛇🕊️🖤🏠🕴️🖤❏🕴️S🌂🖾🏛️ 🖾🍴40🅿️🌸✕🚐SP◉

CROOKHAM

Northumberland
Map ref 5B1

Pretty hamlet taking its name from the winding course of the River Till which flows in the shape of a shepherd's crook. Three castles - Etal, Duddo and Ford - can be seen, and nearby the restored Heatherslaw Mill is of great interest.

The Coach House ⚑

ⴲⴲⴲ HIGHLY COMMENDED

Crookham, Cornhill-on-Tweed TD12 4TD
☎ (01890) 820293 & 820284
Fax (01890) 820284
Spacious rooms, arranged around a courtyard, in rolling country near the Scottish border. Home-cooked, quality fresh food. Rooms specially equipped for disabled guests.
Wheelchair access category 1♿
Bedrooms: 2 single, 2 double, 5 twin
Bathrooms: 7 en-suite, 2 public

Bed & breakfast

per night:	£min	£max
Single	23.00	36.00
Double	46.00	72.00

Half board per

person:	£min	£max
Daily	38.50	52.50

Evening meal 1930 (last orders 1930)
Parking for 12
Open March–November
Cards accepted: Mastercard, Visa

🛇🕊️🖤❏🕴️🖤S🖾🏛️🖾🌸🚐🏧

DARLINGTON

Durham
Map ref 5C3

Largest town in County Durham, standing on the River Skerne and home of the earliest passenger railway which first ran to Stockton in 1825. Now the home of a railway museum. Originally a prosperous market town occupying the site of an Anglo-Saxon settlement, it still holds an open market.
Tourist Information Centre ☎ (01325) 388666

Aberlady Guest House

APPROVED

51 Corporation Road, Darlington, County Durham DL3 6AD
☎ (01325) 461449
Large Victorian house near town centre. Short walking distance to Railway Museum. Within easy reach of 4 golf courses and leisure centre.
Bedrooms: 2 single, 3 twin, 1 triple, 1 family room
Bathrooms: 2 public

Bed & breakfast

per night:	£min	£max
Single	13.50	17.50
Double	27.00	27.00

Parking for 2

The Coachman Hotel

APPROVED

Victoria Road, Darlington, County Durham DL1 5JJ
☎ (01325) 286116
Fax (01325) 382796
Comfortable family-run hotel close to the town centre, railway station and all leisure facilities. Easy access to the A1(M).
Bedrooms: 7 single, 3 double, 8 twin, 1 triple, 1 family room
Bathrooms: 20 en-suite, 4 public

Bed & breakfast

per night:	£min	£max
Single	29.50	45.00
Double	55.00	80.00

Half board per

person:	£min	£max
Daily	40.00	55.00
Weekly	280.00	385.00

Lunch available
Evening meal 1900 (last orders 2200)
Parking for 18
Cards accepted: Mastercard, Visa, Switch/Delta

The Cricketers Hotel ♨

COMMENDED

55 Parkgate, Darlington, County Durham DL1 1RR
☎ (01325) 384 444
Small, family-run hotel close to the town centre. En-suite rooms, friendly bar/lounge and restaurant for 50 people.
Bedrooms: 4 single, 7 double, 4 twin, 1 triple
Bathrooms: 16 en-suite

Bed & breakfast

per night:	£min	£max
Single	30.00	45.00
Double	45.00	60.00

Half board per

person:	£min	£max
Daily	38.50	53.50
Weekly	250.00	300.00

Lunch available
Evening meal 1800 (last orders 2130)
Parking for 18
Cards accepted: Amex, Mastercard, Visa

Grange Hotel

APPROVED

South End, Coniscliffe Road, Darlington, County Durham DL3 7HZ
☎ (01325) 464555
Fax (01325) 464555
Imposing stately mansion built 1804, once the home of Joseph Pease, first Quaker MP and promoter of early railways. Was also a convent from 1905 to 1975. Here we offer you the comfort and contentment of gracious living.
Bedrooms: 2 single, 2 double, 5 twin, 1 triple
Bathrooms: 10 private

Bed & breakfast

per night:	£min	£max
Single	25.00	38.77
Double	40.00	52.87

Evening meal 1700 (last orders 1800)
Parking for 50

Newbus Arms Hotel and Restaurant ♨

COMMENDED

Newbus Arms, Neasham, Darlington, County Durham DL2 1PE
☎ (01325) 721071
Fax (01325) 721770

Country house hotel of immense beauty, dating from 1610. Set in its own grounds, 3.5 miles from Darlington, between Hurworth and Neasham.
Bedrooms: 3 single, 9 double, 4 twin
Bathrooms: 13 en-suite, 2 private, 1 private shower

Bed & breakfast

per night:	£min	£max
Single	49.50	55.00
Double	65.00	85.00

Half board per

person:	£min	£max
Daily	60.00	67.50
Weekly	400.00	500.00

Lunch available
Evening meal 1900 (last orders 2200)
Parking for 80
Cards accepted: Amex, Diners, Mastercard, Visa

Walworth Castle Hotel

COMMENDED

Walworth, Darlington, County Durham DL2 2LY
☎ (01325) 485470
Fax (01325) 462257

12th C castle in 18 acres of lawns and woods, privately owned, offering comfort and food at modest prices. 3 miles west of Darlington off the A68.
Bedrooms: 4 single, 23 double, 5 twin, 4 triple
Bathrooms: 36 en-suite, 2 public

Bed & breakfast

per night:	£min	£max
Single	35.00	65.00
Double	45.00	89.00

Half board per

person:	£min	£max
Daily	45.00	95.00

Lunch available
Evening meal 1900 (last orders 2200)
Parking for 250

Continued ▶

DARLINGTON
Continued

Cards accepted: Amex, Diners, Mastercard, Visa, Switch/Delta

🐎🗝️🛁📞🖥️⬚♿🅿️👤⊘▥🖊️
🍴200🔱⚓🏃✦⚙️🅳🚫 SP 🏠 T

Woodland House
👑👑 COMMENDED
63 Woodland Road, Darlington, County Durham DL3 7BQ
☎ (01325) 461908
Victorian town house built in 1876. Tastefully decorated bedrooms with all amenities.
Bedrooms: 3 single, 1 double, 2 twin, 3 triple
Bathrooms: 3 en-suite, 2 public
Bed & breakfast

per night:	£min	£max
Single	20.00	28.00
Double	34.00	42.00

🐎🖥️⬚♿UL🖊️▥🚗📠🏠

DURHAM
Durham
Map ref 5C2

Ancient city with its Norman castle and cathedral, now a World Heritage site, set on a bluff high over the Wear. A market and university town and regional centre, spreading beyond the market-place on both banks of the river.
Tourist Information Centre ☎ *(0191) 384 3720*

Bay Horse Inn 🏔
👑👑👑 COMMENDED
Brandon Village, Durham DH7 8ST
☎ (0191) 378 0498
Ten stone-built chalets 3 miles from Durham city centre. All have shower, toilet, TV, tea and coffee facilities and telephone. Ample car parking.
Bedrooms: 3 double, 6 twin, 1 family room
Bathrooms: 10 en-suite
Bed & breakfast

per night:	£min	£max
Single	31.00	31.00
Double	40.00	40.00

Lunch available
Evening meal 1900 (last orders 2200)
Parking for 25
Cards accepted: Mastercard, Visa

🐎🛁📠📞🖥️⬚♿🍷🅿️🖊️▥📠🏠✦
🚗 T

Bees Cottage Guest House 🏔
👑 COMMENDED
Bridge Street, Durham DH1 4RT
☎ (0191) 384 5775
Durham's oldest cottage, in city centre and convenient for shops, rail and bus. Hospitality tray, English or vegetarian breakfast, early morning call. All rooms en-suite with TV. No smoking, please. Private parking.
Bedrooms: 1 double, 2 twin, 1 triple
Bathrooms: 4 en-suite
Bed & breakfast

per night:	£min	£max
Single	36.00	36.00
Double	46.00	46.00

Parking for 4

🐎🖥️⬚♿UL S🖊️▥🚗📠🏠

Bowburn Hall Hotel 🏔
👑👑👑 COMMENDED
Bowburn, Durham DH6 5NH
☎ (0191) 377 0311
Fax (0191) 377 3459
Large country house set in 5 acres of private grounds, 3 miles from Durham City.
Bedrooms: 4 single, 11 double, 4 twin
Bathrooms: 19 en-suite, 1 public
Bed & breakfast

per night:	£min	£max
Single	50.00	
Double	65.00	

Lunch available
Evening meal 1830 (last orders 2200)
Parking for 100
Cards accepted: Amex, Diners, Mastercard, Visa, Switch/Delta

🐎📞📠🖥️⬚♿🍷🅿️🖊️▥ TV ▥🚗📠🍴100
✦🚫 SP

Castle View Guest House
👑👑 COMMENDED
4 Crossgate, Durham DH1 4PS
☎ (0191) 386 8852
Fax (0191) 386 8852
250-year-old, listed building in the heart of the old city, with woodland and riverside walks and a magnificent view of the cathedral and castle.
Bedrooms: 1 single, 3 double, 2 twin
Bathrooms: 6 en-suite, 1 public
Bed & breakfast

per night:	£min	£max
Single	38.00	
Double	50.00	

🐎🖥️⬚♿UL🅿️🖊️▥ TV ▥🚗✦🗝️🚗📠🏠

Croxdale Inn
👑👑 COMMENDED
Croxdale, Durham DH6 5HX
☎ (01388) 815727 & 420294
Fax (01388) 815368

Recently refurbished family-run hotel, 3 miles south of the city. Spacious bedrooms, all with private facilities, satellite TV, telephone and hairdryer. Four-poster suite with sauna and jacuzzi. Restaurant serving home-cooked food.
Bedrooms: 4 single, 4 double, 3 twin, 1 triple
Bathrooms: 12 en-suite, 1 public
Bed & breakfast

per night:	£min	£max
Single	28.00	38.00
Double	45.00	58.00

Half board per person:	£min	£max
Daily	38.00	48.00
Weekly	190.00	245.00

Lunch available
Evening meal 1700 (last orders 2200)
Parking for 22
Cards accepted: Mastercard, Visa, Switch/Delta

🐎🛁📠📞⬚♿🍷🗝️🔒 S🖊️▥🚗📠🍴
🔍🚫 SP

Drumforke
👑 COMMENDED
25 Crossgate Peth, Durham DH1 4PZ
☎ (0191) 384 2966
Near the city centre and providing a useful base for touring the beautiful dales of Weardale and Teesdale.
Bedrooms: 2 twin, 1 triple
Bathrooms: 1 public
Bed & breakfast

per night:	£min	£max
Single	20.00	
Double	35.00	

Parking for 4

🐎1 UL🖊️ TV ▥🚗🚗

COLOUR MAPS
Colour maps at the back of this guide pinpoint all places in which you will find accommodation listed.

Hallgarth Manor Hotel ⚑
⚜⚜⚜ COMMENDED

Pittington, Durham DH6 1AB
☎ (0191) 372 1188
Fax (0191) 372 1249

Country house hotel in 4 acres of grounds. Restaurant, lounge, cocktail bar, Tavern bar. Attractively furnished.
Bedrooms: 4 single, 13 double, 6 twin
Bathrooms: 23 en-suite

Bed & breakfast per night:

	£min	£max
Single	48.00	55.00
Double	60.00	75.00

Half board per person:

	£min	£max
Daily	50.00	
Weekly	350.00	

Lunch available
Evening meal 1900 (last orders 2115)
Parking for 300
Cards accepted: Amex, Diners, Mastercard, Visa, Switch/Delta

Hill Rise Guest House ⚑
⚜⚜⚜ HIGHLY COMMENDED

13 Durham Road West, Bowburn, Durham DH6 5AU
☎ (0191) 377 0302
Fax (0191) 377 0302
Conveniently placed 200 yards from A1(M). Family, twin and double rooms with en-suite facilities. Quality home-cooked evening meals available.
Bedrooms: 2 single, 1 twin, 2 triple, 1 family room
Suites available
Bathrooms: 4 en-suite, 1 public

Bed & breakfast per night:

	£min	£max
Single	18.00	25.00
Double	40.00	40.00

Half board per person:

	£min	£max
Daily	28.00	35.00
Weekly	196.00	245.00

Evening meal 1850 (last orders 1900)
Parking for 4

Kensington Hall Hotel ⚑
⚜⚜⚜ COMMENDED

Kensington Terrace, Willington, Crook, County Durham DL15 0PJ
☎ (01388) 745071
Fax (01388) 745800
Comfortable family-run hotel with lounge bar, restaurant and function suite. Excellent meals daily. South-west of Durham on A690 to Crook.
Bedrooms: 3 double, 4 twin, 2 triple, 1 family room
Bathrooms: 10 en-suite

Bed & breakfast per night:

	£min	£max
Single	35.00	35.00
Double	45.00	48.00

Half board per person:

	£min	£max
Daily	45.00	45.00
Weekly	300.00	315.00

Lunch available
Evening meal 1900 (last orders 2145)
Parking for 40
Cards accepted: Amex, Diners, Mastercard, Visa, Switch/Delta

Queens Head Hotel
⚜ APPROVED

Gilesgate, Durham DH1 2JR
☎ (0191) 386 5649
Under a mile from the city centre in a main road position. Bar with pool and darts, beer garden.
Bedrooms: 1 single, 3 double, 3 twin, 1 triple, 1 family room
Bathrooms: 2 en-suite, 2 public

Bed & breakfast per night:

	£min	£max
Single	18.00	26.00
Double	36.00	40.00

Lunch available
Parking for 12

Redhills Hotel ⚑
Redhills Lane, Crossgate Moor, Durham DH1 4AW
☎ (0191) 386 4331
Fax (0191) 386 9612
Small, friendly hotel with well-appointed bedrooms and personal service, only 2 minutes from Durham city centre.
Bedrooms: 5 single, 1 double
Bathrooms: 2 public

Bed & breakfast per night:

	£min	£max
Single	20.00	30.00
Double	25.00	36.00

Half board per person:

	£min	£max
Daily	26.00	42.00
Weekly	175.00	225.00

Lunch available
Evening meal 1900 (last orders 2200)
Parking for 80
Cards accepted: Amex, Diners, Mastercard, Visa

Roadchef Lodge ⚑
⚜⚜⚜ COMMENDED

Durham Motorway Service Area, A1(M), Tursdale Road, Bowburn, Durham DH6 5NP
☎ (0191) 377 3666 & 0800 834719
Fax (0191) 377 1448
CR RoadChef
RoadChef Lodges offer high specification rooms at affordable prices, in popular locations suited to both the business and private traveller. Prices are per room and do not include breakfast.
Bedrooms: 21 double, 16 twin, 1 family room
Bathrooms: 38 en-suite

Bed & breakfast per night:

	£min	£max
Double	43.50	

Parking for 158
Cards accepted: Amex, Diners, Mastercard, Visa, Switch/Delta

Royal County Hotel ⚑
⚜⚜⚜⚜ HIGHLY COMMENDED

Old Elvet, Durham DH1 3JN
☎ (0191) 386 6821
Fax (0191) 386 0704
CR Swallow
Situated in the heart of this cathedral city. Steeped in history the hotel is very well appointed. Choice of restaurants and superbly equipped leisure club.
Wheelchair access category 1
Bedrooms: 35 single, 56 double, 55 twin, 4 family rooms
Suite available
Bathrooms: 150 en-suite

Bed & breakfast per night:

	£min	£max
Single	95.00	115.00
Double	125.00	140.00

Lunch available
Evening meal 1900 (last orders 2215)
Parking for 85
Cards accepted: Amex, Diners, Mastercard, Visa, Switch/Delta

DURHAM
Continued

Three Tuns Hotel ⚌

⚌⚌⚌⚌⚌ COMMENDED

New Elvet, Durham DH1 3AQ
☎ (0191) 386 4326
Fax (0191) 386 1406
Ⓒⓡ Swallow

Originally a coaching inn, the hotel has been tastefully modernised to provide first-class facilities. Within easy walking distance of the magnificent Norman cathedral. Short break packages available.

Bedrooms: 15 single, 12 double, 18 twin, 1 triple, 1 family room
Suite available
Bathrooms: 47 en-suite

Bed & breakfast

per night:	£min	£max
Single	39.00	95.00
Double	55.00	115.00

Half board per

person:	£min	£max
Daily	55.00	113.00
Weekly	250.00	565.00

Lunch available
Evening meal 1900 (last orders 2130)
Parking for 60
Cards accepted: Amex, Diners, Mastercard, Visa, Switch/Delta

🐾📞💷▢🖥🛜📶🅸Ⓢ🏴Ⓜ◑📠🍽350▶🐾 SP🏠Ⓣ

Trevelyan College ⚌

⚌⚌ APPROVED

Elvet Hill Road, Durham DH1 3LN
☎ (0191) 374 3765 & 374 3768
Fax (0191) 374 3789
Email: john.wright@dur.ac.uk
Set in parkland within easy walking distance of Durham City. Comfortable Cloister Bar, TV lounges, ample parking. Standard and en-suite rooms available.
Bedrooms: 253 single, 8 double, 27 twin
Bathrooms: 58 en-suite, 47 public

Bed & breakfast

per night:	£min	£max
Single	18.00	27.50
Double	32.40	49.50

Half board per

person:	£min	£max
Daily	26.30	55.80
Weekly	165.00	225.00

Lunch available
Evening meal 1800 (last orders 1930)
Parking for 100
Open January, March–April, June–September, December

🐾♿🛜📶🅸Ⓢ🏴🖥📶◑📠🍽300▶❄🍽🏠◎

University College (Durham Castle) ⚌

Listed

The Castle, Durham DH1 3RW
☎ (0191) 374 3863
Fax (0191) 374 7470
This 11th C castle is part of a World Heritage site. Now modernised for use as university accommodation with a magnificent dining hall and Norman chapel.
Bedrooms: 65 single, 2 double, 30 twin, 4 family rooms
Bathrooms: 20 en-suite, 5 public

Bed & breakfast

per night:	£min	£max
Single	20.50	30.50

Half board per

person:	£min	£max
Daily	27.75	37.75

Lunch available
Evening meal 1900 (last orders 2230)
Parking for 50
Open March–April, July–September, December

🐾📺♿🛜📶🖥◑📶📠🍽400❄🍽🏠

EAGLESCLIFFE
Tees Valley
Map ref 5C3

Railway suburb of Stockton-on-Tees on the road to Yarm. Preston Hall Park has a museum, zoo, Butterfly World, riverside walks, fishing and picnic areas.

Sunnyside Hotel

⚌⚌ COMMENDED

580-582 Yarm Road, Eaglescliffe, Stockton-on-Tees, Cleveland TS16 0DF
☎ (01642) 780075
Fax (01642) 783789
Friendly family hotel, ideal for touring Cleveland and North Yorkshire, with easy access to main roads, the station and Teesside Airport.
Bedrooms: 7 single, 11 double, 3 twin, 2 triple
Bathrooms: 23 en-suite, 2 public

Bed & breakfast

per night:	£min	£max
Single	25.00	39.00
Double	45.00	59.00

Lunch available
Evening meal 1845 (last orders 2000)
Parking for 20
Cards accepted: Amex, Mastercard, Visa, Switch/Delta

🐾📞💷▢🛜📶🅸Ⓢ🏴🖥📶📠🍽20
DAP SP

EMBLETON
Northumberland
Map ref 5C1

Coastal village beside a golf-course spread along the edge of Embleton Bay. The old church was extensively restored in the 19th C. The vicarage incorporates a medieval pele tower.

The Sportsman ⚌

Listed COMMENDED

Embleton, Alnwick NE66 3XF
☎ (01665) 576588
Fax (01665) 576524
Family-run hotel, recently refurbished. Includes dormitory facilities for golfing parties, etc. Bar meals available.
Bedrooms: 2 single, 1 double, 2 twin, 1 triple, 3 family rooms
Bathrooms: 6 en-suite, 3 private

Bed & breakfast

per night:	£min	£max
Single	20.00	25.00
Double	40.00	50.00

Half board per

person:	£min	£max
Daily	30.00	35.00
Weekly	210.00	245.00

Lunch available
Evening meal 1830 (last orders 2100)
Cards accepted: Amex, Mastercard, Visa, Switch/Delta

🐾2▢♿🛜🅸🖥📶▶❄🍽🐎🚫

FIR TREE
Durham
Map ref 5C2

Attractive Pennine village on the scenic route to Scotland (A68), midway between Edinburgh and York and at the entrance to Weardale. Beautiful dales scenery. Convenient rural stopover for Durham City and cathedral.

Helme Park Hall Hotel ⚌

⚌⚌⚌⚌ HIGHLY COMMENDED

Fir Tree, Crook, County Durham DL13 4NW
☎ (01388) 730970
Fax (01388) 730970

Comfortable, fully refurbished hotel with open fires and warm, welcoming atmosphere. In 5 acres of grounds, with

spectacular views over the dales. A haven of peace and tranquillity.
Bedrooms: 2 single, 7 double, 4 twin
Bathrooms: 13 en-suite

Bed & breakfast per night:	£min	£max
Single	40.00	40.00
Double	65.00	91.50

Lunch available
Evening meal 1900 (last orders 2100)
Parking for 70
Cards accepted: Amex, Mastercard, Visa, Switch/Delta
☎ [S] [TV] 170 [SP] [T]

[Ad] See display advertisement on this page

GATESHEAD

Tyne and Wear
Map ref 5C2

Facing Newcastle across the Tyne, a busy industrial centre which grew rapidly early this century. Now it is a town of glass, steel and concrete buildings. Home of Europe's largest indoor shopping and leisure complex, the MetroCentre.
Tourist Information Centre ☎ (0191) 477 3478

Shaftesbury House Hotel

♛♛ COMMENDED

245 Prince Consort Road, Gateshead NE8 4DT
☎ (0191) 478 2544
Fax (0191) 478 2544
Charming, Victorian, family hotel. Central for MetroCentre, Newcastle City and Arena, Gateshead Stadium, Beamish and local transport. Opposite Gateshead leisure centre. A1 to Gateshead (South), then A167.
Bedrooms: 2 double, 6 twin, 2 triple
Bathrooms: 2 en-suite, 3 public

Bed & breakfast per night:	£min	£max
Single	22.00	32.00
Double	32.00	42.00

Half board per person:	£min	£max
Daily	25.00	40.00
Weekly	161.00	266.00

Evening meal 1800 (last orders 2000)
Parking for 12
[S] [TV] [OAP] [SP] [T]

Swallow Hotel

♛♛♛♛ COMMENDED

High West Street, Gateshead NE8 1PE
☎ (0191) 477 1105
Fax (0191) 478 7214
[CR] Swallow
Modern hotel 1 mile from Newcastle city centre just south of the River Tyne. Leisure complex incorporating pool, sauna, solarium and cardiovascular gym. Well placed for visiting the MetroCentre. Short break packages available.
Bedrooms: 37 single, 29 double, 33 twin, 4 family rooms
Bathrooms: 103 en-suite

Bed & breakfast per night:	£min	£max
Single	85.00	95.00
Double	100.00	110.00

Half board per person:	£min	£max
Daily	100.00	110.00
Weekly	402.50	770.00

Lunch available
Evening meal 1900 (last orders 2200)
Parking for 210
Cards accepted: Amex, Diners, Mastercard, Visa, Switch/Delta
☎ [S] 350 [OAP] [SP] [T]

HALTWHISTLE

Northumberland
Map ref 5B2

Small market town with interesting 12th C church, old inns and blacksmith's smithy. North of the town are several important sites and interpretation centres of Hadrian's Wall. Ideal centre for archaeology, outdoor activity or touring holidays.
Tourist Information Centre ☎ (01434) 322002

Manor House Hotel

♛♛♛ APPROVED

Main Street, Haltwhistle NE49 0BS
☎ (01434) 322588 & 320975

Centrally situated in small town, very near the Roman Wall. Hotel over 400 years old. Recently refurbished.
Bedrooms: 1 double, 4 twin, 1 family room
Bathrooms: 3 en-suite, 1 public, 2 private showers

Bed & breakfast per night:	£min	£max
Single	15.00	20.00
Double	30.00	40.00

Lunch available
Evening meal 1900 (last orders 2130)
Parking for 4
Cards accepted: Amex, Mastercard, Visa
[S] [TV] 20 [OAP]

HALTWHISTLE
Continued

The Spotted Cow Inn
Castle Hill, Haltwhistle NE49 0EN
☎ (01434) 320327
Traditional pub-restaurant with beamed ceilings, dating from 18th C, serving real ales and fresh food cooked to order. En-suite bedrooms with colour TV, tea/coffee facilities. Children welcome.
Bedrooms: 2 double, 1 twin
Bathrooms: 3 en-suite
Bed & breakfast

per night:	£min	£max
Single	20.00	22.50
Double	40.00	45.00

Lunch available
Evening meal 1830 (last orders 2100)
Parking for 10
Cards accepted: Mastercard, Visa, Switch/Delta

HAMSTERLEY FOREST
Durham

See under Barnard Castle, Bishop Auckland

HARTLEPOOL
Tees Valley
Map ref 5C2

Major industrial port north of Tees Bay. Occupying an ancient site, the town's buildings are predominantly modern. Local history can be followed in the Museum of Hartlepool and adjacent historic quay and there is a marina with restored ships.
Tourist Information Centre ☎ (01429) 869706

Grand Hotel
COMMENDED
Swainson Street, Hartlepool, Cleveland TS24 8AA
☎ (01429) 266345
Fax (01429) 265217
Traditional 19th C city centre hotel close to modern enclosed shopping centre. Extensively refurbished and an excellent base for visiting MetroCentre, Beamish and Durham.
Bedrooms: 14 single, 18 double, 13 twin
Suites available
Bathrooms: 45 en-suite

Bed & breakfast per night:	£min	£max
Single	49.50	65.00
Double	60.00	85.00

Half board per person:	£min	£max
Daily	42.50	

Lunch available
Evening meal 1930 (last orders 2200)
Parking for 10
Cards accepted: Amex, Diners, Mastercard, Visa, Switch/Delta

HAYDON BRIDGE
Northumberland
Map ref 5B2

Small town on the banks of the South Tyne with an ancient church, built of stone from sites along the Roman Wall just north. Ideally situated for exploring Hadrian's Wall and the Border country.

Anchor Hotel
COMMENDED
John Martin Street, Haydon Bridge, Hexham NE47 6AB
☎ (01434) 684227
Fax (01434) 684586
Riverside inn, in a village close to the Roman Wall. Ideal centre for touring the North Pennines and Northumberland National Park.
Bedrooms: 5 double, 3 twin, 2 triple
Bathrooms: 10 en-suite, 1 public

Bed & breakfast per night:	£min	£max
Single	36.00	43.50
Double	42.50	55.00

Half board per person:	£min	£max
Daily	39.00	45.00
Weekly	195.00	225.00

Lunch available
Evening meal 1900 (last orders 2045)
Parking for 20
Cards accepted: Amex, Diners, Mastercard, Visa, Switch/Delta

COLOUR MAPS
Colour maps at the back of this guide pinpoint all places in which you will find accommodation listed.

Hadrian Lodge
APPROVED
Hindshield Moss, North Road, Haydon Bridge, Hexham NE47 6NF
☎ (01434) 688688
Fax (01434) 684867
Conversion of single-storey hunting/fishing lodge. In 18 acres with trout lake, near Housesteads Roman Fort and Hadrian's Wall. Cosy residents' bar, tea-room/lounge. Brochure available.
Bedrooms: 1 single, 1 double, 1 twin, 1 triple, 1 family room
Bathrooms: 3 en-suite, 3 public

Bed & breakfast per night:	£min	£max
Single	15.00	18.00
Double	28.00	36.00

Half board per person:	£min	£max
Daily	18.00	23.00
Weekly	95.00	119.00

Parking for 25
Cards accepted: Mastercard, Visa

HEXHAM
Northumberland
Map ref 5B2

Old coaching and market town near Hadrian's Wall. Since pre-Norman times a weekly market has been held in the centre with its market-place and abbey park, and the richly-furnished 12th C abbey church has a superb Anglo-Saxon crypt.
Tourist Information Centre ☎ (01434) 605225

Stotsfold Hall
COMMENDED
Steel, Hexham NE47 0HP
☎ (01434) 673270
Beautiful house surrounded by 15 acres of gardens and woodland with streams and flowers. 6 miles south of Hexham.
Bedrooms: 2 single, 1 double, 1 twin
Bathrooms: 3 public

Bed & breakfast per night:	£min	£max
Single	19.50	19.50
Double	39.00	39.00

Parking for 6

A key to symbols can be found inside the back cover flap.

HOLY ISLAND

Northumberland
Map ref 5B1

Still an idyllic retreat, tiny island and fishing village and cradle of northern Christianity. It is approached from the mainland at low water by a causeway. The clifftop castle (National Trust) was restored by Sir Edwin Lutyens.

Lindisfarne Hotel ⋀

COMMENDED

Holy Island, Berwick-upon-Tweed TD15 2SQ
☎ (01289) 389273
Fax (01289) 389284
Small, comfortable, family-run hotel providing coffees, lunches and evening meals. An ideal place for ornithologists and within walking distance of Lindisfarne Castle and Priory.
Bedrooms: 2 single, 1 double, 1 twin, 3 triple
Bathrooms: 5 en-suite, 1 public

Bed & breakfast

per night:	£min	£max
Single	16.50	33.00
Double	33.00	52.00

Lunch available
Evening meal 1800 (last orders 2030)
Parking for 12
Cards accepted: Amex, Diners, Mastercard, Visa, Switch/Delta

North View ⋀

HIGHLY COMMENDED

Marygate, Holy Island, Berwick-upon-Tweed TD15 2SD
☎ (01289) 389222
400-year-old listed building on historic and beautiful island. Ideally situated for visiting many of Northumberland's tourist attractions.
Bedrooms: 2 double, 1 twin
Bathrooms: 3 en-suite

Bed & breakfast

per night:	£min	£max
Single	25.00	32.00
Double		50.00

Half board per

person:	£min	£max
Daily	35.00	45.00

Lunch available
Evening meal 1900 (last orders 2100)
Parking for 6
Cards accepted: Mastercard, Visa

KIELDER FOREST

Northumberland

See under Bellingham, Kielder Water, Wark

KIELDER WATER

Northumberland
Map ref 5B2

A magnificent man-made lake, the largest in Northern Europe, with over 27 miles of shoreline. On the edge of the Northumberland National Park and near the Scottish border, Kielder can be explored by car, on foot or by ferry.

The Pheasant Inn (by Kielder Water) ⋀

COMMENDED

Stannersburn, Falstone, Hexham NE48 1DD
☎ (01434) 240382
⊕ Logis of GB

Historic inn with beamed ceilings and open fires. Home cooking. Fishing, riding and all water sports nearby. Close to Kielder Water, Hadrian's Wall and the Scottish border.
Bedrooms: 4 double, 3 twin, 1 family room
Bathrooms: 8 en-suite

Bed & breakfast

per night:	£min	£max
Single	22.00	35.00
Double	44.00	56.00

Half board per

person:	£min	£max
Daily	39.00	46.00

Lunch available
Evening meal 1900 (last orders 2100)
Parking for 30
Cards accepted: Mastercard, Visa, Switch/Delta

All accommodation in this guide has been graded, or is awaiting a grading, by a trained Tourist Board inspector.

LANGLEY-ON-TYNE

Northumberland
Map ref 5B2

Small hamlet by a tiny lake, set in beautiful countryside south of Haydon Bridge and the River South Tyne. The road from Haydon Bridge to Langley winds through woodland and past the Derwentwater Memorial and Langley Castle.

Langley Castle ⋀

COMMENDED

Langley-on-Tyne, Hexham NE47 5LU
☎ (01434) 688888
Fax (01434) 684019
Email: langleycastle@dial.pipex.com

14th C castle restored to a magnificent and comfortable hotel. 2 miles south west of Haydon Bridge, 30 minutes from Newcastle and 40 minutes from Newcastle Airport. A69-A686 junction.
Bedrooms: 14 double, 2 twin
Bathrooms: 16 en-suite

Bed & breakfast

per night:	£min	£max
Single	74.50	94.50
Double	99.00	139.00

Half board per

person:	£min	£max
Daily	52.50	72.50

Lunch available
Evening meal 1900 (last orders 2100)
Parking for 100
Cards accepted: Amex, Diners, Mastercard, Visa, Switch/Delta

WELCOME HOST

This is a nationally recognised customer care programme which aims to promote the highest standards of service and a warm welcome. Establishments who are taking part in this initiative are indicated by the ⊛ symbol.

MIDDLESBROUGH

Tees Valley
Map ref 5C3

Boom-town of the mid 19th C, today's Teesside industrial and conference town has a modern shopping complex and predominantly modern buildings. An engineering miracle of the early 20th C is the Transporter Bridge which replaced an old ferry.
Tourist Information Centre ☎ (01642) 243425 or 264330

Baltimore Hotel M

COMMENDED

250 Marton Road, Middlesbrough, Cleveland TS4 2EZ
☎ (01642) 224111
Fax (01642) 226156
Utell International
Close to the heart of both commercial and residential Middlesbrough and 1 mile from the central station. Teesside Airport 18 miles.
Bedrooms: 18 single, 5 double, 7 twin, 1 triple
Suite available
Bathrooms: 31 en-suite
Bed & breakfast per night:

	£min	£max
Single	36.75	89.50
Double	51.50	106.00

Half board per person:

	£min	£max
Daily	41.50	104.25

Lunch available
Evening meal 1830 (last orders 2245)
Parking for 50
Cards accepted: Amex, Diners, Mastercard, Visa, Switch/Delta

MIDDLETON-IN-TEESDALE

Durham
Map ref 5B3

Small stone town of hillside terraces overlooking the river, developed by the London Lead Company in the 18th C. Five miles up-river is the spectacular 70-ft waterfall, High Force.

Teesdale Hotel M

COMMENDED

Middleton-in-Teesdale, Barnard Castle, County Durham DL12 0QG
☎ (01833) 640264 & 640537
Fax (01833) 640651
Tastefully modernised, family-run 18th C coaching inn serving home cooking and fine wines. All rooms with

telephone, radio and TV. Also 4 comfortable holiday cottages in hotel courtyard. Dogs welcome free of charge.
Bedrooms: 2 single, 5 double, 3 twin
Bathrooms: 10 en-suite, 1 public
Bed & breakfast per night:

	£min	£max
Single	38.50	42.50
Double	55.00	65.00

Half board per person:

	£min	£max
Daily	45.00	
Weekly	307.00	

Lunch available
Evening meal 1930 (last orders 2030)
Parking for 24
Cards accepted: Amex, Mastercard, Visa

MORPETH

Northumberland
Map ref 5C2

Market town on the River Wansbeck. There are charming gardens and parks, among them Carlisle Park which lies close to the ancient remains of Morpeth Castle. The chantry building houses the Northumbrian Craft Centre and the bagpipe museum.
Tourist Information Centre ☎ (01670) 511323

Linden Hall Hotel M

HIGHLY COMMENDED

Longhorsley, Morpeth NE65 8XF
☎ (01670) 516611
Fax (01670) 788544
Georgian country house hotel, north of Morpeth, set in a 450-acre estate with extensive leisure facilities including an 18-hole golf-course.
Wheelchair access category 3
Bedrooms: 2 single, 28 double, 20 twin
Suites available
Bathrooms: 50 en-suite, 1 public
Bed & breakfast per night:

	£min	£max
Single	97.50	127.50
Double	130.00	200.00

Lunch available
Evening meal 1900 (last orders 2130)
Parking for 340
Cards accepted: Amex, Diners, Mastercard, Visa, Switch/Delta

NEWCASTLE UPON TYNE

Tyne and Wear
Map ref 5C2

Commercial and cultural centre of the North East, with a large indoor shopping centre, Quayside market, museums and theatres which offer an annual 6 week season by the Royal Shakespeare Company. Norman castle keep, medieval alleys, old Guildhall.
Tourist Information Centre ☎ (0191) 261 0610 or 230 0030 or 261 0691

The Copthorne Newcastle M

HIGHLY COMMENDED

The Close, Quayside, Newcastle upon Tyne, Tyne & Wear NE1 3RT
☎ (0191) 222 0333
Fax (0191) 230 1111
Utell International
Set amidst the historic quayside, all bedrooms, restaurants, bars and leisure club pool overlook the river. Free on-site car parking.
Bedrooms: 132 double, 24 twin
Bathrooms: 156 en-suite
Bed & breakfast per night:

	£min	£max
Single	89.00	176.95
Double	99.00	213.90

Lunch available
Evening meal 1830 (last orders 2215)
Parking for 180
Cards accepted: Amex, Diners, Mastercard, Visa, Switch/Delta

Dene Hotel M

COMMENDED

38-42 Grosvenor Road, Jesmond, Newcastle upon Tyne NE2 2RP
☎ (0191) 281 1502
Fax (0191) 281 8110
In a quiet residential area close to beautiful Jesmond Dene with its small children's zoo. Within easy reach of the city centre. Passenger lift.
Bedrooms: 13 single, 5 double, 5 twin
Bathrooms: 15 en-suite, 2 public, 8 private showers
Bed & breakfast per night:

	£min	£max
Single	25.50	36.50
Double	47.50	52.50

Half board per person:

	£min	£max
Daily	33.00	44.00

Lunch available
Evening meal 1730 (last orders 2000)
Parking for 17

Cards accepted: Amex, Diners,
Mastercard, Visa, Switch/Delta

🐕🛗♿📞🖵🍷📶⛶Ⓢ🍴🖾📺🔌
🖾🅿🍽🕪40🍴 DAP ⌕ SP T ◎

Grosvenor Hotel 🏧
❀❀❀ APPROVED

Grosvenor Road, Jesmond,
Newcastle upon Tyne NE2 2RR
☎ (0191) 281 0543
Fax (0191) 281 9217
*Friendly hotel in quiet residential
suburb, offering a wide range of
facilities. Close to city centre.*
Bedrooms: 17 single, 8 double,
9 twin, 7 triple
Bathrooms: 33 en-suite, 5 public

Bed & breakfast
per night:	£min	£max
Single	25.00	45.00
Double	40.00	60.00

Half board per
person:	£min	£max
Daily	35.00	60.00
Weekly	210.00	360.00

Lunch available
Evening meal 1830 (last orders
2100)
Parking for 30
Cards accepted: Amex, Diners,
Mastercard, Visa, Switch/Delta

🐕🛗♿🍷📞🖵🍷📶Ⓘ🍴📺◗
🖾🍽🕪120 DAP ⌕ SP T

Hospitality Inn 🏧
❀❀❀❀ COMMENDED

Osborne Road, Jesmond, Newcastle
upon Tyne NE2 2AT
☎ (0191) 281 7881
Fax (0191) 281 6241
Ⓡ Mount Charlotte Thistle/Utell
International

*In a quiet residential area of
Newcastle, just 1 mile from the centre
and close to the city's universities and
Jesmond Dene.*
Bedrooms: 10 single, 17 double,
52 twin, 6 triple
Suite available
Bathrooms: 85 en-suite

Bed & breakfast
per night:	£min	£max
Single	40.00	90.00
Double	78.00	150.00

Half board per
person:	£min	£max
Daily	55.00	110.00
Weekly	385.00	770.00

Lunch available

Evening meal 1830 (last orders
2230)
Parking for 45
Cards accepted: Amex, Diners,
Mastercard, Visa, Switch/Delta

🐕🛗♿🍷📞🖵🍷📶Ⓘ🍴🖾◗
🔌🖾🍽🕪100 ⌕ SP T ◎

Imperial Swallow Hotel 🏧
❀❀❀❀ COMMENDED

Jesmond Road, Newcastle upon
Tyne NE2 1PR
☎ (0191) 281 5511
Fax (0191) 281 8472
Ⓡ Swallow
*Elegantly furnished, following recent
major refurbishment. Traditionally
styled bedrooms, cocktail bar and
lounge, a fully equipped leisure club.
Free car park. One mile from
Newcastle city centre, 200 yards from
Jesmond Metro Station. Short break
packages available.*
Bedrooms: 53 single, 45 double,
18 twin, 3 triple, 3 family rooms
Bathrooms: 122 en-suite

Bed & breakfast
per night:	£min	£max
Single	75.00	95.00
Double	85.00	105.00

Half board per
person:	£min	£max
Daily	85.00	110.00

Lunch available
Evening meal 1900 (last orders
2145)
Parking for 130
Cards accepted: Amex, Diners,
Mastercard, Visa, Switch/Delta

🐕🛗♿🍷📞🖵🍷📶Ⓘ🍴📺◗🔌
🖾🍽🕪150 ♨ 🏓 ⚑ ⌕ SP T ◎

Jesmond Park Hotel 🏧
❀❀ COMMENDED

74-76 Queens Road, Jesmond,
Newcastle upon Tyne NE2 2PR
☎ (0191) 281 2821 & 281 1913
Fax (0191) 281 0515
*Clean and friendly hotel offering good
English breakfast, in a quiet area close
to city centre.*
Bedrooms: 8 single, 2 double, 3 twin,
1 triple, 2 family rooms
Bathrooms: 7 en-suite, 3 public

Bed & breakfast
per night:	£min	£max
Single	24.00	33.00
Double	38.00	44.00

Parking for 14
Cards accepted: Mastercard, Visa

🐕🖵📞🖵🍷📶📶🖾📺◗🖾🍽🏵
⚑ SP T

Royal Station Hotel 🏧
❀❀❀❀ COMMENDED

Neville Street, Newcastle upon Tyne
NE1 5DH
☎ (0191) 232 0781
Fax (0191) 222 0786
Ⓡ The Independents
*Opened by Queen Victoria in 1858, the
hotel combines elegant Victorian
architecture with up-to-date facilities.
Fully refurbished, family-run. We take
pride in offering a friendly and
courteous service to all our clients.*
Bedrooms: 43 single, 42 double,
28 twin, 7 triple, 6 family rooms
Bathrooms: 126 en-suite

Bed & breakfast
per night:	£min	£max
Single	60.00	85.00
Double	70.00	90.00

Lunch available
Evening meal 1900 (last orders
2130)
Parking for 100
Cards accepted: Amex, Diners,
Mastercard, Visa, Switch/Delta

🐕🛗♿🍷📞🖵🍷📶🍴◗🔌🖾🍽
🕪180 ⌕ 🛏 T ◎

Surtees Hotel 🏧
❀❀❀❀ COMMENDED

12-16 Dean Street, Newcastle upon
Tyne NE1 1PG
☎ (0191) 261 7771
Fax (0191) 230 1322
Ⓡ Minotel
*City-centre hotel within walking
distance of Eldon Square, the Quayside
and station, with a 24-hour multi-storey
car park adjacent. Cocktail and public
bar, restaurant and nightclub. All
bedrooms are en-suite with satellite TV
and tea-making facilities.*
Bedrooms: 12 single, 9 double,
6 twin
Bathrooms: 27 en-suite

Bed & breakfast
per night:	£min	£max
Single	52.50	67.50
Double	67.50	87.50

Lunch available
Evening meal 1700 (last orders
2230)
Cards accepted: Amex, Diners,
Mastercard, Visa, Switch/Delta

🐕♿📞🖵🍷📶Ⓢ📺◗🔌🖾
🖾🍴🐎⌕ SP T ◎

> Half board prices are given
> per person, but in some cases
> these may be based on
> double/twin occupancy.

NEWCASTLE UPON TYNE

Continued

Swallow Gosforth Park Hotel ⋔

👑👑👑👑 HIGHLY COMMENDED

High Gosforth Park, Newcastle upon Tyne NE3 5HN
☎ (0191) 236 4111
Fax (0191) 236 8192
CR Swallow
Beautifully appointed hotel set in 12 acres of woodland, 5 miles north of city centre. Facilities include restaurants, bars, leisure complex and conference facilities. Short break packages available.
Bedrooms: 110 double, 63 twin, 5 triple
Suites available
Bathrooms: 178 en-suite

Bed & breakfast per night:

	£min	£max
Single	70.00	225.00
Double	85.00	225.00

Half board per person:

	£min	£max
Daily	85.00	230.00
Weekly	595.00	1600.00

Lunch available
Evening meal 1800 (last orders 2230)
Parking for 300
Cards accepted: Amex, Diners, Mastercard, Visa, Switch/Delta

Westland Hotel ⋔

👑👑👑 APPROVED

27 Osborne Avenue, Jesmond, Newcastle upon Tyne NE2 1JR
☎ (0191) 281 0412
Fax (0191) 281 5005
Westland is a well established hotel in a quiet residential area, convenient for city centre, coast, countryside and Gateshead Metro Centre.
Bedrooms: 11 single, 2 double, 2 triple
Bathrooms: 7 en-suite, 3 public

Bed & breakfast per night:

	£min	£max
Single	20.00	26.00
Double	36.00	40.00

Half board per person:

	£min	£max
Daily	27.00	33.00
Weekly	160.00	180.00

Parking for 3
Cards accepted: Amex, Mastercard, Visa

NEWTON AYCLIFFE

Durham
Map ref 5C3

Northern England's first New Town growing from 60 persons in 1947 to over 27,000 today. Leisure centres in the town centre and at Spennymoor offer a wide range of facilities.

Redworth Hall ⋔

👑👑👑👑👑 HIGHLY COMMENDED

Redworth, Newton Aycliffe, County Durham DL5 6NL
☎ (01388) 772442
Fax (01388) 775112
CR Grand Heritage
Beautiful 17th C country house hotel, providing excellent leisure and conference facilities. An ideal venue for business or pleasure.
Wheelchair access category 2 ♿
Bedrooms: 3 single, 35 double, 42 twin, 7 triple, 13 family rooms
Bathrooms: 100 en-suite

Bed & breakfast per night:

	£min	£max
Single	105.00	115.00
Double	125.00	155.00

Half board per person:

	£min	£max
Daily	74.00	148.00
Weekly	521.50	1036.00

Lunch available
Evening meal 1900 (last orders 2200)
Parking for 200
Cards accepted: Amex, Diners, Mastercard, Visa, Switch/Delta

OTTERBURN

Northumberland
Map ref 5B1

Small village set at the meeting of the River Rede with Otter Burn, the site of the Battle of Otterburn in 1388. A peaceful tradition continues in the sale of Otterburn tweeds in this beautiful region, which is ideal for exploring the Border country and the Cheviots.

The Butterchurn Guest House ⋔

👑👑 COMMENDED

Main Street, Otterburn NE19 1NP
☎ (01830) 520585
In village centre, on the River Rede. Central for Roman Wall and Kielder

Water. Within easy reach of Northumberland coast. All rooms en-suite.
Bedrooms: 2 double, 2 twin, 3 triple
Bathrooms: 7 en-suite

Bed & breakfast per night:

	£min	£max
Single	22.00	24.00
Double	34.00	36.00

Parking for 10
Cards accepted: Mastercard, Visa

Redesdale Arms Hotel ⋔

👑👑 COMMENDED

Rochester, Otterburn, Newcastle upon Tyne NE19 1TA
☎ (01830) 520668
Fax (01830) 520063
Family-run old coaching inn, central for Hadrian's Wall and Kielder Forest. All rooms en-suite. Super home-cooked food.
Bedrooms: 3 double, 5 twin, 2 triple
Bathrooms: 10 en-suite

Bed & breakfast per night:

	£min	£max
Single	36.00	41.00
Double	60.00	70.00

Lunch available
Evening meal 1900 (last orders 2200)
Parking for 30
Cards accepted: Amex, Diners, Mastercard, Visa, Switch/Delta

REDCAR

Tees Valley
Map ref 5C3

Lively holiday resort near Teesside with broad sandy beaches, a fine racecourse, a large indoor funfair at Coatham and other seaside amusements. Britain's oldest existing lifeboat can be seen at the Zetland Museum.

Claxton Hotel ⋔

👑👑 COMMENDED

196 High Street, Redcar, Cleveland TS10 3AW
☎ (01642) 486745
Fax (01642) 486522
Hotel facing the sea with traditionally-styled dining room and bar featuring huge inglenook fireplace.
Bedrooms: 3 single, 3 double, 18 twin, 1 family room
Bathrooms: 23 en-suite, 2 public, 2 private showers

Bed & breakfast per night:	£min	£max
Single	20.00	22.50
Double	38.00	40.00

Half board per person:	£min	£max
Daily	26.50	30.00

Evening meal 1730 (last orders 2100)
Parking for 10

☎☺⚓♿🅿Ⓢ🌀TV▥🖥♨☕120🚐

Falcon Hotel M

👑👑 APPROVED

13 Station Road, Redcar, Cleveland
TS10 1AH
☎ (01642) 484300
*Licensed hotel in centre of town with
new extension of en-suite twins and
singles. Within easy reach of the
Cleveland Hills.*
Wheelchair access category 3🚶
Bedrooms: 8 single, 7 twin, 1 triple,
3 family rooms
Bathrooms: 12 en-suite, 3 public

Bed & breakfast per night:	£min	£max
Single	16.00	23.00
Double	27.00	34.00

Half board per person:	£min	£max
Daily	21.50	29.50

Evening meal 1700 (last orders
1900)

☎☺⚓□♿Ⓢ🌀TV▥🖥♨SP

Waterside House

👑 APPROVED

35 Newcomen Terrace, Redcar,
Cleveland TS10 1DB
☎ (01642) 481062
*Large terraced property overlooking the
sea, close to town centre and leisure
centre. Warm, friendly atmosphere with
true Yorkshire hospitality.*
Bedrooms: 2 single, 3 triple, 1 family
room
Bathrooms: 2 public

Bed & breakfast per night:	£min	£max
Single	14.00	16.00
Double	25.00	27.00

Half board per person:	£min	£max
Daily	19.50	22.00
Weekly	136.50	154.00

Evening meal 1700 (last orders
1900)

☎□♿Ⓤ🅻🔒🌀TV▥🚐SP

A key to symbols can be
found inside the back
cover flap.

ROTHBURY

Northumberland
Map ref 5B1

Old market town on the River
Coquet near the Simonside Hills. It
makes an ideal centre for walking
and fishing or for exploring this
beautiful area from the coast to the
Cheviots. Cragside House and
Gardens (National Trust) are open
to the public.

Orchard Guest House M

👑👑 COMMENDED

High Street, Rothbury, Morpeth
NE65 7TL
☎ (01669) 620684
*Charming guesthouse in the middle of
a lovely village, an ideal centre for
visiting all Northumbria's attractions.
Comfortable surroundings.*
Bedrooms: 2 double, 4 twin
Bathrooms: 4 en-suite, 1 private,
3 public

Bed & breakfast per night:	£min	£max
Single	21.00	23.00
Double	42.00	46.00

Open March–October

☎🖥□♿Ⓤ🅻🔒Ⓢ🌀▥🖥♨✿🐾🚐

RUSHYFORD

Durham
Map ref 5C2

Small village on the old Great North
Road.

Eden Arms Swallow Hotel M

👑👑👑👑 COMMENDED

Rushyford, Durham DL17 0LL
☎ (01388) 720541
Fax (01388) 721871
Ⓒ Swallow
*17th C coaching inn with leisure club,
10 miles south of Durham City. Ideal
base for visiting Durham and the Tees
Valley. Short break packages available.*
Bedrooms: 13 single, 14 double,
15 twin, 4 triple
Bathrooms: 46 en-suite

Bed & breakfast per night:	£min	£max
Single	80.00	90.00
Double	95.00	110.00

Half board per person:	£min	£max
Daily	98.50	108.50

Lunch available
Evening meal 1900 (last orders
2130)
Parking for 150

Cards accepted: Amex, Diners,
Mastercard, Visa, Switch/Delta

☎☺⚓🍴♿📞📠□♿🕐🔒Ⓢ✂♨▥
🖥♨100🎱🕐🎾🐾🍴🎣🐾SP🏠T

SEAHOUSES

Northumberland
Map ref 5C1

Small modern resort developed
around a 19th C herring port. Just
offshore, and reached by boat from
here, are the rocky Farne Islands
(National Trust) where there is an
important bird reserve. The bird
observatory occupies a medieval
pele tower.

Beach House Hotel M

👑👑👑 COMMENDED

Sea Front, Seahouses NE68 7SR
☎ (01665) 720337
Fax (01665) 720921
Ⓒ Logis of GB

*Quiet, comfortable and friendly,
family-run hotel overlooking the Farne
Islands. Specialising in imaginative
home cooking and baking.*
Bedrooms: 2 single, 4 double, 6 twin,
2 triple
Bathrooms: 14 en-suite, 2 public

Bed & breakfast per night:	£min	£max
Single	29.50	37.00
Double	59.00	74.00

Half board per person:	£min	£max
Daily	32.00	49.00
Weekly	280.00	299.00

Evening meal 1900 (last orders
2030)
Parking for 16
Open April–October
Cards accepted: Amex, Mastercard,
Visa, Switch/Delta

☎☺⚓📞📠□♿🕐🔒🔒✂♨TV▥🖥♨
✿🐾SP T

COLOUR MAPS

Colour maps at the back of
this guide pinpoint all places
in which you will find
accommodation listed.

SEAHOUSES

Continued

Olde Ship Hotel ⋔

👑 👑 👑 👑 COMMENDED

Seahouses NE68 7RD
☎ (01665) 720200
Fax (01665) 721383
*Hotel with a long-established
reputation for food and drink in
comfortably relaxing old-fashioned
surroundings.*
Bedrooms: 1 single, 9 double, 5 twin,
1 triple
Suites available
Bathrooms: 16 en-suite, 2 public
**Bed & breakfast
per night:**

	£min	£max
Single	30.00	36.50
Double	60.00	73.00

**Half board per
person:**

	£min	£max
Daily	42.50	50.50
Weekly	270.00	320.00

Lunch available
Evening meal 1900 (last orders
2030)
Parking for 12
Open February–November
Cards accepted: Mastercard, Visa,
Switch/Delta

🐾 10 🕊 🗒 📞 🖵 📺 🕯 💷 S 🖊 💈 TV
🛏 🖨 ❄ ✕ 🚲 SP 🎣 ◉

SHOTLEY BRIDGE

Durham
Map ref 5B2

Fashionable suburb of Consett
where German craftsmen settled in
the 17th C. In the 19th C with the
coming of the railway to serve
Consett Iron Works, the village
found fame as a spa. The local
railway line has now been developed
as a walkway and the track follows
the valley to Swalwell.

The Manor House Inn ⋔

Listed COMMENDED

Carterway Heads, Shotley Bridge,
Consett, County Durham DH8 9LX
☎ (01207) 255268
*Small family-run inn, offering warm,
comfortable accommodation. Delicious
food, ales and wines. Overlooking an
Area of Outstanding Natural Beauty
and Derwent reservoir.*
Bedrooms: 2 double, 1 twin, 1 family
room
Bathrooms: 2 public
**Bed & breakfast
per night:**

	£min	£max
Single	24.00	26.00
Double	42.00	45.00

Lunch available

Evening meal 1900 (last orders
2130)
Parking for 50
Cards accepted: Amex, Diners,
Mastercard, Visa, Switch/Delta

🐾 🛏 ⌨ 📞 🖵 🕯 S 🖊 💷 🖨 ❄ 🚲 SP

SOUTH SHIELDS

Tyne and Wear
Map ref 5C2

At the mouth of the Tyne,
shipbuilding and industrial centre
developed around a 19th C coalport
and occupying the site of an
important Roman fort and granary
port. The town's museum has
mementoes of the earliest
self-righting lifeboat, built here in
1789.
*Tourist Information Centre ☎ (0191)
454 6612*

Sea Hotel ⋔

👑 👑 👑 COMMENDED

Sea Road, South Shields NE33 2LD
☎ (0191) 427 0999
Fax (0191) 454 0500
Email: seahot@aol.com
ⓒⓡ Consort
*On the seafront in the heart of
Catherine Cookson country. Popular
restaurant offering French and English
cooking. Secure car park.*
Bedrooms: 20 single, 6 double,
5 twin, 2 triple
Bathrooms: 33 en-suite
**Bed & breakfast
per night:**

	£min	£max
Single	60.00	65.00
Double	75.00	80.00

**Half board per
person:**

	£min	£max
Daily	72.50	77.50

Lunch available
Evening meal 1900 (last orders
2130)
Parking for 70
Cards accepted: Amex, Diners,
Mastercard, Visa, Switch/Delta

🐾 🛏 📞 ⌨ 🖵 📺 🕯 🖐 🍴 📺 ◉ 🖨
🏋 200 SP T

Please mention this guide
when making your booking.

The National Grading and
Classification Scheme is
explained at the back
of this guide.

STANLEY

Durham
Map ref 5C2

Small town on the site of a Roman
cattle camp. At the Beamish North
of England Open Air Museum
numerous set-pieces and displays
recreate industrial and social
conditions prevalent during the
area's past.

Harperley Hotel

👑 👑 APPROVED

Harperley, Stanley, County Durham
DH9 9TY
☎ (01207) 234011
*Converted granary on the outskirts of
Stanley, in the country park area close
to the old water mill. Fishing and
shooting can be arranged.*
Bedrooms: 2 single, 3 double
Bathrooms: 5 en-suite
**Bed & breakfast
per night:**

	£min	£max
Single	30.00	35.00
Double	42.00	48.00

Lunch available
Evening meal 1930 (last orders
2115)
Parking for 200
Cards accepted: Amex, Mastercard,
Visa, Switch/Delta

🐾 📞 🖵 🕯 🖐 S 💷 🖨 🏋 50 ❄ 🚲
DAP 🌲 SP 🎣 T

STOCKTON-ON-TEES

Tees Valley
Map ref 5C3

Teesside town first developed in the
19th C around the ancient market
town with its broad main street
which has been the site of a regular
market since 1310. Green Dragon
Yard has a Georgian theatre and
there is a railway heritage trail
around the town.
*Tourist Information Centre ☎ (01642)
615080*

Parkmore Hotel and Leisure
Club ⋔

👑 👑 👑 👑 HIGHLY COMMENDED

636 Yarm Road, Eaglescliffe,
Stockton-on-Tees, Cleveland
TS16 0DH
☎ (01642) 786815
Fax (01642) 790485
ⓒⓡ Best Western
*Warm, friendly hotel with leisure club,
opposite golf-course near Yarm. Ideal
for visiting North York Moors, the dales,
Durham and York.*
Bedrooms: 18 single, 18 double,
16 twin, 3 triple
Bathrooms: 55 en-suite

Bed & breakfast per night:	£min	£max
Single	50.00	72.00
Double	64.00	90.00

Lunch available
Evening meal 1845 (last orders 2130)
Parking for 100
Cards accepted: Amex, Diners, Mastercard, Visa, Switch/Delta

⌖♿☎▣⌂☕🅟📶🛈Ⓢ✂🅜TV ◗▥🅐♨🏋140🏊✕☂▸ DAP SP T

Swallow Hotel ♨

👑👑👑👑 COMMENDED

John Walker Square, High Street, Stockton-on-Tees, Cleveland TS18 1AQ
☎ (01642) 679721
Fax (01642) 601714
CR Swallow
Smart, modern hotel in Stockton town centre, with Swallow Leisure Club, bar, restaurant and brasserie. An ideal base for visiting the north east for business or pleasure. Short break packages available.
Bedrooms: 3 single, 73 double, 49 twin
Suites available
Bathrooms: 125 en-suite

Bed & breakfast per night:	£min	£max
Single	95.00	125.00
Double	110.00	135.00

Lunch available
Evening meal 1900 (last orders 2200)
Parking for 400
Cards accepted: Amex, Diners, Mastercard, Visa, Switch/Delta

⌖☎▣⌂☕🅟📶🛈Ⓢ✂🅜◐▦▥ ♨🏋300🏊✕☂▸🐾 SP T ◉

SUNDERLAND

Tyne and Wear
Map ref 5C2

Ancient coal and shipbuilding port on Wearside, with important glassworks since the 17th C, although glassmaking here dates back more than 1,000 years.
Tourist Information Centre ☎ (0191) 553 2000 or 553 2001

Anthony Lodge

👑 APPROVED

5 Brookside Terrace, Ashbrook, Sunderland, Tyne & Wear SR2 7RN
☎ (0191) 567 7108
Licensed family-run guesthouse with easy access to town, buses and trains. Parking area to rear.
Bedrooms: 5 single, 1 double, 2 twin
Bathrooms: 1 public, 2 private showers

Bed & breakfast per night:	£min	£max
Single	16.00	32.00
Double	40.00	40.00

Half board per person:	£min	£max
Daily	21.00	50.00
Weekly	147.00	350.00

Evening meal 1700 (last orders 1700)
Parking for 2

⌖▣🅟📶Ⓢ✂🅜TV▥ ♨🏋🐾

Felicitations ♨

👑 APPROVED

94 Ewesley Road, High Barnes, Sunderland, Tyne & Wear SR4 7RJ
☎ (0191) 522 0960 & 551 8915
Refurbished, all rooms spacious and with own hot and cold water. Family and single have own adjacent shower rooms; double has private bathroom with additional WCs. Large, comfortable TV lounge/bar.
Bedrooms: 1 single, 1 double, 1 family
Bathrooms: 1 private, 2 public

Bed & breakfast per night:	£min	£max
Single	18.00	20.00
Double	36.00	40.00

Half board per person:	£min	£max
Daily	25.50	32.50
Weekly	178.50	227.50

Evening meal 1800 (last orders 1930)
Parking for 2

⌖5▣🅟📶🍴 UL 🛈Ⓢ✂🅜TV▥ ♨🏋10❋✕🐾 SP ◉

The Pullman Lodge Hotel ♨

👑👑👑👑 COMMENDED

Whitburn Road, Seaburn, Sunderland, Tyne & Wear SR6 8AA
☎ (0191) 529 2020
Fax (0191) 529 2077
On the coast. Restaurant is in genuine Pullman carriages with sea view. Railway theme throughout. Large children's play area, family room.
Bedrooms: 8 twin, 8 family rooms
Bathrooms: 16 en-suite

Bed & breakfast per night:	£min	£max
Single	35.00	42.50
Double	45.00	50.00

Half board per person:	£min	£max
Daily	43.50	51.00
Weekly	334.50	

Lunch available
Evening meal 1900 (last orders 2230)

Parking for 90
Cards accepted: Amex, Diners, Mastercard, Visa

⌖♿☎▣⌂☕🅟📶🛈Ⓢ🅜▥♨ 🏋240🐾 SP 🏛 T

Swallow Hotel ♨

👑👑👑👑 HIGHLY COMMENDED

Queens Parade, Seaburn, Sunderland, Tyne & Wear SR6 8DB
☎ (0191) 529 2041
Fax (0191) 529 4227
CR Swallow
Highly commended hotel with leisure facilities and spectacular seaside location. Good base for seeing Northumbria's coastline and castles. Short break packages available.
Bedrooms: 3 single, 36 double, 23 twin, 3 family rooms
Bathrooms: 65 en-suite

Bed & breakfast per night:	£min	£max
Single	90.00	105.00
Double	110.00	130.00

Lunch available
Evening meal 1900 (last orders 2145)
Parking for 100
Cards accepted: Amex, Diners, Mastercard, Visa, Switch/Delta

⌖☎▣⌂☕🅟📶🛈Ⓢ✂🅜◐▦▥ ◉♨🏋300🏊✕☂▸🐾 SP T ◉

TYNEMOUTH

Tyne and Wear
Map ref 5C2

At the mouth of the Tyne, old Tyneside resort adjoining North Shields with its fish quay and market. The pier is overlooked by the gaunt ruins of a Benedictine priory and a castle. Splendid sands, amusement centre and park.

Grand Hotel

👑👑👑👑 COMMENDED

Grand Parade, Tynemouth, North Shields NE30 4ER
☎ (0191) 293 6666
Fax (0191) 293 6665

High on the cliffs overlooking beautiful Long Sands beach, this imposing Victorian building was the seaside home of the Duchess of

Continued ▶

TYNEMOUTH

Continued

Northumberland. Building is now completely modernised to offer every comfort.
Bedrooms: 29 double, 7 twin, 8 triple, 2 family rooms
Bathrooms: 46 en-suite

Bed & breakfast per night:

	£min	£max
Single	45.00	80.00
Double	50.00	120.00

Lunch available
Evening meal 1800 (last orders 2130)
Parking for 30
Cards accepted: Amex, Diners, Mastercard, Visa, Switch/Delta

⛺🏨📞📧🖥♿🏧🍴📺◐💷🖥 ⓑ🛏🍴150🏃🚭 SP 🏠 T

WARK

Northumberland
Map ref 5B2

Set in the beautiful North Tyne Valley amid the Northumbrian fells, old village just above the meeting of Warks Burn with the North Tyne. Grey stone houses surround the green with its shady chestnut trees and an iron bridge spans the stream. The mound of a Norman castle occupies the river bank

Battlesteads Hotel ꟺ

👑👑👑 COMMENDED

Wark, Hexham NE48 3LS
☎ (01434) 230209
Fax (01434) 230730
Email: thebattlesteads
@btinternet.com

18th C inn, formerly a farmhouse, in the heart of rural Northumberland, close to the Roman Wall and Kielder Water. An ideal centre for exploring Border country and for relaxing.
Bedrooms: 1 single, 3 double, 5 twin, 1 family room
Bathrooms: 10 en-suite

Bed & breakfast per night:

	£min	£max
Single	30.00	35.00
Double	50.00	60.00

Half board per person:

	£min	£max
Daily	42.00	47.00
Weekly	280.00	300.00

Lunch available
Evening meal 1830 (last orders 2130)
Parking for 50
Cards accepted: Mastercard, Visa, Switch/Delta

⛺🏨📞🖥♿🏧🍴S🖥 🛏80🔔🎵🏃 🖋❄ DAP 🚭 SP 🏠 T ◎

WEST AUCKLAND

Durham
Map ref 5C2

One of County Durham's many "green" villages. A mixture of old and new houses including 2 manor houses borders the extensive village green.

Wheatside Hotel ꟺ

Listed APPROVED

Bildershaw Bank, West Auckland, Bishop Auckland, County Durham DL14 9PL
☎ (01388) 832725 & 832485

Popular, friendly, family-run hotel in beautiful countryside on the main scenic route to Scotland. A warm welcome awaits you.
Bedrooms: 6 single, 4 double, 2 twin
Bathrooms: 12 en-suite, 2 public

Bed & breakfast per night:

	£min	£max
Single	32.00	35.00
Double	48.00	50.00

Half board per person:

	£min	£max
Daily	40.00	45.00
Weekly	210.00	240.00

Lunch available
Evening meal 1800 (last orders 2130)
Parking for 60
Cards accepted: Mastercard, Visa, Switch/Delta

⛺🖥♿🏧S🍴📺🖥🔔❄🏃🚭 SP

The ꟺ symbol after an establishment name indicates that it is a Regional Tourist Board member.

WHITLEY BAY

Tyne and Wear
Map ref 5C2

Traditional seaside resort with long beaches of sand and rock and many pools to explore. St Mary's lighthouse is open to the public.
Tourist Information Centre ☎ (0191) 200 8535

High Point Hotel ꟺ

👑👑 COMMENDED

The Promenade, Whitley Bay NE26 2NJ
☎ (0191) 251 7782
Fax (0191) 251 6318
Prominent, refurbished hotel with panoramic sea views, only 5 minutes' walk from Whitley Bay. Restaurant.
Bedrooms: 3 single, 4 double, 5 twin, 1 triple, 2 family rooms
Bathrooms: 15 en-suite

Bed & breakfast per night:

	£min	£max
Single	52.00	56.00
Double	60.00	65.00

Lunch available
Evening meal 1830 (last orders 2200)
Parking for 20
Cards accepted: Amex, Mastercard, Visa, Switch/Delta

⛺📞🖥♿🏧S🖥◐🖥ⓑ🛏🔔 🍴🚗🚭 SP T

Marlborough Hotel ꟺ

👑👑👑 COMMENDED

20-21 East Parade, The Promenade, Whitley Bay NE26 1AP
☎ (0191) 251 3628
Fax (0191) 251 3628
Traditional seaside hotel with fine sea views. Comfortable, modern accommodation with friendly service.
Wheelchair access category 3♿
Bedrooms: 4 single, 5 double, 4 twin, 1 triple, 1 family room
Bathrooms: 13 en-suite, 2 public

Bed & breakfast per night:

	£min	£max
Single	20.00	35.00
Double	45.00	50.00

Half board per person:

	£min	£max
Daily	29.50	44.50

Evening meal 1800 (last orders 1830)
Parking for 7
Cards accepted: Amex, Mastercard, Visa, Switch/Delta

⛺2♿📞🖥📧🖥♿🏧🖋📺📺🖥 🛏🍴🚗 SP T ◎

Shan-Gri-La ⋀⋀

👑 COMMENDED

29 Esplanade, Whitley Bay
NE26 2AL
☎ (0191) 253 0230
Small family-run guesthouse. Close to all amenities, near seafront and shopping area.
Bedrooms: 4 single, 3 twin, 3 triple
Bathrooms: 2 public

Bed & breakfast

per night:	£min	£max
Single	17.00	20.00
Double	30.00	34.00

Half board per person:

	£min	£max
Daily	23.00	26.00

Evening meal 1800 (last orders 1900)

Windsor Hotel ⋀⋀

👑👑👑👑 COMMENDED

South Parade, Whitley Bay
NE26 2RF
☎ (0191) 251 8888
Fax (0191) 297 0272

Private hotel close to the seafront and town centre. An excellent base in the north east for business or pleasure.
Bedrooms: 4 single, 16 double, 43 twin
Bathrooms: 63 en-suite

Bed & breakfast

per night:	£min	£max
Single	50.00	65.00
Double	50.00	70.00

Lunch available
Evening meal 1800 (last orders 2130)
Parking for 26
Cards accepted: Amex, Diners, Mastercard, Visa, Switch/Delta

York House Hotel ⋀⋀

👑👑👑 COMMENDED

30 Park Parade, Whitley Bay
NE26 1DX
☎ (0191) 252 8313
Fax (0191) 251 3953
Ideally located for exploring historic Northumbria or visiting the excellent shopping facilities at Newcastle and MetroCentre. High standard en-suite accommodation and imaginative menu choice. No charge for children when

sharing. Ground floor bedrooms suitable for disabled. Secure car parking.
Wheelchair access category 3♿
Bedrooms: 4 single, 8 double, 2 twin
Bathrooms: 13 en-suite, 1 private shower

Bed & breakfast

per night:	£min	£max
Single	25.00	35.00
Double	40.00	50.00

Half board per person:

	£min	£max
Daily	35.00	45.00
Weekly	220.00	285.00

Lunch available
Evening meal 1800 (last orders 1930)
Parking for 3
Cards accepted: Amex, Mastercard, Visa, Switch/Delta

WOOLER

Northumberland
Map ref 5B1

Old grey-stone town, market-place for foresters and hill farmers, set at the edge of the north-east Cheviots.

Loreto Guest House ⋀⋀

👑 APPROVED

1 Ryecroft Way, Wooler NE71 6BW
☎ (01668) 281350

Family-run early Georgian house in spacious grounds, in lovely Cheviot village. Central for touring and walking and close to coastline. All home cooking, all rooms en-suite.
Bedrooms: 1 single, 3 double, 1 twin, 1 family room
Bathrooms: 6 en-suite

Bed & breakfast

per night:	£min	£max
Single		18.00
Double		36.00

Half board per person:

	£min	£max
Daily		24.00

Evening meal 1800 (last orders 1830)
Parking for 12

Tankerville Arms Hotel ⋀⋀

👑👑👑 HIGHLY COMMENDED

22 Cottage Road, Wooler
NE71 6AD
☎ (01668) 281581
Fax (01668) 281387

Charming 17th C family-owned coaching inn. All facilities, fine cuisine. Central for beautiful coast, National Trust properties and Scottish borders.
Bedrooms: 2 single, 6 double, 6 twin, 1 triple, 1 family room
Bathrooms: 16 en-suite

Bed & breakfast

per night:	£min	£max
Single	45.50	
Double	76.50	

Half board per person:

	£min	£max
Daily	48.00	

Lunch available
Evening meal 1900 (last orders 2130)
Parking for 104
Cards accepted: Mastercard, Visa

ACCESSIBILITY

Look for the 🦽🚶♿ symbols which indicate accessibility for wheelchair users. These are described in detail at the front of this guide.

WELCOME HOST

This is a nationally recognised customer care programme which aims to promote the highest standards of service and a warm welcome. Establishments who are taking part in this initiative are indicated by the 🏵 symbol.

USE YOUR *i*'s

There are more than 550 Tourist Information Centres throughout England offering friendly help with accommodation and holiday ideas as well as suggestions of places to visit and things to do. There may well be a centre in your home town which can help you before you set out. You'll find addresses in the local Phone Book or simply call Freepages 0800 192 192.

CHECK THE MAPS

The colour maps at the back of this guide show all the cities, towns and villages for which you will find accommodation entries.

Refer to the town index to find the page on which it is listed.

COUNTRY CODE

Always follow the Country Code ✿Enjoy the countryside and respect its life and work ✿Guard against all risk of fire ✿Fasten all gates ✿Keep your dogs under close control ✿Keep to public paths across farmland ✿Use gates and stiles to cross fences, hedges and walls ✿Leave livestock, crops and machinery alone ✿Take your litter home ✿Help to keep all water clean ✿Protect wildlife, plants and trees ✿Take special care on country roads ✿Make no unnecessary noise

NORTH WEST

The North West is an all-round holiday destination. Choose from the glittering excitement of resorts like Blackpool and Morecambe, or the beautiful, untamed countryside of Derbyshire and the West Pennine Moors - perfect for serious walkers and cyclists.

Explore the grand old city of Chester, with its medieval walls, or the colourful heritage of Merseyside, from Liverpool's old docks to Beatlemania. In Greater Manchester visit stately homes or a Victorian sewer. Further afield, find bargains in Lancashire's mill shops and markets.

Why not time your visit to take in one of the region's 450 annual festivals, from the popular transport and tram event to an annual oyster festival?

The counties of Cheshire, Derbyshire
High Peak, Greater Manchester, Lancashire
and Merseyside

FOR MORE INFORMATION CONTACT:
North West Tourist Board
Swan House, Swan Meadow Road,
Wigan Pier, Wigan WN3 5BB
Tel: (01942) 821222 **Fax:** (01942) 820002

Where to Go in the North West –
see pages 120-123
Where to Stay in the North West –
see pages 124-148

NORTH WEST

Where to Go and What to See

You will find hundreds of interesting places to visit during your stay in the North West, just some of which are listed in these pages. The number against each name will help you locate it on the map (page 123). Contact any Tourist Information Centre in the region for more ideas on days out in the North West.

1 Frontierland Western Theme Park
Marine Road West,
Morecambe,
Lancashire LA4 4DG
Tel: (01524) 410024/(01524) 833434
Over 40 thrilling rides and attractions, including the Texas Tornado, Polo Tower, Perculator and Stampede roller coaster. The indoor Fun House complex features live shows in summer.

2 Lancaster Castle
Shire Hall,
Castle Parade,
Lancaster,
Lancashire LA1 1YJ
Tel: (01524) 64998
The hall houses a coat of arms collection, crown court, grand jury room, 'drop room', dungeons and 'Jane Scott's chair'. External tour of castle walls.

3 Blackpool Pleasure Beach
Ocean Boulevard,
Blackpool,
Lancashire FY4 1EZ
Tel: (01253) 341033
Europe's greatest amusement park offers over 145 rides and attractions, including the Space Invader, Big Dipper and the Revolution.

4 Blackpool Sea Life Centre
The Promenade,
Blackpool,
Lancashire FY1 5AA
Tel: (01253) 22445
Tropical sharks up to 8ft in length, housed in a 100,000 gallon water display, with underwater walkway. Also see the Blue Ringed Octopus.

5 Camelot Theme Park and Rare Breeds Farm
Park Hall Road,
Charnock Richard,
Chorley,
Lancashire PR7 5LP
Tel: (01257) 453044/452100
The magical kingdom of Camelot is a world of thrills, fantastic entertainment and family fun, with over 100 rides and attractions, plus medieval entertainment.

6 Wildfowl and Wetland Centre
Martin Mere,
Burscough,
Ormskirk,
Lancashire L40 0TA
Tel: (01704) 895181
45 acres of gardens with over 1,600 ducks, geese and swans.

7 East Lancashire Railway
Bolton Street Station,
Bury,
Lancashire BL9 OEY
Tel: (0161) 764 7790
Eight miles of preserved railway, operated principally by steam. Traction Transport Museum close by.

8 Rufford Old Hall
Rufford,
Ormskirk,
Lancashire L40 1SG
Tel: (01704) 821254
One of the finest 16thC buildings in Lancashire with a magnificent Great Hall, particularly noted for its immense moveable screen.

9 Wigan Pier
Wallgate, Wigan,
Greater Manchester WN3 4EU
Tel: (01942) 323666
Opened by the Queen in 1986. The pier concentrates on life in Wigan in the 1900s. Facilities include a shop, cafe and picnic area.

10 Granada Studios Tour
Water Street,
Greater Manchester M60 9EA
Tel: (0161) 832 9090
Europe's only major television theme park providing a unique insight into the fascinating world behind the television screen.

11 Manchester United Football Club
Museum and Tour Centre,
Old Trafford,
Greater Manchester M16 0RA
Tel: (0161) 877 4002
The official museum and tour of Old Trafford offers every fan a unique insight into the Club.

12 Museum of Science and Industry in Manchester
Liverpool Road,
Castlefield,
Manchester M3 4FP
Tel: (0161) 832 2244/ (0161) 833 0027
The museum is based in the world's oldest passenger railway station with galleries that amaze, amuse and entertain.

13 The Beatles Story
Britannia Vaults,
Albert Dock,
Liverpool,
Merseyside L3 4AA
Tel: (0151) 709 1963
Liverpool's award-winning number one visitor attraction, with a replica of the original Cavern Club.

14 Croxteth Hall and Country Park
Off Muirhead Avenue East,
Liverpool,
Merseyside L12 OHB
Tel: (0151) 228 5311
A 500-acre country park and hall, furnished rooms and walled garden. Farm with rare breeds, miniature railway, gift shop, picnic area, riding centre and adventure playground.

15 Merseyside Maritime Museum
Albert Dock,
Liverpool,
Merseyside L3 4AA
Tel: (0151) 207 0001
Set in the heart of Liverpool's historic waterfront. The museum holds craft demonstrations, working displays and permanent galleries.

16 Tate Gallery
Albert Dock,
Liverpool,
Merseyside L3 4BB
Tel: (0151) 709 3223
The Tate Gallery at Liverpool exhibits the National Collection of modern art.

17 Knowsley Safari Park
Prescot,
Merseyside L34 4AN
Tel: (0151) 430 9009
On a 5-mile drive through the game reserves set in 400 acres of parkland, see lions, tigers, elephants and rhinos. Large picnic areas and children's amusement park.

18 Dunham Massey Hall and Park
Altrincham,
Cheshire WA14 4SJ
Tel: (0161) 941 1025
An 18thC mansion in a 250-acre wooded deer park. Over 30 rooms open to the public. Collections of furniture, paintings and silver. Restaurant and shop.

19 Lyme Park
Disley,
Stockport,
Cheshire SK12 2NX
Tel: (01663) 762023
A National Trust country estate set in 1,377 acres of moorland, woodland and park. This magnificent house has 17 acres of historic gardens.

20 Quarry Bank Mill
Styal,
Wilmslow,
Cheshire SK9 4LA
Tel: (01625) 527468
A Georgian water-powered cotton spinning mill with four floors of displays and demonstrations plus 284 acres of surrounding parkland.

21 CATALYST: The Museum of the Chemical Industry
Gossage Building,
Mersey Road,
Widnes,
Cheshire WA8 0DF
Tel: (0151) 420 1121
Catalyst offers a unique, award-winning formula of interactive exhibits and historical displays. Hands-on exploration will allow you to discover the chemical industry.

22 Cheshire Oaks Designer Outlet Village
Kinsey Road,
Ellesmere Port,
South Wirral L65 9JJ
Tel: (0151) 357 3633
Over 60 individual stores selling famous branded goods.

23 Tatton Park
Knutsford,
Cheshire WA16 6QN
Tel: (01565) 654822/750250
A historic mansion with a 50-acre garden, traditional working farm, medieval manor house and 2,000-acre deer park. A sailing and outdoor centre and adventure playground.

24 Macclesfield Silk Museum
The Heritage Centre,
Roe Street,
Macclesfield,
Cheshire SK11 6UT
Tel: (01625) 613210
Information centre with a town history exhibition and silk museum. The heritage centre was originally built as a Sunday school for the child labourers.

25 Gawsworth Hall
Gawsworth,
Macclesfield,
Cheshire SK11 9RN
Tel: (01260) 223456
A Tudor half-timbered manor house with tilting ground featuring pictures, sculpture, furniture and an open air theatre.

26 Jodrell Bank Science Centre Planetarium and Arboretum,
Lower Withington,
Macclesfield,
Cheshire SK11 9DL
Tel: (01477) 571339
Exhibition and interactive exhibits on astronomy, space, satellites, energy and the environment. Planetarium and the world famous Lovell telescope. Plus a 35-acre arboretum.

27 Chester Zoo
Upton-by-Chester,
Chester,
Cheshire CH2 1LH
Tel: (01244) 380280
A penguin pool with underwater views, tropical house and spectacular displays of spring and summer bedding plants. Chimpanzee house with outdoor enclosure.

28 Beeston Castle
Beeston,
Tarporley,
Cheshire CW6 9TX
Tel: (01829) 260464
A ruined 13thC castle situated on top of the Peckforton Hills with views of the surrounding countryside. Exhibitions featuring the castle's history.

29 Stapeley Water Gardens
London Road,
Stapeley,
Nantwich,
Cheshire CW5 7LH
Tel: (01270) 623868
Large water garden centre filled with display lakes, pools and fountains. Trees and shrubs, pot plants, gifts, garden sundries and pets. Thousands of items on display.

CUMBRIA

NORTH YORKSHIRE

0 ——————— 20 Miles
0 ——————— 30 Kms

1 Morecambe
2 Lancaster

Fleetwood

LANCASHIRE

• Clitheroe
• Nelson

Blackpool **3** **4**

Burnley •
• Accrington

WEST YORKSHIRE

Lytham St Annes

Preston •

Blackburn •

Darwen • • Rawtenstall

Southport

Burscough
5 • Chorley
Charnock
Richard

Ramsbottom

Ormskirk **8** **6**

Bolton • Bury **7** Rochdale

Formby

Skelmersdale
9
Wigan

GREATER MANCHESTER

Oldham

Kirkby

Salford • **10**

MERSEYSIDE

St Helens
11 **12** Manchester

New Brighton
Hoylake
13 **14** **17** Prescot
15 **16** Huyton

Altrincham
Stockport
Cheadle

Birkenhead Liverpool

Warrington
18

19 DERBY-SHIRE
Disley

21 Widnes

Styal **20**
Wilmslow

Ellesmere **22**
Port

Runcorn

Knutsford •

23 Alderley Edge

Northwich

Lower Withington
24 Macclesfield

27 Chester
Winsford

26
Congleton
25 Gawsworth

WALES

CHESHIRE
Sandbach

Beeston **28**
Crewe

Alsager

Kidsgrove

29
Nantwich

STAFFORDSHIRE

FIND OUT MORE

Further information about holidays and attractions in the North West is available from:

North West Tourist Board,
Swan House,
Swan Meadow Road,

Wigan Pier, Wigan WN3 5BB.
Tel: (01942) 821222

These publications are available free from the North West Tourist Board:
■ **North West Welcome Guide**
■ **England's North West**

Discovery Map
■ **Group Travel Guide**
■ **Bed & Breakfast Map**
■ **Caravan and Camping Parks Guide**

WHERE TO STAY (NORTH WEST)

Accommodation entries in this region are listed in alphabetical order of place name,

and then in alphabetical order of establishment.

Map references refer to the colour location maps at the back of this guide.

The first number indicates the map to use; the letter and number which follow refer to the

grid reference on the map.

At-a-glance symbols at the end of each accommodation entry give useful information

about services and facilities. A key to symbols can be found inside the back cover flap.

Keep this open for easy reference.

ALDERLEY EDGE

Cheshire
Map ref 4B2

Picturesque town taking its name from the wooded escarpment towering above the Cheshire plain, with fine views and walks. A romantic local legend tells of the Wizard and sleeping warriors who will save the country in crisis. Excellent shops. Chorley Hall, nearby, boasts a moat.

The Alderley Edge Hotel M

HIGHLY COMMENDED

Macclesfield Road, Alderley Edge SK9 7BJ
☎ (01625) 583033
Fax (01625) 586343
Converted country mansion built originally for one of the Manchester cotton barons. Close to the Edge beauty spot and near the village of Alderley, Jodrell Bank and Gawsworth Hall. Restaurant featuring fish and produce from the hotel bakery. Award-winning head chef.
Wheelchair access category 3
Bedrooms: 32 double
Bathrooms: 32 en-suite

Bed & breakfast

per night:	£min	£max
Single	36.00	98.00
Double	67.00	116.50

Lunch available
Evening meal 1900 (last orders 2200)
Parking for 90
Cards accepted: Amex, Diners, Mastercard, Visa, Switch/Delta

Milverton House Hotel M

APPROVED

Wilmslow Road, Alderley Edge SK9 7QL
☎ (01625) 583615 & 585555
Well-appointed Victorian villa on main road with open country views. Home cooking.
Bedrooms: 1 single, 7 double, 4 twin
Bathrooms: 7 en-suite, 1 private, 4 public

Bed & breakfast

per night:	£min	£max
Single	25.00	35.00
Double	45.00	55.00

Evening meal from 1830
Parking for 16
Cards accepted: Mastercard, Visa

ALTRINCHAM

Greater Manchester
Map ref 4A2

Historic market town developed as a residential area in the 19th C. Preserves the best of the old at its fascinating Old Market Place, with the best of the new on pedestrianised George Street. International fashion and high style interior design rub shoulders with boutiques and speciality shops.
Tourist Information Centre ☎ (0161) 912 5931

Beech Mount Hotel M

APPROVED

46 Barrington Road, Altrincham, Cheshire WA14 1HN
☎ (0161) 928 4523
Fax (0161) 928 1055
Family-run hotel within easy reach of

Manchester Airport and city centre. Convenient for public transport and shopping centre.
Bedrooms: 12 single, 7 double, 10 twin, 3 triple
Bathrooms: 32 en-suite, 2 public

Bed & breakfast

per night:	£min	£max
Single	30.00	33.00
Double	45.00	50.00

Evening meal 1830 (last orders 2030)
Parking for 36
Cards accepted: Mastercard, Visa

Cresta Court Hotel M

COMMENDED

Church Street, Altrincham, Cheshire WA14 4DP
☎ (0161) 927 7272
Fax (0161) 926 9194
Best Western
Privately owned town centre hotel, opened in 1973 and designed to provide all modern facilities. Easy access to M56, M6, M62, M63. 10 minutes to Manchester Airport.
Bedrooms: 114 single, 13 double, 8 twin, 3 triple
Bathrooms: 138 en-suite

Bed & breakfast

per night:	£min	£max
Single	72.50	75.00
Double	92.50	95.00

Half board per

person:	£min	£max
Daily	82.50	85.00
Weekly	577.50	595.00

Lunch available
Evening meal 1830 (last orders 2200)

Parking for 200
Cards accepted: Amex, Diners,
Mastercard, Visa, Switch/Delta

ASHTON-UNDER-LYNE

Greater Manchester
Map ref 4B1

The largest town in the borough of
Tameside, with excellent access to
central Manchester and to the
foothills of Pennines. Famous for its
700-year-old market and the
confluence of 3 canals at Portland
Basin. The Church of St Michael and
All Angels has a spectacular window.
*Tourist Information Centre ☎ (0161)
343 4343*

Lynwood Hotel

👑 👑 COMMENDED

3 Richmond Street,
Ashton-under-Lyne, Lancashire
OL6 7TX
☎ (0161) 330 5358
*Small, comfortable, family-run hotel in
quiet position. Convenient for
motorways, G-Mex, The Arena and
National Cycling Centre. 20 minutes to
Manchester Airport.*
Bedrooms: 2 single, 2 twin
Bathrooms: 2 en-suite, 1 public
Bed & breakfast

per night:	£min	£max
Single	23.00	29.00
Double	40.00	44.00

Parking for 4

York House Hotel 🤟

👑 👑 👑 HIGHLY COMMENDED

York Place, Off Richmond Street,
Ashton-under-Lyne, Lancashire
OL6 7TT
☎ (0161) 330 9000
Fax (0161) 343 1613
CR The Independents
*Refurbished hotel with restaurant and
function room. Emphasis on good food
and fine wines. Garden ("Britain in
Bloom" winner). Ideal base for touring
north of England.*
Bedrooms: 9 single, 18 double,
5 twin, 2 triple
Bathrooms: 34 en-suite
Bed & breakfast

per night:	£min	£max
Single	55.00	59.00
Double	66.00	72.00

Lunch available
Evening meal 1900 (last orders
2130)
Parking for 36

Cards accepted: Amex, Diners,
Mastercard, Visa, Switch/Delta

BIRKENHEAD

Merseyside
Map ref 4A2

Founded in the 12th C by monks
who operated the first Mersey ferry
service, Birkenhead has some fine
Victorian architecture and one of
the best markets in the north west.
Attractions include the famous
Mersey Ferry and Birkenhead Park,
opened in 1847, the first public park
in the country.
*Tourist Information Centre ☎ (0151)
647 6780*

Central Hotel

👑 👑 👑 APPROVED

Clifton Crescent, Birkenhead
L41 2QH
☎ (0151) 647 6347
Fax (0151) 647 5476
CR The Independents
*Town centre hotel opposite railway
station with direct service to Liverpool
and Chester. Near Liverpool tunnel
entrance.*
Bedrooms: 13 single, 8 double,
9 twin, 1 triple
Bathrooms: 27 en-suite, 2 public
Bed & breakfast

per night:	£min	£max
Single	29.00	39.00
Double	39.00	49.00

**Half board per
person:**

	£min	£max
Daily	39.00	49.00
Weekly	250.00	

Lunch available
Evening meal 1830 (last orders
2045)
Parking for 12
Cards accepted: Amex, Diners,
Mastercard, Visa, Switch/Delta

Pine Lodge

👑 👑 COMMENDED

Coral Ridge, Bidston, Birkenhead
L43 7XE
☎ (0151) 652 4138
*Exclusive property with large en-suite
bedrooms. The heated enclosed
swimming pool is set in delightful
wooded gardens adjacent to National
Trust land.*
Bedrooms: 2 single, 1 double, 1 twin,
1 triple
Bathrooms: 5 en-suite

Bed & breakfast

per night:	£min	£max
Single	22.50	25.00
Double	40.00	45.00

Parking for 12

BLACKBURN

Lancashire
Map ref 4A1

North east Lancashire town.
Architecture reflects Victorian
prosperity from the cotton industry.
Daniel Thwaites, founder of
Thwaites Brewery, is buried in St
John's churchyard. Lewis Textile
Museum is dedicated to the history
of the textile industry.
*Tourist Information Centre ☎ (01254)
53277*

Northcote Manor Hotel 🤟

👑 👑 👑 HIGHLY COMMENDED

Northcote Road, Old Langho,
Blackburn BB6 8BE
☎ (01254) 240555
Fax (01254) 246568

*Privately-owned refurbished manor
house with an outstanding restaurant,
offering the best in hospitality. Ideal
location 9 miles from M6 junction 31,
off A59. One night dinner, bed and
breakfast gourmet breaks: £165 for
two.*
Bedrooms: 10 double, 4 twin
Bathrooms: 14 en-suite
Bed & breakfast

per night:	£min	£max
Single	80.00	100.00
Double	100.00	120.00

Lunch available
Evening meal 1900 (last orders
2130)
Parking for 50
Cards accepted: Amex, Diners,
Mastercard, Visa, Switch/Delta

A key to symbols can be
found inside the back
cover flap.

BLACKPOOL

Lancashire
Map ref 4A1

Britain's largest fun resort, with Blackpool Pleasure Beach, 3 piers and the famous Tower. Host to the spectacular autumn illuminations - "the greatest free show on earth". *Tourist Information Centre* ☎ *(01253) 21623*

The Ashbeian Guest House

👑 COMMENDED

49 High Street, Blackpool FY1 2BN
☎ (01253) 26301; changing to (01253) 626301
Just 5 bedrooms, all en-suite. Good public parking. Splendid menus. Terrific value. Just off seafront. A very easy walk to everywhere in the town.
Bedrooms: 1 single, 2 double, 1 triple, 1 family room
Bathrooms: 5 en-suite

Bed & breakfast

per night:	£min	£max
Single	16.00	21.00
Double	32.00	42.00

Half board per

person:	£min	£max
Daily	23.00	28.00
Weekly	116.00	181.00

Evening meal from 1700
Cards accepted: Mastercard, Visa
🛇5🖃🖵♿🕾🄄🅂💇📺🖩 ᐱ 🄰🄿 🆂🄿 🅃

Ashcroft Hotel M

👑 COMMENDED

42 King Edward Avenue, Blackpool FY2 9TA
☎ (01253) 351538
Small, friendly hotel off Queens Promenade, 2 minutes from sea and Gynn Gardens. Offering personal service. Cleanliness assured.
Bedrooms: 3 single, 3 double, 1 twin, 2 triple, 1 family room
Bathrooms: 7 en-suite, 1 public

Bed & breakfast

per night:	£min	£max
Single	16.00	19.00
Double	32.00	38.00

Half board per

person:	£min	£max
Daily	22.00	27.00
Weekly	147.00	182.00

Evening meal from 1700
Parking for 2
Cards accepted: Mastercard, Visa
🛇2🖵♿💇📺🖩 ᐱ 🗶🛺 🄰🄿 🆁 🅃

The Hotel Bambi M

👑 HIGHLY COMMENDED

27 Bright Street, Blackpool FY4 1BS
☎ (01253) 343756
Friendly, family-run guesthouse with good facilities. Ideally situated for Pleasure Beach, Promenade and South Shore shopping area.
Bedrooms: 2 double, 1 twin, 1 triple, 1 family room
Bathrooms: 5 en-suite

Bed & breakfast

per night:	£min	£max
Single	18.00	18.00
Double	33.00	33.00

Parking for 2
Open February–November
Cards accepted: Amex, Diners, Mastercard, Visa
🛇🖵♿🅄🄻🄄🅂💇📺🖩 ᐱ 🗶🛺 🄰🄿

Bedford Hotel

👑 COMMENDED

298-300 North Promenade, Blackpool FY1 2EY
☎ (01253) 23475 & 290163
Fax (01253) 21878
Well-managed family-run hotel on the seafront, with indoor swimming pool, sauna, spa and large, comfortable bedrooms. Choice of menu at all meals. Large, free car park.
Bedrooms: 20 double, 5 twin, 12 triple, 5 family rooms
Suites available
Bathrooms: 42 en-suite

Bed & breakfast

per night:	£min	£max
Single	20.00	80.00
Double	40.00	80.00

Half board per

person:	£min	£max
Daily	25.00	85.00
Weekly	140.00	280.00

Lunch available
Evening meal 1800 (last orders 1900)
Parking for 24
Cards accepted: Amex, Diners, Mastercard, Visa, Switch/Delta
🛇🔥🕾🖃🖵♿🄄🅂💇📺🖩 🡅🖩 ᐱ 🍴50🅟🅠🕾🄿 🄰🄿 🛇 🆂🄿 🅃

Berwyn Hotel M

👑 HIGHLY COMMENDED

1 Finchley Road, Gynn Square, Blackpool FY1 2LP
☎ (01253) 352896
Fax (01253) 594391
Elegant licensed hotel overlooking Gynn Gardens and Queens Promenade. Our standards of cuisine, service and cleanliness are high and our aim is to please.

Bedrooms: 1 single, 14 double, 3 twin, 2 triple
Bathrooms: 20 en-suite

Bed & breakfast

per night:	£min	£max
Single	28.00	34.00
Double	50.00	72.00

Half board per

person:	£min	£max
Daily	36.00	42.00
Weekly	160.00	200.00

Evening meal 1800 (last orders 1830)
Parking for 4
Cards accepted: Mastercard, Visa, Switch/Delta
🛇🕾🖃🖵♿🄄🅂💇📺🖩 ᐱ 🍴40 🡆🗶 🄰🄿 🛇 🆂🄿

Collingwood Hotel M

👑 COMMENDED

8-10 Holmfield Road, Blackpool FY2 9SL
☎ (01253) 352929
Fax (01253) 352929

In a select area just off Queens Promenade and Gynn Gardens. Good reputation for service, home cooking, cleanliness and value for money. All rooms en-suite. Excellence is our standard.
Bedrooms: 2 single, 9 double, 2 twin, 2 triple, 2 family rooms
Bathrooms: 17 en-suite

Bed & breakfast

per night:	£min	£max
Single	18.00	25.00
Double	36.00	50.00

Half board per

person:	£min	£max
Daily	23.00	30.00
Weekly	130.00	165.00

Lunch available
Evening meal from 1700
Parking for 13
Cards accepted: Amex, Diners, Mastercard, Visa
🛇🔥🕾🖃🖵♿🕾🄄🅂💇📺🖩 ᐱ 🡆🗶 🄰🄿 🛇 🆂🄿 🅃

Glenroy Private Hotel

Listed APPROVED

10 Trafalgar Road, Blackpool FY1 6AW
☎ (01253) 344607
Small licensed hotel, 50 yards from the beach. En-suite facilities available. No hidden extras.

Bedrooms: 6 double, 1 triple,
3 family rooms
Bathrooms: 10 en-suite

**Bed & breakfast
per night:**

	£min	£max
Single	16.00	28.00
Double	28.00	48.00

**Half board per
person:**

	£min	£max
Daily	19.00	29.00
Weekly	89.00	99.00

Evening meal from 1700
Cards accepted: Mastercard, Visa
🐴📠🖥☎🛏ℹ️§▥🖨🗝️⚓️🕯️

The Headlands ⚏

🏵🏵🏵🏵 COMMENDED

611-613 South Promenade,
Blackpool FY4 1NJ
☎ (01253) 341179
Fax (01253) 342047
*Superior seafront hotel, all rooms
en-suite. Lift, parking, entertainment.
Weekend breaks, midweek specials.
Excellent service, cuisine, quality. Open
Christmas and New Year.*
Bedrooms: 10 single, 8 double,
14 twin, 10 triple, 1 family room
Bathrooms: 43 en-suite

**Bed & breakfast
per night:**

	£min	£max
Single	29.50	46.60
Double	59.00	87.20

**Half board per
person:**

	£min	£max
Daily	35.00	44.00
Weekly	251.90	334.00

Lunch available
Evening meal 1800 (last orders
2030)
Parking for 40
Cards accepted: Amex, Diners,
Mastercard, Visa, Switch/Delta
🐴☎📠🖥♿ℹ️§✗📺🗝️⚓️▥🛏
🍴♨️👤DAP🖇SP🆃

Imperial Hotel - Forte ⚏

🏵🏵🏵🏵 COMMENDED

North Promenade, Blackpool
FY1 2HB
☎ (01253) 23971
Fax (01253) 751784
Ⓒ Forte/Utell International

*Imposing 19th C Victorian hotel set
back from the North Promenade, with
its own health and fitness club
comprising indoor swimming pool,
sauna, solarium, gymnasium, steam
room, massage and jacuzzi.*

Bedrooms: 26 single, 93 double,
62 twin, 2 family rooms
Suites available
Bathrooms: 183 en-suite

**Bed & breakfast
per night:**

	£min	£max
Single	59.00	114.00
Double	98.00	168.00

Lunch available
Evening meal 1900 (last orders
2200)
Parking for 150
Cards accepted: Amex, Diners,
Mastercard, Visa, Switch/Delta
🐴☎📠🖥♿ℹ️§✗🗝️🕯️▥
⚓️🍴450♨️✗🏌️🎯🖇SP🅿️🆃◎

The Knowlsley Private Hotel

Listed APPROVED

68 Dean Street, Blackpool FY4 1BP
☎ (01253) 343414
*Friendly, family-run hotel in quiet area
of South Shore. Close to beach, shops,
Pleasure Beach. Easy access to M55
and airport.*
Bedrooms: 2 single, 4 double, 2 twin,
2 triple, 2 family rooms
Bathrooms: 7 en-suite, 1 public

**Bed & breakfast
per night:**

	£min	£max
Single	20.00	25.00
Double	30.00	40.00

**Half board per
person:**

	£min	£max
Daily	20.00	25.00
Weekly	140.00	175.00

Evening meal from 1700
Parking for 12
Cards accepted: Mastercard, Visa
🐴☎🖥ℹ️§🗝️📺▥✗🍴♨️DAP🖇SP

May-Dene Licensed Hotel ⚏

Listed APPROVED

10 Dean Street, Blackpool FY4 1AU
☎ (01253) 343464
*In a sun-trap area close to South
Promenade, Sandcastle, Pleasure Beach,
markets and pier. Clean, friendly and
good food.*
Bedrooms: 5 double, 1 triple,
4 family rooms
Bathrooms: 8 en-suite, 2 public

**Bed & breakfast
per night:**

	£min	£max
Single	19.00	30.00
Double	38.00	60.00

**Half board per
person:**

	£min	£max
Daily	25.00	36.00
Weekly	147.00	178.00

Evening meal from 1700
Parking for 5
Cards accepted: Amex, Diners,
Mastercard, Visa
🐴🖥♿ℹ️§🗝️📺▥⚓️✗DAP🖇

The Old Coach House ⚏

🏵🏵🏵 HIGHLY COMMENDED

50 Dean Street, Blackpool FY4 1BP
☎ (01253) 349195
Fax (01253) 344330
*Large detached house set in beautiful
gardens, near the promenade and
South Pier.*
Bedrooms: 3 double, 2 twin, 1 triple,
1 family room
Bathrooms: 7 en-suite

**Bed & breakfast
per night:**

	£min	£max
Single	24.00	31.00
Double	48.00	62.00

**Half board per
person:**

	£min	£max
Daily	32.95	46.95
Weekly	230.65	328.65

Evening meal 1700 (last orders
2100)
Parking for 8
Cards accepted: Amex, Mastercard,
Visa, Switch/Delta
🐴♿☎📠🖥♿ℹ️§✗🗝️▥
⚓️👤♨️✗🎯🆃

Park House Hotel ⚏

🏵🏵🏵🏵 APPROVED

308 North Promenade, Blackpool
FY1 2HA
☎ (01253) 20081
Fax (01253) 290181
*Beautifully situated on promenade
within easy reach of Winter Gardens,
piers, golf-courses, town centre and
Stanley Park.*
Bedrooms: 13 single, 34 double,
35 twin, 14 triple, 8 family rooms
Bathrooms: 104 en-suite, 3 public

**Bed & breakfast
per night:**

	£min	£max
Single	29.10	37.65
Double	52.50	73.90

**Half board per
person:**

	£min	£max
Daily	33.60	42.40
Weekly	182.00	244.30

Lunch available
Evening meal 1800 (last orders
2030)
Parking for 52
Cards accepted: Amex, Mastercard,
Visa, Switch/Delta
🐴☎📠🖥♿ℹ️§🗝️📺🕯️⚓️▥⚓️
🍴160♨️✗DAP🖇SP🆃

Pembroke Private Hotel ⚏

🏵🏵🏵 COMMENDED

11 King Edward Avenue, Blackpool
FY2 9TD
☎ (01253) 351306
Fax (01253) 351306
Warm welcome assured to all at this
Continued ▶

BLACKPOOL

Continued

small, beautifully decorated hotel, which offers a quiet, relaxed atmosphere.
Bedrooms: 4 single, 4 double, 2 twin, 1 triple
Bathrooms: 9 en-suite, 1 public

Bed & breakfast

per night:	£min	£max
Single	17.00	24.00
Double	34.00	48.00

Half board per

person:	£min	£max
Daily	21.00	28.00
Weekly	140.00	150.00

Evening meal 1730 (last orders 1730)
Parking for 6
Open March–October and Christmas

🛏🏕🖥🚭🛗♿️🅂🄿📺🖥🍴🚪🅳🅰🅿️🚫 🆂🅿️

Raffles Hotel ⚒

Listed COMMENDED

73-75 Hornby Road, Blackpool
FY1 4QJ
☎ (01253) 294713
Fax (01253) 294713

Excellent location for theatres, promenade, shops, restaurants, tourist spots and conference venues. Family-run private hotel with character. The proprietor is also the chef.
Bedrooms: 11 double, 3 twin, 2 family rooms
Bathrooms: 12 en-suite, 2 public

Bed & breakfast

per night:	£min	£max
Single	18.00	25.00
Double	36.00	50.00

Evening meal from 1730
Parking for 6

🛏♿️🖥🚭🛗🅂🄿📺🖥🚪🐕🚌 🅳🅰🅿️🚫🆂🅿️

Regent Hotel ⚒

Listed APPROVED

18 Springfield Road, Blackpool
FY1 1QL
☎ (01253) 20299
Comfortable hotel near town centre, North station and all attractions/amenities. En-suite rooms. Disabled welcome. Parking.

Bedrooms: 7 double, 3 triple, 1 family room
Bathrooms: 5 en-suite, 1 public

Bed & breakfast

per night:	£min	£max
Single	10.00	12.00
Double	20.00	30.00

Half board per

person:	£min	£max
Daily	14.00	19.00
Weekly	84.00	112.00

Lunch available
Evening meal from 1700
Cards accepted: Mastercard, Visa

🛏🖥🚭🛗🅂🄿📺🖥🚪🅳🅰🅿️🚫🆂🅿️

The Royal Seabank Hotel

👑👑👑 APPROVED

219-221 Central Promenade, Blackpool FY1 5DL
☎ (01253) 22717 & 22173
Fax (01253) 295148
This recently refurbished hotel enjoys one of the finest positions on the Central Promenade, with unobstructed views of the Irish Sea. Only 700 yards from the Tower.
Bedrooms: 5 single, 18 double, 14 twin, 17 triple, 3 family rooms
Bathrooms: 57 en-suite

Bed & breakfast

per night:	£min	£max
Single	17.50	31.50
Double	31.00	59.00

Half board per

person:	£min	£max
Daily	22.80	34.50
Weekly	159.50	221.50

Evening meal 1730 (last orders 1900)
Cards accepted: Mastercard, Visa, Switch/Delta

🛏🖥🚭🛗🅂📺🖥🚪🍴400🅳🅰🅿️🚫🆂🅿️🅣

St Chads Hotel ⚒

👑👑👑 APPROVED

317-321 Promenade, Blackpool FY1 6BN
☎ (01253) 346348
Fax (01253) 348240
Splendid promenade location offering live entertainment in season. Choice of menu. Home-from-home.
Bedrooms: 7 single, 21 double, 22 twin, 2 triple, 6 family rooms
Bathrooms: 58 en-suite

Bed & breakfast

per night:	£min	£max
Single	20.00	35.00
Double	40.00	70.00

Half board per

person:	£min	£max
Daily	25.00	40.00

Lunch available

Evening meal 1700 (last orders 2030)
Parking for 25
Cards accepted: Mastercard, Visa

🛏🖥📞🛗🅂🚭📺🖥🖥🛗🚪🍴🐕🅳🅰🅿️🚫🆂🅿️🅣

Sunray ⚒

👑👑 COMMENDED

42 Knowle Avenue, Blackpool FY2 9TQ
☎ (01253) 351937
Fax (01253) 593307
Ⓒ Logis of GB
Modern semi in quiet residential part of north Blackpool. Friendly personal service and care. 1.75 miles north of Tower along promenade. Turn right at Uncle Tom's Cabin. Sunray is about 300 yards on left.
Bedrooms: 3 single, 2 double, 2 twin, 2 triple
Bathrooms: 9 en-suite, 1 public

Bed & breakfast

per night:	£min	£max
Single	26.00	29.00
Double	52.00	58.00

Half board per

person:	£min	£max
Daily	38.00	41.00
Weekly	228.00	246.00

Evening meal 1750 (last orders 1500)
Parking for 6
Cards accepted: Amex, Mastercard, Visa

🛏📞🖥🖥🅄🄻🅂📺🖥🚪☀️ 🐕🅳🅰🅿️🆂🅿️🅣

Surrey House Hotel

Listed APPROVED

9 Northumberland Avenue, Blackpool FY2 9SB
☎ (01253) 351743
Friendly, family-run hotel close to promenade, Gynn Gardens and with easy access to town's entertainments. Central heating and en-suite facilities.
Bedrooms: 1 single, 6 double, 2 twin, 2 triple
Bathrooms: 10 en-suite, 1 private, 1 public

Bed & breakfast

per night:	£min	£max
Single	19.00	23.00
Double	38.00	46.00

Half board per

person:	£min	£max
Daily	25.00	29.00
Weekly	175.00	203.00

Evening meal 1700 (last orders 1800)
Parking for 7

🛏🖥🛗🅄🄻🅂📺🖥🚪🐕🚌🅳🅰🅿️ 🚫🆂🅿️

Waverley Hotel

☸☸ COMMENDED

95 Reads Avenue, Blackpool
FY1 4DG
☎ (01253) 21633
*Small, licensed hotel close to Tower,
Winter Gardens, shopping precinct and
promenade. For those special occasions,
book our four-poster or canopied
rooms. Comfort and quality assured, at
prices you can afford.*
Bedrooms: 1 single, 10 double,
1 triple, 1 family room
Bathrooms: 11 en-suite, 1 public
Bed & breakfast

per night:	£min	£max
Single	15.00	30.00
Double	30.00	50.00

Half board per

person:	£min	£max
Daily	21.00	38.00
Weekly	140.00	240.00

Evening meal 1700 (last orders
1800)
Parking for 8
Cards accepted: Mastercard, Visa

The Windsor Hotel

☸☸☸ COMMENDED

21 King Edward Avenue, North
Shore, Blackpool FY2 9TA
☎ (01253) 353735
*Quality furnishings in all bedrooms. Fine
public rooms displaying antiques and
watercolours. Exquisite dining room
serving traditional English cuisine.*
Bedrooms: 3 single, 4 double, 1 twin,
1 triple
Bathrooms: 9 en-suite
Bed & breakfast

per night:	£min	£max
Single	19.50	29.50
Double	39.00	49.00

Half board per

person:	£min	£max
Daily	24.50	29.50
Weekly	119.00	159.00

Evening meal 1700 (last orders
1900)
Parking for 4
Open April–October and Christmas

Windsor Hotel ♠

☸☸ COMMENDED

53 Dean Street, Blackpool FY4 1BP
☎ (01253) 400232 & 346886
Fax (01253) 346886
*Clean, comfortable en-suite rooms.
Four-posters available. Good home
cooking. Guests' individual needs
catered for. Close to promenade and
entertainments.*

Bedrooms: 2 single, 5 double, 3 twin,
2 triple
Bathrooms: 12 en-suite
Bed & breakfast

per night:	£min	£max
Single	16.00	25.00
Double	32.00	46.00

Half board per

person:	£min	£max
Daily	21.00	30.00
Weekly	126.00	144.00

Evening meal 1700 (last orders
1900)
Parking for 8
Cards accepted: Mastercard, Visa,
Switch/Delta

BOLTON

Greater Manchester
Map ref 4A1

On the edge of the West Pennine
Moors and renowned for its
outstanding town centre
architecture and fine shopping
facilities. The Octagon Theatre has
national recognition for its "theatre
in the round". Samuel Crompton,
inventor of the "spinning mule", is
buried here.
*Tourist Information Centre ☎ (01204)
364333*

Commercial Royal Hotel

☸☸☸ COMMENDED

13-15 Bolton Road, Moses Gate,
Farnworth, Bolton BL4 7JN
☎ (01204) 573661
Fax (01204) 862488
*Quality hotel offering the standard of
service and facilities rarely found in
small hotels. Noted English/Italian
restaurant. Two minutes from
motorway network, 15 minutes from
Manchester, 5 minutes from Bolton.*
Bedrooms: 5 single, 4 double,
1 triple
Bathrooms: 6 en-suite, 2 public
Bed & breakfast

per night:	£min	£max
Single	24.00	39.00
Double	29.00	49.00

Evening meal 1800 (last orders
2200)
Parking for 15
Cards accepted: Amex, Diners,
Mastercard, Visa

Please mention this guide
when making your booking.

Last Drop Village Hotel ♠

☸☸☸☸ HIGHLY COMMENDED

Hospital Road, Bromley Cross,
Bolton BL7 9PZ
☎ (01204) 591131
Fax (01204) 304122
CR MacDonald/Utell International
*A collection of 18th C farm buildings
transformed into a "living village", with
2 restaurants, tea shop, leisure club
and hotel. Prices below do not include
breakfast.*
Bedrooms: 43 double, 6 twin,
37 triple
Bathrooms: 86 en-suite
Bed & breakfast

per night:	£min	£max
Single	91.50	101.50
Double	99.50	109.50

Lunch available
Evening meal 1900 (last orders
2130)
Parking for 1000
Cards accepted: Amex, Diners,
Mastercard, Visa, Switch/Delta

BOLTON-BY-BOWLAND

Lancashire
Map ref 4B1

Unspoilt village near the Ribble
Valley with 2 greens, one with stump
of 13th C market cross and stocks.
Whitewashed and greystone
cottages.

Copy Nook Hotel

☸☸☸ COMMENDED

Bolton-by-Bowland, Clitheroe
BB7 4NL
☎ (01200) 447205
Fax (01200) 447004
*Traditional country inn, set in rural
countryside. All the charm and
atmosphere of yesteryear combined
with the modern comforts of today.
Only 3 minutes from A59.*
Bedrooms: 4 double, 2 twin
Bathrooms: 6 en-suite
Bed & breakfast

per night:	£min	£max
Single	30.00	
Double	50.00	

Lunch available
Evening meal 1900 (last orders
2130)
Cards accepted: Amex, Diners,
Mastercard, Visa, Switch/Delta

129

BURNLEY

Lancashire
Map ref 4B1

"A town amidst the Pennines". Towneley Hall has fine period rooms and is home to Burnley's art gallery and museum. The Kay-Shuttleworth collection of lace and embroidery can be seen at Gawthorpe Hall (National Trust). Burnley Mechanics Arts Centre is a well-known jazz and blues venue.
Tourist Information Centre ☎ (01282) 455485

Alexander Hotel ⓜ

👑👑👑 HIGHLY COMMENDED

2 Tarleton Avenue, Todmorden Road, Burnley BB11 3ET
☎ (01282) 422684
Fax (01282) 424094
Ⓒ The Independents
Family-run hotel with accent on personal service. Near the town centre, in quiet residential area close to Towneley Hall.
Bedrooms: 8 single, 5 double, 2 twin, 1 triple
Bathrooms: 13 en-suite, 1 public

Bed & breakfast per night:

	£min	£max
Single	25.00	39.50
Double	42.00	49.00

Half board per person:

	£min	£max
Daily	32.00	48.00
Weekly	230.00	300.00

Lunch available
Evening meal 1815 (last orders 2045)
Parking for 22
Cards accepted: Amex, Mastercard, Visa, Switch/Delta

🐾🛏🔥🌢📞🖥➡🗣🞉⛴Ⓢ🐕📺💻🖭
🖥70🏃❄➰🦢 SP Ⓣ

Ormerod Hotel

👑👑👑 HIGHLY COMMENDED

121-123 Ormerod Road, Burnley BB11 3QW
☎ (01282) 423255
Small bed and breakfast hotel in quiet, pleasant surroundings facing local parks. Recently refurbished, all en-suite facilities. 5 minutes from town centre.
Bedrooms: 4 single, 2 double, 2 twin, 2 triple
Bathrooms: 10 en-suite

Bed & breakfast per night:

	£min	£max
Single	20.00	24.00
Double	36.00	38.00

Parking for 7
🐾🛏🖥♿🕯Ⓤ🏧Ⓢ🐕📺💻🖥Ⓣ

BURWARDSLEY

Cheshire
Map ref 4A2

The Pheasant Inn

👑👑👑 COMMENDED

Higher Burwardsley, Tattenhall, Chester CH3 9PF
☎ (01829) 770434
Fax (01829) 771097
Ⓒ Wayfarer/Logis of GB
300-year-old inn, half-timber and sandstone construction, nestling on the top of the Peckforton Hills. Accommodation in delightfully converted barn affording pleasant views towards Chester.
Bedrooms: 6 double, 2 twin, 2 triple
Bathrooms: 10 en-suite

Bed & breakfast per night:

	£min	£max
Single	45.00	45.00
Double	60.00	80.00

Lunch available
Evening meal 1900 (last orders 2130)
Parking for 60
Cards accepted: Amex, Diners, Mastercard, Visa

🐾🛏🔥📞🖥➡🗣🞉Ⓢ✂🐕📺
💻🖥🚲🍴❄🦢➰ SP 🖭Ⓣ🌐

BURY

Greater Manchester
Map ref 4B1

Famous for its black puddings, huge open market and East Lancashire Steam Railway. Birthplace of Sir Robert Peel, founder of the police force and Prime Minister. Bury Art Gallery has an important collection of Turner and Constable paintings.
Tourist Information Centre ☎ (0161) 253 5111

The Bolholt Country Park Hotel ⓜ

👑👑👑 COMMENDED

Walshaw Road, Bury BL8 1PU
☎ (0161) 764 5239 & 763 7007
Fax (0161) 763 1789
Ⓒ The Independents

Family-run hotel and conference centre in 50 acres of beautiful parkland, lakes and gardens. Large swimming pool and full leisure facilities.

Bedrooms: 14 single, 31 double, 4 twin, 4 triple, 1 family room
Bathrooms: 54 en-suite

Bed & breakfast per night:

	£min	£max
Single	58.00	65.00
Double	73.00	94.00

Half board per person:

	£min	£max
Daily	72.00	79.00

Lunch available
Evening meal 1900 (last orders 2130)
Parking for 150
Cards accepted: Amex, Diners, Mastercard, Visa

🐾🛏🔥🌢📞🖥➡🗣🞉🏧Ⓢ🐕📺💻
🖥🍴180🏃❄➰🏹⚓🦢🎣➰🌂⛳🏐🎠

Normandie Hotel ⓜ

👑👑👑 HIGHLY COMMENDED

Elbut Lane, Birtle, Bury, Lancashire BL9 6UT
☎ (0161) 764 3869 & 764 1170
Fax (0161) 764 4866
Modern, comfortable hotel, noted nationally for the preparation and presentation of modern French/British cooking.
Bedrooms: 7 single, 10 double, 6 twin
Bathrooms: 23 en-suite

Bed & breakfast per night:

	£min	£max
Single	49.00	69.00
Double	59.00	79.00

Half board per person:

	£min	£max
Daily	64.00	84.00

Lunch available
Evening meal 1900 (last orders 2130)
Parking for 60
Cards accepted: Amex, Diners, Mastercard, Visa, Switch/Delta

🐾🛏🔥📞🖥➡🗣🞉Ⓢ✂🐕⚄
🖥💻🖭🍴18❄🍴🦢Ⓣ

The Old Mill Hotel and Restaurant ⓜ

👑👑👑 COMMENDED

Springwood, Ramsbottom, Bury, Lancashire BL0 9DS
☎ (01706) 822991
Fax (01706) 822291
Converted mill with old world appearance but very modern bedrooms. Standing in its own grounds, close to city and country life. Full leisure centre, swimming pool, sauna, whirlpool, solarium and gymnasium.
Bedrooms: 12 single, 13 double, 12 twin
Bathrooms: 37 en-suite

Bed & breakfast

per night:	£min	£max
Single	35.00	49.50
Double	50.00	70.00

Lunch available
Evening meal 1830 (last orders 2230)
Parking for 100
Cards accepted: Amex, Diners, Mastercard, Visa, Switch/Delta

🛏🗝🖐📞📺🖥🖐📶🍴S🅿🛗🖩🚗
⚡150🌯🗡🍵🎯U🟊🐾🦮 SP 🏇

Rostrevor Hotel and Bistro ⋔

COMMENDED
148 Manchester Road, Bury, Lancashire BL9 OTL
☎ (0161) 764 3944
Fax (0161) 764 8266
Small, family-run hotel and bistro opposite open parkland, close to town centre, markets and steam railway. Warm welcome and friendly atmosphere.
Bedrooms: 5 single, 5 double, 4 twin
Bathrooms: 14 en-suite

Bed & breakfast

per night:	£min	£max
Single	29.00	35.00
Double	42.00	48.00

Lunch available
Evening meal 1800 (last orders 2000)
Parking for 14
Cards accepted: Amex, Mastercard, Visa, Switch/Delta

🛏🗝🖨🖐📞📺🖐🍴S🅿TV🖩🚗⚡12
🌸 DAP 🐾 SP 🏇 T

CHEADLE HULME

Greater Manchester
Map ref 4B2

Residential area near Manchester with some older buildings dating from 19th C once occupied by merchants and industrialists from surrounding towns. Several fine timber-framed houses, shopping centre and easy access to Manchester Airport.

Spring Cottage Guest House

Listed HIGHLY COMMENDED
60 Hulme Hall Road, Cheadle Hulme, Stockport, Cheshire SK8 6JZ
☎ (0161) 485 1037
Beautifully furnished Victorian house in historic part of Cheadle Hulme. Convenient for airport, rail station and variety of local restaurants.
Bedrooms: 1 single, 1 double, 4 twin
Bathrooms: 3 en-suite, 1 public

Bed & breakfast

per night:	£min	£max
Single	18.50	27.00
Double	32.50	39.00

Parking for 6
Cards accepted: Mastercard, Visa

🛏🗝🖐📺 UL 🖩🚗❄🦮 SP

CHESTER

Cheshire
Map ref 4A2

Roman and medieval walled city rich in treasures. Black and white buildings are a hallmark, including "The Rows" - two-tier shopping galleries. 900-year-old cathedral and the famous Chester Zoo.
Tourist Information Centre ☎ (01244) 317962 or 351609 or 322220

Belgrave Hotel ⋔

APPROVED
City Road, Chester CH1 3AF
☎ (01244) 312138
Fax (01244) 324951
Near railway station, 5 minutes' walk to city centre. Two bars, entertainment some evenings. En-suite rooms with colour TV, tea/coffee-making facilities.
Bedrooms: 12 single, 4 double, 13 twin, 5 triple
Bathrooms: 34 en-suite

Bed & breakfast

per night:	£min	£max
Single	20.00	35.00
Double	35.00	49.00

Evening meal 1830 (last orders 2100)
Cards accepted: Amex, Mastercard, Visa

🛏🗝📞📺🖐🍴S🖐TV◑🖩🚗 DAP
🦮 SP T

Cheyney Lodge Hotel ⋔

COMMENDED
77-79 Cheyney Road, Chester CH1 4BS
☎ (01244) 381925
Small, friendly hotel of unusual design, featuring indoor garden and fish pond. 10 minutes' walk from city centre and on main bus route. Personally supervised with emphasis on good food.
Bedrooms: 1 single, 4 double, 2 twin, 1 triple
Bathrooms: 8 en-suite

Bed & breakfast

per night:	£min	£max
Single	24.00	24.00
Double	39.00	44.00

Half board per

person:	£min	£max
Daily	28.95	31.95
Weekly	202.65	223.65

Lunch available
Evening meal 1800 (last orders 2000)
Parking for 12
Cards accepted: Mastercard, Visa

🛏🗝🖨📞📺🖐🍴S🖐🖩🚗🚗🗡
SP T

City Walls Hotel and Restaurant

APPROVED
City Walls Road, 14 Stanley Place, Chester CH1 2LU
☎ (01244) 313416
Fax (01244) 313416
® The Independents
Charming Georgian hotel situated on the old city walls, overlooking Chester racecourse. Noted for accommodation, food and service.
Bedrooms: 4 single, 6 double, 2 twin, 4 triple
Bathrooms: 16 en-suite

Bed & breakfast

per night:	£min	£max
Single	40.00	45.00
Double	50.00	60.00

Half board per

person:	£min	£max
Daily	50.00	55.00
Weekly	220.00	280.00

Lunch available
Evening meal 1900 (last orders 2130)
Parking for 3
Cards accepted: Amex, Mastercard, Visa, Switch/Delta

🛏🗝🖐📞📺🖐🍴S🖐TV🖩🚗
🌯 DAP 🐾 SP 🏇

Crabwall Manor Hotel and Restaurant ⋔

HIGHLY COMMENDED
Parkgate Road, Mollington, Chester CH1 6NE
☎ (01244) 851666 & 0800 964470
Fax (01244) 851400
Email: sales@crabwall.u-net.com
Exclusive country house hotel set in 11 acres of formal gardens and parkland, 2 miles north of Chester. Reputation for excellent standards in service and facilities, with excellent food in the conservatory restaurant.
Bedrooms: 4 double, 44 twin
Suites available
Bathrooms: 48 en-suite

Bed & breakfast

per night:	£min	£max
Single	95.00	120.00
Double	110.00	130.00

Lunch available
Evening meal 1900 (last orders 2145)
Parking for 120

Continued ▶

CHESTER
Continued

Cards accepted: Amex, Diners, Mastercard, Visa, Switch/Delta

[symbols] 100 [symbols]

Curzon Hotel ♠
COMMENDED

52-54 Hough Green, Chester
CH4 8JQ
☎ (01244) 678581
Fax (01244) 680866

A warm welcome awaits in this privately owned large Victorian house with beautiful gardens. Close to racecourse, River Dee and golf. Fine cuisine prepared by chef-proprietor Markus Imfeld.
Bedrooms: 1 single, 7 double, 1 twin, 4 triple, 3 family rooms
Bathrooms: 16 en-suite

Bed & breakfast per night:

	£min	£max
Single	40.00	50.00
Double	50.00	70.00

Half board per person:

	£min	£max
Daily	40.00	50.00
Weekly	245.00	315.00

Evening meal 1900 (last orders 2100)
Parking for 60
Cards accepted: Mastercard, Visa, Switch/Delta

[symbols]

Dene Hotel ♠
COMMENDED

Hoole Road, Chester CH2 3ND
☎ (01244) 321165
Fax (01244) 350277
Logis of GB
Hotel in own grounds, adjacent to Alexandra Park and 1 mile from city centre. A la carte restaurant, rooms for non-smokers, ample parking.
Wheelchair access category 3
Bedrooms: 9 single, 23 double, 12 twin, 3 triple, 2 family rooms
Bathrooms: 49 en-suite

Bed & breakfast per night:

	£min	£max
Single	39.50	42.00
Double	51.00	53.00

Half board per person:

	£min	£max
Daily	36.50	
Weekly	219.00	

Lunch available
Evening meal 1900 (last orders 2100)
Parking for 51
Cards accepted: Amex, Mastercard, Visa, Switch/Delta

[symbols] 60 [symbols]

Eaton Hotel ♠
APPROVED

29-31 City Road, Chester CH1 3AE
☎ (01244) 320840
Fax (01244) 320850
Minotel

Ideally situated in the heart of Chester with the advantage of own parking. Friendly atmosphere with traditional standards of service and cuisine.
Bedrooms: 3 single, 5 double, 5 twin, 2 triple, 3 family rooms
Bathrooms: 13 en-suite, 5 private showers

Bed & breakfast per night:

	£min	£max
Single	32.50	42.50
Double	42.50	52.50

Half board per person:

	£min	£max
Daily	29.50	35.00
Weekly	185.00	245.00

Lunch available
Evening meal 1830 (last orders 2000)
Parking for 10
Cards accepted: Amex, Diners, Mastercard, Visa, Switch/Delta

[symbols]

Edwards House Hotel ♠
COMMENDED

61-63 Hoole Road, Chester
CH2 3NJ
☎ (01244) 318055 & 319888
Fax (01244) 319888
Victorian property with well proportioned bedrooms, all en-suite. Convenient for city centre, Chester Zoo, M53/M56 motorways and A55 North Wales trunk road.
Bedrooms: 2 single, 5 double, 3 triple
Bathrooms: 10 en-suite

Bed & breakfast per night:

	£min	£max
Single	22.00	35.00
Double	35.00	50.00

Half board per person:

	£min	£max
Daily	32.00	60.00
Weekly	224.00	420.00

Evening meal 1830 (last orders 1930)
Parking for 10
Cards accepted: Mastercard, Visa

[symbols]

Green Bough Hotel and Restaurant ♠
HIGHLY COMMENDED

60 Hoole Road, Chester CH2 3NL
☎ (01244) 326241 & 0410 353370
Fax (01244) 326265
Comfortable, family-run Victorian hotel with friendly, relaxed atmosphere. Tastefully decorated with many antique furnishings. Restaurant renowned for traditional English cooking.
Wheelchair access category 3
Bedrooms: 2 single, 16 double, 1 twin, 3 triple
Bathrooms: 22 en-suite

Bed & breakfast per night:

	£min	£max
Single	40.00	44.00
Double	50.00	60.00

Half board per person:

	£min	£max
Daily	40.00	45.00

Lunch available
Evening meal 1900 (last orders 2100)
Parking for 21
Cards accepted: Amex, Mastercard, Visa, Switch/Delta

[symbols]

Malvern Guest House
APPROVED

21 Victoria Road, Chester
CH2 2AX
☎ (01244) 380865
Victorian terraced 2-storey town house, within 8 minutes' walk of the cathedral and the city centre.
Bedrooms: 2 single, 1 double, 2 twin, 1 triple, 1 family room
Bathrooms: 2 public

Bed & breakfast per night:

	£min	£max
Single	13.00	
Double	26.00	

Half board per person:	£min	£max
Daily	18.00	
Weekly	115.50	

Evening meal 1800 (last orders 1700)

🐎2🕯🏨♿ⓊⓁ🅼 TV ▥🍴🏃🐎 DAP
🚭 SP

Queen Hotel 🄼

👑👑👑👑 HIGHLY COMMENDED

City Road, Chester CH1 3AH
☎ (01244) 350100
Fax (01244) 318483
Ⓒ Principal/Utell International

Fully modernised hotel that still retains an elegant Victorian air. It is close to the station and all amenities.
Bedrooms: 9 single, 49 double, 60 twin, 10 triple
Suite available
Bathrooms: 128 en-suite

Bed & breakfast per night:

	£min	£max
Single	80.00	130.00
Double	95.00	150.00

Lunch available
Evening meal 1830 (last orders 2130)
Parking for 100
Cards accepted: Amex, Diners, Mastercard, Visa, Switch/Delta
🐎🕯🏦📠🖥🏠♿🎱🛎Ⓢ🖊🅼 TV ◗
✦▥🚗🍴280🌸🚭 SP 🏧 Ⓣ

Stafford Hotel 🄼

👑👑👑 COMMENDED

City Road, Chester CH1 3AE
☎ (01244) 326052
Fax (01244) 311403
Comfortable, family-run hotel, close to city centre and railway station. Restaurant and licensed bar. Parking available. Short breaks available all year. Brochure on request.
Bedrooms: 7 single, 10 double, 4 twin, 1 triple
Bathrooms: 22 en-suite

Bed & breakfast per night:

	£min	£max
Single	34.00	38.00
Double	40.00	50.00

Half board per person:

	£min	£max
Daily	30.00	34.00

Evening meal 1830 (last orders 2045)

Parking for 2
Cards accepted: Amex, Diners, Mastercard, Visa, Switch/Delta
🐎🕯🖥📠🏠♿🎱🛎Ⓢ🖊🅼 TV ▥🍴🏦
🍴70🍴 DAP SP Ⓣ

CHIPPING

Lancashire
Map ref 4A1

Charming, well-preserved 17th C village, on the edge of the Forest of Bowland on the Pendle Witches' Trail. Ancient church, pub, craft shops, superb base for walking and touring the area. Best Kept Village award.

Gibbon Bridge Hotel 🄼

👑👑👑👑 HIGHLY COMMENDED

Forest of Bowland, Chipping, Preston PR3 2TQ
☎ (01995) 61456
Fax (01995) 61277
Privately-owned country house hotel in the heart of some of Lancashire's finest countryside, yet only 20 minutes from M6, exit 32. Award-winning hotel. Excellent dining facilities and executive accommodation, leisure facilities and beauty studio.
Wheelchair access category 3♿
Bedrooms: 3 single, 8 double, 15 twin, 4 triple
Suites available
Bathrooms: 30 en-suite

Bed & breakfast per night:

	£min	£max
Single	70.00	100.00
Double	100.00	220.00

Half board per person:

	£min	£max
Daily	60.00	90.00

Lunch available
Evening meal 1900 (last orders 2030)
Parking for 151
Cards accepted: Amex, Diners, Mastercard, Visa, Switch/Delta
🐎🕯🖥🏦♿🎱🛎Ⓢ🅼 TV ◗
✦▥🚗🍴120🌸🎿🎣🏹⛵🎵✈🐾🍴
🚭 SP 🏧 Ⓣ

The map references refer to the colour maps towards the end of the guide. The first figure is the map number; the letter and figure which follow indicate the grid reference on the map.

CHORLEY

Lancashire
Map ref 4A1

Set between the Pennine moors and the Lancashire Plain, Chorley has been an important town since medieval times, with its "Flat-Iron" and covered markets. The rich heritage includes Astley Hall and Park, Houghton Tower, Rivington Country Park and the Leeds-Liverpool Canal.

Park Hall Hotel, Leisure and Conference Centre 🄼

👑👑👑👑 HIGHLY COMMENDED

Park Hall Road, Charnock Richard, Chorley, Preston PR7 5LP
☎ (01257) 452090
Fax (01257) 451838
Hotel, village and conference centre set in 130 acres of beautiful grounds, close to both the M6 and M61 motorways. Conference and superb leisure facilities.
Bedrooms: 41 double, 42 twin, 53 family rooms
Suites available
Bathrooms: 136 en-suite

Bed & breakfast per night:

	£min	£max
Single		82.50
Double	69.98	79.98

Half board per person:

	£min	£max
Daily	44.99	49.99

Lunch available
Evening meal 1800 (last orders 2145)
Parking for 2500
Cards accepted: Amex, Diners, Mastercard, Visa, Switch/Delta
🐎🏦🕯🖥📠🏠♿🎱🛎Ⓢ🖊🅼 TV
◗✦▥🚗🍴700🌸🎣🏹⛵🎵⛹🎿
✦✈ DAP 🚭 SP 🏧 Ⓣ ⊛

For ideas on places to visit refer to the introduction at the beginning of this section.

Information on accommodation listed in this guide has been supplied by the proprietors. As changes may occur you are advised to check details at the time of booking.

CLAYTON-LE-MOORS

Lancashire
Map ref 4A1

Small industrial town, 5 miles north-east of Blackburn.

Sparth House Hotel ⚠

🏵🏵🏵 COMMENDED

Whalley Road, Clayton-le-Moors, Accrington BB5 5RP
☎ (01254) 872263
Fax (01254) 872263

Privately owned by the Coleman family. Built in 1740 and set in its own peaceful grounds, the hotel offers the perfect location for short stays, conferences and functions alike.
Bedrooms: 2 single, 11 double, 2 twin, 1 triple
Bathrooms: 16 en-suite

Bed & breakfast per night:

	£min	£max
Single	38.00	56.25
Double	50.00	78.50

Half board per person:

	£min	£max
Daily	54.95	73.00
Weekly	346.50	462.00

Lunch available
Evening meal 1900 (last orders 2130)
Parking for 70
Cards accepted: Mastercard, Visa, Switch/Delta

🛏🍽🍷📞🖥📺🧺♿🐕📶💷🔥🅿80⚡🍴🐾DAP📶SP◎

CLITHEROE

Lancashire
Map ref 4A1

Ancient market town with an 800-year-old castle keep and a wide range of award-winning shops. Good base for touring Ribble Valley, Trough of Bowland and Pennine moorland. Country market on Tuesdays and Saturdays.
Tourist Information Centre ☎ (01200) 425566

Brooklyn ⚠

🏵🏵🏵 HIGHLY COMMENDED

32 Pimlico Road, Clitheroe BB7 2AH
☎ (01200) 428268 & 423861
Small, family-run licensed guesthouse,

close to town centre, where the proprietors assure you of a warm and friendly welcome.
Bedrooms: 1 single, 1 double, 2 twin
Bathrooms: 4 en-suite

Bed & breakfast per night:

	£min	£max
Single	23.00	25.00
Double	38.00	40.00

Half board per person:

	£min	£max
Daily	33.00	35.00
Weekly	231.00	245.00

Evening meal 1830 (last orders 1930)
Cards accepted: Amex, Mastercard, Visa, Switch/Delta

🛏🍽🖥📶🔥📞🧺💷🍴📺🖥♿🐾🍴
🚗SP

Middle Flass Lodge Guesthouse and Restaurant ⚠

🏵🏵🏵 COMMENDED

Settle Road, Bolton-by-Bowland, Clitheroe BB7 4NY
☎ (01200) 447259
Fax (01200) 447300

Tasteful barn conversion in beautiful countryside of Forest of Bowland. Chef-prepared cuisine in restaurant open to non-residents. Licensed, ample parking.
Bedrooms: 2 double, 1 twin, 1 triple, 4 family rooms
Bathrooms: 8 en-suite

Bed & breakfast per night:

	£min	£max
Single	25.00	30.00
Double	40.00	50.00

Half board per person:

	£min	£max
Daily	34.00	39.00

Lunch available
Evening meal 1700 (last orders 2000)
Parking for 24
Cards accepted: Visa, Switch/Delta

🛏🍽1🖥🔥📞🖥💷📺🖥♿
🍴35⚡🐾🚗SP

Mitton Hall Lodgings ⚠

🏵🏵🏵 APPROVED

Mitton Road, Mitton, Clitheroe BB7 9PQ
☎ (01254) 826544
Fax (01254) 826386
16th C listed hall in Ribble Valley. Restaurant, pizzeria, tavern, lodgings. Two miles Whalley Abbey, 3 miles Clitheroe Castle, close Trough of Bowland. Eleven miles junction 31 of M6, 7 miles M65.
Bedrooms: 2 single, 6 double, 5 twin, 1 triple
Bathrooms: 14 en-suite

Bed & breakfast per night:

	£min	£max
Single	41.50	51.50
Double	47.00	57.00

Lunch available
Evening meal 1830 (last orders 2230)
Parking for 150
Cards accepted: Amex, Mastercard, Visa, Switch/Delta

🛏🍽🔥📞🖥💷📺🖥♿🅿50🍴
⚡DAP🏠

Shireburn Arms Hotel

🏵🏵🏵 COMMENDED

Whalley Road, Hurst Green, Clitheroe BB7 9QJ
☎ (01254) 826518
Fax (01254) 826208
16th C family-run hotel, with unrivalled views, renowned for food and comfort, log fires, real ale, bar food. Within easy reach of the motorway network.
Bedrooms: 9 double, 3 twin, 1 triple, 1 family room
Bathrooms: 14 en-suite

Bed & breakfast per night:

	£min	£max
Single	40.00	40.00
Double	52.00	55.00

Half board per person:

	£min	£max
Daily	52.00	55.00
Weekly	245.00	

Lunch available
Evening meal 1900 (last orders 2130)
Parking for 80
Cards accepted: Amex, Mastercard, Visa, Switch/Delta

🛏🚿🍷🍽🖥🔥📞🖥💷📺
🖥♿🅿80🚶🍴⚡🐾📶🏠T

For further information on accommodation establishments use the coupons at the back of this guide.

All accommodation in this guide has been graded, or is awaiting a grading, by a trained Tourist Board inspector.

CONGLETON

Cheshire
Map ref 4B2

Important cattle market and silk town on the River Dane, now concerned with general textiles. Nearby are Little Moreton Hall, a Tudor house surrounded by a moat, the Bridestones, remains of a chambered tomb, and Mow Cop, topped by a folly.
Tourist Information Centre ☎ (01260) 271095

Lion & Swan Hotel ⋔

⚛⚛⚛ HIGHLY COMMENDED

Swan Bank, Congleton CW12 1JR
☎ (01260) 273115
Fax (01260) 299270
16th C hotel with oak-beamed restaurant. High standards create an ideal base for business and leisure. 6 miles from M6.
Bedrooms: 4 single, 15 double, 2 twin
Bathrooms: 21 en-suite

Bed & breakfast per night:

	£min	£max
Single	33.00	84.00
Double	54.00	105.00

Half board per person:

	£min	£max
Daily	44.00	96.00

Lunch available
Evening meal 1900 (last orders 2130)
Parking for 53
Cards accepted: Amex, Diners, Mastercard, Visa, Switch/Delta

⛉⚏⚓⚐☎⛉⌨⚕♨🅹⚓⚒📺 ▥ ➲🎨120🏃✳✶ DAP ⚓ SP 🏨

GARSTANG

Lancashire
Map ref 4A1

Picturesque country market town. The gateway to the fells, it stands on the Lancaster Canal and is a popular cruising centre. Close by are the remains of Greenhalgh Castle (no public access) and the Bleasdale Circle. Discovery Centre shows history of Over Wyre and Bowland fringe areas.
Tourist Information Centre ☎ (01995) 602125

Crofters Hotel ⋔

⚛⚛⚛ HIGHLY COMMENDED

A6, Cabus, Garstang, Preston
PR3 1PH
☎ (01995) 604128
Fax (01995) 601646
Family owned and managed hotel with

all modern facilities, situated midway between Preston and Lancaster.
Bedrooms: 1 single, 5 double, 10 twin, 3 triple
Bathrooms: 19 en-suite

Bed & breakfast per night:

	£min	£max
Single	50.00	60.00
Double	60.00	85.00

Lunch available
Evening meal 1900 (last orders 2200)
Parking for 200
Cards accepted: Amex, Diners, Mastercard, Visa, Switch/Delta

⛉⚓⌨⚐♨🅸S⚒🎨⚓ ▥ ➲ 🎨200 ⚓ SP T

Garstang Country Hotel and Golf Club ⋔

⚛⚛⚛⚛ COMMENDED

Garstang Road, Bowgreave, Garstang, Preston PR3 1YE
☎ (01995) 600100
Fax (01995) 600950
The ideal location for business or pleasure, this new family-owned hotel and 18-hole golf course has every amenity for an enjoyable stay. Golf breaks a speciality.
Bedrooms: 4 double, 28 twin
Bathrooms: 32 en-suite

Bed & breakfast per night:

	£min	£max
Single	40.00	50.00
Double	50.00	60.00

Half board per person:

	£min	£max
Daily	55.00	65.00

Lunch available
Evening meal 1900 (last orders 2130)
Parking for 160
Cards accepted: Amex, Diners, Mastercard, Visa, Switch/Delta

⛉⚏⚓⚐⌨⚐♨🅸S⚒🎨📺 ●▥⚓➲🎨300 U🏃✳✶🏊 SP 🏨 T

Guy's Thatched Hamlet ⋔

⚛⚛⚛ COMMENDED

Canalside, St Michael's Road, Bilsborrow, Garstang, Preston PR3 0RS
☎ (01995) 640849 & 640010
Fax (01995) 640141
CR Logis of GB

Friendly, family-run thatched canalside tavern, restaurant, pizzeria, lodgings,

craft shops, cricket ground with thatched pavilion and crown green bowling. Conference centre. Off junction 32 of M6, then 3 miles north on A6 to Garstang.
Bedrooms: 28 double, 20 twin, 5 family rooms
Bathrooms: 53 en-suite

Bed & breakfast per night:

	£min	£max
Single	41.50	55.00
Double	47.50	60.50

Half board per person:

	£min	£max
Daily	35.75	42.25

Lunch available
Evening meal 1800 (last orders 2330)
Parking for 300
Cards accepted: Amex, Mastercard, Visa, Switch/Delta

⛉⚏⚐⌨⚐♨🅸S⚒🎨📺▥ ➲🎨60⚓U🏃✚✳✶ DAP SP 🏨

HOLMES CHAPEL

Cheshire
Map ref 4A2

Large village with some interesting 18th C buildings and St Luke's Church encased in brick hiding the 15th C original.

Holly Lodge Hotel ⋔

⚛⚛⚛ COMMENDED

70 London Road, Holmes Chapel CW4 7AS
☎ (01477) 537033
Fax (01477) 535823
Charming Victorian country hotel, professionally managed and family-owned. Friendly and efficient service. Close to junction 18 of M6. A la carte restaurant, conference and meeting rooms. Four-poster, jacuzzi and water bed.
Bedrooms: 6 single, 21 double, 9 twin, 2 triple
Bathrooms: 38 en-suite

Bed & breakfast per night:

	£min	£max
Single	39.00	69.50
Double	60.00	80.00

Lunch available
Evening meal 1930 (last orders 2145)
Parking for 80
Cards accepted: Amex, Diners, Mastercard, Visa, Switch/Delta

⛉⚏⚓⚐⌨⚐♨🅸S⚒🎨📺 ▥ ➲🎨120U✳⚓ SP ◉

HOYLAKE

Merseyside
Map ref 4A2

Overlooking the North Wales coastline across the River Dee, this residential resort has good beaches, a 4-mile promenade and, nearby, the Royal Liverpool Golf Club. Variety of bird life on Hilbre Islands accessible on foot at low tide.

Kings Gap Court Hotel
APPROVED

Valentia Road, Hoylake, Wirral L47 2AN
☎ (0151) 632 2073
Fax (0151) 632 0247
Old established family hotel close to seafront and many championship golf-courses. Ideal centre for Wales, Chester and Liverpool.
Bedrooms: 3 single, 4 double, 17 twin, 2 triple, 1 family room
Bathrooms: 24 en-suite, 1 private, 2 public

Bed & breakfast

per night:	£min	£max
Single	33.00	36.00
Double	46.00	64.00

Half board per person:

	£min	£max
Daily	31.00	40.00
Weekly	179.00	247.00

Lunch available
Evening meal 1800 (last orders 2000)
Parking for 89
Cards accepted: Mastercard, Visa

KNUTSFORD

Cheshire
Map ref 4A2

Delightful town with many buildings of architectural and historic interest. The setting of Elizabeth Gaskell's "Cranford". Annual May Day celebration and decorative "sanding" of the pavements are unique to the town. Popular Heritage Centre.
Tourist Information Centre ☎ (01565) 632611 or 632210

Longview Hotel and Restaurant
HIGHLY COMMENDED

Manchester Road, Knutsford WA16 0LX
☎ (01565) 632119
Fax (01565) 652402
Period Victorian hotel with many antiques and a relaxed, comfortable atmosphere, overlooking town common.

High quality varied food. Close to exit 19 of M6 and airport.
Bedrooms: 6 single, 9 double, 7 twin, 1 triple
Bathrooms: 23 en-suite

Bed & breakfast

per night:	£min	£max
Single	39.00	55.00
Double	47.50	82.50

Evening meal 1900 (last orders 2100)
Parking for 17
Cards accepted: Amex, Diners, Mastercard, Visa

LANCASTER

Lancashire
Map ref 5A3

Interesting old county town on the River Lune with history dating back to Roman times. Norman castle, St Mary's Church, Customs House, City and Maritime Museums, Ashton Memorial and Butterfly House are among places of note. Good centre for touring the Lake District.
Tourist Information Centre ☎ (01524) 32878

Lancaster House Hotel
HIGHLY COMMENDED

Green Lane, Lancaster LA1 4GJ
☎ (01524) 844822
Fax (01524) 844766
Email: Head Office @lancasterhousehotel.telme.com
Best Western
Elegant country house with extensive leisure facilities, perfectly located for exploring the nearby Lake District, Yorkshire Dales and historic Lancaster. B&B minimum prices below are weekend rates.
Wheelchair access category 2
Bedrooms: 38 double, 42 twin
Bathrooms: 80 en-suite

Bed & breakfast

per night:	£min	£max
Single	77.45	102.45
Double	85.90	110.90

Half board per person:

	£min	£max
Daily	59.50	72.00
Weekly	357.00	432.00

Lunch available
Evening meal 1900 (last orders 2130)
Parking for 100
Cards accepted: Amex, Diners, Mastercard, Visa, Switch/Delta

LANGHO

Lancashire
Map ref 4A1

This parish can trace its history back to Saxon times when in 798 AD a battle was fought at Billangohoh from which the names of Billington and Langho were derived. A flourishing community of mainly cattle farms, near both the River Ribble and the River Calder.

Mytton Fold Hotel and Golf Complex
HIGHLY COMMENDED

Whalley Road, Langho, Blackburn BB6 8AB
☎ (01254) 240662
Fax (01254) 248119
Family-owned, award-winning hotel, 10 miles from exit 31 of M6. Peacefully secluded, yet only 300 yards from the A59. Own private 18-hole golf-course.
Wheelchair access category 3
Bedrooms: 13 double, 14 twin
Bathrooms: 27 en-suite

Bed & breakfast

per night:	£min	£max
Single	39.00	48.00
Double	63.00	74.00

Half board per person:

	£min	£max
Daily	44.00	52.00
Weekly	308.00	364.00

Lunch available
Evening meal 1830 (last orders 2130)
Parking for 200
Cards accepted: Amex, Mastercard, Visa, Switch/Delta

LIVERPOOL

Merseyside
Map ref 4A2

Vibrant city which became prominent in the 18th C as a result of its sugar, spice and tobacco trade with the Americas. Today the historic waterfront is a major attraction. Home to the Beatles, the Grand National and two 20th C cathedrals, as well as many museums and galleries.
Tourist Information Centre ☎ (0151) 709 3631 or 708 8854

Aachen Hotel
COMMENDED

89-91 Mount Pleasant, Liverpool L3 5TB
☎ (0151) 709 3477 & 709 1126
Fax (0151) 709 1126

In city centre close to theatres, shops, cinemas, boat/rail/coach stations. Albert Dock and Maritime Museum close by. Double winner: Best Hotel North West and Best Hotel Merseyside.
Bedrooms: 6 single, 1 double, 5 twin, 5 triple
Bathrooms: 9 en-suite, 2 public
Bed & breakfast

per night:	£min	£max
Single	24.00	32.00
Double	38.00	46.00

Half board per

person:	£min	£max
Daily	32.75	40.75
Weekly	229.25	285.25

Lunch available
Evening meal 1830 (last orders 2030)
Parking for 2
Cards accepted: Amex, Diners, Mastercard, Visa

☎🚭✆📧🖥️♿🌡️🅿️♨️📶🧺📺🅾️💻
🍴🔍❄️ DAP SP 🏠 T ◉

Antrim Hotel ♨

👑👑 APPROVED

73 Mount Pleasant, Liverpool
L3 5TB
☎ (0151) 709 5239 & 709 9212
Fax (0151) 709 7169
Email: antrimhotel@ukbusiness.com
Friendly, family-run city centre hotel, convenient for shops, rail and bus stations, Albert Dock and all major tourist attractions. Twenty minutes from the airport.
Bedrooms: 8 single, 2 double, 8 twin, 2 family rooms
Bathrooms: 7 en-suite, 1 public, 9 private showers
Bed & breakfast

per night:	£min	£max
Single	28.00	40.00
Double	38.00	50.00

Half board per

person:	£min	£max
Daily	37.00	52.00
Weekly	259.00	364.00

Evening meal 1800 (last orders 2000)
Parking for 2
Cards accepted: Amex, Diners, Mastercard, Visa

🚭✆🖥️♿🌡️🅾️📶📺🅾️💻🧺🔍
DAP SP 🏠 T

Atlantic Tower Thistle Hotel ♨

👑👑👑👑 COMMENDED

Chapel Street, Liverpool L3 9RE
☎ (0151) 227 4444
Fax (0151) 236 3973
CR Mount Charlotte Thistle/Utell International
A well known landmark, this modern

hotel overlooks Liverpool's business quarter and has a magnificent view of the River Mersey from its rooms and celebrated restaurant.
Bedrooms: 58 single, 59 double, 109 twin
Suites available
Bathrooms: 226 en-suite
Bed & breakfast

per night:	£min	£max
Single	99.25	106.25
Double	119.50	126.50

Lunch available
Evening meal 1900 (last orders 2200)
Parking for 80
Cards accepted: Amex, Diners, Mastercard, Visa

🚭✆🖥️♿🌡️🅾️📶🧺📺🅾️💻
◉ 🚙🏨🛎️110 🔍❄️ SP 🏠 ◉

Blenheim Guest House ♨

👑👑 COMMENDED

37 Aigburth Drive, Liverpool
L17 4JE
☎ (0151) 727 7380
Fax (0151) 727 5833
Large Victorian villa overlooking Sefton Park, offering first class bed and breakfast accommodation at a very reasonable price. Former family home of Beatle Stu Sutcliffe.
Bedrooms: 2 single, 2 double, 8 twin, 2 triple, 2 family rooms
Bathrooms: 7 en-suite, 4 public
Bed & breakfast

per night:	£min	£max
Single	17.50	25.00
Double	29.00	35.00

Half board per

person:	£min	£max
Daily	22.50	30.00

Parking for 15
Cards accepted: Mastercard, Visa

🚭🚙♿🌡️🅾️📶📺🅾️💻🚙🛎️30
❄️🐕� SP

Blundellsands Hotel ♨

👑👑👑👑 COMMENDED

The Serpentine, Blundellsands, Crosby, Liverpool L23 6YB
☎ (0151) 924 6515
Fax (0151) 931 5364
CR Stagecoach
Majestic Victorian character hotel in a quiet suburb of Crosby. Easy access to Liverpool centre and Southport.
Bedrooms: 12 single, 17 double, 4 twin, 4 triple
Suite available
Bathrooms: 37 en-suite
Bed & breakfast

per night:	£min	£max
Single	66.00	91.00
Double	71.00	96.00

Lunch available

Evening meal 1900 (last orders 2130)
Parking for 250
Cards accepted: Amex, Diners, Mastercard, Visa, Switch/Delta

🚭✆📧🖥️♿🌡️🅾️📶🧺🅾️💻
🚙🛎️300🅿️❄️ SP T

Gladstone Hotel ♨

Lord Nelson Street, Liverpool
L3 5QB
☎ (0151) 709 7050
Fax (0151) 709 2193
CR Forte
Conveniently located in the heart of the city centre, adjacent to Lime Street Station. 6 miles from the airport. Meeting facilities for up to 600 people. Business services available.
Bedrooms: 29 single, 52 double, 69 twin, 4 triple
Suites available
Bathrooms: 154 en-suite
Bed & breakfast

per night:	£min	£max
Single	33.00	80.00
Double	66.00	95.00

Half board per

person:	£min	£max
Daily	43.00	95.00

Lunch available
Evening meal 1830 (last orders 2200)
Parking for 200
Cards accepted: Amex, Diners, Mastercard, Visa, Switch/Delta

🚭✆🖥️♿🌡️🅾️📶🧺📺🅾️◉💻
💻🚙🛎️600🔍 SP T

Green Park Hotel ♨

👑👑👑 APPROVED

4-6 Green Bank Drive, Liverpool
L17 1AN
☎ (0151) 733 3382
Fax (0151) 734 1161
Two miles from city centre and 3 miles from Liverpool Airport.
Bedrooms: 2 single, 6 double, 10 twin, 2 triple
Bathrooms: 20 en-suite, 1 public
Bed & breakfast

per night:	£min	£max
Single	28.00	
Double	38.00	

Half board per

person:	£min	£max
Daily	34.00	

Lunch available
Evening meal 1830 (last orders 2100)
Parking for 25
Cards accepted: Amex, Diners, Mastercard, Visa

🚭🚙✆📧🖥️♿🌡️🅾️📶📺🅾️◉💻🚙
🛎️60🔍 SP

LIVERPOOL

Continued

Holme Leigh Guest House ⚠

Listed | APPROVED
93 Woodcroft Road, Wavertree,
Liverpool L15 2HG
☎ (0151) 734 2216 & 427 9806
*Victorian red brick 3-storey corner
dwelling and fashion shop, facing on to
Lawrence Road. Just 2.5 miles from city
centre.*
Bedrooms: 4 single, 2 double, 4 twin
Bathrooms: 3 en-suite, 1 public
Bed & breakfast

per night:	£min	£max
Single	14.00	19.00
Double	25.00	29.95

Cards accepted: Amex, Mastercard,
Visa

🛬🏧♿🖨🗄⛄Ⓤ🅂✂🎇🍺📿✈
🚐 🆂🅿 🆃 ⊚

Rockland Hotel ⚠

👑👑 APPROVED
View Road, Rainhill, Prescot
L35 0LG
☎ (0151) 426 4603
Fax (0151) 426 0107
*Georgian hotel set in own grounds in
quiet suburban location. Easy access to
motorway (1 mile) and 10 miles from
Liverpool city centre.*
Bedrooms: 4 single, 2 double, 3 twin,
2 triple
Bathrooms: 10 en-suite, 1 public
Bed & breakfast

per night:	£min	£max
Single	25.00	33.50
Double	35.00	44.00

Lunch available
Evening meal 1830 (last orders
2030)
Parking for 30
Cards accepted: Amex, Mastercard,
Visa

🛬🖨⛄🅂🎇🍺📿💷50❄🆂🅿🎇🆃

LOWER WHITLEY

Cheshire
Map ref 4A2

Tall Trees Lodge ⚠

👑👑👑 COMMENDED
Tarporley Road, Lower Whitley,
Warrington WA4 4EZ
☎ (01928) 790824 & 715117
Fax (01928) 791330
*2.5 miles south of junction 10 of the
M56. Take A49 towards Whitchurch.
Little Chef and Mobil garage on site.*
Wheelchair access category 3♿
Bedrooms: 13 double, 1 twin,
6 triple
Bathrooms: 20 en-suite
Bed & breakfast

per night:	£min	£max
Single	39.50	41.50
Double	42.50	46.50

Parking for 40
Cards accepted: Amex, Diners,
Mastercard, Visa, Switch/Delta

🛬🏧♿📞🖨🗄⛄🍴✂◑🍺🚐🚐
⊚

LYTHAM ST ANNES

Lancashire
Map ref 4A1

Pleasant resort famous for its
championship golf-courses, notably
the Royal Lytham and St Annes. Fine
sands and attractive gardens. Some
half-timbered buildings and an old
restored windmill.
Tourist Information Centre ☎ *(01253)
725610*

Chadwick Hotel ⚠

👑👑👑👑 COMMENDED
South Promenade, Lytham St Annes
FY8 1NP
☎ (01253) 720061
Fax (01253) 714455
Ⓒ Logis of GB

*Modern family-run hotel and leisure
complex with reputation for food,
comfort, personal service and value for
money.*
Wheelchair access category 3♿
Bedrooms: 10 single, 11 double,
29 twin, 14 triple, 8 family rooms
Bathrooms: 72 en-suite
Bed & breakfast

per night:	£min	£max
Single	38.00	43.00
Double	52.00	59.00

Half board per person:	£min	£max
Daily	37.50	54.00
Weekly	270.00	378.00

Lunch available
Evening meal 1900 (last orders
2030)
Parking for 40
Cards accepted: Amex, Diners,
Mastercard, Visa, Switch/Delta

🛬🏧🚲📞🖨🗄⛄🍴🎇🅂✂🎇📺
◑🍷🚐📿💷70🚭🔍🎾❄🎯🚶🚏🆂
🆃

Ad See display advertisement on this
page

Dalmeny Hotel ⚠

👑👑👑 COMMENDED
19-33 South Promenade, Lytham St
Annes FY8 1LX
☎ (01253) 712236
Fax (01253) 724447
*The Dalmeny is a rare find these days.
Well-appointed promenade hotel,
managed by the Webb family since
1945.*
Bedrooms: 1 single, 45 double,
12 twin, 36 triple, 15 family rooms
Bathrooms: 109 en-suite

Bed & breakfast per night:	£min	£max
Single	47.00	78.00
Double	66.00	107.00

Half board per person:	£min	£max
Daily	45.00	65.50
Weekly	343.00	717.60

Lunch available
Evening meal 1700 (last orders 2200)
Parking for 160
Cards accepted: Amex, Mastercard, Visa, Switch/Delta

⛵🦯🏑🛆🖵🖐🛈Ⓢ✂🅿📺🌀⊡ 🖩🚗🍴200🌀🏂🏹🐾🌲🛦🚶☂🎿🦌 🅢🅣

The Grand Hotel ⋀

South Promenade, Lytham St Annes FY8 1NB
☎ (01253) 721288
Fax (01253) 714459

On the South Promenade overlooking the bay. Splendid Victorian building offering excellent food and accommodation. Close to championship golf-course.
Bedrooms: 4 single, 17 double, 14 twin, 5 triple
Suites available
Bathrooms: 40 en-suite

Bed & breakfast per night:	£min	£max
Single	55.00	73.00
Double	60.00	90.00

Lunch available
Evening meal 1800 (last orders 2130)
Parking for 152
Cards accepted: Amex, Mastercard, Visa, Switch/Delta

⛵🦯🏑🛆🖵🖐🏑Ⓢ✂🅿🌀⊡🖩 🚗🍴180🐾☂⛛✿🌲🎿🦌🅢🅟🅣◉

Lindum Hotel ⋀

63-67 South Promenade, Lytham St Annes FY8 1LZ
☎ (01253) 721534 & 722516
Fax (01253) 721364
Ⓒⓡ Logis of GB
Family-run, seafront hotel with good reputation for food and comfortable accommodation. Close to fine shops and championship golf-courses.

Bedrooms: 8 single, 30 double, 18 twin, 22 triple
Bathrooms: 78 en-suite, 2 public

Bed & breakfast per night:	£min	£max
Single	30.00	35.00
Double	50.00	56.00

Half board per person:	£min	£max
Daily	35.00	41.00

Lunch available
Evening meal 1800 (last orders 1900)
Parking for 25
Cards accepted: Amex, Mastercard, Visa, Switch/Delta

⛵🦯🖵🛆🖐🛈Ⓢ✂🏑📺🌀⊡🖩 🚗🍴175🌀🐾ⒹⒶⓅ🎿🅢🅟

Cheshire
Map ref 4B2

Cobbled streets and quaint old buildings stand side by side with modern shops and three markets. Centuries of association with the silk industry; museums feature working exhibits and social history. Stunning views of the Peak District National Park.
Tourist Information Centre ☎ (01625) 504114 or 504115

Chadwick House ⋀

55 Beech Lane, Macclesfield SK10 2DS
☎ (01625) 615558 & 0858 154816
Fax/Guests (01625) 610265
Tastefully refurbished large town house, close to town centre and stations. Licensed bar, restaurant, sauna, solarium and gym available. Sky TV in all rooms.
Bedrooms: 6 single, 6 double, 1 twin
Bathrooms: 13 en-suite, 2 public

Bed & breakfast per night:	£min	£max
Single	25.00	40.00
Double	55.00	70.00

Half board per person:	£min	£max
Daily	34.95	49.95

Evening meal from 1930
Parking for 10
Cards accepted: Amex, Diners, Mastercard, Visa

⛵🦯🖵🛆🖐🛈Ⓢ✂🏑📺🖩🚗 🍴20🌀🏂🍴✿

Moorhayes House Hotel ⋀

27 Manchester Road, Tytherington, Macclesfield SK10 2JJ
☎ (01625) 433228
Fax (01625) 433228
Modern, comfortable house in attractive garden, half a mile from town centre. 5 minutes from Peak District National Park, 20 minutes from Manchester and airport.
Bedrooms: 2 single, 6 double, 1 twin
Bathrooms: 7 en-suite, 1 public

Bed & breakfast per night:	£min	£max
Single	25.00	35.00
Double	39.00	44.00

Evening meal 1800 (last orders 1900)
Parking for 14

🦯🏑🛆🖵🖐Ⓤ🛈Ⓢ✂🖩🚗🐾🎿 🅢🅣

Shrigley Hall Hotel Golf and Country Club ⋀

Shrigley Park, Pott Shrigley, Macclesfield SK10 5SB
☎ (01625) 575757
Fax (01625) 573323
Ⓒⓡ Utell International
Country house hotel built in 1825 in the 262-acre estate of Shrigley Park. Overlooks the Cheshire plain and Peak District. 18-hole golf-course and full leisure club.
Bedrooms: 25 single, 92 double, 34 twin, 5 triple
Suite available
Bathrooms: 156 en-suite

Bed & breakfast per night:	£min	£max
Single	99.00	99.00
Double	130.00	130.00

Half board per person:	£min	£max
Daily	120.00	125.00

Lunch available
Evening meal 1900 (last orders 2145)
Parking for 300
Cards accepted: Amex, Diners, Mastercard, Visa, Switch/Delta

⛵🦯🏑🖵🛆🖐🛈Ⓢ✂🏑◉ ⊡🖩🚗🍴250🌀🏂🏹🐾🌲❀⛛Ⓤ♪ 🛦✿🎿🅢🅟🅣

For further information on accommodation establishments use the coupons at the back of this guide.

You are advised to confirm your booking in writing.

MANCHESTER

Greater Manchester
Map ref 4B1

The Gateway to the North, offering one of Britain's largest selections of arts venues and theatre productions, a wide range of chain stores and specialist shops, a legendary, lively nightlife, spectacular architecture and a plethora of eating and drinking places.
Tourist Information Centre ☎ *(0161) 234 3157 or 234 3158 or 436 3344*

Bentley Guest House ⋔

👑 COMMENDED

64 Hill Lane, Blackley, Manchester
M9 6PF
☎ (0161) 795 1115
Comfortable, friendly house, 10 minutes from M62 and close to shops and bus for city centre. Private parking, garden, patio. Personal attention, freshly-cooked meals, dinner optional.
Bedrooms: 1 single, 2 double
Bathrooms: 1 en-suite, 1 public
Bed & breakfast

per night:	£min	£max
Single	16.00	20.00
Double	30.00	40.00

Half board per

person:	£min	£max
Daily	26.00	36.00
Weekly	182.00	252.00

Evening meal 1800 (last orders 2000)
Parking for 3

The Drop Inn Hotel ⋔

👑👑👑 APPROVED

393 Wilmslow Road, Withington, Manchester M20 4WA
☎ (0161) 286 1919
Fax (0161) 286 8880
Hotel with private baths and showers. Special rates for weekend breaks.
Bedrooms: 10 single, 8 double, 10 twin
Bathrooms: 28 private, 1 public
Bed & breakfast

per night:	£min	£max
Single	35.00	
Double	45.00	

Lunch available
Evening meal 1600 (last orders 2300)
Parking for 45
Cards accepted: Mastercard, Visa, Switch/Delta

Elm Grange Hotel ⋔

👑👑👑 COMMENDED

559-561 Wilmslow Road, Withington, Manchester M20 4GJ
☎ (0161) 445 3336
Fax (0161) 445 3336
Ⓖ The Independents
On main bus routes to city centre and airport. Cleanliness, service, value for money. Convenient for theatres, shops, restaurants, hospitals and university. Special weekend discounts. Restaurant open evenings.
Bedrooms: 13 single, 5 double, 11 twin
Bathrooms: 19 en-suite, 3 public
Bed & breakfast

per night:	£min	£max
Single	25.50	41.00
Double	38.00	58.00

Half board per

person:	£min	£max
Daily	36.00	52.50
Weekly	248.00	360.00

Lunch available
Evening meal 1800 (last orders 2000)
Parking for 41
Cards accepted: Amex, Mastercard, Visa, Switch/Delta

Granada Hotel

👑👑 APPROVED

404 Wilmslow Road, Withington, Manchester M20 9BM
☎ (0161) 286 9551 & 434 3480
Fax (0161) 286 9553
Comfortable hotel close to Manchester city centre and airport. En-suite rooms, colour TV, telephone, hairdryer. Lounge, bar and restaurant.
Bedrooms: 3 single, 2 double, 3 twin, 2 triple
Bathrooms: 10 private
Bed & breakfast

per night:	£min	£max
Single	35.00	45.00
Double	50.00	60.00

Half board per

person:	£min	£max
Daily	50.00	60.00
Weekly	250.00	280.00

Evening meal 1800 (last orders 2330)
Parking for 20
Cards accepted: Amex, Diners, Mastercard, Visa

Holiday Inn Garden Court ⋔

👑👑👑 COMMENDED

Outward Lane, Manchester Airport, Manchester M90 4HL
☎ (0161) 498 0333 & Freefone 0800 897121 (reservations)
Fax (0161) 498 0222
All rooms comfortably sleep up to 4 people. 200 metres from airport, with complimentary transfer to and from airport. Discounted long-term parking on airport complex.
Bedrooms: 85 double, 78 twin
Bathrooms: 163 en-suite
Bed & breakfast

per night:	£min	£max
Single	51.00	63.00
Double	57.00	69.00

Evening meal 1800 (last orders 2245)
Parking for 160
Cards accepted: Amex, Diners, Mastercard, Visa, Switch/Delta

Imperial Hotel ⋔

👑👑 COMMENDED

157 Hathersage Road, Manchester M13 0HY
☎ (0161) 225 6500
Fax (0161) 225 6500
A well-maintained hotel run by the same owner for over 10 years, offering reasonably priced accommodation. Close to university and hospitals.
Bedrooms: 13 single, 5 double, 9 twin
Bathrooms: 21 en-suite, 3 public
Bed & breakfast

per night:	£min	£max
Single	30.00	38.00
Double	38.00	48.00

Evening meal 1830 (last orders 2030)
Parking for 30
Cards accepted: Amex, Diners, Mastercard, Visa

Hotel Montana/The Acropolis Restaurant ⋔

👑👑 APPROVED

59 Palatine Road, West Didsbury, Manchester M20 9LJ
☎ (0161) 445 6427 & 445 0062
Fax (0161) 448 9458
Family-run hotel with pleasant atmosphere. Greek and Mediterranean restaurant and tapas bar. Sky TV. Large secure car park. 3 miles city centre and airport.
Bedrooms: 7 single, 5 double, 9 twin, 1 triple
Bathrooms: 18 en-suite, 3 public

Bed & breakfast per night:	£min	£max
Single	30.00	35.00
Double	52.00	65.00

Half board per person:	£min	£max
Daily	45.00	55.00
Weekly	280.00	300.00

Evening meal 1800 (last orders 2200)
Parking for 40
Cards accepted: Diners, Mastercard

 80 DAP SP T

Novotel Manchester West M

COMMENDED

Worsley Brow, Worsley, Manchester
M28 2YA
☎ (0161) 799 3535
Fax (0161) 703 8207
CR Novotel

*New hotel, restaurant, banqueting and
conference centre. Ideal for business or
pleasure. Junction 13 on M62.
Restaurant open 0600-midnight. For
early risers, breakfast available from
0430.*
Wheelchair access category 2
Bedrooms: 38 single, 38 double,
38 twin, 5 triple
Bathrooms: 119 en-suite

Bed & breakfast per night:	£min	£max
Single	77.50	82.50
Double	82.50	91.00

Half board per person:	£min	£max
Daily	93.50	98.50

Lunch available
Evening meal 1800 (last orders
2359)
Parking for 133
Cards accepted: Amex, Diners,
Mastercard, Visa, Switch/Delta

220

The Palace Hotel M

HIGHLY COMMENDED

Oxford Street, Manchester
M60 7HA
☎ (0161) 288 1111
Fax (0161) 288 2222
CR Principal/Utell International
*Character listed building in city centre,
designed in country house hotel style.*
Bedrooms: 5 single, 103 double,
53 twin, 10 family rooms
Bathrooms: 171 en-suite

Bed & breakfast per night:	£min	£max
Single	94.00	
Double	94.00	

Lunch available
Evening meal 1750 (last orders
2130)
Cards accepted: Amex, Diners,
Mastercard, Visa, Switch/Delta

1000 SP T

The Portland Thistle Hotel M

HIGHLY COMMENDED

Portland Street, Piccadilly Gardens,
Manchester M1 6DP
☎ (0161) 228 3400
Fax (0161) 228 6347
CR Mount Charlotte Thistle/Utell
International
*Traditional style hotel, combining old
world charm with full modern facilities,
including a leisure spa and the recently
acclaimed Winstons Restaurant.
Overlooks Piccadilly Gardens in the
heart of the city's commercial and
shopping area.*
Bedrooms: 107 single, 75 double,
11 twin, 12 triple
Suites available
Bathrooms: 205 en-suite

Bed & breakfast per night:	£min	£max
Single	108.00	122.00
Double	135.50	144.00

Lunch available
Evening meal 1900 (last orders
2200)
Parking for 30
Cards accepted: Amex, Diners,
Mastercard, Visa, Switch/Delta

300

The Royals Hotel M

Altrincham Road, Wythenshawe,
Manchester M22 4BJ
☎ (0161) 998 9011
Fax (0161) 998 4641
CR Consort
*At the heart of Manchester's motorway
network, 2 miles from Manchester
Airport. Recently renovated mock-Tudor
building in own grounds with beautiful
Conservatory Restaurant. Ample car
parking.*
Bedrooms: 9 single, 9 double, 8 twin,
1 triple, 6 family rooms
Bathrooms: 33 en-suite

Bed & breakfast per night:	£min	£max
Single	52.00	60.00
Double	66.00	72.00

Lunch available
Evening meal 1900 (last orders
2145)
Parking for 100
Cards accepted: Amex, Diners,
Mastercard, Visa

100 SP T

Wilmslow Hotel M

APPROVED

356 Wilmslow Road, Fallowfield,
Manchester M14 6AB
☎ (0161) 225 3030 & 224 5815
Fax (0161) 257 2854
*Comfortable, family-run hotel with Sky
TV in all rooms. Special group and long
term rates available. Convenient for
Manchester University, city centre,
airport, railway stations and M56,
M63.*
Bedrooms: 14 single, 4 double,
6 twin, 1 triple, 3 family rooms
Bathrooms: 14 en-suite, 3 public,
2 private showers

Bed & breakfast per night:	£min	£max
Single	16.65	30.65
Double	28.30	35.50

Half board per person:	£min	£max
Daily	30.00	57.00
Weekly	210.00	399.00

Evening meal 1830 (last orders
2100)
Parking for 35
Cards accepted: Mastercard, Visa

40 SP T

MANCHESTER AIRPORT

*See under Alderley Edge, Altrincham,
Cheadle Hulme, Knutsford, Manchester,
Mobberley, Sale, Salford, Stockport,
Wilmslow*

MAWDESLEY

Lancashire
Map ref 4A1

Mawdsleys Eating House and Hotel

👑👑👑 COMMENDED

Hall Lane, Mawdesley, Ormskirk
L40 2QZ
☎ (01704) 822552 & 821874
Fax (01704) 822096
In the picturesque village of Mawdesley, which has been voted "best kept village". Its peaceful setting will be appreciated by business people and pleasure travellers alike.
Bedrooms: 39 double, 6 twin
Bathrooms: 45 en-suite
Bed & breakfast

per night:	£min	£max
Single	43.50	45.50
Double	53.00	55.00

Lunch available
Evening meal 1900 (last orders 2200)
Parking for 100
Cards accepted: Amex, Diners, Mastercard, Visa, Switch/Delta
🛏🛁⚓📞📺🖥🐕❓💷📱🖩🛏🖨

MOBBERLEY

Cheshire
Map ref 4A2

The Hinton

👑👑👑 HIGHLY COMMENDED

Town Lane, Mobberley, Knutsford
WA16 7HH
☎ (01565) 873484
Fax (01565) 873484
Bed and breakfast for both business and private guests. Within easy reach of M6, M56, Manchester Airport and InterCity rail network. Ideal touring base, on the B5085 between Knutsford and Wilmslow.
Bedrooms: 3 single, 2 double, 1 twin
Bathrooms: 4 en-suite, 1 public
Bed & breakfast

per night:	£min	£max
Single	30.00	35.00
Double	42.00	48.00

Evening meal 1800 (last orders 1900)
Parking for 10
Cards accepted: Amex, Diners, Mastercard, Visa
🛏📞📺🖥📱🖩🛏🖨

Please check prices and other details at the time of booking.

MORETON

Merseyside
Map ref 4A2

Leasowe Castle Hotel and Conference Centre 🅰

👑👑👑 COMMENDED

Leasowe Road, Moreton, Wirral
L46 3RF
☎ (0151) 606 9191
Fax (0151) 678 5551
Email: leasowe.castle
@mail.cybase.co.uk

16th C building converted to a hotel. All rooms with direct-dial telephone, trouser press and hairdryer. 3 bars, health club, a la carte restaurant. Golf-course adjacent.
Bedrooms: 25 double, 25 twin
Bathrooms: 50 en-suite
Bed & breakfast

per night:	£min	£max
Single	42.50	59.50
Double	59.50	66.50

Half board per

person:	£min	£max
Daily	59.45	75.95
Weekly	416.15	531.65

Lunch available
Evening meal 1900 (last orders 2200)
Parking for 200
Cards accepted: Amex, Diners, Mastercard, Visa, Switch/Delta
🛏📞📺🖥📱🖩🛏🖨

NEW BRIGHTON

Merseyside
Map ref 4A2

This resort on the Mersey Estuary has 7 miles of coastline, with fishing off the sea wall and pleasant walks along the promenade. Attractions include New Palace Amusements, Floral Pavilion Theatre, ten pin bowling and good sports facilities.

Sea Level Hotel

👑 APPROVED

126 Victoria Road, New Brighton, Wallasey L45 9LD
☎ (0151) 639 3408
Fax (0151) 639 3408
Homely, family-run hotel offering a

warm welcome and wholesome food. Light meals available until 11pm.
Bedrooms: 8 single, 3 double, 2 twin, 2 triple
Bathrooms: 1 en-suite, 3 public
Bed & breakfast

per night:	£min	£max
Single	17.50	23.50
Double	30.90	47.00

Half board per

person:	£min	£max
Daily	22.40	30.45
Weekly	135.00	180.00

Evening meal 1845 (last orders 2000)
Parking for 10
Cards accepted: Mastercard, Visa
🛏♿📞📺🖥📱🖩🛏🖨
T

Sherwood Guest House

👑👑 COMMENDED

55 Wellington Road, New Brighton, Wirral L45 2ND
☎ (0151) 639 5198
Family guesthouse facing promenade and Irish Sea. Close to station.
Bedrooms: 1 single, 2 double, 2 twin, 2 triple
Bathrooms: 2 en-suite, 2 public
Bed & breakfast

per night:	£min	£max
Single	13.00	15.00
Double	25.00	30.00

Half board per

person:	£min	£max
Daily	18.00	20.00
Weekly	115.00	140.00

Evening meal 1800 (last orders 1900)
🛏📺🖥📱🖩🛏🖨

OLDHAM

Greater Manchester
Map ref 4B1

The magnificent mill buildings which made Oldham one of the world's leading cotton-spinning towns still dominate the landscape. Ideally situated on the edge of the Peak District, it is now a centre of culture, sport and shopping. Art gallery has fine collections.
Tourist Information Centre ☎ (0161) 627 1024

Hotel Smokies Park 🅰

👑👑👑👑 HIGHLY COMMENDED

Ashton Road, Bardsley, Oldham
OL8 3HX
☎ (0161) 624 3405
Fax (0161) 627 5262
©® Consort
Beautifully-appointed hotel with spacious en-suite bedrooms. Good

function facilities for up to 500 people. Nightclub, trimnasium and ample free parking.
Bedrooms: 34 double, 16 twin
Bathrooms: 50 en-suite

Bed & breakfast per night:	£min	£max
Single	35.00	65.00
Double	50.00	85.00

Lunch available
Evening meal 1900 (last orders 2200)
Parking for 120
Cards accepted: Amex, Diners, Mastercard, Visa, Switch/Delta
150

PARKGATE

Cheshire
Map ref 4A2

Once a busy port on the Dee Estuary, Parkgate was the scene of Handel's departure for the great performance of 'Messiah' in Dublin in 1741. The George Inn where he stayed is now Mostyn House School.

Parkgate Hotel

COMMENDED

Boathouse Lane, Parkgate, South Wirral L64 6RD
☎ (0151) 336 5001
Fax (0151) 336 8504
Rural Wirral hotel on the edge of the unspoilt Dee Marshes conservation area, set in landscaped gardens. Just 20 minutes' drive from Chester.
Bedrooms: 1 single, 11 double, 12 twin, 3 triple
Bathrooms: 27 en-suite

Bed & breakfast per night:	£min	£max
Single	25.00	35.00
Double	50.00	60.00

Half board per person:	£min	£max
Daily	40.00	40.00
Weekly	280.00	280.00

Lunch available
Evening meal 1900 (last orders 2200)
Parking for 125
Cards accepted: Amex, Mastercard, Visa, Switch/Delta
100

Establishments should be open throughout the year, unless otherwise stated.

PRESTON

Lancashire
Map ref 4A1

Scene of decisive Royalist defeat by Cromwell in the Civil War and later of riots in the Industrial Revolution. Local history exhibited in Harris Museum. Famous for its Guild and the celebration that takes place every 20 years.
Tourist Information Centre ☎ (01772) 253731

Olde Duncombe House

HIGHLY COMMENDED

Garstang Road, Bilsborrow, Preston PR3 0RE
☎ (01995) 640336
Fax (01995) 640336

Traditional cottage-style bed and breakfast establishment set in rural surroundings alongside the picturesque Lancaster canal. 4 miles north of M6, junction 32.
Bedrooms: 2 single, 4 double, 2 twin, 1 triple
Bathrooms: 9 en-suite

Bed & breakfast per night:	£min	£max
Single	32.50	39.50
Double	45.00	49.50

Lunch available
Evening meal 1800 (last orders 2030)
Parking for 12
Cards accepted: Amex, Mastercard, Visa

Tulketh Hotel

COMMENDED

209 Tulketh Road, Ashton, Preston PR2 1ES
☎ (01772) 728096 & 726250
Fax (01772) 723743
The Independents
Hotel of fine quality and with personal service, in a quiet residential area. A la carte menu. 5 minutes from town centre, 10 minutes from M6 motorway.
Bedrooms: 5 single, 2 double, 5 twin
Bathrooms: 11 en-suite, 1 private

Bed & breakfast per night:	£min	£max
Single	35.00	38.50
Double	45.00	49.50

Half board per person:	£min	£max
Daily	40.00	52.55
Weekly	266.00	349.00

Evening meal 1830 (last orders 1930)
Parking for 12
Cards accepted: Amex, Diners, Mastercard, Visa, Switch/Delta

RADCLIFFE

Greater Manchester
Map ref 4A1

By the River Irwell, originally a coal and cotton town. The ruins of the medieval Radcliffe Tower can still be seen.

Hawthorn Hotel & Restaurant

APPROVED

139-143 Stand Lane, Radcliffe, Manchester M26 1JR
☎ (0161) 723 2706
Fax (0161) 723 2706
Comfortable family hotel with restaurant, convenient for M62 junction 17, motorway netwook and Metrolink system. Close to Bury, Bolton and Manchester.
Bedrooms: 1 single, 4 double, 7 twin, 1 triple, 1 family room
Bathrooms: 14 en-suite, 1 public

Bed & breakfast per night:	£min	£max
Single	29.50	35.50
Double	39.50	47.00

Half board per person:	£min	£max
Daily	39.45	45.45

Evening meal 1800 (last orders 2000)
Parking for 9
Cards accepted: Amex, Mastercard, Visa, Switch/Delta
60

RIBBLE VALLEY

See under Chipping, Clitheroe, Langho

ACCESSIBILITY

Look for the symbols which indicate accessibility for wheelchair users. These are described in detail at the front of this guide.

SADDLEWORTH

Greater Manchester
Map ref 4B1

The stone-built villages of Saddleworth are peppered with old mill buildings and possess a unique Pennine character. The superb scenery of Saddleworth Moor provides an ideal backdrop for canal trips, walking and outdoor pursuits. *Tourist Information Centre* ☎ *(01457) 870336*

La Pergola Hotel and Restaurant ♨

⚜⚜⚜⚜ COMMENDED

Rochdale Road, Denshaw, Oldham OL3 5UE
☎ (01457) 871040
Fax (01457) 873804
Ⓒ The Independents
Country hotel set in Pennine hills, only 5 minutes M62. All bedrooms en-suite with TV, telephone, hairdryer and trouser press (non-smoking available). Lounge bar with log fire, restaurant and pizzeria.
Bedrooms: 2 single, 15 double, 7 twin, 2 triple
Suite available
Bathrooms: 26 en-suite
Bed & breakfast

per night:	£min	£max
Single	40.00	50.00
Double	55.00	75.00

Lunch available
Evening meal 1830 (last orders 2200)
Parking for 65
Cards accepted: Amex, Mastercard, Visa, Switch/Delta
🛇🅰♿📞📧🖥🎧♨️🅱🅂✂🅿📺◗🖩🛄🅿️🎯200🅿✻❀❄SP T

SALE

Greater Manchester
Map ref 4B2

Located between Manchester and Altrincham, Sale owes its name to the 12th C landowner Thomas de Sale. It is now home to Trafford Water Sports Centre and Park which offers the best in aquatic leisure and countryside activities.

Cornerstones

⚜⚜⚜ HIGHLY COMMENDED

230 Washway Road, Sale, Cheshire M33 4RA
☎ (0161) 283 6909 & 881 0901
Fax (0161) 283 6909

Elegantly refurbished, offering every comfort and service. Ideally situated on the A56 only minutes from city and airport. 5 minutes' walk to Metro station.
Bedrooms: 3 single, 3 double, 3 twin
Bathrooms: 5 en-suite, 4 private showers
Bed & breakfast

per night:	£min	£max
Single	23.00	30.00
Double	46.00	50.00

Half board per person:	£min	£max
Daily	38.00	43.00

Evening meal 1830 (last orders 1930)
Parking for 10
Cards accepted: Mastercard, Visa
🛇🅰♿📞📧🖥🎧♨️🅱🅂✂🅿📺🖩🛄🎯25🅿✻❀🐾SP 🏳

SALFORD

Greater Manchester
Map ref 4B1

Industrial city close to Manchester with Roman Catholic cathedral and university. Lowry often painted Salford's industrial architecture and much of his work is in the local art gallery. Salford Quays provide a backdrop to pubs, walkways and a large cinema complex.

Hazeldean Hotel ♨

⚜⚜⚜ APPROVED

467 Bury New Road, Kersal Bar, Salford, Lancashire M7 3NE
☎ (0161) 792 6667 & 792 2079
Fax (0161) 792 6668
Ⓒ Minotel
Renovated Victorian mansion in residential area of Salford. Two miles exit 17 M62, 2.5 miles city centre on A56. Most rooms en-suite. Fully stocked bar leading on to beautiful garden. Restaurant, TV lounge.
Bedrooms: 10 single, 4 double, 5 twin, 2 triple
Bathrooms: 17 en-suite, 2 public
Bed & breakfast

per night:	£min	£max
Single	30.00	45.00
Double	47.50	55.00

Lunch available
Evening meal 1830 (last orders 2030)

Parking for 25
Cards accepted: Amex, Diners, Mastercard, Visa, Switch/Delta
🛇🅰♿📞📧🖥🎧♨️🅱🅂✂🅿📺🖩🛄🎯40🐾✻🐾SP T

White Lodge Private Hotel

⚜ APPROVED

87-89 Great Cheetham Street West, Broughton, Salford M7 9JA
☎ (0161) 792 3047
Small, family-run hotel, close to city centre amenities and sporting facilities.
Bedrooms: 3 single, 3 double, 3 twin
Bathrooms: 2 public
Bed & breakfast

per night:	£min	£max
Single	20.00	
Double	36.00	

Parking for 6
🛇♿2🅂🅿📺🖩🛄🚗

SAMLESBURY

Lancashire
Map ref 4A1

Swallow Hotel ♨

⚜⚜⚜⚜ COMMENDED

Preston New Road, Samlesbury, Preston PR5 0UL
☎ (01772) 877351
Fax (01772) 877424
Ⓒ Swallow
Hotel and leisure club, ideal for business and family use, overlooking Ribble Valley countryside, 1 mile from the M6. Short break packages available.
Bedrooms: 24 single, 36 double, 18 twin
Bathrooms: 78 en-suite
Bed & breakfast

per night:	£min	£max
Single	80.00	95.00
Double	110.00	130.00

Lunch available
Evening meal 1900 (last orders 2130)
Parking for 300
Cards accepted: Amex, Diners, Mastercard, Visa
🛇🅰♿📞📧🖥🎧♨️🅱🅂✂🅿◗🖩🛄🎯250♿🐾✻🐾♻🅿SP T ♿

SANDBACH

Cheshire
Map ref 4A2

Small Cheshire town, originally important for salt production. Contains narrow, winding streets, timbered houses and a cobbled market-place. Town square has 2 Anglo-Saxon crosses to commemorate the conversion to Christianity of the King of Mercia's son.

Saxon Cross Hotel 🏛

👑👑👑 COMMENDED

M6 junction 17, Holmes Chapel Road, Sandbach CW11 1SE
☎ (01270) 763281
Fax (01270) 768723
Conveniently situated in the heart of Cheshire at junction 17 of M6. Just 1 mile from the quaint town of Sandbach.
Wheelchair access category 3♿
Bedrooms: 10 single, 10 double, 18 twin, 14 triple
Bathrooms: 52 en-suite

Bed & breakfast per night:	£min	£max
Single	40.00	62.50
Double	55.00	77.00

Lunch available
Evening meal 1930 (last orders 2200)
Parking for 200
Cards accepted: Amex, Diners, Mastercard, Visa, Switch/Delta
🐴🛏📞📠🖥☕💨🔒[S]⚡🪑[TV]◐▥⛟Ƭ150⚑❀[OAP]🚫🐕[SP][T]

SOUTHPORT

Merseyside
Map ref 4A1

Delightful Victorian resort noted for gardens, sandy beaches and 6 golf-courses, particularly Royal Birkdale. Attractions include the Atkinson Art Gallery, Southport Railway Centre, Pleasureland and the annual Southport Flower Show. Excellent shopping, particularly in Lord Street's elegant boulevard.
Tourist Information Centre ☎ (01704) 533333

Ambassador Private Hotel

👑👑👑 COMMENDED

13 Bath Street, Southport PR9 0DP
☎ (01704) 530459 & 543998
Fax (01704) 536269
Delightful small quality hotel with residential licence, 200 yards from promenade and conference facilities. All bedrooms en-suite. Pets welcome.
Bedrooms: 4 double, 2 twin, 2 triple
Bathrooms: 8 en-suite, 2 public

Bed & breakfast per night:	£min	£max
Single	30.00	30.00
Double	50.00	50.00

Half board per person:	£min	£max
Daily	35.00	45.00
Weekly	190.00	190.00

Lunch available
Evening meal 1800 (last orders 1900)
Parking for 6
Cards accepted: Amex, Mastercard, Visa
🐴4🛏📠🖥☕💨🔒[S]⚡🪑▥⛟🚌

Dukes Folly Hotel 🏛

👑👑👑👑 COMMENDED

11 Duke Street, Southport PR8 1LS
☎ (01704) 533355
Fax (01704) 530065
Licensed family-run hotel noted for its high standards and friendly atmosphere. On the corner of Duke Street and Lord Street and within easy reach of all local amenities.
Bedrooms: 5 single, 7 double, 7 twin
Bathrooms: 19 en-suite

Bed & breakfast per night:	£min	£max
Single	38.50	50.00
Double	62.00	70.00

Half board per person:	£min	£max
Daily	48.50	60.00

Evening meal 1800 (last orders 2050)
Parking for 10
Cards accepted: Amex, Mastercard, Visa
🐴🛏📞📠🖥☕💨🔒[S]⚡🪑[TV]▥⛟Ƭ🤸

Leicester Hotel

👑👑 APPROVED

24 Leicester Street, Southport PR9 0EZ
☎ (01704) 530049
Fax (01704) 530049
Email: leicester.hotel@mail.cybase.co.uk
Family-run hotel with personal attention, clean and comfortable, close to all amenities. Car park. Licensed bar. TV in all rooms. En-suite available.
Bedrooms: 2 single, 3 double, 3 twin
Bathrooms: 3 en-suite, 2 public

Bed & breakfast per night:	£min	£max
Single	17.50	25.00
Double	35.00	40.00

Half board per person:	£min	£max
Daily	23.50	30.00

Evening meal from 1800
Parking for 8
Cards accepted: Diners, Mastercard, Visa
🐴🖥☕🔒[S]🪑[TV]▥⛟Ƭ⚑🚌[OAP][SP]

Metropole Hotel 🏛

👑👑👑 COMMENDED

3 Portland Street, Southport PR8 1LL
☎ (01704) 536836
Fax (01704) 549041
Fully licensed, privately owned family hotel. Centrally located, 50 yards from famous Lord Street shopping boulevard. Close to Royal Birkdale Golf Course.
Bedrooms: 13 single, 3 double, 5 twin, 3 triple
Bathrooms: 21 en-suite, 2 public

Bed & breakfast per night:	£min	£max
Single	30.00	35.00
Double	52.00	60.00

Lunch available
Evening meal 1900 (last orders 2030)
Parking for 12
Cards accepted: Amex, Mastercard, Visa, Switch/Delta
🐴📞📠🖥☕🔒[S]🪑[TV]▥⛟⚑[OAP]🚫🐕[SP][T]

Rosedale Hotel 🏛

👑👑👑 COMMENDED

11 Talbot Street, Southport PR8 1HP
☎ (01704) 530604
Fax (01704) 530604
Well-established, centrally situated private hotel with licensed bar and reading room. All bedrooms have colour TV with satellite link. Weekly rates available.
Bedrooms: 4 single, 2 double, 3 twin, 1 family room
Bathrooms: 7 en-suite, 1 public

Bed & breakfast per night:	£min	£max
Single	19.00	22.00
Double	40.00	44.00

Evening meal 1800 (last orders 1600)
Parking for 8
Cards accepted: Mastercard, Visa, Switch/Delta
🐴🖥☕🔒[S]🪑[TV]▥⛟❀✈[SP][T]

Please mention this guide when making your booking.

SOUTHPORT
Continued

Scarisbrick Hotel ⚑
👑👑👑 COMMENDED

239 Lord Street, Southport
PR8 1NZ
☎ (01704) 543000
Fax (01704) 533335
Ⓡ The Independents
*Prominent town-centre traditional hotel.
A la carte and table d'hote restaurant,
several bars, function rooms and
conference suites.
Wheelchair access category 3*
Bedrooms: 7 single, 40 double,
24 twin, 6 triple
Bathrooms: 77 en-suite

Bed & breakfast per night:

	£min	£max
Single	45.00	70.00
Double	80.00	125.00

Half board per person:

	£min	£max
Daily	57.50	85.00
Weekly	252.00	462.00

Lunch available
Evening meal 1830 (last orders 2130)
Parking for 65
Cards accepted: Amex, Diners, Mastercard, Visa, Switch/Delta

Stutelea Hotel and Leisure Club ⚑
👑👑👑👑 HIGHLY COMMENDED

Alexandra Road, Southport
PR9 0NB
☎ (01704) 544220
Fax (01704) 500232
Email: Stutlea@mail.cybase.co.uk
*Charming, licensed hotel in pleasant
gardens. Heated indoor swimming pool,
sauna, jacuzzi, gymnasium, steam room,
solarium and games room. Convenient
for promenade, marina, golf-courses
and shopping centre. Also self-catering
apartments. Half-board prices shown
are for a minimum 2-night stay.
Bedrooms: 8 double, 9 twin, 3 triple
Bathrooms: 20 en-suite, 4 public

Bed & breakfast per night:

	£min	£max
Single	50.00	60.00
Double	80.00	85.00

Half board per person:

	£min	£max
Daily	47.50	50.00

Lunch available
Evening meal 1900 (last orders 2100)
Parking for 16

Cards accepted: Amex, Diners, Mastercard, Visa, Switch/Delta

STOCKPORT
Greater Manchester
Map ref 4B2

Once an important cotton-spinning and manufacturing centre, Stockport has an impressive railway viaduct, a shopping precinct built over the River Mersey and a new leisure complex. Lyme Hall and Vernon Park Museum nearby.
Tourist Information Centre ☎ (0161) 474 3320 or 474 3321

Pymgate Lodge Hotel ⚑
👑👑 COMMENDED
147 Styal Road, Gatley, Stockport, Cheshire SK8 3TG
☎ (0161) 436 4103
Fax (0161) 499 9171

*Within 1 mile of Manchester Airport.
Every bedroom overlooks garden or
open fields. Decorated and furnished to
a high standard. Licensed a la carte
restaurant. Courtesy tray in each room.
All bedrooms non-smoking.
Bedrooms: 5 twin, 3 triple
Bathrooms: 6 en-suite, 1 public

Bed & breakfast per night:

	£min	£max
Single	38.00	44.50
Double	46.00	50.00

Half board per person:

	£min	£max
Daily	46.50	49.95
Weekly	325.50	395.15

Lunch available
Evening meal 1800 (last orders 2130)
Parking for 14
Cards accepted: Amex, Mastercard, Visa

COLOUR MAPS
Colour maps at the back of this guide pinpoint all places in which you will find accommodation listed.

URMSTON
Greater Manchester
Map ref 4A2

Manor Hey Hotel
👑👑 COMMENDED
130 Stretford Road, Urmston, Manchester M41 9LT
☎ (0161) 748 3896
Fax (0161) 746 7183
*Comfortable and friendly family-run
hotel. Five minutes to Trafford Park, 15
minutes to Manchester Airport.
Bedrooms: 1 double, 10 twin, 1 triple
Bathrooms: 12 en-suite

Bed & breakfast per night:

	£min	£max
Single	30.00	45.00
Double	45.00	60.00

Half board per person:

	£min	£max
Daily	40.45	55.45

Lunch available
Evening meal 1830 (last orders 2030)
Parking for 50
Cards accepted: Mastercard, Visa

WADDINGTON
Lancashire
Map ref 4A1

One of the area's best-known villages, with a stream and public gardens gracing the main street.

The Moorcock Inn ⚑
👑👑 COMMENDED
Slaidburn Road, Waddington, Clitheroe BB7 3AA
☎ (01200) 422333
Fax (01200) 429184

*Friendly, family-run inn with panoramic
views of Ribble Valley. En-suite rooms.
Fresh home-cooked food available in
bar and restaurant. Banqueting
facilities.
Bedrooms: 1 double, 10 twin
Bathrooms: 10 en-suite, 1 private

Bed & breakfast per night:

	£min	£max
Single	35.00	35.00
Double	55.00	55.00

Lunch available

Evening meal 1900 (last orders 2130)
Parking for 250
Cards accepted: Mastercard, Visa
🛏🍴🖃🗔🕯🍷🖱🛋🗗✂🎿🖎💻🅿🛄🛎140 🕕🅿❀🚗🐾SP

WARRINGTON

Cheshire
Map ref 4A2

Has prehistoric and Roman origins. Once the "beer capital of Britain" because so much beer was brewed here. Developed in the 18th and 19th C as a commercial and industrial town. The cast-iron gates in front of the town hall were originally destined for Sandringham. *Tourist Information Centre ☎ (01925) 442180*

The Park Royal International Hotel, Health and Leisure Spa ♙

👑👑👑👑 HIGHLY COMMENDED

Stretton Road, Stretton, Warrington WA4 4NS
☎ (01925) 730706
Fax (01925) 730740
Ⓒ Best Western

Set in the heart of the Cheshire countryside, 2 minutes from junction 10 M56. Special weekend rates available. Newly opened health and leisure spa.
Wheelchair access category 3♿
Bedrooms: 2 single, 73 double, 35 twin, 2 triple, 2 family rooms
Suites available
Bathrooms: 114 en-suite

Bed & breakfast per night:

	£min	£max
Single	60.00	100.45
Double	120.00	248.80

Lunch available
Evening meal 1900 (last orders 2200)
Parking for 400
Cards accepted: Amex, Diners, Mastercard, Visa, Switch/Delta
🛏🍴🛎🖃🗔🕯🍷🖱🅂✂🎿🖎📺◑🖹💻🖵🛋🅿🛎400🎱🏹🛶🎯🐾❀🚬SP T

Rockfield Hotel ♙

👑👑👑 HIGHLY COMMENDED

Alexandra Road, Grappenhall, Warrington WA4 2EL
☎ (01925) 262898
Fax (01925) 263343
Elegant Edwardian house, full of character and tastefully modernised. Swiss family owned. Award-winning restaurant with Swiss and English cuisine. 5 minutes from M6 junction 20, off A50.

Bedrooms: 5 single, 6 double, 1 twin
Bathrooms: 11 en-suite, 1 private

Bed & breakfast per night:

	£min	£max
Single	30.00	51.00
Double	45.00	65.00

Half board per person:

	£min	£max
Daily	38.00	

Lunch available
Evening meal 1900 (last orders 2100)
Parking for 30
Cards accepted: Mastercard, Visa, Switch/Delta
🛏🍴🕯🖃🗔🕯🍷🖱🅂✂🎿🖎📺💻🛋🛎20❀🚗🐾SP T

WIGAN

Greater Manchester
Map ref 4A1

Although a major industrial town, Wigan is an ancient settlement which received a royal charter in 1246. Famous for its pier distinguished in Orwell's "Road to Wigan Pier". The pier has now been developed as a major tourist attraction.
Tourist Information Centre ☎ (01942) 825677

Coaching Inn Hotel ♙

👑👑👑 APPROVED

Warrington Road, Lower Ince, Wigan, Lancashire WN3 4NJ
☎ (01942) 866330
Fax (01942) 749990

Approximately one mile from town centre on good regular bus route. All rooms are en-suite with tea-making facilities, TV and office desks. Secure car park.
Bedrooms: 12 single, 2 double, 3 twin, 1 triple
Bathrooms: 18 en-suite

Bed & breakfast per night:

	£min	£max
Single	22.00	25.00
Double	39.00	43.00

Half board per person:

	£min	£max
Daily	25.00	27.00

Lunch available
Evening meal 1900 (last orders 2130)

Parking for 24
Cards accepted: Mastercard, Visa, Switch/Delta
🛏🗔🕯🍷🖱🅂🖎📺🖵🛋🍴🕯❀🏹🔔T◉

WILLINGTON

Cheshire
Map ref 4B3

Willington Hall Hotel ♙

👑👑👑👑 COMMENDED

Willington, Tarporley CW6 0NB
☎ (01829) 752321
Fax (01829) 752596

Country house hotel set in its own park with good views over surrounding countryside.
Bedrooms: 2 single, 3 double, 5 twin
Bathrooms: 10 en-suite, 1 public

Bed & breakfast per night:

	£min	£max
Single	46.00	56.00
Double	78.00	82.00

Lunch available
Evening meal 1930 (last orders 2130)
Parking for 60
Cards accepted: Amex, Diners, Mastercard, Visa, Switch/Delta
🛏🗔5🕯🖃🗔🕯🍷🖱🅂🖎💻🛋🍴20🍷🕕❀🏹

WILMSLOW

Cheshire
Map ref 4B2

Nestling in the valleys of the Rivers Bollin and Dane, Wilmslow retains an intimate village atmosphere. Easy-to-reach attractions include Quarry Bank Mill at Styal. Lindow Man was discovered on a nearby common. Romany's Caravan sits in a memorial garden.

Belfry Hotel ♙

👑👑👑👑 HIGHLY COMMENDED

Stanley Road, Handforth, Wilmslow SK9 3LD
☎ (0161) 437 0511
Fax (0161) 499 0597
Email: andrew.beech@the-belfry-hotel.co.uk
Ⓒ Utell International
Modern hotel on B5358 (old A34), noted for good food and service.

Continued ▶

WILMSLOW

Continued

Convenient for business in Manchester and Wilmslow area. 10 minutes from Manchester Airport (courtesy transport available with prior notice). Minimum prices shown are weekend rates.
Bedrooms: 25 single, 30 double, 18 twin, 7 triple
Suites available
Bathrooms: 80 en-suite

Bed & breakfast

per night:	£min	£max
Single	40.00	95.00
Double	80.00	110.00

Half board per

person:	£min	£max
Daily	60.00	115.00

Lunch available
Evening meal 1900 (last orders 2200)
Parking for 150
Cards accepted: Amex, Diners, Mastercard, Visa, Switch/Delta

Dean Bank Hotel 𝔐

COMMENDED

Adlington Road, Wilmslow SK9 2BT
☎ (01625) 524268
Fax (01625) 549715
Family-run, countryside hotel in a peaceful setting, ideal for leisure breaks, long or short stay business accommodation and Manchester Airport. Home-cooked evening meals.
Wheelchair access category 1
Bedrooms: 1 single, 5 double, 6 twin, 5 triple
Bathrooms: 17 en-suite

Bed & breakfast

per night:	£min	£max
Single	32.00	37.50
Double	44.00	49.50

Half board per

person:	£min	£max
Daily	40.50	46.00

Evening meal 1730 (last orders 1930)
Parking for 24
Cards accepted: Amex, Mastercard, Visa

Fern Bank Guest House

COMMENDED

188 Wilmslow Road, Handforth, Wilmslow SK9 3JX
☎ (01625) 523729
Fax (01625) 539515
Detached Victorian house, built 1881, standing in its own grounds. Tastefully furnished with antiques, large

south-facing conservatory. Manchester Airport 10 minutes by car. Long-stay car parking next door.
Bedrooms: 2 single, 1 double, 1 twin
Bathrooms: 4 en-suite, 1 public

Bed & breakfast

per night:	£min	£max
Single	30.00	35.00
Double	40.00	45.00

Parking for 6

Hollow Bridge Guest House 𝔐

HIGHLY COMMENDED

90 Manchester Road, Wilmslow SK9 2JY
☎ (01625) 537303
Fax (01625) 528718
Newly refurbished house, en-suite bedrooms, garden room dining, reading room. Homely atmosphere. Manchester Airport and motorway 10 minutes away, 5 minutes from Wilmslow centre.
Bedrooms: 2 single, 1 double, 1 twin
Bathrooms: 4 en-suite

Bed & breakfast

per night:	£min	£max
Single	35.00	35.00
Double	40.00	40.00

Parking for 7
Cards accepted: Mastercard, Visa

Lisieux

HIGHLY COMMENDED

199 Wilmslow Road, Handforth, Wilmslow SK9 3JX
☎ (01625) 522113
Fax (01625) 526313
Deceptively large, homely bungalow with high standard of accommodation. Extensive breakfast menu available early morning. 3 miles from Manchester Airport.
Bedrooms: 1 single, 1 double, 1 twin
Bathrooms: 2 en-suite, 1 private, 1 public

Bed & breakfast

per night:	£min	£max
Single	27.00	29.00
Double	37.00	41.00

Half board per

person:	£min	£max
Daily	42.00	44.00
Weekly	280.00	294.00

Evening meal 1800 (last orders 1900)
Parking for 5

Rylands Farm Guest House 𝔐

COMMENDED

Altrincham Road, Wilmslow SK9 4LT
☎ (01625) 535646 & 548041
Fax (01625) 535646
Family-run guesthouse with many exposed beams, colour co-ordinated en-suite rooms, secure parking. Free travel to airport. Only 7 minutes from junction 6, M56.
Bedrooms: 4 double, 2 twin
Bathrooms: 6 en-suite

Bed & breakfast

per night:	£min	£max
Single	33.00	33.00
Double	39.50	39.50

Evening meal 1745 (last orders 1745)
Parking for 18
Cards accepted: Mastercard, Visa

Stanneylands Hotel 𝔐

HIGHLY COMMENDED

Stanneylands Road, Wilmslow SK9 4EY
☎ (01625) 525225
Fax (01625) 537282
Email: gordonbeech
@thestanneylandshotel.co.uk
Utell International
The ideal blend of comfort and facilities makes Stanneylands a perfect setting for business meetings or entertaining in the exclusive restaurant.
Bedrooms: 7 single, 11 double, 14 twin
Suites available
Bathrooms: 32 en-suite

Bed & breakfast

per night:	£min	£max
Single	55.00	130.00
Double	100.00	150.00

Lunch available
Evening meal 1900 (last orders 2200)
Parking for 80
Cards accepted: Amex, Diners, Mastercard, Visa, Switch/Delta

WIRRAL

Merseyside

See under Birkenhead, Hoylake, Moreton, New Brighton, Parkgate

Yorkshire

The wide open spaces of Yorkshire and North East Lincolnshire promise a stunning variety of holiday experiences. The breathtaking landscape offers everything from the serenity of the Wolds and the Dales, to picturesque Herriot country, Brontë country, and the dramatic North Yorkshire moors.

Ancient York is a fine touring base and has fascinating Roman and Viking remains. There are pretty coastal spots, too, including the family resort of Cleethorpes, and the colourful port of Whitby at the heart of Captain Cook country.

There's excellent shopping and night life in the region's big towns, while Grimsby has the National Fishing Heritage Centre and hosts an annual seafood festival.

The counties of East Riding of Yorkshire, North East Lincolnshire, North Lincolnshire, North Yorkshire, South Yorkshire and West Yorkshire

FOR MORE INFORMATION CONTACT:
Yorkshire Tourist Board
312 Tadcaster Road, York YO2 2HF
Tel: (01904) 707961 or 707070 (24 hour brochure line)
Fax: (01904) 701414

Where to Go in Yorkshire –see pages 150-153
Where to Stay in Yorkshire –see pages 154-207

YORKSHIRE

Where to Go and What to See

You will find hundreds of interesting places to visit during your stay in Yorkshire, just some of which are listed in these pages. The number against each name will help you locate it on the map (page 153). Contact any Tourist Information Centre in the region for more ideas on days out in Yorkshire.

1 Music in Miniature Exhibition
Albion Road,
Robin Hood's Bay, Whitby,
North Yorkshire YO22 4SH
Tel: (01947) 880512
Exhibition of 50 one-twelfth scale dioramic models set in illuminated recesses - depicting man's love of music from stone age to space age.

2 The Honey Farm
Racecourse Road,
East Ayton, Scarborough,
North Yorkshire YO13 9HT
Tel: (01723) 864001
Working honey farm with an extensive exhibition of live honey bees. Guided tour with a description of the life and history of bees. Farm shop. Cafe.

3 Scarborough Millennium
Harbourside, Scarborough,
North Yorkshire YO11 1PG
Tel: (01723) 501000
A time travel experience unlike any other. An epic adventure through 1,000 years from 966 to 1966.

4 North Yorkshire Moors Railway
Pickering Station, Pickering,
North Yorkshire YO18 7AJ
Tel: (01751) 472508
Operates the route between Grosmont and Pickering, through some of the most magnificent scenery of the North York Moors National Park.

5 Castle Howard
Coneysthorpe,
York YO6 7DA
Tel: (01653) 648444
Set in 1,000 acres of magnificent parkland with nature walks, scenic lake and stunning rose gardens. Attractions include important furniture and works of art.

6 Island Heritage Pott Hall Farm
Healey, Ripon,
North Yorkshire HG4 4LT
Tel: (01765) 689651
A working dales farm producing natural, undyed woollen products from its own flock of rare breed, primitive sheep. See lambing, shearing, spinning. Shop.

7 Fountains Abbey and Studley Royal
Ripon,
North Yorkshire HG4 3DY
Tel: (01765) 608888
Largest monastic ruin in Britain, founded by Cistercian monks in 1132. Landscape garden laid out 1720-40 with lake, formal watergarden and temples. Deer park.

8 **White Scar Caves**
Ingleton, Carnforth,
Lancashire LA6 3AW
Tel: (01524) 241244
Britain's longest show cave,
underground waterfalls and
streams, massive ice-age cavern,
floodlighting.

9 **Yorkshire Dales Falconry**
and Conservation Centre
Crows Nest,
Giggleswick, Settle,
North Yorkshire LA2 8AS
Tel: (01729) 825164/822832
Falconry centre with many species
of birds of prey from around the
world including vultures, eagles,
hawks, falcons and owls. Free flying
displays, lecture room and aviaries.

10 **Skipton Castle**
Skipton,
North Yorkshire BD23 1AQ
Tel: (01756) 792442
One of the most complete and well-
preserved medieval castles in
England. Explore massive round
towers and see beautiful Conduit
Court with its famous yew.

11 **Jorvik Viking Centre**
Coppergate,
York YO1 1NT
Tel: (01904) 643211/613711
Travel back in time in a timecar to
a recreation of Viking York. See
excavated remains of Viking houses
and a display of objects found.

12 **National Railway Museum**
Leeman Road,
York YO2 4XJ
Tel: (01904) 621261
Experience nearly 200 years of
technical and social history on
the railways and see how
they shaped the world.

13 **York Castle Museum**
The Eye of York,
York YO1 1RY
Tel: (01904) 653611
England's most popular museum of
everyday life including reconstructed
streets and period rooms,
Edwardian park, costume and
jewellery, arms and armour, craft
workshops.

14 **Harewood House**
Harewood, Leeds LS17 9LQ
Tel: (0113) 288 6331
18thC Carr/Adam house, Capability
Brown landscape, fine Sevres and
Chinese porcelain, English and
Italian paintings, Chippendale
furniture. Exotic bird garden.

15 **National Museum of**
Photography, Film & Television
Pictureville, Bradford,
West Yorkshire BD1 1NQ
Tel: (01274) 727488
Museum housing the largest cinema
screen (Imax) in Britain, 64 x 52 ft.
Fly on a magic carpet, operate a TV
camera, or become a newsreader
for a day.

16 **Transperience**
Transperience Way,
Low Moor, Bradford,
West Yorkshire
BD12 7HQ
Tel: (01274) 690909
With historic vehicle rides
and state of the art

interactive technology, travel on a
unique journey through the past,
present and future of transport.

17 **Royal Armouries Museum**
Leeds LS10 1LT
Tel: (0113) 220 1900
See the thrill of jousting
tournaments and the terror of the
battlefield recaptured. The museum
includes one of the world's finest
collections of arms and armour.

18 **Tetley's Brewery Wharf**
The Waterfront, Leeds LS1 1QG
Tel: (0113) 242 0666/243 1888
A unique development which brings
to life the story through the ages of
probably the greatest British
traditions - the pub.

19 Hull & East Riding Museum
33 High Street, Hull
Tel: (01482) 613902/613925
The museum explores the story of Hull and the East Riding area, covering geology and archaeology. Also features the Hasholme Boat - over 3,000 years old.

20 National Fishing Heritage Centre
Alexandra Dock,
Grimsby,
North East Lincolnshire
DN31 1UZ
Tel: (01472) 323345
Spectacular 1950s steam trawler experience. See, hear, smell and touch a series of recreated environments. Museum displays, shop, aquarium and historic fishing vessels.

21 Cleethorpes Coast Light Railway
Kingsway Station, Cleethorpes,
North East Lincolnshire
DN35 0AG
Tel: (01472) 604657/602118
A delightful scenic railway journey from Kingsway Station with panoramic views of the Humber Estuary.

22 Pleasure Island Family Theme Park
Kings Road, Cleethorpes,
North East Lincolnshire
DN35 0PL
Tel: (01472) 211511
The East coast's biggest fun day out, with over 50 rides and attractions, many undercover. Shows from around the world.

23 Barnsley Metrodome Leisure Complex
Queens Road, Barnsley,
South Yorkshire S71 1AN
Tel: (01226) 730060
One of the North's largest leisure facilities with five pools, dry sports and leisure complex.

24 Yorkshire Sculpture Park
West Bretton, Wakefield,
West Yorkshire WF4 4LG
Tel: (01924) 830302
International open-air gallery with changing exhibitions of contemporary sculpture, set in 260 acres of beautiful 18thC landscaped grounds.

25 Eureka! The Museum for Children
Discovery Road, Halifax,
West Yorkshire HX1 2NE
Tel: (01422) 330069/
(01426) 983191
First museum of its kind designed especially for children up to the age of 12. There are over 400 hands-on exhibits to touch, listen to, feel and smell as well as look.

26 Kirklees Light Railway
Railway Station,
Park Mill Way, Clayton,
West Huddersfield HD8 9XJ
Tel: (01484) 865727
A 15-inch gauge steam railway with original Lancashire and Yorkshire station. Steam and diesel locomotives and enclosed carriages. Shop and cafe. Children's play area.

27 National Coal Mining Museum for England
Caphouse Collier, New Road,
Overton, Wakefield,
West Yorkshire WF4 4RH
Tel: (01924) 848806
Award-winning museum of the English coalfields, including guided underground tour in authentic old workings, surface displays, working steam winder.

28 Heeley City Farm
Richards Road,
Sheffield S2 3DT
Tel: (0114) 258 0482
Four-acre farm with horses, cows, goats, pigs, sheep, ducks, chickens, turkeys, bees, rabbits, herb gardens, organic gardens, wild flowers. Cafe. Garden centre.

29 Rother Valley Country Park
Mansfield Road, Wales Bar,
Sheffield S31 8PE
Tel: (0114) 247 1452
Watersports centre, visitor and craft centres, nature reserve, special events, shop, cafe and walks.

FIND OUT MORE

Further information about holidays and attractions in the Yorkshire region is available from **Yorkshire Tourist Board,** 312 Tadcaster Road, York YO2 2HF. Tel: (01904) 707961 or 707070 (24 hour brochure line) These publications are available free from the Yorkshire Tourist Board:

■ **Yorkshire Holidays and Short Breaks** - information on the region, including hotels, self-catering, caravan and camping parks

■ **Yorkshire - a Great Day Out** - the official guide of what to do, where to go, what to see, where to eat and how to get there, the list goes on!

■ **Bed & Breakfast Touring Map** - forming part of a 'family' of maps covering England, this guide provides information on bed and breakfast establishments in the Yorkshire region

■ **What's on** - listing of events. Published three times a year

WHERE TO STAY (YORKSHIRE)

Accommodation entries in this region are listed in alphabetical order of place name, and then in alphabetical order of establishment.

Map references refer to the colour location maps at the back of this guide.

The first number indicates the map to use; the letter and number which follow refer to the grid reference on the map.

At-a-glance symbols at the end of each accommodation entry give useful information about services and facilities. A key to symbols can be found inside the back cover flap.

Keep this open for easy reference.

APPLETON-LE-MOORS

North Yorkshire
Map ref 5C3

A charming, unspoilt village in the North York Moors National Park. 23 miles inland from Scarborough and 33 miles north of York, it is an excellent centre for the coast, Herriot country, the North Yorkshire Moors Railway and many delightful walks and places of historic interest.

Appleton Hall Country House Hotel ⋒

HIGHLY COMMENDED

Appleton-le-Moors, York YO6 6TF
☎ (01751) 417227 & 417452
Fax (01751) 417540

Victorian country house set in 2 acres of mature lawns and award-winning gardens. A hideaway place offering elegance, comfort and tranquillity.
Bedrooms: 2 single, 5 double, 2 twin
Suites available
Bathrooms: 9 en-suite
Bed & breakfast

per night:	£min	£max
Single	40.00	55.00
Double	80.00	110.00

Half board per

person:	£min	£max
Daily	55.00	70.00
Weekly	340.00	385.00

Lunch available

Evening meal 1830 (last orders 2030)
Parking for 20
Cards accepted: Amex, Mastercard, Visa, Switch/Delta

ARDSLEY

South Yorkshire
Map ref 4B1

Ardsley House Hotel ⋒

HIGHLY COMMENDED

Doncaster Road, Ardsley, Barnsley S71 5EH
☎ (01226) 309955
Fax (01226) 205374
Ⓖ Best Western
18th C manor house, tastefully converted to a private hotel. Extensive conference and banqueting facilities. French and English cooking.
Bedrooms: 17 single, 22 double, 23 twin, 11 triple
Bathrooms: 73 en-suite
Bed & breakfast

per night:	£min	£max
Single	35.00	75.00
Double	70.00	100.00

Half board per

person:	£min	£max
Daily	48.00	93.50

Lunch available
Evening meal 1900 (last orders 2230)
Parking for 250
Cards accepted: Amex, Diners, Mastercard, Visa, Switch/Delta

ARKENGARTHDALE

North Yorkshire
Map ref 5B3

Picturesque Yorkshire dale, once an important and prosperous lead-mining valley developed by Charles Bathurst in the 18th C.

The White House ⋒

COMMENDED

Arkle Town, Arkengarthdale, Richmond DL11 6RB
☎ (01748) 884203
Fax (01748) 884088
Family-run guesthouse with panoramic views of this secluded dale. Close to Richmond and Barnard Castle and 3 miles from Reeth in Swaledale. An ideal touring and walking centre. Reduced rates for two or more nights.
Bedrooms: 2 double, 1 twin
Bathrooms: 2 en-suite, 1 public
Bed & breakfast

per night:	£min	£max
Double	37.00	39.00

Half board per

person:	£min	£max
Daily	29.50	30.50
Weekly	192.00	198.50

Evening meal 1830 (last orders 1200)
Parking for 5
Open March–November
Cards accepted: Mastercard, Visa

A key to symbols can be found inside the back cover flap.

ASKRIGG

North Yorkshire
Map ref 5B3

The name of this dales village means "ash tree ridge". It is centred on a steep main street of high, narrow 3-storey houses and thrived on cotton and later wool in 18th C. Once famous for its clock making.

Kings Arms Hotel and Clubroom Restaurant

♕♕♕ COMMENDED

Askrigg, Leyburn DL8 3HQ
☎ (01969) 650258
Fax (01969) 650635
Email: rayliz
@jagaskrigg.prestel.co.uk.
Logis of GB
Yorkshire Life "Hotel of the Year" and Herriot pub. Famous for comfort, atmosphere, good food, fine wine, real ales. Central for dales, moors and Lakes.
Bedrooms: 10 double, 1 twin
Bathrooms: 11 en-suite

Bed & breakfast
per night:	£min	£max
Single	50.00	75.00
Double	79.00	120.00

Half board per
person:	£min	£max
Daily	59.50	80.00

Lunch available
Evening meal 1830 (last orders 2100)
Parking for 15
Cards accepted: Amex, Mastercard, Visa, Switch/Delta

Winville Hotel & Restaurant

♕♕♕ APPROVED

Main Street, Askrigg, Leyburn DL8 3HG
☎ (01969) 650515
Fax (01969) 650594
Logis of GB

19th C Georgian residence in the centre of Herriot village. Some rooms have views of the dales. Conservatory, private gardens.
Bedrooms: 4 double, 2 twin, 4 triple
Bathrooms: 10 en-suite

Bed & breakfast
per night:	£min	£max
Single	32.00	36.00
Double	44.00	52.00

Half board per
person:	£min	£max
Daily	37.50	45.50
Weekly	240.00	260.00

Lunch available
Evening meal 1900 (last orders 2130)
Parking for 18
Cards accepted: Diners, Mastercard, Visa

AUSTWICK

North Yorkshire
Map ref 5B3

Picturesque dales village with pleasant cottages, a green, an old cross and an Elizabethan Hall.

The Traddock

♕♕♕ COMMENDED

Austwick, Settle LA2 8BY
☎ (015242) 51224
Fax (015242) 51224
A well-known Yorkshire gem. This Georgian country house hotel is situated in the walkers' paradise of the Yorkshire Dales. Emphasis on comfort, good food and wines.
Bedrooms: 1 single, 4 double, 3 twin, 2 triple, 1 family room
Bathrooms: 11 en-suite, 1 public

Bed & breakfast
per night:	£min	£max
Single	40.00	
Double	70.00	

Half board per
person:	£min	£max
Daily	55.00	
Weekly	300.00	

Lunch available
Evening meal 1900 (last orders 2030)
Parking for 22
Cards accepted: Mastercard, Visa

Woodview Guest House

The Green, Austwick, Lancaster LA2 8BB
☎ (015242) 51268
One of the oldest (c 1700) farmhouses in Austwick, an elegant Grade II listed building on The Green. All rooms en-suite. Packed lunch available.
Bedrooms: 2 double, 1 twin, 3 triple
Bathrooms: 6 en-suite

Bed & breakfast
per night:	£min	£max
Single	35.00	40.00
Double	44.00	48.00

Half board per
person:	£min	£max
Daily	34.50	34.50
Weekly	225.00	225.00

Evening meal 1800 (last orders 1930)
Parking for 6

BAINBRIDGE

North Yorkshire
Map ref 5B3

This Wensleydale grey-stone village, with fine views of the River Bain, reputedly England's shortest river, was once a Roman settlement, some of it still visible. Boating and water-skiing on nearby Semerwater. Ancient foresters' custom of hornblowing still continues.

Riverdale House Country Hotel

♕♕♕ COMMENDED

Bainbridge, Leyburn DL8 3EW
☎ (01969) 650311 & 663381
Tastefully-appointed, comfortable house, with special emphasis on food. In the centre of a lovely village in Upper Wensleydale, the area used for the filming of the James Herriot stories.
Bedrooms: 6 double, 4 twin, 2 triple
Bathrooms: 10 en-suite, 1 private, 1 public

Bed & breakfast
per night:	£min	£max
Double	52.00	

Lunch available
Evening meal 1930 (last orders 2030)
Parking for 4
Open March–October

BEDALE

North Yorkshire
Map ref 5C3

Ancient church of St Gregory and Georgian Bedale Hall occupy commanding positions over this market town situated in good hunting country. The hall, which contains interesting architectural features including great ballroom and flying-type staircase, now houses a library and museum.

Elmfield House
👑 👑 👑 COMMENDED

Arrathorne, Bedale DL8 1NE
☎ (01677) 450558
Fax (01677) 450557
Country house in own grounds with special emphasis on standards and home cooking. All rooms en-suite. Bar, games room, solarium. Ample secure parking.
Bedrooms: 4 double, 3 twin, 2 triple
Bathrooms: 9 en-suite

Bed & breakfast per night:

	£min	£max
Single	29.50	31.50
Double	42.00	48.00

Half board per person:

	£min	£max
Daily	32.50	35.50
Weekly	227.00	248.00

Evening meal from 1830
Parking for 10
Cards accepted: Mastercard, Visa

BEVERLEY

East Riding of Yorkshire
Map ref 4C1

Beverley's most famous landmark is its beautiful medieval Minster with Percy family tomb. Many attractive squares and streets, notably Wednesday and Saturday Market and North Bar Gateway. Famous racecourse.
Tourist Information Centre ☎ (01482) 867430

Eastgate Guest House M
👑 COMMENDED

7 Eastgate, Beverley, East Riding of Yorkshire HU17 0DR
☎ (01482) 868464
Fax (01482) 871899
Family-run Victorian guesthouse, established and run by the same proprietor for 29 years. Close to the town centre, Beverley Minster, Museum of Army Transport and railway station.

Bedrooms: 6 single, 3 double, 3 twin, 3 triple, 3 family rooms
Bathrooms: 7 en-suite, 3 public

Bed & breakfast per night:

	£min	£max
Single	19.50	30.00
Double	32.00	44.00

Tickton Grange Hotel & Restaurant M
👑 👑 👑 👑 COMMENDED

Tickton Grange, Tickton, Beverley, East Riding of Yorkshire HU17 9SH
☎ (01964) 543666
Fax (01964) 542556
Ⓒ Logis of GB
Family-run Georgian country house set in rose gardens, 2 miles from historic Beverley. Country house cooking.
Bedrooms: 3 single, 10 double, 3 twin, 1 triple
Bathrooms: 17 en-suite

Bed & breakfast per night:

	£min	£max
Single	50.00	60.00
Double	67.50	77.50

Lunch available
Evening meal 1900 (last orders 2130)
Parking for 65
Cards accepted: Amex, Diners, Mastercard, Visa, Switch/Delta

BINGLEY

West Yorkshire
Map ref 4B1

Bingley Five-Rise is an impressive group of locks on the Leeds and Liverpool Canal. Town claims to have first bred the Airedale terrier originally used for otter hunting. Among fine Georgian houses is Myrtle Grove where John Wesley stayed. East Riddlesden Hall is nearby.

Five Rise Locks Hotel M
👑 👑 👑 HIGHLY COMMENDED

Beck Lane, Bingley BD16 4DD
☎ (01274) 565296
Fax (01274) 568828
Delightful Victorian mill owner's house set in its own grounds, with excellent views and terraced gardens. Relaxed atmosphere complemented by interesting menus and wine list.
Bedrooms: 7 double, 2 twin
Bathrooms: 9 en-suite

Bed & breakfast per night:

	£min	£max
Single	32.50	46.00
Double	46.00	55.00

Half board per person:

	£min	£max
Daily	35.50	58.50

Evening meal 1930 (last orders 2100)
Parking for 15
Cards accepted: Mastercard, Visa, Switch/Delta

Oakwood Hall Hotel M
👑 👑 👑 COMMENDED

Lady Lane, Bingley BD16 4AW
☎ (01274) 564123 & 563569
Fax (01274) 561477
Impressive listed building in quiet woodland. Individually designed bedrooms, some with four-poster beds. 4 ground floor bedrooms. Relaxed place to visit, serving fine food.
Bedrooms: 1 single, 15 double, 4 twin
Bathrooms: 20 en-suite

Bed & breakfast per night:

	£min	£max
Single	55.00	65.00
Double	80.00	90.00

Lunch available
Evening meal 1900 (last orders 2200)
Parking for 120
Cards accepted: Amex, Diners, Mastercard, Visa, Switch/Delta

BOLTON ABBEY

North Yorkshire
Map ref 4B1

This hamlet is best known for its priory situated near a bend in the River Wharfe. It was founded in 1151 by Alicia de Romilly and before that was site of Anglo-Saxon manor. Popular with painters, amongst them Landseer.

Devonshire Arms Country House Hotel M
👑 👑 👑 👑 👑 DE LUXE

Bolton Abbey, Skipton BD23 6AJ
☎ (01756) 710441
Fax (01756) 710564
Traditional country house hotel in Yorkshire Dales. Open fires, lounges furnished with antiques from Chatsworth. Leisure, health and beauty therapy club. Winner of silver award for "Hotel of the Year" in England for Excellence 1993.

Wheelchair access category 3
Bedrooms: 22 double, 19 twin
Suite available
Bathrooms: 41 en-suite

Bed & breakfast

per night:	£min	£max
Single	115.00	130.00
Double	160.00	260.00

Lunch available
Evening meal 1900 (last orders 2145)
Parking for 150
Cards accepted: Amex, Diners, Mastercard, Visa, Switch/Delta

BOROUGHBRIDGE

North Yorkshire
Map ref 5C3

On the River Ure, Boroughbridge was once an important coaching centre with 22 inns and in the 18th C a port for Knaresborough's linens. It has fine old houses, many trees and a cobbled square with market cross. Nearby stand 3 megaliths known as the Devil's Arrows.

Crown Hotel

COMMENDED

Horsefair, Boroughbridge, York Y05 9LB
☎ (01423) 322328
Fax (01423) 324512
The Independents/Consort
Fully-modernised 12th C coaching inn, 1 mile from A1. Ideal base for Yorkshire Dales, Herriot country, York and Harrogate. Good restaurant.
Bedrooms: 5 single, 14 double, 22 twin, 1 triple
Bathrooms: 42 en-suite

Bed & breakfast

per night:	£min	£max
Single	52.50	
Double	73.50	

Half board per

person:	£min	£max
Daily	68.25	

Lunch available
Evening meal 1900 (last orders 2130)
Parking for 60
Cards accepted: Amex, Diners, Mastercard, Visa

You are advised to confirm your booking in writing.

BRADFORD

West Yorkshire
Map ref 4B1

City founded on wool, with fine Victorian and modern buildings. Attractions include the cathedral, city hall, Cartwright Hall, Lister Park, Moorside Mills Industrial Museum and National Museum of Photography, Film and Television. *Tourist Information Centre* ☎ (01274) 753678

Cedar Court Hotel Bradford

HIGHLY COMMENDED

Mayo Avenue (top of the M606), Off Rooley Lane, Bradford BD5 8HZ
☎ (01274) 406606
Fax (01274) 406600

First purpose-built hotel in Bradford for 20 years. Situated at the top of the M606. The ideal location. Prices are for Friday or Saturday night.
Bedrooms: 86 double, 33 twin, 7 triple
Suites available
Bathrooms: 126 en-suite

Bed & breakfast

per night:	£min	£max
Single	35.00	60.00
Double	50.00	70.00

Half board per

person:	£min	£max
Daily	42.50	57.50

Lunch available
Evening meal 1800 (last orders 2200)
Parking for 320
Cards accepted: Amex, Diners, Mastercard, Visa, Switch/Delta

Please check prices and other details at the time of booking.

For ideas on places to visit refer to the introduction at the beginning of this section.

Ivy Guest House

Listed APPROVED

3 Melbourne Place, Bradford BD5 0HZ
☎ (01274) 727060 & (0421) 509207
Fax (01274) 306347
Email: 101524-3725 @compuserve.com
Large, detached, listed house built of Yorkshire stone. Car park and gardens. Close to city centre, National Museum of Photography, Film and Television and Alhambra Theatre.
Bedrooms: 3 single, 2 double, 4 twin, 1 triple
Bathrooms: 3 public

Bed & breakfast

per night:	£min	£max
Single	18.00	18.00
Double	30.00	30.00

Lunch available
Evening meal 1800 (last orders 2000)
Parking for 15
Cards accepted: Amex, Diners, Mastercard, Visa, Switch/Delta

New Beehive Inn

APPROVED

171 Westgate, Bradford BD1 3AA
☎ (01274) 721784
Edwardian gaslit oak-panelled inn, full of character, close to centre of Bradford. Antique furniture and individually furnished bedrooms.
Bedrooms: 1 single, 4 double, 2 twin, 1 triple
Bathrooms: 8 en-suite, 2 public

Bed & breakfast

per night:	£min	£max
Single	27.00	
Double	42.00	

Half board per

person:	£min	£max
Daily	37.00	

Lunch available
Evening meal 1900 (last orders 1900)
Parking for 22
Cards accepted: Visa

The symbols in each entry give information about services and facilities. A key to these symbols appears at the back of this guide.

BRADFORD

Continued

Novotel Bradford

👑👑👑👑 APPROVED

Adjacent M606, Merrydale Road,
Bradford BD4 6SA
☎ (01274) 683683
Fax (01274) 651342
CR Novotel

*10 minutes' drive from Bradford city
and 2 minutes from the M62, with
easy access to Leeds/Bradford Airport.
B&B prices below are for room only.*
Wheelchair access category 3
Bedrooms: 58 double, 58 twin,
11 triple
Suite available
Bathrooms: 127 en-suite

Bed & breakfast

per night:	£min	£max
Single	53.00	57.00
Double	53.00	57.00

Half board per

person:	£min	£max
Daily	70.00	75.00

Lunch available
Evening meal 1800 (last orders
2359)
Parking for 200
Cards accepted: Amex, Diners,
Mastercard, Visa, Switch/Delta

🐾🧺📞🖥⛳♿☎⬛🔊✂📺🕐📶
📖🚗🛏♨250 ⚲🔍❄ DAP ⬧ SP

Park Drive Hotel Ⓜ

👑👑👑 COMMENDED

12 Park Drive, Heaton, Bradford
BD9 4DR
☎ (01274) 480194
Fax (01274) 484869
CR The Independents

*"It's like staying in the country!" This
elegant Victorian residence in delightful
woodland setting is just 1.5 miles from
the city centre and has parking inside
the grounds.*
Bedrooms: 5 single, 3 double, 2 twin,
1 triple
Bathrooms: 11 en-suite

Bed & breakfast

per night:	£min	£max
Single	30.00	47.00
Double	48.00	57.00

Half board per

person:	£min	£max
Daily	36.00	59.00

Evening meal 1900 (last orders
2030)
Parking for 9
Cards accepted: Amex, Mastercard,
Visa

🐾🧺📞🖥♿☎⬛🔊✂🕐📺🛏🚗♨16
❄🚗 DAP SP ⌂ T

Park Grove Hotel and Restaurant

👑👑👑 COMMENDED

Park Grove, Frizinghall, Bradford
BD9 4JY
☎ (01274) 543444
Fax (01274) 495619
CR Minotel

*Victorian establishment in a secluded
preserved area of Bradford, 1.5 miles
from the city centre. Gateway to the
dales.*
Bedrooms: 6 single, 5 double, 1 twin,
2 triple
Bathrooms: 14 en-suite

Bed & breakfast

per night:	£min	£max
Single	35.00	46.00
Double	45.00	58.00

Half board per

person:	£min	£max
Daily	35.00	45.00

Evening meal 1800 (last orders
2330)
Parking for 8
Cards accepted: Amex, Diners,
Mastercard, Visa, Switch/Delta

🐾4🧺📞🖥♿☎⬛🔊✂📺🛏🚗
🕐❄✗ DAP ⬧ SP T

Pennington Midland Hotel Ⓜ

👑👑👑 COMMENDED

Forster Square, Bradford BD1 4HU
☎ (01274) 735735 & 0836 261557
Fax (01274) 720003
Email: Sales
@penningtonmidland.co.uk

*Totally refurbished owner-managed
Victorian city centre hotel. Free secure
parking, adjacent Intercity station and
direct motorway link. Spacious rooms,
ornate plasterwork, glittering
chandeliers and two of the finest
ballrooms in Yorkshire make the venue
way ahead of the rest. All-day
restaurant, 24-hour room service,
friendly staff.*
www.penningtonmidland.co.uk
Bedrooms: 20 single, 56 double,
15 twin
Bathrooms: 91 en-suite

Bed & breakfast

per night:	£min	£max
Single	35.00	59.00
Double	49.00	69.00

Lunch available
Evening meal 1100 (last orders
2300)
Parking for 70
Cards accepted: Amex, Diners,
Mastercard, Visa, Switch/Delta

🐾🧺📞📧🖥♿☎⬛🔊✂📺🕐⬧
📖🍽🚗♨400 ⚲⋃🔍⬧ SP ⌂ T

BRANDESBURTON

East Riding of Yorkshire
Map ref 4D1

The village church retains work
from the Norman period through to
the 15th C, and the shaft of a
medieval cross stands on the village
green.

Burton Lodge Hotel Ⓜ

👑👑👑 HIGHLY COMMENDED

Brandesburton, Driffield, East
Yorkshire YO25 8RU
☎ (01964) 542847
Fax (01964) 542847
CR Logis of GB

*Charming country hotel situated in own
grounds adjoining 18-hole parkland
golf-course. 7 miles from Beverley on
A165.*
Bedrooms: 2 single, 2 double, 3 twin,
1 triple, 1 family room
Bathrooms: 9 en-suite

Bed & breakfast

per night:	£min	£max
Single	32.00	36.00
Double	42.00	48.00

Half board per

person:	£min	£max
Daily	34.50	37.00

Evening meal 1900 (last orders
2100)
Parking for 15
Cards accepted: Amex, Mastercard,
Visa, Switch/Delta

🐾🧺📞🖥♿☎⬛🔊✂📺🛏
🚗🔍⋃❄🚗 SP

For further information on
accommodation establishments
use the coupons at the
back of this guide.

BRIDLINGTON

East Riding of Yorkshire
Map ref 5D3

Lively seaside resort with long sandy beaches, Leisure World and busy harbour with fishing trips in cobles. Priory church of St Mary whose Bayle Gate is now a museum. Mementoes of flying pioneer, Amy Johnson, in Sewerby Hall. Harbour Museum and Aquarium.
Tourist Information Centre ☎ (01262) 673474

Bay Court Hotel ⚠

⚜⚜ COMMENDED

35a Sands Lane, Bridlington, East Riding of Yorkshire YO15 2JG
☎ (01262) 676288 & (0589) 380295 (Mobile)
Small, high quality licensed hotel, 50 yards from beach, offering tasteful accommodation and a friendly welcome. Lounge with open fires, south-facing sun patio that provides a haven in which to relax and enjoy sea views. Convenient for cliff walks, moors, Wolds villages, stately homes and beaches/coves.
Bedrooms: 2 single, 3 double, 2 twin
Bathrooms: 2 en-suite, 1 public

Bed & breakfast per night:

	£min	£max
Single	19.00	19.00
Double	38.00	50.00

Half board per person:

	£min	£max
Daily	26.00	32.00

Lunch available
Evening meal 1830 (last orders 1930)
Parking for 7
Cards accepted: Mastercard, Visa

🛏🐶🔥📺💷🍽♨🚫📺💻🖤🅿♨🏊15
🔗🅿❄📠♨ SP

Bay Ridge Hotel ⚠

⚜⚜⚜ COMMENDED

11 Summerfield Road, Bridlington, East Riding of Yorkshire YO15 3LF
☎ (01262) 673425
Friendly, comfortable and caring family-run hotel near the South Beach and Spa Complex. Good value for money, all mod cons.
Bedrooms: 2 single, 6 double, 2 twin, 4 triple
Bathrooms: 12 en-suite, 2 private, 1 public

Bed & breakfast per night:

	£min	£max
Single	19.50	21.00
Double	39.00	42.00

Half board per person:

	£min	£max
Daily	25.50	26.50
Weekly	150.00	160.00

Lunch available
Evening meal 1745 (last orders 1815)
Parking for 7
Cards accepted: Mastercard, Visa

🛏🐶🔥💷🍽♨📺💻🖤🅿♨🔍
🔗🅿📠♨ SP 🅣

Expanse Hotel ⚠

⚜⚜⚜ COMMENDED

North Marine Drive, Bridlington, East Riding of Yorkshire YO15 2LS
☎ (01262) 675347
Fax (01262) 604928

In a unique position overlooking the beach and sea, with panoramic views of the bay and Heritage Coast.
Bedrooms: 13 single, 11 double, 20 twin, 4 triple
Bathrooms: 48 en-suite

Bed & breakfast per night:

	£min	£max
Single	29.50	48.00
Double	45.00	75.00

Half board per person:

	£min	£max
Weekly	210.00	290.00

Lunch available
Evening meal 1830 (last orders 2100)
Parking for 30
Cards accepted: Amex, Diners, Mastercard, Visa, Switch/Delta

🛏🐶🔥☎💷🍽💷🖤🅿♨
♨40🅿✈🚫 SP 🅣

Rags Restaurant & Dyl's Hotel ⚠

⚜⚜⚜ COMMENDED

South Pier, Southcliff Road, Bridlington, East Yorkshire YO15 3AN
☎ (01262) 400355 & 674791
En-suite rooms with corner baths, 3 rooms with harbour view. Restaurant with sea views and bistro bar.
Bedrooms: 3 double, 3 twin
Bathrooms: 6 en-suite

Bed & breakfast per night:

	£min	£max
Single	25.00	40.00
Double	40.00	100.00

Lunch available
Evening meal 1800 (last orders 2230)

Parking for 15
Cards accepted: Diners, Mastercard, Visa, Switch/Delta

🐶📞🔥♨🅿💷🖤🍽60🅿✈
📠 DAP SP 🏢

The Tennyson Hotel

⚜⚜ HIGHLY COMMENDED

19 Tennyson Avenue, Bridlington, North Humberside YO15 2EU
☎ (01262) 604382
Fax (01262) 604382
Fine cuisine in attractive surroundings, close to sea and Leisure World. Complimentary newspaper and toiletries.
Bedrooms: 3 double, 3 twin
Bathrooms: 4 en-suite, 1 private, 2 public

Bed & breakfast per night:

	£min	£max
Single	20.00	24.95
Double	32.00	40.00

Lunch available
Evening meal 1800 (last orders 2030)
Parking for 2
Cards accepted: Amex, Diners, Mastercard, Visa, Switch/Delta

🛏9📠🖤🔥♨💷🍽♨🖤
♨16🅿🅿❄📠🅣◎

BURNSALL

North Yorkshire
Map ref 5B3

Attractive village of grey-stone buildings with massive 5-arched bridge over the River Wharfe, popular for fishing, boating and walking excursions. Annual feast day games, notably fell race held round maypole on the village green in August.

Fell Hotel ⚠

⚜⚜⚜ COMMENDED

Burnsall, Skipton BD23 6BT
☎ (01756) 720209
Fax (01756) 720605

The hotel stands in well-tended gardens overlooking the River Wharfe with views of the surrounding fells and the village of Burnsall.
Bedrooms: 9 double, 1 twin, 3 triple
Bathrooms: 13 en-suite

Continued ▶

BURNSALL

Continued

Bed & breakfast per night:

	£min	£max
Single	33.50	36.50
Double	58.00	64.00

Half board per person:

	£min	£max
Daily	43.00	46.00
Weekly	301.00	322.00

Lunch available
Evening meal 1900 (last orders 2100)
Parking for 60
Cards accepted: Mastercard, Visa, Switch/Delta

🛏🏠♿📞🖥⛵🍸Ⓢ☇🎜📺🔥 ▦ 🚗🍴80 🔍 U🡒❄🐾🈺 SP ⊚

CASTLETON

North Yorkshire
Map ref 5C3

Eskdale village, site of castle built by deBrus circa 1089. Castleton Moors are rich in prehistoric remains.

Moorlands Hotel ⋀

👑👑👑 APPROVED

Castleton, Whitby YO21 2DB
☎ (01287) 660206
Fax (01287) 660317
Family-run hotel/freehouse offering home cooking and a well stocked bar. In the national park with magnificent views of the Esk Valley and the North York Moors. Ideal for walking and touring.
Bedrooms: 2 single, 2 double, 3 twin, 1 triple
Bathrooms: 6 en-suite, 2 public

Bed & breakfast per night:

	£min	£max
Single	23.00	33.00
Double	56.00	76.00

Lunch available
Evening meal 1700 (last orders 2200)
Parking for 15
Cards accepted: Amex, Diners, Mastercard, Visa, Switch/Delta

🛏🏠♿📞Ⓢ☇🎜📺▦🚗🍴20 🔍 U🡒❄🚐 DAP 🈺 SP

National gradings and classifications were correct at the time of going to press but are subject to change. Please check at the time of booking.

CATTERICK

North Yorkshire
Map ref 5C3

A military camp since Roman times, known then as Cataractonium, Catterick used to be a major coaching stop on the Great North Road. Crowds once gathered to watch cock-fighting where nowadays they come to Catterick for horse-racing.

Rose Cottage Guest House ⋀

👑👑 COMMENDED

26 High Street, Catterick, Richmond DL10 7LJ
☎ (01748) 811164
Small, friendly stone-built guesthouse. En-suite facilities, guest lounge, private parking. Convenient for Richmond and Yorkshire Dales. Midway London/Edinburgh, A1(M) 1 kilometre. Open all year. Evening meal on request (May-September).
Bedrooms: 1 single, 2 twin, 1 triple
Bathrooms: 2 en-suite, 1 public

Bed & breakfast per night:

	£min	£max
Single	20.50	27.00
Double	38.00	42.00

Half board per person:

	£min	£max
Daily	29.00	35.50
Weekly	203.00	248.50

Evening meal 1730 (last orders 1830)
Parking for 4

🛏📞🖥🏠♿🔌Ⓤ Ⓛ Ⓢ☇🎜▦🚗🚐 ⊚

CLECKHEATON

West Yorkshire
Map ref 4B1

West Yorkshire town 4 miles north-west of Dewsbury.

Prospect Hall Hotel ⋀

👑👑👑 COMMENDED

Prospect Road, Cleckheaton BD19 3HD
☎ (01274) 873022
Fax (01274) 870376
Hall, converted to provide a well-appointed hotel, close to the M62, Bronte country, the dales and Peak District. Reduced prices for B&B at weekends.
Bedrooms: 7 single, 30 double, 3 twin
Bathrooms: 40 en-suite

Bed & breakfast per night:

	£min	£max
Single	40.00	46.50
Double	56.50	56.50

Half board per person:

	£min	£max
Daily	50.50	60.45

Lunch available
Evening meal 1900 (last orders 2130)
Parking for 200
Cards accepted: Amex, Diners, Mastercard, Visa, Switch/Delta

🛏🏠♿📞🖥🔌☇🍸Ⓢ☇🎜📺◐ ▦ 🚗🍴70 ❄ DAP 🈺

DEWSBURY

West Yorkshire
Map ref 4B1

Although this town is most famous for its woollen products, its history stretches back to Saxon times. Robin Hood is reputed to have died and been buried in the Cistercian convent in Kirklees Park nearby.

Heath Cottage Hotel & Restaurant

👑👑👑 HIGHLY COMMENDED

Wakefield Road, Dewsbury WF12 8ET
☎ (01924) 465399
Fax (01924) 459405
Impressive Victorian house in well-kept gardens. On the A638, 2.5 miles from M1 junction 40. Conference/banquet facilities. Large car park.
Bedrooms: 10 single, 13 double, 1 twin, 3 triple
Bathrooms: 27 en-suite

Bed & breakfast per night:

	£min	£max
Single	37.00	55.00
Double	55.00	65.00

Half board per person:

	£min	£max
Daily	49.95	67.95

Lunch available
Evening meal 1830 (last orders 2130)
Parking for 65
Cards accepted: Mastercard, Visa, Switch/Delta

🛏🏠♿📞🖥🔌☇Ⓢ☇🎜📺▦ ⊚ 🚗🍴80 🔍❄🍴✗🈺 SP

The map references refer to the colour maps towards the end of the guide.
The first figure is the map number; the letter and figure which follow indicate the grid reference on the map.

DONCASTER

South Yorkshire
Map ref 4C1

Ancient Roman town famous for its heavy industries, butterscotch and racecourse (St Leger), also centre of agricultural area. Attractions include 18th C Mansion House, Cusworth Hall Museum, Doncaster Museum, St George's Church, The Dome and Doncaster Leisure Park.
Tourist Information Centre ☎ (01302) 734309

Almel Hotel ⚊

👑 APPROVED

20 Christchurch Road, Doncaster DN1 2QL
☎ (01302) 365230
Fax (01302) 341434
Licensed hotel in the town centre, close to racecourse and leisure park. Coach parties welcome.
Bedrooms: 12 single, 1 double, 15 twin, 1 triple, 1 family room
Bathrooms: 15 en-suite, 3 public, 9 private showers
Bed & breakfast per night:

	£min	£max
Single	21.00	30.00
Double	36.00	42.00

Half board per person:

	£min	£max
Daily	27.50	36.50

Evening meal 1700 (last orders 1930)
Parking for 8
Cards accepted: Amex, Mastercard, Visa, Switch/Delta

Regent Hotel ⚊

👑👑👑 COMMENDED

Regent Square, Doncaster DN1 2DS
☎ (01302) 364180 & 364336
Fax (01302) 322331
Family-run hotel overlooking Regents Park. Two public bars, cocktail bar and a good restaurant. All rooms en-suite.
Bedrooms: 20 single, 9 double, 15 twin, 5 triple
Bathrooms: 49 en-suite
Bed & breakfast per night:

	£min	£max
Single	40.00	68.50
Double	65.00	75.00

Half board per person:

	£min	£max
Daily	50.00	80.00

Lunch available
Evening meal 1800 (last orders 2200)
Parking for 26

Cards accepted: Amex, Diners, Mastercard, Visa, Switch/Delta

DRIFFIELD

East Riding of Yorkshire
Map ref 4C1

Lively market town on edge of Wolds with fine Early English church, All Saints. Popular with anglers for its trout streams which flow into the River Hull. Its 18th C canal is lined with barges and houseboats.

The Old Rectory ⚊

👑👑👑 HIGHLY COMMENDED

Cowlam, Driffield, East Riding of Yorkshire YO25 0AD
☎ (01377) 267617
Fax (01377) 267403

Victorian rectory set in the traditional riding of East Yorkshire. We offer classic good food, log fires and elegant en-suite rooms. In the heart of unspoilt countryside.
Bedrooms: 1 double, 2 twin
Bathrooms: 2 en-suite, 1 private
Bed & breakfast per night:

	£min	£max
Double	55.00	59.00

Half board per person:

	£min	£max
Daily	47.50	49.50

Evening meal 1900 (last orders 2100)
Parking for 12

WELCOME HOST

This is a nationally recognised customer care programme which aims to promote the highest standards of service and a warm welcome. Establishments who are taking part in this initiative are indicated by the symbol.

EASINGWOLD

North Yorkshire
Map ref 5C3

Market town of charm and character with a cobbled square and many fine Georgian buildings.

The George ⚊

👑👑 COMMENDED

Market Place, Easingwold, York YO6 3AD
☎ (01347) 821698
Fax (01347) 823448
18th C coaching inn overlooking cobbled square in delightful Georgian market town. 15 minutes York, dales, moors. Good food. Cask beers.
Bedrooms: 8 double, 5 twin, 1 triple, 1 family room
Bathrooms: 15 en-suite
Bed & breakfast per night:

	£min	£max
Single	35.00	45.00
Double	50.00	70.00

Half board per person:

	£min	£max
Daily	42.50	47.50

Lunch available
Evening meal 1900 (last orders 2130)
Parking for 8
Cards accepted: Mastercard, Visa, Switch/Delta

Old Farmhouse Country Hotel & Restaurant ⚊

👑👑 COMMENDED

Raskelf, York YO6 3LF
☎ (01347) 821971
Former farmhouse converted to a comfortable country hotel, offering home cooking, open fires and a warm, friendly welcome. In Herriot country, 3 miles from Easingwold and 15 miles from York.
Bedrooms: 1 single, 7 double, 1 twin, 1 triple
Bathrooms: 10 en-suite
Bed & breakfast per night:

	£min	£max
Single	32.00	35.00
Double	56.00	60.00

Half board per person:

	£min	£max
Daily	41.00	43.00
Weekly	273.00	287.00

Evening meal 1930 (last orders 2030)
Parking for 10

ELLERBY

North Yorkshire
Map ref 5C3

Hamlet 3 miles south of Staithes.

Ellerby Hotel ⋔

👑 👑 👑 COMMENDED

Ellerby, Saltburn-by-the-Sea,
Cleveland TS13 5LP
☎ (01947) 840342
Fax (01947) 841221

*Residential country inn within the
North York Moors National Park, 9
miles north of Whitby, 1 mile inland
from Runswick Bay.*
Wheelchair access category 3⧖
Bedrooms: 5 double, 4 triple
Bathrooms: 9 en-suite
**Bed & breakfast
per night:**

	£min	£max
Single	35.00	37.00
Double	54.00	58.00

Lunch available
Evening meal 1900 (last orders
2200)
Parking for 60
Cards accepted: Mastercard, Visa,
Switch/Delta

🛏🕭📞🖭💻⚓🕯📵Ⓢ✂🎿▥🖂
🍽40🏴🌸🐎 SP 🏰

FILEY

North Yorkshire
Map ref 5D3

Resort with elegant Regency
buildings along the front and 6 miles
of sandy beaches bounded by
natural breakwater, Filey Brigg.
Starting point of the Cleveland Way.

The Downcliffe House
Hotel ⋔

👑 👑 👑 HIGHLY COMMENDED

The Beach, Filey YO14 9LA
☎ (01723) 513310
Fax (01723) 516141
*Recently refurbished seafront hotel with
magnificent views over Filey Bay. All
rooms en-suite with telephone, satellite
TV and tea-making facilities.*
Bedrooms: 1 single, 6 double, 1 twin,
1 triple, 1 family room
Bathrooms: 10 en-suite

**Bed & breakfast
per night:**

	£min	£max
Single	30.00	36.00
Double	60.00	72.00

**Half board per
person:**

	£min	£max
Daily	42.00	52.00
Weekly	250.00	350.00

Lunch available
Evening meal 1800 (last orders
2100)
Parking for 8
Open February–December
Cards accepted: Mastercard, Visa,
Switch/Delta

🛏5📞🖭💻🍵⚓🕯Ⓢ✂▥ TV ▥
🖂✗🐎🔌 SP 🏰

Sea Brink Hotel ⋔

👑 👑 👑 COMMENDED

3 The Beach, Filey YO14 9LA
☎ (01723) 513257
Fax (01723) 514139
*Seafront hotel overlooking the beach.
Magnificent views, delightful en-suite
rooms with all facilities. Licensed
restaurant/coffee shop. German
spoken.*
Bedrooms: 5 double, 4 family rooms
Bathrooms: 7 en-suite, 2 private,
1 public
**Bed & breakfast
per night:**

	£min	£max
Single	27.00	30.00
Double	50.00	56.00

**Half board per
person:**

	£min	£max
Daily	37.00	40.00
Weekly	204.00	225.00

Lunch available
Evening meal 1830 (last orders
1930)
Cards accepted: Mastercard, Visa,
Switch/Delta

🛏📞🖭💻🍵⚓🕯Ⓢ✂▥ TV ▥🖂
🍽🔌 SP

Seafield Hotel ⋔

👑 👑 👑 COMMENDED

9-11 Rutland Street, Filey YO14 9JA
☎ (01723) 513715
*Small, friendly and comfortable hotel in
the centre of Filey, close to the beach
and all amenities. Car park. Family
rooms.*
Bedrooms: 4 double, 4 triple,
5 family rooms
Bathrooms: 13 en-suite, 1 public
**Bed & breakfast
per night:**

	£min	£max
Single	19.00	21.00
Double	38.00	42.00

**Half board per
person:**

	£min	£max
Daily	25.00	27.00
Weekly	165.00	179.00

Evening meal 1800 (last orders
1600)
Parking for 7
Cards accepted: Mastercard, Visa
🛏🕭📞🖭💻🍵🕯▥ TV ▥🖂
🍽20🏴✗🐎 DAP SP 🔘

FLAMBOROUGH

East Riding of Yorkshire
Map ref 5D3

Village with strong seafaring
tradition, high on chalk headland
dominated by cliffs of Flamborough
Head, a fortress for over 2000 years.
St Oswald's Church is in the oldest
part of Flamborough.

Flaneburg Hotel ⋔

👑 👑 👑 APPROVED

North Marine Road, Flamborough,
Bridlington, East Riding of Yorkshire
YO15 1LF
☎ (01262) 850284
Fax (01262) 850284
*Taking its name from ancient
Flamborough, the hotel offers comfort,
good food and a flavour of the region.
Under the personal supervision of the
proprietors. Ideal for bird watching,
walking, rambling or golf. Good base for
touring East Coast and moors.*
Bedrooms: 1 single, 6 double, 2 twin,
3 triple, 1 family room
Bathrooms: 10 en-suite, 2 public
**Bed & breakfast
per night:**

	£min	£max
Single	24.00	27.00
Double	48.00	54.00

**Half board per
person:**

	£min	£max
Daily	34.00	37.00
Weekly	209.00	229.00

Lunch available
Evening meal 1800 (last orders
2200)
Parking for 35
Cards accepted: Mastercard, Visa,
Switch/Delta

🛏🖭💻🍵Ⓢ▥ TV ▥🖂🍽35🌸
✗ DAP 🔌 SP Ⓣ

Please mention this guide
when making your booking.

All accommodation in this
guide has been graded, or is
awaiting a grading, by a trained
Tourist Board inspector.

GOATHLAND

North Yorkshire
Map ref 5D3

Spacious village with several large greens grazed by sheep, an ideal centre for walking the North York Moors. Nearby are several waterfalls, among them Mallyan Spout. Plough Monday celebrations held in January. Location for filming of TV "Heartbeat" series.

Fairhaven Country Hotel ⚠

🏨🏨 COMMENDED

The Common, Goathland, Whitby YO22 5AN
☎ (01947) 896361
Edwardian country house with superb moorland views in the centre of Goathland village. Warm hospitality and fine food in a relaxed atmosphere.
Bedrooms: 2 single, 2 double, 2 twin, 2 triple, 1 family room
Bathrooms: 4 en-suite, 3 public

Bed & breakfast

per night:	£min	£max
Single	20.00	31.00
Double	40.00	50.00

Half board per

person:	£min	£max
Daily	32.00	37.00
Weekly	210.00	245.00

Evening meal 1900 (last orders 1730)
Parking for 10
Cards accepted: Mastercard, Visa, Switch/Delta

🛏♿🍽🛢🚿🖄📺🏧🖨🚗🍴21🔌✳

Inn on the Moor ⚠

🏨🏨🏨 COMMENDED

Goathland, Whitby YO22 5LZ
☎ (01947) 896296
Fax (01947) 896484
Country house hotel overlooking the Yorkshire Moors. A warm welcome, pleasant service, English food, fresh air and peace. All rooms have colour TV, 8 with four-poster beds, 2 family suites. "Heartbeat" country.
Bedrooms: 18 double, 5 twin, 2 family rooms
Bathrooms: 25 en-suite, 1 public

Bed & breakfast

per night:	£min	£max
Single	32.00	42.00
Double	60.00	76.00

Half board per

person:	£min	£max
Daily	40.00	48.00
Weekly	240.00	288.00

Lunch available
Evening meal 1900 (last orders 2030)
Parking for 50

Cards accepted: Amex, Diners, Mastercard, Visa

🛏♿🍽📞🖄🛢🖍🍴⚓🍀🖄📺🏧🖨
🍴50🔌∪🕊❋✳ SP T ◉

Mallyan Spout Hotel ⚠

🏨🏨🏨 COMMENDED

Goathland, Whitby YO22 5AN
☎ (01947) 896486 & 896206
Fax (01947) 896327

Comfortable hotel with old-fashioned comforts, welcoming log fires and good dining facilities. An ideal centre for walking the North York Moors. "Heartbeat" country.
Bedrooms: 4 single, 12 double, 7 twin
Bathrooms: 21 en-suite, 2 private

Bed & breakfast

per night:	£min	£max
Single	50.00	65.00
Double	65.00	130.00

Half board per

person:	£min	£max
Daily	50.00	80.00

Lunch available
Evening meal 1900 (last orders 2100)
Parking for 100
Cards accepted: Amex, Mastercard, Visa, Switch/Delta

🛏♿🍽📞🖄🛢🖍🍀🖄🏧🖨
🖨🍴16∪🕊❋ DAP ❋ SP 🏠 T

Whitfield House Hotel ⚠

🏨🏨🏨 COMMENDED

Darnholm, Goathland, Whitby YO22 5LA
☎ (01947) 896215 & 896214

17th C farmhouse providing modern comforts amidst old world charm. Peaceful location. Cottage-style en-suite bedrooms (non-smoking) with every amenity.
Bedrooms: 1 single, 6 double, 2 triple
Bathrooms: 9 en-suite

Bed & breakfast

per night:	£min	£max
Single	26.00	28.00
Double	52.00	56.00

Cards accepted: Amex, Diners, Mastercard, Visa

Half board per

person:	£min	£max
Daily	37.50	39.50
Weekly	260.50	270.50

Lunch available
Evening meal 1900 (last orders 1730)
Parking for 10
Cards accepted: Mastercard, Visa

🛏5📞🖄🛢🛢🖍🛢🖍🏧🖨🚗🚐
SP 🏠

GOOLE

North Lincolnshire
Map ref 4C1

This busy port on the River Ouse developed with the opening of the Aire and Calder Canal in 1826 and is reminiscent of the Netherlands with its red brick buildings and flat, watery landscape. Goole Museum houses Garside Local History Collection.

Clifton Hotel

🏨🏨🏨 COMMENDED

Boothferry Road, Goole, East Riding of Yorkshire DN14 6AL
☎ (01405) 761336
Fax (01405) 762350
Ⓒ The Independents
Small, comfortable and friendly family-run hotel convenient for Humberside, York, East Yorkshire and Lincolnshire. One mile from M62 motorway.
Bedrooms: 4 single, 3 double, 1 twin, 1 family room
Bathrooms: 8 en-suite, 1 private

Bed & breakfast

per night:	£min	£max
Single	26.00	40.00
Double	40.00	48.00

Half board per

person:	£min	£max
Daily	31.00	

Lunch available
Evening meal 1900 (last orders 2100)
Parking for 8
Cards accepted: Amex, Diners, Mastercard, Visa

🛏📞🖄🛢🖍🛢🖍🖄📺🏧🖨🚗🍴40
✳ DAP SP T

ACCESSIBILITY

Look for the ♿🧑‍🦽🚶 symbols which indicate accessibility for wheelchair users. These are described in detail at the front of this guide.

GRASSINGTON

North Yorkshire
Map ref 5B3

Tourists visit this former lead-mining village to see its "smiddy", antique and craft shops and Upper Wharfedale Museum of country trades. Popular with fishermen and walkers. Numerous prehistoric sites. Grassington Feast in October. National Park Centre.

Ashfield House Hotel M

HIGHLY COMMENDED

Summers Fold, Grassington, Skipton BD23 5AE
☎ (01756) 752584
Fax (01756) 752584
Quiet and secluded 17th C private hotel near the village square. Open fires and creative home cooking using only fresh produce.
Bedrooms: 4 double, 3 twin
Bathrooms: 6 en-suite, 1 private

Bed & breakfast

per night:	£min	£max
Single	26.00	45.00
Double	52.00	60.00

Half board per

person:	£min	£max
Daily	38.00	55.00
Weekly	250.00	290.00

Evening meal 1900 (last orders 1900)
Parking for 9
Open February–December
Cards accepted: Mastercard, Visa

Clarendon Hotel M

COMMENDED

Hebden, Grassington, Skipton BD23 5DE
☎ (01756) 752446
Yorkshire Dales village inn serving good food and ales. Personal supervision at all times. Steaks and fish dishes are specialities. Seven nights for the price of six.
Bedrooms: 2 double, 1 twin
Bathrooms: 3 en-suite

Bed & breakfast

per night:	£min	£max
Single	30.00	
Double	40.00	50.00

Lunch available
Evening meal 1900 (last orders 2100)
Parking for 30

Grassington House Hotel M

COMMENDED

5 The Square, Grassington, Skipton BD23 5AQ
☎ (01756) 752406
Fax (01756) 752135

Friendly, family-run Georgian hotel in the Yorkshire Dales. Renowned for comfort and food. Pets welcome. Ideal touring and walking base. Special terms for weekly stays.
Bedrooms: 1 single, 6 double, 2 twin, 1 triple
Bathrooms: 10 en-suite

Bed & breakfast

per night:	£min	£max
Single	26.00	29.00
Double	52.00	58.00

Half board per

person:	£min	£max
Daily	37.50	38.50

Lunch available
Evening meal 1830 (last orders 2100)
Parking for 24
Cards accepted: Mastercard, Visa, Switch/Delta

Tennant Arms Hotel M

COMMENDED

Kilnsey, Skipton BD23 5PS
☎ (01756) 752301
17th C coaching inn nestling alongside Kilnsey Crag, offering comfortable, attractive accommodation for those wishing to experience the beauty of Wharfedale.
Bedrooms: 5 double, 3 twin, 2 triple
Bathrooms: 10 en-suite

Bed & breakfast

per night:	£min	£max
Single	29.95	35.75
Double	47.00	

Half board per

person:	£min	£max
Daily	35.75	35.75
Weekly	227.00	227.00

Lunch available
Evening meal 1900 (last orders 2130)
Parking for 40
Cards accepted: Mastercard, Visa

GRIMSBY

North East Lincolnshire
Map ref 4D1

Founded 1,000 years ago by a Danish fisherman named Grim, Grimsby is today a major fishing port and docks. It has modern shopping precincts and National Fishing Heritage Centre, voted England's top tourist attraction in 1992.
Tourist Information Centre ☎ *(01472) 323222*

Millfields M

COMMENDED

53 Bargate, Grimsby, North East Lincolnshire DN34 5AD
☎ (01472) 356068
Fax (01472) 250286
CR Minotel/The Independents
Exclusive yet competitively priced hotel with a wide range of leisure facilities, situated close to the commercial and retail centre of Grimsby.
Wheelchair access category 3
Bedrooms: 13 double, 9 twin
Bathrooms: 22 en-suite

Bed & breakfast

per night:	£min	£max
Single	37.50	49.00
Double	47.50	67.50

Half board per

person:	£min	£max
Daily	52.00	64.00

Lunch available
Evening meal 1900 (last orders 2100)
Parking for 50
Cards accepted: Amex, Diners, Mastercard, Visa, Switch/Delta

All accommodation in this guide has been graded, or is awaiting a grading, by a trained Tourist Board inspector.

Information on accommodation listed in this guide has been supplied by the proprietors. As changes may occur you are advised to check details at the time of booking.

HALIFAX

West Yorkshire
Map ref 4B1

Founded on the cloth trade, and famous for its building society, textiles, carpets and toffee. Most notable landmark is Piece Hall where wool merchants traded, now restored to house shops, museums and art gallery. Home also to Eureka! The Museum for Children.
Tourist Information Centre ☎ (01422) 368725

The Hobbit ⚏

👑👑👑 COMMENDED

Hob Lane, Norland, Sowerby Bridge HX6 3QL
☎ (01422) 832202
Fax (01422) 835381
Ⓒ The Independents

Country hotel with panoramic views. Restaurant and bistro have reputation for good food at affordable prices. Friendly inn-type atmosphere. "Murder Mysteries" featured regularly.
Bedrooms: 2 single, 7 double, 9 twin, 3 triple
Bathrooms: 21 en-suite

Bed & breakfast

per night:	£min	£max
Single	32.00	59.00
Double	45.00	73.00

Lunch available
Evening meal 1700 (last orders 2200)
Parking for 100
Cards accepted: Amex, Diners, Mastercard, Visa, Switch/Delta

🐕🛁🖿📞🖂🖵❑👜🛎Ⓢ🖊🗔📺🎬📠🛏🏧80⛴⊃♪✿✕🚭 SP T

Rock Inn Hotel & Churchills Restaurant ⚏

👑👑👑 COMMENDED

Holywell Green, Halifax HX4 9BS
☎ (01422) 379721
Fax (01422) 379110
Privately-owned hostelry offering all the attractions of a wayside inn plus the sophistication of a first class hotel and conference centre. Rural setting yet only 1.5 miles from junction 24 of M62. Open all day for conservatory dining.
Bedrooms: 14 double, 2 twin, 1 triple, 1 family room
Bathrooms: 18 en-suite

Bed & breakfast

per night:	£min	£max
Single	45.00	72.00
Double	59.00	85.00

Lunch available
Evening meal 1200 (last orders 2200)
Parking for 125
Cards accepted: Amex, Diners, Mastercard, Visa, Switch/Delta

🐕🛁🖿📞🖂🖵❑👜🛎Ⓢ🖊🗔📠🏧200⛴⊃♪✿✕🚭 SP T

HARROGATE

North Yorkshire
Map ref 4B1

A major conference, exhibition and shopping centre, renowned for its spa heritage and award winning floral displays, spacious parks and gardens. Famous for antiques, toffee, fine shopping and excellent tea shops, also its Royal Pump Rooms and Baths.
Tourist Information Centre ☎ (01423) 537300

Abbatt & Young's Hotel ⚏

👑👑👑 COMMENDED

15 York Road, (Off Swan Road), Harrogate HG1 2QL
☎ (01423) 567336 & 521231
Fax (01423) 500042
Victorian property in a quiet conservation area. Attractive gardens, private car park. Within walking distance of town centre and Valley Gardens.
Bedrooms: 4 single, 2 double, 2 twin, 1 family room
Bathrooms: 9 en-suite

Bed & breakfast

per night:	£min	£max
Single	38.00	50.00
Double	56.00	80.00

Half board per person:

	£min	£max
Daily	41.50	53.50
Weekly	266.00	350.00

Evening meal 1800 (last orders 2030)
Parking for 9
Cards accepted: Mastercard, Visa, Switch/Delta

🐕🛁📞🖂🖵❑👜🛎Ⓢ🗔📺🎬📠🛏✿ DAP SP T

Half board prices are given per person, but in some cases these may be based on double/twin occupancy.

Acacia Lodge

👑👑 HIGHLY COMMENDED

21 Ripon Road, Harrogate HG1 2JL
☎ (01423) 560752 & 503725
Warm, lovingly restored Victorian house in select town centre area. Fine furnishings/antiques, beautiful lounge with open fire, all rooms en-suite. Award-winning breakfasts, ample floodlit parking. Entirely non-smoking.
Bedrooms: 1 double, 2 twin, 2 triple
Bathrooms: 5 en-suite

Bed & breakfast

per night:	£min	£max
Single	38.00	54.00
Double	48.00	60.00

Parking for 6

🐕5🖂🖵❑👜🛎Ⓢ🖊🗔📺🏧◎🛏✿✕🐾🚭 SP T

Alamah ⚏

👑👑👑 COMMENDED

88 Kings Road, Harrogate HG1 5JX
☎ (01423) 502187
Fax (01423) 566175
Comfortable rooms, personal attention, friendly atmosphere and full English breakfast. 300 metres from town centre. Garages/parking.
Bedrooms: 2 single, 2 double, 2 twin, 1 family room
Bathrooms: 5 en-suite, 2 private showers

Bed & breakfast

per night:	£min	£max
Single	24.00	27.00
Double	44.00	50.00

Evening meal 1830 (last orders 1400)
Parking for 8

🐕3🖂🖵❑👜🛎 UL 🖊🗔🏧🛏🐾 SP T

Albany Hotel ⚏

👑👑👑 COMMENDED

22-23 Harlow Moor Drive, Harrogate HG2 0JY
☎ (01423) 565890
Fax (01423) 565890
Comfortable, small hotel with friendly relaxing atmosphere, overlooking the beautiful Valley Gardens. All rooms have en-suite facilities. Excellent value for discerning guests.
Bedrooms: 4 single, 3 double, 4 twin, 3 triple
Bathrooms: 14 en-suite, 1 public

Bed & breakfast

per night:	£min	£max
Single	25.00	34.00
Double	48.00	64.00

Cards accepted: Amex, Diners, Mastercard, Visa

🐕🖂🖵❑👜🛎🗔🏧🛏✕ SP T

HARROGATE
Continued

The Alexander

👑👑 HIGHLY COMMENDED

88 Franklin Road, Harrogate
HG1 5EN
☎ (01423) 503348
Fax (01423) 540230
*Friendly, family-run elegant Victorian
guesthouse with some en-suite facilities.
Ideal for conference centre and
Harrogate town. Good touring centre
for dales. Non-smokers only, please.*
Bedrooms: 2 single, 1 double,
2 triple
Bathrooms: 3 en-suite, 1 public
**Bed & breakfast
per night:**

	£min	£max
Single	22.00	24.00
Double	44.00	44.00

Parking for 2

Alvera Court Hotel 🏨

👑👑👑 COMMENDED

76 Kings Road, Harrogate HG1 5JX
☎ (01423) 505735
Fax (01423) 507996
*Extensively refurbished Victorian
residence placing special emphasis on
comfort and personal service. Directly
opposite the conference centre.*
Bedrooms: 5 single, 1 double, 2 twin,
4 triple
Bathrooms: 12 en-suite
**Bed & breakfast
per night:**

	£min	£max
Single	29.00	42.00
Double	58.00	84.00

**Half board per
person:**

	£min	£max
Daily	44.50	51.50
Weekly	311.00	361.00

Evening meal 1930 (last orders
1400)
Parking for 8
Cards accepted: Mastercard, Visa,
Switch/Delta

Anro 🏨

👑👑 COMMENDED

90 Kings Road, Harrogate HG1 5JX
☎ (01423) 503087
*In a central position, 2 minutes from
the conference centre and near Valley
Gardens, town, bus and rail stations.
Ideal for touring the dales. Home
cooking.*
Bedrooms: 3 single, 1 double, 2 twin,
1 family room
Bathrooms: 4 en-suite, 1 public

**Bed & breakfast
per night:**

	£min	£max
Single	22.00	
Double	44.00	

**Half board per
person:**

	£min	£max
Daily	35.00	

Evening meal 1815 (last orders
1630)

Arden House Hotel 🏨

👑👑👑 COMMENDED

69-71 Franklin Road, Harrogate
HG1 5EH
☎ (01423) 509224
Fax (01423) 561170
*Family-run hotel with a warm, friendly
atmosphere and real home cooking.
Close to the town centre. Trouser press
and hairdryer in all rooms.*
Bedrooms: 4 single, 5 double, 4 twin,
1 triple
Bathrooms: 14 en-suite

**Bed & breakfast
per night:**

	£min	£max
Single	30.00	
Double	55.00	

**Half board per
person:**

	£min	£max
Daily	45.00	
Weekly	250.00	

Evening meal 1900 (last orders
2000)
Parking for 10
Cards accepted: Amex, Diners,
Mastercard, Visa, Switch/Delta

Ascot House Hotel 🏨

👑👑👑 COMMENDED

53 Kings Road, Harrogate HG1 5HJ
☎ (01423) 531005
Fax (01423) 503523
ⓇMinotel
*Delightful, refurbished hotel near town
centre assuring you of a friendly
welcome and an enjoyable stay. Quality
cuisine. Parking. Ring for colour
brochure.*
Bedrooms: 3 single, 7 double, 7 twin,
1 triple
Bathrooms: 18 en-suite

**Bed & breakfast
per night:**

	£min	£max
Single	48.50	56.50
Double	69.00	89.00

**Half board per
person:**

	£min	£max
Daily	46.00	51.00
Weekly	276.00	306.00

Evening meal 1900 (last orders
2045)

Parking for 14
Cards accepted: Amex, Diners,
Mastercard, Visa

Ashbrooke House Hotel 🏨

👑👑 HIGHLY COMMENDED

140 Valley Drive, Harrogate
HG2 0JS
☎ (01423) 564478
*Elegant Edwardian town house hotel,
close to town, conference centre and
countryside, offering quality
accommodation. Children and pets
most welcome.*
Bedrooms: 3 single, 1 double, 2 twin,
1 triple
Bathrooms: 4 en-suite, 2 public,
1 private shower

**Bed & breakfast
per night:**

	£min	£max
Single	23.00	25.00
Double	45.00	48.00

Cards accepted: Mastercard, Visa,
Switch/Delta

Ashley House Hotel 🏨

👑👑 COMMENDED

36-40 Franklin Road, Harrogate
HG1 5EE
☎ (01423) 507474
Fax (01423) 560858
Email: ashleyhousehotel@btinternet
*Ron and Linda welcome you to their
comfortable home in a quiet street
close to the town centre. Friendly
atmosphere, personal service, delicious
meals and cosy bar.*
Bedrooms: 5 single, 7 double, 6 twin
Bathrooms: 18 en-suite

**Bed & breakfast
per night:**

	£min	£max
Single	32.50	40.00
Double	50.00	70.00

**Half board per
person:**

	£min	£max
Daily	35.00	50.00
Weekly	250.00	300.00

Evening meal 1900 (last orders
2000)
Parking for 6
Cards accepted: Amex, Diners,
Mastercard, Visa, Switch/Delta

The National Grading and
Classification Scheme is
explained at the back
of this guide.

Balmoral Hotel & Henry's Restaurant ♒

👑👑👑 HIGHLY COMMENDED

Franklin Mount, Harrogate HG1 5EJ
☎ (01423) 508208
Fax (01423) 530652
Exclusive town house with beautifully furnished rooms and a relaxed, tranquil ambience. Nine four-poster rooms. Award-winning restaurant with modern English menu. Special weekend rates.
Bedrooms: 5 single, 12 double,
4 twin
Bathrooms: 21 en-suite

Bed & breakfast

per night:	£min	£max
Single	68.00	92.00
Double	84.00	170.00

Half board per

person:	£min	£max
Daily	60.00	75.00

Lunch available
Evening meal 1900 (last orders 2100)
Parking for 20
Cards accepted: Amex, Mastercard, Visa, Switch/Delta

🐾♿👤🍴📠🖥👷♨♫🛉Ⓢ✂🔌▦ 🖨 ♟35▶✳ SP T

Bay Horse Inn ♒

👑👑👑 COMMENDED

Burnt Yates, Harrogate HG3 3EJ
☎ (01423) 770230
Ⓒ Wayfarer
Renowned 18th C inn with oak beams, open log fires and restaurant serving traditional English fare. In Nidderdale between Ripley and Pateley Bridge. Ideal base for racing in Yorkshire, golf courses and shooting parties.
Bedrooms: 4 double, 6 twin, 2 triple
Bathrooms: 12 en-suite

Bed & breakfast

per night:	£min	£max
Single	40.00	40.00
Double	55.00	60.00

Lunch available
Evening meal 1900 (last orders 2200)
Parking for 80
Cards accepted: Mastercard, Visa, Switch/Delta

🐾♿👤🍴📠🖥👷♨♫Ⓢ✂🔌▦🖨 ♟40●▶✳ DAP ◿ SP T

The symbols in each entry give information about services and facilities. A key to these symbols appears at the back of this guide.

The Boar's Head Hotel ♒

👑👑👑👑 HIGHLY COMMENDED

Ripley Castle Estate, Ripley, Harrogate HG3 3AY
☎ (01423) 771888
Fax (01423) 771509
Ⓒ Grand Heritage

At the heart of the historic Ripley Castle estate, overlooking the cobbled market square. Renowned restaurant and fine village pub. One of the great inns of England. Daily half board price based on minimum 2 nights.
Wheelchair access category 3🧍
Bedrooms: 5 double, 20 twin
Bathrooms: 25 en-suite

Bed & breakfast

per night:	£min	£max
Single	85.00	95.00
Double	98.00	120.00

Half board per

person:	£min	£max
Daily	67.50	75.00

Lunch available
Evening meal 1900 (last orders 2130)
Parking for 43
Cards accepted: Amex, Diners, Mastercard, Visa, Switch/Delta

🐾♿👤🍴📠🖥👷♨Ⓢ🔌Ⓞ▦ ♟85●∪♩▶✳◿ SP 🅿 T

Britannia Lodge Hotel ♒

👑👑👑 COMMENDED

16 Swan Road, Harrogate HG1 2SA
☎ (01423) 508482
Fax (01423) 526840

Beautiful 19th C town house with delightful gardens and private parking in select Harrogate area. Elegant, cosy lounge and bar with open fire, pretty bedrooms, all en-suite. Only 5 minutes' walk to town centre and Valley Gardens.
Bedrooms: 4 single, 3 twin, 5 triple
Bathrooms: 12 en-suite

Bed & breakfast

per night:	£min	£max
Single	38.00	55.00
Double	54.00	75.00

Half board per

person:	£min	£max
Daily	39.00	50.50
Weekly	275.00	340.00

Evening meal 1800 (last orders 2030)
Parking for 7
Cards accepted: Amex, Mastercard, Visa

🐾♿👤🍴🖥👷♨Ⓢ✂🔌 TV ▦🖨 ♟✳✗🚐 SP 🅿 T

Cavendish Hotel ♒

👑👑👑 COMMENDED

3 Valley Drive, Harrogate HG2 0JJ
☎ (01423) 509637
Overlooking the beautiful Valley Gardens in a quiet location yet close to conference centre and extensive shopping area. Ideal for business or pleasure.
Bedrooms: 3 single, 4 double, 2 twin
Bathrooms: 9 en-suite

Bed & breakfast

per night:	£min	£max
Single	28.00	35.00
Double	50.00	65.00

Evening meal 1900 (last orders 2030)
Cards accepted: Mastercard, Visa

🐾♿👤🍴🖥👷♨Ⓢ✂🔌▦🖨♟✳

The Coppice ♒

👑👑👑 COMMENDED

9 Studley Road, Harrogate HG1 5JU
☎ (01423) 569626
Fax (01423) 569005

A warm and friendly welcome awaits. Quiet location, excellent food and service. Five minutes' walk to elegant town centre, 2 minutes to conference centre and a short drive to the dales.
Bedrooms: 1 single, 2 double, 1 twin, 1 triple
Bathrooms: 5 en-suite

Bed & breakfast

per night:	£min	£max
Single	23.00	38.00
Double	40.00	46.00

Half board per

person:	£min	£max
Daily	36.50	51.50

Evening meal 1800 (last orders 1900)
Cards accepted: Amex, Diners, Mastercard, Visa

🐾♿5👤🍴📠🖥👷 UL Ⓢ✂🔌▦🖨✗ 🚐◿ SP ◉

HARROGATE
Continued

Delaine Hotel ⋔

⚜⚜ HIGHLY COMMENDED

17 Ripon Road, Harrogate HG1 2JL
☎ (01423) 567974
Fax (01423) 561723

Family-run hotel set in beautiful award-winning gardens. Very attractive en-suite rooms. Delicious home-cooked fare. An ideal choice for your holiday.
Bedrooms: 1 single, 5 double, 2 twin, 2 triple
Bathrooms: 10 en-suite

Bed & breakfast per night:

	£min	£max
Single	37.00	39.00
Double	54.00	58.00

Half board per person:

	£min	£max
Daily	40.95	42.95

Evening meal 1830 (last orders 1900)
Parking for 14
Cards accepted: Amex, Mastercard, Visa

🛇🕭🚻🖤📞📺🖳⚓🏵❖🖬📺

🖬❖✕🖾🚗 DAP ⚊ SP

Eton House

⚜ APPROVED

3 Eton Terrace, Knaresborough Road, Harrogate HG2 7SU
☎ (01423) 886850
Still here after 20 years, this homely guesthouse with spacious comfortable rooms, all with TV and tea/coffee facilities. Situated on A59 on the edge of the Stray and close to town.
Bedrooms: 1 single, 1 double, 2 triple, 3 family rooms
Bathrooms: 2 en-suite, 2 public

Bed & breakfast per night:

	£min	£max
Single	16.00	18.00
Double	36.00	44.00

Parking for 10

🛇🖵🖤 UL S 🖾 📺🖬

Garden House Hotel ⋔

⚜⚜⚜ COMMENDED

14 Harlow Moor Drive, Harrogate HG2 0JX
☎ (01423) 503059
Small, family-run, Victorian hotel overlooking Valley Gardens, in a quiet location with unrestricted parking. Home cooking using fresh produce only.
Bedrooms: 3 single, 2 double, 2 twin
Bathrooms: 5 en-suite, 2 private showers

Bed & breakfast per night:

	£min	£max
Single	22.00	
Double	47.00	

Half board per person:

	£min	£max
Daily	34.50	
Weekly	217.00	

Evening meal 1900 (last orders 1200)
Cards accepted: Amex, Diners, Mastercard, Visa

🛇⚜2🖤🖵🚻❖🏵S🖾📺🖬⚊✕
SP T ◉

Imperial Hotel ⋔

⚜⚜⚜⚜ COMMENDED

Prospect Place, Harrogate HG1 1LA
☎ (01423) 565071
Fax (01423) 500082
CR Principal/Utell International
Recently refurbished and situated in the heart of this historic spa town, this hotel was once the home of Lord Carnarvon. Half board price below is based on double/twin occupancy for minimum 2-night stay, with free entry into some local attractions.
Bedrooms: 12 single, 22 double, 51 twin
Suite available
Bathrooms: 85 en-suite

Bed & breakfast per night:

	£min	£max
Single	80.00	
Double	95.00	

Half board per person:

	£min	£max
Daily	43.00	

Lunch available
Evening meal 1900 (last orders 2130)
Parking for 45
Cards accepted: Amex, Diners, Mastercard, Visa, Switch/Delta

🛇📞🖤🖵🚻❖🏵S🖾📺◑⚊⊞🖬
⚊🍽200🖑🏵🚗⚊ SP 🏬 T

Kimberley Hotel ⋔

⚜⚜ COMMENDED

11-19 Kings Road, Harrogate HG1 5JY
☎ (01423) 505613
Fax (01423) 530276
Email: kimberley@ecosse-it.co.uk
Free-standing Victorian terraced house, 100 yards from Harrogate Conference Centre. Within 5 minutes' walk of town centre and railway station.
Bedrooms: 5 single, 24 double, 16 twin, 3 triple
Bathrooms: 48 en-suite

Bed & breakfast per night:

	£min	£max
Single	32.00	78.00
Double	64.00	105.40

Parking for 40
Cards accepted: Amex, Diners, Mastercard, Visa, Switch/Delta

🛇🕭🚻📞🖵🖤🏵🖾📺◑⚊⊞
🖬⚊🍽90🖑🏵 SP T

Low Hall Hotel and Restaurant ⋔

⚜⚜⚜⚜ COMMENDED

Ripon Road, Killinghall, Harrogate HG3 2AY
☎ (01423) 508598
Fax (01423) 560848
Charming, privately-owned country hotel, set in attractive gardens. Excellent restaurant and bar meals. 2 miles north of Harrogate.
Bedrooms: 2 single, 4 double, 1 twin
Bathrooms: 7 en-suite

Bed & breakfast per night:

	£min	£max
Single	45.00	75.00
Double	55.00	85.00

Lunch available
Evening meal 1900 (last orders 2130)
Parking for 50
Cards accepted: Amex, Diners, Mastercard, Visa

🛇10🕭🚻📞🖵🖤🏵🖾📺
🖬⚊🍽100❖✕🚗⚊ SP 🏬 T

Lynton House ⋔

⚜ COMMENDED

42 Studley Road, Harrogate HG1 5JU
☎ (01423) 504715
In a central, quiet, tree-lined avenue, 100 yards from exhibition halls and close to Valley Gardens. Personal supervision. Non-smokers only, please.
Bedrooms: 2 single, 2 double, 1 twin
Bathrooms: 1 public

Map references apply to the colour maps at the back of this guide.

Bed & breakfast

per night:	£min	£max
Single	18.00	20.00
Double	36.00	37.00

Open March–November

🛇9🖵♿ⓊⓁⓈ🗲📺🖵✈🏇 DAP ♨

Ruskin Hotel and Restaurant

👑👑👑 HIGHLY COMMENDED

1 Swan Road, Harrogate HG1 2SS
☎ (01423) 502045
Fax (01423) 506131
Small, enchanting Victorian hotel, full of graceful charm and character in lovely mature gardens. Close to conference centre and town. Beautiful antique furnished bedrooms, all en-suite including four-poster, offering every comfort and facility. Delightful licensed restaurant. Private car park.
Bedrooms: 2 single, 3 double, 2 triple
Bathrooms: 7 en-suite

Bed & breakfast

per night:	£min	£max
Single	40.00	59.00
Double	60.00	95.00

Half board per

person:	£min	£max
Daily	44.00	73.00

Lunch available
Evening meal 1900 (last orders 2100)
Parking for 10
Cards accepted: Amex, Mastercard, Visa

🛇5🖵🎱🕮🖵🖵♿🛡Ⓢ🗲📺🖵
🍴❄✿ DAP SP ♨ T ◉

St George Swallow Hotel ♨

👑👑👑👑 COMMENDED

Ripon Road, Harrogate HG1 2SY
☎ (01423) 561431
Fax (01423) 530037
Ⓒℝ Swallow
Traditional hotel, tastefully restored, with leisure complex including pool, sauna, solarium, spa bath and exercise gym. Close to the Valley Gardens and other historic attractions. Short break packages available.
Wheelchair access category 3♿
Bedrooms: 35 single, 28 double, 13 twin, 8 triple, 6 family rooms
Suite available
Bathrooms: 85 en-suite

Bed & breakfast

per night:	£min	£max
Single	90.00	105.00
Double	110.00	125.00

Half board per

person:	£min	£max
Daily	107.50	

Lunch available
Evening meal 1900 (last orders 2130)
Parking for 63

Cards accepted: Amex, Diners, Mastercard, Visa, Switch/Delta

🛇🖵🎱♿🖵🖵♿🛡Ⓢ🗲🕮◐🖼
🖵🖵🍴150🎱🍴✈🏇❄✿ SP T

Spring Lodge Guest House ♨

👑 COMMENDED

22 Spring Mount, Harrogate HG1 2HX
☎ (01423) 506036
In a quiet cul-de-sac, a few minutes' walk from the town centre, bus/railway stations, Royal Hall, conference centre and gardens. Ideal for tourists and business visitors.
Bedrooms: 1 single, 4 double, 1 triple
Bathrooms: 2 en-suite, 1 public, 2 private showers

Bed & breakfast

per night:	£min	£max
Single	17.00	28.00
Double	32.00	42.00

Half board per

person:	£min	£max
Daily	25.00	31.00
Weekly	170.00	190.00

Evening meal 1900 (last orders 2100)
Parking for 1

🛇🖵🎱♿🛡Ⓢ🗲📺🖵🖵🏇 SP ◉

Studley Hotel and Le Breton Restaurant ♨

👑👑👑 COMMENDED

Swan Road, Harrogate HG1 2SE
☎ (01423) 560425
Fax (01423) 530967
Small, friendly hotel, ideally situated near Valley Gardens, shops and conference/exhibition centre. Le Breton French Restaurant has genuine charcoal grill. Excellent value table d'hote dinner and a la carte menu with extensive wine list. Half-board prices apply to weekend breaks.
Bedrooms: 15 single, 10 double, 11 twin
Bathrooms: 36 en-suite

Bed & breakfast

per night:	£min	£max
Single	68.00	85.00
Double	88.00	98.00

Half board per

person:	£min	£max
Daily	55.00	60.00

Lunch available
Evening meal 1900 (last orders 2200)
Parking for 14
Cards accepted: Amex, Diners, Mastercard, Visa, Switch/Delta

🛇🖵🎱♿🖵🖵♿🛡Ⓢ🗲🕮📺◐🖼🖵
🖵🍴16❄ SP T

Valley Hotel ♨

👑👑👑 COMMENDED

93-95 Valley Drive, Harrogate HG2 0JP
☎ (01423) 504868
Fax (01423) 531940
Email: valley@harrogate.com
Hotel overlooking Valley Gardens, offering a warm welcome both to tourists and business people. Licensed restaurant.
Bedrooms: 4 single, 3 double, 5 twin, 2 triple, 2 family rooms
Bathrooms: 16 en-suite

Bed & breakfast

per night:	£min	£max
Single	30.00	40.00
Double	50.00	65.00

Half board per

person:	£min	£max
Daily	34.00	40.00
Weekly	238.00	280.00

Lunch available
Evening meal 1800 (last orders 2030)
Parking for 3
Cards accepted: Amex, Diners, Mastercard, Visa

🛇🖵🎱♿🛡Ⓢ🗲🕮🖼🖵🖵 SP
T

White Hart Hotel ♨

👑👑👑 COMMENDED

Cold Bath Road, Harrogate HG2 0NF
☎ (01423) 505681
Fax (01423) 568354
Grade II listed building in the centre of Harrogate, overlooking West Park Stray. Recently upgraded and refurbished. Large car park.
Bedrooms: 37 single, 4 double, 13 twin
Bathrooms: 54 en-suite

Bed & breakfast

per night:	£min	£max
Single	51.50	
Double	77.50	

Lunch available
Evening meal 1830 (last orders 2030)
Parking for 85
Cards accepted: Mastercard, Visa

🖵🎱♿🛡Ⓢ🗲🕮◐🖼🖵🖵
🍴100🍴✈ DAP

ACCESSIBILITY

Look for the ♿♿♿ symbols which indicate accessibility for wheelchair users. These are described in detail at the front of this guide.

HAWES

North Yorkshire
Map ref 5B3

The capital of Upper Wensleydale on the famous Pennine Way, renowned for great cheeses. Popular with walkers. Dales National Park Information Centre and Folk Museum. Nearby is spectacular Hardraw Force waterfall.

Stone House Hotel ⚘

ಠ ಠ ಠ COMMENDED

Sedbusk, Hawes DL8 3PT
☎ (01969) 667571
Fax (01969) 667720

Fine Edwardian country house hotel in a beautiful old English garden with panoramic views of Upper Wensleydale.
Bedrooms: 1 single, 10 double, 7 twin, 1 triple
Bathrooms: 19 en-suite, 1 public

Bed & breakfast per night:

	£min	£max
Single	29.00	50.00
Double	58.00	83.00

Half board per person:

	£min	£max
Daily	45.95	57.45
Weekly	289.49	361.95

Evening meal 1900 (last orders 2000)
Parking for 30
Open February–December
Cards accepted: Mastercard, Visa, Switch/Delta

🐎🛏🕭🖵🐾🧺📶S✂🕮🏛🖨 ⚓🎀50🔍🔎♺🟙⬜SP🎏Ⓣ

Tarney Fors Country Guest House ⚘

ಠ ಠ ಠ COMMENDED

Tarney Fors, Hawes DL8 3LS
☎ (01969) 667475
Grade II listed building. Former dales farmhouse situated in open countryside, yet with easy access. In heart of Dales National Park. Lunches and cream teas available. Parking.
Bedrooms: 2 double, 1 twin
Bathrooms: 2 en-suite, 1 private

Bed & breakfast per night:

	£min	£max
Double	44.00	50.00

Half board per person:

	£min	£max
Daily	36.50	39.50

Lunch available
Evening meal from 1900
Parking for 9
Open March–November
Cards accepted: Mastercard, Visa

🐎🛏7📶🕭🐾📶S✂🕮📺🧺🖨⚓🎀 🍴🚲SP🎏◎

White Hart Inn ⚘

🛏 APPROVED

Main Street, Hawes DL8 3QL
☎ (01969) 667259
17th C coaching inn with a friendly welcome, offering traditional fare. Open fires, Yorkshire ales. Central for exploring the dales.
Bedrooms: 1 single, 4 double, 2 twin
Bathrooms: 2 public

Bed & breakfast per night:

	£min	£max
Single	18.50	25.00
Double	35.00	40.00

Lunch available
Evening meal 1900 (last orders 2100)
Parking for 7
Cards accepted: Amex, Mastercard, Visa

🐎🐾📶S🕮📺🍽20🔍SP

HAWORTH

West Yorkshire
Map ref 4B1

This Pennine town is famous as home of the Bronte family. The Parsonage is now a Bronte Museum where furniture and possessions of the family are displayed. Moors and Bronte waterfalls nearby and steam trains on the Keighley and Worth Valley Railway pass through.
Tourist Information Centre ☎ *(01535) 642329*

The Apothecary Guest House & Tea Rooms ⚘

🛏 APPROVED

86 Main Street, Haworth, Keighley BD22 8DA
☎ (01535) 643642
Fax (01535) 643642
At the top of Haworth Main Street opposite the famous Bronte church, 1 minute from the Parsonage and moors.
Bedrooms: 1 single, 4 double, 1 twin, 1 triple
Bathrooms: 6 en-suite, 1 private

Bed & breakfast per night:

	£min	£max
Single	18.00	19.00
Double	34.00	39.00

Parking for 7
Cards accepted: Mastercard, Visa

🐎🛏🖵🐾📶S✂🕮🏛🖨🟙❄🚲 SP🎏◎

Bronte Hotel

Listed APPROVED

Lees Lane, Haworth, Keighley BD22 8RA
☎ (01535) 644112
Fax (01535) 646725
On the edge of the moors, 5 minutes' walk from the station and 15 minutes' walk to the Parsonage, the former home of the Brontes.
Bedrooms: 3 single, 3 double, 2 twin, 3 triple
Bathrooms: 8 en-suite, 1 public

Bed & breakfast per night:

	£min	£max
Single	20.00	30.00
Double	40.00	46.00

Lunch available
Evening meal 1900 (last orders 2130)
Parking for 30
Cards accepted: Mastercard, Visa

🐎🛏🖵🕭📶S📺🏛🍽SP

Ferncliffe

ಠ ಠ ಠ COMMENDED

Hebden Road, Haworth, Keighley BD22 8RS
☎ (01535) 643405
Well-appointed, private hotel with panoramic views overlooking Haworth and the Worth Valley Steam Railway. Personal attention and good food.
Bedrooms: 2 single, 2 double, 1 twin, 1 triple
Bathrooms: 6 en-suite

Bed & breakfast per night:

	£min	£max
Single	19.50	24.00
Double	39.00	42.00

Half board per person:

	£min	£max
Daily	29.00	35.00
Weekly	203.00	245.00

Lunch available
Evening meal 1900 (last orders 2100)
Parking for 12
Cards accepted: Mastercard, Visa

🐎🛏🖵🐾📶S✂🕮📺🏛⚓∪ ▶❄🚲DAF SP

Old White Lion Hotel ⚘

ಠ ಠ ಠ COMMENDED

Haworth, Keighley BD22 8DU
☎ (01535) 642313
Fax (01535) 646222
Family-run, centuries old coaching inn. Candlelit restaurant using local fresh produce, cooked to order. Old world bars serving home-made bar meals

and traditional ales. Special rates available all year. Confirmed prices on application.
Bedrooms: 3 single, 8 double, 1 twin, 2 triple
Bathrooms: 14 en-suite

Bed & breakfast

per night:	£min	£max
Single	60.00	70.00
Double	85.00	95.00

Lunch available
Evening meal 1900 (last orders 2130)
Parking for 8
Cards accepted: Amex, Diners, Mastercard, Visa

🚗🍽️📞📠🖥️📻⌨️✂️🛏️📺🖥️🍺
🍴60✈️ SP 🏧 ◉

HEBDEN BRIDGE

West Yorkshire
Map ref 4B1

Originally a small town on packhorse route, Hebden Bridge grew into a booming mill town in 18th C with rows of "up-and-down" houses of several storeys built against hillsides. Ancient "pace-egg play" custom held on Good Friday.
Tourist Information Centre ☎ *(01422) 843831*

Carlton Hotel 🏦
👑👑👑👑 HIGHLY COMMENDED
Albert Street, Hebden Bridge
HX7 8ES
☎ (01422) 844400
Fax (01422) 843117
Victorian emporium converted and lovingly restored to provide comfort and tranquillity from the town set below. Varied and interesting shops to hand and excellent walking nearby.
Bedrooms: 3 single, 9 double, 4 twin
Bathrooms: 16 en-suite

Bed & breakfast

per night:	£min	£max
Single	49.00	59.00
Double	65.00	75.00

Lunch available
Evening meal 1900 (last orders 2130)
Cards accepted: Amex, Mastercard, Visa, Switch/Delta

🚗🍽️📞📠🖥️📻⌨️✂️🛏️🖥️
🍺🍴150▸✎ SP 🇹

Nutclough House Hotel 🏦
👑👑👑 APPROVED
Keighley Road, Hebden Bridge
HX7 8EZ
☎ (01422) 844361
Family-run hotel offering an extensive menu with large vegetarian selection. 800 yards from town centre. Large car park.

Bedrooms: 3 double, 1 twin, 1 family room
Bathrooms: 4 en-suite, 1 private

Bed & breakfast

per night:	£min	£max
Single	20.00	25.00
Double	30.00	40.00

Lunch available
Evening meal 1800 (last orders 2000)
Parking for 20

🖥️♿🍽️📻🖥️📠🔍⌨️✈️🚜

White Lion Hotel 🏦
👑👑👑 COMMENDED
Bridge Gate, Hebden Bridge
HX7 8EX
☎ (01422) 842197
Fax (01422) 846619

Family-run inn, dating back to 1657, well known for a wide range of cask ales and good home-cooked food.
Bedrooms: 5 double, 2 twin, 1 triple, 2 family rooms
Bathrooms: 10 en-suite

Bed & breakfast

per night:	£min	£max
Single	35.00	35.00
Double	40.00	45.00

Lunch available
Evening meal 1200 (last orders 2100)
Parking for 10
Cards accepted: Mastercard, Visa, Switch/Delta

🚗♿🖥️🍽️📻🖥️✂️🛏️🍺🍴50✿✈️
🚜🏧

HELMSLEY

North Yorkshire
Map ref 5C3

Pretty town on the River Rye at the entrance to Ryedale and the North York Moors, with large square and remains of 12th C castle, several inns and All Saints' Church.

Carlton Lodge 🏦
👑👑 COMMENDED
Bondgate, Helmsley, York YO6 5EY
☎ (01439) 770557
Fax (01439) 770623
Email: carlton.lodge@dial.pipex.com
Within the North York Moors National Park, convivial resident directors offer good food in a superb walking and touring area.

Bedrooms: 2 single, 7 double, 3 twin
Bathrooms: 10 en-suite, 1 public

Bed & breakfast

per night:	£min	£max
Single	35.00	40.00
Double	69.00	75.00

Half board per

person:	£min	£max
Daily	49.00	55.00
Weekly	285.00	295.00

Lunch available
Evening meal 1900 (last orders 2030)
Parking for 60
Cards accepted: Mastercard, Visa

🚗♿🍽️📞🖥️📻🖥️🍺📠✂️🛏️🖥️
🍴160⋃▸✿🐾 DAP ✎ SP 🇹 ◉

The Crown Hotel 🏦
👑👑👑 COMMENDED
Market Place, Helmsley, York
YO6 5BJ
☎ (01439) 770297
Fax (01439) 771595
16th C inn with a Jacobean dining room offering traditional country cooking. Special breaks available. Dogs welcome. Run by the same family for 36 years.
Bedrooms: 5 single, 4 double, 4 twin, 1 triple
Bathrooms: 12 en-suite, 1 public

Bed & breakfast

per night:	£min	£max
Single	28.00	35.00
Double	56.00	70.00

Half board per

person:	£min	£max
Daily	38.00	49.00

Lunch available
Evening meal 1915 (last orders 2000)
Parking for 15
Cards accepted: Mastercard, Visa, Switch/Delta

🚗♿🍽️📞🖥️🍺📻🖥️✂️🛏️🖥️🍺🍴
⋃▸✿🐾 SP 🇹

Feathers Hotel 🏦
👑👑👑 APPROVED
Market Place, Helmsley, York
YO6 5BH
☎ (01439) 770275
Fax (01439) 771101
Fronting on to Helmsley Market Place, the hotel could not be more centrally or pleasantly situated.
Bedrooms: 9 double, 6 twin
Bathrooms: 13 en-suite, 2 public

Bed & breakfast

per night:	£min	£max
Single	35.00	45.00
Double	70.00	90.00

Lunch available

Continued ▶

HELMSLEY
Continued

Evening meal 1900 (last orders
2100)
Parking for 12
Cards accepted: Amex, Diners,
Mastercard, Visa, Switch/Delta
⌂⌖🖳♨⑂Ⓢ🅿📺🛏🖨🛎100
◉🅿❀◫SP🏬

Pheasant Hotel 🅜
⌂⌂⌂ COMMENDED
Harome, Helmsley, York YO6 5JG
☎ (01439) 771241
Fax (01439) 771744
ⓒ Logis of GB
*In a quiet rural village, with a terrace
and gardens overlooking the village
pond. Oak-beamed bar in a former
blacksmith's shop, English food and log
fires. Children over 12 years are
welcome. Heated indoor swimming
pool.*
Wheelchair access category 3🚶
Bedrooms: 1 single, 5 double, 6 twin
Bathrooms: 12 en-suite
**Half board per
person:**

	£min	£max
Daily	55.00	65.00
Weekly	385.00	455.00

Lunch available
Evening meal 1930 (last orders
2030)
Parking for 20
Open March–December
🖧♨📞🖳♨Ⓢ✂🅿🛏🖨🎱✎
🅿❀🚐SP◫

HORNSEA
East Riding of Yorkshire
Map ref 4D1

Small holiday town situated on a
strip of land between the beach
bordering the North Sea and
Hornsea Mere, a large natural
freshwater lake. Some sailing and
fishing permitted on protected
nature reserve. Hornsea Freeport
retail and pottery attracts many
visitors.

Merlstead Private Hotel 🅜
⌂⌂⌂ COMMENDED
59 Eastgate, Hornsea, East Riding of
Yorkshire HU18 1NB
☎ (01964) 533068
Fax (01964) 536975
*Large, well-built, family-run property
offering comfortable, spacious
accommodation with a warm and
friendly atmosphere, close to the sea.*
Bedrooms: 1 double, 3 twin, 1 triple
Bathrooms: 5 en-suite

**Bed & breakfast
per night:**

	£min	£max
Single	30.00	32.00
Double	45.00	48.00

**Half board per
person:**

	£min	£max
Daily	42.50	44.50
Weekly	255.00	267.00

Lunch available
Evening meal 1700 (last orders
1900)
Parking for 4
Cards accepted: Mastercard, Visa
⌂⌖♨⑂Ⓢ📺🛏🖨🅿❀🚐
DAP◫

HOVINGHAM
North Yorkshire
Map ref 5C3

Peaceful village of golden stone
cottages, below Hambleton Hills,
clustering around Hovingham Hall,
home of Duchess of Kent's family.
Built by Sir Thomas Worsley in
1760, the Hall is open to the public
by appointment.

Worsley Arms Hotel 🅜
⌂⌂⌂ HIGHLY COMMENDED
Hovingham, York YO6 4LA
☎ (01653) 628234
Fax (01653) 628130
*Georgian coaching inn set in village
birthplace of the Duchess of Kent.
Sitting rooms with beautiful decor and
open log fires. Food is a highlight, with
local produce and game in abundance.
Andrew Jones combines the best of
traditional and modern cooking.*
Bedrooms: 4 single, 6 double, 9 twin
Bathrooms: 19 en-suite

**Bed & breakfast
per night:**

	£min	£max
Single	55.00	65.00
Double	75.00	85.00

**Half board per
person:**

	£min	£max
Daily	75.00	85.00

Lunch available
Evening meal 1900 (last orders
2130)
Parking for 57
Cards accepted: Amex, Diners,
Mastercard, Visa, Switch/Delta
⌂🖧📞🖳♨⑂Ⓢ✂🅿📺◐🛏
🖨🎱50🏹🎣♒◡🎵✎❀SP◫🎯

The National Grading and
Classification Scheme is
explained at the back
of this guide.

HOWDEN
East Riding of Yorkshire
Map ref 4C1

Small town near the River Ouse,
dominated by partly-ruined
medieval church of St Peter's which
has ancient origins but has been
rebuilt in a range of architectural
styles over the centuries.

Wellington Hotel 🅜
⌂⌂⌂ COMMENDED
31 Bridgegate, Howden, East
Yorkshire DN14 7JG
☎ (01430) 430258
Fax (01430) 432139
*16th C coaching inn with modern
facilities in historic market town.
Popular restaurant, bars and beer
garden. Ideal for business or pleasure.*
Bedrooms: 3 single, 3 double, 4 twin
Bathrooms: 8 en-suite, 2 private

**Bed & breakfast
per night:**

	£min	£max
Single	25.00	29.50
Double	35.00	45.00

Lunch available
Evening meal 1830 (last orders
2200)
Parking for 60
Cards accepted: Amex, Mastercard,
Visa
⌂📞🖳♨Ⓢ🛏🖨🛎60❀🏬SP🏬
◫

HUDDERSFIELD
West Yorkshire
Map ref 4B1

Founded on wool and cloth, has a
famous choral society. Town centre
redeveloped, but several good
Victorian buildings remain, including
railway station, St Peter's Church,
Tolson Memorial Museum, art
gallery and nearby Colne Valley
Museum.
Tourist Information Centre ☎ (01484)
223200

Ashfield Hotel 🅜
⌂⌂ COMMENDED
93 New North Road, Huddersfield
HD1 5ND
☎ (01484) 425916
Fax (01484) 425916
*Family-run licensed hotel with emphasis
on home-cooked food and friendly
service. Half a mile from town centre
and within 2 miles of M62.*
Bedrooms: 6 single, 3 double, 2 twin,
3 triple
Bathrooms: 4 en-suite, 3 public,
3 private showers

Bed & breakfast per night:	£min	£max
Single	20.00	27.00
Double	34.00	50.00

Half board per person:	£min	£max
Daily	25.00	37.00

Evening meal 1830 (last orders 2000)
Parking for 20
Cards accepted: Amex, Diners, Mastercard, Visa, Switch/Delta

Briar Court Hotel ♠
♚♚♚ COMMENDED

Halifax Road, Birchencliffe, Huddersfield HD3 3NT
☎ (01484) 519902
Fax (01484) 431812

Yorkshire-stone hotel renowned for friendly and efficient service and high standards. Two restaurants, one being the famous Da Sandro Ristorante, very popular with local and regional guests. In the heart of the countryside close to, yet quietly removed from, exit 24 of M62.
Bedrooms: 2 single, 40 double, 2 twin, 1 triple, 2 family rooms
Suites available
Bathrooms: 47 en-suite

Bed & breakfast per night:	£min	£max
Single	45.00	70.00
Double	55.00	84.00

Lunch available
Evening meal 1800 (last orders 2300)
Parking for 140
Cards accepted: Amex, Diners, Mastercard, Visa, Switch/Delta

The symbol ⓒⓡ and a group name following an hotel address indicates that bookings can be made through a central reservations office. These offices are listed in the information pages at the back of this guide.

Flying Horse Country Hotel ♠
♚♚♚ COMMENDED

Nettleton Hill Road, Scapegoat Hill, Huddersfield HD7 4NY
☎ (01484) 642368
Fax (01484) 642866
ⓒⓡ Minotel

Country hotel within walking distance of moors, 2 miles from M62, exit 23.
Bedrooms: 1 single, 17 double, 15 twin
Bathrooms: 33 en-suite

Bed & breakfast per night:	£min	£max
Single	30.00	54.95
Double	50.00	64.95

Lunch available
Evening meal 1900 (last orders 2145)
Parking for 113
Cards accepted: Amex, Diners, Mastercard, Visa

Hilton National Huddersfield/Halifax ♠
♚♚♚ HIGHLY COMMENDED

M62 Exit 24, Ainley Top, Huddersfield HD3 3RH
☎ (01422) 375431
Fax (01422) 310067
ⓒⓡ Utell International
Imposing modern hotel, with attractive leisure club, surrounded by the rugged Pennines. Close to Haworth (Bronte country) and Holmfirth (Summer Wine country).
Bedrooms: 45 double, 63 twin, 6 family rooms
Suite available
Bathrooms: 114 en-suite

Bed & breakfast per night:	£min	£max
Single	40.00	98.00
Double	50.00	107.00

Half board per person:	£min	£max
Daily	49.00	116.00

Lunch available
Evening meal 1900 (last orders 2200)
Parking for 220
Cards accepted: Amex, Diners, Mastercard, Visa, Switch/Delta

Huddersfield Hotel and Rosemary Lane Bistro ♠
♚♚♚ COMMENDED

33-47 Kirkgate, Huddersfield HD1 1QT
☎ (01484) 512111
Fax (01484) 435262
Past winner of "Yorkshire In Bloom". Free secure car park. Continental-style brasserie, traditional pub and nightclub within the complex. Renowned for friendliness.
Bedrooms: 20 single, 13 double, 10 twin, 1 triple, 1 family room
Suite available
Bathrooms: 45 en-suite

Bed & breakfast per night:	£min	£max
Single	25.00	50.00
Double	40.00	70.00

Half board per person:	£min	£max
Daily	37.00	67.00

Lunch available
Evening meal 1800 (last orders 2300)
Parking for 120
Cards accepted: Amex, Diners, Mastercard, Visa, Switch/Delta

HULL

Kingston upon Hull
Map ref 4C1

Busy seaport with a modern city centre and excellent shopping facilities. Maritime traditions in the town, docks museum, and the home of William Wilberforce, the slavery abolitionist, whose house is now a museum. The Humber Bridge is 5 miles west.
Tourist Information Centre ☎ (01482) 223559 or 702118

Conway-Roseberry Hotel
♚♚♚ COMMENDED

86 Marlborough Avenue, Hull HU5 3JT
☎ (01482) 445256
Fax (01482) 445256
Homely guesthouse set in tree-lined avenue of Victorian houses in quiet conservation area. Emphasis on food, cleanliness and comfort. High standard of service in a friendly atmosphere.
Bedrooms: 1 single, 2 double, 1 twin
Bathrooms: 2 en-suite, 1 public, 2 private showers

Bed & breakfast per night:	£min	£max
Single	17.00	27.00
Double	34.00	38.00

Continued ▶

HULL
Continued

Half board per person:

	£min	£max
Daily	24.00	34.00
Weekly	168.00	238.00

Lunch available
Evening meal 1800 (last orders 1900)
Cards accepted: Mastercard, Visa

The Earlsmere Hotel ⋔
Listed COMMENDED

76-78 Sunnybank, Off Spring Bank West, Hull HU3 1LQ
☎ (01482) 341977
Fax (01482) 473714
Small family-run hotel in a quiet area overlooking the private grounds of Hymers College. Local buses 50 metres from door, city centre 1 mile, Humberside Airport 25 minutes' drive.
Bedrooms: 2 single, 4 double, 3 triple
Bathrooms: 6 en-suite, 1 public, 3 private showers
Bed & breakfast per night:

	£min	£max
Single	17.50	28.00
Double	30.00	40.00

Cards accepted: Mastercard, Visa

Kingstown Hotel ⋔
HIGHLY COMMENDED

Hull Road, Hedon, Hull HU12 8DJ
☎ (01482) 890461
Fax (01482) 890713
Stylish, select and very friendly. Ideally placed for visiting Hull and Holderness. Large kiddies' indoor/outdoor play areas. Extensive dining facilities.
Wheelchair access category 1 &
Bedrooms: 10 single, 19 double, 5 twin
Bathrooms: 34 en-suite
Bed & breakfast per night:

	£min	£max
Single	45.00	62.00
Double	55.00	75.00

Half board per person:

	£min	£max
Daily	55.00	80.00

Lunch available
Evening meal 1200 (last orders 2200)
Parking for 96
Cards accepted: Amex, Diners, Mastercard, Visa, Switch/Delta

Quality Royal Hotel ⋔
COMMENDED

Ferensway, Hull HU1 3UF
☎ (01482) 325087
Fax (01482) 323172
Large Victorian city centre hotel with direct access to coach and railway stations, refurbished to a high standard and with an indoor leisure centre. Rooms feature en-suite bathroom, colour TV, radio/alarm, tea and coffee hospitality tray.
Wheelchair access category 2 &
Bedrooms: 46 single, 46 double, 63 twin
Bathrooms: 155 en-suite
Bed & breakfast per night:

	£min	£max
Single	73.50	80.85
Double	96.60	111.80

Half board per person:

	£min	£max
Daily	46.75	109.25
Weekly	327.25	764.75

Lunch available
Evening meal 1830 (last orders 2200)
Parking for 125
Cards accepted: Amex, Diners, Mastercard, Visa, Switch/Delta

ILKLEY
West Yorkshire
Map ref 4B1

This moorland town is famous for its ballad. The 16th C manor house, now a museum, displays local prehistoric and Roman relics. Popular walk leads up Heber's Ghyll to Ilkley Moor, with the mysterious Swastika Stone and White Wells, 18th C plunge baths.
Tourist Information Centre ☎ (01943) 602319

Crescent Hotel ⋔
COMMENDED

Brook Street, Ilkley LS29 8DG
☎ (01943) 600012 & 600062
Fax (01943) 607186
Fully modernised hotel with family rooms and self-catering suites. In a central position in town. Convenient for the dales. Meals can also be provided for residents at The Box Tree, an award-winning restaurant.
Bedrooms: 1 single, 4 double, 15 twin
Bathrooms: 20 en-suite
Bed & breakfast per night:

	£min	£max
Single	46.00	60.00
Double	55.00	72.00

Half board per person:

	£min	£max
Daily	61.00	75.00

Lunch available
Evening meal 1830 (last orders 2045)
Parking for 25
Cards accepted: Amex, Mastercard, Visa

Grove Hotel ⋔
COMMENDED

66 The Grove, Ilkley LS29 9PA
☎ (01943) 600298
Fax (01943) 600298
Small, friendly, private hotel offering well-appointed accommodation. Convenient for Ilkley town centre, shops and gardens. Short breaks available all year.
Bedrooms: 1 single, 3 double, 2 triple
Bathrooms: 6 en-suite, 1 public
Bed & breakfast per night:

	£min	£max
Single	30.00	42.00
Double	40.00	54.00

Half board per person:

	£min	£max
Daily	33.00	40.00
Weekly	231.00	280.00

Lunch available
Evening meal 1900 (last orders 1930)
Parking for 5
Cards accepted: Amex, Diners, Mastercard, Visa, Switch/Delta

Rombalds Hotel and Restaurant ⋔
HIGHLY COMMENDED

West View, Wells Road, Ilkley LS29 9JG
☎ (01943) 603201
Fax (01943) 816586

Elegant Georgian restoration on the edge of Ilkley Moor, 600 yards from the town centre. Award-winning restaurant.
Bedrooms: 3 single, 9 double, 2 twin, 1 triple
Suites available
Bathrooms: 15 en-suite

Bed & breakfast per night:	£min	£max
Single	52.50	97.50
Double	65.00	115.00

Half board per person:	£min	£max
Daily	50.45	70.45
Weekly	303.00	423.00

Lunch available
Evening meal 1830 (last orders 2130)
Parking for 22
Cards accepted: Amex, Diners, Mastercard, Visa, Switch/Delta

⌂☏▣▢♦⛴🅂✕🄫TV▥🖨
🍴70⛶❄🚭SP🎪T

INGLETON

North Yorkshire
Map ref 5B3

Thriving tourist centre for fell-walkers, climbers and pot-holers. Popular walks up beautiful Twiss Valley to Ingleborough Summit, Whernside, White Scar Caves and waterfalls.

Bridge End Guest House

👑👑 COMMENDED

Mill Lane, Ingleton, Carnforth, Lancashire LA6 3EP
☎ (015242) 41413
Georgian house pleasantly situated adjacent to the entrance to the waterfalls walk. It features a cantilevered patio over the River Doe and retains an elegant staircase. All rooms en-suite. Vegetarians welcome.
Bedrooms: 1 single, 1 double, 1 triple
Bathrooms: 3 en-suite

Bed & breakfast per night:	£min	£max
Single	19.00	22.00
Double	34.00	40.00

Half board per person:	£min	£max
Daily	24.00	32.00
Weekly	168.00	224.00

Lunch available
Evening meal 1830 (last orders 2030)
Parking for 10
Cards accepted: Mastercard, Visa

⌂▣▢♦ UL🄸🅂✕🄫TV▥🖨✕
🚐 DAP🚭SP🎪

Ferncliffe Guest House ⋀

👑👑👑 COMMENDED

55 Main Street, Ingleton, Carnforth, Lancashire LA6 3HJ
☎ (015242) 42405
Lovely detached Victorian house in quiet location, with a growing

reputation for good food and high standard of accommodation. All rooms en-suite.
Bedrooms: 1 double, 4 twin
Bathrooms: 5 en-suite

Bed & breakfast per night:	£min	£max
Single	30.00	30.00
Double	44.00	44.00

Half board per person:	£min	£max
Daily	34.50	42.00
Weekly	218.00	275.00

Evening meal 1830 (last orders 2030)
Parking for 5
Open February–October

⌂12▢♦ UL🄸🅂✕🄫TV▥🖨🚗❄
🚐 DAP🚭SP

Ingleborough View ⋀

👑👑 HIGHLY COMMENDED

Main Street, Ingleton, Carnforth, Lancashire LA6 3HH
☎ (015242) 41523
Attractive stone-built house overlooking river. Renowned for food, comfort and hospitality. Ideally situated for local walks and touring dales and Lake District.
Bedrooms: 3 double, 1 twin
Bathrooms: 2 en-suite, 2 private

Bed & breakfast per night:	£min	£max
Single	20.00	25.00
Double	35.00	40.00

Parking for 4

⌂▣▢♦ UL🄸🅂✕🄫TV▥🖨
❄✕🚐SP

Langber Country Guest House ⋀

👑 APPROVED

Tatterthorne Road, Ingleton, Carnforth LA6 3DT
☎ (015242) 41587
Detached country house in hilltop position with panoramic views. Good touring centre for dales, lakes and coast. Comfortable accommodation. Friendly service - everyone welcome.
Bedrooms: 1 single, 2 double, 1 twin, 2 triple, 1 family room
Bathrooms: 4 en-suite, 1 public

Bed & breakfast per night:	£min	£max
Single	16.50	22.00
Double	32.00	42.00

Half board per person:	£min	£max
Daily	22.50	32.00
Weekly	138.00	170.00

Evening meal 1830 (last orders 1700)
Parking for 6

⌂☏♦ UL🄸🅂✕🄫TV▥🖨♦❄SP
◉

Springfield Private Hotel ⋀

👑👑👑 COMMENDED

Main Street, Ingleton, Carnforth, Lancashire LA6 3HJ
☎ (015242) 41280
Detached Victorian villa in its own grounds with a fountain and conservatory. Private fishing.
Bedrooms: 3 double, 1 twin, 1 family room
Bathrooms: 5 en-suite, 1 public

Bed & breakfast per night:	£min	£max
Single	21.00	21.00
Double	42.00	42.00

Half board per person:	£min	£max
Daily	31.25	31.25
Weekly	196.00	196.00

Evening meal 1830 (last orders 1700)
Parking for 12
Cards accepted: Mastercard, Visa, Switch/Delta

⌂▢♦ UL🄸🅂✕🄫TV▥🖨🍴🎣
❄🚐 DAP SP T◉

KETTLEWELL

North Yorkshire
Map ref 5B3

Set in the spectacular scenery of the Yorkshire Dales National Park in Wharfedale, this former market town is a convenient stopping place for climbers and walkers. Dramatic rock formation of Kilnsey Crag is 3 miles south.

Langcliffe Country Guest House ⋀

👑👑👑 COMMENDED

Kettlewell, Skipton BD23 5RJ
☎ (01756) 760243 & 760896
Detached guesthouse in the heart of the Yorkshire Dales with peaceful surroundings and magnificent scenery. Ideal for touring and walking in the national park. Home cooking.
Bedrooms: 2 double, 2 twin, 1 family room
Bathrooms: 4 en-suite, 1 private shower

Bed & breakfast per night:	£min	£max
Single	40.00	40.00
Double	60.00	60.00

Continued ▶

KETTLEWELL

Continued

Half board per person:

	£min	£max
Daily	45.00	45.00
Weekly	295.00	300.00

Evening meal 1900 (last orders 2030)
Parking for 7
Cards accepted: Mastercard, Visa

⛺🛏️🍴📞📠🖥️💷♨️🔍Ⓢ✂🍴🖥️ 🍺🌸🐾🐕SP

KILBURN

North Yorkshire
Map ref 5C3

Attractive village of stone cottages with tiled roofs in the Hambleton Hills. Famous for its White Horse cut by local schoolmaster, Thomas Hodgson, in 1857 and for the mouse carved in oak which is the famous trade mark of Robert Thompson. Mouseman Visitors' Centre.

The Forresters Arms Hotel ⋔

👑👑👑 COMMENDED
Kilburn YO6 4AH
☎ (01347) 868550 & 868386
Fax (01347) 868386
ⒸⓇ Wayfarer
Set in the North York Moors National Park in Herriot country. 12th C inn next door to the famous "Mousey" Thompson.
Bedrooms: 7 double, 3 twin
Bathrooms: 10 en-suite

Bed & breakfast per night:

	£min	£max
Single	38.00	38.00
Double	49.00	58.00

Half board per person:

	£min	£max
Daily	48.00	48.00
Weekly	190.00	226.00

Lunch available
Evening meal 1900 (last orders 2130)
Parking for 40
Cards accepted: Amex, Mastercard, Visa, Switch/Delta

⛺🛏️🍴📞💷🖥️💷♨️🔍Ⓢ🖥️🍴 🍴20🍷🐕🐾SP🅣

COLOUR MAPS

Colour maps at the back of this guide pinpoint all places in which you will find accommodation listed.

KIRKBYMOORSIDE

North Yorkshire
Map ref 5C3

Attractive market town with remains of Norman castle. Good centre for exploring moors. Nearby are wild daffodils of Farndale.

George & Dragon Hotel ⋔

👑👑👑 COMMENDED
Market Place, Kirkbymoorside, York YO6 6AA
☎ (01751) 433334
Fax (01751) 433334
Inn of character adjacent to the North York Moors. Extensively modernised bedrooms, all with colour TV, en-suite bathrooms. Ideal touring location. Good Pub Guide "Newcomer of the Year Award 1995".
Bedrooms: 1 single, 12 double, 3 twin, 2 triple, 1 family room
Bathrooms: 19 en-suite

Bed & breakfast per night:

	£min	£max
Single	45.00	49.00
Double	79.00	89.00

Lunch available
Evening meal 1830 (last orders 2115)
Parking for 20
Cards accepted: Mastercard, Visa, Switch/Delta

⛺🛏️🍴📞💷🖥️♨️🔍Ⓢ✂🖥️🍴 🍴40🚻🚶♨🌸🐾SP🅟🅣◎

KNARESBOROUGH

North Yorkshire
Map ref 4B1

Picturesque market town on the River Nidd, famous for its 11th C castle ruins, overlooking town and river gorge. Attractions include oldest chemist's shop in country, prophetess Mother Shipton's cave, Dropping Well and Court House Museum. Boating on river.

Abbeyfield House

👑👑 COMMENDED
25 Park Grove, Knaresborough HG5 9ET
☎ (01423) 866867
Just 2 miles from the town centre, a large older-type house, built in 1901, which has been modernised to a good standard.
Bedrooms: 2 double
Bathrooms: 2 en-suite

Bed & breakfast per night:

	£min	£max
Single	30.00	30.00
Double	36.00	36.00

Parking for 2

⛺🛏️📞♨️🔍UL✂🖥️TV🖥️🛏️🍴🐾🐕SP

Ebor Mount ⋔

👑👑 COMMENDED
18 York Place, Knaresborough HG5 0AA
☎ (01423) 863315
Fax (01423) 863315
Charming 18th C townhouse with private car park, providing bed and breakfast accommodation in recently refurbished rooms. Ideal touring centre.
Bedrooms: 1 single, 4 double, 1 twin, 2 triple
Bathrooms: 8 en-suite, 1 public

Bed & breakfast per night:

	£min	£max
Single	19.00	38.00
Double	38.00	42.00

Parking for 10
Cards accepted: Mastercard, Visa, Switch/Delta

⛺📞💷📠♨️🔍UL✂🍴🐕🐾🏠 🅣

General Tarleton Inn ⋔

👑👑👑 COMMENDED
Boroughbridge Road, Ferrensby, Knaresborough HG5 0QB
☎ (01423) 340284
Fax (01423) 340288

All rooms elegantly furnished. Freehouse, traditional ales. Warm family welcome.
Bedrooms: 3 double, 12 twin
Bathrooms: 15 en-suite

Bed & breakfast per night:

	£min	£max
Single	55.00	
Double	62.50	

Half board per person:

	£min	£max
Daily	82.00	

Lunch available
Evening meal 1800 (last orders 2200)
Parking for 100
Cards accepted: Mastercard, Visa, Switch/Delta

⛺🛏️🍴📞💷🖥️💷♨️🔍Ⓢ✂🖥️🍴 🍴40🌸🐾SP🅣

Newton House Hotel ⚐

‹‹‹ COMMENDED

5-7 York Place, Knaresborough
HG5 0AD
☎ (01423) 863539
Fax (01423) 869748
Charming, family-run, 17th C former coaching inn, situated 2 minutes' walk from the market square, castle and river. 10 minutes Harrogate, 20 minutes York, 30 minutes the dales.
Bedrooms: 1 single, 6 double, 3 twin, 2 triple
Bathrooms: 11 en-suite, 1 private
Bed & breakfast per night:

	£min	£max
Single	32.50	45.00
Double	50.00	60.00

Half board per person:

	£min	£max
Daily	35.00	51.25
Weekly	245.00	315.00

Evening meal 1900 (last orders 2000)
Parking for 10
Cards accepted: Mastercard, Visa, Switch/Delta

Yorkshire Lass ⚐

‹‹‹ APPROVED

High Bridge, Harrogate Road, Knaresborough HG5 8DA
☎ (01423) 862962
Fax (01423) 869091
Detached inn on main Harrogate/York road, with attractive bedrooms overlooking River Nidd. Real ales, wines, large selection of whiskies. Specialising in traditional Yorkshire dishes. Special seasonal rates available.
Bedrooms: 1 single, 2 double, 2 twin, 1 triple
Bathrooms: 6 en-suite
Bed & breakfast per night:

	£min	£max
Single	30.00	39.50
Double	40.00	55.00

Half board per person:

	£min	£max
Daily	37.50	45.00
Weekly	262.50	

Lunch available
Evening meal 1700 (last orders 2200)
Parking for 34
Cards accepted: Amex, Mastercard, Visa, Switch/Delta

Please mention this guide when making your booking.

LEEDS

West Yorkshire
Map ref 4B1

Large city with excellent modern shopping centre and splendid Victorian architecture. Museums and galleries including Temple Newsam House (the Hampton Court of the North), Tetley's Brewery Wharf and the Royal Armouries Museum; also home of Opera North.
Tourist Information Centre ☎ (0113) 242 5242

Aintree Hotel ⚐

‹‹‹ COMMENDED

38 Cardigan Road, Headingley, Leeds LS6 3AG
☎ (0113) 275 8290
Small, comfortable licensed family hotel in tree-lined road, overlooking Headingley Cricket Ground. Close to university, public transport and shopping centre, 1.5 miles from city centre.
Bedrooms: 6 single, 1 double, 2 twin
Bathrooms: 5 en-suite, 2 public
Bed & breakfast per night:

	£min	£max
Single	24.00	32.00
Double	37.00	43.00

Half board per person:

	£min	£max
Daily	34.50	42.50

Evening meal 1800 (last orders 1000)
Parking for 10
Cards accepted: Mastercard, Visa

Aragon Hotel

‹‹‹

250 Stainbeck Lane, Meanwood, Leeds LS7 2PS
☎ (0113) 275 9306
Fax (0113) 275 7166
CR The Independents
Converted, late Victorian house in quiet, wooded surroundings, 2 miles from the city centre. TV, telephone and tea-making facilities in all bedrooms. Weekly half board rates negotiable.
Bedrooms: 3 single, 7 double, 3 twin
Bathrooms: 11 en-suite, 2 public
Bed & breakfast per night:

	£min	£max
Single	27.00	41.00
Double	40.00	48.00

Half board per person:

	£min	£max
Daily	28.00	49.00

Evening meal 1900 (last orders 2100)

Parking for 27
Cards accepted: Amex, Diners, Mastercard, Visa

Ascot Grange Hotel ⚐

‹‹‹ COMMENDED

126-130 Otley Road, Headingley, Leeds LS16 5JX
☎ (0113) 2934444
Fax (0113) 2935555
Newly refurbished throughout to a high standard. All rooms en-suite. Two miles from city centre, close to Beckets Park and Yorkshire County Cricket Ground. Warm welcome from friendly staff.
Bedrooms: 5 single, 9 double, 6 family rooms
Bathrooms: 20 en-suite
Bed & breakfast per night:

	£min	£max
Single	37.00	
Double	46.00	

Half board per person:

	£min	£max
Daily	47.50	

Lunch available
Cards accepted: Amex, Diners, Mastercard, Visa, Switch/Delta

Broomhurst Hotel ⚐

‹‹‹ COMMENDED

12 Chapel Lane, Off Cardigan Road, Headingley, Leeds LS6 3BW
☎ (0113) 278 6836 & 278 5764
Fax (0113) 230 7099
Small, comfortable, hotel in a quiet, pleasantly wooded conservation area, 1.5 miles from the city centre. Convenient for Yorkshire County Cricket Ground and university. Warm welcome from friendly staff.
Bedrooms: 8 single, 4 double, 2 twin, 2 triple, 2 family rooms
Bathrooms: 12 en-suite, 3 public
Bed & breakfast per night:

	£min	£max
Single	25.00	36.00
Double	41.00	46.00

Half board per person:

	£min	£max
Daily	35.50	46.50

Lunch available
Evening meal 1800 (last orders 0900)
Parking for 16
Cards accepted: Diners, Mastercard, Visa, Switch/Delta

Cardigan Private Hotel ⋀⋀

👑👑 COMMENDED

36 Cardigan Road, Headingley, Leeds
LS6 3AG
☎ (0113) 278 4301
Fax (0113) 230 7792
*Family-run hotel, next to Headingley
Cricket/Rugby League Ground. Near
public transport and shopping facilities,
1.5 miles from city centre. Evening
meals available Monday to Thursday
only.*
Bedrooms: 5 single, 1 double, 2 twin,
1 triple, 1 family room
Bathrooms: 6 en-suite, 2 public

Bed & breakfast

per night:	£min	£max
Single	25.00	36.00

Half board per person:

	£min	£max
Daily	37.00	48.00

Evening meal from 1830
Parking for 11
Cards accepted: Mastercard, Visa

⏳🛋🖥📠🛏♿🆂✕🅜 TV 📟 📠 ✈ 🐾 🆂🅿
🏵

Cliff Lawn Hotel

👑👑 COMMENDED

Cliff Road, Headingley, Leeds
LS6 2ET
☎ (0113) 278 5442 & 275 6192
Fax (0113) 278 5442
*Large Victorian mansion set in well
kept grounds . In a quiet location,
approximately 1 mile from Leeds city
centre.*
Bedrooms: 10 single, 7 double,
5 twin, 1 triple
Bathrooms: 12 en-suite, 3 public,
2 private showers

Bed & breakfast

per night:	£min	£max
Single	31.72	41.12
Double	47.00	56.40

Evening meal 1800 (last orders
2000)
Parking for 20
Cards accepted: Mastercard, Visa,
Switch/Delta

⏳🛋🖥♿🆂🅜 TV 📟 📠 🍴120 🕯
🔌🏵🆂🅿

Fairbairn House ⋀⋀

👑 APPROVED

71-75 Clarendon Road, Leeds
LS2 9PL
☎ (0113) 233 6633
Fax (0113) 246 0899
Email: faimat@lucs-01acuk
*Victorian mansion, dating from 1850,
with modern bedroom extension.
Within easy reach of Leeds city centre.*

Bedrooms: 22 single, 8 double
Bathrooms: 20 en-suite, 3 public

Bed & breakfast

per night:	£min	£max
Single	20.00	44.00
Double	40.00	44.00

Half board per person:

	£min	£max
Daily	32.50	56.50

Lunch available
Evening meal 1830 (last orders
1930)
Parking for 79
Cards accepted: Mastercard, Visa

🖥📠♿🆂✕🅜 TV ☕📟 📠🍴80
🏵🆂🅿🏵

Harewood Arms Hotel ⋀⋀

👑👑👑👑 HIGHLY COMMENDED

Harrogate Road, Harewood, Leeds
LS17 9LH
☎ (0113) 288 6566
Fax (0113) 288 6064
*Stone-built hotel and restaurant of
character with a rural aspect, 8 miles
from Harrogate and Leeds. Opposite
Harewood House and close to all
amenities, including golf and racing.*
Bedrooms: 2 single, 10 double,
10 twin, 2 triple
Bathrooms: 24 en-suite

Bed & breakfast

per night:	£min	£max
Single	45.00	65.00
Double	60.00	78.00

Half board per person:

	£min	£max
Daily	44.85	60.95

Lunch available
Evening meal 1900 (last orders
2200)
Parking for 60
Cards accepted: Amex, Diners,
Mastercard, Visa, Switch/Delta

⏳🛋🕯📞🖥♿🆂🅜 ☕📟 📠
🍴20🍴🏵🆂🅿🏵🔲

Pinewood Hotel ⋀⋀

👑👑👑 COMMENDED

78 Potternewton Lane, Leeds
LS7 3LW
☎ (0113) 262 2561 & 262 8485

*Extremely attractively decorated and
very well furnished, with many extra
touches enhancing guests' comfort. A
most comfortable welcome in a small
hotel of distinction.*
Bedrooms: 5 single, 3 double, 2 twin
Bathrooms: 10 en-suite

Bed & breakfast

per night:	£min	£max
Single	20.00	36.00
Double	35.00	44.00

Half board per person:

	£min	£max
Daily	27.50	46.00

Evening meal 1830 (last orders
1000)
Cards accepted: Amex, Mastercard,
Visa

⏳🛋🖥📠♿🆂✕🅜 TV 📟 📠
🍴18🐾🆂🅿🏵🔲

St Michael's Tower Hotel ⋀⋀

👑 APPROVED

5 St Michael's Villas, Cardigan Road,
Headingley, Leeds LS6 3AF
☎ (0113) 275 5557 & 275 6039
Fax (0113) 230 7491
*Comfortable, licensed hotel, 1.5 miles
from city centre and close to
Headingley Cricket Ground and
university. Easy access to Yorkshire
countryside. Warm welcome from
friendly staff.*
Bedrooms: 7 single, 7 double, 7 twin,
1 triple, 1 family room
Bathrooms: 12 en-suite, 4 public

Bed & breakfast

per night:	£min	£max
Single	24.00	31.00
Double	34.00	38.00

Half board per person:

	£min	£max
Daily	34.50	41.50

Evening meal 1830 (last orders
2000)
Parking for 26
Cards accepted: Mastercard, Visa

⏳🛋🖥♿🆂🅜 TV 📟 📠✈🆂🅿

Stakis Leeds ⋀⋀

👑👑👑 COMMENDED

Ring Road, Mill Green View,
Seacroft, Leeds LS14 5QF
☎ (0113) 273 2323
Fax (0113) 232 3018
Email: reservations@stakis.co.uk
*Ideal for both business and holiday
makers. On the main Leeds to York
road with easy access to the airport
and motorways. Half board rate based
on a minimum 2-night stay.*
Bedrooms: 22 single, 26 double,
50 twin, 2 family rooms
Suites available
Bathrooms: 100 en-suite

Bed & breakfast

per night:	£min	£max
Single	27.00	82.00
Double	54.00	92.00

Half board per person:

	£min	£max
Daily	40.00	102.00
Weekly	280.00	714.00

Lunch available
Evening meal 1900 (last orders 2200)
Parking for 120
Cards accepted: Amex, Diners, Mastercard, Visa, Switch/Delta

🐕♿✆⌨🖵👜🌺🏷§🍴📺◑🖊
📼🅰️🚬🍺🛏325 DAP 🐾 SP T

De Vere Oulton Hall ᴧᴧ

👑👑👑👑 HIGHLY COMMENDED

Rothwell Lane, Oulton, Woodlesford, Leeds LS26 8HN
☎ (0113) 282 1000
Fax (0113) 282 8066
Fully renovated hall in the heart of Yorkshire, south-east of Leeds. Adjacent to a golf-course. Full leisure club.
Bedrooms: 88 double, 64 twin
Suites available
Bathrooms: 152 en-suite
Bed & breakfast

per night:	£min	£max
Single	125.00	135.00
Double	145.00	155.00

Lunch available
Evening meal 1900 (last orders 2200)
Parking for 220
Cards accepted: Amex, Diners, Mastercard, Visa

🐕♿✆⌨🖵👜🌺🏷§🍴📺◑🖊
📼🏊🛏338 🏌️🎾🎿🏇🐾🚬 SP 🏰
T ◎

LEEDS/BRADFORD AIRPORT

See under Bingley, Bradford, Leeds, Pool in Wharfedale

LEEMING BAR

North Yorkshire
Map ref 5C3

Just off the A1 between dales and moors.

White Rose Hotel ᴧᴧ

👑👑👑 COMMENDED

Leeming Bar, Northallerton DL7 9AY
☎ (01677) 422707 & 424941
Fax (01677) 425123
Family-run private hotel and restaurant ideally situated in village half a mile from A1 motorway. Central for Yorkshire Dales, "Heartbeat" country, coastal resorts. Pets welcome.
Bedrooms: 9 single, 1 double, 6 twin, 2 triple
Bathrooms: 18 en-suite
Bed & breakfast

per night:	£min	£max
Single	17.50	32.50
Double	32.00	45.00

Half board per

person:	£min	£max
Daily	22.50	37.50

Lunch available
Evening meal 1900 (last orders 2130)
Parking for 40
Cards accepted: Amex, Diners, Mastercard, Visa, Switch/Delta

🐕♿✆⌨🖵👜🌺🏷§🍴🖊💷📼
🛏50 🍺🏳️ DAP 🐾 SP T

LEYBURN

North Yorkshire
Map ref 5B3

Attractive dales market town where Mary Queen of Scots was reputedly captured after her escape from Bolton Castle. Fine views over Wensleydale from nearby.
Tourist Information Centre ☎ *(01969) 623069 or 622773*

Golden Lion Hotel & Licensed Restaurant ᴧᴧ

👑👑👑 APPROVED

Market Place, Leyburn DL8 5AS
☎ (01969) 622161
Fax (01969) 623836
Small family-run hotel in the market place of a busy dales town. A good base for touring the surrounding countryside.
Wheelchair access category 3 ♿
Bedrooms: 3 single, 4 double, 3 twin, 4 triple
Bathrooms: 13 en-suite, 2 public
Bed & breakfast

per night:	£min	£max
Single	21.00	30.00
Double	42.00	60.00

Half board per

person:	£min	£max
Daily	34.00	42.00
Weekly	182.00	249.00

Lunch available
Evening meal 1900 (last orders 2100)
Parking for 12
Cards accepted: Amex, Mastercard, Visa, Switch/Delta

🐕♿✆⌨🖵👜🌺🏷§🍴🖊💷📼🛏🍺
🏳️🚶🏰 DAP SP 🏰 T

Secret Garden House ᴧᴧ

👑👑👑 COMMENDED

Grove Square, Leyburn DL8 5AE
☎ (01969) 623589
Georgian house with secluded walled garden and conservatory, in market town, the heart of James Herriot country. Free off-street parking.
Bedrooms: 3 double, 1 twin
Bathrooms: 4 en-suite
Bed & breakfast

per night:	£min	£max
Single	19.50	25.50
Double	39.00	51.00

Evening meal 1930 (last orders 2000)
Parking for 10
Cards accepted: Mastercard, Visa

🐕🛏12♿⌨🖵👜🏷§🍴🖊📺🚬📼🍺♣
🚐 SP

LIVERSEDGE

West Yorkshire
Map ref 4B1

Typical West Yorkshire town 3 miles north-west of Dewsbury.

Healds Hall Hotel ᴧᴧ

👑👑👑 COMMENDED

Leeds Road, Liversedge WF15 6JA
☎ (01924) 409112
Fax (01924) 401895

Family-run hotel with award-winning restaurant. Large gardens. On A62, near M1 and M62. Ideal for dales. Special weekend breaks available.
Bedrooms: 5 single, 11 double, 5 twin, 4 triple
Bathrooms: 25 en-suite
Bed & breakfast

per night:	£min	£max
Single	30.00	53.00
Double	50.00	75.00

Half board per

person:	£min	£max
Daily	35.00	68.00
Weekly	245.00	525.00

Lunch available
Evening meal 1900 (last orders 2100)
Parking for 60
Cards accepted: Amex, Diners, Mastercard, Visa, Switch/Delta

🐕♿✆⌨🖵👜🌺🏷§🍴🖊📺◑
📼🍺🛏100 ♣ SP 🏰 T

LONG PRESTON

North Yorkshire
Map ref 4B1

Village surrounded by limestone country and overlooking Ribblesdale.

Plough Inn ⚑

⚑⚑⚑ COMMENDED

Wigglesworth, Skipton BD23 4RJ
☎ (01729) 840243 & 840638
Fax (01729) 840243
Once an inn and working farm which was part of a large country estate, now converted to provide high standard accommodation in a rural setting.
Bedrooms: 7 double, 4 twin, 1 triple
Bathrooms: 12 en-suite

Bed & breakfast

per night:	£min	£max
Single	34.00	38.00
Double	55.00	65.00

Half board per

person:	£min	£max
Daily	42.50	49.00
Weekly	225.00	260.00

Lunch available
Evening meal 1900 (last orders 2130)
Parking for 50
Cards accepted: Amex, Diners, Mastercard, Visa

🐎🔧♿️📞🖥📺💷🗇🛈⚲🖂▥◨ ⏲150♻️❄️✈️🚲🚭 SP

MALHAM

North Yorkshire
Map ref 5B3

Hamlet of stone cottages amid magnificent rugged limestone scenery in the Yorkshire Dales National Park. Malham Cove is a curving, sheer white cliff 240 ft high. Malham Tarn, one of Yorkshire's few natural lakes, belongs to the National Trust. National Park Centre.

Beck Hall Guest House ⚑

⚑ APPROVED

Malham, Skipton BD23 4DJ
☎ (01729) 830332
Family-run guesthouse set in a spacious riverside garden. Homely atmosphere, four-poster beds, log fires, large car park.
Bedrooms: 11 double, 3 twin
Bathrooms: 9 en-suite, 2 private, 1 public

Bed & breakfast

per night:	£min	£max
Single	17.00	26.00
Double	32.00	40.00

Half board per

person:	£min	£max
Daily	23.25	27.25

Lunch available
Evening meal 1900 (last orders 2000)
Parking for 30

🐎🖥♿️🖂▥◨⏲❄️⚑ 🏠

MALTON

North Yorkshire
Map ref 5D3

Thriving farming town on the River Derwent with large livestock market. Famous for racehorse training. The local museum has Roman remains and the Eden Camp Modern History Theme Museum transports visitors back to wartime Britain. Castle Howard within easy reach.
Tourist Information Centre ☎ (01653) 600048

The George Hotel ⚑

⚑⚑ COMMENDED

19 Yorkersgate, Malton YO17 0AA
☎ (01653) 692884 & (0468) 344337
Family-run hotel, dating from 16th C, now totally refurbished. In town centre location with own car park. Families welcome. Special diets.
Bedrooms: 1 double, 1 twin, 1 triple, 1 family room
Suite available
Bathrooms: 4 en-suite

Bed & breakfast

per night:	£min	£max
Double	42.00	46.00

Lunch available
Evening meal 1800 (last orders 2030)
Parking for 12
Cards accepted: Mastercard, Visa, Switch/Delta

🐎🖥📞🖥♿️📺🛈 S 🖂◈❄️✈️🚲🚭 SP 🏠

Newstead Grange ⚑

⚑⚑⚑ HIGHLY COMMENDED

Norton, Malton YO17 9PJ
☎ (01653) 692502
Fax (01653) 696951
Elegant Georgian country house in 2.5 acres, 1.5 miles from Malton on the Beverley road. Antique furniture. Non-smoking establishment. Children 10 years and over and sometimes younger children by arrangement.
Bedrooms: 4 double, 4 twin
Bathrooms: 8 en-suite

Bed & breakfast

per night:	£min	£max
Single	37.00	43.00
Double	57.00	74.00

Half board per

person:	£min	£max
Daily	42.00	56.00
Weekly	265.00	310.00

Evening meal 1930 (last orders 1945)
Parking for 15
Open February–November
Cards accepted: Mastercard, Visa

🐎⏲10🖥🖥♿️🐾 S ⚲🖂▥🚗🛥⏲20 ❄️✈️🚲 SP 🏠

Wentworth Arms Hotel ⚑

⚑⚑ APPROVED

Town Street, Old Malton, Malton YO17 0HD
☎ (01653) 692618
Former coaching inn, built early 1700s and run by the same family for 100 years. 20 miles from York. An excellent base for touring the Yorkshire Dales, North York Moors and the East Coast.
Bedrooms: 3 double, 2 twin
Bathrooms: 4 en-suite, 1 public

Bed & breakfast

per night:	£min	£max
Single	22.00	23.00
Double	44.00	46.00

Lunch available
Evening meal 1800 (last orders 2045)
Parking for 30
Cards accepted: Mastercard, Visa

🖥♿️🐾🛈▥◨✈️🚲🏠

MIDDLEHAM

North Yorkshire
Map ref 5C3

Town famous for racehorse training, with cobbled squares and houses of local stone. Norman castle, once principal residence of Warwick the Kingmaker and later Richard III. Ruins of Jervaulx Abbey nearby.

Black Swan Hotel ⚑

⚑⚑ COMMENDED

Market Place, Middleham DL8 4NP
☎ (01969) 622221
Fax (01969) 622221
Ⓒ Consort
Unspoilt 17th C inn, with open fires and beamed ceilings, allied to 20th C comforts. Emphasis on food.
Bedrooms: 1 single, 4 double, 1 twin, 1 triple
Bathrooms: 7 en-suite

Bed & breakfast

per night:	£min	£max
Single	27.00	32.00
Double	48.00	65.00

Half board per

person:	£min	£max
Daily	33.00	42.00

Lunch available

Evening meal 1830 (last orders
2100)
Parking for 3
Cards accepted: Mastercard, Visa

Millers House Hotel 𝕄
Ⱶ Ⱶ Ⱶ HIGHLY COMMENDED

Middleham, Leyburn DL8 4NR
☎ (01969) 622630
Fax (01969) 623570
*Yorkshire's Hotel of the Year runner-up
96/97. Elegant Georgian country house
in heart of dales. Privately owned and
run, offering a warm welcome, quality
and comfort. Noted restaurant. 20
minutes from A1.*
Bedrooms: 1 single, 3 double, 3 twin
Bathrooms: 6 en-suite, 1 private

Bed & breakfast
per night:	£min	£max
Single	37.50	37.50
Double	75.00	90.00

Half board per
person:	£min	£max
Daily	54.50	62.00
Weekly	350.00	400.00

Evening meal 1900 (last orders
2030)
Parking for 8
Open February–December
Cards accepted: Mastercard, Visa,
Switch/Delta

MONK FRYSTON

North Yorkshire
Map ref 4C1

Village dating back to Saxon times.
The prefix "Monk" denotes its
former ownership by monks of
Selby Abbey. Interesting church,
lodge and several early thatched
cottages.

Monk Fryston Hall Hotel 𝕄
Ⱶ Ⱶ Ⱶ Ⱶ HIGHLY COMMENDED

Monk Fryston, Leeds LS25 5DU
☎ (01977) 682369
Fax (01977) 683544
Ⓒ Best Western
*Old manor house with peaceful,
comfortable accommodation on the
A63 just off the A1. Friendly
atmosphere and English cooking.
Weekend half board reduction for
minimum 2-night stay.*
Bedrooms: 5 single, 15 double,
6 twin, 2 triple
Bathrooms: 28 en-suite

Bed & breakfast
per night:	£min	£max
Single	72.00	75.00
Double	98.00	105.00

Half board per
person:	£min	£max
Daily	80.00	85.00

Lunch available
Evening meal 1900 (last orders
2130)
Parking for 60
Cards accepted: Amex, Diners,
Mastercard, Visa, Switch/Delta

MORLEY

West Yorkshire
Map ref 4B1

On the outskirts of Leeds, just off
the M62 and close to the M1. The
Town Hall dominates the town.

Old Vicarage Guest House 𝕄
Ⱶ Ⱶ Ⱶ COMMENDED

Bruntcliffe Road, Morley, Leeds
LS27 0JZ
☎ (0113) 253 2174
Fax (0113) 253 3549
*Within minutes of motorways, providing
a Yorkshire welcome with home
comforts in an authentic Victorian
setting. Weekend rates available.*
Bedrooms: 11 single, 4 double,
2 twin
Bathrooms: 17 en-suite

Bed & breakfast
per night:	£min	£max
Single	27.00	48.00
Double	44.00	62.00

Evening meal 1800 (last orders
1945)
Parking for 21
Cards accepted: Amex, Mastercard,
Visa, Switch/Delta

NEWBY WISKE

North Yorkshire
Map ref 5C3

Village on the River Wiske in the
Vale of Mowbray.

Solberge Hall 𝕄
Ⱶ Ⱶ Ⱶ Ⱶ HIGHLY COMMENDED

Newby Wiske, Northallerton
DL7 9ER
☎ (01609) 779191
Fax (01609) 780472
Ⓒ Best Western
*Victorian country house in the heart of
Herriot country, convenient for the*

*moors and dales. Daily half-board
prices based on 2-night stay.*
Bedrooms: 4 single, 16 double,
5 twin
Bathrooms: 25 en-suite

Bed & breakfast
per night:	£min	£max
Single	68.00	78.00
Double	93.00	103.00

Half board per
person:	£min	£max
Daily	60.00	63.00
Weekly	420.00	441.00

Lunch available
Evening meal 1930 (last orders
2130)
Parking for 80
Cards accepted: Amex, Diners,
Mastercard, Visa, Switch/Delta

NORTHALLERTON

North Yorkshire
Map ref 5C3

Formerly a staging post on coaching
route to the North and later a
railway town. Today a lively market
town and administrative capital of
North Yorkshire. Parish church of
All Saints dates from 1200.
*Tourist Information Centre ☎ (01609)
776864*

Alverton Guest House 𝕄
Ⱶ Ⱶ Ⱶ COMMENDED

26 South Parade, Northallerton
DL7 8SG
☎ (01609) 776207
*Family-run guesthouse convenient for
county town facilities and ideal for
touring the dales, moors and coastal
areas.*
Bedrooms: 2 single, 1 double, 1 twin,
1 triple
Bathrooms: 3 en-suite, 1 public

Bed & breakfast
per night:	£min	£max
Single	17.00	23.00
Double	35.00	38.00

Half board per
person:	£min	£max
Daily	26.95	32.95
Weekly	183.00	230.00

Evening meal 1700 (last orders
1830)
Parking for 5

Map references apply to
the colour maps at the
back of this guide.

PATELEY BRIDGE

North Yorkshire
Map ref 5C3

Small market town at centre of Upper Nidderdale. Flax and linen industries once flourished in this remote and beautiful setting.

Grassfields Country House Hotel M

🏵🏵🏵 COMMENDED

Low Wath Road, Pateley Bridge, Harrogate HG3 5HL
☎ (01423) 711412

Georgian building in 2 acres of lawns and trees, within level walking distance of Pateley Bridge. A fine wine cellar and wholesome Yorkshire food.
Bedrooms: 1 single, 4 double, 3 twin, 1 triple
Bathrooms: 9 en-suite

Bed & breakfast per night:	£min	£max
Single	25.00	35.00
Double	40.00	60.00

Half board per person:	£min	£max
Daily	39.00	49.00
Weekly	252.00	322.00

Lunch available
Evening meal 1900 (last orders 2000)
Parking for 15
Cards accepted: Mastercard, Visa

Yorke Arms Hotel M

🏵🏵🏵🏵 HIGHLY COMMENDED

Ramsgill, Harrogate HG3 5RL
☎ (01423) 755243
Fax (01423) 755330
18th C hostelry on village green. In the heart of unspoilt Nidderdale at the head of Gouthwaite Reservoir Nature Reserve. All bedrooms en-suite.
Bedrooms: 3 single, 3 double, 5 twin, 2 triple
Bathrooms: 13 en-suite

Bed & breakfast per night:	£min	£max
Single	50.00	65.00
Double	70.00	110.00

Half board per person:	£min	£max
Daily	60.00	75.00

Lunch available
Evening meal 1900 (last orders 2100)
Parking for 30
Cards accepted: Mastercard, Visa, Switch/Delta

PICKERING

North Yorkshire
Map ref 5D3

Market town and tourist centre on edge of North York Moors. Parish church has complete set of 15th C wall paintings depicting lives of saints. Part of 12th C castle still stands. Beck Isle Museum. The North York Moors Railway begins here.
Tourist Information Centre ☎ (01751) 473791

Bramwood Guest House M

🏵🏵🏵 HIGHLY COMMENDED

19 Hallgarth, Pickering YO18 7AW
☎ (01751) 474066
Charming 18th C house. All rooms tastefully furnished en-suite. Individual dining tables, guest lounge. Friendly and relaxed atmosphere. No smoking. Private parking.
Bedrooms: 4 double, 1 twin
Bathrooms: 5 en-suite

Bed & breakfast per night:	£min	£max
Single	25.00	
Double	40.00	45.00

Half board per person:	£min	£max
Daily	32.00	

Evening meal 1830 (last orders 1430)
Parking for 6

Forest & Vale Hotel M

🏵🏵🏵🏵 COMMENDED

Malton Road, Pickering YO18 7DL
☎ (01751) 472722
Fax (01751) 472972
Ⓒ Consort

Old manor house with comfortable accommodation, good food and pleasant staff. Central for Yorkshire Moors, East Coast and York.
Bedrooms: 2 single, 9 double, 3 twin, 3 triple

Bathrooms: 17 en-suite

Bed & breakfast per night:	£min	£max
Single	40.00	55.00
Double	50.00	75.00

Half board per person:	£min	£max
Daily	40.00	52.00
Weekly	280.00	364.00

Lunch available
Evening meal 1900 (last orders 2100)
Parking for 75
Cards accepted: Amex, Diners, Mastercard, Visa

Fox and Hounds Country Inn M

🏵🏵🏵 COMMENDED

Sinnington, York YO6 6SQ
☎ (01751) 431577
Fax (01751) 431577

Once an old coaching inn. Open fires and period furniture. In tranquil rural setting west of Pickering. Fishing, riding, golf and riverside walks close by.
Bedrooms: 1 single, 6 double, 2 twin, 1 family room
Bathrooms: 10 en-suite

Bed & breakfast per night:	£min	£max
Double	40.00	58.00

Half board per person:	£min	£max
Daily	38.00	48.00

Lunch available
Evening meal 1830 (last orders 2130)
Parking for 30
Cards accepted: Mastercard, Visa, Switch/Delta

Heathcote House M

🏵🏵🏵 COMMENDED

100 Eastgate, Pickering YO18 7DW
☎ (01751) 476991
Fax (01751) 476991
Early Victorian house 5 minutes from town centre. Ideal for walking and touring. All bedrooms have en-suite. Optional dinners. Relaxed, friendly atmosphere. Secluded parking. Non-smoking throughout.
Bedrooms: 3 double, 2 twin
Bathrooms: 5 en-suite, 1 public

Bed & breakfast

per night:	£min	£max
Single	25.00	26.50
Double	40.00	43.00

Half board per

person:	£min	£max
Daily	32.00	38.50
Weekly	210.00	242.00

Evening meal 1900 (last orders 1100)
Parking for 7
Open February–December
Cards accepted: Mastercard, Visa, Switch/Delta

🛇🚗 ⬚📺 ➿ 🛇 🏴

Old Manse Guest House ⚞

HIGHLY COMMENDED

Middleton Road, Pickering
YO18 8AL
☎ (01751) 476484
Fax (01751) 477124
Edwardian house set in large garden with orchard and private car park. All rooms en-suite. 4 minutes' walk to steam railway and town centre.
Bedrooms: 5 double, 3 twin
Bathrooms: 8 en-suite

Bed & breakfast

per night:	£min	£max
Single	18.00	20.00
Double	36.00	40.00

Half board per

person:	£min	£max
Daily	28.00	30.00
Weekly	196.00	210.00

Evening meal 1800 (last orders 1900)
Parking for 8

🛇🔟⬚➿ 🛇📺➿🏴

Sunnyside ⚞

HIGHLY COMMENDED

Carr Lane, Middleton, Pickering
YO18 8PD
☎ (01751) 476104
Fax (01751) 476104
Large, south-facing chalet bungalow with private parking and a garden, in an open country aspect. Some ground floor rooms.
Bedrooms: 1 double, 1 twin, 1 triple
Bathrooms: 3 en-suite

Bed & breakfast

per night:	£min	£max
Single	24.00	25.00
Double	36.00	38.00

Evening meal from 1930
Parking for 4
Open March–October
Cards accepted: Mastercard, Visa

🛇🚗⬚➿ 🛇➿🏴

Close to the A1, this town has a long history, being one of the oldest boroughs in the country. Famous for its castle and locally-processed liquorice, used for sweets and medicines. Also well-known for its racecourse.

Rogerthorpe Manor Country House Hotel ⚞

COMMENDED

Thorpe Lane, Badsworth, Pontefract WF9 1AB
☎ (01977) 643839
Fax (01977) 641571

Impressive Grade II listed country manor in its own grounds. Tastefully restored and ideally located near Pontefract, the A1 and M62.
Bedrooms: 4 single, 4 double, 5 twin, 1 triple
Suites available
Bathrooms: 14 en-suite

Bed & breakfast

per night:	£min	£max
Single	48.00	60.00
Double	55.00	90.00

Half board per

person:	£min	£max
Daily	35.00	60.00
Weekly	215.00	490.00

Lunch available
Evening meal 1930 (last orders 2130)
Parking for 90
Cards accepted: Amex, Diners, Mastercard, Visa, Switch/Delta

🛇🚗➿⬚➿🛇📺➿🏴
🍽200 ⬚🎵🎿🏴➿📺🏴🛇

Monkman's Bistro with Bedrooms

HIGHLY COMMENDED

Pool Bank, Pool in Wharfedale, Otley LS21 1EH
☎ (0113) 284 1105
Fax (0113) 284 3115
Fine Georgian mansion 9 miles from Harrogate, Leeds and Bradford.

Exceptionally warm welcome and renowned modern bistro cuisine.
Bedrooms: 1 single, 3 double, 2 twin
Bathrooms: 6 en-suite

Bed & breakfast

per night:	£min	£max
Single	63.00	73.00
Double	70.00	80.00

Lunch available
Evening meal 1830 (last orders 2200)
Parking for 65
Cards accepted: Mastercard, Visa, Switch/Delta

🛇🐎➿⬚➿🛇📺➿🏴
🚗🏴🏴

Splendidly-positioned small coastal resort with magnificent views over Robin Hood's Bay. Its Old Peak is the end of the famous Lyke Wake Walk or "corpse way".

Bide-a-While ⚞

Listed APPROVED

3 Loring Road, Ravenscar, Scarborough YO13 OLY
☎ (01723) 870643
Small guesthouse offering clean, comfortable accommodation in a homely atmosphere. Home cooking with fresh produce. Sea views from all rooms. On the edge of North York Moors and ideal for exploring the dales.
Bedrooms: 1 double, 2 family rooms
Bathrooms: 1 public

Bed & breakfast

per night:	£min	£max
Single	18.50	22.50
Double	33.00	37.00

Half board per

person:	£min	£max
Daily	23.00	26.50

Evening meal 1700 (last orders 1830)
Parking for 6

🛇➿⬚➿ 🛇📺➿ 🛇
🏴🚗➿

You are advised to confirm your booking in writing.

A key to symbols can be found inside the back cover flap.

RAVENSCAR

Continued

Crag Hill ♨

APPROVED

Ravenhall Road, Ravenscar,
Scarborough YO13 ONA
☎ (01723) 870925
*Magnificent coastal views. Golf and
pony trekking available locally. TV in all
rooms. Ideal for walking and touring.
Please send for brochure.*
Bedrooms: 3 double, 2 twin, 2 family
rooms
Bathrooms: 4 en-suite, 1 public
Bed & breakfast

per night:	£min	£max
Double	34.00	40.00

Half board per

person:	£min	£max
Daily	26.00	29.00
Weekly	175.00	196.00

Lunch available
Evening meal from 1830
Parking for 9

REETH

North Yorkshire
Map ref 5B3

Once a market town and
lead-mining centre, Reeth today
serves holiday-makers in Swaledale
with its folk museum and 18th C
shops and inns lining the green at
High Row.

Kings Arms Hotel

Listed **APPROVED**

High Row, Reeth, Richmond
DL11 6SY
☎ (01748) 884259
Ⓒ Consort
*Traditional Yorkshire inn dating from
1730 with spectacular views of
Swaledale from the inglenook bar or
residents' bedrooms overlooking the
village green.*
Bedrooms: 2 double, 1 twin, 1 family
room
Bathrooms: 4 private showers
Bed & breakfast

per night:	£min	£max
Single	20.00	24.50
Double	40.00	90.00

Half board per

person:	£min	£max
Daily	25.00	30.00
Weekly	150.00	180.00

Lunch available

Evening meal 1830 (last orders
2130)
Cards accepted: Mastercard, Visa,
Switch/Delta

RICHMOND

North Yorkshire
Map ref 5C3

Market town on edge of Swaledale
with 11th C castle, Georgian and
Victorian buildings surrounding
cobbled market-place. Green
Howards' Museum is in the former
Holy Trinity Church. Attractions
include the Georgian Theatre,
Richmondshire Museum and Easby
Abbey.
*Tourist Information Centre ☎ (01748)
850252*

Bridge House Hotel ♨

COMMENDED

Catterick Bridge, Richmond
DL10 7PE
☎ (01748) 818331
Fax (01748) 818331

The Bridge House Hotel

*Riverside coaching hotel dating back to
the 15th C. Easily accessible from the
A1. Situated midway between the dales
and the North York Moors.*
Bedrooms: 2 single, 6 double, 6 twin,
2 triple
Bathrooms: 13 en-suite, 1 public
Bed & breakfast

per night:	£min	£max
Single	40.00	45.00
Double	60.00	65.00

Half board per

person:	£min	£max
Daily	55.00	60.00
Weekly	385.00	420.00

Lunch available
Evening meal 1830 (last orders
2130)
Parking for 70
Cards accepted: Amex, Diners,
Mastercard, Visa, Switch/Delta

King's Head Hotel ♨

COMMENDED

Market Place, Richmond DL10 4HS
☎ (01748) 850220
Fax (01748) 850635
Ⓒ Consort/The Independents

*Beautiful Georgian hotel in historic
market town. Ideal for touring Herriot
country/Yorkshire Dales. High standard
of accommodation and service. Freshly
prepared cuisine, extensive wine list.*
Bedrooms: 5 single, 14 double,
8 twin, 1 triple
Bathrooms: 28 en-suite
Bed & breakfast

per night:	£min	£max
Single	49.00	55.00
Double	75.00	99.00

Half board per

person:	£min	£max
Daily	53.45	70.95

Lunch available
Evening meal 1900 (last orders
2115)
Parking for 25
Cards accepted: Amex, Diners,
Mastercard, Visa, Switch/Delta

The Restaurant on the Green ♨

Listed **COMMENDED**

5-7 Bridge Street, Richmond
DL10 4RW
☎ (01748) 826229

*Grade II listed William and Mary
property with Georgian sundials at foot
of Castle bluff. Near town centre, River
Swale and countryside. Family run.
Bedrooms with colour TV, beverage tray,
en-suite or private bathroom. Good
food, fine wines. No smoking.*
Bedrooms: 1 double, 1 twin
Bathrooms: 1 en-suite, 1 private
Bed & breakfast

per night:	£min	£max
Single		29.00
Double		37.00

Evening meal 1900 (last orders
2030)
Cards accepted: Mastercard, Visa

Please check prices and other
details at the time of booking.

RIPON

North Yorkshire
Map ref 5C3

Small, ancient city with impressive cathedral containing Saxon crypt which houses church treasures from all over Yorkshire. "Setting the Watch" tradition kept nightly by horn-blower in Market Square. Fountains Abbey nearby.

Bishopton Grove House

👑 COMMENDED
Bishopton, Ripon HG4 2QL
☎ (01765) 600888
Restored Georgian house in a lovely rural corner of Ripon, near the River Laver and Fountains Abbey.
Bedrooms: 2 double, 1 twin
Bathrooms: 1 en-suite, 2 public
Bed & breakfast

per night:	£min	£max
Single	20.00	22.00
Double	35.00	36.00

Half board per person:

	£min	£max
Daily	26.50	27.50

Evening meal 1800 (last orders 1930)
Parking for 5

🛇🖵🗖📺🔌📺🚗🏠

ROSEDALE ABBEY

North Yorkshire
Map ref 5C3

Sturdy hamlet built around Cistercian nunnery in the reign of Henry II, in the middle of Rosedale, largest of the moorland valleys.

Milburn Arms Hotel 🅼

👑👑👑 COMMENDED
Rosedale Abbey, Pickering
YO18 8RA
☎ (01751) 417312
Fax (01751) 417312

Historic inn, in a picturesque conservation area village, central to the national park and 15 miles from the Yorkshire Heritage Coast. Restaurant noted for enjoyable, well-prepared food.
Bedrooms: 9 double, 2 twin
Bathrooms: 11 en-suite

Bed & breakfast

per night:	£min	£max
Single	42.00	48.00
Double	68.00	80.00

Lunch available
Evening meal 1900 (last orders 2130)
Parking for 30
Cards accepted: Diners, Mastercard, Visa

🛇🖥🖻📞🖵🗖🔌🖓📶ⓈⒾ📺💻🖨
🍽14☎♨🖐♪🕯✿⛲🅾🚿 SP 🏠🅣◎

ROTHERHAM

South Yorkshire
Map ref 4B2

In the Don Valley, Rotherham became an important industrial town in 19th C with discovery of coal and development of iron and steel industry by Joshua Walker who built Clifton House, now the town's museum. Magnificent 15th C All Saints Church is town's showpiece.
Tourist Information Centre ☎ (01709) 823611

Best Western Elton Hotel 🅼

👑👑👑 HIGHLY COMMENDED
Main Street, Bramley, Rotherham
S66 0SF
☎ (01709) 545681
Fax (01709) 549100
Ⓒ Best Western
200-year-old, stone-built, Yorkshire house with a modern extension and a restaurant. Half a mile from junction 1 of M18, 2 miles from M1. Minimum prices below for one-day stays apply at weekends only.
Wheelchair access category 3🧍
Bedrooms: 9 single, 12 double, 4 twin, 4 triple
Bathrooms: 29 en-suite
Bed & breakfast

per night:	£min	£max
Single	48.50	72.50
Double	67.00	92.00

Half board per person:

	£min	£max
Daily	69.00	93.00
Weekly	543.00	603.00

Lunch available
Evening meal 1900 (last orders 2130)
Parking for 50
Cards accepted: Amex, Diners, Mastercard, Visa, Switch/Delta

🛇🖥🖻📞🖵🗖🔌🖓📶ⓈⒾ📺💻◐🛆
💻🍽40✿🅾🚿 SP 🏠🅣

Carlton Park Hotel 🅼

👑👑👑 COMMENDED
102-104 Moorgate Road,
Rotherham S60 2BG
☎ (01709) 849955
Fax (01709) 368960
Ⓒ Utell International
Modern hotel with conference facilities, extensive leisure facilities, a restaurant and public bar. In a residential area, close to M1 and M18 motorways.
Bedrooms: 38 single, 11 double, 21 twin, 6 triple
Suites available
Bathrooms: 76 en-suite
Bed & breakfast

per night:	£min	£max
Single	35.00	70.00
Double	70.00	100.00

Half board per person:

	£min	£max
Daily	47.00	85.00
Weekly	329.00	595.00

Lunch available
Evening meal 1900 (last orders 2145)
Parking for 122
Cards accepted: Amex, Diners, Mastercard, Visa

🛇🖥🖻📞🖵🗖🔌🖓📶ⓈⒾ📺📺◑
🖨💻🛆🍽250♨🏊🗡▶🚿 SP

Consort Hotel Banqueting & Conference Suite 🅼

👑👑👑 COMMENDED
Brampton Road, Thurcroft,
Rotherham S66 9JA
☎ (01709) 530022
Fax (01709) 531529
Ⓒ Consort
At the junction of M1 and M18 (access exits 31 and 33 of M1 and exit 1 of M18).
Bedrooms: 10 double, 7 twin, 1 family room
Bathrooms: 18 en-suite
Bed & breakfast

per night:	£min	£max
Single	30.00	60.00
Double	45.00	70.00

Half board per person:

	£min	£max
Daily	44.00	44.00

Lunch available
Evening meal 1800 (last orders 2130)
Parking for 96
Cards accepted: Amex, Diners, Mastercard, Visa

🛇🖥🖻📞🖵🗖🔌🖓📶ⓈⒾ📺◐💻
🖨🍽300🗡 SP 🅣

ROTHERHAM
Continued

Swallow Hotel ⋒

𝔚𝔚𝔚𝔚 COMMENDED

West Bawtry Road, Rotherham
S60 4NA
☎ (01709) 830630
Fax (01709) 830549
ᴄᴿ Swallow
*Modern, 4-storey building with
extensive conference and banqueting
facilities and leisure complex. Easy
access from junction 33 of M1.*
Bedrooms: 71 double, 27 twin,
2 family rooms
Suites available
Bathrooms: 100 en-suite

Bed & breakfast

per night:	£min	£max
Single	75.00	90.00
Double	85.00	105.00

Lunch available
Evening meal 1900 (last orders
2145)
Parking for 252
Cards accepted: Amex, Diners,
Mastercard, Visa, Switch/Delta

🛥🕭🖭🎦🖵🖂🛆🎇🏋🖊◐🖂🖩
🛋🎍280🗗🗙🖘U↻🠨🛇SP⊤◎

RUNSWICK

North Yorkshire
Map ref 5D3

Holiday and fishing village on the
west side of Runswick Bay.

Cliffemount Hotel ⋒

𝔚𝔚𝔚 COMMENDED

Runswick Bay, Runswick,
Saltburn-by-the-Sea, Cleveland
TS13 5HU
☎ (01947) 840103
Fax (01947) 841025
*Relaxing hotel on the clifftop with
panoramic views of Runswick Bay. 9
miles north of Whitby. Noted for
cuisine.*
Bedrooms: 1 single, 8 double,
2 triple
Bathrooms: 10 en-suite, 1 private

Bed & breakfast

per night:	£min	£max
Single	25.00	42.50
Double	49.00	70.00

Half board per

person:	£min	£max
Daily	35.00	60.00
Weekly	245.00	420.00

Lunch available
Evening meal 1900 (last orders
2130)

Parking for 30
Cards accepted: Mastercard, Visa,
Switch/Delta

🛥🕭🖭🎦🖵🖂🛆🖊🖂S🖩🛆🎇🚗🖥SP

The Firs ⋒

Listed APPROVED

26 Hinderwell Lane, Runswick,
Saltburn-by-the-Sea, Cleveland
TS13 5HR
☎ (01947) 840433
*In a coastal village, 8 miles north of
Whitby. All rooms en-suite, with colour
TV, tea/coffee facilities. Evening meals
by arrangement. Autumn and winter
midweek breaks available.*
Bedrooms: 1 double, 1 twin, 2 triple,
1 family room
Bathrooms: 5 en-suite

Bed & breakfast

per night:	£min	£max
Single	26.00	
Double	40.00	

Half board per

person:	£min	£max
Daily	29.50	

Evening meal from 1800
Parking for 6

🛥3🖵🖊UL🖂S🖩TV🖩🛆🚗

SCARBOROUGH

North Yorkshire
Map ref 5D3

Large, popular East Coast seaside
resort, formerly a spa town.
Beautiful gardens and two splendid
sandy beaches. Castle ruins date
from 1100; fine Georgian and
Victorian houses. Scarborough
Millennium depicts 1,000 years of
town's history. Sea Life Centre.
Tourist Information Centre ☎ *(01723)
373333*

Ambassador Hotel ⋒

𝔚𝔚𝔚 COMMENDED

Centre of the Esplanade,
Scarborough YO11 2AY
☎ (01723) 362841
Fax (01723) 362841

*Victorian hotel offering en-suite
bedrooms, sea views, indoor heated
swimming pool, spa, sauna, solarium,
entertainment, lift and free parking.*
Bedrooms: 9 single, 17 double,
29 twin, 3 triple, 1 family room
Bathrooms: 59 en-suite

Bed & breakfast

per night:	£min	£max
Single	27.00	42.00
Double	54.00	84.00

Half board per

person:	£min	£max
Daily	31.50	52.00
Weekly	245.00	336.00

Lunch available
Evening meal 1800 (last orders
2030)
Cards accepted: Amex, Mastercard,
Visa, Switch/Delta

🛥🕭🖭🕭🖵🖂🖊🖂🖊🖂S🖩🏋🖩
🖩🛆🎍120🗗🗙🖘🎇🖂DAP🖥SP⊤

Avoncroft Hotel ⋒

𝔚𝔚𝔚

5-7 Crown Terrace, South Cliff,
Scarborough YO11 2BL
☎ (01723) 372737
Fax (01723) 372737
*Listed Georgian terrace overlooking
Crown Gardens. Close to spa and
sports facilities. Convenient for town
centre and all entertainments.*
Bedrooms: 7 single, 10 double,
5 twin, 12 triple
Bathrooms: 20 en-suite, 5 public

Bed & breakfast

per night:	£min	£max
Single	20.50	26.50
Double	41.00	53.00

Half board per

person:	£min	£max
Daily	27.00	33.00
Weekly	175.50	214.50

Lunch available
Evening meal 1730 (last orders
1815)
Open February–December

🛥🕭🖵🖂S🖩🏋TV🖩🛆🔍🖂DAP SP
🏠⊤

East Ayton Lodge Country
Hotel and Restaurant ⋒

𝔚𝔚𝔚 COMMENDED

Moor Lane, East Ayton, Scarborough
YO13 9EW
☎ (01723) 864227
Fax (01723) 862680

*Country hotel and restaurant in a
beautiful 3-acre setting by the River
Derwent, in the North York Moors
National Park, only 3 miles from
Scarborough.*
Bedrooms: 17 double, 11 twin,
2 triple, 1 family room
Bathrooms: 31 en-suite

Bed & breakfast per night:	£min	£max
Single	49.00	49.00
Double	50.00	99.50

Half board per person:	£min	£max
Daily	50.00	72.50
Weekly	250.00	350.00

Lunch available
Evening meal 1800 (last orders 2100)
Parking for 50
Open February–December
Cards accepted: Mastercard, Visa, Switch/Delta

Esplanade Hotel

COMMENDED

Belmont Road, Scarborough
YO11 2AA
☎ (01723) 360382
Fax (01723) 376137
The Independents
Welcoming period-style hotel in good position on Scarborough's South Cliff. Close to beach, spa and town centre. Landau restaurant, parlour bar and roof terrace.
Bedrooms: 18 single, 19 double, 26 twin, 8 triple, 2 family rooms
Bathrooms: 73 en-suite, 4 public

Bed & breakfast per night:	£min	£max
Single	44.00	44.00
Double	82.00	92.00

Half board per person:	£min	£max
Daily	49.00	59.00
Weekly	310.00	355.00

Lunch available
Evening meal 1830 (last orders 2100)
Parking for 24
Open March–December
Cards accepted: Amex, Diners, Mastercard, Visa, Switch/Delta

Excelsior Private Hotel

APPROVED

1 Marlborough Street, Scarborough
YO12 7HG
☎ (01723) 360716
North Bay seafront corner, superb views. Traditionally cooked fresh produce and home-made bread by hosts Irene and Raymond Brown. Reduced rates for 3 or more nights, over 60s discounts. Totally non-smoking.
Bedrooms: 2 single, 4 double, 1 triple, 1 family room
Bathrooms: 6 en-suite, 1 public

Bed & breakfast per night:	£min	£max
Single	20.00	22.50
Double	40.00	45.00

Half board per person:	£min	£max
Daily	25.00	27.50
Weekly	130.00	150.00

Evening meal from 1730
Open April–October

The Gresham Hotel

COMMENDED

18 Lowdale Avenue, Northstead, Scarborough YO12 6JW
☎ (01723) 372117

Beautifully appointed, detached, licensed hotel in imposing position next to Peasholm Park. Ideal for North Cliff golf-course. A warm welcome awaits.
Bedrooms: 6 single, 6 double, 1 twin
Bathrooms: 5 en-suite, 2 public

Bed & breakfast per night:	£min	£max
Single	17.00	21.00
Double	34.00	42.00

Half board per person:	£min	£max
Daily	25.00	29.00
Weekly	166.00	192.00

Evening meal from 1800
Parking for 4
Open March–October

Holmelea Guest House

Listed APPROVED

8 Belle Vue Parade, Scarborough
YO11 1SU
☎ (01723) 360139 (Voice/Fax/Text for people with hearing difficulties)
Fax (01723) 360139
All rooms with CH, divans, duvets, tea/coffee making, colour TV with satellite/video link, radio alarm and hairdryer. Now facilities for deaf and hard of hearing, including Minicom.
Bedrooms: 2 single, 1 double, 2 twin, 1 family room
Bathrooms: 1 public

Please mention this guide when making your booking.

Bed & breakfast per night:	£min	£max
Single	13.00	15.00
Double	26.00	30.00

Cards accepted: Mastercard, Visa, Switch/Delta

Lysander Hotel

COMMENDED

22 Weydale Avenue, Scarborough
YO12 6AX
☎ (01723) 373369
In a peaceful setting between Peasholm Park and Northstead Gardens. Close to the beach, swimming pools, boating lakes, golf and theatres.
Bedrooms: 4 single, 7 double, 5 twin, 2 triple
Bathrooms: 16 en-suite, 1 public

Bed & breakfast per night:	£min	£max
Single	20.00	25.00
Double	40.00	50.00

Half board per person:	£min	£max
Daily	26.00	32.00
Weekly	173.00	213.00

Evening meal 1800 (last orders 1900)
Parking for 12
Open April–October and Christmas
Cards accepted: Mastercard, Visa

Manor Heath Hotel

COMMENDED

67 Northstead Manor Drive, Scarborough YO12 6AF
☎ (01723) 365720
Detached hotel with pleasant gardens and a private car park, overlooking Peasholm Park and the sea. Close to all North Bay attractions.
Bedrooms: 1 single, 6 double, 2 triple, 5 family rooms
Bathrooms: 14 en-suite, 1 public

Bed & breakfast per night:	£min	£max
Single	20.00	22.50
Double	40.00	45.00

Half board per person:	£min	£max
Daily	25.00	27.50
Weekly	165.00	180.00

Evening meal from 1800
Parking for 12
Cards accepted: Mastercard, Visa, Switch/Delta

SCARBOROUGH
Continued

Northcote Non-Smoking Hotel M

👑👑

114 Columbus Ravine, Scarborough
YO12 7QZ
☎ (01723) 367758
Modern, semi-detached private hotel with bedrooms on 2 floors only. Special offers available for senior citizens. All rooms en-suite and with colour TV. Non-smokers only, please. Families welcome.
Bedrooms: 1 single, 4 double, 2 twin, 1 triple, 1 family room
Bathrooms: 9 en-suite, 1 public
Bed & breakfast per night:

	£min	£max
Single	16.50	20.00
Double	33.00	40.00

Half board per person:

	£min	£max
Daily	22.00	25.00
Weekly	135.00	150.00

Evening meal from 1730
Parking for 5
Open March–November

Ox Pasture Hall M

👑👑👑 HIGHLY COMMENDED

Lady Ediths Drive, Throxenby,
Scarborough YO15 5TD
☎ (01723) 365295
Fax (01723) 355156

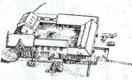

Grade II listed hotel set in 30 acres. Panoramic views. Ground floor spacious quality accommodation. Good food and resident proprietors.
Bedrooms: 1 single, 8 double, 5 twin, 2 triple, 1 family room
Suite available
Bathrooms: 17 en-suite
Bed & breakfast per night:

	£min	£max
Single	31.50	36.50
Double	53.00	63.00

Half board per person:

	£min	£max
Daily	41.50	46.50
Weekly	261.50	293.00

Lunch available
Evening meal 1830 (last orders 2100)
Parking for 40

Cards accepted: Mastercard, Visa, Switch/Delta

Red Lea Hotel M

👑👑👑 COMMENDED

Prince of Wales Terrace,
Scarborough YO11 2AJ
☎ (01723) 362431
Fax (01723) 371230
Traditional hotel with sea views, close to the Spa Centre. Restaurant, bar, lounges, lift and colour TVs. Solarium and indoor heated swimming pool.
Bedrooms: 19 single, 11 double, 27 twin, 7 triple, 4 family rooms
Bathrooms: 68 en-suite
Bed & breakfast per night:

	£min	£max
Single	33.00	35.00
Double	66.00	70.00

Half board per person:

	£min	£max
Daily	45.00	48.00
Weekly	300.00	310.00

Lunch available
Evening meal 1830 (last orders 2000)
Cards accepted: Amex, Mastercard, Visa, Switch/Delta

Ryndle Court Private Hotel M

👑👑👑 COMMENDED

47 Northstead Manor Drive,
Scarborough YO12 6AF
☎ (01723) 375188 & 0860 711517
Fax (01723) 375188
Pleasantly situated overlooking Peasholm Park and near the sea. All rooms en-suite with TV and tea-making facilities. Residents' bar, car park.
Bedrooms: 1 single, 6 double, 2 twin, 3 triple, 2 family rooms
Bathrooms: 14 en-suite
Bed & breakfast per night:

	£min	£max
Single	27.00	30.00
Double	54.00	56.00

Half board per person:

	£min	£max
Daily	34.00	36.00
Weekly	180.00	205.00

Lunch available
Evening meal 1730 (last orders 1700)
Parking for 10
Cards accepted: Amex, Mastercard, Visa

Sunningdale Private Hotel M

👑👑👑 COMMENDED

105 Peasholm Drive, Scarborough
YO12 7NB
☎ (01723) 372041 & 0850 784347
Fax (01723) 354691
Modern, detached hotel facing Peasholm Park and close to all north side attractions. Short, level walk to North Beach.
Bedrooms: 2 single, 5 double, 5 triple
Bathrooms: 12 en-suite, 1 public
Bed & breakfast per night:

	£min	£max
Single	24.00	26.00
Double	48.00	52.00

Half board per person:

	£min	£max
Daily	31.00	33.00
Weekly	210.00	220.00

Evening meal 1800 (last orders 1900)
Cards accepted: Amex, Mastercard, Visa, Switch/Delta

Wharncliffe Hotel

👑👑 COMMENDED

26 Blenheim Terrace, Scarborough
YO12 7HD
☎ (01723) 374635
Panoramic sea views - cleanliness assured - friendly atmosphere. All rooms en-suite with colour TV, radio/alarm and tea/coffee facilities. Close to town centre and amenities.
Bedrooms: 7 double, 1 twin, 2 triple, 2 family rooms
Bathrooms: 12 en-suite
Bed & breakfast per night:

	£min	£max
Single	25.00	26.00
Double	40.00	42.00

Half board per person:

	£min	£max
Daily	27.00	28.00
Weekly	189.00	

Evening meal 1800 (last orders 1200)
Parking for 1
Open March–September

The symbols in each entry give information about services and facilities. A key to these symbols appears at the back of this guide.

SCUNTHORPE

North Lincolnshire
Map ref 4C1

Consisted of 5 small villages until
1860 when extensive ironstone
beds were discovered. Today an
industrial "garden town" with some
interesting modern buildings.
Nearby Normanby Hall contains
fine examples of Regency furniture.

Beverley Hotel

🏰🏰🏰 APPROVED

55 Old Brumby Street, Scunthorpe,
North Lincolnshire DN16 2AJ
☎ (01724) 282212
Fax (01724) 270422
*In the pleasant, quiet residential district
of Old Brumby off the A18, close to
Scunthorpe town centre.*
Bedrooms: 5 single, 3 double, 5 twin,
2 triple
Bathrooms: 15 en-suite

Bed & breakfast

per night:	£min	£max
Single	38.50	42.00
Double	48.50	52.00

Lunch available
Evening meal 1830 (last orders
1930)
Parking for 15
Cards accepted: Mastercard, Visa,
Switch/Delta

🛇🛆🔥📞💻🖥♨🅿💷🗝📺💻🔌
▶❀

Briggate Lodge Inn 𝗔𝗔

🏰🏰🏰🏰 HIGHLY COMMENDED

Ermine Street, Broughton, Brigg,
Scunthorpe, North Lincolnshire
DN20 0NQ
☎ (01652) 650770
Fax (01652) 650495

*Close to junction 4 of the M180, within
easy reach of Lincoln, Hull and York, a
beautifully-appointed hotel set in
mature woodland, with 27-hole
championship golf complex and floodlit
driving range.*
Bedrooms: 2 single, 41 double,
7 twin
Bathrooms: 50 en-suite

Bed & breakfast

per night:	£min	£max
Single	47.00	81.00
Double	57.00	89.00

Lunch available

Evening meal 1900 (last orders
2200)
Parking for 300
Cards accepted: Amex, Diners,
Mastercard, Visa, Switch/Delta

🛇🛆🔥📞💻🖥♨🅿💷🗝🖥◐💷
💻🔌🍴250🛇🏊❀✎🅂🅿🏡🆃

Wortley House Hotel 𝗔𝗔

🏰🏰🏰 COMMENDED

Rowland Road, Scunthorpe, North
Lincolnshire DN16 1SU
☎ (01724) 842223
Fax (01724) 280646
*Friendly, modern hotel, close to the
town centre, but with easy access to
the M18, MI and Humber Bridge. Ideal
base for touring Humberside and
Lincolnshire.*
Bedrooms: 16 single, 17 double,
3 twin, 2 triple
Bathrooms: 38 en-suite

Bed & breakfast

per night:	£min	£max
Single	47.50	67.50
Double	52.50	70.00

Half board per

person:	£min	£max
Daily	60.50	80.50

Lunch available
Evening meal 1900 (last orders
2130)
Parking for 100
Cards accepted: Amex, Diners,
Mastercard, Visa, Switch/Delta

🛇🔥📞💻🖥♨💷🗝🖥◐💷💻🔌
🍴300 OAP ✎🅿🆃

SELBY

North Yorkshire
Map ref 4C1

Small market town on the River
Ouse, believed to have been
birthplace of Henry I, with a
magnificent abbey containing much
fine Norman and Early English
architecture.
*Tourist Information Centre ☎ (01757)
703263*

Hazeldene Guest House 𝗔𝗔

Listed APPROVED

34 Brook Street, Doncaster Road,
Selby YO8 0AR
☎ (01757) 704809
Fax (01757) 709300
*Large Victorian detached house on
A19, convenient for York, Leeds and
Hull. En-suite or standard rooms,
recently refurbished. All non-smoking.*
Bedrooms: 3 single, 2 double, 3 twin,
1 family room
Bathrooms: 3 en-suite, 2 public

Bed & breakfast

per night:	£min	£max
Single	18.00	27.00
Double	34.00	44.00

Parking for 6

🛇🛆2🔥📞♨🅄🅻🅂✎💻🏡🗙🏡

Loftsome Bridge Coaching House

🏰🏰🏰🏰 HIGHLY COMMENDED

Loftsome Bridge, Wressle, Selby
YO8 7EN
☎ (01757) 630070
Fax (01757) 630070
*Nestling alongside the tranquil River
Derwent, just 5 minutes from the M62
and a leisurely 20-minute drive from
York. Dating back to 1782, this
family-run country house hotel boasts a
hand-carved Chippendale four-poster
bed.*
Bedrooms: 10 double, 4 twin,
1 family room
Bathrooms: 15 en-suite

Bed & breakfast

per night:	£min	£max
Single	35.00	40.00
Double	45.00	50.00

Half board per

person:	£min	£max
Daily	51.95	56.95

Lunch available
Evening meal 1900 (last orders
2200)
Parking for 80
Cards accepted: Mastercard, Visa

🛇🛆🔥📞💻🖥♨💷🗝🖥💻🔌
❀🗙🏡🏡

SETTLE

North Yorkshire
Map ref 5B3

Town of narrow streets and
Georgian houses in an area of great
limestone hills and crags. Panoramic
view from Castleberg Crag which
stands 300 ft above town.
*Tourist Information Centre ☎ (01729)
825192*

Falcon Manor Hotel 𝗔𝗔

🏰🏰🏰🏰 COMMENDED

Skipton Road, Settle BD24 9BD
☎ (01729) 823814
Fax (01729) 822087
*Privately-owned country house hotel,
Grade II listed, in the dales market
town of Settle. Ideal for walking,
motoring and the Settle to Carlisle
Railway.*
Bedrooms: 11 double, 5 twin,
3 triple
Bathrooms: 19 en-suite

Continued ▶

SETTLE

Continued

Bed & breakfast per night:

	£min	£max
Single	55.00	70.00
Double	80.00	104.00

Half board per person:

	£min	£max
Daily	52.00	70.00

Lunch available
Evening meal 1900 (last orders 2130)
Parking for 80
Cards accepted: Diners, Mastercard, Visa

⛺🚶♿🍴🖳🗀👟🍵🛈🔒✂🎿🖭 🖬🍺🅿85↺�“❀🌸🏤

Maypole Inn ♨

⛺⛺⛺ COMMENDED

Maypole Green, Main Street, Long Preston, Skipton BD23 4PH
☎ (01729) 840219
Email: landlord@maypole.co.uk
17th C inn, with open fires, on the village green. Easy access to many attractive walks in the surrounding dales. 4 miles from Settle.
Bedrooms: 1 single, 2 double, 1 twin, 1 triple, 1 family room
Bathrooms: 6 en-suite

Bed & breakfast per night:

	£min	£max
Single	26.00	35.00
Double	39.00	43.00

Lunch available
Evening meal 1830 (last orders 2100)
Parking for 25
Cards accepted: Amex, Diners, Mastercard, Visa

⛺🚶🍴🖳🗀👟🍵🛈🅂✂🎿TV🖬🍺 🅿60🌸❀🛨🐕🏤🆃⊕

New Inn Hotel ♨

⛺⛺⛺ COMMENDED

Clapham, Lancaster LA2 8HH
☎ (015242) 51203
Fax (015242) 51496
Ⓖ Wayfarer
18th C coaching inn in a picturesque Yorkshire Dales village 6 miles north of Settle, in dramatic river, waterfall and fell country.
Bedrooms: 11 double, 4 twin, 1 family room
Bathrooms: 16 en-suite

Bed & breakfast per night:

	£min	£max
Single	45.00	
Double	65.00	

Half board per person:

	£min	£max
Daily	47.50	
Weekly	280.00	

Lunch available
Evening meal 1900 (last orders 2030)
Parking for 50
Cards accepted: Amex, Mastercard, Visa, Switch/Delta

⛺🚶🚲🖳🗀👟🍵🛈🅂✂🎿🖬 🍴50↺🕭✎↗✾🆄🖳🛨🏤🆃

Whitefriars Country Guest House ♨

⛺⛺ COMMENDED

Church Street, Settle BD24 9JD
☎ (01729) 823753
Historic family-run guesthouse, set in spacious gardens, in heart of Settle. Ideal for exploring the Dales, Settle-Carlisle Railway. Non-smokers only, please.
Bedrooms: 1 single, 3 double, 3 twin, 1 triple, 1 family room
Bathrooms: 3 en-suite, 2 public

Bed & breakfast per night:

	£min	£max
Single	17.50	
Double	35.00	44.00

Half board per person:

	£min	£max
Daily	28.00	33.00
Weekly	173.25	204.60

Evening meal 1900 (last orders 2000)
Parking for 9

⛺👟🛈🅂✂🎿TV🖬🍺❀🛨🐕🆄 🏤

SHEFFIELD

South Yorkshire
Map ref 4B2

Local iron ore and coal gave Sheffield its prosperous steel and cutlery industries. The modern city centre has many interesting buildings - cathedral, Cutlers' Hall, Crucible Theatre, Graves and Mappin Art Galleries - and Meadowhall Shopping Centre nearby.
Tourist Information Centre ☎ (0114) 273 4671 or 273 4672

Etruria House Hotel

⛺⛺ APPROVED

91 Crookes Road, Broomhill, Sheffield S10 5BD
☎ (0114) 266 2241 & 267 0853
Fax (0114) 267 0853
Family-run hotel in elegant Victorian house, close to all amenities and city centre. Ideal base for Peak District.

Bedrooms: 5 single, 3 double, 2 twin, 1 triple
Bathrooms: 7 en-suite, 2 public

Bed & breakfast per night:

	£min	£max
Single	26.00	35.00
Double	40.00	49.00

Parking for 13
Cards accepted: Mastercard, Visa

⛺🚶♿🖳🗀👟🍵Ⓤ🅂🍴TV🖬🍺 ❀🚑SP🏤🆃

Ivory House Hotel ♨

⛺⛺ APPROVED

34 Wostenholm Road, Sheffield S7 1LJ
☎ (0114) 255 1853
Fax (0114) 255 1578
Within easy reach of both the city centre and countryside. Personal service from the family management. TV and tea/coffee facilities in all rooms.
Bedrooms: 5 single, 1 twin, 1 triple, 1 family room
Bathrooms: 2 en-suite, 3 public

Bed & breakfast per night:

	£min	£max
Single	18.00	22.00
Double	30.00	34.00

Parking for 8

⛺🗀👟🛈🅂🖭TV🖬🍺🔍🛨🆄SP

Lindrick Hotel ♨

⛺⛺ COMMENDED

226-230 Chippinghouse Road, Sheffield S7 1DR
☎ (0114) 258 5041
Fax (0114) 255 4758
Family-run hotel with parking at the front and rear, only minutes from the city centre.
Bedrooms: 16 single, 3 double, 2 twin, 2 triple
Bathrooms: 15 en-suite, 2 public

Bed & breakfast per night:

	£min	£max
Single	21.00	38.00
Double	42.00	48.00

Evening meal 1800 (last orders 2045)
Parking for 22
Cards accepted: Amex, Mastercard, Visa, Switch/Delta

⛺🚶♿🍴🖳🗀👟🍵🛈🅂✂🎿TV🖬🍺 SP

Peace Guest House ♨

Listed APPROVED

92 Brocco Bank, Sheffield S11 8RS
☎ (0114) 268 5110 & 267 0760
Established for 15 years. Close to Endcliffe Park, university, hospitals and Peak District Route.
Bedrooms: 3 single, 1 double, 2 twin, 1 triple

Bathrooms: 2 public, 2 private showers

Bed & breakfast per night:

	£min	£max
Single	15.00	18.00
Double	28.00	32.00

Half board per person:

	£min	£max
Daily	25.00	28.00

Evening meal 1700 (last orders 1900)
Parking for 6

🐴☐🖥Ⓤ🖊✂🏃📺🛏 🞄🗙🏍

St Pellegrino

Listed **APPROVED**

2 Oak Park, Off Manchester Road, Sheffield S10 5DE
☎ (0114) 268 1953 & 266 0151
Comfortable, family-run hotel near university and city centre, yet you can still enjoy the spacious beauty of peaceful surroundings.
Bedrooms: 3 single, 2 double, 3 twin, 3 triple
Bathrooms: 4 en-suite, 1 private, 2 public

Bed & breakfast per night:

	£min	£max
Single	20.00	28.00
Double	38.00	42.00

Parking for 22

🐴☐🖊♿🏃📺🛏 🞄🗙20❧✿🐕 OAP 🐾 SP T

Swallow Hotel 🅰

👑👑👑👑 HIGHLY COMMENDED

Kenwood Road, Sheffield S7 1NQ
☎ (0114) 258 3811
Fax (0114) 255 4744
Ⓒ Swallow
Set in extensive landscaped grounds with its own leisure club, this hotel is ideal for the Peaks, Meadowhall and Chatsworth. Short break packages available.
Bedrooms: 25 single, 58 double, 35 twin
Bathrooms: 118 en-suite

Bed & breakfast per night:

	£min	£max
Single	105.00	125.00
Double	120.00	135.00

Half board per person:

	£min	£max
Daily	115.00	125.00

Lunch available
Evening meal 1900 (last orders 2145)
Parking for 200
Cards accepted: Amex, Diners, Mastercard, Visa, Switch/Delta

🐴♿✉📞🖥☐🖊Ⓢ✂❍⊞ 🛏🞄🗙200🐎🗙🕯❧🌙🐾 SP 🎣 T ♿

Whitley Hall Hotel 🅰

👑👑👑👑 HIGHLY COMMENDED

Elliott Lane, Grenoside, Sheffield S35 8NR
☎ (0114) 245 4444
Fax (0114) 245 5414

Elizabethan mansion with 30 acres of gardens, lakes and woodlands, only a few miles from the centres of Sheffield, Rotherham and Barnsley. Food a speciality with full a la carte and daily menus. Open to non-residents.
Bedrooms: 2 single, 8 double, 7 twin, 1 family room
Suite available
Bathrooms: 18 en-suite

Bed & breakfast per night:

	£min	£max
Single	65.00	78.00
Double	86.00	103.00

Half board per person:

	£min	£max
Daily	63.00	98.00

Lunch available
Evening meal 1900 (last orders 2130)
Parking for 100
Cards accepted: Amex, Diners, Mastercard, Visa, Switch/Delta

🐴🏨📞✉🖥☐♿Ⓢ🖊❍🛏🞄 🞄70🚶🝙❧🐾 SP 🎣

SHELLEY

West Yorkshire
Map ref 4B1

West Yorkshire village south of Huddersfield and close to Kirklees Light Railway.

Three Acres Inn and Restaurant

Listed **COMMENDED**

Roydhouse, Shelley, Huddersfield HD8 8LR
☎ (01484) 602606
Fax (01484) 608411
Attractive country inn, convenient for all Yorkshire's major conurbations and motorway network. Restaurant, traditional beers.
Bedrooms: 6 single, 9 double, 2 twin, 2 triple
Bathrooms: 19 en-suite

Bed & breakfast per night:

	£min	£max
Single	30.00	50.00
Double	45.00	65.00

Lunch available

Evening meal 1900 (last orders 2130)
Parking for 100
Cards accepted: Amex, Mastercard, Visa, Switch/Delta

🐴♿✉🖥☐♿🛏Ⓢ🛏🞄20❧🗙 🏍 SP

SKIPTON

North Yorkshire
Map ref 4B1

Pleasant market town at gateway to dales, with farming community atmosphere, a Palladian Town Hall, parish church and fully roofed castle at the top of the High Street.
Tourist Information Centre ☎ *(01756) 792809*

Devonshire Hotel 🅰

Listed **APPROVED**

Newmarket Street, Skipton BD23 2HR
☎ (01756) 793078 & 426640
Fax (01756) 793078
Family-run, country market town hotel with an attractive garden and children's play area. All bedrooms have TV. Resident proprietors. Real ale. An ideal base for touring the dales and Yorkshire countryside.
Bedrooms: 1 single, 7 double, 4 twin, 1 triple, 2 family rooms
Bathrooms: 6 en-suite, 4 public

Bed & breakfast per night:

	£min	£max
Single	20.00	30.00
Double	34.00	50.00

Half board per person:

	£min	£max
Daily	28.00	38.00
Weekly	196.00	266.00

Lunch available
Evening meal 1800 (last orders 2000)
Parking for 28
Cards accepted: Mastercard, Visa, Switch/Delta

🐴☐🖥♿🛏🞄🛏🞄100✿ OAP SP

SKIPTON

Continued

Hanover International Hotel & Club Skipton ⚑

⚜⚜⚜⚜ COMMENDED

Keighley Road, Skipton BD23 2TA
☎ (01756) 700100
Fax (01756) 700107

Situated at the gateway to the dales. Individually designed rooms and suites, Waterside Restaurant, conference facilities for up to 400 people. Leisure centre with indoor pool and squash courts. Registered children's nursery.

Wheelchair access category 3⚐
Bedrooms: 26 double, 29 twin, 20 triple
Bathrooms: 75 en-suite

Bed & breakfast

per night:	£min	£max
Single	76.00	80.00
Double	86.00	90.00

Half board per

person:	£min	£max
Daily	55.00	115.00

Lunch available
Evening meal 1900 (last orders 2200)
Parking for 200
Cards accepted: Amex, Diners, Mastercard, Visa, Switch/Delta

Tempest Arms Hotel & Restaurant ⚑

⚜⚜⚜ COMMENDED

Elslack, Skipton BD23 3AY
☎ (01282) 842450
Fax (01282) 843331

18th C stone-built inn on the A56 between Earby and Skipton. Surrounded by green fields and edged with a stream, giving character to this traditional Yorkshire pub. Special half board daily rate of £74 per room (2 people) for minimum 2-night stay.

Bedrooms: 6 double, 2 twin, 2 triple
Bathrooms: 10 en-suite

Bed & breakfast

per night:	£min	£max
Single	49.50	49.50
Double	57.50	57.50

Lunch available
Evening meal 1830 (last orders 2130)
Parking for 80
Cards accepted: Amex, Mastercard, Visa

Unicorn Hotel ⚑

⚜⚜⚜ COMMENDED

Devonshire Place, Keighley Road, Skipton BD23 2LP
☎ (01756) 794146 & 793376

Centrally situated, with double-glazing to ensure peace and tranquillity. Ideal base for touring Bronte country and the Yorkshire Dales. Recently refurbished to a high standard. Half board prices based on minimum 2-night stay.

Bedrooms: 6 double, 2 twin, 1 family room
Bathrooms: 9 en-suite

Bed & breakfast

per night:	£min	£max
Single	42.00	44.00
Double	49.00	52.00

Half board per

person:	£min	£max
Daily	32.00	34.00

Evening meal 1900 (last orders 2100)
Cards accepted: Amex, Mastercard, Visa, Switch/Delta

THIRSK

North Yorkshire
Map ref 5C3

Thriving market town with cobbled square surrounded by old shops and inns and also with a local museum. St Mary's Church is probably the best example of Perpendicular work in Yorkshire.

Angel Inn ⚑

⚜⚜⚜ COMMENDED

Long Street, Topcliffe, Thirsk YO7 3RW
☎ (01845) 577237
Fax (01845) 578000

Well-appointed, attractive village inn, renowned for good food and traditional ales. Ideal centre for touring York and Herriot country.

Bedrooms: 2 single, 8 double, 4 twin, 1 family room
Bathrooms: 15 en-suite

Bed & breakfast

per night:	£min	£max
Single	39.00	42.50
Double	55.00	60.00

Lunch available
Evening meal 1830 (last orders 2130)
Parking for 150
Cards accepted: Mastercard, Visa, Switch/Delta

Fourways Guest House ⚑

⚜⚜ APPROVED

Town End, Thirsk YO7 1PY
☎ (01845) 522601

Guesthouse close to the town centre, 2 minutes' walk from the surgery of famous vet and author, the late James Herriot. Centrally located for touring North York Moors and Yorkshire Dales.

Bedrooms: 3 single, 3 double, 3 twin, 1 triple
Bathrooms: 7 en-suite, 1 public

Bed & breakfast

per night:	£min	£max
Single	16.00	18.00
Double	32.00	36.00

Half board per

person:	£min	£max
Daily	23.00	25.00
Weekly	145.00	157.00

Lunch available
Evening meal 1830 (last orders 1930)
Parking for 10
Cards accepted: Mastercard, Visa

Golden Fleece ⚑

⚜⚜⚜ COMMENDED

Market Place, Thirsk YO7 1LL
☎ (01845) 523108
Fax (01845) 523996
Ⓒⓡ Consort

Situated in the market place within easy reach of the Yorkshire Dales and Moors, this old coaching inn has a friendly atmosphere and serves traditional ales and fine fare.

Bedrooms: 1 single, 14 double, 2 twin, 1 triple
Bathrooms: 18 en-suite

Bed & breakfast

per night:	£min	£max
Single	55.00	
Double	75.00	

Half board per

person:	£min	£max
Daily	47.50	70.00

Lunch available
Evening meal 1900 (last orders 2100)
Parking for 30
Cards accepted: Amex, Diners, Mastercard, Visa, Switch/Delta

National gradings and classifications were correct at the time of going to press but are subject to change. Please check at the time of booking.

Old Red House

👑👑 APPROVED

Station Road, Carlton Miniott,
Thirsk YO7 4LT
☎ (01845) 524383
*Two-storey Georgian building, with a
bar lounge and open fire.*
Bedrooms: 1 single, 3 double, 1 twin,
1 triple, 4 family rooms
Bathrooms: 10 en-suite
Bed & breakfast

per night:	£min	£max
Single	20.00	22.00
Double	34.00	36.00

Half board per person:	£min	£max
Daily	27.00	32.00
Weekly	150.00	160.00

Lunch available
Evening meal 1900 (last orders
2100)
Parking for 30
Cards accepted: Amex, Diners,
Mastercard, Visa

THORNTON WATLASS

North Yorkshire
Map ref 5C3

Picturesque village in Lower
Wensleydale.

The Buck Inn

👑👑👑 COMMENDED

Thornton Watlass, Ripon HG4 4AH
☎ (01677) 422461
Fax (01677) 422447
*Friendly village inn overlooking the
delightful cricket green in a small
village, 3 miles from Bedale on the
Masham road, and close to the A1.
Ideal centre for exploring both the
dales and North York Moors.*
Bedrooms: 1 single, 3 double, 2 twin,
1 triple
Bathrooms: 5 en-suite, 1 public
Bed & breakfast

per night:	£min	£max
Single	34.00	
Double	52.00	

Half board per person:	£min	£max
Daily	37.00	

Lunch available
Evening meal 1830 (last orders
2130)
Parking for 40
Cards accepted: Amex, Diners,
Mastercard, Visa, Switch/Delta

THWAITE

North Yorkshire
Map ref 5B3

Quiet village, ideal for walking the
fells of Great Shunner, Kisdon, High
Seat, Rogan's Seat and Lovely Seat.
Magnificent scenery.

Kearton Guest House

Listed APPROVED

Thwaite, Richmond DL11 6DR
☎ (01748) 886277
Fax (01748) 886590
*In the charming village of Thwaite in
Swaledale, within easy reach of York,
the Lake District, Herriot country and
the Yorkshire Dales.*
Bedrooms: 1 single, 4 double, 1 twin,
6 triple, 1 family room
Bathrooms: 4 public, 10 private
showers
Bed & breakfast

per night:	£min	£max
Single		21.00
Double		42.00

Half board per person:	£min	£max
Daily		27.00
Weekly		189.00

Lunch available
Evening meal from 1830
Parking for 40
Open March–December
Cards accepted: Mastercard, Visa,
Switch/Delta

WAKEFIELD

West Yorkshire
Map ref 4B1

Thriving city with cathedral church
of All Saints boasting 247-ft spire.
Old Bridge, a 9-arched structure,
has fine medieval chantry chapels of
St Mary's. Fine Georgian
architecture and good shopping
centre (The Ridings). National Coal
Mining Museum for England nearby.
*Tourist Information Centre ☎ (01924)
305000 or 305001*

Cedar Court Hotel

👑👑👑👑 COMMENDED

Denby Dale Road, Calder Grove,
Wakefield WF4 3QZ
☎ (01924) 276310 & 261459
Fax (01924) 280221
*International hotel, designed for
ultimate customer satisfaction. Close to
the M1 and M62 motorways, halfway
between London and Scotland. Suitable
for business people, conferences,
private functions and holidaymakers.*

Bedrooms: 126 double, 23 twin,
1 triple
Suites available
Bathrooms: 150 en-suite
Bed & breakfast

per night:	£min	£max
Single	50.00	110.00
Double	60.00	120.00

Lunch available
Evening meal 1800 (last orders
2200)
Parking for 350
Cards accepted: Amex, Diners,
Mastercard, Visa

Dimple Well Lodge Hotel

👑👑👑👑 HIGHLY COMMENDED

The Green, Ossett WF5 8JX
☎ (01924) 264352
Fax (01924) 274024
Email: joandsandy@dimple-well-
lodge-hotel.co.uk
*Family-run, Georgian house hotel in
own picturesque gardens, offering
charm and character. Close to M1
(junction 40) and M62.*
Bedrooms: 5 single, 5 double, 1 twin
Bathrooms: 11 en-suite
Bed & breakfast

per night:	£min	£max
Single	43.00	43.00
Double	55.00	55.00

Half board per person:	£min	£max
Daily	55.00	55.00

Evening meal 1900 (last orders
2030)
Parking for 20
Cards accepted: Amex, Mastercard,
Visa

Parklands Hotel

👑👑👑

143 Horbury Road, Wakefield
WF2 8TY
☎ (01924) 377407
Fax (01924) 290348

*Elegant Victorian former vicarage
overlooking 680 acres of beautiful
parkland. Family-run for over 28 years,
providing a high standard of service
and cuisine and well-appointed en-suite
bedrooms.*

Continued ▶

WAKEFIELD

Continued

Bedrooms: 9 single, 2 double, 2 twin
Bathrooms: 11 en-suite, 2 private
showers
Bed & breakfast

per night:	£min	£max
Single	32.50	42.50
Double	42.50	48.50

Lunch available
Evening meal 1845 (last orders
2115)
Parking for 20
Cards accepted: Amex, Diners,
Mastercard, Visa, Switch/Delta

Waterton Park Hotel

HIGHLY COMMENDED

Walton Hall, Walton, Wakefield
WF2 6PW
☎ (01924) 257911
Fax (01924) 240082
CR Best Western
*Georgian mansion, situated on an
island and surrounded by a 26-acre
lake. Well-equipped bedrooms,
restaurant, swimming pool, steamroom,
sauna, solarium, fly-fishing, fitness-room,
coffee shop, 18-hole golf.*
Bedrooms: 3 single, 31 double,
8 twin
Bathrooms: 42 en-suite
Bed & breakfast

per night:	£min	£max
Single	60.00	120.00
Double	70.00	150.00

Half board per

person:	£min	£max
Daily	115.00	140.00

Lunch available
Evening meal 1900 (last orders
2130)
Parking for 130
Cards accepted: Amex, Diners,
Mastercard, Visa, Switch/Delta

The symbol CR and a group
name following an hotel
address indicates that
bookings can be made
through a central reservations
office. These offices are listed
in the information pages at
the back of this guide.

WEST WITTON

North Yorkshire
Map ref 5B3

*Popular Wensleydale village, where
the burning of "Owd Bartle", effigy
of an 18th C pig rustler, is held in
August.*

Ivy Dene Country Guesthouse

COMMENDED

Main Street, West Witton, Leyburn
DL8 4LP
☎ (01969) 622785
*17th C country guesthouse, beautifully
situated in Yorkshire Dales National
Park. Quality en-suite accommodation
in a friendly, informal atmosphere.
Super home-cooked meals prepared
from fresh produce. Short break
discounts.*
Bedrooms: 3 double, 1 twin, 1 triple
Bathrooms: 4 en-suite, 1 private
Bed & breakfast

per night:	£min	£max
Single	28.00	34.00
Double	44.00	48.00

Half board per

person:	£min	£max
Daily	35.00	37.00
Weekly	229.60	242.20

Evening meal 1900 (last orders
1700)
Parking for 6

Wensleydale Heifer

HIGHLY COMMENDED

West Witton, Leyburn DL8 4LS
☎ (01969) 622322
Fax (01969) 624183
CR Consort/Logis of GB

*17th C inn situated in Yorkshire Dales
National Park. Seafood restaurant and
bistro. Four-poster bedrooms. Special
breaks. Dogs welcome. Rustic country
cooking.*
Bedrooms: 8 double, 5 twin, 1 triple,
1 family room
Suite available
Bathrooms: 15 en-suite
Bed & breakfast

per night:	£min	£max
Single	54.00	54.00
Double	70.00	90.00

Half board per

person:	£min	£max
Daily	52.50	62.50

Lunch available
Evening meal 1900 (last orders
2130)
Parking for 40
Cards accepted: Amex, Diners,
Mastercard, Visa, Switch/Delta

WETHERBY

West Yorkshire
Map ref 4B1

*Prosperous market town on the
River Wharfe, noted for
horse-racing.*
Tourist Information Centre ☎ (0113)
247 7253

Jarvis Wetherby Hotel

COMMENDED

Leeds Road, Wetherby LS22 5HE
☎ (01937) 583881
Fax (01937) 580062
CR Jarvis/Utell International
*Oasis amid Yorkshire Dales. Just off A1
hub for York, Leeds and Harrogate.
Modern hotel, run with Jarvis flair and
Italian charm.*
Bedrooms: 17 double, 53 twin,
2 triple
Bathrooms: 72 en-suite
Bed & breakfast

per night:	£min	£max
Single	39.00	89.95
Double	78.00	110.90

Lunch available
Evening meal 1900 (last orders
2145)
Parking for 125
Cards accepted: Amex, Diners,
Mastercard, Visa, Switch/Delta

Prospect House

Listed APPROVED

8 Caxton Street, Wetherby
LS22 6RU
☎ (01937) 582428
*Established 35 years. En-suite rooms
available. Near York, Harrogate, Dales,
Herriot country. Midway
London/Edinburgh. Restaurants nearby.
Pets welcome.*
Bedrooms: 1 single, 3 double, 2 twin
Bathrooms: 4 en-suite, 1 public
Bed & breakfast

per night:	£min	£max
Single	20.00	25.00
Double	45.00	50.00

Parking for 6

WHITBY

North Yorkshire
Map ref 5D3

Quaint holiday town with narrow streets and steep alleys at the mouth of the River Esk. Captain James Cook, the famous navigator, lived in Grape Lane. 199 steps lead to St Mary's Church and St Hilda's Abbey overlooking harbour. Dracula connections. Sandy beach.
Tourist Information Centre ☎ (01947) 602674

Glendale Guest House

🏆 COMMENDED

16 Crescent Avenue, Whitby
YO21 3ED
☎ (01947) 604242
Family-run Victorian guesthouse. Clean and comfortable with a pleasant atmosphere. Emphasis on food.
Bedrooms: 1 single, 5 double
Bathrooms: 5 en-suite, 2 public

Bed & breakfast
per night:	£min	£max
Single	17.00	19.00
Double	38.00	40.00

Half board per
person:	£min	£max
Daily	27.00	29.00
Weekly	170.00	190.00

Evening meal 1600 (last orders 1730)
Parking for 6
Open March–November

Larpool Hall Country Hotel and Restaurant ⋀

🏆 COMMENDED

Larpool Lane, Whitby YO22 4ND
☎ (01947) 602737
Fax (01947) 820204
Email: larpool.hall@onyxnet.co.uk
Ⓒ The Independents

Georgian mansion set in 14 acres overlooking Esk Valley, offering peace and tranquillity. One mile from town centre.
Bedrooms: 3 single, 10 double, 3 twin, 1 triple
Bathrooms: 17 en-suite

Bed & breakfast
per night:	£min	£max
Single	45.00	65.00
Double	79.00	130.00

Half board per
person:	£min	£max
Daily	54.95	
Weekly	345.00	

Lunch available
Evening meal 1900 (last orders 2100)
Parking for 20
Cards accepted: Amex, Diners, Mastercard, Visa

Saxonville Hotel ⋀

🏆 COMMENDED

Ladysmith Avenue, Whitby
YO21 3HX
☎ (01947) 602631
Fax (01947) 820523
Family-owned hotel, in operation since 1946, proud of its cuisine and friendly atmosphere.
Bedrooms: 3 single, 10 double, 9 twin, 2 triple
Bathrooms: 24 en-suite

Bed & breakfast
per night:	£min	£max
Single	32.50	40.00
Double	65.00	80.00

Half board per
person:	£min	£max
Daily	41.50	48.00
Weekly	265.00	310.00

Lunch available
Evening meal 1900 (last orders 2030)
Parking for 20
Open April–October
Cards accepted: Mastercard, Visa, Switch/Delta

Seacliffe Hotel ⋀

🏆 COMMENDED

12 North Promenade, West Cliff, Whitby YO21 3JX
☎ (01947) 603139 & 0500 202229
Fax (01947) 603139
Friendly, family-run hotel overlooking the sea. Seafood a speciality in the a la carte restaurant. Golf nearby.
Bedrooms: 1 single, 13 double, 2 twin, 3 triple, 1 family room
Bathrooms: 20 en-suite, 1 public

Bed & breakfast
per night:	£min	£max
Single	32.50	37.50
Double	59.00	63.00

Evening meal 1800 (last orders 2100)
Parking for 8
Cards accepted: Amex, Diners, Mastercard, Visa, Switch/Delta

Stakesby Manor ⋀

🏆 COMMENDED

Manor Close, High Stakesby, Whitby YO21 1HL
☎ (01947) 602773 & 602140
Fax (01947) 602773
Ⓒ Minotel
Georgian house dating back to 1710, in its own grounds, on the outskirts of Whitby in the North York Moors National Park. Facing south with views of the moors.
Bedrooms: 8 double, 2 twin
Bathrooms: 10 en-suite

Bed & breakfast
per night:	£min	£max
Single	45.00	45.00
Double	64.00	68.00

Half board per
person:	£min	£max
Daily	38.00	46.00
Weekly	266.00	322.00

Lunch available
Evening meal 1900 (last orders 2130)
Parking for 30
Cards accepted: Amex, Mastercard, Visa, Switch/Delta

YORK

North Yorkshire
Map ref 4C1

Ancient walled city nearly 2000 years old containing many well-preserved medieval buildings. Its Minster has over 100 stained glass windows. Attractions include Castle Museum, National Railway Museum, Jorvik Viking Centre and York Dungeon.
Tourist Information Centre ☎ (01904) 621756 or 621757 or 620557

Aaron Guest House ⋀

Listed COMMENDED

42 Bootham Crescent, Bootham, York YO3 7AH
☎ (01904) 625927

Attractive and well-decorated family guesthouse, a short walk from city centre. Most rooms en-suite. Ample parking.

Continued ▶

YORK
Continued

Bedrooms: 1 single, 3 double, 1 twin,
1 triple
Bathrooms: 4 en-suite, 1 public

Bed & breakfast per night:

	£min	£max
Single	16.00	25.00
Double	30.00	44.00

Half board per person:

	£min	£max
Daily	25.00	31.00
Weekly	170.00	210.00

Parking for 3

Abbey Guest House ⋀
Listed COMMENDED
14 Earlsborough Terrace, Marygate,
York YO3 7BQ
☎ (01904) 627782
*Small family-run guesthouse on the
banks of the River Ouse, 450 yards
from the city centre. En-suite rooms
available.*
Bedrooms: 2 single, 3 double,
1 family room
Bathrooms: 2 en-suite, 2 public

Bed & breakfast per night:

	£min	£max
Single	18.00	25.00
Double	36.00	50.00

Parking for 7
Cards accepted: Amex, Mastercard,
Visa

Abbots Mews Hotel ⋀
♛♛♛ APPROVED
6 Marygate Lane, Bootham, York
YO3 7DE
☎ (01904) 634866 & 622395
Fax (01904) 612848
*Converted Victorian coachmen's
cottages, quietly located in a mews,
with easy access to the city centre.*
Bedrooms: 7 single, 18 double,
15 twin, 9 triple
Bathrooms: 49 en-suite, 1 public

Bed & breakfast per night:

	£min	£max
Single	25.00	40.00
Double	40.00	51.00

Half board per person:

	£min	£max
Daily	30.00	45.00

Lunch available
Evening meal 1900 (last orders
2130)
Parking for 30

Cards accepted: Amex, Diners,
Mastercard, Visa, Switch/Delta

Ad See display advertisement on this
page

Alfreda Guest House ⋀
♛♛ COMMENDED
61 Heslington Lane, Fulford, York
YO1 4HN
☎ (01904) 631698
*Double-fronted, Edwardian residence in
1.5 acres, close to Fulford Golf Course
and York University. Large parking area
with security lighting.*
Bedrooms: 3 double, 3 twin, 2 triple,
2 family rooms
Bathrooms: 8 en-suite, 1 public

Bed & breakfast per night:

	£min	£max
Single	20.00	35.00
Double	30.00	50.00

Parking for 21
Cards accepted: Amex, Mastercard,
Visa

Alhambra Court Hotel

👑👑👑👑 [COMMENDED]

31 St Mary's, Bootham, York
YO3 7DD
☎ (01904) 628474
Fax (01904) 610690

Early Georgian town house in a quiet cul-de-sac near the city centre. Family-run hotel with bar, restaurant, open to non-residents. Lift and parking.
Bedrooms: 3 single, 9 double, 7 twin, 3 triple, 2 family rooms
Bathrooms: 24 en-suite

Bed & breakfast per night:	£min	£max
Single	32.00	42.00
Double	45.00	65.00

Half board per person:	£min	£max
Daily	35.00	
Weekly	210.00	

Evening meal 1800 (last orders 2100)
Parking for 20
Cards accepted: Mastercard, Visa, Switch/Delta
[S] [TV] [OAP] [SP] [T]

Ambassador

👑👑👑👑 [HIGHLY COMMENDED]

123-125 The Mount, York YO2 2DA
☎ (01904) 641316
Fax (01904) 640259
[CR] Consort
Listed building in 2 acres of garden on York's main approach road from the south and west. Only 5 minutes from the railway station, city centre and racecourse. Lift to most bedrooms. B&B prices are per room.
Bedrooms: 17 double, 8 twin
Bathrooms: 25 en-suite

Bed & breakfast per night:	£min	£max
Single		102.00
Double		120.00

Half board per person:	£min	£max
Daily		79.50
Weekly		556.50

Evening meal 1830 (last orders 2130)
Parking for 30
Cards accepted: Amex, Mastercard, Visa, Switch/Delta
[S]
50 [SP] [T]

Ambleside Guest House

👑👑 [COMMENDED]

62 Bootham Crescent, Bootham, York YO3 7AH
☎ (01904) 637165
Fax (01904) 637165

Tastefully furnished Victorian town house, 5 minutes' walk to city centre. Most rooms en-suite. Cleanliness and hospitality guaranteed at all times. All rooms no smoking.
Bedrooms: 6 double, 1 twin, 1 triple
Bathrooms: 6 en-suite, 1 public

Bed & breakfast per night:	£min	£max
Double	36.00	48.00

Open February–December
10 [UL] [S] [TV]
[OAP]

Arndale Hotel

👑👑 [HIGHLY COMMENDED]

290 Tadcaster Road, York YO2 2ET
☎ (01904) 702424

Delightful Victorian house, directly overlooking racecourse. Beautiful enclosed walled gardens giving a country atmosphere within the city. Antiques, fresh flowers, four-poster beds, whirlpool baths. Enclosed gated car park.
Bedrooms: 7 double, 2 twin, 1 triple
Bathrooms: 10 en-suite

Bed & breakfast per night:	£min	£max
Single	39.00	49.00
Double	47.00	69.00

Parking for 20
Cards accepted: Mastercard, Visa
8
[SP] [T]

COLOUR MAPS

Colour maps at the back of this guide pinpoint all places in which you will find accommodation listed.

Ascot House

👑👑 [COMMENDED]

80 East Parade, York YO3 7YH
☎ (01904) 426826
Fax (01904) 431077

A most attractive Victorian villa, 15 minutes' walk from city centre. All double rooms are en-suite. Some have four-poster or canopy beds. Private car park. Licensed.
Bedrooms: 1 single, 8 double, 2 twin, 3 triple, 1 family room
Bathrooms: 12 en-suite, 1 private, 2 public

Bed & breakfast per night:	£min	£max
Single	18.00	22.00
Double	36.00	45.00

Parking for 12
Cards accepted: Diners, Mastercard, Visa
[S] [TV]
[SP] [T]

Ashbourne House Hotel

👑👑👑 [COMMENDED]

139 Fulford Road, York YO1 4HG
☎ (01904) 639912
Fax (01904) 631332
Charming, comfortable, family-owned and run licensed private hotel. On main route into York from the south and within walking distance of city centre.
Bedrooms: 3 double, 2 twin, 1 family room
Bathrooms: 5 en-suite, 1 private

Bed & breakfast per night:	£min	£max
Single	34.00	38.00
Double	40.00	50.00

Half board per person:	£min	£max
Daily	35.00	45.00
Weekly	245.00	315.00

Evening meal 1900 (last orders 1800)
Parking for 6
Cards accepted: Amex, Diners, Mastercard, Visa
[S]
[SP] [T]

For ideas on places to visit refer to the introduction at the beginning of this section.

YORK
Continued

Ashcroft Hotel ▲▲
👑👑👑 COMMENDED
294 Bishopthorpe Road, York
YO2 1LH
☎ (01904) 659286 & 629543
Fax (01904) 640107
ⓒ Minotel

Victorian former mansion in 2 acres of
wooded grounds overlooking the River
Ouse, only 1 mile from the city centre.
All bedrooms are en-suite and have
colour TV, radio, telephone,
coffee/tea-making facilities, hairdryer
and trouser press.
Bedrooms: 1 single, 7 double, 4 twin,
1 triple, 2 family rooms
Bathrooms: 15 en-suite

Bed & breakfast

per night:	£min	£max
Single	40.00	48.00
Double	50.00	85.00

Half board per

person:	£min	£max
Daily	44.50	54.50
Weekly	311.50	360.00

Lunch available
Evening meal 1900 (last orders
2130)
Parking for 40
Cards accepted: Amex, Diners,
Mastercard, Visa, Switch/Delta
🐎5🏦🚻📞📺🖥🔌♨🛏📺🖥💻 ➶
🍴70 ➷❄🚭 SP T

Avondale ▲▲
👑 APPROVED
61 Bishopthorpe Road, York
YO2 1NX
☎ (01904) 633989
Small, friendly guesthouse, close to city
centre. All rooms en-suite with TV and
tea/coffee facilities. Non-smoking.
Bedrooms: 3 double, 1 twin, 1 triple
Bathrooms: 5 en-suite

Bed & breakfast

per night:	£min	£max
Double	30.00	40.00

Cards accepted: Mastercard, Visa
🐎📺🔌UL S ✂💻 ➷🍴🐕🚗 ⊚

Bedford Hotel ▲▲
👑👑 COMMENDED
108-110 Bootham, York YO3 7DG
☎ (01904) 624412
Family-run hotel, a short walk along
historic Bootham to the famous York
Minster and city centre. Evening meals
available.
Bedrooms: 4 single, 6 double, 2 twin,
3 triple, 1 family room
Bathrooms: 16 en-suite

Bed & breakfast

per night:	£min	£max
Single	33.00	38.00
Double	46.00	56.00

Parking for 14
Cards accepted: Amex, Mastercard,
Visa, Switch/Delta
🐎📞🔌♨🛏📺🖥💻➷🍴🚗 SP 🏨 T
⊚

Beechwood Close Hotel ▲▲
👑👑👑 COMMENDED
19 Shipton Road, Clifton, York
YO3 6RE
☎ (01904) 658378
Fax (01904) 647124
Email: bchc@dial.pipex.com
ⓒ Minotel
Spacious, detached, family-run hotel set
among trees, located on the A19,
1 mile north of the city centre.
Restaurant, bar, lounge, attractive
gardens, car park.
Bedrooms: 3 single, 4 double, 2 twin,
5 triple
Bathrooms: 14 en-suite

Bed & breakfast

per night:	£min	£max
Single	43.50	48.00
Double	70.00	75.00

Half board per

person:	£min	£max
Daily	44.75	52.25
Weekly	306.25	358.75

Lunch available
Evening meal 1900 (last orders
2100)
Parking for 36
Cards accepted: Amex, Diners,
Mastercard, Visa, Switch/Delta
🐎📞🖥📺🔌♨🛏 S 🛏💻➷🍴60
❄🐕🚗 SP T

Bloomsbury Hotel ▲▲
👑👑 COMMENDED
127 Clifton, York YO3 6BL
☎ (01904) 634031

An elegantly appointed large Victorian
town house, centrally situated, with
large private car park. Recently totally
refurbished. Completely non-smoking.
Bedrooms: 2 single, 3 double, 3 twin,
2 triple
Bathrooms: 10 en-suite

Bed & breakfast

per night	£min	£max
Single	35.00	65.00
Double	45.00	65.00

Parking for 8
Cards accepted: Mastercard, Visa,
Switch/Delta
🐎🏦📺🔌♨🔌UL S ✂📺📺💻➷
🍴12 ➷🚭🚗 GAP SP

Blue Bridge Hotel ▲▲
👑 APPROVED
Fishergate, York YO1 4AP
☎ (01904) 621193
Fax (01904) 671571
Friendly, private hotel with a relaxed
atmosphere and a warm welcome.
Short riverside walk to city. Private car
park.
Bedrooms: 2 single, 6 double, 3 twin,
5 triple
Bathrooms: 14 en-suite, 1 public

Bed & breakfast

per night	£min	£max
Single	35.00	48.00
Double	50.00	58.00

Parking for 20
Cards accepted: Mastercard, Visa
🐎🏦📞📺📺🔌♨🛏 S ✂🛏💻➷
🍴12 SP

Bootham Bar Hotel ▲▲
Listed APPROVED
4 High Petergate, York YO1 2EH
☎ (01904) 658516
ⓒ Consort

Hotel garden is bordered by the city
walls, 150 yards from York Minster.
Excellent full English breakfasts.
Luggage lift. Parking available on
request.
Bedrooms: 3 single, 7 double, 1 twin,
2 triple, 1 family room
Bathrooms: 9 en-suite, 2 private,
1 public

Bed & breakfast

per night	£min	£max
Single	20.00	20.00
Double	40.00	58.00

Lunch available
Parking for 6
Cards accepted: Mastercard, Visa

Bootham Guest House ⚜

APPROVED

56 Bootham Crescent, York
YO3 7AH
☎ (01904) 672123
*Family-run guesthouse in a quiet
crescent off the main thoroughfare.
Only a few minutes' walk from the city
centre and Minster.*
Bedrooms: 2 single, 3 double, 1 twin,
1 triple
Bathrooms: 5 en-suite, 1 public
Bed & breakfast

per night:	£min	£max
Single	18.00	20.00
Double	38.00	40.00

Parking for 4

Bootham Park Hotel ⚜

COMMENDED

9 Grosvenor Terrace, Bootham,
York YO3 7AG
☎ (01904) 644262
Fax (01904) 645647
*Elegant Victorian house 5 minutes'
walk from York Minster and tourist
attractions. En-suite rooms with
hairdryer, alarm clock, colour TV, drinks
tray and telephone. Parking.*
Bedrooms: 3 double, 1 twin, 1 triple,
1 family room
Bathrooms: 6 en-suite
Bed & breakfast

per night:	£min	£max
Single	28.00	37.00
Double	38.00	56.00

Parking for 6
Cards accepted: Mastercard, Visa

Bowen House ⚜

COMMENDED

4 Gladstone Street, Huntington
Road, York YO3 7RF
☎ (01904) 636881
Fax (01904) 636881
*Within a short walk of York Minster
and city centre, this late Victorian,
family-run guesthouse combines high
quality facilities with old-style charm.
Private car park. Traditional or
vegetarian breakfasts. Non-smoking
throughout.*
Bedrooms: 1 single, 2 double, 1 twin,
1 family room
Bathrooms: 3 en-suite, 1 public,
1 private shower

Bed & breakfast

per night:	£min	£max
Single	20.00	25.00
Double	32.00	45.00

Parking for 4
Cards accepted: Mastercard, Visa

Briar Lea Guest House ⚜

APPROVED

8 Longfield Terrace, Bootham, York
YO3 7DJ
☎ (01904) 635061 & (0589) 178956
*Victorian house with all rooms en-suite,
5 minutes' walk from the city centre
and railway station.*
Bedrooms: 1 double, 1 twin, 1 triple,
1 family room
Bathrooms: 4 en-suite
Bed & breakfast

per night:	£min	£max
Double	34.00	44.00

Parking for 2

Carlton House Hotel ⚜

COMMENDED

134 The Mount, York YO2 2AS
☎ (01904) 622265
Fax (01904) 637157
Email: carltonuk@aol.com
*Hotel in Georgian terraced home,
family-run for 50 years. Just outside city
walls, close to all attractions and
amenities.*
Bedrooms: 1 single, 6 double, 1 twin,
4 triple, 1 family room
Bathrooms: 13 en-suite, 1 public
Bed & breakfast

per night:	£min	£max
Single	27.00	28.00
Double	48.00	50.00

Parking for 7

Carousel Guest House ⚜

Listed APPROVED

83 Eldon Street, off Stanley Street,
Haxby Road, York YO3 7NH
☎ (01904) 646709
*Warm, friendly, licensed guesthouse in
central location. All rooms en-suite with
tea/coffee making facilities and colour
TV. Parking.*
Bedrooms: 2 single, 4 double, 1 twin,
1 triple, 1 family room
Bathrooms: 9 en-suite
Bed & breakfast

per night:	£min	£max
Single	16.50	17.50
Double	30.00	33.00

Evening meal 1730 (last orders
1000)
Parking for 15

Cavalier Private Hotel ⚜

COMMENDED

39 Monkgate, York YO3 7PB
☎ (01904) 636615
Fax (01904) 636615
*Small family-run hotel close to the city
centre, only yards from the ancient Bar
Walls and many of York's famous
historic landmarks.*
Bedrooms: 2 single, 4 double,
2 triple, 2 family rooms
Bathrooms: 7 en-suite, 3 public
Bed & breakfast

per night:	£min	£max
Single	23.00	25.00
Double	44.00	52.00

Parking for 3
Cards accepted: Amex, Mastercard,
Visa

Chelmsford Place Guest House

APPROVED

85 Fulford Road, York YO1 4BD
☎ (01904) 624491
Fax (01904) 674491
*Small, friendly guesthouse offering
comfortable en-suite accommodation
at a moderate price. Ten minutes' walk
from York centre.*
Bedrooms: 3 double, 1 twin, 1 triple,
1 family room
Bathrooms: 5 en-suite, 1 public
Bed & breakfast

per night:	£min	£max
Single	17.00	25.00
Double	28.00	45.00

Parking for 4
Cards accepted: Mastercard, Visa

Chilton Guest House ⚜

Listed COMMENDED

1 Claremont Terrace, Gillygate, York
YO3 7EJ
☎ (01904) 612465
*Small guesthouse in city centre, close to
the city's historic attractions. All rooms
en-suite with hairdryer, tea/coffee tray,
colour TV with satellite, direct-dial
telephone.*
Bedrooms: 1 double, 1 twin, 1 triple
Bathrooms: 3 en-suite

Continued ▶

YORK

Continued

Bed & breakfast

per night:	£min	£max
Single	25.00	30.00
Double	36.00	42.00

Parking for 2

🛌5🕭☎💻📺♿🗑UL S✂🛏🐕✕ 🚐 DAP SP

City Guest House 🏔

👑👑 COMMENDED

68 Monkgate, York YO3 7PF
☎ (01904) 622483
Small, friendly, family-run B & B in attractive Victorian town-house. Ideally situated 5 minutes' walk to York Minster and close to attractions. Private parking. Cosy en-suite rooms. Restaurants nearby. Non-smoking.
Bedrooms: 1 single, 4 double, 1 twin, 1 family room
Bathrooms: 6 en-suite, 1 private shower

Bed & breakfast

per night:	£min	£max
Single	16.00	22.00
Double	28.00	44.00

Parking for 4
Cards accepted: Mastercard, Visa

🛌🖾📻💻📺♿UL S✂🛏🛏🚐 SP T

Clarence Gardens Hotel 🏔

👑👑👑 APPROVED

Haxby Road, York YO3 7JS
☎ (01904) 624252
Fax (01904) 671293
Comfortable accommodation with emphasis on service. 10 minutes' walk to the city centre and York Minster. Large private car park.
Bedrooms: 1 single, 4 double, 8 twin, 1 triple, 4 family rooms
Bathrooms: 18 en-suite

Bed & breakfast

per night:	£min	£max
Single	20.00	43.00
Double	40.00	60.00

Half board per

person:	£min	£max
Daily	28.00	42.95
Weekly	196.00	300.65

Evening meal 1900 (last orders 2015)
Parking for 60
Cards accepted: Amex, Mastercard, Visa

🛌🐕🖾💻📺♿S🍴🗑🛏🐕⚓🛎✕ 🚐♿SP T

Cornmill Lodge 🏔

👑👑 COMMENDED

120 Haxby Road, York YO3 7JP
☎ (01904) 620566
Well-appointed guesthouse only 12 minutes' walk from York Minster. Most rooms en-suite. No smoking indoors. Car park. Launderette nearby. Friendly welcome.
Bedrooms: 1 single, 2 double, 2 twin
Bathrooms: 3 en-suite, 2 private showers

Bed & breakfast

per night:	£min	£max
Single	17.00	21.00
Double	32.00	40.00

Parking for 4
Open February–November

🛌4🖾📻💻♿UL S✂🛏 TV 🗑🚐 ✕🚐SP

Cottage Hotel 🏔

👑👑👑 COMMENDED

1 Clifton Green, York YO3 6LH
☎ (01904) 643711
Fax (01904) 611230

Enchanting family-run hotel within 10 minutes' walking distance of the city centre, overlooking the beautiful Clifton Green.
Bedrooms: 2 single, 9 double, 5 twin, 3 triple
Bathrooms: 19 en-suite

Bed & breakfast

per night:	£min	£max
Single	30.00	45.00
Double	45.00	75.00

Half board per

person:	£min	£max
Daily	29.50	42.50

Evening meal 1830 (last orders 2030)
Parking for 12
Cards accepted: Amex, Diners, Mastercard, Visa, Switch/Delta

🛌🐕🖾🕭💻📺♿S🛏🗑🛏🚐 DAP 🍴SP

Craig-Y-Don 🏔

👑 APPROVED

3 Grosvenor Terrace, Bootham, York YO3 7AG
☎ (01904) 637186 & 0850 202795
Fax (01904) 637186
Under the Oliver ownership since 1979, where guests have become friends. Early booking is advisable to prevent disappointment.

Bedrooms: 3 single, 3 double, 2 twin
Bathrooms: 1 en-suite, 3 public

Bed & breakfast

per night:	£min	£max
Single	16.00	20.00
Double	32.00	40.00

Parking for 5
Open January–November
Cards accepted: Mastercard, Visa

🛌10♿💻📺♿UL S🗑🚐SP

Crook Lodge 🏔

👑👑👑 COMMENDED

26 St Mary's, Bootham, York YO3 7DD
☎ (01904) 655614
Early Victorian residence 450 yards from city centre. Bedrooms all en-suite with colour TV, radio. Private car park. Special breaks, dinner, bed and breakfast. No smoking.
Bedrooms: 1 single, 4 double, 2 twin
Bathrooms: 7 en-suite

Bed & breakfast

per night:	£min	£max
Single	25.00	28.00
Double	40.00	50.00

Half board per

person:	£min	£max
Daily	29.00	37.00

Evening meal 1800 (last orders 1000)
Parking for 8
Open February–December

🖾📻💻📺♿🗑S✂🛏🚐⚓🍴✕🚐 SP

Crossways Guest House

Listed APPROVED

23 Wigginton Road, York YO3 7HJ
☎ (01904) 637250
Ten minutes' walk from city centre. En-suite rooms with colour TV. Garden. Warm welcome and hearty breakfast.
Bedrooms: 4 double, 1 twin
Bathrooms: 5 en-suite

Bed & breakfast

per night:	£min	£max
Single	20.00	25.00
Double	36.00	40.00

Half board per

person:	£min	£max
Daily	29.00	34.00

Evening meal 1730 (last orders 1730)
Parking for 2
Cards accepted: Mastercard, Visa

🛌🖾💻♿UL🛏🚐❋✕🚐

Establishments should be open throughout the year, unless otherwise stated.

Curzon Lodge and Stable Cottages ⚑

👑👑 HIGHLY COMMENDED

23 Tadcaster Road, Dringhouses, York YO2 2QG
☎ (01904) 703157

Delightful 17th C listed house and old stables overlooking racecourse within historic city. Country antiques, beams, fresh flowers, cottagey bedrooms all en-suite, four-posters and brass beds. Cosy and informal. Floodlit parking in grounds. Restaurants one minute's walk.
Bedrooms: 1 single, 4 double, 3 twin, 1 triple, 1 family room
Bathrooms: 10 en-suite

Bed & breakfast per night:

	£min	£max
Single	30.00	42.00
Double	45.00	62.00

Parking for 16
Cards accepted: Mastercard, Visa, Switch/Delta

Dean Court Hotel ⚑

👑👑👑 HIGHLY COMMENDED

Duncombe Place, York YO1 2EF
☎ (01904) 625082
Fax (01904) 620305
CR Best Western

Elegant Victorian hotel, superbly situated next to York Minster in the centre of the city. Tearooms, restaurant, bar and conference facilities. Secure car park with free valet service. Half board price based on minimum 2-night stay.
Bedrooms: 10 single, 19 double, 8 twin, 1 triple, 2 family rooms
Suites available
Bathrooms: 40 en-suite

Bed & breakfast per night:

	£min	£max
Single	75.00	85.00
Double	115.00	145.00

Half board per person:

	£min	£max
Daily	69.50	87.00

Lunch available
Evening meal 1900 (last orders 2130)
Parking for 30
Cards accepted: Amex, Diners, Mastercard, Visa, Switch/Delta

Elmbank ⚑

👑👑👑👑 COMMENDED

The Mount, York YO2 2DD
☎ (01904) 610653
Fax (01904) 627139
CR Consort

City hotel with a country house atmosphere, close to York city centre, the Knavesmire and racecourse. Half board daily rate based on minimum 2-night stay.
Bedrooms: 9 single, 14 double, 26 twin, 8 triple, 1 family room
Bathrooms: 55 en-suite, 1 public

Bed & breakfast per night:

	£min	£max
Single	49.00	69.00
Double	55.00	95.00

Half board per person:

	£min	£max
Daily	40.00	56.00
Weekly	240.00	336.00

Lunch available
Evening meal 1830 (last orders 2130)
Parking for 20
Cards accepted: Amex, Diners, Mastercard, Visa, Switch/Delta

Four Seasons Hotel ⚑

👑👑👑 HIGHLY COMMENDED

7 St Peter's Grove, Bootham, York YO3 6AQ
☎ (01904) 622621
Fax (01904) 620976

Delightful, high-quality Victorian hotel, in quiet tree-lined grove. Only 5 minutes' walk from city centre. All rooms en-suite. Private car park.
Bedrooms: 2 double, 1 twin, 1 triple, 1 family room
Bathrooms: 5 en-suite

Bed & breakfast per night:

	£min	£max
Double	52.00	58.00

Parking for 8
Open February–December
Cards accepted: Mastercard, Visa

Fourposter Lodge Hotel

👑👑👑 COMMENDED

68-70 Heslington Road, Barbican Road, York YO1 5AU
☎ (01904) 651170 & 0802 383991

Victorian villa, lovingly restored and furnished for your comfort. Just 10 minutes' walk from historic York with all its fascinations.
Bedrooms: 8 double, 1 twin, 1 triple
Bathrooms: 9 en-suite, 1 private, 1 public

Half board per person:

	£min	£max
Daily	20.00	56.00

Evening meal 1830 (last orders 2000)
Parking for 8
Cards accepted: Amex, Mastercard, Visa

Galtres Lodge Hotel ⚑

👑👑 COMMENDED

54 Low Petergate, York YO1 2HZ
☎ (01904) 622478
Fax (01904) 627804
Georgian brick building of character, with views of the rose window of York Minster from some rooms.
Bedrooms: 3 single, 5 double, 3 twin, 1 triple
Bathrooms: 4 en-suite, 2 public

Bed & breakfast per night:

	£min	£max
Single	20.00	25.00
Double	45.00	65.00

Lunch available
Evening meal 1700 (last orders 2100)
Cards accepted: Mastercard, Visa, Switch/Delta

TOWN INDEX

This can be found at the back of the guide. If you know where you want to stay, the index will give you the page number listing all accommodation in your chosen town, city or village.

George Hotel ⋀
☗☗☗ COMMENDED

6 St George's Place, Tadcaster Road,
York YO2 2DR
☎ (01904) 625056
Fax (01904) 625009
Small family-run hotel in a quiet cul-de-sac near the racecourse and convenient for the city centre. Good car parking facilities.
Bedrooms: 5 double, 3 triple,
2 family rooms
Bathrooms: 10 en-suite
Bed & breakfast

per night:	£min	£max
Single	20.00	30.00
Double	35.00	50.00

Evening meal 1900 (last orders 2100)
Parking for 9
Cards accepted: Amex, Diners, Mastercard, Visa

Gleneagles Lodge Guest House ⋀
☗☗ APPROVED

27 Nunthorpe Avenue, York
YO2 1PF
☎ (01904) 637000
Fax (01904) 637000
In a cul-de-sac close to the station, city centre and museums. Within easy walking distance of the racecourse.
Bedrooms: 2 double, 1 twin, 2 family rooms
Bathrooms: 4 en-suite, 1 public
Bed & breakfast

per night:	£min	£max
Single	25.00	30.00
Double	42.00	45.00

Granby Lodge Hotel ⋀
Listed APPROVED

41-43 Scarcroft Road, York
YO2 1DA
☎ (01904) 653291
Fax (01904) 653291
Victorian family hotel offering all modern comforts and a mezzanine bar-lounge. Most rooms en-suite. Car park.
Bedrooms: 8 single, 20 double,
23 twin, 3 family rooms
Bathrooms: 32 en-suite, 6 public
Bed & breakfast

per night:	£min	£max
Single	18.00	23.00
Double	35.00	42.50

Half board per person:

	£min	£max
Daily	26.00	31.00

Evening meal 1800 (last orders 1900)
Parking for 30
Cards accepted: Amex, Diners, Mastercard, Visa

Grange Hotel ⋀
☗☗☗☗ HIGHLY COMMENDED

Clifton, York YO3 6AA
☎ (01904) 644744
Fax (01904) 612453
Classical, Regency town house hotel with all bedrooms individually decorated with antiques and English chintz. Within easy walking distance of York Minster.
Bedrooms: 3 single, 9 double,
17 twin, 1 triple
Suite available
Bathrooms: 30 en-suite
Bed & breakfast

per night:	£min	£max
Single	99.00	130.00
Double	108.00	190.00

Half board per person:

	£min	£max
Daily	78.00	

Lunch available
Evening meal 1800 (last orders 2230)
Parking for 26
Cards accepted: Amex, Diners, Mastercard, Visa, Switch/Delta

Grange Lodge ⋀
☗ APPROVED

52 Bootham Crescent, Bootham,
York YO3 7AH
☎ (01904) 621137
Attractive, tastefully furnished Victorian town house with a friendly atmosphere. Special emphasis is given to food, cleanliness and hospitality. Basic and en-suite rooms available. Evening meal by arrangement.
Bedrooms: 1 single, 3 double, 1 twin,
2 triple
Bathrooms: 4 en-suite, 1 public
Bed & breakfast

per night:	£min	£max
Single	16.00	20.00
Double	32.00	40.00

Half board per person:

	£min	£max
Daily	24.00	28.00
Weekly	160.00	190.00

Evening meal from 1800

Greenside
☗☗ APPROVED

124 Clifton, York YO3 6BQ
☎ (01904) 623631

Owner-run guesthouse, fronting Clifton Green, ideally situated for all York's attractions. Offers many facilities and a homely atmosphere.
Bedrooms: 1 single, 3 double, 2 twin,
2 triple
Bathrooms: 3 en-suite, 2 public
Bed & breakfast

per night:	£min	£max
Single	16.00	
Double	24.00	

Half board per person:

	£min	£max
Daily	25.50	

Evening meal 1800 (last orders 1800)
Parking for 6

Hazelmere Guest House ⋀
Listed APPROVED

65 Monkgate, York YO3 7PA
☎ (01904) 655947
Fax (01904) 626142
Georgian cottages, tastefully linked to retain their original character. Very close to York Minster and to several restaurants. Established for over 30 years. All rooms on first floor level. Private parking.
Bedrooms: 2 single, 2 double, 2 twin,
2 triple
Bathrooms: 1 en-suite, 1 private,
2 public
Bed & breakfast

per night:	£min	£max
Single	14.00	19.00
Double	28.00	42.00

Parking for 7

The Hazelwood ⋀
☗☗ COMMENDED

24-25 Portland Street, Gillygate,
York YO3 7EH
☎ (01904) 626548
Fax (01904) 628032
Situated in centre of York, only 400 yards from Minster, in an extremely quiet location with own car park. Elegant Victorian house. Non-smoking.

Bedrooms: 1 single, 7 double, 3 twin,
1 triple, 1 family room
Bathrooms: 13 en-suite

Bed & breakfast

per night:	£min	£max
Single	25.00	49.00
Double	39.00	59.00

Parking for 11
Cards accepted: Mastercard, Visa

🛏6♿🖭🕻🖵🗨♦🕯🍷ⓈⒾ↙🖬▥🗻
❄✗🚗⚓ SP 🏛 T

Hedley House 🏨
👑👑👑 COMMENDED
3-4 Bootham Terrace, York
YO3 7DH
☎ (01904) 637404
Family-run hotel close to the city centre.
1 ground floor bedroom. All rooms
en-suite. Home cooking, special diets
catered for.
Bedrooms: 2 single, 5 double, 5 twin,
2 triple, 1 family room
Bathrooms: 15 en-suite

Bed & breakfast

per night:	£min	£max
Single	20.00	34.00
Double	36.00	60.00

Half board per

person:	£min	£max
Daily	30.00	40.00

Evening meal 1830 (last orders
1900)
Parking for 18
Cards accepted: Amex, Diners,
Mastercard, Visa, Switch/Delta

🛏♿🖭🖵♦🕯Ⓘ↙🖬▥🗻✗ SP T

Heworth Court Hotel 🏨
👑👑👑 COMMENDED
76-78 Heworth Green, York
YO3 7TQ
☎ (01904) 425156
Fax (01904) 415290

Privately-owned, family-run hotel close
to York Minster and surrounding
countryside. Special short breaks. Bar,
restaurant, car park, lounge. Brochure
available.
Wheelchair access category 3🕭
Bedrooms: 5 single, 14 double,
4 triple, 2 family rooms
Bathrooms: 25 en-suite

Bed & breakfast

per night:	£min	£max
Single	44.00	54.00
Double	44.00	78.00

Half board per

person:	£min	£max
Daily	30.00	42.00
Weekly	175.00	245.00

Lunch available
Evening meal 1830 (last orders
2130)
Parking for 26
Cards accepted: Amex, Diners,
Mastercard, Visa, Switch/Delta

🛏♿🕻🖭🖵♦🕯↙🖬▥🗻
🍷16▶✗🚗⚓ SP T

Hobbits Hotel 🏨
👑👑 COMMENDED
9 St Peter's Grove, York YO3 6AQ
☎ (01904) 624538 & 642926
Fax (01904) 651765
Find a friendly and comfortable
welcome in this lovely old house, in a
quiet cul-de-sac 10 minutes' walk from
centre.
Bedrooms: 2 single, 2 double, 1 twin,
1 triple
Bathrooms: 6 en-suite

Bed & breakfast

per night:	£min	£max
Single	25.00	30.00
Double	50.00	55.00

Parking for 5
Cards accepted: Diners, Mastercard,
Visa

🛏🖭🖵♦Ⓘ↙🖬▥🗻🗻 OAP SP
🏛◉

Hollies 🏨
Listed APPROVED
141 Fulford Road, York YO1 4HG
☎ (01904) 634279
Comfortable family-run guesthouse,
close to university and golf-course and
with easy access to city centre.
Tea/coffee facilities, colour TV in all
rooms, some en-suite. Car parking.
Bedrooms: 2 double, 2 triple,
1 family room
Bathrooms: 2 en-suite, 1 public

Bed & breakfast

per night:	£min	£max
Single	16.00	22.00
Double	32.00	38.00

Parking for 5

🛏3♿🖵♦🗏↙🗻🗻🚗 SP

Holly Lodge 🏨
👑👑 COMMENDED
206 Fulford Road, York YO1 4DD
☎ (01904) 646005
Listed Georgian building on the A19,
convenient for both the north and
south and within walking distance of
the city centre. Close to university, golf
course and Barbican centre. Quiet
rooms and private car park.

Bedrooms: 3 double, 1 twin, 1 family
room
Bathrooms: 5 en-suite

Bed & breakfast

per night:	£min	£max
Single	30.00	50.00
Double	40.00	60.00

Parking for 5
Cards accepted: Amex, Mastercard,
Visa

🛏♿🖵♦ⓊⒾ↙🖬▥🗻❄✗
🚗 SP 🏛

Holmwood House Hotel 🏨
👑👑👑 HIGHLY COMMENDED
112-114 Holgate Road, York
YO2 4BB
☎ (01904) 626183
Fax (01904) 670899
Two listed Victorian town houses, 5
minutes from city walls, lovingly
redecorated and elegantly furnished.
Offering comfort in attractive
non-smoking, en-suite rooms.
Bedrooms: 8 double, 2 twin, 1 triple
Bathrooms: 11 en-suite

Bed & breakfast

per night:	£min	£max
Single	45.00	60.00
Double	55.00	70.00

Parking for 9
Cards accepted: Amex, Mastercard,
Visa, Switch/Delta

🛏8♿🖭🕻🖭🖵♦🕯🍷Ⓘ↙🖬▥
🗻❄✗🚗⚓ SP 🏛 T

Jacobean Lodge Hotel 🏨
👑👑👑 COMMENDED
Plainville Lane, Wigginton, York
YO3 8RG
☎ (01904) 762749
Fax (01904) 768403

Converted 17th C farmhouse, 4 miles
north of York. Set in picturesque
gardens with ample parking. Warm,
friendly atmosphere and traditional
cuisine.
Bedrooms: 2 single, 9 double, 1 twin,
2 triple
Bathrooms: 14 en-suite

Bed & breakfast

per night:	£min	£max
Single	30.00	35.00
Double	52.00	60.00

Lunch available
Evening meal 1900 (last orders
2200)

Continued ▶

YORK
Continued

Parking for 70
Cards accepted: Mastercard, Visa, Switch/Delta

Jarvis Abbey Park ⚏
♛♛♛ COMMENDED
77 The Mount, York YO2 2BN
☎ (01904) 658301
Fax (01904) 621224
Ⓒℝ Jarvis/Utell International
Explore York from this centrally located yet quiet hotel. Friendly service with a full bar and English restaurant. All rooms en-suite and most refurbished in 1997.
Bedrooms: 9 single, 28 double, 34 twin, 8 triple, 6 family rooms
Bathrooms: 85 en-suite

Bed & breakfast per night:

	£min	£max
Single	44.50	93.50
Double	89.00	122.00

Half board per person:

	£min	£max
Daily	45.00	108.25

Lunch available
Evening meal 1830 (last orders 2130)
Parking for 30
Cards accepted: Amex, Diners, Mastercard, Visa, Switch/Delta

Jorvik Hotel ⚏
♛♛♛ APPROVED
50-52 Marygate, Bootham, York YO3 7BH
☎ (01904) 653511
Fax (01904) 627009
Well-appointed central hotel overlooking the walls of St Mary's Abbey and Museum Gardens. Close to York Minster and shopping areas.
Bedrooms: 1 single, 12 double, 8 twin, 1 triple
Bathrooms: 22 en-suite

Bed & breakfast per night:

	£min	£max
Single	28.00	35.00
Double	42.00	65.00

Half board per person:

	£min	£max
Daily	30.00	41.00
Weekly	189.00	259.00

Evening meal 1730 (last orders 2100)
Parking for 12
Cards accepted: Mastercard, Visa

Judges Lodging ⚏
♛♛♛ HIGHLY COMMENDED
9 Lendal, York YO1 2AQ
☎ (01904) 623587 & 638733
Fax (01904) 679947
Georgian town house of exceptional historic importance, set in the centre of this ancient city. Lavishly decorated and furnished. Private parking.
Bedrooms: 2 single, 6 double, 4 twin, 2 triple
Suites available
Bathrooms: 14 en-suite

Bed & breakfast per night:

	£min	£max
Single	75.00	95.00
Double	95.00	140.00

Half board per person:

	£min	£max
Daily	62.50	85.00

Lunch available
Evening meal 1830 (last orders 2130)
Parking for 12
Cards accepted: Amex, Diners, Mastercard, Visa, Switch/Delta

Keys House ⚏
Listed COMMENDED
137 Fulford Road, York YO1 4HG
☎ (01904) 658488
Comfortable Edwardian house providing spacious bedrooms with showers and WCs. Own key provided. Reductions for 3 or more nights. Walled car park.
Bedrooms: 2 double, 3 triple
Bathrooms: 5 en-suite

Bed & breakfast per night:

	£min	£max
Single	24.00	40.00
Double	28.00	50.00

Parking for 5
Cards accepted: Mastercard, Visa

ACCESSIBILITY
Look for the ♿ symbols which indicate accessibility for wheelchair users. These are described in detail at the front of this guide.

Kilima Hotel ⚏
♛♛♛ COMMENDED
129 Holgate Road, York YO2 4DE
☎ (01904) 625787
Fax (01904) 612083
Lovingly furbished 19th C rectory with a fine restaurant serving a la carte and table d'hote. Walking distance to city centre. Private car park.
Bedrooms: 4 single, 7 double, 3 twin, 1 family room
Bathrooms: 15 en-suite

Bed & breakfast per night:

	£min	£max
Single	50.00	50.00
Double	78.00	90.00

Half board per person:

	£min	£max
Daily	53.50	63.00
Weekly	374.50	441.00

Lunch available
Evening meal 1830 (last orders 2130)
Parking for 20
Cards accepted: Amex, Diners, Mastercard, Visa, Switch/Delta

Knavesmire Manor Hotel ⚏
♛♛♛ COMMENDED
302 Tadcaster Road, York YO2 2HE
☎ (01904) 702941
Fax (01904) 709274
Ⓒℝ Logis of GB

Once a Rowntree family home, overlooking York Racecourse whilst close to the city centre. Award-winning Brasserie restaurant. Walled gardens and car park. Private tropical pool and spa.
Bedrooms: 3 single, 9 double, 5 twin, 3 triple, 1 family room
Bathrooms: 21 en-suite

Bed & breakfast per night:

	£min	£max
Single	39.50	59.00
Double	49.00	79.00

Half board per person:

	£min	£max
Daily	34.50	47.50
Weekly	210.00	260.00

Evening meal 1900 (last orders 2200)
Parking for 26
Cards accepted: Amex, Diners, Mastercard, Visa, Switch/Delta

Linden Lodge ♨

ⓦⓦ COMMENDED

6 Nunthorpe Avenue, Scarcroft
Road, York YO2 1PF
☎ (01904) 620107
Fax (01904) 620985

*Victorian town house in a quiet
cul-de-sac, 10 minutes' walk from
racecourse, rail station and city centre.
Easy access A64.*
Bedrooms: 2 single, 7 double, 2 twin,
2 family rooms
Bathrooms: 9 en-suite, 1 public

Bed & breakfast per night:	£min	£max
Single	20.00	30.00
Double	40.00	55.00

Cards accepted: Amex, Mastercard,
Visa

The Manor Country House ♨

ⓦⓦ HIGHLY COMMENDED

Acaster Malbis, York YO2 1UL
☎ (01904) 706723
Fax (01904) 706723

*Atmospheric manor in rural tranquillity,
bordering river. Off the beaten track
yet close for city, racecourse and A64.
Private fishing in lake. En-suite rooms
with full facilities. Wonderful
conservatory dining room with view of
lake and gardens.*
Bedrooms: 1 single, 4 double, 2 twin,
3 triple
Bathrooms: 10 en-suite

Bed & breakfast per night:	£min	£max
Single	38.00	42.00
Double	52.00	64.00

Evening meal 1900 (last orders
2030)
Parking for 15

> You are advised to confirm
> your booking in writing.

Middlethorpe Hall ♨

ⓦⓦⓦⓦ DE LUXE

Bishopthorpe Road, Middlethorpe,
York YO2 1QB
☎ (01904) 641241
Fax (01904) 620176

*Handsomely appointed and beautifully
furnished Queen Anne country house
with a fine kitchen and carefully
chosen wine list. In 27 acres of green
gardens bordering the racecourse, 1.5
miles from the centre of York.*
Bedrooms: 4 single, 14 double,
12 twin
Suites available
Bathrooms: 30 en-suite

Bed & breakfast per night:	£min	£max
Single	95.00	110.00
Double	131.00	215.00

Lunch available
Evening meal 1930 (last orders
2145)
Parking for 70
Cards accepted: Amex, Mastercard,
Visa, Switch/Delta

Midway House Hotel ♨

ⓦⓦ COMMENDED

145 Fulford Road, York YO1 4HG
☎ (01904) 659272
Fax (01904) 659272

*Non-smoking, family-run hotel. Spacious
en-suite bedrooms with four-poster and
ground floor rooms available. Close to
city centre and university. Private
parking.*
Bedrooms: 8 double, 2 twin, 2 triple
Bathrooms: 11 en-suite, 1 private,
1 public

Bed & breakfast per night:	£min	£max
Single	27.00	45.00
Double	36.00	60.00

Evening meal 1900 (last orders
1900)
Parking for 14
Cards accepted: Amex, Diners,
Mastercard, Visa

Moorland House ♨

ⓦⓦ APPROVED

1A Moorland Road, Fulford Road,
York YO1 4HF
☎ (01904) 629354

*Purpose-built guesthouse with car park,
close to city centre, golf club and
university. Pleasant and quiet en-suite
ground floor rooms with colour TV and
hot drink facilities.*
Bedrooms: 2 twin, 2 triple, 1 family
room
Bathrooms: 5 en-suite

Bed & breakfast per night:	£min	£max
Single	24.00	40.00
Double	32.00	52.00

Parking for 4
Cards accepted: Mastercard, Visa,
Switch/Delta

Newington Hotel ♨

ⓦⓦ COMMENDED

147-157 Mount Vale, York YO2 2DJ
☎ (01904) 625173 & 623090
Fax (01904) 679937
Ⓡ Inter Europe
*Hotel in a fine Georgian terrace, next
to York's famous racecourse and within
walking distance of city centre. Car
park, indoor swimming pool, sauna.*
Bedrooms: 4 single, 21 double,
11 twin, 7 triple
Bathrooms: 43 en-suite

Bed & breakfast per night:	£min	£max
Single	30.00	42.00
Double	50.00	64.00

Half board per person:	£min	£max
Daily	36.00	43.00
Weekly	269.00	269.00

Lunch available
Evening meal 1800 (last orders
2115)
Parking for 32
Cards accepted: Amex, Mastercard,
Visa, Switch/Delta

Novotel York ♨

ⓦⓦⓦⓦ COMMENDED

Fishergate, York YO1 4AD
☎ (01904) 611660
Fax (01904) 610925
Ⓡ Novotel
*Completely refurbished city centre
hotel. All rooms with private facilities,
including 4 for disabled guests. Garden
brasserie restaurant open 0600 to
2400. Bar, indoor swimming pool.
Wheelchair access category 2♿*
Bedrooms: 31 single, 31 double,
31 twin, 31 triple
Bathrooms: 124 en-suite

Bed & breakfast per night:	£min	£max
Single	70.00	85.00
Double	85.00	95.00

Half board per person:	£min	£max
Daily	70.00	80.00
Weekly	490.00	560.00

Lunch available

Continued ▶

YORK
Continued

Evening meal 1800 (last orders 2200)
Parking for 150
Cards accepted: Amex, Diners, Mastercard, Visa, Switch/Delta

Papillon Hotel
Listed APPROVED
43 Gillygate, York YO3 7EA
☎ (01904) 636505
Small, friendly city centre guesthouse with personal attention at all times. 300 yards from York Minster. En-suite available. No smoking, please. Car parking. Phone for details.
Bedrooms: 2 single, 1 double, 2 twin, 3 triple
Bathrooms: 3 en-suite, 2 public

Bed & breakfast per night:

	£min	£max
Single	20.00	25.00
Double	38.00	50.00

Parking for 7

Park View Guest House
Listed COMMENDED
34 Grosvenor Terrace, Bootham, York YO3 7AG
☎ (01904) 620437
Fax (01904) 620437
Family-run Victorian house with views of York Minster, close to city centre off the A19. Reductions for children sharing.
Bedrooms: 1 single, 3 double, 2 triple, 1 family room
Bathrooms: 3 en-suite, 1 public

Bed & breakfast per night:

	£min	£max
Single	16.00	20.00
Double	32.00	42.00

Priory Hotel
COMMENDED
126-128 Fulford Road, York YO1 4BE
☎ (01904) 625280
Fax (01904) 625280
Family hotel in a residential area with adjacent riverside walk to the city centre.
Bedrooms: 1 single, 9 double, 3 twin, 2 triple, 3 family rooms
Bathrooms: 18 en-suite

Bed & breakfast per night:

	£min	£max
Single	35.00	40.00
Double	45.00	50.00

Half board per person:

	£min	£max
Daily	32.50	35.00

Evening meal 1830 (last orders 2130)
Parking for 24
Cards accepted: Amex, Mastercard, Visa, Switch/Delta

Romley Guest House
APPROVED
2 Millfield Road, Scarcroft Road, York YO2 1NQ
☎ (01904) 652822
Comfortable, friendly, family-run guesthouse offering a licensed bar and a variety of other facilities. 10 minutes from city centre.
Bedrooms: 3 single, 1 double, 1 twin, 1 triple, 1 family room
Bathrooms: 1 public, 2 private showers

Bed & breakfast per night:

	£min	£max
Single	14.00	19.00
Double	28.00	38.00

Royal York Hotel
HIGHLY COMMENDED
Station Road, York YO2 2AA
☎ (01904) 653681
Fax (01904) 653271
Ⓡ Principal/Utell International

Set in 3 acres of private grounds, this refurbished, magnificent Victorian hotel is in the centre of historic York. Major attractions within a short walking distance. Prices shown are based on minimum 2-night stay.
Bedrooms: 29 single, 59 double, 57 twin, 3 triple, 10 family rooms
Suites available
Bathrooms: 158 en-suite

Bed & breakfast per night:

	£min	£max
Single	49.00	60.00
Double	98.00	116.00

Half board per person:

	£min	£max
Daily	59.00	70.00
Weekly	354.00	420.00

Lunch available

Evening meal 1900 (last orders 2145)
Parking for 120
Cards accepted: Amex, Diners, Mastercard, Visa, Switch/Delta

St Paul's Hotel
COMMENDED
120 Holgate Road, York YO2 4BB
☎ (01904) 611514

Close to York's many attractions, this small, family-run hotel has a warm atmosphere and serves a hearty breakfast. Come as a guest and leave as a friend.
Bedrooms: 1 single, 1 double, 1 twin, 1 triple, 2 family rooms
Bathrooms: 6 en-suite

Bed & breakfast per night:

	£min	£max
Single	25.00	35.00
Double	36.00	65.00

Evening meal 1800 (last orders 2100)
Parking for 12

Savages Hotel
COMMENDED
15 St Peter's Grove, Clifton, York YO3 6AQ
☎ (01904) 610818
Fax (01904) 627729
Victorian hotel in quiet tree-lined street close to city centre and all attractions. Comfortable, well equipped bedrooms (some ground floor) and traditional restaurant serving fine food. Wheelchair access category 3
Bedrooms: 3 single, 9 double, 5 twin, 1 triple, 2 family rooms
Bathrooms: 20 en-suite

Bed & breakfast per night:

	£min	£max
Single	25.00	40.00
Double	50.00	70.00

Half board per person:

	£min	£max
Daily	30.00	45.00

Evening meal 1800 (last orders 2100)

Parking for 14
Cards accepted: Amex, Diners, Mastercard, Visa, Switch/Delta

Swallow Hotel

HIGHLY COMMENDED

Tadcaster Road, York YO2 2QQ
☎ (01904) 701000
Fax (01904) 702308
Ⓒ Swallow

Set on the edge of York racecourse on the Knavesmire. A traditional hotel with extensive leisure facilities, attractive bedrooms and a restaurant overlooking the hotel grounds. Short break packages available.
Wheelchair access category 1
Bedrooms: 7 single, 42 double, 47 twin, 10 triple, 7 family rooms
Suite available
Bathrooms: 113 en-suite

Bed & breakfast per night:

	£min	£max
Single	99.00	110.00
Double	115.00	135.00

Half board per person:

	£min	£max
Daily	70.00	120.00
Weekly	430.00	1088.00

Lunch available
Evening meal 1900 (last orders 2200)
Parking for 200
Cards accepted: Amex, Diners, Mastercard, Visa, Switch/Delta

Tower Guest House

COMMENDED

2 Feversham Crescent, Wigginton Road, York YO3 7HQ
☎ (01904) 655571 & 635924
Comfortable and spacious 19th C guesthouse with friendly, informative hosts. Strolling distance from York Minster and city centre attractions.
Bedrooms: 1 single, 3 double, 1 twin, 1 triple
Bathrooms: 6 en-suite

Bed & breakfast per night:

	£min	£max
Single	18.00	25.00
Double	35.00	40.00

Evening meal 1730 (last orders 1830)
Parking for 6
Cards accepted: Mastercard, Visa

Tyburn House

COMMENDED

11 Albemarle Road, York YO2 1EN
☎ (01904) 655069
Family-owned and run guesthouse overlooking the racecourse. In a quiet and beautiful area, close to the city centre and railway station.
Bedrooms: 2 single, 3 double, 3 twin, 3 triple, 2 family rooms
Bathrooms: 11 en-suite, 1 private, 1 private shower

Bed & breakfast per night:

	£min	£max
Single	25.00	30.00
Double	44.00	60.00

Open February–October

Warrens Guest House

COMMENDED

30 Scarcroft Road, York YO2 1NF
☎ (01904) 643139
Centrally situated guesthouse. All rooms en-suite with colour TV and tea/coffee-making facilities. Full English breakfast. Four-poster beds available, also some ground-floor bedrooms. Private car park with CCTV.
Bedrooms: 1 single, 1 double, 2 twin, 1 triple, 1 family room
Bathrooms: 5 en-suite, 1 private

Bed & breakfast per night:

	£min	£max
Single	25.00	35.00
Double	38.00	45.00

Parking for 8
Open March–November

Winston House

APPROVED

4 Nunthorpe Drive, Bishopthorpe Road, York YO2 1DY
☎ (01904) 653171
Close to racecourse and 10 minutes' walk to city centre and railway station. Character en-suite room with all facilities. Private car park.
Bedrooms: 1 double
Bathrooms: 1 en-suite

Bed & breakfast per night:

	£min	£max
Double	30.00	34.00

Parking for 6

York Pavilion Hotel

HIGHLY COMMENDED

45 Main Street, Fulford, York YO1 4PJ
☎ (01904) 622099
Fax (01904) 626939
Ⓒ Best Western

Charming Georgian country house near city centre. Excellent restaurant, individually designed en-suite bedrooms, car parking, all within mature, walled grounds.
Bedrooms: 22 double, 10 twin, 2 triple
Bathrooms: 34 en-suite

Bed & breakfast per night:

	£min	£max
Single	88.00	90.00
Double	111.00	115.00

Lunch available
Evening meal 1830 (last orders 2130)
Parking for 45
Cards accepted: Amex, Diners, Mastercard, Visa, Switch/Delta

The map references refer to the colour maps towards the end of the guide. The first figure is the map number; the letter and figure which follow indicate the grid reference on the map.

WELCOME HOST

This is a nationally recognised customer care programme which aims to promote the highest standards of service and a warm welcome. Establishments who are taking part in this initiative are indicated by the ⊕ symbol.

COUNTRY CODE

Always follow the Country Code

🍀 Enjoy the countryside and respect its life and work 🍀 Guard against all risk of fire 🍀 Fasten all gates 🍀 Keep your dogs under close control 🍀 Keep to public paths across farmland 🍀 Use gates and stiles to cross fences, hedges and walls 🍀 Leave livestock, crops and machinery alone 🍀 Take your litter home 🍀 Help to keep all water clean 🍀 Protect wildlife, plants and trees 🍀 Take special care on country roads 🍀 Make no unnecessary noise

CHECK THE MAPS

The colour maps at the back of this guide show all the cities, towns and villages for which you will find accommodation entries.

Refer to the town index to find the page on which it is listed.

ENQUIRY COUPONS

To help you obtain further information about advertisers and accommodation featured in this guide you will find enquiry coupons at the back. Send these directly to the establishments in which you are interested. Remember to complete both sides of the coupon.

HEART OF ENGLAND

The exciting diversity of the Heart of England takes in rural, industrial, social, and artistic heritage, where unspoiled landscapes and black-and-white villages contrast with mellow market towns and major cities.

The region is home to the Cotswolds, the Malverns, the beautiful Wye valley, the marches of Hereford and Shropshire, and traditional brewing and pottery centres like Stafford and Burton-on-Trent.

Try popular local delicacies like Bakewell tarts and cheeses from Leicester. Tour famous Sherwood Forest or marvel at Northampton's unforgettable hot air balloon festival. England's heart beats fast in Coventry and Birmingham, both excellent touring bases and packed with things to do and see.

The counties of Derbyshire, Gloucestershire, Hereford & Worcester, Leicestershire, Northamptonshire, Nottinghamshire, Rutland, Shropshire, Staffordshire, Warwickshire and West Midlands

FOR MORE INFORMATION CONTACT:
Heart of England Tourist Board
Lark Hill Road, Worcester WR5 2EZ
Tel: (01905) 763436 **Fax:** (01905) 763450

Where to Go in the Heart of England –
see pages 210-214
Where to Stay in the Heart of England –
see pages 215-293

HEART OF ENGLAND

Where to Go and What to See

You will find hundreds of interesting places to visit during your stay in the Heart of England, just some of which are listed in these pages. The number against each name will help you locate it on the map (page 214). Contact any Tourist Information Centre in the region for more ideas on days out in the Heart of England.

1 Chatsworth House and Garden
Bakewell,
Derbyshire DE45 1PP
Tel: (01246) 582204
Built in 1687-1707 with a collection of fine pictures, books, drawings and furniture. Garden laid out by Capability Brown with fountains, cascades, a farmyard and playground.

2 The Heights of Abraham
Matlock Bath, Matlock,
Derbyshire DE4 3PD
Tel: (01629) 582365
A cable car ride across the Derwent Valley gives access to the Alpine Centre with refreshments, superb views, woodland, prospect tower and two show caves.

3 Peak District Mining Museum
The Pavilion, Matlock Bath,
Derbyshire DE4 3NR
Tel: (01629) 583834
Exhibition on 2,500 years of lead mining with displays on geology, mines and miners, tools and engines. The climbing shafts make it suitable for children.

4 The National Tramway Museum
Crich, Matlock,
Derbyshire DE4 5DP
Tel: (01773) 852565
Over 70 trams from Britain and overseas from 1873-1957 with tram rides on a one mile route, a period street scene, depots, a power station, workshops and exhibitions.

5 Midland Railway Centre
Butterley Station, Ripley,
Derby DE5 3QZ
Tel: (01773) 747674/570140
Over 25 locomotives and over 80 items of historic rolling stock of Midland and LMS origin with a steam-hauled passenger service, museum site, country and farm park.

6 **American Adventure World**
Pit Lane, Ilkeston,
Derbyshire DE7 5SX
Tel: (01773) 531521
*The new American Adventure
World has action and
entertainment for all ages. Ride the
missile white-knuckle rollercoasters,
rapid rides motion master and see
the Sooty Show.*

7 **Newark Air Museum**
The Airfield,
Winthorpe, Newark,
Nottinghamshire NG24 2NY
Tel: (01636) 707170
*Aircraft parts and memorabilia with
exhibition hall showing Anson,
Prentice, Swift, Provost, Vulcan,
Vampire, Meteors, Varsity and
Sycamores. Book and model shop.*

8 **White Post Modern Farm
Centre**
Farnsfield, Newark,
Nottinghamshire NG22 8HL
Tel: (01623) 882977
*A working farm with over 4,000
farm animals, an 8,000 egg
incubator, free-range hens, lambs,
lakes, picnic areas, tea gardens and
an indoor countryside night walk.*

9 **The Canal Museum**
Canal Street, Nottingham,
Tel: (0115) 959 8835
*A former canal warehouse with
landing areas and wharves, displays
on the history of the River Trent,
canal and river transport, bridges,
floods and natural history.*

10 **Nottingham Industrial
Museum**
Courtyard Buildings,
Wollaton Park,
Nottingham NG8 2AE
Tel: (0115) 928 4602
*An 18thC stables presenting the
history of Nottingham's industries:
printing, pharmacy, hosiery and
lace. There is also a Victorian beam
engine, a horse gin and transport.*

11 **The Tales of Robin Hood**
30-38 Maid Marian Way,
Nottingham NG1 6GF
Tel: (0115) 9414414/9483284
*Join the world's greatest medieval
adventure hide-out in the Sheriff's
eerie cave. Ride through the
magical green wood and play the
Silver Arrow game.*

12 **Belvoir Castle**
Belvoir,
Lincolnshire NG32 1PD
Tel: (01476) 870262
*The present castle is the fourth to
be built on this site and dates from
1816. Art treasures include works
by Poussin, Rubens, Holbein and
Reynolds. Queens Royal Lancers
display.*

13 **Alton Towers Theme Park**
Alton,
Stoke-on-Trent,
Staffordshire ST10 4DB
Tel: (0990) 204060/
(01538) 703344
*Theme Park with over 125 rides
and attractions including Nemesis,
Haunted House, Runaway Mine
Train, Congo River Rapids, Log
Flume and Toyland Tours.*

14 **Spode Museum and Visitor
Centre**
Spode Works, Church Street,
Stoke-on-Trent,
Staffordshire ST4 1BX
Tel: (01782) 744011
*Watch the various processes in the
making of bone china. Samples can
be bought at the Spode Shop.*

15 **Wedgwood Visitor Centre**
Barlaston,
Stoke-on-Trent,
Staffordshire ST12 9ES
Tel: (01782) 204141/204218
*Located in the Wedgwood factory
which lies within a 500-acre country
estate. You can see potters and
decorators at work. Museum
and shop.*

16 **Ye Olde Pork Pie Shoppe**
10 Nottingham Street,
Melton Mowbray,
Leicestershire LE13 1NW
Tel: (01664) 62341
*Pork pie shop and bakery in a
17thC building. History of the shop
and the Melton Mowbray pork pie
industry. Traditional hand raising
demonstration.*

17 **Rutland Water**
Whitwell, Oakham,
Leicestershire LE15 8PX
Tel: (01780) 460321/
(01480) 846427
*Water and land based recreational
facilities. Pleasure cruiser, church
museum, butterfly and aquatic
centre.*

18 **Twycross Zoo**
Twycross, Atherstone,
Warwickshire CV9 3PX
Tel: (01827) 880250/880440
*Gorillas, orangutans, chimpanzees,
a modern gibbon complex,
elephants, lions, cheetahs, giraffes,
a reptile house, pets corner
and rides.*

19 **Drayton Manor Theme Park
and Zoo**
Tamworth,
Staffordshire B78 3TW
Tel: (01827) 287979
*Family theme park with 250 acres
of parkland and lakes. Open plan
zoo. Amusement park with 50
rides. Wristbands for unlimited rides
or discount tickets.*

20 **The Shrewsbury Quest**
193 Abbey Foregate,
Shrewsbury,
Shropshire SY2 6AH
Tel: (01743) 243324/355990
*12thC historical site. Visitors are
invited to solve three mysteries,
creating manuscripts and playing
medieval garden games.*

21 **Ironbridge Gorge Museum**
Ironbridge, Telford,
Shropshire TF8 7AW
Tel: (01925) 433522
*World's first cast-iron bridge,
Museum of the River Visitor Centre,
Tar Tunnel, Jackfield Tile Museum,
Coalport China Museum, Rosehill
House, Blists Hill Museum and
Museum of Iron.*

22 **Acton Scott Historic
Working Farm**
Wenlock Lodge,
Acton Scott Church, Stretton,
Shropshire SY6 6QN
Tel: (01694) 781306/781307
*Living history in the Shropshire Hills
- dairy farming, milking, butter
making and craft demonstrations.*

23 **Black Country Living
Museum**
Tipton Road, Dudley,
West Midlands DY1 4SQ
Tel: (0121) 557 9643
*Midlands open air museum with
shops, chapel, canal trip into
limestone cavern, underground
mining experience and electric
tramway. Britain's industrial past
brought to life.*

24 **Stanford Hall and Motor
Cycle Museum**
Lutterworth,
Leicestershire LE17 6DH
Tel: (01788) 860250
*A William and Mary house on the
River Avon with family costumes,
furniture, pictures, a replica 1898
flying machine, motorcycle museum,
rose garden and nature trail.*

25 **National Sea Life Centre**
The Water's Edge,
Brindleyplace,
Birmingham B1 2HL
Tel: (0121) 633 4700/643 6777
*Over 55 fascinating displays.
The opportunity to come face-to-
face with hundreds of fascinating
sea creatures from sharks to
shrimps.*

26 **National Motorcycle
Museum**
Coventry Road,
Bickenhill, Solihull,
West Midlands B92 OEJ
Tel: (01675) 443311
*Collection of 650 British machines
from 1898-1993, housed in a
new high architectural standard
building.*

27 **Brandon Marsh Nature
Centre**
Brandon Lane, Coventry,
West Midlands CV3 3GW
Tel: (01203) 302912
*Two-hundred acre nature reserve
with lakes, marshes and woodland.
Ideal place to see natural wildlife.
Nature trail with disabled access.
Nature centre with displays and
shop.*

28 **Cadbury World**
Linden Road, Bournville,
Birmingham,
West Midlands B30 2LD
Tel: (0121) 451 4180/4159
*Story of chocolate from Aztec times
to present day. Chocolate-making
demonstration and children's
fantasy factory.*

29 **Rugby School Museum**
10 Little Church Street,
Rugby,
Warwickshire CV21 3AW
Tel: (01788) 574117/565871
*Tells the story of the school, scene of
Tom Brown's Schooldays, and
contains memorabilia of the game of
rugby invented on the School Close.*

30 Holdenby House, Gardens and Falconry Centre
Holdenby,
Northampton NN6 8DJ
Tel: (01604) 770074
The remains of an Elizabethan palace and garden by Rosemary Verey with a fragrant border, falconry centre, armoury, a 17thC homestead, tearoom and shop.

31 Warwick Castle
Warwick,
Warwickshire CV34 4QU
Tel: (01926) 406600/495421
Set in 60 acres of grounds with state rooms, armoury, dungeon, torture chamber, clock tower. Exhibits include 'A Royal Weekend Party 1898' and 'Kingmaker - a preparation for battle'.

32 Shakespeare's Birthplace
Henley Street,
Stratford-upon-Avon,
Warwickshire CV37 6QW
Tel: (01789) 204016
Beginning with an evocation of the busy market town into which he was born, the exhibition covers Shakespeare's home background, school, marriage and theatre career in London.

33 Elgar's Birthplace Museum
Crown East Lane,
Lower Broadheath,
Worcester,
Worcestershire WR2 6RH
Tel: (01905) 333224
Cottage where Edward Elgar was born, housing a museum of photographs, musical scores, letters and records associated with the composer.

34 Mappa Mundi & Chained Library Exhibition
Hereford Cathedral,
5 The Cloister,
Hereford HR1 2NG
Tel: (01432) 359880
The new library of Hereford Cathedral is open to the public. See the unique Mappa Mundi, the largest and most complete map in the world, drawn in 1289.

35 Eastnor Castle
Eastnor, Ledbury,
Herefordshire HR8 1RD
Tel: (01531) 633160/632302
Medieval in appearance, the castle stands at the end of the Malvern Hills. Fine collections of armour, pictures, tapestries and Italian furniture.

36 The National Birds of Prey Centre
Newent,
Gloucestershire GL18 1JJ
Tel: (01531) 820286
Large collection of birds of prey. Flying demonstrations daily

(weather permitting), with eagles, falcons, hawks, owls and vultures.

37 World of Butterflies
Jubilee Park, Symonds Yat,
West Ross-on-Wye,
Herefordshire HR9 6DA
Tel: (01600) 890471
A collection of butterflies flying freely in their natural environment inside a large tropical glass house.

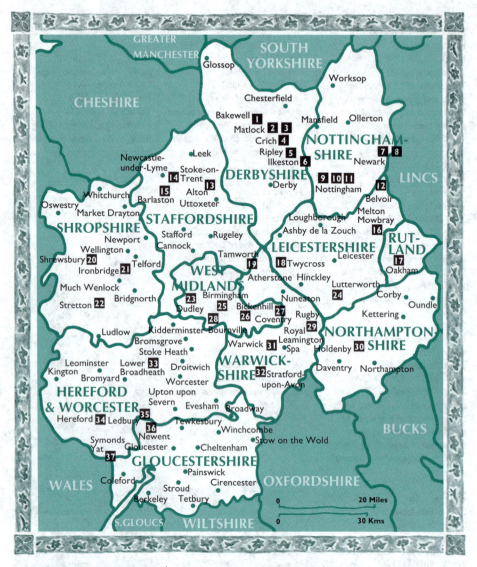

FIND OUT MORE

Further information about holidays and attractions in the Heart of England is available from:

Heart of England Tourist Board,
Lark Hill Road,
Worcester WR5 2EZ.
Tel: (01905) 763436 (24 hours)
These publications are available free from the Heart of England Tourist Board:

■ **Bed & Breakfast Touring Map**
■ **Great Escapes - short breaks and leisure holidays for all seasons**
■ **Events list**

Also available are:
Places to Visit in the Heart of England - a comprehensive guide to over 750 varied attractions and things to see, also great ideas for where to go in winter, (over £40 in discount vouchers included). £3.99
■ **Cotswolds Map** £2.95
■ **Cotswold/Wyndean Map** £3.25
■ **Shropshire/Staffordshire Map** £3.25
Please add *60p* postage for up to 3 items, plus *25p* for each additional 3 items.

WHERE TO STAY (HEART OF ENGLAND)

Accommodation entries in this region are listed in alphabetical order by place name, and then by establishment. As West Oxfordshire and Cherwell are also promoted under Heart of England, places in the area with accommodation are listed in this section. See South of England for full West Oxfordshire and Cherwell entries.

Map references refer to the colour location maps at the back of this guide. The first number indicates the map to use; the letter and number which follow refer to the grid reference on the map.

At-a-glance symbols at the end of each accommodation entry give useful information about services and facilities. A key to symbols can be found inside the back cover flap.

ABBOTS SALFORD

Warwickshire
Map ref 2B1

This hamlet gets its name from the place where the Salt Way forded the River Avon and from the Abbots of Evesham who owned Salford Hall.

Salford Hall Hotel M

HIGHLY COMMENDED

Abbots Salford, Evesham,
Worcestershire WR11 5UT
☎ (01386) 871300
Fax (01386) 871301
CR Best Western

Historic, noble manor house, lovingly restored, situated 8 miles west of Stratford-upon-Avon. Atmospheric charm and character of times past, combined with modern comfort.
Bedrooms: 2 single, 23 double,
8 twin
Bathrooms: 33 en-suite

Bed & breakfast

per night:	£min	£max
Single	75.00	120.00
Double	110.00	160.00

Half board per

person:	£min	£max
Daily	65.00	90.00
Weekly	390.00	450.00

Lunch available
Evening meal 1930 (last orders 2130)
Parking for 50
Cards accepted: Amex, Diners, Mastercard, Visa, Switch/Delta

ADDERBURY

Oxfordshire
Map ref 2C1

Red Lion Inn
See South of England region for full entry details

ALCESTER

Warwickshire
Map ref 2B1

Town has Roman origins and many old buildings around the High Street. It is close to Ragley Hall, the 18th C Palladian mansion with its magnificent baroque Great Hall.

Icknield House M

APPROVED

54 Birmingham Road, Alcester
B49 5EG
☎ (01789) 763287 & 763681
Fax (01789) 763287
Comfortable, well-furnished Victorian house of character, on the Birmingham road, a few hundred yards off A435. Close to Warwick and the Cotswolds and 10 minutes from Stratford-upon-Avon. Excellent touring centre.
Bedrooms: 2 single, 2 double, 1 twin,
1 triple
Bathrooms: 3 en-suite, 1 public,
1 private shower

Bed & breakfast

per night:	£min	£max
Single	18.00	25.00
Double	36.00	40.00

Half board per

person:	£min	£max
Daily	25.00	32.00

Evening meal 1830 (last orders 1930)
Parking for 8

Kings Court Hotel M

COMMENDED

Kings Coughton,
Stratford-upon-Avon B49 5QQ
☎ (01789) 763111
Fax (01789) 400242

Delightful bedrooms set around main part of the hotel, which is a listed Tudor farmhouse. Excellent home-cooked bar and restaurant meals. Close to Stratford-upon-Avon and the Cotswolds.
Bedrooms: 6 single, 18 double,
17 twin, 1 triple
Bathrooms: 42 en-suite

Bed & breakfast

per night:	£min	£max
Single	31.00	52.00
Double	52.00	78.00

Lunch available
Evening meal 1900 (last orders 2200)
Parking for 100
Cards accepted: Amex, Mastercard, Visa, Switch/Delta

ALCESTER

Continued

Throckmorton Arms Hotel M

ᗏᗏᗏ COMMENDED

Coughton, Alcester B49 5HX
☎ (01789) 762879
Fax (01789) 762654
*Small family-owned and managed
country hotel of quality. Friendly
atmosphere, log fires, air conditioning.
Bar meals and restaurant. Ideally
located for Stratford-upon-Avon and
Cotswolds. On A435 between Studley
and Alcester. Exit junction 3, M42.*
Bedrooms: 5 double, 5 twin
Bathrooms: 10 en-suite

Bed & breakfast

per night:	£min	£max
Single	27.50	45.00
Double	45.00	60.00

Lunch available
Evening meal 1800 (last orders
2145)
Parking for 70
Cards accepted: Amex, Diners,
Mastercard, Visa, Switch/Delta

ᗆᗒᘁᕮᕳ🖵ᗏᖘᗏᏚᕝ📺⌨🛏🅿⛵14
ᑌᖘ🗡🚜🛥 SP

ALREWAS

Staffordshire
Map ref 4B3

Delightful village of black and white
cottages, past which the
willow-fringed Trent runs. The Trent
and Mersey Canal enhances the
scene and Fradley Junction, a mile
away, is one of the most charming
inland waterway locations in the
country.

Claymar Hotel M

ᗏᗏᗏᗏ COMMENDED

118a Main Street, Alrewas, Burton
upon Trent DE13 7AE
☎ (01283) 790202 & 791281
Fax (01283) 791465
*Homely inn and Rafters Restaurant.
Bar food also available. Sunday lunches
available in Rafters.*
Bedrooms: 2 single, 10 double,
4 twin, 3 triple
Bathrooms: 19 en-suite

Bed & breakfast

per night:	£min	£max
Single	35.00	
Double	45.00	

Lunch available
Evening meal 1900 (last orders
2130)
Parking for 50
Cards accepted: Mastercard, Visa

ᗆᗒᘁᕮᕳ🖵ᗏᖘᏚᗏ📺◉⌨
🛏🅿⛵20ᖘ🌼🚜🛥 SP T

ALTON

Staffordshire
Map ref 4B2

Alton Castle, an impressive 19th C
building, dominates the village which
is set in spectacular scenery. Nearby
is Alton Towers, a romantic 19th C
ruin with innumerable tourist
attractions within one of England's
largest theme parks in its 800 acres
of magnificent gardens.

Fernlea Guest House M

ᗏᗏ COMMENDED

Cedar Hill, Alton, Stoke-on-Trent
ST10 4BH
☎ (01538) 702327
*Stone country guesthouse in the heart
of village. Homely, friendly atmosphere
guaranteed. Families most welcome.
Walking distance to pub/restaurants.*
Bedrooms: 1 double, 1 triple,
1 family room
Bathrooms: 3 en-suite

Bed & breakfast

per night:	£min	£max
Single	20.00	25.00
Double	32.00	40.00

Parking for 3
Open February–November

ᗆᕮᕳ🖵ᗏᖘ🅄🄻Ꮪᕝ📺⌨🗡🐾🚜

ASHBOURNE

Derbyshire
Map ref 4B2

Market town on the edge of the
Peak District National Park and an
excellent centre for walking. Its
impressive church with 212-ft spire
stands in an unspoilt old street.
Ashbourne is well-known for
gingerbread and its Shrovetide
football match.
Tourist Information Centre ☎ *(01335)
343666*

Callow Hall Country House
Hotel & Restaurant M

ᗏᗏᗏ HIGHLY COMMENDED

Mappleton, Ashbourne DE6 2AA
☎ (01335) 343403 & 342412
Fax (01335) 343624

*Half a mile from the centre of
Ashbourne and set in an elevated
position in unspoilt countryside,*

surrounded by its own woodland and
overlooking the valleys of Bentley Brook
and River Dove.
Bedrooms: 10 double, 6 twin
Suite available
Bathrooms: 16 en-suite

Bed & breakfast

per night:	£min	£max
Single	70.00	95.00
Double	105.00	130.00

Half board per

person:	£min	£max
Daily	85.50	98.00
Weekly	516.25	568.75

Evening meal 1900 (last orders
2130)
Parking for 50
Cards accepted: Amex, Diners,
Mastercard, Visa

ᗆᗒᘁᕮᕳ🖵ᗏᖘᏚᕝ🗡🚜⌨
🛏⛵40ᑌᗏᖘ🌼🚜 SP 🏮

Hanover International Hotel
and Club Ashbourne M

ᗏᗏᗏᗏ COMMENDED

Derby Road, Ashbourne DE6 1XH
☎ (01335) 346666
Fax (01335) 346549

*Purpose-built hotel offering en-suite
cottage-style bedrooms, luxury leisure
centre, two restaurants and bars.
Within easy reach of Alton Towers and
ideally located for exploring the Peak
District, including Dovedale, Haddon
Hall and Chatsworth.*
Bedrooms: 2 single, 25 double,
10 twin, 8 triple, 5 family rooms
Suites available
Bathrooms: 50 en-suite

Bed & breakfast

per night:	£min	£max
Single	68.50	78.50
Double	93.00	113.00

Half board per

person:	£min	£max
Daily	86.50	96.50

Lunch available
Evening meal 1900 (last orders
2200)
Parking for 200
Cards accepted: Amex, Diners,
Mastercard, Visa, Switch/Delta

ᗆᗒᘁᕮᕳ🖵ᗏᖘᏚᕝ🚜◉🛏
⌨🛏⛵200🚲🗡🍴🎱ᑌ🌼🗡 SP T

Lichfield Guest House 🏮

👑 HIGHLY COMMENDED

Bridge View, Mayfield, Ashbourne
DE6 2HN
☎ (01335) 344422
Fax (01335) 344422
Georgian house set in 2 acres of landscaped gardens. Magnificent views over River Dove and valleys. Convenient for Alton Towers, Chatsworth and the Peaks. Non-smoking.
Bedrooms: 1 single, 1 double, 1 twin, 1 family room
Bathrooms: 2 en-suite, 1 public

Bed & breakfast per night:

	£min	£max
Single	20.00	20.00
Double	38.00	45.00

Parking for 10

🛇🚗📞📺♿🔥🇸🎢🐴📺📖🅿❄🐕🚌

ASHBY-DE-LA-ZOUCH

Leicestershire
Map ref 4B3

Lovely market town with late 15th C church, impressive ruined 15th C castle, an interesting small museum and a wide, sloping main street with Georgian buildings. Twycross Zoo is nearby.
Tourist Information Centre ☎ (01530) 411767

Smisby Manor

👑👑 COMMENDED

Annwell Lane, Ashby-de-la-Zouch
LE65 2TA
☎ (01530) 415881
Fax (01530) 411914

16th C manor house overlooking Ivanhoe tournament fields. Large lawned gardens. Close to Calke Abbey, Staunton Harold, and convenient for Alton Towers and Donington Park.
Bedrooms: 2 single, 2 double
Bathrooms: 4 en-suite

Bed & breakfast per night:

	£min	£max
Single	35.00	40.00
Double	55.00	

Lunch available
Evening meal 1800 (last orders 2130)
Parking for 30
Cards accepted: Mastercard, Visa

🛇🏠🚗🇸📺🔥🅿🚪30♿🎵❄🗡🚌🏏🆚🏡

ASHFORD IN THE WATER

Derbyshire
Map ref 4B2

Limestone village in attractive surroundings of the Peak District approached by 3 bridges over the River Wye. There is an annual well-dressing ceremony and the village was well-known in the 18th C for its black marble quarries.

Chy-an-Dour 🏮

👑👑 HIGHLY COMMENDED

Vicarage Lane, Ashford in the Water, Bakewell DE45 1QN
☎ (0162981) 3162
Bungalow overlooking a pretty village and offering a friendly welcome. An ideal base for visiting the nearby stately homes and Derbyshire Dales.
Bedrooms: 2 double, 1 twin
Bathrooms: 3 en-suite

Bed & breakfast per night:

	£min	£max
Single	30.00	45.00
Double	42.00	55.00

Parking for 3

🍴🚗📞♿🇸🗡🔥❄🚌 DAP SP T

Riverside Country House Hotel 🏮

👑👑👑 HIGHLY COMMENDED

Fennel Street, Ashford in the Water, Bakewell DE4 1QF
☎ (01629) 814275
Fax (01629) 812873
17th C manor house with its own river frontage and an acre of garden which supplies home produce. Panelled bar, antiques, four-poster beds and an inglenook fireplace with log fires.
Bedrooms: 10 double, 5 twin
Bathrooms: 15 en-suite

Bed & breakfast per night:

	£min	£max
Single	75.00	95.00
Double	85.00	170.00

Half board per person:

	£min	£max
Daily	75.00	98.00
Weekly	500.00	655.00

Lunch available
Evening meal 1900 (last orders 2130)
Parking for 25
Cards accepted: Amex, Diners, Mastercard, Visa, Switch/Delta

🛇🏠🚗🍷📞♿🎢🇸🗡📺🔥🅿🚪20♿❄🚌🆚 SP 🏨

Please mention this guide when making your booking.

BAKEWELL

Derbyshire
Map ref 4B2

Pleasant market town, famous for its pudding. It is set in beautiful countryside on the River Wye and is an excellent centre for exploring the Derbyshire Dales, the Peak District National Park, Chatsworth and Haddon Hall.
Tourist Information Centre ☎ (01629) 813227

Castle Cliffe Private Hotel 🏮

👑👑 COMMENDED

Monsal Head, Bakewell DE45 1NL
☎ (01629) 640258
Fax (01629) 640258
Victorian stone house overlooking beautiful Monsal Dale. Noted for its friendly atmosphere, good food and exceptional views.
Bedrooms: 1 single, 2 double, 4 twin, 2 family rooms
Bathrooms: 6 en-suite, 2 public, 3 private showers

Bed & breakfast per night:

	£min	£max
Single	30.00	37.50
Double	48.00	55.00

Half board per person:

	£min	£max
Daily	37.50	50.00
Weekly	235.00	270.00

Evening meal 1900 (last orders 1700)
Parking for 15
Cards accepted: Mastercard, Visa

🛇♿🇸🗡📺🔥📺🔥🅿🚪15♿❄🏏🚌🆚 SP ◎

East Lodge Country House Hotel and Restaurant 🏮

👑👑👑👑 HIGHLY COMMENDED

Rowsley, Matlock DE4 2EF
☎ (01629) 734474
Fax (01629) 733949
Ⓒ Logis of GB
Tastefully furnished country house hotel and restaurant, set in 10 acres of grounds close to Chatsworth, Haddon Hall and the market town of Bakewell.
Bedrooms: 3 single, 6 double, 6 twin
Bathrooms: 15 en-suite

Bed & breakfast per night:

	£min	£max
Single	63.00	
Double	85.00	

Half board per person:

	£min	£max
Daily	63.00	

Lunch available

Continued ▶

BAKEWELL

Continued

Evening meal 1930 (last orders 2100)
Parking for 30
Cards accepted: Amex, Mastercard, Visa, Switch/Delta

🛍️♿🅿️🍴📞🖥️🐾🎣Ⓢ🖳🔥🍴
🍸70♿⚙️✈️🚲🐾 SP 🏧 T

BANBURY

Oxfordshire
Map ref 2C1

Banbury House Hotel
Prospect House Guest House
See South of England region for full entry details

BARTON UNDER NEEDWOOD

Staffordshire
Map ref 4B3

Fairfield Guest House 🏩

👑👑 HIGHLY COMMENDED

55 Main Street, Barton under Needwood, Burton upon Trent DE13 8AB
☎ (01283) 716396
Fax (01827) 61594
Spacious, early-Victorian residence, recently carefully restored, with modern facilities but retaining many original features.
Bedrooms: 2 double, 1 twin
Bathrooms: 3 en-suite

Bed & breakfast

per night:	£min	£max
Single	30.00	35.00
Double	45.00	50.00

Half board per

person:	£min	£max
Daily	40.00	45.00

Evening meal 1830 (last orders 2000)
Parking for 3
Cards accepted: Mastercard, Visa

🛍️🖳🐾🎣📞Ⓢ✂️🖳TV🖳🍴16
🔥✈️🚲🏠

> You are advised to confirm your booking in writing.

> A key to symbols can be found inside the back cover flap.

BEESTON

Nottinghamshire
Map ref 4C2

Within easy reach of Nottingham's city centre, with its castle, museums, shopping and entertainments, and close to the university.

The Grove Guesthouse

Listed APPROVED

8 Grove Street, Beeston, Nottingham NG9 1JL
☎ (0115) 925 9854
Small, friendly Victorian guesthouse, close to GPT, Plessey, Boots, university and tennis centre. Four miles from M1 junction 25, 6 miles East Midlands International Airport.
Bedrooms: 4 single, 1 twin
Bathrooms: 2 public

Bed & breakfast

per night:	£min	£max
Single	15.00	21.00
Double	25.00	32.00

Parking for 5

🛍️🐾UL✂️TV🖳🏠✈️🚲 SP T

BERKSWELL

West Midlands
Map ref 4B3

Pretty village with an unusual set of 5-holed stocks on the green. It has some fine houses, cottages, a 16th C inn and a windmill open to the public Sunday afternoons, May to end September. The Norman church is one of the finest in the area, with many interesting features.

Nailcote Hall Hotel and Restaurant 🏩

👑👑👑 HIGHLY COMMENDED

Nailcote Lane, Berkswell, Coventry CV7 7DE
☎ (01203) 466174
Fax (01203) 470720

Historic country house hotel and restaurant. Ideally located for Heart of England visitors. Situated on the B4101 Knowle to Coventry road.
Bedrooms: 25 double, 13 twin
Bathrooms: 38 en-suite

Bed & breakfast

per night:	£min	£max
Single	120.00	120.00
Double	130.00	130.00

Half board per

person:	£min	£max
Daily		149.00

Lunch available
Evening meal 1900 (last orders 2130)
Parking for 130
Cards accepted: Amex, Diners, Mastercard, Visa, Switch/Delta

🛍️♿🅿️🍴📞🖥️🐾🎣Ⓢ🖳TV🖳●
🔥🖳🅿️100🏊✈️🐾🎣♿U🅿️🔥✈️
🖳 SP 🏧 T

BIBURY

Gloucestershire
Map ref 2B1

Village on the River Coln with stone houses and the famous 17th C Arlington Row, former weavers' cottages. Arlington Mill is now a folk museum. Trout farm and Bansley House Gardens nearby are open to the public.

The Swan Hotel 🏩

👑👑👑👑 DE LUXE

Bibury, Cirencester GL7 5NW
☎ (01285) 740695
Fax (01285) 740473
De luxe family-run hotel, with riverside gardens, cosy parlours, noted restaurant, sumptuous bedrooms all with extravagant bathrooms (3 with four-posters and jacuzzis). Centrally located for touring the Cotswolds, Stratford, Oxford and Bath.
Bedrooms: 13 double, 4 twin, 1 family room
Bathrooms: 18 en-suite

Bed & breakfast

per night:	£min	£max
Single	97.00	97.00
Double	140.00	210.00

Half board per

person:	£min	£max
Daily	170.00	240.00

Lunch available
Evening meal 1930 (last orders 2130)
Parking for 20
Cards accepted: Amex, Mastercard, Visa, Switch/Delta

🛍️🅿️🍴📞🖥️🎣Ⓢ✂️🖳🖳🅿️🖳
🍸50♿🎣🅿️✈️🔥✈️🖳 SP 🏧 T

BICESTER

Oxfordshire
Map ref 2C1

Littlebury Hotel
See South of England region for full entry details

BIGGIN-BY-HARTINGTON

Derbyshire
Map ref 4B2

Biggin Hall

♛♛♛ [COMMENDED]

Biggin-by-Hartington, Buxton
SK17 0DH
☎ (01298) 84451
Fax (01298) 84681

17th C hall, Grade II listed, sympathetically modernised. Set tranquilly in the Peak District National Park. Fresh home cooking and comforts. Beautiful, uncrowded walks from the grounds.

Bedrooms: 7 double, 7 twin, 3 triple, 1 family room
Bathrooms: 18 en-suite

Bed & breakfast per night:	£min	£max
Single	30.00	45.00
Double	40.00	80.00

Half board per person:	£min	£max
Daily	30.00	55.00

Evening meal 1900 (last orders 1900)
Parking for 30
Cards accepted: Amex, Mastercard, Switch/Delta
12 [S] [TV] 20 [SP] [T]

BIRMINGHAM

West Midlands
Map ref 4B3

Britain's second city, whose attractions include Centenary Square and the ICC with Symphony Hall, the NEC, the City Art Gallery, Barber Institute of Fine Arts, 17th C Aston Hall, science and railway museums, Jewellery Quarter, Cadbury World, 2 cathedrals and Botanical Gardens.
Tourist Information Centre ☎ (0121) 643 2514 or 780 4321 or 693 6300

Arden Hotel and Leisure Club

♛♛♛♛ [HIGHLY COMMENDED]

Coventry Road, Bickenhill, Solihull
B92 0EH
☎ (01675) 443221
Fax (01675) 443221
[CR] The Independents

Perfect location next to NEC, railway, airport and motorway network. Privately owned and managed. Leisure complex includes swimming pool, sauna and jacuzzi. Free car parking.

Bedrooms: 28 single, 14 double, 98 twin, 6 triple
Bathrooms: 146 en-suite

Bed & breakfast per night:	£min	£max
Single	73.00	82.00
Double	89.00	106.00

Half board per person:	£min	£max
Daily	89.00	97.00

Lunch available
Evening meal 1800 (last orders 2200)
Parking for 300
Cards accepted: Amex, Diners, Mastercard, Visa, Switch/Delta
☎ [S] 220 [SP] [T]

Ashdale House Hotel

♛♛ [COMMENDED]

39 Broad Road, Acocks Green, Birmingham B27 7UX
☎ (0121) 706 3598
Fax (0121) 706 3598
Email: Ashdale@waverider

Furnished to enhance its Victorian character, this quiet, friendly hotel is in an attractive location overlooking a park. Delicious organic English breakfasts and alternatives are our speciality. If needed a courtesy car is usually available to welcome you.

Bedrooms: 7 single, 2 triple
Bathrooms: 4 en-suite, 2 public

Bed & breakfast per night:	£min	£max
Single	20.00	25.00
Double	32.00	38.00

Parking for 3
Cards accepted: Mastercard, Visa, Switch/Delta
[UL] [S] [TV] [DAP] [SP] [T]

Asquith House Hotel & Restaurant

♛♛♛ [COMMENDED]

19 Portland Road, Edgbaston, Birmingham B16 9UN
☎ (0121) 454 5282 & 454 6699
Fax (0121) 456 4668

Listed building (1854) of architectural interest, converted into an exclusive licensed hotel and restaurant. Well suited for mini-conferences and business meetings. Weddings a speciality.

Bedrooms: 2 single, 2 double, 5 twin, 1 triple
Bathrooms: 10 en-suite

Bed & breakfast per night:	£min	£max
Single	60.50	72.00
Double	77.55	83.00

Half board per person:	£min	£max
Daily	80.45	91.95

Lunch available
Evening meal 1930 (last orders 2130)
Parking for 10
Cards accepted: Amex, Mastercard, Visa
3 ☎ [S] [TV] 45 [SP] [T]

Atholl Lodge

♛♛ [APPROVED]

16 Elmdon Road, Acocks Green, Birmingham B27 6LH
☎ (0121) 707 4417
Fax (0121) 707 4417

Friendly guesthouse in a quiet location on the south side of Birmingham. The National Exhibition Centre, airport and town centre are all within easy reach.

Bedrooms: 4 single, 1 double, 4 twin, 1 triple
Bathrooms: 2 en-suite, 3 public

Bed & breakfast per night:	£min	£max
Single	20.00	26.00
Double	36.00	44.00

Lunch available
Evening meal 1700 (last orders 2100)
Parking for 10
[UL] [S] [TV] [DAP] [SP] [T]

Bridge House Hotel

♛♛♛ [COMMENDED]

49 Sherbourne Road, Acocks Green, Birmingham B27 6DX
☎ (0121) 706 5900 (Bookings line)
Fax (0121) 624 5900

Comfortably appointed private hotel with a range of facilities including pleasant dining room with a la carte menu, 2 licensed residential bars, TV lounge, patio and garden. Large secure car park. Executive rooms available.

Bedrooms: 15 single, 14 double, 14 twin, 1 triple
Bathrooms: 44 en-suite, 1 public

Bed & breakfast per night:	£min	£max
Single	37.60	42.00
Double		53.00

Evening meal 1900 (last orders 2100)
Parking for 70
Cards accepted: Amex, Diners, Mastercard, Visa, Switch/Delta
☎ [S] [TV] 60 [SP]

BIRMINGHAM
Continued

Central Guest House
Listed COMMENDED
1637 Coventry Road, South Yardley,
Birmingham B26 1DD
☎ (0121) 706 7757
Fax (0121) 706 7757
*Well established with warm and
friendly atmosphere. Central to all
amenities, airport, National Exhibition
Centre, railway, city centre. Good full
English breakfast. Home from home.*
Bedrooms: 1 single, 3 twin, 1 triple
Bathrooms: 4 en-suite, 1 private

Bed & breakfast

per night:	£min	£max
Single	17.50	22.00
Double	35.00	45.00

Parking for 4

Chamberlain Hotel M
Listed COMMENDED
Alcester Street, Birmingham B12 0PJ
☎ (0121) 606 9000
Fax (0121) 606 9001
Email: info@chamberlain.co.uk
The Independents
*Restored and refurbished Grade II
listed Victorian building of character, 1
mile from city centre. Extensive
conference and banqueting facilities.*
Bedrooms: 69 single, 118 double,
63 twin
Bathrooms: 250 en-suite

Bed & breakfast

per night:	£min	£max
Single		35.00
Double		40.00

Half board per

person:	£min	£max
Daily		45.00
Weekly		315.00

Lunch available
Evening meal 1800 (last orders
2200)
Parking for 180
Cards accepted: Amex, Diners,
Mastercard, Visa, Switch/Delta

Elmdon Guest House
COMMENDED
2369 Coventry Road, Sheldon,
Birmingham B26 3PN
☎ (0121) 742 1626 & 688 1720
Fax (0121) 688 1720
*Family-run guesthouse with en-suite
facilities. TV in all rooms, including Sky.
On main A45 close to the National
Exhibition Centre, airport, railway and
city centre.*
Bedrooms: 2 single, 4 twin, 1 triple

Bathrooms: 5 en-suite, 1 public

Bed & breakfast

per night:	£min	£max
Single	20.00	26.00
Double	36.00	45.00

Half board per

person:	£min	£max
Daily	20.50	36.50
Weekly	143.50	255.50

Lunch available
Evening meal 1830 (last orders
1930)
Parking for 7
Cards accepted: Mastercard, Visa

Fountain Court Hotel
COMMENDED
339-343 Hagley Road, Edgbaston,
Birmingham B17 8NH
☎ (0121) 429 1754
Fax (0121) 429 1209
*Small family-run hotel with friendly
service and easy access to city centre.*
Bedrooms: 11 single, 6 double,
2 twin, 4 triple
Bathrooms: 23 en-suite

Bed & breakfast

per night:	£min	£max
Single	39.00	45.00
Double	45.00	55.00

Half board per

person:	£min	£max
Daily	53.95	59.95
Weekly	323.70	359.70

Lunch available
Evening meal 1830 (last orders
2030)
Parking for 20
Cards accepted: Amex, Diners,
Mastercard, Visa, Switch/Delta

Greenway House Hotel
978 Warwick Road, Acocks Green,
Birmingham B27 6QG
☎ (0121) 706 1361 & 624 8356
Fax (0121) 706 1361
*Small, comfortable, privately-run
friendly hotel, close to the city centre,
motorways, airport and National
Exhibition Centre. Special weekend
tariffs from £16.*
Bedrooms: 8 single, 3 double, 2 twin,
1 triple
Bathrooms: 7 en-suite, 2 public,
1 private shower

Bed & breakfast

per night:	£min	£max
Single	18.00	24.00
Double	30.00	34.00

Half board per

person:	£min	£max
Daily	20.50	22.50

Lunch available
Evening meal 1830 (last orders
1930)
Parking for 18

Hagley Court Hotel M
COMMENDED
229 Hagley Road, Edgbaston,
Birmingham B16 9RP
☎ (0121) 454 6514
Fax (0121) 456 2722
*A private hotel and restaurant, all
rooms en-suite with TV, telephone.
English breakfast. 1.5 miles from city
centre.*
Bedrooms: 8 single, 16 double,
3 twin
Bathrooms: 27 en-suite

Bed & breakfast

per night:	£min	£max
Single	32.00	52.00
Double	42.00	70.00

Half board per

person:	£min	£max
Daily	45.00	65.00

Evening meal 1800 (last orders
2130)
Parking for 27
Cards accepted: Amex, Diners,
Mastercard, Visa, Switch/Delta

Heath Lodge Hotel M
APPROVED
Coleshill Road, Marston Green,
Birmingham B37 7HT
☎ (0121) 779 2218
Fax (0121) 779 2218

*Licensed family-run hotel, quietly
situated and less than 2 miles from the
National Exhibition Centre and
Birmingham Airport. Most rooms
en-suite.*
Bedrooms: 9 single, 3 double, 6 twin
Bathrooms: 13 en-suite, 1 public,
1 private shower

Bed & breakfast

per night:	£min	£max
Single	30.00	42.00
Double	42.00	48.00

Evening meal 1830 (last orders
2030)

Parking for 24
Cards accepted: Amex, Diners,
Mastercard, Visa

🛏 5 👤 ♿ 📞 🖵 🗕 ♨ 🛡 🅂 🗲 🗡 📺 ▥
🖪 🖍 120 ❀ DAP SP T

Ibis Birmingham

👑👑👑 COMMENDED

Ladywell Walk, Birmingham B5 4ST
☎ (0121) 622 6010
Fax (0121) 622 6020
*In the heart of the city, close to the
main line railway station and within
easy access of motorway and
international airport links. Adjacent to
the Chinese quarter, theatre district,
shopping and restaurants.*
Bedrooms: 94 double, 60 twin,
5 family rooms
Bathrooms: 159 en-suite

**Bed & breakfast
per night:**

	£min	£max
Single	50.50	51.50
Double	56.00	57.00

Lunch available
Evening meal 1900 (last orders
2200)
Cards accepted: Amex, Diners,
Mastercard, Visa, Switch/Delta

🛏 🖍 📞 🖵 🗕 ♨ 🗡 🗲 🗵 ▥ 🖪 🖍 120
🐾 SP T

Kensington Guest House Hotel

👑👑👑 COMMENDED

785 Pershore Road, Selly Park,
Birmingham B29 7LR
☎ (0121) 472 7086 & 414 1874
Fax (0121) 472 5520

*Family atmosphere. Full central heating,
evening meals, discount for long stay,
ground floor rooms. Four-poster bed in
bridal suite. Close to all amenities.*
Bedrooms: 5 single, 7 double, 8 twin,
5 triple, 4 family rooms
Bathrooms: 17 en-suite, 5 public,
10 private showers

**Bed & breakfast
per night:**

	£min	£max
Single	30.00	35.00
Double	40.00	45.00

**Half board per
person:**

	£min	£max
Daily	38.00	53.00
Weekly	266.00	371.00

Evening meal 1800 (last orders
2000)

Parking for 34
Cards accepted: Amex, Diners,
Mastercard, Visa, Switch/Delta

🛏 👤 ♿ 🏨 🖵 🗕 ♨ 🛡 🅂 🗲 🗡 📺 ▥ 🖪
❀ DAP 🐾 SP T

Lyndhurst Hotel M

👑👑 APPROVED

135 Kingsbury Road, Erdington,
Birmingham B24 8QT
☎ (0121) 373 5695
Fax (0121) 373 5695
*Within half a mile of M6 (junction 6)
and within easy reach of the city and
National Exhibition Centre.
Comfortable bedrooms, spacious
restaurant. Personal service in a quiet
friendly atmosphere.*
Bedrooms: 10 single, 2 double,
2 twin
Bathrooms: 13 en-suite, 1 private

**Bed & breakfast
per night:**

	£min	£max
Single	25.00	39.50
Double	39.50	52.50

**Half board per
person:**

	£min	£max
Daily	35.00	51.50

Evening meal 1800 (last orders
2000)
Parking for 12
Cards accepted: Amex, Diners,
Mastercard, Visa

🛏 👤 🖵 🗕 ♨ 🐾 🛡 🅂 🗲 🗡 📺 ▥ 🖪
🖍 30 ❀ 🐾 SP T

Rollason Wood Hotel M

👑👑 APPROVED

130 Wood End Road, Erdington,
Birmingham B24 8BJ
☎ (0121) 373 1230
Fax (0121) 382 2578
*Friendly, family-run hotel, 1 mile from
M6, exit 6. Convenient for city centre,
NEC and convention centre. A la carte
restaurant and bar.*
Bedrooms: 19 single, 3 double,
8 twin, 5 triple
Bathrooms: 11 en-suite, 5 public,
6 private showers

**Bed & breakfast
per night:**

	£min	£max
Single	17.85	36.25
Double	30.00	52.00

Evening meal 1800 (last orders
2030)
Parking for 43
Cards accepted: Amex, Diners,
Mastercard, Visa

🛏 👤 🖵 🗕 ♨ 🛡 🅂 🗲 🗡 📺 ◐ ▥ 🖪 🖍
SP T

Please check prices and other
details at the time of booking.

Sheriden House Hotel M

👑👑👑 COMMENDED

82 Handsworth Wood Road,
Handsworth Wood, Birmingham
B20 2PL
☎ (0121) 523 5960 & 554 2185
Fax (0121) 551 4761
*Private hotel 3.5 miles from
Birmingham city centre, ICC and
National Indoor Arena. 20 minutes
from NEC, 5 minutes from M5 and
M6. Car park.*
Bedrooms: 2 single, 3 double, 5 twin,
1 triple
Bathrooms: 9 en-suite, 1 public,
1 private shower

**Bed & breakfast
per night:**

	£min	£max
Single	28.00	41.00
Double	40.00	56.00

**Half board per
person:**

	£min	£max
Daily	41.00	54.00

Lunch available
Evening meal 1830 (last orders
2100)
Parking for 30
Cards accepted: Amex, Mastercard,
Visa, Switch/Delta

🛏 🏨 📞 🖵 🗕 ♨ 🛡 🅂 🗲 🗡 📺 ◐ ▥ 🖪
🖍 50 ❀ 🗡 🐾 SP T

Swallow Hotel M

👑👑👑👑👑 DE LUXE

Hagley Road, Five Ways, Birmingham
B16 8SJ
☎ (0121) 452 1144
Fax (0121) 456 3442
CR Swallow
*Luxurious hotel with air-conditioning,
award-winning food, an
Egyptian-themed leisure club and
excellent service. Short break packages
available.*
Wheelchair access category 3 ♿
Bedrooms: 14 single, 44 double,
40 twin
Suites available
Bathrooms: 98 en-suite

**Bed & breakfast
per night:**

	£min	£max
Single	150.00	165.00
Double	170.00	299.00

Lunch available
Evening meal 1800 (last orders
2230)
Parking for 70
Cards accepted: Amex, Diners,
Mastercard, Visa, Switch/Delta

🛏 🏨 📞 🖵 🗕 ♨ 🛡 🗲 🗡 ◐ 🛡 ▥ ◉
🖪 🖍 28 🗡 🍷 🐾 🐾 SP 🏨 T ◉

Please mention this guide
when making your booking.

BIRMINGHAM
Continued

Wentworth Hotel

⬥⬥⬥ APPROVED

103 Wentworth Road, Harborne,
Birmingham B17 9SU
☎ (0121) 427 2839 & 427 6818
Fax (0121) 427 2839
*Family-run hotel, all bedrooms en-suite
with tea and coffee facilities. Victorian
building with bar and restaurant in
Victorian style. Sky TV.*
Bedrooms: 6 single, 2 double, 4 twin
Bathrooms: 12 en-suite
Bed & breakfast

per night:	£min	£max
Single	28.00	35.00
Double	45.00	55.00

Half board per person:	£min	£max
Daily	40.00	45.00

Evening meal 1800 (last orders
1930)
Parking for 10
Cards accepted: Amex, Mastercard,
Visa, Switch/Delta

Westbourne Lodge Hotel Ⓜ

⬥⬥⬥ COMMENDED

27-29 Fountain Road, Edgbaston,
Birmingham B17 8NJ
☎ (0121) 429 1003
Fax (0121) 429 7436
Ⓒ The Independents
*Family-run hotel, all rooms en-suite.
Good food. Ideal for city, National
Exhibition Centre, International
Convention Centre, National Indoor
Arena and airport. Free parking.*
Bedrooms: 9 single, 3 double, 2 twin,
3 triple
Bathrooms: 17 en-suite
Bed & breakfast

per night:	£min	£max
Single	38.00	48.00
Double	48.00	58.00

Half board per person:	£min	£max
Daily	48.00	63.00
Weekly	280.00	370.00

Lunch available
Evening meal 1900 (last orders
2100)
Parking for 14
Cards accepted: Amex, Mastercard,
Visa, Switch/Delta

The Westley Hotel Ⓜ

⬥⬥⬥⬥ HIGHLY COMMENDED

Westley Road, Acocks Green,
Birmingham B27 7UJ
☎ (0121) 706 4312
Fax (0121) 706 2824
Ⓒ Best Western
*Close to National Exhibition Centre
and International Convention Centre.
Two restaurants, theme bar and
banqueting. Convenient for
Stratford-upon-Avon and Warwick. 3
miles junction 5 of M42.*
Bedrooms: 8 single, 7 double,
20 twin, 1 triple
Suite available
Bathrooms: 36 en-suite
Bed & breakfast

per night:	£min	£max
Single	39.50	75.25
Double	39.50	91.85

Lunch available
Evening meal 1900 (last orders
2200)
Parking for 200
Cards accepted: Amex, Diners,
Mastercard, Visa, Switch/Delta

Woodville House Ⓜ

Listed APPROVED

39 Portland Road, Edgbaston,
Birmingham B16 9HN
☎ (0121) 454 0274
Fax (0121) 421 4340
*High standard accommodation, 1 mile
from city centre. Full English breakfast.
All rooms have colour TV and
tea/coffee-making facilities. En-suite
bedrooms available.*
Bedrooms: 4 single, 2 double, 2 twin,
1 triple
Bathrooms: 2 en-suite, 4 public
Bed & breakfast

per night:	£min	£max
Single		16.00
Double	30.00	35.00

Parking for 12

BIRMINGHAM AIRPORT
West Midlands

*See under Berkswell, Birmingham,
Coleshill, Coventry, Hampton in Arden,
Meriden, Solihull*

For further information on
accommodation establishments
use the coupons at the
back of this guide.

BISHOP'S CASTLE
Shropshire
Map ref 4A3

A 12th C Planned Town with a
castle site at the top of the hill and a
church at the bottom of the main
street. Many interesting buildings
with original timber frames hidden
behind present day houses. On the
Welsh border close to the Clun
Forest in quiet, unspoilt countryside.

The Boars Head Hotel Ⓜ

⬥⬥⬥ COMMENDED

Church Street, Bishop's Castle
SY9 5AE
☎ (01588) 638521 & 0468 882248
Fax (01588) 630126
Email: 101327.1457
@compuserve.com
Ⓒ Wayfarer
*Old world inn, with en-suite
accommodation in original stables.
Comfortable dining area serves wide
choice of bar meals. A la carte
restaurant also available.*
Bedrooms: 1 double, 2 twin, 1 family
room
Bathrooms: 4 en-suite
Bed & breakfast

per night:	£min	£max
Single	33.00	38.00
Double	50.00	60.00

Half board per person:	£min	£max
Daily	60.00	70.00
Weekly	360.00	420.00

Lunch available
Evening meal 1830 (last orders
2130)
Parking for 20
Cards accepted: Amex, Diners,
Mastercard, Visa, Switch/Delta

BLAKENEY
Gloucestershire
Map ref 2B1

Village in wooded hills near the
Forest of Dean and the Severn
Estuary. It is close to Lydney where
the Dean Forest Railway has full size
railway engines, a museum and
steam days.

Viney Hill Country Guesthouse Ⓜ

Blakeney GL15 4LT
☎ (01594) 516000
Fax (01594) 516018
*Detached period farmhouse south-west
of Gloucester, set in delightful gardens
of approximately half an acre. Lovely*

rural setting with extensive views of surrounding countryside.
Bedrooms: 4 double, 2 twin
Bathrooms: 6 en-suite

Bed & breakfast per night:

	£min	£max
Single	30.00	32.00
Double	44.00	48.00

Half board per person:

	£min	£max
Daily	37.00	39.00

Evening meal 1900 (last orders 1700)
Parking for 7
Cards accepted: Mastercard, Visa, Switch/Delta

BLEDINGTON

Gloucestershire
Map ref 2B1

Village close to the Oxfordshire border, with a pleasant green and a beautiful church.

Kings Head Inn & Restaurant ♒

👑👑👑 COMMENDED

The Green, Bledington, Oxford
OX7 6XQ
☎ (01608) 658365
Fax (01608) 658902

15th C inn located in the heart of the Cotswolds, facing the village green. Authentic lounge bars, notable restaurant. Delightful en-suite rooms.
Bedrooms: 10 double, 2 twin
Bathrooms: 12 en-suite

Bed & breakfast per night:

	£min	£max
Single	40.00	45.00
Double	60.00	75.00

Lunch available
Evening meal 1900 (last orders 2200)
Parking for 60
Cards accepted: Mastercard, Visa, Switch/Delta

For ideas on places to visit refer to the introduction at the beginning of this section.

BLYTH

Nottinghamshire
Map ref 4C2

Village on the old Great North Road. A busy staging post in Georgian times with many examples of Georgian Gothic architecture. The remains of a Norman Benedictine priory survive as the parish church.

The Charnwood Hotel ♒

👑👑👑 HIGHLY COMMENDED

Sheffield Road, Blyth, Worksop
S81 8HF
☎ (01909) 591610
Fax (01909) 591429
Ⓒ Best Western
On the A634 Sheffield road between the villages of Blyth and Oldcotes. Stands in 3 acres of landscaped gardens with a natural wildlife pond.
Bedrooms: 2 single, 23 double, 9 twin
Bathrooms: 34 en-suite

Bed & breakfast per night:

	£min	£max
Single	60.00	60.00
Double	75.00	75.00

Half board per person:

	£min	£max
Daily	77.95	77.95

Lunch available
Evening meal 1900 (last orders 2145)
Parking for 75
Cards accepted: Amex, Diners, Mastercard, Visa, Switch/Delta

BOBBINGTON

Staffordshire
Map ref 4B3

Blakelands Country Guest House and Restaurant ♒

👑👑 COMMENDED

Halfpenny Green, Bobbington, Stourbridge, West Midlands
DY7 5DP
☎ (01384) 221464
Fax (01384) 221585
Dating from 1722, with original rooms and period features. Set in 6 acres of grounds including walled gardens, orchards and carp lake.
Bedrooms: 6 double, 2 twin
Bathrooms: 8 en-suite

Bed & breakfast per night:

	£min	£max
Single	38.00	43.00
Double	66.00	71.00

Evening meal 1900 (last orders 2100)

Parking for 100
Cards accepted: Mastercard, Visa, Switch/Delta

BOURTON-ON-THE-WATER

Gloucestershire
Map ref 2B1

The River Windrush flows through this famous Cotswold village which has a green, and cottages and houses of Cotswold stone. Its many attractions include a model village, Birdland, a Motor Museum and the Cotswold Perfumery.

Bourton Lodge Hotel ♒

👑👑👑 COMMENDED

Whiteshoots Hill, Bourton-on-the-Water, Cheltenham
GL54 2LE
☎ (01451) 820387
Fax (01451) 821635
Email: bourton@star.co.uk
Ⓒ Logis of GB
Family-run hotel with friendly atmosphere and traditional home cooking. Panoramic views of surrounding countryside from most bedrooms. Bourton-on-the-Water close by. Within easy driving distance of Cirencester, Cheltenham and Stratford.
Bedrooms: 7 double, 1 twin, 1 triple, 1 family room
Bathrooms: 10 en-suite

Bed & breakfast per night:

	£min	£max
Single	43.50	48.50
Double	65.00	85.00

Half board per person:

	£min	£max
Daily	47.50	57.50

Lunch available
Evening meal 1900 (last orders 2100)
Parking for 30
Cards accepted: Amex, Mastercard, Visa, Switch/Delta

The map references refer to the colour maps towards the end of the guide. The first figure is the map number; the letter and figure which follow indicate the grid reference on the map.

BOURTON-ON-THE-WATER
Continued

Dial House ⚋

ⴲ ⴲ ⴲ ⴲ HIGHLY COMMENDED

The Chestnuts, High Street,
Bourton-on-the-Water, Cheltenham
GL54 2AN
☎ (01451) 822244
Fax (01451) 810126
*17th C hotel in 1.5 acres of beautiful
walled garden, peacefully situated in
village centre. Log fires, four-posters,
noted a la carte restaurant. Special
winter offers.*
Bedrooms: 1 single, 6 double, 3 twin
Bathrooms: 9 en-suite, 1 private
**Bed & breakfast
per night:**

	£min	£max
Single	30.00	45.00
Double	60.00	110.00

**Half board per
person:**

	£min	£max
Daily	58.50	68.00
Weekly	346.00	409.00

Lunch available
Evening meal 1900 (last orders
2100)
Parking for 18
Cards accepted: Amex, Mastercard,
Visa, Switch/Delta

🛏🖭📞📧🖵❄🗑🛈🔒✂🔌🚭🖩 🖵
☎20🅿↻❄🚭 SP 🏕 T

Old Manse Hotel ⚋

ⴲ ⴲ ⴲ COMMENDED

Victoria Street,
Bourton-on-the-Water, Cheltenham
GL54 2BX
☎ (01451) 820082
Fax (01451) 810381

*Listed 18th C village centre hotel
fronting the River Windrush. A la carte,
table d'hote and vegetarian menus, real
ales, four-poster with whirlpool spa, log
fire. Special break and winter rates
available.*
Bedrooms: 9 double, 3 twin
Bathrooms: 12 en-suite
**Bed & breakfast
per night:**

	£min	£max
Single	39.50	74.50
Double	59.00	119.00

**Half board per
person:**

	£min	£max
Daily	42.75	76.45

Lunch available

Evening meal 1830 (last orders
2130)
Parking for 12
Cards accepted: Amex, Diners,
Mastercard, Visa, Switch/Delta

🛏🖭📞📧🖵❄🗑🛈🔒✂🔌🖩
🖵☎30🅿🚭🚭 SP 🏕

Old New Inn ⚋

ⴲ ⴲ ⴲ COMMENDED

Bourton-on-the-Water, Cheltenham
GL54 2AF
☎ (01451) 820467
Fax (01451) 810236
Email: 106206.2571
@compuserve.com

*This local inn with its pictures and
traditional log fires retains the
character and ambience which has
been built up over the last 200 years.*
Bedrooms: 3 single, 9 double, 4 twin,
1 triple
Bathrooms: 12 en-suite, 4 public
**Bed & breakfast
per night:**

	£min	£max
Single	30.00	36.00
Double	60.00	72.00

**Half board per
person:**

	£min	£max
Daily	48.00	55.00

Lunch available
Evening meal 1930 (last orders
2030)
Parking for 32
Cards accepted: Mastercard, Visa,
Switch/Delta

🛏🖭📞📧❄🛈🔒🔌TV🖩🖵🌸🚭
SP 🏕 T

BRIDGNORTH

Shropshire
Map ref 4A3

Red sandstone riverside town in 2
parts - High and Low - linked by a
cliff railway. Much of interest
including a ruined Norman keep,
half-timbered 16th C houses,
Midland Motor Museum and Severn
Valley Railway.
*Tourist Information Centre ☎ (01746)
763358*

The Croft Hotel ⚋

ⴲ ⴲ ⴲ APPROVED

St. Mary's Street, Bridgnorth
WV16 4DW
☎ (01746) 762416 & 767155
*Listed building with a wealth of oak

beams, in an old street. Family-run and
an ideal centre for exploring the
delightful Shropshire countryside.*
Bedrooms: 3 single, 4 double, 1 twin,
4 triple
Bathrooms: 10 en-suite, 1 public
**Bed & breakfast
per night:**

	£min	£max
Single	23.50	40.00
Double	40.00	50.00

**Half board per
person:**

	£min	£max
Daily	35.00	50.00
Weekly	205.00	310.00

Lunch available
Evening meal 1800 (last orders
2030)
Cards accepted: Amex, Mastercard,
Visa

🛏🖭📞📧🖵🛈🔒✂🔌TV🖩🖵🌸🚭
🅿❄🚭 DAP SP 🏕

Mill Hotel ⚋

ⴲ ⴲ ⴲ ⴲ HIGHLY COMMENDED

Alveley, Bridgnorth WV15 6HL
☎ (01746) 780437
Fax (01746) 780850
*Beautiful hotel in a delightful, tranquil
setting. En-suite bedrooms overlook the
mill pool and landscaped gardens.
Superb waterside restaurant.*
Bedrooms: 2 single, 13 double,
6 twin
Suite available
Bathrooms: 21 en-suite
**Bed & breakfast
per night:**

	£min	£max
Single	58.00	78.00
Double	69.50	100.00

**Half board per
person:**

	£min	£max
Daily	82.50	102.50
Weekly	577.50	717.50

Lunch available
Evening meal 1900 (last orders
2215)
Parking for 200
Cards accepted: Amex, Diners,
Mastercard, Visa, Switch/Delta

🛏🖭📞📧🖵❄🗑🛈🔒✂🔌🞉
🖩🖵☎200♨↻🎵❄✕🎣 SP 🏕 T

Old Vicarage Hotel ⚋

ⴲ ⴲ ⴲ ⴲ DE LUXE

Worfield, Bridgnorth WV15 5JZ
☎ (01746) 716497
Fax (01746) 716552
Ⓖ Logis of GB

Country house hotel in a quiet,

peaceful location, ideal for business or pleasure, close to Ironbridge Gorge and Severn Valley Railway. Half board daily prices are based on minimum 2-night stay.
Wheelchair access category 2
Bedrooms: 8 double, 5 twin, 1 triple
Suite available
Bathrooms: 14 en-suite

Bed & breakfast

per night:	£min	£max
Single	70.00	95.00
Double	107.50	152.50

Half board per

person:	£min	£max
Daily	157.50	217.50
Weekly	980.00	1295.00

Lunch available
Evening meal 1930 (last orders 2130)
Parking for 30
Cards accepted: Amex, Diners, Mastercard, Visa

Parlors Hall Hotel

COMMENDED

Mill Street, Low Town, Bridgnorth WV15 5AL
☎ (01746) 761931
Fax (01746) 767058
15th C residence of the Parlor family, built in 1419, with fine carved wood fireplaces and 18th C panelled lounge.
Bedrooms: 2 single, 8 double, 1 twin, 2 triple
Bathrooms: 13 en-suite

Bed & breakfast

per night:	£min	£max
Single	39.00	39.00
Double	48.00	48.00

Half board per

person:	£min	£max
Daily	49.90	57.95
Weekly	349.30	405.65

Lunch available
Evening meal 1900 (last orders 2200)
Parking for 26
Cards accepted: Mastercard, Visa

Please mention this guide when making your booking.

Establishments should be open throughout the year, unless otherwise stated.

BROADWAY

Hereford and Worcester
Map ref 2B1

Beautiful Cotswold village called the "Show village of England", with 16th C stone houses and cottages. Near the village is Broadway Tower with magnificent views over 12 counties and a country park with nature trails and adventure playground.

Broadway Hotel

COMMENDED

The Green, Broadway, Worcestershire WR12 7AA
☎ (01386) 852401
Fax (01386) 853879
Email: andrew@thebroadway.u-net.com

Grade II listed 16th C family-run hotel in the heart of picturesque village. Combines old world charm with the comforts and amenities of a modern hotel.
Bedrooms: 2 single, 10 double, 6 twin
Bathrooms: 18 en-suite

Bed & breakfast

per night:	£min	£max
Single	47.50	
Double	80.00	

Lunch available
Evening meal 1900 (last orders 2100)
Parking for 24
Cards accepted: Amex, Diners, Mastercard, Visa, Switch/Delta

Collin House Hotel & Restaurant

COMMENDED

Collin Lane, Broadway, Worcestershire WR12 7PB
☎ (01386) 858354 & 852544
16th C, secluded Cotswold hotel, with traditional atmosphere and charm. Four-poster bedrooms, inglenook fireplaces. Fine views, extensive gardens. Noted for good food.
Bedrooms: 1 single, 3 double, 3 twin
Bathrooms: 6 en-suite, 1 private shower

Bed & breakfast

per night:	£min	£max
Single	46.00	46.00
Double	88.00	98.00

Lunch available
Evening meal 1900 (last orders 2100)
Parking for 30
Cards accepted: Mastercard, Visa

Eastbank

Station Drive, Broadway, Worcestershire WR12 7DF
☎ (01386) 852659
Quiet location, half a mile from village. All rooms fully en-suite (bath/shower), with colour TV and beverage facilities. Homely atmosphere. Free brochure.
Bedrooms: 2 double, 2 twin, 2 triple
Bathrooms: 6 en-suite

Bed & breakfast

per night:	£min	£max
Single	20.00	40.00
Double	40.00	55.00

Parking for 6

Leasow House

HIGHLY COMMENDED

Laverton Meadow, Broadway, Worcestershire WR12 7NA
☎ (01386) 584526
Fax (01386) 584596
Email: bmeeking@compuserve.com
17th C Cotswold-stone farmhouse tranquilly set in open countryside close to Broadway village.
Bedrooms: 3 double, 2 twin, 2 triple
Bathrooms: 7 en-suite

Bed & breakfast

per night:	£min	£max
Double	53.00	62.00

Parking for 10
Cards accepted: Amex, Mastercard, Visa

The Lygon Arms

HIGHLY COMMENDED

Broadway, Worcestershire WR12 7DU
☎ (01386) 852255
Fax (01386) 858611
Email: info@the-lygon-arms.co.uk
16th C coaching inn set in the heart of the Cotswolds, with all the comforts of the 20th C. Well situated for touring the Cotswolds and Shakespeare country.
Bedrooms: 2 single, 48 double, 9 twin, 6 triple
Bathrooms: 65 en-suite

Bed & breakfast

per night:	£min	£max
Single	185.00	162.50
Double	190.00	

Continued ▶

BROADWAY
Continued

Half board per person:

	£min	£max
Daily	125.00	

Lunch available
Evening meal 1930 (last orders 2115)
Parking for 153
Cards accepted: Amex, Diners, Mastercard, Visa, Switch/Delta

The Old Rectory ♠
DE LUXE

Church Street, Willersey, Broadway, Worcestershire WR12 7PN
☎ (01386) 853729
Fax (01386) 858061

Award-winning guesthouse. A combination of the standards of a good hotel with the warmth of a private home - the ultimate in B & B, in exceptionally quiet surroundings.
Bedrooms: 5 double, 1 twin, 2 triple
Bathrooms: 6 en-suite, 2 private
Bed & breakfast per night:

	£min	£max
Single	45.00	75.00
Double	60.00	95.00

Evening meal from 1900
Parking for 10
Cards accepted: Mastercard, Visa, Switch/Delta

Olive Branch Guest House ♠
COMMENDED

78 High Street, Broadway, Worcestershire WR12 7AJ
☎ (01386) 853440
Fax (01386) 853440
Email: mark@olivebr.u-net.com
16th C house with modern amenities close to centre of village. Traditional English breakfast served. Reduced rates for 3 nights or more.
Bedrooms: 2 single, 3 double, 2 twin, 1 triple
Suite available
Bathrooms: 6 en-suite, 1 public

Bed & breakfast per night:

	£min	£max
Single	19.00	19.50
Double	40.00	56.00

Parking for 8
Cards accepted: Amex

Pathlow House ♠
Listed COMMENDED

82 High Street, Broadway, Worcestershire WR12 7AJ
☎ (01386) 853444
Comfortable period house, central for village amenities.
Bedrooms: 4 double, 1 twin, 1 family room
Bathrooms: 5 en-suite, 1 private
Bed & breakfast per night:

	£min	£max
Double	42.00	46.00

Parking for 6

Southwold Guest House ♠
COMMENDED

Station Road, Broadway, Worcestershire WR12 7DE
☎ (01386) 853681 & 0589 950833
Fax (01386) 854610

Warm welcome, friendly service, good cooking at this large Edwardian house, only 4 minutes' walk from village centre. Reductions for 2 or more nights; bargain winter breaks.
Bedrooms: 1 single, 4 double, 2 twin, 1 family room
Suite available
Bathrooms: 6 en-suite, 2 public
Bed & breakfast per night:

	£min	£max
Single	17.00	20.00
Double	34.00	44.00

Parking for 8
Cards accepted: Amex, Mastercard, Visa, Switch/Delta

White Acres Guesthouse ♠
HIGHLY COMMENDED

Station Road, Broadway, Worcestershire WR12 7DE
☎ (01386) 852320
Spacious Victorian house with en-suite bedrooms, 3 with four-poster beds. Off-road parking. 4 minutes' walk from village centre. Reductions for 3 or more nights. Bargain winter breaks.

Bedrooms: 5 double, 1 twin
Bathrooms: 6 en-suite
Bed & breakfast per night:

	£min	£max
Double	38.00	42.00

Parking for 8
Open March–October

Windrush House ♠
HIGHLY COMMENDED

Station Road, Broadway, Worcestershire WR12 7DE
☎ (01386) 853577
Edwardian guesthouse on the A44, 300 yards from the village centre, offering personal service. Evening meals by arrangement. 10 per cent reduction in tariff after 2 nights. A no-smoking establishment.
Bedrooms: 4 double, 1 twin
Bathrooms: 5 en-suite
Bed & breakfast per night:

	£min	£max
Single	25.00	25.00
Double	36.00	44.00

Parking for 5

BROMSGROVE
Hereford and Worcester
Map ref 4B3

This market town near the Lickey Hills has an interesting museum and craft centre and 14th C church with fine tombs and a Carillon tower. The Avoncroft Museum of Buildings is nearby where many old buildings have been re-assembled, having been saved from destruction.
Tourist Information Centre ☎ (01527) 831809

Bromsgrove Country Hotel ♠
COMMENDED

249 Worcester Road, Stoke Heath, Bromsgrove, Worcestershire B61 7JA
☎ (01527) 835522
Fax (01527) 871257
A quiet, elegant, Victorian residence with modern amenities, suitable for business or pleasure. Close to the M6/M42/M5 junctions and historic countryside. A pleasant stay ensured under the personal supervision of the proprietors.
Bedrooms: 4 double, 2 twin, 3 triple
Bathrooms: 8 en-suite, 1 private, 1 public
Bed & breakfast per night:

	£min	£max
Single	40.00	45.00
Double	45.00	49.00

Half board per person:	£min	£max
Daily	55.00	60.00

Evening meal 1930 (last orders 1400)
Parking for 20
Cards accepted: Mastercard, Visa

❄♿🏧🖥♨🛁🍴🅂🔌📺🎱🛏♿
🛩🚗 SP ⊚

Pine Lodge Hotel 𝖠

👑👑👑👑👑 HIGHLY COMMENDED

Kidderminster Road, Bromsgrove,
Worcestershire B61 9AB
☎ (01527) 576600
Fax (01527) 878981
Email: pinelodge
@bromsgrove.telme.com
Ⓒ Consort

With convenient access to the
motorway network, in beautiful
countryside. This Spanish design hotel
has 2 restaurants, lounge bar, 12
conference and banqueting suites and
leisure club. Close to NEC, Birmingham,
Cadbury World and Warwick Castle.
Bedrooms: 15 single, 70 double,
12 twin, 17 triple
Suites available
Bathrooms: 114 en-suite

Bed & breakfast per night:	£min	£max
Single	32.50	112.00
Double	65.00	122.00

Half board per person:	£min	£max
Daily	48.00	

Lunch available
Evening meal 1900 (last orders
2200)
Parking for 250
Cards accepted: Amex, Diners,
Mastercard, Visa, Switch/Delta

❄♿🏧🖥♨🛁🍴🅂🍴📺◐
🖥🛏♨🚗🍴200♨🎾🍴🎣♨🐾 DAP SP T

The map references refer
to the colour maps towards
the end of the guide.
The first figure is the
map number; the letter and
figure which follow indicate
the grid reference
on the map.

Gloucestershire
Map ref 2B1

Village with a church full of
interesting features including a 15th
C glass east window. The rectory,
also 15th C, is one of the oldest in
England. Nearby is Snowshill Manor,
owned by the National Trust.

Buckland Manor 𝖠

👑👑👑👑 DE LUXE

Buckland, Broadway, Worcestershire
WR12 7LY
☎ (01386) 852626
Fax (01386) 853557
13th C Cotswold manor in 10 acres, in
idyllic secluded valley. Log fires, central
heating. Tennis, riding, and complete
tranquillity.
Bedrooms: 8 double, 5 twin
Bathrooms: 13 en-suite

Bed & breakfast per night:	£min	£max
Single	175.00	315.00
Double	185.00	325.00

Lunch available
Evening meal 1930 (last orders
2045)
Parking for 30
Cards accepted: Amex, Diners,
Mastercard, Visa, Switch/Delta

❄🍴12♿🖥✆🍴♨🛁🅂🎱🛏♨🚗🎣
♨🎿🏇❄🍴🚗🐾🎣🎣

Oxfordshire
Map ref 2B1

Elm House Hotel
Golden Pheasant Hotel
The Highway Hotel
Romany Inn
See South of England region for full entry
details

Staffordshire
Map ref 4B3

An important brewing town with
the Bass Museum of Brewing, where
the Bass shire horses are stabled.
There are 3 bridges with views over
the river and some interesting
public buildings including the 18th C
St Modwen's Church.
Tourist Information Centre ☎ (01283)
516609 or 508589

The Delter Hotel

👑👑 COMMENDED

5 Derby Road, Burton upon Trent
DE14 1RU
☎ (01283) 535115
Fax (01283) 535115

Conveniently situated hotel, resident
proprietors. Comfortable en-suite
bedrooms, private licensed dining room,
offering home cooking, cosy cellar bar
and friendly atmosphere.
Bedrooms: 1 single, 1 double, 3 twin
Bathrooms: 5 en-suite

Bed & breakfast per night:	£min	£max
Single	28.50	28.50
Double	39.50	42.50

Evening meal 1900 (last orders
1800)
Parking for 8
Cards accepted: Mastercard, Visa

❄🍴🛁♨🅂📺🛏♨🚗🍴🛩🚗

The Queens Hotel 𝖠

👑👑👑👑 COMMENDED

1 Bridge Street, Burton upon Trent
DE14 1SY
☎ (01283) 564993
Fax (01283) 517556
A hotel within Burton's oldest licensed
house. Choice of restaurants, bars and
extensive conference and meeting
facilities. Close to Alton Towers.
Bedrooms: 10 single, 14 double,
3 twin
Suites available
Bathrooms: 27 en-suite

Bed & breakfast per night:	£min	£max
Single	29.50	67.00
Double	39.50	89.50

Half board per person:	£min	£max
Daily	39.50	77.00

Lunch available
Evening meal 1900 (last orders
2230)
Parking for 52
Cards accepted: Amex, Mastercard,
Visa, Switch/Delta

❄🍴✆🏧🖥♨🍴♨🅂🎱♨🖥🚗
🍴100🍴🛩🎣 SP 🏇 T

Riverside Hotel 𝖠

👑👑👑👑 COMMENDED

Riverside Drive, Branston, Burton
upon Trent DE14 3EP
☎ (01283) 511234
Fax (01283) 511441
Character hotel with restaurant
offering a wide choice of food, in
peaceful surroundings with own river
frontage.
Bedrooms: 16 single, 6 double
Bathrooms: 22 en-suite

Bed & breakfast per night:	£min	£max
Single	28.00	60.00
Double	56.00	70.00

Continued ▶

BURTON UPON TRENT

Continued

Half board per person:	£min	£max
Daily	45.95	77.95
Weekly	349.65	449.65

Lunch available
Evening meal 1900 (last orders 2200)
Parking for 110
Cards accepted: Amex, Mastercard, Visa, Switch/Delta

🛇🐾♿🕯️🖥️☐🛁🕹️⌂🅂🕪⌕💻 ☎150 ⏲📷✷🗲🚫 SP T

BUTTERTON

Staffordshire
Map ref 4B2

Village close to Thor's Cave, Hartington and the beautiful scenery of Dovedale.

The Old School Tea Room and En-suite Bed & Breakfast

👑 COMMENDED

Pot Hooks Lane, Butterton, Leek ST13 7SY
☎ (01538) 304320

Tastefully converted Victorian village school in beautiful Peak Park. Approximately 20 minutes from Alton Towers. Homely ground-floor en-suite B&B.
Bedrooms: 1 double, 1 family room
Bathrooms: 2 en-suite

Bed & breakfast per night:	£min	£max
Double	36.00	40.00

Lunch available
Parking for 6

🛇🐾♿☐🛁🕹️Ⓤ🅂🗲💻🚗✷🚐🚫 SP ◎

You are advised to confirm your booking in writing.

Establishments should be open throughout the year, unless otherwise stated.

BUXTON

Derbyshire
Map ref 4B2

The highest market town in England and one of the oldest spas, with an elegant Crescent, Poole's Cavern, Opera House and attractive Pavilion Gardens. An excellent centre for exploring the Peak District.
Tourist Information Centre ☎ (01298) 25106

Buxton View 👭

👑👑👑 COMMENDED

74 Corbar Road, Buxton SK17 6RJ
☎ (01298) 79222
Guesthouse built from local stone, offering a friendly and relaxed atmosphere. In a quiet area with a commanding view over the town and surrounding hills, yet only a few minutes' walk from the town's amenities.
Bedrooms: 1 single, 2 double, 1 twin, 1 triple
Bathrooms: 4 en-suite, 1 private

Bed & breakfast per night:	£min	£max
Single	19.00	20.00
Double	38.00	40.00

Half board per person:	£min	£max
Daily	28.00	30.00
Weekly	189.00	189.00

Evening meal 1900 (last orders 2000)
Parking for 7
Open February–November

🛇🐾♿☐🛁🕹️Ⓤ🅂🗲🎇💻🚗✷ 🚐 SP ◎

Fairhaven 👭

Listed APPROVED

1 Dale Terrace, Buxton SK17 6LU
☎ (01298) 24481
Fax (01298) 24481
Within easy reach of the Opera House, Pavilion Gardens, 2 golf courses and the many and varied attractions of Derbyshire's Peak District.
Bedrooms: 1 single, 1 double, 1 twin, 2 triple, 1 family room
Bathrooms: 1 public

Bed & breakfast per night:	£min	£max
Single	17.00	
Double	30.00	

Half board per person:	£min	£max
Daily	25.00	
Weekly	168.00	

Evening meal 1800 (last orders 1600)
Cards accepted: Amex, Mastercard, Visa

🛇🐾♿☐🛁🕹️Ⓤ🅂🗲💻🚗🚐

Ford Side House 👭

👑👑👑 COMMENDED

125 Lightwood Road, Buxton SK17 6RW
☎ (01298) 72842
Elegant, Edwardian house for non-smokers, in premier residential area yet close to all amenities. Stylish accommodation and delicious home cooking with flair.
Bedrooms: 2 double, 1 twin
Bathrooms: 3 en-suite

Bed & breakfast per night:	£min	£max
Single	19.00	30.00
Double	38.00	38.00

Half board per person:	£min	£max
Daily	30.00	30.00
Weekly	197.00	210.00

Evening meal from 1900
Parking for 3
Open March–October

🛇☎10☐🛁🕹️🅂🗲🎇💻🚗⏲ 🚐 SP T

Grosvenor House Hotel 👭

👑👑👑 COMMENDED

1 Broad Walk, Buxton SK17 6JE
☎ (01298) 72439
Fax (01298) 72439
Privately-run, Victorian residence enjoying splendid views of Pavilion Gardens/theatre. Homely and peaceful atmosphere. Bedrooms non-smoking. Home-cooked traditional English food. Comfort and hospitality assured.
Bedrooms: 5 double, 1 twin, 2 triple
Bathrooms: 8 en-suite

Bed & breakfast per night:	£min	£max
Single	42.50	47.50
Double	50.00	70.00

Half board per person:	£min	£max
Daily	40.00	50.00
Weekly	250.00	300.00

Lunch available
Evening meal 1845 (last orders 1845)

🛇☎8☐🛁🕹️🅂🗲🎇💻🚗 ☎18⏲📷✕🚐🚫 SP ◎

Map references apply to the colour maps at the back of this guide.

Hawthorn Farm Guesthouse

👑👑 COMMENDED

Fairfield Road, Buxton SK17 7ED
☎ (01298) 23230
A 400-year-old former farmhouse which has been in the family for 10 generations. Full English breakfast. En-suite rooms available. Tea/coffee facilities, colour TV.
Bedrooms: 4 single, 2 double, 2 twin, 4 triple
Bathrooms: 5 en-suite, 2 public

Bed & breakfast

per night:	£min	£max
Single	21.00	22.00
Double	42.00	48.00

Parking for 15
Open April–October

Lakenham Guesthouse 🅰

👑👑👑 COMMENDED

11 Burlington Road, Buxton
SK17 9AL
☎ (01298) 79209
Elegant Victorian house in own grounds overlooking Pavilion Gardens. Furnished in Victorian manner and offering personal service in a friendly, relaxed atmosphere.
Bedrooms: 2 double, 2 twin, 2 family rooms
Bathrooms: 6 en-suite

Bed & breakfast

per night:	£min	£max
Single	30.00	
Double	44.00	

Evening meal from 1800
Parking for 10

Old Hall Hotel 🅰

👑👑👑 COMMENDED

The Square, Buxton SK17 6BD
☎ (01298) 22841
Fax (01298) 72437
This historic hotel, reputed to be the oldest in England, offers a warm and friendly service. Ideally located opposite Pavilion Gardens (with 23 acres parkland and spa water swimming pool) and Edwardian Theatre, we serve pre and post theatre dinner in our restaurant and wine bar. A visit is recommended.
Bedrooms: 5 single, 19 double, 8 twin, 4 triple
Bathrooms: 34 en-suite, 2 private showers

Bed & breakfast

per night:	£min	£max
Single	55.00	60.00
Double	80.00	85.00

Half board per person:

	£min	£max
Daily	67.50	
Weekly	335.00	360.00

Lunch available
Evening meal 1800 (last orders 2300)
Cards accepted: Amex, Diners, Mastercard, Visa, Switch/Delta

Portland Hotel and Park Restaurant 🅰

👑👑👑 COMMENDED

32 St John's Road, Buxton
SK17 6XQ
☎ (01298) 71493 & 22462
Fax (01298) 27464
Ⓖ Logis of GB
Situated just 100 yards from Buxton's famous Opera House, the hotel and its noted restaurant make the perfect base for touring the Peak District.
Bedrooms: 6 single, 11 double, 7 twin, 1 triple
Bathrooms: 25 en-suite

Bed & breakfast

per night:	£min	£max
Single	48.00	54.60
Double	65.00	70.00

Half board per person:

	£min	£max
Daily	46.00	55.00
Weekly	300.00	360.00

Lunch available
Evening meal 1845 (last orders 2130)
Parking for 17
Cards accepted: Amex, Diners, Mastercard, Visa, Switch/Delta

Staden Grange Country House 🅰

👑👑👑 HIGHLY COMMENDED

Staden Lane, Staden, Buxton
SK17 9RZ
☎ (01298) 24965
Fax (01298) 72067
Ⓖ Minotel
250-acre dairy farm. Spacious residence 1.5 miles from Buxton, in a magnificent scenic area. It has been carefully extended and enjoys uninterrupted views over open farmland. Ground floor rooms available.
Bedrooms: 7 double, 4 twin
Bathrooms: 10 en-suite, 1 public, 1 private shower

Bed & breakfast

per night:	£min	£max
Single	42.00	45.50
Double	60.00	66.00

Half board per person:

	£min	£max
Daily	42.95	50.95

Evening meal 1830 (last orders 2000)
Parking for 30
Cards accepted: Amex, Diners, Mastercard, Visa

Castle Ashby is a fine Elizabethan mansion open for special events, product launches and conferences and set in landscaped grounds which are open to the public in summer. The church has many monuments to the Compton family.

The Falcon 🅰

👑👑👑 COMMENDED

Castle Ashby, Northampton
NN7 1LF
☎ (01604) 696200
Fax (01604) 696673
Email: falcon@castleashby.co.uk
Ⓖ Best Western
Proprietor-managed country cottage hotel. Ideal touring centre for Oxford, Cambridge, Stratford, Warwick and National Exhibition Centre. Good restaurant and bar open daily. Sky TV in all rooms.
Bedrooms: 4 single, 10 double, 2 twin
Bathrooms: 16 en-suite, 1 public

Bed & breakfast

per night:	£min	£max
Single	65.00	
Double	75.00	

Half board per person:

	£min	£max
Daily	57.00	
Weekly	399.00	

Lunch available
Evening meal 1930 (last orders 2130)
Parking for 60
Cards accepted: Amex, Mastercard, Visa, Switch/Delta

COLOUR MAPS

Colour maps at the back of this guide pinpoint all places in which you will find accommodation listed.

CASTLE DONINGTON

Leicestershire
Map ref 4C3

A Norman castle once stood here. The world's largest collection of single-seater racing cars is displayed at Donington Park alongside the racing circuit, and an Aeropark Visitor Centre can be seen at nearby East Midlands International Airport.

Delven Hotel ⚠

APPROVED

12 Delven Lane, Castle Donington, Derby DE7 2LJ
☎ (01332) 810153 & 850507
Small, family-run hotel, 1 mile from Donington race track and 2 miles from East Midlands International Airport.
Bedrooms: 2 double, 4 twin, 1 triple
Bathrooms: 3 public, 2 private showers

Bed & breakfast
per night:

	£min	£max
Single	18.00	23.00
Double	36.00	39.00

Parking for 5
Cards accepted: Mastercard, Visa

Donington Manor Hotel ⚠

👑👑👑

High Street, Castle Donington, Derby DE74 2PP
☎ (01332) 810253
Fax (01332) 850330
CR The Independents

This 18th C coaching inn with modern bedroom extensions has French and English menus, is 2 miles from junction 24 of the M1 and is close to Donington Park motor circuit and East Midlands International Airport.
Bedrooms: 2 single, 12 double, 11 twin, 1 family room
Bathrooms: 26 en-suite

Bed & breakfast
per night:

	£min	£max
Single	65.00	75.00
Double	75.00	85.00

Lunch available
Evening meal 1900 (last orders 2130)

Parking for 60
Cards accepted: Amex, Diners, Mastercard, Visa, Switch/Delta

Donington Park Farmhouse Hotel ⚠

👑👑👑 COMMENDED

Melbourne Road, Isley Walton, Castle Donington, Derby DE74 2RN
☎ (01332) 862409
Fax (01332) 862364
Email: park.farmhouse @dial.pipex.com
CR Logis of GB
Half-timbered 17th C farmhouse, in its own grounds. Spacious rooms, farmhouse suppers. Located at competitors' entrance to Donington Park.
Wheelchair access category 2 ♿
Bedrooms: 2 single, 3 double, 3 twin, 2 triple, 1 family room
Bathrooms: 10 en-suite, 1 private

Bed & breakfast
per night:

	£min	£max
Single	49.00	55.00
Double	65.00	75.00

Evening meal 1800 (last orders 2030)
Parking for 15
Cards accepted: Amex, Diners, Mastercard, Visa

Four-Poster Guesthouse

👑👑 APPROVED

73 Clapgun Street, Castle Donington, Derby DE7 2LF
☎ (01332) 810335 & 812418
Fax (01332) 812418
Some four-poster beds are available in this old-world accommodation in a quiet location opposite the church.
Bedrooms: 3 single, 3 double, 2 twin, 3 family rooms
Bathrooms: 5 en-suite, 2 public

Bed & breakfast
per night:

	£min	£max
Single	15.00	25.00
Double	36.00	50.00

Parking for 12

Little Chimneys Guesthouse

👑👑 COMMENDED

19 The Green, Diseworth, Castle Donington, Derby DE7 2QN
☎ (01332) 812458
Modern building in the pleasant village of Diseworth, close to the M1, East Midlands International Airport and Donington race track.
Bedrooms: 4 twin, 1 triple
Bathrooms: 5 private

Bed & breakfast
per night:

	£min	£max
Single		24.50
Double		36.50

Evening meal 1700 (last orders 2000)
Parking for 7
Cards accepted: Mastercard, Visa

Morton House Hotel

👑

78 Bondgate, Castle Donington, Derby DE7 2NR
☎ (01332) 812415
Fax (01332) 812415
Family-run private hotel with friendly atmosphere and lounge bar, only 1.5 miles from M1, junction 24, and East Midlands International Airport. 1 mile from Donington Park race circuit.
Bedrooms: 2 single, 3 double, 1 twin, 1 triple
Bathrooms: 2 private, 2 public

Bed & breakfast
per night:

	£min	£max
Single	21.00	25.00
Double	38.00	45.00

Half board per person:

	£min	£max
Daily	25.00	30.00

Evening meal 1830 (last orders 2000)
Parking for 10
Cards accepted: Mastercard, Visa

CASTLETON

Derbyshire
Map ref 4B2

Large village in a spectacular Peak District setting with ruined Peveril Castle and 4 great show caverns, where the Blue John stone and lead were mined. One cavern offers a mile-long underground boat journey.

Ye Olde Cheshire Cheese Inn ⚠

Listed COMMENDED

How Lane, Castleton, Sheffield S30 2WJ
☎ (01433) 620330 & 0836 369636

17th C inn in the heart of the Peak District. En-suite rooms. Restaurant

with 30 home-made dishes, including
roast wild boar, pheasant, game pie.
Two beamed lounge bars with real ale -
no pool tables or machines! Family-run.
Bedrooms: 2 single, 6 double, 1 twin
Bathrooms: 2 en-suite, 7 private

Bed & breakfast

per night:	£min	£max
Single	25.00	25.00
Double	45.00	60.00

Lunch available
Evening meal 1800 (last orders
2100)
Parking for 65
Cards accepted: Mastercard, Visa

CHELTENHAM

Gloucestershire
Map ref 2B1

Cheltenham was developed as a spa
town in the 18th C and has some
beautiful Regency architecture, in
particular the Pittville Pump Room.
It holds international music and
literature festivals and is also famous
for its race meetings and cricket.
Tourist Information Centre ☎ (01242)
522878

Barn End

Listed COMMENDED

23 Cheltenham Road, Bishop's
Cleeve, Cheltenham GL52 4LU
☎ (01242) 672404
*Large, spacious and comfortable
detached house. Convenient for
Cheltenham (4 miles) and its
racecourse (2 miles), also Tewkesbury,
Stratford and Cotswolds. Horse riding,
walking and golf on Cleeve Common (1
mile).*
Bedrooms: 1 double, 2 twin
Bathrooms: 1 en-suite, 1 public

Bed & breakfast

per night:	£min	£max
Single	38.00	50.00
Double	38.00	50.00

Parking for 7

Beechworth Lawn Hotel ⋔

HIGHLY COMMENDED

133 Hales Road, Cheltenham
GL52 6ST
☎ (01242) 522583
Fax (01242) 522583
*Carefully modernised and
well-appointed, detached Victorian
hotel, set in conifer and shrub gardens.
Convenient for shopping centre and all
amenities.*
Bedrooms: 2 double, 4 twin, 2 triple
Bathrooms: 6 en-suite, 1 public

Bed & breakfast

per night:	£min	£max
Single	25.00	35.00
Double	45.00	52.00

Half board per

person:	£min	£max
Daily	39.00	49.00

Evening meal 1800 (last orders
1900)
Parking for 12

Carlton Hotel ⋔

COMMENDED

Parabola Road, Cheltenham
GL50 3AQ
☎ (01242) 514453
Fax (01242) 226487
*In quiet, first class position, 250 yards
from famous Promenade and
award-winning parks. Emphasis on
traditional friendly service. Tasteful
bedrooms offer today's guest all
modern comforts. Excellent restaurant
and bar facilities. Half board prices
below apply at weekends only.*
Bedrooms: 16 single, 16 double,
43 twin
Bathrooms: 75 en-suite

Bed & breakfast

per night:	£min	£max
Single	40.00	62.50
Double	65.00	83.50

Half board per

person:	£min	£max
Daily	39.50	41.50

Lunch available
Evening meal 1900 (last orders
2130)
Parking for 85
Cards accepted: Amex, Diners,
Mastercard, Visa, Switch/Delta

Central Hotel ⋔

COMMENDED

7-9 Portland Street, Cheltenham
GL52 2NZ
☎ (01242) 582172 & 524789
*Family-run hotel close to town centre,
shops, coach station, racecourse,
cinema and theatre. Fully-licensed bar
and restaurant.*
Bedrooms: 2 single, 4 double, 6 twin,
2 triple
Bathrooms: 7 en-suite, 2 public,
1 private shower

Bed & breakfast

per night:	£min	£max
Single	25.00	36.00
Double	42.00	52.00

Half board per

person:	£min	£max
Daily	37.00	47.00

Lunch available
Evening meal 1900 (last orders
2030)
Parking for 5
Cards accepted: Amex, Diners,
Mastercard, Visa

Charlton Kings Hotel ⋔

HIGHLY COMMENDED

London Road, Charlton Kings,
Cheltenham GL52 6UU
☎ (01242) 231061
Fax (01242) 241900

*2.5 miles from town centre in an area
of outstanding beauty. Friendly staff,
interesting menus and quality
accommodation.*
Bedrooms: 2 single, 8 double, 2 twin,
1 triple, 1 family room
Bathrooms: 14 en-suite

Bed & breakfast

per night:	£min	£max
Single	35.50	55.50
Double	84.00	94.00

Half board per

person:	£min	£max
Daily	59.00	64.00
Weekly	301.00	322.00

Lunch available
Evening meal 1900 (last orders
2045)
Parking for 26
Cards accepted: Amex, Mastercard,
Visa, Switch/Delta

The Cheltenham Park Hotel ⋔

COMMENDED

Cirencester Road, Charlton Kings,
Cheltenham GL53 8EA
☎ (01242) 222021
Fax (01242) 254880
*Stylish Regency hotel in own colourful
gardens in the heart of the Cotswolds.
On the edge of Cheltenham, the hotel
enjoys splendid views over the adjoining
golf course and Cotswold Hills. Leisure
club with pool, spa bath, steam room,
sauna and gyms.*
Bedrooms: 17 single, 58 double,
68 twin, 2 family rooms
Suite available
Bathrooms: 145 en-suite

Continued ▶

CHELTENHAM

Continued

Bed & breakfast per night:	£min	£max
Single	89.00	99.00
Double	110.00	130.00

Half board per person:	£min	£max
Daily	60.00	110.00

Lunch available
Evening meal 1930 (last orders 2145)
Parking for 74
Cards accepted: Amex, Diners, Mastercard, Visa

⛱🛴🕭🖃🖵🕩🎅🍴🛈⌖🕼▥ 🖴🍴350🎣🎄🗝🗘🕻🌼 DAP 🗞 SP 🏤 T

The Frogmill ⚠

👑👑👑 COMMENDED

Shipton Oliffe, Andoversford, Cheltenham GL54 4HT
☎ (01242) 820547
Fax (01242) 820237
Magnificent building set in 5 acres by the River Coln. Turning ornamental waterwheel in the garden. 4 miles from Cheltenham, 9 miles from Gloucester.
http://www.epinet.co.uk/90/hotels/frogmill
Bedrooms: 6 double, 6 twin, 4 family rooms
Bathrooms: 16 en-suite

Bed & breakfast per night:	£min	£max
Single	39.00	45.00
Double	61.50	80.00

Lunch available
Evening meal 1830 (last orders 2145)
Parking for 200
Cards accepted: Amex, Diners, Mastercard, Visa

⛱🛴🕭🖃🖵🕩🎅🛈⌖🕼▥🖴 🍴200🌼 SP 🏤 T

George Hotel ⚠

👑👑👑 COMMENDED

41-49 St Georges Road, Cheltenham GL50 3DZ
☎ (01242) 235751
Fax (01242) 224359
Regency building, centrally situated. Close to Promenade and Montpellier shops.
Bedrooms: 8 single, 21 double, 10 twin
Bathrooms: 39 en-suite

Bed & breakfast per night:	£min	£max
Single	44.00	56.00
Double	58.00	68.00

Lunch available

Evening meal 1900 (last orders 2115)
Parking for 28
Cards accepted: Amex, Diners, Mastercard, Visa, Switch/Delta

⛱🛴🕭🖃🖵🕩🎅🍴🛈⌖🕼📺◑▥ 🖴🍴48 DAP 🗞 SP 🏤 T

Hanover House ⚠

👑👑👑 COMMENDED

65 St Georges Road, Cheltenham GL50 3DU
☎ (01242) 529867
Fax (01242) 222779
Well-appointed and spacious accommodation in elegant, listed Victorian Cotswold-stone house. Close to theatre, town hall, gardens and shopping facilities.
Bedrooms: 1 single, 3 double, 1 twin, 1 triple
Bathrooms: 3 en-suite, 1 public

Bed & breakfast per night:	£min	£max
Single	23.00	38.00
Double	48.00	58.00

Evening meal 1830 (last orders 0900)
Parking for 4
Cards accepted: Amex

⛱5🖃🖵🕩🛈⌖🕼📺▥🖴🌼🎄 🕹 SP 🏤 T

Hollington House Hotel ⚠

👑👑👑 COMMENDED

115 Hales Road, Cheltenham GL52 6ST
☎ (01242) 256652
Fax (01242) 570280
Ⓡ The Independents

Easy to find, 700 yards from London road/A40. Plenty of free on-site parking. Victorian house, spacious en-suite bedrooms, a la carte menus, licensed bar. Standards maintained by resident proprietors. Special interest tours arranged in our own mini-bus. Nous parlons francais. Chakap bahasa sidikit. Wir sprechen Deutsch.
Bedrooms: 2 single, 2 double, 1 twin, 1 triple, 3 family rooms
Bathrooms: 8 en-suite, 1 private

Bed & breakfast per night:	£min	£max
Single	30.00	45.00
Double	45.00	65.00

Evening meal 1900 (last orders 1900)
Parking for 14

Cards accepted: Amex, Mastercard, Visa, Switch/Delta

⛱3🛴🖃🖵🕩🎅🛈⌖🕼▥🖴 🍴25🙂🌼🎄 DAP 🗞 SP T

Ivy Dene House Hotel ⚠

👑👑 COMMENDED

145 Hewlett Road, Cheltenham GL52 6TS
☎ (01242) 521726 & 521776
Ideal base for exploring the Cotswolds. A charming corner house in its own grounds, situated in a residential area within walking distance of the town.
Bedrooms: 3 single, 1 twin, 4 triple, 1 family room
Bathrooms: 5 en-suite, 2 public

Bed & breakfast per night:	£min	£max
Single	20.00	25.00
Double	40.00	45.00

Parking for 6

⛱🖵🕩🛈📺▥🖴

Lonsdale House ⚠

👑👑 COMMENDED

Montpellier Drive, Cheltenham GL50 1TX
☎ (01242) 232379
Fax (01242) 232379
Regency house situated 5 minutes' walk from the town hall, Promenade, shopping centre, parks and theatre. Easy access to all main routes.
Bedrooms: 4 single, 2 double, 1 twin, 2 triple, 1 family room
Bathrooms: 3 en-suite, 1 private, 3 public

Bed & breakfast per night:	£min	£max
Single	19.00	30.00
Double	38.00	44.00

Parking for 6
Cards accepted: Mastercard, Visa, Switch/Delta

⛱🖃🖵🕩🛈⌖🕼▥🖴🌼🎄 🏤 T

Milton House ⚠

👑👑👑 HIGHLY COMMENDED

12 Royal Parade, Bayshill Road, Cheltenham GL50 3AY
☎ (01242) 582601
Fax (01242) 222326
Beautiful Regency listed building with individually styled spacious bedrooms, set among tree-lined avenues, only 4 minutes' stroll from the Promenade.
Bedrooms: 2 single, 3 double, 1 twin, 2 triple
Bathrooms: 8 en-suite

Bed & breakfast per night:	£min	£max
Single	38.50	45.00
Double	52.00	68.00

Evening meal 1930 (last orders 1930)
Parking for 6
Cards accepted: Amex, Diners, Mastercard, Visa, Switch/Delta

Moorend Park Hotel 🅜

👑👑👑👑 COMMENDED

11 Moorend Road, Cheltenham
GL53 0LA
☎ (01242) 224441
Fax (01242) 572413
Ⓒ The Independents
Elegant Victorian house, recently renovated and refurbished. Ample private parking. Fine Swiss orientated cuisine. Close to town centre and M5 (junction 11A).
Bedrooms: 1 single, 2 double, 3 twin, 2 triple, 1 family room
Bathrooms: 9 en-suite

Bed & breakfast
per night:	£min	£max
Single	35.00	45.00
Double	45.00	55.00

Half board per
person:	£min	£max
Daily	38.00	60.00

Lunch available
Evening meal 1900 (last orders 2030)
Parking for 25
Cards accepted: Amex, Mastercard, Visa, Switch/Delta

4 Pittville Crescent

👑 COMMENDED

Cheltenham GL52 2QZ
☎ (01242) 575567
Email: sparrey@tr250.demon.co.uk
Lovely Regency house with large airy rooms, beautifully situated overlooking charming parkland. 5 minutes from town centre.
Bedrooms: 1 single, 2 twin
Bathrooms: 1 public

Bed & breakfast
per night:	£min	£max
Single	17.50	19.50
Double	35.00	39.00

Parking for 20

The Prestbury House Hotel and Restaurant 🅜

👑👑👑 COMMENDED

The Burgage, Prestbury, Cheltenham
GL52 3DN
☎ (01242) 529533
Fax (01242) 227076
300-year-old Georgian country manor house set in 4 acres of secluded grounds beneath Cleeve Hill. Only 1 mile from Cheltenham centre.
Wheelchair access category 3♿
Bedrooms: 1 single, 10 double, 6 twin
Bathrooms: 17 en-suite

Bed & breakfast
per night:	£min	£max
Single	50.00	70.00
Double	65.00	88.00

Half board per
person:	£min	£max
Daily	75.00	95.00

Lunch available
Evening meal 1900 (last orders 2100)
Parking for 50
Cards accepted: Amex, Diners, Mastercard, Visa, Switch/Delta

Regency House Hotel 🅜

👑👑 HIGHLY COMMENDED

50 Clarence Square, Pittville, Cheltenham GL50 4JR
☎ (01242) 582718
Fax (01242) 262697
Email: regency1.demon.co.uk
Restored Regency house in a quiet Georgian square. Near Pittville Park but only minutes' walk from all town centre amenities.
Bedrooms: 5 double, 3 triple
Bathrooms: 8 en-suite

Bed & breakfast
per night:	£min	£max
Single	34.00	46.00
Double	46.00	58.00

Half board per
person:	£min	£max
Daily	44.00	56.00
Weekly	220.00	251.50

Evening meal 1800 (last orders 1930)
Parking for 5
Cards accepted: Amex, Mastercard, Visa

St. Michaels 🅜

👑👑 COMMENDED

4 Montpellier Drive, Cheltenham
GL50 1TX
☎ (01242) 513587
Fax (01242) 513587

Elegant Edwardian guesthouse offering delightful non-smoking accommodation with parking, five minutes' walk from town centre. Excellent breakfast menu and a warm welcome.
Bedrooms: 2 double, 1 twin, 2 triple
Bathrooms: 3 en-suite, 1 public

Bed & breakfast
per night:	£min	£max
Single	25.00	35.00
Double	36.00	48.00

Parking for 3
Cards accepted: Mastercard, Visa

Savoy Hotel 🅜

👑👑👑👑 COMMENDED

Bayshill Road, Cheltenham
GL50 3AS
☎ (01242) 527788
Fax (01242) 226412
Ⓒ Best Western
Located in a quiet tree-lined avenue in the prestigious Montpellier area of this Regency spa town. Excellent English restaurant. Parking.
Bedrooms: 16 single, 17 double, 8 twin
Suite available
Bathrooms: 41 en-suite

Bed & breakfast
per night:	£min	£max
Single	52.00	60.00
Double	80.00	85.00

Half board per
person:	£min	£max
Daily	64.00	72.00
Weekly	384.00	432.00

Evening meal 1830 (last orders 2130)
Parking for 40
Cards accepted: Amex, Mastercard, Visa, Switch/Delta

CHELTENHAM

Continued

Stretton Lodge Hotel ⋀

☺☺☺ HIGHLY COMMENDED

Western Road, Cheltenham
GL50 3RN
☎ (01242) 570771
Fax (01242) 528724
Ⓡ Logis of GB
Nestling in the heart of Cheltenham, a family-managed Victorian hotel with parking. En-suite bedrooms, home-cooked dinners and personal service ensure a relaxing stay.
Bedrooms: 1 single, 2 double, 1 twin, 1 triple
Bathrooms: 5 en-suite
Bed & breakfast

per night:	£min	£max
Single	38.50	55.00
Double	55.00	72.00

Half board per

person:	£min	£max
Daily	40.00	56.00
Weekly	265.00	350.00

Lunch available
Evening meal 1700 (last orders 1930)
Parking for 6
Cards accepted: Amex, Mastercard, Visa, Switch/Delta
🐾📞🖥️⌨️♿🎣🛍️🔒🗝️✂️🎿📺📺🛏️🗜️
🍴30❄️🚐 OAP SP 🏡 T

White House Hotel

☺☺☺ COMMENDED

Gloucester Road, Staverton, Cheltenham GL51 0ST
☎ (01452) 713226
Fax (01452) 857590
Peacefully located hotel, just a few minutes' drive from Cheltenham or Gloucester city centre. Ideal base for the Cotswolds.
Bedrooms: 1 single, 6 double, 37 twin, 3 triple, 2 family rooms
Suites available
Bathrooms: 49 en-suite
Bed & breakfast

per night:	£min	£max
Single	40.00	80.00
Double	80.00	98.00

Lunch available
Evening meal 1900 (last orders 2130)
Parking for 150
Cards accepted: Amex, Diners, Mastercard, Visa, Switch/Delta
🐎♿🚗📞🖥️⌨️♿🎣🛍️🔒🗝️●🛏️
🛏️🍴200▶❄️ OAP 🚐 SP T 🌐

CHESTERFIELD

Derbyshire
Map ref 4B2

Famous for the twisted spire of its parish church, Chesterfield has some fine modern buildings and excellent shopping facilities, including a large, traditional open-air market. Hardwick Hall and Bolsover Castle are nearby.
Tourist Information Centre ☎ *(01246) 345777*

Abbeydale Hotel ⋀

☺☺☺ COMMENDED

Cross Street, Chesterfield S40 4TD
☎ (01246) 277849
Fax (01246) 558223
Ⓡ Minotel/Logis of GB
Resident proprietors. Quiet location within walking distance of town centre, close to Peak District and Chatsworth. Short breaks available.
Wheelchair access category 3♿
Bedrooms: 3 single, 7 double, 1 twin, 1 triple
Bathrooms: 12 en-suite
Bed & breakfast

per night:	£min	£max
Single	42.00	47.00
Double	60.00	60.00

Lunch available
Evening meal 1900 (last orders 2030)
Parking for 12
Cards accepted: Amex, Diners, Mastercard, Visa
🐾♿♿📞🖥️🖥️♿🎣🛍️🔒🗝️✂️📺📺🛏️🛏️
🍴15 ✗ SP T 🌐

Abigails ⋀

☺☺ COMMENDED

62 Brockwell Lane, Chesterfield S40 4EE
☎ (01246) 279391
Relax taking breakfast in the conservatory overlooking Chesterfield and surrounding moorlands. Garden with pond and waterfall, private car park.
Bedrooms: 2 single, 3 double, 2 twin
Bathrooms: 7 en-suite
Bed & breakfast

per night:	£min	£max
Single	21.50	24.00
Double	39.50	39.50

Half board per

person:	£min	£max
Daily	32.00	34.50
Weekly	208.95	224.70

Evening meal from 1830
Parking for 7
🐾♿📞🖥️🖥️♿🎣🛍️UL🔒🗝️✂️📺📺🛏️
🛏️❄️🚐 SP 🌐

Clarendon Guesthouse ⋀

☺☺ COMMENDED

32 Clarence Road, West Bars, Chesterfield S40 1LN
☎ (01246) 235004
Victorian town residence, near town centre, cricket ground, leisure facilities and Peak District National Park. Special diets catered for.
Bedrooms: 2 single, 1 double, 1 twin
Bathrooms: 3 en-suite, 1 private, 1 public
Bed & breakfast

per night:	£min	£max
Single	14.00	17.50
Double	32.00	32.00

Half board per

person:	£min	£max
Daily	20.50	24.00
Weekly	129.00	143.00

Evening meal 1800 (last orders 2000)
Parking for 1
🐾🖥️⌨️♿🎣UL🛍️🔒🗝️✂️📺📺🛏️🗜️●🌸
🚐🐾 SP T

Ringwood Hall Hotel and Conference Centre ⋀

☺☺☺ COMMENDED

Brimington, Chesterfield S43 1DQ
☎ (01246) 280077
Fax (01246) 472241
Email: ringwood@enterprise.net
Country house hotel, c 1804, in its own grounds. A bowling green and various other activities available. Conferences and functions are a speciality.
Bedrooms: 1 single, 15 double, 8 twin
Bathrooms: 24 en-suite
Bed & breakfast

per night:	£min	£max
Single	50.00	90.00
Double	57.00	95.00

Half board per

person:	£min	£max
Daily	60.00	100.00

Lunch available
Evening meal 1830 (last orders 2100)
Parking for 170
Cards accepted: Amex, Diners, Mastercard, Visa, Switch/Delta
🐾🚗♿📞🖥️⌨️♿🎣🛍️🔒🗝️✂️📺📺●
🛏️🛏️🍴160❄️🐾 SP 🏡 T

Sandpiper Hotel ⋀

☺☺☺ COMMENDED

Sheffield Road, Sheep Bridge, Chesterfield S41 9EH
☎ (01246) 450550 & 0421 536797
Fax (01246) 452805
Ⓡ The Independents
In a prime location with easy access to Chesterfield, Sheffield and the Peak

District. Sky TV, full restaurant, conference and banqueting facilities.
Bedrooms: 8 double, 16 twin, 3 triple, 1 family room
Bathrooms: 28 en-suite

Bed & breakfast

per night:	£min	£max
Single	35.00	49.00
Double	45.00	62.00

Half board per

person:	£min	£max
Daily	32.50	41.00

Lunch available
Evening meal 1900 (last orders 2200)
Parking for 220
Cards accepted: Amex, Diners, Mastercard, Visa, Switch/Delta

⊗ ⛄ & ⚄ ⌨ 📟 ♿ 🔌 📶 S ▥ ▱ ♨60 ▶ SP

The Van Dyk Hotel Ⓜ

👑👑 COMMENDED

Worksop Road, Clowne, Chesterfield S43 4TD
☎ (01246) 810219
Fax (01246) 819566

Elegant country house hotel in beautiful countryside, with 2 bars, a restaurant, banqueting and conference facilities. Approximately 1 mile from M1 junction 30.
Bedrooms: 8 single, 1 double, 5 twin, 2 triple
Bathrooms: 16 en-suite

Bed & breakfast

per night:	£min	£max
Single	45.00	48.00
Double	55.00	

Half board per

person:	£min	£max
Daily	55.00	63.00
Weekly	335.00	378.00

Lunch available
Evening meal 1900 (last orders 2130)
Parking for 100
Cards accepted: Amex, Mastercard, Visa

⊗ & ⛄ ⌨ 📟 ♿ 🔌 📶 S ▥ ▱ ♨120 ❀
DAP SP T

CHESTERTON

Oxfordshire
Map ref 2C1

Bignell Park Hotel
See South of England region for full entry details

CHIPPING CAMPDEN

Gloucestershire
Map ref 2B1

Outstanding Cotswold wool town with many old stone gabled houses, a splendid church and 17th C almshouses. Nearby are Kiftsgate Court Gardens and Hidcote Manor Gardens (National Trust).

Malt House Ⓜ

👑👑👑 HIGHLY COMMENDED

Broad Campden, Chipping Campden GL55 6UU
☎ (01386) 840295
Fax (01386) 841334
Listed 16th C Cotswold home set in 7.5 acres of secluded gardens. Bedrooms individually decorated, four-poster room available. Public rooms furnished with English antiques and with log fires. Noted restaurant serving a table d'hote evening menu.
Bedrooms: 4 double, 3 twin, 1 triple
Bathrooms: 8 en-suite

Bed & breakfast

per night:	£min	£max
Single	49.50	69.50
Double	75.00	95.00

Half board per

person:	£min	£max
Daily	61.00	72.50

Evening meal from 1930
Parking for 10
Cards accepted: Amex, Mastercard, Visa, Switch/Delta

⊗ & ⛄ ⌨ 📟 ♿ 🔌 📶 S ✂ ⍾ ▥ ▱ ♨16 ⏰ ❀ 🚗 ⚓ SP ♠ ◉

Three Ways House Ⓜ

👑👑👑👑 COMMENDED

Chapel Lane, Mickleton, Chipping Campden GL55 6SB
☎ (01386) 438429
Fax (01386) 438118
Ⓖ Logis of GB
Cotswold village hotel close to Chipping Campden, Broadway and Stratford-upon-Avon. Comfortable bedrooms, cosy bar, good food and friendly service. Known as "Home of the Pudding Club" for many years.
Bedrooms: 3 single, 14 double, 19 twin, 3 triple, 2 family rooms
Bathrooms: 41 en-suite

Bed & breakfast

per night:	£min	£max
Single	60.00	
Double	87.00	

Half board per

person:	£min	£max
Daily	59.00	

Lunch available
Evening meal 1900 (last orders 2130)

Parking for 40
Cards accepted: Amex, Diners, Mastercard, Visa, Switch/Delta

⊗ ⛄ & ⌨ 📟 ♿ 🔌 S ✂ ⍾ ▥ ▱ ♨85 ⏰ ❀ ⚓ SP T

CHIPPING NORTON

Oxfordshire
Map ref 2C1

Southcombe Lodge Guest House
See South of England region for full entry details

CHURCH STRETTON

Shropshire
Map ref 4A3

Church Stretton lies under the eastern slope of the Longmynd surrounded by hills. It is ideal for walkers, with marvellous views, golf and gliding. Wenlock Edge is not far away.

Belvedere Guest House Ⓜ

👑👑👑 COMMENDED

Burway Road, Church Stretton SY6 6DP
☎ (01694) 722232
Fax (01694) 722232
Quiet detached house set in its own grounds, convenient for Church Stretton town centre and Longmynd Hills. Adequate parking.
Bedrooms: 3 single, 3 double, 2 twin, 3 triple, 1 family room
Bathrooms: 6 en-suite, 4 public

Bed & breakfast

per night:	£min	£max
Single	23.00	28.00
Double	46.00	50.00

Half board per

person:	£min	£max
Daily	33.00	38.00
Weekly	214.90	227.50

Evening meal 1900 (last orders 1800)
Parking for 8
Cards accepted: Mastercard, Visa, Switch/Delta

⊗ ⌨ ♿ 📶 📶 S ▥ TV ▱ ▱ ⏰ ❀ 🚗 SP T

The symbols in each entry give information about services and facilities. A key to these symbols appears at the back of this guide.

CHURCH STRETTON

Continued

Denehurst Hotel & Leisure Centre ♨

👑👑👑 COMMENDED

Shrewsbury Road, Church Stretton SY6 6EU
☎ (01694) 722699
Fax (01694) 724110
In the heart of beautiful Shropshire, with a comfortable, friendly family atmosphere. En-suite rooms. Suitable for all the family. Leisure facilities, including indoor pool.
Bedrooms: 1 single, 7 double, 6 twin, 2 triple
Bathrooms: 16 en-suite, 1 public

Bed & breakfast

per night:	£min	£max
Single	35.00	40.00
Double	55.00	60.00

Half board per

person:	£min	£max
Daily	47.50	52.50

Lunch available
Evening meal 1900 (last orders 2030)
Parking for 70
Cards accepted: Mastercard, Visa

Longmynd Hotel ♨

👑👑👑👑 COMMENDED

Cunnery Road, Church Stretton SY6 6AG
☎ (01694) 722244
Fax (01694) 722718
Email: neil@neilski.demon.co.uk
Family-run country hotel commanding panoramic views of the south Shropshire highlands. Situated in an Area of Outstanding Natural Beauty. Self-catering lodges available.
Bedrooms: 6 single, 22 double, 13 twin, 6 triple, 3 family rooms
Bathrooms: 50 en-suite, 2 public

Bed & breakfast

per night:	£min	£max
Single	48.00	50.00
Double	84.00	120.00

Half board per

person:	£min	£max
Daily	42.00	72.50
Weekly	259.00	350.00

Lunch available
Evening meal 1845 (last orders 2100)
Parking for 100
Cards accepted: Amex, Diners, Mastercard, Visa, Switch/Delta

CIRENCESTER

Gloucestershire
Map ref 2B1

"Capital of the Cotswolds", Cirencester was Britain's second most important Roman town with many finds housed in the Corinium Museum. It has a very fine Perpendicular church and old houses around the market place.
Tourist Information Centre ☎ (01285) 654180

Crown of Crucis ♨

👑👑👑 COMMENDED

Ampney Crucis, Cirencester GL7 5RS
☎ (01285) 851806
Fax (01285) 851735
Privately owned 16th C Cotswold hotel with elegant bedrooms. Quiet riverside location, 2.5 miles east of Cirencester on A417. Excellent local reputation for quality food and service.
Bedrooms: 9 double, 16 twin
Bathrooms: 25 en-suite

Bed & breakfast

per night:	£min	£max
Single	38.00	54.00
Double	56.00	78.00

Half board per

person:	£min	£max
Daily	52.00	69.00
Weekly	276.00	420.00

Lunch available
Evening meal 1800 (last orders 2200)
Parking for 80
Cards accepted: Amex, Diners, Mastercard, Visa, Switch/Delta

Eliot Arms Hotel Free House ♨

👑👑👑 COMMENDED

Clarks Hay, South Cerney, Cirencester GL7 5UA
☎ (01285) 860215
Fax (01285) 861121

Dating from the 16th C, a comfortable Cotswold freehouse hotel, 2.5 miles from Cirencester, just off the A419. Reputation for fine food and hospitality. Riverside gardens.
Bedrooms: 1 single, 5 double, 4 twin, 2 triple
Suites available

Bathrooms: 12 en-suite

Bed & breakfast

per night:	£min	£max
Single	38.00	40.00
Double	49.50	55.00

Lunch available
Evening meal 1830 (last orders 2200)
Parking for 30
Cards accepted: Amex, Mastercard, Visa, Switch/Delta

King's Head Hotel ♨

👑👑👑 COMMENDED

Market Place, Cirencester GL7 2NR
☎ (01285) 653322
Fax (01285) 655103
GB Logis of GB/The Independents
Comfortable town centre hotel (historic coaching inn) with old world charm. Secret passage. English cuisine. Lift and night porter.
Wheelchair access category 3 ♿
Bedrooms: 15 single, 20 double, 26 twin, 2 triple, 3 family rooms
Bathrooms: 66 en-suite

Bed & breakfast

per night:	£min	£max
Single		75.00
Double		89.00

Lunch available
Evening meal 1900 (last orders 2100)
Parking for 100
Cards accepted: Amex, Diners, Mastercard, Visa, Switch/Delta

Warwick Cottage Guest House

👑👑👑 COMMENDED

75 Victoria Road, Cirencester GL7 1ES
☎ (01285) 656279 & 0976 257137
Attractive Victorian townhouse, 5 minutes from the town centre. Good base for touring the Cotswolds. Family rooms available as doubles or twins. Singles by arrangement. Bargain breaks available.
Bedrooms: 2 double, 2 triple
Bathrooms: 3 en-suite, 1 public

Bed & breakfast

per night:	£min	£max
Double	32.00	36.00

Half board per

person:	£min	£max
Daily	23.50	25.50
Weekly	144.00	165.00

Evening meal from 1830
Parking for 4

CLEARWELL

Gloucestershire
Map ref 2A1

Attractive village in the Forest of
Dean, noted for its castle, built in
1735 and one of the oldest
Georgian Gothic houses in England.
The old mines in Clearwell Caves
are open to the public.

Tudor Farmhouse Hotel and Restaurant

HIGHLY COMMENDED

Clearwell, Coleford GL16 8JS
☎ (01594) 833046
Fax (01594) 837093
*Charming 13th C listed house with
original oak panelling and unique spiral
staircase. Accommodation with suites in
annexe. Award-winning restaurant.*
Bedrooms: 2 single, 6 double, 1 twin,
4 triple
Suites available
Bathrooms: 13 en-suite

Bed & breakfast

per night:	£min	£max
Double	57.00	90.00

Half board per person:

	£min	£max
Daily	41.25	57.50
Weekly	255.00	345.00

Evening meal 1900 (last orders
2100)
Parking for 20
Cards accepted: Amex, Mastercard,
Visa, Switch/Delta

Wyndham Arms ⚠

HIGHLY COMMENDED

Clearwell, Coleford GL16 8JT
☎ (01594) 833666
Fax (01594) 836450
Ⓒ Logis of GB
*Stay free on Sundays in this historic
hotel. Under the competent
management of the Stanford family
since 1973.*
Bedrooms: 2 single, 4 double, 9 twin,
2 triple
Bathrooms: 17 en-suite

Bed & breakfast

per night:	£min	£max
Single	52.50	52.50
Double	61.00	65.00

Half board per person:

	£min	£max
Daily	40.00	50.00
Weekly	267.00	267.00

Lunch available
Evening meal 1900 (last orders
2130)

Parking for 52
Cards accepted: Amex, Diners,
Mastercard, Visa, Switch/Delta

CLEEVE HILL

Gloucestershire
Map ref 2B1

Settlement with wonderful all-round
views and public golf course, above
Cheltenham on the road to
Winchcombe and Broadway.

Rising Sun Hotel ⚠

COMMENDED

Cleeve Hill, Cheltenham GL52 3PX
☎ (01242) 676281 & 672002
Fax (01242) 673069
Ⓒ Countryside/The Independents
*Spectacular hilltop location with
panoramic Cotswolds views, close to
racecourse and golf-course. Ideal for
exploring the Cotswolds. Half board
prices shown apply at weekends.*
Bedrooms: 3 single, 15 double,
6 twin
Bathrooms: 24 en-suite

Bed & breakfast per night:

	£min	£max
Single	36.50	62.00
Double	48.00	82.00

Half board per person:

	£min	£max
Daily	31.00	42.00

Lunch available
Evening meal 1800 (last orders
2200)
Parking for 70
Cards accepted: Amex, Diners,
Mastercard, Visa, Switch/Delta

CLEOBURY MORTIMER

Shropshire
Map ref 4A3

Village with attractive timbered and
Georgian houses and a church with
a wooden spire. It is close to the
Clee Hills with marvellous views.

The Redfern Hotel ⚠

COMMENDED

Cleobury Mortimer, Kidderminster,
Worcestershire DY14 8AA
☎ (01299) 270395
Fax (01299) 271011
Email: jon@red-fern.demon.co.uk
Ⓒ Minotel/Logis of GB
*18th C stone-built hotel in ancient
market town, bordering 6,000-acre
Forest of Wyre. Conservation area.*

Four-poster bed and room with
whirlpool bathroom available.
Bedrooms: 5 double, 5 twin, 1 triple
Bathrooms: 10 en-suite, 1 private

Bed & breakfast per night:

	£min	£max
Single	48.00	65.00
Double	70.00	84.00

Half board per person:

	£min	£max
Daily	52.75	65.00
Weekly	280.00	385.00

Lunch available
Evening meal 1930 (last orders
2200)
Parking for 20
Cards accepted: Amex, Diners,
Mastercard, Visa, Switch/Delta

COALVILLE

Leicestershire
Map ref 4B3

North-west Leicestershire town,
home of Snibston Discovery Park
and close to Twycross Zoo and
Charnwood Forest area.
Tourist Information Centre ☎ (01530)
813608

Hermitage Park Hotel ⚠

COMMENDED

Whitwick Road, Coalville, Leicester
LE67 3FA
☎ (01530) 814814
Fax (01530) 814202
*Modern hotel, located in the heart of
the National Forest, offering a
comfortable atrium bar and restaurant,
leisure suite and friendly professional
service.*
Bedrooms: 21 double, 4 twin
Suite available
Bathrooms: 25 en-suite

Bed & breakfast per night:

	£min	£max
Single	35.00	69.50
Double	39.50	79.50

Half board per person:

	£min	£max
Daily	45.00	79.50

Lunch available
Evening meal 1900 (last orders
2230)
Parking for 48
Cards accepted: Amex, Mastercard,
Visa, Switch/Delta

COLEFORD

Gloucestershire
Map ref 2A1

Small town in the Forest of Dean with the ancient iron mines at Clearwell Caves nearby, where mining equipment and geological samples are displayed. There are several forest trails in the area.
Tourist Information Centre ☎ *(01594) 812388*

Forest House Hotel ⋔

☀☀☀ APPROVED

Cinder Hill, Coleford GL16 8HQ
☎ (01594) 832424
18th C listed former home of industrial steel pioneers. Spacious, comfortable rooms, imaginative cuisine. Close to town centre. Ideal touring/outdoor pursuits base.
Bedrooms: 2 single, 3 double, 2 twin
Bathrooms: 2 en-suite, 2 public
Bed & breakfast

per night:	£min	£max
Single	17.00	25.00
Double	34.00	40.00

Half board per

person:	£min	£max
Daily	28.00	36.00

Evening meal 1900 (last orders 1900)
Parking for 10
⌂з⬜♨♙⚓↙⋔TV▥↠⚐瓞

COLESHILL

Warwickshire
Map ref 4B3

Close to Birmingham's many attractions including the 17th C Aston Hall with its plasterwork and furnishings, the Railway Museum and Sarehole Mill, an 18th C water-powered mill restored to working order.

Coleshill Hotel ⋔

☀☀☀ COMMENDED

152 High Street, Coleshill,
Birmingham B46 3BG
☎ (01675) 465527
Fax (01675) 464013
Ⓒℝ The Independents/Countryside
In traditional coaching inn style with restaurant, lounge bar and function/conference facilities. 5 minutes' drive from the National Exhibition Centre. Half board prices shown apply at weekends.
Bedrooms: 2 single, 11 double, 10 twin
Bathrooms: 23 en-suite

Bed & breakfast

per night:	£min	£max
Single	33.50	75.00
Double	42.00	85.00

Half board per

person:	£min	£max
Daily	28.00	36.00

Lunch available
Evening meal 1900 (last orders 2200)
Parking for 48
Cards accepted: Amex, Diners, Mastercard, Visa, Switch/Delta
⌂⚡♦⚓⬜♙☎⒔Ⓢ◉▥⚐
🍴150∪ℙ✿↠SP▥T

COTSWOLDS

*See under Bibury, Bledington, Bourton-on-the-Water, Broadway, Buckland, Cheltenham, Chipping Campden, Cirencester, Cleeve Hill, Fairford, Gloucester, Lechlade, Moreton-in-Marsh, Northleach, Nympsfield, Painswick, Slimbridge, Stow-on-the-Wold, Stroud, Tetbury, Tewkesbury, Wotton-under-Edge
See also Cotswolds in South of England region*

COVENTRY

West Midlands
Map ref 4B3

Modern city with a long history. It has many places of interest including the post-war and ruined medieval cathedrals, art gallery and museums, some 16th C almshouses, St Mary's Guildhall, Lunt Roman fort and the Belgrade Theatre.
Tourist Information Centre ☎ *(01203) 832303 or 832304*

Ashleigh House

☀☀ COMMENDED

17 Park Road, Coventry CV1 2LH
☎ (01203) 223804
Recently renovated guesthouse only 100 yards from the railway station. All city amenities within 5 minutes' walk.
Bedrooms: 3 single, 3 double, 2 twin, 2 triple
Bathrooms: 8 en-suite, 1 public
Bed & breakfast

per night:	£min	£max
Single	18.00	25.00
Double	28.00	36.00

Evening meal 1700 (last orders 1900)
Parking for 12
⌂⬜♨♙↠TV▥⚐🍴↠OAP SP

Chester House

Listed

3 Chester Street, Coventry
CV1 4DH
☎ (01203) 223857

Large white stone house with double bays, the first house off the main Holyhead road.
Bedrooms: 1 single, 3 triple, 1 family room
Bathrooms: 1 en-suite, 2 public
Bed & breakfast

per night:	£min	£max
Single	14.00	18.00
Double	28.00	36.00

Half board per

person:	£min	£max
Daily	19.00	23.00
Weekly	130.00	145.00

Evening meal 1800 (last orders 2000)
Parking for 4
⌂⬜♨♙UL⚓TV▥↠🚗瓞

Coombe Abbey ⋔

☀☀☀ HIGHLY COMMENDED

Brinklow Road, Binley, Coventry
CV3 2AB
☎ (01203) 450450
Fax (01203) 635101
Historic country house hotel, dating back to the 11th C. Quality bedrooms, atmospheric public areas. Set in 500 acres of parkland.
Bedrooms: 49 double, 14 twin
Suites available
Bathrooms: 63 en-suite
Bed & breakfast

per night:	£min	£max
Single	115.00	125.00
Double	125.00	160.00

Half board per

person:	£min	£max
Daily	77.50	87.50

Lunch available
Evening meal 1900 (last orders 2200)
Parking for 300
Cards accepted: Amex, Diners, Mastercard, Visa, Switch/Delta
⌂⚡♦⚓⬜♙☎Ⓢ↙◉▣▥
⚐🍴120ℙ✿↠SP瓞T

Falcon Hotel ⋔

☀☀☀

13-19 Manor Road, Coventry
CV1 2LH
☎ (01203) 258615
Fax (01203) 520680
Close to Coventry railway station, ideal for the travelling businessman. Ten minutes from NEC, M6 motorway and Birmingham Airport. Large free car park. Shops, social and cultural activities readily at hand.
Bedrooms: 6 single, 2 double, 3 twin, 3 triple, 1 family room
Bathrooms: 15 en-suite
Bed & breakfast

per night:	£min	£max
Single	45.00	49.99
Double	60.00	65.00

Half board per person:	£min	£max
Daily	55.00	60.00

Lunch available
Evening meal 1900 (last orders 2100)
Parking for 50
Cards accepted: Amex, Mastercard, Visa

🦽🛏📞🖰🖵🚾♿🔒🍴📺◐🛏 🛌🍴50🅿✳🐾 DAP ⚲ SP T

Merrick Lodge Hotel ⚠

👑👑👑 COMMENDED

80-82 St. Nicholas Street, Coventry
CV1 4BP
☎ (01203) 553940
Fax (01203) 550112

Former manor house, 5 minutes' walk from city centre. Table d'hôte and a la carte restaurant, 3 bars. Comfortable, well-equipped, en-suite bedrooms. Superb base for visiting the area. Private functions and conferences also catered for.
Bedrooms: 4 single, 8 double, 9 twin, 4 triple, 1 family room
Bathrooms: 25 en-suite, 1 private shower

Bed & breakfast per night:	£min	£max
Single	35.00	55.00
Double	55.00	85.00

Half board per person:	£min	£max
Daily	40.00	75.00
Weekly	280.00	525.00

Lunch available
Evening meal 1830 (last orders 2300)
Parking for 60
Cards accepted: Amex, Mastercard, Visa, Switch/Delta

🦽🛏🛋🖵🖰♿🔒🍴📺◐🖰 🛏🍴180🅿✳ DAP ⚲ SP T

Northanger House ⚠

👑 APPROVED

35 Westminster Road, Coventry
CV1 3GB
☎ (01203) 226780
Friendly home 5 minutes from the city centre. Close to railway and bus stations, and convenient for NEC and NAC.
Bedrooms: 4 single, 1 twin, 2 triple, 2 family rooms
Bathrooms: 3 public

Bed & breakfast per night:	£min	£max
Single	15.00	17.00
Double	28.00	32.00

Half board per person:	£min	£max
Daily	19.00	21.00
Weekly	130.00	137.00

Evening meal from 1900

🦽🛌🖵🖰♿ UL 🔒🍴📺🖰🛏🖰 T

Novotel Coventry ⚠

👑👑👑👑 COMMENDED

M6, Junction 3, Wilsons Lane, Longford, Coventry CV6 6HL
☎ (01203) 365000
Fax (01203) 362422
CR Novotel
Coventry and the Novotel, a venue for business, holiday weekends or as a relaxing stop-over between journeys.
Bedrooms: 98 triple
Bathrooms: 98 en-suite

Bed & breakfast per night:	£min	£max
Single	50.00	
Double	50.00	

Lunch available
Evening meal 1800 (last orders 2359)
Parking for 120
Cards accepted: Amex, Diners, Mastercard, Visa, Switch/Delta

🦽🛏📞🖵🖰♿🔒🍴📺◐🖻🖰 ⊜🛏🍴200🏊🐾✳ SP T

CRESSBROOK

Derbyshire
Map ref 4B2

Delightful dale with stone hall and pleasant houses, steep wooded slopes and superb views.

Cressbrook Hall ⚠

👑👑 COMMENDED

Cressbrook, Buxton SK17 8SY
☎ (01298) 871289 & 0500 121248
Fax (01298) 871845
Accommodation with a difference. Enjoy this magnificent family home built in 1835, set in 23 acres, with spectacular views around the compass.
Wheelchair access category 3♿
Bedrooms: 2 double, 1 twin
Bathrooms: 3 en-suite

Bed & breakfast per night:	£min	£max
Double	62.00	80.00

Evening meal 1830 (last orders 1930)
Parking for 10
Cards accepted: Mastercard, Visa

🦽🛏🖰♿🔒🍴📺◐🖰🛏🗞 ☎♉✳🐾🚐 SP ♎

DEDDINGTON

Oxfordshire
Map ref 2C1

The Deddington Arms Holcombe Hotel & Restaurant
See South of England region for full entry details

DERBY

Derbyshire
Map ref 4B2

Modern industrial city but with ancient origins. There is a wide range of attractions including several museums (notably Royal Crown Derby), a theatre, a concert hall, and the cathedral with fine ironwork and Bess of Hardwick's tomb. *Tourist Information Centre ☎ (01332) 255802*

European Inn ⚠

💷💷💷 COMMENDED

Midland Road, Derby DE1 2SL
☎ (01332) 292000
Fax (01332) 293940
CR The Independents

Stylish, modern hotel with en-suite bedrooms. Full English buffet-style breakfast, restaurant on site. Near Derby rail station and 10 minutes off M1.
Bedrooms: 66 double, 22 twin
Bathrooms: 88 en-suite

Bed & breakfast per night:	£min	£max
Single	48.50	48.50
Double	54.50	54.50

Parking for 90
Cards accepted: Amex, Diners, Mastercard, Visa, Switch/Delta

🦽🛋🖵🖰♿🔒◐🖻🖰🛏 🍴80 ⚲ SP T

Please check prices and other details at the time of booking.

For ideas on places to visit refer to the introduction at the beginning of this section.

DERBY

Continued

International Hotel & Restaurant ⚠

👑👑👑👑 **COMMENDED**

Burton Road (A5250), Derby
DE23 6AD
☎ (01332) 369321
Fax (01332) 294430
Situated close to the city centre, this privately owned hotel makes an excellent base from which to explore the Peak District Park. Good quality restaurant offers an extensive selection of fare.
Bedrooms: 12 single, 40 double, 6 twin, 4 triple
Bathrooms: 62 en-suite

Bed & breakfast per night:

	£min	£max
Single	36.00	55.00
Double	47.50	66.00

Half board per person:

	£min	£max
Daily	36.50	71.50
Weekly	157.50	385.00

Lunch available
Evening meal 1900 (last orders 2215)
Parking for 120
Cards accepted: Amex, Diners, Mastercard, Visa, Switch/Delta
🛏🛁&📞🖥🖂🌭🍴🍷📶S▶🅿◐🔲🖩
🍽♨60▶ DAP 🐾 SP

Hotel Ristorante 'La Gondola'

👑👑👑👑 **COMMENDED**

220 Osmaston Road, Derby
DE23 8JX
☎ (01332) 332895
Fax (01332) 384512
Privately owned hotel with bar, restaurant and private car park. Close to the city centre and all amenities.
Bedrooms: 11 double, 2 twin, 6 triple, 1 family room
Bathrooms: 20 en-suite

Bed & breakfast per night:

	£min	£max
Single	48.50	58.50
Double	52.00	63.00

Half board per person:

	£min	£max
Daily	38.50	71.00

Lunch available
Evening meal 1900 (last orders 2200)
Parking for 70
Cards accepted: Amex, Diners, Mastercard, Visa, Switch/Delta
🛏🛁&🖥🌭🍷📶S📺◐🖩🖂
🍽120▶🐾SP T

Rose & Thistle ⚠

21 Charnwood Street, Derby
DE1 2GU
☎ (01332) 344103
Eight bedrooms, all with TV and tea/coffee facilities. Children welcome.
Bedrooms: 2 single, 5 double, 1 triple
Bathrooms: 3 public

Bed & breakfast per night:

	£min	£max
Single	18.00	20.00
Double	20.00	34.00

Evening meal 1700 (last orders 1900)
🛒🖥🌭UL🏠S🍴🐾

ELLESMERE

Shropshire
Map ref 4A2

Small market town with old streets and houses and situated close to 9 lakes. The largest, the Mere, has many waterfowl and recreational facilities and some of the other meres have sailing and fishing.

The Ellesmere Hotel ⚠

👑👑👑 **APPROVED**

High Street, Ellesmere SY12 0ES
☎ (01691) 622055
Fax (01691) 622055
17th C coaching inn in the centre of an attractive market town. En-suite rooms. Restaurant, lounge and bar serving wholesome, hearty food. Quality wines, spirits and cask conditioned ales.
Bedrooms: 3 single, 7 double, 2 twin
Bathrooms: 12 en-suite

Bed & breakfast per night:

	£min	£max
Single	27.00	30.00
Double	46.90	48.95

Half board per person:

	£min	£max
Daily	31.45	50.00
Weekly	140.00	210.00

Lunch available
Evening meal 1700 (last orders 2130)
Parking for 20
Cards accepted: Mastercard, Visa
🛏📞🖥🌭🍷🏠S🍴🍽📺🖩🖂
🍽70🔍🐾SP🎱

National gradings and classifications were correct at the time of going to press but are subject to change. Please check at the time of booking.

EVESHAM

Hereford and Worcester
Map ref 2B1

Market town in the centre of a fruit-growing area. There are pleasant walks along the River Avon and many old houses and inns. A fine 16th C bell tower stands between 2 churches near the medieval Almonry Museum.
Tourist Information Centre ☎ (01386) 446944

Evesham Hotel ⚠

👑👑👑👑 **HIGHLY COMMENDED**

Cooper's Lane, Off Waterside, Evesham, Worcestershire
WR11 6DA
☎ (01386) 765566 & 0800 716969
Fax (01386) 765443
Family-run Tudor mansion in 2.5-acre garden, offering unusual food and wine and all modern facilities. Ideal touring centre. Indoor pool designed for fun. Daily half-board prices based on minimum 2-night stay.
Bedrooms: 6 single, 22 double, 11 twin, 1 family room
Bathrooms: 40 en-suite

Bed & breakfast per night:

	£min	£max
Single	58.00	66.00
Double	76.00	90.00

Half board per person:

	£min	£max
Daily	49.00	63.00
Weekly	355.00	440.00

Lunch available
Evening meal 1900 (last orders 2130)
Parking for 45
Cards accepted: Amex, Diners, Mastercard, Visa, Switch/Delta
🛏🛁&📞🖥🌭🍷🏠S📶🍴🖩🖂
🍽12♨✳🐾SP🎱 T

The Mill at Harvington ⚠

👑👑👑👑 **HIGHLY COMMENDED**

Anchor Lane, Harvington, Evesham, Worcestershire WR11 5NR
☎ (01386) 870688
Fax (01386) 870688

Peaceful, owner-run, riverside hotel tastefully converted from beautiful house and mill. In acres of gardens, quarter of a mile from Evesham to Stratford road.
Bedrooms: 12 double, 3 twin

Bathrooms: 15 en-suite

Bed & breakfast

per night:	£min	£max
Single	58.00	64.00
Double	79.00	115.00

Half board per

person:	£min	£max
Daily	52.00	75.00

Lunch available
Evening meal 1900 (last orders 2045)
Parking for 45
Cards accepted: Amex, Diners, Mastercard, Visa, Switch/Delta

🛇 10 🖥 📞 🖂 🖵 ♿ 🖎 🅸 🆂 ⌿ 🅜 🖩
🛏 🍽20 ⚡ ♞ ♒ ✈ ☼ ✗ 🐎 SP 🏠 T

Park View Hotel M

♛ APPROVED

Waterside, Evesham,
Worcestershire WR11 6BS
☎ (01386) 442639
Email: mike.spires@btinternet.com
Family-run hotel offering comfortable accommodation in a friendly atmosphere. Riverside situation, close to town centre. Ideal base for touring the Cotswolds and Shakespeare country.
Bedrooms: 10 single, 4 double, 10 twin, 1 triple, 1 family room
Bathrooms: 7 public

Bed & breakfast

per night:	£min	£max
Single	20.50	24.00
Double	37.00	41.00

Evening meal 1800 (last orders 1900)
Parking for 50
Cards accepted: Amex, Diners, Mastercard, Visa

🛇 🅸 🆂 🅜 📺 🛏 🍽30 SP T

The Waterside Hotel M

♛♛♛ HIGHLY COMMENDED

56 Waterside, Evesham,
Worcestershire WR11 6JZ
☎ (01386) 442420
Fax (01386) 446272
Friendly and personal service. Popular restaurant with extensive menu. Bedrooms with top of the range beds. Enviable position overlooking river and parks.
Bedrooms: 2 single, 8 double, 4 twin, 1 triple
Bathrooms: 15 en-suite, 1 public

Bed & breakfast

per night:	£min	£max
Single	40.60	54.60
Double	52.00	75.00

Half board per

person:	£min	£max
Weekly	255.00	297.00

Lunch available
Evening meal 1830 (last orders 2130)
Parking for 30

Cards accepted: Amex, Mastercard, Visa

🛇 🖣 📞 🖂 🖵 ♿ 🖎 🅸 🆂 ⌿ 🅜 📺 🖩
🛏 🍽12 ⚡ ☼ 🐎 DAP SP T

FAIRFORD

Gloucestershire
Map ref 2B1

Small town with a 15th C wool church famous for its complete 15th C stained glass windows, interesting carvings and original wall paintings. It is an excellent touring centre and the Cotswolds Wildlife Park is nearby.

Bull Hotel M

♛♛♛ COMMENDED

Market Place, Fairford GL7 4AA
☎ (01285) 712535 & 712217
Fax (01285) 713782

15th C family-run Cotswold hotel with a la carte restaurant. Rooms with private facilities, TV, Teasmaid, telephone. Private fishing.
Bedrooms: 3 single, 13 double, 5 twin, 1 family room
Bathrooms: 17 en-suite, 2 private, 2 public, 1 private shower

Bed & breakfast

per night:	£min	£max
Single	29.50	49.50
Double	39.50	69.50

Half board per

person:	£min	£max
Daily	37.50	57.50
Weekly	210.00	280.00

Lunch available
Evening meal 1800 (last orders 2115)
Parking for 20
Cards accepted: Amex, Diners, Mastercard, Visa, Switch/Delta

🛇 🖣 🐎 📞 🖂 🖵 ♿ 🅸 🆂 ⌿ 🅜 ● 🖩
🛏 🍽60 ⚡ ✈ ☼ DAP ✗ SP 🏠 T

ACCESSIBILITY

Look for the ♿♿♿ symbols which indicate accessibility for wheelchair users. These are described in detail at the front of this guide.

FINEDON

Northamptonshire
Map ref 3A2

Large ironstone village with interesting Victorian houses and cottages and an ironstone 14th C church. The inn claims to be the oldest in England.

Tudor Gate Hotel M

♛♛♛ COMMENDED

35 High Street, Finedon,
Wellingborough NN9 5JN
☎ (01933) 680408
Fax (01933) 680745
CR The Independents
Converted from a 17th C farmhouse, with 3 four-poster beds. Close to new A1/M1 link. 30 antique businesses within walking distance and a wide range of leisure activities locally.
Wheelchair access category 3♿
Bedrooms: 4 single, 20 double, 3 twin
Bathrooms: 27 en-suite

Bed & breakfast

per night:	£min	£max
Single	45.00	78.00
Double	55.00	100.00

Half board per

person:	£min	£max
Daily	65.00	98.00
Weekly	325.00	490.00

Lunch available
Evening meal 1900 (last orders 2145)
Parking for 40
Cards accepted: Amex, Diners, Mastercard, Visa, Switch/Delta

🛇 🖣 🐎 📞 🖵 ♿ 🖎 🅸 🆂 ⌿ 🅜 ● 🖩
🛏 🍽65 ∪ ⑂ ☼ ✗ SP 🏠 T

FOREST OF DEAN

See under Blakeney, Clearwell, Coleford, Newent

Half board prices are given per person, but in some cases these may be based on double/twin occupancy.

Information on accommodation listed in this guide has been supplied by the proprietors. As changes may occur you are advised to check details at the time of booking.

GLOUCESTER

Gloucestershire
Map ref 2B1

A Roman city and inland port, its cathedral is one of the most beautiful in Britain. Gloucester's many attractions include museums and the restored warehouses in the Victorian docks containing the National Waterways Museum, Robert Opie Packaging Collection and other attractions.
Tourist Information Centre ☎ *(01452) 421188*

Brookthorpe Lodge ⚏

⚜⚜ COMMENDED

Stroud Road, Brookthorpe, Gloucester GL4 0UQ
☎ (01452) 812645

Three-storey Georgian house on the outskirts of Gloucester, set in lovely countryside at the foot of the Cotswold Escarpment.
Bedrooms: 3 single, 2 double, 3 twin, 2 family rooms
Bathrooms: 6 en-suite, 2 private, 2 public

Bed & breakfast per night:

	£min	£max
Single	20.00	
Double	43.00	

Half board per person:

	£min	£max
Daily	30.00	
Weekly	210.00	

Evening meal 1800 (last orders 2100)
Parking for 15

Cheltenham/Gloucester Moat House ⚏

⚜⚜⚜⚜ HIGHLY COMMENDED

Shurdington Road, Brockworth, Gloucester GL3 4PB
☎ (01452) 519988
Fax (01452) 519977
ⓒⓡ Queens Moat/Utell International
Recently built hotel with leisure facilities, set in extensive landscaped grounds. Directly accessible from M5, junction 11a. Rates shown below apply Friday-Sunday only. From Monday-Thursday, rate is £90 for room only.
Bedrooms: 55 double, 41 twin

Suites available
Bathrooms: 96 en-suite

Bed & breakfast per night:

	£min	£max
Single	48.00	100.00
Double	96.00	125.00

Half board per person:

	£min	£max
Daily	58.00	120.00

Lunch available
Evening meal 1900 (last orders 2200)
Parking for 212
Cards accepted: Amex, Diners, Mastercard, Visa, Switch/Delta

Denmark Hotel ⚏

⚜⚜⚜ COMMENDED

36 Denmark Road, Gloucester GL1 3JQ
☎ (01452) 303808
Small family hotel close to city centre.
Bedrooms: 7 single, 2 double, 1 triple
Bathrooms: 5 en-suite, 2 public

Bed & breakfast per night:

	£min	£max
Single	21.00	29.00
Double	35.00	44.00

Half board per person:

	£min	£max
Daily	30.00	31.00
Weekly	189.00	215.00

Evening meal 1800 (last orders 1900)
Parking for 15

Hatherley Manor Hotel ⚏

⚜⚜⚜⚜ COMMENDED

Down Hatherley Lane, Gloucester GL2 9QA
☎ (01452) 730217
Fax (01452) 731032
ⓒⓡ Lyric
Beautiful hotel in 37 acres, with notable restaurant. Mini-breaks available. Ideal base for visiting Cotswolds and Cheltenham.
Bedrooms: 8 single, 43 double, 5 twin
Bathrooms: 56 en-suite

Bed & breakfast per night:

	£min	£max
Single	35.00	90.00
Double	45.00	110.00

Half board per person:

	£min	£max
Daily	38.00	73.00
Weekly	228.00	511.00

Lunch available
Evening meal 1900 (last orders 2130)

Parking for 250
Cards accepted: Amex, Diners, Mastercard, Visa, Switch/Delta

Jarvis Gloucester Hotel and Country Club ⚏

⚜⚜⚜⚜ COMMENDED

Matson Lane, Robinswood Hill, Gloucester GL4 6EA
☎ (01452) 525653
Fax (01452) 307212
ⓒⓡ Jarvis/Utell International
Hotel and country club specialising in golf, skiing and leisure activities, within the boundaries of the Roman city of Gloucester. Convenient for touring the Cotswolds and the Wye Valley.
Bedrooms: 9 single, 34 double, 57 twin, 7 triple
Suites available
Bathrooms: 107 en-suite

Bed & breakfast per night:

	£min	£max
Single	45.00	107.50
Double	90.00	152.00

Half board per person:

	£min	£max
Daily	42.00	117.45
Weekly	315.00	907.00

Lunch available
Evening meal 1900 (last orders 2200)
Parking for 400
Cards accepted: Amex, Diners, Mastercard, Visa, Switch/Delta

Notley House and Coach House ⚏

⚜⚜⚜ COMMENDED

93 Hucclecote Road, Hucclecote, Gloucester GL3 3TR
☎ (01452) 611584
Fax (01452) 371229
Affordable quality accommodation. Ideal for historic Gloucester and the Cotswolds. Tastefully furnished en-suite rooms, suites with four-poster bed.
Bedrooms: 1 single, 2 double, 2 twin, 1 triple, 1 family room
Bathrooms: 5 en-suite, 2 private showers

Bed & breakfast per night:

	£min	£max
Single	23.50	41.50
Double	38.00	60.00

Half board per person:

	£min	£max
Daily	26.00	70.00
Weekly	164.00	440.00

Evening meal 1900 (last orders 2000)
Parking for 8
Cards accepted: Mastercard, Visa

🛏🏨📠🖥♿🕾⬆📵🅢⚡🍽📺📶
🅿❋✕🏠

Pembury Guest House ⚠

😊😊 COMMENDED

9 Pembury Road, St. Barnabas,
Gloucester GL4 9UE
☎ (01452) 521856
Fax (01452) 303418
*Licensed family-run detached house,
close to ski-slope and golfing facilities.
Ideal base for Cotswolds, Gloucester
Docks and cathedral.*
Bedrooms: 1 single, 4 double, 3 twin,
2 triple
Bathrooms: 5 en-suite, 1 public,
2 private showers

Bed & breakfast per night:	£min	£max
Single	18.00	26.00
Double	32.00	37.00

Evening meal 1900 (last orders
1930)
Parking for 10
Cards accepted: Mastercard, Visa,
Switch/Delta

🛏🏨🕾🖥♿🕾📵🅢📺🅞🏠
❋✕ SP

Rotherfield House Hotel ⚠

😊😊😊 COMMENDED

5 Horton Road, Gloucester
GL1 3PX
☎ (01452) 410500
Fax (01452) 381922
*Elegant Victorian detached property in
quiet side road location, 1 mile from
city centre and minutes from M5.
Family business. Choice of
freshly-cooked dishes.*
Bedrooms: 8 single, 2 double, 1 twin,
2 triple
Bathrooms: 6 en-suite, 2 private,
2 public

Bed & breakfast per night:	£min	£max
Single	22.00	34.00
Double	48.00	48.00

Half board per person:	£min	£max
Daily	32.00	44.00
Weekly	192.00	264.00

Evening meal 1845 (last orders
1915)
Parking for 9
Cards accepted: Amex, Diners,
Mastercard, Visa

🛏🕾🖥♿🕾🅢📺🏠📠❋🚗 SP
T

Village in the Abberley Hills beside
the shell of the once sumptuous
palace of Witley Court, home of the
Earl of Dudley.

Hundred House Hotel ⚠

😊😊😊 COMMENDED

Great Witley, Worcester WR6 6HS
☎ (01299) 896888
Fax (01299) 896588
*Family-owned country hotel, on A443
Worcester to Tenbury road, 8 miles
from M5 junction 5. Close to
golf-courses and places of historic
interest.*
Bedrooms: 2 single, 14 double,
8 twin, 2 triple
Bathrooms: 26 en-suite

Bed & breakfast per night:	£min	£max
Single	40.00	45.00
Double	55.00	60.00

Half board per person:	£min	£max
Daily	37.00	47.00

Lunch available
Evening meal 1900 (last orders
2145)
Parking for 120
Cards accepted: Amex, Mastercard,
Visa, Switch/Delta

🛏🍴🏨🕾📠🖥♿🕾🅢⚡🍽🖥♿
📠⛵120🔍🅄🅿❋✕ OAP SP 🏠 T

GRINDLEFORD

Derbyshire
Map ref 4B2

Good centre for walking, at the
eastern end of the Hope Valley.
Longshaw Estate is nearby with
1500 acres of moorland and
woodland.

Maynard Arms Hotel ⚠

😊😊 HIGHLY COMMENDED

Main Road, Grindleford S30 1HP
☎ (01433) 630321
Fax (01433) 630445
*Established hotel with a relaxed,
friendly atmosphere and extensive
facilities. Picturesque gardens with
lovely views of Hope Valley and Peak
Park. Excellent walking country.*
Bedrooms: 8 double, 2 twin
Suites available
Bathrooms: 10 en-suite

Bed & breakfast per night:	£min	£max
Single	59.00	79.00
Double	69.00	89.00

Half board per person:	£min	£max
Daily	44.50	54.50

Lunch available
Evening meal 1900 (last orders
2130)
Parking for 80
Cards accepted: Amex, Mastercard,
Visa, Switch/Delta

🛏🏨🕾📠🖥♿🕾📵🅢⚡🍽🖥🏠
🍴140🅄❋🚗🏃 SP 🏠 T

HAMPTON IN ARDEN

West Midlands
Map ref 4B3

Midway between Birmingham and
Coventry and with the National
Exhibition Centre on the doorstep.

The Hollies ⚠

😊😊 COMMENDED

Kenilworth Road, Hampton in
Arden, Solihull B92 0LW
☎ (01675) 442941 & 442681
Fax (01675) 442941

*Excellent accommodation just 2.5 miles
from NEC and Birmingham
International Airport. Sky TV, ample
parking.*
Bedrooms: 1 single, 4 double, 2 twin,
1 triple
Bathrooms: 6 en-suite, 1 public

Bed & breakfast per night:	£min	£max
Single	20.00	25.00
Double	36.00	45.00

Parking for 10

🛏🏨🖥♿🕾📵🅄🅢📵🍽📺📺🏠
🍴25❋ T ◎

HARRINGWORTH

Northamptonshire
Map ref 3A1

Village with a medieval cross, a 12th C church, an inn and old manor house. The 82 arches of the 19th C Welland railway viaduct dominate the valley, which forms the Northamptonshire/Leicestershire border.

White Swan Ⓜ

👑 👑 👑 COMMENDED

Seaton Road, Harringworth, Corby NN17 3AF
☎ (01572) 747543
Fax (01572) 747323
Ⓒ Logis of GB
15th C coaching inn offering en-suite accommodation, in a delightful village, close to many historic sites. Home-cooked food and real ales.
Bedrooms: 1 single, 4 double, 1 twin
Bathrooms: 6 en-suite

Bed & breakfast per night:

	£min	£max
Single	38.50	
Double	52.00	

Lunch available
Evening meal 1900 (last orders 2200)
Parking for 8
Cards accepted: Amex, Mastercard, Visa, Switch/Delta

🛇🕿🛈📞🖵🖧♿🦽📶Ⓢ✄🅿🚗Ⅱ12 ⚓↻Ⓤ🏹✗🚌🔐SP🏮Ⓣ

HAYFIELD

Derbyshire
Map ref 4B2

Village set in spectacular scenery at the highest point of the Peak District with the best approach to the Kinder Scout plateau via the Kinder Downfall. An excellent centre for walking. Three reservoirs close by.

The Royal Hotel Ⓜ

👑 👑 👑 COMMENDED

Market Street, Hayfield, Stockport, Cheshire SK12 5EP
☎ (01663) 742721
Fax (01663) 742997

Centrally located in Hayfield at the foot of Kinder Scout in the High Peak district. Built in 1755, comprises oak

panelled pub and restaurant with log fires, function room and accommodation.
Bedrooms: 2 double, 1 twin
Bathrooms: 3 en-suite, 1 public

Bed & breakfast per night:

	£min	£max
Single	32.00	35.00
Double	47.50	50.00

Half board per person:

	£min	£max
Daily	40.00	45.00
Weekly	275.00	300.00

Lunch available
Evening meal 1900 (last orders 2145)
Parking for 100
Cards accepted: Mastercard, Visa, Switch/Delta

🛇🕿🖧📞🖵♿🦽Ⓢ✄🅿📺📶🚗 Ⅱ100⚓↻Ⓤ🏹✗🚌ᴅᴀᴘSP🏮

HENLEY-IN-ARDEN

Warwickshire
Map ref 2B1

Old market town which in Tudor times stood in the Forest of Arden. It has many ancient inns, a 15th C Guildhall and parish church. Coughton Court with its Gunpowder Plot connections is nearby.

Ardencote Manor Hotel and Country Club

👑 👑 👑 👑 COMMENDED

Lye Green Road, Claverdon, Warwick CV35 8LS
☎ (01926) 843111
Fax (01926) 842646

Historic former gentleman's residence, sympathetically refurbished, set in 40 acres of gardens and grounds. Extensive leisure and sports facilities. Easy access to M40, M42 and Shakespeare country.
Bedrooms: 6 single, 8 double, 4 twin
Bathrooms: 18 en-suite

Bed & breakfast per night:

	£min	£max
Single	87.50	
Double	135.00	

Half board per person:

	£min	£max
Daily	100.00	

Lunch available
Evening meal 1930 (last orders 2130)

Parking for 150
Cards accepted: Amex, Diners, Mastercard, Visa

🛇🦽🕿🖧📞🖵♿🦽📶Ⓢ🅿♿Ⓞ📶,🅴 🅿Ⅱ35🎿✗🚣⚓🏹♿Ⓤ↻♪↟🌻🏹 SP🏮Ⓣ

Henley Hotel Ⓜ

👑 👑 👑 COMMENDED

Tanworth Lane, Henley-in-Arden B95 5RA
☎ (01564) 794551
Fax (01564) 795044
Although a modern building, the hotel is full of character, enhanced by its delightful situation beside the River Alne. Explore Shakespeare country or visit the NEC, both only 15 minutes away.
Bedrooms: 5 single, 22 double, 4 twin, 2 triple
Suites available
Bathrooms: 33 en-suite

Bed & breakfast per night:

	£min	£max
Single	33.50	40.75
Double	43.00	60.00

Half board per person:

	£min	£max
Daily	33.45	41.95

Lunch available
Evening meal 1900 (last orders 2130)
Parking for 40
Cards accepted: Mastercard, Visa, Switch/Delta

🛇🦽🕿🖧📞🖵♿🦽📶Ⓢ✄🅿📺Ⓞ 📶,🅴🅿Ⅱ50Ⓤ♪↟🌻ᴅᴀᴘ🔐SP

HEREFORD

Hereford and Worcester
Map ref 2A1

Agricultural county town, its cathedral containing much Norman work and a large chained library. Among the city's varied attractions are several museums including the Cider Museum and the Old House.
Tourist Information Centre ☎ *(01432) 268430*

Aylestone Court Hotel Ⓜ

👑 👑 👑 HIGHLY COMMENDED

Aylestone Hill, Hereford HR1 1HS
☎ (01432) 341891 & 359342
Fax (01432) 267691
Three-storey Georgian building, listed Grade II, tastefully renovated throughout. Spacious, comfortable public rooms and en-suite bedrooms. Lawns and gardens. 4 minutes' walk to city centre.
Bedrooms: 7 double, 3 twin, 1 triple
Bathrooms: 11 en-suite

Bed & breakfast per night:	£min	£max
Single	30.00	45.00
Double	48.00	58.00

Half board per person:	£min	£max
Daily	42.00	50.00
Weekly	260.00	315.00

Evening meal 1830 (last orders 2030)
Parking for 18
Cards accepted: Amex, Mastercard, Visa

🐴♿📞🖥📺💷🅿️📺📻💼🍴
🍴25❄️🚐 SP 🔥

Belmont Lodge and Golf Course ⋀

👑👑 COMMENDED

Belmont, Hereford HR2 9SA
☎ (01432) 352666
Fax (01432) 358090
Comfortable hotel situated off the A465, 2 miles south of Hereford city centre. Overlooking the River Wye and Herefordshire countryside, offering beautiful views.
Bedrooms: 26 twin, 4 triple
Bathrooms: 30 en-suite, 2 public

Bed & breakfast per night:	£min	£max
Single	44.50	47.50
Double	59.50	62.50

Half board per person:	£min	£max
Daily	42.75	60.50

Lunch available
Evening meal 1900 (last orders 2130)
Parking for 120
Cards accepted: Amex, Diners, Mastercard, Visa, Switch/Delta

🐴♿🚗📞📺💷🅿️📺🔆💼
🍴60🔍⚓☀️ SP 🔥 T

The Bowens Country House ⋀

👑👑👑 COMMENDED

Fownhope, Hereford HR1 4PS
☎ (01432) 860430
Fax (01432) 860430

Georgian country house in peaceful village. Tastefully furnished en-suite rooms with TV and tea trays. Home cooking. 4 ground-floor rooms. Lovely garden, putting green and grass tennis court. Superb views and walking. Cream teas.

Bedrooms: 1 single, 4 double, 2 twin, 1 triple, 2 family rooms
Bathrooms: 10 en-suite

Bed & breakfast per night:	£min	£max
Single	25.00	32.50
Double	50.00	65.00

Half board per person:	£min	£max
Daily	37.00	45.00
Weekly	230.00	280.00

Lunch available
Evening meal 1900 (last orders 2100)
Parking for 16
Cards accepted: Mastercard, Visa, Switch/Delta

🐴♿📞📺💷🅿️🔆💼📻💳
❄️🚐 SP 🔥

Castle Pool Hotel ⋀

👑👑👑 COMMENDED

Castle Street, Hereford HR1 2NW
☎ (01432) 356321
Fax (01432) 356321
Ⓖ Logis of GB
The hotel garden is part of the old castle moat. Located minutes from the cathedral, river and sports facilities.
Bedrooms: 8 single, 8 double, 8 twin, 2 triple
Bathrooms: 26 en-suite

Bed & breakfast per night:	£min	£max
Single	38.00	52.00
Double	58.00	82.00

Half board per person:	£min	£max
Daily	56.50	67.00
Weekly	350.00	410.00

Lunch available
Evening meal 1930 (last orders 2130)
Parking for 14
Cards accepted: Amex, Diners, Mastercard, Visa

🐴♿🚗📞📺💷🅿️📺💼🍴
🍴40🍴❄️🚐 SP 🔥

Cedar Guest House ⋀

👑 APPROVED

123 Whitecross Road, Whitecross, Hereford HR4 0LS
☎ (01432) 267235
Situated on touring route, approximately 1 mile from Hereford, this Georgian family guesthouse has private parking.
Bedrooms: 2 double, 1 twin, 2 triple, 1 family room
Bathrooms: 1 public, 3 private showers

Bed & breakfast per night:	£min	£max
Single	19.00	21.00
Double	34.00	36.00

Parking for 10

🐴♿📺📺💷🅿️📺💼📻❄️✈️
🚐

Collins House ⋀

👑👑 COMMENDED

19 St Owen Street, Hereford HR1 2JB
☎ (01432) 272416
Fax (01432) 357717
Fully restored early Georgian town house, c1722, combining comfort, character and convenience in historic town centre. Private parking. No smoking, please.
Bedrooms: 1 double, 2 twin
Bathrooms: 3 en-suite

Bed & breakfast per night:	£min	£max
Single	30.00	30.00
Double	40.00	40.00

Parking for 3
Cards accepted: Mastercard, Visa

🐴5📞📺📺💷🅿️🔆📺💼
🍴❄️✈️🚐 SP 🔥 T

Hedley Lodge ⋀

👑👑 COMMENDED

Belmont Abbey, Hereford HR2 9RZ
☎ (01432) 277475
Fax (01432) 277597
Guesthouse set within the historic estate of Belmont Abbey, a Benedictine monastery on the A465 Hereford to Abergavenny road.
Bedrooms: 8 twin
Bathrooms: 8 en-suite

Bed & breakfast per night:	£min	£max
Single	18.50	35.00
Double	50.00	55.00

Half board per person:	£min	£max
Daily	27.00	

Lunch available
Evening meal 1900 (last orders 1930)
Parking for 200

🐴♿📺💷🅿️💷🔆📺📺💼🍴150
❄️✈️ DAP 🚐 SP 🔥

The symbols in each entry give information about services and facilities. A key to these symbols appears at the back of this guide.

HEREFORD

Continued

Merton Hotel ♏

👑👑👑👑 APPROVED

Commercial Road, Hereford
HR1 2BD
☎ (01432) 265925 & 0860 550288
Fax (01432) 354983
Email: 106317.2760
@compuserve.com
Georgian origin, this charming town house hotel has been modernised to provide comfortable, well-appointed accommodation with elegant "Governor's" restaurant.
Bedrooms: 8 single, 5 double, 3 twin, 1 triple
Bathrooms: 17 en-suite

Bed & breakfast per night:

	£min	£max
Single	45.00	55.00
Double	60.00	70.00

Half board per person:

	£min	£max
Daily	60.00	70.00
Weekly	385.00	

Lunch available
Evening meal 1830 (last orders 2130)
Parking for 4
Cards accepted: Amex, Diners, Mastercard, Visa, Switch/Delta

The New Priory Hotel ♏

👑👑👑 APPROVED

Stretton Sugwas, Hereford
HR4 7AR
☎ (01432) 760264 & 761809
Fax (01432) 761809
Really friendly family hotel set in pleasant peaceful surroundings, 2 miles from the centre of Hereford. Good home-cooked food, lots of historical interest. En-suite four-poster rooms.
Bedrooms: 2 single, 5 double, 1 twin
Bathrooms: 6 en-suite, 1 public

Bed & breakfast per night:

	£min	£max
Single	25.00	45.00
Double	45.00	70.00

Half board per person:

	£min	£max
Daily	35.00	45.00
Weekly	220.00	280.00

Lunch available
Evening meal 1900 (last orders 2145)
Parking for 60
Cards accepted: Mastercard, Visa

Pilgrim Hotel ♏

👑👑👑 COMMENDED

Ross Road, Much Birch, Hereford
HR2 8HJ
☎ (01981) 540742
Fax (01981) 540620
Ⓒℝ The Independents

Country house hotel combining modern facilities with old world charm. Popular with country lovers and golfers. Set in 4 acres of grounds, south of Hereford.
Bedrooms: 1 single, 9 double, 8 twin, 2 triple
Bathrooms: 20 en-suite

Bed & breakfast per night:

	£min	£max
Single	39.50	52.00
Double	45.00	59.50

Half board per person:

	£min	£max
Daily	44.50	49.50
Weekly	273.00	297.00

Lunch available
Evening meal 1900 (last orders 2200)
Parking for 40
Cards accepted: Amex, Diners, Mastercard, Visa

Priory Lodge

Listed APPROVED

76 Broomy Hill, Hereford HR4 0LQ
☎ (01432) 273988
Family residence with pleasant garden, in quiet area close to city boundary and River Wye. Private bathroom and sitting room. Cold lunches available.
Bedrooms: 1 single, 1 twin
Bathrooms: 1 public

Bed & breakfast per night:

	£min	£max
Single	12.00	14.00
Double	23.00	26.00

Half board per person:

	£min	£max
Daily	17.00	19.00
Weekly	98.00	100.00

Lunch available
Evening meal 1930 (last orders 2100)
Parking for 2
Cards accepted: Visa

The Somerville ♏

👑👑👑 COMMENDED

12 Bodenham Road, Hereford
HR1 2TS
☎ (01432) 273991
Quiet guesthouse with views, convenient for city centre and station. Well-appointed bedrooms. No lunches. Children welcome. Ample parking.
Bedrooms: 4 single, 3 double, 2 twin, 1 triple
Bathrooms: 6 en-suite, 3 public

Bed & breakfast per night:

	£min	£max
Single	18.00	25.00
Double	32.00	40.00

Half board per person:

	£min	£max
Daily	28.50	
Weekly	199.50	

Evening meal 1830 (last orders 1900)
Parking for 10
Cards accepted: Amex, Mastercard, Visa, Switch/Delta

Three Counties Hotel ♏

👑👑👑 COMMENDED

Belmont Road, Hereford HR2 7BP
☎ (01432) 299955
Fax (01432) 275114
Excellently appointed hotel set in 3.5 acres. Emphasis on traditional, friendly service. Tasteful bedrooms, restaurant and bar offer today's guest all modern comforts. Ideal base for touring Wye Valley. Town centre 1 mile.
Bedrooms: 17 double, 43 twin
Bathrooms: 60 en-suite

Bed & breakfast per night:

	£min	£max
Single	25.00	72.00
Double	50.00	74.50

Lunch available
Evening meal 1900 (last orders 2130)
Parking for 250
Cards accepted: Amex, Diners, Mastercard, Visa, Switch/Delta

HINCKLEY

Leicestershire
Map ref 4B3

The town has an excellent leisure centre. Bosworth Battlefield, with its Visitor Centre and Battle Trail, is 5 miles away.
Tourist Information Centre ☎ (01455) 635106

Sketchley Grange Hotel Ⓜ
HIGHLY COMMENDED
Sketchley Lane, Burbage, Hinckley LE10 3HU
☎ (01455) 251133
Fax (01455) 631384
Ⓒ Best Western
Country house hotel set in green fields, yet only 2 minutes from the M69. Friendly and efficient service assured. Located on the border of Leicestershire/Warwickshire.
Bedrooms: 7 single, 13 double, 13 twin, 5 triple
Bathrooms: 38 en-suite

Bed & breakfast per night:	£min	£max
Single	60.00	90.00
Double	80.00	120.00

Lunch available
Evening meal 1900 (last orders 2145)
Parking for 200
Cards accepted: Amex, Diners, Mastercard, Visa, Switch/Delta

HOCKLEY HEATH

West Midlands
Map ref 4B3

Village near the National Trust property of Packwood House, with its well-known yew garden, and Kenilworth.

Nuthurst Grange Country House Hotel & Restaurant Ⓜ
HIGHLY COMMENDED
Nuthurst Grange Lane, Hockley Heath, Warwickshire B94 5NL
☎ (0156478) 3972
Fax (0156478) 3919
Located close to motorway network in rural setting of 7.5 acres. Relaxed country house atmosphere with acclaimed restaurant. Bedrooms en-suite with whirlpool baths. Single price is for sole occupancy of double room.
Bedrooms: 10 double, 5 twin
Bathrooms: 15 en-suite

Bed & breakfast per night:	£min	£max
Single	120.00	
Double	140.00	165.00

Lunch available
Evening meal 1900 (last orders 2130)
Parking for 86
Cards accepted: Amex, Diners, Mastercard, Visa, Switch/Delta

HOPE

Derbyshire
Map ref 4B2

Village in the Hope Valley which is an excellent base for walking in the Peak District and for fishing and shooting. There is a well-dressing ceremony each June and its August sheep dog trials are well-known. Castleton Caves are nearby.

Moorgate
APPROVED
Edale Road, Hope, Sheffield S30 2RF
☎ (01433) 621219
Distinctive country guesthouse in the heart of the Peak District. En-suite facilities available. Boot and drying room. Packed lunches. Ideal for walking and touring.
Bedrooms: 8 single, 3 double, 15 twin
Bathrooms: 11 en-suite, 8 public

Bed & breakfast per night:	£min	£max
Single	18.50	24.00
Double	37.00	48.00

Half board per person:	£min	£max
Daily	27.00	37.00

Lunch available
Evening meal from 1900
Parking for 30
Cards accepted: Mastercard, Visa, Switch/Delta

Please check prices and other details at the time of booking.

The National Grading and Classification Scheme is explained at the back of this guide.

IRONBRIDGE

Shropshire
Map ref 4A3

Small town on the Severn where the Industrial Revolution began. It has the world's first iron bridge built in 1779. The Ironbridge Gorge Museum, of exceptional interest, comprises a rebuilt turn-of-the-century town and sites spread over 6 square miles.
Tourist Information Centre ☎ (01952) 432166

Broseley Guest House Ⓜ
COMMENDED
The Square, Broseley TF12 5EW
☎ (01952) 882043
Well-appointed spacious accommodation in the centre of Broseley, 1 mile from Ironbridge and convenient for Telford business centres.
Bedrooms: 2 single, 2 double, 1 twin, 1 triple
Bathrooms: 6 en-suite

Bed & breakfast per night:	£min	£max
Single	26.00	30.00
Double	42.00	48.00

Evening meal (last orders 1800)
Cards accepted: Mastercard, Visa

Hundred House Hotel, Restaurant and Country Inn Ⓜ
HIGHLY COMMENDED
Bridgnorth Road, (A442), Norton, Shifnal, Telford TF11 9EE
☎ (01952) 730353
Fax (01952) 730355
Ⓒ Logis of GB
Homely, family-run hotel, with atmospheric historic bars, interesting bar food and intimate restaurant. Antique patchwork themed bedrooms with all facilities. Beautiful, relaxing cottage gardens.
Bedrooms: 2 single, 2 double, 1 twin, 5 triple
Bathrooms: 10 en-suite

Bed & breakfast per night:	£min	£max
Single	65.00	80.00
Double	80.00	100.00

Half board per person:	£min	£max
Daily	60.00	67.50
Weekly	378.00	425.00

Lunch available
Evening meal 1800 (last orders 2200)

Continued ▶

IRONBRIDGE
Continued

Parking for 30
Cards accepted: Amex, Mastercard, Visa, Switch/Delta

🐶♿🛴📞🖥️🗔♨️🎤🅿️🛄💻🖨️♟20🏌️❄️ 🐴🚭 SP 🎣 T

The Library House
👑👑 HIGHLY COMMENDED

11 Severn Bank, Ironbridge, Telford
TF8 7AN
☎ (01952) 432299
Fax (01952) 433967
Fascinating 18th C house, 60 metres from the Ironbridge, where you are assured of a friendly, personal welcome, comfortable rooms and home cooking. Free car park passes available.
Bedrooms: 1 double, 2 triple
Bathrooms: 2 en-suite, 1 private
Bed & breakfast

per night:	£min	£max
Single	38.00	40.00
Double	48.00	50.00

🐶🛴📞🗔♨️🎤🅾️S✂️📺💻🖨️❄️ 🐴🎣

Madeley Court Hotel 𝍔
👑👑👑👑 HIGHLY COMMENDED

Castlefields Way, Madeley, Telford
TF7 5DW
☎ (01952) 680068
Fax (01952) 684275
CR Lyric
Country house style hotel converted from 16th C manor house in the heart of the Ironbridge Gorge. Telford and motorway network 5 minutes' drive.
Bedrooms: 7 single, 31 double, 8 twin, 1 triple
Bathrooms: 47 en-suite
Bed & breakfast

per night:	£min	£max
Single	60.00	128.00
Double	75.00	150.00

Half board per

person:	£min	£max
Daily	55.00	105.00
Weekly	330.00	735.00

Lunch available
Evening meal 1900 (last orders 2145)
Parking for 200
Cards accepted: Amex, Diners, Mastercard, Visa, Switch/Delta

🐶♿🛴🍷📞🖥️🗔♨️🎤🅾️S✂️📺🅾️ 💻🖨️♟200🚶🏌️❄️🚭 SP 🎣

Please mention this guide when making your booking.

Severn Lodge 𝍔
👑👑 DE LUXE

New Road, Ironbridge, Telford
TF8 7AS
☎ (01952) 432148
Fax (01952) 432148
Georgian house set in a lovely garden and situated a few yards from the famous iron bridge and River Severn.
Bedrooms: 2 double, 1 twin
Bathrooms: 2 en-suite, 1 private
Bed & breakfast

per night:	£min	£max
Single	39.00	39.00
Double	52.00	52.00

Parking for 22

🐶♟12🗔📞♨️🎤🅾️UL🅾️S✂️📺 🖨️❄️🏌️🐴🎣

Tontine Hotel
👑👑👑 COMMENDED

The Square, Ironbridge, Telford
TF8 7AL
☎ (01952) 432127
Fax (01952) 432094

Family hotel with personal service and attention, built 200 years ago by the makers of the first iron bridge.
Bedrooms: 2 single, 4 double, 2 twin, 2 triple, 2 family rooms
Bathrooms: 7 en-suite, 2 public
Bed & breakfast

per night:	£min	£max
Single	20.00	34.00
Double	38.00	52.00

Lunch available
Evening meal 1800 (last orders 2100)
Parking for 5
Cards accepted: Amex, Mastercard, Visa

🐶♿🛴📞🖥️🗔♨️🅾️S💻🖨️🅾️♟🏌️🚭🐴🎣

Valley Hotel 𝍔
👑👑👑👑 COMMENDED

Ironbridge, Telford TF8 7DW
☎ (01952) 432247
Fax (01952) 432308
CR Consort/The Independents

Georgian listed building situated in World Heritage Site of Ironbridge.

Riverside location with large car park. All Ironbridge Gorge Museum attractions are within walking distance of the hotel.
Bedrooms: 9 single, 24 double, 2 twin
Bathrooms: 35 en-suite
Bed & breakfast

per night:	£min	£max
Single	55.00	70.00
Double	70.00	85.00

Lunch available
Evening meal 1900 (last orders 2200)
Parking for 100
Cards accepted: Amex, Diners, Mastercard, Visa

🐶♿🛴🍷📞🖥️🗔♨️🎤🅾️S✂️🅾️🅾️ 💻🖨️♟200❄️🏌️🚭 SP 🎣 T

KEGWORTH

Leicestershire
Map ref 4C3

Village on the River Soar close to East Midlands International Airport and Donington Park racing circuit. It has a 14th C church with a fine nave and chantry roof. The nearby churches of Staunton Harold, Melbourne and Breedon-on-the-Hill are of exceptional interest.

Kegworth House 𝍔
👑👑👑 HIGHLY COMMENDED

42 High Street, Kegworth, Derby
DE74 2DA
☎ (01509) 672575
Fax (01509) 670645
Fine 250-year-old Georgian residence, set in lovely grounds with walled garden and orchard. Delightful individual rooms with all facilities. Excellent cuisine.
Bedrooms: 5 double
Bathrooms: 5 en-suite
Bed & breakfast

per night:	£min	£max
Single	37.50	49.00
Double	49.00	65.00

Half board per

person:	£min	£max
Daily	52.50	64.00

Evening meal 1800 (last orders 2000)
Parking for 10
Cards accepted: Mastercard, Visa

🐶🛴📞🖥️🗔♨️🎤🅾️UL🅾️S✂️🅾️💻❄️ 🏌️🐴🎣

The 𝍔 symbol after an establishment name indicates that it is a Regional Tourist Board member.

KENILWORTH

Warwickshire
Map ref 4B3

The main feature of the town is the ruined 12th C castle. It has many royal associations but was damaged by Cromwell. A good base for visiting Coventry, Leamington Spa and Warwick.
Tourist Information Centre ☎ (01926) 852595 or 850708

Abbey Guest House ♠

👑 COMMENDED

41 Station Road, Kenilworth
CV8 1JD
☎ (01926) 512707
Fax (01926) 859148
Cosy Victorian house, 10 minutes from National Agricultural Centre, 15 minutes from NEC. Ideally placed for Warwick, Stratford-upon-Avon, Coventry and the Cotswolds.
Bedrooms: 1 single, 2 double, 3 twin, 1 triple
Bathrooms: 3 en-suite, 1 public

Bed & breakfast per night:

	£min	£max
Single	21.00	25.00
Double	36.00	42.00

Parking for 2

Castle Laurels Hotel ♠

👑👑👑 COMMENDED

22 Castle Road, Kenilworth
CV8 1NG
☎ (01926) 856179
Fax (01926) 854954
Victorian house in conservation area beside Kenilworth Castle and Abbey Fields. Convenient for Warwick, Leamington Spa, Coventry, National Exhibition Centre and National Agricultural Centre. Non-smokers only, please.
Bedrooms: 3 single, 4 double, 3 twin, 1 triple
Bathrooms: 11 en-suite

Bed & breakfast per night:

	£min	£max
Single	33.00	40.00
Double	53.00	66.00

Evening meal 1800 (last orders 1930)
Parking for 14
Cards accepted: Mastercard, Visa

The Cottage Inn ♠

👑👑 APPROVED

36 Stoneleigh Road, Kenilworth
CV8 2GD
☎ (01926) 853900
Traditional English pub located centrally for Warwick, Leamington, Stratford-upon-Avon, Coventry, Birmingham Airport, the National Exhibition Centre and the Royal Agricultural Showground at Stoneleigh. Home-made bar meals and snacks.
Bedrooms: 1 single, 3 double, 2 twin
Bathrooms: 6 en-suite

Bed & breakfast per night:

	£min	£max
Single	20.00	29.00
Double	30.00	40.00

Lunch available
Evening meal 1800 (last orders 1000)
Parking for 12
Cards accepted: Mastercard, Visa, Switch/Delta

Enderley Guest House ♠

👑👑 APPROVED

20 Queens Road, Kenilworth
CV8 1JQ
☎ (01926) 855388 & 850450
Family-run guesthouse, quietly situated near town centre and convenient for Warwick, Stratford-upon-Avon, Stoneleigh, Warwick University and National Exhibition Centre.
Bedrooms: 2 double, 1 twin, 1 triple
Bathrooms: 4 en-suite

Bed & breakfast per night:

	£min	£max
Single	26.00	40.00
Double	39.00	45.00

Parking for 2

Ferndale Guest House ♠

👑👑 COMMENDED

45 Priory Road, Kenilworth
CV8 1LL
☎ (01926) 853214
Fax (01926) 858336
Delightfully modernised Victorian house. Attractive en-suite bedrooms with colour TV, tea/coffee facilities. Ideal for NEC, NAC and Warwick University. Private parking.
Bedrooms: 1 single, 1 double, 3 twin, 2 triple
Bathrooms: 7 en-suite

Bed & breakfast per night:

	£min	£max
Single	21.00	25.00
Double	36.00	36.00

Parking for 8

Hollyhurst Guest House ♠

👑👑 COMMENDED

47 Priory Road, Kenilworth
CV8 1LL
☎ (01926) 853882
High standard family-run guesthouse in quiet location close to town centre. Easy access to National Exhibition Centre, Royal Showground and tourist areas of Stratford-upon-Avon, Warwick and Coventry.
Bedrooms: 1 single, 1 double, 3 twin, 2 triple
Bathrooms: 3 en-suite, 2 public

Bed & breakfast per night:

	£min	£max
Single	21.00	
Double	40.00	

Parking for 9

Victoria Lodge Hotel

👑👑👑 HIGHLY COMMENDED

180 Warwick Road, Kenilworth
CV8 1HU
☎ (01926) 512020
Fax (01926) 858703
Prestigious small hotel with a warming ambience. Beautiful bedrooms, with individual appeal and character, are complemented by traditional hospitality. Non-smoking.
Bedrooms: 1 single, 5 double, 1 twin
Bathrooms: 7 en-suite

Bed & breakfast per night:

	£min	£max
Single	37.50	42.50
Double	52.50	52.50

Lunch available
Evening meal 1700 (last orders 1930)
Parking for 10
Cards accepted: Amex, Mastercard, Visa, Switch/Delta

For further information on accommodation establishments use the coupons at the back of this guide.

National gradings and classifications were correct at the time of going to press but are subject to change. Please check at the time of booking.

You are advised to confirm your booking in writing.

KIDDERMINSTER

Hereford and Worcester
Map ref 4B3

The town is the centre for carpet manufacturing. It has a medieval church with good monuments and a statue of Sir Rowland Hill, a native of the town and founder of the penny post. West Midlands Safari Park is nearby. Severn Valley Railway station.

Cedars Hotel ⚠

`COMMENDED`

Mason Road, Kidderminster,
Worcestershire DY11 6AG
☎ (01562) 515595
Fax (01562) 751103
Ⓒ Minotel

Charming conversion of a Georgian building close to the River Severn, Severn Valley Railway and Worcestershire countryside. 15 minutes from M5.
Bedrooms: 2 single, 8 double, 6 twin, 4 triple, 2 family rooms
Bathrooms: 22 en-suite

Bed & breakfast per night:

	£min	£max
Single	33.25	55.25
Double	45.75	67.50

Evening meal 1900 (last orders 2030)
Parking for 23
Cards accepted: Amex, Diners, Mastercard, Visa

Gainsborough House Hotel ⚠

`COMMENDED`

Bewdley Hill, Kidderminster,
Worcestershire DY11 6BS
☎ (01562) 820041
Fax (01562) 66179
Ⓒ Lyric

Traditional hotel close to River Severn. The Severn Valley Railway, West Midlands Safari Park and Worcestershire countryside are all close at hand. 15 minutes from M5.
Bedrooms: 1 single, 12 double, 24 twin, 5 triple
Bathrooms: 42 en-suite

Bed & breakfast per night:

	£min	£max
Single	30.00	80.00
Double	40.00	90.00

Half board per person:

	£min	£max
Daily	35.00	63.00
Weekly	210.00	441.00

Lunch available
Evening meal 1900 (last orders 2200)
Parking for 127
Cards accepted: Amex, Diners, Mastercard, Visa, Switch/Delta

The Granary Hotel and Restaurant ⚠

`COMMENDED`

Shenstone, Kidderminster,
Worcestershire DY10 4BS
☎ (01562) 777535
Fax (01562) 777722
Ⓒ The Independents

Family-owned restaurant and hotel renowned for food and good service. Close to Severn Valley Railway and safari park. Rural location.
Wheelchair access category 3 ♿
Bedrooms: 5 double, 13 twin
Bathrooms: 18 en-suite

Bed & breakfast per night:

	£min	£max
Single	42.50	62.50
Double	45.00	65.00

Half board per person:

	£min	£max
Daily	35.00	57.50

Lunch available
Evening meal 1900 (last orders 2115)
Parking for 95
Cards accepted: Amex, Diners, Mastercard, Visa, Switch/Delta

ACCESSIBILITY

Look for the ♿ symbols which indicate accessibility for wheelchair users. These are described in detail at the front of this guide.

KINETON

Warwickshire
Map ref 2C1

Attractive old village in rolling countryside. 1 mile from site of famous battle of Edgehill. Medieval church of St Peter.

The Castle ⚠

`Listed` `COMMENDED`

Edgehill, Kineton, Banbury,
Oxfordshire OX15 6DJ
☎ (01295) 670255
"Folly" built by Sanderson-Miller, copy of Guy's Tower at Warwick Castle erected to commemorate 100th anniversary of Battle of Edgehill (1642), traditionally where King Charles I stood.
Bedrooms: 2 twin
Bathrooms: 2 en-suite

Bed & breakfast per night:

	£min	£max
Single	35.00	
Double	59.50	

Lunch available
Evening meal 1830 (last orders 2100)
Parking for 25
Cards accepted: Amex, Diners, Mastercard, Visa, Switch/Delta

KINGTON

Hereford and Worcester
Map ref 2A1

Market town on the Welsh border, with Offa's Dyke close by. The Hergest Croft Gardens are well-known for their beautiful displays of azaleas and rhododendrons during May and June.

Burton Hotel ⚠

`APPROVED`

Mill Street, Kington, Herefordshire HR5 3BQ
☎ (01544) 230323
Fax (01544) 230323
Attractively modernised, authentic coaching inn, in centre of small market town near Welsh border and Offa's Dyke footpath.
Bedrooms: 1 single, 5 double, 3 twin, 6 triple
Bathrooms: 15 en-suite

Bed & breakfast per night:

	£min	£max
Single	42.00	50.00
Double	55.00	60.00

Half board per person:

	£min	£max
Daily	44.00	56.00
Weekly	262.00	315.00

Lunch available
Evening meal 1930 (last orders 2130)
Parking for 45
Cards accepted: Amex, Diners, Mastercard, Visa

LANGAR

Nottinghamshire
Map ref 4C2

Small village standing on a small escarpment. Has a fine, Early English style church and a strong village atmosphere.

Langar Hall ⋀

COMMENDED

Langar, Nottingham NG13 9HG
☎ (01949) 860559
Fax (01949) 861045

Charming small hotel in peaceful rural setting, 12 miles south-east of Nottingham. Central for touring or as a stop-off for travellers between north and south.
Bedrooms: 9 double, 1 twin
Bathrooms: 10 private

Bed & breakfast per night:

	£min	£max
Single	75.00	85.00
Double	85.00	150.00

Half board per person:

	£min	£max
Daily	100.00	120.00

Lunch available
Evening meal 1900 (last orders 2130)
Parking for 20
Cards accepted: Amex, Diners, Mastercard, Visa

All accommodation in this guide has been graded, or is awaiting a grading, by a trained Tourist Board inspector.

LEAMINGTON SPA

Warwickshire
Map ref 4B3

18th C spa town with many fine Georgian and Regency houses. Tea can be taken in the 19th C Pump Room. The attractive Jephson Gardens are laid out alongside the river and there is a museum and art gallery.
Tourist Information Centre ☎ (01926) 311470

Adams Hotel

COMMENDED

22 Avenue Road, Leamington Spa CV31 3PQ
☎ (01926) 450742
Fax (01926) 313110
Privately owned 17th C listed hotel, with modern bedrooms, standing back from the road in a typical Regency setting.
Bedrooms: 3 single, 4 double, 3 twin
Bathrooms: 10 en-suite

Bed & breakfast per night:

	£min	£max
Single	38.95	56.00
Double	52.90	68.75

Half board per person:

	£min	£max
Daily	44.00	49.50

Evening meal 1800 (last orders 2000)
Parking for 10
Cards accepted: Amex, Diners, Mastercard, Visa

Beech Lodge Hotel ⋀

COMMENDED

28 Warwick New Road, Leamington Spa CV32 5JJ
☎ (01926) 422227
Elegant Regency building with spacious lounge, dining room and residents' bar. All bedrooms with colour TV, radio, telephone and tea/coffee-making facilities.
Bedrooms: 7 single, 6 double, 1 twin
Bathrooms: 12 en-suite, 1 public

Bed & breakfast per night:

	£min	£max
Single	30.00	44.00
Double	47.00	60.00

Half board per person:

	£min	£max
Daily	38.00	58.00
Weekly	245.00	340.00

Lunch available
Evening meal 1900 (last orders 2000)

Parking for 14
Cards accepted: Amex, Diners, Mastercard, Visa

Charnwood Guest House ⋀

APPROVED

47 Avenue Road, Leamington Spa CV31 3PF
☎ (01926) 831074
Attractive Victorian house near railway station and town centre. All rooms have colour TV and tea/coffee.
Bedrooms: 1 single, 2 double, 2 twin, 1 triple
Bathrooms: 2 en-suite, 2 public, 1 private shower

Bed & breakfast per night:

	£min	£max
Single	17.00	27.00
Double	32.00	37.00

Half board per person:

	£min	£max
Daily	27.00	37.00
Weekly	189.00	259.00

Evening meal 1800 (last orders 1200)
Parking for 5
Cards accepted: Mastercard, Visa

Eaton Court Hotel ⋀

COMMENDED

1-7 St Marks Road, Leamington Spa CV32 6DL
☎ (01926) 885848
Fax (01926) 885848
Privately owned and run hotel with spacious en-suite rooms and comfortable facilities including function rooms and licensed restaurant.
Bedrooms: 10 single, 12 double, 10 twin, 2 triple, 2 family rooms
Bathrooms: 36 en-suite

Bed & breakfast per night:

	£min	£max
Single	40.00	55.00
Double	60.00	75.00

Half board per person:

	£min	£max
Daily	55.00	70.00
Weekly	355.00	460.00

Lunch available
Evening meal 1900 (last orders 2130)
Parking for 36
Cards accepted: Amex, Diners, Mastercard, Visa

LEAMINGTON SPA

Continued

Falstaff Hotel

👑👑👑 COMMENDED

16-20 Warwick New Road,
Leamington Spa CV32 5JQ
☎ (01926) 312044
Fax (01926) 450574
Elegant Regency hotel offering every modern convenience to the business traveller. Ideally located in the Heart of England.
Bedrooms: 27 single, 16 double,
18 twin
Bathrooms: 61 en-suite
Bed & breakfast

per night:	£min	£max
Single	30.00	65.00
Double	40.00	75.00

Half board per

person:	£min	£max
Daily	33.00	50.00
Weekly	200.00	300.00

Lunch available
Evening meal 1900 (last orders 2115)
Parking for 80
Cards accepted: Amex, Diners, Mastercard, Visa, Switch/Delta

Milverton House Hotel ♠

👑👑👑 COMMENDED

1 Milverton Terrace, Leamington Spa
CV32 5BE
☎ (01926) 428335
Graceful, modernised, 145-year-old building, licensed and centrally heated, within walking distance of the town centre. Home-cooked food.
Bedrooms: 2 single, 3 double, 4 twin,
1 triple
Bathrooms: 6 en-suite, 2 public,
1 private shower
Bed & breakfast

per night:	£min	£max
Single	20.00	
Double	34.00	

Evening meal 1900 (last orders 1900)
Parking for 6
Cards accepted: Mastercard, Visa

Half board prices are given per person, but in some cases these may be based on double/twin occupancy.

Victoria Park Hotel ♠

👑👑👑 COMMENDED

12 Adelaide Road, Leamington Spa
CV31 3PW
☎ (01926) 424195
Fax (01926) 421521
Victorian house close to bus and railway stations and town centre. Park, Pump Room, gardens, bowls, tennis and river all three minutes' walk away.
Bedrooms: 11 single, 3 double,
1 twin, 1 triple
Bathrooms: 14 en-suite, 1 public
Bed & breakfast

per night:	£min	£max
Single	30.00	36.00
Double	42.00	50.00

Half board per

person:	£min	£max
Daily	44.50	50.50
Weekly	311.50	353.50

Lunch available
Evening meal 1830 (last orders 1920)
Parking for 12
Cards accepted: Amex, Diners, Mastercard, Visa

LECHLADE

Gloucestershire
Map ref 2B1

Attractive village on the River Thames and a popular spot for boating. It has a number of fine Georgian houses and a 15th C church. Nearby is Kelmscott Manor, with its William Morris furnishings, and 18th C Buscot House (National Trust).

Cambrai Lodge ♠

Listed COMMENDED

Oak Street, Lechlade GL7 3AY
☎ (01367) 253173 & 0860 150467
Friendly, family-run guesthouse, recently modernised, close to River Thames. Ideal base for touring the Cotswolds. Four-poster bedroom, garden and ample parking.
Bedrooms: 2 single, 2 double
Bathrooms: 2 en-suite, 1 public
Bed & breakfast

per night:	£min	£max
Single	21.00	30.00
Double	34.00	42.00

Parking for 11

Please check prices and other details at the time of booking.

New Inn Hotel ♠

👑👑👑 APPROVED

Market Square, Lechlade-on-Thames,
Lechlade GL7 3AB
☎ (01367) 252296
Fax (01367) 252315
Situated in a tranquil riverside setting, offering a comfortable blend of traditional hospitality and all modern advantages. Private parking.
Bedrooms: 2 single, 16 double,
12 twin
Bathrooms: 30 en-suite
Bed & breakfast

per night:	£min	£max
Single	40.00	49.00
Double	45.00	69.00

Half board per

person:	£min	£max
Daily	30.00	45.00
Weekly	170.00	295.00

Lunch available
Evening meal 1900 (last orders 2200)
Parking for 40
Cards accepted: Amex, Diners, Mastercard, Visa, Switch/Delta

LEDBURY

Hereford and Worcester
Map ref 2B1

Town with cobbled streets and many black and white timbered houses, including the 17th C market house and old inns. Nearby is Eastnor Castle with an interesting collection of tapestries and armour.
Tourist Information Centre ☎ *(01531) 636147*

Feathers Hotel ♠

👑👑👑👑 COMMENDED

High Street, Ledbury, Herefordshire
HR8 1DS
☎ (01531) 635266
Fax (01531) 632001
Ⓡ Logis of GB
Traditional Elizabethan coaching inn, situated in the centre of Ledbury. Ideal for touring Malverns and the Marches.
Bedrooms: 4 double, 4 twin, 3 triple
Bathrooms: 11 en-suite
Bed & breakfast

per night:	£min	£max
Single		65.00
Double	85.00	95.00

Lunch available
Evening meal 1830 (last orders 2130)
Parking for 20

Cards accepted: Amex, Diners, Mastercard, Visa, Switch/Delta

🐕🛏🕭🖳🖵👤♿🎧🛈Ⓢ🅟📺◐🗎
🛢🍴100🎿∪🏃🛶 SP🏕

Old silk and textile town, with some interesting buildings and a number of inns dating from the 17th C. Its art gallery has displays of embroidery. Brindley Mill, designed by James Brindley, has been restored as a museum.
Tourist Information Centre ☎ (01538) 483741

Three Horseshoes Inn & Restaurant 🅜

👑👑 COMMENDED

Buxton Road, Blackshaw Moor, Leek ST13 8TW
☎ (01538) 300296
Fax (01538) 300320
Ⓒ Logis of GB

Log fire, slate floor, oak and pine beams, good food and wines. Cottage-style rooms. Convenient for Peak District National Park and Alton Towers.
Bedrooms: 4 double, 2 twin
Bathrooms: 6 en-suite
Bed & breakfast per night:

	£min	£max
Single	45.00	55.00
Double	50.00	65.00

Half board per person:

	£min	£max
Daily	45.00	55.00

Lunch available
Evening meal 1900 (last orders 2100)
Parking for 100
Cards accepted: Amex, Mastercard, Visa, Switch/Delta

🐕🛏🕭🖳🖵👤🛈Ⓢ✗🎧📺🗎🛢∪
🏃🌸 SP🇹◉

Modern industrial city with a wide variety of attractions including Roman remains, ancient churches, Georgian houses and a Victorian clock tower. Excellent shopping precincts, arcades and market, museums, theatres, concert hall and sports and leisure centres.
Tourist Information Centre ☎ (0116) 265 0555

Beaumaris Guesthouse

👑 APPROVED

18 Westcotes Drive, Leicester LE3 0QR
☎ (0116) 254 0261
Friendly, family-run guesthouse, away from heavy traffic, yet on a bus route to town and within 15 minutes' walking distance of it.
Bedrooms: 2 single, 1 double, 2 twin, 1 triple
Bathrooms: 2 public
Bed & breakfast per night:

	£min	£max
Single	17.00	20.00
Double	25.00	30.00

🐕🖵Ⓤ🅛Ⓢ📺🗎🛢🚐

Burlington Hotel 🅜

👑👑👑 COMMENDED

Elmfield Avenue, Stoneygate, Leicester LE2 1RB
☎ (0116) 270 5112
Fax (0116) 270 4207
A friendly welcome awaits you at this family-run hotel. Situated in a quiet residential area close to the city centre.
Bedrooms: 9 single, 4 double, 2 twin, 1 triple
Bathrooms: 11 en-suite, 1 public, 4 private showers
Bed & breakfast per night:

	£min	£max
Single	30.00	40.00
Double	44.00	48.00

Evening meal 1845 (last orders 2015)
Parking for 18
Cards accepted: Amex, Mastercard, Visa

🐕🕭🖵👤🛈🎧📺🗎🛢🍴20🌸
🏸 SP🇹

Glenfield Lodge Hotel

👑 APPROVED

4 Glenfield Road, Leicester LE3 6AP
☎ (0116) 262 7554

Small, friendly hotel with an interesting ornamental courtyard, home-cooked food and cosy, relaxed surroundings. Close to city centre.
Bedrooms: 6 single, 3 double, 4 twin, 2 triple
Bathrooms: 3 public
Bed & breakfast per night:

	£min	£max
Single	15.50	15.50
Double	27.00	27.00

Evening meal 1730 (last orders 1830)
Parking for 3

🐕🖴Ⓤ🅛🎧📺🗎🛢🌸🚐

The Grand Hotel 🅜

👑👑👑👑 COMMENDED

Granby Street, Leicester LE1 6ES
☎ (0116) 255 5599
Fax (0116) 254 4736
Ⓒ Jarvis/Utell International
Recently refurbished city centre hotel, close to railway station, theatres, cinemas, shops and sporting venues.
Bedrooms: 25 single, 42 double, 25 twin
Suite available
Bathrooms: 92 en-suite
Bed & breakfast per night:

	£min	£max
Single	80.00	110.00
Double	90.00	140.00

Half board per person:

	£min	£max
Daily	55.00	

Lunch available
Evening meal 1900 (last orders 2200)
Parking for 132
Cards accepted: Amex, Diners, Mastercard, Visa, Switch/Delta

🐕🛏🕭🖳🖵👤♿🎧🛈Ⓢ✗🎧◐⬛
🗎🛢🍴450🛶 SP🏕

LEICESTER
Continued

Holiday Inn Leicester ♠
👑👑👑👑 COMMENDED

129 St Nicholas Circle, Leicester
LE1 5LX
☎ (0116) 253 1161
Fax (0116) 251 3169
City centre hotel with extensive leisure facilities. Ideal for sporting and cultural attractions. Three miles from M1 junction 21, with free resident parking. Major refurbishment completed in 1996.
Bedrooms: 89 double, 99 twin
Bathrooms: 188 en-suite

Bed & breakfast

per night:	£min	£max
Single	59.00	122.00
Double	59.00	142.00

Half board per

person:	£min	£max
Daily	48.00	140.50

Lunch available
Evening meal 1830 (last orders 2200)
Parking for 700
Cards accepted: Amex, Diners, Mastercard, Visa

Leicester Stage Hotel ♠
👑👑👑👑 COMMENDED

Leicester Road (A50), Wigston,
Leicester LE18 1JW
☎ (0116) 288 6161
Fax (0116) 281 1874
ⒸⓇ Consort
On the A50, 3 miles south of the city centre and the M1/M69, this friendly, privately-owned hotel has en-suite bedrooms, a health and leisure club, indoor heated pool, excellent bar and restaurant.
Bedrooms: 37 double, 39 twin
Bathrooms: 76 en-suite

Bed & breakfast

per night:	£min	£max
Single	40.00	87.50
Double	49.00	96.00

Half board per

person:	£min	£max
Daily	55.95	104.45
Weekly	548.65	645.65

Lunch available
Evening meal 1900 (last orders 2200)
Parking for 200
Cards accepted: Amex, Diners, Mastercard, Visa, Switch/Delta

Spindle Lodge Hotel
👑👑👑 COMMENDED

2 West Walk, Leicester LE1 7NA
☎ (0116) 233 8801
Fax (0116) 233 8804
Victorian house with friendly atmosphere, within easy walking distance of city centre, university, station, civic and entertainment centres.
Bedrooms: 5 single, 3 double, 3 twin, 2 triple
Bathrooms: 7 en-suite, 3 public

Bed & breakfast

per night:	£min	£max
Single	29.50	41.00
Double	50.00	62.00

Evening meal 1830 (last orders 1800)
Parking for 7
Cards accepted: Mastercard, Visa, Switch/Delta

Waltham House ♠
👑 APPROVED

500 Narborough Road, Leicester
LE3 2FU
☎ (0116) 289 1129
Victorian detached house. Close M1/M69 junction and approximately 2 miles from city centre. Very large rooms. Warm, friendly welcome assured.
Bedrooms: 1 single, 1 double, 1 triple
Bathrooms: 1 en-suite, 1 public

Bed & breakfast

per night:	£min	£max
Single	19.00	22.00
Double	35.00	36.00

Parking for 4

LEOMINSTER
Hereford and Worcester
Map ref 2A1

The town owed its prosperity to wool and has many interesting buildings, notably the timber-framed Grange Court, a former town hall. The impressive Norman priory church has 3 naves and a ducking stool. Berrington Hall (National Trust) is nearby.
Tourist Information Centre ☎ (01568) 616460

Copper Hall ♠
👑 COMMENDED

South Street, Leominster,
Herefordshire HR6 8JN
☎ (01568) 611622
Comfortable 17th C house with spacious garden. Good English cooking

and homely atmosphere. Convenient touring centre for Wales, Wye Valley and the Malverns.*
Bedrooms: 1 double, 2 twin, 1 triple
Bathrooms: 1 public

Bed & breakfast

per night:	£min	£max
Single	20.00	25.00
Double	40.00	40.00

Half board per

person:	£min	£max
Daily	30.00	35.00

Evening meal 1800 (last orders 1900)
Parking for 6

Royal Oak Hotel ♠
👑👑👑 APPROVED

South Street, Leominster,
Herefordshire HR6 8JA
☎ (01568) 612610
Fax (01568) 612710
ⒸⓇ Minotel
Grade II listed Georgian coaching house dating from 1723, with log fires in winter, real ales and an emphasis on good food and wines at reasonable prices.
Bedrooms: 2 single, 9 double, 5 twin, 2 triple
Bathrooms: 18 en-suite

Bed & breakfast

per night:	£min	£max
Single	31.50	35.00
Double	45.00	55.00

Half board per

person:	£min	£max
Daily	32.75	41.75
Weekly	206.30	263.00

Lunch available
Evening meal 1830 (last orders 2130)
Parking for 25
Cards accepted: Amex, Diners, Mastercard, Visa

Talbot Hotel ♠
👑👑👑 APPROVED

West Street, Leominster,
Herefordshire HR6 8EP
☎ (01568) 616347
Fax (01568) 614880
ⒸⓇ Best Western
15th C coaching inn with oak beams and log fire, now offering 20th C facilities. Ideal location for touring Mid-Wales, Shropshire and Herefordshire.
Bedrooms: 2 single, 8 double, 7 twin, 2 triple, 1 family room
Bathrooms: 20 en-suite

Bed & breakfast per night:	£min	£max
Single	40.00	47.00
Double	54.00	66.00

Lunch available
Evening meal 1900 (last orders 2130)
Parking for 25
Cards accepted: Amex, Diners, Mastercard, Visa

☎🍴📶🖥♿🅂♨📺◑🛖🌷
🍴150🚶🅿♫ SP 🏤 T

LICHFIELD

Staffordshire
Map ref 4B3

Lichfield is Dr Samuel Johnson's birthplace and commemorates him with a museum and statue. The 13th C cathedral has 3 spires and the west front is full of statues. Among the attractive town buildings is the Heritage Centre. The Regimental Museum is in Whittington Barracks. *Tourist Information Centre ☎ (01543) 252109*

Broad Lane Guest House

👑 COMMENDED

35 Broad Lane, Lichfield WS14 9SU
☎ (01543) 262301
Detached, modern house, situated 1 mile from city centre.
Bedrooms: 1 twin
Bathrooms: 1 private

Bed & breakfast per night:	£min	£max
Single	18.00	20.00
Double	30.00	32.00

Half board per person:	£min	£max
Daily	23.00	23.00
Weekly	133.00	133.00

Evening meal 1800 (last orders 2000)
Parking for 1

🍴📶🖥♿🅂♨ UL ⅄📺◑🛖🌷🛏🐕

Coppers End 🅜

👑 COMMENDED

Walsall Road, Muckley Corner, Lichfield WS14 0BG
☎ (01543) 372910
Fax (01543) 372910

Detached guesthouse of character and charm in its own grounds. Rural location with easy access to M6, Birmingham, Lichfield and M1.

Residential licence. Telephone for weekly half-board rates.
Bedrooms: 1 single, 2 double, 2 twin
Bathrooms: 1 en-suite, 1 public

Bed & breakfast per night:	£min	£max
Single	23.00	30.00
Double	36.00	42.00

Half board per person:	£min	£max
Daily	30.50	37.50

Evening meal 1900 (last orders 2030)
Parking for 10
Cards accepted: Amex, Diners, Mastercard, Visa, Switch/Delta

☎🍴📶🖥♿🅂⅄📺◑🛖🌷
🌷🛏 SP 🏤

Little Barrow Hotel 🅜

👑👑👑 COMMENDED

Beacon Street, Lichfield WS13 7AR
☎ (01543) 414500
Fax (01543) 415734
Popular hotel just a short distance from the centre of town and close to the cathedral. Bedrooms are well designed and the restaurant enjoys a good reputation.
Bedrooms: 2 single, 6 double, 16 twin
Bathrooms: 24 en-suite

Bed & breakfast per night:	£min	£max
Single	45.00	55.00
Double	55.00	65.00

Half board per person:	£min	£max
Daily	59.50	69.50

Lunch available
Evening meal 1900 (last orders 2130)
Parking for 70
Cards accepted: Amex, Diners, Mastercard, Visa, Switch/Delta

☎📶🖥📶♿🅂📺◑🛖🌷🛏
🍴100🚶🅿⅄✕ SP

Oakleigh House Hotel 🅜

👑👑👑 COMMENDED

25 St. Chad's Road, Lichfield WS13 7LZ
☎ (01543) 262688 & 255573
Fax (01543) 418556

Country house hotel standing in its own grounds, alongside a small lake, just behind Lichfield Cathedral.
Bedrooms: 4 single, 2 double, 4 twin
Bathrooms: 8 en-suite, 1 public

Bed & breakfast per night:	£min	£max
Single	35.00	45.00
Double	55.00	70.00

Half board per person:	£min	£max
Daily	42.00	60.00
Weekly	255.00	385.00

Lunch available
Evening meal 1900 (last orders 2100)
Parking for 20
Cards accepted: Mastercard, Visa

☎🍂🏠🍴📶🖥♿🐕🅂⅄🛖
🛏🍴20🌷🚐

The Olde Corner House Hotel 🅜

👑👑👑 COMMENDED

Walsall Road, Muckley Corner, Lichfield WS14 0BG
☎ (01543) 372182
Fax (01543) 372211

17th C and Victorian premises furnished to a high standard. Ideal for tourists and business. Easy access to motorway network. Fully licensed.
Bedrooms: 4 single, 16 double, 3 twin
Bathrooms: 23 en-suite

Bed & breakfast per night:	£min	£max
Single	28.00	45.00
Double	55.00	65.00

Half board per person:	£min	£max
Daily	37.00	60.00

Lunch available
Evening meal 1800 (last orders 2200)
Parking for 66
Cards accepted: Amex, Mastercard, Visa, Switch/Delta

☎🍂🏠🍴📶🖥♿🐕🅂⅄🛖
🛏🍴10⚓✕🚐♫ SP T

Please mention this guide when making your booking.

For ideas on places to visit refer to the introduction at the beginning of this section.

LOUGHBOROUGH

Leicestershire
Map ref 4C3

Industrial town famous for its bell foundry and 47-bell Carillon Tower. The Great Central Railway operates steam railway rides of over 8 miles through the attractive scenery of Charnwood Forest.
Tourist Information Centre ☎ (01509) 218113

Demontfort Hotel ♨

👑👑 COMMENDED

88 Leicester Road, Loughborough
LE11 2AQ
☎ (01509) 216061
Fax (01509) 233667
One of Loughborough's oldest hotels. Family-run, warm, friendly service, rooms tastefully decorated, restaurant, bar, lounge. Close to town centre, university and Steam Trust.
Bedrooms: 1 single, 3 double, 2 twin, 3 triple
Bathrooms: 4 en-suite, 1 public, 2 private showers

Bed & breakfast per night:

	£min	£max
Single	23.00	30.00
Double	32.00	45.00

Half board per person:

	£min	£max
Daily	29.00	40.00

Lunch available
Evening meal 1830 (last orders 2000)
Cards accepted: Amex, Mastercard, Visa, Switch/Delta

Forest Rise Hotel

👑👑👑 COMMENDED

55 Forest Road, Loughborough
LE11 3NW
☎ (01509) 215928
Fax (01509) 210506
Friendly personal service. Excellent order throughout. Easy access to M1 motorway, university and town centre. Car parking at rear.
Bedrooms: 8 single, 10 double, 1 twin, 3 triple
Bathrooms: 18 en-suite, 4 private showers

Bed & breakfast per night:

	£min	£max
Single	32.00	43.00
Double	51.00	59.50

Evening meal 1900 (last orders 2100)
Parking for 25
Cards accepted: Mastercard, Visa, Switch/Delta

Garendon Lodge Guesthouse ♨

👑👑👑 COMMENDED

136 Leicester Road, Loughborough
LE11 2AQ
☎ (01509) 211120 & 0585 582449

Spacious Victorian guesthouse, completely refurbished. In quiet surroundings but within 5 minutes of the town centre and nearby Charnwood Forest.
Bedrooms: 2 single, 3 double
Bathrooms: 5 en-suite

Bed & breakfast per night:

	£min	£max
Single	25.00	28.00
Double	35.00	38.00

Half board per person:

	£min	£max
Daily	30.50	35.50

Lunch available
Evening meal 1800 (last orders 2000)
Parking for 6
Cards accepted: Amex

Garendon Park Hotel ♨

👑👑👑 COMMENDED

92 Leicester Road, Loughborough
LE11 2AQ
☎ (01509) 236557
Fax (01509) 265559
You are assured of a warm, friendly welcome and high standards in bright, comfortable surroundings. Five minutes from town centre. Local attractions include Great Central Railway, Bell Foundry and surrounding countryside.
Bedrooms: 3 single, 2 double, 3 twin, 1 triple
Bathrooms: 7 en-suite, 1 public

Bed & breakfast per night:

	£min	£max
Single	23.00	35.00
Double	30.00	45.00

Half board per person:

	£min	£max
Daily	28.50	43.50

Evening meal 1830 (last orders 2030)
Cards accepted: Amex, Mastercard, Visa, Switch/Delta

Great Central Hotel and Master Cutler Restaurant ♨

👑👑👑 APPROVED

Great Central Road, Loughborough
LE11 1RW
☎ (01509) 263405
Fax (01509) 264130
Friendly, family-owned pub/hotel offering excellent value food/accommodation/functions. Draught beer only £1 a pint - open all day.
Bedrooms: 3 single, 9 double, 5 twin, 1 triple, 2 family rooms
Bathrooms: 20 en-suite

Bed & breakfast per night:

	£min	£max
Single	25.00	30.00
Double	35.00	40.00

Half board per person:

	£min	£max
Daily	29.00	40.00
Weekly	205.00	350.00

Lunch available
Evening meal 1900 (last orders 2200)
Parking for 30
Cards accepted: Mastercard, Visa, Switch/Delta

The Highbury Guesthouse ♨

👑👑👑 COMMENDED

146 Leicester Road, Loughborough
LE11 0BJ
☎ (01509) 230545
Fax (01509) 233086
Guesthouse on the A6 road from Loughborough to Leicester. Within 5 minutes' walking distance of the town centre. Convenient for steam railway, junction 23 of M1, university, airport and Donington Park.
Bedrooms: 4 single, 4 double, 3 triple
Bathrooms: 7 en-suite, 1 private, 1 public, 3 private showers

Bed & breakfast per night:

	£min	£max
Single	19.00	26.00
Double	32.00	36.00

Half board per person:

	£min	£max
Daily	24.00	31.00
Weekly	150.00	190.00

Evening meal 1800 (last orders 2000)
Parking for 12

Jarvis Kings Head Hotel 🅜
☆☆☆☆☆ COMMENDED
High Street, Loughborough
LE11 2QL
☎ (01509) 233222
Fax (01509) 262911
🆑 Jarvis/Utell International

Georgian-style hotel located midway between Leeds and London, only 3 miles off M1. Many interesting places to visit in the nearby English shires.
Bedrooms: 18 single, 34 double, 26 twin
Bathrooms: 78 en-suite

Bed & breakfast per night:

	£min	£max
Single	37.50	85.00
Double	75.00	95.00

Half board per person:

	£min	£max
Daily	45.00	100.00

Lunch available
Evening meal 1900 (last orders 2130)
Parking for 80
Cards accepted: Amex, Diners, Mastercard, Visa, Switch/Delta

Peachnook 🅜
Listed APPROVED
154 Ashby Road, Loughborough
LE11 3AG
☎ (01509) 264390 & 204390
Small, friendly guesthouse built around 1890. Near all amenities. TV and tea-making facilities in all rooms. Ironing facilities.
Bedrooms: 1 twin, 2 triple
Bathrooms: 2 en-suite, 1 public

Bed & breakfast per night:

	£min	£max
Single	13.00	27.00
Double	30.00	38.00

LUDLOW
Shropshire
Map ref 4A3

Outstandingly interesting border town with a magnificent castle high above the River Teme, 2 half-timbered old inns and an impressive 15th C church. The Reader's House, with its 3-storey Jacobean porch, should also be seen. *Tourist Information Centre ☎ (01584) 875053*

Cecil Guest House 🅜
☆☆☆ COMMENDED
Sheet Road, Ludlow SY8 1LR
☎ (01584) 872442
Fax (01584) 872442
Attractive guesthouse 15 minutes' walk from town centre and station. Good fresh food and comfortable accommodation.
Bedrooms: 2 single, 2 double, 4 twin, 1 triple
Bathrooms: 4 en-suite, 2 public

Bed & breakfast per night:

	£min	£max
Single	19.00	30.00
Double	38.00	52.00

Half board per person:

	£min	£max
Daily	31.00	42.00
Weekly	191.70	235.80

Evening meal 1900 (last orders 0900)
Parking for 11
Cards accepted: Mastercard, Visa

Cliffe Hotel 🅜
☆☆☆ COMMENDED
Dinham, Ludlow SY8 2JE
☎ (01584) 872063
Fax (01584) 873991
Hotel in its own garden conveniently placed on the edge of town, near the castle, river and forest.
Bedrooms: 1 single, 4 double, 4 twin
Bathrooms: 9 en-suite

Bed & breakfast per night:

	£min	£max
Single	30.00	35.00
Double	52.00	58.00

Lunch available
Evening meal 1900 (last orders 2030)
Parking for 50
Cards accepted: Amex, Mastercard, Visa

Dinham Hall Hotel & Restaurant 🅜
☆☆☆☆ COMMENDED
Dinham, By The Castle, Ludlow SY8 1EJ
☎ (01584) 876464
Fax (01584) 876019
🆑 Best Western
Splendid Georgian residence opposite Ludlow Castle and with open views of the countryside from all rooms. Restaurant noted for cuisine.
Bedrooms: 2 single, 6 double, 4 twin
Bathrooms: 12 en-suite

Bed & breakfast per night:

	£min	£max
Single	65.00	75.00
Double	95.00	125.00

Half board per person:

	£min	£max
Daily	65.00	80.00
Weekly	409.50	504.00

Lunch available
Evening meal 1900 (last orders 2100)
Parking for 16
Cards accepted: Amex, Diners, Mastercard, Visa, Switch/Delta

Dinham Weir Hotel and Restaurant 🅜
☆☆☆ COMMENDED
Dinham Bridge, Ludlow SY8 1EH
☎ (01584) 874431
🆑 Logis of GB

Beautifully situated on the banks of the River Teme. All bedrooms with riverside views. Intimate candelit restaurant.
Bedrooms: 4 double, 2 twin
Bathrooms: 6 en-suite

Bed & breakfast per night:

	£min	£max
Single	30.00	55.00
Double	65.00	85.00

Half board per person:

	£min	£max
Daily	45.00	62.50
Weekly	252.00	325.00

Lunch available
Evening meal 1900 (last orders 2030)
Parking for 8
Cards accepted: Amex, Mastercard, Visa

LUDLOW
Continued

The Feathers at Ludlow

⌂⌂⌂ HIGHLY COMMENDED
Bull Ring, Ludlow SY8 1AA
☎ (01584) 875261
Fax (01584) 876030
Ⓡ Regal

Historic inn with Jacobean interior and exterior, sited within the medieval walls of Ludlow, historic capital of the English/Welsh Marches.
Wheelchair access category 3⅃
Bedrooms: 11 single, 15 double, 11 twin, 2 triple
Suites available
Bathrooms: 39 en-suite

Bed & breakfast per night:

	£min	£max
Single	64.25	64.25
Double	88.50	113.50

Half board per person:

	£min	£max
Daily	52.00	67.00
Weekly	327.60	422.10

Lunch available
Evening meal 1900 (last orders 2100)
Parking for 32
Cards accepted: Amex, Diners, Mastercard, Visa, Switch/Delta
⌂⌂⌂⌂⌂⌂⌂⌂⌂⌂⌂⌂⌂⌂⌂⌂⌂⌂ T90⌂⌂ SP ⌂ T

The Moor Hall

⌂⌂⌂ HIGHLY COMMENDED
Cleedownton, Ludlow SY8 3EG
☎ (01584) 823209 & 823333
Fax (01584) 823387

Built c1789 and set in 5 acres of mature grounds with pools, amid unspoilt countryside and yet close to Ludlow. Relaxed, informal atmosphere. Fishing.
Bedrooms: 2 double, 1 twin
Bathrooms: 3 en-suite

Bed & breakfast per night:

	£min	£max
Single	22.00	28.00
Double	25.00	30.00

Half board per person:

	£min	£max
Daily	40.00	45.00

Evening meal 1900 (last orders 2000)
Parking for 12
⌂⌂⌂⌂⌂⌂⌂⌂⌂⌂⌂ T25⌂⌂⌂⌂⌂⌂⌂⌂ SP ⌂ T

Number Twenty Eight

⌂⌂⌂ HIGHLY COMMENDED
28 Lower Broad Street, Ludlow SY8 1PQ
☎ (01584) 876996
Fax (01584) 876996
Email: ross.no28@etinternet.com
Period town houses of great charm and character, centrally situated in old Ludlow town, near river. All rooms individually furnished, providing en-suite accommodation.
Bedrooms: 4 double, 1 twin, 1 triple
Bathrooms: 6 en-suite, 1 public

Bed & breakfast per night:

	£min	£max
Single	35.00	60.00
Double	50.00	65.00

Evening meal 1930 (last orders 2030)
Cards accepted: Amex, Mastercard, Visa
⌂⌂⌂⌂⌂⌂⌂⌂⌂⌂ S ⌂⌂⌂⌂⌂⌂ SP ⌂ T ⌂

Overton Grange Hotel

⌂⌂⌂ COMMENDED
Old Hereford Road, Ludlow SY8 4AD
☎ (01584) 873500
Fax (01584) 873524

Country house hotel in its own grounds, with commanding views over the Shropshire countryside. Noted for cuisine and comfort.
Bedrooms: 1 single, 10 double, 4 twin, 1 triple
Bathrooms: 13 en-suite, 2 public

Bed & breakfast per night:

	£min	£max
Single	40.00	65.00
Double	81.00	92.00

Half board per person:

	£min	£max
Daily	54.00	64.00
Weekly	350.00	

Lunch available
Evening meal 1900 (last orders 2145)
Parking for 80
Cards accepted: Amex, Diners, Mastercard, Visa, Switch/Delta
⌂⌂⌂⌂⌂⌂⌂⌂ S ⌂⌂⌂⌂⌂⌂⌂⌂ T160⌂⌂⌂⌂ DAF ⌂ SP ⌂

MACKWORTH

Derbyshire
Map ref 4B2

An old Roman road lies between Mackworth and Markeaton. Built on the side is All Saints Church with a rare tower.

The Mackworth Hotel

⌂⌂⌂ COMMENDED
Ashbourne Road, Mackworth, Derby DE22 4LY
☎ (01332) 824324
Fax (01332) 824692
Hotel with ample car parking, in a rural setting. Recently refurbished restaurant and bedrooms. Within easy reach of city centre, Peak District and Alton Towers.
Bedrooms: 4 single, 5 double, 1 twin, 3 triple, 1 family room
Bathrooms: 14 en-suite

Bed & breakfast per night:

	£min	£max
Single	32.00	49.00
Double	50.00	70.00

Half board per person:

	£min	£max
Daily	40.00	70.00
Weekly	280.00	490.00

Lunch available
Evening meal 1800 (last orders 2145)
Parking for 80
Cards accepted: Amex, Mastercard, Visa, Switch/Delta
⌂⌂⌂⌂⌂⌂⌂⌂⌂ S ⌂⌂⌂⌂⌂ ⌂ T ⌂⌂⌂⌂ SP T

The map references refer to the colour maps towards the end of the guide. The first figure is the map number; the letter and figure which follow indicate the grid reference on the map.

MALVERN

Hereford and Worcester
Map ref 2B1

Spa town in Victorian times, its water is today bottled and sold worldwide. 6 resorts, set on the slopes of the Hills, form part of Malvern. Great Malvern Priory has splendid 15th C windows. It is an excellent walking centre.
Tourist Information Centre ☎ (01684) 892289 or 862345

Bredon House Hotel
👑👑 COMMENDED

34 Worcester Road, Malvern, Worcestershire WR14 4AA
☎ (01684) 566990
Fax (01684) 575323
Quiet, relaxed and friendly family-run hotel with spectacular views. 100 yards from town centre, Winter Gardens and theatre. Wonderful walks. Car park, pets welcome.
Bedrooms: 2 single, 2 double, 2 twin, 2 triple, 1 family room
Bathrooms: 9 en-suite

Bed & breakfast

per night:	£min	£max
Single	35.00	45.00
Double	45.00	65.00

Parking for 10
Cards accepted: Amex, Mastercard, Visa

🛇📞🖵☎🖥♦🖎🛆🛈Ⓢ⚡🅜🛆🚗 🅳🅰🅿 🆂🅿 🏠 🆃

Colwall Park Hotel 🏔
👑👑👑👑 HIGHLY COMMENDED

Walwyn Road, Colwall, Malvern, Worcestershire WR13 6QG
☎ (01684) 540206 & 541033
Fax (01684) 540847

Charming country house hotel set on the western side of the Malvern Hills. Well-appointed bedrooms. Good views of the hills and mature hotel garden. Enjoy award-winning cuisine in relaxing and comfortable surroundings.
Bedrooms: 3 single, 9 double, 7 twin, 2 triple, 2 family rooms
Suites available
Bathrooms: 23 en-suite

Bed & breakfast

per night:	£min	£max
Single	59.50	75.00
Double	89.50	105.00

Half board per

person:	£min	£max
Daily	59.50	79.50
Weekly	416.50	477.00

Lunch available
Evening meal 1930 (last orders 2100)
Parking for 40
Cards accepted: Amex, Diners, Mastercard, Visa, Switch/Delta

🛇📞🖵☎🖥♦🖎🛈Ⓢ⚡🅜🆃🆅◖🖿 🛆🍴120 ⓊⰂ❀🔆🅢🅟🆃◉

Cotford Hotel 🏔
👑👑👑 COMMENDED

Graham Road, Malvern, Worcestershire WR14 2HU
☎ (01684) 572427 & 574680
Fax (01684) 572952
Peaceful situation near town centre and hills. Ample car parking, good food, good service and value for money.
Bedrooms: 8 single, 3 double, 1 twin, 4 triple
Bathrooms: 16 en-suite, 1 public

Bed & breakfast

per night:	£min	£max
Single	40.00	45.00
Double	60.00	65.00

Half board per

person:	£min	£max
Daily	45.00	60.00

Evening meal 1900 (last orders 2100)
Parking for 14
Cards accepted: Mastercard, Visa, Switch/Delta

🛇📞🖵☎🖥♦🖈Ⓢ⚡🅜🖿🛆🍴14 ◖❀🚗🅢🅟🏠🆃

The Cottage in the Wood Hotel 🏔
👑👑👑 HIGHLY COMMENDED

Holywell Road, Malvern Wells, Malvern, Worcestershire WR14 4LG
☎ (01684) 575859
Fax (01684) 560662
Ⓒ Best Western

Set high on the Malvern Hills with 30-mile views to the Cotswolds. All en-suite. Family owned and run. Exceptional food. Daily half board prices based on minimum 2-night stay. Weekly is 7 nights for price of 6. Breaks available all week, all year.
Bedrooms: 16 double, 4 twin
Bathrooms: 20 en-suite

Bed & breakfast

per night:	£min	£max
Single	70.00	76.00
Double	89.00	140.00

Half board per

person:	£min	£max
Daily	52.00	80.00
Weekly	312.00	480.00

Lunch available
Evening meal 1900 (last orders 2100)
Parking for 40
Cards accepted: Amex, Mastercard, Visa, Switch/Delta

🛇♨🖨🛆☎🖥♦🖈🛈Ⓢ⚡🅜🖿 🛆🍴16 🎋ⓊⰂ❀🚗🅢🅟🏠🆃🌀

Elm Bank 🏔
👑👑 COMMENDED

52 Worcester Road, Malvern, Worcestershire WR14 4AB
☎ (01684) 566051
Elegant late Regency house, with en-suite bedrooms enjoying breathtaking views. Close to town centre, Malvern Hills and Three Counties Showground.
Bedrooms: 3 double, 1 twin, 2 triple
Bathrooms: 5 en-suite, 1 private

Bed & breakfast

per night:	£min	£max
Single	24.00	35.00
Double	35.00	48.00

Parking for 9
Cards accepted: Amex

🛇🖵♦🖈⚡🅜🖿🛆🚗🛈🅢🅟🏠 🌀

Great Malvern Hotel 🏔
👑👑 COMMENDED

Graham Road, Malvern, Worcestershire WR14 2HN
☎ (01684) 563411
Fax (01684) 560514
In Malvern's central conservation area, close to the Priory and Winter Gardens, this early Victorian hotel was refurbished in 1997. Run by the proprietors.
Bedrooms: 1 single, 8 double, 2 twin, 3 triple
Bathrooms: 13 en-suite, 1 private

Bed & breakfast

per night:	£min	£max
Single	40.00	51.00
Double	65.00	75.00

Lunch available
Evening meal 1800 (last orders 2100)
Parking for 9
Cards accepted: Amex, Diners, Mastercard, Visa

🛇📞🖵☎🖥♦🖎🛈Ⓢ⚡🅜🎚🖿🛆 🍴50▶⚔🅢🅟🏠🆃

MALVERN

Continued

Harcourt Cottage 🅰🅰

⌂⌂⌂ COMMENDED

252 West Malvern Road, West Malvern, Malvern, Worcestershire WR14 4DQ
☎ (01684) 574561
Nestling on the west side of the Malvern Hills, well placed for walking holidays or as a base for touring. English and French cuisine.
Bedrooms: 2 double, 1 twin
Bathrooms: 3 en-suite

Bed & breakfast

per night:	£min	£max
Double	38.00	40.00

Half board per person:

	£min	£max
Daily	28.00	29.00
Weekly	180.00	185.00

Evening meal 1845 (last orders 1800)
Parking for 3
🛏🚭🛁♨S✕🎿🅿TV▥🖨❋✗🚗
SP

Holdfast Cottage Hotel 🅰🅰

⌂⌂⌂ HIGHLY COMMENDED

Marlbank Road, Little Malvern, Malvern, Worcestershire WR13 6NA
☎ (01684) 310288
Fax (01684) 311117
Ⓒ Logis of GB

Small oak-beamed country house set in 2 acres of gardens at the foot of the Malvern Hills. Pretty bedrooms, log fires, wonderful views. Award-winning restaurant.
Bedrooms: 1 single, 5 double, 2 twin
Bathrooms: 8 en-suite, 1 public

Bed & breakfast

per night:	£min	£max
Single	42.00	
Double	84.00	

Half board per person:

	£min	£max
Daily	56.00	58.00
Weekly	336.00	348.00

Evening meal 1900 (last orders 2100)
Parking for 20
Cards accepted: Mastercard, Visa, Switch/Delta
🛏🚭📞🖷🖵♨🕮🛎S✕🎿▥🖨
🍴12❋✗🚗❄SP🏠T◎

Malvern Hills Hotel 🅰🅰

⌂⌂⌂⌂ COMMENDED

British Camp, Wynd's Point, Malvern, Worcestershire WR13 6DW
☎ (01684) 540237 & 540690
Fax (01684) 540327

Enchanting hotel sitting atop the Malvern Hills. Magnificent views, prettily decorated en-suite rooms, oak panelled lounge, friendly and efficient staff.
Bedrooms: 2 single, 6 double, 7 twin, 2 triple
Bathrooms: 17 en-suite

Bed & breakfast

per night:	£min	£max
Single	40.00	50.00
Double	65.00	75.00

Half board per person:

	£min	£max
Daily	55.00	70.00
Weekly	350.00	400.00

Lunch available
Evening meal 1900 (last orders 2130)
Parking for 30
Cards accepted: Mastercard, Visa
🛏🚭📞🖷🖵♨🕮🛎S✕🎿TV
🍴❋60❋DAP❄SP🏠T

Mount Pleasant Hotel 🅰🅰

⌂⌂⌂ COMMENDED

Belle Vue Terrace, Malvern, Worcestershire WR14 4PZ
☎ (01684) 561837
Fax (01684) 569968
Ⓒ Logis of GB/The Independents

Georgian building with Orangery, in 1.5 acres of garden with beautiful views. Close to theatre and shops and with direct access to Malvern Hills.
Bedrooms: 3 single, 7 double, 5 twin
Bathrooms: 14 en-suite, 1 private, 1 public

Bed & breakfast

per night:	£min	£max
Single	42.50	54.50
Double	62.50	82.50

Half board per person:

	£min	£max
Daily	42.50	49.50
Weekly	250.00	305.00

Lunch available
Evening meal 1900 (last orders 2130)
Parking for 20
Cards accepted: Amex, Diners, Mastercard, Visa
🛏🚭📞🖷🖵♨🕮🛎S▥🖨🍴80
❋✗DAP❄SP🏠T

MANSFIELD

Nottinghamshire
Map ref 4C2

Ancient town, now an industrial and shopping centre, with a popular market, in the heart of Robin Hood country. There is an impressive 19th C railway viaduct, 2 interesting churches, an 18th C Moot Hall and a museum and art gallery.

The Fringe Hotel and Leisure Complex 🅰🅰

⌂⌂⌂ COMMENDED

Briar Lane, Mansfield NG18 3HS
☎ (01623) 641337
Fax (01623) 27521
Modern, well-equipped hotel with extensive leisure facilities including squash, tennis, gymnasium and sunbeds. Comfortable, pleasant interior and friendly service.
Bedrooms: 6 single, 3 double, 6 twin
Bathrooms: 15 en-suite

Bed & breakfast

per night:	£min	£max
Single	25.00	47.00
Double	50.00	60.00

Half board per person:

	£min	£max
Daily	35.00	57.00

Lunch available
Evening meal 1900 (last orders 2200)
Parking for 140
Cards accepted: Amex, Mastercard, Visa, Switch/Delta
🛏🚭📞🖷🖵♨🕮🛎S🎿TV▥🖨
🍴30❋✗♣🎣♨✗SP

Pine Lodge Hotel 🅰🅰

⌂⌂⌂ COMMENDED

281-283 Nottingham Road, Mansfield NG18 4SE
☎ (01623) 22308
Fax (01623) 656819
Friendly and informal. Good food, good value, excellent service.
Bedrooms: 5 single, 5 double, 7 twin, 2 triple
Bathrooms: 19 en-suite

Bed & breakfast per night:	£min	£max
Single	25.00	49.95
Double	40.00	59.95

Half board per person:	£min	£max
Daily	33.00	63.00
Weekly	281.00	

Lunch available
Evening meal 1900 (last orders 2100)
Parking for 35
Cards accepted: Amex, Diners, Mastercard, Visa, Switch/Delta

🐎🏛🛁&📞🖂🖵👤🛐Ⓢ💆📺🖳🖊
🍴40🌀❀✶🐾🌿 SP T

MARKET DRAYTON

Shropshire
Map ref 4A2

Old market town with black and white buildings and 17th C houses, also acclaimed for its gingerbread. Hodnet Hall is in the vicinity with its beautiful landscaped gardens covering 60 acres.
Tourist Information Centre ☎ (01630) 652139

The Bear Hotel 🄼

😃😃😃 COMMENDED

Hodnet, Market Drayton TF9 3NH
☎ (01630) 685214 & 685788
Fax (01630) 685787

Privately owned 16th C inn, with the character of a bygone age but 20th C comforts, and a warm and friendly atmosphere. Oak-beamed, open fires.
Bedrooms: 1 single, 3 double, 2 twin
Bathrooms: 6 en-suite

Bed & breakfast per night:	£min	£max
Single	30.00	32.50
Double	50.00	60.00

Half board per person:	£min	£max
Daily	40.00	

Lunch available
Evening meal 1900 (last orders 2145)
Parking for 100
Cards accepted: Amex, Mastercard, Visa, Switch/Delta

🐎🏛📞🖂🖵👤🛐Ⓢ💆📺🖳🖊
🍴100🍺🙂☕❀✶🐾🌿 DAP 🌿 SP 🏮 T

MARKFIELD

Leicestershire
Map ref 4C3

Field Head Hotel 🄼

Markfield Lane, Markfield, Leicester LE67 9PS
☎ (01530) 245454
Fax (01530) 243740
® Countryside
Located on the A50, 1 mile from junction 22 off the M1. Originally an old farmhouse, the hotel has been built in local stone. Half board prices shown apply at weekends.
Wheelchair access category 3 ♿
Bedrooms: 11 double, 16 twin, 1 triple
Bathrooms: 28 private

Bed & breakfast per night:	£min	£max
Single	33.50	69.00
Double	42.00	79.00

Half board per person:	£min	£max
Daily	28.00	36.00

Lunch available
Evening meal 1900 (last orders 2200)
Parking for 90
Cards accepted: Amex, Diners, Mastercard, Visa, Switch/Delta

🐎🏛🛁📞🖂🖵👤🛐Ⓢ💆📺Ⓞ
🖳🖊🍴60🍴❀✶🌿 SP 🏮

MATLOCK

Derbyshire
Map ref 4B2

The town lies beside the narrow valley of the River Derwent surrounded by steep wooded hills. Good centre for exploring Derbyshire's best scenery.

Jackson Tor House Hotel 🄼

😃😃 APPROVED

76 Jackson Road, Matlock DE4 3JQ
☎ (01629) 582348
Fax (01629) 582348
Family-run hotel overlooking Matlock. Ideal for touring the National Park, many historic houses and picturesque countryside.
Bedrooms: 11 single, 7 double, 9 twin, 2 family rooms
Bathrooms: 13 en-suite, 7 public

Bed & breakfast per night:	£min	£max
Single	15.00	30.00
Double	30.00	60.00

Half board per person:	£min	£max
Daily	23.00	38.00

Evening meal 1930 (last orders 2030)
Parking for 25
Cards accepted: Mastercard, Visa

🐎🏛🛁📞🖵👤🛐Ⓢ💆📺🖳✶🍴🏮

Lane End House 🄼

😃😃 HIGHLY COMMENDED

Green Lane, Tansley, Matlock DE4 5FJ
☎ (01629) 583981
Fax (01629) 583981
Georgian farmhouse, c.1730. Non-smoking. Every comfort, super healthy food and good wine cellar. Idyllically situated with spectacular views to Riber Castle. Close to Chatsworth, Haddon, Hardwick.
Bedrooms: 3 double, 1 twin
Bathrooms: 2 en-suite, 2 private

Bed & breakfast per night:	£min	£max
Single	30.00	35.00
Double	46.00	57.00

Evening meal 1930 (last orders 1900)
Parking for 6
Cards accepted: Mastercard, Visa

🐎🏛🛁📞🖂🖵👤🛐Ⓢ💆📺🖳🖊
🍽❀🐾 DAP SP T

Riber Hall 🄼

😃😃😃 HIGHLY COMMENDED

Matlock DE4 5JU
☎ (01629) 582795
Fax (01629) 580475
Enjoy pure tranquillity in the intimate atmosphere of this historic Derbyshire country house. B&B prices shown include Continental breakfast (full English £8 pp extra). Half board prices include full English breakfast.
Bedrooms: 14 double
Bathrooms: 14 en-suite

Bed & breakfast per night:	£min	£max
Single	87.50	101.50
Double	108.00	153.00

Half board per person:	£min	£max
Daily	84.00	106.50

Lunch available
Evening meal 1900 (last orders 2130)
Parking for 50
Cards accepted: Amex, Diners, Mastercard, Visa, Switch/Delta

🐎10🏛📞🖂🖵👤🛐Ⓢ💆
🖳🖊🍴20☕❀✶🐾 SP 🏮 T

Establishments should be open throughout the year, unless otherwise stated.

MATLOCK

Continued

Robertswood ♠

ꗬ ꗬ ꗬ COMMENDED

Farley Hill, Matlock DE4 3LL
☎ (01629) 55642
Fax (01629) 55642
Spacious Victorian residence on the edge of Matlock, with panoramic views. Near Chatsworth. All bedrooms en-suite. Friendly, warm welcome.
Bedrooms: 6 double, 2 twin
Bathrooms: 8 en-suite

Bed & breakfast per night:

	£min	£max
Single	35.00	38.00
Double	46.00	50.00

Half board per person:

	£min	£max
Daily	35.00	37.00
Weekly	245.00	259.00

Evening meal 1830 (last orders 1900)
Parking for 12
Cards accepted: Mastercard, Visa

☐▨⌨❄♦🛡S⌇꜀TV▥◨🖊
♿✿✈🚲SP

The Tavern

Listed COMMENDED

Nottingham Road, Tansley, Matlock DE4 5FR
☎ (01629) 57735 & 57840
17th C country village inn serving real ales and with extensive lunch and dinner menus. Close to the main road, M1 and numerous places of local interest.
Bedrooms: 1 double, 1 twin
Bathrooms: 2 en-suite

Bed & breakfast per night:

	£min	£max
Single	25.00	25.00
Double	35.00	35.00

Half board per person:

	£min	£max
Daily	32.50	32.50
Weekly	199.00	199.00

Lunch available
Evening meal 1830 (last orders 2130)
Parking for 60
Cards accepted: Mastercard, Visa

☐⌨♦S▥◨🖊✈🚲🐾🏯

COLOUR MAPS

Colour maps at the back of this guide pinpoint all places in which you will find accommodation listed.

Winstaff Guesthouse ♠

ꗬ ꗬ COMMENDED

Derwent Avenue, (Off Old English Road), Matlock DE4 3LX
☎ (01629) 582593
In a pleasant, quiet cul-de-sac, with a garden backing on to the River Derwent and the park, central for many tourist attractions. Private forecourt parking. Colour TV in all rooms.
Bedrooms: 5 double, 1 twin, 1 triple
Bathrooms: 3 en-suite, 1 public

Bed & breakfast per night:

	£min	£max
Single	18.00	20.50
Double	36.00	41.00

Parking for 6

☐▨♦UL🛡S⌇꜀TV▥◨🖊✿
OAP☕

MATLOCK BATH

Derbyshire
Map ref 4B2

19th C spa town with many attractions including several caverns to visit, a lead mining museum and a family fun park. There are marvellous views over the surrounding countryside from the Heights of Abraham, to which a cable car gives easy access.
Tourist Information Centre ☎ (01629) 55082

Hodgkinsons Hotel ♠

ꗬ ꗬ COMMENDED

150 South Parade, Matlock Bath, Matlock DE4 3NR
☎ (01629) 582170
Fax (01629) 584891
Georgian hotel, beautifully restored, with original features. Open fires, antique shop and hairdressing salon. Terraced garden with lovely views.
Bedrooms: 1 single, 6 double
Bathrooms: 7 en-suite

Bed & breakfast per night:

	£min	£max
Single	30.00	35.00
Double	50.00	90.00

Half board per person:

	£min	£max
Daily	49.50	94.50
Weekly	270.00	774.00

Evening meal 1930 (last orders 2100)
Parking for 6
Cards accepted: Amex, Mastercard, Visa, Switch/Delta

☐▨🍴⌨☐♦S▥◑▥◨🖊
♿✿SP🏯Ⓣ

Temple Hotel ♠

ꗬ ꗬ ꗬ ꗬ COMMENDED

Temple Walk, Matlock Bath, Matlock DE4 3PG
☎ (01629) 583911
Fax (01629) 580851

The hotel nestles comfortably amid "Little Switzerland" scenery of picturesque Matlock Bath, overlooking the Vale of the River Derwent from a steep, wooded hillside. All bedrooms en-suite with colour TV.
Bedrooms: 1 single, 10 double, 3 twin
Bathrooms: 14 en-suite

Bed & breakfast per night:

	£min	£max
Single	39.00	45.00
Double	61.00	66.00

Half board per person:

	£min	£max
Daily	44.00	47.00

Lunch available
Evening meal 1800 (last orders 2100)
Parking for 45
Cards accepted: Amex, Diners, Mastercard, Visa

☐▨🍴⌨☐♦🛡S⌇꜀◑▥◨🖊
🛎60▸✿✈🚲🏯

MEDBOURNE

Leicestershire
Map ref 4C3

Picturesque village with medieval bridge.

Homestead House

ꗬ ꗬ HIGHLY COMMENDED

5 Ashley Road, Medbourne, Market Harborough LE16 8DL
☎ (01858) 565724
Fax (01858) 565324
In an elevated position overlooking the Welland Valley on the outskirts of Medbourne, a picturesque village dating back to Roman times.
Bedrooms: 3 twin
Bathrooms: 3 en-suite

Bed & breakfast per night:

	£min	£max
Single	24.00	26.00
Double	38.00	40.00

Half board per person:

	£min	£max
Daily	34.00	

Evening meal 1800 (last orders 2000)
Parking for 6
Cards accepted: Mastercard, Visa

MELTON MOWBRAY

Leicestershire
Map ref 4C3

Close to the attractive Vale of Belvoir and famous for its pork pies and Stilton cheese which are the subjects of special displays in the museum. It has a beautiful church with a tower 100 ft high.
Tourist Information Centre ☎ (01664) 480992

Quorn Lodge Hotel

COMMENDED

46 Asfordby Road, Melton Mowbray LE13 0HR
☎ (01664) 66660 & 62590
Fax (01664) 480660
Originally a hunting lodge. Short walk from busy market town. Family owned and run. Restaurant overlooking garden serving a la carte and table d'hote meals. Large car park.
Bedrooms: 6 single, 8 double, 3 twin, 1 triple
Bathrooms: 18 en-suite

Bed & breakfast per night:

	£min	£max
Single	37.50	49.50
Double	50.00	65.00

Half board per person:

	£min	£max
Daily	40.50	48.00

Lunch available
Evening meal 1900 (last orders 2100)
Parking for 33
Cards accepted: Mastercard, Visa, Switch/Delta

Sysonby Knoll Hotel

COMMENDED

Asfordby Road, Melton Mowbray LE13 0HP
☎ (01664) 63563
Fax (01664) 410364
Logis of GB
Friendly, family-run hotel set in its own grounds with river frontage. Tastefully extended, offering comfortable accommodation and good food, both lunchtime and evening. Dogs welcome.
Bedrooms: 6 single, 10 double, 6 twin, 2 triple
Bathrooms: 24 en-suite

Bed & breakfast per night:

	£min	£max
Single	38.00	54.50
Double	54.00	63.00

Lunch available
Evening meal 1900 (last orders 2100)
Parking for 30
Cards accepted: Amex, Diners, Mastercard, Visa, Switch/Delta

MERIDEN

West Midlands
Map ref 4B3

Village halfway between Coventry and Birmingham. Said to be the centre of England, marked by a cross on the green.

Meriden Hotel

APPROVED

Main Road, Meriden, Solihull, Coventry CV7 7NH
☎ (01676) 522005
Fax (01676) 523744
Family-run hotel near National Exhibition Centre and Birmingham Airport. Convenient for Coventry, Birmingham, Solihull and surrounding districts.
Bedrooms: 6 single, 4 double, 5 twin
Bathrooms: 12 en-suite, 3 private

Bed & breakfast per night:

	£min	£max
Single	34.00	40.00
Double	55.00	70.00

Lunch available
Evening meal 1800 (last orders 2200)
Parking for 15
Cards accepted: Amex, Diners, Mastercard, Visa, Switch/Delta

MORETON-IN-MARSH

Gloucestershire
Map ref 2B1

Attractive town of Cotswold stone with 17th C houses, an ideal base for touring the Cotswolds. Some of the local attractions include Batsford Park Arboretum, the Jacobean Chastleton House and Sezincote Garden.

Blue Cedar House

COMMENDED

Stow Road, Moreton-in-Marsh GL56 0DW
☎ (01608) 650299
Attractive detached residence set in

half-acre garden in the Cotswolds, with pleasantly decorated, well-equipped accommodation and garden room. Complimentary tea/coffee. Close to village centre.
Bedrooms: 1 single, 1 double, 1 twin, 1 family room
Bathrooms: 2 en-suite, 2 public

Bed & breakfast per night:

	£min	£max
Single	19.00	
Double	36.00	44.00

Half board per person:

	£min	£max
Daily	27.00	31.00

Evening meal 1800 (last orders 1800)
Parking for 7
Open February–November

Moreton House

APPROVED

Moreton-in-Marsh GL56 0LQ
☎ (01608) 650747
Fax (01608) 652747
Family-run guesthouse providing full English breakfast and optional evening meal. Tea shop, open 6 days a week, lounge bar with restaurant. Ideal for touring the Cotswolds. Children and dogs welcome.
Bedrooms: 2 single, 7 double, 2 twin
Bathrooms: 7 en-suite, 2 public

Bed & breakfast per night:

	£min	£max
Single	22.00	22.00
Double	42.00	60.00

Half board per person:

	£min	£max
Daily	32.00	40.00
Weekly	212.80	266.00

Lunch available
Evening meal 1800 (last orders 2030)
Parking for 5
Cards accepted: Mastercard, Visa

Map references apply to the colour maps at the back of this guide.

The National Grading and Classification Scheme is explained at the back of this guide.

MUCH WENLOCK

Shropshire
Map ref 4A3

Small town close to Wenlock Edge in beautiful scenery and full of interest. In particular there are the remains of an 11th C priory with fine carving and the black and white 16th C Guildhall.

Gaskell Arms Hotel ⚑
👑👑 APPROVED

Much Wenlock TF13 6HF
☎ (01952) 727212
Fax (01952) 727736
17th C coaching inn built of stone and brick, with beamed ceilings, log fires. Family-run freehouse. Situated on outskirts of small medieval town and Wenlock Edge, close to Ironbridge.
Bedrooms: 7 double, 3 twin, 1 family room
Bathrooms: 6 en-suite, 2 public

Bed & breakfast

per night:	£min	£max
Single	29.00	39.00
Double	48.00	60.00

Half board per

person:	£min	£max
Daily	34.00	55.00
Weekly	215.00	355.00

Lunch available
Evening meal 1900 (last orders 2200)
Parking for 31
Cards accepted: Amex, Mastercard, Visa, Switch/Delta

🛉🌤📞🖵🖥🐾🗔📺🖵🖧♿️🍴🎱20♿️❄
✖️ OAP SP 🏠 T

Raven Hotel & Restaurant ⚑
👑👑👑 HIGHLY COMMENDED

Barrow Street, Much Wenlock
TF13 6EN
☎ (01952) 727251
Fax (01952) 728416

A fine coaching inn which has provided hospitality since 1700. Beautifully appointed accommodation, making this an ideal base for discovering Shropshire. Close to Ironbridge Gorge.
Bedrooms: 1 single, 11 double, 3 twin
Suite available
Bathrooms: 15 en-suite

Bed & breakfast

per night:	£min	£max
Single	48.00	55.00
Double	85.00	110.00

Half board per

person:	£min	£max
Daily	68.00	80.00

Lunch available
Evening meal 1900 (last orders 2115)
Parking for 30
Cards accepted: Amex, Diners, Mastercard, Visa, Switch/Delta

🛉🌤📞🖵🖥🐾🗔♿️S✖️🖵🖧🖵
🍴15♿️❄✖️🚗 SP 🏠

NEWARK

Nottinghamshire
Map ref 4C2

The town has many fine old houses and ancient inns near the large, cobbled market-place. Substantial ruins of the 12th C castle, where King John died, dominate the riverside walk and there are several interesting museums. Sherwood Forest is nearby.
Tourist Information Centre ☎ (01636) 78962

The Grange Hotel ⚑
👑👑👑 COMMENDED

73 London Road, Newark
NG24 1RZ
☎ (01636) 703399
Fax (01636) 702328
Family-run hotel with en-suite rooms, candlelit restaurant and excellent food. Spacious restaurant and bar with good selection of wines and malt whiskies. Car park.
Bedrooms: 2 single, 9 double, 3 twin, 1 triple
Bathrooms: 15 en-suite

Bed & breakfast

per night:	£min	£max
Single	45.00	55.00
Double	62.50	72.95

Half board per

person:	£min	£max
Daily	57.95	67.95

Lunch available
Evening meal 1900 (last orders 2100)
Parking for 18
Cards accepted: Amex, Mastercard, Visa, Switch/Delta

🛉🌤📞🖵🖥🐾🗔♿️S✖️🖵📺🖧
🖵🍴20👣❄✖️🚗 SP

> Please mention this guide when making your booking.

South Parade Hotel ⚑
👑👑 COMMENDED

117 Balderton Gate, Newark
NG24 1RY
☎ (01636) 703008
Fax (01636) 605593
🆗 The Independents
Family-run Georgian listed hotel in quiet location, 5 minutes' walk from market place. Good home-cooked food. All rooms, restaurant and bar recently renovated, refurbished and redecorated. Car park.
Bedrooms: 5 single, 5 double, 1 twin, 2 triple, 1 family room
Bathrooms: 13 en-suite, 1 private, 3 public

Bed & breakfast

per night:	£min	£max
Single	39.50	42.00
Double	54.00	64.50

Half board per

person:	£min	£max
Daily	52.00	55.00

Lunch available
Evening meal 1900 (last orders 2045)
Parking for 14
Cards accepted: Amex, Mastercard, Visa, Switch/Delta

🛥🛉📞🖵🖥🐾🗔S✖️📺🖧◐
🖵🍴20 SP 🏠 T

Willow Tree Inn ⚑
👑👑 COMMENDED

Front Street, Barnby-in-the-Willows, Newark NG24 2SA
☎ (01636) 626613
Fax (01636) 626060

17th C village inn, conveniently placed for historic Lincoln, Grantham, Newark and Sherwood. Known locally for good food and ales. Off the A17 and A1.
Bedrooms: 3 single, 1 double, 3 triple
Bathrooms: 7 en-suite

Bed & breakfast

per night:	£min	£max
Single	35.00	
Double	45.00	

Lunch available
Evening meal 1900 (last orders 2130)
Parking for 50
Cards accepted: Amex, Mastercard, Visa

🛥🛉🖵🖥🐾🗔S✖️🖵🍴120♿️♿️
❄🚗🐾🏠

NEWCASTLE-UNDER-LYME

Staffordshire
Map ref 4B2

Industrial town whose museum and art gallery give evidence of its past. The Guildhall was built in the 18th C and there is the modern University of Keele.
Tourist Information Centre ☎ (01782) 297313

Borough Arms Hotel Ⓜ

🏵🏵🏵 APPROVED

King Street, Newcastle-under-Lyme ST5 1HX
☎ (01782) 629421
Fax (01782) 712388
Ⓒ Consort
Former coaching inn, on the outskirts of Newcastle-under-Lyme and close to the Potteries and Alton Towers.
Bedrooms: 26 single, 6 double, 10 twin, 1 triple, 2 family rooms
Bathrooms: 45 en-suite

Bed & breakfast

per night:	£min	£max
Single	30.00	49.00
Double	45.00	65.00

Half board per person:

	£min	£max
Daily	45.00	60.00

Lunch available
Evening meal 1900 (last orders 2130)
Parking for 45
Cards accepted: Amex, Diners, Mastercard, Visa, Switch/Delta
🛇🕭🖦🖵📞♿🛈Ⓢ📺◐🛏🍴90 ✠ DAP SP

NEWENT

Gloucestershire
Map ref 2B1

Small town with the largest collection of birds of prey in Europe at the Falconry Centre. Flying demonstrations daily. Glass workshop where visitors can watch glass being blown. There is a "seconds" shop. North of the village is the Three Choirs Vineyards.
Tourist Information Centre ☎ (01531) 822468

George Hotel

🏵🏵 APPROVED

Church Street, Newent GL18 1PU
☎ (01531) 820203
Fax (01531) 822899
Family-run 17th C coaching house in Newent town centre, offering bed and breakfast (some en-suite) and extensive bar and restaurant menus. In Good Beer Guide.

Bedrooms: 2 double, 5 twin, 2 triple
Bathrooms: 3 en-suite, 4 public

Bed & breakfast

per night:	£min	£max
Single	18.00	25.00
Double	30.00	37.00

Lunch available
Evening meal 1900 (last orders 2200)
Parking for 12
Cards accepted: Mastercard, Visa
🛇🖵♿🛈Ⓢ📺🛏📞🍴120 DAP 🛇 SP 🏠

Old Court Hotel

🏵🏵 APPROVED

Church Street, Newent GL18 1AB
☎ (01531) 820522

Magnificent manor house in 1 acre of walled gardens. Friendly, relaxed atmosphere in elegant surroundings. Super food. Four poster available. Central for Wye Valley and Cotswolds.
Bedrooms: 3 double, 1 twin, 1 triple
Bathrooms: 4 en-suite, 1 private

Bed & breakfast

per night:	£min	£max
Single	25.00	39.50
Double	45.00	69.50

Half board per person:

	£min	£max
Daily	38.75	53.25
Weekly	236.25	313.25

Evening meal 1930 (last orders 2030)
Parking for 21
Cards accepted: Amex, Mastercard, Visa, Switch/Delta
🛇🖦🗝🖵♿🏧🛈Ⓢ✂🛏🍴40 ✿🐎🛇 SP 🏠

NEWPORT

Shropshire
Map ref 4A3

Small market town on the Shropshire Union Canal has a wide High Street and a church with some interesting monuments. Newport is close to Aqualate Mere which is the largest lake in Staffordshire.

Norwood House Hotel and Restaurant Ⓜ

🏵🏵🏵 APPROVED

Pave Lane, Newport TF10 9LQ
☎ (01952) 825896
Hotel of character just off the A41

Whitchurch to Wolverhampton road, close to Lilleshall National Sports Centre.
Bedrooms: 1 single, 2 double, 2 twin, 1 triple
Bathrooms: 6 en-suite

Bed & breakfast

per night:	£min	£max
Single	25.00	30.00
Double	35.00	39.00

Lunch available
Evening meal 1900 (last orders 2200)
Parking for 26
Cards accepted: Amex, Mastercard, Visa
🛇🖦♿🛈Ⓢ🛏🖦🛏 DAP SP

NORTHAMPTON

Northamptonshire
Map ref 2C1

A bustling town and a shoe manufacturing centre, with excellent shopping facilities, several museums and parks, a theatre and a concert hall. Several old churches include 1 of only 4 round churches in Britain.
Tourist Information Centre ☎ (01604) 22677

Aarandale Regent Hotel and Guesthouse Ⓜ

🏵 APPROVED

6-8 Royal Terrace, Barrack Road (A508), Northampton NN1 3RF
☎ (01604) 31096
Fax (01604) 21035
Small and cosy, family-run hotel/guesthouse within easy walking distance of town centre, bus and train stations.
Bedrooms: 4 single, 6 double, 6 twin, 4 triple
Bathrooms: 5 public

Bed & breakfast

per night:	£min	£max
Single	22.00	26.00
Double	35.00	41.00

Evening meal 1930 (last orders 2130)
Parking for 14
Cards accepted: Amex, Diners, Mastercard, Visa
🛇🖦🖵♿🛈Ⓢ🛏📺🛏🛏 DAP SP Ⓣ

NORTHAMPTON

Continued

Broomhill Country House Hotel and Restaurant 🅰

👑👑👑👑 COMMENDED

Holdenby Road, Spratton, Northampton NN6 8LD
☎ (01604) 845959
Fax (01604) 845834

Converted Victorian country house with some splendid views. As a welcomed guest you will be offered relaxed, old fashioned hospitality, while chef will tempt you with his interesting and varied menus. 6 miles north of Northampton, 6 miles from A14.

Bedrooms: 2 single, 4 double, 7 twin
Bathrooms: 13 en-suite

Bed & breakfast per night:	£min	£max
Single	37.00	65.00
Double	65.00	75.00

Lunch available
Evening meal 1900 (last orders 2145)
Parking for 100
Cards accepted: Amex, Diners, Mastercard, Visa

🐎📞📠🖥☕🔒[S]♨👔🍸45 🏃🔑
U⛳✿[SP][T]

Lime Trees Hotel 🅰

👑👑👑👑 COMMENDED

8 Langham Place, Barrack Road, Northampton NN2 6AA
☎ (01604) 32188
Fax (01604) 233012
[CR] The Independents

Delightful hotel in conservation area. Owner-managed with great care. Fine restaurant. Secure courtyard car park. Half a mile from town centre.

Bedrooms: 7 single, 13 double, 1 twin, 2 triple
Bathrooms: 23 en-suite, 1 public

Bed & breakfast per night:	£min	£max
Single	45.00	69.00
Double	57.50	85.00

Half board per person:	£min	£max
Daily	60.00	87.00

Lunch available
Evening meal 1900 (last orders 2100)
Parking for 24
Cards accepted: Amex, Diners, Mastercard, Visa, Switch/Delta

🐎🛏📠📞📠🖥☕💨🔒[S]🚭[R][TV]
◐♨👔🍸60[DAP][SP]🏛[T]

Poplars Hotel

👑👑👑 COMMENDED

Cross Street, Moulton, Northampton NN3 7RZ
☎ (01604) 643983
Fax (01604) 790233

Personal attention is given at this small country hotel in the heart of Northamptonshire. Within easy reach of many tourist attractions.

Bedrooms: 6 single, 4 double, 1 twin, 7 family rooms
Bathrooms: 14 en-suite, 2 public, 4 private showers

Bed & breakfast per night:	£min	£max
Single	25.00	42.50
Double	47.50	55.00

Evening meal 1830 (last orders 2000)
Parking for 21
Cards accepted: Amex, Mastercard, Visa

🐎🛏📞🖥☕💨🔒[S]🚭[R][TV]♨👔
U✿[SP]🏛[T]

NORTHLEACH

Gloucestershire
Map ref 2B1

Village famous for its beautiful 15th C wool church with its lovely porch and interesting interior. There are also some fine houses including a 17th C wool merchant's house containing Keith Harding's World of Mechanical Music. The Cotswold Countryside Collection is in the former prison.

Northfield Bed & Breakfast 🅰

👑👑👑 COMMENDED

Cirencester Road (A429), Northleach, Cheltenham GL54 3JL
☎ (01451) 860427
Email: nrth-fieldo@aol.com

Detached family house in the country with large gardens and home-grown produce. Excellent centre for visiting the Cotswolds and close to local services.

Bedrooms: 1 double, 2 family rooms
Bathrooms: 3 en-suite

Bed & breakfast per night:	£min	£max
Single	26.00	28.00
Double	45.00	48.00

Half board per person:	£min	£max
Daily	40.00	

Evening meal 1800 (last orders 1900)
Parking for 10

🐎🛏📠🖥☕💨🔒[S]🚭[R][TV]♨👔
U✿🐕🚐[SP]

NORTHMOOR

Oxfordshire
Map ref 2C1

The Ferryman Inn

See South of England region for full entry details

NOTTINGHAM

Nottinghamshire
Map ref 4C2

Attractive modern city with a rich history. Outside its castle, now a museum, is Robin Hood's statue. Attractions include "The Tales of Robin Hood"; the Lace Hall; Wollaton Hall; museums and excellent facilities for shopping, sports and entertainment.
Tourist Information Centre ☎ (0115) 947 0661

Clifton Hotel 🅰

👑👑 APPROVED

126 Nottingham Road, Long Eaton, Nottingham NG10 2BZ
☎ (0115) 973 4277

Friendly, family-run hotel close to M1, exit 25. 10 minutes from Donington Racecourse, East Midlands International Airport, Derby and Nottingham.

Bedrooms: 5 single, 2 double, 1 twin, 2 triple
Bathrooms: 2 en-suite, 2 public

Bed & breakfast per night:	£min	£max
Single	19.00	26.00
Double	28.00	34.00

Half board per person:	£min	£max
Daily	27.00	42.00

Evening meal 1830 (last orders 1730)
Parking for 25

🐎🛏🖥☕🔒[S][R][TV]♨👔🐕🚐

A key to symbols can be found inside the back cover flap.

National gradings and classifications were correct at the time of going to press but are subject to change. Please check at the time of booking.

Fairhaven Private Hotel

👑 APPROVED

19 Meadow Road, Beeston Rylands,
Nottingham NG9 1JP
☎ (0115) 922 7509
*Family-run private hotel close to the
university and rail station, midway
between the M1 and Nottingham city
centre.*
Bedrooms: 5 single, 4 double, 2 twin,
1 triple
Bathrooms: 4 en-suite, 3 public

Bed & breakfast per night:	£min	£max
Single	21.00	30.00
Double	30.00	44.00

Evening meal 1800 (last orders
1400)
Parking for 12

Forte Posthouse Nottingham City ⋔

👑👑 COMMENDED

St James Street, Nottingham
NG1 6BN
☎ (0115) 947 0131
Fax (0115) 948 4366
Ⓡ Forte/Utell International
*Modern city centre hotel, with variety of
dining/bar experiences, ideally placed
for theatres, shopping and such major
attractions as Nottingham Castle. Half
board prices below are weekend rates.*
Bedrooms: 93 single, 13 double,
24 twin
Bathrooms: 130 en-suite

Bed & breakfast per night:	£min	£max
Single	78.00	88.00
Double	88.00	98.00

Half board per person:	£min	£max
Daily	42.00	49.50

Lunch available
Evening meal 1900 (last orders
2230)
Cards accepted: Amex, Diners,
Mastercard, Visa, Switch/Delta

Grantham Hotel ⋔

👑 COMMENDED

24-26 Radcliffe Road, West
Bridgford, Nottingham NG2 5FW
☎ (0115) 981 1373
Fax (0115) 981 8567
*Family-run licensed hotel offering
modern accommodation in a
comfortable atmosphere. Convenient
for the centre of Nottingham, Trent
Bridge and the National Water Sports
Centre.*
Bedrooms: 13 single, 2 double,
4 twin, 2 triple, 1 family room
Bathrooms: 14 en-suite, 2 public

Bed & breakfast per night:	£min	£max
Single	21.00	29.00
Double	39.00	42.00

Half board per person:	£min	£max
Daily	26.95	35.95
Weekly	135.00	155.00

Evening meal 1800 (last orders
1900)
Parking for 20
Cards accepted: Amex, Mastercard,
Visa, Switch/Delta

Greenwood Lodge City Guesthouse ⋔

👑👑👑 HIGHLY COMMENDED

Third Avenue, Sherwood Rise,
Nottingham NG7 6JH
☎ (0115) 962 1206
Fax (0115) 962 1206

*Warm and welcoming Victorian house,
1 mile from city centre. All rooms
en-suite with tea/coffee facilities,
trouser press, TV and telephone.*
Bedrooms: 1 single, 3 double, 1 twin
Bathrooms: 5 en-suite

Bed & breakfast per night:	£min	£max
Single	29.00	40.00
Double	45.00	55.00

Half board per person:	£min	£max
Daily	39.00	50.00
Weekly	271.00	385.00

Evening meal 1800 (last orders
1930)
Parking for 5
Cards accepted: Mastercard, Visa

The Nottingham Gateway Hotel ⋔

👑👑👑 HIGHLY COMMENDED

Nuthall Road, Nottingham
NG8 6AZ
☎ (0115) 979 4949
Fax (0115) 979 4744

Privately owned hotel with impressive

*glass architectural features. Ground
floor entrance, free and easy car
parking, carvery and Thai restaurant
providing comfort and personal service.
Convenient for numerous places of
interest including Tales of Robin Hood
and the Lace Hall.*
Wheelchair access category 3♿
Bedrooms: 69 double, 31 twin,
8 triple
Bathrooms: 108 en-suite

Bed & breakfast per night:	£min	£max
Single	32.00	72.00
Double	50.00	85.00

Half board per person:	£min	£max
Daily	44.00	84.00
Weekly	300.00	450.00

Lunch available
Evening meal 1830 (last orders
2230)
Parking for 250
Cards accepted: Amex, Diners,
Mastercard, Visa, Switch/Delta

Swans Hotel and Restaurant ⋔

👑👑👑 COMMENDED

84-90 Radcliffe Road, West
Bridgford, Nottingham NG2 5HH
☎ (0115) 981 4042
Fax (0115) 945 5745

*Ideally placed for all Nottingham's
major sporting facilities. Good value,
excellent service, wonderful food.*
Bedrooms: 5 single, 19 double,
3 twin, 2 triple, 1 family room
Suite available
Bathrooms: 30 en-suite

Bed & breakfast per night:	£min	£max
Single	35.00	50.00
Double	45.00	65.00

Half board per person:	£min	£max
Daily	49.00	65.00
Weekly	143.00	163.00

Lunch available
Evening meal 1900 (last orders
2100)
Parking for 30
Cards accepted: Amex, Diners,
Mastercard, Visa, Switch/Delta

NUNEATON

Warwickshire
Map ref 4B3

Busy town with an art gallery and museum which has a permanent exhibition of the work of George Eliot. The library also has an interesting collection of material. Arbury Hall, a fine example of Gothic architecture, is nearby.
Tourist Information Centre ☎ (01203) 384027

La Tavola Calda **M**

APPROVED

70 Midland Road, Abbey Green, Nuneaton CV11 5DY
☎ (01203) 383195 & 0850 279908
Fax (01203) 381816
Family-run Italian restaurant and hotel.
Bedrooms: 1 single, 5 twin, 2 triple
Bathrooms: 8 en-suite
Bed & breakfast

per night:	£min	£max
Single	18.00	20.00
Double	32.00	32.00

Half board per person:	£min	£max
Daily	28.50	

Evening meal 1900 (last orders 2200)
Parking for 30
Cards accepted: Amex, Diners, Mastercard, Visa

NYMPSFIELD

Gloucestershire
Map ref 2B1

Pretty village high up in the Cotswolds, with a simple mid-Victorian church and a prehistoric long barrow nearby.

Rose and Crown Inn **M**

COMMENDED

Nympsfield, Stonehouse GL10 3TU
☎ (01453) 860240
Fax (01453) 860240
Email: roseandcrowninn@btinternet
Logis of GB
300-year-old inn, in quiet Cotswold village, close to Cotswold Way. Easy access to M4/M5.
Bedrooms: 1 double, 3 triple
Bathrooms: 3 en-suite, 1 private
Bed & breakfast

per night:	£min	£max
Single	30.00	34.00
Double	51.00	58.00

Half board per person:	£min	£max
Daily	37.00	52.00

Lunch available
Evening meal (last orders 2130)
Parking for 30
Cards accepted: Amex, Diners, Mastercard, Visa, Switch/Delta

OAKHAM

Leicestershire
Map ref 4C3

Pleasant former county town of Rutland. Fine 12th C Great Hall, part of its castle, with a historic collection of horseshoes. An octagonal Butter Cross stands in the market-place and Rutland County Museum, Rutland Farm Park and Rutland Water are of interest.
Tourist Information Centre ☎ (01572) 724329

Barnsdale Country Club and Hotel **M**

HIGHLY COMMENDED

Barnsdale, Exton, Oakham LE15 8AB
☎ (01572) 757901 & 722209
Fax (01572) 756235
The Independents/Best Western

Set in 60 acres overlooking Rutland Water, offering extensive leisure and sporting facilities and a gourmet restaurant. Self-catering lodges also available.
Bedrooms: 3 single, 40 double, 6 twin
Bathrooms: 49 en-suite, 3 public
Bed & breakfast

per night:	£min	£max
Single	46.75	54.75
Double	93.50	109.50

Lunch available
Evening meal 1900 (last orders 2200)
Parking for 200
Cards accepted: Amex, Diners, Mastercard, Visa, Switch/Delta

A key to symbols can be found inside the back cover flap.

Barnsdale Lodge Hotel **M**

HIGHLY COMMENDED

The Avenue, Exton, Oakham LE15 8AH
☎ (01572) 724678
Fax (01572) 724961
Country farmhouse hotel furnished in Edwardian style. On the side of Rutland Water, 2 miles from Oakham.
Bedrooms: 8 single, 12 double, 7 twin, 2 triple
Suites available
Bathrooms: 29 en-suite
Bed & breakfast

per night:	£min	£max
Single	58.00	65.00
Double	75.00	94.50

Lunch available
Evening meal 1900 (last orders 2145)
Parking for 107
Cards accepted: Mastercard, Visa, Switch/Delta

Boultons Country House Hotel **M**

COMMENDED

4 Catmos Street, Oakham LE15 6HW
☎ (01572) 722844
Fax (01572) 724473
Email: bhotbedd@sprynet.co.uk
Consort

In the county of Rutland. Unspoilt surroundings with many attractions, including Rutland Water. Country house ambience, pub circa 1604 and intimate restaurant.
Bedrooms: 7 single, 12 double, 6 twin
Bathrooms: 25 en-suite
Bed & breakfast

per night:	£min	£max
Single	60.00	
Double	80.00	

Half board per person:	£min	£max
Daily	47.50	50.00
Weekly		285.00

Lunch available
Evening meal 1900 (last orders 2130)
Parking for 15
Cards accepted: Amex, Diners, Mastercard, Visa, Switch/Delta

ONNELEY

Staffordshire
Map ref 4A2

Village on the line between Shropshire and Staffordshire counties, within easy reach of Bridgemere Garden World.

The Wheatsheaf Inn at Onneley

⛉⛉⛉ COMMENDED

Bar Hill Road, Onneley, Madeley CW3 9QF
☎ (01782) 751581
Fax (01782) 751499
18th C country inn with bars, Spanish restaurant, conference and function facilities. On A525, 7 miles from Newcastle-under-Lyme. Close to Potteries, Keele University and M6. Convenient for Alton Towers and Chester.
Bedrooms: 4 double, 1 twin
Bathrooms: 5 en-suite

Bed & breakfast per night:	£min	£max
Single	45.00	45.00
Double	50.00	60.00

Half board per person:	£min	£max
Daily	57.50	

Lunch available
Evening meal 1800 (last orders 2130)
Parking for 150
Cards accepted: Amex, Diners, Mastercard, Visa, Switch/Delta

OSWESTRY

Shropshire
Map ref 4A3

Town close to the Welsh border, the scene of many battles. To the north are the remains of a large Iron Age hill fort. An excellent centre for exploring Shropshire and Offa's Dyke.
Tourist Information Centre ☎ (01691) 662488 or 662753

Pen-y-Dyffryn Country Hotel

⛉⛉⛉ HIGHLY COMMENDED

Rhyd-y-Croesau, Oswestry SY10 7DT
☎ (01691) 653700
Fax (01691) 653700

You are advised to confirm your booking in writing.

Peaceful, stone-built Georgian former rectory in 5 acres of grounds in Shropshire/Welsh border hills. Fully licensed, extensive a la carte menu. Quiet and relaxed atmosphere. Shrewsbury and Chester 30 minutes.
Bedrooms: 1 single, 3 double, 3 twin, 1 triple
Bathrooms: 8 en-suite

Bed & breakfast per night:	£min	£max
Single	42.00	49.00
Double	65.00	74.00

Half board per person:	£min	£max
Daily	48.00	52.00
Weekly	280.00	320.00

Evening meal 1900 (last orders 2100)
Parking for 38
Cards accepted: Amex, Mastercard, Visa, Switch/Delta

Sebastians Hotel & Restaurant

⛉⛉ HIGHLY COMMENDED

45 Willow Street, Oswestry SY11 1AQ
☎ (01691) 655444
Fax (01691) 653452
16th C small hotel with beautifully decorated and furnished en-suite bedrooms. Award-winning restaurant with table d'hote and a la carte menus, featuring the finest French cuisine. Original oak beams and panelling. Chef/patron, Mark Sebastian Fisher.
Bedrooms: 2 double, 1 twin
Bathrooms: 3 en-suite

Bed & breakfast per night:	£min	£max
Single	36.95	39.95
Double	49.90	55.90

Half board per person:	£min	£max
Daily	54.90	

Lunch available
Evening meal 1830 (last orders 2200)
Parking for 3
Cards accepted: Amex, Mastercard, Visa, Switch/Delta

Sweeney Hall Hotel

⛉⛉⛉ HIGHLY COMMENDED

Morda, Oswestry SY10 9EU
☎ (01691) 652450
Fax (01691) 652805
A haven for gracious living, offering top class hospitality in an ocean of tranquillity overlooking a panorama of unspoilt countryside.
Bedrooms: 1 single, 4 double, 4 twin
Bathrooms: 6 en-suite, 3 private showers

Bed & breakfast per night:	£min	£max
Single	30.00	45.00
Double	40.00	65.00

Half board per person:	£min	£max
Daily	33.95	46.45

Lunch available
Evening meal 1900 (last orders 2130)
Parking for 50
Cards accepted: Amex, Diners, Mastercard, Visa, Switch/Delta

PAINSWICK

Gloucestershire
Map ref 2B1

Picturesque wool town with inns and houses dating from the 14th C. Painswick Rococo Garden is open to visitors from January to November, and the house is a Palladian mansion. The churchyard is famous for its yew trees.

The Falcon Hotel

⛉⛉⛉ COMMENDED

New Street, Painswick, Stroud GL6 6UN
☎ (01452) 814222 & 812228
Fax (01452) 813377
Famous old coaching inn and posting house dating from 1554, situated in the heart of the village of Painswick. Recently refurbished to very high standards, with antique furniture and many original oil paintings. Renowned restaurant.
Bedrooms: 2 double, 4 twin, 2 triple
Bathrooms: 6 en-suite, 1 public

Bed & breakfast per night:	£min	£max
Single	35.00	50.00
Double	48.50	64.00

Half board per person:	£min	£max
Daily	33.50	58.50
Weekly	225.00	400.00

Lunch available

Continued ▶

PAINSWICK

Continued

Evening meal 1900 (last orders
2130)
Parking for 32
Cards accepted: Amex, Mastercard,
Visa, Switch/Delta

PEAK DISTRICT

*See under Ashbourne, Ashford in the
Water, Bakewell, Biggin-by-Hartington,
Butterton, Buxton, Castleton, Cressbrook,
Grindleford, Hayfield, Hope, Rowsley*

PENKRIDGE

Staffordshire
Map ref 4B3

Small town south of Stafford in the
wide valley of the Penk has a stately
church with many monuments to
the Littleton family.

Hatherton Country Hotel & Leisure Centre

COMMENDED
Pinfold Lane, Penkridge, Stafford
ST19 5QP
☎ (01785) 712459
Fax (01785) 715532
Lyric
*Listed building set in its own extensive
grounds. Leisure facilities include indoor
pool, squash, sauna and gym. Walking
distance to picturesque Penkridge
village. Leisure breaks.*
Bedrooms: 13 double, 32 twin,
2 triple
Suite available
Bathrooms: 47 en-suite

Bed & breakfast

per night:	£min	£max
Single	30.00	75.00
Double	40.00	102.00

Half board per

person:	£min	£max
Daily	35.00	70.00
Weekly	210.00	490.00

Lunch available
Evening meal 1900 (last orders
2130)
Parking for 150
Cards accepted: Amex, Diners,
Mastercard, Visa

Please check prices and other
details at the time of booking.

QUORN

Leicestershire
Map ref 4C3

The Great Central Railway, a
preserved steam railway, runs
through attractively wooded
countryside at the edge of this
village.

Quorn Grange Hotel and Restaurant

COMMENDED
Quorn Grange, 88 Wood Lane,
Quorn, Loughborough LE12 8DB
☎ (01509) 412167
Fax (01509) 415621
*Old country house on the edge of
Bradgate Park, set in its own gardens.*
Bedrooms: 10 double, 5 twin
Suite available
Bathrooms: 15 en-suite

Bed & breakfast

per night:	£min	£max
Single	50.00	85.35
Double	68.00	106.70

Lunch available
Evening meal 1900 (last orders
2200)
Parking for 100
Cards accepted: Amex, Diners,
Mastercard, Visa, Switch/Delta

REDDITCH

Hereford and Worcester
Map ref 4B3

Town has remains of a Cistercian
Abbey which have been excavated
to reveal the Abbey's history. Forge
Mill Needle Museum, with a
restored water wheel, is close by.
*Tourist Information Centre ☎ (01527)
60806*

Hotel Montville and Granny's Restaurant

101 Mount Pleasant, Southcrest,
Redditch, Worcestershire B97 4JE
☎ (01527) 544411
Fax (01527) 544341
Email: hotel-montville
@compuserve.com

*Perfect location for NEC, Birmingham
station and airport, Stratford,*

Cotswolds, M5, M6, M42 and M40.
*Privately owned and managed. Free car
parking.*
Bedrooms: 10 single, 3 double,
1 twin, 2 triple
Bathrooms: 15 en-suite, 1 private
shower

Bed & breakfast

per night:	£min	£max
Single	30.00	60.00
Double	50.00	52.50

Half board per

person:	£min	£max
Daily	40.00	70.00
Weekly	240.00	420.00

Lunch available
Evening meal 1800 (last orders
2200)
Parking for 12
Cards accepted: Amex, Diners,
Mastercard, Visa, Switch/Delta

REDMILE

Leicestershire
Map ref 4C2

Vale of Belvoir village, overlooked by
the hilltop castle.

Peacock Farm Guesthouse and Country Restaurant

COMMENDED
Redmile, Nottingham NG13 0GQ
☎ (01949) 842475
Fax (01949) 43127
Logis of GB
*Nicky, Peter and Marjorie Need
welcome you to their old farmhouse in
the delightful Vale of Belvoir, close to
the castle. A small licensed restaurant
is attached, and there is a small
covered pool, play room and gardens.*
Bedrooms: 1 single, 2 double, 2 twin,
3 triple, 2 family rooms
Bathrooms: 9 en-suite, 2 public

Bed & breakfast

per night:	£min	£max
Single	35.00	49.00

Half board per

person:	£min	£max
Daily	39.00	49.50

Lunch available
Evening meal 1900 (last orders
2100)
Parking for 40
Cards accepted: Amex, Diners,
Mastercard, Visa, Switch/Delta

ROSS-ON-WYE

Hereford and Worcester
Map ref 2A1

Attractive market town with a 17th C market hall, set above the River Wye. There are lovely views over the surrounding countryside from the Prospect and the town is close to Goodrich Castle and the Welsh border. *Tourist Information Centre ☎ (01989) 562768*

The Arches Hotel

⛲⛲ COMMENDED

Walford Road, Ross-on-Wye, Herefordshire HR9 5PT
☎ (01989) 563348
Small, family-run hotel, set in half an acre of lawned gardens, 10 minutes' walk from town centre. Warm, friendly atmosphere. All rooms furnished to a high standard and with views of the garden. Victorian-style conservatory in which to relax.
Bedrooms: 1 single, 4 double, 1 twin, 1 triple
Bathrooms: 4 en-suite, 2 public

Bed & breakfast

per night:	£min	£max
Single	20.00	25.00
Double	38.00	44.00

Half board per person:

	£min	£max
Daily	30.00	35.00
Weekly	191.00	227.00

Evening meal from 1900
Parking for 10

Bridge House Hotel ⋀

⛲⛲⛲ COMMENDED

Wilton, Ross-on-Wye, Herefordshire HR9 6AA
☎ (01989) 562655
Fax (01989) 567652
Riverside hotel with panoramic views from the gardens and pride in its comfort and cuisine. All rooms en-suite. Break terms available.
Bedrooms: 4 double, 3 twin, 1 triple
Bathrooms: 8 en-suite, 1 public

Bed & breakfast

per night:	£min	£max
Single	33.50	35.00
Double	52.00	55.00

Half board per person:

	£min	£max
Daily	40.00	44.00
Weekly	230.00	250.00

Evening meal 1800 (last orders 2030)

Parking for 12
Cards accepted: Mastercard, Visa, Switch/Delta

The Chase Hotel ⋀

⛲⛲ HIGHLY COMMENDED

Gloucester Road, Ross-on-Wye, Herefordshire HR9 5LH
☎ (01989) 763161
Fax (01989) 768330
Georgian country house set in 11 acres of lovely grounds. Short walk to town centre. Enthusiastic staff provide a professional service in a friendly and relaxed atmosphere. Ideal touring centre.
Bedrooms: 17 double, 21 twin, 1 triple
Bathrooms: 39 en-suite

Bed & breakfast

per night:	£min	£max
Single	70.00	85.00
Double	85.00	120.00

Half board per person:

	£min	£max
Daily	95.00	110.00

Lunch available
Evening meal 1900 (last orders 2145)
Parking for 200
Cards accepted: Amex, Diners, Mastercard, Visa, Switch/Delta

Pencraig Court Hotel ⋀

⛲⛲⛲ HIGHLY COMMENDED

Pencraig, Ross-on-Wye, Herefordshire HR9 6HR
☎ (01989) 770306 & 770416
Fax (01989) 770040
Email: michael.cliffordf@rfdc.ac.uk

Georgian country house hotel, privately owned, providing both English and French cooking. Elegant restaurant and extensive wine cellars. Large attractive garden with glorious views overlooking River Wye. Special breaks available.
Bedrooms: 1 single, 4 double, 4 twin, 2 triple
Bathrooms: 11 en-suite

Bed & breakfast

per night:	£min	£max
Single	40.00	50.00
Double	50.00	70.00

Half board per person:

	£min	£max
Daily	42.50	56.50
Weekly	315.00	

Lunch available
Evening meal 1900 (last orders 2100)
Parking for 20
Cards accepted: Mastercard, Visa, Switch/Delta

Pengethley Manor ⋀

⛲⛲⛲ COMMENDED

Ross-on-Wye, Herefordshire HR9 6LL
☎ (01989) 730211
Fax (01989) 730238
Ⓒ Best Western
Elegant Georgian country house in superb gardens with magnificent views over Herefordshire countryside. Extensive wine list. Restaurant specialises in fresh local produce.
Bedrooms: 2 single, 11 double, 10 twin, 1 triple
Suites available
Bathrooms: 24 en-suite

Bed & breakfast

per night:	£min	£max
Single	75.00	115.00
Double	60.00	80.00

Half board per person:

	£min	£max
Daily	75.00	95.00
Weekly	450.00	570.00

Lunch available
Evening meal 1900 (last orders 2130)
Parking for 70
Cards accepted: Amex, Diners, Mastercard, Visa, Switch/Delta

For further information on accommodation establishments use the coupons at the back of this guide.

The symbols in each entry give information about services and facilities. A key to these symbols appears at the back of this guide.

ROSS-ON-WYE

Continued

Sunnymount Hotel ⚠

⚜ ⚜ ⚜ COMMENDED

Ryefield Road, Ross-on-Wye,
Herefordshire HR9 5LU
☎ (01989) 563880
*Warm, comfortable hotel in quiet
location on edge of town, offering
French and English cooking with
home-grown and local produce freshly
cooked for each meal. Special breaks
always available.*
Bedrooms: 3 single, 3 double, 3 twin
Bathrooms: 7 en-suite, 1 public
**Bed & breakfast
per night:**

	£min	£max
Single	28.00	29.00
Double	49.00	51.00

**Half board per
person:**

	£min	£max
Daily	43.00	44.00
Weekly	230.00	270.00

Evening meal 1900 (last orders
1730)
Parking for 7
Cards accepted: Amex, Mastercard,
Visa

🛏☕🛁Ⓢ✂🅜📺🖬🖤🐾🐎DAP
SP🏡Ⓣ⊚

ROWSLEY

Derbyshire
Map ref 4B2

Village at the meeting point of the
Rivers Wye and Derwent, and on
the edge of the Haddon and
Chatsworth estates. 19th C
water-powered flour mill, working
and open to visitors, with craft
workshops.

Grouse and Claret ⚠

⚜ COMMENDED

Station Road, Rowsley, Matlock
DE4 2EL
☎ (01629) 733233
*A delightful country inn, in the heart of
the Peak District, providing a friendly,
comfortable atmosphere and easy
access to attractions.*
Bedrooms: 2 single, 3 double
Bathrooms: 2 public
**Bed & breakfast
per night:**

	£min	£max
Single	20.00	
Double	35.00	

Lunch available
Evening meal 1800 (last orders
2130)
Parking for 77
Cards accepted: Mastercard, Visa

🛏🦮📇🗻🍷✂🖬🖤🐾🐎Ⓣ

RUGBY

Warwickshire
Map ref 4C3

Town famous for its public school
which gave its name to Rugby Union
football and which featured in "Tom
Brown's Schooldays".
Tourist Information Centre ☎ *(01788)
535348*

The Golden Lion Inn of
Easenhall ⚠

⚜ ⚜ COMMENDED

Easenhall, Rugby CV23 0JA
☎ (01788) 832265
Fax (01788) 832878
*Individually styled bedrooms, all
en-suite, in a traditional 16th C building
in beautiful village surroundings. Bar
and restaurant, wholesome food, secure
parking.*
Bedrooms: 2 single, 1 double, 1 twin
Bathrooms: 4 en-suite
**Bed & breakfast
per night:**

	£min	£max
Single	40.00	40.00
Double	44.00	69.00

Lunch available
Evening meal 1800 (last orders
2200)
Parking for 60
Cards accepted: Amex, Mastercard,
Visa, Switch/Delta

🛏🦮5🍷📇🗻🖤♿🖐🗻✂🖬🖤📱🏇14Ụ
🏇🐾🐎DAP🔌SP🏡Ⓣ⊚

White Lion Inn ⚠

⚜ ⚜ APPROVED

Coventry Road, Pailton, Rugby
CV23 0QD
☎ (01788) 832359
Fax (01788) 832359
*17th C coaching inn, recently
refurbished but retaining all old world
features. Close to Rugby and
Stratford. Within 2 miles of motorways.*
Bedrooms: 9 twin
Bathrooms: 3 en-suite, 2 public
**Bed & breakfast
per night:**

	£min	£max
Single	18.50	25.00
Double	37.00	45.00

Lunch available
Evening meal 1830 (last orders
2200)
Parking for 60
Cards accepted: Mastercard, Visa

🛏🦮📇🗻🍷Ⓢ✂🅜📺🖬🖤📱🏇30🐾
ỤDAP

RUTLAND WATER

Rutland

See under Oakham

ST BRIAVELS

Gloucestershire
Map ref 2A1

Village with remains of a 13th C
castle, set above the Wye Valley in
the Forest of Dean. Tintern, with its
magnificent abbey ruins, is nearby.

The Florence Country
Hotel ⚠

⚜ ⚜ ⚜ COMMENDED

Bigsweir, St Briavels, Lower Wye
Valley, Lydney GL15 6QQ
☎ (01594) 530830

*Overlooking the River Wye at Bigsweir,
in 5 acres of woodland. Area of
outstanding beauty. Adjacent to Offa's
Dyke path.*
Bedrooms: 1 single, 2 double, 1 twin,
1 triple
Bathrooms: 5 en-suite
**Bed & breakfast
per night:**

	£min	£max
Single	30.00	30.00
Double	50.00	60.00

**Half board per
person:**

	£min	£max
Daily	34.00	37.00
Weekly	230.00	250.00

Lunch available
Evening meal 1930 (last orders
1930)
Parking for 13
Cards accepted: Mastercard, Visa,
Switch/Delta

🛏🦮🅔📇🗻🖤♿🍷Ⓢ✂🅜🖬🖤📱🐾
🗻SP🏡

SEVERN STOKE

Hereford and Worcester
Map ref 2B1

Village to the south of Worcester
with a picturesque group of houses
surrounding the church and
magnificent views across the Severn
to the Malvern Hills.

The Old School House Hotel
& Restaurant ⚠

⚜ ⚜ HIGHLY COMMENDED

Severn Stoke, Worcester WR8 9JA
☎ (01905) 371368
Fax (01905) 371591

A warm welcome awaits at this 17th C farmhouse/Victorian school near Worcester. Award-winning restaurant, gardens, outdoor pool. Wonderful views of the Malverns. Easy car parking. Winter discounts available.
Bedrooms: 2 single, 8 double, 2 twin, 1 family room
Bathrooms: 13 en-suite
Bed & breakfast

per night:	£min	£max
Single	39.50	60.00
Double	60.00	80.00

Lunch available
Evening meal 1900 (last orders 2130)
Parking for 80
Cards accepted: Diners, Mastercard, Visa, Switch/Delta

SHERWOOD FOREST

See under Mansfield, Newark, Worksop

SHIFNAL

Shropshire
Map ref 4A3

Small market town, once an important staging centre for coaches on the Holyhead road. Where industrialism has not prevailed, the predominating architectural impression is Georgian, though some timber-framed houses survived the Great Fire of 1591.

Village Farm Lodge

COMMENDED

Sheriffhales, Shifnal TF11 8RD
☎ (01952) 462763 & 0585 254528
Fax (01952) 201310
Tastefully converted farm buildings in Sheriffhales village, situated on the B4379 off the A5. Minutes from Telford and Ironbridge Gorge.
Bedrooms: 1 single, 2 double, 3 twin, 1 triple, 1 family room
Bathrooms: 8 en-suite
Bed & breakfast

per night:	£min	£max
Single	28.50	
Double	39.00	

Parking for 8
Cards accepted: Amex, Mastercard, Visa

SHIPTON-UNDER-WYCHWOOD

Oxfordshire
Map ref 2B1

The Shaven Crown Hotel

See South of England region for full entry details

SHREWSBURY

Shropshire
Map ref 4A3

Beautiful historic town on the River Severn retaining many fine old timber-framed houses. Its attractions include Rowley's Museum with Roman finds, remains of a castle, Clive House Museum, St Chad's 18th C round church, rowing on the river and the Shrewsbury Flower Show in August.
Tourist Information Centre ☎ (01743) 350761

Abbot's Mead Hotel

COMMENDED

9-10 St. Julian Friars, Shrewsbury SY1 1XL
☎ (01743) 235281
Fax (01743) 369133
Email: abbotsmead@studio.erta.net
Georgian town house between town centre and the River Severn. All bedrooms have private facilities, colour TV, tea/coffee makers, direct dial telephone. Car parking.
Bedrooms: 10 double, 4 twin
Bathrooms: 14 en-suite, 1 public
Bed & breakfast

per night:	£min	£max
Single	34.00	37.00
Double	48.00	54.00

Half board per

person:	£min	£max
Daily	38.50	48.00

Evening meal 1900 (last orders 2130)
Parking for 10
Cards accepted: Amex, Mastercard, Visa, Switch/Delta

The symbols in each entry give information about services and facilities. A key to these symbols appears at the back of this guide.

Albright Hussey Hotel and Restaurant

HIGHLY COMMENDED

Ellesmere Road, Shrewsbury SY4 3AF
☎ (01939) 290571 & 290523
Fax (01939) 291143

Historic 16th C moated manor house, only 2 miles from Shrewsbury town centre. Renowned for fine food, fine wines and impeccable and friendly service. In the heart of Shropshire countryside yet only 5 minutes from M54 motorway link.
Bedrooms: 10 double, 4 twin
Suite available
Bathrooms: 14 en-suite
Bed & breakfast

per night:	£min	£max
Single	65.00	80.00
Double	85.00	130.00

Half board per

person:	£min	£max
Daily	55.00	68.50
Weekly	385.00	479.50

Lunch available
Evening meal 1900 (last orders 2200)
Parking for 80
Cards accepted: Amex, Diners, Mastercard, Visa, Switch/Delta

Cromwells Hotel & Wine Bar

Listed APPROVED

11 Dogpole, Shrewsbury SY1 1EN
☎ (01743) 361440
Fax (01743) 361440
15th C coaching inn in Shrewsbury town centre, offering comfortable, well-maintained character bedrooms. Cosy restaurant, with excellent local reputation, and lively wine bar.
Bedrooms: 2 single, 2 double, 1 twin, 2 triple
Bathrooms: 2 public
Bed & breakfast

per night:	£min	£max
Single	23.00	28.00
Double	37.00	40.00

Lunch available
Evening meal 1900 (last orders 2200)
Cards accepted: Amex, Mastercard, Visa, Switch/Delta

SHREWSBURY

Continued

Hawkstone Park Hotel, Golf, Historic Park & Follies and Leisure Centre ♨

HIGHLY COMMENDED

Weston-under-Redcastle,
Shrewsbury SY4 5UY
☎ (01939) 200611 & 200204
Fax (01939) 200311
Fine example of a country house hotel, built in 1752, set in over 400 acres of English Heritage designated Grade I listed landscape with panoramic views over golf courses and beyond to the forgotten masterpiece - an Historic Park and Follies with dramatic scenery, high cliffs and grotto caves. North of Shrewsbury off A49.
Bedrooms: 6 single, 28 double,
29 twin, 2 triple
Suites available
Bathrooms: 65 en-suite, 8 public
Bed & breakfast

per night:	£min	£max
Single	59.00	78.00
Double	59.00	78.00

Half board per

person:	£min	£max
Daily	46.50	56.00
Weekly	292.95	352.80

Lunch available
Evening meal 1930 (last orders
2145)
Parking for 300
Cards accepted: Amex, Diners,
Mastercard, Visa, Switch/Delta

The Mermaid Hotel

COMMENDED

Atcham, Shrewsbury SY5 6QG
☎ (01743) 761220
Fax (01743) 761292
Grade II listed manor house on the banks of the River Severn. Two miles from Shrewsbury and 7 miles from Telford.
Bedrooms: 2 single, 11 double,
4 twin, 1 family room
Bathrooms: 18 en-suite
Bed & breakfast

per night:	£min	£max
Single	29.95	45.00
Double	45.00	65.00

Half board per

person:	£min	£max
Daily	32.50	

Lunch available
Evening meal 1830 (last orders
2130)

Parking for 100
Cards accepted: Amex, Diners,
Mastercard, Visa, Switch/Delta

Sandford House Hotel

HIGHLY COMMENDED

St. Julian Friars, Shrewsbury
SY1 1XL
☎ (01743) 343829
Fax (01743) 343829
Family-run Grade II listed town house, close to the river, with pleasant walks and access to good fishing. Easy parking and within a few minutes of the town centre.
Bedrooms: 2 single, 4 double, 3 twin,
2 triple
Bathrooms: 9 en-suite, 1 public,
1 private shower
Bed & breakfast

per night:	£min	£max
Single		35.00
Double		50.00

Parking for 3
Cards accepted: Mastercard, Visa,
Switch/Delta

Sydney House Hotel

COMMENDED

Coton Crescent, Coton Hill,
Shrewsbury SY1 2LJ
☎ (01743) 354681 & 0500 130243
Fax (01743) 354681
Logis of GB
Edwardian town house, 10 minutes' walk from town centre and railway station. Most rooms en-suite, all with direct dial telephone, colour TV, hot drink facilities and hairdryer. Restaurant and licensed bar.
Bedrooms: 2 single, 2 double, 2 twin,
1 family room
Bathrooms: 4 en-suite, 2 public
Bed & breakfast

per night:	£min	£max
Single	35.00	50.00
Double	46.00	68.00

Half board per

person:	£min	£max
Daily	46.00	66.00
Weekly	255.00	400.00

Evening meal 1930 (last orders
2100)
Parking for 7
Cards accepted: Amex, Mastercard,
Visa

Please mention this guide
when making your booking.

SLIMBRIDGE

Gloucestershire
Map ref 2B1

The Wildfowl and Wetlands Trust Centre was founded by Sir Peter Scott and has the world's largest collection of wildfowl. Of special interest are the wild swans and the geese which wander around the grounds.

Tudor Arms Lodge

COMMENDED

Shepherds Patch, Slimbridge,
Gloucester GL2 7BP
☎ (01453) 890306
Fax (01453) 890103
Recently-built lodge adjoining an 18th C freehouse, alongside Gloucester and Sharpness Canal. Renowned Slimbridge Wildfowl and Wetlands Trust Centre only 800 yards away.
Bedrooms: 4 double, 5 twin, 2 triple,
1 family room
Bathrooms: 12 en-suite
Bed & breakfast

per night:	£min	£max
Single	34.00	36.50
Double	44.00	46.50

Lunch available
Evening meal 1900 (last orders
2200)
Parking for 70
Cards accepted: Amex, Mastercard,
Visa, Switch/Delta

SOLIHULL

West Midlands
Map ref 4B3

On the outskirts of Birmingham. Some Tudor houses and a 13th C church remain amongst the new public buildings and shopping centre. The 16th C Malvern Hall is now a school and the 15th C Chester House at Knowle is now a library.
Tourist Information Centre ☎ (0121) 704 6130 or 704 6134

Cedarwood House ♨

COMMENDED

347 Lyndon Road, Solihull B92 7QT
☎ (0121) 743 5844
Private guesthouse, all bedrooms elegantly furnished, en-suite facilities. Within 2 miles of the National Exhibition Centre, airport, station and Solihull centre.
Bedrooms: 4 single, 1 twin
Bathrooms: 5 en-suite

Bed & breakfast per night:	£min	£max
Single	27.50	40.00
Double	40.00	50.00

Parking for 6

The Edwardian Guest House ⚜

HIGHLY COMMENDED

7 St Bernards Road, Olton, Solihull
B92 7AU
☎ (0121) 706 2138
Edwardian guesthouse of character. A warm welcome, good food. Excellent accommodation and delightful garden. 1.25 miles Solihull, 10 minutes NEC, airport and railway, 5 minutes junction 5 of M42. No smoking, please.
Bedrooms: 2 twin
Bathrooms: 2 en-suite

Bed & breakfast per night:	£min	£max
Single	30.00	35.00
Double	50.00	60.00

Parking for 7

St. John's Swallow Hotel ⚜

HIGHLY COMMENDED

651 Warwick Road, Solihull
B91 1AT
☎ (0121) 711 3000
Fax (0121) 705 6629
Swallow
Newly refurbished hotel with leisure facilities, close to Solihull town centre. A good touring base for Stratford, Warwick and Coventry. Short break packages available.
Bedrooms: 14 single, 58 double, 100 twin, 5 family rooms
Suites available
Bathrooms: 177 en-suite

Bed & breakfast per night:	£min	£max
Single	50.00	115.00
Double	70.00	125.00

Lunch available
Evening meal 1900 (last orders 2145)
Parking for 380
Cards accepted: Amex, Diners, Mastercard, Visa, Switch/Delta

For ideas on places to visit refer to the introduction at the beginning of this section.

SOUTH NORMANTON

Derbyshire
Map ref 4C2

Village near the Nottinghamshire border and close to Hardwick Hall, Newstead Abbey and the National Tramway Museum at Crich.

Swallow Hotel ⚜

HIGHLY COMMENDED

Carter Lane East, Junction 28 of M1, South Normanton DE55 2EH
☎ (01773) 812000
Fax (01773) 580032
Swallow
Modern hotel at junction 28 of M1 motorway. Ideal for Peak District, Chatsworth House, Sherwood Forest, Alton Towers (discounted tickets available). Leisure facilities. Short break packages available.
Wheelchair access category 3
Bedrooms: 54 single, 66 double, 41 twin
Bathrooms: 161 en-suite

Bed & breakfast per night:	£min	£max
Single	55.00	95.00
Double	75.00	120.00

Half board per person:	£min	£max
Daily	75.00	115.00

Lunch available
Evening meal 1900 (last orders 2200)
Parking for 280
Cards accepted: Amex, Diners, Mastercard, Visa

STEEPLE ASTON

Oxfordshire
Map ref 2C1

Hopcrofts Holt Hotel
Westfield Farm Motel
See South of England region for full entry details

Establishments should be open throughout the year, unless otherwise stated.

All accommodation in this guide has been graded, or is awaiting a grading, by a trained Tourist Board inspector.

STOKE-ON-TRENT

Staffordshire
Map ref 4B2

Famous for its pottery. Factories of several famous makers, including Josiah Wedgwood, can be visited. The City Museum has one of the finest pottery and porcelain collections in the world.
Tourist Information Centre ☎ (01782) 284600

George Hotel

HIGHLY COMMENDED

Swan Square, Burslem, Stoke-on-Trent ST6 2AE
☎ (01782) 577544
Fax (01782) 837496

Attractive neo-Georgian building in Burslem's elegant Swan Square. Conveniently situated between the Midlands, Liverpool and Manchester.
Bedrooms: 7 single, 17 double, 11 twin, 2 triple
Bathrooms: 37 en-suite

Bed & breakfast per night:	£min	£max
Single	50.00	70.00
Double	60.00	90.00

Half board per person:	£min	£max
Daily	55.00	75.00

Lunch available
Evening meal 1900 (last orders 2100)
Parking for 22
Cards accepted: Amex, Diners, Mastercard, Visa, Switch/Delta

Haydon House Hotel ⚜

HIGHLY COMMENDED

Haydon Street, Basford, Stoke-on-Trent ST4 6JD
☎ (01782) 711311
Fax (01782) 717470
Country house in the city. Fine food and service. Executive accommodation, including suites. A landmark in Staffordshire.
Bedrooms: 7 single, 7 double, 7 twin, 2 triple
Bathrooms: 23 en-suite

Continued ▶

STOKE-ON-TRENT
Continued

Bed & breakfast

per night:	£min	£max
Single	38.00	59.50
Double	58.00	69.50

Half board per

person:	£min	£max
Daily	57.00	76.50

Lunch available
Evening meal 1900 (last orders 2145)
Parking for 50
Cards accepted: Amex, Diners, Mastercard, Visa, Switch/Delta

🐂🕭🛆🖭📞🖃💻🖥♨🦮🛎🛇🖂🖩▦⬛➰
🍴100▶🐾 SP T

Jarvis Clayton Lodge Hotel ⋀
👑👑👑👑 COMMENDED
Clayton Road,
Newcastle-under-Lyme ST5 4AF
☎ (01782) 613093
Fax (01782) 711896
ⒸⓇ Jarvis/Utell International
Conveniently located for M6, Potteries and Alton Towers, offering a quiet and comfortable setting overlooking the Lyme Valley. Top-rate conference and events facilities available.
Bedrooms: 11 single, 18 double, 20 twin, 1 triple
Suite available
Bathrooms: 50 en-suite
Bed & breakfast

per night:	£min	£max
Single	37.50	87.50
Double	65.00	97.50

Half board per

person:	£min	£max
Daily	42.50	105.00

Lunch available
Evening meal 1900 (last orders 2200)
Parking for 408
Cards accepted: Amex, Diners, Mastercard, Visa, Switch/Delta

🐂🕭📞🖃💻🖥♨🦮🛎🛇🖂📺◐▦⬛➰
🍴300✿🐾 SP T

Sneyd Arms Hotel ⋀
👑👑
Tower Square, Tunstall,
Stoke-on-Trent ST6 5AA
☎ (01782) 826722
Fax (01782) 826722

Residential town centre hotel,

---

restaurant and public house with function suite, gym, sauna and sunbeds. En-suite and budget accommodation available.
Bedrooms: 4 single, 3 double, 4 twin, 2 triple
Bathrooms: 5 en-suite, 1 private, 2 public
Bed & breakfast

per night:	£min	£max
Single	20.00	35.00
Double	36.00	47.00

Lunch available
Evening meal 1900 (last orders 2100)
Parking for 2
Cards accepted: Amex, Diners, Mastercard, Visa

🐂🖃♨🛎🛇🖩▦➰🐾🔍❦✕🚃⬛
SP

Verdon Guest House ⋀
Listed APPROVED
44 Charles Street, Hanley,
Stoke-on-Trent ST1 3JY
☎ (01782) 264244
Large, friendly guesthouse almost in town centre and close to bus station. Convenient for all pottery factory visits, museum and Festival Park. Alton Towers 20 minutes, M6 10 minutes. All rooms with cable TV, some en-suite.
Bedrooms: 2 double, 2 twin, 5 triple, 1 family room
Bathrooms: 4 en-suite, 3 public
Bed & breakfast

per night:	£min	£max
Single	17.00	17.00
Double	30.00	38.00

Parking for 8
Cards accepted: Mastercard, Visa

🐂🛆🖃💻♨⑮🛇🖩▦➰🚃

STONE
Staffordshire
Map ref 4B2

Town on the River Trent with the remains of a 12th C Augustinian priory. It is surrounded by pleasant countryside. Trentham Gardens with 500 acres of parklands and recreational facilities is within easy reach.

Stone House Hotel
👑👑👑 HIGHLY COMMENDED
Stone ST15 0BQ
☎ (01785) 815531
Fax (01785) 814764
Elegant building, set in its own delightful grounds, offers extensive leisure facilities, including tennis courts and swimming pool.
Bedrooms: 9 single, 29 double, 8 twin, 1 triple
Bathrooms: 47 en-suite

Bed & breakfast

per night:	£min	£max
Single	60.00	81.00
Double	70.00	90.00

Half board per

person:	£min	£max
Daily	52.00	98.00

Lunch available
Evening meal 1900 (last orders 2200)
Parking for 150
Cards accepted: Amex, Diners, Mastercard, Visa

🐂🦽🛆🕭📞🖃💻🖥♨🦮🛎🛇🖂🖩📺
◐▦➰🍴180🐾✕🐾🔍❦▶➰ DAP 🚫
SP T

STOW-ON-THE-WOLD
Gloucestershire
Map ref 2B1

Attractive Cotswold wool town with a large market-place and some fine houses, especially the old grammar school. There is an interesting church dating from Norman times. Stow-on-the-Wold is surrounded by lovely countryside and Cotswold villages.
Tourist Information Centre ☎ *(01451) 831082*

Auld Stocks Hotel ⋀
👑👑👑👑 COMMENDED
The Square, Stow-on-the-Wold,
Cheltenham GL54 1AF
☎ (01451) 830666
Fax (01451) 870014
ⒸⓇ The Independents

17th C Grade II listed hotel facing quiet village green on which the original penal stocks still stand. Refurbished to combine modern comforts with original charm and character. Friendly and caring staff make this an ideal base for exploring the Cotswolds.
Bedrooms: 1 single, 14 double, 2 twin, 1 triple
Bathrooms: 18 en-suite
Bed & breakfast

per night:	£min	£max
Single	37.50	
Double	75.00	80.00

Half board per

person:	£min	£max
Daily	52.50	57.50

Lunch available
Evening meal 1900 (last orders 2130)

Parking for 14
Cards accepted: Mastercard, Visa, Switch/Delta

Corsham Field Farmhouse

APPROVED

Bledington Road, Stow-on-the-Wold, Cheltenham GL54 1JH
☎ (01451) 831750

100-acre mixed farm. Homely farmhouse with breathtaking views. Ideally situated for exploring the Cotswolds. En-suite and standard rooms. TVs, guest lounge, tea/coffee facilities. Good pub food 5 minutes' walk away.

Bedrooms: 2 double, 2 twin, 3 family rooms
Bathrooms: 5 en-suite, 1 public

Bed & breakfast per night:	£min	£max
Single	15.00	25.00
Double	30.00	40.00

Parking for 10

Farmers Lodge Hotel and Restaurant

COMMENDED

Fosse Way, Stow-on-the-Wold, Cheltenham GL54 1JX
☎ (01451) 870539
Fax (01451) 870639

New, privately owned and operated budget lodge in central Cotswold location. All rooms en-suite. Adjoining bar and restaurant.

Bedrooms: 9 double, 4 twin, 5 family rooms
Bathrooms: 18 en-suite

Bed & breakfast per night:	£min	£max
Single	45.00	55.00
Double	45.00	55.00

Half board per person:	£min	£max
Daily	58.85	77.35

Lunch available
Evening meal 1900 (last orders 2200)
Parking for 60
Cards accepted: Mastercard, Visa, Switch/Delta

Half board prices are given per person, but in some cases these may be based on double/twin occupancy.

Fosse Manor Hotel

HIGHLY COMMENDED

Stow-on-the-Wold, Cheltenham GL54 1JX
☎ (01451) 830354
Fax (01451) 832486
Consort

Rurally located Cotswold manor house in beautiful gardens. Tastefully decorated throughout. Elegant restaurant serving traditional and continental cuisine. Central to all Cotswold attractions.

Bedrooms: 3 single, 8 double, 3 twin, 3 triple
Suite available
Bathrooms: 17 en-suite

Bed & breakfast per night:	£min	£max
Single	57.00	80.00
Double	110.00	170.00

Half board per person:	£min	£max
Daily	67.00	85.00

Lunch available
Evening meal 1900 (last orders 2130)
Parking for 55
Cards accepted: Amex, Diners, Mastercard, Visa, Switch/Delta

Grapevine Hotel

HIGHLY COMMENDED

Sheep Street, Stow-on-the-Wold, Cheltenham GL54 1AU
☎ (01451) 830344
Fax (01451) 832278
Email: enquiries@vines.co.uk
Best Western

Exceptional small hotel in antique centre of Cotswolds. Accent on food and hospitality. Lovely furnishings complement the romantic, vine-clad conservatory restaurant. Daily half board minimum price based on 2-night stay.

Bedrooms: 3 single, 7 double, 10 twin, 2 triple
Bathrooms: 22 en-suite

Bed & breakfast per night:	£min	£max
Single	80.00	100.00
Double	120.00	160.00

Half board per person:	£min	£max
Daily	65.00	85.00
Weekly	350.00	470.00

Lunch available
Evening meal 1900 (last orders 2130)
Parking for 23
Cards accepted: Amex, Diners, Mastercard, Visa, Switch/Delta

Horse and Groom Inn

COMMENDED

Upper Oddington, Moreton-in-Marsh GL56 0XH
☎ (01451) 830584
Fax (01451) 870494

16th C old world character inn off A436. In quiet village yet only 2 miles from Stow-on-the-Wold and close to motorway and trunk roads. En-suite rooms, lunchtime and evening meals. Families welcome.

Bedrooms: 5 double, 2 twin
Bathrooms: 7 en-suite

Bed & breakfast per night:	£min	£max
Single	40.00	50.00
Double	55.00	70.00

Lunch available
Evening meal 1830 (last orders 2130)
Parking for 40
Cards accepted: Mastercard, Visa, Switch/Delta

Old Farmhouse Hotel

COMMENDED

Lower Swell, Stow-on-the-Wold, Cheltenham GL54 1LF
☎ (01451) 830232 & 0500 657842
Fax (01451) 870962
Email: oldfarm@globalnet.co.uk

Sympathetically converted 16th C Cotswold-stone farmhouse in a quiet hamlet, 1 mile west of Stow-on-the-Wold. Warm and unpretentious hospitality.
http://www.scws.com/webcraft/hotels/Old_Farmhouse

Continued ▶

STOW-ON-THE-WOLD
Continued

Bedrooms: 7 double, 4 twin, 2 family rooms
Suites available
Bathrooms: 11 en-suite, 1 public

Bed & breakfast

per night:	£min	£max
Single	20.00	75.00
Double	40.00	95.00

Half board per person:

	£min	£max
Daily	37.00	92.00
Weekly	259.00	644.00

Lunch available
Evening meal 1900 (last orders 2100)
Parking for 25
Cards accepted: Mastercard, Visa, Switch/Delta

Stow Lodge Hotel ⚏
HIGHLY COMMENDED

The Square, Stow-on-the-Wold, Cheltenham GL54 1AB
☎ (01451) 830485
Fax (01451) 831671

Family-run, Grade II listed manor house in pretty gardens overlooking market square. Open fires in bar and lounge, en-suite comfortably furnished bedrooms, candlelit restaurant with interesting wine list, private car park.
Bedrooms: 1 single, 9 double, 9 twin, 2 triple
Bathrooms: 21 en-suite

Bed & breakfast

per night:	£min	£max
Single	45.00	95.00
Double	65.00	105.00

Half board per person:

	£min	£max
Weekly	230.00	360.00

Evening meal 1900 (last orders 2100)
Parking for 30
Open February–December
Cards accepted: Diners, Mastercard, Visa, Switch/Delta

Unicorn Hotel ⚏
COMMENDED

Sheep Street, Stow-on-the-Wold, Cheltenham GL54 1HQ
☎ (01451) 830257
Fax (01451) 831090
ⓒ Forte

17th C coaching inn, well placed for touring the Cotswolds. Its hospitality is second to none, with an award-winning restaurant. The inn is full of old world charm.
Bedrooms: 2 single, 14 double, 4 twin
Bathrooms: 20 en-suite

Bed & breakfast

per night:	£min	£max
Single	54.00	74.00
Double	108.00	148.00

Half board per person:

	£min	£max
Daily	64.00	84.00

Lunch available
Evening meal 1900 (last orders 2130)
Parking for 50
Cards accepted: Amex, Diners, Mastercard, Visa, Switch/Delta

STRATFORD-UPON-AVON
Warwickshire
Map ref 2B1

Famous as Shakespeare's home town, Stratford's many attractions include his birthplace, New Place where he died, the Royal Shakespeare Theatre and Gallery, "The World of Shakespeare" 30 minute theatre and Hall's Croft (his daughter's house).
Tourist Information Centre ☎ (01789) 293127

Aberfoyle Guest House ⚏
Listed COMMENDED

3 Evesham Place, Stratford-upon-Avon CV37 6HT
☎ (01789) 295703
Charming bijou Edwardian residence with spacious bedrooms, near town centre. English breakfast. Garage. Non-smokers only, please.
Bedrooms: 1 double, 1 triple
Bathrooms: 2 en-suite

Bed & breakfast

per night:	£min	£max
Single	22.00	25.00
Double	38.00	42.00

Parking for 2

Ambleside Guest House ⚏
Listed APPROVED

41 Grove Road, Stratford-upon-Avon CV37 6PB
☎ (01789) 297239 & 295670
Fax (01789) 295670
Picturesque guesthouse, offering a warm welcome to all. Overlooking Firs Park and close to town centre. Delightfully furnished rooms. Private parking.
Bedrooms: 1 single, 2 double, 1 twin, 2 triple
Bathrooms: 3 en-suite, 1 public

Bed & breakfast

per night:	£min	£max
Single	23.00	28.00
Double	40.00	48.00

Parking for 11
Cards accepted: Mastercard, Visa, Switch/Delta

Amelia Linhill Guesthouse ⚏
Listed APPROVED

35 Evesham Place, Stratford-upon-Avon CV37 6HT
☎ (01789) 292879
Fax (01789) 414478
Comfortable Victorian guesthouse offering warm welcome and good food. 5 minutes' walk from town centre and theatres and convenient for Cotswolds. Baby sitting service.
Bedrooms: 1 single, 1 double, 3 twin, 2 triple, 1 family room
Bathrooms: 2 en-suite, 2 public

Bed & breakfast

per night:	£min	£max
Single	14.00	20.00
Double	30.00	50.00

Half board per person:

	£min	£max
Daily	21.50	24.00
Weekly	140.00	150.00

Lunch available
Evening meal 1700 (last orders 1930)

Billesley Manor Hotel ⚏
HIGHLY COMMENDED

Billesley, Alcester, Stratford-upon-Avon B49 6NF
☎ (01789) 279955
Fax (01789) 764145
ⓒ Utell International/Queens Moat

Elizabethan manor set in 11 acres of gardens, 4 miles from Stratford-upon-Avon on the A46. Fine oak-panelled restaurant.
Bedrooms: 1 single, 23 double, 17 twin
Suites available
Bathrooms: 41 en-suite

Bed & breakfast per night:	£min	£max
Single	80.00	125.00
Double	160.00	270.00

Half board per person:	£min	£max
Daily	100.00	160.00

Lunch available
Evening meal 1930 (last orders 2130)
Parking for 100
Cards accepted: Amex, Diners, Mastercard, Visa, Switch/Delta
☎ [S] [T] 100 [SP] [T]

Brook Lodge

HIGHLY COMMENDED
192 Alcester Road,
Stratford-upon-Avon CV37 9DR
☎ (01789) 295988
Fax (01789) 295988

Immaculately maintained guesthouse, convenient for all local attractions. Prettily decorated and comfortable en-suite bedrooms. Highest standards throughout. Large car park.
Bedrooms: 4 double, 1 twin, 2 triple
Bathrooms: 6 en-suite, 1 private

Bed & breakfast per night:	£min	£max
Single	25.00	45.00
Double	38.00	50.00

Parking for 10
Cards accepted: Amex, Mastercard, Visa, Switch/Delta
5 [UL] [S] [TV] [SP] [T]

Carlton Guest House

COMMENDED
22 Evesham Place,
Stratford-upon-Avon CV37 6HT
☎ (01789) 293548
Elegantly furnished house combining Victorian origins with all modern facilities. 5 minutes' walk to the theatre and town centre. Private parking.
Bedrooms: 2 single, 2 double, 1 twin, 1 triple
Bathrooms: 3 en-suite, 1 public

Bed & breakfast per night:	£min	£max
Single	21.00	21.00
Double	42.00	48.00

Parking for 3
[UL] [S]

Charlecote Pheasant Country Hotel

COMMENDED
Charlecote CV35 9EW
☎ (01789) 279954
Fax (01789) 470222
[CR] Utell International
19th C farmhouse converted into a comfortable hotel, opposite Charlecote Park. Set in beautiful Warwickshire countryside, 4 miles from Stratford-upon-Avon and Warwick.
Continued ▶

STRATFORD-UPON-AVON
Continued

Bedrooms: 5 single, 16 double,
6 twin, 40 triple
Suites available
Bathrooms: 67 en-suite

Bed & breakfast

per night:	£min	£max
Double	60.00	75.00

Half board per person:

	£min	£max
Daily	40.00	52.50

Lunch available
Evening meal 1900 (last orders
2200)
Parking for 130
Cards accepted: Amex, Diners,
Mastercard, Visa

The Coach House Hotel ⚑

☒☒☒ COMMENDED

16/17 Warwick Road,
Stratford-upon-Avon CV37 6YW
☎ (01789) 204109 & 299468
Fax (01789) 415916
Email: kiwiauon@aol.com.uk
Ⓡ Logis of GB
*Family-run hotel within 6 minutes' walk
of town centre. Adjacent to sports
centre and golf-courses. Vaulted Cellar
Restaurant.*
Bedrooms: 4 single, 11 double,
6 twin, 1 triple, 1 family room
Bathrooms: 22 en-suite, 1 public

Bed & breakfast

per night:	£min	£max
Single	30.00	55.00
Double	48.00	98.00

Half board per person:

	£min	£max
Daily	43.00	68.00
Weekly	301.00	476.00

Lunch available
Evening meal 1730 (last orders
2200)
Parking for 32
Cards accepted: Amex, Diners,
Mastercard, Visa, Switch/Delta

Courtland Hotel ⚑

☒☒ APPROVED

12 Guild Street,
Stratford-upon-Avon CV37 6RE
☎ (01789) 292401
Fax (01789) 292401
*Personal attention in elegant Georgian
house. Town centre situation at rear of
Shakespeare's birthplace and 3-4*

---

*minutes from theatre. Home-made
preserves, antique furniture.*
Bedrooms: 2 single, 2 double, 1 twin,
2 family rooms
Bathrooms: 3 en-suite, 2 public

Bed & breakfast

per night:	£min	£max
Single	22.00	38.00
Double	38.00	56.00

Parking for 3
Cards accepted: Amex, Mastercard,
Visa

Craig Cleeve House ⚑

☒☒ COMMENDED

67-69 Shipston Road,
Stratford-upon-Avon CV37 7LW
☎ (01789) 296573
Fax (01789) 299452
*Licensed family hotel close to the town
centre and theatre, offering friendly
service and value for money in
comfortable surroundings.*
Bedrooms: 2 single, 7 double, 5 twin,
1 family room
Bathrooms: 9 en-suite, 2 public

Bed & breakfast

per night:	£min	£max
Single	21.00	48.00
Double	40.00	54.00

Parking for 15
Cards accepted: Amex, Diners,
Mastercard, Visa, Switch/Delta

Curtain Call ⚑

142 Alcester Road,
Stratford-upon-Avon CV37 9DR
☎ (01789) 267734
Fax (01789) 267734
*Ten-minute walk from town. En-suite
rooms and four-poster bed available,
colour TV in all rooms, relaxed
atmosphere - all at reasonable prices.*
Bedrooms: 2 single, 2 double, 1 twin
Bathrooms: 3 en-suite, 1 public

Bed & breakfast

per night:	£min	£max
Single	16.00	21.00
Double	32.00	48.00

Half board per person:

	£min	£max
Daily	21.00	29.00
Weekly	147.00	203.00

Evening meal 1830 (last orders
2030)
Parking for 5
Cards accepted: Mastercard, Visa,
Switch/Delta

Dukes Hotel ⚑

☒☒☒☒ COMMENDED

Payton Street, Stratford-upon-Avon
CV37 6UA
☎ (01789) 269300 & 297921
Fax (01789) 414700
Ⓡ Logis of GB

*Listed Georgian town house, furnished
with antiques, in town centre location.
Own garden and car park. Privately
owned and operated. French and
German spoken.*
Bedrooms: 4 single, 10 double,
8 twin
Suites available
Bathrooms: 22 en-suite

Bed & breakfast

per night:	£min	£max
Single	50.00	54.50
Double	69.50	115.00

Half board per person:

	£min	£max
Daily	57.50	65.00

Lunch available
Evening meal 1800 (last orders
2130)
Parking for 30
Cards accepted: Amex, Diners,
Mastercard, Visa, Switch/Delta

Dylan Guesthouse ⚑

Listed APPROVED

10 Evesham Place,
Stratford-upon-Avon CV37 6HT
☎ (01789) 204819
*Located in the town, 5 minutes' walk
from shops and the Royal Shakespeare
Theatre. We are a no-smoking
establishment.*
Bedrooms: 1 single, 2 double, 1 twin,
1 triple
Bathrooms: 5 en-suite

Bed & breakfast

per night:	£min	£max
Single	20.00	25.00
Double	38.00	44.00

Parking for 5

> Map references apply to
> the colour maps at the
> back of this guide.

East Bank House

👑👑 [COMMENDED]

19 Warwick Road,
Stratford-upon-Avon CV37 6YW
☎ (01789) 292758
Fax (01789) 292758

Fine Victorian house set in well-tended grounds just 3 minutes' walk from town centre. Friendly, good food and good value.

Wheelchair access category 3♿
Bedrooms: 6 double, 3 twin, 1 triple
Bathrooms: 8 en-suite, 1 public

Bed & breakfast per night:	£min	£max
Single	32.00	50.00
Double	40.00	64.00

Parking for 5
Cards accepted: Mastercard, Visa, Switch/Delta
🐎 🛏 📺 ☕ [UL] [S] 🚭 [R] [SP]

Eastnor House Hotel

👑👑 [COMMENDED]

Shipston Road, Stratford-upon-Avon CV37 7LN
☎ (01789) 268115
Fax (01789) 266516

Comfortable Victorian private hotel, oak panelled and tastefully furnished. Spacious bedrooms with private bathrooms. Centrally located by River Avon, theatre 350 metres.

Bedrooms: 3 double, 2 twin, 2 triple, 2 family rooms
Bathrooms: 9 en-suite

Bed & breakfast per night:	£min	£max
Single	20.00	50.00
Double	50.00	64.00

Parking for 9
Cards accepted: Amex, Mastercard, Visa, Switch/Delta
🐎 🛏 📺 ☕ [S] 🚭 [R] 12 [OAP] [SP] [T]

Falcon Hotel

👑👑👑👑 [COMMENDED]

Chapel Street, Stratford-upon-Avon CV37 6HA
☎ (01789) 279953
Fax (01789) 414260
[CR] Utell International

A magnificently preserved 16th C timbered inn, with a skilfully blended modern extension, large enclosed garden and ample car parking, situated in the heart of Stratford.

Bedrooms: 5 single, 23 double, 31 twin, 13 triple, 1 family room
Bathrooms: 73 en-suite

Bed & breakfast per night:	£min	£max
Single	60.00	99.00
Double	70.00	145.00

Half board per person:	£min	£max
Daily	52.00	75.00
Weekly	315.00	441.00

Lunch available
Evening meal 1800 (last orders 2100)
Parking for 124
Cards accepted: Amex, Diners, Mastercard, Visa, Switch/Delta
🐎 ☎ 📺 ☕ [S] 🚭 [R] [TV] 200 [OAP] [SP] [T]

Grosvenor Hotel

👑👑👑👑 [COMMENDED]

Warwick Road,
Stratford-upon-Avon CV37 6YT
☎ (01789) 269213
Fax (01789) 266087

Independently-owned Georgian hotel, 5 minutes' walk from town centre, theatres, Shakespeare's birthplace and River Avon. Unique restaurant decor, private car park.

Wheelchair access category 3♿
Bedrooms: 7 single, 35 double, 17 twin, 7 triple, 1 family room
Suites available
Bathrooms: 67 en-suite

Bed & breakfast per night:	£min	£max
Single	78.50	81.50
Double	95.00	98.00

Lunch available
Evening meal 1800 (last orders 2130)
Parking for 50
Cards accepted: Amex, Diners, Mastercard, Visa, Switch/Delta
🐎 🛏 ☎ 📺 ☕ [S] 🚭 [R] 80 [OAP] [SP] [T]

A key to symbols can be found inside the back cover flap.

Hampton Lodge Guest House

👑👑 [COMMENDED]

38 Shipston Road,
Stratford-upon-Avon CV37 7LP
☎ (01789) 299374
Fax (01789) 299374

Comfortable guesthouse. All en-suite rooms with usual facilities. 5 minutes' walk town centre and RSC Theatre. Friendly reception. Private parking.

Bedrooms: 1 single, 2 double, 1 twin, 2 triple
Bathrooms: 6 en-suite

Bed & breakfast per night:	£min	£max
Single	28.00	35.00
Double	36.00	46.00

Evening meal 1800 (last orders 1930)
Parking for 8
Cards accepted: Amex, Mastercard, Visa, Switch/Delta
🐎 🛏 ☎ 📺 ☕ [UL] [S] 🚭 [R] [TV] [SP]

Hardwick House

👑👑 [COMMENDED]

1 Avenue Road,
Stratford-upon-Avon CV37 6UY
☎ (01789) 204307
Fax (01789) 296760

Family-run Victorian guesthouse in a quiet area, a short walk to town, theatre, Shakespearean properties. Non-smoking bedrooms. Large car park.

Bedrooms: 2 single, 7 double, 2 twin, 2 triple, 1 family room
Bathrooms: 13 en-suite, 1 private, 1 public

Bed & breakfast per night:	£min	£max
Single	28.00	38.00
Double	38.00	64.00

Parking for 12
Cards accepted: Amex, Mastercard, Visa, Switch/Delta
🐎 🛏 📺 ☕ [UL] [S] 🚭 [R] [SP] [T]

COLOUR MAPS

Colour maps at the back of this guide pinpoint all places in which you will find accommodation listed.

Melita Private Hotel

COMMENDED

37 Shipston Road,
Stratford-upon-Avon CV37 7LN
☎ (01789) 292432
Fax (01789) 204867

*Appointed to a high and comfortable
standard, managed by caring
proprietors offering a warm, friendly
atmosphere. Close to town centre and
an ideal base for Cotswolds and
National Exhibition Centre. Lounge bar
and beautiful award-winning garden.*
Bedrooms: 3 single, 4 double, 3 twin,
1 triple, 1 family room
Bathrooms: 10 en-suite, 2 private
Bed & breakfast

per night:	£min	£max
Single	32.00	54.00
Double	49.00	78.00

Parking for 12
Cards accepted: Amex, Mastercard,
Visa, Switch/Delta

Moonlight Bed & Breakfast ⋀

Listed COMMENDED

144 Alcester Road,
Stratford-upon-Avon CV37 9DR
☎ (01789) 298213
*Small family guesthouse near town
centre, offering comfortable
accommodation at reasonable prices.
Tea/coffee-making facilities and colour
TV. En-suite rooms available.*
Bedrooms: 1 single, 1 double, 1 twin,
1 triple
Bathrooms: 2 en-suite, 1 public
Bed & breakfast

per night:	£min	£max
Single	15.00	17.00
Double	30.00	34.00

Parking for 4

Moonraker House ⋀

COMMENDED

40 Alcester Road,
Stratford-upon-Avon CV37 9DB
☎ (01789) 299346 & 267115
Fax (01789) 295504
Email: moonraker.spencer
@virgin.net
Ⓒ Minotel

*Family-run, near town centre.
Beautifully co-ordinated decor
throughout. Some rooms with
four-poster beds and garden terrace
available for non-smokers.*
www.stratford-upon-avon.co.uk/
moonraker.htm
Bedrooms: 16 double, 2 twin,
4 triple
Bathrooms: 22 en-suite
Bed & breakfast

per night:	£min	£max
Single	35.00	45.00
Double	45.00	70.00

Parking for 24
Cards accepted: Mastercard, Visa

Moss Cottage ⋀

COMMENDED

61 Evesham Road,
Stratford-upon-Avon CV37 9BA
☎ (01789) 294770
Fax (01789) 294770
*Pauline and Jim Rush welcome you to
their charming detached cottage.
Walking distance theatre/town.
Spacious en-suite accommodation.
Hospitality tray, TV. Parking.*
Bedrooms: 2 double
Bathrooms: 2 en-suite
Bed & breakfast

per night:	£min	£max
Single	25.00	35.00
Double	34.00	46.00

Parking for 3

The Myrtles Bed and Breakfast ⋀

Listed COMMENDED

6 Rother Street,
Stratford-upon-Avon CV37 6LU
☎ (01789) 295511
*Victorian 3-storey building in town
centre. En-suite bedrooms, breakfast
room and patio garden.*
Bedrooms: 2 double, 1 twin
Bathrooms: 3 en-suite
Bed & breakfast

per night:	£min	£max
Single	30.00	45.00
Double	45.00	50.00

Cards accepted: Mastercard, Visa

Newlands ⋀

COMMENDED

7 Broad Walk, Stratford-upon-Avon
CV37 6HS
☎ (01789) 298449
Fax (01789) 298449
*Sue Boston's home is a short walk to
the Royal Shakespeare Theatre, town*

*centre and Shakespeare properties,
and has some forecourt parking.*
Bedrooms: 1 single, 1 double,
2 triple
Bathrooms: 3 en-suite, 1 public
Bed & breakfast

per night:	£min	£max
Single	19.00	21.00
Double	40.00	46.00

Parking for 2
Cards accepted: Mastercard, Visa,
Switch/Delta

Oxstalls Farm

COMMENDED

Warwick Road,
Stratford-upon-Avon CV37 0NS
☎ (01789) 205277
*Beautifully situated 60-acre stud farm
overlooking the Welcome Hills and
golf-course. 1 mile from
Stratford-upon-Avon town centre and
the Royal Shakespeare Theatre.*
Bedrooms: 1 single, 11 double,
4 twin, 7 triple
Bathrooms: 16 en-suite, 1 public,
3 private showers
Bed & breakfast

per night:	£min	£max
Single	17.50	35.00
Double	35.00	60.00

Parking for 20

Ad See display advertisement on
page 279

Parkfield ⋀

COMMENDED

3 Broad Walk, Stratford-upon-Avon
CV37 6HS
☎ (01789) 293313
Fax (01789) 293313
*Delightful Victorian house. Quiet
location, 5 minutes' walk from theatre
and town. Some rooms en-suite. Colour
TV, tea and coffee facilities and parking.
Choice of breakfast, including
vegetarian. A non-smoking house.*
Bedrooms: 1 single, 1 double, 1 twin,
4 triple
Bathrooms: 5 en-suite, 1 public
Bed & breakfast

per night:	£min	£max
Single	19.00	19.00
Double	36.00	42.00

Parking for 7
Cards accepted: Diners, Mastercard,
Visa

Payton Hotel ⚜

👑👑 HIGHLY COMMENDED

6 John Street, Stratford-upon-Avon
CV37 6UB
☎ (01789) 266442
Fax (01789) 266442

Listed Georgian house in centre of
Stratford, in quiet location. Theatre 3
minutes' walk. Four-poster or Victorian
antique beds.
Bedrooms: 3 double, 2 twin
Bathrooms: 4 en-suite, 1 private
shower

Bed & breakfast

per night:	£min	£max
Single	38.00	42.00
Double	56.00	64.00

Parking for 3
Cards accepted: Amex, Mastercard,
Visa

Peartree Cottage ⚜

👑👑👑 HIGHLY COMMENDED

7 Church Road, Wilmcote,
Stratford-upon-Avon CV37 9UX
☎ (01789) 205889
Fax (01789) 262862
Elizabethan house, furnished with
antiques, set in beautiful garden
overlooking Mary Arden's house. Pub
and restaurant within walking distance.
Bedrooms: 4 double, 2 twin, 1 triple
Bathrooms: 7 en-suite

Bed & breakfast

per night:	£min	£max
Single	30.00	32.00
Double	45.00	50.00

Parking for 8

For ideas on places to visit
refer to the introduction at
the beginning of this section.

The National Grading and
Classification Scheme is
explained at the back
of this guide.

Ravenhurst ⚜

👑👑 COMMENDED

2 Broad Walk, Stratford-upon-Avon
CV37 6HS
☎ (01789) 292515
Quietly situated, a few minutes' walk
from the town centre and places of
historic interest. Comfortable home,
with substantial breakfast provided.
Four-poster available.
Bedrooms: 4 double, 1 twin
Bathrooms: 5 en-suite

Bed & breakfast

per night:	£min	£max
Double	40.00	50.00

Parking for 4
Cards accepted: Amex, Diners,
Mastercard, Visa

The Stag at Redhill ⚜

👑👑 COMMENDED

Alcester Road, Stratford-upon-Avon
B49 6NQ
☎ (01789) 764634
Fax (01789) 764431

16th C coaching inn in 4 acres of
landscaped gardens, 2 miles from
Stratford-upon-Avon. En-suite bedrooms
with all amenities. Smoking and
non-smoking restaurant renowned for
splendid food.
Bedrooms: 4 single, 5 double, 3 twin
Bathrooms: 12 en-suite

Bed & breakfast

per night:	£min	£max
Single	40.00	48.75
Double	50.00	66.00

Lunch available
Evening meal 1900 (last orders
2130)
Parking for 92
Cards accepted: Amex, Diners,
Mastercard, Visa

The symbols in each entry
give information about
services and facilities.
A key to these symbols
appears at the back
of this guide.

Stratford Court Hotel ⚜

👑👑👑 HIGHLY COMMENDED

20 Avenue Road,
Stratford-upon-Avon CV37 6UX
☎ (01789) 297799
Fax (01789) 262449

Quietly situated Edwardian house,
furnished with antiques and set in
beautiful gardens with car park. Enjoy
the relaxed atmosphere yet only 10
minutes' walk from the town and
theatres.
Bedrooms: 4 single, 5 double, 2 twin,
2 triple
Bathrooms: 13 en-suite

Bed & breakfast

per night:	£min	£max
Single	45.00	55.00
Double	75.00	140.00

Half board per

person:	£min	£max
Daily	60.50	70.50

Lunch available
Evening meal 1800 (last orders
2030)
Parking for 32
Cards accepted: Mastercard, Visa

Stratford Manor Hotel ⚜

👑👑👑👑 HIGHLY COMMENDED

Warwick Road,
Stratford-upon-Avon CV37 0PY
☎ (01789) 731173
Fax (01789) 731131
⊂ℝ Best Western
A warm welcome awaits you. Superb
leisure facilities. Ideal base for exploring
Cotswolds and Stratford-upon-Avon.
Bedrooms: 38 double, 66 twin
Bathrooms: 104 en-suite

Bed & breakfast

per night:	£min	£max
Single	99.50	119.50
Double	125.00	145.00

Half board per

person:	£min	£max
Daily	121.50	141.50

Lunch available
Evening meal 1900 (last orders
2130)
Parking for 220
Cards accepted: Amex, Diners,
Mastercard, Visa, Switch/Delta

STRATFORD-UPON-AVON

Continued

Stratford Victoria ♨

👑👑👑👑 HIGHLY COMMENDED

Arden Street, Stratford-upon-Avon
CV37 6NX
☎ (01789) 271000
Fax (01789) 271001
*Newly-constructed, Victorian-style hotel
close to the centre of
Stratford-upon-Avon. Brasserie
restaurant, bar, gym, whirlpool spa and
conference facilities.*
Bedrooms: 10 single, 37 double,
2 twin, 9 triple, 42 family rooms
Suite available
Bathrooms: 100 en-suite

Bed & breakfast

per night:	£min	£max
Single	75.00	135.00
Double	95.00	155.00

Half board per

person:	£min	£max
Daily	57.50	80.00
Weekly	450.00	500.00

Lunch available
Evening meal 1800 (last orders
2200)
Parking for 95
Cards accepted: Amex, Diners,
Mastercard, Visa, Switch/Delta
🐕♿🍴📞🖥️⏰🎱💺Ⓢ✂🎵◐
🏬▥🛜🛎️140✕⛵⛳❀🖂SP Ⓣ

Twelfth Night ♨

👑👑👑 COMMENDED

Evesham Place, Stratford-upon-Avon
CV37 6HT
☎ (01789) 414595
*Somewhere special. Once owned by the
Royal Shakespeare Company, this
beautifully restored Victorian villa
provides nostalgia and superior
accommodation for the discerning.
Non-smokers only, please.*
Bedrooms: 6 double
Bathrooms: 6 en-suite

Bed & breakfast

per night:	£min	£max
Double	45.00	58.00

Parking for 7
Cards accepted: Mastercard, Visa
📞🖥️⏰🎱UL Ⓢ✂🎵🏬🖂✕🛜
🛎️

COLOUR MAPS

Colour maps at the back of
this guide pinpoint all places
in which you will find
accommodation listed.

Victoria Spa Lodge ♨

👑👑 HIGHLY COMMENDED

Bishopton Lane,
Stratford-upon-Avon CV37 9QY
☎ (01789) 267985
Fax (01789) 204728
*Elegant 19th C English home in
country setting, overlooking canal 1.5
miles from town centre. Your hosts are
Paul and D'reen Tozer.*
Bedrooms: 3 double, 1 twin, 3 family
rooms
Bathrooms: 7 en-suite, 1 public

Bed & breakfast

per night:	£min	£max
Single	35.00	45.00
Double	45.00	55.00

Parking for 12
Cards accepted: Mastercard, Visa
🐕🍴🖥️⏰🎱UL🎵✂🎵🏬🖂❀✕
🛜🛎️ Ⓣ

STRETTON

Staffordshire
Map ref 4B3

On the outskirts of Burton upon
Trent, beside the Trent and Mersey
Canal and River Dove, alongside the
Roman road - Ryknild Street.

Dovecliff Hall ♨

👑👑👑👑 HIGHLY COMMENDED

Dovecliff Road, Stretton, Burton
upon Trent DE13 0DJ
☎ (01283) 531818
Fax (01283) 516546
*Magnificent Georgian house, with
breathtaking views, overlooking the
River Dove and set in 7 acres of
landscaped gardens in open
countryside. Half a mile from A38.*
Bedrooms: 1 single, 5 double, 1 twin
Bathrooms: 7 en-suite

Bed & breakfast

per night:	£min	£max
Single	55.00	85.00
Double	95.00	105.00

Lunch available
Evening meal 1900 (last orders
2130)
Parking for 40
Cards accepted: Amex, Diners,
Mastercard, Visa, Switch/Delta
🐕📞🍴🖥️🎱Ⓢ🎵🏬🖂🛜60▶❀
✕🛜SP🛎️

The ♨ symbol after an
establishment name indicates
that it is a Regional
Tourist Board member.

STROUD

Gloucestershire
Map ref 2B1

This old town, surrounded by
attractive hilly country, has been
producing broadcloth for centuries
and the local museum has an
interesting display on the subject.
Many of the mills have been
converted into craft centres and for
other uses.
*Tourist Information Centre ☎ (01453)
765768*

Ashleigh House ♨

👑 COMMENDED

Bussage, Stroud GL6 8AZ
☎ (01453) 883944
Fax (01453) 886931
*Ideal Cotswold touring centre in
peaceful setting, offering good food,
cleanliness and comfort. All rooms
en-suite.*
Bedrooms: 3 double, 3 twin, 3 triple
Bathrooms: 9 en-suite

Bed & breakfast

per night:	£min	£max
Single		32.00
Double		50.00

Half board per

person:	£min	£max
Daily		45.50

Evening meal 1830 (last orders
1900)
Parking for 10
Open March–November
🐕8♿🍴🖥️🎱Ⓢ✂🎵🏬🖂❀✕
🛜

Bell Hotel & Restaurant ♨

👑👑 COMMENDED

Wallbridge, Stroud GL5 3JA
☎ (01453) 763556
Fax (01453) 758611
*Friendly, family-run hotel. All rooms with
TV, tea/coffee facilities and telephone.
Bridal suite. A la carte restaurant.
Garden and bar on canal.*
Bedrooms: 1 single, 7 double, 3 twin,
1 triple
Bathrooms: 10 en-suite, 1 public

Bed & breakfast

per night:	£min	£max
Single	32.00	50.00
Double	45.00	70.00

Half board per

person:	£min	£max
Daily	42.00	64.00

Lunch available
Evening meal 1900 (last orders
2130)
Parking for 25

Cards accepted: Diners, Mastercard, Visa

🛏🛅🍴📞🖭♿⬆🎿Ⓢ⌕📺🗑 ⬛🛏📍35 ⚲∪🏃☀❀ ᴅᴀᴘ 🐾 SP 🏵 Ⓣ

Downfield Hotel 🅜
🏆🏆🏆 COMMENDED
134 Cainscross Road, Stroud
GL5 4HN
☎ (01453) 764496
Fax (01453) 753150

Imposing hotel in quiet location. Home cooking. 1 mile from town centre, 5 miles from M5 motorway, junction 13, on main A419 road.
Bedrooms: 4 single, 9 double, 7 twin, 1 triple
Bathrooms: 11 en-suite, 3 public

Bed & breakfast per night:	£min	£max
Single	20.00	29.00
Double	33.00	39.00

Evening meal 1830 (last orders 2000)
Parking for 23
Cards accepted: Amex, Diners, Mastercard, Visa, Switch/Delta

🛏🛅🍴⬆🛅Ⓢ⌕📺🗑🛏🐾

SYMONDS YAT EAST
Hereford and Worcester
Map ref 2A1

Well-known beauty spot where the River Wye loops back on itself in a narrow gorge. It is close to the ruins of Goodrich Castle, the Forest of Dean and the Welsh border.

Royal Hotel 🅜
🏆🏆🏆🏆 APPROVED
Symonds Yat East, Ross-on-Wye, Herefordshire HR9 6JL
☎ (01600) 890238
Fax (01600) 890238
Quiet country house in Alpine-type setting, next to the River Wye. Ideal touring location. Only 6 miles from Ross-on-Wye and Monmouth.
Bedrooms: 1 single, 15 double, 4 twin
Bathrooms: 20 en-suite

Bed & breakfast per night:	£min	£max
Single	30.00	45.00
Double	60.00	70.00

Lunch available
Evening meal 1900 (last orders 2100)

Parking for 90
Cards accepted: Amex, Diners, Mastercard, Visa, Switch/Delta

🛏🛅12🍴📞🖭⬆Ⓢ⌕🗑🛏🛏80 ∪🎵❀🐾🐾 SP 🏵

SYMONDS YAT WEST
Hereford and Worcester
Map ref 2A1

Jubilee Maze and Exhibition was created here in 1977 to commemorate Queen Elizabeth II's Jubilee, and there are other attractions beside the river. The area of Symonds Yat is a world-renowned beauty spot.

Riversdale Lodge Hotel
🏆🏆 COMMENDED
Symonds Yat West, Ross-on-Wye, Herefordshire HR9 6BL
☎ (01600) 890445
Fax (01600) 890445
High standard accommodation, set in 2 acres on the banks of the River Wye. Spectacular views of the rapids and gorge. Traditional food.
Bedrooms: 3 double, 1 twin, 1 family room
Bathrooms: 5 en-suite, 1 public

Bed & breakfast per night:	£min	£max
Single	25.00	30.00
Double	50.00	50.00

Half board per person:	£min	£max
Daily	37.00	40.00
Weekly	259.00	280.00

Lunch available
Evening meal 1900 (last orders 1300)
Parking for 11

🛏🛅📖⬆🛅🎿⌕📺🗑🛏🐾⏍🏃 ❀🐾Ⓣ

Woodlea Hotel 🅜
🏆🏆 COMMENDED
Symonds Yat West, Ross-on-Wye, Herefordshire HR9 6BL
☎ (01600) 890206
Fax (01600) 890206
Family-run Victorian country house hotel set in a secluded woodland valley close to River Wye. Only one and half miles from A40, between Ross and Monmouth. Excellent food and wines, friendly welcome.
Bedrooms: 1 single, 4 double, 1 twin, 1 triple, 1 family room
Bathrooms: 6 en-suite, 2 public

Bed & breakfast per night:	£min	£max
Single	25.00	41.50
Double	50.00	63.00

Half board per person:	£min	£max
Daily	38.00	44.50
Weekly	241.50	

Evening meal 1900 (last orders 1830)
Parking for 9
Cards accepted: Mastercard, Visa

🛏🛅🍴📖⬆Ⓢ⌕📺🗑🛏🐾❀🐾🐾 SP 🎖

TELFORD
Shropshire
Map ref 4A3

New Town named after Thomas Telford, the famous engineer who designed many of the country's canals, bridges and viaducts. It is close to Ironbridge with its monuments and museums to the Industrial Revolution, including restored 18th C buildings.
Tourist Information Centre ☎ (01952) 291370

Arleston Inn Hotel
🏆🏆🏆 COMMENDED
Arleston Lane, Wellington, Telford TF1 2LA
☎ (01952) 501881
Fax (01952) 506429
Tudor-style building with many exposed beamed ceilings. M54, 5 minutes from junction 6. A la carte and bar menus.
Bedrooms: 2 single, 4 double, 1 twin
Bathrooms: 7 en-suite

Bed & breakfast per night:	£min	£max
Single	38.00	38.00
Double	48.00	48.00

Lunch available
Evening meal 1900 (last orders 2200)
Parking for 40
Cards accepted: Mastercard, Visa

🛏📞🖭⬆🛅Ⓢ🔵🗑🛏🛏❀🍴❀ 🐾 SP 🏵

Falcon Hotel 🅜
🏆🏆 APPROVED
Holyhead Road, Wellington, Telford TF1 2DD
☎ (01952) 255011
Small, family-run 18th C coaching hotel, 10 miles from Shrewsbury, 4 miles from Ironbridge, 18 miles from M6 at the end of M54 (exit 7).
Bedrooms: 2 single, 4 double, 4 twin, 1 family room
Bathrooms: 7 en-suite, 2 public

Bed & breakfast per night:	£min	£max
Single	27.00	38.00
Double	35.00	47.00

Continued ▶

TELFORD

Continued

Lunch available
Evening meal 1900 (last orders 2100)
Parking for 30
Cards accepted: Mastercard, Visa

The Oaks Hotel & Restaurant ⚑

👑👑👑 COMMENDED

Redhill, St Georges, Telford
TF2 9NZ
☎ (01952) 620126
Fax (01952) 620257
Family-owned hotel, 2.5 miles from Telford town centre. Restaurant, public bar. En-suite bedrooms with telephone, colour TV, tea/coffee facilities.
Bedrooms: 6 single, 3 double, 3 twin
Bathrooms: 12 en-suite

Bed & breakfast

per night:	£min	£max
Single	42.00	45.00
Double	50.00	53.00

Lunch available
Evening meal 1900 (last orders 2130)
Parking for 40
Cards accepted: Amex, Diners, Mastercard, Visa

Park House Hotel ⚑

👑👑👑👑 COMMENDED

Park Street, Shifnal TF11 9BA
☎ (01952) 460128
Fax (01952) 461658
CR MacDonald/Utell International
Magnificent character hotel converted from 2 17th C country houses. Located just a few minutes' drive from exit 4 of M54. 40 minutes from Birmingham. Leisure facilities.
Bedrooms: 5 single, 30 double, 19 twin
Bathrooms: 54 en-suite

Bed & breakfast

per night:	£min	£max
Single	55.00	98.00
Double	70.00	124.00

Half board per

person:	£min	£max
Daily	55.00	118.95
Weekly	315.00	

Lunch available
Evening meal 1900 (last orders 2130)
Parking for 180
Cards accepted: Amex, Diners, Mastercard, Visa, Switch/Delta

Stone House ⚑

👑👑👑 COMMENDED

Shifnal Road, Priorslee, Telford
TF2 9NN
☎ (01952) 290119
Fax (01952) 290119
Comfortable guesthouse, convenient for M54, station, town centre, Ironbridge and university. Personal attention assured. Good home cooking.
Bedrooms: 2 double, 3 twin
Bathrooms: 5 en-suite

Bed & breakfast

per night:	£min	£max
Single	24.00	26.00
Double	38.00	40.00

Half board per

person:	£min	£max
Daily	34.00	36.00
Weekly		252.00

Evening meal 1800 (last orders 1900)
Parking for 4

TETBURY

Gloucestershire
Map ref 2B2

Small market town with 18th C houses and an attractive 17th C Town Hall. It is a good touring centre with many places of interest nearby including Badminton House and Westonbirt Arboretum.

Hunters Hall Inn ⚑

👑👑👑 COMMENDED

Kingscote, Tetbury GL8 8XZ
☎ (01453) 860393
Fax (01453) 860707
16th C coaching inn with open fireplaces and beamed ceilings. The old stable block has been converted into bedrooms. On the A4135 between Tetbury and Dursley.
Bedrooms: 6 double, 5 twin, 1 triple
Bathrooms: 12 en-suite

Bed & breakfast

per night:	£min	£max
Single	45.00	50.00
Double	60.00	70.00

Half board per

person:	£min	£max
Daily	60.00	
Weekly	280.00	

Lunch available
Evening meal 1900 (last orders 2145)
Parking for 100
Cards accepted: Amex, Mastercard, Visa, Switch/Delta

Tavern House ⚑

👑👑👑 DE LUXE

Willesley, Tetbury GL8 8QU
☎ (01666) 880444
Fax (01666) 880254

Grade II listed Cotswold stone house (formerly a staging post) on the A433 Bath road, 1 mile from Westonbirt Arboretum and 4 miles from Tetbury.
Bedrooms: 3 double, 1 twin
Bathrooms: 4 en-suite

Bed & breakfast

per night:	£min	£max
Single	42.50	47.50
Double	57.00	67.00

Parking for 4
Cards accepted: Mastercard, Visa

TEWKESBURY

Gloucestershire
Map ref 2B1

Tewkesbury's outstanding possession is its magnificent church, built as an abbey, with a great Norman tower and beautiful 14th C interior. The town stands at the confluence of the Severn and Avon and has many medieval houses, inns and several museums.
Tourist Information Centre ☎ (01684) 295027

Jessop House Hotel ⚑

👑👑👑 COMMENDED

65 Church Street, Tewkesbury
GL20 5RZ
☎ (01684) 292017
Fax (01684) 273076
CR Logis of GB/Minotel
Georgian house facing the abbey and medieval cottages, peacefully overlooking Tewkesbury's "Ham".
Bedrooms: 3 double, 4 twin, 1 triple
Bathrooms: 8 en-suite

Bed & breakfast

per night:	£min	£max
Single		55.00
Double		75.00

Evening meal 1900 (last orders 2030)
Parking for 6
Cards accepted: Amex, Mastercard, Visa

THEDDINGWORTH

Leicestershire
Map ref 4C3

Village close to the Civil War battlefield of Naseby with its Battle and Farm Museum.

Hothorpe Hall ⚇

⚜⚜⚜ COMMENDED

Theddingworth, Lutterworth
LE17 6QX
☎ (01858) 880257
Fax (01858) 880979

Family-run hotel/conference centre in Georgian country house in a delightful, quiet rural setting. 12 acres of gardens and grounds. Car parking. 5 miles from Market Harborough.
Wheelchair access category 1&
Bedrooms: 2 single, 4 double, 28 twin, 3 triple, 17 family rooms
Bathrooms: 35 en-suite, 7 public

Bed & breakfast

per night:	£min	£max
Single	18.75	23.50
Double	30.50	34.00

Half board per person:

	£min	£max
Daily	26.70	31.45
Weekly	140.18	165.11

Lunch available
Evening meal 1800 (last orders 1900)
Parking for 70
Cards accepted: Mastercard, Visa, Switch/Delta

🐎🐟&♿🖭📞 🔌♻♨🔥 S ⚡📺 ◑ ☎ 🔥
🖨 ⛟150 ● ❀ ↘ SP 🎫

ULLINGSWICK

Hereford and Worcester
Map ref 2A1

Village close to Hereford with its many attractions including the cathedral and the Cider Museum.

The Steppes ⚇

⚜⚜⚜⚜ HIGHLY COMMENDED

Ullingswick, Hereford HR1 3JG
☎ (01432) 820424
Fax (01432) 820042
17th C listed building with oak beams, log fires and inglenook fireplaces. Cordon Bleu cuisine. Intimate atmosphere. En-suite accommodation in restored barns.

Bedrooms: 4 double, 2 twin
Bathrooms: 6 en-suite

Bed & breakfast

per night:	£min	£max
Single	45.00	55.00
Double	80.00	90.00

Half board per person:

	£min	£max
Daily	64.00	69.00
Weekly	375.00	400.00

Evening meal 1930 (last orders 2030)
Parking for 8
Open February–December
Cards accepted: Amex, Mastercard, Visa, Switch/Delta

🐎12&♿📞🖭📦♻🔥 S ⚡🔥🖨 🖨❀🐕↘ SP 🎫

UPPINGHAM

Leicestershire
Map ref 4C3

Quiet market town dominated by its famous public school which was founded in 1584. It has many stone houses and is surrounded by attractive countryside.

Lake Isle Hotel ⚇

⚜⚜⚜ HIGHLY COMMENDED

16 High Street East, Uppingham, Oakham LE15 9PZ
☎ (01572) 822951
Fax (01572) 822951
This 18th C hotel absorbs more than a little of Uppingham's charm. The personal touch will make your stay extra special with weekly changing menus and a list of over 300 wines.
Bedrooms: 1 single, 9 double, 2 twin
Suites available
Bathrooms: 12 en-suite

Bed & breakfast

per night:	£min	£max
Single	45.00	52.00
Double	65.00	80.00

Lunch available
Evening meal 1930 (last orders 2130)
Parking for 7
Cards accepted: Amex, Diners, Mastercard, Visa

🐎♿📞🖭📦♻🔊 S ⚡🖨⏺ 🖨 ❀🐕↘ SP 🎫

Rutland House ⚇

⚜⚜ COMMENDED

61 High Street East, Uppingham
LE15 9PY
☎ (01572) 822497
Fax (01572) 822497
Family-run B & B. All rooms en-suite. Close to Rutland Water. Full English or continental breakfast. Well-placed for exploring Rutland's villages and countryside.
Bedrooms: 2 double, 2 twin, 1 triple
Bathrooms: 5 en-suite

Bed & breakfast

per night:	£min	£max
Single	30.00	30.00
Double	40.00	40.00

Parking for 3
Cards accepted: Mastercard, Visa

🐎5&♿🖭📦♻ UL S ⚡🖨 🖨 🎫

UPTON-UPON-SEVERN

Hereford and Worcester
Map ref 2B1

Attractive country town on the banks of the Severn and a good river cruising centre. It has many pleasant old houses and inns, and the pepperpot landmark is now the Heritage Centre.
Tourist Information Centre ☎ (01684) 594200

Bridge House ⚇

⚜⚜⚜ HIGHLY COMMENDED

Welland Stone, Upton-upon-Severn, Worcester WR8 0RW
☎ (01684) 593046
Fax (01684) 593046
The house, originally a cottage, benefits from extensive and tasteful renovation, with each room enjoying lovely views over the countryside.
Bedrooms: 2 double, 1 twin
Bathrooms: 3 en-suite

Bed & breakfast

per night:	£min	£max
Single	20.00	25.00
Double	40.00	50.00

Half board per person:

	£min	£max
Daily	35.00	40.00
Weekly	200.00	230.00

Parking for 8

🐎5🎪🖭📦♻🔊 UL S ⚡🖨📺 🖨 🖨❀🐕 DAP SP

Map references apply to the colour maps at the back of this guide.

UPTON-UPON-SEVERN

Continued

Tiltridge Farm and Vineyard ♙

♕♕ HIGHLY COMMENDED

Upper Hook Road,
Upton-upon-Severn, Worcester
WR8 0SA
☎ (01684) 592906
Fax (01684) 594142
*9-acre vineyard and farm. Fully
renovated period farmhouse close to
Upton and Malvern showground. Warm
welcome, bumper breakfast and wine
from our own vineyard!*
Bedrooms: 2 double, 1 twin
Bathrooms: 3 en-suite
Bed & breakfast

per night:	£min	£max
Single	23.00	25.00
Double	36.00	40.00

Parking for 12

🛇🍽📞📟🖥♿📶🔌🗲🕇📺 🎞 🕭🍴❋🛲
SP 🏠

UTTOXETER

Staffordshire
Map ref 4B2

Small market town, famous for its
racecourse. There are half-timbered
buildings around the Market Square.

Bank House Hotel ♙

♕♕♕ COMMENDED

Church Street, Uttoxeter ST14 8AG
☎ (01889) 566922
Fax (01889) 567565
Ⓒℝ Consort
*Listed Georgian town house, tastefully
converted, with restaurant, lounge bar
and conference facilities.*
Bedrooms: 3 single, 5 double,
2 triple
Bathrooms: 10 en-suite
Bed & breakfast

per night:	£min	£max
Single	44.50	59.50
Double	59.50	79.50

Half board per

person:	£min	£max
Daily	44.75	54.75

Lunch available
Evening meal 1830 (last orders
2130)
Parking for 16
Cards accepted: Amex, Diners,
Mastercard, Visa, Switch/Delta

🛇🍴📞📟🖥♿📶🔌🗲🕇📺🎞🕭
🛲🕇50 ∪🏃❋ SP 🏠 T ◉

WALSALL

West Midlands
Map ref 4B3

Industrial town with a magnificent
collection of pictures and antiquities
in its museum and art gallery.
Walsall Leather Museum and Jerome
K Jerome birthplace. It has a fine
arboretum with lakes and walks and
illuminations each September.

Beverley Hotel ♙

♕♕♕ COMMENDED

58 Lichfield Road, (A461), Walsall
WS4 2DJ
☎ (01922) 22999 & 614967
Fax (01922) 724187
*Hotel close to motorway network, with
special facilities and rates for group
bookings. Convenient for National
Exhibition Centre.*
Bedrooms: 7 single, 10 double,
14 twin, 2 triple
Bathrooms: 33 en-suite
Bed & breakfast

per night:	£min	£max
Single	40.00	70.00
Double	45.00	80.00

Half board per

person:	£min	£max
Daily	55.00	85.00
Weekly	385.00	595.00

Lunch available
Evening meal 1800 (last orders
2130)
Parking for 66
Cards accepted: Amex, Mastercard,
Visa, Switch/Delta

🛇🍴🛏📞📟🖥♿📶🔌S🗲📺
◉🎞🛲🕇60🍴🗡♜🏃❋🛲 SP T

The Fairlawns at Aldridge ♙

♕♕♕ COMMENDED

Little Aston Road, Aldridge, Walsall
WS9 0NU
☎ (01922) 55122
Fax (01922) 743210
Ⓒℝ Best Western
*Modern hotel in its own grounds, in a
quiet, rural location, 20 minutes from
Birmingham and 30 minutes from the
National Exhibition Centre. Award
winning restaurant specialising in fresh
fish.*
Bedrooms: 3 single, 20 double,
6 twin, 6 triple, 1 family room
Suites available
Bathrooms: 36 en-suite
Bed & breakfast

per night:	£min	£max
Single	49.50	97.50
Double	59.50	105.00

Lunch available
Evening meal 1900 (last orders
2200)

Parking for 82
Cards accepted: Amex, Diners,
Mastercard, Visa, Switch/Delta

🛇🍴🐾📞📟🖥♿📶🔌🕇S🗲📺◗
🎞🛲🕇80∪🏃❋ DAP SP 🔲T

WARWICK

Warwickshire
Map ref 2B1

Castle rising above the River Avon,
15th C Beauchamp Chapel attached
to St Mary's Church, medieval Lord
Leycester's Hospital almshouses and
several museums. Nearby is
Ashorne Hall Nickelodeon and the
National Heritage museum at
Gaydon.
*Tourist Information Centre ☎ (01926)
492212*

The Croft ♙

♕♕♕ COMMENDED

Haseley Knob, Warwick CV35 7NL
☎ (01926) 484447
Fax (01926) 484447
*Friendly family atmosphere in
picturesque rural setting. In Haseley
Knob village off the A4177 between
Balsall Common and Warwick,
convenient for NEC, National
Agricultural Centre, Stratford and
Coventry. 15 minutes from Birmingham
Airport.*
Bedrooms: 1 single, 1 double, 1 twin,
2 triple
Bathrooms: 5 en-suite, 2 public
Bed & breakfast

per night:	£min	£max
Single	21.00	32.00
Double	39.00	44.00

Evening meal 1800 (last orders
1900)
Parking for 10
Cards accepted: Mastercard, Visa,
Switch/Delta

🛇🐾📞📟🖥♿📶🖥 UL 📶🗲📺🎞
🛲❋🐾 SP T ◉

The Glebe at Barford ♙

♕♕♕♕ HIGHLY COMMENDED

Church Street, Barford, Warwick
CV35 8BS
☎ (01926) 624218
Fax (01926) 624625
*Country village location, 1 mile junction
15 of M40, 7 miles
Stratford-upon-Avon. Four-poster beds,
traditional cuisine, fine wines, leisure
club. All en-suite facilities.*
Bedrooms: 4 single, 12 double,
10 twin, 9 triple
Suites available
Bathrooms: 35 en-suite

Bed & breakfast per night:	£min	£max
Single		90.00
Double		110.00

Half board per person:	£min	£max
Daily		60.00

Lunch available
Evening meal 1930 (last orders 2200)
Parking for 67
Cards accepted: Amex, Diners, Mastercard, Visa, Switch/Delta

🛇🏃♿📞📺🗖📶🐾🎣ⓈⓊ◑⊡ 📶📠🖥♟130✂✕🎿🏹∪▶❄ⓈⓅ🏇 Ⓣ

Lord Leicester Hotel ⋀⋀
👑👑👑 APPROVED

17 Jury Street, Warwick CV34 4EJ
☎ (01926) 491481
Fax (01926) 491561
Historic Georgian hotel in Warwick centre. Renowned cuisine in elegant and comfortable surroundings. Easy drive to NEC, walking distance to castle.
Bedrooms: 13 single, 25 double, 7 twin, 2 triple, 4 family rooms
Bathrooms: 51 en-suite

Bed & breakfast per night:	£min	£max
Single	30.00	49.50
Double	60.00	69.50

Lunch available
Evening meal 1900 (last orders 2130)
Parking for 50
Cards accepted: Amex, Diners, Mastercard, Visa, Switch/Delta

🛇🏃♿📞📺🗖📶🐾♟Ⓢ🎿🍺📺◑ ⊡📶🖥♟200∪▶Ⓓ🅐🅟❄ⓈⓅ🏇Ⓣ

Northleigh House ⋀⋀
👑👑 HIGHLY COMMENDED

Five Ways Road, Hatton, Warwick CV35 7HZ
☎ (01926) 484203 & 0374 101894
Fax (01926) 484006

Comfortable, peaceful country house where the elegant rooms are individually designed and have en-suite bathroom, fridge, kettle and remote-control TV.
Bedrooms: 1 single, 5 double, 1 twin
Bathrooms: 7 en-suite

Bed & breakfast per night:	£min	£max
Single		33.00
Double		46.00

Bed & breakfast per night:	£min	£max
Single	33.00	40.00
Double	46.00	58.00

Parking for 8
Open February–November
Cards accepted: Mastercard, Visa

🛇🏃♿📞🗖📶🐾🎣ⓊⓈ🎿🍺📺🖥 🖥❄🏇

The Old Fourpenny Shop Hotel ⋀⋀
👑👑 HIGHLY COMMENDED

27-29 Crompton Street, Warwick CV34 6HJ
☎ (01926) 491360
Fax (01926) 411892
Recently refurbished, offering real ale, real food and friendly hospitality. Situated in a quiet side street, close to town centre.
Bedrooms: 2 single, 5 double, 3 twin, 1 triple
Bathrooms: 11 en-suite

Bed & breakfast per night:	£min	£max
Single	35.00	37.50
Double	59.50	65.00

Half board per person:	£min	£max
Daily	45.00	47.50

Lunch available
Evening meal 1900 (last orders 2130)
Parking for 13
Cards accepted: Amex, Diners, Mastercard, Visa, Switch/Delta

🛇♟10🏃♿📞🗖📶🐾♟🍺🎿🍺📺 🖥🖥▶❄ⓈⓅ🏇

Old Rectory ⋀⋀
👑👑👑 COMMENDED

Vicarage Lane, Sherbourne, Warwick CV35 8AB
☎ (01926) 624562
Fax (01926) 624995

Georgian country house with beams and inglenooks, furnished with antiques. En-suite bedrooms, many with brass beds, all with direct-dial telephone and colour TV. Four poster and spa bath available. A la carte restaurant, bar, hearty breakfast. Half a mile from M40, junction 15.
Bedrooms: 2 single, 6 double, 3 twin, 2 triple, 1 family room
Bathrooms: 12 en-suite, 2 private

Bed & breakfast per night:	£min	£max
Single	33.00	45.00
Double	40.00	65.00

Half board per person:	£min	£max
Daily	35.00	45.00

Evening meal 1900 (last orders 2030)
Parking for 16
Cards accepted: Diners, Mastercard, Visa, Switch/Delta

🛇🏃♿📞🗖📶🐾♟Ⓢ🎿🍺🖥🖥10 ❄Ⓓ🅐🅟🏇Ⓣ

Shrewley House ⋀⋀
👑👑 HIGHLY COMMENDED

Hockley Road, Shrewley, Warwick CV35 7AT
☎ (01926) 842549 & 0468 315204
Fax (01926) 842216
Listed 17th C farmhouse and home set amidst beautiful 1.5 acre gardens. King-sized four-poster bedrooms, all en-suite, with many thoughtful extras. Four miles from Warwick.
Bedrooms: 3 double
Bathrooms: 3 en-suite

Bed & breakfast per night:	£min	£max
Single	37.00	
Double	52.00	

Evening meal (last orders 1930)
Parking for 17
Cards accepted: Mastercard, Visa

🛇🏃♿📞🗖📶🐾🎣ⓊⒶⓈ🎿🍺📺 📶🖥∪❄✕🚗🏇

Northamptonshire
Map ref 2C1

Old village steeped in history, with thatched cottages and several antique shops.

Globe Hotel ⋀⋀
👑👑 COMMENDED

High Street, Weedon, Northampton NN7 4QD
☎ (01327) 340336
Fax (01327) 349058
19th C countryside inn. Old world atmosphere and freehouse hospitality with good English cooking, available all day. Meeting rooms. Close to M1, Stratford and many tourist spots. Send for information pack.
Bedrooms: 4 single, 6 double, 5 twin, 3 triple
Bathrooms: 18 en-suite

Bed & breakfast per night:	£min	£max
Single	32.00	45.00
Double	45.00	55.00

Continued ▶

WEEDON

Continued

Half board per person:

	£min	£max
Daily	40.00	56.00

Lunch available
Evening meal (last orders 2200)
Parking for 40
Cards accepted: Amex, Diners, Mastercard, Visa, Switch/Delta

⌂♨♿☎🖥▢⌨♠🛎Ⓢ✂🅟🖩
🖼🏛30♣🅿 DAP SP 🏠 Ⓣ

WELLESBOURNE

Warwickshire
Map ref 2B1

Picturesque village with several noteworthy inns. The River Dene, which divides the place in two, once separated Wellesbourne Hastings from Wellesbourne Mountford, but now both parts are regarded as one village.

Walton Hall Members ♏

👑👑👑 COMMENDED

Walton, Wellesbourne, Warwick CV35 9HU
☎ (01789) 842424
Fax (01789) 470418

Victorian country mansion only 7 miles from Stratford-upon-Avon. Well-appointed apartments, hotel or self-catering. 22 sports and leisure facilities.
Bedrooms: 88 triple
Bathrooms: 88 en-suite
Bed & breakfast per night:

	£min	£max
Single	80.00	110.00
Double	110.00	140.00

Half board per person:

	£min	£max
Daily	100.00	130.00
Weekly	700.00	900.00

Lunch available
Evening meal 1900 (last orders 2200)
Parking for 250
Cards accepted: Amex, Diners, Mastercard, Visa

⌂♨1♿🖥☎🖥▢⌨♠🛎Ⓢ✂🖩
📺🍴⬤🖼🏛120♂✕🏹🐾♣⚲U
♪🎵🚲🏇❄🐾✈ SP 🏠 Ⓣ

WELLINGBOROUGH

Northamptonshire
Map ref 3A2

Manufacturing town, mentioned in the Domesday Book, with some old buildings and inns, in one of which Cromwell stayed on his way to Naseby. It has attractive gardens in the centre of the town and 2 interesting churches.
Tourist Information Centre ☎ (01933) 228101

High View Hotel ♏

👑👑👑

156 Midland Road, Wellingborough NN8 1NG
☎ (01933) 278733
Fax (01933) 225948
Large, detached, modernised building with pleasant gardens. In quiet tree-lined area near town centre and railway station. All rooms en-suite.
Bedrooms: 5 single, 5 double, 4 twin
Bathrooms: 14 en-suite
Bed & breakfast per night:

	£min	£max
Single	28.00	45.00
Double	45.00	51.00

Evening meal 1830 (last orders 2030)
Parking for 10
Cards accepted: Amex, Diners, Mastercard, Visa, Switch/Delta

⌂♨4♿🖥☎🖥▢⌨♠🛎Ⓢ✂🖩 📺🖩
🖼❄✕ SP Ⓣ

Oak House Private Hotel ♏

👑👑👑 APPROVED

8-11 Broad Green, Wellingborough NN8 4LE
☎ (01933) 271133
Fax (01933) 271133
Ⓒ The Independents
Small, homely hotel with a comfortable atmosphere, on the edge of the town centre. Double-glazed. Enclosed car park.
Bedrooms: 5 single, 5 double, 6 twin
Bathrooms: 15 en-suite, 1 private shower
Bed & breakfast per night:

	£min	£max
Single	28.00	32.50
Double	38.00	42.00

Half board per person:

	£min	£max
Daily	29.50	41.00

Evening meal 1815 (last orders 1200)
Parking for 9
Cards accepted: Amex, Diners, Mastercard, Visa

⌂♨♿🖥☎🖥▢⌨♠🛎Ⓢ📺🖩🖼🚗🚲

WEM

Shropshire
Map ref 4A3

Small town connected with Judge Jeffreys who lived in Lowe Hall. Well known for its ales.

Soulton Hall ♏

👑👑👑 COMMENDED

Wem, Shrewsbury SY4 5RS
☎ (01939) 232786
Fax (01939) 234097

Super home cooking and en-suite rooms at this Tudor manor house ensure a relaxing holiday. Moated Domesday site in grounds, private riverside and woodland walks.
Bedrooms: 1 single, 3 double, 1 twin, 1 triple
Suite available
Bathrooms: 5 en-suite, 1 private
Bed & breakfast per night:

	£min	£max
Single	33.50	40.50
Double	52.00	66.00

Half board per person:

	£min	£max
Daily	51.50	58.50
Weekly	278.00	321.50

Evening meal 1900 (last orders 2030)
Parking for 23
Cards accepted: Diners, Mastercard, Visa

⌂♨♿🖥☎🖥▢⌨♠🛎Ⓢ✂🖩🚗
🍴10U♪🎵✏🏹❄🚜🐾✈ SP 🏠 Ⓣ ⓦ

WENLOCK EDGE

Shropshire
Map ref 4A3

A hill running from Craven Arms north-east to Much Wenlock, with attractive views across the south Shropshire Hills.

The Wenlock Edge Inn ♏

👑👑👑 COMMENDED

Hilltop, Wenlock Edge, Much Wenlock TF13 6DJ
☎ (01746) 785678
Fax (01746) 785285
Ⓒ Logis of GB

Family-run freehouse of Wenlock limestone, built about 1700. Peaceful location, fine views. Four miles from Much Wenlock on B4371.
Bedrooms: 2 double, 1 twin
Bathrooms: 3 en-suite
Bed & breakfast

per night:	£min	£max
Single	40.00	50.00
Double	65.00	75.00

Lunch available
Evening meal 1900 (last orders 2100)
Parking for 40
Cards accepted: Amex, Mastercard, Visa, Switch/Delta

☎ 8 🛆 🖭 🗗 ♦ 🕯 📷 🕊 🗡 🐾 TV 🕮 🖮
🗘 🐾 SP 🏮

WEOBLEY
Hereford and Worcester
Map ref 2A1

One of the most beautiful Herefordshire villages, full of framed houses, at the heart of the Black and White Trail. It is dominated by the church which has a fine spire.

Ye Olde Salutation Inn 🚇
👑👑👑 HIGHLY COMMENDED
Market Pitch, Weobley, Hereford
HR4 8SJ
☎ (01544) 318443
Fax (01544) 318216

Traditional black and white country inn overlooking the main Broad Street. Quality home-cooked bar meals and a la carte menu. Inglenook fireplace. Homely atmosphere.
Bedrooms: 2 single, 1 double, 1 twin, 1 family room
Bathrooms: 5 en-suite, 1 public
Bed & breakfast

per night:	£min	£max
Single	37.00	42.50
Double	60.00	85.00

Lunch available
Evening meal 1900 (last orders 2130)
Parking for 20

Cards accepted: Amex, Diners, Mastercard, Visa, Switch/Delta

☎ 14 🚽 🖭 🗗 ♦ 🕯 📷 🗞 🗡 🐾 TV 🕮
🖀 🍴 12 🏹 ♦ ∪ ⌚ 🐾 🐾 SP 🏮

WESTON-UNDER-REDCASTLE
Shropshire
Map ref 4A3

Picturesque Shropshire village in the heart of the beautiful historic Hawkstone Park and Follies, between Whitchurch and Shrewsbury off the A49.

Windmill Cottage Guesthouse
Listed COMMENDED
Weston-under-Redcastle, Shrewsbury SY4 5UX
☎ (01939) 200219
Grade II listed 17th C black and white property with original exposed beams externally and internally. Nearby are Hawkstone Hall, Park and Follies and Hodnet Hall Garden. Ideal for golfers, walkers and countryside lovers.
Bedrooms: 2 twin
Bathrooms: 2 en-suite
Bed & breakfast

per night:	£min	£max
Single	24.99	
Double	40.00	

Lunch available
Parking for 10

☎ 10 🗗 ♦ 🕯 ∪ 🗎 🖭 🗞 S 🕮 🖀 🗗 🏹 🐾 🏮

WILLINGTON
Derbyshire

The Willington
28 Hall Lane, Willington, Derby
DE65 6DR
☎ (01283) 702104
Fax (01283) 701570

The main pub/restaurant dates back to the late 1700s. The whole complex has been recently refurbished to a high standard. Just off main A38 between Burton and Derby.
Bedrooms: 6 double, 5 triple
Bathrooms: 11 private
Bed & breakfast

per night:	£min	£max
Single	37.50	40.00
Double	48.50	53.50

Half board per

person:	£min	£max
Daily	45.00	47.50

Lunch available
Evening meal 1800 (last orders 2200)
Parking for 50
Cards accepted: Mastercard, Visa

☎ 🛆 🖭 🗗 ♦ 🕯 🖃 S 🗞 TV 🕮
🕮 🖀 🍴 90 🕯 🛠 🐾 DAP 🗞 SP 🏮 T

WITNEY
Oxfordshire
Map ref 2C1

Greystones Lodge Hotel
The Marlborough Hotel
See South of England region for full entry details

WOLVERHAMPTON
West Midlands
Map ref 4B3

Modern industrial town with a long history, a fine parish church and an excellent art gallery. There are several places of interest in the vicinity including Moseley Old Hall and Wightwick Manor with its William Morris influence.
Tourist Information Centre ☎ (01902) 312051

Ely House 🚇
👑👑👑 COMMENDED
53 Tettenhall Road, Wolverhampton
WV3 9NB
☎ (01902) 311311
Fax (01902) 21098
ℂℝ Minotel/The Independents
Fine imposing Georgian building, fully restored, in a good central position adjacent to motorway network. Ideal base for touring the West Midlands.
Bedrooms: 6 single, 6 double, 7 twin
Bathrooms: 19 en-suite
Bed & breakfast

per night:	£min	£max
Single	46.00	46.00
Double	56.00	56.00

Lunch available
Evening meal 1900 (last orders 2100)
Parking for 16
Cards accepted: Amex, Diners, Mastercard, Visa, Switch/Delta

☎ 🛆 🖭 🗗 ♦ 🕯 📷 S 🗞 TV 🕮 🖀
🐾 SP 🏮 T

Map references apply to the colour maps at the back of this guide.

WOLVERHAMPTON
Continued

Featherstone Farm
Listed COMMENDED
New Road, Featherstone,
Wolverhampton WV10 7NW
☎ (01902) 725371 & 0836 315258
Fax (01902) 731741
*17th C farmhouse with listed
barn/stables completely refurbished.
Open fires. Near M6, M54 and close
to Weston Hall. Restaurant offering
Indian cuisine.*
Bedrooms: 2 single, 3 double, 3 twin,
1 triple
Suites available
Bathrooms: 9 en-suite, 1 public
Bed & breakfast

per night:	£min	£max
Single	35.00	45.00
Double	45.00	55.00

Half board per

person:	£min	£max
Daily	45.00	65.00
Weekly	315.00	415.00

Lunch available
Evening meal 1800 (last orders
2100)
Parking for 62
Cards accepted: Mastercard, Visa,
Switch/Delta
🛇🛆🖭📞📭🖵🛉🍽🛈✕🅿🗺📺◑
🛏🎖30❄🅙🆐 SP 🎬 T

Fox Hotel International
COMMENDED APPROVED
118 School Street, Wolverhampton
WV3 0NR
☎ (01902) 21680
Fax (01902) 711654
*Town centre, free parking, nearby
shopping. All rooms en-suite, satellite
TV, direct-dial telephone. Bar, restaurant
and conference room.*
Bedrooms: 26 single, 6 double
Bathrooms: 32 en-suite
Bed & breakfast

per night:	£min	£max
Single	30.00	43.00
Double	49.00	59.00

Half board per

person:	£min	£max
Daily	40.00	45.00
Weekly	210.00	260.00

Lunch available
Evening meal 1700 (last orders
2200)
Parking for 20
Cards accepted: Amex, Diners,
Mastercard, Visa, Switch/Delta
🛇🖁🖭📞📭🖵🛉🍽🛈🆂✕🅿📺◑
🛏🎖100✕🅐🗺 SP T

Patshull Park Hotel Golf and Country Club
COMMENDED
Patshull Park, Pattingham,
Wolverhampton WV6 7HR
☎ (01902) 700100
Fax (01902) 700874
*Modern, attractive country hotel set in
picturesque estate with own golf-course
and fishing lakes. Health and fitness
complex includes sauna, indoor pool
and solarium. 6 miles from junction 3
of M54.*
Bedrooms: 7 double, 38 twin,
4 triple
Suite available
Bathrooms: 49 en-suite, 4 public
Bed & breakfast

per night:	£min	£max
Single	62.50	75.00
Double	62.50	75.00

Half board per

person:	£min	£max
Daily	48.75	55.00
Weekly	341.25	385.00

Lunch available
Evening meal 1930 (last orders
2130)
Parking for 200
Cards accepted: Amex, Diners,
Mastercard, Visa, Switch/Delta
🛇🛆📞📭🖵🛉🍽🛈✕🅿📺◑
🛏🎖160🐾✕🔍🎾🖐♩♪❄🗺 SP
🎬

WOODSTOCK
Oxfordshire
Map ref 2C1

Gorselands Farmhouse Auberge
*See South of England region for full entry
details*

WORCESTER
Hereford and Worcester
Map ref 2B1

Lovely riverside city dominated by
its Norman and Early English
cathedral, King John's burial place.
Many old buildings including the
15th C Commandery and the 18th
C Guildhall. There are several
museums and the Royal Worcester
porcelain factory.
Tourist Information Centre ☎ *(01905)
726311 or 722480*

Bank House Hotel, Golf & Country Club
COMMENDED
Hereford Road, Bransford,
Worcester WR6 5JD
☎ (01886) 833551
Fax (01886) 832461
CR Best Western

*Sympathetically converted country
house hotel and golf course set in 123
acres of countryside, 3 miles from
Worcester. On A4103 Worcester to
Hereford road, close to many local
attractions.*
Bedrooms: 11 single, 32 double,
23 twin
Suites available
Bathrooms: 66 en-suite
Bed & breakfast

per night:	£min	£max
Single	67.50	67.50
Double	90.00	90.00

Half board per

person:	£min	£max
Daily	85.00	85.00

Lunch available
Evening meal 1900 (last orders
2145)
Parking for 300
Cards accepted: Amex, Diners,
Mastercard, Visa, Switch/Delta
🛇🛆🖁📞📭🖵🛉🍽🛈🆂✕🅿📺◑
🛏🚗🎖400🐾✕🔍🎾🖐♩❄🗺 SP
🎬 T

Loch Ryan Hotel
COMMENDED
119 Sidbury, Worcester WR5 2DH
☎ (01905) 351143
Fax (01905) 351143
*Historic hotel, once home of Bishop
Gore, close to cathedral, Royal
Worcester Porcelain factory and
Commandery. Attractive terraced
garden. Imaginative food. Holders of
Heartbeat and Worcester City clean
food awards.*
Bedrooms: 1 single, 4 double, 4 twin,
1 family room
Bathrooms: 10 en-suite
Bed & breakfast

per night:	£min	£max
Single	42.00	
Double	58.00	

Half board per

person:	£min	£max
Daily	45.00	

Evening meal 1800 (last orders
1900)
Parking for 10
Cards accepted: Amex, Diners,
Mastercard, Visa
🛇🖵🛉🍽🛈🆂✕🅿📺◑🛏🚗🎖❄
✕🅐🗺 SP 🎬

COLOUR MAPS

Colour maps at the back of
this guide pinpoint all places
in which you will find
accommodation listed.

The Manor Arms Hotel ⚊

⚊⚊⚊ COMMENDED

Abberley Village, Worcester
WR6 6BN
☎ (01299) 896507
Fax (01299) 896723
Email: 100432,3616
@compuserve.com
*Fully licensed 300-year-old inn, with old
oak beams and lots of character.
Within easy reach of Worcester,
Birmingham and National Exhibition
Centre. A la carte restaurant and bar
food always available.*
Bedrooms: 4 single, 3 double,
1 family room
Bathrooms: 8 en-suite

Bed & breakfast per night:	£min	£max
Single	35.00	35.00
Double	45.00	60.00

Half board per person:	£min	£max
Daily	40.00	50.00
Weekly	200.00	280.00

Lunch available
Evening meal 1900 (last orders
2130)
Parking for 30
Cards accepted: Mastercard, Visa,
Switch/Delta

The Maximillian Hotel ⚊

⚊⚊ APPROVED

Shrub Hill Road, Shrub Hill,
Worcester WR4 9EF
☎ (01905) 23867 & 21694
Fax (01905) 724935
*Warm and friendly, 6 minutes' walk
from city centre, 2 minutes from Shrub
Hill station. 2 miles from M5, junction
6 or 7. Ample car parking.*
Bedrooms: 4 single, 5 double, 4 twin
Bathrooms: 13 en-suite

Bed & breakfast per night:	£min	£max
Single	38.50	38.50
Double	51.00	51.00

Half board per person:	£min	£max
Daily	40.00	40.00
Weekly	280.00	280.00

Lunch available
Evening meal 1900 (last orders
2330)
Parking for 15
Cards accepted: Amex, Diners,
Mastercard, Visa

Ye Olde Talbot Hotel ⚊

Friar Street, Worcester WR1 2NA
☎ (01905) 23573
Fax (01905) 612760
CR Countryside
*Originally an old courtroom, located
close to the town centre and the
cathedral, to which it once belonged.
Half board prices shown apply at
weekends.*
Bedrooms: 10 single, 15 double,
4 twin
Bathrooms: 29 en-suite

Bed & breakfast per night:	£min	£max
Single	33.50	60.00
Double	42.00	65.00

Half board per person:	£min	£max
Daily	28.00	36.00

Lunch available
Evening meal 1900 (last orders
2200)
Parking for 8
Cards accepted: Amex, Diners,
Mastercard, Visa, Switch/Delta

Market town close to the Dukeries,
where a number of Ducal families
had their estates, some of which, like
Clumber Park, may be visited. The
upper room of the 14th C
gatehouse of the priory housed the
country's first elementary school in
1628.
*Tourist Information Centre ☎ (01909)
501148*

Sherwood Guesthouse ⚊

⚊⚊ COMMENDED

57 Carlton Road, Worksop S80 1PP
☎ (01909) 474209 & 478214
*In Robin Hood country, near M1 and
A1 and close to station and town
centre. Comfortable rooms with TV and
tea/coffee facilities.*
Bedrooms: 1 single, 4 twin, 2 triple
Bathrooms: 2 en-suite, 2 public

Bed & breakfast per night:	£min	£max
Single	18.00	22.00
Double	36.00	40.00

For ideas on places to visit
refer to the introduction at
the beginning of this section.

Small town in the southern
Cotswolds. Berkeley Castle is within
easy reach.

Burrows Court ⚊

⚊⚊ COMMENDED

Nibley Green, North Nibley, Dursley
GL11 6AZ
☎ (01453) 546230
*18th C country house in idyllic setting.
Peaceful, quiet and relaxing. All en-suite,
exposed beams, acre of gardens. Ideal
for Cotswolds and Bath.*
Bedrooms: 3 double, 1 twin, 2 triple
Bathrooms: 6 en-suite

Bed & breakfast per night:	£min	£max
Single	29.00	34.00
Double	40.00	50.00

Parking for 20
Open February–November
Cards accepted: Mastercard, Visa

*See under Hereford, Ross-on-Wye, St
Briavels, Symonds Yat East, Symonds Yat
West*

The symbol CR and a group
name following an hotel
address indicates that
bookings can be made
through a central reservations
office. These offices are listed
in the information pages at
the back of this guide.

WELCOME HOST

This is a nationally recognised
customer care programme
which aims to promote
the highest standards of
service and a warm welcome.
Establishments who are taking
part in this initiative are
indicated by the ⊕ symbol.

USE YOUR *i*'s

There are more than 550 Tourist Information Centres throughout England offering friendly help with accommodation and holiday ideas as well as suggestions of places to visit and things to do. There may well be a centre in your home town which can help you before you set out. You'll find addresses in the local Phone Book or simply call Freepages 0800 192 192.

AT-A-GLANCE SYMBOLS

Symbols at the end of each accommodation entry give useful information about services and facilities. A key to symbols can be found inside the back cover flap.

Keep this open for easy reference.

COUNTRY CODE

Always follow the Country Code ⚘ Enjoy the countryside and respect its life and work ⚘ Guard against all risk of fire ⚘ Fasten all gates ⚘ Keep your dogs under close control ⚘ Keep to public paths across farmland ⚘ Use gates and stiles to cross fences, hedges and walls ⚘ Leave livestock, crops and machinery alone ⚘ Take your litter home ⚘ Help to keep all water clean ⚘ Protect wildlife, plants and trees ⚘ Take special care on country roads ⚘ Make no unnecessary noise

EAST OF ENGLAND

Traditional seaside resorts from Skegness to Southend-on-Sea, beautiful Constable country, the Norfolk Broads, lavender fields and heritage towns - these and much more await you in the East of England.

Discover some of the country's richest treasures - Lincoln and Norwich cathedrals, Cambridge, Royal Sandringham and Woburn Abbey. Or take a leisurely cruise on the region's waterways, teeming with wildlife. It's ideal cycling country, too.

Events to enjoy include a day at Newmarket races, plus a chance to tour the National Stud. Spalding, in the heart of the Lincolnshire fenland, stages a spectacular floral festival each Spring. There's also the famous music festival at Aldeburgh, or cheese rolling at Stilton!

The counties of Bedforshire, Cambridgeshire, Essex, Hertfordshire, Lincolnshire, Norfolk and Suffolk

FOR MORE INFORMATION CONTACT:
East of England Tourist Board
Toppesfield Hall, Hadleigh, Suffolk IP7 5DN
Tel: (01473) 822922 **Fax:** (01473) 823063

Where to Go in the East of England – see pages 296-299
Where to Stay in the East of England – see pages 300-342

eAST OF ENGLAND

Where to Go and What to See

You will find hundreds of interesting places to visit during your stay in the East of England, just some of which are listed in these pages. The number against each name will help you locate it on the map (page 299). Contact any Tourist Information Centre in the region for more ideas on days out in the East of England.

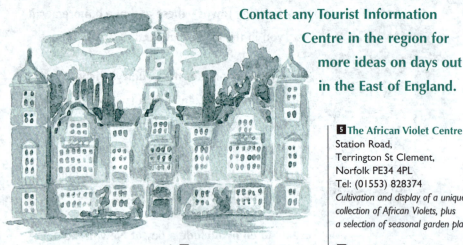

5 The African Violet Centre
Station Road,
Terrington St Clement,
Norfolk PE34 4PL
Tel: (01553) 828374
Cultivation and display of a unique collection of African Violets, plus a selection of seasonal garden plants.

3 Belton House, Park and Gardens
Belton,
Lincolnshire NG32 2LS
Tel: (01476) 566116
The crowning achievement of restoration country house architecture, built in 1685-88 for Sir John Brownlow with alterations by James Wyatt in 1777.

6 Sandringham
Sandringham, King's Lynn,
Norfolk PE35 6EN
Tel: (01553) 772675
The country retreat of HM The Queen. Delightful house and 60 acres of grounds and lakes. Museum of royal vehicles and royal memorabilia.

1 Gainsborough Old Hall
Parnell Street, Gainsborough,
Lincolnshire DN21 2NB
Tel: (01427) 612669
A late medieval timber-framed manor house, built about 1460 with a fine medieval kitchen.

2 Museum of Lincolnshire Life
Burton Road,
Lincoln LN1 3LY
Tel: (01522) 528448
The region's largest social history museum showing the agricultural, industrial and social history of Lincolnshire from a teapot to a World War I tank and a Victorian room.

4 Springfields Show Gardens
Camelgate, Spalding,
Lincolnshire PE12 6ET
Tel: (01775) 724843/713253
One of Britain's premier show gardens; in spring there is a spectacle of tulips, daffodils and hyacinths and in summer, a bedding plant display.

7 Tales of the Old Gaol House
The Old Gaol House,
Saturday Market Place,
King's Lynn, Norfolk PE30 5DQ
Tel: (01553) 763044
A personal stereo tour of the Old Gaol House tells the true stories of Lynn's infamous murderers, highwaymen and witches.

8 Pensthorpe Waterfowl Park

Pensthorpe, Fakenham,
Norfolk NR21 OLN
Tel: (01328) 851465
One of the largest waterfowl and wildfowl collections in the world with information centre, conservation shop, adventure play area, walks, nature trails and a licensed restaurant.

9 Inspire Hands-On-Science Centre

St Michael's Church,
Coslany Street, Norwich,
Norfolk NR3 3DT
Tel: (01603) 612612
Hands-on science centre housed in a medieval church. Suitable for all ages, it allows everyone to explore and discover the wonders of science.

10 Pleasurewood Hills Family Theme Park

Corton, Lowestoft,
Suffolk NR32 5DZ
Tel: (01502) 508200
Log flume, chair lift, cine 180, two railways, pirate ship, fort, Aladdin's cave, parrot, sealion shows, roller coaster, waveswinger, Eye in the Sky and Star Ride Enterprise.

11 Ely Cathedral

The College, Ely,
Cambridgeshire CB7 4DL
Tel: (01353) 667735
One of England's finest cathedrals with fine buildings. Guided tours and tours of the Monastic Octagon and West Tower. Brass rubbing centre and stained glass museum.

12 Oliver Cromwell's House

29 St Marys Street, Ely,
Cambridgeshire CB7 4HF
Tel: (01353) 662062
The family home of Oliver Cromwell with a 17thC kitchen, parlour and a 'haunted bedroom'. Tourist Information Centre, souvenirs and a craft shop.

13 West Stow Country Park and Anglo-Saxon Village

Icklingham Road, West Stow,
Bury St Edmunds,
Suffolk IP28 6HG
Tel: (01284) 728718
Reconstructions of six pagan Anglo-Saxon buildings with a seventh in the process of reconstruction. Information point with displays of excavation plans.

14 Bruisyard Vineyard and Herb Centre

Church Road, Bruisyard,
Saxmundham,
Suffolk IP17 2EF
Tel: (01728) 638281
A 10-acre vineyard showing summer work and maintenance of the vines, a tour of the winery and herb garden. A video show and display of winemaking is also provided.

15 Framlingham Castle

Framlingham, Woodbridge,
Suffolk IP13 9BP
Tel: (01728) 724189/621448
12thC curtain walls, 13 towers, Tudor brick chimneys and a wall walk. Built by the Bigod family, the Earls of Norfolk. Home of Mary Tudor in 1553.

16 National Horseracing Museum

99 High Street, Newmarket,
Suffolk CB8 8JL
Tel: (01638) 667333
Five galleries telling the development of horseracing and the individuals involved. A display of sporting art includes loans from the Tate gallery. Also a 'hands-on' gallery.

17 Imperial War Museum

Duxford Airfield, Duxford,
Cambridgeshire CB2 4QR
Tel: (01223) 835000
Over 140 aircraft on display with tanks, vehicles and guns, a ride on the simulator, an adventure playground, shops and a restaurant.

18 Shuttleworth Collection
Old Warden Aerodrome,
Biggleswade,
Bedfordshire SG18 9EP
Tel: (01767) 627288/627502
A unique historical collection of aircraft from a 1909 Bleriot to a 1942 Spitfire in flying condition. Cars dating from an 1898 Panhard in running order.

19 The Swiss Garden
Biggleswade Road, Old Warden,
Biggleswade, Bedfordshire
Tel: (01234) 228671
An attractive garden dating from the 19thC, taking its name from the tiny Swiss thatched cottage in the centre.

20 Colne Valley Railway
Yeldham Road,
Castle Hedingham,
Essex CO9 3DZ
Tel: (01787) 461174
An award-winning station and a ride in the loveliest part of the Colne Valley. A large, interesting collection of operational heritage rolling stock.

21 Colchester Zoo
Stanway, Maldon Road,
Colchester,
Essex CO3 5SL
Tel: (01206) 330253/331292
See 170 species of animals, 40 acres of gardens and lakes and award-winning animal enclosures. Picnic areas, a road train, two play areas, pony rides and a large soft play area.

22 The Working Silk Museum
New Mills, South Street,
Braintree, Essex CM7 3GB
Tel: (01376) 553393
A show of textiles (ancient textile machines restored and working) a mill shop and looms. Working looms with weaving demonstrations on the hour on Monday - Friday and Saturday mornings.

23 Hyde Hall
Rettendon,
Chelmsford,
Essex CM3 8ET
Tel: (01245) 400256
Royal Horticultural Society 8-acre garden with all-year-round interest including greenhouses, roses, flowering shrubs, perennial borders and alpines.

24 Paradise Wildlife Park
White Stubbs Lane,
Broxbourne,
Hertfordshire EN10 7QA
Tel: (01992) 468001
Britain's most interactive wildlife park with many animal activities daily. Also an adventure playground, children's rides, woodland railway and catering facilities.

25 Hatfield House
Hatfield Park, Hatfield,
Hertfordshire AL9 5NQ
Tel: (01707) 262823
Jacobean house built in 1611 and Old Palace built in 1497. Famous paintings, fine furniture and the possessions of Queen Elizabeth I. Extensive park and gardens.

26 The Gardens of the Rose
Chiswell Green, St Albans,
Hertfordshire AL2 3NR
Tel: (01727) 850461
Royal National Rose Society garden with 20 acres of showground and trial grounds for new varieties of rose. Roses of all types displayed, with 1,700 different varieties.

27 Luton Hoo - The Wernher Collection
The Mansion House, Luton Hoo,
Luton, Bedfordshire LU1 3TQ
Tel: (01582) 22955
An historic house built in 1767 exhibiting paintings, tapestries, bronzes, ivories, porcelain, jewellery by Carl Faberge and mementoes of the Russian imperial family.

28 Stockwood Craft Museum and Gardens
Stockwood Park, Farley, Hill,
Luton, Bedfordshire LU1 4BH
Tel: (01582) 738714/746739
Housed in an 18thC stable block and featuring Bedfordshire craft displays and workshops, including a blacksmith, wheelwright, saddler, shoemaker and thatcher.

N. LINCS

N.E. LINCS

1 Gainsborough

Mablethorpe

LINCOLNSHIRE

2 Lincoln   Ingoldmells

Skegness

Sleaford   Boston

Wells-next-the-Sea   Sherringham

Cromer

3 Belton   North Walsham

Terrington St Clement   Fakenham   Pensthorpe **8**

Bourne   **4** Spalding   **5**   **6** **7** King's Lynn   **NORFOLK**   Caister-on-Sea

Market   Wisbech   Swaffham   East Dareham   Great

Deeping   Oxborough   Yarmouth

LEICS   Peterborough   March   Wymondham   **9** Norwich

Whittlesey   Attleborough   **10**

Yaxley   Chatteris   Lowestoft

NORTHANTS   Huntingdon   Ely **11** **12** Lakenheath   Diss   Bungay   Southwold

St Ives   Mildenhall   Halesworth

CAMBRIDGESHIRE   Bury St **13**   **SUFFOLK**   **14** Bruisyard

St Neots   Cambridge   **16** Edmunds   Stowmarket   **15** Framlingham

Newmarket   Aldeburgh

Bedford Sandy   Great Shelford

BEDFORD   Duxford **17**   Haverhill   Ipswich

SHIRE   **18** **19**   Sudbury   Hadleigh

Leighton   Biggleswade   **20**   Harwich

Buzzard **29** **27** **28**   Hitchin   Castle Hedingham

Luton   **HERTFORD**   **22** **ESSEX**   **21** Colchester

Hertford   Braintree   Coggeshall

SHIRE   Harlow   Witham   Clacton-on-Sea

Hemel   **26** **25** **24**   Chelmsford   West

Hempstead   Hatfield   Broxbourne   **23** Maldon   Mersea

St Albans   Brentwood   Ingatestone   Burnham-on-Crouch

BUCKS Watford   Basildon

Stanford-le-Hope

Grays   Southend-on-Sea

0 — 20 Miles
0 — 30 Kms

---

29 **Leighton Buzzard Railway**
Page's Park Station,
Billington Road, Leighton
Buzzard, Bedfordshire LU7 8TN
Tel: (01525) 373888
*A preserved industrial railway with
steam locomotives from around the
world and a diesel collection. This
2ft guage railway, built in 1919,
offers a return trip of 5.5 miles.*

FIND OUT MORE
Further information about
holidays and attractions in
the East of England is
available from:
East of England Tourist Board,
Toppesfield Hall,
Hadleigh, Suffolk IP7 5DN.
Tel: (01473) 822922

These publications are available
from the East of England Tourist
Board (post free):
■ **Touring Map** - Bed &
Breakfast and Camping and
Caravanning
■ **Places to Stay**
Also available are (prices include
postage and packaging):
■ **East Anglia Guide 1998** *£4.50*

WHERE TO STAY (EAST OF ENGLAND)

Accommodation entries in this region are listed in alphabetical order of place name, and then in alphabetical order of establishment.

Map references refer to the colour location maps at the back of this guide.

The first number indicates the map to use; the letter and number which follow refer to the grid reference on the map.

At-a-glance symbols at the end of each accommodation entry give useful information about services and facilities. A key to symbols can be found inside the back cover flap.

Keep this open for easy reference.

ALDEBURGH

Suffolk
Map ref 3C2

A prosperous port in the 16th C, now famous for the Aldeburgh Music Festival held annually in June. The 16th C Moot Hall, now a museum, is a timber-framed building once used as an open market.

Uplands Hotel M

COMMENDED
Victoria Road, Aldeburgh IP15 5DX
☎ (01728) 452420
Fax (01728) 454872
Comfortable family-run hotel with en-suite rooms. Restaurant using local produce overlooks award-winning gardens.
Bedrooms: 4 single, 5 double, 9 twin, 2 triple
Bathrooms: 17 en-suite, 3 private, 1 public
Bed & breakfast per night:

	£min	£max
Single	33.50	50.00
Double	65.00	70.00

Half board per person:

	£min	£max
Daily	47.00	60.00
Weekly	280.00	350.00

Evening meal 1900 (last orders 2030)
Parking for 20
Cards accepted: Amex, Diners, Mastercard, Visa

White Lion Hotel M

COMMENDED
Market Cross Place, Aldeburgh IP15 5BJ
☎ (01728) 452720
Fax (01728) 452986
Best Western
Imposing hotel standing directly on the seafront of totally unspoilt fishing town of great charm, famous for classical music concerts. Single room half-board supplement £18 per night.
Bedrooms: 2 single, 21 double, 14 twin, 1 triple
Bathrooms: 38 en-suite
Bed & breakfast per night:

	£min	£max
Single	59.50	69.50
Double	84.00	104.00

Half board per person:

	£min	£max
Daily	54.00	64.00
Weekly	358.00	428.00

Lunch available
Evening meal 1900 (last orders 2100)
Parking for 15
Cards accepted: Amex, Diners, Mastercard, Visa, Switch/Delta

AYLMERTON

Norfolk
Map ref 3B1

Felbrigg Lodge M

Aylmerton, North Norfolk NR11 8RA
☎ (01263) 837588
Fax (01263) 838012
Hidden in 4 acres of spectacular gardens and woods. Large, comfortable bedrooms, well appointed with every facility and all en-suite. Delicious dinners. 10 minutes from Holt.
Bedrooms: 1 double, 2 twin
Bathrooms: 3 en-suite
Bed & breakfast per night:

	£min	£max
Single	38.00	58.00
Double	60.00	80.00

Half board per person:

	£min	£max
Daily	50.00	60.00

Parking for 4
Cards accepted: Mastercard, Visa

AYLSHAM

Norfolk
Map ref 3B1

Small town on the River Bure with an attractive market place and interesting church. Nearby is Blickling Hall (National Trust). Also the terminus of the Bure Valley narrow gauge steam railway which runs on 9 miles of the old Great Eastern trackbed, between Wroxham and Aylsham.
Tourist Information Centre ☎ (01263) 733903

The Aylsham Motel M

COMMENDED
Norwich Road, Aylsham, Norwich NR11 6JH
☎ (01263) 734851
Fax (01263) 734851
Family-run motel. Relaxed and friendly atmosphere in peaceful surroundings. All rooms en-suite. Close to North Norfolk coast and Broads. Bar and a la carte meals available.

Bedrooms: 3 double, 10 twin,
2 triple
Bathrooms: 15 en-suite

Bed & breakfast

per night:	£min	£max
Single	29.00	35.00
Double	40.00	50.00

Half board per

person:	£min	£max
Weekly	156.00	180.00

Lunch available
Evening meal 1900 (last orders
2130)
Parking for 100
Cards accepted: Amex, Mastercard,
Visa, Switch/Delta

🐕♿♨📞🖥♨Ⓢ✁📺📠💺✗100
♨❀⚡SP T

The Old Pump House ⋒

♛♛♛ HIGHLY COMMENDED

Holman Road, Aylsham, Norwich
NR11 6BY
☎ (01263) 733789

Creature comforts, steps everywhere,
home cooking. Rambling 1750s house
beside the thatched pump, a minute
from church and marketplace. Pine
shuttered breakfast room overlooks
peaceful garden. Non-smoking.
Bedrooms: 3 double, 2 twin
Bathrooms: 4 en-suite, 1 public

Bed & breakfast

per night:	£min	£max
Single	18.00	25.00
Double	36.00	44.00

Half board per

person:	£min	£max
Daily	28.00	35.00
Weekly	165.00	165.00

Evening meal from 1800
Parking for 7

🐕📞♨UL❀Ⓢ✁📺📠💺❀
🚐SP ♨

BACTON-ON-SEA

Norfolk
Map ref 3C1

Seacroft Private Hotel ⋒

♛♛♛ APPROVED

Beach Road, Bacton-on-Sea,
Norwich NR12 OHS
☎ (01692) 650302
Large Victorian house close to shops
and beach. Home cooking and
personal supervision. Off B1159, via
Seacroft caravan park.

Bedrooms: 2 single, 3 double, 2 twin,
1 triple, 1 family room
Bathrooms: 6 en-suite, 3 public

Bed & breakfast

per night:	£min	£max
Single	19.50	28.00
Double	39.00	56.00

Half board per

person:	£min	£max
Daily	32.00	40.00
Weekly	200.00	250.00

Evening meal 1800 (last orders
2000)
Parking for 15
Open February–December
Cards accepted: Mastercard, Visa

🐕♿📧🖥♨🚩Ⓢ📠📺💺❀✗
🚐 DAP SP T

BARNHAM BROOM

Norfolk
Map ref 3B1

Barnham Broom Hotel, Golf, Conference & Leisure Centre ⋒

♛♛♛ HIGHLY COMMENDED

Honingham Road, Barnham Broom,
Norwich NR9 4DD
☎ (01603) 759393
Fax (01603) 758224
Ⓑ Best Western

In 250 acres of beautiful countryside,
with a relaxed and friendly atmosphere.
Excellent sports facilities, 2 18-hole
golf-courses. Large conference complex,
indoor heated pool.
Bedrooms: 1 single, 8 double,
36 twin, 1 triple, 7 family rooms
Bathrooms: 53 en-suite

Bed & breakfast

per night:	£min	£max
Single	68.00	72.00
Double	90.00	95.00

Half board per

person:	£min	£max
Daily	84.25	86.00
Weekly	350.00	360.00

Lunch available
Evening meal 1900 (last orders
2130)
Parking for 200
Cards accepted: Amex, Diners,
Mastercard, Visa, Switch/Delta

🐕♿📧🖥♨🚩Ⓢ✗Ⓞ📠💺
💺150♨✗🏹🎿♀Ↄ♿❀✗❀SP T

For further information on
accommodation establishments
use the coupons at the
back of this guide.

BASILDON

Essex
Map ref 3B3

One of the New Towns planned
after World War II. It overlooks the
estuary of the River Thames and is
set in undulating countryside. The
main feature is the town square
with a traffic-free pedestrian
concourse.

The Chichester Hotel

♛♛♛ COMMENDED

Old London Road, Wickford
SS11 8UE
☎ (01268) 560555
Fax (01268) 560580
Picturesque family-run hotel with
restaurant, dinner-dance restaurant
and functions complex. Surrounded by
farmland in the Basildon, Chelmsford,
Southend triangle.
Bedrooms: 17 single, 10 double,
8 twin
Bathrooms: 35 en-suite

Bed & breakfast

per night:	£min	£max
Single	47.50	57.50
Double	59.50	59.50

Lunch available
Evening meal 1900 (last orders
2130)
Parking for 41
Cards accepted: Amex, Diners,
Mastercard, Visa

♿📞📧🖥♨🚩📺🏛Ⓞ📠💺✗
SP T

BATTLESBRIDGE

Essex
Map ref 3B3

The Cottages Guest House

Listed COMMENDED

The Cottages, Beeches Road,
Battlesbridge, Wickford SS11 8TJ
☎ (01702) 232105
Rural cottage, close to Southend,
Chelmsford and Basildon. Good views.
Half a mile from Battlesbridge Antique
Centre. Extensive parking. Bridal room,
licensed bar.
Bedrooms: 1 single, 1 double, 3 twin
Bathrooms: 1 public

Bed & breakfast

per night:	£min	£max
Single	20.00	25.00
Double	35.00	45.00

Half board per

person:	£min	£max
Daily	25.00	35.00

Continued ▶

BATTLESBRIDGE

Continued

Evening meal 1800 (last orders 2030)
Parking for 14
🛇🌳🏠💷👤🅿🍴🗚📺🛏🚇🚶🅿🍴❄

BECCLES

Suffolk
Map ref 3C1

Fire destroyed the town in the 16th C and it was rebuilt in Georgian red brick. The River Waveney, on which the town stands, is popular with boating enthusiasts and has an annual regatta. Home of Beccles and District Museum.

Colville Arms Motel

👑👑 APPROVED

Lowestoft Road, Worlingham, Beccles NR34 7EF
☎ (01502) 712571
Fax (01502) 712571
Quiet village location, all rooms en-suite, bar, restaurant, large car park. Half hour to Norwich, Lowestoft, Yarmouth, Broads and Blue Flag beaches. Daily half board price shown is for single occupancy, based on minimum 3-night stay.
Bedrooms: 2 double, 2 twin, 1 triple
Bathrooms: 5 en-suite

Bed & breakfast

per night:	£min	£max
Single	22.50	26.00
Double	30.00	36.00

Half board per person:

	£min	£max
Daily	28.50	
Weekly	147.00	

Lunch available
Evening meal 1900 (last orders 2200)
Parking for 40
Cards accepted: Mastercard, Visa
🛇🌳🏠💷👤🍴🛡S📺🛏🚇🔍🅿🎵🅿❄🚐🚭 SP

Please mention this guide when making your booking.

All accommodation in this guide has been graded, or is awaiting a grading, by a trained Tourist Board inspector.

BEDFORD

Bedfordshire
Map ref 2D1

Busy county town with interesting buildings and churches near the River Ouse which has pleasant riverside walks. Many associations with John Bunyan including Bunyan Meeting House, museum and statue. The Bedford Museum and Cecil Higgins Art Gallery are of interest.
Tourist Information Centre ☎ *(01234) 215226*

Bedford Oak House

👑 APPROVED

33 Shakespeare Road, Bedford MK40 2DX
☎ (01234) 266972
Fax (01234) 266972

Comfortable motor hotel bed and breakfast accommodation in a large mock-Tudor house, close to the railway station and town centre. En-suite facilities and large car park.
Bedrooms: 3 single, 10 double, 1 twin
Bathrooms: 12 en-suite, 1 public

Bed & breakfast

per night:	£min	£max
Single	30.00	35.00
Double	38.00	45.00

Evening meal (last orders 1900)
Parking for 15
Cards accepted: Amex, Diners, Mastercard, Visa
🛇🌳🏠💷👤🛡🚇📺🛏🚇🅿🍴🎯30🏸🚐 SP

1 Ravensden Grange

👑👑 COMMENDED

Sunderland Hill, Ravensden, Bedford MK44 2SH
☎ (01234) 771771
Well-appointed accommodation in spacious Georgian manor house overlooking lawns with great cedar trees. Cooking, comfort, hospitality all first class.
Bedrooms: 1 single, 1 double, 1 twin
Bathrooms: 2 private, 2 public

Bed & breakfast

per night:	£min	£max
Single	20.00	20.00
Double	36.00	36.00

Half board per person:

	£min	£max
Daily		35.00
Weekly		245.00

Lunch available
Evening meal 1830 (last orders 1200)
Parking for 10
🛇🌳3🏠👤🛡Ⓤ🛡S🔍🗚📺🛏🅿🍴❄♿🚐🚭🏠Ⓣ

BISHOP'S STORTFORD

Hertfordshire
Map ref 2D1

Fine old town on the River Stort with many interesting buildings, particularly Victorian, and an imposing parish church. The vicarage where Cecil Rhodes was born is now a museum.
Tourist Information Centre ☎ *(01279) 655831*

The Cottage 🏍

👑👑 HIGHLY COMMENDED

71 Birchanger Lane, Birchanger, Bishop's Stortford CM23 5QA
☎ (01279) 812349
Fax (01279) 812349
17th C listed house with panelled rooms and wood stove. Conservatory dining room overlooks large, mature garden. Quiet village setting yet near M11 junction 8 and Stansted Airport.
Bedrooms: 3 single, 6 double, 6 twin
Bathrooms: 11 en-suite, 2 private, 1 public

Bed & breakfast

per night:	£min	£max
Single	26.00	40.00
Double	50.00	50.00

Parking for 15
Cards accepted: Mastercard, Visa
🛇🌳🏠💷👤🛡S🔍🗚🛏🅿🍴❄🏸🚐 SP 🏠Ⓣ

Woodlands Lodge

👑👑 COMMENDED

Dunmow Road, Bishop's Stortford CM23 5QX
☎ (01279) 504784
Fax (01279) 461474
Charming, detached family home offering comfortable, pleasant and friendly accommodation. In own grounds with ample parking. Easy reach of Stansted Airport and M11, junction 8.
Bedrooms: 1 double, 2 twin, 1 triple
Bathrooms: 4 en-suite

Bed & breakfast

per night:	£min	£max
Single	30.00	32.00
Double	46.00	48.00

Parking for 14
Cards accepted: Mastercard, Visa, Switch/Delta

BLAKENEY

Norfolk
Map ref 3B1

Picturesque village on the north coast of Norfolk and a former port and fishing village. 15th C Guildhall. Marshy creeks extend towards Blakeney Point (National Trust) and are a paradise for naturalists, with trips to the reserve and to see the seals from Blakeney Quay.

Flintstones Guesthouse

Listed COMMENDED

Wiveton, Holt NR25 7TL
☎ (01263) 740337
Attractive licensed guesthouse in picturesque rural surroundings near village green. 1 mile from Cley and Blakeney with good sailing and bird-watching. All rooms with private facilities. Non-smokers only, please.
Bedrooms: 1 single, 1 double, 3 triple
Bathrooms: 3 en-suite, 2 private
Bed & breakfast

per night:	£min	£max
Single	21.00	22.00
Double	34.00	38.00

Evening meal 1900 (last orders 1700)
Parking for 5

Morston Hall

HIGHLY COMMENDED

Morston, Holt NR25 7AA
☎ (01263) 741041
Fax (01263) 740419
17th C country house hotel with delightful gardens, 2 miles from Blakeney. Fine restaurant, fully licensed. Attractive bedrooms. Peaceful.
Bedrooms: 5 double, 1 twin
Bathrooms: 6 en-suite
Half board per

person:	£min	£max
Daily	80.00	90.00

Lunch available
Evening meal 1930 (last orders 2100)
Parking for 50
Open February–December
Cards accepted: Amex, Mastercard, Visa, Switch/Delta

White Horse Hotel

COMMENDED

4 High Street, Blakeney, Holt NR25 7AL
☎ (01263) 740574
Fax (01263) 741303
Old Norfolk inn near picturesque harbour, offering traditional food and real beer. Restaurant closed Sunday/Monday evenings. Bar food 7 days a week. Local fish and game used. Service not included in prices shown.
Bedrooms: 2 single, 4 double, 1 twin, 2 triple
Bathrooms: 9 en-suite
Bed & breakfast

per night:	£min	£max
Single	30.00	30.00
Double	60.00	70.00

Lunch available
Evening meal 1900 (last orders 2130)
Parking for 15
Cards accepted: Amex, Mastercard, Visa, Switch/Delta

BOSTON

Lincolnshire
Map ref 3A1

Historic town famous for its church tower, the Boston Stump, 272 ft high. Still a busy port, the town is full of interest and has links with Boston, Massachusetts, through the Pilgrim Fathers. The cells where they were imprisoned can be seen in the medieval Guildhall.
Tourist Information Centre ☎ (01205) 356656

Comfort Friendly Inn

COMMENDED

Junction A17/A52, Donnington Road, Bicker Bar Roundabout, Boston PE20 3AN
☎ (01205) 820118
Fax (01205) 820228
Conveniently located at the junction of the A17/A52. Well-equipped bedrooms, all-day restaurant, meeting and conference facilities, ample free car parking. Special short-break weekends from £23.25 per person per night; £33.00 per person, including dinner.
Bedrooms: 20 double, 35 twin
Bathrooms: 55 en-suite
Bed & breakfast

per night:	£min	£max
Single	25.00	48.00
Double	50.00	54.00

Half board per

person:	£min	£max
Daily	35.00	45.00

Lunch available

Evening meal 1830 (last orders 2200)
Parking for 70
Cards accepted: Amex, Diners, Mastercard, Visa, Switch/Delta

Ye Olde Magnet Tavern

Listed COMMENDED

South Square, Boston PE21 6HX
☎ (01205) 369186
Traditional 17th C English pub with cask ales, serving home-cooked food in a friendly atmosphere. Opposite the historic Guildhall Museum and within easy reach of all local amenities.
Bedrooms: 1 single, 2 double, 1 twin
Bathrooms: 4 en-suite
Bed & breakfast

per night:	£min	£max
Single	31.75	34.00
Double	41.50	46.00

Lunch available
Evening meal 1800 (last orders 2000)
Parking for 3
Cards accepted: Mastercard, Visa

BRAINTREE

Essex
Map ref 3B2

The Heritage Centre in the Town Hall describes Braintree's former international importance in wool, silk and engineering. St Michael's parish church includes some Roman bricks. Braintree market was first chartered in 1199.
Tourist Information Centre ☎ (01376) 550066

White Hart Hotel

COMMENDED

Bocking End, Braintree CM7 9AB
☎ (01376) 321401
Fax (01376) 552628
Email: greaves@cix.co.uk.
Stagecoach
Warm and cosily furnished, town centre hotel, created around an original 16th C coaching inn. Excellent base for visiting East Anglia.
Bedrooms: 3 single, 14 double, 6 twin, 8 triple
Bathrooms: 31 en-suite
Bed & breakfast

per night:	£min	£max
Single	36.00	65.45
Double	52.00	82.90

Lunch available
Evening meal 1800 (last orders 2200)

Continued ▶

BRAINTREE

Continued

Parking for 51
Cards accepted: Amex, Diners, Mastercard, Visa, Switch/Delta

🛏🐕📞💷🖥🕳💷📺🗝🛎⌑🌙💻🖨
🍴40🏊🎿✕⚲ SP🅿T

BRENTWOOD

Essex
Map ref 2D2

The town grew up in the late 12th C and developed as a staging post, being strategically placed close to the London to Chelmsford road. Deer roam by the lakes in the 428-acre park at South Weald, part of Brentwood's attractive Green Belt.
Tourist Information Centre ☎ (01277) 200300

Brentwood Guesthouse

👑 APPROVED

75/77 Rose Valley, Brentwood
CM14 4HJ
☎ (01277) 262713 & 0410 523757
Fax (01277) 211146
Victorian detached guesthouse, recently refurbished. Close to Brentwood centre and local parks. 2 minutes' walk from rail station (London 25 minutes), 1 mile to M25. TV in all rooms, en-suite rooms available.
Bedrooms: 2 single, 4 double, 2 twin, 2 triple
Bathrooms: 8 en-suite, 3 public

Bed & breakfast per night:

	£min	£max
Single	25.00	45.00
Double	45.00	50.00

Parking for 10
Cards accepted: Mastercard, Visa

🛏🐕📞🖥💷🕳💷🗝🛎⌑🌙💻🖨🍴25✕
T

Marygreen Manor Hotel ᛗ

👑👑👑 HIGHLY COMMENDED

London Road, Brentwood
CM14 4NR
☎ (01277) 225252
Fax (01277) 262809

Original Tudor building dating back to 1512. Hunting lodge visited by Catherine of Aragon. Old world garden. B&B prices below are per room.

Bedrooms: 16 double, 17 twin
Bathrooms: 33 en-suite

Bed & breakfast per night:

	£min	£max
Single	108.50	117.00
Double	119.50	128.50

Lunch available
Evening meal 1915 (last orders 2215)
Parking for 100
Cards accepted: Amex, Diners, Mastercard, Visa, Switch/Delta

🛏🐕📞💷🖥💷🕳💷📺🗝🛎🌙💻🖨🍴60❀⚲ SP🅿

BUNGAY

Suffolk
Map ref 3C1

Market town and yachting centre on the River Waveney with the remains of a great 12th C castle. In the market-place stands the Butter Cross, rebuilt in 1689 after being largely destroyed by fire. Nearby at Earsham is the Otter Trust.

The Kings Head Hotel

👑👑 APPROVED

Market Place, Bungay NR35 1AF
☎ (01986) 893583
Fax (01986) 893583
17th C coaching inn, centre of delightful Waveney Valley market town. Central for Norwich, the Broads, Suffolk coast and countryside. Bar, restaurant and ballroom.
Bedrooms: 6 single, 2 double, 5 twin, 1 family room
Bathrooms: 8 en-suite, 2 public

Bed & breakfast per night:

	£min	£max
Single	25.00	40.00
Double	40.00	55.00

Half board per person:

	£min	£max
Daily	32.50	47.00
Weekly	200.00	280.00

Lunch available
Evening meal 1900 (last orders 2200)
Parking for 23
Cards accepted: Amex, Diners, Mastercard, Visa, Switch/Delta

🛏🐕🖥💷🕳💷🗝🛎📺💻🖨🍴100
🌙🅿❀🚗 DAP ⚲ SP🅿T

COLOUR MAPS

Colour maps at the back of this guide pinpoint all places in which you will find accommodation listed.

BURY ST EDMUNDS

Suffolk
Map ref 3B2

Ancient market and cathedral town which takes its name from the martyred Saxon King, St Edmund. Bury St Edmunds has many fine buildings including the Athenaeum and Moyses Hall, reputed to be the oldest Norman house in the county.
Tourist Information Centre ☎ (01284) 764667 or 757083

Angel Hotel ᛗ

👑👑👑 HIGHLY COMMENDED

Angel Hill, Bury St Edmunds
IP33 1LT
☎ (01284) 753926
Fax (01284) 750092

Attractive Georgian hotel with individually decorated bedrooms. Four-posters and suites available. Ballroom and conference rooms. Bar food and noted restaurant.
Bedrooms: 11 single, 19 double, 12 twin
Suite available
Bathrooms: 42 en-suite

Bed & breakfast per night:

	£min	£max
Single	38.00	72.50
Double	76.00	93.00

Half board per person:

	£min	£max
Daily	63.00	

Lunch available
Evening meal 1900 (last orders 2200)
Parking for 58
Cards accepted: Amex, Diners, Mastercard, Visa, Switch/Delta

🛏🐕📞💷🖥💷🕳💷📺🗝🛎⌑🌙💻
🖨🍴120🔱✓⚲ SP🅿T

Butterfly Hotel ᛗ

👑👑👑 COMMENDED

A14 Bury East Exit, Moreton Hall, Bury St Edmunds IP32 7BW
☎ (01284) 760884
Fax (01284) 755476
Modern building with rustic style and decor, around open central courtyard. Special weekend rates available.
Bedrooms: 32 single, 19 double, 14 twin
Bathrooms: 65 en-suite

Bed & breakfast per night:	£min	£max
Single	51.95	61.95
Double	58.90	68.90

Half board per person:	£min	£max
Daily	64.45	74.45

Lunch available
Evening meal 1800 (last orders 2200)
Parking for 70
Cards accepted: Amex, Diners, Mastercard, Visa, Switch/Delta
🐕♿📞🖥⬜☕🍴🔥⬛Ⓢ🔑🧺⬤🛏️▣
🍳40✱T

Dunston Guesthouse/Hotel ♏

👑👑 COMMENDED

8 Springfield Road, Bury St Edmunds IP33 3AN
☎ (01284) 767981
Attractive Victorian guesthouse/hotel providing high standard accommodation, quietly situated half a mile from town centre. Licensed, sun lounge, garden and car park. Groups welcome.
Bedrooms: 6 single, 3 double, 3 twin, 3 triple
Bathrooms: 7 en-suite, 3 private, 3 public

Bed & breakfast per night:	£min	£max
Single	20.00	27.50
Double	40.00	45.00

Parking for 12
🐕♿📞🖥⬜☕🍴Ⓢ🔑🧺TV⬛🛏️
✱🍴

The Grange Hotel ♏

👑👑👑 COMMENDED

Barton Road, Thurston, Bury St Edmunds IP31 3PQ
☎ (01359) 231260
Fax (01359) 231260

Family-owned country house hotel with chef/proprietor, 4 miles from Bury St Edmunds.
Bedrooms: 2 single, 8 double, 2 twin, 1 triple
Suite available
Bathrooms: 13 en-suite

Bed & breakfast per night:	£min	£max
Single	37.00	48.00
Double	52.00	69.00

Lunch available

Evening meal 1900 (last orders 2130)
Parking for 80
Cards accepted: Mastercard, Visa
🐕♿📞🖥♿☕🍴⬛Ⓢ🧺⬛🛏️🍴120✱
🚗 SP T

CAMBRIDGE

Cambridgeshire
Map ref 2D1

A most important and beautiful city on the River Cam with 31 colleges forming one of the oldest universities in the world. Numerous museums, good shopping centre, restaurants, good theatres, cinema and fine bookshops.
Tourist Information Centre ☎ (01223) 322640

Arbury Lodge Guesthouse

Listed COMMENDED

82 Arbury Road, Cambridge CB4 2JE
☎ (01223) 364319 & 566988
Fax (01223) 566988
Comfortable family-run guesthouse, about 20 minutes' walk to city centre and colleges. Easy access from A14. Large car park and garden.
Bedrooms: 2 single, 1 double, 2 twin
Bathrooms: 2 en-suite, 4 public

Bed & breakfast per night:	£min	£max
Single	22.00	25.00
Double	36.00	46.00

Parking for 8
🐕🖥☕🔥UL⬛Ⓢ⬤⬛🛏️✱🍴🚗

Arundel House Hotel ♏

👑👑 COMMENDED

Chesterton Road, Cambridge CB4 3AN
☎ (01223) 367701
Fax (01223) 367721
Elegant, privately-owned 19th C terraced hotel. Beautiful location overlooking River Cam and open parkland, near city centre and colleges. Reputation for some of the best food in the area.
Bedrooms: 43 single, 33 double, 23 twin, 5 triple, 1 family room
Bathrooms: 99 en-suite, 8 public

Bed & breakfast per night:	£min	£max
Single	39.50	67.00
Double	59.00	89.00

Lunch available
Evening meal 1830 (last orders 2130)
Parking for 70
Cards accepted: Amex, Diners, Mastercard, Visa, Switch/Delta
🐕♿📞🖥⬜☕🍴⬛Ⓢ🔑🧺⬛
🛏️🍴50✱🍴 SP 🎠

Ashley Hotel ♏

👑👑👑 APPROVED

74 Chesterton Road, Cambridge CB4 1ER
☎ (01223) 350059
Well-appointed small hotel with modern facilities, close to city centre. Nearby Arundel House Hotel's facilities available to Ashley residents (under same ownership).
Bedrooms: 2 single, 3 double, 3 twin, 2 triple
Bathrooms: 8 en-suite, 2 public

Bed & breakfast per night:	£min	£max
Single	29.50	39.50
Double	49.50	59.50

Parking for 16
Cards accepted: Mastercard, Visa, Switch/Delta
🐕♿📞🖥⬜☕🔥UL⬛🛏️TV⬤⬛
🛏️✱🍴🚗 SP

Ashtrees Guesthouse

Listed COMMENDED

128 Perne Road, Cambridge CB1 3RR
☎ (01223) 411233
Comfort and an enjoyable stay are the priorities. Individually decorated rooms to a high standard. Home cooking. Garden and car park.
Bedrooms: 2 single, 3 double, 1 twin, 1 triple
Bathrooms: 1 en-suite, 1 public

Bed & breakfast per night:	£min	£max
Single	19.00	32.00
Double	36.00	43.00

Half board per person:	£min	£max
Daily	28.00	40.00

Evening meal 1830 (last orders 1830)
Parking for 6
Cards accepted: Mastercard, Visa
🐕♿🖥☕🔥UL⬛🧺🛏️✱🍴🚗

Assisi Guesthouse ♏

👑👑 APPROVED

193 Cherry Hinton Road, Cambridge CB1 4BX
☎ (01223) 246648 & 211466
Fax (01223) 412900

Warm, welcoming, family-run guesthouse, ideally situated for the city,
Continued ▶

CAMBRIDGE

Continued

colleges and Addenbrookes Hospital. All modern facilities. Large car park.
Bedrooms: 4 single, 5 double, 6 twin, 1 triple
Bathrooms: 16 en-suite
Bed & breakfast

per night:	£min	£max
Single	29.00	31.00
Double	39.00	42.00

Parking for 15
Cards accepted: Amex, Mastercard, Visa

Aylesbray Lodge Guesthouse
COMMENDED
5 Mowbray Road, Cambridge
CB1 4SR
☎ (01223) 240089
Fax (01223) 240089

All rooms are en-suite, tastefully decorated and have complimentary extras. Four poster rooms, satellite TV. Car parking.
Bedrooms: 1 single, 2 double, 1 twin, 1 family room
Bathrooms: 5 en-suite
Bed & breakfast

per night:	£min	£max
Single	28.00	28.00
Double	40.00	45.00

Evening meal 1800 (last orders 1900)
Parking for 7
Cards accepted: Amex, Diners, Mastercard, Visa, Switch/Delta

Bridge Hotel (Motel) ⚑
APPROVED
Clayhythe, Waterbeach, Cambridge
CB5 9NZ
☎ (01223) 860252
Fax (01223) 440448

Picturesque 17th C riverside hotel with motel rooms, between A45 and A10

(B1047), 4 miles from Cambridge. Fishing, walking, boating.
Bedrooms: 3 single, 20 double, 5 twin
Suites available
Bathrooms: 28 en-suite
Bed & breakfast

per night:	£min	£max
Single	35.00	
Double	55.00	65.00

Lunch available
Evening meal 1830 (last orders 2130)
Parking for 50
Cards accepted: Amex, Mastercard, Visa, Switch/Delta

Brooklands Guesthouse
COMMENDED
95 Cherry Hinton Road, Cambridge
CB1 4BS
☎ (01223) 242035
Fax (01223) 242035
Friendly guesthouse, well decorated. All rooms en-suite and with telephone. Satellite TV, jacuzzi, sauna, four-poster bed.
Bedrooms: 3 double, 2 twin
Bathrooms: 5 private
Bed & breakfast

per night:	£min	£max
Single	28.00	30.00
Double	38.00	45.00

Evening meal 1830 (last orders 1900)
Parking for 5
Cards accepted: Amex, Diners, Mastercard, Visa, Switch/Delta

Cam Guesthouse
Listed COMMENDED
17 Elizabeth Way, Cambridge
CB4 1DD
☎ (01223) 354512
Guesthouse close to the River Cam, within 15 minutes' walking distance of the city centre and 5 minutes from Grafton shopping centre. En-suite jacuzzi bath.
Bedrooms: 3 single, 3 double, 2 triple, 1 family room
Bathrooms: 1 en-suite, 3 public
Bed & breakfast

per night:	£min	£max
Single	24.00	30.00
Double	40.00	55.00

Parking for 6

Cristinas
COMMENDED
47 St Andrews Road, Cambridge
CB4 1DH
☎ (01223) 365855 & 327700
Fax (01223) 365855
Small family-run business in quiet location, a short walk from city centre and colleges.
Bedrooms: 5 double, 3 twin, 1 triple
Bathrooms: 7 en-suite, 1 public
Bed & breakfast

per night:	£min	£max
Single	35.00	42.00
Double	42.00	49.00

Parking for 8

Dresden Villa Guesthouse ⚑
APPROVED
34 Cherry Hinton Road, Cambridge
CB1 4AA
☎ (01223) 247539
Fax (01223) 410640

Family-run guesthouse offering friendly service. All rooms en-suite, tea/coffee, satellite TV. Easy access to city colleges, hospital.
Bedrooms: 6 single, 3 double, 2 twin, 2 triple
Bathrooms: 13 en-suite, 1 public
Bed & breakfast

per night:	£min	£max
Single	26.00	28.00
Double	40.00	44.00

Half board per

person:	£min	£max
Daily	36.00	38.00
Weekly	252.00	266.00

Evening meal 1900 (last orders 2000)
Parking for 8

Fairways Guesthouse
APPROVED
141-143 Cherry Hinton Road, Cambridge CB1 4BX
☎ (01223) 246063
Fax (01223) 212093
Charming Victorian house. Family and en-suite rooms available. Direct dial telephone, clock/radio in all rooms. Close to Addenbrookes Hospital, station and golf-course and 1 mile from city centre. English/continental breakfast, bar/lounge.

Bedrooms: 4 single, 4 double, 4 twin,
1 triple, 2 family rooms
Bathrooms: 8 en-suite, 2 public

Bed & breakfast

per night:	£min	£max
Single	20.00	29.00
Double	35.00	45.00

Parking for 20
Cards accepted: Mastercard, Visa,
Switch/Delta

Gonville Hotel M

COMMENDED

Gonville Place, Cambridge CB1 1LY
☎ (01223) 366611
Fax (01223) 315470
Ⓒ Best Western
*Occupies one of the most favoured
positions in Cambridge, overlooking
Parkers Piece and close to most of the
colleges and shopping areas.*
Bedrooms: 24 single, 19 double,
21 twin, 1 triple
Bathrooms: 65 en-suite

Bed & breakfast

per night:	£min	£max
Single	82.50	
Double	107.00	

Half board per

person:	£min	£max
Daily	70.45	99.45
Weekly	312.00	696.15

Lunch available
Evening meal 1900 (last orders
2045)
Parking for 80
Cards accepted: Amex, Diners,
Mastercard, Visa, Switch/Delta

Hamden Guesthouse

89 High Street, Cherry Hinton,
Cambridge CB1 4LU
☎ (01223) 413263
*The owner of this guesthouse
guarantees you will not be
disappointed with the comfortable
en-suite bedrooms, most of which have
garden view. Full English breakfast. Bus
service to city centre. Shops, pubs and
restaurant within walking distance.
Easy access to M11 and A14.*
Bedrooms: 1 single, 1 double, 1 twin,
1 triple, 1 family room
Bathrooms: 5 private

Bed & breakfast

per night:	£min	£max
Single	25.00	28.00
Double	40.00	45.00

Parking for 7

Hamilton Hotel

APPROVED

156 Chesterton Road, Cambridge
CB4 1DA
☎ (01223) 365664
Fax (01223) 314866
*Family-run private hotel about 1 mile
from city centre. TVs, telephones,
en-suites, tea and coffee-making
facilities. Bar, meals, car park.*
Bedrooms: 5 single, 5 double, 5 twin,
3 triple
Bathrooms: 14 en-suite, 1 public

Bed & breakfast

per night:	£min	£max
Single	22.00	35.00
Double	40.00	57.50

Half board per

person:	£min	£max
Daily	30.00	45.00

Evening meal 1830 (last orders
2000)
Parking for 18
Cards accepted: Amex, Diners,
Mastercard, Visa, Switch/Delta

Holiday Inn (Cambridge) M

HIGHLY COMMENDED

Downing Street, Cambridge
CB2 3DT
☎ (01223) 464466
Fax (01223) 464440
*Centrally located, fully air-conditioned
hotel. Bloomsbury's Bar Restaurant
with theatre-style kitchen open all day.
Quinn's Irish pub - an alternative venue
at the hotel for food and drink.*
Wheelchair access category 2♿
Bedrooms: 85 double, 112 twin
Suites available
Bathrooms: 197 en-suite

Bed & breakfast

per night:	£min	£max
Single		118.00
Double		145.00

Half board per

person:	£min	£max
Daily	85.00	146.00

Lunch available
Evening meal 1830 (last orders
2230)
Parking for 68
Cards accepted: Amex, Diners,
Mastercard, Visa, Switch/Delta

Half board prices are given
per person, but in some cases
these may be based on
double/twin occupancy.

Lensfield Hotel M

53 Lensfield Road, Cambridge
CB2 1EN
☎ (01223) 355017
Fax (01223) 312022
*Family-run hotel in central location for
all parts of the city's splendour - the
"Bridges and Backs", Botanical
Gardens, colleges, entertainment and
shopping.*
Bedrooms: 7 single, 11 double,
10 twin, 2 triple
Bathrooms: 27 en-suite, 4 public

Bed & breakfast

per night:	£min	£max
Single	40.00	48.00
Double	60.00	68.00

Half board per

person:	£min	£max
Daily	50.00	58.00

Evening meal 1830 (last orders
2100)
Parking for 11
Cards accepted: Amex, Diners,
Mastercard, Visa, Switch/Delta

Southampton House

Listed COMMENDED

7 Elizabeth Way, Cambridge
CB4 1DE
☎ (01223) 357780
Fax (01223) 314297
*Victorian property with friendly
atmosphere, only 8 minutes' walk along
riverside to city centre, colleges and
new shopping mall.*
Bedrooms: 1 single, 1 double,
2 triple, 1 family room
Bathrooms: 5 en-suite

Bed & breakfast

per night:	£min	£max
Single	25.00	37.00
Double	38.00	48.00

Parking for 8

WELCOME HOST

This is a nationally recognised
customer care programme
which aims to promote
the highest standards of
service and a warm welcome.
Establishments who are taking
part in this initiative are
indicated by the 🌐 symbol.

CAWSTON

Norfolk
Map ref 3B1

Village with one of the finest churches in the country. St Agnes, built in the Perpendicular style, was much patronised by Michael de la Pole, Earl of Suffolk (1414), and has a magnificent hammer-beam roof and numerous carved angels.

Grey Gables Country House Hotel & Restaurant

👑👑👑 COMMENDED

Norwich Road, Cawston, Norwich
NR10 4EY
☎ (01603) 871259

Former rectory in pleasant, rural setting, 10 miles from Norwich, coast and Broads. Wine cellar, emphasis on food. Comfortably furnished with many antiques.
Bedrooms: 2 single, 5 double, 1 twin
Bathrooms: 6 en-suite, 1 public

Bed & breakfast

per night:	£min	£max
Single	21.00	40.00
Double	54.00	60.00

Half board per

person:	£min	£max
Daily	35.00	60.00
Weekly	226.00	246.00

Lunch available
Evening meal 1900 (last orders 2100)
Parking for 15
Cards accepted: Mastercard, Visa
🏇🛁✆📟☐🖂♦🕯🍽⑤🌙📺🏨 🍷♈12 📞♈☼🚗 SP 🏠 T

CHATTERIS

Cambridgeshire
Map ref 3A2

Cross Keys Inn Hotel ♏

👑👑 COMMENDED

12-16 Market Hill, Chatteris
PE16 6BA
☎ (01354) 693036 & 692644
Fax (01354) 693036

Elizabethan coaching inn built around 1540, Grade II listed. A la carte menu and bar meals. Friendly atmosphere, oak-beamed lounge with log fires. Ideally placed in the heart of the Fens.
Bedrooms: 2 double, 4 twin, 1 triple
Bathrooms: 5 en-suite, 1 public

Bed & breakfast

per night:	£min	£max
Single	21.00	32.50
Double	32.50	55.00

Half board per

person:	£min	£max
Daily	40.00	40.00

Lunch available
Evening meal 1900 (last orders 2200)
Parking for 10
Cards accepted: Amex, Diners, Mastercard, Visa, Switch/Delta
🏇🛁✆📟☐♦🕯🍽⑤🌙📺🏨 🍷♈☼ OAP SP 🏠 T

CHELMSFORD

Essex
Map ref 3B3

The county town of Essex, originally a Roman settlement, Caesaromagus, thought to have been destroyed by Boudicca. Growth of the town's industry can be traced in the excellent museum in Oaklands Park. 15th C parish church has been Chelmsford Cathedral since 1914. *Tourist Information Centre* ☎ *(01245) 283400*

Beechcroft Private Hotel ♏

👑👑 COMMENDED

211 New London Road, Chelmsford
CM2 0AJ
☎ (01245) 352462 & 250861
Fax (01245) 347833
Central hotel offering clean and comfortable accommodation with friendly service. Under family ownership and management. Within walking distance of town centre.

Bedrooms: 12 single, 3 double, 3 twin, 1 triple, 1 family room
Bathrooms: 9 en-suite, 4 public

Bed & breakfast

per night:	£min	£max
Single	31.00	37.40
Double	45.00	51.00

Parking for 15
Cards accepted: Mastercard, Visa
🏇🛁✆☐♦ UL 🕯📺🏨 🍷🚌

Boswell House Hotel ♏

👑👑👑 COMMENDED

118 Springfield Road, Chelmsford
CM2 6LF
☎ (01245) 287587
Fax (01245) 287587
Victorian town house in central location, offering high-standard accommodation in friendly and informal surroundings. Family atmosphere with home cooking.
Bedrooms: 5 single, 6 double, 2 triple
Bathrooms: 13 en-suite

Bed & breakfast

per night:	£min	£max
Single	45.00	48.00
Double	60.00	65.00

Half board per

person:	£min	£max
Daily	57.00	60.00

Lunch available
Evening meal 1900 (last orders 2030)
Parking for 15
Cards accepted: Amex, Diners, Mastercard, Visa
🏇🛁✆📟☐♦🕯🍽⑤🌙📺🏨 📞☼🍽🏠

The Chelmer Hotel

Listed APPROVED

2-4 Hamlet Road, Chelmsford
CM2 0EU
☎ (01245) 353360 & 609055
Fax (0181) 574 3912
Friendly and homely atmosphere. Close to all amenities and priding itself as the most economic hotel in Chelmsford.
Bedrooms: 2 single, 1 double, 2 twin, 2 triple
Bathrooms: 2 public

Bed & breakfast

per night:	£min	£max
Single	19.00	20.50
Double	33.00	35.00

Parking for 2
🏇🛁✆📟 UL ⑤🌙📺🏨 🐾🚭 T

County Hotel ♏

👑👑👑 COMMENDED

Rainsford Road, Chelmsford
CM1 2QA
☎ (01245) 491911
Fax (01245) 492762
Privately owned hotel, 10 minutes' walk

*from town centre. Families welcome -
free cots, extra beds. Popular
restaurant offering £18 - £20
three-course meal.*
Bedrooms: 18 single, 7 double,
10 twin
Suite available
Bathrooms: 35 en-suite
**Bed & breakfast
per night:**

	£min	£max
Single	28.00	30.00
Double	56.00	60.00

Lunch available
Evening meal 1830 (last orders
2100)
Parking for 120
Cards accepted: Amex, Diners,
Mastercard, Visa, Switch/Delta

Miami Hotel ⚑
🏆🏆🏆 APPROVED
Princes Road, Chelmsford CM2 9AJ
☎ (01245) 264848 & 269603
Fax (01245) 259860
Ⓒ The Independents
*Family-run hotel, 1 mile from town
centre. All rooms are twin/double size
(let as singles when required).*
Bedrooms: 22 single, 23 double,
10 twin
Bathrooms: 55 en-suite
**Bed & breakfast
per night:**

	£min	£max
Single	40.00	60.00
Double	50.00	71.00

**Half board per
person:**

	£min	£max
Daily	37.50	52.50
Weekly	237.50	327.50

Lunch available
Evening meal 1830 (last orders
2130)
Parking for 80
Cards accepted: Amex, Diners,
Mastercard, Visa, Switch/Delta

Tanunda Hotel
🏆🏆 APPROVED
217-219 New London Road,
Chelmsford CM2 0AJ
☎ (01245) 354295
Fax (01245) 345503
*Well-positioned commercial hotel with
homely atmosphere. Snacks available.*
Bedrooms: 8 single, 6 double, 6 twin
Bathrooms: 11 en-suite, 3 public
**Bed & breakfast
per night:**

	£min	£max
Single	30.00	45.00
Double	43.50	53.00

Parking for 20
Cards accepted: Amex, Diners,
Mastercard, Visa, Switch/Delta

CHESHUNT
Hertfordshire
Map ref 2D1

Cheshunt Marriott Hotel
🏆🏆🏆🏆 COMMENDED
Halfhide Lane, Turnford, Broxbourne
EN10 6NG
☎ (01992) 451245
Fax (01992) 440120
Ⓒ Utell International
*Only minutes' drive from the M25
motorway, the Cheshunt Marriott offers
an ideal base for exploring London and
the South East. Prices shown are for
room only.*
Wheelchair access category 1♿
Bedrooms: 104 double, 38 twin
Suites available
Bathrooms: 142 en-suite
**Bed & breakfast
per night:**

	£min	£max
Single	94.00	94.00

Lunch available
Evening meal 1830 (last orders
2200)
Parking for 200
Cards accepted: Amex, Diners,
Mastercard, Visa, Switch/Delta

CLACTON-ON-SEA
Essex
Map ref 3B3

Developed in the 1870s into a
popular holiday resort with pier,
pavilion, funfair, theatres and
traditional amusements. The
Martello Towers on the seafront
were built like many others in the
early 19th C to defend Britain
against Napoleon.
*Tourist Information Centre ☎ (01255)
423400*

Sandrock Hotel ⚑
🏆🏆🏆 COMMENDED
1 Penfold Road, Marine Parade
West, Clacton-on-Sea CO15 1JN
☎ (01255) 428215
Fax (01255) 428215
*Private hotel in central position, just off
seafront and close to town.
Comfortable bedrooms with
co-ordinated soft furnishings. Excellent,
freshly cooked food. Licensed. Car park.*

Bedrooms: 5 double, 2 twin, 1 triple
Bathrooms: 8 en-suite
**Bed & breakfast
per night:**

	£min	£max
Single	22.00	24.50
Double	44.00	49.00

**Half board per
person:**

	£min	£max
Daily	32.00	34.50
Weekly	185.00	200.00

Lunch available
Evening meal 1830 (last orders
1900)
Parking for 6
Cards accepted: Amex, Diners,
Mastercard, Visa, Switch/Delta

CLEY NEXT THE SEA
Norfolk
Map ref 3B1

Due to land reclamation the village
has not been "next the sea" since
the 17th C. Behind the old quay the
main street winds between
flint-built houses. The marshes
between Cley and Salthouse are
bird reserves. Cley Windmill is a
160-year-old tower mill converted
into a guesthouse.

Cley Windmill ⚑
🏆🏆 APPROVED
Cley next the Sea, Holt NR25 7NN
☎ (01263) 740209 & 741324
Fax (01263) 740209

*Unusual, dramatic building which
enjoys superb views over Cley marshes.
Wonderfully comfortable and relaxed
atmosphere within.*
Bedrooms: 1 single, 4 double, 2 twin
Bathrooms: 5 en-suite, 2 public
**Bed & breakfast
per night:**

	£min	£max
Single	30.00	69.00
Double	56.00	69.00

**Half board per
person:**

	£min	£max
Daily	43.00	84.00
Weekly	262.50	553.00

Evening meal 1930 (last orders
1930)
Parking for 12
Cards accepted: Mastercard, Visa,
Switch/Delta

CODICOTE

Hertfordshire
Map ref 2D1

The Bell Inn & Motel
👑👑👑 COMMENDED

High Street, Codicote SG4 8XD
☎ (01438) 820278
Fax (01438) 821671

Beautiful bungalow-styled executive bedrooms, all en-suite. Full a la carte restaurant and traditional country pub serving excellent bar meals and real ales. Very close to A1M, M25 and M1. Family-run and very welcoming.
Bedrooms: 9 double, 16 twin
Bathrooms: 25 en-suite

Bed & breakfast per night:

	£min	£max
Single	42.50	52.50
Double	49.50	59.50

Half board per person:

	£min	£max
Daily	37.50	42.50
Weekly	325.00	

Lunch available
Evening meal 1900 (last orders 2200)
Parking for 60
Cards accepted: Amex, Diners, Mastercard, Visa, Switch/Delta

🐶👪🌛📞🚪🗔👆🖤🖁ⓈⅪ📺
🔟📼🍴40🖑🖣❉🛪🕱 SP

COGGESHALL

Essex
Map ref 3B2

The National Trust property "Paycocke's" is at Coggeshall. It is a 16th century half-timbered merchant's house featuring a richly-carved interior.

The White Hart Hotel ⚞
👑👑👑 HIGHLY COMMENDED

Market End, Coggeshall, Colchester CO6 1NH
☎ (01376) 561654
Fax (01376) 561789
Tudor inn dating from 1432, built on a Roman road and signed off the A120 and A12, 7 miles west of Colchester.
Bedrooms: 2 single, 14 double, 2 twin
Bathrooms: 18 en-suite

Bed & breakfast per night:

	£min	£max
Single	49.20	66.50
Double	77.60	97.00

Lunch available
Evening meal 1900 (last orders 2200)
Parking for 41
Cards accepted: Amex, Mastercard, Visa, Switch/Delta

🐶📞🚪🗔👆🖁Ⓢ🍴📼🍴35❉
🛪🚜 SP 🏠

COLCHESTER

Essex
Map ref 3B2

Britain's oldest recorded town standing on the River Colne and famous for its oysters. Numerous historic buildings, ancient remains and museums. Plenty of parks and gardens, extensive shopping centre, theatre and zoo.
Tourist Information Centre ☎ (01206) 282920

Butterfly Hotel ⚞
👑👑👑 COMMENDED

A12-A120 Ardleigh Junction, Old Ipswich Road, Colchester CO7 7QY
☎ (01206) 230900
Fax (01206) 231095
Purpose-built hotel in traditional style. Modern coaching inn by the water's edge on the outskirts of Colchester at the junction of A12 and A120.
Bedrooms: 22 single, 12 double, 12 twin, 4 family rooms
Suites available
Bathrooms: 50 en-suite

Bed & breakfast per night:

	£min	£max
Single	51.95	61.95
Double	58.90	68.90

Half board per person:

	£min	£max
Daily	64.45	74.45

Lunch available
Evening meal 1800 (last orders 2200)
Parking for 75
Cards accepted: Amex, Diners, Mastercard, Visa, Switch/Delta

🐶👪📞🚪🗔👆🖤ⓈⅪ📺◑🔟
📼🍴80❉ SP T

Colchester Mill Hotel ⚞

East Street, Colchester CO1 2TS
☎ (01206) 865022
Fax (01206) 860851
Converted flour mill set alongside the River Colne, just a few minutes from the ancient town centre of Colchester. The quayside restaurant overlooks the river and has a reputation locally for good food and service.

Bedrooms: 6 single, 34 double, 15 twin, 2 triple, 4 family rooms
Bathrooms: 59 en-suite, 2 private

Bed & breakfast per night:

	£min	£max
Single	45.00	52.50
Double	65.00	90.00

Half board per person:

	£min	£max
Daily	55.00	58.00

Lunch available
Evening meal 1900 (last orders 2200)
Parking for 200
Cards accepted: Amex, Diners, Mastercard, Visa

🐶👪📞🚪🗔👆🖟🖁ⓈⅪ◑🔟
🔟📼🍴80❉🖣 DAP 🕱 SP 🏠 T

The Lodge ⚞
👑👑👑 COMMENDED

The Essex Golf & Country Club, Earls Colne, Colchester CO6 2NS
☎ (01787) 224466
Fax (01787) 224410
Modern hotel at The Essex Golf and Country Club. West of Colchester in some of the most beautiful countryside in the country.
Bedrooms: 12 double, 30 twin
Bathrooms: 42 en-suite

Bed & breakfast per night:

	£min	£max
Single	52.50	72.50
Double	55.00	75.00

Half board per person:

	£min	£max
Daily	45.00	65.00

Lunch available
Evening meal 1830 (last orders 2130)
Parking for 100
Cards accepted: Mastercard, Visa, Switch/Delta

🐶👪📞🗔👆🖤ⓈⅪ◑🔟📼
🍴315♟🛪🖣🔍🎣♪🖣❉🛪🕱 SP T

Peveril Hotel ⚞
👑 APPROVED

51 North Hill, Colchester CO1 1PY
☎ (01206) 574001
Fax (01206) 574001
Friendly, family-run hotel with fine restaurant and bar. All rooms have colour TV and all facilities. Some en-suite available.
Bedrooms: 5 single, 7 double, 4 twin, 1 triple
Suites available
Bathrooms: 3 en-suite, 3 public

Bed & breakfast per night:

	£min	£max
Single	25.00	40.00
Double	36.00	47.00

Half board per person:	£min	£max
Daily	31.00	46.00
Weekly	217.00	322.00

Lunch available
Evening meal 1900 (last orders 2145)
Parking for 24
Cards accepted: Amex, Diners, Mastercard, Visa

🛏🍴🖥📠🗜�</>💷 S ▥ ⬛ 🔌 ⊠ SP

Rose & Crown ▲▲

👑👑👑 COMMENDED

East Street, Colchester CO1 2TZ
☎ (01206) 866677
Fax (01206) 866616
Ⓒ Logis of GB

The oldest inn in the oldest recorded town in England. Early 15th C inn with charming en-suite bedrooms, log fire bar and noted restaurant. On Ipswich road 2 miles off A12 and half a mile from town centre.
Bedrooms: 1 single, 23 double, 2 twin, 4 triple
Bathrooms: 30 en-suite

Bed & breakfast per night:	£min	£max
Single		62.00
Double		62.00

Lunch available
Evening meal 1900 (last orders 2200)
Parking for 60
Cards accepted: Amex, Diners, Mastercard, Visa, Switch/Delta

🛏🍴🖥🐾📠🗜�</>💷 S 🖉 🔌 TV ◖
▥ ⬛ 🍴120 ✿ ⊠ DAP 🔌 SP 🏠 T

The Salisbury

Listed APPROVED

112 Butt Road, Colchester CO3 3DL
☎ (01206) 572338 & 508508
Fax (01206) 797265
Family-run hotel near town centre. Fully licensed restaurant/bar, private meeting facilities, pool, darts. Specialises in small, informal dinner parties.
Bedrooms: 3 single, 2 double, 2 twin, 1 triple
Bathrooms: 8 en-suite

Bed & breakfast per night:	£min	£max
Single	30.00	40.00
Double	50.00	60.00

Lunch available
Evening meal 1930 (last orders 2100)

Parking for 40
Cards accepted: Amex, Mastercard, Visa

🛏🖥🐾📠🗜💷 S 🖉 TV ▥ ⬛ ⚑ 🗜 ✈ 🔌
✈ DAP SP

Scheregate Hotel ▲▲

APPROVED

36 Osborne Street, via St John's Street, Colchester CO2 7DB
☎ (01206) 573034
Interesting 15th C building, centrally situated, providing accommodation at moderate prices.
Bedrooms: 12 single, 6 double, 8 twin, 1 triple, 1 family room
Bathrooms: 8 en-suite, 5 public

Bed & breakfast per night:	£min	£max
Single	18.00	30.00
Double	40.00	50.00

Parking for 28
Cards accepted: Mastercard, Visa

🛏🐾🖥📠🔌💷 S 🖉 TV 🔌 ▥ ⬛ ✈ T

Wivenhoe House Hotel and Conference Centre ▲▲

👑👑👑👑 COMMENDED

Wivenhoe Park, Colchester CO4 3SQ
☎ (01206) 863666
Fax (01206) 868532
Email: fossy@essex.ac.uk

Georgian mansion in 200 acres of parkland on the outskirts of Colchester. Prices are per room.
Bedrooms: 7 single, 10 double, 30 twin
Bathrooms: 47 en-suite

Bed & breakfast per night:	£min	£max
Single	54.80	65.80
Double	54.80	65.80

Half board per person:	£min	£max
Daily		72.65

Lunch available
Evening meal 1900 (last orders 2045)
Parking for 80
Cards accepted: Amex, Diners, Mastercard, Visa, Switch/Delta

🛏🐾📠🖥📠🗜🔌💷 S TV ◖
▥ ⬛ 🍴80 🗜 ✿ 🔌 SP 🏠 T

On the River Bure, with an RAF station nearby. The village is attractive with many pleasant 18th C brick houses and a thatched church.

The Norfolk Mead Hotel ▲▲

👑👑👑 COMMENDED

The Mead, Coltishall, Norwich NR12 7DN
☎ (01603) 737531
Fax (01603) 737521

Beautiful Georgian country house set in 12 secluded acres of parkland and gardens with river frontage. Boating, birdlife, fishing, outdoor swimming pool and restaurant.
Bedrooms: 6 double, 3 twin, 2 family rooms
Bathrooms: 11 en-suite

Bed & breakfast per night:	£min	£max
Single	55.00	75.00
Double	69.00	99.00

Half board per person:	£min	£max
Daily	49.00	64.00
Weekly	294.00	354.00

Lunch available
Evening meal 1900 (last orders 2100)
Parking for 50
Cards accepted: Amex, Mastercard, Visa, Switch/Delta

🛏🐾🖥📠🗜🔌🔌💷 S 🖉 🔌 ▥ ⬛
🍴30 🏊 ⛵ ✿ 🐕 🔌 SP 🏠 T

WELCOME HOST

This is a nationally recognised customer care programme which aims to promote the highest standards of service and a warm welcome. Establishments who are taking part in this initiative are indicated by the 🏵 symbol.

CROMER

Norfolk
Map ref 3C1

Once a small fishing village and now famous for its fishing boats that still work off the beach and offer freshly caught crabs. Excellent bathing on sandy beaches fringed by cliffs. The town boasts a fine pier, theatre, museum and a lifeboat station.
Tourist Information Centre ☎ (01263) 512497

Cliftonville Hotel ♨
👑👑👑 COMMENDED

Seafront, Runton Road, Cromer
NR27 9AS
☎ (01263) 512543
Fax (01263) 515700
Beautifully restored Edwardian hotel on the seafront. En-suite bedrooms all with sea view. All-day coffee shop/bar, Boltons Seafood Bistro and fine a la carte restaurant.
Wheelchair access category 3 ♿
Bedrooms: 8 single, 10 double, 9 twin, 2 triple, 1 family room
Bathrooms: 30 en-suite, 1 public

Bed & breakfast per night:

	£min	£max
Single	25.00	55.00
Double	50.00	110.00

Half board per person:

	£min	£max
Daily	35.00	65.00
Weekly	240.00	390.00

Lunch available
Evening meal 1800 (last orders 2200)
Parking for 20
Cards accepted: Amex, Mastercard, Visa, Switch/Delta

The Grove Guesthouse ♨
👑👑 COMMENDED

95 Overstrand Road, Cromer
NR27 0DJ
☎ (01263) 512412
Fax (01263) 513416
Georgian holiday home in 3 acres, with beautiful walks through fields and woods to the cliffs and beach. We also have self-catering cottages in a range of converted barns which are very popular.
Bedrooms: 1 single, 4 double, 2 twin, 2 family rooms
Bathrooms: 9 en-suite

Bed & breakfast per night:

	£min	£max
Single	23.00	23.00
Double	46.00	46.00

Half board per person:

	£min	£max
Daily	31.00	
Weekly	199.00	

Evening meal 1830 (last orders 1830)
Parking for 15
Open April–September

Hotel De Paris ♨
👑👑👑 APPROVED

High Street, Cromer NR27 9HG
☎ (01263) 513141
Fax (01263) 515217
Large hotel of historic and architectural interest, overlooking pier and close to shops.
Bedrooms: 10 single, 14 double, 27 twin, 5 triple
Bathrooms: 56 en-suite, 1 public

Bed & breakfast per night:

	£min	£max
Single	22.00	29.00
Double	44.00	58.00

Lunch available
Evening meal 1800 (last orders 1900)
Parking for 12
Open March–December
Cards accepted: Mastercard, Visa

DISS

Norfolk
Map ref 3B2

Old market town built around 3 sides of the Mere, a 6-acre stretch of water. Although modernised, some interesting Tudor, Georgian and Victorian buildings around the market-place remain. St Mary's church has a fine knapped flint chancel.
Tourist Information Centre ☎ (01379) 650523

Malt House ♨
👑👑 DE LUXE

Denmark Hill, Palgrave, Diss
IP22 1AE
☎ (01379) 642107
Fax (01379) 640315
17th C malt house, beautifully renovated and with all modern amenities. Candlelit dinners in elegant dining room, after-dinner coffee in beamed lounge. 1 acre of landscaped garden with walled kitchen garden. 10 minutes' walk Diss, 2 miles Bressingham Gardens.
Bedrooms: 2 double, 1 twin
Bathrooms: 3 en-suite

Bed & breakfast per night:

	£min	£max
Single	35.00	
Double	60.00	60.00

Parking for 6
Cards accepted: Diners, Mastercard, Visa

DUNSTABLE

Bedfordshire
Map ref 2D1

Modern town with remains of a 12th C Augustinian priory in the parish church. The Dunstable Downs are famous for gliding and in the parkland of Whipsnade Zoo on the edge of the Downs many animals roam freely.
Tourist Information Centre ☎ (01582) 471012

Old Palace Lodge Hotel
👑👑👑 COMMENDED

Church Street, Dunstable LU5 4RT
☎ (01582) 662201
Fax (01582) 696422

Parts of hotel are believed to date back to the lodge at Norman palace of Dunstable circa 1100 AD. Hotel lies on edge of Chilterns, 6 miles from Luton Airport.
Bedrooms: 5 single, 52 double, 11 twin
Bathrooms: 68 en-suite

Bed & breakfast per night:

	£min	£max
Single	58.75	82.50
Double	68.75	92.50

Half board per person:

	£min	£max
Daily	44.50	95.00

Lunch available
Evening meal 1900 (last orders 2145)
Parking for 70
Cards accepted: Amex, Diners, Mastercard, Visa, Switch/Delta

A key to symbols can be found inside the back cover flap.

ELY

Cambridgeshire
Map ref 3A2

Until the 17th C, when the Fens were drained, Ely was an island. The cathedral, completed in 1189, dominates the surrounding area. One particular feature is the central octagonal tower with a fan-vaulted timber roof and wooden lantern.
Tourist Information Centre ☎ (01353) 662062

Lamb Hotel M
⌂⌂⌂⌂ COMMENDED
2 Lynn Road, Ely CB7 4EJ
☎ (01353) 663574
Fax (01353) 662023
CR Consort
In the shadows of Ely Cathedral, this fully modernised former coaching inn has been used by travellers since the 14th C.
Bedrooms: 7 single, 5 double, 13 twin, 6 triple, 1 family room
Bathrooms: 32 en-suite

Bed & breakfast per night:

	£min	£max
Single	62.00	72.00
Double	84.00	94.00

Lunch available
Evening meal 1900 (last orders 2130)
Parking for 23
Cards accepted: Amex, Diners, Mastercard, Visa, Switch/Delta
🐕🛁🕭📞🖵💷♿🏧🛡⌖📺◑🖩
🖨🕭50🅿 OAP ⌗ SP ♨ T

Nyton Hotel M
⌂⌂⌂ APPROVED
7 Barton Road, Ely CB7 4HZ
☎ (01353) 662459
Fax (01353) 666619
In a quiet, residential area overlooking Fenland countryside and adjoining golf-course. Close to city centre and cathedral.
Bedrooms: 2 single, 4 double, 2 twin, 2 family rooms
Bathrooms: 10 en-suite

Bed & breakfast per night:

	£min	£max
Single	38.00	40.00
Double	50.00	60.00

Lunch available
Evening meal 1900 (last orders 2030)
Parking for 25
Cards accepted: Amex, Diners, Mastercard, Visa
🐕🛁🕭📞🖵💷♿🏧🛡⌖🖩◑🖩
🕭40🚹♿⌗ SP T

EYE

Suffolk
Map ref 3B2

"Eye" means island and this town was once surrounded by marsh. The fine church of SS Peter and Paul has a tower over 100 ft high and a carving of the Archangel Gabriel can be seen on the 16th C Guildhall.

The Cornwallis Arms M
⌂⌂⌂⌂ COMMENDED
Brome, Eye IP23 8AJ
☎ (01379) 870326
Fax (01379) 870051
Family-run country house hotel with medieval origins set in beautiful spacious grounds with water garden. Well-appointed bedrooms with four-poster beds. Characterful bar and elegant restaurant.
Bedrooms: 10 double, 1 twin
Bathrooms: 11 en-suite

Bed & breakfast per night:

	£min	£max
Single	60.00	85.00
Double	85.00	120.00

Half board per person:

	£min	£max
Daily	70.00	100.00

Lunch available
Evening meal 1900 (last orders 2130)
Parking for 150
Cards accepted: Amex, Diners, Mastercard, Visa, Switch/Delta
🐕🛁🕭📞🖵💷♿🏧🛡⌖🖩◑🖩
🕭80🚹⌗🐾♨ SP ♨

FAKENHAM

Norfolk
Map ref 3B1

Attractive, small market town dates from Saxon times and was a Royal Manor until the 17th C. Its market place has 2 old coaching inns, both showing traces of earlier work behind Georgian facades, and the parish church has a commanding 15th C tower.

The Old Brick Kilns Guest House M
⌂⌂⌂ HIGHLY COMMENDED
Little Barney Lane, Little Barney, Fakenham NR21 ONL
☎ (01328) 878305
Fax (01328) 878948
Private 7-acre park with fishing pond (David Bellamy Gold Conservation Award 1996), home cooking with fresh produce (Heartbeat award). No pets and no smoking, please.
Bedrooms: 1 single, 1 double, 1 twin
Bathrooms: 3 en-suite

Bed & breakfast per night:

	£min	£max
Single	20.00	24.00
Double	40.00	48.00

Half board per person:

	£min	£max
Daily	35.00	39.00
Weekly	245.00	245.00

Evening meal 1800 (last orders 1000)
Parking for 8
Cards accepted: Mastercard, Visa, Switch/Delta
🐕🛁🕭📞🖵💷♿🏧🛡⌖📺🖩🖨
🕭30♦⌖✿🐾🏧

Wensum Lodge Hotel M
⌂⌂⌂ COMMENDED
Bridge Street, Fakenham NR21 9AY
☎ (01328) 862100
Fax (01328) 863365
Riverside location. Private gardens, freshly prepared a la carte menu. All bedrooms en-suite with colour TV.
Bedrooms: 2 single, 3 double, 4 twin
Bathrooms: 9 en-suite

Bed & breakfast per night:

	£min	£max
Single	40.00	50.00
Double	55.00	65.00

Half board per person:

	£min	£max
Daily	50.00	60.00
Weekly	350.00	420.00

Lunch available
Evening meal 1830 (last orders 2200)
Parking for 30
Cards accepted: Amex, Diners, Mastercard, Visa, Switch/Delta
🐕🛁🕭📞🖵💷♿🏧🛡⌖🖩◑🖨
🕭150♦⌖✿🚹 OAP ♨ SP ♨

FELIXSTOWE

Suffolk
Map ref 3C2

Seaside resort that developed at the end of the 19th C. Lying in a gently curving bay with a 2-mile-long beach and backed by a wide promenade of lawns and floral gardens.
Tourist Information Centre ☎ (01394) 276770

Brook Hotel M
⌂⌂⌂⌂ COMMENDED
Orwell Road, Felixstowe IP11 7PF
☎ (01394) 278441
Fax (01394) 670422
Well-appointed hotel, close to town centre and seaside, offering freshly

Continued ▶

FELIXSTOWE

Continued

prepared snacks, mouth-watering carvery, cask ales and fine wines.
Bedrooms: 2 single, 17 double, 5 twin, 1 family room
Suite available
Bathrooms: 24 en-suite, 1 private

Bed & breakfast

per night:	£min	£max
Single	45.00	58.00
Double	58.00	70.00

Half board per person:

	£min	£max
Daily	52.95	72.95

Lunch available
Evening meal 1900 (last orders 2130)
Parking for 15
Cards accepted: Amex, Diners, Mastercard, Visa, Switch/Delta

🛌🏸🚻📠📞🖥📺🍽💺🦽🛁🍴🔌♿🛏 80 🏇❄🐾 DAP SP

Dolphin Hotel M

👑 APPROVED

41 Beach Station Road, Felixstowe
IP11 8EY
☎ (01394) 282261
Private hotel, 5 minutes from beach and 10 minutes from town centre.
Bedrooms: 3 single, 3 double, 2 twin, 1 triple
Bathrooms: 2 en-suite, 2 public

Bed & breakfast

per night:	£min	£max
Single	16.00	24.00
Double	24.00	38.00

Lunch available
Evening meal 1900 (last orders 2100)
Parking for 24
Cards accepted: Amex, Mastercard, Visa

🛌🚻📠📞🖥💺 S 🛏🍴🚗🚐

Fludyer Arms Hotel M

👑👑 APPROVED

Undercliff Road East, Felixstowe
IP11 7LU
☎ (01394) 283279
Fax (01394) 670754
Closest hotel to the sea in Felixstowe. Two fully licensed bars and family room overlooking the sea. All rooms have superb sea views. Colour TV. Specialises in home-cooked food, with children's and vegetarian menus available.
Bedrooms: 3 single, 4 double, 2 twin
Bathrooms: 5 en-suite, 1 public

Bed & breakfast

per night:	£min	£max
Single	18.00	26.00
Double	32.00	40.00

Lunch available

Evening meal 1900 (last orders 2100)
Parking for 14
Cards accepted: Mastercard, Visa

🛌🚻📠📞🖥🍴🔌♿🛏🍴📞🐾🚗

Orwell Hotel

👑👑👑👑 COMMENDED

Hamilton Road, Felixstowe
IP11 7DX
☎ (01394) 285511
Fax (01394) 670687
Elegant, late-Victorian hotel dating back to 1898.
Bedrooms: 7 single, 12 double, 34 twin, 5 triple
Bathrooms: 58 en-suite

Bed & breakfast

per night:	£min	£max
Single		50.00
Double		65.00

Half board per person:

	£min	£max
Daily		42.50
Weekly		235.00

Lunch available
Evening meal 1900 (last orders 2145)
Parking for 215
Cards accepted: Amex, Diners, Mastercard, Visa, Switch/Delta

🛌🚻📞📠📞🖥💺🍴 S 🛏🍴♿🔌🛏🍴 200 🏇❄🐾 SP T

Waverley Hotel M

👑👑👑 COMMENDED

Wolsey Gardens, Felixstowe
IP11 7DF
☎ (01394) 282811
Fax (01394) 670185
Beautifully refurbished clifftop hotel with spectacular views of the sea and promenade. Half board price based on a minimum 2-night stay.
Bedrooms: 5 single, 8 double, 6 twin, 1 triple
Bathrooms: 19 en-suite, 1 private

Bed & breakfast

per night:	£min	£max
Single	40.00	55.00
Double		64.95

Half board per person:

	£min	£max
Daily		45.00

Lunch available
Evening meal 1900 (last orders 2130)
Parking for 26
Cards accepted: Amex, Diners, Mastercard, Visa

🛌🚻📠📞🖥💺📞 S 🛏🍴♿🔌🛏 85 ♿❄ SP T

FRESSINGFIELD

Suffolk
Map ref 3C2

Chippenhall Hall M

👑👑👑 HIGHLY COMMENDED

Fressingfield, Eye IP21 5TD
☎ (01379) 588180 & 586733
Fax (01379) 586272
Listed Tudor manor, film location, heavily beamed and with inglenook fireplaces, in 7 secluded acres. Fine food and wines. 1 mile south of Fressingfield on B1116.
Bedrooms: 3 double
Bathrooms: 3 en-suite

Bed & breakfast

per night:	£min	£max
Single	53.00	59.00
Double	59.00	65.00

Half board per person:

	£min	£max
Daily	52.50	56.00
Weekly	348.00	375.00

Lunch available
Evening meal 1930 (last orders 1600)
Parking for 12
Cards accepted: Mastercard, Visa

📠📞🖥💺 S 🛏🍴📺🔌🛏🚗🐾🏇⛱♿
🏇❄🐾🚗🐕🍴

GARBOLDISHAM

Norfolk
Map ref 3B2

Ingleneuk Lodge M

👑👑👑 COMMENDED

Hopton Road, Garboldisham, Diss
IP22 2RQ
☎ (01953) 681541
Fax (01953) 681633

Modern single-level home, family-run. South-facing patio, riverside walk. Very friendly atmosphere. On B1111, 1 mile south of village.
Wheelchair access category 2 ♿
Bedrooms: 1 single, 1 double, 2 twin
Bathrooms: 4 en-suite

Bed & breakfast

per night:	£min	£max
Single	33.00	33.00
Double	51.00	51.00

Parking for 20
Cards accepted: Amex, Mastercard, Visa, Switch/Delta
🛇🛆⛏♨�🅂✂🕮⛁🅿🚡12✿�
SP T

GRANTHAM

Lincolnshire
Map ref 3A1

On the old Great North Road (A1), Grantham's splendid parish church has a fine spire and chained library. Sir Isaac Newton was educated here and his statue stands in front of the museum which includes displays on Newton and other famous local people.
Tourist Information Centre ☎ (01476) 566444

Kings Hotel ♒

♛♛♛♛ COMMENDED

North Parade, Grantham
NG31 8AU
☎ (01476) 590800
Fax (01476) 590800
CR Logis of GB
Privately owned hotel serving Grantham and the East Midlands, with a tradition of good hospitality and great value since 1974.
Wheelchair access category 3🡇
Bedrooms: 10 double, 10 twin, 1 family room
Suite available
Bathrooms: 21 en-suite
Bed & breakfast per night:

	£min	£max
Single	35.00	55.00
Double	45.00	65.00

Lunch available
Evening meal 1900 (last orders 2200)
Parking for 50
Cards accepted: Amex, Diners, Mastercard, Visa, Switch/Delta
🛇🛆⛏♨♨⛉□♨🅂✂🕮●
⛁🅿100🅿✿DAP SP T ◉

One of Britain's major seaside resorts with 5 miles of seafront and every possible amenity including an award winning leisure complex offering a huge variety of all-weather facilities. Busy harbour and fishing centre.

Burlington Palm Court Hotel ♒

♛♛♛ COMMENDED

North Drive, Great Yarmouth
NR30 1EG
☎ (01493) 844568
Fax (01493) 331848
Sea views, heated indoor pool, sauna, solarium, lift and car park, in a resort with sandy beaches and crammed with history.
Wheelchair access category 3🡇
Bedrooms: 9 single, 17 double, 29 twin, 9 triple, 8 family rooms
Bathrooms: 72 en-suite, 1 public
Bed & breakfast per night:

	£min	£max
Single	40.00	50.00
Double	64.00	75.00

Half board per person:

	£min	£max
Daily	42.00	66.00
Weekly	238.00	266.00

Lunch available
Evening meal 1800 (last orders 2000)
Parking for 47
Open February–December
Cards accepted: Amex, Diners, Mastercard, Visa, Switch/Delta
🛇⛏⛉□♨♨🅂🕮TV▣🕮⛁
🍴120🛆♨♨🖊🐾✂SP T

The Corner House Hotel

♛♛♛♛ COMMENDED

Albert Square, Great Yarmouth
NR30 3JH
☎ (01493) 842773
Bay-fronted Victorian house adjacent to seafront, enjoying a high reputation for good cooking and personal, courteous service.
Bedrooms: 5 double, 2 twin, 1 triple
Bathrooms: 8 en-suite, 2 public
Bed & breakfast per night:

	£min	£max
Single	19.00	25.00
Double	38.00	50.00

Half board per person:

	£min	£max
Daily	24.00	33.00
Weekly	165.00	209.00

Evening meal 1715 (last orders 1715)
Parking for 8
Open March–September
🛇⛆⛏□♨♨🅂🅂TV🕮⛁🖊
🚡DAP SP ⛉

Horse & Groom Motel ♒

♛♛♛ COMMENDED

Rollesby, Great Yarmouth
NR29 5ER
☎ (01493) 740624
Fax (01493) 740022
CR The Independents

Recently built motel on A149 in Norfolk Broads area. All rooms en-suite with satellite TV and tea/coffee facilities. Prices are per room.
Wheelchair access category 2🡇
Bedrooms: 13 double, 3 twin, 4 family rooms
Bathrooms: 20 en-suite

Continued ▶

GREAT YARMOUTH

Continued

Bed & breakfast

per night:	£min	£max
Single		39.00
Double	41.50	49.00

Lunch available
Evening meal 1800 (last orders 2115)
Parking for 50
Cards accepted: Amex, Mastercard, Visa, Switch/Delta

Imperial Hotel

COMMENDED

North Drive, Great Yarmouth
NR30 1EQ
☎ (01493) 851113
Fax (01493) 852229
Modern, comfortable accommodation is offered in this family-run seafront hotel, locally renowned for fine food, wine and service. Overnight half-board prices are for mini-breaks.
Bedrooms: 4 single, 22 double, 10 twin, 3 triple
Bathrooms: 39 en-suite

Bed & breakfast

per night:	£min	£max
Single	45.00	65.00
Double	77.00	90.00

Half board per

person:	£min	£max
Daily	41.00	52.00
Weekly	256.00	314.00

Lunch available
Evening meal 1900 (last orders 2200)
Parking for 39
Cards accepted: Amex, Diners, Mastercard, Visa, Switch/Delta

Regency Dolphin Hotel

COMMENDED

Albert Square, Great Yarmouth
NR30 3JH
☎ (01493) 855070
Fax (01493) 853798
CR MacDonald
Friendly, relaxing hotel with many amenities. Suites, presidential suite, jacuzzis, heated swimming pool in summer. Short breaks available. Pets welcome by arrangement. Weekend rate £38.50 per person per night.
Bedrooms: 6 single, 32 double, 6 twin, 4 triple
Bathrooms: 48 en-suite

Bed & breakfast

per night:	£min	£max
Single	60.00	65.00
Double	80.00	85.00

Half board per

person:	£min	£max
Daily	38.50	45.00
Weekly	270.00	300.00

Lunch available
Evening meal 1830 (last orders 2200)
Parking for 24
Cards accepted: Amex, Diners, Mastercard, Visa, Switch/Delta

Southern Hotel

APPROVED

46 Queens Road, Great Yarmouth
NR30 3JR
☎ (01493) 843313
Fax (01493) 853047
Comfortable and friendly hotel within easy walking distance of seafront and attractions.
Bedrooms: 3 single, 11 double, 1 twin, 6 triple
Bathrooms: 15 en-suite, 3 public

Bed & breakfast

per night:	£min	£max
Single	16.00	20.00
Double	32.00	38.00

Half board per

person:	£min	£max
Daily	20.00	25.00
Weekly	120.00	155.00

Evening meal from 1745
Parking for 8
Open March–October

Spindrift Private Hotel

APPROVED

36 Wellesley Road, Great Yarmouth
NR30 1EU
☎ (01493) 858674
Fax (01493) 858674
Attractively situated small private hotel, close to all amenities and with Beach Coach Station and car park at rear. Front bedrooms overlook gardens and sea.
Bedrooms: 2 single, 2 double, 1 twin, 1 triple, 1 family room
Bathrooms: 5 en-suite, 2 private

Bed & breakfast

per night:	£min	£max
Single	20.00	32.00
Double	34.00	42.00

Cards accepted: Amex, Mastercard, Visa

Trotwood Private Hotel

COMMENDED

2 North Drive, Great Yarmouth
NR30 1ED
☎ (01493) 843971
Opposite bowling greens on seafront, giving unrivalled sea views. Close to Britannia Pier and all amenities. En-suite bedrooms, licensed bar, own car park.
Bedrooms: 8 double, 1 twin
Bathrooms: 8 en-suite, 1 private shower

Bed & breakfast

per night:	£min	£max
Single	24.00	32.00
Double	42.00	53.00

Parking for 11
Cards accepted: Mastercard, Visa

GRIMSTHORPE

Lincolnshire
Map ref 3A1

Hamlet situated at the edge of the huge deer park which surrounds Grimsthorpe Castle, a palatial mansion, partly rebuilt in 1722 by Vanbrugh, open during the summer.

Black Horse Inn

HIGHLY COMMENDED

Grimsthorpe, Bourne PE10 0LY
☎ (01778) 591247
Fax (01778) 591373
A coaching inn since 1717, nestling in the shadow of Grimsthorpe Castle. A hostelry of individuality from its furnishings to its food. All guests treated personally.
Bedrooms: 4 double, 2 twin
Bathrooms: 5 en-suite, 1 private, 1 public

Bed & breakfast

per night:	£min	£max
Single	40.00	49.00
Double	55.00	80.00

Lunch available
Evening meal 1900 (last orders 2130)
Parking for 41
Cards accepted: Mastercard, Visa, Switch/Delta

The National Grading and Classification Scheme is explained at the back of this guide.

HARLOW

Essex
Map ref 2D1

Although one of the New Towns, it was planned so that it could develop alongside the existing old town. It has a museum of local history and a nature reserve with nature trails and study centre.

Churchgate Manor Hotel ₥

₩₩₩₩ HIGHLY COMMENDED

Churchgate Street Village, Old Harlow, Harlow CM17 0JT
☎ (01279) 420246
Fax (01279) 437720
ⓒⱤ Best Western
Spacious hotel in secluded grounds with large indoor leisure complex and swimming pool. Close to M11, M25 and Stansted Airport. 16th C restaurant and bars. Extensive conference facilities for up to 200 persons. Special value weekend breaks.
Bedrooms: 22 single, 24 double, 24 twin, 15 triple
Bathrooms: 85 en-suite

Bed & breakfast per night:	£min	£max
Single	62.00	85.00
Double	66.00	95.00

Lunch available
Evening meal 1900 (last orders 2145)
Parking for 120
Cards accepted: Amex, Diners, Mastercard, Visa, Switch/Delta
⚅☆♿&♨▯🖥♦♀🛈S✂🕊Ⓞ🖥
🖥🅿🍽200🐎✕🎣🏹♨✺ SP 🏮Ⓣ

Harlow Moat House ₥

₩₩₩₩ COMMENDED

Southern Way, Harlow CM18 7BA
☎ (01279) 829988
Fax (01279) 635094
ⓒⱤ Queens Moat/Utell International
Modern 120-bedroomed hotel with comprehensive conference facilities. Ideally located for business people and tourists.
Bedrooms: 30 double, 90 twin
Bathrooms: 120 en-suite

Bed & breakfast per night:	£min	£max
Single	85.00	95.00
Double	95.00	105.00

Lunch available
Evening meal 1900 (last orders 2200)
Parking for 180
Cards accepted: Amex, Diners, Mastercard, Visa, Switch/Delta
⚅☆♿&♨▯🖥♦♀🛈S✂🕊ⓉⓋⓄ
🖥🅿🍽160♦ SP Ⓣ

HARPENDEN

Hertfordshire
Map ref 2D1

Delightful country town with many scenic walks through surrounding woods and fields. Harpenden train station provides a fast service into London.

Milton Hotel ₥

₩₩ APPROVED

25 Milton Road, Harpenden AL5 5LA
☎ (01582) 762914
Family-run, comfortable hotel in residential area close to mainline station, junctions 9/10 of M1 and convenient for M25. Large car park.
Bedrooms: 3 single, 2 double, 2 twin
Bathrooms: 3 en-suite, 2 public

Bed & breakfast per night:	£min	£max
Single	22.00	
Double	38.00	

Evening meal 1900 (last orders 2100)
Parking for 9
⚅🐎▯🖥♦S✂ⓉⓋ🖥♦🅿🍽30✺🏹

HARWICH

Essex
Map ref 3C2

Port where the Rivers Orwell and Stour converge and enter the North Sea. The old town still has a medieval atmosphere with its narrow streets. To the south is the seaside resort of Dovercourt with long sandy beaches.
Tourist Information Centre ☎ *(01255) 506139*

The Pier at Harwich ₥

₩₩₩ COMMENDED

The Quay, Harwich CO12 3HH
☎ (01255) 241212
Fax (01255) 551922
Two restaurants both with excellent views of twin estuaries of Stour and Orwell rivers, serving the freshest fish available from the quay opposite. En-suite accommodation.
Bedrooms: 4 double, 2 twin
Bathrooms: 6 en-suite

Bed & breakfast per night:	£min	£max
Single	52.50	67.50
Double	75.00	85.00

Lunch available
Evening meal 1800 (last orders 2130)
Parking for 10
Cards accepted: Mastercard, Visa
⚅☆🕊▯♦🛈S🖥♦🅿🍽50✕🚐

HATFIELD

Hertfordshire
Map ref 2D1

The old town is dominated by the great Jacobean Hatfield House, built for Robert Cecil and still in the Cecil family. It has many interesting exhibits and extensive gardens open to the public.

Comet Hotel

₩₩₩₩ COMMENDED

301 St Albans Road West, Hatfield AL10 9RH
☎ (01707) 265411
Fax (01707) 264019
ⓒⱤ Jarvis/Utell International
A hotel in the style of the 1930s, combining traditional comfort and service with modern design. Ideally located for London and Hertfordshire countryside. Minimum prices shown below apply at weekends only.
Bedrooms: 14 single, 63 double, 24 twin
Bathrooms: 101 en-suite

Bed & breakfast per night:	£min	£max
Single	35.00	75.00
Double	70.00	109.00

Half board per person:	£min	£max
Daily	42.50	85.00

Lunch available
Evening meal 1900 (last orders 2145)
Parking for 190
Cards accepted: Amex, Diners, Mastercard, Visa, Switch/Delta
⚅☆♿&♨▯🖥♦♀🛈S✂🕊ⓉⓋⓄ
🖥🅿🍽120Ⓤ🕊✺ OAP ♨🏮

HEMEL HEMPSTEAD

Hertfordshire
Map ref 2D1

Pleasant market town greatly expanded since the 1950s but with older origins. The High Street has pretty cottages and 18th C houses and the Norman parish church has a fine 14th C timber spire. The Grand Union Canal runs nearby.
Tourist Information Centre ☎ *(01442) 234222*

The Bobsleigh Inn ₥

₩₩₩ COMMENDED

Hempstead Road, Bovingdon, Hemel Hempstead HP3 0DS
☎ (01442) 833276 & 832000
Fax (01442) 832471
Privately owned country hotel with
Continued ▶

HEMEL HEMPSTEAD

Continued

*reputation for good food and service.
Easy access M1 and M25. 30 minutes
from Luton and London Heathrow
airports.*
Wheelchair access category 3
Bedrooms: 5 single, 27 double,
5 twin, 5 triple, 1 family room
Bathrooms: 43 en-suite

Bed & breakfast
per night:	£min	£max
Single	40.00	85.00
Double	60.00	120.00

Half board per
person:	£min	£max
Daily	59.95	104.95

Lunch available
Evening meal 1900 (last orders
2130)
Parking for 63
Cards accepted: Amex, Diners,
Mastercard, Visa, Switch/Delta

HERTFORD

Hertfordshire
Map ref 2D1

Old county town with attractive
cottages and houses and fine public
buildings. The remains of the ancient
castle, childhood home of Elizabeth
I, now form the council offices and
the grounds are open to the public.
Tourist Information Centre ☎ (01992)
584322

Hall House

DE LUXE
Broad Oak End, Off Bramfield Road,
Hertford SG14 2JA
☎ (01992) 582807
*Tranquil, 15th C country house, rebuilt
in woodland setting on the edge of
Hertford town. Non-smokers only,
please.*
Bedrooms: 3 double
Bathrooms: 2 en-suite, 1 private,
1 public

Bed & breakfast
per night:	£min	£max
Single	48.00	48.00
Double	65.00	65.00

Half board per
person:	£min	£max
Daily	52.50	68.00
Weekly	367.50	476.00

Evening meal from 1900
Parking for 6
Cards accepted: Mastercard, Visa

HEVINGHAM

Norfolk
Map ref 3B1

Marsham Arms Inn

COMMENDED
Holt Road, Hevingham, Norwich
NR10 5NP
☎ (01603) 754268
Fax (01603) 754839
*Set in peaceful Norfolk countryside
within reach of Norwich, the Broads
and the coast. Comfortable and
spacious accommodation, good food
and a fine selection of ales.*
Bedrooms: 3 double, 5 twin
Bathrooms: 8 en-suite

Bed & breakfast
per night:	£min	£max
Single	38.00	45.00
Double	49.50	55.00

Lunch available
Evening meal 1800 (last orders
2200)
Parking for 100
Cards accepted: Amex, Mastercard,
Visa, Switch/Delta

HITCHIN

Hertfordshire
Map ref 2D1

Once a flourishing wool town. Full
of interest, with many fine old
buildings around the market square.
These include the 17th C
almshouses, old inns and the
Victorian Corn Exchange.

Firs Hotel

APPROVED
83 Bedford Road, Hitchin SG5 2TY
☎ (01462) 422322
Fax (01462) 432051

*Family-run establishment in welcoming
surroundings, with own Italian
restaurant. Convenient for visiting
London, Luton Airport, Bedford and
Stevenage.*
Bedrooms: 15 single, 2 double,
11 twin, 2 triple
Bathrooms: 22 en-suite, 3 public

Bed & breakfast
per night:	£min	£max
Single	31.00	49.00
Double	48.00	59.00

Half board per
person:	£min	£max
Daily	41.50	59.50
Weekly	290.50	416.50

Evening meal 1900 (last orders
2130)
Parking for 26
Cards accepted: Amex, Diners,
Mastercard, Visa, Switch/Delta

The Lord Lister Hotel

COMMENDED
1 Park Street, Hitchin SG4 9AH
☎ (01462) 432712 & 459451
Fax (01462) 438506
*Charming Victorian house hotel with
friendly and helpful staff. Individually
furnished rooms some non-smoking.
Restaurant, bar, car park. Close to town
centre.*
Bedrooms: 4 single, 11 double,
3 twin, 3 triple
Bathrooms: 12 en-suite, 1 private,
1 public, 6 private showers

Bed & breakfast
per night:	£min	£max
Single	35.00	55.00
Double	45.00	70.00

Half board per
person:	£min	£max
Daily	40.00	65.00
Weekly	240.00	390.00

Lunch available
Evening meal 1800 (last orders
2200)
Parking for 11
Cards accepted: Amex, Diners,
Mastercard, Visa, Switch/Delta

Redcoats Farmhouse Hotel

COMMENDED
Redcoats Green, Hitchin SG4 7JR
☎ (01438) 729500
Fax (01438) 723322
Email: redcoatsfarmhouse
@ukbusiness.com
The Independents/Logis of GB
*15th C farmhouse in open countryside
offering secluded comfort and fresh
food. Luton Airport is 20 minutes away.*
Bedrooms: 1 single, 10 double,
2 twin, 1 triple
Bathrooms: 13 en-suite, 1 private,
1 public

Bed & breakfast
per night:	£min	£max
Single	44.00	90.00
Double	54.00	95.00

Half board per
person:	£min	£max
Daily	64.00	110.00

Lunch available
Evening meal 1900 (last orders
2100)

Parking for 40
Cards accepted: Amex, Diners,
Mastercard, Visa, Switch/Delta

HORNCASTLE

Lincolnshire
Map ref 4D2

Pleasant market town near the
Lincolnshire Wolds, which was once
a walled Roman settlement. It was
the scene of a decisive Civil War
battle, relics of which can be seen in
the church. Tennyson's bride lived
here.

Admiral Rodney Hotel M

COMMENDED

North Street, Horncastle LN9 5DX
☎ (01507) 523131
Fax (01507) 523104
*Located in pleasant market town just
off main Lincoln to Skegness road -
ideal touring base. Large car park,
en-suite bedrooms, fine restaurant.*
Bedrooms: 19 double, 9 twin,
1 triple, 2 family rooms
Bathrooms: 31 en-suite

Bed & breakfast per night:

	£min	£max
Single	38.00	50.00
Double	50.00	72.00

Half board per person:

	£min	£max
Daily	32.50	57.00

Lunch available
Evening meal 1900 (last orders
2130)
Parking for 70
Cards accepted: Amex, Diners,
Mastercard, Visa, Switch/Delta

HORNING

Norfolk
Map ref 3C1

Riverside village and well-known
Broadland centre. Occasional
glimpses of the river can be caught
between picturesque thatched
cottages.

Petersfield House Hotel M

COMMENDED

Lower Street, Horning, Norwich
NR12 8PF
☎ (01692) 630741
Fax (01692) 630745
*Set slightly back from the banks of the
River Bure, the hotel occupies one of
the choicest positions on the Broads.
Weekend breaks available.*

Bedrooms: 3 single, 9 double, 5 twin,
1 family room
Bathrooms: 18 en-suite

Bed & breakfast per night:

	£min	£max
Single	58.00	63.00
Double	75.00	85.00

Half board per person:

	£min	£max
Daily	49.50	54.50
Weekly	346.50	381.50

Lunch available
Evening meal 1930 (last orders
2130)
Parking for 25
Cards accepted: Amex, Diners,
Mastercard, Visa

HUNSTANTON

Norfolk
Map ref 3B1

Seaside resort which faces the
Wash. The shingle and sand beach is
backed by striped cliffs and many
unusual fossils can be found here.
The town is predominantly
Victorian. The Oasis family leisure
centre has indoor and outdoor
pools.
*Tourist Information Centre ☎ (01485)
532610*

The Linksway Country House Hotel

COMMENDED

Golf Course Road, Old Hunstanton,
Hunstanton PE36 6JE
☎ (01485) 532209 & 0860 330178
Fax (01485) 532209
*In quiet location overlooking
Hunstanton Golf Course. Close to
beach and RSPB bird sanctuaries.*
Bedrooms: 2 single, 2 double, 8 twin,
2 family rooms
Bathrooms: 13 en-suite, 1 private

Bed & breakfast per night:

	£min	£max
Single	22.00	36.00
Double	40.00	65.00

Half board per person:

	£min	£max
Daily	36.50	50.00
Weekly	245.00	297.00

Evening meal 1900 (last orders
2000)
Parking for 15
Open March–December
Cards accepted: Mastercard, Visa

HUNTINGDON

Cambridgeshire
Map ref 3A2

Attractive, interesting town which
abounds in associations with the
Cromwell family. The town is
connected to Godmanchester by a
beautiful 14th C bridge over the
River Great Ouse.
*Tourist Information Centre ☎ (01480)
388588*

Old Bridge Hotel M

HIGHLY COMMENDED

1 High Street, Huntingdon
PE18 6TQ
☎ (01480) 452681
Fax (01480) 411017
*Beautifully decorated Georgian town
hotel by the River Ouse. Oak-panelled
dining room and terrace brasserie with
award-winning wine list, real ales and
log fires. Privately owned.*
Bedrooms: 5 single, 16 double,
4 twin
Bathrooms: 25 en-suite

Bed & breakfast per night:

	£min	£max
Single	79.50	99.50
Double	89.50	139.50

Half board per person:

	£min	£max
Daily	79.50	140.00

Lunch available
Evening meal 1830 (last orders
2230)
Parking for 70
Cards accepted: Amex, Diners,
Mastercard, Visa, Switch/Delta

Prince of Wales M

COMMENDED

Potton Road, Hilton, Huntingdon
PE18 9NG
☎ (01480) 830257
Fax (01480) 830257
*Traditional village inn renowned for its
traditional ales and good value food.
Convenient for St Ives, Huntingdon, St
Neots and Cambridge. On B1040,
south-east of Huntingdon.*
Bedrooms: 2 single, 1 double, 1 twin
Bathrooms: 4 en-suite

Bed & breakfast per night:

	£min	£max
Single	25.00	37.50
Double	40.00	50.00

Lunch available
Evening meal 1900 (last orders
2115)

Continued ▶

HUNTINGDON

Continued

Parking for 9
Cards accepted: Amex, Diners, Mastercard, Visa, Switch/Delta

⌖5📞🖃🖵♿🌙🍴🗄🎫💻🕯❀🚐 SP T

IPSWICH

Suffolk
Map ref 3B2

Interesting county town and major port on the River Orwell. Birthplace of Cardinal Wolsey. Christchurch Mansion, set in a fine park, contains a good collection of furniture and pictures, with works by Gainsborough, Constable and Munnings.
Tourist Information Centre ☎ (01473) 258070

Anglesea Hotel 🏔

👑👑 APPROVED

10 Oban Street, Ipswich IP1 3PH
☎ (01473) 255630 & 0850 052764
Fax (01473) 255630
Victorian house, tastefully refurbished as a small hotel, in quiet conservation area. Within easy walking distance of town centre. Meals always available at a time to suit guests.
Bedrooms: 1 single, 1 double, 2 twin, 2 triple, 1 family room
Bathrooms: 7 en-suite

Bed & breakfast per night:	£min	£max
Single	35.00	
Double	45.00	

Evening meal 1830 (last orders 2100)
Parking for 9
Cards accepted: Amex, Diners, Mastercard, Visa

⌖10📞🖃🖵♿🛡S🎫TV💻🗄❀🚐🐾SP

Claydon Country House Hotel and Restaurant 🏔

👑👑👑 COMMENDED

Ipswich Road, Claydon, Ipswich IP6 0AR
☎ (01473) 830382
Fax (01473) 832476
Hotel with all en-suite bedrooms and 50 seater restaurant. A la carte and table d' hote menus, excellent wines, beers and cocktail bar. Set in small village of Claydon just outside Ipswich on A45.
Bedrooms: 1 single, 10 double, 3 twin
Bathrooms: 14 en-suite

Bed & breakfast per night:	£min	£max
Single	48.00	54.00
Double	53.00	59.00

Lunch available
Evening meal 1830 (last orders 2130)
Parking for 60
Cards accepted: Amex, Mastercard, Visa

⌖🦽🖃📞🖃🖵♿🌙🛡S🎫TV🕯💻🗄🍴30❀🐶🚐🐾SP

The Marlborough at Ipswich 🏔

👑👑👑 COMMENDED

Henley Road, Ipswich IP1 3SP
☎ (01473) 257677
Fax (01473) 226927
CR Best Western

Quietly situated hotel opposite Christchurch Park and Mansion. Victorian restaurant overlooking floodlit gardens. All rooms, including a suite and several with balconies, are individually decorated.
Bedrooms: 4 single, 13 double, 5 twin
Suite available
Bathrooms: 22 en-suite

Bed & breakfast per night:	£min	£max
Single	68.00	
Double	72.00	92.00

Half board per person:	£min	£max
Daily	56.50	56.50

Lunch available
Evening meal 1930 (last orders 2130)
Parking for 60
Cards accepted: Amex, Diners, Mastercard, Visa, Switch/Delta

⌖🦽🖃📞🖃🖵♿🌙🍴🔏🎫💻🗄🍴60🕯❀🐾SP T

Novotel Ipswich 🏔

👑👑👑 COMMENDED

Greyfriars Road, Ipswich IP1 1UP
☎ (01473) 232400
Fax (01473) 232414
CR Novotel
Town centre situation, access from A12/A14. 2 minutes from mainline station. All bedrooms have king-size bed and couch, radio, TV. Conference facilities, restaurant, bar. Minimum daily prices below are weekend rates.

Wheelchair access category 3♿
Bedrooms: 100 double
Bathrooms: 100 en-suite

Bed & breakfast per night:	£min	£max
Single	41.00	77.75
Double	48.00	86.50

Half board per person:	£min	£max
Daily	49.00	91.25
Weekly	343.00	512.00

Lunch available
Evening meal 1800 (last orders midnight)
Parking for 50
Cards accepted: Amex, Diners, Mastercard, Visa, Switch/Delta

⌖📞🖃🖵♿🌙🛡S🍴🎫TV💻🗄🍴180🕯❀🐾SP T

KING'S LYNN

Norfolk
Map ref 3B1

A busy town with many outstanding buildings. The Guildhall and Town Hall are both built of flint in a striking chequer design. Behind the Guildhall in the Old Gaol House the sounds and smells of prison life 2 centuries ago are recreated.
Tourist Information Centre ☎ (01553) 763044

The Beeches Guesthouse

👑👑 APPROVED

2 Guanock Terrace, King's Lynn PE30 5QT
☎ (01553) 766577
Fax (01553) 776664
Detached Victorian house, all rooms with TV, tea/coffee facilities and telephone. Most rooms en-suite. Full English breakfast and 3-course evening meal with coffee.
Bedrooms: 2 double, 3 twin, 2 triple
Bathrooms: 4 en-suite, 2 private, 1 public

Bed & breakfast per night:	£min	£max
Single	20.00	28.00
Double	36.00	42.00

Half board per person:	£min	£max
Daily	25.00	36.50
Weekly	160.00	245.00

Evening meal 1830 (last orders 1930)
Parking for 3
Cards accepted: Amex, Mastercard, Visa

⌖📞🖵♿🌙🛡🎫TV💻🗄❀🚐

Butterfly Hotel M

⚜⚜⚜ COMMENDED

A10-A47 Roundabout, Hardwick
Narrows, King's Lynn PE30 4NB
☎ (01553) 771707
Fax (01553) 768027
*Modern building with rustic style and
decor, set around an open central
courtyard. Special weekend rates
available.*
Bedrooms: 23 single, 15 double,
12 twin
Bathrooms: 50 en-suite

Bed & breakfast per night:	£min	£max
Single	51.95	61.95
Double	58.90	68.90

Half board per person:	£min	£max
Daily	64.45	74.45

Lunch available
Evening meal 1800 (last orders
2200)
Parking for 70
Cards accepted: Amex, Diners,
Mastercard, Visa, Switch/Delta

The Duke's Head M

⚜⚜⚜⚜ COMMENDED

Tuesday Market Place, King's Lynn
PE30 1JS
☎ (01553) 774996
Fax (01553) 763556
Ⓡ Regal
*One of the finest classical buildings in
the town. Overlooking the delightful
market square, it holds a prime
position from which to enjoy this
interesting town. Daily half-board prices
below are based on minimum 2-night
stay.*
Bedrooms: 18 single, 37 double,
14 twin, 2 triple
Bathrooms: 71 en-suite

Bed & breakfast per night:	£min	£max
Single	39.00	74.00
Double	66.00	98.00

Half board per person:	£min	£max
Daily	40.00	50.00
Weekly	252.00	315.00

Lunch available
Evening meal 1900 (last orders
2145)
Parking for 40
Cards accepted: Amex, Diners,
Mastercard, Visa, Switch/Delta

Havana Guesthouse

⚜⚜ COMMENDED

117 Gaywood Road, King's Lynn
PE30 2PU
☎ (01553) 772331
*Comfortable bedrooms with colour
co-ordinated soft furnishings. Some
rooms non-smoking. Ground floor
en-suites. Ample private parking. 10
minutes' walk to town centre.*
Bedrooms: 1 single, 2 double, 3 twin,
1 triple
Bathrooms: 4 en-suite, 1 public

Bed & breakfast per night:	£min	£max
Single	17.00	25.00
Double	32.00	38.00

Parking for 8

Knights Hill Hotel M

⚜⚜⚜ COMMENDED

Knights Hill Village, South Wootton,
King's Lynn PE30 3HQ
☎ (01553) 675566
Fax (01553) 675568
Ⓡ Best Western
*Sympathetically restored farm complex
offering a choice of accommodation
styles, 2 restaurants, a country pub and
an extensive health club. Special breaks
available. Minimum weekly half board
rate is for two people sharing.*
Bedrooms: 5 single, 37 double,
13 twin
Bathrooms: 55 en-suite

Bed & breakfast per night:	£min	£max
Single	82.00	102.00
Double	99.00	124.00

Half board per person:	£min	£max
Weekly	354.00	574.00

Lunch available
Evening meal 1900 (last orders
2200)
Parking for 350
Cards accepted: Amex, Diners,
Mastercard, Visa, Switch/Delta

Maranatha Guesthouse M

⚜⚜ APPROVED

115 Gaywood Road, Gaywood,
King's Lynn PE30 2PU
☎ (01553) 774596
*Large carrstone and brick residence
with gardens front and rear, 10
minutes' walk from town centre,
Lynnsport and Queen Elizabeth
Hospital. Direct road to Sandringham
and the coast.*
Bedrooms: 2 single, 2 double, 2 twin,
1 triple
Bathrooms: 3 en-suite, 1 private,
1 public

Bed & breakfast per night:	£min	£max
Single	17.00	
Double	30.00	

Half board per person:	£min	£max
Daily	20.00	

Lunch available
Evening meal 1800 (last orders
1800)
Parking for 9

Russet House Hotel M

⚜⚜⚜ COMMENDED

53 Goodwins Road, Vancouver
Avenue, King's Lynn PE30 5PE
☎ (01553) 773098
Fax (01553) 773098
*Lovely old house with pretty en-suite
rooms. Four-poster available. Bar, dining
room, gardens, ample parking. Good
food.*
Bedrooms: 3 single, 5 double, 2 twin,
2 triple
Bathrooms: 12 en-suite

Bed & breakfast per night:	£min	£max
Single	30.00	48.00
Double	50.00	70.00

Evening meal 1900 (last orders
2100)
Parking for 14
Cards accepted: Amex, Diners,
Mastercard, Visa, Switch/Delta

The map references refer
to the colour maps towards
the end of the guide.
The first figure is the
map number; the letter and
figure which follow indicate
the grid reference
on the map.

The symbol Ⓡ and a group
name following an hotel
address indicates that
bookings can be made
through a central reservations
office. These offices are listed
in the information pages at
the back of this guide.

KING'S LYNN

Continued

Stuart House Hotel

👑👑👑 COMMENDED

35 Goodwins Road, King's Lynn
PE30 5QX
☎ (01553) 772169
Fax (01553) 774788
Email: stuarthousehotel
@ukbusiness.com

Warm welcome and friendly
atmosphere, coupled with home-cooked
fresh food served in the bar and
restaurant. Quiet, central location next
to the town park.
Bedrooms: 1 single, 8 double, 6 twin,
2 family rooms
Bathrooms: 17 en-suite, 1 public

Bed & breakfast

per night:	£min	£max
Single	30.00	45.00
Double	45.00	90.00

Lunch available
Evening meal 1900 (last orders
2130)
Parking for 30
Cards accepted: Mastercard, Visa,
Switch/Delta

The Tudor Rose Hotel ♏

👑👑👑 COMMENDED

St. Nicholas Street, Off Tuesday
Market Place, King's Lynn PE30 1LR
☎ (01553) 762824
Fax (01553) 764894
Ⓒ The Independents
Built around 1500 by a local merchant
and extended in 1640, the hotel offers
comfortable accommodation, traditional
British cooking and a choice of 4 real
ales in 2 bars.
Bedrooms: 5 single, 5 double, 3 twin
Bathrooms: 11 en-suite, 2 private

Bed & breakfast

per night:	£min	£max
Single	30.00	38.50
Double	50.00	55.00

Lunch available
Evening meal 1900 (last orders
2100)
Cards accepted: Amex, Diners,
Mastercard, Visa, Switch/Delta

LAVENHAM

Suffolk
Map ref 3B2

A former prosperous wool town of
timber-framed buildings with the
cathedral-like church and its tall
tower. The market-place is 13th C
and the Guildhall now houses a
museum.

Angel Hotel ♏

👑👑👑 HIGHLY COMMENDED

Market Place, Lavenham, Sudbury
CO10 9QZ
☎ (01787) 247388
Fax (01787) 248344

Family-run 15th C inn overlooking
famous Guildhall. Freshly cooked local
food, menu changing daily. Saturday
night stays must include dinner.
Bedrooms: 6 double, 1 twin, 1 triple
Bathrooms: 8 en-suite

Bed & breakfast

per night:	£min	£max
Single	39.50	39.50
Double	65.00	65.00

Half board per

person:	£min	£max
Daily	40.00	55.00
Weekly		280.00

Lunch available
Evening meal 1845 (last orders
2115)
Parking for 5
Cards accepted: Amex, Mastercard,
Visa, Switch/Delta

For ideas on places to visit
refer to the introduction at
the beginning of this section.

National gradings and
classifications were correct
at the time of going to press
but are subject to change.
Please check at the time
of booking.

The Great House Restaurant and Hotel ♏

👑👑👑👑 HIGHLY COMMENDED

Market Place, Lavenham, Sudbury
CO10 9QZ
☎ (01787) 247431
Fax (01787) 248007
Famous and historic 15th C house with
covered outside courtyard, quietly and
ideally located, full of warmth and oak
furniture for a relaxing stay. Menu
changing daily.
Bedrooms: 2 double, 2 twin
Suites available
Bathrooms: 4 en-suite

Bed & breakfast

per night:	£min	£max
Single	50.00	
Double	55.00	88.00

Half board per

person:	£min	£max
Daily	44.45	

Lunch available
Evening meal 1900 (last orders
2130)
Parking for 10
Cards accepted: Mastercard, Visa

LEADENHAM

Lincolnshire
Map ref 3A1

Village on the Lincoln Edge, noted
for its fine church spire.

George Hotel ♏

👑👑 APPROVED

High Street, Leadenham, Lincoln
LN5 0PN
☎ (01400) 272251
Fax (01400) 272091
17th C coaching inn where the owners
take pride in the international menu
and their collection of over 500
whiskies from all over the world.
Bedrooms: 2 single, 2 double, 3 twin
Bathrooms: 2 en-suite, 1 private,
2 public

Bed & breakfast

per night:	£min	£max
Single	20.00	30.00
Double	30.00	40.00

Half board per

person:	£min	£max
Daily	27.50	37.50

Lunch available
Evening meal 1900 (last orders
2145)
Parking for 150
Cards accepted: Amex, Diners,
Mastercard, Visa, Switch/Delta

LEISTON

Suffolk
Map ref 3C2

Busy industrial town near the coast. The abbey sited here in 1363 was for hundreds of years used as a farm until it was restored in 1918.

White Horse Hotel M
♛♛♛

Station Road, Leiston IP16 4HD
☎ (01728) 830694
Fax (01728) 833105
18th C Georgian hotel with a relaxed and informal atmosphere, only 2 miles from the sea, in the heart of bird-watching country.
Bedrooms: 3 single, 6 double, 4 twin
Bathrooms: 11 en-suite, 2 public

Bed & breakfast per night:

	£min	£max
Single	25.00	33.50
Double	45.00	52.00

Lunch available
Evening meal 1930 (last orders 2200)
Parking for 16
Cards accepted: Amex, Diners, Mastercard, Visa

LINCOLN

Lincolnshire
Map ref 4C2

Ancient city dominated by the magnificent 11th C cathedral with its triple towers. A Roman gateway is still used and there are medieval houses lining narrow, cobbled streets. Other attractions include the Norman castle, several museums and the Usher Gallery. *Tourist Information Centre ☎ (01522) 529828*

Branston Hall Hotel M
♛♛♛ COMMENDED

Lincoln Road, Branston, Lincoln LN4 1PD
☎ (01522) 793305
Fax (01522) 790549

Magnificent country house hotel set in over 80 acres of wooded parkland and lakes, on the B1188, 3 miles south of Lincoln.

Bedrooms: 9 single, 21 double, 5 twin, 1 triple, 1 family room
Suite available
Bathrooms: 37 en-suite

Bed & breakfast per night:

	£min	£max
Single	62.50	
Double	80.00	100.00

Half board per person:

	£min	£max
Daily		60.00

Lunch available
Evening meal 1900 (last orders 2145)
Parking for 70
Cards accepted: Amex, Diners, Mastercard, Visa, Switch/Delta

[Ad] See display advertisement on this page

ACCESSIBILITY

Look for the symbols which indicate accessibility for wheelchair users. These are described in detail at the front of this guide.

BRANSTON HALL HOTEL

AA approved Country House Hotel

Branston Hall Hotel is a magnificent country manor house which enjoys a fine reputation for its warm welcome and hospitality. Steeped in history, the Hall is situated in 88 acres of private wooded parkland, private lakes and with commanding views and gardens famous for their interest and splendour. Branston Hall Hotel provides the ultimate oasis of tranquillity and true country living, yet only 5 miles from Lincoln City centre. Within the hotel, all rooms have en suite bathrooms, tea/coffee making facilities, direct dial telephone, TV text and radio. Amongst the traditional oak paneled splendour of yesteryear, is the famed Lakeside Restaurant which is internationally acclaimed independently of the hotel.

Bedrooms 29 (29 en suite) Prices £38.75 bed and breakfast, based on double occupancy.
Mini breaks available (minimum 2 persons, 2 nights) on dinner, bed and breakfast £45

TEL (01522) 793305 Branston Hall Hotel, Lincoln Road, Branston, Lincoln, LN4 1PD FAX (01522) 790549

Castle Hotel ⚐

👑👑👑 COMMENDED

Westgate, Lincoln LN1 3AS
☎ (01522) 538801
Fax (01522) 575457

Privately owned traditional English hotel offering hospitality at its best. Listed building in Lincoln's historic heart. Impressive castle and cathedral views. Ample free parking. A unique welcome, and one we're confident you'll wish to experience again. Half-board daily prices are for a minimum 2-night stay.
Bedrooms: 4 single, 9 double, 5 twin, 1 triple
Bathrooms: 19 en-suite

Bed & breakfast
per night:	£min	£max
Single	55.00	65.00
Double	65.00	75.00

Half board per
person:	£min	£max
Daily	42.50	62.50
Weekly	285.00	390.00

Lunch available
Evening meal 1900 (last orders 2130)
Parking for 20
Cards accepted: Mastercard, Visa, Switch/Delta

Damon's Motel ⚐

👑👑👑 HIGHLY COMMENDED

997 Doddington Road, Lincoln LN6 3SE
☎ (01522) 887733
Fax (01522) 887734
Purpose-built, 2-storey motel on the Lincoln ring road. Adjacent restaurant, indoor pool, gym, solarium. Satellite TV.
Wheelchair access category 3
Bedrooms: 24 double, 18 twin, 5 triple
Bathrooms: 47 en-suite

Bed & breakfast
per night:	£min	£max
Single	42.00	45.00
Double	46.50	49.50

Lunch available
Evening meal 1500 (last orders 2200)

Parking for 47
Cards accepted: Amex, Diners, Mastercard, Visa, Switch/Delta

Grand Hotel ⚐

👑👑👑 COMMENDED

St Mary's Street, Lincoln LN5 7EP
☎ (01522) 524211
Fax (01522) 537661
The Independents/Best Western
Family-owned hotel, in the centre of beautiful historic city. Getaway breaks available throughout the year. Half board prices below are based on a minimum 2-night stay.
Bedrooms: 19 single, 14 double, 13 twin, 2 triple
Bathrooms: 48 en-suite

Bed & breakfast
per night:	£min	£max
Single	52.00	67.50
Double	60.00	75.00

Half board per
person:	£min	£max
Daily	43.50	49.50

Lunch available
Evening meal 1900 (last orders 2100)
Parking for 30
Cards accepted: Amex, Diners, Mastercard, Visa, Switch/Delta

Hillcrest Hotel ⚐

👑👑 COMMENDED

15 Lindum Terrace, Lincoln LN2 5RT
☎ (01522) 510182
Fax (01522) 510182
Logis of GB
Victorian rectory overlooking gardens and park. Peaceful location, 5 minutes' walk to cathedral and city. Short breaks available all year for a minimum 2-night stay.
Bedrooms: 6 single, 6 double, 1 twin, 4 triple
Bathrooms: 17 en-suite

Bed & breakfast
per night:	£min	£max
Single	37.00	49.00
Double	65.00	70.00

Lunch available
Evening meal 1915 (last orders 2045)
Parking for 7
Cards accepted: Amex, Mastercard, Visa, Switch/Delta

Hollies Hotel ⚐

👑👑👑 COMMENDED

65 Carholme Road, Lincoln LN1 1RT
☎ (01522) 522419
Fax (01522) 522419
Privately-owned Victorian residence of considerable charm and character. A short and picturesque walk to the town, tourist areas and Brayford Marina.
Bedrooms: 2 single, 4 double, 2 twin, 1 triple, 1 family room
Bathrooms: 6 en-suite, 1 private, 2 public

Bed & breakfast
per night:	£min	£max
Single	30.00	48.00
Double	55.00	70.00

Half board per
person:	£min	£max
Daily	38.00	45.00
Weekly	245.00	255.00

Lunch available
Evening meal 1900 (last orders 2100)
Parking for 8
Cards accepted: Amex, Mastercard, Visa

D'Isney Place Hotel ⚐

Listed COMMENDED

Eastgate, Lincoln LN2 4AA
☎ (01522) 538881
Fax (01522) 511321
Small family-run hotel near the cathedral, with individually styled bedrooms and an emphasis on comfort and privacy.
Bedrooms: 1 single, 10 double, 3 twin, 2 triple, 1 family room
Bathrooms: 17 en-suite

Bed & breakfast
per night:	£min	£max
Single	57.00	67.00
Double	72.00	92.00

Parking for 20
Cards accepted: Amex, Diners, Mastercard, Visa, Switch/Delta

Tennyson Hotel ⚐

👑👑 COMMENDED

7 South Park Avenue, Lincoln LN5 8EN
☎ (01522) 521624
Fax (01522) 521624
Hotel with a comfortable atmosphere, overlooking the South Park, 1 mile from the city centre. Personally supervised. Leisure breaks available.
Bedrooms: 2 single, 3 double, 1 twin, 2 triple
Bathrooms: 8 en-suite

Bed & breakfast per night:	£min	£max
Single	29.00	33.00
Double	37.50	40.00

Parking for 8
Cards accepted: Amex, Diners, Mastercard, Visa

Washingborough Hall Country House Hotel ⋀
COMMENDED
Church Hill, Washingborough, Lincoln LN4 1BE
☎ (01522) 790340
Fax (01522) 792936
Minotel/The Independents
Stone-built, former manor house in grounds of 3 acres, in a pleasant village 2.5 miles from the historic cathedral city of Lincoln.
Bedrooms: 6 double, 6 twin
Bathrooms: 12 en-suite, 1 public

Bed & breakfast per night:	£min	£max
Single	56.50	69.00
Double	79.50	91.50

Half board per person:	£min	£max
Weekly	280.00	320.00

Evening meal 1900 (last orders 2030)
Parking for 50
Cards accepted: Amex, Diners, Mastercard, Visa, Switch/Delta

LONG MELFORD
Suffolk
Map ref 3B2

One of Suffolk's loveliest villages, remarkable for the length of its main street. Holy Trinity Church is considered to be the finest village church in England. The National Trust own the Elizabethan Melford Hall and nearby Kentwell Hall is also open to the public.

The George & Dragon ⋀
COMMENDED
Long Melford, Sudbury CO10 9JB
☎ (01787) 371285
Fax (01787) 312428
Email: geodrg.@ mail.global net.co.uk.
English country inn offering traditional service and hospitality. The best in both beer and food.
Bedrooms: 2 double, 3 twin, 1 triple
Bathrooms: 5 en-suite, 1 private shower

Bed & breakfast per night:	£min	£max
Single	35.00	35.00
Double	50.00	50.00

Half board per person:	£min	£max
Daily		50.00

Lunch available
Evening meal 1800 (last orders 2200)
Parking for 20
Cards accepted: Mastercard, Visa, Switch/Delta

Perseverance Hotel
Listed APPROVED
Station Road, Long Melford, Sudbury CO10 9HN
☎ (01787) 375862
Public house with converted outbuildings providing additional chalet-style accommodation.
Bedrooms: 1 single, 1 double, 3 twin, 1 triple
Bathrooms: 3 en-suite, 1 public

Bed & breakfast per night:	£min	£max
Single	16.00	28.00
Double	32.00	40.00

Half board per person:	£min	£max
Daily	22.00	34.00
Weekly	140.00	210.00

Lunch available
Evening meal 1900 (last orders 2100)

LOWESTOFT
Suffolk
Map ref 3C1

Seaside town with wide sandy beaches. Important fishing port with picturesque fishing quarter. Home of the famous Lowestoft porcelain and birthplace of Benjamin Britten. East Point Pavilion's exhibition describes the Lowestoft story.
Tourist Information Centre ☎ (01502) 523000

Aarland House
COMMENDED
36 Lyndhurst Road, Lowestoft NR32 4PD
☎ (01502) 585148
For a quiet retreat, England's most easterly guesthouse. Hospitality trays in rooms. En-suite available. Caroline and Tony Barley welcome you.

Bedrooms: 1 single, 4 double, 2 twin, 1 triple
Bathrooms: 1 private, 2 public, 3 private showers

Bed & breakfast per night:	£min	£max
Single	18.00	27.50
Double	35.50	39.50

Evening meal from 1800
Parking for 1

Albany Hotel ⋀
COMMENDED
400 London Road South, Lowestoft NR33 0BQ
☎ (01502) 574394
Small, family-run private hotel. 3 minutes from sandy beach and Kensington Gardens and a short distance from main shopping precinct.
Bedrooms: 2 single, 1 double, 1 twin, 1 triple, 2 family rooms
Bathrooms: 4 en-suite, 1 public

Bed & breakfast per night:	£min	£max
Single	16.00	22.00
Double	34.00	34.00

Half board per person:	£min	£max
Daily	22.00	28.00
Weekly	142.00	142.00

Evening meal 1800 (last orders 1500)
Parking for 1
Cards accepted: Amex, Diners, Mastercard, Visa

Longshore Guesthouse
Listed COMMENDED
7 Wellington Esplanade, Lowestoft NR33 0QQ
☎ (01502) 565037
Fax (01502) 582032
Family-run guesthouse in south Lowestoft, 5 minutes from town centre and close to Oulton Broad. Friendly atmosphere. Most rooms are en-suite and most have sea views. Dogs welcome.
Bedrooms: 2 single, 2 double, 1 twin, 1 triple
Bathrooms: 4 en-suite, 2 private

Bed & breakfast per night:	£min	£max
Single	20.00	32.00
Double	40.00	42.00

Parking for 5
Cards accepted: Amex, Diners, Mastercard, Visa, Switch/Delta

MANNINGTREE

Essex
Map ref 3B2

On the estuary of the River Stour. The village has many interesting Georgian and Victorian buildings and the Strand attracts swans in great numbers.

Thorn Hotel

🏛🏛 COMMENDED

High Street, Mistley, Manningtree CO11 1HE
☎ (01206) 392821
Fax (01206) 392133
Situated close to the picturesque River Stour, the hotel has recently been refurbished. All rooms en-suite. Children welcome.
Bedrooms: 2 single, 2 double
Bathrooms: 4 private

Bed & breakfast per night:

	£min	£max
Single	30.00	35.00
Double	45.00	50.00

Half board per person:

	£min	£max
Daily	40.00	45.00

Lunch available
Evening meal 1900 (last orders 2130)
Parking for 6
Cards accepted: Mastercard, Visa

🛇🖥♿🎱🗝✕⊙🛏 ⚓🍽30►✕
🚲 SP 🏠 T

MARGARETTING

Essex
Map ref 3B3

Ivy Hill Hotel 🅼

🏛🏛 COMMENDED

Writtle Road, Margaretting, Ingatestone CM4 OEH
☎ (01277) 353040
Fax (01277) 355038

Converted mansion house in the countryside near the A12. Complex includes conference centre, banqueting, bar and elegant restaurant.
Bedrooms: 24 double, 10 twin
Bathrooms: 34 en-suite

Bed & breakfast per night:

	£min	£max
Single	75.00	85.00
Double	80.00	120.00

Half board per person:

	£min	£max
Daily	100.00	110.00
Weekly	700.00	770.00

Lunch available
Evening meal 1900 (last orders 2200)
Parking for 160
Cards accepted: Amex, Diners, Mastercard, Visa, Switch/Delta

🛇♿🎱🗝✕🖥🔽🐾🍴🛒Ⓢ🅼TV⊙
🛏 ⚓🍽150 🔧✎❋✿✕☂ SP 🏠

MILDENHALL

Suffolk
Map ref 3B2

Town that has grown considerably in size in the last 20 years but still manages to retain a pleasant small country town centre. Mildenhall and District Museum deals with local history, particularly RAF Mildenhall and the Mildenhall Treasure.

Riverside Hotel 🅼

🏛🏛🏛 COMMENDED

Mill Street, Mildenhall, Bury St Edmunds IP28 7DP
☎ (01638) 717274
Grade II Regency-style manor house in picturesque riverside setting. Recently refurbished to a high standard. Easter, Christmas and New Year breaks.
Bedrooms: 3 single, 8 double, 6 twin, 3 triple
Bathrooms: 20 en-suite

Bed & breakfast per night:

	£min	£max
Single	53.00	62.00
Double	82.00	84.00

Lunch available
Evening meal 1830 (last orders 2100)
Parking for 50
Cards accepted: Amex, Diners, Mastercard, Visa, Switch/Delta

🛇♿🎱🗝✕🖥🔽🐾🍴Ⓢ🅼🔊
🛏⚓🍽60 🔧❋✿✕☂ SP 🏠 T

The Smoke House 🅼

🏛🏛🏛 COMMENDED

Beck Row, Mildenhall, Bury St Edmunds IP28 8DH
☎ (01638) 713223
Fax (01638) 712202
Ⓒ Best Western
Listed Tudor/Georgian manor house with inglenook fireplaces and comfortable, well-equipped rooms. 2 bars, licensed restaurant, barbecue in season. Conference centre.
Wheelchair access category 3🚶
Bedrooms: 4 double, 84 twin, 16 triple
Bathrooms: 104 en-suite

Bed & breakfast per night:

	£min	£max
Single	80.00	110.00
Double	100.00	130.00

Half board per person:

	£min	£max
Daily	60.00	75.00
Weekly	385.00	490.00

Lunch available
Evening meal 1700 (last orders 2200)
Parking for 200
Cards accepted: Amex, Diners, Mastercard, Visa, Switch/Delta

🛇♿🎱🗝✕🖥🔽🐾♿🍴Ⓢ🅼TV
⊙🛏Ⓢ⚓🍽120 🔍❋U🔽❋✿✕☂
SP 🏠 T

NEATISHEAD

Norfolk
Map ref 3C1

The Barton Angler Country Inn 🅼

🏛🏛🏛 COMMENDED

Irstead Road, Neatishead, Norwich NR12 8XP
☎ (01692) 630740
Fax (01692) 631122

The inn, part of which is nearly 500 years old, has extensive gardens and is situated in the heart of Norfolk countryside adjacent to lovely Barton Broad.
Bedrooms: 3 single, 3 double, 1 twin
Bathrooms: 5 en-suite, 1 public

Bed & breakfast per night:

	£min	£max
Single	20.00	35.00
Double	58.00	80.00

Lunch available
Evening meal 1900 (last orders 2100)
Parking for 30
Cards accepted: Amex, Mastercard, Visa

🛇🖥♿🗝✕🖥🔽🐾Ⓢ✂🅼TV🛏 ⚓
🍽36U🔽❋✿✕🚲 SP 🏠 T

COLOUR MAPS

Colour maps at the back of this guide pinpoint all places in which you will find accommodation listed.

Regency Guesthouse

⛤ ⛤ COMMENDED

The Street, Neatishead, Norwich
NR12 8AD
☎ (01692) 630233
*Peaceful Broads village. Ideal nature
rambles, wildlife, bird-watching. 6 miles
coast/10 miles Norwich. Accent on
personal service. Renowned for
generous English breakfasts. Laura
Ashley rooms with tea-making facilities,
TV. Wild duck speciality in village
pub/restaurant a few yards' walk.*
Bedrooms: 2 double, 2 twin
Bathrooms: 3 en-suite, 2 public

**Bed & breakfast
per night:**

	£min	£max
Single	21.00	
Double	39.00	44.00

Parking for 8
Cards accepted: Diners

NEEDHAM MARKET

Suffolk
Map ref 3B2

Interesting town on the Ipswich to
Bury St Edmunds road containing
Georgian houses in the High Street,
the Friends' Meeting House, the
17th C timber-framed grammar
school and the "Bull Inn" with
carved corner-post.

The Annex

Listed COMMENDED

17 High Street, Needham Market,
Ipswich IP6 8AL
☎ (01449) 720687
Fax (01449) 722230
*Close to all local amenities and
recreational facilities. Family suites
available if required. Payphone for
guests' use. Private car park.*
Bedrooms: 1 single, 1 double, 1 twin
Bathrooms: 2 public

**Bed & breakfast
per night:**

	£min	£max
Single	20.00	25.00
Double	35.00	35.00

Parking for 4

ACCESSIBILITY

Look for the symbols
which indicate accessibility for
wheelchair users. These are
described in detail at the
front of this guide.

NEWMARKET

Suffolk
Map ref 3B2

Centre of the English horse-racing
world and the headquarters of the
Jockey Club and National Stud.
Racecourse and horse sales. The
National Horse Racing Museum
traces the history and development
of the Sport of Kings.
Tourist Information Centre ☎ *(01638)
667200*

Bedford Lodge Hotel
Conference and Leisure ⋔

⛤⛤⛤⛤ HIGHLY COMMENDED

Bury Road, Newmarket CB8 7BX
☎ (01638) 663175
Fax (01638) 667391
Ⓡ Best Western
*A former hunting lodge and one of
Suffolk's most attractive country hotels.
A striking combination of the classic
and the new, offering every modern
convenience, including fitness centre,
indoor swimming pool, sauna, steam
room and beauty salon. Close to town
and racecourse. Daily half board price
based on minimum 2-night stay.*
Bedrooms: 43 double, 13 twin
Suites available
Bathrooms: 56 en-suite

**Bed & breakfast
per night:**

	£min	£max
Single	75.00	78.50
Double	97.00	102.00

**Half board per
person:**

	£min	£max
Daily	59.50	63.75
Weekly	416.50	446.25

Lunch available
Evening meal 1900 (last orders
2130)
Parking for 90
Cards accepted: Amex, Diners,
Mastercard, Visa, Switch/Delta

Heath Court Hotel ⋔

⛤⛤⛤ COMMENDED

Moulton Road, Newmarket
CB8 8DY
☎ (01638) 667171
Fax (01638) 666533
*Hotel of high standards in a quiet
central position. Ideal location for
touring, horseracing and local
countryside.*
Wheelchair access category 3 ⋔
Bedrooms: 16 single, 13 double,
10 twin, 2 triple
Suites available
Bathrooms: 41 en-suite

**Bed & breakfast
per night:**

	£min	£max
Single	68.00	78.00
Double	80.00	120.00

Lunch available
Evening meal 1900 (last orders
2145)
Parking for 70
Cards accepted: Amex, Diners,
Mastercard, Visa, Switch/Delta

NORFOLK BROADS

*See under Aylsham, Beccles, Bungay,
Cawston, Coltishall, Great Yarmouth,
Hevingham, Horning, Lowestoft,
Neatishead, Norwich, Oulton Broad,
Rollesby, Wroxham*

NORWICH

Norfolk
Map ref 3C1

Beautiful cathedral city and county
town on the River Wensum with
many fine museums and medieval
churches. Norman castle, Guildhall
and interesting medieval streets.
Good shopping centre and market.
Tourist Information Centre ☎ *(01603)
666071*

Aberdale Lodge

Listed APPROVED

211 Earlham Road, Norwich
NR2 3RQ
☎ (01603) 502100
*Family-run Victorian guesthouse in
historic city of Norwich. Easy reach of
city centre, Norfolk Broads, heritage
coastline and countryside.*
Bedrooms: 3 single, 1 double, 1 twin,
1 family room
Bathrooms: 1 public

**Bed & breakfast
per night:**

	£min	£max
Single	15.50	15.50
Double	31.00	31.00

Cards accepted: Diners

Annesley House Hotel ⋔

⛤⛤⛤ HIGHLY COMMENDED

6 Newmarket Road, Norwich
NR2 2LA
☎ (01603) 624553
Fax (01603) 621577
Ⓡ Consort
*Three listed Georgian buildings,
restored and refurbished to a high
standard. Set in landscaped grounds in
a conservation area, yet just a stroll to
the city centre.*

Continued ▶

NORWICH

Continued

Bedrooms: 8 single, 16 double, 2 twin
Bathrooms: 26 en-suite

Bed & breakfast

per night:	£min	£max
Single	50.00	80.00
Double	65.00	85.00

Half board per person:

	£min	£max
Daily	67.00	

Evening meal 1900 (last orders 2100)
Parking for 24
Cards accepted: Amex, Diners, Mastercard, Visa, Switch/Delta

🐎🐕♿🕯📧🖵☎🎱Ⓢ🛏💻🖊❄
✕🚐 SP ♿ T

Becklands

👑👑 COMMENDED

105 Holt Road, Horsford, Norwich
NR10 3AB
☎ (01603) 898582 & 898020
Fax (01603) 891649
Quietly located modern house overlooking open countryside. 5 miles north of Norwich. Central for the Broads and coastal areas.
Bedrooms: 4 single, 3 double, 2 twin
Bathrooms: 7 en-suite, 3 public

Bed & breakfast

per night:	£min	£max
Single	18.00	20.00
Double	36.00	38.00

Parking for 30
Cards accepted: Diners, Mastercard, Visa

🐎♿📧🖵☎🎱 UL Ⓢ 🛏 TV 💻🖊❄✕
🚐

Beeches Hotel & Victorian Gardens ᴀᴀ

👑👑👑 HIGHLY COMMENDED

4-6 Earlham Road, Norwich
NR2 3DB
☎ (01603) 621167
Fax (01603) 620151
Email: beeches.hotel@paston.co.uk
Ⓒʀ The Independents

Welcoming hotel, with unique and tranquil English Heritage wooded gardens. Tastefully restored and refurbished to offer high standards of

comfort in a relaxed, informal atmosphere. An oasis in the heart of historic Norwich.
Wheelchair access category 2♿
Bedrooms: 8 single, 14 double, 3 twin
Bathrooms: 25 en-suite

Bed & breakfast

per night:	£min	£max
Single	50.00	60.00
Double	65.00	80.00

Half board per person:

	£min	£max
Daily	44.50	47.00
Weekly	285.00	346.00

Evening meal 1830 (last orders 2100)
Parking for 24
Cards accepted: Amex, Diners, Mastercard, Visa, Switch/Delta

🐎♿🕯📧🖵☎🎱Ⓢ🖊❄☀💻🖵
🍴40❄✕ SP ♿ T

Conifers Hotel ᴀᴀ

👑 APPROVED

162 Dereham Road, Norwich
NR2 3AH
☎ (01603) 628737
Friendly hotel, close to city centre, university, sports village and showground. All rooms have colour TV, tea/coffee, coffee facilities.
Bedrooms: 4 single, 1 double, 3 twin
Bathrooms: 1 en-suite, 3 public

Bed & breakfast

per night:	£min	£max
Single	19.00	25.00
Double	36.00	40.00

Parking for 4

🐎♿📧🖵☎🎱 UL Ⓢ TV 💻🖵
🚐

The Corner House ᴀᴀ

👑👑 COMMENDED

62 Earlham Road, Norwich
NR2 3DF
☎ (01603) 627928
Large Victorian house with friendly atmosphere, 10 minutes from city centre. TV, coffee/tea facilities in all bedrooms, residents' lounge area. Car parking.
Bedrooms: 2 double, 1 triple
Bathrooms: 2 en-suite, 1 private

Bed & breakfast

per night:	£min	£max
Single	20.00	25.00
Double	35.00	36.00

Parking for 4

🐎📧🖵☎🎱 UL Ⓢ🖊❄🛏 TV 💻🖵
❄🚐

Crofters Hotel ᴀᴀ

👑👑👑 COMMENDED

2 Earlham Road, Norwich NR2 3DA
☎ (01603) 613287
Fax (01603) 766864

Tastefully restored Victorian house set in beautiful landscaped gardens. Comfortable accommodation at affordable rates in central Norwich. Private car park.
Bedrooms: 6 double, 5 twin, 1 triple
Bathrooms: 12 en-suite

Bed & breakfast

per night:	£min	£max
Single	42.00	56.00
Double	56.00	75.00

Half board per person:

	£min	£max
Daily	52.00	66.00
Weekly	312.00	395.00

Lunch available
Evening meal 1800 (last orders 2100)
Parking for 20
Cards accepted: Mastercard, Visa, Switch/Delta

♿🕯📧☎🎱Ⓢ🛏 TV ◐💻🖵
🍴30❄🚐

Edmar Lodge

👑👑👑 COMMENDED

64 Earlham Road, Norwich
NR2 3DF
☎ (01603) 615599
Fax (01603) 632977
A warm welcome awaits you. Most rooms en-suite with cable TV, tea/coffee facilities, hairdryer, etc. Close to city centre and UEA, with 2 car parks. Excellent breakfasts.
Bedrooms: 1 single, 1 double, 1 twin, 1 triple
Bathrooms: 3 en-suite, 1 public

Bed & breakfast

per night:	£min	£max
Single	18.00	28.00
Double	30.00	40.00

Parking for 6

🐎♿🕯📧🖵☎🎱 UL Ⓢ🖊❄🖵
❄✕🚐 OAP ❄ SP T

Elm Farm Chalet Hotel ᴀᴀ

👑👑👑 COMMENDED

St Faiths NR10 3HH
☎ (01603) 898366
Fax (01603) 897129
Situated in quiet, pretty village 4 miles north of Norwich. Ideal base for touring

Norfolk and Suffolk. En-suite chalet bedrooms. Restaurant in farmhouse. Licensed.
Wheelchair access category 3๋
Bedrooms: 4 single, 6 double, 6 twin, 1 family room
Bathrooms: 15 en-suite, 2 private

Bed & breakfast

per night:	£min	£max
Single	31.00	36.00
Double	50.50	56.00

Half board per

person:	£min	£max
Daily	42.00	48.00
Weekly	294.00	336.00

Lunch available
Evening meal 1830 (last orders 1930)
Parking for 20
Cards accepted: Amex, Mastercard, Visa

🛏🖐✆💷🖵📞🍴♿🕪🖻📺📺🖥🖭🖴
🍴❄🎾🚐 SP

Forte Posthouse Norwich ⋀

👑👑👑 COMMENDED
Ipswich Road, Norwich NR4 6EP
☎ (01603) 456431
Fax (01603) 506400
ⓒ Forte
Recently refurbished hotel, with a health club, on the southern side of the city. Convenient for both town and country.
Bedrooms: 89 double, 21 twin, 6 triple
Bathrooms: 116 en-suite

Bed & breakfast

per night:	£min	£max
Single	29.00	79.00
Double	58.00	88.00

Half board per

person:	£min	£max
Daily	39.00	99.00
Weekly	259.00	693.00

Lunch available
Evening meal 1830 (last orders 2230)
Parking for 200
Cards accepted: Amex, Diners, Mastercard, Visa, Switch/Delta

🛏🖐✆💷🖵📞🕪📞🍴♿🕪🖻📺◐
🖭🖴🍴110🏊🎾🎣⛳🚶❄🚐 SP T

Fuchsias Guesthouse ⋀

Listed COMMENDED
139 Earlham Road, Norwich NR2 3RG
☎ (01603) 451410
Fax (01603) 259696
Friendly, family-run guesthouse, convenient for city centre, university and surrounding countryside. Special diets available. Own keys.

Bedrooms: 1 single, 2 double, 2 twin, 1 triple
Suite available
Bathrooms: 1 en-suite, 2 public

Bed & breakfast

per night:	£min	£max
Single	20.00	25.00
Double	35.00	40.00

🛏🖵🖐🍴🕪🖻📞♿◐🖭🖴🚗🍴🚐 SP

The Gables Guesthouse

👑👑 HIGHLY COMMENDED
527 Earlham Road, Norwich NR4 7HN
☎ (01603) 456666
Fax (01603) 250320
High standard of accommodation with a friendly and relaxed atmosphere, snooker table and car park. Close to city and UEA.
Bedrooms: 5 double, 4 twin, 1 triple
Bathrooms: 10 en-suite, 1 public

Bed & breakfast

per night:	£min	£max
Single	35.00	35.00
Double	50.00	55.00

Parking for 11
Cards accepted: Mastercard, Visa, Switch/Delta

🛏🖐✆🖵🖐🕪🍴🕪🖻📺📺🖭🖴
🍴❄🎾🚐

The Georgian House Hotel ⋀

👑👑👑 APPROVED
32-34 Unthank Road, Norwich NR2 2RB
☎ (01603) 615655
Fax (01603) 765689
ⓒ Minotel/The Independents

Comfortable we may be, expensive we are not. Two tastefully furnished linked Victorian houses, set in beautiful gardens, form the heart of this popular hotel. Ample parking, intimate bar and relaxed restaurant.
Bedrooms: 10 single, 10 double, 5 twin, 2 triple
Bathrooms: 27 en-suite

Bed & breakfast

per night:	£min	£max
Single	40.00	45.00
Double	50.00	55.00

Half board per

person:	£min	£max
Daily	57.00	75.00

Lunch available
Evening meal 1830 (last orders 2030)
Parking for 30

Cards accepted: Amex, Diners, Mastercard, Visa, Switch/Delta

🛏🖐🖻🕪🖵🖵📞🍴♿🕪🖻📺
🖭🖴🍴🚐 DAP SP 🏠 T

Marlborough House Hotel ⋀

👑👑👑 APPROVED
22 Stracey Road, Norwich NR1 1EZ
☎ (01603) 628005
Fax (01603) 628005
Long established family hotel, close to city centre, Castle Mall, museum, cathedral and Elm Hill. 3 minutes from railway station. Full central heating. All double, twin and family rooms are en-suite. Tea and coffee-making facilities, licensed bar, car park.
Bedrooms: 5 single, 3 double, 2 twin, 1 triple
Bathrooms: 6 en-suite, 2 public

Bed & breakfast

per night:	£min	£max
Single	20.00	30.00
Double	40.00	45.00

Half board per

person:	£min	£max
Daily	27.00	37.00
Weekly	189.00	259.00

Evening meal 1730 (last orders 1900)
Parking for 10

🛏🖐🖵🕪🖻📺🖭🖭🖴🍴 DAP ♿
SP

Hotel Nelson ⋀

👑👑👑👑 HIGHLY COMMENDED
Prince of Wales Road, Norwich NR1 1DX
☎ (01603) 760260
Fax (01603) 620008
Modern, purpose-built hotel on the riverside close to railway station and city centre. Easy access to the Broads and coast. Leisure club with indoor swimming pool. B&B prices shown do not include breakfast.
Bedrooms: 27 single, 67 double, 38 twin
Bathrooms: 132 en-suite

Bed & breakfast

per night:	£min	£max
Single	75.00	80.00
Double	82.00	87.00

Half board per

person:	£min	£max
Daily	53.00	58.00

Lunch available
Evening meal 1845 (last orders 2145)
Parking for 214
Cards accepted: Amex, Diners, Mastercard, Visa

🛏🖐✆🕪🖵🖵🖐🕪🖻📺📺◐
📳🖭🖴🍴190🏊🎾🎣❄🍴♿ SP

NORWICH
Continued

Hotel Norwich 🅼
🅦🅦🅦🅦 COMMENDED

121-131 Boundary Road, Norwich
NR3 2BA
☎ (01603) 787260
Fax (01603) 400466
Ⓒ Best Western
Modern hotel conveniently located on the ring road, with easy access to the city centre, countryside, coastlines and Norfolk Broads. Leisure centre with indoor pool.
Wheelchair access category 2🅖
Bedrooms: 18 single, 42 double, 38 twin, 8 triple
Suites available
Bathrooms: 106 en-suite

Bed & breakfast
per night:	£min	£max
Single	69.50	79.50
Double	79.50	89.50

Half board per person:
	£min	£max
Daily	49.50	81.50
Weekly	297.00	459.00

Lunch available
Evening meal 1900 (last orders 2200)
Parking for 221
Cards accepted: Amex, Diners, Mastercard, Visa

Norwich Sport Village Hotel 🅼
🅦🅦🅦 COMMENDED

Drayton High Road, Hellesdon, Norwich NR6 5DU
☎ (01603) 789469
Fax (01603) 406845
Ⓒ Inter Europe
Situated on outer Norwich Ring Road on the A1067. Providing sports facilities, including tennis, squash, badminton, snooker, health centre, sauna and £4.5m Aquapark. Three bars and three restaurants. Many facilities free to residents. Non-smoking rooms.
Bedrooms: 11 double, 42 twin, 2 family rooms
Bathrooms: 55 en-suite

Bed & breakfast
per night:	£min	£max
Single	64.00	70.00
Double	76.00	85.00

Half board per person:
	£min	£max
Daily	83.00	89.00

Lunch available
Evening meal 1830 (last orders 2130)

Parking for 1200
Cards accepted: Amex, Diners, Mastercard, Visa, Switch/Delta

Old Rectory 🅼
🅦🅦🅦 COMMENDED

North Walsham Road, Crostwick, Norwich NR12 7BG
☎ (01603) 738513
Fax (01603) 738712
Old Victorian rectory with bedroom extension, set amidst 3.5 acres of mature trees. Well placed for the Broads and 5 miles from Norwich. Homely accommodation.
Wheelchair access category 3🅖
Bedrooms: 5 double, 6 twin, 2 family rooms
Bathrooms: 13 en-suite

Bed & breakfast
per night:	£min	£max
Single	34.00	36.00
Double	47.50	50.00

Half board per person:
	£min	£max
Daily	44.50	46.50
Weekly	311.50	325.50

Evening meal 1830 (last orders 1930)
Parking for 45
Cards accepted: Mastercard, Visa

The Old Rectory 🅼
🅦🅦🅦 HIGHLY COMMENDED

103 Yarmouth Road, Thorpe St Andrew, Norwich NR7 0HF
☎ (01603) 700772

Delightful Georgian house in an acre of gardens overlooking the Yare valley. Personally run by the owners who offer traditional hospitality in a friendly atmosphere.
Bedrooms: 7 double, 1 twin
Bathrooms: 8 en-suite

Bed & breakfast
per night:	£min	£max
Single	55.00	65.00
Double	70.00	80.00

Half board per person:
	£min	£max
Daily	70.00	80.00
Weekly	350.00	400.00

Evening meal 1900 (last orders 2000)
Parking for 18
Cards accepted: Amex, Mastercard, Visa

Stakis Norwich 🅼
🅦🅦🅦🅦 COMMENDED

Norwich Airport, Cromer Road, Norwich NR6 6JA
☎ (01603) 410544
Fax (01603) 487701
Fine hotel in quiet location 5 minutes from city centre. Modern facilities including leisure area with indoor swimming pool and fully equipped gymnasium. Ideally located for Norfolk Broads.
Bedrooms: 4 single, 70 double, 30 twin, 4 triple
Bathrooms: 108 en-suite

Bed & breakfast
per night:	£min	£max
Single	49.00	77.00
Double	68.00	90.00

Lunch available
Evening meal 1900 (last orders 2230)
Parking for 320
Cards accepted: Amex, Diners, Mastercard, Visa, Switch/Delta

Wedgewood House 🅼
🅦🅦 APPROVED

42 St Stephens Road, Norwich NR1 3RE
☎ (01603) 625730
Fax (01603) 615035
Family-run hotel, close to coach station and within walking distance of shops and places of interest. Parking.
Bedrooms: 2 single, 5 double, 2 twin, 3 triple, 1 family room
Bathrooms: 8 en-suite, 2 private, 1 public

Bed & breakfast
per night:	£min	£max
Single	20.00	24.00
Double	42.00	46.00

Parking for 5
Cards accepted: Amex, Mastercard, Visa

The 🅼 symbol after an establishment name indicates that it is a Regional Tourist Board member.

OULTON BROAD

Suffolk
Map ref 3C1

Oulton Broad is the most southerly of the Broads and the centre of a very busy boating industry.

Broadlands Hotel M

👑👑 APPROVED

Bridge Road, Oulton Broad,
Lowestoft NR32 3LN
☎ (01502) 516031 & 572157
Fax (01502) 501454
*Modern hotel near Oulton Broad,
gateway to Norfolk and Suffolk Broads.
Own indoor swimming pool and leisure
facilities. Traditional English fare served
in beautiful restaurant. Mini-breaks
available.*
Bedrooms: 2 single, 29 double,
19 twin
Bathrooms: 50 en-suite

Bed & breakfast

per night:	£min	£max
Single	45.00	55.00
Double	55.00	65.00

Half board per

person:	£min	£max
Daily	34.00	39.00
Weekly	238.00	273.00

Lunch available
Evening meal 1900 (last orders
2130)
Parking for 40
Cards accepted: Amex, Diners,
Mastercard, Visa, Switch/Delta

Parkhill Hotel

👑👑👑 COMMENDED

Parkhill, Oulton, Lowestoft
NR32 5DQ
☎ (01502) 730322
Fax (01502) 731695
*Peaceful wooded grounds with gardens
and lawns. The hotel offers a friendly
and homely atmosphere. Minimum
B&B prices below are for weekends.*
Bedrooms: 7 single, 8 double, 3 twin
Suites available
Bathrooms: 18 en-suite

Bed & breakfast

per night:	£min	£max
Single	45.00	70.00
Double	60.00	90.00

Half board per

person:	£min	£max
Daily	43.00	55.00
Weekly	280.00	350.00

Lunch available
Evening meal 1900 (last orders
2130)
Parking for 154

Cards accepted: Amex, Diners,
Mastercard, Visa, Switch/Delta

PETERBOROUGH

Cambridgeshire
Map ref 3A1

Prosperous and rapidly expanding cathedral city on the edge of the Fens on the River Nene. Catherine of Aragon is buried in the cathedral. City Museum and Art Gallery. Ferry Meadows Country Park has numerous leisure facilities.
Tourist Information Centre ☎ (01733) 452336

The Bell Inn Hotel M

👑👑👑 HIGHLY COMMENDED

Great North Road, Stilton,
Peterborough PE7 3RA
☎ (01733) 241066
Fax (01733) 245173

*Old coaching inn, restored as a hotel
including restaurant, village bar and
banqueting facilities. 6 miles south of
Peterborough off A1.*
Bedrooms: 2 single, 15 double,
1 twin, 1 triple
Bathrooms: 19 en-suite

Bed & breakfast

per night:	£min	£max
Single	45.00	74.00
Double	59.00	99.00

Lunch available
Evening meal 1900 (last orders
2130)
Parking for 30
Cards accepted: Amex, Mastercard,
Visa, Switch/Delta

Butterfly Hotel M

👑👑👑 COMMENDED

Thorpe Meadows, Off Longthorpe
Parkway, Peterborough PE3 6GA
☎ (01733) 64240
Fax (01733) 65538
*By the water's edge at Thorpe
Meadows, this modern hotel maintains
all the traditional values of design and
comfort. Special weekend rates
available.*
Bedrooms: 33 single, 18 double,
15 twin, 4 triple
Bathrooms: 70 en-suite

Bed & breakfast

per night:	£min	£max
Single	51.95	66.45
Double	58.90	73.40

Half board per

person:	£min	£max
Daily	64.45	85.90

Lunch available
Evening meal 1800 (last orders
2200)
Parking for 80
Cards accepted: Amex, Diners,
Mastercard, Visa, Switch/Delta

Dalwhinnie Lodge Hotel M

👑👑 APPROVED

31-33 Burghley Road, Peterborough
PE1 2QA
☎ (01733) 65968 & 565968
Fax (01733) 890838
*We believe we are the best hotel of our
kind for location, comfort and value for
money. High standards and a warm
welcome guaranteed. 5 minutes from
city centre, bus and train station. Ample
parking.*
Bedrooms: 4 single, 4 double, 2 twin
Bathrooms: 3 en-suite, 2 public,
2 private showers

Bed & breakfast

per night:	£min	£max
Single	25.00	35.00
Double	35.00	45.00

Half board per

person:	£min	£max
Daily	31.00	40.00

Evening meal 1830 (last orders
2100)
Parking for 14
Cards accepted: Amex, Diners,
Mastercard, Visa, Switch/Delta

Hawthorn House Hotel

👑👑👑 COMMENDED

89 Thorpe Road, Peterborough
PE3 6JQ
☎ (01733) 340608
Fax (01733) 340608
*City centre licensed hotel. High
standard of accommodation and
service. Tastefully furnished en-suite
rooms with TV and tea-making
facilities.*
Bedrooms: 3 single, 3 double, 2 twin
Bathrooms: 8 en-suite

Bed & breakfast

per night:	£min	£max
Single	25.00	38.50
Double	45.00	51.50

Evening meal 1830 (last orders
2030)

Continued ▶

PETERBOROUGH

Continued

Parking for 5
Cards accepted: Amex, Diners,
Mastercard, Visa

[symbols]

Orton Hall Hotel ⚑

👑👑👑 COMMENDED

The Village, Orton Longueville,
Peterborough PE2 7DN
☎ (01733) 391111
Fax (01733) 231912
Ⓒⓡ Best Western

*17th C manor house set in 20 acres of
mature parkland. En-suite bedrooms,
some with four-poster beds. Huntly
Restaurant or country pub for a choice
of dining. Minimum half board daily
price below based on 2-night weekend
stay.*
Bedrooms: 9 single, 32 double,
7 twin, 2 triple
Bathrooms: 50 en-suite

Bed & breakfast

per night:	£min	£max
Single	73.00	105.50
Double	110.90	135.90

Half board per

person:	£min	£max
Daily	49.50	119.95
Weekly	297.00	

Lunch available
Evening meal 1830 (last orders
2130)
Parking for 200
Cards accepted: Amex, Diners,
Mastercard, Visa, Switch/Delta

[symbols] 120

Queensgate Hotel ⚑

👑👑👑 COMMENDED

5 Fletton Avenue, Peterborough
PE2 8AX
☎ (01733) 62572 & 53181
Fax (01733) 558982

*City centre hotel 5 minutes' walk from
Rivergate Centre, main shopping area,
Cathedral and theatre. Character
building refurbished in 1996. Ample car
parking.*
Bedrooms: 6 single, 8 double, 3 twin,
2 triple
Bathrooms: 19 en-suite

Bed & breakfast

per night:	£min	£max
Single	35.00	59.50
Double	49.50	69.50

Half board per

person:	£min	£max
Daily	50.00	74.50

Lunch available

Evening meal 1830 (last orders
2045)
Parking for 20
Cards accepted: Amex, Diners,
Mastercard, Visa, Switch/Delta

[symbols]

Thomas Cook Bluebell Lodge Leisure Centre

👑👑👑 COMMENDED

P O Box 36, Thorpe Wood,
Peterborough PE3 6SB
☎ (01733) 502555 & 503008
Fax (01733) 502020

*Friendly, efficient service is provided at
this modern hotel. Bar, restaurant and
leisure facilities available.*
Bedrooms: 2 double, 9 twin, 2 triple
Bathrooms: 13 en-suite

Bed & breakfast

per night:	£min	£max
Single	30.00	52.88
Double	40.00	65.80

Lunch available
Evening meal 1830 (last orders
2200)
Parking for 250
Cards accepted: Mastercard, Visa

[symbols] 150

ROLLESBY

Norfolk
Map ref 3C1

Rollesby Broad forms part of the
Ormesby Broad complex and fine
views can be seen from the road
which runs through the middle.

The Old Court House ⚑

👑👑 COMMENDED

Court Road, Rollesby, Great
Yarmouth NR29 5HG
☎ (01493) 369665

*18th C workhouse set in 4 acres in a
peaceful, rural location near the Broads.
Family-run with private bar and home
cooking. Large games area. Bicycles for
hire. Tennis, fishing and riding nearby.*
Bedrooms: 2 double, 1 twin, 1 triple,
3 family rooms
Bathrooms: 5 en-suite, 2 public

Bed & breakfast

per night:	£min	£max
Single	20.00	37.00
Double	30.00	46.00

Half board per

person:	£min	£max
Daily	25.00	47.00
Weekly	190.00	292.00

Evening meal 1830 (last orders
1900)
Parking for 20
Open February–October

[symbols]

SAFFRON WALDEN

Essex
Map ref 2D1

Takes its name from the saffron
crocus once grown around the
town. The church of St Mary has
superb carvings, magnificent roofs
and brasses. A town maze can be
seen on the common. Two miles
south-west is Audley End, a
magnificent Jacobean mansion
owned by English Heritage.
Tourist Information Centre ☎ *(01799)
510444*

The Cricketers

👑👑👑 HIGHLY COMMENDED

Clavering, Saffron Walden
CB11 4QT
☎ (01799) 550442
Fax (01799) 550882

*16th C freehouse with beamed and
attractively-decorated interior.
Well-established restaurant and bar
meals. Accommodation adjacent. Half
board prices below are for single
occupancy.*
Bedrooms: 2 double, 4 twin
Bathrooms: 6 en-suite

Bed & breakfast

per night:	£min	£max
Single	60.00	60.00
Double	80.00	80.00

Half board per

person:	£min	£max
Daily	68.00	83.00

Lunch available
Evening meal 1900 (last orders
2200)
Parking for 45
Cards accepted: Amex, Mastercard,
Visa, Switch/Delta

[symbols]

COLOUR MAPS

Colour maps at the back of
this guide pinpoint all places
in which you will find
accommodation listed.

Queens Head Inn

ᗯᗯᗯ COMMENDED

Littlebury, Saffron Walden
CB11 4TD
☎ (01799) 522251
Fax (01799) 513522
ⒸⓇ Logis of GB
*Family-run freehouse and hotel close to
Audley End. All rooms en-suite. Good
Pub Guide "Best Pub in Essex" 1995.
Interesting and unusual menu.*
Bedrooms: 2 single, 2 double, 1 twin,
1 family room
Bathrooms: 6 en-suite

Bed & breakfast per night:	£min	£max
Single	32.95	41.90
Double	49.95	67.85

Half board per person:	£min	£max
Weekly	245.00	308.00

Lunch available
Evening meal 1900 (last orders
2100)
Parking for 30
Cards accepted: Amex, Diners,
Mastercard, Visa, Switch/Delta

Saffron Hotel ♨

ᗯᗯᗯ COMMENDED

10-18 High Street, Saffron Walden
CB10 1AY
☎ (01799) 522676
Fax (01799) 513979
*16th C hotel in market town. South of
Cambridge, close to Duxford Air
Museum and Stansted Airport. Noted
restaurant.*
Bedrooms: 3 single, 10 double,
3 twin, 1 triple
Bathrooms: 14 en-suite, 3 private

Bed & breakfast per night:	£min	£max
Single	45.00	55.00
Double	65.00	85.00

Half board per person:	£min	£max
Daily	42.50	

Lunch available
Evening meal 1830 (last orders
2130)
Parking for 8
Cards accepted: Amex, Diners,
Mastercard, Visa

For further information on
accommodation establishments
use the coupons at the
back of this guide.

Hertfordshire
Map ref 2D1

As Verulamium this was one of the
largest towns in Roman Britain and
its remains can be seen in the
museum. The Norman cathedral
was built from Roman materials to
commemorate Alban, the first
British Christian martyr.
*Tourist Information Centre ☎ (01727)
864511*

The Apples Hotel

ᗯᗯᗯ COMMENDED

133 London Road, St Albans
AL1 1TA
☎ (01727) 844111
Fax (01727) 861100
ⒸⓇ The Independents
*Family-run hotel in beautiful gardens
within easy reach of city centre, station
and major motorways. Heated
swimming pool. Facilities for disabled.*
Bedrooms: 1 single, 5 double, 3 twin,
1 triple
Bathrooms: 10 en-suite

Bed & breakfast per night:	£min	£max
Single	43.00	50.00
Double	55.00	69.00

Half board per person:	£min	£max
Daily	42.50	49.50

Lunch available
Evening meal 1930 (last orders
2100)
Parking for 10
Cards accepted: Amex, Diners,
Mastercard, Visa, Switch/Delta

Jarvis Aubrey Park Hotel

ᗯᗯᗯ COMMENDED

Hemel Hempstead Road, Redbourn,
St Albans AL3 7AF
☎ (01582) 792105
Fax (01582) 792001
ⒸⓇ Jarvis/Utell International
*Elegant, well-appointed, friendly hotel
set in 6 acres of well-kept gardens and
woodland. Only 25 miles north of
London via the M1.*
Bedrooms: 88 double, 31 twin
Bathrooms: 119 en-suite

Bed & breakfast per night:	£min	£max
Single	50.00	105.00
Double	60.00	115.00

Half board per person:	£min	£max
Daily	40.00	130.00
Weekly	280.00	910.00

Lunch available

Evening meal 1900 (last orders
2145)
Parking for 160
Cards accepted: Amex, Diners,
Mastercard, Visa, Switch/Delta

Sopwell House Hotel and Country Club ♨

ᗯᗯᗯᗯ HIGHLY COMMENDED

Cottonmill Lane, Sopwell, St Albans
AL1 2HQ
☎ (01727) 864477
Fax (01727) 844741
ⒸⓇ Best Western
*Elegant Georgian country house in
rural surroundings only 1 mile from the
city centre. Country club and health
spa with special weekend breaks.*
Bedrooms: 12 single, 60 double,
20 twin, 6 family rooms
Suites available
Bathrooms: 98 en-suite

Bed & breakfast per night:	£min	£max
Single	77.25	124.70
Double	110.25	184.90

Half board per person:	£min	£max
Daily	100.75	198.45

Lunch available
Evening meal 1930 (last orders
2200)
Parking for 200
Cards accepted: Amex, Diners,
Mastercard, Visa, Switch/Delta

Cambridgeshire
Map ref 3A2

Picturesque market town with a
narrow 6-arched bridge spanning
the River Ouse on which stands a
bridge chapel. There are numerous
Georgian and Victorian buildings
and the Norris Museum has a good
local collection.

The Dolphin Hotel ♨

ᗯᗯᗯᗯ COMMENDED

Bridgefoot, London Road, St Ives,
Huntingdon PE17 4EP
☎ (01480) 466966 & 497497
Fax (01480) 495597
*Modern hotel on banks of the River
Great Ouse, with panoramic views
across surrounding meadows. 2
minutes' walk from historic town centre
and just 20 minutes' drive from centre*
Continued ▶

ST IVES

Continued

of Cambridge and the Imperial War Museum at Duxford. Extensive restaurant menus.
Bedrooms: 2 single, 12 double, 31 twin, 2 family rooms
Bathrooms: 47 en-suite
Bed & breakfast per night:

	£min	£max
Single	62.00	65.00
Double	80.00	90.00

Half board per person:

	£min	£max
Daily	78.00	

Lunch available
Evening meal 1900 (last orders 2130)
Parking for 200
Cards accepted: Amex, Diners, Mastercard, Visa

🐴♿📞🖭🖵🕯🍷🎱🎀◑🖩🛄🖊
🍴150 ✦❋✕ SP

The Golden Lion Hotel ⚠

👑👑 APPROVED

Market Hill, St Ives, Huntingdon PE17 4AL
☎ (01480) 492100
Fax (01480) 497109

16th C coaching inn of great historic interest in the town centre. Good facilities for business people and tourists, full a la carte menu. 15 minutes' drive to Cambridge. Weekend rates available.
Bedrooms: 5 single, 9 double, 3 twin, 2 triple, 1 family room
Bathrooms: 20 en-suite
Bed & breakfast per night:

	£min	£max
Single	36.00	41.00
Double	46.00	51.00

Lunch available
Evening meal 1900 (last orders 2200)
Parking for 4
Cards accepted: Diners, Mastercard, Visa

🐴📞🖵🕯🍷S🖾📺🖩🛄🍴15🔦
SP🏠T

Please check prices and other details at the time of booking.

Slepe Hall Hotel ⚠

👑👑👑 COMMENDED

Ramsey Road, St Ives, Huntingdon PE17 4RB
☎ (01480) 463122
Fax (01480) 300706
Former private Victorian girls' school converted in 1966. Now a Grade II listed building, 5 minutes' walk from the River Great Ouse and historic town centre. Extensive bar and restaurant menus.
Bedrooms: 2 single, 4 double, 8 twin, 1 triple
Bathrooms: 15 en-suite
Bed & breakfast per night:

	£min	£max
Single	52.00	67.00
Double	70.00	90.00

Lunch available
Evening meal 1900 (last orders 2130)
Parking for 70
Cards accepted: Amex, Diners, Mastercard, Visa, Switch/Delta

🐴♿📞🖭🖵🕯🍷S🖊✕🖾🛄🖊
🍴200❋🚐 SP🏠T

ST NEOTS

Cambridgeshire
Map ref 2D1

Pleasant market town on the River Ouse with a large square which grew up around a 10th C priory. There are many interesting buildings and St Mary's is one of the largest medieval churches in the county. *Tourist Information Centre ☎ (01480) 388788*

Abbotsley Golf Hotel ⚠

👑👑👑 COMMENDED

Eynesbury, Hardwicke, St Neots, Huntingdon PE19 4XN
☎ (01480) 474000
Fax (01480) 471018
Charming country hotel amidst its own 2 excellent 18-hole golf-courses. Golf Monthly: "The design is a revelation, the presentation superb". Non-golfers just as welcome!
Bedrooms: 2 single, 13 twin, 2 triple
Bathrooms: 17 en-suite
Bed & breakfast per night:

	£min	£max
Single	40.00	40.00
Double	70.00	70.00

Half board per person:

	£min	£max
Daily	55.00	55.00

Lunch available
Evening meal 1930 (last orders 2130)
Parking for 140

Cards accepted: Mastercard, Visa, Switch/Delta

🐴♿📞🖭🖵🕯🍷🎱🍷S🖾📺🖩🛄
🍴60🎣⛳🕺❋❄ SP🏠T

SANDRINGHAM

Norfolk
Map ref 3B1

Famous as the country retreat of Her Majesty the Queen. The house and grounds are open to the public at certain times.

Park House ⚠

👑👑👑 COMMENDED

Sandringham, King's Lynn PE35 6EH
☎ (01485) 543000
Fax (01485) 540663
Country house hotel for people with physical disabilities and their relatives, friends or carers. Full 24-hour care available. Excellent leisure facilities.
Wheelchair access category 1♿
Bedrooms: 8 single, 8 twin
Bathrooms: 16 en-suite, 2 public
Bed & breakfast per night:

	£min	£max
Single	46.00	67.00
Double	74.00	116.00

Half board per person:

	£min	£max
Daily	59.00	80.00
Weekly	345.00	558.00

Lunch available
Evening meal 1830 (last orders 1930)
Parking for 30
Cards accepted: Amex, Mastercard, Visa

🐴♿📞🖭🖵🕯🍷S🖊✕🖾♨🖩🛄
🏊🎣❄✕🚐🐾🏠

SAXMUNDHAM

Suffolk
Map ref 3C2

The church of St John the Baptist has a hammer-beam roof and contains a number of good monuments.

The Bell Hotel

👑👑 APPROVED

High Street, Saxmundham IP17 1AF
☎ (01728) 602331
Fax (01728) 833105
Recently refurbished 18th C coaching inn. The principal building in Saxmundham, a tranquil hamlet town just off the main A12.
Bedrooms: 3 single, 3 double, 6 twin, 1 triple, 1 family room
Bathrooms: 8 en-suite, 1 public, 6 private showers

Bed & breakfast per night:

	£min	£max
Single	25.00	30.00
Double	40.00	45.00

Lunch available
Evening meal 1900 (last orders 2200)
Parking for 20
Cards accepted: Amex, Diners, Mastercard, Visa

🏠🕐📞🖥️ ♨️📺 🖥️ 🅿️🏋️30 🚭 SP 🏨

SHERINGHAM

Norfolk
Map ref 3B1

Holiday resort with Victorian and Edwardian hotels and a sand and shingle beach where the fishing boats are hauled up. The North Norfolk Railway operates from Sheringham station during the summer. Other attractions include museums, theatre and Splash Fun Pool.

The Bay Leaf Guest House
👑 COMMENDED
10 St. Peters Road, Sheringham NR26 8QY
☎ (01263) 823779
Charming Victorian guesthouse with licensed bar, open all year. Conveniently situated in the town. Near golf-course and woodlands, adjacent to steam railway and 5 minutes from sea.
Bedrooms: 2 double, 2 twin, 2 triple
Bathrooms: 6 en-suite

Bed & breakfast per night:

	£min	£max
Single	17.00	22.00
Double	34.00	44.00

Half board per person:

	£min	£max
Daily	24.00	30.00
Weekly	165.00	190.00

Evening meal 1800 (last orders 1930)
Parking for 4
Cards accepted: Mastercard, Visa

🏠8🔥📞🖥️ ♨️📺 🖥️ 🅿️🌸 🏨 DAP SP T

Beaumaris Hotel ⚊
👑👑👑 COMMENDED
15 South Street, Sheringham NR26 8LL
☎ (01263) 822370
Fax (01263) 821421
Family-run hotel established in 1947. Reputation for personal service and English cuisine. Quietly located close to beach, shops and golf club.
Bedrooms: 5 single, 10 double, 7 twin
Bathrooms: 22 en-suite

Bed & breakfast per night:

	£min	£max
Single	30.00	40.00
Double	60.00	80.00

Half board per person:

	£min	£max
Daily	44.00	
Weekly	245.00	320.00

Lunch available
Evening meal 1900 (last orders 2030)
Parking for 20
Open March–December
Cards accepted: Amex, Diners, Mastercard, Visa, Switch/Delta

🏠🔥📞🖥️ ♨️📺 🖥️ 🅿️🌸🚂 SP

Olivedale Guesthouse ⚊
👑👑 COMMENDED
20 Augusta Street, Sheringham NR26 8LA
☎ (01263) 825871
Charming family home, close to town centre, sea and amenities. Ideal base for exploring this beautiful area. All rooms have colour TV, radio/alarm, tea/coffee facilities.
Bedrooms: 1 single, 3 double, 1 twin
Bathrooms: 1 en-suite, 1 private, 1 public

Bed & breakfast per night:

	£min	£max
Single	20.00	24.00
Double	40.00	48.00

Parking for 4

🏠10📞🖥️ ♨️📺 🖥️ 🅿️🍴🚂

Southlands Hotel ⚊
👑👑👑 COMMENDED
South Street, Sheringham NR26 8LL
☎ (01263) 822679
Fax (01263) 822679

Privately owned hotel ideally situated close to town, seafront and golf-courses.
Bedrooms: 2 single, 9 double, 6 twin
Bathrooms: 17 en-suite

Bed & breakfast per night:

	£min	£max
Single	31.00	33.00
Double	62.00	66.00

Half board per person:

	£min	£max
Daily	40.00	42.00
Weekly	252.00	255.00

Lunch available

Evening meal 1845 (last orders 2000)
Parking for 20
Open March–October
Cards accepted: Mastercard, Visa

🏠📞🖥️ ♨️📺 🖥️ 🅿️🏋️120 ♨🌸

SKEGNESS

Lincolnshire
Map ref 4D2

Famous seaside resort with 6 miles of sandy beaches and bracing air. Attractions include swimming pools, bowling greens, gardens, Natureland Marine Zoo, golf-courses and a wide range of entertainment at the Embassy Centre. Nearby is Gibraltar Point Nature Reserve.
Tourist Information Centre ☎ (01754) 764821

Crown Hotel ⚊
Listed COMMENDED
Drummond Road, Skegness PE25 3AB
☎ (01754) 610760
Fax (01754) 610847
A family-run hotel in a quiet part of Skegness, near Gibraltar Point and Seacroft Golf Club.
Bedrooms: 1 single, 4 double, 13 twin, 8 triple, 1 family room
Suite available
Bathrooms: 26 en-suite, 1 private

Bed & breakfast per night:

	£min	£max
Single	40.50	45.00
Double	59.40	66.00

Half board per person:

	£min	£max
Weekly	227.70	253.00

Lunch available
Evening meal 1900 (last orders 2130)
Parking for 80
Cards accepted: Amex, Diners, Mastercard, Visa, Switch/Delta

🏠📞🖥️ ♨️📺 🖥️ 🅿️🏋️180 🌸 SP T

Grosvenor House Hotel ⚊
👑👑 COMMENDED
North Parade, Skegness PE25 2TE
☎ (01754) 763376
Fax (01754) 764650
The hotel is midway along the seafront, near the bathing pool, bowling greens, Sun Castle and the Embassy Conference Centre.
Bedrooms: 9 single, 9 double, 3 twin, 11 triple, 1 family room
Bathrooms: 23 en-suite, 4 public

SKEGNESS
Continued

Bed & breakfast per night:

	£min	£max
Single	23.60	30.45
Double	47.20	60.90

Half board per person:

	£min	£max
Daily	32.55	39.90
Weekly	201.60	238.35

Lunch available
Evening meal 1830 (last orders 1915)
Parking for 6
Open April–October
Cards accepted: Amex, Diners, Mastercard, Visa

Saxby Hotel ♙
COMMENDED
12 Saxby Avenue, Skegness
PE25 3LG
☎ (01754) 763905
Fax (01754) 763905
Family-run hotel on a corner in a quiet residential area of Skegness. 300 yards from seafront and close to all amenities.
Wheelchair access category 3
Bedrooms: 1 single, 10 double, 2 twin, 2 triple
Bathrooms: 11 en-suite, 2 public

Bed & breakfast per night:

	£min	£max
Single	25.00	26.00
Double	50.00	52.00

Half board per person:

	£min	£max
Daily	32.00	33.00
Weekly	161.00	170.00

Lunch available
Evening meal 1800 (last orders 1900)
Parking for 8
Cards accepted: Amex, Diners, Mastercard, Visa, Switch/Delta

The Vine ♙
COMMENDED
Vine Road, Seacroft, Skegness
PE25 3DB
☎ (01754) 610611 & 763018
Fax (01754) 769845

Attractive, detached brick-built property in this popular seaside resort.
Bedrooms: 3 single, 10 double, 3 twin, 4 triple, 1 family room
Bathrooms: 20 en-suite, 1 private shower

Bed & breakfast per night:

	£min	£max
Single	45.00	55.00
Double	65.00	75.00

Half board per person:

	£min	£max
Daily	55.00	65.00

Lunch available
Evening meal 1900 (last orders 2100)
Parking for 40
Cards accepted: Amex, Diners, Mastercard, Visa, Switch/Delta

SLEAFORD
Lincolnshire
Map ref 3A1

Market town whose parish church has one of the oldest stone spires in England and particularly fine tracery round the windows.
Tourist Information Centre ☎ (01529) 414294

The Lincolnshire Oak Hotel ♙
COMMENDED
East Road, Sleaford NG34 7EH
☎ (01529) 413807
Fax (01529) 413710
Situated on the edge of a market town, this comfortable hotel offers an ideal central base for exploring Lincolnshire. Excellent food and wines.
Bedrooms: 5 single, 7 double, 2 twin
Bathrooms: 14 en-suite

Bed & breakfast per night:

	£min	£max
Single	45.00	47.00
Double	59.00	65.00

Half board per person:

	£min	£max
Daily	39.00	63.00
Weekly	273.00	441.00

Lunch available
Evening meal 1900 (last orders 2100)
Parking for 60
Cards accepted: Amex, Mastercard, Visa, Switch/Delta

The Tally Ho Inn
COMMENDED
Aswarby, Sleaford NG34 8SA
☎ (01529) 455205

Traditional, friendly 17th C listed country inn. En-suite rooms in carefully converted stables, a la carte restaurant and bar meals. Plenty of welcoming atmosphere and character.
Bedrooms: 2 double, 4 twin
Bathrooms: 6 en-suite

Bed & breakfast per night:

	£min	£max
Single	30.00	33.00
Double	45.00	50.00

Lunch available
Evening meal 1900 (last orders 2200)
Parking for 50
Cards accepted: Mastercard, Visa, Switch/Delta

SOUTHEND-ON-SEA
Essex
Map ref 3B3

On the Thames Estuary and the nearest seaside resort to London. Famous for its pier and unique pier trains. Other attractions include Peter Pan's Playground, indoor swimming pools, indoor rollerskating and ten pin bowling.
Tourist Information Centre ☎ (01702) 215120

Balmoral Hotel
COMMENDED
32-36 Valkyrie Road,
Southend-on-Sea SSO 8BU
☎ (01702) 342947
Fax (01702) 337828
Highly appealing hotel, designer furnished in 1995. En-suite rooms, excellent bar, restaurant, 24-hour service. Near station, buses, shops and sea. Secure parking.
Bedrooms: 10 single, 13 double, 6 twin
Suite available
Bathrooms: 29 en-suite

Bed & breakfast per night:

	£min	£max
Single	39.00	80.00
Double	60.00	80.00

Half board per person:

	£min	£max
Daily	48.95	
Weekly	308.00	

Lunch available
Evening meal 1830 (last orders 2130)
Parking for 28
Cards accepted: Amex, Mastercard, Visa, Switch/Delta

Haven House Hotel

APPROVED

47 Heygate Avenue,
Southend-on-Sea SS1 2AN
☎ (01702) 619246
Central location, modern building, car park.
Bedrooms: 2 single, 2 double, 4 twin, 1 triple
Bathrooms: 1 public, 9 private showers

Bed & breakfast

per night:	£min	£max
Single	19.00	
Double	30.00	32.00

Parking for 5

Roslin Hotel M

COMMENDED

Thorpe Esplanade, Thorpe Bay,
Southend-on-Sea SS1 3BG
☎ (01702) 586375
Fax (01702) 586663

Hotel overlooking the Thames Estuary in residential Thorpe Bay. Within easy reach of Southend and 45 minutes from London.
Bedrooms: 16 single, 8 double, 10 twin, 4 triple
Bathrooms: 38 en-suite

Bed & breakfast

per night:	£min	£max
Single	42.00	59.00
Double	60.00	70.00

Lunch available
Evening meal 1830 (last orders 2200)
Parking for 34
Cards accepted: Amex, Diners, Mastercard, Visa, Switch/Delta

Tower Hotel and Restaurant

APPROVED

146 Alexandra Road,
Southend-on-Sea SS1 1HE
☎ (01702) 348635
Fax (01702) 433044
The Independents
Restored Victorian hotel in conservation area, 10 minutes' walk from Cliff Gardens, the sea, Cliffs Pavilion Theatre, High Street and British Rail.
Bedrooms: 12 single, 14 double, 2 twin, 2 triple, 1 family room
Bathrooms: 31 en-suite, 1 public

Bed & breakfast

per night:	£min	£max
Single	36.00	43.00
Double	50.00	65.00

Half board per

person:	£min	£max
Daily	33.00	50.00
Weekly	200.00	350.00

Lunch available
Evening meal 1800 (last orders 2200)
Parking for 3
Cards accepted: Amex, Diners, Mastercard, Visa, Switch/Delta

SOUTHWOLD

Suffolk
Map ref 3C2

Pleasant and attractive seaside town with a triangular market square and spacious greens around which stand flint, brick and colour-washed cottages. The parish church of St Edmund is one of the greatest churches in Suffolk.

The Angel Inn

COMMENDED

39 High Street, Wangford, Beccles
NR34 8RL
☎ (01502) 578636
Fax (01502) 578535

16th C, Grade II listed village inn, carefully renovated in 1995, with log fires and en-suite rooms.
Bedrooms: 4 double, 1 family room
Bathrooms: 5 en-suite

Bed & breakfast

per night:	£min	£max
Single	40.00	40.00
Double	49.00	58.00

Half board per

person:	£min	£max
Daily	25.00	30.00

Lunch available
Evening meal 1800 (last orders 2200)
Parking for 30
Cards accepted: Amex, Diners, Mastercard, Visa, Switch/Delta

SPALDING

Lincolnshire
Map ref 3A1

Fenland town famous for its bulbfields. A spectacular Flower Parade takes place at the beginning of May each year and the tulips at Springfields show gardens are followed by displays of roses and bedding plants in summer. Interesting local museum.
Tourist Information Centre ☎ (01775) 725468 or 761161

Cley Hall Hotel M

COMMENDED

22 High Street, Spalding PE11 1TX
☎ (01775) 725157
Fax (01775) 710785
Georgian manor house by the River Welland, 500 metres from town centre, with unique candlelit cellar restaurant. Own car park.
Bedrooms: 6 single, 3 double, 2 twin
Bathrooms: 11 en-suite

Bed & breakfast

per night:	£min	£max
Single	30.00	48.00
Double	50.00	60.00

Half board per

person:	£min	£max
Daily	40.00	58.00

Lunch available
Evening meal 1900 (last orders 2130)
Parking for 20
Cards accepted: Amex, Diners, Mastercard, Visa, Switch/Delta

Travel Stop M

APPROVED

Locks Mill Farm, 50 Cowbit Road,
Spalding PE11 2RJ
☎ (01775) 767290 & 767716
Fax (01775) 767716
Converted from farm buildings, the motel complements the 17th C farmhouse. Three-quarters of a mile from centre of Spalding on A1073 Peterborough road. Most units are on ground floor with own porches and all are equipped with refrigerator and colour TV.
Bedrooms: 3 single, 5 double, 2 twin
Bathrooms: 10 en-suite, 2 public

Bed & breakfast

per night:	£min	£max
Single	25.00	45.00
Double	35.00	70.00

Continued ▶

SPALDING

Continued

Parking for 25
Cards accepted: Amex, Mastercard, Visa

🐎♿🚪📞🖤🌸♠📺🛏🧺♨️🍴🐾🖤📺🛏⬛
🛏🕯️☼❄OAP SP 🏠 T

STAMFORD

Lincolnshire
Map ref 3A1

Exceptionally beautiful and historic town with many houses of architectural interest, several notable churches and other public buildings all in the local stone. Burghley House, built by William Cecil, is a magnificent Tudor mansion on the edge of the town.
Tourist Information Centre ☎ *(01780) 755611*

Abbey House and Coach House ⋀

👑👑 COMMENDED

West End Road, Maxey, Peterborough PE6 9EJ
☎ (01778) 344642

Grade II listed former rectory, dating in part from 1190 AD, located in quiet, predominantly stone, village east of Stamford. Attractive gardens. Ideal for touring the Eastern Shires.
Bedrooms: 1 single, 4 double, 3 twin, 1 triple, 1 family room
Bathrooms: 10 en-suite, 1 public
Bed & breakfast

per night:	£min	£max
Single	23.00	34.00
Double	38.00	49.00

Parking for 12

🐎6♿📞🛏♨🛡♠️♨️📺🛏
🖤🍴☼✕🐾🏠

Dolphin Guesthouse ⋀

👑 APPROVED

12 East Street, Stamford PE9 1QD
☎ (01780) 755494 & 757515
Fax (01780) 757515
En-suite accommodation next to the Dolphin Inn, renowned for its cask ales, friendliness and food. Off-road secure car parking and only 100 yards from the town centre.
Bedrooms: 4 double, 3 twin, 1 triple, 1 family room
Suites available
Bathrooms: 7 en-suite, 1 public
Bed & breakfast

per night:	£min	£max
Single	18.00	25.00
Double	36.00	40.00

Lunch available
Evening meal 1800 (last orders 2130)
Parking for 5
Cards accepted: Mastercard, Visa, Switch/Delta

🐎♿🚪📞🛏♨🛡♠️♨️📺🛏⬛
🍴30☼🐾🖤 SP T

Garden House Hotel ⋀

👑👑👑 COMMENDED

St Martins, Stamford PE9 2LP
☎ (01780) 763359
Fax (01780) 763339
CR Minotel

Charming 18th C town house converted to a hotel, where guests are treated as such by their hosts. Features a conservatory full of floral extravaganza and a meandering garden of 1 acre.
Wheelchair access category 3🚶
Bedrooms: 2 single, 9 double, 8 twin, 1 triple
Bathrooms: 20 en-suite
Bed & breakfast

per night:	£min	£max
Single	45.00	65.00
Double	65.00	85.00

Half board per person:

	£min	£max
Daily	45.00	55.00

Lunch available
Evening meal 1900 (last orders 2130)
Parking for 25
Cards accepted: Amex, Mastercard, Visa, Switch/Delta

🐎♿🚪📞📞🛏♨🛡♠️🛏⬛⬛
🍴40☼🐾🖤 SP 🏠 ◎

The Priory ⋀

👑👑👑 HIGHLY COMMENDED

Church Road, Ketton, Stamford PE9 3RD
☎ (01780) 720215
Fax (01780) 721881
Email: Priory.a0504924 @infotrade.co.uk

Listed 16th C country house in peaceful setting. Award- winning bed and breakfast. En-suite rooms with every comfort overlook splendid gardens. Resident chef. Choice of menus. Brochure available.
www.rutland-on-line.co.uk/Priory
Bedrooms: 2 double, 1 twin
Bathrooms: 3 en-suite
Bed & breakfast

per night:	£min	£max
Single	55.00	58.00
Double	69.00	80.00

Half board per person:

	£min	£max
Daily	54.00	59.50
Weekly	334.00	369.00

Lunch available
Evening meal 1900 (last orders 2000)
Parking for 10
Cards accepted: Mastercard, Visa

🐎📞🚪📞🛏♨🛡♠️♨️📺🛏⬛
🍴12🖤🌸☼✕🐾 SP 🏠 T

STOKE-BY-NAYLAND

Suffolk
Map ref 3B2

Picturesque village with a fine group of half-timbered cottages near the church of St Mary, the tower of which was one of Constable's favourite subjects. In School Street are the Guildhall and the Maltings, both 16th C timber-framed buildings.

The Angel Inn ⋀

👑👑👑 HIGHLY COMMENDED

Polstead Street, Stoke-by-Nayland, Colchester CO6 4SA
☎ (01206) 263245
Fax (01206) 263373
Beautifully restored freehouse and restaurant in the historic village of Stoke-by-Nayland, in the heart of Constable country.
Bedrooms: 5 double, 1 twin
Bathrooms: 6 en-suite

Bed & breakfast per night:	£min	£max
Single	46.00	46.00
Double	59.50	59.50

Lunch available
Evening meal 1830 (last orders 2100)
Parking for 25
Cards accepted: Amex, Diners, Mastercard, Visa, Switch/Delta
☎10 ♿ ℂ ☐ ⬥ 🖐 🅸 Ⓢ ⭤ ⬛ ✕ 🚲
🏠 Ⓣ

STOWMARKET

Suffolk
Map ref 3B2

Small market town where routes converge. There is an open-air museum of rural life at the Museum of East Anglian Life.
Tourist Information Centre ☎ (01449) 676800

Cedars Hotel 🏔

☗☗☗ COMMENDED

Needham Road, Stowmarket
IP14 2AJ
☎ (01449) 612668
Fax (01449) 674704
Ⓡ The Independents
Originally a 16th C farmhouse, now a family-run hotel, ideal for those wishing to tour Suffolk. Good food available in comfortable, informal atmosphere. Ample parking.
Bedrooms: 5 single, 13 double, 4 twin, 1 family room
Bathrooms: 23 en-suite

Bed & breakfast per night:	£min	£max
Single	42.00	45.00
Double	47.00	50.00

Lunch available
Evening meal 1900 (last orders 2130)
Parking for 80
Cards accepted: Amex, Diners, Mastercard, Visa, Switch/Delta
☎ ♿ ℂ ▣ ☐ ⬥ 🖐 🅸 Ⓢ ⭤ ⬛ 🍴150
❄ SP 🏠

TITCHWELL

Norfolk
Map ref 3B1

Briarfields

☗☗☗ COMMENDED

Main Street, Titchwell, King's Lynn
PE31 8BB
☎ (01485) 210742
Fax (01485) 210933

Traditional, privately owned hotel, overlooking Titchwell RSPB Reserve, salt marshes and beaches. Renowned for comfort and excellent menus. Ideally situated for birdwatching, beach walking, golf or visiting places of local interest. Special breaks all-year-round.
Bedrooms: 10 double, 5 twin, 2 family rooms
Bathrooms: 17 en-suite

Bed & breakfast per night:	£min	£max
Single	35.50	
Double	66.00	

Half board per person:	£min	£max
Daily	47.95	
Weekly	296.00	

Lunch available
Evening meal 1845 (last orders 2100)
Parking for 40
Cards accepted: Mastercard, Visa, Switch/Delta
☎ ♿ 🔔 ℂ ☐ ⬥ 🖐 🅸 Ⓢ ⭤ 🅿 📺 ⬛
⬛ 🍴25 ⛳ ❄ ✕ ❄ SP Ⓣ

TIVETSHALL ST MARY

Norfolk
Map ref 3B2

The Old Ram Coaching Inn

☗☗☗ HIGHLY COMMENDED

Ipswich Road, Tivetshall St Mary,
Norwich NR15 2DE
☎ (01379) 676794
Fax (01379) 608399
17th C coaching inn (15 miles south of Norwich) with oak beams and log fires. En-suite accommodation, extensive menu.
Bedrooms: 8 double, 2 family rooms
Bathrooms: 10 en-suite

Bed & breakfast per night:	£min	£max
Single	49.00	51.50
Double	68.00	70.50

Lunch available
Evening meal 1700 (last orders 2200)
Parking for 150
Cards accepted: Mastercard, Visa, Switch/Delta
☎ ♿ ℂ ▣ ☐ ⬥ 🖐 🅸 Ⓢ ⭤ 🅿 ◑ ⬛
⬛ 🍴 ⛳ ❄ ✕ ❄ DAP ❄ SP 🏠

UPWELL

Cambridgeshire
Map ref 3A1

The Olde Mill Hotel 🏔

☗☗☗ APPROVED

Town Street, Upwell, Wisbech
PE14 9AF
☎ (01945) 772614
Fax (01945) 772614

Converted mill which has been tastefully extended. In a small town on the outskirts of Wisbech, providing a good base for touring the Fens. Close to Norfolk coast. Minimum B&B prices below do not include breakfast.
Bedrooms: 3 double, 1 twin, 3 triple
Bathrooms: 7 en-suite

Bed & breakfast per night:	£min	£max
Single	25.00	31.00
Double	40.00	52.00

Half board per person:	£min	£max
Daily	41.00	50.00
Weekly	275.00	300.00

Lunch available
Evening meal 1830 (last orders 2145)
Parking for 150
Cards accepted: Amex, Diners, Mastercard, Visa, Switch/Delta
☎ ☐ ⬥ 🖐 🅸 Ⓢ ⭤ 🅿 📺 ⬛ ⬛ 🍴50
🎵 ❄ DAP ❄ SP 🏠

The symbols in each entry give information about services and facilities. A key to these symbols appears at the back of this guide.

National gradings and classifications were correct at the time of going to press but are subject to change. Please check at the time of booking.

WELLS-NEXT-THE-SEA

Norfolk
Map ref 3B1

Seaside resort and small port on the north coast. The Buttlands is a large tree-lined green surrounded by Georgian houses and from here narrow streets lead to the quay.

Crown Hotel ⚜

👑👑👑 APPROVED

The Buttlands, Wells-next-the-Sea NR23 1EX
☎ (01328) 710209
Fax (01328) 711432
Famous old coaching inn set amongst Norfolk's finest coastal scenery.
Bedrooms: 1 single, 6 double, 4 twin, 3 triple, 1 family room
Bathrooms: 11 en-suite, 1 public
Bed & breakfast

per night:	£min	£max
Single	45.00	55.00
Double	60.00	70.00

Lunch available
Evening meal 1900 (last orders 2130)
Parking for 10
Cards accepted: Amex, Diners, Mastercard, Visa

🛏📞💷🖵📺♿️🛋⬛📶Ⓢ📺▥🖨🅿🐾
⬛ SP 🏤

The Normans

👑👑 COMMENDED

Invaders Court, Standard Road, Wells-next-the-Sea NR23 1JW
☎ (01328) 710657
Fax (01328) 710468

Listed Georgian house 100 yards from the quay. All rooms en-suite with colour TV and tea/coffee. Some rooms have views over saltmarshes to the sea. Dogs welcome.
Bedrooms: 5 double, 1 twin, 1 triple
Bathrooms: 7 en-suite, 1 public
Bed & breakfast

per night:	£min	£max
Single	30.00	30.00
Double	40.00	55.00

Parking for 12

🛏📺10🖵♿️🛋Ⓢ✂🛏📺▥🖨
🐾 SP 🏤

WEST MERSEA

Essex
Map ref 3B3

Weatherboarded and Georgian brick cottages still remain as evidence of the old fishing, oyster and sailing centre and the small museum includes fishing exhibits.

The Blackwater Hotel and Restaurant Le Champagne ⚜

👑👑 HIGHLY COMMENDED

20-22 Church Road, West Mersea, Colchester CO5 8QH
☎ (01206) 383338
Fax (01206) 383038
Originally a Victorian coaching inn, located in the heart of the village close to West Mersea beach.
Bedrooms: 1 single, 5 double, 3 twin
Bathrooms: 6 en-suite, 3 private
Bed & breakfast

per night:	£min	£max
Single	50.00	70.00
Double	60.00	80.00

Half board per person:	£min	£max
Daily	64.00	84.00
Weekly	308.00	588.00

Lunch available
Evening meal 1800 (last orders 2200)
Parking for 12
Open February–December
Cards accepted: Amex, Mastercard, Visa, Switch/Delta

🛏📞💷🖵♿️Ⓢ🛏▥🖨🍽25∪ﬞ
☀🚗🐾 SP 🆃

WHITTLESFORD

Cambridgeshire
Map ref 2D1

Red Lion Hotel ⚜

👑👑 APPROVED

Station Road East, Whittlesford, Cambridge CB2 4NL
☎ (01223) 832047 & 832115
Fax (01223) 837576
Traditional 13th C English inn with modern facilities. Well situated for Cambridge with excellent road and rail connections. 1 mile from Duxford Imperial War Museum.
Bedrooms: 7 single, 6 double, 1 twin, 2 triple, 2 family rooms
Bathrooms: 18 en-suite
Bed & breakfast

per night:	£min	£max
Single	35.00	39.00
Double	49.00	54.00

Lunch available
Evening meal 1900 (last orders 2130)
Parking for 75

Cards accepted: Amex, Diners, Mastercard, Visa, Switch/Delta

🛏📪📞💷🖵♿️🛏Ⓢ✂🛏▥🖨
🍽80🔍☀🚗 DAP SP 🏤 🆃

WIX

Essex
Map ref 3B2

New Farm House ⚜

👑👑👑 COMMENDED

Spinnell's Lane, Wix, Manningtree CO11 2UJ
☎ (01255) 870365
Fax (01255) 870837

Modern comfortable farmhouse in large garden, 10 minutes' drive to Harwich and convenient for Constable country. From Wix village crossroads, take Bradfield Road, turn right at top of hill; first house on left.
Bedrooms: 3 single, 1 double, 3 twin, 5 family rooms
Bathrooms: 7 en-suite, 2 public
Bed & breakfast

per night:	£min	£max
Single	22.00	26.00
Double	42.00	45.00

Half board per person:	£min	£max
Daily	35.00	39.00

Evening meal 1830 (last orders 1730)
Parking for 18
Cards accepted: Amex, Mastercard, Visa

🛏♿️💷🖵♿️Ⓢ✂🛏📺▥🖨🍽
☀🐾

All accommodation in this guide has been graded, or is awaiting a grading, by a trained Tourist Board inspector.

ACCESSIBILITY

Look for the 👩‍🦽🚶‍♂️♿️ symbols which indicate accessibility for wheelchair users. These are described in detail at the front of this guide.

WOODBRIDGE

Suffolk
Map ref 3C2

Once a busy seaport, the town is now a sailing centre on the River Deben. There are many buildings of architectural merit including the Bell and Angel Inns. The 18th C Tide Mill is now restored and open to the public.
Tourist Information Centre ☎ (01394) 382240

Seckford Hall Hotel ⚞

☗☗☗☗☗ HIGHLY COMMENDED

Woodbridge IP13 6NU
☎ (01394) 385678
Fax (01394) 380610
Elizabethan country house hotel with four-poster beds, spa baths, indoor heated swimming pool and 18-hole golf-course. Excellent cuisine in 2 restaurants.
Bedrooms: 3 single, 14 double, 10 twin, 1 triple, 4 family rooms
Suites available
Bathrooms: 32 en-suite
Bed & breakfast
per night:

	£min	£max
Single	79.00	115.00
Double	110.00	150.00

Lunch available
Evening meal 1915 (last orders 2130)
Parking for 102
Cards accepted: Amex, Diners, Mastercard, Visa

WOODHALL SPA

Lincolnshire
Map ref 4D2

Attractive town which was formerly a spa. It has excellent sporting facilities with a championship golf-course and is surrounded by pine woods.

Claremont Guesthouse ⚞

☗☗ APPROVED

9-11 Witham Road, Woodhall Spa LN10 6RW
☎ (01526) 352000
Homely B&B in unspoilt Victorian guesthouse within easy reach of the town's sporting and leisure facilities. All rooms have TV and tea/coffee making facilities. Off-street car parking, garden for use of guests.
Bedrooms: 2 single, 1 double, 1 twin, 4 triple, 1 family room
Bathrooms: 2 en-suite, 1 private, 2 public

Bed & breakfast
per night:

	£min	£max
Single	15.00	20.00
Double	30.00	40.00

Evening meal from 1800
Parking for 6

Eagle Lodge Hotel ⚞

☗☗☗ APPROVED

The Broadway, Woodhall Spa LN10 6ST
☎ (01526) 353231
Fax (01526) 352797
Mock Tudor country house hotel, close to many good golf-courses and a short drive from Lincoln, Boston and the East Coast. Good food, real ales and a good atmosphere.
Bedrooms: 5 single, 7 double, 9 twin, 1 triple, 1 family room
Bathrooms: 22 en-suite, 1 private
Bed & breakfast
per night:

	£min	£max
Single	25.00	39.50
Double	44.00	60.00

Half board per person:

	£min	£max
Daily	28.00	35.00

Lunch available
Evening meal 1900 (last orders 2130)
Parking for 28
Cards accepted: Amex, Diners, Mastercard, Visa, Switch/Delta

Pitchaway Guesthouse

☗☗ COMMENDED

The Broadway, Woodhall Spa LN10 6SQ
☎ (01526) 352969
A warm welcome, home cooking and personal service await you at this family-run guesthouse. Close to the golf links, recreation park and wooded walks.
Bedrooms: 2 single, 1 double, 2 twin, 1 triple, 1 family room
Bathrooms: 2 en-suite, 2 public
Bed & breakfast
per night:

	£min	£max
Single	16.00	
Double	32.00	36.00

Half board per person:

	£min	£max
Daily	24.00	

Lunch available
Evening meal 1930 (last orders 0900)
Parking for 8

WROXHAM

Norfolk
Map ref 3C1

Yachting centre on the River Bure which houses the headquarters of the Norfolk Broads Yacht Club. The church of St Mary has a famous doorway and the manor house nearby dates back to 1623.

The Broads Hotel ⚞

☗☗☗☗ COMMENDED

Station Road, Wroxham, Norwich NR12 8UR
☎ (01603) 782869
Fax (01603) 784066
Family hotel in the heart of Broadland, 2 minutes from shops, boat hire and fishing. Ideal touring base for the coast and the city of Norwich.
Bedrooms: 7 single, 17 double, 3 twin, 1 family room
Bathrooms: 28 private
Bed & breakfast
per night:

	£min	£max
Single	35.00	40.00
Double	52.00	62.00

Half board per person:

	£min	£max
Daily	45.00	50.00
Weekly	280.00	310.00

Lunch available
Evening meal 1900 (last orders 2130)
Parking for 40
Cards accepted: Amex, Diners, Mastercard, Visa

Information on accommodation listed in this guide has been supplied by the proprietors. As changes may occur you are advised to check details at the time of booking.

The symbols in each entry give information about services and facilities. A key to these symbols appears at the back of this guide.

WYMONDHAM

Norfolk
Map ref 3B1

Thriving historic market town of charm and architectural interest. The octagonal market cross, 12th C abbey and 15th C Green Dragon inn blend with streetscapes spanning three centuries. An excellent touring base.

Abbey Hotel

COMMENDED

10 Church Street, Wymondham
NR18 0PH
☎ (01953) 602148
Fax (01953) 606247
CR Best Western

Quiet location opposite 12th C abbey. Character Victorian town house with friendly, relaxed atmosphere. Proprietor-run with high rate of repeat business.

Bedrooms: 3 single, 10 double, 9 twin, 1 triple
Bathrooms: 23 en-suite

Bed & breakfast per night:

	£min	£max
Single	55.00	60.00
Double	75.00	88.00

Half board per person:

	£min	£max
Daily	71.00	76.00
Weekly	215.00	260.00

Lunch available
Evening meal 1900 (last orders 2130)
Parking for 4
Cards accepted: Amex, Diners, Mastercard, Visa, Switch/Delta

🛇🛏🕭📞🖃📺🗔👃🔌🛎🆂🎍🎲🖳🝙
🍴40🅿🗇 🆂🅿🏛🆃

Wymondham Consort Hotel ♔

COMMENDED

28 Market Street, Wymondham
NR18 0BB
☎ (01953) 606721
Fax (01953) 601361
CR Consort

Totally refurbished. Restaurant award. Walled gardens and secure private car parking.
Bedrooms: 5 single, 9 double, 5 twin, 1 triple
Bathrooms: 20 en-suite

Bed & breakfast per night:

	£min	£max
Single	45.00	55.00
Double	60.00	68.00

Half board per person:

	£min	£max
Daily	46.00	50.00

Lunch available
Evening meal 1900 (last orders 2130)
Parking for 16
Cards accepted: Amex, Diners, Mastercard, Visa, Switch/Delta

🛇🛏🕭📞🖃📺👃🔌🛎🆂🗲🖳📺
🌓🖳🛥🍴30🅿✳🌸🗇 DAP🆂🏛🆃

AT-A-GLANCE SYMBOLS

Symbols at the end of each accommodation entry give useful information about services and facilities. A key to symbols can be found inside the back cover flap.

Keep this open for easy reference.

ENQUIRY COUPONS

To help you obtain further information about advertisers and accommodation featured in this guide you will find enquiry coupons at the back. Send these directly to the establishments in which you are interested. Remember to complete both sides of the coupon.

WEST COUNTRY

Go west for an area of natural beauty that's rich in history, legend and perhaps magic too. Land's End, vast Exmoor and Dartmoor, Tintagel, home of King Arthur, and prehistoric Stonehenge wait to be explored. Thatched cottages, coastal artists' colonies, and elegant cities like Bath or Wells are typical of this unspoilt area.

Spring comes early to the delightful Isles of Scilly, while the magnificent coastline of Devon and Cornwall is home to beach resorts as well as tiny, sheltered coves and, for the adventurous, the best surfing in the country.

For the true flavour of the west, don't forget those tasty local delights - Devon cream, scrumpy and Cheddar cheese.

The counties of Bath and North East Somerset, Bristol, Cornwall, Devon, Dorset (Western), Isles of Scilly, North Somerset, Somerset, South Gloucestershire and Wiltshire

FOR MORE INFORMATION CONTACT:
West Country Tourist Board
60 St Davids Hill, Exeter EX4 4SY
Tel: (01392) 425426 **Fax:** (01392) 420891
Email: post@wctb.co.uk

Where to Go in the West Country – see pages 344-348
Where to Stay in the West Country – see pages 349-434

WEST COUNTRY

Where to Go and What to See

You will find hundreds of interesting places to visit during your stay in the West Country, just some of which are listed in these pages. The number against each name will help you locate it on the map (pages 346-347). Contact any Tourist Information Centre in the region for more ideas on days out in the West Country.

1 Sheldon Manor
Chippenham,
Wiltshire SN14 0RG
Tel: (01249) 653120
Ancient manor house with fine example of 13thC porch. Early English oak furniture and Nailsea glass. A 15thC detached chapel and connoisseur gardens.

2 Bowood House & Gardens
Calne,
Wiltshire SN11 OLZ
Tel: (01249) 812102
An 18thC house by Robert Adam with collections of paintings, watercolours, Victoriana, Indiana and porcelain. Landscaped park with lake, terraces, waterfall and grottos.

3 The Exploratory Hands-on Science Centre
Bristol Old Station,
Temple Meads,
Bristol BS1 6QU
Tel: (0117) 907 9000
Exhibition of lights, lenses, lasers, bubbles, bridges, illusions, gyroscopes and much more all housed in Brunel's original engine shed and drawing office.

4 Harveys Wine Museum
12 Denmark Street,
Bristol BS1 5DQ
Tel: (0117) 9275036
Wine museum in original 13thC cellars displaying artefacts connected with the production and enjoyment of wines, especially glass, silver and corkscrews.

5 Museum of Costume
Assembly Rooms,
Bennett Street, Bath BA1 2QH
Tel: (01225) 477789
Displays of fashionable dress for men, women and children, from 16thC to present day.

6 Roman Baths Museum
Pump Room,
Abbey Church Yard,
Bath BA1 1LZ
Tel: (01225) 477000/477785
Roman baths and temple precinct, hot springs and Roman temple. Jewellery, coins, curses and votive offerings from the sacred spring.

7 Weston-super-Mare Sea Life Centre
Marine Parade,
Weston-super-Mare BS23 1BE
Tel: (01934) 641603
All aspects of British marine life housed on Britain's first pier for 85 years.

8 Rode Bird Gardens
Rode, Bath,
Somerset BA3 6QW
Tel: (01373) 830326
Hundreds of exotic birds in lovely natural surroundings, 17 acres of woodland, gardens, lakes, children's play area, pets corner, clematis collection. Miniature steam railway.

9 Wookey Hole Caves and Papermill
Wookey Hole, Wells,
Somerset BA5 1BB
Tel: (01749) 672243
Spectacular caves and legendary home of the Witch of Wookey. Working Victorian papermill including Fairground Memories, Old Penny Arcade, Magical Mirror Maze and Cave Diving Museum.

10 Wells Cathedral
Wells
Somerset BA5 2PA
Tel: (01749) 674483
Dating from the 12thC and built in the Early English Gothic style. Magnificent West Front with 296 medieval groups of sculpture. Chapter House and Lady Chapel.

11 Longleat
Warminster,
Wiltshire BA12 7NW
Tel: (01985) 844400
Great Elizabethan house with lived-in atmosphere. Important libraries and Italian ceilings. Capability Brown designed parkland. Safari Park.

12 Stonehenge
Amesbury, Salisbury,
Wiltshire SP4 7DE
Tel: (01980) 23108/624715
World famous pre-historic monument built as a ceremonial centre. Started 5,000 years ago and remodelled several times.

13 Wilton House
Wilton, Salisbury,
Wiltshire SP2 0BJ
Tel: (01722) 743115
Home of the Earls of Pembroke for nearly 450 years. Famous Double and Single Cube rooms. Art collection. Adventure playground. Woodland walk. Wareham Bears.

14 Clarks Village
Farm Road, Street,
Somerset BA16 0BB
Tel: (01458) 840064
Factory shopping village including over 40 high street name outlets plus a variety of attractions including shoe museum, landscaped walkways, children's play area, pottery, studio.

15 Cannington College Heritage Gardens and Plant Centre
Cannington, Bridgwater,
Somerset TA5 2LS
Tel: (01278) 652226
The gardens have been established for 75 years and house extensive plant collections including eight national collections. Glasshouses open to visitors.

16 Sheppy's Cider Farm Centre
Three Bridges,
Bradford-on-Tone, Taunton,
Somerset TA4 1ER
Tel: (01823) 461233
Wander through orchards, visit the press room and farm/cider museum. Three farm trails. Children's play area. Licensed tea room open in season.

17 Fleet Air Arm Museum
Royal Naval Air Station,
Yeovilton, Ilchester,
Somerset BA22 8HT
Tel: (01935) 840565
Forty historic naval aircraft, displays, models, uniforms and other artefacts. Concorde, WWI, WWII, Wrens, Kamikaze, Harrier, Korea and Aircraft Carrier exhibitions.

18 Clovelly Village
Clovelly, Bideford,
Devon EX39 5SY
Tel: (01237) 431200/431781
Unspoilt fishing village on North Devon coast with steep cobbled street and no vehicular access. Donkeys and sledges are the only means of transport.

19 Rosemoor Garden
Rosemoor, Torrington,
Devon EX38 8PH
Tel: (01805) 624067
Royal Horticultural Society garden with trees, shrubs, roses, alpines and arboretum. Nursery of uncommon and rare plants. Eight acres being expanded to 40 acres.

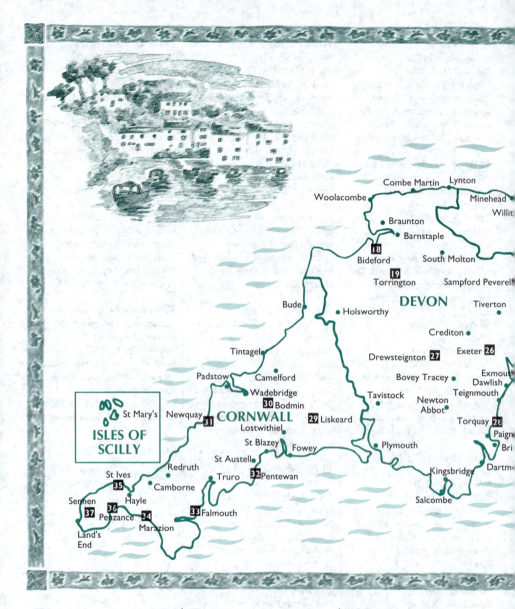

Combe Martin
Lynton
Minehead
Willit
Woolacombe
Braunton
Barnstaple
18
Bideford
South Molton
19
Torrington
Sampford Peverel
DEVON
Tiverton
Bude
Holsworthy
Crediton
Tintagel
Drewsteignton **27**
Exeter **26**
Padstow
Camelford
Bovey Tracey
Exmout
Dawlish
Wadebridge
Tavistock
Teignmouth
30 Bodmin
Newton
Abbot
Torquay **28**
St Mary's
Newquay
31
CORNWALL
29 Liskeard
Paign
Lostwithiel
Bri
**ISLES OF
SCILLY**
St Blazey
Fowey
Plymouth
St Austell
Dartm
Redruth
Truro
32 Pentewan
Kingsbridge
St Ives
Camborne
35
Sennen
Hayle
Salcombe
37
36
Penzance
34
33 Falmouth
Land's
End
Marazion

GLOUCESTER-SHIRE

OXFORDSHIRE

Portishead

Chipping Sodbury
SOUTH GLOUCESTERSHIRE

• Malmesbury

• Wootton Bassett

Swindon

BERKSHIRE

BRISTOL
3 4 Kingswood
Bristol

NORTH SOMERSET

Wester-per-Mare **7**

Banwell

Bath **5 6**

1 Chippenham

2 Calne

• Lacock

• Avebury

BATH & NORTH EAST SOMERSET

Bradford on Avon

• Devizes

WILTSHIRE

urnham-on-Sea

Cheddar

Wookey Hole **9**

• Midsomer

Rode

Frome **8**

• Trowbridge

10

• Wells

Shepton Mallet

11 • Warminster

12

15 Bridgwater

SOMERSET

14 Street

Wincanton

Amesbury

13 Wilton

• Salisbury

16 Taunton

17 Ilchester

Wellington

Yeovil

Ilminster

20 Sherborne

HAMPSHIRE

Chard **21**

DORSET (western)

oniton

Axminster

Beaminster

Athelhampton

DORSET (eastern)

ttery St Mary

eaton

Bridport

Higher Bockhampton **23**

22

Lyme Regis

24

dmouth

25 Dorchester

Abbotsbury

Weymouth

ISLE OF WIGHT

Fortuneswell

0 _____ 20 Miles

0 _____ 30 Kms

---

23 Hardy's Cottage and Garden
Higher Bockhampton,
Dorchester, Dorset DT2 8QJ
Tel: (01305) 262366
A small thatched cottage where the novelist and poet Thomas Hardy was born in 1840, built by his great grandfather and little altered.

24 The Tutankhamun Exhibition
High West Street, Dorchester,
Dorset DT1 1UW
Tel: (01305) 269571
Tutankhamun's tomb perfectly reconstructed for the first time outside of Egypt. Facsimiles of his magnificent treasures including his golden burial mask.

25 Abbotsbury Sub-Tropical Gardens
Bullers Way, Abbotsbury,
Weymouth, Dorset DT3 4LA
Tel: (01305) 871387
Twenty acres of woodland valley. Exotic plants from all over the world thrive. Bird aviary and children's play area.

26 Crealy Park
Sidmouth Road, Clyst St Mary,
Exeter,
Devon EX5 1DR
Tel: (01395) 233200
*One of Devon's largest animal
farms. Milk a cow, feed a lamb and
pick up a piglet. Adventure
playgrounds. Dragonfly lake and
farm trails.*

27 Castle Drogo
Drewsteignton,
Exeter,
Devon EX6 6PB
Tel: (01647) 433306
*Granite castle, built between 1910
and 1930 by Sir Edwin Lutyens,
overlooking the wooded gorge of
the River Teign. Views of Dartmoor.*

28 Babbacombe Model Village
Hampton Avenue,
Babbacombe,
Torquay,
Devon TQ1 3LA
Tel: (01803) 315315/328669
*Over 400 models, many with sound
and animation, within four acres
of award-winning gardens. See
modern towns, villages, railways
and rural areas. 'City of Lights' -
illuminations.*

**29 Dobwalls Family
Adventure Park**
Dobwalls, Liskeard,
Cornwall PL14 6HD
Tel: (01579) 320325/320578
*Two miles of scenically dramatic
miniature railway based on an
American railroad. Children's
Adventureland. Krazee Kavern.*

30 Lanhydrock
Bodmin,
Cornwall PL30 5AD
Tel: (01208) 73320
*A 17thC house largely rebuilt after
fire in 1881. 116ft gallery with
magnificent plaster ceiling
illustrating scenes from the Old
Testament. Park, gardens, walks.*

31 Newquay Sea Life Centre
Towan Promenade, Newquay,
Cornwall TR7 1DU
Tel: (01637) 878134
*Journey beneath the ocean waves
and encounter thousands of marine
creatures - everything from shrimps
and starfish to conger eels and
octopus.*

32 The Lost Gardens of Heligan
Heligan, Pentewan, St Austell,
Cornwall PL26 6EN
Tel: (01726) 844157/843566
*The largest garden restoration
project undertaken since the war.
New attraction, The Lost Valley,
covers 35 acres.*

33 Pendennis Castle
Falmouth, Cornwall TR11 4LP
Tel: (01326) 316594
*Well-preserved coastal fort erected
in 1540s by Henry VIII, and added
to by Elizabeth I.*

34 St Michael's Mount
Marazion, Cornwall TR17 0HT
Tel: (01736) 710507
*Originally the site of a Benedictine
chapel, the castle on its rock dates
from the 14thC. Fine views towards
Land's End and the Lizard. Reached
by foot, or ferry at high tide in
summer.*

35 Tate Gallery - St Ives
Porthmeor Beach, St Ives,
Cornwall TR26 1TG
Tel: (01736) 796226
*A major new gallery showing
changing groups of work from the
Tate Gallery's pre-eminent collection
of St Ives painting and sculpture.*

**36 The Minack Theatre and
Exhibition Centre**
Porthcurno, Penzance,
Cornwall TR19 6JU
Tel: (01736) 810694/810181
*Open-air cliffside theatre with
breathtaking views, presenting a
16-week season of plays and*

*musicals. Exhibition centre telling
the theatre's story.*

37 Lands End
The Custom House,
Sennen, Penzance,
Cornwall TR19 7AA
Tel: (01736) 871501/871780
*Spectacular cliffs with breathtaking
vistas. Superb multi-sensory Last
Labyrinth Show, Land's End Hotel,
art gallery, exhibitions and much
more.*

FIND OUT MORE

Further information about
holidays and attractions in the
West Country is available from:
**West Country Tourist
Board,**
60 St Davids Hill,
Exeter EX4 4SY.
Tel: (01392) 425426
Fax: (01392) 420891
Email: post@wctb.co.uk

These publications are available
free from the West Country
Tourist Board:
■ **Great Escapes in England's
West Country**
■ **Bed & Breakfast Touring
Map**
■ **West Country Inspected
Holiday Homes**
■ **Commended Hotels and
Guesthouses**
■ **Glorious Gardens of the
West Country**
■ **Camping and Caravan
Touring Map**
■ **Tourist Attraction Touring
Map**
■ **Trencherman's West
Country, Good Food Guide**

WHERE TO STAY (WEST COUNTRY)

Accommodation entries in this region are listed in alphabetical order of place name, and then in alphabetical order of establishment.

Map references refer to the colour location maps at the back of this guide.

The first number indicates the map to use; the letter and number which follow refer to the grid reference on the map.

At-a-glance symbols at the end of each accommodation entry give useful information about services and facilities. A key to symbols can be found inside the back cover flap.

Keep this open for easy reference.

ABBOTSBURY

Dorset
Map ref 2A3

Beautiful village near Chesil Beach, with a long main street of mellow stone and thatched cottages and the ruins of a Benedictine monastery. High above the village on a hill is a prominent 15th C chapel. Abbotsbury's famous swannery and sub-tropical gardens lie just outside the village.

Swan Lodge ♠♠

COMMENDED
Rodden Row, Abbotsbury,
Weymouth DT3 4JL
☎ (01305) 871249
Fax (01305) 871249
Situated on the B3157 coastal road between Weymouth and Bridport. Swan Inn public house opposite, where food is served all day, is under the same ownership.
Bedrooms: 2 double, 2 twin, 1 triple
Bathrooms: 4 en-suite, 1 public

Bed & breakfast per night:

	£min	£max
Single	30.00	36.00
Double	44.00	56.00

Lunch available
Evening meal 1800 (last orders 2200)
Parking for 10
Cards accepted: Mastercard, Visa

ALLERFORD

Somerset
Map ref 1D1

Village with picturesque stone and thatch cottages and a packhorse bridge, set in the beautiful Vale of Porlock.

Fern Cottage ♠♠

COMMENDED
Allerford, Minehead TA24 8HN
☎ (01643) 862215
Fax (01643) 862215

Large 16th C traditional Exmoor cottage in National Trust wooded vale. Dramatic scenery and wildlife. Fine classic cooking and comprehensive wine list. Special breaks available.
Bedrooms: 2 double, 2 triple
Bathrooms: 3 en-suite, 1 private

Bed & breakfast per night:

	£min	£max
Single	30.00	30.00
Double	53.00	53.00

Half board per person:

	£min	£max
Daily	39.00	39.00
Weekly	245.70	245.70

Evening meal 1900 (last orders 1800)

Parking for 7
Cards accepted: Mastercard, Visa, Switch/Delta

AMESBURY

Wiltshire
Map ref 2B2

Standing on the banks of the River Avon, this is the nearest town to Stonehenge on Salisbury Plain. The area is rich in prehistoric sites. *Tourist Information Centre ☎ (01980) 622833*

Antrobus Arms Hotel

COMMENDED
15 Church Street, Amesbury,
Salisbury SP4 7EU
☎ (01980) 623163
Fax (01980) 622112
Logis of GB

Traditional hotel with highly acclaimed "Fountain Restaurant". Walled Victorian garden. Near Stonehenge, A303 half a mile, Salisbury 5 miles. Well situated for visiting countryside steeped in history and rich in culture.
Bedrooms: 7 single, 7 double, 5 twin, 1 family room
Bathrooms: 14 en-suite, 2 public

Continued ▶

AMESBURY

Continued

Bed & breakfast per night:

	£min	£max
Single	35.00	46.00
Double	75.00	120.00

Half board per person:

	£min	£max
Daily	48.50	133.50

Lunch available
Evening meal 1900 (last orders 2130)
Parking for 60
Cards accepted: Amex, Diners, Mastercard, Visa, Switch/Delta

🛏🍴🖨📞🖵💻♿🏐🎯Ⓢ🅿🛗📶📧🖼
🍽50🎸🔍♻↺♪🏷❋🐾 DAP 🐾 SP 📶 T 🌐

ASHBURTON

Devon
Map ref 1C2

Formerly a thriving wool centre and important as one of Dartmoor's four stannary towns. Today's busy market town has many period buildings. Ancient tradition is maintained in the annual ale-tasting and bread-weighing ceremony. Good centre for exploring Dartmoor or the south Devon coast.

Gages Mill

👑👑 COMMENDED

Buckfastleigh Road, Ashburton, Newton Abbot TQ13 7JW
☎ (01364) 652391

14th C former millhouse set in beautiful countryside on edge of Dartmoor. Comfortable accommodation, quality home cooking, large well-kept gardens.
Bedrooms: 1 single, 6 double, 1 twin
Bathrooms: 7 en-suite, 1 private shower

Bed & breakfast per night:

	£min	£max
Single	19.50	23.00
Double	39.00	46.00

Half board per person:

	£min	£max
Daily	31.50	35.00
Weekly	210.00	220.50

Evening meal 1900 (last orders 1900)
Parking for 10
Open March–November

🐲🍴5♿🖨🍴📞🏐Ⓢ🅿🛗 TV 🖼🛗📧
🏐🐾🐾🍴🐾🐾 SP 📶

Holne Chase Hotel and Restaurant ♏

👑👑👑 HIGHLY COMMENDED

Tavistock Road, Ashburton, Newton Abbot TQ13 7NS
☎ (01364) 631471
Fax (01364) 631453
Stunning estate setting inside Dartmoor National Park. River Dart for fishing. Excellent cuisine, comfortable, friendly hospitality, peaceful, relaxing. Lovely gardens and walks. Half board prices based on minimum 2-night stay.
Bedrooms: 1 single, 9 double, 8 twin
Suites available
Bathrooms: 18 en-suite

Bed & breakfast per night:

	£min	£max
Single	60.00	65.00
Double	115.00	160.00

Half board per person:

	£min	£max
Daily	65.50	90.00

Lunch available
Evening meal 1915 (last orders 2100)
Parking for 30
Cards accepted: Amex, Diners, Mastercard, Visa, Switch/Delta

🐲♿🍴📞🖨🖵♿🏐Ⓢ🅿🛗🖼
🍽30↺♪🏐❋🐾 DAP 🐾 SP 📶 T

ASHWATER

Devon
Map ref 1C2

Village 6 miles south-east of Holsworthy, with a pleasant village green dominated by its church.

Blagdon Manor Country Hotel ♏

👑👑👑 DE LUXE

Ashwater EX21 5DF
☎ (01409) 211224
Fax (01409) 211634
17th C manor house, nestling in 8 acres with superb views of rural Devon. Central for exploring Devon and Cornwall. Country house party atmosphere, fine wine and exquisite food. Warm and cosy with open log fires.
Bedrooms: 5 double, 2 twin
Bathrooms: 7 en-suite

Bed & breakfast per night:

	£min	£max
Single	60.00	70.00
Double	95.00	110.00

Half board per person:

	£min	£max
Daily	78.50	88.50

Evening meal 2000 (last orders 2000)
Parking for 8
Cards accepted: Amex, Mastercard, Visa, Switch/Delta

🐲📞🍴🖨🖵♿🏐🎯Ⓢ🖼🛗🍴14🎸
↺♪🏐❋🐾🐾 SP 📶

BADMINTON

South Gloucestershire
Map ref 2B2

Small village close to Badminton House, a 17th to 18th C Palladian mansion which has been the seat of the Dukes of Beaufort for centuries. The 3-day Badminton Horse Trials are held in the Great Park every May.

Bodkin House Hotel ♏

👑👑 COMMENDED

A46, Bath to Stroud Road, Badminton, South Gloucestershire GL9 1AF
☎ (01454) 238310
Fax (01454) 238422
Ⓒℝ Logis of GB
Ideal for Bath and Cotswolds. Beautifully restored 17th C Cotswold coaching inn, providing large, well-appointed en-suite bedrooms. Renowned for its good food.
Bedrooms: 7 double, 2 twin, 2 triple
Bathrooms: 11 en-suite

Bed & breakfast per night:

	£min	£max
Single	46.00	49.95
Double	66.00	70.00

Half board per person:

	£min	£max
Daily	46.00	48.00
Weekly	290.00	300.00

Lunch available
Evening meal 1900 (last orders 2130)
Parking for 30
Cards accepted: Amex, Diners, Mastercard, Visa, Switch/Delta

🐲♿🐲📞🖨🖵♿🏐Ⓢ🅿♿◐
🖼🛗🍴60↺🅿❋🐾🐾 SP 📶 T 🌐

Petty France Hotel ♏

👑👑👑 COMMENDED

A46, Dunkirk, Badminton GL9 1AF
☎ 0500 824889 (Freephone)
Fax (01454) 238768
Email: hotel@pettyfrance.telme.com
Ⓒℝ Consort
Informal country house atmosphere on the edge of the Cotswolds. Good

walking, many sights to visit, convenient
for Bath and Bristol.
Bedrooms: 2 single, 12 double,
5 twin, 1 triple
Bathrooms: 20 en-suite

**Bed & breakfast
per night:**

	£min	£max
Single	69.00	89.00
Double	89.00	130.00

**Half board per
person:**

	£min	£max
Daily	59.00	79.00
Weekly	385.00	525.00

Lunch available
Evening meal 1900 (last orders
2130)
Parking for 91
Cards accepted: Amex, Diners,
Mastercard, Visa, Switch/Delta

Devon
Map ref 1C1

At the head of the Taw Estuary,
once a ship-building and textile
town, now an agricultural centre
with attractive period buildings, a
modern civic centre and leisure
centre. Attractions include Queen
Anne's Walk, a charming
colonnaded arcade and Pannier
Market.
*Tourist Information Centre ☎ (01271)
375000*

Barnstaple Hotel ᴍ
COMMENDED

Braunton Road, Barnstaple
EX31 1LE
☎ (01271) 76221
Fax (01271) 24101
ⓒ Brend
*Located outside the town centre, an
ideal base for touring North Devon.
Excellent facilities include indoor and
outdoor swimming pools with sun
terrace, a gymnasium, meeting rooms
and two full sized snooker tables.*
Bedrooms: 24 double, 33 twin,
3 triple
Suite available
Bathrooms: 58 en-suite

**Bed & breakfast
per night:**

	£min	£max
Single	47.00	62.00
Double	67.00	87.00

**Half board per
person:**

	£min	£max
Daily	48.50	77.00
Weekly	315.00	500.00

Lunch available
Evening meal 1900 (last orders
2130)
Parking for 200

Cards accepted: Amex, Diners,
Mastercard, Visa, Switch/Delta

The Park Hotel ᴍ
COMMENDED

Taw Vale, Barnstaple EX32 8NJ
☎ (01271) 72166
Fax (01271) 23157
ⓒ Brend
*Overlooking parkland and River Taw, a
short walk to town centre. Leisure
facilities available at sister hotel, the
Barnstaple Hotel.*
Bedrooms: 7 single, 16 double,
19 twin
Bathrooms: 42 en-suite

**Bed & breakfast
per night:**

	£min	£max
Single	42.00	57.00
Double	60.00	82.00

**Half board per
person:**

	£min	£max
Daily	45.00	72.00
Weekly	315.00	470.00

Lunch available
Evening meal 1900 (last orders
2130)
Parking for 90
Cards accepted: Amex, Diners,
Mastercard, Visa, Switch/Delta

Royal and Fortescue Hotel ᴍ
HIGHLY COMMENDED

Boutport Street, Barnstaple
EX31 1HG
☎ (01271) 42289
Fax (01271) 42289
ⓒ Brend
*Traditional market town hotel centrally
located. Extensive refurbishments have
retained the hotel's coaching inn charm
while adding fine modern facilities, the
latest being "The Bank", a stylish bistro.*
Bedrooms: 4 single, 18 double,
20 twin, 5 triple
Bathrooms: 47 en-suite

**Bed & breakfast
per night:**

	£min	£max
Single	44.00	59.00
Double	63.00	85.00

**Half board per
person:**

	£min	£max
Daily	46.50	74.00
Weekly	315.00	473.00

Lunch available
Evening meal 1900 (last orders
2100)
Parking for 55
Cards accepted: Amex, Diners,
Mastercard, Visa, Switch/Delta

Bath & North East Somerset
Map ref 2B2

Georgian spa city beside the River
Avon. Important Roman site with
impressive reconstructed baths,
uncovered in 19th C. Bath Abbey
built on site of monastery where
first king of England was crowned
(AD 973). Fine architecture in
mellow local stone. Pump Room and
museums.
*Tourist Information Centre ☎ (01225)
477101*

Apsley House Hotel
HIGHLY COMMENDED

141 Newbridge Hill, Bath BA1 3PT
☎ (01225) 336966
Fax (01225) 425462
*Elegant William IV period house
approximately 1 mile from the town
centre. Beautifully furnished. Caring
personal service and comfort.*
Bedrooms: 5 double, 2 twin, 1 triple
Bathrooms: 8 en-suite

**Bed & breakfast
per night:**

	£min	£max
Single	45.00	55.00
Double	55.00	90.00

Evening meal 1930 (last orders
2100)
Parking for 10
Cards accepted: Amex, Mastercard,
Visa, Switch/Delta

Ashley Villa Hotel

26 Newbridge Road, Bath BA1 3JZ
☎ (01225) 421683 & 428887
Fax (01225) 313604
*Comfortably furnished licensed hotel
with relaxing informal atmosphere,
close to city centre. All rooms en-suite.
Swimming pool. Car park.*
Bedrooms: 2 single, 7 double, 2 twin,
3 triple
Bathrooms: 14 en-suite

**Bed & breakfast
per night:**

	£min	£max
Single	49.00	49.00
Double	59.00	75.00

Evening meal 1830 (last orders
1930)
Parking for 10
Cards accepted: Amex, Mastercard,
Visa, Switch/Delta

BATH
Continued

The Bath Spa Hotel ⚠

👑👑👑👑 HIGHLY COMMENDED

Sydney Road, Bath BA2 6JF
☎ (01225) 444424
Fax (01225) 444006
ℂℝ Utell International/Forte
*Georgian former mansion, set in 7
acres of landscaped gardens, 10
minutes' walk from the centre of Bath.
Exceptional comfort is combined with
attentive service and friendly
informality. Rates shown below based
on a minimum 2-night stay.*
Bedrooms: 7 single, 45 double,
46 twin
Suites available
Bathrooms: 98 en-suite

Bed & breakfast

per night:	£min	£max
Double	79.00	109.00

Half board per

person:	£min	£max
Daily	99.00	139.00

Lunch available
Evening meal 1830 (last orders
2200)
Parking for 156
Cards accepted: Amex, Diners,
Mastercard, Visa, Switch/Delta

The Bath Tasburgh Hotel ⚠

👑👑👑 HIGHLY COMMENDED

Warminster Road, Bath BA2 6SH
☎ (01225) 425096
Fax (01225) 463842
*Victorian mansion in lovely gardens
with spectacular views. Convenient for
city centre. All rooms en-suite and well
appointed. Four-poster and family
bedrooms. Evening meals. Warm
hospitality. Parking.*
Bedrooms: 1 single, 7 double, 1 twin,
3 family rooms
Bathrooms: 12 en-suite

Bed & breakfast

per night:	£min	£max
Single	48.00	55.00
Double	65.00	78.00

Half board per

person:	£min	£max
Daily	49.00	55.50
Weekly	336.00	378.00

Evening meal 1930 (last orders
2000)
Parking for 15
Cards accepted: Amex, Mastercard,
Visa, Switch/Delta

Brompton House ⚠

👑👑👑 HIGHLY COMMENDED

Saint Johns Road, Bath BA2 6PT
☎ (01225) 420972
Fax (01225) 420505
Email: brompton-house
@compuserve.com

*Charming Georgian rectory in beautiful
secluded gardens. 6-7 minutes' level
walk to city centre. Car park. No
smoking.*
Bedrooms: 2 single, 9 double, 5 twin,
2 family rooms
Bathrooms: 18 en-suite

Bed & breakfast

per night:	£min	£max
Single	32.00	55.00
Double	60.00	80.00

Parking for 18
Cards accepted: Amex, Mastercard,
Visa, Switch/Delta

Carfax Hotel ⚠

👑👑👑 COMMENDED

Great Pulteney Street, Bath
BA2 4BS
☎ (01225) 462089
Fax (01225) 443257
*In a famous Georgian street,
surrounded by beautiful Bath hills. The
rear of Carfax overlooks Henrietta
Park. A well maintained, listed building.*
Bedrooms: 13 single, 12 double,
10 twin, 3 triple
Bathrooms: 33 en-suite, 2 public

Bed & breakfast

per night:	£min	£max
Single	29.50	60.50
Double	51.50	78.25

Half board per

person:	£min	£max
Daily	33.50	45.50
Weekly	217.00	284.00

Evening meal 1830 (last orders
1930)
Parking for 17
Cards accepted: Amex, Mastercard,
Visa, Switch/Delta

Cheriton House

👑👑 COMMENDED

9 Upper Oldfield Park, Bath
BA2 3JX
☎ (01225) 429862
Fax (01225) 428403

*Victorian house in quiet location set in
attractive gardens overlooking Bath.
Within 12 minutes' walk of city centre.*
Bedrooms: 6 double, 3 twin
Bathrooms: 9 en-suite

Bed & breakfast

per night:	£min	£max
Single	38.00	44.00
Double	56.00	62.00

Parking for 9
Cards accepted: Amex, Diners,
Mastercard, Visa, Switch/Delta

Chesterfield Hotel ⚠

👑👑 COMMENDED

11 Great Pulteney Street, Bath
BA2 4BR
☎ (01225) 460953
Fax (01225) 448770

*Centrally situated Grade I listed
Georgian building. Family-run hotel with
individually decorated en-suite rooms at
reasonable B & B rates. Limited garage
parking by prior arrangement only.*
Bedrooms: 4 single, 12 double,
2 twin, 2 triple
Bathrooms: 20 en-suite

Bed & breakfast

per night:	£min	£max
Single	35.00	45.00
Double	60.00	85.00

Parking for 14
Cards accepted: Amex, Diners,
Mastercard, Visa

Combe Grove Manor Hotel and Country Club ⚠

👑👑👑👑 HIGHLY COMMENDED

Bras99knocker Hill, Monkton Combe,
Bath BA2 7HS
☎ (01225) 834644
Fax (01225) 834961
ℂℝ Grand Heritage

Beautiful 18th C manor house and more recently built garden lodge. 2 miles from centre of Bath and with excellent sports facilities. Prices are per room.
Bedrooms: 27 double, 11 twin, 2 triple
Suites available
Bathrooms: 40 en-suite
Bed & breakfast

per night:	£min	£max
Single	99.00	270.00
Double	99.00	270.00

Half board per

person:	£min	£max
Daily	130.00	300.00

Lunch available
Evening meal 1900 (last orders 2130)
Parking for 200
Cards accepted: Amex, Diners, Mastercard, Visa, Switch/Delta

Dukes Hotel ⋀
Great Pulteney Street, Bath BA2 4DN
☎ (01225) 463512
Fax (01225) 483733
Ⓒ Logis of GB

Elegantly refurbished, family-run Grade 1 Georgian town-house hotel, in city centre. Restaurant offers finest local produce and reasonably priced wines carefully selected by a Master of Wine.
Bedrooms: 4 single, 11 double, 4 twin, 4 triple
Bathrooms: 23 en-suite
Bed & breakfast

per night:	£min	£max
Single	55.00	75.00
Double	65.00	95.00

Half board per

person:	£min	£max
Daily	45.00	60.00

Evening meal 1845 (last orders 2030)

Cards accepted: Amex, Diners, Mastercard, Visa, Switch/Delta

Edgar Hotel
APPROVED
64 Great Pulteney Street, Bath BA2 4DN
☎ (01225) 420619
Georgian town house hotel, close to city centre and Roman Baths. Privately run. All rooms with en-suite facilities.
Bedrooms: 2 single, 9 double, 4 twin, 1 triple
Suites available
Bathrooms: 16 en-suite
Bed & breakfast

per night:	£min	£max
Single	30.00	45.00
Double	40.00	65.00

Cards accepted: Mastercard, Visa

Forres Guest House
172 Newbridge Road, Lower Weston, Bath BA1 3LE
☎ (01225) 427698
Edwardian family guesthouse with helpful hosts, who are ex-teachers and love Bath. River Avon and Cotswold Way close by. Traditional and vegetarian breakfasts. Colour TV and beverages in all rooms.
Bedrooms: 3 double, 2 triple
Bathrooms: 4 en-suite, 1 private
Bed & breakfast

per night:	£min	£max
Double	40.00	50.00

Parking for 5
Open April–October

Gainsborough Hotel ⋀
COMMENDED
Weston Lane, Bath BA1 4AB
☎ (01225) 311380
Fax (01225) 447411
Ⓒ The Independents

Spacious and comfortable country house hotel in own lovely grounds, near the botanical gardens and within easy walking distance of the city. High ground, nice views, own large car park. 5-course breakfast, friendly staff, warm welcome.
Bedrooms: 2 single, 6 double, 6 twin, 2 triple, 1 family room
Bathrooms: 17 en-suite

Bed & breakfast

per night:	£min	£max
Single	30.00	46.00
Double	50.00	70.00

Parking for 18
Cards accepted: Amex, Mastercard, Visa

Georges Hotel ⋀
APPROVED
2 South Parade, Bath BA2 4AA
☎ (01225) 464923
Fax (01225) 425471
In city centre, close to Abbey, Roman Baths and shops. 200 yards from bus and train stations and adjacent to public car park.
Bedrooms: 9 double, 3 twin, 3 triple, 4 family rooms
Bathrooms: 19 en-suite
Bed & breakfast

per night:	£min	£max
Single	40.00	50.00
Double	55.00	85.00

Lunch available
Evening meal 1800 (last orders 2300)
Cards accepted: Amex, Mastercard, Visa, Switch/Delta

Georgian Guest House
Listed APPROVED
34 Henrietta Street, Bath BA2 6LR
☎ (01225) 424103
Central Bath. Grade I listed Georgian town house, next to Henrietta Park and only 2 minutes' walk to town centre. 1 minute from famous Pulteney Bridge and restaurants.
Bedrooms: 2 single, 3 double, 2 twin, 2 triple, 1 family room
Bathrooms: 3 en-suite, 1 public, 4 private showers
Bed & breakfast

per night:	£min	£max
Single	20.00	35.00
Double	40.00	60.00

Cards accepted: Amex, Mastercard, Visa

Haringtons Hotel ⋀
COMMENDED
8-10 Queen Street, Bath BA1 1HE
☎ (01225) 461728
Fax (01225) 444804
Enjoy warm hospitality, good food and wine in this charming hotel set in a
Continued ▶

BATH

Continued

picturesque cobbled street in the very heart of Bath. Just minutes from the Roman Baths, theatre, premiere shopping and major attractions.
Bedrooms: 10 double, 1 twin, 2 triple
Bathrooms: 13 en-suite
Bed & breakfast

per night:	£min	£max
Single	55.00	70.00
Double	65.00	85.00

Half board per person:

	£min	£max
Daily	45.00	60.00

Lunch available
Evening meal 1800 (last orders 2100)
Cards accepted: Amex, Diners, Mastercard, Visa, Switch/Delta

Haute Combe Hotel
⚜⚜ COMMENDED

174/176 Newbridge Road, Bath BA1 3LE
☎ (01225) 420061 & 339064
Fax (01225) 420061
Email: ID/101352.42 @compuserve.com
Fully-equipped non-smoking en-suite rooms in comfortable, period surroundings. Easy access to city attractions. Special off-season rates. Telephone for brochure.
Bedrooms: 2 single, 3 double, 2 twin, 3 triple, 2 family rooms
Bathrooms: 11 en-suite, 1 private
Bed & breakfast

per night:	£min	£max
Single	39.00	49.00
Double	49.00	69.00

Evening meal 1900 (last orders 1800)
Parking for 12
Cards accepted: Amex, Diners, Mastercard, Visa, Switch/Delta

Henrietta Hotel
⚜⚜

32 Henrietta Street, Bath BA2 6LR
☎ (01225) 447779
Fax (01225) 466916
Privately-run Georgian town house hotel, close to city centre and Roman Baths. All rooms with en-suite facilities.
Bedrooms: 7 double, 2 twin, 1 triple
Bathrooms: 10 en-suite

Bed & breakfast

per night:	£min	£max
Single	30.00	45.00
Double	40.00	65.00

Cards accepted: Mastercard, Visa

Holly Lodge ⚊
⚜⚜ DE LUXE

8 Upper Oldfield Park, Bath BA2 3JZ
☎ (01225) 424042
Fax (01225) 481138
Elegant Victorian house set in its own grounds, enjoying magnificent views of the city.
Bedrooms: 1 single, 4 double, 2 twin
Bathrooms: 7 en-suite
Bed & breakfast

per night:	£min	£max
Single	48.00	55.00
Double	75.00	89.00

Parking for 8
Cards accepted: Amex, Diners, Mastercard, Visa, Switch/Delta

Kennard Hotel ⚊
⚜⚜ HIGHLY COMMENDED

11 Henrietta Street, Bath BA2 6LL
☎ (01225) 310472
Fax (01225) 460054
Email: kennard@dircon.co.uk
Georgian town house hotel of charm and character in a quiet street. A few minutes' level walk to the Abbey and Roman Baths.
Bedrooms: 2 single, 9 double, 1 twin, 1 family room
Bathrooms: 11 en-suite, 1 public
Bed & breakfast

per night:	£min	£max
Single	35.00	45.00
Double	65.00	85.00

Cards accepted: Amex, Diners, Mastercard, Visa, Switch/Delta

Laura Place Hotel ⚊
⚜⚜ COMMENDED

3 Laura Place, Great Pulteney Street, Bath BA2 4BH
☎ (01225) 463815
Fax (01225) 310222
18th C town house, centrally located in Georgian square. 2 minutes from Roman Baths, Pump Rooms and abbey.
Bedrooms: 6 double, 1 twin, 1 family room
Suite available
Bathrooms: 7 en-suite, 1 private
Bed & breakfast

per night:	£min	£max
Double	62.00	90.00

Parking for 10
Open March–December
Cards accepted: Amex, Mastercard, Visa

Leighton House ⚊
⚜⚜ HIGHLY COMMENDED

139 Wells Road, Bath BA2 3AL
☎ (01225) 314769 & 420210
Fax (01225) 443079

Marilyn and Colin extend a warm welcome at their elegant, spacious, detached Victorian home, with car park and just a 10 minute walk to the city centre.
Bedrooms: 3 double, 4 twin, 1 family room
Bathrooms: 8 en-suite
Bed & breakfast

per night:	£min	£max
Single	47.00	60.00
Double	62.00	75.00

Parking for 8
Cards accepted: Mastercard, Visa, Switch/Delta

Lucknam Park
⚜⚜⚜⚜⚜ HIGHLY COMMENDED

Colerne, Chippenham, Wiltshire SN14 8AZ
☎ (01225) 742777
Fax (01225) 743536
Ⓒ Utell International
Built in 1720, Lucknam Park is a magnificent Georgian country house hotel with extensive leisure facilities. Set in 500 acres of parkland north-east of Bath. Half board price based on minimum 2-night stay at weekends.
Bedrooms: 1 single, 27 double, 14 twin
Suites available
Bathrooms: 42 en-suite
Bed & breakfast

per night:	£min	£max
Single	157.00	
Double	208.00	

Half board per person:

	£min	£max
Daily	139.50	

Lunch available

Evening meal 1930 (last orders 2130)
Parking for 70
Cards accepted: Amex, Diners, Mastercard, Visa, Switch/Delta

Meadowland

DE LUXE

36 Bloomfield Park, Bath BA2 2BX
☎ (01225) 311079
Fax (01452) 304507

Set in quiet, secluded grounds and offering the highest standard in de-luxe en-suite accommodation, Meadowland is elegantly furnished and decorated. Private parking, lovely gardens, non-smoking only. A peaceful retreat for discerning travellers.
Bedrooms: 2 double, 1 twin
Bathrooms: 3 en-suite

Bed & breakfast

per night:	£min	£max
Single	40.00	45.00
Double	58.00	65.00

Parking for 6
Cards accepted: Mastercard, Visa

Old Malt House Hotel ⋔

COMMENDED

Radford, Timsbury, Bath BA3 1QF
☎ (01761) 470106
Fax (01761) 472726
Ⓒ Minotel/Logis of GB

Six miles south of Bath, in beautiful unspoilt countryside. Built in 1835 as a brewery malt house, now a hotel with character and comfort.
Bedrooms: 1 single, 4 double, 5 twin, 2 triple
Bathrooms: 12 en-suite

Bed & breakfast

per night:	£min	£max
Single	33.00	39.50
Double	66.00	69.00

Half board per person:

	£min	£max
Daily	49.50	56.00
Weekly	281.75	

Lunch available
Evening meal 1900 (last orders 2030)

Parking for 26
Cards accepted: Amex, Diners, Mastercard, Visa

Parade Park Hotel

COMMENDED

10 North Parade, Bath BA2 4AL
☎ (01225) 463384
Fax (01225) 442322

Centrally situated, friendly bed and breakfast hotel. The Roman Baths and many of the city's finest restaurants are on the doorstep, railway and bus stations are 3 minutes' walk. All rooms have TV, tea/coffee and telephone.
Bedrooms: 7 single, 7 double, 2 twin, 2 family rooms
Bathrooms: 12 en-suite, 2 public

Bed & breakfast

per night:	£min	£max
Single	30.00	60.00
Double	55.00	75.00

Cards accepted: Mastercard, Visa, Switch/Delta

Rosemary House ⋔

COMMENDED

63 Wellsway, Bath BA2 4RT
☎ (01225) 425667

Elegant small Edwardian house, in elevated location close to city centre on A367 Exeter road. Wide choice of traditional or vegetarian breakfasts cooked to order.
Bedrooms: 2 double, 1 twin
Bathrooms: 3 en-suite

Bed & breakfast

per night:	£min	£max
Single	25.00	39.00
Double	35.00	55.00

Open February–December

Hotel Saint Clair

COMMENDED

1 Crescent Gardens, Upper Bristol Road, Bath BA1 2NA
☎ (01225) 425543 & (01378) 834592
Fax (01225) 425543

Small family hotel 5 minutes' walk from city, 2 minutes from Royal Crescent. Large public car park 1 minute away. One-night stays welcome.

Bedrooms: 4 double, 2 twin, 2 triple, 1 family room
Bathrooms: 7 en-suite, 1 public

Bed & breakfast

per night:	£min	£max
Single	22.00	38.00
Double	34.00	52.00

Cards accepted: Mastercard, Visa

Siena Hotel ⋔

HIGHLY COMMENDED

24/25 Pulteney Road, Bath BA2 4EZ
☎ (01225) 425495
Fax (01225) 469029

Attractive hotel, set in landscaped gardens overlooking Bath Abbey, offering quality accommodation, excellent cuisine, licensed bar and private car parking.
Bedrooms: 2 single, 6 double, 2 twin, 3 triple, 2 family rooms
Bathrooms: 15 en-suite

Bed & breakfast

per night:	£min	£max
Single	42.50	57.50
Double	57.50	87.50

Parking for 14
Cards accepted: Amex, Diners, Mastercard, Visa, Switch/Delta

Somerset House Hotel and Restaurant ⋔

HIGHLY COMMENDED

35 Bathwick Hill, Bath BA2 6LD
☎ (01225) 466451 & 463471
Fax (01225) 317188
Ⓒ Logis of GB

A restaurant with rooms, this Regency house (1827) is owned and run by the Seymour family. Large garden. Good views of city. Non-smoking house. Lunch available on Sundays in winter.
Bedrooms: 1 single, 2 double, 2 twin, 5 triple
Bathrooms: 10 en-suite

Continued ▶

BATH
Continued

Bed & breakfast per night:	£min	£max
Single	20.50	48.00
Double	41.00	64.00

Half board per person:	£min	£max
Daily	43.50	51.00
Weekly	270.00	281.00

Evening meal 1900 (last orders 1830)
Parking for 15
Cards accepted: Amex, Mastercard, Visa

Sydney Gardens Hotel
COMMENDED

Sydney Road, Bath BA2 6NT
☎ (01225) 464818
Elegant, spacious, Victorian house in a scenic parkland setting, 10 minutes' walk from the city centre. All facilities, car parking.
Bedrooms: 3 double, 2 twin, 1 triple
Bathrooms: 6 en-suite

Bed & breakfast per night:	£min	£max
Single	45.00	59.00
Double	59.00	69.00

Parking for 6
Cards accepted: Amex, Mastercard, Visa, Switch/Delta

Villa Magdala Hotel
HIGHLY COMMENDED

Henrietta Road, Bath BA2 6LX
☎ (01225) 466329
Fax (01225) 483207
Email: villa@btinternet.com

Charming Victorian town house hotel enjoying a peaceful setting overlooking Henrietta Park. Only 5 minutes' level walk to Roman Baths. Parking in grounds.
Bedrooms: 2 single, 9 double, 5 twin, 1 triple
Bathrooms: 17 en-suite

Bed & breakfast per night:	£min	£max
Single	50.00	65.00
Double	60.00	90.00

Parking for 20
Cards accepted: Amex, Mastercard, Visa, Switch/Delta

Wentworth House Hotel
COMMENDED

106 Bloomfield Road, Bath BA2 2AP
☎ (01225) 339193
Fax (01225) 310460

Imposing Victorian mansion standing in secluded gardens with stunning views. Free car park. Walking distance city. High standard, licensed lounge, outdoor swimming pool. Light evening snacks available.
Bedrooms: 11 double, 6 twin, 1 triple
Bathrooms: 16 en-suite, 2 private

Bed & breakfast per night:	£min	£max
Single	40.00	45.00
Double	50.00	70.00

Parking for 20
Cards accepted: Amex, Mastercard, Visa

Williams Guest House
Listed APPROVED

81 Wells Road, Bath BA2 3AN
☎ (01225) 312179
Long established non-smoking guesthouse, run from a Victorian town house with good views to the front. Four minutes' walk to the city, British Rail and National Express stations. Private parking available. A warm welcome awaits.
Bedrooms: 1 single, 2 double
Bathrooms: 1 public, 1 private shower

Bed & breakfast per night:	£min	£max
Single	20.00	25.00
Double	40.00	45.00

Parking for 5

A key to symbols can be found inside the back cover flap.

BIDEFORD
Devon
Map ref 1C1

The home port of Sir Richard Grenville, the town with its 17th C merchants' houses flourished as a shipbuilding and cloth town. The bridge of 24 arches was built about 1460. Charles Kingsley stayed here while writing Westward Ho!
Tourist Information Centre ☎ (01237) 477676 or 421853

The Mount Hotel
COMMENDED

Northdown Road, Bideford EX39 3LP
☎ (01237) 473748
Small, family-run hotel over 200 years old, with character and charm. Home cooking. Peaceful garden. Short walk to town centre and quay. Ideal base for touring North Devon and "Tarka" country. No smoking, please.
Bedrooms: 2 single, 3 double, 2 twin, 1 triple
Bathrooms: 7 en-suite, 1 private shower

Bed & breakfast per night:	£min	£max
Single	21.00	26.00
Double	40.00	44.00

Half board per person:	£min	£max
Daily	28.00	36.00
Weekly	200.00	250.00

Evening meal 1830 (last orders 1700)
Parking for 4
Cards accepted: Mastercard, Visa

Riversford Hotel
APPROVED

Limers Lane, Bideford EX39 2RG
☎ (01237) 474239
Fax (01237) 421661
Peace and tranquillity, overlooking the River Torridge. Delightful restaurant offering home-cooked foods (fresh fish a speciality). Individual en-suite bedrooms with character and river views, four-poster bedrooms. Take A386 from Bideford to Northam then turn right into Limers Lane.
Bedrooms: 6 double, 7 twin, 1 family room
Bathrooms: 14 en-suite

Bed & breakfast per night:	£min	£max
Single	40.00	40.00
Double	60.00	80.00

Half board per person:	£min	£max
Daily	45.00	50.00
Weekly	266.00	298.00

Lunch available
Evening meal 1800 (last orders 2100)
Parking for 22
Cards accepted: Amex, Diners, Mastercard, Visa, Switch/Delta

🏢🔥5♿📞🖥️🍴♨️🅂📺🌙⬆️ 🍴🛥️🏌️60⛵🎣✂️❀ DAP 🚫 SP T

Royal Hotel ♨
👑👑👑 COMMENDED

Barnstaple Street, Bideford
EX39 4AE
☎ (01237) 472005
Fax (01237) 478957
CR Brend

Overlooking historic Bideford Bridge and the River Torridge. Bideford's leading hotel with locally renowned restaurant and well-appointed lounges.
Bedrooms: 5 single, 10 double, 14 twin, 1 triple
Bathrooms: 30 en-suite, 3 public

Bed & breakfast per night:	£min	£max
Single	42.00	57.00
Double	60.00	82.00

Half board per person:	£min	£max
Daily	45.00	72.00
Weekly	315.00	470.00

Lunch available
Evening meal 1900 (last orders 2100)
Parking for 35
Cards accepted: Amex, Diners, Mastercard, Visa, Switch/Delta

🏢🔥♿📞🖥️♨️🅂📺🌙⬆️🍴 🛥️🍴✂️🚫 SP 🏢 T

Sunset Hotel
👑👑 COMMENDED

Landcross, Bideford EX39 5JA
☎ (01237) 472962
Small, quality country hotel in peaceful, picturesque location, specialising in home cooking. Delightful en-suite bedrooms with beverages and colour TV. Book with confidence. A non-smoking establishment.
Bedrooms: 1 double, 1 twin, 1 triple, 1 family room
Bathrooms: 4 en-suite

Bed & breakfast per night:	£min	£max
Single	25.00	30.00
Double	46.00	50.00

Half board per person:	£min	£max
Daily	34.50	35.50
Weekly	220.00	224.00

Evening meal 1900 (last orders 1900)
Parking for 10
Open March–October
Cards accepted: Mastercard, Visa

🐴🖥️♨️🍽️🅂✂️📺🌙💻🍴 ❀🚗 DAP SP 🏢

Yeoldon Country House Hotel and Restaurant ♨
👑👑👑 HIGHLY COMMENDED

Durrant Lane, Northam, Bideford
EX39 2RL
☎ (01237) 474400
Fax (01237) 476618
CR Logis of GB

Victorian country house overlooking river. Quality English and continental cuisine and an interesting wine list. Hospitable owners, friendly and efficient staff. Individually decorated rooms.
Bedrooms: 7 double, 3 twin
Bathrooms: 10 en-suite

Bed & breakfast per night:	£min	£max
Single	45.00	57.00
Double	75.00	95.00

Lunch available
Evening meal 1900 (last orders 2100)
Parking for 22
Cards accepted: Amex, Diners, Mastercard, Visa, Switch/Delta

🐴🖥️📞🖥️♨️🅂✂️🍴💻🛥️ 🍴50⛵🎣❀🚗🚫 SP T

BIGBURY-ON-SEA

Devon
Map ref 1C3

Small resort on Bigbury Bay at the mouth of the River Avon. Wide sands, rugged cliffs. Burgh Island can be reached on foot at low tide.

The Henley Hotel ♨
👑👑👑 COMMENDED

Folly Hill, Bigbury-on-Sea, Kingsbridge TQ7 4AR
☎ (01548) 810240
Fax (01548) 810020
CR Logis of GB
Small, comfortable hotel on the edge of the sea. Spectacular views with private steps through garden down to lovely beach. A non-smoking establishment.
Bedrooms: 2 single, 4 double, 2 twin
Bathrooms: 8 en-suite

Bed & breakfast per night:	£min	£max
Single	27.00	37.00
Double	54.00	64.00

Half board per person:	£min	£max
Daily	42.00	48.00
Weekly	274.00	291.00

Lunch available
Evening meal 1900 (last orders 2130)
Parking for 10
Open April–October
Cards accepted: Amex, Mastercard, Visa

🐴🔥📞🖥️♨️🍽️🅂✂️🍴📺🌙💻 🛥️🍴❀🚗🚫 SP T

BODMIN

Cornwall
Map ref 1B2

County town south-west of Bodmin Moor with a ruined priory and church dedicated to St Petroc. Nearby are Lanhydrock House and Pencarrow House.
Tourist Information Centre ☎ (01208) 76616

Mount Pleasant Moorland Hotel ♨
👑👑👑 HIGHLY COMMENDED

Mount, Bodmin PL30 4EX
☎ (01208) 821342
Fax (01208) 821417

Charming countryside hotel with friendly, relaxing atmosphere. Residents' bar, TV, sun-lounges. Delicious home cooking. Gardens, safe parking and beautiful secluded swimming pool.
Bedrooms: 1 single, 3 double, 1 twin, 1 triple, 1 family room
Bathrooms: 6 en-suite, 1 private

Bed & breakfast per night:	£min	£max
Single	20.00	26.00
Double	40.00	52.00

Half board per person:	£min	£max
Daily	32.00	38.00
Weekly	200.00	225.00

Evening meal 1900 (last orders 1700)
Parking for 10

Continued ▶

BODMIN
Continued

Open April–September
Cards accepted: Mastercard, Visa,
Switch/Delta

Tredethy Country Hotel M
👑👑👑 COMMENDED
Hellandbridge, Bodmin PL30 4QS
☎ (01208) 841262
Fax (01208) 841707
Ⓒℝ Logis of GB
Gracious living with spacious rooms, log fires in winter and absolute peace and quiet in beautiful surroundings. From Bodmin take the Launceston road, then the Helland turn-off to Helland Bridge. Tredethy is up the hill over the bridge.
Bedrooms: 1 single, 7 double, 3 twin
Bathrooms: 11 en-suite

Bed & breakfast
per night:	£min	£max
Single	36.00	46.00
Double	60.00	80.00

Half board per
person:	£min	£max
Daily	44.00	54.00
Weekly	280.00	360.00

Lunch available
Evening meal 1900 (last orders 2030)
Parking for 60
Cards accepted: Amex, Diners, Mastercard, Visa, Switch/Delta

BOSCASTLE
Cornwall
Map ref 1B2

Small, unspoilt village in Valency Valley. Active as a port until onset of railway era, its natural harbour affords rare shelter on this wild coast. Attractions include spectacular blow-hole, Celtic field strips, part-Norman church. Nearby St Juliot Church was restored by Thomas Hardy.

Bottreaux House Hotel and Restaurant M
👑👑👑 HIGHLY COMMENDED
Boscastle PL35 0BG
☎ (01840) 250231
Charming old house with panoramic views overlooking unspoilt harbour village. Specialising in comfort and cuisine. On B3266 Camelford to Boscastle road.

Bedrooms: 4 double, 2 twin, 1 family room
Bathrooms: 7 en-suite
Bed & breakfast
per night:	£min	£max
Single	20.00	28.00
Double	38.00	51.00

Half board per
person:	£min	£max
Daily	30.00	35.00
Weekly	187.00	266.00

Evening meal 1900 (last orders 2100)
Parking for 8
Cards accepted: Amex, Mastercard, Visa, Switch/Delta

The Old Coach House M
Tintagel Road, Boscastle PL35 0AS
☎ (01840) 250398
Fax (01840) 250346
Relax in beautiful 300-year-old former coach house. All rooms en-suite with colour TV, teamaker, hairdryer, etc. Friendly and helpful owners. Good parking.
Bedrooms: 1 single, 3 double, 1 twin, 1 triple
Bathrooms: 6 en-suite
Bed & breakfast
per night:	£min	£max
Single	17.00	25.00
Double	34.00	50.00

Parking for 9
Open February–November
Cards accepted: Amex, Mastercard, Visa

Tolcarne House Hotel and Restaurant M
👑👑👑 HIGHLY COMMENDED
Tintagel Road, Boscastle PL35 0AS
☎ (01840) 250654
Fax (01840) 250654
Delightful late Victorian house in spacious grounds with lovely views to the dramatic Cornish coastline. All rooms en-suite. Restaurant and bar. Warm welcome.
Bedrooms: 1 single, 5 double, 2 twin
Bathrooms: 8 en-suite, 1 public
Bed & breakfast
per night:	£min	£max
Single	28.00	30.00
Double	44.00	60.00

Half board per
person:	£min	£max
Daily	36.00	44.00
Weekly	230.00	280.00

Evening meal 1900 (last orders 2100)

Parking for 15
Open March–October
Cards accepted: Mastercard, Visa

BOVEY TRACEY
Devon
Map ref 1D2

Standing by the river just east of Dartmoor National Park, this old town has good moorland views. Its church, with a 14th C tower, holds one of Devon's finest medieval rood screens.

Edgemoor Hotel M
👑👑👑 HIGHLY COMMENDED
Haytor Road, Lowerdown Cross, Bovey Tracey TQ13 9LE
☎ (01626) 832466
Fax (01626) 834760
Email: Edgemoor@Binternet.com
Country house hotel in peaceful wooded setting on edge of Dartmoor National Park. Good food. Elegance without pretension.
Bedrooms: 3 single, 9 double, 3 twin, 1 triple, 1 family room
Bathrooms: 17 en-suite
Bed & breakfast
per night:	£min	£max
Single	46.50	52.50
Double	75.95	89.95

Half board per
person:	£min	£max
Daily	47.99	57.50
Weekly	670.00	700.00

Lunch available
Evening meal 1900 (last orders 2100)
Parking for 50
Cards accepted: Amex, Diners, Mastercard, Visa, Switch/Delta

For ideas on places to visit refer to the introduction at the beginning of this section.

Information on accommodation listed in this guide has been supplied by the proprietors. As changes may occur you are advised to check details at the time of booking.

BRIDGWATER

Somerset
Map ref 1D1

Former medieval port on the River
Parrett, now small industrial town
with mostly 19th C or modern
architecture. Georgian Castle Street
leads to West Quay and site of 13th
C castle razed to the ground by
Cromwell. Birthplace of
Cromwellian Admiral Robert Blake
is now museum. Arts centre.

Apple Tree Inn Hotel and Restaurant ⋀

💥💥💥 COMMENDED

Keenthorne, Nether Stowey,
Bridgwater TA5 1HZ
☎ (01278) 733238
Fax (01278) 732693
Email: applehotel@msn.co.

*Small family hotel easily located on the
main A39, surrounded by rolling
Quantock Hills. Large car park and
gardens. Well known restaurant. Near
Nether Stowey, some 6 miles west of
Bridgwater.*
Bedrooms: 2 single, 3 double, 3 twin,
3 triple
Bathrooms: 11 en-suite, 2 public

Bed & breakfast

per night:	£min	£max
Single	37.50	42.50
Double	47.50	52.50

Half board per

person:	£min	£max
Daily	36.75	42.75
Weekly	240.00	275.00

Lunch available
Evening meal 1830 (last orders
2200)
Parking for 50
Cards accepted: Mastercard, Visa,
Switch/Delta

🛇🖐🖧🖩🌢🗂️💻🖥️🧺✕🗺️⛽
🍴30⛳🎣☼❄🚲🐾🚭 SP 🅿️ T

Friarn Court Hotel ⋀

💥💥💥 COMMENDED

37 St Mary Street, Bridgwater
TA6 3LX
☎ (01278) 452859
Fax (01278) 452988
*Comfortable friendly hotel with
restaurant and cosy bar, ideal base for
business or pleasure. Double price is
for special weekend breaks. Colour
brochure.*

Wheelchair access category 2♿
Bedrooms: 2 single, 7 double, 6 twin,
1 triple
Bathrooms: 16 en-suite

Bed & breakfast

per night:	£min	£max
Single	39.90	59.90
Double	45.00	69.90

Lunch available
Evening meal 1900 (last orders
2100)
Parking for 14
Cards accepted: Amex, Diners,
Mastercard, Visa

🛇🖐🖧🖩🗝️💻🖥️🌢🗂️🍴📶✕🅿️📺
◑🖥️🛁🍴80 SP 🅿️ T

Quantock View House

Bridgwater Road, North Petherton,
Bridgwater TA6 6PR
☎ (01278) 663309 & 0860 137638
Fax (01278) 663309
*Comfortable, family-run guesthouse in
central Somerset. En-suite facilities
available. Close to hills and coast, yet
only minutes from M5, junction 24.*
Bedrooms: 1 double, 1 twin, 1 triple,
1 family room
Bathrooms: 3 en-suite, 1 private
shower

Bed & breakfast

per night:	£min	£max
Single	15.00	18.00
Double	30.00	36.00

Half board per

person:	£min	£max
Daily	22.00	25.00
Weekly	135.00	160.00

Evening meal 1830 (last orders
1500)
Parking for 5
Cards accepted: Mastercard, Visa

🛇🖐🖧🗂️🌢 UL 🖩 S 🅿️ 📺 🖥️🗺️🚲

Walnut Tree Hotel ⋀

💥💥💥💥 HIGHLY COMMENDED

North Petherton, Bridgwater
TA6 6QA
☎ (01278) 662255
Fax (01278) 663946
🅶🅡 Best Western/The Independents
*Set in the heart of Somerset. 18th C
coaching inn on A38, 1 mile from M5
exit 24. A welcome stopover for
businessmen and tourists.*
Bedrooms: 2 single, 23 double,
8 twin
Suites available
Bathrooms: 33 en-suite

Bed & breakfast

per night:	£min	£max
Single	37.00	80.00
Double	52.00	86.00

Half board per

person:	£min	£max
Daily	49.00	

Lunch available

Evening meal 1900 (last orders
2200)
Parking for 74
Cards accepted: Amex, Diners,
Mastercard, Visa, Switch/Delta

🛇🖐🖧🖩🗝️💻🖥️🌢🗂️ S ◑🖥️🗺️
🍴80 ⛳⛽🚲🐾🚭 SP

BRIDPORT

Dorset
Map ref 2A3

Market town and chief producer of
nets and ropes just inland of
dramatic Dorset coast. Old, broad
streets built for drying and twisting
and long gardens for rope-walks.
Grand arcaded Town Hall and
Georgian buildings. Local history
museum has Roman relics.
Tourist Information Centre ☎ *(01308)
424901*

Britmead House ⋀

💥💥💥 HIGHLY COMMENDED

West Bay Road, Bridport DT6 4EG
☎ (01308) 422941
Fax (01308) 422516

*Elegant, spacious, tastefully decorated
house. Lounge and dining room
overlooking garden. West Bay
Harbour/Coastal Path, 10 minutes'
walk away. Renowned for hospitality,
delicious meals and comfort.*
Bedrooms: 4 double, 3 twin
Bathrooms: 6 en-suite, 1 private

Bed & breakfast

per night:	£min	£max
Single	25.00	36.00
Double	40.00	58.00

Half board per

person:	£min	£max
Daily	33.50	42.50
Weekly	206.50	241.50

Evening meal 1900 (last orders
1700)
Parking for 8
Cards accepted: Amex, Diners,
Mastercard, Visa

🛇5🖐🗝️💻🖥️🌢🗂️ S 🅿️✕🗺️🖩🗺️
🅿️❄🚲 SP T

Establishments should be
open throughout the year,
unless otherwise stated.

BRIDPORT
Continued

Haddon House Hotel M

👑👑👑 COMMENDED

West Bay, Bridport DT6 4EL
☎ (01308) 423626 & 425323
Fax (01308) 427348
CR Logis of GB

*Country house hotel, renowned for
cuisine, situated 500 yards from
picturesque harbour, coast and golf
course. Well situated for touring
Dorset, Devon and Somerset.*
Bedrooms: 2 single, 6 double, 3 twin,
2 triple
Bathrooms: 13 en-suite

Bed & breakfast

per night:	£min	£max
Double	49.00	75.00

Lunch available
Evening meal 1900 (last orders
2100)
Parking for 44
Cards accepted: Amex, Diners,
Mastercard, Visa

🖰🛏🕭📞📺🖵🛆🕯🗓️§🗓️🖩🖃
🍴40⟋🌣🌂 SP 🏰 T

Roundham House Hotel M

👑👑👑 HIGHLY COMMENDED

Roundham Gardens, West Bay Road,
Bridport DT6 4BD
☎ (01308) 422753
Fax (01308) 421145
CR Logis of GB

*Attractive stone house in elevated
position, within own 1-acre gardens,
giving superb country and sea views.
Noted for excellent food (using
home-grown and local produce) and
hospitality.*
Bedrooms: 1 single, 3 double, 2 twin,
2 family rooms
Bathrooms: 8 en-suite

Bed & breakfast

per night:	£min	£max
Single	33.00	35.00
Double	55.00	65.00

Half board per

person:	£min	£max
Daily	47.00	52.00
Weekly	275.00	280.00

Lunch available
Evening meal 1900 (last orders
2030)
Parking for 12
Open March–December
Cards accepted: Mastercard, Visa

🖰📞🖵🛆🕯§🗓️🖩🖃🛆⟋🌣
OAP 🌂 SP T Ⓐ

BRISTOL

Map ref 2A2

Famous for maritime links, historic
harbour, Georgian terraces and
Brunel's Clifton suspension bridge.
Many attractions including SS Great
Britain, Bristol Zoo, museums and
art galleries and top name
entertainments. Events include
Balloon Fiesta and Regatta.
*Tourist Information Centre ☎ (0117)
926 0767*

Alcove Guest House

👑 APPROVED

508/510 Fishponds Road, Bristol
BS16 3DT
☎ (0117) 965 3886 & 965 2436
Fax (0117) 965 3886
*Clean and comfortable accommodation
with personal service. Easy access from
M32, M4. Private car park.*
Bedrooms: 1 single, 3 double, 3 twin,
1 triple, 1 family room
Bathrooms: 3 en-suite, 4 public

Bed & breakfast

per night:	£min	£max
Single	23.00	28.00
Double	34.00	42.00

Parking for 9

🖰🛏🖵 UL § 🖩🛆🖃 T

Arches Hotel

👑 COMMENDED

132 Cotham Brow, Cotham, Bristol
BS6 6AE
☎ (0117) 9247398
Fax (0117) 9247398
*Small friendly private hotel close to
central stations and 100 yards from
main A38. Option of traditional or
vegetarian breakfast.*
Bedrooms: 3 single, 4 double, 1 twin,
2 triple
Bathrooms: 2 en-suite, 2 public

Map references apply to
the colour maps at the
back of this guide.

Bed & breakfast

per night:	£min	£max
Single	22.50	32.50
Double	39.50	46.00

Cards accepted: Amex, Diners,
Mastercard, Visa, Switch/Delta

🖰🛏🖵🕯🗓️ UL § ⟋🖩🛆🖃🛺
SP Ⓖ

The Bowl Inn and
Restaurant M

👑👑 COMMENDED

16 Church Road, Lower
Almondsbury, Almondsbury, Bristol
BS12 4DT
☎ (01454) 612757
Fax (01454) 619910
Email: thebowl@3wa.co.uk

*12th C building, once a priory, nestling
on the edge of the Severn Vale. 3
minutes from M4/M5 interchange.*
Bedrooms: 6 double, 4 twin
Bathrooms: 10 en-suite

Bed & breakfast

per night:	£min	£max
Single	32.45	70.00
Double	52.25	108.00

Half board per

person:	£min	£max
Daily	48.95	92.95

Lunch available
Evening meal 1830 (last orders
2200)
Parking for 40
Cards accepted: Amex, Diners,
Mastercard, Visa, Switch/Delta

🖰4🖾📞🖵🛆🕯🗓️§⟋🖩🛆🖃
🍴30🌣🍴🛺 SP 🏰

Courtlands Hotel

👑👑👑 COMMENDED

1 Redland Court Road, Redland,
Bristol BS6 7EE
☎ (0117) 9424432
Fax (0117) 9232432

*Comfortable, family-run town-house
hotel. Located in a quiet residential
area overlooking Redland Grove. Close
to all the main attractions.*

Bedrooms: 5 single, 10 double,
4 twin, 3 triple, 1 family room
Bathrooms: 23 en-suite

Bed & breakfast

per night:	£min	£max
Single	44.00	46.00
Double	54.00	56.00

Lunch available
Evening meal 1900 (last orders
2000)
Parking for 15
Cards accepted: Mastercard, Visa

⛱🛁📞🖂☐🐾🍴📶🅿️Ⓢ🕒📺🔲
🍴Ⓣ30❄️🐕️SP🏫Ⓣ

Glenroy Hotel
⚜⚜⚜ COMMENDED

Victoria Square, Clifton, Bristol
BS8 4EW
☎ (0117) 9739058
Fax (0117) 9739058
Email: reservations@
glenroyhotel.demon.co.uk
Ⓒ Consort
*Two large, detached, early Victorian
houses, in one of Bristol's most
attractive squares. Restaurant open
Monday-Friday and for Sunday lunch.
Restricted menu available on Saturday
and Sunday evenings.*
Bedrooms: 14 single, 14 double,
8 twin, 8 triple
Bathrooms: 44 en-suite

Bed & breakfast

per night:	£min	£max
Single	53.00	73.00
Double	73.00	83.00

Half board per

person:	£min	£max
Daily	64.00	74.00

Evening meal 1830 (last orders
2130)
Parking for 16
Cards accepted: Amex, Diners,
Mastercard, Visa, Switch/Delta

⛱🛁📞🖂☐🐾🍴Ⓢ🕒📺🔲
🍴45 SP🏫Ⓣ◎

Henbury Lodge Hotel Ⓜ
⚜⚜⚜⚜ COMMENDED

Station Road, Henbury, Bristol
BS10 7QQ
☎ (0117) 9502615
Fax (0117) 9509532
*One mile from junction 17 off M5, 15
minutes' drive from city centre. Local
interest includes Blaise Castle and
Blaise Hamlet. Various special diets
catered for.*
Bedrooms: 1 single, 12 double,
2 twin, 4 triple
Bathrooms: 19 en-suite, 1 public

Bed & breakfast

per night:	£min	£max
Single	38.00	72.00
Double	56.00	82.00

Half board per

person:	£min	£max
Daily	55.00	89.00

Lunch available
Evening meal 1900 (last orders
2130)
Parking for 24
Cards accepted: Amex, Diners,
Mastercard, Visa, Switch/Delta

⛱🛁📞🖂☐🐾🍴Ⓢ🕒📺🔲
🍴32🐕🏫🎾❄️🌸OAPSP🏫Ⓣ

Jurys Bristol Hotel Ⓜ
⚜⚜⚜⚜ COMMENDED

Prince Street, Bristol BS1 4QF
☎ (0117) 9230333
Fax (0117) 9230300
Ⓒ Best Western/Utell International
*Modern hotel, recently refurbished,
overlooking quay and close to city
centre. Special weekend rates.
Restaurant, lounge bar and waterfront
tavern.*
Bedrooms: 20 single, 81 double,
86 twin
Bathrooms: 187 en-suite

Bed & breakfast

per night:	£min	£max
Single	84.00	114.00
Double	94.00	124.00

Lunch available
Evening meal 1830 (last orders
2215)
Parking for 400
Cards accepted: Amex, Diners,
Mastercard, Visa, Switch/Delta

⛱📞🖂☐🐾🍴Ⓢ🕒📺◐🔲
🍴320🐕SPⓉ

Mayfair Hotel
⚜⚜ COMMENDED

5 Henleaze Road,
Westbury-on-Trym, Bristol BS9 4EX
☎ (0117) 9622008 & 9493924
*Small hotel run by owners, situated
close to the downs and within easy
reach of both the city centre and
motorway.*
Bedrooms: 4 single, 2 double, 2 twin,
1 triple
Bathrooms: 3 en-suite, 2 public

Bed & breakfast

per night:	£min	£max
Single	28.00	36.00
Double	42.00	46.00

Parking for 9
Cards accepted: Mastercard

⛱☐🐾🍴UL📺◐🔲🚗

For further information on
accommodation establishments
use the coupons at the
back of this guide.

Oakfield Hotel
⚜ APPROVED

52 Oakfield Road, Clifton, Bristol
BS8 2BG
☎ (0117) 9735556 & 9733643
*Georgian facade with open views at
front and back. Well proportioned
rooms. Closed at Christmas.*
Bedrooms: 10 single, 3 double,
10 twin, 4 triple
Bathrooms: 7 public

Bed & breakfast

per night:	£min	£max
Single	27.00	28.00
Double	37.00	38.00

Half board per

person:	£min	£max
Daily	33.50	34.50
Weekly	234.50	241.50

Evening meal 1800 (last orders
1900)
Parking for 9

⛱🛁☐🐾UL📶Ⓢ📺🔲🚗

8 Southover Close
Listed COMMENDED

Westbury-on-Trym, Bristol
BS9 3NG
☎ (0117) 9500754
*Semi-detached house in quiet
cul-de-sac 3 miles from centre of
Bristol - off main Falcondale Road, just
outside Westbury village.*
Bedrooms: 1 single, 1 double
Bathrooms: 1 public

Bed & breakfast

per night:	£min	£max
Single	16.00	
Double	30.00	

Parking for 4
Open January–November

📺🖂☐🐾🍴UL📶🍴📺🔲🚗❄️✈
🚗

Sunderland Guest House Ⓜ
Listed APPROVED

4 Sunderland Place, (off St Paul's
Road), Clifton, Bristol BS8 1NA
☎ (0117) 9737249
*Small friendly guesthouse, well situated
for Bristol centre or Clifton village.
Within 5 minutes' walk of BBC, Bristol
University, Victoria Rooms. Close to
coach and train stations.*
Bedrooms: 5 single, 2 double, 2 twin,
1 triple
Bathrooms: 1 private, 2 public,
2 private showers

Bed & breakfast

per night:	£min	£max
Single	32.00	36.00
Double	44.00	55.00

⛱🛁☐🐾UL⒮🍴🔲🚗🏫

BRISTOL
Continued

Swallow Royal Hotel M
😛😛😛😛 HIGHLY COMMENDED
College Green, Bristol BS1 5TA
☎ (0117) 9255100 & 9255200
Fax (0117) 9251515
CR Swallow
Enjoys a prime position in the centre of Bristol. Exceptionally well-appointed, with air-conditioning, award-winning food and a Roman-themed leisure club. Short break packages available.
Wheelchair access category 3
Bedrooms: 16 single, 104 double, 108 twin, 14 triple
Suites available
Bathrooms: 242 en-suite
Bed & breakfast per night:

	£min	£max
Single	116.00	133.00
Double	143.00	158.00

Lunch available
Evening meal 1900 (last orders 2230)
Parking for 200
Cards accepted: Amex, Diners, Mastercard, Visa, Switch/Delta

The Town and Country Lodge
😛😛😛 COMMENDED
A38 Bridgwater Road, Bristol
BS13 8AG
☎ (01275) 392441
Fax (01275) 393362
CR The Independents

Recently refurbished hotel in glorious rural surroundings halfway between city centre and Bristol Airport. Restaurant with extensive menu. Function and conference rooms.
Bedrooms: 10 single, 12 double, 10 twin, 4 triple
Suites available
Bathrooms: 36 en-suite
Bed & breakfast per night:

	£min	£max
Single	39.00	52.50
Double	54.00	69.50

Half board per person:

	£min	£max
Daily	59.50	65.00
Weekly	350.00	350.00

Lunch available

Evening meal 1800 (last orders 2230)
Parking for 300
Cards accepted: Amex, Mastercard, Visa, Switch/Delta

Westbury Park Hotel
😛😛 HIGHLY COMMENDED
37 Westbury Road, Bristol BS9 3AU
☎ (0117) 9620465
Fax (0117) 9628607
Friendly, family-run hotel on Durdham Downs, close to city centre and M5, junction 17.
Bedrooms: 1 single, 5 double, 2 twin
Bathrooms: 8 en-suite
Bed & breakfast per night:

	£min	£max
Single	29.00	39.00
Double	45.00	52.00

Parking for 5
Cards accepted: Amex, Diners, Mastercard, Visa

BRIXHAM
Devon
Map ref 1D2

Famous for its trawling fleet in the 19th C, a steeply-built fishing port overlooking the harbour and fish market. A statue of William of Orange recalls his landing here before deposing James II. There is an aquarium and museum. Good cliff views and walks.
Tourist Information Centre ☎ (01803) 852861

The Berry Head Hotel M
😛😛 COMMENDED
Berry Head Road, Brixham TQ5 9AJ
☎ (01803) 853225
Fax (01803) 882084
Steeped in history, nestling on water's edge in 6 acres of grounds and in an Area of Outstanding Natural Beauty.
Bedrooms: 1 single, 6 double, 6 twin, 3 family rooms
Bathrooms: 16 en-suite
Bed & breakfast per night:

	£min	£max
Single	35.00	45.00
Double	70.00	104.00

Half board per person:

	£min	£max
Daily	40.00	65.00
Weekly	250.00	420.00

Lunch available
Evening meal 1900 (last orders 2130)
Parking for 202

Cards accepted: Amex, Diners, Mastercard, Visa

Richmond House Hotel M
😛😛 COMMENDED
Higher Manor Road, Brixham
TQ5 8HA
☎ (01803) 882391
Fax (01803) 882391
Detached Victorian house with well-appointed accommodation, sun-trap garden and adjacent car park. En-suite available. Convenient for shops and harbour, yet quiet location. First left after Golden Lion.
Bedrooms: 1 single, 4 double, 1 triple
Bathrooms: 4 en-suite, 1 private, 1 public
Bed & breakfast per night:

	£min	£max
Single	16.00	18.00
Double	32.00	40.00

Parking for 2
Cards accepted: Mastercard, Visa

BUDE
Cornwall
Map ref 1C2

Resort on dramatic Atlantic coast. High cliffs give spectacular sea and inland views. Golf-course, cricket pitch, folly, surfing, coarse-fishing and boating. Mother-town Stratton was base of Royalist Sir Bevil Grenville.
Tourist Information Centre ☎ (01288) 354240

Atlantic House Hotel M
😛😛 COMMENDED
Summerleaze Crescent, Bude
EX23 8HJ
☎ (01288) 352451
Fax (01288) 356666
Superb location overlooking beach, downs and town. Renowned for good food and fine wines. Five-choice menu daily in award winning restaurant.
Bedrooms: 1 single, 7 double, 2 twin, 3 family rooms
Bathrooms: 13 en-suite, 2 public
Bed & breakfast per night:

	£min	£max
Single	22.65	24.00
Double	43.30	51.50

Half board per person:

	£min	£max
Daily	35.90	39.00
Weekly	226.60	251.00

Lunch available

Evening meal 1830 (last orders 2000)
Parking for 10
Open March–November
Cards accepted: Mastercard, Visa, Switch/Delta

Bude Haven Hotel

COMMENDED

Flexbury Avenue, Bude EX23 8NS
☎ (01288) 352305

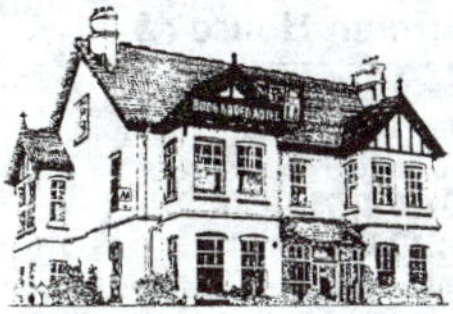

Edwardian family hotel with friendly, relaxing atmosphere in quiet area. Convenient for beach, town and golf-course. Comfort, hospitality and good food assured.
Bedrooms: 2 single, 5 double, 4 twin, 1 triple
Bathrooms: 12 en-suite

Bed & breakfast per night:	£min	£max
Single	25.00	27.00
Double	40.00	50.00

Half board per person:	£min	£max
Daily	30.00	37.00
Weekly	177.00	195.00

Evening meal 1830 (last orders 1900)
Parking for 8
Cards accepted: Amex, Mastercard, Visa

Camelot Hotel

COMMENDED

Downs View, Bude EX23 8RE
☎ (01288) 352361
Fax (01288) 355470)

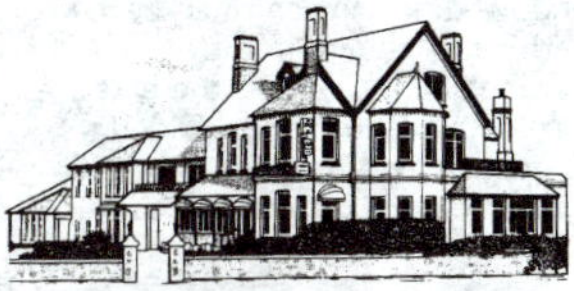

Comfortable family-run hotel situated close to the famous Crooklets Beach and overlooking a championship golf-course.
Bedrooms: 2 single, 6 double, 12 twin, 1 triple
Bathrooms: 21 en-suite

Bed & breakfast per night:	£min	£max
Single	24.00	28.00
Double	48.00	56.00

Half board per person:	£min	£max
Daily	36.00	40.00
Weekly	220.00	250.00

Evening meal 1900 (last orders 2030)
Parking for 21
Open February–November
Cards accepted: Mastercard, Visa

Cliff Hotel

HIGHLY COMMENDED

Crooklets Beach, Bude EX23 8NG
☎ (01288) 353110
Fax (01288) 353110

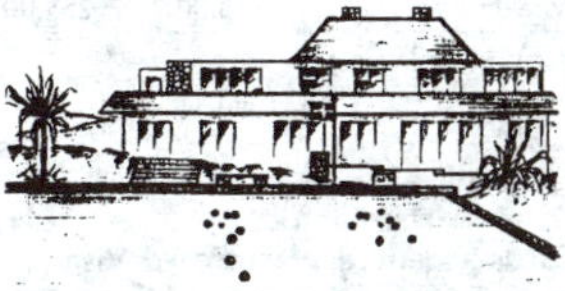

Indoor pool, mini-gym, putting, tennis court, bowling green, 5 acres next to National Trust cliffs, 200 yards from the beach. Chef/proprietor.
Bedrooms: 2 single, 3 double, 1 twin, 9 triple
Bathrooms: 15 en-suite

Bed & breakfast per night:	£min	£max
Single	22.50	28.50
Double	45.00	57.00

Half board per person:	£min	£max
Daily	31.50	38.50
Weekly	215.00	265.00

Lunch available
Evening meal 1830 (last orders 2030)
Parking for 15
Open April–September
Cards accepted: Mastercard, Visa, Switch/Delta

Please mention this guide when making your booking.

A key to symbols can be found inside the back cover flap.

The Falcon Hotel

HIGHLY COMMENDED

Breakwater Road, Bude EX23 8SD
☎ (01288) 352005
Fax (01288) 356359

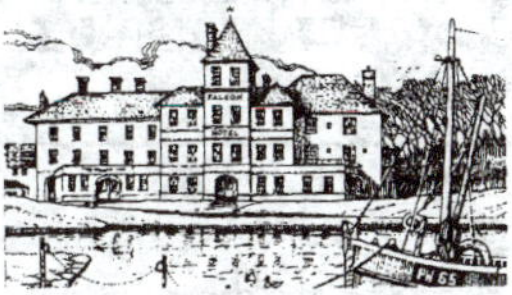

Character hotel in lovely position overlooking the Bude Canal. Close to beaches and shops. Self-catering apartments also available.
Bedrooms: 4 single, 14 double, 5 twin
Suites available
Bathrooms: 23 en-suite

Bed & breakfast per night:	£min	£max
Single	34.00	36.00
Double	68.00	72.00

Half board per person:	£min	£max
Daily	47.50	49.50
Weekly	285.00	297.00

Lunch available
Evening meal 1900 (last orders 2100)
Parking for 40
Cards accepted: Amex, Diners, Mastercard, Visa, Switch/Delta

Maer Lodge Hotel

APPROVED

Maer Down Road, Crooklets Beach, Bude EX23 8NG
☎ (01288) 353306
Fax (01288) 354005
Email: maerlodgehotel@btinternet.com
CR Minotel/Logis of GB
In own grounds in semi-rural setting overlooking the seaward end of the golf-course, near Crooklets surfing beach.
Bedrooms: 2 single, 9 double, 4 twin, 1 triple, 3 family rooms
Bathrooms: 19 en-suite, 1 public

Bed & breakfast per night:	£min	£max
Single	29.00	34.00
Double	52.00	62.00

Half board per person:	£min	£max
Daily	34.00	42.00
Weekly	203.00	238.00

Evening meal 1900 (last orders 2030)
Parking for 20

Continued ▶

BUDE

Continued

Cards accepted: Amex, Diners, Mastercard, Visa, Switch/Delta

🛁🖐🌣🏧🖨🗙🛒🕯🕭📺❄✕🐾 🍴🔍☕⛲❄🐾 SP T

Meva-Gwin Hotel Ⓜ

👑👑👑 COMMENDED

Upton, Bude EX23 0LY
☎ (01288) 352347
Fax (01288) 352347
On Marine Drive between Bude and Widemouth Bay. Coastal and rural views from all rooms, friendly atmosphere, traditional English cooking.
Bedrooms: 2 single, 4 double, 1 twin, 2 triple, 3 family rooms
Bathrooms: 11 en-suite, 1 public

Bed & breakfast
per night:	£min	£max
Single	22.00	24.00
Double	44.00	48.00

Half board per
person:	£min	£max
Daily	30.95	32.95
Weekly	185.00	195.00

Lunch available
Evening meal 1830 (last orders 1830)
Parking for 44
Open April–September
Cards accepted: Mastercard, Visa

🛁🖨🗙🛒🕭📺🖱❄✕ SP 🏦

Old Rectory

👑👑 HIGHLY COMMENDED

Marhamchurch, Bude EX23 0ER
☎ (01288) 361379
Offering spacious, quality en-suite accommodation, 2 minutes to Atlantic Highway (A39). Spectacular unspoilt coastline. Plentiful home cooking. No smoking.
Bedrooms: 2 double, 1 twin
Bathrooms: 3 en-suite

Bed & breakfast
per night:	£min	£max
Single	18.00	
Double	36.00	

Half board per
person:	£min	£max
Daily	28.00	
Weekly	196.00	

Evening meal 1830 (last orders 1830)
Parking for 4
Open March–November

🛁🔟🖨🗙🛒🕭UL✕📺🖱❄✕ 🐾🏦

Hotel Penarvor

👑👑👑 COMMENDED

Crooklets Beach, Bude EX23 8NE
☎ (01288) 352036
Fax (01288) 355027
Email: hotel-Penarvor
@compuserve.com
On the edge of National Trust coastline, with views across the magnificent sweep of Bude Bay, only 50 yards from the beach. Professionally prepared English and French cuisine.
Bedrooms: 3 single, 9 double, 4 twin
Bathrooms: 15 en-suite, 1 private shower

Bed & breakfast
per night:	£min	£max
Single	23.00	27.00
Double	46.00	54.00

Half board per
person:	£min	£max
Daily	32.00	39.00
Weekly	215.00	255.00

Lunch available
Evening meal 1900 (last orders 2030)
Parking for 20
Open March–October
Cards accepted: Mastercard, Visa

🛁🖐🌣🖨🗙🛒🕭🕯S✕📺🖱🔍 ▶❄OAP SP T

Stratton Gardens Hotel

👑👑👑 COMMENDED

Cot Hill, Stratton, Bude EX23 9DN
☎ (01288) 352500
Fax (01288) 352500

Charming 16th C Grade II listed hotel personally run by resident proprietors. Lovely home-cooked food. Quiet location in conservation area.
Bedrooms: 3 double, 1 twin, 1 triple
Bathrooms: 5 en-suite, 1 public

Bed & breakfast
per night:	£min	£max
Single	20.00	30.00
Double	40.00	50.00

Half board per
person:	£min	£max
Daily	29.00	35.00

Lunch available
Evening meal 1930 (last orders 2030)
Parking for 12
Cards accepted: Mastercard, Visa, Switch/Delta

🛁🔢5🗙🕭🕯S✕📺🖱🏧🍴35❄ ✕🐾 SP 🏦

BURNHAM-ON-SEA

Somerset
Map ref 1D1

Small Victorian resort famous for sunsets and sandy beaches, a few minutes from junction 22 of the M5. Ideal base for touring Somerset, Cheddar and Bath. Good sporting facilities, championship golf-course.
Tourist Information Centre ☎ (01278) 787852

Laburnum House Ⓜ

👑👑👑 COMMENDED

Sloway Lane, West Huntspill, Highbridge TA9 3RJ
☎ (01278) 781830
Fax (01278) 781612
Rural location near beaches. Indoor swimming pool, clay pigeon shooting, tennis court, water skiing. Restaurant. Situated in quiet location on edge of nature reserve. 3 miles from Burnham-on-Sea.
Bedrooms: 7 double, 11 twin, 7 triple
Bathrooms: 25 en-suite

Bed & breakfast
per night:	£min	£max
Single	34.00	38.00
Double	38.00	48.00

Half board per
person:	£min	£max
Daily	27.00	32.00
Weekly	135.00	160.00

Lunch available
Evening meal 1900 (last orders 2130)
Parking for 200
Cards accepted: Mastercard, Visa

🛁🖐🌣🖨🗙🛒🕭🕯S✕📺🖱🔍🏧 🍴110🗄🔍🎣🔍♪✕✎❄🐾 SP T

CALNE

Wiltshire
Map ref 2B2

Prosperity from wool in the 15th C endowed this ancient market town with a fine church in the Perpendicular style. To the east are chalk downlands and at Oldbury Castle, an Iron Age fort, a 17th C white horse is carved into the hillside.

Lansdowne Strand Hotel and Restaurant Ⓜ

👑👑👑 COMMENDED

The Strand, Calne SN11 0EH
☎ (01249) 812488
Fax (01249) 815323
Ⓒ® Consort
16th C coaching inn noted for cuisine and high standard of accommodation.

Retains all original features. Ideal touring centre for Cotswolds and Wiltshire.
Bedrooms: 2 single, 12 double, 9 twin, 3 family rooms
Bathrooms: 26 en-suite

Bed & breakfast

per night:	£min	£max
Single	50.00	57.00
Double	60.00	74.00

Half board per person:

	£min	£max
Daily	42.00	67.00

Lunch available
Evening meal 1900 (last orders 2130)
Parking for 20
Cards accepted: Amex, Diners, Mastercard, Visa, Switch/Delta

⛏🐴🛎📞📠🖥♿🏋🛇Ⓢ✂🛏🖿🞑
🍴80♻🏃🚴 SP 🏠Ⓣ⊚

CARBIS BAY

Cornwall
Map ref 1B3

Overlooking St Ives Bay and with fine beaches.

Tregorran Hotel 🅜
🏅🏅 APPROVED
Headland Road, Carbis Bay, St Ives TR26 2NU
☎ (01736) 795889
Mediterranean-style villa hotel in own grounds overlooking St Ives Bay, with panoramic sea views, safe beaches and tropical garden.
Bedrooms: 7 double, 2 twin, 1 triple, 6 family rooms
Bathrooms: 16 en-suite, 1 public

Bed & breakfast

per night:	£min	£max
Single	19.50	36.00
Double	39.00	72.00

Half board per person:

	£min	£max
Daily	29.00	45.50
Weekly	203.00	318.50

Evening meal 1830 (last orders 1915)
Parking for 18
Open April–September
Cards accepted: Amex, Mastercard, Visa, Switch/Delta

⛏🐴🖥♿🛇Ⓢ✂🛏🖵🞑🖿🞑❀🔍
🞏❄ DAP SP Ⓣ

White House Hotel
🏅🏅 COMMENDED
The Valley, Carbis Bay, St Ives TR26 2QY
☎ (01736) 797405 & 797426
Relaxed and friendly family-run hotel situated at the bottom of a woody

valley, 150 yards to Carbis Bay beach. Cosy a la carte restaurant.
Bedrooms: 4 double, 2 twin, 1 triple, 1 family room
Bathrooms: 8 en-suite, 1 public

Bed & breakfast

per night:	£min	£max
Single	30.00	40.00
Double	40.00	60.00

Half board per person:

	£min	£max
Daily	33.00	43.00
Weekly	199.50	238.00

Lunch available
Evening meal 1900 (last orders 2130)
Parking for 10
Open March–October
Cards accepted: Mastercard, Visa, Switch/Delta

⛏🐴📞🖥♿🛇🏋🖵🞑🖿❀🐕✕
🚆 SP

CARLYON BAY

Cornwall
Map ref 1B3

Residential and retirement suburb near St Austell, with fine clifftop golf-course.

Carlyon Bay Hotel 🅜
🏅🏅🏅🏅 HIGHLY COMMENDED
Sea Road, Carlyon Bay, St Austell PL25 3RD
☎ (01726) 812304
Fax (01726) 814938
Ⓒ Brend
High standard accommodation, complemented by extensive leisure facilites, including an 18-hole golf-course. Seasonal break rates available.
Bedrooms: 13 single, 16 double, 41 twin, 2 triple
Bathrooms: 72 en-suite, 1 public

Bed & breakfast

per night:	£min	£max
Single	68.00	83.00
Double	130.00	198.00

Half board per person:

	£min	£max
Daily	77.00	111.00
Weekly	350.00	777.00

Lunch available
Evening meal 1900 (last orders 2100)
Parking for 74
Cards accepted: Amex, Diners, Mastercard, Visa, Switch/Delta

⛏📞🖥♿🛇Ⓢ🏋🖵🞑◐🞑⛊🖿
🞑🍴70🚲🏊🏃🔍🞏♻♻❀✕🚆
🞏 SP Ⓣ

CASTLE CARY

Somerset
Map ref 2B2

One of south Somerset's most attractive market towns, with a picturesque winding high street of golden stone and thatch, market-house and famous round 18th C lock-up.

George Hotel 🅜
🏅🏅🏅 COMMENDED
Market Place, Castle Cary BA7 7AH
☎ (01963) 350761
Fax (01963) 350035
15th C thatched coaching inn with en-suite rooms, 2 bars and noted restaurant. Centrally located for many National Trust houses and gardens, Cheddar, Wells, Glastonbury and Bath.
Bedrooms: 4 single, 7 double, 3 twin, 1 family room
Bathrooms: 15 en-suite

Bed & breakfast

per night:	£min	£max
Single	40.00	45.00
Double	70.00	85.00

Half board per person:

	£min	£max
Daily	54.00	64.00

Lunch available
Evening meal 1900 (last orders 2100)
Parking for 10
Cards accepted: Amex, Mastercard, Visa, Switch/Delta

⛏🐴📞🖥♿🛇Ⓢ✂🛏🖿🞑
🍴20♻ SP 🏠Ⓣ

The Horse Pond Inn and Motel 🅜
🏅🏅 COMMENDED
The Triangle, Castle Cary BA7 7BD
☎ (01963) 350318 & 351762/4
17th C coaching inn with its old stables converted to spacious motel units, within a few steps of the main building.
Bedrooms: 1 double, 2 twin, 3 triple
Suites available
Bathrooms: 3 en-suite, 3 private, 2 public

Bed & breakfast

per night:	£min	£max
Single	30.00	35.00
Double	38.00	40.00

Half board per person:

	£min	£max
Daily	40.00	45.00
Weekly	224.00	250.00

Lunch available
Evening meal 1900 (last orders 2100)

Continued ▶

CASTLE CARY
Continued

Parking for 24
Cards accepted: Mastercard, Visa,
Switch/Delta

🛇🛉♿🖵📞♨🔒⟨S⟩✂🛏🖼 ⟐🍴120 🔍
▶ ⟨SP⟩ 🏠

CHAGFORD
Devon
Map ref 1C2

Handsome stone houses, some from
the Middle Ages, grace this former
stannary town on northern
Dartmoor. It is a popular centre for
walking expeditions and for tours of
the antiquities on the rugged moor.
There is a splendid 15th C granite
church, said to be haunted by the
poet Godolphin.

Easton Court Hotel ⋀

⟨👑👑👑⟩ COMMENDED

Easton Cross, Chagford, Newton
Abbot TQ13 8JL
☎ (01647) 433469
Fax (01647) 433654
Email: stay@easton.co.uk

*Thatched 15th C hotel of great charm
and character on the edge of
Dartmoor, offering peace, comfort and
good food.*
Bedrooms: 6 double, 2 twin
Bathrooms: 8 en-suite
Bed & breakfast

per night:	£min	£max
Single	45.00	52.00
Double	80.00	90.00

Half board per

person:	£min	£max
Daily	64.00	69.00
Weekly	329.00	364.00

Evening meal 1930 (last orders
2030)
Parking for 16
Open February–December
Cards accepted: Amex, Mastercard,
Visa

🛇12♿🛉📞🖵🖵♨🔒⟨S⟩✂🛏🖼
🖥❄🐾🚫⟨SP⟩🏠⟨T⟩

You are advised to confirm
your booking in writing.

Gidleigh Park ⋀

⟨👑👑👑⟩ DE LUXE

Chagford TQ13 8HH
☎ (01647) 432367 & 432225
Fax (01647) 432574
Email: gidleighpark@gidleigh.co.uk
*Luxurious hotel and restaurant on the
banks of the River Teign. Regarded by
many as having the finest restaurant
between Bath and Land's End.*
Bedrooms: 1 double, 13 twin
Suites available
Bathrooms: 14 en-suite
Half board per

person:	£min	£max
Daily	167.50	212.50

Lunch available
Evening meal 1900 (last orders
2100)
Parking for 25
Cards accepted: Amex, Diners,
Mastercard, Visa, Switch/Delta

🛇📞🖵🖵♨🔒⟨S⟩✂🛏⟐🍴22🔍
🖥🐾🚫⟨SP⟩🏠

Glendarah House ⋀

⟨👑👑⟩ HIGHLY COMMENDED

Chagford, Newton Abbot
TQ13 8BZ
☎ (01647) 433270
Fax (01647) 433483
*Comfortable Victorian house with
beautiful views in peaceful location, a
short walk from village centre. Friendly
service, en-suite rooms with all facilities.*
Bedrooms: 3 double, 3 twin
Bathrooms: 6 en-suite
Bed & breakfast

per night:	£min	£max
Single	25.00	35.00
Double	45.00	60.00

Parking for 7
Cards accepted: Mastercard, Visa,
Switch/Delta

🛇10♿🖵♨🔒⟨S⟩✂🛏🖼 🖥❄🐕
🐾⟨SP⟩

Mill End ⋀

⟨👑👑👑⟩ HIGHLY COMMENDED

Sandy Park, Chagford, Newton
Abbot TQ13 8JN
☎ (01647) 432282
Fax (01647) 433106

*Family-owned, situated in the Dartmoor
National Park on the banks of the
River Teign. 3 miles from A30, Whiddon
Down, on A382.*

Bedrooms: 2 single, 5 double, 8 twin,
2 triple
Bathrooms: 15 en-suite, 2 private
Bed & breakfast

per night:	£min	£max
Single	47.00	52.00
Double	65.00	95.00

Half board per

person:	£min	£max
Daily	48.00	75.00
Weekly	378.00	483.00

Lunch available
Evening meal 1930 (last orders
2100)
Parking for 21
Cards accepted: Amex, Mastercard,
Visa, Switch/Delta

🛇♿🛉📞🖵🖵♨🔒⟨S⟩🖼⟨TV⟩🛏 🖥
🍴⟐📞♪❄🚗🚫⟨SP⟩🏠⟨T⟩

Thornworthy House ⋀

⟨👑👑⟩ COMMENDED

Chagford, Newton Abbot
TQ13 8EY
☎ (01647) 433297
Fax (01647) 433297

*Peaceful moorland setting for country
lovers in search of real comfort and
personal service. Stylish home cooking
and fine wines.*
Bedrooms: 1 single, 1 double, 1 twin
Bathrooms: 2 en-suite, 1 public
Bed & breakfast

per night:	£min	£max
Single	25.50	30.50
Double	55.00	66.00

Half board per

person:	£min	£max
Daily	40.50	50.50
Weekly	262.50	318.50

Evening meal 2000 (last orders
2030)
Parking for 8

🛇🖵♨🔒✂🛏⟨TV⟩🖼 🖥📞♪❄
🚗⟨SP⟩

Please check prices and other
details at the time of booking.

For ideas on places to visit
refer to the introduction at
the beginning of this section.

Three Crowns Hotel ♙

High Street, Chagford, Newton
Abbot TQ13 8AJ
☎ (01647) 433444
Fax (01647) 433117

*13th C hotel of character in
picturesque village within Dartmoor
National Park. Good cuisine. Function
room. Four-poster beds. Log fires.*
Bedrooms: 1 single, 10 double,
3 twin
Bathrooms: 14 en-suite, 3 public

Bed & breakfast per night:	£min	£max
Single	30.00	45.00
Double	50.00	65.00

Half board per person:	£min	£max
Daily	42.50	50.00
Weekly	250.00	290.00

Lunch available
Evening meal 1900 (last orders
2130)
Parking for 21
Cards accepted: Amex, Diners,
Mastercard, Visa, Switch/Delta

🐎🖭📞🖵👶🍴🕭💺✂🔌📺🗄🖴
🍽150🔍♺♪🏃✳🛇🐾SP🏤T

CHARMOUTH

Dorset
Map ref 1D2

Set back from the fossil-rich cliffs, a
small coastal town where Charles II
came to the Queen's Armes when
seeking escape to France. Just south
at low tide, the sandy beach rewards
fossil-hunters; at Black Ven an
ichthyosaurus (now in London's
Natural History Museum) was
found.

Hensleigh Hotel ♙

Lower Sea Lane, Charmouth,
Bridport DT6 6LW
☎ (01297) 560830
*Family-run hotel with a reputation for
friendly service, comfort, hospitality and
delicious food. Situated just 300 metres
from beach.*
Bedrooms: 2 single, 4 double, 4 twin,
1 triple
Bathrooms: 11 en-suite

Bed & breakfast per night:	£min	£max
Single	25.00	27.00
Double	50.00	54.00

Half board per person:	£min	£max
Daily	39.00	41.00
Weekly	245.00	260.00

Evening meal 1830 (last orders
1930)
Parking for 15
Open March–October
Cards accepted: Amex, Mastercard,
Visa

🐎3🖭📞👶🍴🕭💺✂🔌🗄🖴🍴✳🐾
SP T

Newlands House

Stonebarrow Lane, Charmouth,
Bridport DT6 6RA
☎ (01297) 560212
*House of character, comfortably
furnished and giving an ambience of
quiet relaxation, offers you excellent
home-cooked food. Set in large gardens
and orchard 5 minutes from the
Heritage Coastal Path. No smoking
except in bar lounge. About 2.5 miles
east of Lyme Regis.*
Bedrooms: 3 single, 4 double, 3 twin,
2 family rooms
Bathrooms: 11 en-suite, 1 public

Bed & breakfast per night:	£min	£max
Single	23.75	27.00
Double	47.50	54.00

Half board per person:	£min	£max
Daily	38.25	41.50
Weekly	241.00	261.00

Evening meal 1900 (last orders
1930)
Parking for 15
Open March–October

🐎6🖵👶🍴🕭💺✂🔌📺🗄🖴🍴✳
🚜SP

The White House Hotel ♙

2 Hillside, The Street, Charmouth,
Bridport DT6 6PJ
☎ (01297) 560411
Fax (01297) 560702
Ⓒ Logis of GB
*Listed Regency house with many
original period features including
Regency windows and bow doors.
Warmly furnished for peace and
relaxation.*
Bedrooms: 1 single, 7 double, 2 twin
Bathrooms: 9 en-suite, 1 private
shower

Bed & breakfast per night:	£min	£max
Single	46.00	56.00
Double	77.00	112.00

Half board per person:	£min	£max
Daily	53.00	60.00
Weekly	322.00	371.00

Lunch available
Evening meal 1900 (last orders
2200)
Parking for 15
Open February–October, December
Cards accepted: Amex, Diners,
Mastercard, Visa, Switch/Delta

🐎14🖭📞🕭🖵👶♺🕭💺✂🔌🌑
🗄🖴🍴♺U🏃✳🚜DAP🛇SP🏤T

CHEW STOKE

Bath & North East Somerset
Map ref 2A2

Attractive village in the Mendip Hills
with an interesting Tudor rectory
and the remains of a Roman villa. To
the south is the Chew Valley
reservoir with its extensive leisure
facilities.

Orchard House ♙

Bristol Road, Chew Stoke, Bristol
BS18 8UB
☎ (01275) 333143
Fax (01275) 333754
*Comfortable accommodation in a
carefully modernised Georgian house
and coach house annexe. Home
cooking using local produce.*
Bedrooms: 1 single, 2 double, 3 twin,
1 family room
Bathrooms: 5 en-suite, 1 private,
2 public

Bed & breakfast per night:	£min	£max
Single	18.00	22.00
Double	36.00	44.00

Half board per person:	£min	£max
Daily	28.00	32.00

Evening meal 1830 (last orders
1000)
Parking for 9

🐎🖭👶🍴🕭💺📺🗄🖴🍴✳🐾🚜◉

The symbols in each entry
give information about
services and facilities.
A key to these symbols
appears at the back
of this guide.

CHIDEOCK

Dorset
Map ref 1D2

Village of sandstone thatched
cottages in a valley near the
dramatic Dorset coast. The church
holds an interesting processional
cross in mother-of-pearl and the
manor house close by is associated
with the Victorian Roman Catholic
church. Seatown has a pebble beach
and limestone cliffs.

Chideock House Hotel M

👑👑👑 APPROVED

Main Street, Chideock, Bridport
DT6 6JN
☎ (01297) 489242

*15th C thatched family-run hotel. On
the A35, 3 miles west of Bridport and
less than 1 mile from the sea.
Oak-beamed restaurant and bar
serving "real food" in comfortable
surroundings. Reputed headquarters of
General Fairfax.*
Bedrooms: 7 double, 2 twin, 2 triple
Bathrooms: 8 en-suite, 3 private
**Bed & breakfast
per night:**

	£min	£max
Single	35.00	70.00
Double	55.00	75.00

**Half board per
person:**

	£min	£max
Daily	45.00	60.00
Weekly	280.00	390.00

Evening meal 1900 (last orders
2100)
Parking for 20
Cards accepted: Amex, Mastercard,
Visa, Switch/Delta
🛏🐎🖥📞🔌⬛🕮🖩⛓🔥🚗✕
SP 🏠 T

CHIPPENHAM

Wiltshire
Map ref 2B2

Ancient market town with modern
industry. Notable early buildings
include the medieval Town Hall and
the gabled 15th C Yelde Hall, now a
local history museum. On the
outskirts Hardenhuish has a
charming hilltop church by the
Georgian architect John Wood of
Bath.
*Tourist Information Centre ☎ (01249)
657733*

The Bramleys

Listed COMMENDED

73 Marshfield Road, Chippenham
SN15 1JR
☎ (01249) 653770
*Large Victorian listed building, close to
town centre. Family-run with relaxed
friendly atmosphere. All home cooking.*
Bedrooms: 1 single, 3 twin, 1 triple
Bathrooms: 1 public
**Bed & breakfast
per night:**

	£min	£max
Single	15.00	16.00
Double	30.00	32.00

Parking for 4
🐎🖥🔌⬛UL🕮S✕🖩TV🖩⬛🚗✕
🐕🏠T

CHIPPING SODBURY

South Gloucestershire
Map ref 2B2

Old market town, its buildings a
mixture of Cotswold stone and
mellowed brickwork. The 15th C
church and the market cross are of
interest. Horton Court (National
Trust) stands 4 miles north-east and
preserves a very rare Norman hall.

The Sodbury House Hotel M

👑👑 COMMENDED

Badminton Road, Old Sodbury,
South Gloucestershire BS17 6LU
☎ (01454) 312847
Fax (01454) 273105
CR The Independents
*Former farmhouse in extensive,
well-kept grounds, offering informal but
quality accommodation. Easy access
M4/M5. Stepping-stone to Bath, Bristol,
Cotswolds and South Wales.*
Bedrooms: 7 single, 3 double, 2 twin,
2 triple
Bathrooms: 14 en-suite
**Bed & breakfast
per night:**

	£min	£max
Single	43.00	67.00
Double	64.00	90.00

Parking for 30

Cards accepted: Amex, Mastercard,
Visa, Switch/Delta
🐎🛏📞🖥⬛🔌🕮🖩S✕🖩🖩🚗
🍴35 UↃ🔥🐕 SP ◎

CLEVEDON

North Somerset
Map ref 1D1

Handsome Victorian resort on
shingly shores of Severn Estuary.
Pier, golf links with ruined folly,
part-Norman clifftop church.
Tennyson and Thackeray stayed at
nearby Clevedon Court just to the
east. Medieval with later additions,
the manor overlooks terraces with
rare plants.

Walton Park Hotel M

👑👑👑 COMMENDED

1 Wellington Terrace, Clevedon
BS21 7BL
☎ (01275) 874253
Fax (01275) 343577
CR Consort
*Country house hotel overlooking the
Severn Estuary. 2 miles from M5
junction 20. Ideal base for touring the
West Country. Daily half board prices
are based on a minimum 2-night stay.*
Bedrooms: 10 single, 8 double,
22 twin
Bathrooms: 40 en-suite
**Bed & breakfast
per night:**

	£min	£max
Single	42.00	65.00
Double	73.50	80.00

**Half board per
person:**

	£min	£max
Daily	49.50	52.00
Weekly	346.50	364.00

Lunch available
Evening meal 1930 (last orders
2130)
Parking for 50
Cards accepted: Amex, Diners,
Mastercard, Visa, Switch/Delta
🐎📞⬛🖥🔌⬛🕮S✕🖩◎🔆⬛🖩
⬛🍴150 UↃ🔥🐕 SP 🏠T

CLOVELLY

Devon
Map ref 1C1

Clinging to wooded cliffs, fishing village with steep cobbled street zigzagging, or cut in steps, to harbour. Carrying sledges stand beside whitewashed flower-decked cottages. Charles Kingsley's father was rector of the church set high up near the Hamlyn family's Clovelly Court.

The New Inn

High Street, Clovelly, Bideford EX39 5TQ
☎ (01237) 431303
Fax (01237) 431636

17th C inn hidden deep within the cobbled streets of this historic village. Newly restored. Lovely bedrooms. Rare views. Wonderful atmosphere.
Bedrooms: 1 single, 7 double
Bathrooms: 8 en-suite
Bed & breakfast

per night:	£min	£max
Single	30.00	55.00
Double	60.00	80.00

Half board per

person:	£min	£max
Daily	48.00	58.00
Weekly	224.00	301.00

Lunch available
Evening meal 1900 (last orders 2100)
Cards accepted: Mastercard, Visa, Switch/Delta

Red Lion Hotel

The Quay, Clovelly, Bideford EX39 5TF
☎ (01237) 431237
Fax (01237) 431044

Newly refurbished ancient inn. Dramatic quayside setting in unique heritage village. Splendid bedrooms. Stunning sea views. Seafood a speciality.

Bedrooms: 7 double, 2 twin, 2 triple
Bathrooms: 11 en-suite
Bed & breakfast

per night:	£min	£max
Single	37.00	57.00
Double	74.00	85.00

Half board per

person:	£min	£max
Daily	55.00	59.00
Weekly	252.00	336.00

Lunch available
Evening meal 1900 (last orders 2030)
Parking for 11
Cards accepted: Amex, Mastercard, Visa, Switch/Delta

COMBE MARTIN

Devon
Map ref 1C1

On the edge of the Exmoor National Park, this seaside village is set in a long narrow valley with its natural harbour lying between towering cliffs. The main beach is a mixture of sand, rocks and pebbles and the lack of strong currents ensures safe bathing.

Saffron House Hotel

COMMENDED
King Street, Combe Martin, Ilfracombe EX34 0BX
☎ (01271) 883521
17th C hotel set in own grounds close to beaches and Exmoor. Well-appointed en-suite rooms. Heated pool. Children and pets very welcome. Ideal touring centre.
Bedrooms: 4 double, 1 twin, 2 triple, 2 family rooms
Bathrooms: 7 en-suite, 1 public
Bed & breakfast

per night:	£min	£max
Single	19.00	21.00
Double	36.00	40.00

Half board per

person:	£min	£max
Daily	27.00	29.00
Weekly	165.00	189.00

Evening meal from 1830
Parking for 10
Open January–November
Cards accepted: Mastercard, Visa, Switch/Delta

You are advised to confirm your booking in writing.

Sandy Cove Hotel

APPROVED
Old Coast Road, Berrynarbor, Ilfracombe EX34 9SR
☎ (01271) 882243 & 882888
Fax (01271) 883830

In many acres of own grounds incorporating garden, cliffs, own beach and woods. Overlooks Combe Martin Bay, the beaches, sea and Exmoor. Outdoor/indoor pools, sauna, sunbed, gym equipment and whirlpool.
Bedrooms: 2 single, 16 double, 5 twin, 10 triple
Bathrooms: 33 en-suite
Bed & breakfast

per night:	£min	£max
Single	25.00	46.00
Double	50.00	92.00

Half board per

person:	£min	£max
Daily	35.00	73.00
Weekly	294.00	403.00

Lunch available
Evening meal 1900 (last orders 2130)
Parking for 70

CRANTOCK

Cornwall
Map ref 1B2

Pretty village of thatched cottages and seaside bungalows. Village stocks, once used against smugglers, are in the churchyard and the pub has a smugglers' hideout.

Crantock Bay Hotel

COMMENDED
Crantock, Newquay TR8 5SE
☎ (01637) 830229
Fax (01637) 831111
Minotel
Long established family hotel on headland, with grounds leading directly on to beach. National Trust land nearby. Wonderful walking country.
Bedrooms: 9 single, 8 double, 15 twin, 2 family rooms
Bathrooms: 34 en-suite
Half board per

person:	£min	£max
Daily	51.00	59.00
Weekly	325.00	385.00

Continued ▶

CRANTOCK

Continued

Lunch available
Evening meal 1900 (last orders
2030)
Parking for 36
Open March–November
Cards accepted: Amex, Diners,
Mastercard, Visa, Switch/Delta

CREDITON

Devon
Map ref 1D2

Ancient town in fertile valley, once
prosperous from wool, now active
in cider-making. Said to be the
birthplace of St Boniface. The 13th
C Chapter House, the church
governors' meeting place, holds a
collection of armour from the Civil
War.

Coombe House Country Hotel M

COMMENDED

Coleford, Crediton EX17 5BY
☎ (01363) 84487
Fax (01363) 84722
Logis of GB
*Georgian manor house in 5 acres.
Rural heart of Devon between
Dartmoor and Exmoor, equidistant
north and south coasts and 15 minutes
from Exeter. Croquet, swimming, tennis.*
Bedrooms: 9 double, 6 twin
Bathrooms: 15 en-suite
Bed & breakfast

per night:	£min	£max
Single	49.50	59.50
Double	72.50	84.50

Half board per

person:	£min	£max
Daily	55.75	79.00
Weekly	279.00	395.00

Lunch available
Evening meal 1900 (last orders
2100)
Parking for 90
Cards accepted: Mastercard, Visa,
Switch/Delta

The National Grading and
Classification Scheme is
explained at the back
of this guide.

CREWKERNE

Somerset
Map ref 1D2

This charming little market town on
the Dorset border nestles in
undulating farmland and orchards in
a conservation area. Built of local
sandstone with Roman and Saxon
origins. The magnificent St
Bartholomew's Church dates from
15th C; St Bartholomew's Fair is
held in September.

Broadview Gardens M

DE LUXE

East Crewkerne, Crewkerne
TA18 7AG
☎ (01460) 73424
Fax (01460) 73424
*Unusual Colonial bungalow, a winner of
awards for quality, friendliness and
traditional English cooking. En-suite
rooms overlooking acre of beautiful
secluded gardens. Dorset border,
perfect touring base.*
Bedrooms: 1 double, 2 twin
Bathrooms: 2 en-suite, 1 private
Bed & breakfast

per night:	£min	£max
Single	35.00	46.00
Double	50.00	56.00

Half board per

person:	£min	£max
Daily	39.00	42.00
Weekly	273.00	294.00

Evening meal 1830 (last orders
1200)
Parking for 6
Cards accepted: Mastercard, Visa,
Switch/Delta

The George Hotel and Restaurant M

APPROVED

Market Square, Crewkerne
TA18 7LP
☎ (01460) 73650
Fax (01460) 72974
Email: thegeorgehotelcrewkerne
@ukbusiness.comm
*Recently refurbished 17th C Grade II
listed coaching inn in the market
square. Ideally located for touring. Fine
food, real ales, warm welcome!*
Bedrooms: 3 single, 6 double, 2 twin,
1 triple, 1 family room
Bathrooms: 10 en-suite, 2 public,
1 private shower
Bed & breakfast

per night:	£min	£max
Single	24.00	38.00
Double	48.00	70.00

Half board per

person:	£min	£max
Daily	35.00	

Lunch available
Evening meal 1900 (last orders
2130)
Cards accepted: Amex, Diners,
Mastercard, Visa, Switch/Delta

CROYDE

Devon
Map ref 1C1

Pretty village with thatched cottages
near Croyde Bay. To the south
stretch Saunton Sands and their
dunelands Braunton Burrows with
interesting flowers and plants,
nature reserve and golf-course. Cliff
walks and bird-watching at Baggy
Point, west of the village.

Croyde Bay House Hotel M

HIGHLY COMMENDED

Moor Lane, Croyde, Braunton
EX33 1PA
☎ (01271) 890270
*Small, friendly hotel beside beach,
where comfort, good food and personal
care are still found. Beautifully
positioned sun deck and sun lounge.
Peaceful garden, car parking.*
Bedrooms: 3 double, 2 twin, 2 triple
Bathrooms: 7 en-suite
Half board per

person:	£min	£max
Daily	44.00	54.00
Weekly	295.00	335.00

Evening meal 1915 (last orders
2000)
Parking for 7
Open March–November
Cards accepted: Amex, Mastercard,
Visa, Switch/Delta

WELCOME HOST

This is a nationally recognised
customer care programme
which aims to promote
the highest standards of
service and a warm welcome.
Establishments who are taking
part in this initiative are
indicated by the ✿ symbol.

CULLOMPTON

Devon
Map ref 1D2

Market town on former coaching routes, with pleasant tree-shaded cobbled pavements and some handsome 17th C houses. Earlier prosperity from the wool industry is reflected in the grandness of the church with its fan-vaulted aisle built by a wool-stapler in 1526.

Rullands M

⚜⚜ COMMENDED
Rull Lane, Cullompton EX15 1NQ
☎ (01884) 33356
Fax (01884) 35890
Ⓒ Logis of GB
15th C country house amidst beautiful Devon countryside. En-suite facilities. Delicious home cooking and choice wines. 5 minutes junction 28 of M5.
Bedrooms: 2 single, 2 double, 1 triple
Bathrooms: 4 en-suite, 1 private shower

Bed & breakfast per night:	£min	£max
Single	27.50	35.00
Double	50.00	50.00

Half board per person:	£min	£max
Daily	45.00	47.50

Evening meal 1915 (last orders 2130)
Parking for 30
Cards accepted: Amex, Mastercard, Visa, Switch/Delta

🛇🖾🏠🗃📞☐🖥♿🍴🎦Ⓢ✂🌙🚿🖳🗲
🍴20❄✽🌳🚲 SP 🏠

DARTMOOR

See under Ashburton, Bovey Tracey, Chagford, Horrabridge, Lydford, Moretonhampstead, Okehampton, Two Bridges, Yelverton

Map references apply to the colour maps at the back of this guide.

ACCESSIBILITY

Look for the ♿ symbols which indicate accessibility for wheelchair users. These are described in detail at the front of this guide.

DARTMOUTH

Devon
Map ref 1D3

Ancient port at mouth of Dart. Has fine period buildings, notably town houses near Quay and Butterwalk of 1635. Harbour castle ruin. In 12th C Crusader fleets assembled here. Royal Naval College dominates from Hill. Carnival, June; Regatta, August.
Tourist Information Centre ☎ (01803) 834224

Ford House M

⚜⚜⚜ HIGHLY COMMENDED
44 Victoria Road, Dartmouth
TQ6 9DX
☎ (01803) 834047 & 0378 771971
Fax (01803) 834047
All the assets of a hotel but the intimacy of a guesthouse. Centrally located. Twin or king-sized beds. Breakfast served until noon.
Bedrooms: 3 double, 1 twin
Bathrooms: 3 en-suite, 1 private

Bed & breakfast per night:	£min	£max
Single	35.00	70.00
Double	50.00	70.00

Half board per person:	£min	£max
Daily	60.00	95.00
Weekly	420.00	665.00

Lunch available
Evening meal 1900 (last orders 2100)
Parking for 5
Open March–October
Cards accepted: Amex, Mastercard, Visa

🛇🖾📞☐🖥♿🔌Ⓤ🎦🖳🛋🗲❄
🚲 DAP SP 🏠

Stoke Lodge Hotel M

⚜⚜⚜ COMMENDED
Stoke Fleming, Dartmouth
TQ6 0RA
☎ (01803) 770523
Fax (01803) 770851
Country house hotel with sea and village views. Heated indoor and outdoor swimming pools and leisure facilities, including all-weather tennis court.
Bedrooms: 2 single, 8 double, 8 twin, 7 triple
Bathrooms: 25 en-suite

Bed & breakfast per night:	£min	£max
Single	45.00	49.50
Double	74.00	85.00

Half board per person:	£min	£max
Daily	49.50	55.00
Weekly	259.00	380.00

Lunch available
Evening meal 1900 (last orders 2100)
Parking for 50
Cards accepted: Amex, Mastercard, Visa

🛇🖾🏠📞☐🖥♿🍴Ⓢ✂🌙🖳
🍴100🐾☎🎣🔌🐕❄🌳🚲🌙 SP 🏠
Ⓣ

Victoria Hotel M

⚜⚜⚜ COMMENDED
27-29 Victoria Road, Dartmouth
TQ6 9RT
☎ (01803) 832572 & 832573
Fax (01803) 835815
Small, elegant hotel in town centre with en-suite rooms. Candlelit restaurant serving finest local produce, prepared with flair. 2 bars. Friendly and efficient staff.
Bedrooms: 7 double, 3 twin
Suite available
Bathrooms: 10 en-suite

Bed & breakfast per night:	£min	£max
Single	30.00	50.00
Double	60.00	130.00

Half board per person:	£min	£max
Daily	30.00	55.00
Weekly	210.00	385.00

Lunch available
Evening meal 1900 (last orders 2130)
Parking for 1
Cards accepted: Mastercard, Visa

🏠📞☐🖥♿🎣Ⓢ✂🌙🖳🛋Ⓤ⛵
🚲🌙 SP ©

DEVIZES

Wiltshire
Map ref 2B2

Old market town standing on the Kennet and Avon Canal. Rebuilt Norman castle, good 18th C buildings. St John's church has 12th C work and Norman tower. Museum of Wiltshire's archaeology and natural history reflects wealth of prehistoric sites in the county.
Tourist Information Centre ☎ (01380) 729408

Black Swan Hotel

⚜⚜⚜ APPROVED
Market Place, Devizes SN10 1JQ
☎ (01380) 723259
Fax (01380) 729966
Welcoming, family-run hotel in picturesque market town, central for many of Wiltshire's historic sights. Excellent food, well-appointed en-suite rooms, friendly service.

Continued ▶

DEVIZES
Continued

Bedrooms: 1 single, 5 double, 4 twin
Bathrooms: 10 en-suite

Bed & breakfast

per night:	£min	£max
Single	40.00	40.00
Double	60.00	80.00

Lunch available
Evening meal 1900 (last orders 2200)
Parking for 13
Cards accepted: Mastercard, Visa, Switch/Delta

The Castle Hotel M
COMMENDED

New Park Street, Devizes
SN10 1DS
☎ (01380) 729300
Fax (01380) 729155
Well-appointed accommodation in a busy market town. A la carte restaurant and popular bar. All rooms en-suite.
Bedrooms: 5 single, 5 double, 7 twin, 1 family room
Suite available
Bathrooms: 18 en-suite

Bed & breakfast

per night:	£min	£max
Single	40.00	45.00
Double	55.00	65.00

Half board per

person:	£min	£max
Daily	40.00	55.00

Lunch available
Evening meal 1830 (last orders 2100)
Parking for 6
Cards accepted: Amex, Mastercard, Visa, Switch/Delta

Spout Cottage
HIGHLY COMMENDED

Stert, Devizes SN10 3JD
☎ (01380) 724336
Delightfully situated thatched cottage in secluded valley. Idyllic peaceful retreat. Well-appointed centrally heated rooms, inglenook fireplace, beamed ceilings. Delicious, imaginative food.
Bedrooms: 1 single, 1 twin
Bathrooms: 2 public

Bed & breakfast

per night:	£min	£max
Single	18.50	20.00
Double	33.00	36.00

Half board per

person:	£min	£max
Daily	36.00	38.00

Lunch available
Evening meal from 2000
Parking for 4

DORCHESTER
Dorset
Map ref 2B3

Busy medieval county town destroyed by fires in 17th and 18th C. Cromwellian stronghold and scene of Judge Jeffreys' Bloody Assize after Monmouth Rebellion of 1685. Tolpuddle Martyrs were tried in Shire Hall. Museum has Roman and earlier exhibits and Hardy relics.
Tourist Information Centre ☎ (01305) 267992

Wessex Royale Hotel
COMMENDED

32 High West Street, Dorchester
DT1 1UP
☎ (01305) 262660
Fax (01305) 251941

Georgian town centre hotel, recently refurbished to a high standard, with extensive restaurant, bar and function facilities.
Bedrooms: 3 single, 17 double, 6 twin, 2 triple
Suite available
Bathrooms: 27 en-suite

Bed & breakfast

per night:	£min	£max
Single	25.00	40.00
Double	39.00	59.00

Half board per

person:	£min	£max
Daily	45.00	59.00
Weekly	315.00	413.00

Lunch available
Evening meal 1830 (last orders 2130)
Parking for 5
Cards accepted: Amex, Diners, Mastercard, Visa, Switch/Delta

Yalbury Cottage Hotel and Restaurant
HIGHLY COMMENDED

Lower Bockhampton, Dorchester
DT2 8PZ
☎ (01305) 262382
Fax (01305) 266412

17th C thatched hotel in beautiful countryside 2 miles east of Dorchester near Hardy's Cottage. Comfortable, oak-beamed lounge and excellent restaurant with friendly, attentive service. Well-equipped en-suite bedrooms.
Bedrooms: 6 twin, 1 triple, 1 family room
Bathrooms: 8 en-suite

Bed & breakfast

per night:	£min	£max
Single	46.00	46.00
Double	72.00	72.00

Half board per

person:	£min	£max
Daily	55.00	65.00
Weekly	336.00	406.00

Evening meal 1900 (last orders 2100)
Parking for 19
Open February–December
Cards accepted: Mastercard, Visa, Switch/Delta

DULVERTON
Somerset
Map ref 1D1

Set among woods and hills of south-west Exmoor, a busy riverside town with a 13th C church. The Rivers Barle and Exe are rich in salmon and trout. The information centre at the Exmoor National Park Headquarters at Dulverton is open throughout the year.

Dassels Country House
COMMENDED

Dassels, Dulverton TA22 9RZ
☎ (01398) 341561
Fax (01398) 341203

Georgian style country guesthouse, magnificently situated on the Devon/Somerset border, with panoramic views.
Bedrooms: 1 single, 3 double, 3 twin, 3 triple
Bathrooms: 10 en-suite

Bed & breakfast per night:	£min	£max
Single	30.00	35.00
Double	46.00	56.00

Half board per person:	£min	£max
Daily	33.00	38.00
Weekly	210.00	245.00

Evening meal 1900 (last orders 2100)
Parking for 16
Cards accepted: Amex, Mastercard, Visa, Switch/Delta

🐎♿📞📺👶🕯️🗝️⬛🅂✂🗝️📺🛏️🖼️ 🍴20♺🌸🔖 SP

Exton House Hotel 👥

👑👑👑 HIGHLY COMMENDED

Exton, Dulverton TA22 9JT
☎ (01643) 851365
Fax (01643) 851213
Former rectory in a delightful rural setting on side of the Exe Valley. Turn off A396 at Bridgetown and we are half a mile on right.
Bedrooms: 1 single, 5 double, 3 twin
Bathrooms: 8 en-suite, 1 private

Bed & breakfast per night:	£min	£max
Single	27.00	35.00
Double	46.00	62.00

Half board per person:	£min	£max
Daily	40.00	45.00
Weekly	256.00	301.00

Evening meal 1930 (last orders 1400)
Parking for 10
Cards accepted: Mastercard, Visa

🐎♿📞📺👶🗝️⬛🅂✂🖼️🛏️🖼️🍴30 🔔♫✿🚗🔖 SP ♻

EAST PRAWLE

Devon
Map ref 1C3

The Forge on the Green

👑👑 HIGHLY COMMENDED

East Prawle, Kingsbridge TQ7 2BU
☎ (01548) 511210
Fax (01548) 511210
Acclaimed country cottage with picturesque views to the sea. Superbly appointed interior, en-suite spa bath, emperor bed, all facilities to make an extremely comfortable stay. Imaginative table d'hote evening meal £12.50, supper £7.00.
Bedrooms: 2 double
Bathrooms: 2 en-suite

Bed & breakfast per night:	£min	£max
Single	25.00	30.00
Double	38.00	45.00

Half board per person:	£min	£max
Daily	40.00	43.00
Weekly	250.00	275.00

Evening meal 1800 (last orders 2000)

📞📧📺👶🗝️🗝️🅄🅇⬛🅂✂📺🌙🛏️🖼️ 🚗 SP

EXEBRIDGE

Somerset
Map ref 1D1

Village on the River Exe, 2 miles north-west of Bampton. The Exmoor National Park is north of the village.

The Anchor Inn and Hotel 👥

👑👑👑 HIGHLY COMMENDED

Exebridge, Dulverton TA22 9AZ
☎ (01398) 323433
Fax (01398) 323808
Charming residential country inn/hotel on the banks of the River Exe, with its own fishing. Stable restaurant overlooking river. Ideal base for exploring Exmoor.
Bedrooms: 1 single, 3 double, 2 twin
Bathrooms: 6 en-suite

Bed & breakfast per night:	£min	£max
Single	37.00	
Double	66.00	76.00

Half board per person:	£min	£max
Daily	49.00	54.00
Weekly	297.50	335.00

Lunch available
Evening meal 1900 (last orders 2100)
Parking for 100
Cards accepted: Mastercard, Visa, Switch/Delta

🐎♿📞📧📺👶🗝️⬛🅂📺🛏️🖼️🚗 🍴60🔔♫✿🚗 DAP SP

A key to symbols can be found inside the back cover flap.

Information on accommodation listed in this guide has been supplied by the proprietors. As changes may occur you are advised to check details at the time of booking.

EXETER

Devon
Map ref 1D2

University city rebuilt after the 1940s around its cathedral. Attractions include 13th C cathedral with fine west front; notable waterfront buildings; Guildhall; Royal Albert Memorial Museum; underground passages; Northcott Theatre.
Tourist Information Centre ☎ (01392) 265700

Barton Cross Hotel

👑👑👑 HIGHLY COMMENDED

Huxham, Stoke Canon, Exeter EX5 4EJ
☎ (01392) 841245
Fax (01392) 841942

Harmonious blend of 17th C charm and 20th C comfort. International standard accommodation with superb cuisine in glorious Devon countryside, just 4 miles north of Exeter.
Bedrooms: 1 single, 3 double, 2 twin
Bathrooms: 6 en-suite

Bed & breakfast per night:	£min	£max
Single	63.50	69.50
Double	78.50	85.00

Half board per person:	£min	£max
Daily	69.50	83.50

Lunch available
Evening meal 1900 (last orders 2130)
Parking for 30
Cards accepted: Amex, Mastercard, Visa, Switch/Delta

🐎♿📞📧📺👶🗝️🅂✂📺 🖼️🚗🍴20🔔♻✿🚗🔖 SP ⊤

Devon Hotel 👥

👑👑👑 COMMENDED

Exeter-by-Pass, Matford, Exeter EX2 8XU
☎ (01392) 259268
Fax (01392) 413142
Ⓒ Brend
Set in beautiful countryside, yet offering easy accessibility to the M5 and the centre of Exeter. Recent refurbishment has seen the addition of a further banquetting suite and "Carriages", a stylish bistro.

Continued ▶

EXETER

Continued

Bedrooms: 7 single, 15 double, 17 twin, 2 family rooms
Bathrooms: 41 en-suite

Bed & breakfast

per night:	£min	£max
Single	44.00	59.00
Double	63.00	85.00

Half board per person:

	£min	£max
Daily	46.50	74.00
Weekly	315.00	490.00

Lunch available
Evening meal 1900 (last orders 2100)
Parking for 200
Cards accepted: Amex, Diners, Mastercard, Visa, Switch/Delta

🐕🛌🦽📞🖃🖵🛉🕿🛈Ⓢ✂◑🖾🎔
🍴200❄️🕙 SP 🏠 T

Ebford House Hotel 🏵

👑👑👑 COMMENDED

Exmouth Road, Ebford, Exeter
EX3 0QH
☎ (01392) 877658
Fax (01392) 874424
Ⓒ Logis of GB

Beautiful Georgian country house surrounded by lovely gardens, fine views. Noted restaurant. Relax in our leisure area. Convenient for 8 golf courses, sea, sand and moors.
Bedrooms: 3 single, 11 double, 2 twin
Bathrooms: 16 en-suite

Bed & breakfast

per night:	£min	£max
Single	61.00	73.50
Double	80.00	100.00

Half board per person:

	£min	£max
Daily	80.00	94.50
Weekly	560.00	661.50

Lunch available
Evening meal 1830 (last orders 2130)
Parking for 45
Cards accepted: Amex, Mastercard, Visa, Switch/Delta

🐕🛌🦽📞🖃🖵🛉🕿🛈Ⓢ✂🏍◐
🖾🎔🍴45🕙✕Ủ↑✓❄️ SP 🏠 T ◎

Fairwinds Hotel 🏵

👑👑 COMMENDED

Kennford, Exeter EX6 7UD
☎ (01392) 832911
Fax (01392) 832911
Friendly little "no-smoking" hotel, offering real value for money in beautiful rural surroundings. Comfortable, well-equipped en-suite

bedrooms. Excellent choice of home-made food. Perfect touring base.
Bedrooms: 1 single, 3 double, 2 twin, 1 triple
Bathrooms: 6 en-suite, 1 private shower

Bed & breakfast

per night:	£min	£max
Single	35.00	39.00
Double	45.00	52.00

Half board per person:

	£min	£max
Daily	35.00	42.00
Weekly	195.00	250.00

Evening meal 1830 (last orders 1930)
Parking for 9
Open January–November
Cards accepted: Mastercard, Visa

🐕🛌🦽📞🖃🖵🛉🕿🛈Ⓢ✂🖾🎔
❄️✕🏍 DAP SP

Gipsy Hill Hotel and Restaurant 🏵

👑👑👑 COMMENDED

Gipsy Hill Lane, Pinhoe, Exeter
EX1 3RN
☎ (01392) 465252
Fax (01392) 464302
Ⓒ Consort

Peaceful country house hotel with magnificent views. 1 mile from M5, junction 30, and 2 miles from Exeter, just off the A30. Adjacent M5 junction 29 (under construction).
Bedrooms: 9 single, 16 double, 10 twin, 2 triple, 1 family room
Bathrooms: 38 en-suite

Bed & breakfast

per night:	£min	£max
Single	37.50	75.00
Double	70.00	95.00

Half board per person:

	£min	£max
Daily		92.50

Lunch available
Evening meal 1900 (last orders 2115)
Parking for 100
Cards accepted: Amex, Mastercard, Visa, Switch/Delta

🐕🛌🦽📞🖃🖵🛉🕿🛈Ⓢ◑🖾
🖾🎔🍴120❄️ SP T

Please check prices and other details at the time of booking.

Globe Hotel 🏵

👑👑👑 COMMENDED

Fore Street, Topsham, Exeter
EX3 0HR
☎ (01392) 873471
Fax (01392) 873879

Family-run 16th C coaching inn, situated in the beautiful and historic estuary town of Topsham (exit 30, M5). Exeter 4 miles.
Bedrooms: 1 single, 6 double, 7 twin, 3 triple
Bathrooms: 17 en-suite

Bed & breakfast

per night:	£min	£max
Single	38.00	
Double	53.00	60.00

Lunch available
Evening meal 1900 (last orders 2130)
Parking for 14
Cards accepted: Amex, Mastercard, Visa, Switch/Delta

🐕🛌🏍📞🖃🛉🛈Ⓢ🖾🖾🍴60🏍
🏠

The Great Western Hotel 🏵

👑👑👑 COMMENDED

Station Approach, St David's, Exeter
EX4 4NU
☎ (01392) 274039
Fax (01392) 425529
Ⓒ Minotel

Hotel has easy access to railway station. Bar, restaurant, lounge, conference room and car park.
Bedrooms: 23 single, 7 double, 9 twin, 1 triple
Bathrooms: 30 en-suite, 5 public

Bed & breakfast

per night:	£min	£max
Single	32.00	36.00
Double	48.00	52.00

Half board per person:

	£min	£max
Daily	40.00	46.00
Weekly	252.00	294.00

Lunch available
Evening meal 1900 (last orders 2130)
Parking for 25
Cards accepted: Amex, Diners, Mastercard, Visa, Switch/Delta

🐕📞🖃🖵🛉🕿🛈Ⓢ✂🖾 TV 🖾🖾
🍴80 DAP 🕙 SP T

The Lord Haldon Hotel ⚕

👑👑👑 COMMENDED

Dunchideock, Exeter EX6 7YF
☎ (01392) 832483
Fax (01392) 833765
Ⓒ The Independents

Family-run, historic former mansion within own grounds, offering panoramic views. 5 miles south-west of Exeter and well placed for Dartmoor and coast.
Bedrooms: 10 double, 5 twin,
3 triple, 1 family room
Bathrooms: 19 en-suite, 1 public
Bed & breakfast

per night:	£min	£max
Single	42.50	46.50
Double	68.50	79.50

Half board per person:	£min	£max
Daily	60.00	64.00
Weekly	299.50	

Lunch available
Evening meal 1900 (last orders 2200)
Parking for 80
Cards accepted: Mastercard, Visa

🐴🚳🛎📞📺♨🅿🚭Ⓢ✂📺◐
▥🖊🍴250🔍∪🏳✓❀🐾 SP 🎪
🆃 ◉

Park View Hotel ⚕

👑👑 COMMENDED

8 Howell Road, Exeter EX4 4LG
☎ (01392) 271772
Fax (01392) 253047
Charming family-run hotel, noted for peace and quiet and high standards, near city centre and stations. Tea/coffee, colour TV and telephone in all rooms.
Bedrooms: 3 single, 7 double, 3 twin,
2 triple
Bathrooms: 8 en-suite, 2 private,
2 public
Bed & breakfast

per night:	£min	£max
Single	20.00	30.00
Double	35.00	45.00

Parking for 6
Cards accepted: Amex, Mastercard, Visa

🐴🚳📞📺♨ⓊⓁ🔒✂📺📺▥🖊🚪❀
📺

St Andrews Hotel ⚕

👑👑👑 COMMENDED

28 Alphington Road, Exeter
EX2 8HN
☎ (01392) 276784
Fax (01392) 250249
Ⓒ Logis of GB

A warm welcome awaits you at this long established family-run hotel. Whilst retaining the features of a large Victorian house it provides all the facilities of a modern hotel. Brochure and tariff on request. Weekend breaks available all year.
Wheelchair access category 3♿
Bedrooms: 4 single, 7 double, 3 twin,
2 triple
Bathrooms: 16 en-suite
Bed & breakfast

per night:	£min	£max
Single	39.00	46.00
Double	50.00	60.00

Lunch available
Evening meal 1900 (last orders 2030)
Parking for 20
Cards accepted: Amex, Diners, Mastercard, Visa, Switch/Delta

🐴🚳🛎📞📺♨🍴🔒Ⓢ✂🚭▥🖊🚪
🍴14🚗 SP

The Southgate Hotel ⚕

👑👑👑👑 HIGHLY COMMENDED

Southernhay East, Exeter EX1 1QF
☎ (01392) 412812 & 413549
Fax (01392) 413549
Ⓒ Forte
Part of the Forte Heritage Collection, the Southgate is an elegant hotel offering first class facilities including a health club with indoor pool.
Bedrooms: 56 double, 48 twin,
6 triple
Suite available
Bathrooms: 110 en-suite
Half board per

person:	£min	£max
Daily	59.00	78.00

Lunch available
Evening meal 1900 (last orders 2200)
Parking for 115
Cards accepted: Amex, Diners, Mastercard, Visa

🐴🚳📞📺♨🍴🔒Ⓢ✂◐▥🖊
🚪🍴150🏊🏋❀∪🚭 SP 🎪🆃

Somerset
Map ref 1D1

Sheltered village on the River Exe close to Exmoor. Attractive old houses, shops and inns face the village green and the Methodist chapel has 2 windows by Burne-Jones. A footpath north-eastward leads to Dunkery Beacon, Exmoor's highest point.

Exmoor White Horse Hotel ⚕

👑👑👑 COMMENDED

Exford, Minehead TA24 7PY
☎ (01643) 831229
Fax (01643) 831246

Old world inn standing on the green beside the River Exe in beautiful Exmoor village. Local blacksmith at work in village, with the rolling moors just up the road.
Bedrooms: 12 double, 3 twin,
3 triple
Bathrooms: 18 en-suite
Bed & breakfast

per night:	£min	£max
Single	25.00	46.00
Double	50.00	92.00

Half board per person:	£min	£max
Daily	35.00	73.00
Weekly	290.00	330.00

Lunch available
Evening meal 1900 (last orders 2130)
Parking for 30

🐴🚳🛎📞📺♨🍴Ⓢ✂🚭📺▥🚪
🍴∪🚣❀🚗 SP 🆃◉

See under Allerford, Combe Martin, Dulverton, Exebridge, Exford, Lynmouth, Lynton, Porlock, Wheddon Cross

EXMOUTH

Devon
Map ref 1D2

Developed as a seaside resort in George III's reign, set against the woods of the Exe Estuary and red cliffs of Orcombe Point. Extensive sands, small harbour, chapel and almshouses, a model railway and A la Ronde, a 16-sided house.
Tourist Information Centre ☎ (01395) 222299

The Devoncourt Hotel ᛘ

ᛞᛞᛞᛞ COMMENDED

Douglas Avenue, Exmouth EX8 2EX
☎ (01395) 272277
Fax (01395) 269315

The ideal family resort, spectacular sea views over golden sandy beaches. Set in 4 acres of sub-tropical gardens, with full leisure complex, 2 pools, tennis, putting, croquet and much more. Sky TV, baby listening. 8 miles from Exeter/M5.
Bedrooms: 6 single, 11 double, 6 twin, 17 triple, 11 family rooms
Suites available
Bathrooms: 51 en-suite

Bed & breakfast

per night:	£min	£max
Single	50.00	75.00
Double	80.00	115.00

Half board per

person:	£min	£max
Daily	50.00	67.50
Weekly	315.00	425.25

Lunch available
Evening meal 1900 (last orders 2130)
Parking for 54
Cards accepted: Amex, Diners, Mastercard, Visa, Switch/Delta

FALMOUTH

Cornwall
Map ref 1B3

Busy port and fishing harbour, popular resort on the balmy Cornish Riviera. Henry VIII's Pendennis Castle faces St Mawes Castle across the broad natural harbour and yacht basin Carrick Roads, which receives 7 rivers.
Tourist Information Centre ☎ (01326) 312300

Hotel Anacapri ᛘ

ᛞᛞ APPROVED

Gyllyvase Road, Sea Front, Falmouth TR11 4DJ
☎ (01326) 311454
Fax (01326) 311454

Overlooking the beach and Falmouth Bay. Pretty bedrooms, all en-suite with colour TV. English breakfast and 5-course dinner. Bar.
Bedrooms: 1 single, 7 double, 7 twin, 1 triple
Bathrooms: 16 en-suite

Bed & breakfast

per night:	£min	£max
Single	27.00	
Double	47.00	

Half board per

person:	£min	£max
Daily	32.90	36.43
Weekly	230.30	255.00

Evening meal 1830 (last orders 1930)
Parking for 16
Cards accepted: Amex, Diners, Mastercard, Visa

Carthion Hotel ᛘ

ᛞᛞᛞ COMMENDED

Cliff Road, Falmouth TR11 4AP
☎ (01326) 313669
Fax (01326) 212828
Family hotel, situated in pleasant gardens, with a panoramic view of the sea from Pendennis Point to the Manacles.
Bedrooms: 2 single, 8 double, 4 twin, 4 triple
Bathrooms: 18 en-suite

Bed & breakfast

per night:	£min	£max
Single	27.00	41.00
Double	50.00	80.00

Half board per

person:	£min	£max
Daily	35.00	53.00
Weekly	231.00	357.00

Lunch available
Evening meal 1900 (last orders 2000)
Parking for 12
Cards accepted: Amex, Diners, Mastercard, Visa, Switch/Delta

Falmouth Beach Resort Hotel ᛘ

ᛞᛞᛞ COMMENDED

Gyllyngvase Beach, Seafront, Falmouth TR11 4NA
☎ (01326) 318084
Fax (01326) 319147
Ⓒ Consort

Modern hotel, right by the beach, with lifts to most floors. No steps/stairs from seafront to public rooms. Superb sea views. Leisure complex and tennis.
Bedrooms: 15 single, 34 double, 55 twin, 23 family rooms
Suites available
Bathrooms: 127 en-suite

Bed & breakfast

per night:	£min	£max
Single	40.00	55.00
Double	70.00	89.00

Half board per

person:	£min	£max
Daily	42.00	49.00
Weekly	275.00	399.00

Lunch available
Evening meal 1900 (last orders 2100)
Parking for 120
Cards accepted: Amex, Diners, Mastercard, Visa, Switch/Delta

The symbols in each entry give information about services and facilities. A key to these symbols appears at the back of this guide.

National gradings and classifications were correct at the time of going to press but are subject to change. Please check at the time of booking.

Green Lawns Hotel ⋀⋀

ⓦⓦⓦⓦ HIGHLY COMMENDED

Western Terrace, Falmouth
TR11 4QJ
☎ (01326) 312734
Fax (01326) 211427
Email: green.lawns@dial.pipex.com.
Ⓒⓡ The Independents

*Elegant chateau-style hotel situated
between the main beaches and town,
with indoor leisure complex.
Honeymoon and executive suites.*
Bedrooms: 6 single, 16 double,
9 twin, 2 triple, 6 family rooms
Bathrooms: 39 en-suite

Bed & breakfast

per night:	£min	£max
Single	49.00	88.00
Double	88.00	126.00

Half board per

person:	£min	£max
Daily	67.00	106.00
Weekly	385.00	480.00

Lunch available
Evening meal 1845 (last orders
2145)
Parking for 60
Cards accepted: Amex, Diners,
Mastercard, Visa, Switch/Delta
🛏🕭🖧📞🖂🖵♿🐾🅿ⓢ✂🅜📺
◑🎱🖨🛢♨250⌨✗🗡✿🅚🌂🔌♪
✻🐾 SP 🎏 T

Greenbank Hotel

ⓦⓦⓦⓦ HIGHLY COMMENDED

Harbourside, Falmouth TR11 2SR
☎ (01326) 312440
Fax (01326) 211362
*Privately-owned, historic hotel with
panoramic views across one of the
world's finest harbours. Uninterrupted
views of yachting and shipping.*
Bedrooms: 9 single, 16 double,
32 twin, 4 triple
Bathrooms: 60 en-suite, 1 private,
1 public

Bed & breakfast

per night:	£min	£max
Single	64.00	70.00
Double	110.00	160.00

Lunch available
Evening meal 1900 (last orders
2145)
Parking for 70
Cards accepted: Amex, Diners,
Mastercard, Visa
🛏🕭📞🖂🖵♿🅜ⓢ✂🗡◑🖹📺🖨🛢
♨100⌨✗ SP 🎏

Grove Hotel

ⓦⓦⓦ APPROVED

Grove Place, Falmouth TR11 4AU
☎ (01326) 319577
Fax (01326) 319577
*Harbourside Georgian hotel offering a
warm welcome, good food and good
value. Central to all local amenities.
Public car and dinghy parks opposite.*
Bedrooms: 2 single, 2 double, 3 twin,
6 triple, 2 family rooms
Bathrooms: 13 en-suite, 2 public

Bed & breakfast

per night:	£min	£max
Single	20.00	25.00
Double	40.00	42.00

Half board per

person:	£min	£max
Daily	29.00	34.00

Evening meal 1900 (last orders
2100)
Open January–November
Cards accepted: Amex, Diners,
Mastercard, Visa, Switch/Delta
🛏🕭📞🖵♿🅜ⓢ✂🗡📺🖨🛢♨30
◑✿ SP 🎏

Gyllyngdune Manor Hotel ⋀⋀

ⓦⓦⓦⓦ COMMENDED

Melvill Road, Falmouth TR11 4AR
☎ (01326) 312978
Fax (01326) 211881
*Old Georgian manor house situated in
an acre of beautiful gardens. 10
minutes' walk from town centre, 2
minutes' walk from beach overlooking
Falmouth Bay.*
Bedrooms: 3 single, 13 double,
10 twin, 4 triple
Bathrooms: 30 en-suite

Bed & breakfast

per night:	£min	£max
Single	30.00	55.00
Double	60.00	110.00

Half board per

person:	£min	£max
Daily	43.00	68.00
Weekly	301.00	430.00

Lunch available
Evening meal 1900 (last orders
2100)
Parking for 20
Cards accepted: Amex, Diners,
Mastercard, Visa, Switch/Delta
🛏🕭📞🖂🖵♿🅜ⓢ✂🗡◑🅜
🛢🖨✗🔌🎱♨✿🅓🐾 DAP 🌂 SP 🎏 T

Madeira Hotel ⋀⋀

ⓦⓦⓦ APPROVED

Sea Front, Falmouth TR11 4NY
☎ (01326) 313531
Fax (01326) 319143
*Well-situated with views over Falmouth
Bay. Entertainment most evenings.*

Bedrooms: 6 single, 16 double,
19 twin, 8 triple
Bathrooms: 49 en-suite, 2 public

Bed & breakfast

per night:	£min	£max
Single	25.00	32.00
Double	44.00	58.00

Half board per

person:	£min	£max
Daily	34.00	41.00
Weekly	165.00	220.00

Lunch available
Evening meal 1800 (last orders
1900)
Parking for 20
Open March–November and
Christmas
Cards accepted: Mastercard, Visa
🛏🕭🖧🖵♿🅜ⓢ✂🅚◑🔌🖹🛢
✻🐾🌂 SP

Park Grove Hotel ⋀⋀

ⓦⓦⓦ COMMENDED

Kimberley Park Road, Falmouth
TR11 2DD
☎ (01326) 313276
Fax (01326) 211926
*Family-run, long established hotel,
centrally situated for harbour, beaches
and town centre. Spacious restaurant
serving excellent cuisine. Large car
park.*
Bedrooms: 3 single, 5 double, 6 twin,
5 triple
Bathrooms: 12 en-suite, 5 private,
2 public, 2 private showers

Bed & breakfast

per night:	£min	£max
Single	21.00	27.00
Double	50.00	54.00

Half board per

person:	£min	£max
Daily	27.00	33.00
Weekly	189.00	231.00

Lunch available
Evening meal 1830 (last orders
1930)
Parking for 23
Cards accepted: Amex, Mastercard,
Visa, Switch/Delta
🛏1🖧📞🖂🖵♿🅜ⓢ🅚📺🅜
🛢♨10♪🔌✿🌂 SP T

Royal Duchy Hotel ⋀⋀

ⓦⓦⓦⓦⓦ HIGHLY COMMENDED

Cliff Road, Falmouth TR11 4NX
☎ (01326) 313042
Fax (01326) 319420
Ⓒⓡ Brend
*Falmouth's first and foremost hotel
situated overlooking the bay. High
standard accommodation with
extensive leisure facilities. Varied
seasonal break rates available.*

Continued ▶

FALMOUTH

Continued

Bedrooms: 5 single, 17 double, 17 twin, 4 triple, 1 family room
Suites available
Bathrooms: 43 en-suite

Bed & breakfast per night:

	£min	£max
Single	53.00	81.00
Double	98.00	182.00

Half board per person:

	£min	£max
Daily	61.00	103.00
Weekly	300.00	721.00

Lunch available
Evening meal 1900 (last orders 2100)
Parking for 56
Cards accepted: Amex, Diners, Mastercard, Visa, Switch/Delta

🐴♿🛢📠🖥👤🍴📶ⓢ🎱♨️⬦🖥
🛢🍽180🔗🚲🎿🏹⚘🍴🏸🐎 SP T

Tresillian House Hotel M

👑👑 COMMENDED
3 Stracey Road, Falmouth
TR11 4DW
☎ (01326) 312425 & 311139
Family-run hotel in a quiet area, close to safe beaches, town and harbours. Traditional English menus.
Bedrooms: 2 single, 3 double, 3 twin, 4 triple
Bathrooms: 12 en-suite

Bed & breakfast per night:

	£min	£max
Single	20.00	22.00
Double	40.00	44.00

Half board per person:

	£min	£max
Daily	27.75	31.00
Weekly	176.05	198.45

Lunch available
Evening meal 1830 (last orders 1915)
Parking for 8
Open March–October
Cards accepted: Amex, Mastercard, Visa

🐴📠🖥👤🍴📶ⓢ🎱🖥⬛⚘
🏸🐎 SP T ◉

Wickham Guest House

👑👑 APPROVED
21 Gyllyngvase Terrace, Falmouth
TR11 4DL
☎ (01326) 311140
Small guesthouse in quiet road a few minutes' walk from main beaches. Most rooms with sea views, some with colour TV and some en-suite.
Bedrooms: 2 single, 2 double, 1 twin, 1 family room
Bathrooms: 3 en-suite, 1 public

Bed & breakfast per night:

	£min	£max
Single	17.50	17.50
Double	35.00	39.00

Half board per person:

	£min	£max
Daily	26.00	28.00
Weekly	170.00	180.00

Evening meal 1845 (last orders 1700)
Parking for 2

🐴🖥👤UL🍴ⓢ🎿🖥TV🖥⚘🏹🐎
🎿

FONTHILL GIFFORD

Wiltshire
Map ref 2B3

Village north of Tisbury. The 18th C architect, James Wyatt, built the now ruined Fonthill Abbey. Old Wardour Castle, 4 miles south.

Beckford Arms M

👑👑👑 COMMENDED
Fonthill Gifford, Tisbury, Salisbury SP3 6PX
☎ (01747) 870385
Fax (01747) 851496
Ⓒ Wayfarer

Tastefully refurbished, stylish and comfortable 18th C inn, between Tisbury and Hindon in area of outstanding beauty. 2 miles A303. Convenient for Salisbury and Shaftesbury.
Bedrooms: 3 single, 4 double, 1 twin
Bathrooms: 5 en-suite, 3 private showers

Bed & breakfast per night:

	£min	£max
Single	34.50	34.50
Double	54.50	59.50

Half board per person:

	£min	£max
Daily	39.00	
Weekly	227.50	

Lunch available
Evening meal 1900 (last orders 2200)
Parking for 42
Cards accepted: Amex, Mastercard, Visa, Switch/Delta

🐴📠🖥👤🍴📶ⓢ🖥🛢📠30🔍
U⚘🎿 SP 🏹 T

FOWEY

Cornwall
Map ref 1B3

Set on steep slopes at the mouth of the Fowey River, important clayport and fishing town. Ruined forts guarding the shore recall days of "Fowey Gallants" who ruled local seas. The lofty church rises above the town. Ferries to Polruan and Bodinnick; August Regatta.
Tourist Information Centre ☎ (01726) 833616

Carnethic House Hotel M

👑👑👑 COMMENDED
Lambs Barn, Fowey PL23 1HQ
☎ (01726) 833336
Fax (01726) 833336
Regency house in 1.5 acres of mature gardens. Heated pool. Home cooking with local fish a speciality. Informal atmosphere.
Bedrooms: 1 single, 4 double, 1 twin, 2 triple
Bathrooms: 6 en-suite, 1 private, 1 public, 1 private shower

Bed & breakfast per night:

	£min	£max
Single	30.00	40.00
Double	50.00	70.00

Half board per person:

	£min	£max
Daily	40.00	50.00
Weekly	270.00	330.00

Evening meal 1930 (last orders 2030)
Parking for 20
Open February–November
Cards accepted: Amex, Diners, Mastercard, Visa, Switch/Delta

🐴♿📠🖥👤🍴📶ⓢ🎿🖥◉🛢🖥
🔍🏹U👤⚘🐎 SP 🏹 T

Cormorant Hotel M

👑👑👑 COMMENDED
Golant, Fowey PL23 1LL
☎ (01726) 833426
Fax (01726) 833426
Ⓒ Logis of GB

Small, attractive, family-run hotel with magnificent views of the Fowey estuary. Noted for hospitality and food. Indoor heated swimming pool. Special rates for short breaks all year round.
Bedrooms: 7 double, 4 twin
Bathrooms: 11 en-suite

Bed & breakfast per night:	£min	£max
Single	44.00	54.00
Double	88.00	98.00

Half board per person:	£min	£max
Daily	60.00	70.00

Lunch available
Evening meal 1900 (last orders 2100)
Parking for 15
Cards accepted: Amex, Mastercard, Visa, Switch/Delta

🐕📞🖭🖥♿🏸🛈⚲⤢🅿📠📡
♻🖱🚐♨ SP T

Marina Hotel ⓜ
HIGHLY COMMENDED
Esplanade, Fowey PL23 1HY
☎ (01726) 833315
Fax (01726) 832779
Privately-run, comfortably appointed Georgian hotel of character with river views and some balcony rooms. Own moorings, waterside garden and restaurant.
Bedrooms: 5 double, 5 twin
Bathrooms: 10 en-suite

Bed & breakfast per night:	£min	£max
Single	40.00	52.00
Double	54.00	90.00

Half board per person:	£min	£max
Daily	42.00	62.00
Weekly	266.00	378.00

Evening meal 1900 (last orders 2030)
Open March–December
Cards accepted: Amex, Mastercard, Visa, Switch/Delta

🐕8♿📞🖭🖥♿🛈⚲⤢🅿📠🚗
♻🚐 SP

Old market town with modern light industry, its medieval centre watered by the River Frome. Above Cheap Street with its flagstones and watercourse is the church showing work of varying periods. Interesting buildings include 18th C wool merchants' houses.
Tourist Information Centre ☎ (01373) 467271

Fourwinds Guest House ⓜ
COMMENDED
19 Bath Road, Frome BA11 2HJ
☎ (01373) 462618
Fax (01373) 453029
Comfortable and friendly guesthouse

with all the amenities of a small hotel. Half a mile north of town centre.
Wheelchair access category 3♿
Bedrooms: 1 single, 2 double, 2 twin, 1 family room
Bathrooms: 4 en-suite, 2 public

Bed & breakfast per night:	£min	£max
Single	25.00	30.00
Double	40.00	50.00

Half board per person:	£min	£max
Daily	35.00	42.00

Evening meal 1800 (last orders 1900)
Parking for 12
Cards accepted: Mastercard, Visa, Switch/Delta

🐕4♿📞🖭🖥♿🛈⚲⤢🅿📠
❄🖱🚐

Mendip Lodge Hotel
Bath Road, Frome BA11 2HP
☎ (01373) 463223
Fax (01373) 463990
CR Best Western

Set in 3.5 acres overlooking Mendip Hills, near Bath, Wells and Longleat. Restaurant and terrace for dining al fresco.
Bedrooms: 6 single, 10 double, 14 twin, 4 triple, 6 family rooms
Bathrooms: 40 en-suite

Bed & breakfast per night:	£min	£max
Single		50.00
Double		70.00

Half board per person:	£min	£max
Daily		42.50
Weekly		212.50

Lunch available
Evening meal 1900 (last orders 2130)
Parking for 75
Cards accepted: Amex, Diners, Mastercard, Visa, Switch/Delta

🐕♿📞🖭🖥♿🛈🅂🍴🖵📠🍷90
❄🖱 SP T

COLOUR MAPS

Colour maps at the back of this guide pinpoint all places in which you will find accommodation listed.

Hamlet on high, wild country near Hartland Point. Just west, the parish church tower makes a magnificent landmark; the light, unrestored interior holds one of Devon's finest rood screens. There are spectacular cliffs around Hartland Point and the lighthouse.

Hartland Quay Hotel ⓜ
👑👑 APPROVED
Hartland, Bideford EX39 6DU
☎ (01237) 441218
Small family-run hotel overlooking the rugged Atlantic coastline. Coastal walks. Important geological area.
Bedrooms: 2 single, 4 double, 4 twin, 3 triple, 1 family room
Bathrooms: 10 en-suite, 3 public

Bed & breakfast per night:	£min	£max
Single	21.00	22.00
Double	42.00	44.00

Half board per person:	£min	£max
Daily	30.00	32.00
Weekly	185.00	215.00

Lunch available
Evening meal 1900 (last orders 2000)
Parking for 100
Open February–November
Cards accepted: Mastercard, Visa

🐕🖥♿🛈🅂🖵 TV

Former mining town with modern light industry on the Hayle Estuary. Most buildings are Georgian or early Victorian, with some Regency houses along the canal.

Penellen Hotel ⓜ
👑👑 APPROVED
Riviere Towans, Hayle TR27 5AF
☎ (01736) 753777
Small family beachside hotel overlooking St Ives Bay, offering sea-bathing and glorious views. Ideal centre for touring. Restaurant, safe parking.
Bedrooms: 6 double, 2 twin, 2 family rooms
Bathrooms: 10 en-suite, 1 public

Bed & breakfast per night:	£min	£max
Single	20.00	28.00
Double	36.00	50.00

Continued ➤

HAYLE

Continued

Half board per person:

	£min	£max
Daily	25.00	35.00
Weekly	175.00	245.00

Lunch available
Evening meal 1830 (last orders 2130)
Parking for 20

HELSTON

Cornwall
Map ref 1B3

Handsome town with steep, main street and narrow alleys. In medieval times it was a major port and stannary town. Most buildings date from Regency and Victorian periods. The famous May dance, the Furry, is thought to have pre- Christian origins. A museum occupies the old Butter Market.
Tourist Information Centre ☎ *(01326) 565431*

Gwealdues Hotel

👑👑👑 COMMENDED

Falmouth Road, Helston TR13 8JX
☎ (01326) 572808 & 573331
Fax (01326) 561388
Ⓒ The Independents
Licensed modern hotel with en-suite rooms. Bar meals and a la carte restaurant. Satellite TV lounge. Beer garden with fishpond and waterfall.
Bedrooms: 3 single, 9 double, 2 twin, 2 triple, 1 family room
Bathrooms: 15 en-suite, 1 private, 1 public

Bed & breakfast per night:

	£min	£max
Single	30.00	45.00
Double	40.00	60.00

Lunch available
Evening meal 1930 (last orders 2100)
Parking for 60
Cards accepted: Amex, Mastercard, Visa, Switch/Delta

The **M** symbol after an establishment name indicates that it is a Regional Tourist Board member.

HONITON

Devon
Map ref 1D2

Old coaching town in undulating farmland. Formerly famous for lace-making, it is now an antiques trade centre and market town. Small museum.
Tourist Information Centre ☎ *(01404) 43716*

The Belfry Country Hotel M

👑👑👑 HIGHLY COMMENDED

Yarcombe, Honiton EX14 9BD
☎ (01404) 861234 & 861588
Fax (01404) 861579
Ⓒ Minotel

Tastefully converted Victorian village school in picturesque valley with lovely views. Relaxed and friendly atmosphere, all rooms en-suite, scrumptious award-winning home cooking. Log fire. No children under 12.
Bedrooms: 3 double, 2 twin, 1 triple
Bathrooms: 6 en-suite

Bed & breakfast per night:

	£min	£max
Single	34.00	44.00
Double	68.00	68.00

Half board per person:

	£min	£max
Daily	47.95	54.45
Weekly	273.00	308.00

Evening meal 1900 (last orders 2100)
Parking for 10
Cards accepted: Amex, Mastercard, Visa, Switch/Delta

Home Farm Hotel and Restaurant M

👑👑👑 COMMENDED

Wilmington, Honiton EX14 9JR
☎ (01404) 831278 & 831246
Fax (01404) 831411
Ⓒ Logis of GB
Thatched 16th C farmhouse hotel in lovely countryside. Restaurant uses local produce to serve food of high standard. Bar with light meals. Log fires. 6 miles from sea.
Bedrooms: 3 single, 4 double, 2 twin, 4 triple
Suite available
Bathrooms: 13 en-suite, 1 public

Bed & breakfast per night:

	£min	£max
Single	32.00	
Double	60.00	

Half board per person:

	£min	£max
Daily	44.50	
Weekly	280.00	

Lunch available
Evening meal 1900 (last orders 2130)
Parking for 20
Cards accepted: Amex, Diners, Mastercard, Visa, Switch/Delta

Honiton Motel M

👑👑 COMMENDED

Turks Head Corner, Exeter Road, Honiton EX14 8BL
☎ (01404) 43440 & 45400
Fax (01404) 47767
Comfortable, friendly licensed motel. Ideal touring base or for a one-night stay. Midway stop between Cornwall and the North.
Bedrooms: 1 single, 4 double, 8 twin, 2 triple
Bathrooms: 15 en-suite

Bed & breakfast per night:

	£min	£max
Single	32.00	34.00
Double	49.50	50.00

Half board per person:

	£min	£max
Daily	40.50	42.50
Weekly	260.00	

Lunch available
Evening meal 1900 (last orders 2100)
Parking for 150
Cards accepted: Amex, Mastercard, Visa, Switch/Delta

HOPE COVE

Devon
Map ref 1C3

Sheltered by the 400-ft headland of Bolt Tail, Hope Cove lies close to a small resort with thatched cottages, Inner Hope. Between Bolt Tail and Bolt Head lie 6 miles of beautiful National Trust cliffs.

Lantern Lodge Hotel

👑👑👑 HIGHLY COMMENDED

Hope Cove, Kingsbridge TQ7 3HE
☎ (01548) 561280
Fax (01548) 561736
Small, privately run, cliff-top hotel.

Bedrooms: 10 double, 3 twin,
1 triple
Bathrooms: 14 en-suite
Half board per person:

	£min	£max
Daily	47.00	65.00
Weekly	310.00	410.00

Evening meal 1900 (last orders
2030)
Parking for 20
Open March–November
Cards accepted: Mastercard, Visa,
Switch/Delta

HORRABRIDGE

Devon
Map ref 1C2

Beside the River Walkham at the
south-west edge of Dartmoor.

Overcombe Hotel ⏴

COMMENDED

Horrabridge, Yelverton PL20 7RA
☎ (01822) 853501 & 853602
Fax (01822) 853501
*Situated in west Dartmoor, between
Plymouth and Tavistock. Ideal for
walking and touring. Friendly,
comfortable hotel offering personal
service.*
Bedrooms: 1 single, 5 double, 3 twin,
2 triple
Bathrooms: 10 en-suite, 1 private
Bed & breakfast per night:

	£min	£max
Single	23.00	28.00
Double	46.00	51.00

Half board per person:

	£min	£max
Daily	37.00	42.00
Weekly	214.00	241.00

Lunch available
Evening meal 1930 (last orders
1915)
Parking for 10
Cards accepted: Mastercard, Visa

You are advised to confirm
your booking in writing.

For further information on
accommodation establishments
use the coupons at the
back of this guide.

ILFRACOMBE

Devon
Map ref 1C1

Resort of Victorian grandeur set on
hillside between cliffs with sandy
coves. At the mouth of the harbour
stands an 18th C lighthouse, built
over a medieval chapel. There are
fine formal gardens and a museum.
Chambercombe Manor, an
interesting old house, is nearby.
*Tourist Information Centre ☎ (01271)
863001*

Beechwood Hotel

COMMENDED

Torrs Park, Ilfracombe EX34 8AZ
☎ (01271) 863800
Fax (01271) 893800

*Small Victorian mansion peacefully
situated in own garden and woodlands
bordering National Trust coastline.
Splendid views over town to the sea.*
Bedrooms: 1 single, 6 double, 2 twin
Bathrooms: 9 en-suite, 2 public
Bed & breakfast per night:

	£min	£max
Single	20.00	25.00
Double	40.00	44.00

Half board per person:

	£min	£max
Daily	28.00	30.00
Weekly	195.00	210.00

Evening meal 1900 (last orders
1900)
Parking for 8
Cards accepted: Mastercard, Visa,
Switch/Delta

Capstone Hotel and Restaurant ⏴

St James Place, Ilfracombe EX34 9BJ
☎ (01271) 863540
Fax (01271) 862277
*Family-run hotel with restaurant on
ground floor. Close to harbour and all
amenities. Local seafood a speciality.*
Bedrooms: 1 single, 7 double, 1 twin,
3 family rooms
Bathrooms: 11 en-suite, 1 private
Bed & breakfast per night:

	£min	£max
Single	14.00	17.00
Double	27.00	35.00

Half board per person:

	£min	£max
Daily	24.00	28.00
Weekly	150.00	180.00

Lunch available
Evening meal 1800 (last orders
2200)
Parking for 4
Open April–October
Cards accepted: Amex, Mastercard,
Visa, Switch/Delta

Elmfield Hotel

COMMENDED

Torrs Park, Ilfracombe EX34 8AZ
☎ (01271) 863377
Fax (01271) 866828
*Stands in 1-acre of gardens, with car
parking. Heated indoor swimming pool,
jacuzzi, sauna and solarium. Two
bedrooms have four-posters.*
Bedrooms: 2 single, 8 double, 4 twin
Bathrooms: 14 en-suite
Bed & breakfast per night:

	£min	£max
Single	32.00	35.00
Double	64.00	70.00

Half board per person:

	£min	£max
Daily	37.00	39.00
Weekly	225.00	248.00

Lunch available
Evening meal 1900 (last orders
1930)
Parking for 15
Open April–October and Christmas
Cards accepted: Mastercard, Visa

Epchris Hotel ⏴

APPROVED

Torrs Park, Ilfracombe EX34 8AZ
☎ (01271) 862751

*Old stone house with a country feel,
near centre of Ilfracombe and Torrs
Walks. Bar, lovely terraced gardens,
swimming pool.*
Bedrooms: 1 single, 1 double,
2 triple, 5 family rooms
Bathrooms: 9 en-suite, 1 public
Bed & breakfast per night:

	£min	£max
Single	19.00	22.00
Double	38.00	44.00

Continued ▶

ILFRACOMBE
Continued

Half board per person:	£min	£max
Daily	26.50	30.50
Weekly	184.00	208.00

Lunch available
Evening meal from 1830
Parking for 8
Open January–October, December
Cards accepted: Mastercard, Visa

The Ilfracombe Carlton Hotel 𝕸

♛♛♛ COMMENDED

Runnacleave Road, Ilfracombe EX34 8AR
☎ (01271) 862446 & 863711
Fax (01271) 865379

Premier resort hotel in central location adjacent to beach and seafront. Comfortable rooms with good facilities. Buttery, dancing, 1 non-smoking lounge.
Bedrooms: 10 single, 18 double, 14 twin, 6 triple
Bathrooms: 48 en-suite, 2 public

Bed & breakfast per night:	£min	£max
Single	27.50	29.50
Double	50.00	50.00

Half board per person:	£min	£max
Daily	32.50	35.00
Weekly	205.00	220.00

Lunch available
Evening meal 1900 (last orders 2030)
Parking for 25
Open March–December
Cards accepted: Amex, Diners, Mastercard, Visa

ACCESSIBILITY

Look for the ♿ symbols which indicate accessibility for wheelchair users. These are described in detail at the front of this guide.

Imperial Hotel 𝕸

♛♛♛ APPROVED

Wilder Road, Ilfracombe EX34 9AL
☎ (01271) 862536
Fax (01271) 862571
On seafront close to all amenities and a few minutes' walk from beautiful harbour. Entertainment 5 nights a week.
Bedrooms: 16 single, 41 double, 39 twin, 8 triple
Bathrooms: 104 en-suite

Bed & breakfast per night:	£min	£max
Single	19.00	28.00
Double	38.00	56.00

Half board per person:	£min	£max
Daily	20.00	28.00
Weekly	135.00	190.00

Lunch available
Evening meal 1800 (last orders 1900)
Parking for 12
Open March–October, December
Cards accepted: Mastercard, Visa

Lyncott

56 St Brannock's Road, Ilfracombe EX34 8EQ
☎ (01271) 862425

Devon's romantic Atlantic coast. "Lyncott" combines elegance, moderate terms and old fashioned hospitality. Delightful en-suite bedrooms. Scrumptious fare!
Bedrooms: 4 double, 1 twin, 2 triple
Bathrooms: 5 en-suite, 2 private, 2 public

Bed & breakfast per night:	£min	£max
Single	13.50	17.00
Double	27.00	34.00

Half board per person:	£min	£max
Daily	23.50	27.00
Weekly	140.00	160.00

Evening meal 1830 (last orders 1200)
Parking for 7

Merlin Court Hotel 𝕸

♛♛♛ APPROVED

Torrs Park, Ilfracombe EX34 8AY
☎ (01271) 862697

Listed detached hotel, peacefully situated in own lovely terraced gardens and ideally located for exploring beautiful North Devon. Four-poster bed available. Car park.
Bedrooms: 7 double, 2 triple, 4 family rooms
Bathrooms: 12 en-suite, 1 public

Bed & breakfast per night:	£min	£max
Single	19.99	21.99
Double	39.98	43.98

Half board per person:	£min	£max
Daily	26.50	27.50
Weekly	175.00	185.00

Evening meal 1830 (last orders 1900)
Parking for 14
Cards accepted: Amex, Mastercard, Visa

Sherborne Lodge Hotel 𝕸

♛♛ COMMENDED

Torrs Park, Ilfracombe EX34 8AY
☎ (01271) 862297
Friendly, licensed family hotel with parking in beautiful Torrs Park. Short walk to seafront, harbour and all amenities. Golfing, shooting, walking and fishing days arranged.
Bedrooms: 1 single, 7 double, 3 twin, 1 family room
Bathrooms: 6 en-suite, 2 public

Bed & breakfast per night:	£min	£max
Single	15.50	18.00
Double	31.00	36.00

Half board per person:	£min	£max
Daily	23.50	26.00
Weekly	149.00	169.00

Lunch available
Evening meal 1830 (last orders 1900)
Parking for 12
Cards accepted: Mastercard, Visa, Switch/Delta

The Torrs Hotel M
APPROVED

Torrs Park, Ilfracombe EX34 8AY
☎ (01271) 862334
Victorian mansion with fine views. Quiet location beside the National Trust Torrs Coastal Walk. Close to seafront and town centre.
Bedrooms: 6 double, 3 twin, 5 triple
Bathrooms: 14 en-suite

Bed & breakfast

per night:	£min	£max
Single	20.00	23.00
Double	40.00	46.00

Half board per person:

	£min	£max
Daily	28.00	36.00
Weekly	196.00	217.00

Lunch available
Evening meal 1830 (last orders 1930)
Parking for 14
Open February–November
Cards accepted: Mastercard, Visa, Switch/Delta

ILLOGAN
Cornwall
Map ref 1B3

Former mining village 2 miles north-west of Redruth and close to the coast. The Victorian engineer and benefactor, Sir Richard Tangye, was born here in 1833.

Aviary Court Hotel
HIGHLY COMMENDED

Marys Well, Illogan, Redruth TR16 4QZ
☎ (01209) 842256
Fax (01209) 843744
Logis of GB
Charming country house hotel set in over 2 acres of secluded gardens. Portreath 5 minutes by car or a 20 minute woodland walk.
Bedrooms: 4 double, 1 twin, 1 triple
Bathrooms: 6 en-suite

Bed & breakfast

per night:	£min	£max
Single	40.00	44.00
Double	56.00	60.00

Half board per person:

	£min	£max
Daily	53.00	57.00
Weekly	246.00	258.00

Evening meal 1900 (last orders 2030)
Parking for 25
Cards accepted: Amex, Diners, Mastercard, Visa

ISLES OF SCILLY
Map ref 1A3

Picturesque group of islands and granitic rocks south-west of Land's End. Peaceful and unspoilt, they are noted for natural beauty, romantic maritime history, silver sands, early flowers and sub-tropical gardens on Tresco. Main island is St Mary's.
Tourist Information Centre ☎ (01720) 422536

Bell Rock Hotel
COMMENDED

Church Street, St Mary's, Isles of Scilly TR21 0JS
☎ (01720) 422575
Fax (01720) 423093
Warm welcome and friendly, informal service. All en-suite, heated indoor pool, wide choice of good food, fully licensed. In central position, 100 yards from beaches.
Bedrooms: 5 single, 11 double, 4 twin, 2 triple, 1 family room
Bathrooms: 23 en-suite

Bed & breakfast

per night:	£min	£max
Single	27.00	57.00
Double	54.00	114.00

Half board per person:

	£min	£max
Daily	39.00	62.00
Weekly	273.00	434.00

Lunch available
Evening meal 1830 (last orders 2030)
Cards accepted: Mastercard, Visa

St Martins on the Isle M
HIGHLY COMMENDED

St Martin's, Isles of Scilly TR25 0QW
☎ (01720) 422092
Fax (01720) 422298

Hotel designed like a cluster of cottages. Well-appointed sea-view rooms and suites. Fine restaurant. In idyllic position next to its own beach.
Bedrooms: 20 double, 10 family rooms
Suites available
Bathrooms: 30 en-suite, 2 public

Half board per person:

	£min	£max
Daily	100.00	185.00
Weekly	700.00	1295.00

Lunch available
Evening meal 1915 (last orders 2045)
Open March–October
Cards accepted: Amex, Diners, Mastercard, Visa, Switch/Delta

IVYBRIDGE
Devon
Map ref 1C2

Town set in delightful woodlands on the River Erme. Brunel designed the local railway viaduct. South Dartmoor Leisure Centre.
Tourist Information Centre ☎ (01752) 897035

Ermewood House Hotel
COMMENDED

Totnes Road, Ermington, Ivybridge PL21 9NS
☎ (01548) 830741
Fax (01548) 830982
Logis of GB
Country house hotel overlooking the River Erme, run under the personal direction of Mike and Claire Loseby.
Bedrooms: 3 single, 4 double, 2 twin
Bathrooms: 9 en-suite

Bed & breakfast

per night:	£min	£max
Single	36.50	38.50
Double	59.00	75.00

Half board per person:

	£min	£max
Daily	43.60	51.60
Weekly	269.50	343.00

Evening meal 1900 (last orders 2030)
Parking for 20
Cards accepted: Mastercard, Visa, Switch/Delta

Please check prices and other details at the time of booking.

For ideas on places to visit refer to the introduction at the beginning of this section.

KEYNSHAM

Bath & North East Somerset
Map ref 2B2

Busy town on the River Avon between Bath and Bristol.

Grasmere Court Hotel [AA]

[COMMENDED]

22-24 Bath Road, Keynsham, Bristol BS18 1SN
☎ (0117) 9862662
Fax (0117) 9862762

Well-appointed hotel with high standard of decor and accommodation. Private facilities. Situated on A4 between Bath and Bristol.

Bedrooms: 2 single, 9 double, 3 twin, 2 family rooms
Bathrooms: 16 en-suite

Bed & breakfast per night:	£min	£max
Single	35.00	52.00
Double	48.00	64.00

Evening meal 1830 (last orders 1930)
Parking for 18
Cards accepted: Amex, Mastercard, Visa, Switch/Delta
[S] [TV] [SP]

LANDS END

Cornwall
Map ref 1A3

The most westerly point of the English mainland, 8 miles south-west of Penzance. Spectacular cliffs with marvellous views. Exhibitions and multi-sensory Last Labyrinth Show.

The Lands End Hotel [AA]

[COMMENDED]

Lands End, Sennen, Penzance TR19 7AA
☎ (01736) 871844
Fax (01736) 871599
[CR] Consort

Situated on the cliff tops at Lands End. The sea views are breathtaking!

Bedrooms: 4 single, 13 double, 13 twin, 3 family rooms
Suite available
Bathrooms: 33 en-suite

Bed & breakfast per night:	£min	£max
Single	49.00	87.00
Double	98.00	164.00

Half board per person:	£min	£max
Daily	69.00	102.00
Weekly	448.00	679.00

Lunch available
Evening meal 1900 (last orders 2130)
Parking for 1000
Cards accepted: Amex, Mastercard, Visa, Switch/Delta
[S]
160 [SP] [T]

LAUNCESTON

Cornwall
Map ref 1C2

Medieval "Gateway to Cornwall", county town until 1838, founded by the Normans under their hilltop castle near the original monastic settlement. This market town, overlooked by its castle ruin, has a square with Georgian houses and an elaborately-carved granite church.
Tourist Information Centre ☎ (01566) 772321 or 772333

Glencoe Villa

[APPROVED]

13 Race Hill, Launceston PL15 9BB
☎ (01566) 773012 & 775819

Large 3-storey, hilltop Victorian-type house with superb views across Tamar Valley. 4 minutes from town centre.

Bedrooms: 1 double, 1 twin, 1 triple, 1 family room
Bathrooms: 2 private, 1 public

Bed & breakfast per night:	£min	£max
Single	15.00	25.00
Double	26.00	38.00

Parking for 10
Cards accepted: Mastercard, Visa
[UL] [S] [TV]

LISKEARD

Cornwall
Map ref 1C2

Former stannary town with a livestock market and light industry, at the head of a valley running to the coast. Handsome Georgian and Victorian residences and a Victorian Guildhall reflect the prosperity of the mining boom. The large church has an early 20th C tower and a Norman font.

Elnor Guest House

[COMMENDED]

1 Russell Street, Liskeard PL14 4BP
☎ (01579) 342472

Home-from-home with friendly family atmosphere in 100-year-old town house between the station and market town.

Bedrooms: 4 single, 1 double, 1 twin, 3 triple
Bathrooms: 7 en-suite, 1 public

Bed & breakfast per night:	£min	£max
Single	17.00	20.00
Double	34.00	40.00

Half board per person:	£min	£max
Daily	28.00	31.00
Weekly	182.00	203.00

Evening meal 1800 (last orders 1800)
Parking for 6
[TV]

The Pencubitt Country House Hotel [AA]

[COMMENDED]

Station Road, Liskeard PL14 4EB
☎ (01579) 342694

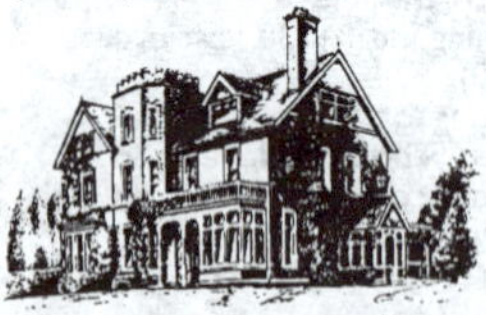

Beautiful Victorian mansion house in 2 acres of mature gardens. Private, superb views. Award-winning cuisine by chef/proprietor. Family-owned and run.

Bedrooms: 3 single, 3 double, 2 twin, 1 family room
Bathrooms: 9 en-suite

Bed & breakfast per night:	£min	£max
Single	30.00	40.00
Double	60.00	80.00

Half board per person:	£min	£max
Daily	50.00	60.00
Weekly	280.00	350.00

Evening meal 1900 (last orders 2030)
Parking for 25
Cards accepted: Mastercard, Visa
[S] 40
[SP]

Establishments should be open throughout the year, unless otherwise stated.

Information on accommodation listed in this guide has been supplied by the proprietors. As changes may occur you are advised to check details at the time of booking.

THE LIZARD

Cornwall
Map ref 1B3

Ending in England's most southerly point, a treeless peninsula with rugged, many-coloured cliffs and deep shaded valleys facing the Helford River. Kynance Cove, famous for serpentine cliffs and lovely sands.

Lizard Hotel

COMMENDED

Penmenner Road, The Lizard,
Helston TR12 7NP
☎ (01326) 290305
Small hotel set in 1.5 acres of lawned grounds with superb view across Kynance Cove. Short break/weekly reductions.
Bedrooms: 1 single, 4 double, 1 twin,
1 triple
Bathrooms: 2 en-suite, 1 public,
5 private showers

Bed & breakfast

per night:	£min	£max
Single	17.50	24.00
Double	35.00	48.00

Half board per

person:	£min	£max
Daily	31.00	37.00
Weekly	210.00	224.00

Evening meal 1930 (last orders
1800)
Parking for 10
Cards accepted: Mastercard, Visa

LONG SUTTON

Somerset
Map ref 2A3

Village 2 miles south-west of Somerton with village green flanked by the stone-built 13th C church, manor, shop and pub.

The Devonshire Arms Hotel

COMMENDED

Long Sutton, Langport TA10 9LP
☎ (01458) 241271 & 0385 348800
Fax (01458) 241037
ⓒ Minotel/Logis of GB
Built as a hunting lodge by the Duke of Devonshire in 1787.
Bedrooms: 5 double, 3 twin, 1 triple
Bathrooms: 9 en-suite

Bed & breakfast

per night:	£min	£max
Single	40.00	45.00
Double	55.00	85.00

Lunch available

Evening meal 1830 (last orders
2200)
Parking for 10
Cards accepted: Amex, Mastercard,
Visa, Switch/Delta

LOOE

Cornwall
Map ref 1C2

Small resort developed around former fishing and smuggling ports occupying the deep estuary of the East and West Looe Rivers. Narrow winding streets, with old inns; museum and art gallery are housed in interesting old buildings. Shark fishing centre, boat trips; busy harbour.

Commonwood Manor Hotel

HIGHLY COMMENDED

St Martins Road, Looe PL13 1LP
☎ (01503) 262929
Fax (01503) 262632
Email: commonwood
@compuserve.com

Spacious and relaxing country house hotel. Set in 6-acre estate overlooking Looe River valley and countryside beyond, yet only 5 minutes' walk to harbour and town.
Bedrooms: 1 single, 6 double, 3 twin,
1 family room
Suite available
Bathrooms: 11 en-suite

Bed & breakfast

per night:	£min	£max
Single	31.00	38.00
Double	62.00	76.00

Half board per

person:	£min	£max
Daily	44.00	54.00
Weekly	311.50	343.00

Lunch available
Evening meal 1900 (last orders
2000)
Parking for 20
Cards accepted: Amex, Mastercard,
Visa, Switch/Delta

Coombe Farm

HIGHLY COMMENDED

Widegates, Looe PL13 1QN
☎ (01503) 240223
Fax (01503) 240895

Lovely country house in wonderful tranquil setting with superb views to the sea. Delicious food, log fires and warm, friendly hospitality. 3.5 miles east of Looe on B3253.
Bedrooms: 3 double, 3 twin, 2 triple,
2 family rooms
Bathrooms: 10 en-suite

Bed & breakfast

per night:	£min	£max
Single	23.00	29.00
Double	46.00	58.00

Half board per

person:	£min	£max
Daily	38.00	44.00
Weekly	252.00	294.00

Evening meal 1900 (last orders
1900)
Parking for 12
Open March–October
Cards accepted: Amex, Diners,
Mastercard, Visa, Switch/Delta

Fieldhead Hotel

HIGHLY COMMENDED

Portuan Road, Hannafore, West
Looe, Looe PL13 2DR
☎ (01503) 262689
Fax (01503) 264114
ⓒ Minotel/The Independents
Turn-of-the-century house set in lovely gardens in quiet area, with panoramic views of the sea and bay. Intimate candlelit restaurant.
www.chycor.co.uk.fieldhead
Bedrooms: 1 single, 9 double, 3 twin,
1 triple
Bathrooms: 14 en-suite

Bed & breakfast

per night:	£min	£max
Single	38.50	38.50
Double	60.00	78.00

Half board per

person:	£min	£max
Daily	48.00	52.00
Weekly	270.00	335.00

Lunch available
Evening meal 1830 (last orders
2030)
Parking for 14

Continued ▶

LOOE
Continued

Open February–December
Cards accepted: Amex, Mastercard,
Visa, Switch/Delta
🛇🜂5🜂🜂🜂🜂🜂🜂🜂🜂🜂🜂 TV
🜂🜂🜂24🜂🜂🜂🜂🜂🜂🜂 SP T ◉

Kantara Guest House ⚠
COMMENDED
7 Trelawney Terrace, Looe
PL13 2AG
☎ (01503) 262093
*Licensed guesthouse close to beach
and shops. Informal, friendly
atmosphere. Ideal family holiday setting
and touring base. Satellite TV in all
rooms.*
Bedrooms: 1 single, 1 double, 1 twin,
1 triple, 2 family rooms
Bathrooms: 2 public

Bed & breakfast

per night:	£min	£max
Single	12.00	15.50
Double	24.00	31.00

Half board per

person:	£min	£max
Daily	22.00	25.50
Weekly	150.00	174.00

Evening meal 1800 (last orders
1900)
Parking for 1
Cards accepted: Amex, Mastercard,
Visa
🛇🜂🜂🜂🜂🜂🜂🜂 TV 🜂🜂14🜂
🜂🜂 SP T

The Panorama Hotel ⚠
COMMENDED
Hannafore Road, Looe PL13 2DE
☎ (01503) 262123
Fax (01503) 265654
Email: panorama @ west
looe.avel.co.uk.
*Family-run hotel, good food, friendly
atmosphere. Magnificent setting
overlooking harbour, beach and miles
of beautiful coastline.*
Bedrooms: 2 single, 4 double, 1 twin,
2 triple, 1 family room
Bathrooms: 10 en-suite, 1 public

Bed & breakfast

per night:	£min	£max
Single	23.50	33.50
Double	47.00	67.00

Half board per

person:	£min	£max
Daily	35.00	46.00
Weekly	211.00	272.00

Evening meal 1830 (last orders
1900)

Parking for 8
Cards accepted: Amex, Diners,
Mastercard, Visa, Switch/Delta
🛇🜂🜂🜂🜂🜂🜂🜂 S 🜂 TV 🜂🜂🜂
🜂🜂🜂🜂🜂 SP T ◉

LOSTWITHIEL
Cornwall
Map ref 1B2

Cornwall's ancient capital which
gained its Royal Charter in 1189. Tin
from the mines around the town
was smelted and coined in the
Duchy Palace. Norman Restormel
Castle, with its circular keep and
deep moat, overlooks the town.

Lostwithiel Golf and Country Club ⚠
👑👑👑 COMMENDED
Lower Polscoe, Lostwithiel
PL22 0HQ
☎ (01208) 873550
Fax (01208) 873479
*Overlooking the beautiful River Fowey
valley in idyllic setting. Charm, character
and high levels of comfort and service.
Bedrooms are converted from Cornish
stone farm buildings.*
Bedrooms: 2 single, 3 double,
13 twin
Suites available
Bathrooms: 18 en-suite

Bed & breakfast

per night:	£min	£max
Single	33.00	40.00
Double	66.00	80.00

Half board per

person:	£min	£max
Daily	48.00	55.00
Weekly	273.00	329.00

Lunch available
Evening meal 1900 (last orders
2130)
Parking for 150
Cards accepted: Amex, Diners,
Mastercard, Visa
🛇🜂🜂🜂🜂🜂🜂🜂 S 🜂 TV 🜂 🜂
🜂🜂150🜂🜂🜂🜂🜂🜂🜂🜂 SP T

Restormel Lodge Hotel ⚠
👑👑👑 COMMENDED
19 Castle Hill, Lostwithiel
PL22 0DD
☎ (01208) 872223
Fax (01208) 873568
Ⓒ Consort
*Set in the beautiful Fowey Valley. Warm,
spacious well-equipped bedrooms.
Imaginative menus of delicious food
and friendly, efficient service.*
Bedrooms: 2 single, 14 double,
13 twin, 3 triple
Bathrooms: 32 en-suite

Bed & breakfast

per night:	£min	£max
Single	48.00	50.00
Double	66.00	68.00

Half board per

person:	£min	£max
Daily	33.00	43.00
Weekly	230.00	310.00

Lunch available
Evening meal 1900 (last orders
2130)
Parking for 45
Cards accepted: Amex, Diners,
Mastercard, Visa
🛇🜂🜂🜂🜂🜂🜂🜂 S 🜂 🜂
🜂100🜂🜂🜂🜂 SP

LYDFORD
Devon
Map ref 1C2

Former important tin mining centre,
a small village on edge of West
Dartmoor. Remains of Norman
castle where all falling foul of
tinners' notorious "Lydford Law"
were incarcerated. Bridge crosses
River Lyd where it rushes through a
mile-long gorge of boulders and
trees.

Lydford House Hotel ⚠
👑👑👑 HIGHLY COMMENDED
Lydford, Okehampton EX20 4AU
☎ (01822) 820347
Fax (01822) 820442
Ⓒ Minotel
*Family-run country house hotel,
peacefully set in own grounds on edge
of Dartmoor. Superb touring centre.
Own riding stables.*
Bedrooms: 2 single, 3 double, 3 twin,
2 triple, 2 family rooms
Suite available
Bathrooms: 11 en-suite, 1 private

Bed & breakfast

per night:	£min	£max
Single		36.00
Double		72.00

Half board per

person:	£min	£max
Daily		49.00
Weekly		286.00

Lunch available
Evening meal 1900 (last orders
2030)
Parking for 30
Cards accepted: Mastercard, Visa
🛇🜂5🜂🜂🜂🜂🜂🜂🜂 S 🜂🜂🜂
🜂🜂15🜂🜂🜂🜂🜂 OAP SP 🜂 T

Please mention this guide
when making your booking.

Moor View House 𝄞

Vale Down, Lydford, Okehampton
EX20 4BB
☎ (01822) 820220

*Family-run country house hotel on edge
of Dartmoor, peacefully set in 2 acres
of gardens. Fine food, sound wine, log
fires. Walking, fishing, riding, shooting
and golf. Excellent touring centre.*
Bedrooms: 1 single, 2 double,
1 triple
Bathrooms: 4 en-suite

**Bed & breakfast
per night:**

	£min	£max
Single	40.00	50.00
Double	70.00	95.00

**Half board per
person:**

	£min	£max
Daily	60.00	70.00
Weekly	328.00	355.00

Evening meal 1900 (last orders
2000)
Parking for 15

🛠12📟🖵👪🕯🗜🆂✂️🎦🛏
🔌🚶☂️✳️🚗🐾 SP 🎣

LYME REGIS

Dorset
Map ref 1D2

Pretty, historic fishing town and
resort set against the fossil-rich cliffs
of Lyme Bay. In medieval times it
was an important port and cloth
centre. The Cobb, a massive stone
breakwater, shelters the ancient
harbour which is still lively with
boats.
Tourist Information Centre ☎ *(01297)
442138*

Hotel Buena Vista 𝄞

Pound Street, Lyme Regis DT7 3HZ
☎ (01297) 442494

*Regency house with a country house
atmosphere in an unrivalled position
overlooking the bay. Close to the town
and beaches.*

Bedrooms: 4 single, 9 double, 4 twin,
1 family room
Bathrooms: 17 en-suite, 1 private

**Bed & breakfast
per night:**

	£min	£max
Single	37.00	45.00
Double	64.00	104.00

**Half board per
person:**

	£min	£max
Daily	43.00	64.00
Weekly	291.00	384.00

Evening meal 1900 (last orders
2000)
Parking for 20
Open February–November
Cards accepted: Amex, Diners,
Mastercard, Visa, Switch/Delta

🛠♿🖵📟👪🕯🗜🆂✂️🎦🛏🔌🚗✳️
SP 🅃

The Dower House Hotel 𝄞

Rousdon, Lyme Regis DT7 3RB
☎ (01297) 21047
Fax (01297) 24748

*Originally a dower house, now a
country house hotel in its own idyllic
grounds. Open fires. Emphasis on good
food and comfort.*
Bedrooms: 1 single, 3 double, 2 twin,
3 triple
Bathrooms: 9 en-suite, 1 public

**Bed & breakfast
per night:**

	£min	£max
Single	38.00	48.00
Double	60.00	80.00

**Half board per
person:**

	£min	£max
Daily	45.00	60.00
Weekly	275.00	341.00

Lunch available
Evening meal 1900 (last orders
2100)
Parking for 48
Cards accepted: Amex, Diners,
Mastercard, Visa

🛠♿🖵📟👪🕯🗜🆂🎦🛏💻🔌
🍴🚶☂️✳️🚗🐾 SP 🎣🅃

Kersbrook Hotel and Restaurant 𝄞

Pound Road, Lyme Regis DT7 3HX
☎ (01297) 442596 & 442576
Fax (01297) 442596
Ⓒ Minotel
*Thatched, 18th C listed hotel and
restaurant in its own picturesque*

---

*gardens, set high above Lyme Bay. For
those who prefer peace and tranquillity.*
Bedrooms: 2 single, 6 double, 2 twin
Bathrooms: 10 en-suite

**Bed & breakfast
per night:**

	£min	£max
Single	50.00	60.00
Double	65.00	75.00

**Half board per
person:**

	£min	£max
Daily	52.00	
Weekly	300.00	340.00

Lunch available
Evening meal 1930 (last orders
2100)
Parking for 16
Open February–November
Cards accepted: Amex, Mastercard,
Visa, Switch/Delta

🛠♿🖵👪🕯🗜🆂✂️🎦🛏💻🔌🎣20
🚶🍴⚓🏌️☂️✳️🚗 SP 🎣🅃

Lydwell House 𝄞

Lyme Road, Uplyme, Lyme Regis
DT7 3TJ
☎ (01297) 443522
*Delightful Victorian house in attractive
gardens, ideally located for coast and
country walks. Short distance to Lyme
Regis town centre and beaches.*
Bedrooms: 1 single, 1 double, 1 twin,
2 family rooms
Bathrooms: 2 en-suite, 1 public

**Bed & breakfast
per night:**

	£min	£max
Single	17.00	19.00
Double	36.00	44.00

**Half board per
person:**

	£min	£max
Daily	29.00	32.00
Weekly	149.00	210.00

Evening meal 1800 (last orders
2000)
Parking for 7

🛠👪♿🗜✂️🎦🛏🔌🚗✳️🚗⚓🅃

Orchard Country Hotel 𝄞

Rousdon, Lyme Regis DT7 3XW
☎ (01297) 442972
*Good food, comfortable
accommodation, gentle relaxing
atmosphere and a friendly welcome
are assured. Ideal base for motorists
and walkers.*
Bedrooms: 2 single, 5 double, 5 twin
Bathrooms: 9 en-suite, 3 private

**Bed & breakfast
per night:**

	£min	£max
Single	30.00	40.00
Double	60.00	80.00

Evening meal 1930 (last orders
2015)
Parking for 15

Continued ▶

LYME REGIS

Continued

Open March–December
Cards accepted: Mastercard, Visa, Switch/Delta
8 [S] [TV] [SP] [T]

Rotherfield

[COMMENDED]

View Road, Lyme Regis DT7 3AA
☎ (01297) 445585

Exceptionally spacious, comfortable accommodation, own car park, home cooking, licensed, panoramic sea and countryside views. Warm welcome assured. Completely refurbished.

Bedrooms: 2 single, 2 double, 2 twin, 1 family room
Bathrooms: 3 en-suite, 2 public

Bed & breakfast per night:	£min	£max
Single	17.50	19.00
Double	35.00	38.00

Half board per person:	£min	£max
Daily	28.50	30.00
Weekly	192.50	210.00

Evening meal 1850 (last orders 1950)
Parking for 7
[TV] 16 [OAP] [SP]

Swallows Eaves Hotel

[HIGHLY COMMENDED]

Colyford, Colyton, Devon EX13 6QJ
☎ (01297) 553184

Attractive award-winning hotel for discerning guests, in an Area of Outstanding Natural Beauty. Quality rooms and interesting food. Special breaks. Ideal centre for visiting gardens and National Trust properties.

Bedrooms: 1 single, 3 double, 4 twin
Bathrooms: 8 en-suite

Bed & breakfast per night:	£min	£max
Single	38.00	48.00
Double	56.00	76.00

Half board per person:	£min	£max
Daily	42.00	57.00
Weekly	290.00	340.00

Lunch available
Evening meal 1900 (last orders 2000)
Parking for 10
Open February–November
Cards accepted: Amex, Mastercard, Visa, Switch/Delta
[S] 10 [SP] [T]

Thatch Lodge Hotel

[HIGHLY COMMENDED]

The Street, Charmouth, near Lyme Regis DT6 6PQ
☎ (01297) 560407
Fax (01297) 560407

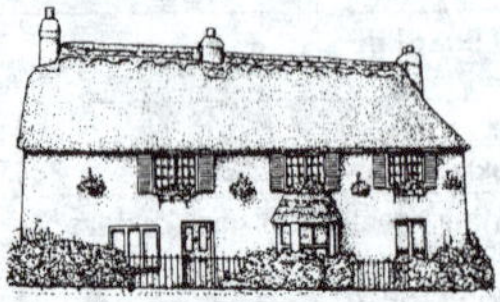

"Perfect small hotel" - Daily Mail. "Picture postcard" 14th C thatched hotel offering tranquillity, discerning quality, superb chef inspired cuisine. World famous fossil beach 3 minutes' walk away. Non smoking throughout.

Bedrooms: 6 double, 1 twin
Bathrooms: 6 en-suite, 1 private

Bed & breakfast per night:	£min	£max
Single	39.50	57.50
Double	54.00	90.00

Half board per person:	£min	£max
Daily	45.50	64.50

Evening meal 2000
Parking for 10
Open January, March–December
Cards accepted: Mastercard, Visa, Switch/Delta
[S] [SP]

LYNMOUTH

Devon
Map ref 1C1

Resort set beneath bracken-covered cliffs and pinewood gorges where 2 rivers meet, and cascade between boulders to the town. Lynton, set on cliffs above, can be reached by water-operated cliff railway from the Victorian esplanade. Valley of the Rocks, to the west, gives dramatic walks.

Bath Hotel

[COMMENDED]

Lynmouth EX35 6EL
☎ (01598) 752238
Fax (01598) 752544

Friendly, family-run hotel by picturesque Lynmouth harbour. Ideal centre for exploring Exmoor National Park.

Bedrooms: 1 single, 12 double, 8 twin, 3 triple
Bathrooms: 24 en-suite

Bed & breakfast per night:	£min	£max
Single	28.50	38.50
Double	57.00	77.00

Half board per person:	£min	£max
Daily	37.00	55.00
Weekly	220.00	329.00

Lunch available
Evening meal 1900 (last orders 2030)
Parking for 17
Open February–December
Cards accepted: Amex, Diners, Mastercard, Visa, Switch/Delta
[S] [SP] [T]

Tregonwell Riverside Guesthouse

[COMMENDED]

1 Tors Road, Lynmouth EX35 6ET
☎ (01598) 753369

Elegant, Victorian former sea captain's house on riverside, alongside waterfalls, cascades, dramatic scenery, enchanting harbour, in romantic old world smugglers' village. Nature lovers' and walkers' paradise.

Bedrooms: 5 double, 1 twin, 1 triple
Bathrooms: 4 en-suite, 2 private, 1 public

Bed & breakfast per night:	£min	£max
Single	19.50	25.00
Double	39.00	50.00

Evening meal 1800 (last orders 1815)
Parking for 9
[UL] [S] [TV] [OAP] [SP]

LYNTON

Devon
Map ref 1C1

Hilltop resort on Exmoor coast linked to its seaside twin, Lynmouth, by a water-operated cliff railway which descends from the town hall. Spectacular surroundings of moorland cliffs with steep chasms of conifer and rocks through which rivers cascade.
Tourist Information Centre ☎ (01598) 752225

Alford House Hotel

Alford Terrace, Lynton EX35 6AT
☎ (01598) 752359

Elegant Georgian hotel with spectacular views over Lynton and Exmoor coastline. Delightful en-suite rooms, some four-poster beds. Relaxing and peaceful, warm hospitality, outstanding food and fine wine. Non-smokers.

Bedrooms: 1 single, 5 double, 2 twin
Bathrooms: 8 en-suite, 1 public

Bed & breakfast

per night:	£min	£max
Single	23.00	28.00
Double	46.00	56.00

Half board per person:

	£min	£max
Daily	39.00	44.00
Weekly	259.00	293.00

Evening meal 1900 (last orders 1500)
Open February–November and Christmas
Cards accepted: Mastercard, Visa

🏨🍽️📺♨️S✕🎵📺🛏️🅿️❄️✗ 🚗♨️ SP T

Chough's Nest Hotel

⌒⌒ COMMENDED

North Walk, Lynton EX35 6HJ
☎ (01598) 753315
Detached cliffside retreat with 2-acre grounds and magnificent sea views. Good food. Value for money. Within walking distance of shops.
Bedrooms: 2 single, 7 double, 1 twin, 2 triple
Bathrooms: 12 en-suite

Bed & breakfast

per night:	£min	£max
Single	29.00	29.00
Double	58.00	64.00

Half board per person:

	£min	£max
Daily	40.00	44.00
Weekly	270.00	295.00

Lunch available
Evening meal 1900 (last orders 2000)
Parking for 10
Open March–October
Cards accepted: Diners, Mastercard, Visa, Switch/Delta

🛏️2🏨📺♨️🎵🅰️S✕🎵📺🛏️🅿️❄️✗ SP 🏨 T

The Exmoor Sandpiper Inn ⋀

⌒⌒⌒ COMMENDED

Countisbury, Lynton EX35 6NE
☎ (01598) 741263
Fax (01598) 741358

Beamed character inn/hotel, part 13th C, amidst thousands of acres of rolling

Exmoor hills. A few hundred yards from Countisbury sea cliffs and 1 mile from Lynmouth harbour.
Bedrooms: 9 double, 1 twin, 4 triple, 2 family rooms
Bathrooms: 16 en-suite

Bed & breakfast

per night:	£min	£max
Single	25.00	46.00
Double	50.00	92.00

Half board per person:

	£min	£max
Daily	35.00	73.00
Weekly	290.00	330.00

Lunch available
Evening meal 1900 (last orders 2130)
Parking for 50

🛏️🏨📺♨️S🎵📺🛏️🅿️🔔⋃♩ ❄️🚗✗ SP 🏨 T ◉

Ingleside Hotel ⋀

⌒⌒⌒ COMMENDED

Lynton EX35 6HW
☎ (01598) 752223
Family-run hotel with high standards in elevated position overlooking village. Ideal centre for exploring Exmoor.
Bedrooms: 4 double, 1 twin, 2 triple
Bathrooms: 7 en-suite

Bed & breakfast

per night:	£min	£max
Single	24.00	27.00
Double	48.00	54.00

Half board per person:

	£min	£max
Daily	36.00	39.00
Weekly	238.00	259.00

Evening meal 1900 (last orders 1800)
Parking for 10
Open March–October
Cards accepted: Mastercard, Visa

🛏️12🍽️📺♨️🎵S✕🛏️📺🛏️🅿️❄️✗ 🚗 DAP SP T

Kingford House ⋀

⌒⌒⌒ HIGHLY COMMENDED

Longmead, Lynton EX35 6DQ
☎ (01598) 752361
Private hotel close to Valley of Rocks. Attractive, comfortable rooms, good home-cooked meals with choice of menu. Individual attention assured.
Bedrooms: 2 single, 3 double, 1 twin
Bathrooms: 5 en-suite, 1 private

Bed & breakfast

per night:	£min	£max
Single	18.00	21.00
Double	36.00	42.00

Half board per person:

	£min	£max
Daily	29.50	32.50

Evening meal 1900 (last orders 1700)
Parking for 8
Open February–December

🛏️8🍽️📺♨️🎵🅰️S✕🎵📺🛏️🅿️ ❄️✗🚗✗ SP

Longmead House Hotel ⋀

⌒⌒⌒ HIGHLY COMMENDED

9 Longmead, Lynton EX35 6DQ
☎ (01598) 752523

Delightful old house set in a large garden, quietly situated towards the "Valley of Rocks". Comfortable, pretty en-suite bedrooms. No smoking. Home cooking a speciality.
Bedrooms: 1 single, 4 double, 1 twin, 1 triple
Bathrooms: 5 en-suite, 1 public

Bed & breakfast

per night:	£min	£max
Single	17.00	20.00
Double	34.00	44.00

Half board per person:

	£min	£max
Daily	30.00	35.00
Weekly	175.00	217.00

Evening meal 1900 (last orders 1530)
Parking for 8
Open March–October
Cards accepted: Mastercard, Visa, Switch/Delta

🛏️♨️🅰️S✕🎵📺🛏️❄️✗🚗 SP T

Rockvale Hotel

⌒⌒ COMMENDED

Lee Road, Lynton EX35 6HW
☎ (01598) 752279 & 753343
Quiet, very sunny central location with panoramic views. Pretty en-suite rooms, bar and large level car park. Award-winning home cooking and hospitality. Non-smoking.
Bedrooms: 1 single, 5 double, 2 triple
Bathrooms: 6 en-suite, 2 private

Bed & breakfast

per night:	£min	£max
Single	20.00	22.00
Double	44.00	48.00

Half board per person:

	£min	£max
Daily	34.00	38.00
Weekly	232.00	258.00

Evening meal 1900 (last orders 1600)

Continued ▶

LYNTON

Continued

Parking for 10
Open March–October
Cards accepted: Mastercard, Visa,
Switch/Delta

⛵🅿4📞📠🖥♿🍴🔒Ⓢ✂🅿📺🛏🚗
☀✕🚲 SP

Sandrock Hotel ♠

👑👑👑 COMMENDED

Longmead, Lynton EX35 6DH
☎ (01598) 753307
Fax (01598) 752665

*Relaxing Edwardian hotel with modern
comforts, in delightful sunny position
close to Exmoor's superb coastal
scenery and beauty spots.*
Bedrooms: 2 single, 4 double, 3 twin
Bathrooms: 7 en-suite, 1 public

Bed & breakfast
per night:	£min	£max
Single	19.50	23.00
Double	43.00	49.00

Half board per
person:	£min	£max
Daily	31.00	37.50
Weekly	217.00	262.50

Evening meal 1900 (last orders
2000)
Parking for 9
Cards accepted: Amex, Mastercard,
Visa, Switch/Delta

⛵📞📠🖥♿🍴🔒Ⓢ🅿📺🛏🚗🔍🚲
OAP SP T

Seawood Hotel

👑👑👑 HIGHLY COMMENDED

North Walk Drive, Lynton
EX35 6HJ
☎ (01598) 752272
*Family-run country house hotel nestling
on wooded cliffs overlooking Lynmouth
Bay and headland. Varied menu and
friendly service.*
Bedrooms: 1 single, 9 double, 2 twin
Bathrooms: 12 en-suite, 2 public

Bed & breakfast
per night:	£min	£max
Single	27.00	29.00
Double	54.00	58.00

Half board per
person:	£min	£max
Daily	39.00	41.00
Weekly	259.00	269.00

Evening meal 1900 (last orders
1930)
Parking for 10
Open April–October

⛵🅿12🛏🖥♿🍷🔒Ⓢ✂🅿📺🛏🚗☀
🚲 SP 🏠 T

MALMESBURY

Wiltshire
Map ref 2B2

Overlooking the River Avon, an old
town dominated by its great church,
once a Benedictine abbey. The
surviving Norman nave and porch
are noted for fine sculptures, 12th C
arches and musicians' gallery.
Tourist Information Centre ☎ (01666)
823748

Knoll House Hotel

👑👑👑 COMMENDED

Swindon Road, Malmesbury
SN16 9LU
☎ (01666) 823114
Fax (01666) 823897
Ⓒ Minotel/The Independents

*Ideally located with easy access to M4,
Bath, Cheltenham and Cotswolds.
Country house with fine restaurant and
outdoor heated pool.*
Bedrooms: 9 single, 10 double,
3 twin
Bathrooms: 22 en-suite

Bed & breakfast
per night:	£min	£max
Single		60.00
Double		80.00

Lunch available
Evening meal 1900 (last orders
2130)
Parking for 60
Cards accepted: Amex, Mastercard,
Visa, Switch/Delta

⛵🅿📞📠🖥♿🍷🔒Ⓢ📺🛏🚗
📺50🔜⛵∪🏃☀ OAP 🚲 SP

*The symbols in each entry
give information about
services and facilities.
A key to these symbols
appears at the back
of this guide.*

Mayfield House Hotel ♠

👑👑👑 COMMENDED

Crudwell, Malmesbury SN16 9EW
☎ (01666) 577409 & 577198
Fax (01666) 577977
Ⓒ Consort
*Delightful country hotel with 2 acres of
walled garden. Award-winning
restaurant, with warm and friendly
service. Close to M4, ideal for touring
Cotswolds and Bath.*
Bedrooms: 4 single, 8 double, 7 twin,
1 triple
Bathrooms: 20 en-suite

Bed & breakfast
per night:	£min	£max
Single	44.00	44.00
Double	65.00	

Half board per
person:	£min	£max
Daily	29.00	40.00
Weekly	199.00	211.00

Lunch available
Evening meal 1900 (last orders
2130)
Parking for 50
Cards accepted: Amex, Diners,
Mastercard, Visa, Switch/Delta

⛵🅿♿📞📠🖥♿🍷🔒Ⓢ📺🛏🚗📺30☀
🚲 SP 🏠 T

MAWGAN PORTH

Cornwall
Map ref 1B2

Holiday village occupying a steep
valley on the popular coastal route
to Newquay. Golden sands, rugged
cliffs and coves. Nearby Bedruthan
Steps offers exhilarating cliff walks
and views. The chapel of a
Carmelite nunnery, once the home
of the Arundells, may be visited.

Tredragon Hotel ♠

👑👑👑 COMMENDED

Mawgan Porth, Newquay TR8 4DQ
☎ (01637) 860213
Fax (01637) 860269
Ⓒ Logis of GB

*Grounds lead directly to sandy cove.
Magnificent coastal walks/views. Relax
in our indoor pool complex. Excellent
food and wine. Open all year. Ideal for
short breaks.*
Bedrooms: 2 single, 9 double, 5 twin,
13 family rooms
Bathrooms: 29 en-suite

Bed & breakfast per night:	£min	£max
Single	18.50	35.00
Double	31.00	70.00

Half board per person:	£min	£max
Daily	37.00	61.50
Weekly	259.00	450.00

Lunch available
Evening meal 1900 (last orders 2000)
Parking for 32
Cards accepted: Amex, Mastercard, Visa, Switch/Delta

🛇♿📞💷🖨️☎⚓📶🛈🅂🄿📺🛏️🚗
🍴50🏌️🏇⚓🎣🏃🚶🌸🐕🐾🅳🄰🄿 ⚓ 🆂🄿 🅃

MAWNAN SMITH

Cornwall
Map ref 1B3

Budock Vean Golf and Country House Hotel ♏

👑👑👑👑 COMMENDED

Mawnan Smith, Falmouth TR11 5LG
☎ (01326) 250288
Fax (01326) 250892

Enjoy the quiet dignity of this country house hotel. Set in 65 acres of sub-tropical gardens and parkland. Own golf-course, tennis courts and indoor pool.
Bedrooms: 6 single, 16 double, 30 twin, 2 triple
Suite available
Bathrooms: 54 en-suite

Bed & breakfast per night:	£min	£max
Single	45.00	75.00
Double	90.00	150.00

Half board per person:	£min	£max
Daily	55.00	85.00
Weekly	343.00	553.00

Lunch available
Evening meal 1900 (last orders 2100)
Parking for 100
Open February–December
Cards accepted: Diners, Mastercard, Visa, Switch/Delta

🛇♿📞💷🖨️☎⚓📶🛈🅂🄿✂🎿🅗⊙🍴
🛏️🚗🍴100🏌️⚓🏇🎣🚶🌸🐕🐾🆂🄿
🄵🄸🅃

MELKSHAM

Wiltshire
Map ref 2B2

Small industrial town standing on the banks of the River Avon. Old weavers' cottages and Regency houses are grouped around the attractive church which has traces of Norman work. The 18th C Round House, once used for dyeing fleeces, is now a craft centre.
Tourist Information Centre ☎ (01225) 707424

Conigre Farm Hotel and Restaurant ♏

👑👑👑 COMMENDED

Semington Road, Melksham
SN12 6BZ
☎ (01225) 702229
Fax (01225) 707392
Charming 17th C farmhouse and stable block tastefully converted to provide individually decorated en-suite accommodation and popular restaurant. 400 yards to town centre.
Bedrooms: 3 single, 5 double, 1 twin
Bathrooms: 8 en-suite, 1 private, 1 public

Bed & breakfast per night:	£min	£max
Single	43.00	49.00
Double	59.00	69.00

Half board per person:	£min	£max
Daily	35.00	61.50
Weekly	220.50	387.45

Lunch available
Evening meal 1900 (last orders 2145)
Parking for 15
Cards accepted: Mastercard, Visa, Switch/Delta

🛇♿📞💷🖨️☎⚓📶🛈🅂🄿🛏️🚗
🍴40🚶🌸🐾🆂🄿🄵🄸🅃

The Kings Arms Hotel ♏

👑👑👑 COMMENDED

Market Place, Melksham SN12 6EX
☎ (01225) 707272
Fax (01225) 702085
Combines old world atmosphere with modern amenities and is an ideal centre for touring historic Wiltshire.
Bedrooms: 6 single, 5 double, 2 twin
Bathrooms: 10 en-suite, 2 public

Bed & breakfast per night:	£min	£max
Single	32.00	47.00
Double	52.00	52.00

Lunch available
Evening meal 1900 (last orders 2100)

Parking for 45
Cards accepted: Amex, Diners, Mastercard, Visa, Switch/Delta

🛇📞💷🖨️☎⚓📶🛈🅂🄿🛏️🚗⚓🍴60
🅳🄰🄿⚓🆂🄿🄵🄸🅃

Longhope Guest House

👑👑 APPROVED

9 Beanacre Road, Melksham
SN12 8AG
☎ (01225) 706737
Fax (01225) 706737
Situated in its own grounds on the A350 Melksham - Chippenham road. Half a mile from Melksham town centre, 10 miles from M4 junction 17.
Bedrooms: 1 single, 1 double, 1 twin, 2 triple
Bathrooms: 6 en-suite

Bed & breakfast per night:	£min	£max
Single	23.00	25.00
Double	40.00	

Evening meal 1830 (last orders 1900)
Parking for 12

🛇♿💷🖨️☎📶🅄🅻🛈🅂🄿📺🛏️🚗✗
🐾🅳🄰🄿🆂🄿

MERE

Wiltshire
Map ref 2B2

Small town with a grand Perpendicular church surrounded by Georgian houses, with old inns and a 15th C chantry house. On the chalk downs overlooking the town is an Iron Age fort.
Tourist Information Centre ☎ (01747) 861211

Chetcombe House Hotel

👑👑👑 COMMENDED

Chetcombe Road, Mere, Warminster BA12 6AZ
☎ (01747) 860219
Fax (01747) 860111
Ⓡ Logis of GB
Country house hotel set in 1 acre of mature gardens, close to Stourhead House and Garden. Ideal touring centre. Home-cooked local produce a speciality.
Bedrooms: 1 single, 2 double, 2 twin
Bathrooms: 5 en-suite

Bed & breakfast per night:	£min	£max
Single	29.00	33.00
Double	50.00	50.00

Half board per person:	£min	£max
Daily	39.50	47.50
Weekly	240.00	285.00

Continued ▶

MERE

Continued

Lunch available
Evening meal 1900 (last orders 1700)
Parking for 10
Cards accepted: Amex, Mastercard, Visa

🐎🖥♨♿🗄Ⓢ✂🏛🖾♨🚃 SP T

Meltone House M

⚜ HIGHLY COMMENDED

The Causeway, Shaftesbury Road, Mere, Warminster BA12 6BW
☎ (01747) 861383
Comfortable house with beautiful views. Large car park and garden. About 1 mile from Mere on the Shaftesbury road.
Bedrooms: 1 single, 2 double
Bathrooms: 1 en-suite, 1 private, 1 public
Bed & breakfast

per night:	£min	£max
Single	17.50	20.00
Double	32.00	35.00

Parking for 6

🐎8🖥♨♿🗄 UL 🖾♨🐕🚃

Talbot Hotel

⚜⚜⚜ APPROVED

The Square, Mere BA12 6DR
☎ (01747) 860427
Fax (01747) 861210
16th C coaching inn with interesting features. Ideal for visits to Stourhead, Longleat, Stonehenge, Salisbury, Bath, Sherborne and Cheddar areas. Two-night breaks available.
Bedrooms: 1 single, 2 double, 1 twin, 3 triple
Bathrooms: 6 en-suite, 1 private
Bed & breakfast

per night:	£min	£max
Single	25.00	32.50
Double	45.00	53.00

Lunch available
Evening meal 1830 (last orders 2130)
Parking for 20
Cards accepted: Amex, Mastercard, Visa

🐎2🖥♨♿🗄Ⓢ✂🏛🖾♨🍷15 🚃🔌 SP 🎦

COLOUR MAPS

Colour maps at the back of this guide pinpoint all places in which you will find accommodation listed.

MEVAGISSEY

Cornwall
Map ref 1B3

Small fishing town, a favourite with holidaymakers. Earlier prosperity came from pilchard fisheries, boat-building and smuggling. By the harbour are fish cellars, some converted, and a local history museum is housed in an old boat-building shed. Handsome Methodist chapel; shark fishing, sailing.

Seapoint House Hotel M

⚜⚜⚜ COMMENDED

Battery Terrace, Mevagissey, St Austell PL26 6QS
☎ (01726) 842684
Fax (01726) 842266
Family-run hotel with beautiful views overlooking the bay and harbour. All bedrooms with en-suite facilities, colour TV and hot drinks.
Bedrooms: 3 double, 1 twin, 2 triple, 3 family rooms
Suite available
Bathrooms: 9 en-suite, 1 public
Bed & breakfast

per night:	£min	£max
Single	25.00	45.00
Double	50.00	70.00

Half board per

person:	£min	£max
Daily	40.00	60.00
Weekly	170.00	275.00

Lunch available
Evening meal 1900 (last orders 1900)
Parking for 11
Open March–December
Cards accepted: Amex, Mastercard, Visa

🐎🖪♨📞🖥♨♿Ⓢ✂🏛🎦Ⓟ🖾 🔌🍷50🔍↺∪🐕♨🚃🚭 SP T

Spa Hotel

⚜⚜⚜ COMMENDED

Polkirt Hill, Mevagissey, St Austell PL26 6UY
☎ (01726) 842244
Detached hotel with own grounds, in a traffic-free position away from the bustle, yet within walking distance of the village. Weekend and midweek bookings available.
Bedrooms: 4 double, 2 twin, 3 triple, 2 family rooms
Bathrooms: 11 en-suite
Bed & breakfast

per night:	£min	£max
Single	22.50	27.50
Double	45.00	55.00

Half board per

person:	£min	£max
Daily	32.50	37.50
Weekly	220.00	255.00

Evening meal 1900 (last orders 2000)
Parking for 16
Open March–October
Cards accepted: Amex, Mastercard, Visa, Switch/Delta

🐎♿🖥♨♿🗄Ⓢ✂🏛🎦🖾🔌🔍♨ 🚃 GAP T

Steep House M

⚜⚜

Portmellon Cove, Mevagissey, St Austell PL26 6PH
☎ (01726) 843732

Comfortable house with large garden and covered (summertime) pool. Superb seaside views, licensed, free off-road parking.
Bedrooms: 1 single, 5 double, 1 twin, 1 triple
Bathrooms: 2 en-suite, 1 private, 2 public
Bed & breakfast

per night:	£min	£max
Single	20.00	24.00
Double	36.00	

Parking for 12
Cards accepted: Amex, Mastercard, Visa

🐎10🖥♨♿🗄✂🏛🎦🖾♨↺♨🐕🚃 SP

Tremarne Hotel M

⚜⚜⚜ COMMENDED

Polkirt, Mevagissey, St Austell PL26 6UY
☎ (01726) 842213
Fax (01726) 843420
In a quiet secluded area with views of sea and country. Within easy reach of Mevagissey harbour and Portmellon bathing beach.
Bedrooms: 2 single, 7 double, 3 twin, 1 triple, 1 family room
Bathrooms: 14 en-suite
Bed & breakfast

per night:	£min	£max
Single	25.00	30.00
Double	50.00	60.00

Half board per

person:	£min	£max
Daily	40.00	45.00
Weekly	265.00	300.00

Evening meal 1900 (last orders 1930)

Parking for 13
Open March–October
Cards accepted: Amex, Diners,
Mastercard, Visa, Switch/Delta

🐎📞💷🖨🖐♿🐾Ⓢ⚲🅜🛏🏠🚲❄
🚐 SP T ◎

Trevalsa Court Hotel M

👑👑👑 COMMENDED

Polstreath Hill, Mevagissey, St Austell
PL26 6TH
☎ (01726) 842468
*Clifftop position with superb sea views
and access to beach, in peaceful
surroundings. Ideal for touring. Ample
car parking. Accent on fresh food,
vegetarian/special diets. Ground floor
room ideal for semi-disabled persons.*
Bedrooms: 2 single, 8 double, 4 twin,
1 triple
Bathrooms: 15 en-suite

Bed & breakfast

per night:	£min	£max
Single	25.00	35.00
Double	50.00	70.00

Half board per

person:	£min	£max
Daily	39.00	49.00
Weekly	246.00	309.00

Lunch available
Evening meal 1830 (last orders
1830)
Parking for 40
Open February–November
Cards accepted: Mastercard, Visa

🐎📞🖐Ⓢ⚲🅜TV🛏🏠🚲❄
🚐 SP

MIDSOMER NORTON

Bath & North East Somerset
Map ref 2B2

Small town in pleasant rural setting
in the valley of the River Somer.

Centurion Hotel M

👑👑👑👑 COMMENDED

Charlton Lane, Midsomer Norton,
Bath BA3 4BD
☎ (01761) 417711
Fax (01761) 418357
*Ideally situated hotel, midway between
Bath and Wells. Well-appointed
bedrooms, golf, squash, swimming pool,
indoor and outdoor bowls.*
Bedrooms: 15 double, 27 twin,
2 triple
Suite available
Bathrooms: 44 en-suite

Bed & breakfast

per night:	£min	£max
Single	55.00	
Double	65.00	

Half board per

person:	£min	£max
Daily	40.00	
Weekly	235.00	

Lunch available
Evening meal 1930 (last orders
2130)
Parking for 100
Cards accepted: Amex, Diners,
Mastercard, Visa, Switch/Delta

🐎📞💷🖨🖐♿🐾Ⓢ⚲🅜◎🛏
🏠🍽150🔍❄🏹🎿UↃ❄🐾⚲ SP T

MINEHEAD

Somerset
Map ref 1D1

Victorian resort with spreading
sands developed around old fishing
port on the coast below Exmoor.
Former fishermen's cottages stand
beside the 17th C harbour; cobbled
streets climb the hill in steps to the
church. Boat trips, steam railway.
Hobby Horse festival 1 May.
Tourist Information Centre ☎ *(01643)
702624*

Channel House Hotel M

👑👑👑 HIGHLY COMMENDED

Church Path, Off Northfield Road,
Minehead TA24 5QG
☎ (01643) 703229

*Hotel specialising in first class food and
service. Beautiful gardens in peaceful
location. The bedrooms will suit those
who appreciate quality. Perfect for
exploring Exmoor.*
Bedrooms: 2 double, 5 twin, 1 triple
Bathrooms: 8 en-suite

Bed & breakfast

per night:	£min	£max
Single	62.00	80.00
Double	100.00	100.00

Half board per

person:	£min	£max
Daily	60.00	60.00
Weekly	339.50	357.00

Evening meal 1900 (last orders
2030)
Parking for 10
Open March–November and
Christmas
Cards accepted: Diners, Mastercard,
Visa, Switch/Delta

🐎📞💷🖨🖐🐾Ⓢ🅜◎🛏🏠
UↃ❄🏹🚐 DAP ⚲ SP T

Kildare Lodge M

👑👑👑 COMMENDED

Townsend Road, Minehead
TA24 5RQ
☎ (01643) 702009
Fax (01643) 706516
CR The Independents
*Family-run, Edwin Lutyens designed,
Grade II listed building. Elegant a la
carte restaurant; character-filled
licensed bar; bar meals; well appointed
en-suite accommodation, including
family rooms.*
Bedrooms: 1 single, 4 double, 2 twin,
2 family rooms
Bathrooms: 9 en-suite, 1 public

Bed & breakfast

per night:	£min	£max
Single	19.00	37.00
Double	38.00	74.00

Half board per

person:	£min	£max
Daily	26.00	45.00
Weekly	170.00	260.00

Lunch available
Evening meal 1900 (last orders
2100)
Parking for 28
Cards accepted: Amex, Diners,
Mastercard, Visa

🐎📞💷🖨🖐🐾Ⓢ🅜TV🛏🏠
🍽50UↃ❄ DAP ⚲ SP 🚲 T

Mayfair Hotel

👑👑👑 COMMENDED

25 The Avenue, Minehead
TA24 5AY
☎ (01643) 702719
*Victorian house hotel with lovely decor
and furnishings. All rooms en-suite and
with refrigerator. Family run, home
cooking. On level, 3 minutes from sea
and shops. No smoking.*
Bedrooms: 2 single, 4 double, 2 twin,
5 triple
Bathrooms: 12 en-suite, 1 private

Bed & breakfast

per night:	£min	£max
Single	25.00	26.00
Double	48.00	52.00

Half board per

person:	£min	£max
Daily	34.00	36.00
Weekly	183.00	194.00

Evening meal 1830 (last orders
1900)
Parking for 14
Open March–October
Cards accepted: Mastercard, Visa

🐎📞💷🖨🖐🐾Ⓢ⚲🅜🛏🏠🚲❄
🏹 DAP SP

MORETONHAMPSTEAD

Devon
Map ref 1C2

Small market town with a row of
17th C almshouses standing on the
Exeter road. Surrounding moorland
is scattered with ancient
farmhouses, prehistoric sites.

Manor House Hotel and Golf Course ♨

COMMENDED

Moretonhampstead, Newton Abbot
TQ13 8RE
☎ (01647) 440355
Fax (01647) 440961
ⓒⓡ Principal/Utell International
*This beautiful Jacobean manor is set in
270 acres of estate and is home to a
par-69 championship golf course.*
Bedrooms: 23 single, 28 double,
36 twin, 3 triple
Suite available
Bathrooms: 90 en-suite, 2 public

Bed & breakfast

per night:	£min	£max
Single	75.00	80.00
Double	105.00	135.00

Half board per

person:	£min	£max
Daily	65.00	85.00

Lunch available
Evening meal 1930 (last orders
2130)
Parking for 70
Cards accepted: Amex, Diners,
Mastercard, Visa, Switch/Delta

MORTEHOE

Devon
Map ref 1C1

Old coastal village with small,
basically Norman church. Wild cliffs,
inland combes; sand and surf at
Woolacombe.

Lundy House Hotel ♨

Chapel Hill, Mortehoe, Woolacombe
EX34 7DZ
☎ (01271) 870372 & 870469
Fax (01271) 871001
Email: walkinharmony@msn.com

Magnificently situated on coastal path

with spectacular sea views. Traditional
home cooking, licensed bar/lounge. Pets
welcome. Bargain breaks.
Bedrooms: 1 single, 4 double,
3 triple, 1 family room
Bathrooms: 6 en-suite, 1 public

Bed & breakfast

per night:	£min	£max
Single	17.50	20.00
Double	35.00	45.00

Half board per

person:	£min	£max
Daily	27.00	32.00
Weekly	179.00	215.00

Lunch available
Evening meal 1930 (last orders
1700)
Parking for 9
Cards accepted: Mastercard, Visa,
Switch/Delta

MOUSEHOLE

Cornwall
Map ref 1A3

Old fishing port completely rebuilt
after destruction in the 16th C by
Spanish raiders. Twisting lanes and
granite cottages with luxuriant
gardens rise steeply from the
harbour; just south is a private bird
sanctuary.

Carn Du Hotel

Raginnis Hill, Mousehole, Penzance
TR19 6SS
☎ (01736) 731233
*Elegant Victorian house in an elevated
position above Mousehole. Cosy lounge,
delightful cocktail bar and licensed
restaurant specialising in seafood and
local vegetables. Terraced gardens.*
Bedrooms: 1 single, 3 double, 3 twin
Bathrooms: 6 en-suite, 1 private

Bed & breakfast

per night:	£min	£max
Single	25.00	30.00
Double	50.00	60.00

Half board per

person:	£min	£max
Daily	40.95	45.95
Weekly	240.00	270.00

Lunch available
Evening meal 1900 (last orders
2030)
Parking for 12
Cards accepted: Amex, Mastercard,
Visa

MULLION

Cornwall
Map ref 1B3

Small holiday village with a
golf-course, set back from the coast.
The church has a serpentine tower
of 1500, carved roof and beautiful
medieval bench-ends. Beyond
Mullion Cove, with its tiny harbour,
wild untouched cliffs stretch
south-eastward toward Lizard Point.

Mullion Cove Hotel ♨

COMMENDED

Mullion, Helston TR12 7EP
☎ (01326) 240328
Fax (01326) 240998
*Beautiful late-Victorian hotel with
spectacular harbour and coastal views.
Outstanding food and fine wines.
Guaranteed warmth and relaxation.*
Bedrooms: 6 single, 13 double,
12 twin, 4 triple
Suites available
Bathrooms: 23 en-suite, 6 public

Bed & breakfast

per night:	£min	£max
Single	25.00	75.00
Double	40.00	150.00

Half board per

person:	£min	£max
Daily	33.00	80.00
Weekly	230.00	560.00

Lunch available
Evening meal 1930 (last orders
2045)
Parking for 50
Cards accepted: Amex, Mastercard,
Visa, Switch/Delta

Polurrian Hotel, Apartments and Leisure Club ♨

HIGHLY COMMENDED

Polurrian Cove, Mullion, Helston
TR12 7EN
☎ (01326) 240421
Fax (01326) 240083
*Idyllic setting for family-run hotel with
own beach, surrounded by National
Trust coastline. Indoor leisure club and
outdoor amenities. Personal service.*
Bedrooms: 18 double, 17 twin,
4 triple
Suite available
Bathrooms: 39 en-suite, 1 public

Bed & breakfast

per night:	£min	£max
Single	35.00	50.00
Double	70.00	100.00

Half board per

person:	£min	£max
Daily	45.00	90.00
Weekly	270.00	575.00

Lunch available
Evening meal 1900 (last orders 2100)
Parking for 60
Open February–December
Cards accepted: Amex, Diners, Mastercard, Visa

[symbols]

NEWQUAY

Cornwall
Map ref 1B2

Popular resort spread over dramatic cliffs around its old fishing port. Many beaches with abundant sands, caves and rock pools; excellent surf. Pilots' gigs are still raced from the harbour and on the headland stands the stone Huer's House from the pilchard-fishing days.
Tourist Information Centre ☎ *(01637) 871345*

Aloha Hotel
👑👑 APPROVED
122/124 Henver Road, Newquay
TR7 3EQ
☎ (01637) 878366
Email: 106176.437
@compuserve.com.
Friendly licensed hotel with en-suite rooms and home comforts. Well situated for beaches and touring Cornwall. Conservatory and garden overlooking Trencreek Valley.
Bedrooms: 2 single, 5 double, 3 triple, 3 family rooms
Bathrooms: 6 en-suite, 2 public, 4 private showers

Bed & breakfast
per night:	£min	£max
Single	13.00	20.00
Double	26.00	40.00

Half board per
person:	£min	£max
Daily	19.00	26.00
Weekly	132.00	172.00

Evening meal 1830 (last orders 1000)
Parking for 14
Cards accepted: Amex, Diners, Mastercard, Visa

[symbols]

Chichester M
👑 COMMENDED
14 Bay View Terrace, Newquay
TR7 2LR
☎ (01637) 874216
Comfortable, licensed establishment convenient for shops, beaches and gardens. Showers in most bedrooms, many extras. Walking, mineral

collecting and Discover Cornwall holidays provided in spring and autumn.
Bedrooms: 2 single, 2 double, 2 twin, 1 triple
Bathrooms: 1 public, 5 private showers

Bed & breakfast
per night:	£min	£max
Single	14.00	14.00
Double	28.00	28.00

Half board per
person:	£min	£max
Daily	19.00	19.00
Weekly	132.00	132.00

Evening meal from 1830
Parking for 6
Open March–November

[symbols]

Corisande Manor Hotel M
👑👑👑 COMMENDED
Riverside Avenue, Pentire, Newquay
TR7 1PL
☎ (01637) 872042
Fax (01637) 874557
Unique turreted Austrian design, quietly situated, commanding an unrivalled position in 3-acre secluded grounds with private foreshore. Extensive wine cellar, chef/proprietor.
Bedrooms: 2 single, 7 double, 2 twin
Bathrooms: 10 en-suite, 1 private

Bed & breakfast
per night:	£min	£max
Single	29.00	39.00
Double	55.00	75.00

Half board per
person:	£min	£max
Daily	39.00	49.00
Weekly	235.00	295.00

Evening meal 1900 (last orders 1930)
Parking for 19
Cards accepted: Mastercard, Visa

[symbols]

Edgcumbe Hotel
👑👑👑 APPROVED
Narrowcliff, Newquay TR7 2RR
☎ (01637) 872061
Fax (01637) 879490
Email: edgcumbe@silverquick.com
Family hotel on seafront, only 5 minutes' level walking to town centre. Good congenial atmosphere, friendly staff and renowned for excellent fare.
Bedrooms: 9 single, 31 double, 8 twin, 13 triple, 27 family rooms
Bathrooms: 88 en-suite, 2 public

Bed & breakfast
per night:	£min	£max
Single	34.00	
Double	68.00	

Half board per
person:	£min	£max
Daily	.	50.00
Weekly	153.00	303.00

Lunch available
Evening meal 1900 (last orders 2030)
Parking for 50
Cards accepted: Amex, Mastercard, Visa, Switch/Delta

[symbols]

Eliot-Cavendish Hotel M
👑👑👑 APPROVED
Edgcumbe Avenue, Newquay
TR7 2NH
☎ (01637) 878177
Fax (01637) 852053
Large family hotel situated close to beaches. Heated outdoor pool, sauna and solarium. Extensive parking.
Bedrooms: 6 single, 37 double, 22 twin, 11 triple
Bathrooms: 76 en-suite

Bed & breakfast
per night:	£min	£max
Single	22.00	28.00
Double	38.00	50.00

Half board per
person:	£min	£max
Daily	28.00	34.00
Weekly	135.00	190.00

Lunch available
Evening meal 1800 (last orders 1900)
Parking for 35
Open January, March–December
Cards accepted: Mastercard, Visa

[symbols]

The Esplanade Hotel M
👑👑👑 COMMENDED
9 Esplanade Road, Pentire, Newquay
TR7 1PS
☎ (01637) 873333
Fax (01637) 851413
Email: foh@esplanade.demon.co.uk
Modern hotel overlooking beautiful Fistral Bay. Good food, friendly service and excellent facilities for a happy, relaxing holiday.
Bedrooms: 6 single, 21 double, 10 twin, 17 triple, 20 family rooms
Bathrooms: 74 en-suite, 2 public

Bed & breakfast
per night:	£min	£max
Single	20.00	50.00
Double	40.00	100.00

Half board per
person:	£min	£max
Daily	23.00	55.00
Weekly	130.00	300.00

Continued ▶

NEWQUAY
Continued

Lunch available
Evening meal 1900 (last orders 2030)
Parking for 32
Open February–December
Cards accepted: Amex, Mastercard, Visa, Switch/Delta

🐕♨🛢☎🖥🖵♿🛗🛈Ⓢ🍴🕭Ⓞ✣📠
🛢⛴250🏊🍴🍷🕯🎣🐾🌸 DAP 🎿 SP

Pendeen Hotel
♚♚♚ COMMENDED

Alexandra Road, Porth, Newquay TR7 3ND
☎ (01637) 873521
Fax (01637) 873521
Well established hotel, in its own grounds, 2 miles from Newquay and close to beach. Good food served with friendly and efficient service.
Bedrooms: 2 single, 8 double, 2 twin, 2 triple, 1 family room
Bathrooms: 15 en-suite

Bed & breakfast

per night:	£min	£max
Single	21.50	26.00
Double	39.00	48.00

Half board per

person:	£min	£max
Daily	25.00	32.50
Weekly	139.00	195.00

Evening meal 1830 (last orders 1930)
Parking for 15
Open January–October
Cards accepted: Amex, Mastercard, Visa

🐕♨🛢🖵♿🎣🛈Ⓢ🕭🕅🖵🛢✣🍴
🚤 SP T

Philema Hotel ⚫⚫
♚♚ COMMENDED

1 Esplanade Road, Pentire, Newquay TR7 1PY
☎ (01637) 872571
Fax (01637) 873188
Furnished to a high standard with magnificent views overlooking Fistral Beach and golf-course. Friendly informal hotel with good facilities, including indoor pool, leisure complex and apartments.
Bedrooms: 2 single, 8 double, 3 twin, 5 triple, 11 family rooms
Suites available
Bathrooms: 29 en-suite, 2 public

Bed & breakfast

per night:	£min	£max
Single	20.00	35.00
Double	42.00	64.00

Half board per

person:	£min	£max
Daily	24.00	40.00
Weekly	154.00	200.00

Evening meal 1830 (last orders 1930)
Parking for 38
Open March–October
Cards accepted: Mastercard, Visa, Switch/Delta

🐕♨🛢🖥🖵♿🛈Ⓢ🕭🖵🛢🍴
🛢🏊🎣🐾🚤 SP

Trebarwith Hotel
♚♚♚ COMMENDED

Newquay TR7 1BZ
☎ (01637) 872288
Fax (01637) 875431

On the sea edge with 350 feet of private sea frontage, in a central position away from traffic noise. Same ownership since 1964.
Bedrooms: 3 single, 20 double, 12 twin, 6 family rooms
Bathrooms: 38 en-suite, 3 private

Half board per

person:	£min	£max
Daily	24.00	52.00
Weekly	168.00	305.00

Lunch available
Evening meal 1915 (last orders 2030)
Parking for 40
Open March–October
Cards accepted: Mastercard, Visa, Switch/Delta

🐕♨🛢🖥🖵♿🛈Ⓢ🕅Ⓞ🖵
🛢🏊🎣🍷🐾🌸🍴 SP T

Tregarn Hotel
♚♚ COMMENDED

Pentire Crescent, Newquay TR7 1PX
☎ (01637) 874292
Fax (01637) 850116
Family hotel with facilities for all weathers. Entertainment most nights. Few minutes' walk to Fistral Beach and the River Gannel estuary.
Bedrooms: 4 single, 11 double, 5 twin, 9 triple, 10 family rooms
Bathrooms: 36 en-suite, 2 public

Bed & breakfast

per night:	£min	£max
Single	16.00	33.00
Double	32.00	66.00

Half board per

person:	£min	£max
Daily	21.00	38.00
Weekly	147.00	266.00

Lunch available
Evening meal 1830 (last orders 2000)
Parking for 30
Open March–December
Cards accepted: Mastercard, Visa

🐕♨🛢🖥🖵♿🛈Ⓢ🕅🕅🖵
🍴🛢🎣🍷🐾🌸🎿 SP

Tregurrian Hotel ⚫⚫
♚♚ APPROVED

Watergate Bay, Newquay TR8 4AB
☎ (01637) 860280
Fax (01637) 860280
On coast road between Newquay and Padstow, just 100 yards from golden sandy beach in an area reputed to have some of the finest beaches and coastline in Europe.
Bedrooms: 4 single, 11 double, 4 twin, 3 triple, 6 family rooms
Suites available
Bathrooms: 22 en-suite, 2 public

Bed & breakfast

per night:	£min	£max
Single	22.00	28.00
Double	40.00	52.00

Half board per

person:	£min	£max
Daily	30.00	35.50
Weekly	156.00	230.00

Lunch available
Evening meal 1845 (last orders 1930)
Parking for 25
Open March–October
Cards accepted: Mastercard, Visa

🐕♨🛢🖥🖵♿🛈Ⓢ🕅🖵🛢✣🍷
🌸 DAP SP T

Trevalsa Hotel
♚♚♚ COMMENDED

Watergate Road, Porth, Newquay TR7 3LX
☎ (01637) 873336
Fax (01637) 878843
Modern, licensed hotel above beautiful Whipsiderry beach. Panoramic views of Newquay's coastline. Golf, fishing, wind-surfing, surfing, coastal and countryside walks.
Bedrooms: 4 single, 10 double, 2 twin, 5 triple, 3 family rooms
Bathrooms: 22 en-suite, 2 public

Bed & breakfast

per night:	£min	£max
Single	19.00	26.00
Double	36.00	52.00

Half board per

person:	£min	£max
Daily	22.00	32.00
Weekly	149.00	209.00

Lunch available
Evening meal 1900 (last orders 1930)
Parking for 21
Open March–October
Cards accepted: Amex, Mastercard, Visa, Switch/Delta

Whipsiderry Hotel

HIGHLY COMMENDED

Trevelgue Road, Porth, Newquay TR7 3LY
☎ (01637) 874777
Fax (01637) 874777

Set in own grounds overlooking Porth Beach and Newquay Bay. Noted for fine cuisine. Watch the badgers feed and play only a few feet away.

Bedrooms: 2 single, 12 double, 1 twin, 1 triple, 4 family rooms
Bathrooms: 12 en-suite, 8 private, 2 public

Bed & breakfast per night:	£min	£max
Single	18.50	28.50
Double	37.00	57.00

Half board per person:	£min	£max
Daily	32.00	42.00
Weekly	215.00	289.00

Evening meal 1830 (last orders 2000)
Parking for 30
Open March–October, December
Cards accepted: Amex, Mastercard, Visa

Windward Hotel

HIGHLY COMMENDED

Alexandra Road, Porth, Newquay TR7 3NB
☎ (01637) 873185 & 852436
Fax (01637) 852436

Modern hotel of fine quality with large car park and situated on coastal road to Padstow overlooking Porth Bay. 1.5 miles north of Newquay.

Bedrooms: 10 double, 1 twin, 1 triple, 2 family rooms
Bathrooms: 14 en-suite

Bed & breakfast per night:	£min	£max
Single	25.00	30.00
Double	40.00	60.00

Half board per person:	£min	£max
Daily	30.00	35.00
Weekly	130.00	199.00

Lunch available
Evening meal 1830 (last orders 1900)
Parking for 14
Open March–October
Cards accepted: Amex, Mastercard, Visa, Switch/Delta

NEWTON ABBOT

Devon
Map ref 1D2

Lively market town at the head of the Teign Estuary. A former railway town, well placed for moorland or seaside excursions. Interesting old houses nearby include Bradley Manor, dating from the 15th C, and Forde House, visited by Charles I and William of Orange.
Tourist Information Centre ☎ (01626) 67494

Hazelwood Hotel

COMMENDED

33a Torquay Road, Newton Abbot TQ12 2LW
☎ (01626) 66130
Fax (01626) 65021

Attractive, turn-of-the-century building in quiet residential location, 5 minutes' walk from town centre, rail and coach stations. Licensed restaurant, residents' lounge, garden, car park.

Bedrooms: 1 single, 4 double, 3 twin
Bathrooms: 7 en-suite, 1 public, 1 private shower

Bed & breakfast per night:	£min	£max
Single	30.00	35.00
Double	40.00	49.00

Half board per person:	£min	£max
Daily	40.50	48.95

Lunch available
Evening meal 1830 (last orders 1930)
Parking for 10
Cards accepted: Mastercard, Visa, Switch/Delta

WELCOME HOST

This is a nationally recognised customer care programme which aims to promote the highest standards of service and a warm welcome. Establishments who are taking part in this initiative are indicated by the symbol.

OKEHAMPTON

Devon
Map ref 1C2

Busy market town near the high tors of northern Dartmoor. The Victorian church, with William Morris windows and a 15th C tower, stands on the site of a Saxon church. A Norman castle ruin overlooks the river to the west of the town. Museum of Dartmoor Life in a restored mill.

Heathfield House

COMMENDED

Klondyke Road, Okehampton EX20 1EW
☎ (01837) 54211 & 0850 881547
Fax (01837) 54211

Friendly country guesthouse specialising in the personal touch. Noted for cuisine. The ideal stopover for business or pleasure. Comfort assured. Heated pool. Non-smoking.

Bedrooms: 1 single, 1 double, 1 twin, 1 family room
Bathrooms: 3 en-suite, 1 private

Bed & breakfast per night:	£min	£max
Single	30.00	35.00
Double	50.00	56.00

Lunch available
Evening meal (last orders 2000)
Parking for 8
Open January–November
Cards accepted: Mastercard, Visa

White Hart Hotel

COMMENDED

Fore Street, Okehampton EX20 1HD
☎ (01837) 52730 & 54514
Fax (01837) 53979

Town centre 17th C, coaching inn. Fully licensed freehouse with bars, restaurant, function suites and car parking. Under new management.

Bedrooms: 2 single, 11 double, 6 twin, 1 triple
Bathrooms: 20 en-suite

Bed & breakfast per night:	£min	£max
Single	35.00	
Double	50.00	

Lunch available
Evening meal 1900 (last orders 2100)
Parking for 28
Cards accepted: Mastercard, Visa, Switch/Delta

OLD SODBURY

South Gloucestershire
Map ref 2B2

Cross Hands Hotel ♨
COMMENDED
Old Sodbury, Bristol BS17 6RJ
☎ (01454) 313000
Fax (01454) 324409
Two miles from M4 (exit 18) towards
Stroud. In 6 acres, with a garden and
orchard. A la carte restaurant and large
meeting rooms with private bar for
over 100 delegates.
Bedrooms: 9 single, 9 double, 6 twin
Bathrooms: 20 en-suite, 2 public

Bed & breakfast per night:	£min	£max
Single	35.00	69.45
Double	57.50	99.50

Lunch available
Evening meal 1830 (last orders
2230)
Parking for 200
Cards accepted: Amex, Diners,
Mastercard, Visa, Switch/Delta

OTTERY ST MARY

Devon
Map ref 1D2

Former wool town with modern
light industry set in countryside on
the River Otter. The Cromwellian
commander, Fairfax, made his
headquarters here briefly during the
Civil War. The interesting church,
dating from the 14th C, is built to
cathedral plan.

Fluxton Farm Hotel ♨
APPROVED
Ottery St Mary EX11 1RJ
☎ (01404) 812818
Former farmhouse in beautiful country
setting. Comfortable en-suite bedrooms,
2 sitting rooms, large gardens.
Home-cooked food served in candlelit
dining room. Log fires in season. Cat
lovers' paradise.
Bedrooms: 3 single, 3 double, 4 twin,
2 triple
Bathrooms: 10 en-suite, 1 public

Bed & breakfast per night:	£min	£max
Single	23.00	24.50
Double	46.00	49.00

Half board per person:	£min	£max
Daily	30.00	32.50
Weekly	195.00	210.00

Evening meal 1850 (last orders
1800)
Parking for 20

Salston Manor Hotel ♨
COMMENDED
Ottery St Mary, Exeter EX11 1RQ
☎ (01404) 815581
Fax (01404) 815581
Welcoming country house hotel in the
heart of East Devon, with amenities for
all the family. Indoor pool, squash,
sauna, solarium. Ideal for business or
pleasure.
Bedrooms: 3 single, 7 double, 4 twin,
12 triple, 1 family room
Bathrooms: 27 en-suite

Bed & breakfast per night:	£min	£max
Single	37.50	50.00
Double	60.00	75.00

Half board per person:	£min	£max
Daily	39.50	47.50
Weekly	262.00	360.00

Lunch available
Evening meal 1900 (last orders
2100)
Parking for 100
Cards accepted: Mastercard, Visa,
Switch/Delta

Venn Ottery Barton Hotel ♨
COMMENDED
Venn Ottery, Ottery St Mary
EX11 1RZ
☎ (01404) 812733
Fax (01404) 814713
16th C country hotel. Great food, jolly
atmosphere, special interest holidays,
short breaks, etc. Lovely gardens, ample
parking. Ground floor rooms available.
Bedrooms: 2 single, 5 double, 7 twin,
3 triple
Bathrooms: 12 en-suite, 2 public

Bed & breakfast per night:	£min	£max
Single	32.00	36.00
Double	60.00	75.00

Half board per person:	£min	£max
Daily	42.00	50.00
Weekly	265.00	320.00

Evening meal 1900 (last orders
2100)
Parking for 16
Cards accepted: Mastercard, Visa

PADSTOW

Cornwall
Map ref 1B2

Old town encircling its harbour on
the Camel Estuary. The 15th C
church has notable bench-ends.
There are fine houses on North
Quay and Raleigh's Court House on
South Quay. Tall cliffs and golden
sands along the coast and ferry to
Rock. Famous 'Obby 'Oss Festival
on 1 May.
Tourist Information Centre ☎ (01841)
533449

Green Waves Hotel
COMMENDED
Trevone, Padstow PL28 8RD
☎ (01841) 520114
Long established, small, family-run hotel
in quiet cul-de-sac. Set in garden facing
south to the sea. All rooms have colour
TV and tea-making facilities. Half-size
snooker table available.
Bedrooms: 2 single, 11 double,
6 twin
Bathrooms: 19 en-suite, 1 public

Bed & breakfast per night:	£min	£max
Single	26.00	30.00
Double	52.00	60.00

Half board per person:	£min	£max
Daily	37.00	42.00
Weekly	200.00	250.00

Evening meal 1900 (last orders
2000)
Parking for 16
Open April–October
Cards accepted: Mastercard, Visa

Trevone Bay Hotel ♨
COMMENDED
Trevone Bay, Padstow PL28 8QS
☎ (01841) 520243
Fax (01841) 521195
You will find friendship, relaxation and
good food in our spotless, family-run
hotel. Tranquil village position
overlooking beach/coastal footpath.
Bedrooms: 3 single, 3 double, 3 twin,
1 triple, 3 family rooms
Bathrooms: 13 en-suite

Bed & breakfast per night:	£min	£max
Single	26.00	32.00
Double	44.00	60.00

Half board per person:	£min	£max
Daily	31.00	38.00
Weekly	185.00	225.00

Lunch available
Evening meal 1900 (last orders
1930)

Parking for 12
Open April–October
Cards accepted: Mastercard, Visa

Woodlands Country House

COMMENDED

Treator, Padstow PL28 8RU
☎ (01841) 532426
Fax (01841) 532426
Delightful country house in rural setting near beaches and golf-courses, offering picturesque walks, modern amenities and choice of cuisine.
Bedrooms: 5 double, 2 twin, 2 triple
Bathrooms: 9 en-suite

Bed & breakfast per night:

	£min	£max
Single	26.00	30.00
Double	46.00	50.00

Evening meal 1830 (last orders 1700)
Parking for 15
Open March–October

PAIGNTON

Devon
Map ref 1D2

Lively seaside resort with a pretty harbour on Torbay. Bronze Age and Saxon sites are occupied by the 15th C church, which has a Norman door and font. The beautiful Chantry Chapel was built by local landowners, the Kirkhams.
Tourist Information Centre ☎ (01803) 558383

Lyncourt Hotel

COMMENDED

14 Elmsleigh Park, Paignton TQ4 5AT
☎ (01803) 557124 & (0410) 209291
Situated in a quiet tree-lined road on a level location a short distance from shops, beaches and leisure facilities.
Bedrooms: 3 single, 3 double, 3 twin, 1 triple, 1 family room
Bathrooms: 6 en-suite, 2 public

Bed & breakfast per night:

	£min	£max
Single	14.00	20.00
Double	26.00	40.00

Half board per person:

	£min	£max
Daily	19.00	26.00
Weekly	115.00	160.00

Evening meal 1800 (last orders 1815)
Parking for 3
Cards accepted: Mastercard, Visa

Redcliffe Hotel

COMMENDED

Marine Drive, Paignton TQ3 2NL
☎ (01803) 526397
Fax (01803) 528030
Email: Redclfe@aol.com
The Independents
Choice location in 3 acres of grounds directly adjoining the beach. Heated outdoor swimming pool and new indoor leisure complex.
Bedrooms: 12 single, 23 double, 22 twin, 2 triple
Bathrooms: 59 en-suite, 1 public

Bed & breakfast per night:

	£min	£max
Single	40.00	50.00
Double	80.00	100.00

Half board per person:

	£min	£max
Daily	45.00	60.00
Weekly	280.00	364.00

Evening meal 1900 (last orders 2030)
Parking for 100
Cards accepted: Amex, Mastercard, Visa, Switch/Delta

South Sands Hotel

COMMENDED

12 Alta Vista Road, Paignton TQ4 6BZ
☎ (01803) 557231 & 0500 432153
Fax (01803) 529947
Family-run, wonderful fresh food. Superb, peaceful location overlooking sea, beach, park and close to harbour. Large car park. Dogs and children very welcome.
Bedrooms: 2 single, 3 double, 1 twin, 5 triple, 8 family rooms
Bathrooms: 17 en-suite, 2 private

Bed & breakfast per night:

	£min	£max
Single	20.00	30.00
Double	40.00	60.00

Half board per person:

	£min	£max
Daily	28.00	38.00
Weekly	165.00	230.00

Lunch available
Evening meal 1800 (last orders 2130)
Parking for 17
Open April–October and Christmas
Cards accepted: Mastercard, Visa

Summerhill Hotel

COMMENDED

Braeside Road, Goodrington Sands, Goodrington, Paignton TQ4 6BX
☎ (01803) 558101
Fax (01803) 558101
Comfortable hotel with spacious, secluded, suntrap gardens, adjacent to sandy beaches and park. Close to harbour, leisure centre and water theme park.
Bedrooms: 2 single, 10 double, 5 twin, 9 triple
Bathrooms: 25 en-suite, 1 private

Bed & breakfast per night:

	£min	£max
Single	20.00	27.00
Double	40.00	54.00

Half board per person:

	£min	£max
Daily	28.00	35.00
Weekly	180.00	225.00

Lunch available
Evening meal 1830 (last orders 1900)
Parking for 36
Open March–November

Torbay Court Hotel

COMMENDED

Steartfield Road, Paignton TQ3 2BG
☎ (01803) 663332
Fax (01803) 522680
Situated in a quiet, secluded position. A few yards' level walk to the seafront. Close to park and amenities.
Bedrooms: 11 single, 16 double, 27 twin, 3 triple, 1 family room
Bathrooms: 58 en-suite, 2 public

Bed & breakfast per night:

	£min	£max
Single	13.00	19.00

Half board per person:

	£min	£max
Weekly	128.00	173.90

Lunch available
Evening meal 1800 (last orders 1830)
Parking for 16
Open March–December

National gradings and classifications were correct at the time of going to press but are subject to change. Please check at the time of booking.

PAIGNTON

Continued

Torbay Holiday Motel ⋀

COMMENDED

Totnes Road, Paignton TQ4 7PP
☎ (01803) 558226
Fax (01803) 663375
On the A385 in peaceful countryside, close to all amenities of Torbay. Ideal base for touring Devon.
Bedrooms: 2 single, 7 double, 5 twin, 2 triple
Bathrooms: 16 en-suite

Bed & breakfast

per night:	£min	£max
Single	30.00	33.00
Double	48.00	54.00

Half board per

person:	£min	£max
Daily	30.00	33.00
Weekly	210.00	231.00

Lunch available
Evening meal 1830 (last orders 2100)
Parking for 100
Cards accepted: Amex, Mastercard, Visa

Wynncroft Hotel ⋀

HIGHLY COMMENDED

2 Elmsleigh Park, Paignton TQ4 5AT
☎ (01803) 525728
Centrally situated hotel, with traditional cuisine from an a la carte menu, in the comfort of a refurbished Victorian home.
Bedrooms: 6 double, 3 twin, 2 triple
Bathrooms: 9 en-suite, 1 public, 2 private showers

Bed & breakfast

per night:	£min	£max
Single	18.00	29.00
Double	36.00	58.00

Half board per

person:	£min	£max
Daily	26.00	37.00
Weekly	156.00	222.00

Lunch available
Evening meal 1800 (last orders 1900)
Parking for 8
Open January–November
Cards accepted: Mastercard, Visa

Map references apply to the colour maps at the back of this guide.

PENZANCE

Cornwall
Map ref 1A3

Resort and fishing port on Mount's Bay with mainly Victorian promenade and some fine Regency terraces. Former prosperity came from tin trade and pilchard fishing. Grand Georgian style church by harbour. Georgian Egyptian building at head of Chapel Street and Morrab Gardens.
Tourist Information Centre ☎ (01736) 362207

Estoril Hotel ⋀

COMMENDED

46 Morrab Road, Penzance
TR18 4EX
☎ (01736) 362468 & 367471
Fax (01736) 367471
Elegant Victorian house offering comfortable, comprehensive accommodation. A warm welcome and personal service in peaceful and immaculate surroundings await you.
Bedrooms: 1 single, 4 double, 3 twin, 1 triple, 1 family room
Bathrooms: 10 en-suite

Bed & breakfast

per night:	£min	£max
Single	24.00	27.50
Double	48.00	55.00

Half board per

person:	£min	£max
Daily	36.00	40.00
Weekly	252.00	273.00

Lunch available
Evening meal 1845 (last orders 1930)
Parking for 4
Open February–November
Cards accepted: Mastercard, Visa

Keigwin Hotel ⋀

APPROVED

Alexandra Road, Penzance
TR18 4LZ
☎ (01736) 363930
Smoke-free, quiet, comfortable, family-run hotel, close to all amenities. Good cooking, on-street parking, colour TV. Pre-booking advised.
Bedrooms: 2 single, 4 double, 1 twin, 1 triple
Bathrooms: 4 en-suite, 1 private, 1 public

Bed & breakfast

per night:	£min	£max
Single	14.00	18.00
Double	29.00	37.00

Half board per

person:	£min	£max
Daily	28.00	32.00
Weekly	189.00	215.00

Evening meal 1800 (last orders 0900)
Cards accepted: Mastercard, Visa

Lynwood Guest House ⋀

APPROVED

41 Morrab Road, Penzance
TR18 4EX
☎ (01736) 365871
Fax (01736) 365871
Email: lynwood@connexions.co.uk
Lynwood offers a warm welcome and is situated between promenade and town centre, close to all amenities. Prices shown are for standard rooms (supplement for en-suite).
Bedrooms: 1 single, 2 double, 1 twin, 1 triple, 1 family room
Bathrooms: 2 en-suite, 3 public

Bed & breakfast

per night:	£min	£max
Single	11.50	16.50
Double	23.00	33.00

Cards accepted: Amex, Diners, Mastercard, Visa

Mount Haven Hotel and Restaurant ⋀

COMMENDED

Turnpike Road, Marazion, Penzance
TR17 0DQ
☎ (01736) 710249
Fax (01736) 711658
Email: mount_haven_cornwall@compuserve.com
Ⓒ Minotel/Logis of GB

Well-situated detached hotel in own grounds overlooking St Michael's Mount and Mount's Bay. Ideal touring centre for West Cornwall.
Bedrooms: 3 single, 7 double, 2 twin, 5 triple
Bathrooms: 17 en-suite

Bed & breakfast

per night:	£min	£max
Single	38.00	46.00
Double	58.00	76.00

Half board per

person:	£min	£max
Daily	48.00	60.00
Weekly	231.00	364.00

Lunch available

Evening meal 1900 (last orders 2100)
Parking for 30
Cards accepted: Amex, Mastercard, Visa

♿🛏🖥📞💻♨🞰🍴⒮🎿♨🛗🚐
🍽15❀🚲 SP T

Penmorvah Hotel ᴀ
�☆☆☆ APPROVED

Alexandra Road, Penzance
TR18 4LZ
☎ (01736) 363711
350 yards from promenade in tree-lined avenue. Easy reach of town centre and an ideal location for touring.
Bedrooms: 2 single, 1 double, 1 twin, 4 triple
Bathrooms: 8 en-suite

Bed & breakfast per night:	£min	£max
Single	15.00	20.00
Double	30.00	40.00

Half board per person:	£min	£max
Daily	25.00	30.00
Weekly	155.00	195.00

Evening meal 1830 (last orders 1700)
Cards accepted: Amex, Mastercard, Visa

♿🛏🖥📞💻♨⒮🎿♨🛗🚐 OAP SP T

The Sea and Horses Hotel ᴀ
☆☆☆ COMMENDED

6 Alexandra Terrace, Sea Front, Penzance TR18 4NX
☎ (01736) 361961
Fax (01736) 330499
In quiet seafront location enjoying breathtaking views across Mount's Bay to St Micheal's Mount. Former Victorian gentlemen's residence retaining original features. Excellent cuisine and wines.
Bedrooms: 3 single, 1 double, 3 twin, 3 triple, 1 family room
Bathrooms: 9 en-suite, 2 private

Bed & breakfast per night:	£min	£max
Single	28.00	
Double	56.00	

Half board per person:	£min	£max
Daily	39.50	
Weekly	250.00	

Lunch available
Evening meal 1900 (last orders 2030)
Parking for 12
Cards accepted: Amex, Diners, Mastercard, Visa, Switch/Delta

♿🚪📞🖥💻♨🞰⒮🎿♨TV◐
🛗🚐🍽15▸🐾 OAP 🏌 SP 🏵 T ◎

Tarbert Hotel ᴀ
☆☆☆ COMMENDED

11 Clarence Street, Penzance
TR18 2NU
☎ (01736) 363758
Fax (01736) 331336
Email: 100734.257
@compuserve.com
Ⓒᴿ Minotel/Logis of GB/The Independents
Georgian hotel, centrally located, with emphasis on quality and personal service. Restaurant featuring a la carte with fish specialities. Short breaks available.
Bedrooms: 2 single, 6 double, 4 twin
Bathrooms: 12 en-suite

Bed & breakfast per night:	£min	£max
Single	29.00	33.00
Double	50.00	66.00

Half board per person:	£min	£max
Daily	41.00	49.00
Weekly	246.00	294.00

Evening meal 1900 (last orders 2030)
Parking for 5
Open February–December
Cards accepted: Amex, Mastercard, Visa

♿7🛏📞🖥💻♨🞰⒮🎿♨🛗🚐
❀🍴🚲 SP 🏵 T

Treventon Guest House
☆☆ COMMENDED

Alexandra Place, Penzance
TR18 4NE
☎ (01736) 363521

Genuine Cornish granite guesthouse, 200 yards' walk to promenade. Homely atmosphere. Our guest book is your guarantee.
Bedrooms: 1 single, 3 double, 2 twin, 1 triple
Bathrooms: 4 en-suite, 1 public

Bed & breakfast per night:	£min	£max
Single	14.00	18.00
Double	28.00	36.00

♿5🖥♨UL♨TV🛗🍴 OAP SP

A key to symbols can be found inside the back cover flap.

Warwick House Hotel ᴀ
☆☆☆ COMMENDED

17 Regent Terrace, Penzance
TR18 4DW
☎ (01736) 363881
Family-run hotel near the sea, station and heliport. Tastefully decorated rooms, most en-suite and with sea views. Car parking.
Bedrooms: 1 single, 3 double, 1 twin, 1 triple
Bathrooms: 4 en-suite, 1 public

Bed & breakfast per night:	£min	£max
Single	17.00	19.00
Double	34.00	38.00

Half board per person:	£min	£max
Daily	29.50	31.50
Weekly	206.50	220.50

Evening meal 1830 (last orders 1900)
Parking for 10
Open January–November
Cards accepted: Mastercard, Visa, Switch/Delta

♿5🖥♨UL♨⒮🎿♨🛗🚐❀🚐
🏠

Woodstock House
☆☆ COMMENDED

29 Morrab Road, Penzance
TR18 4AZ
☎ (01736) 369049
Fax (01736) 369049
Email: woodstocp@aol.com.
Well-appointed, centrally situated guesthouse. Helpful, friendly service. Tea-making facilities, radio and TV. Standard and en-suite rooms available.
Bedrooms: 2 single, 2 double, 2 twin, 1 triple
Bathrooms: 3 en-suite, 1 public, 1 private shower

Bed & breakfast per night:	£min	£max
Single	12.00	18.00
Double	24.00	36.00

Cards accepted: Amex, Diners, Mastercard, Visa

♿10🖥📞🖥♨UL⒮🎿♨TV🛗
🚐🐾 SP

The symbol Ⓒᴿ and a group name following an hotel address indicates that bookings can be made through a central reservations office. These offices are listed in the information pages at the back of this guide.

PERRANPORTH

Cornwall
Map ref 1B2

Small seaside resort developed around a former mining village. Today's attractions include exciting surf, rocks, caves and extensive sand dunes.

Beach Dunes Hotel M

👑👑👑 COMMENDED

Ramoth Way, Perranporth TR6 0BY
☎ (01872) 572263
Fax (01872) 573824
Email: beachdunes@thenet.co.uk
Situated in the sand dunes and adjoining the golf-course, overlooking Perranporth beach and its 3 miles of golden sands.
Bedrooms: 4 double, 2 triple,
2 family rooms
Bathrooms: 8 en-suite

Bed & breakfast

per night:	£min	£max
Single	26.50	29.00
Double	53.00	58.00

Half board per

person:	£min	£max
Daily	36.00	40.00
Weekly	220.00	260.00

Lunch available
Evening meal 1830 (last orders 2000)
Parking for 15
Open January–October
Cards accepted: Amex, Diners, Mastercard, Visa, Switch/Delta

Chyan Kerensa Guest House M

👑👑 COMMENDED

Cliff Road, Perranporth TR6 0DR
☎ (01872) 572470
Fax (01872) 572470
Comfortable licensed guesthouse directly overlooking miles of surfing beach. Rooms with panoramic sea views. 200 yards from beach and village centre. Children and pets welcome.
Bedrooms: 3 single, 3 double, 1 twin, 1 triple, 1 family room
Suites available
Bathrooms: 3 en-suite, 3 public

Bed & breakfast

per night:	£min	£max
Single	16.00	23.00
Double	32.00	46.00

Parking for 2

Ponsmere Hotel M

👑👑 COMMENDED

Ponsmere Road, Perranporth
TR6 0BW
☎ (01872) 572225
Fax (01872) 572225
A family hotel with plenty of facilities for children, situated by Perranporth's golden beach. Well placed for touring Cornwall.
Bedrooms: 9 single, 16 double,
6 twin, 46 family rooms
Bathrooms: 77 en-suite

Bed & breakfast

per night:	£min	£max
Single	18.00	25.00
Double	36.00	50.00

Half board per

person:	£min	£max
Daily	27.00	36.00
Weekly	199.00	245.00

Evening meal 1830 (last orders 2000)
Parking for 80
Open April–October and Christmas
Cards accepted: Mastercard, Visa, Switch/Delta

PIDDLETRENTHIDE

Dorset
Map ref 2B3

The Poachers Inn M

👑👑👑 COMMENDED

Piddletrenthide, Dorchester
DT2 7QX
☎ (01300) 348358

Inn situated in lovely Piddle Valley on B3143. En-suite rooms with colour TV, telephone, tea/coffee. Restaurant. Stay 2 nights half board October–March, get third night free.
Bedrooms: 9 double, 1 twin, 2 family rooms
Bathrooms: 12 en-suite

Bed & breakfast

per night:	£min	£max
Double	46.00	50.00

Half board per

person:	£min	£max
Daily	33.00	35.00
Weekly	230.00	245.00

Lunch available

Evening meal 1700 (last orders 2130)
Parking for 30
Cards accepted: Mastercard, Visa

PLYMOUTH

Devon
Map ref 1C2

Devon's largest city, major port and naval base. Old houses on the Barbican and ambitious architecture in modern centre, with aquarium, museum and art gallery, the Dome - a heritage centre on the Hoe. Superb coastal views over Plymouth Sound from the Hoe.
Tourist Information Centre ☎ (01752) 264849 or 266030

Athenaeum Lodge

Listed HIGHLY COMMENDED

4 Athenaeum Street, The Hoe,
Plymouth PL1 2RH
☎ (01752) 665005
Elegant Georgian Grade II listed guesthouse, furnished to a high standard. In a central position for the Hoe, historic Barbican and ferry port. Reputation for comfort and hospitality. Free private parking. Non-smoking.
Bedrooms: 4 double, 3 twin, 3 triple
Bathrooms: 5 en-suite, 1 private, 2 public

Bed & breakfast

per night:	£min	£max
Single	16.00	32.00
Double	30.00	38.00

Parking for 5
Cards accepted: Mastercard, Visa

Berkeleys of St James

👑👑 COMMENDED

4 St James Place East, The Hoe,
Plymouth PL1 3AS
☎ (01752) 221654
Non-smoking, charming Victorian house in secluded square on Plymouth Hoe. Quality stay assured. Awarded healthy options/ eats award 1997/8. En-suite accommodation.
Bedrooms: 1 single, 3 double,
1 triple
Bathrooms: 4 en-suite, 1 private

Bed & breakfast

per night:	£min	£max
Single	21.00	30.00
Double	34.00	40.00

Parking for 4
Cards accepted: Amex, Diners, Mastercard, Visa, Switch/Delta

The Grand Hotel

COMMENDED

Elliot Street, The Hoe, Plymouth PL1 2PT
☎ (01752) 661195
Fax (01752) 600653
CR MacDonald/Utell International

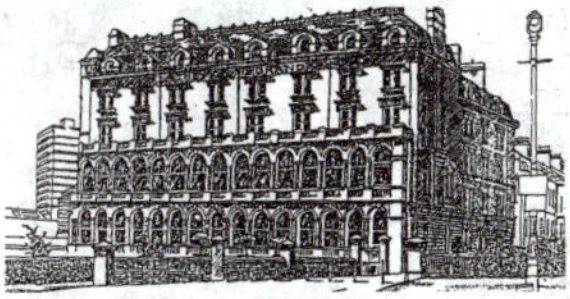

Victorian hotel on Plymouth Hoe. Magnificent sea views, close to city centre and historic Barbican. Leisure breaks available all year round. Live entertainment every Saturday. Balcony rooms and suites.
Bedrooms: 38 double, 34 twin, 3 triple, 2 family rooms
Suites available
Bathrooms: 77 en-suite

Bed & breakfast per night:	£min	£max
Single	40.00	120.00
Double	55.00	140.00

Half board per person:	£min	£max
Daily	37.50	65.00

Lunch available
Evening meal 1900 (last orders 2200)
Parking for 70
Cards accepted: Amex, Diners, Mastercard, Visa, Switch/Delta
S TV 70 SP T

Grosvenor Park Hotel

COMMENDED

114-116 North Road East, Plymouth PL4 6AH
☎ (01752) 229312
Fax (01752) 252777
Popular, comfortable, recently refurbished hotel offering good food and drink and great value. Nearest hotel to the station and all city centre amenities. Look no further! Golf, bowls and diving package breaks a speciality.
Bedrooms: 5 single, 5 double, 5 twin, 1 family room
Bathrooms: 10 en-suite, 2 public

Bed & breakfast per night:	£min	£max
Single	20.00	26.00
Double	36.00	38.00

Half board per person:	£min	£max
Daily	25.00	32.00
Weekly	175.00	220.00

Lunch available
Evening meal 1900 (last orders 2000)
Parking for 6
Cards accepted: Amex, Mastercard, Visa
S TV T

Invicta Hotel

HIGHLY COMMENDED

11/12 Osborne Place, Lockyer Street, The Hoe, Plymouth PL1 2PU
☎ (01752) 664997
Fax (01752) 664994
Elegant Victorian hotel opposite Sir Francis Drake bowling green and famous Plymouth Hoe. Very close to the city centre and historic Barbican.
Bedrooms: 4 single, 6 double, 7 twin, 3 triple, 3 family rooms
Bathrooms: 21 en-suite, 1 public

Bed & breakfast per night:	£min	£max
Single	40.00	43.00
Double	50.00	53.00

Half board per person:	£min	£max
Daily	34.50	35.50
Weekly	207.00	213.00

Lunch available
Evening meal 1900 (last orders 2100)
Parking for 10
Cards accepted: Amex, Mastercard, Visa
12 S TV 55 OAP SP

Lamplighter Hotel

COMMENDED

103 Citadel Road, The Hoe, Plymouth PL1 2RN
☎ (01752) 663855
Fax (01752) 228139
Small friendly hotel on Plymouth Hoe, 5 minutes' walk from the city centre and seafront.
Bedrooms: 5 double, 2 twin, 1 triple, 1 family room
Bathrooms: 7 en-suite, 2 private

Bed & breakfast per night:	£min	£max
Single	18.00	25.00
Double	28.00	35.00

Parking for 4
Cards accepted: Mastercard, Visa
UL S TV

Millstones Country Hotel

COMMENDED

436-438 Tavistock Road, Roborough, Plymouth PL6 7HQ
☎ (01752) 773734
Fax (01752) 769435
Elegant country hotel set in an acre of delightful lawned gardens with private parking. Located 4 miles north of the centre of Plymouth on main A386 road.
Bedrooms: 2 single, 5 double, 2 twin
Bathrooms: 9 en-suite, 1 public

Bed & breakfast per night:	£min	£max
Single	55.00	55.00
Double	65.00	75.00

Half board per person:	£min	£max
Daily	47.00	
Weekly	329.00	

Evening meal 1930 (last orders 2100)
Parking for 16
Cards accepted: Amex, Diners, Mastercard, Visa
S TV 16

New Continental Hotel

COMMENDED

Millbay Road, Plymouth PL1 3LD
☎ (01752) 220782
Fax (01752) 227013

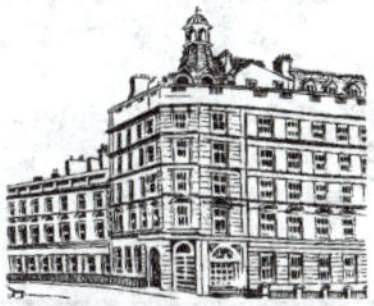

Beautifully refurbished Grade II listed Victorian building in city centre. Within easy walking distance of the shops, Barbican and Hoe. Adjacent to Pavilions conference centre. Superb indoor leisure complex. Leisure breaks available.
Bedrooms: 22 single, 37 double, 14 twin, 2 triple, 24 family rooms
Suites available
Bathrooms: 99 en-suite

Bed & breakfast per night:	£min	£max
Single	53.00	75.00
Double	63.00	130.00

Half board per person:	£min	£max
Daily	42.00	
Weekly	258.00	

Lunch available
Evening meal 1800 (last orders 2200)
Parking for 100
Cards accepted: Amex, Mastercard, Visa, Switch/Delta
S 400 SP T

You are advised to confirm your booking in writing.

Rosaland Hotel ♠

👑 👑 👑 COMMENDED

32 Houndiscombe Road, Plymouth
PL4 6HQ
☎ (01752) 664749
Fax (01752) 256984
*Victorian private hotel in quiet
residential area, close to centre,
university and railway station.
Well-appointed rooms with satellite TV.
Licensed bar. Warm welcome assured.*
Bedrooms: 3 single, 2 double, 1 twin,
2 triple
Bathrooms: 4 en-suite, 2 public,
1 private shower

Bed & breakfast

per night:	£min	£max
Single	17.00	25.00
Double	30.00	37.00

Half board per

person:	£min	£max
Daily	26.00	34.00

Evening meal 1800 (last orders
1800)
Parking for 3
Cards accepted: Amex, Diners,
Mastercard, Visa

St Mellion Hotel, Golf and Country Club ♠

👑 👑 👑 HIGHLY COMMENDED

St Mellion, Saltash, Cornwall
PL12 6SD
☎ (01579) 351351
Fax (01579) 350116
*The compass pivot of Devon and
Cornwall. The visitor's perfect choice,
with world-class golf, new leisure
facilities, award-winning food and
lodge/hotel accommodation. At St
Mellion on A388, north-west of
Plymouth.*
Bedrooms: 8 double, 16 twin
Bathrooms: 24 en-suite

Bed & breakfast

per night:	£min	£max
Single	58.00	95.00
Double	66.00	138.00

Half board per

person:	£min	£max
Daily	50.00	98.00

Lunch available
Evening meal 1930 (last orders
2130)
Parking for 400
Cards accepted: Amex, Diners,
Mastercard, Visa, Switch/Delta

Squires Guest House

Listed HIGHLY COMMENDED

7 St James Place East, The Hoe,
Plymouth PL1 3AS
☎ (01752) 261459
Fax (01752) 261459
*Elegant Victorian establishment in a
quiet secluded square on Plymouth
Hoe. Converted to a high standard.
Within easy walking distance of all
amenities. Winner of Chairman's Cup
for Excellence, awarded by Plymouth
Marketing Bureau.*
Bedrooms: 2 single, 4 double,
2 triple
Bathrooms: 3 en-suite, 2 private,
1 public, 1 private shower

Bed & breakfast

per night:	£min	£max
Single	18.00	25.00
Double	30.00	36.00

Parking for 4
Cards accepted: Amex, Diners,
Mastercard, Visa

Strathmore Hotel ♠

👑 👑 👑 COMMENDED

Elliot Street, The Hoe, Plymouth
PL1 2PR
☎ (01752) 662101
Fax (01752) 223690

*A warm and friendly welcome awaits
you at this ideally situated hotel - close
to city centre.*
Bedrooms: 18 single, 15 double,
15 twin, 5 triple, 1 family room
Bathrooms: 54 en-suite

Bed & breakfast

per night:	£min	£max
Single	34.00	39.00
Double	44.00	49.00

Evening meal 1800 (last orders
2100)
Cards accepted: Amex, Mastercard,
Visa, Switch/Delta

The Teviot Guest House ♠

Listed HIGHLY COMMENDED

20 North Road East, Plymouth
PL4 6AS
☎ (01752) 262656
Fax (01752) 251660
*Early Victorian town house situated
close to university, rail, bus and ferry
terminals. Within a short walking
distance of Plymouth Hoe and
Barbican. Catering for non-smokers.*
Bedrooms: 1 single, 2 double, 2 twin,
1 triple
Bathrooms: 2 en-suite, 1 public,
3 private showers

Bed & breakfast

per night:	£min	£max
Single	18.00	26.00
Double	32.00	40.00

Parking for 2
Cards accepted: Amex, Mastercard,
Visa

Picturesque fishing village clinging to
steep valley slopes about its
harbour. A river splashes past
cottages and narrow lanes twist
between. The harbour mouth,
guarded by jagged rocks, is closed by
heavy timbers during storms.

Claremont Hotel ♠

👑 👑 👑 APPROVED

The Coombes, Polperro, Looe
PL13 2RG
☎ (01503) 272241
Fax (01503) 272241
ⓒ Logis of GB

*Family-run hotel in the heart of fishing
village. Splendid coastal walks and
places of interest nearby.
Award-winning restaurant, sun-trap
patio. Off-season breaks.*
Bedrooms: 7 double, 1 twin, 1 triple,
1 family room
Bathrooms: 10 en-suite

Bed & breakfast

per night:	£min	£max
Single	18.95	30.95
Double	37.90	55.90

Half board per

person:	£min	£max
Daily	31.00	40.00
Weekly	195.00	255.00

Lunch available
Evening meal 1900 (last orders
2000)
Parking for 16

Open April–December
Cards accepted: Amex, Mastercard,
Visa, Switch/Delta

Penryn House 🅜

COMMENDED

The Coombes, Polperro, Looe
PL13 2RQ
☎ (01503) 272157
Fax (01503) 273055

*Charming Victorian hotel offering
comfortable en-suite accommodation
and fine dining in candlelit restaurant.
Fabulous coastal walks and National
Trust properties. "Murder Mystery"
weekends.*
Bedrooms: 9 double, 1 twin
Bathrooms: 10 en-suite, 1 public

Bed & breakfast
per night:	£min	£max
Single	28.00	36.00
Double	40.00	56.00

Half board per
person:	£min	£max
Daily	33.00	41.00
Weekly	217.00	280.00

Lunch available
Evening meal 1830 (last orders
2130)
Parking for 14
Cards accepted: Diners, Mastercard,
Visa

POLZEATH

Cornwall
Map ref 1B2

Small resort on Padstow Bay and
the widening Camel Estuary, with
excellent sands and bathing. Pentire
Head (National Trust), a notable
viewpoint, lies to the north.

Seascape Hotel 🅜

COMMENDED

Polzeath PL27 6SX
☎ (01208) 863638
Fax (01208) 862940
*Renowned for food and a high degree
of comfort, with magnificent sea views.
Honeymoon and Christmas specials.
Four-poster and balcony rooms
available. Children over 12 years
welcome.*

Bedrooms: 13 double, 2 twin
Bathrooms: 15 en-suite

Bed & breakfast
per night:	£min	£max
Single	25.00	30.00
Double	50.00	60.00

Half board per
person:	£min	£max
Daily	35.00	40.00
Weekly	245.00	280.00

Evening meal 1900 (last orders
1800)
Parking for 18
Open February–October, December
Cards accepted: Mastercard, Visa

PORLOCK

Somerset
Map ref 1D1

Village set between steep Exmoor
hills and the sea at the head of
beautiful Porlock Vale. The narrow
street shows a medley of building
styles. South westward is Porlock
Weir with its old houses and tiny
harbour and further along the shore
at Culbone is England's smallest
church.

Anchor and Ship Hotel 🅜

COMMENDED

Porlock Harbour, Porlock, Minehead
TA24 8PB
☎ (01643) 862753
Fax (01643) 862843

*Attractive, quiet, comfortable hotel on
water's edge. Picturesque harbour amid
Exmoor's magnificent scenery and
coastline. Wildlife everywhere, ancient
villages, medieval castle, smugglers'
coves.*
Bedrooms: 2 single, 13 double,
4 twin, 2 triple
Bathrooms: 20 en-suite, 1 private

Bed & breakfast
per night:	£min	£max
Single	49.00	65.00
Double	82.00	115.00

Half board per
person:	£min	£max
Daily	59.75	79.75
Weekly	336.00	468.00

Lunch available
Evening meal 1900 (last orders
2115)
Parking for 30

Open February–December
Cards accepted: Amex, Mastercard,
Visa, Switch/Delta

Porlock Vale House

HIGHLY COMMENDED

Porlock Weir, Minehead TA24 8NY
☎ (01643) 862338
Fax (01643) 862338
*Formerly a hunting lodge, now a small
friendly hotel. Magnificent location, with
25 acres of grounds sweeping down to
the sea and with wonderful views
across Porlock Bay.*
Bedrooms: 10 double, 5 twin
Bathrooms: 14 en-suite, 1 private,
2 public

Bed & breakfast
per night:	£min	£max
Single	50.00	60.00
Double	73.00	83.00

Half board per
person:	£min	£max
Daily	55.00	65.00
Weekly	295.00	330.00

Lunch available
Evening meal 1900 (last orders
1930)
Parking for 20
Cards accepted: Amex, Mastercard,
Visa, Switch/Delta

PORT GAVERNE

Cornwall
Map ref 1B2

Small village sheltering in a narrow
inlet on the dramatic north Cornish
coast. In the 19th C the shingle
beach was a loading site for slate
from the nearby Delabole quarry.

Port Gaverne Hotel 🅜

COMMENDED

Port Gaverne, Port Isaac PL29 3SQ
☎ (01208) 880244 & 0500 657867
Fax (01208) 880151
*17th C hotel and restaurant in a tiny
paradise on the North Cornwall coast.
Half board daily price below based on
minimum 2-day stay.*
Bedrooms: 3 single, 7 double, 2 twin,
5 triple
Bathrooms: 16 en-suite, 1 private

Bed & breakfast
per night:	£min	£max
Single	48.00	52.00
Double	96.00	104.00

Continued ▶

PORT GAVERNE

Continued

Half board per person:	£min	£max
Daily	55.00	65.00
Weekly	371.00	413.00

Lunch available
Evening meal 1900 (last orders 2130)
Parking for 20
Open February–December
Cards accepted: Amex, Diners, Mastercard, Visa, Switch/Delta

⛵📞💻🖥️♿🎣🍵Ⓢ✂️🎦🖥️ ⬛
🍽️50🅿️❄️🚲⚡Ⓢ🅿️👜

PORT ISAAC

Cornwall
Map ref 1B2

Old fishing port of whitewashed cottages, twisting stairways and narrow alleys. A stream splashes down through the centre of the harbour. Nearby stands a 19th C folly, Doyden Castle, with a magnificent view of the coast.

The Cornish Arms 𝖠𝖠

👑👑👑 COMMENDED

Pendoggett, St Kew, Bodmin
PL30 3HH
☎ (01208) 880263
Fax (01208) 880335
Ⓒ Wayfarer/Logis of GB
Delightful 16th C coaching inn, surrounded by unspoilt countryside with views down to north Cornish coast. Noted for food. Charming, spacious bedrooms. Special breaks available.
Bedrooms: 4 double, 3 twin
Bathrooms: 6 en-suite, 1 public

Bed & breakfast per night:	£min	£max
Single	35.00	50.00
Double	49.00	80.00

Half board per person:	£min	£max
Daily	34.95	39.95

Lunch available
Evening meal 1915 (last orders 2130)
Parking for 40
Cards accepted: Amex, Diners, Mastercard, Visa, Switch/Delta

⛵📞💻🖥️♿🎣🍵Ⓢ✂️🎦🖥️ ⬛
🍽️14🅿️♉️☂️❄️🚲Ⓢ🅿️👜🅣

For ideas on places to visit refer to the introduction at the beginning of this section.

PORTHLEVEN

Cornwall
Map ref 1B3

Old fishing port with handsome Victorian buildings overlooking Mount's Bay. An extensive, shingly beach reaches south-east towards the Loe Bar, where the pebbles make a lake on the landward side.

Harbour Inn 𝖠𝖠

👑👑👑 COMMENDED

Commercial Road, Porthleven, Helston TR13 9JD
☎ (01326) 573876
150-year-old inn on harbour edge. Restaurant open 7 days a week. Most bedrooms en-suite, many with harbour views.
Bedrooms: 1 single, 6 double, 2 twin, 1 family room
Bathrooms: 8 en-suite, 1 public, 2 private showers

Bed & breakfast per night:	£min	£max
Single		32.50
Double	40.00	59.00

Half board per person:	£min	£max
Daily	30.95	40.45
Weekly		286.50

Lunch available
Evening meal 1830 (last orders 2130)
Parking for 10
Cards accepted: Amex, Diners, Mastercard, Visa

⛵📞💻🖥️♿🎣🍵Ⓢ✂️🎦🖥️ ⬛🛬
🚲Ⓢ🅣

PORTLAND

Dorset
Map ref 2B3

Joined by a narrow isthmus to the coast, a stony promontory sloping from the lofty landward side to a lighthouse on Portland Bill at its southern tip. Villages are built of the white limestone for which the "isle" is famous.

Alessandria Hotel and Italian Restaurant 𝖠𝖠

👑👑👑 APPROVED

71 Wakeham Easton, Portland, Weymouth DT5 1HW
☎ (01305) 822270 & 820108
Fax (01305) 820561
Italy on Portland. Warm and friendly Italian hospitality from chef/proprietor Giovanni. Spacious en-suite bedrooms with all facilities. Food prepared and cooked to order. Three bedrooms on ground floor.

Bedrooms: 6 single, 3 double, 3 twin, 2 triple, 1 family room
Suite available
Bathrooms: 10 en-suite, 1 private, 3 public, 1 private shower

Bed & breakfast per night:	£min	£max
Single	25.00	35.00
Double	45.00	60.00

Half board per person:	£min	£max
Daily	40.00	50.00
Weekly	220.00	245.00

Evening meal 1900 (last orders 2100)
Parking for 19
Cards accepted: Amex, Mastercard, Visa, Switch/Delta

⛵📞♿🎣💻🖥️♿🎣🍵Ⓢ✂️🎦🎦🖥️ ⬛
🍽️20🚲⚡📅❄️🅿️🅣◎

PORTLOE

Cornwall
Map ref 1B3

Old fishing village and small resort where majestic cliffs rise from Veryan Bay. Unspoilt National Trust coast stretches south-westward to Nare Head.

Lugger Hotel and Restaurant 𝖠𝖠

👑👑👑 HIGHLY COMMENDED

Portloe, Truro TR2 5RD
☎ (01872) 501322
Fax (01872) 501691
17th C smugglers' inn, at the water's edge in a quiet, picturesque cove, where fishing boats moor alongside. Hotel does not cater for children under 12 years of age.
Bedrooms: 3 single, 9 double, 7 twin
Suites available
Bathrooms: 19 en-suite

Bed & breakfast per night:	£min	£max
Single	55.00	55.00
Double	110.00	110.00

Half board per person:	£min	£max
Daily	60.00	75.00
Weekly	420.00	

Lunch available
Evening meal 1900 (last orders 2130)
Parking for 25
Open March–October
Cards accepted: Amex, Diners, Mastercard, Visa, Switch/Delta

⛵12♿🎣📞💻🖥️♿🎣🍵Ⓢ✂️🎦
🖥️👜🌀♉️☂️❄️✖️🚲Ⓢ🅿️🅣

PORTSCATHO

Cornwall
Map ref 1B3

Coastal village spreading along low cliffs of Gerrans Bay on the eastern side of the Roseland Peninsula. Seaside buildings show a variety of styles from late Georgian houses to small, interestingly-designed modern blocks.

Gerrans Bay Hotel ⚠

COMMENDED

12 Tregassick Road, Portscatho, Truro TR2 5ED
☎ (01872) 580338
Fax (01872) 580250
Set in superb countryside, near sandy beaches. Noted for food. Personal service, en-suite rooms.
Bedrooms: 2 single, 5 double, 5 twin, 2 family rooms
Bathrooms: 12 en-suite, 2 private

Bed & breakfast
per night:	£min	£max
Single	29.00	38.00
Double	54.00	76.00

Half board per
person:	£min	£max
Daily	49.00	53.50
Weekly	300.00	330.00

Lunch available
Evening meal 1930 (last orders 2000)
Parking for 16
Open April–October
Cards accepted: Amex, Mastercard, Visa, Switch/Delta

RADSTOCK

Bath & North East Somerset
Map ref 2B2

Thriving small town ideally situated for touring the Mendip Hills.

The Rookery ⚠

APPROVED

Wells Road, Radstock, Bath BA3 3RS
☎ (01761) 432626
Fax (01761) 432626
Homely, family-run guesthouse with licensed restaurant, situated between Bath and Wells. Ideal for touring the West Country. All rooms en-suite.
Bedrooms: 3 double, 3 twin, 3 triple
Bathrooms: 9 en-suite

Bed & breakfast
per night:	£min	£max
Single	25.00	30.00
Double	45.00	53.00

Evening meal 1900 (last orders 2100)
Parking for 25
Cards accepted: Amex, Diners, Mastercard, Visa

RANGEWORTHY

South Gloucestershire
Map ref 2B2

Rangeworthy Court Hotel ⚠

COMMENDED

Church Lane, Wotton Road, Rangeworthy, Bristol BS17 5ND
☎ (01454) 228347
Fax (01454) 228945
17th C country manor house with relaxing, peaceful atmosphere and popular restaurant. Less than 20 minutes from M4, M5 and Bristol.
Bedrooms: 3 single, 7 double, 2 twin, 2 triple
Bathrooms: 14 en-suite

Bed & breakfast
per night:	£min	£max
Single	55.00	58.00
Double	68.00	80.00

Half board per
person:	£min	£max
Daily	42.00	52.00

Lunch available
Evening meal 1900 (last orders 2100)
Parking for 40
Cards accepted: Amex, Diners, Mastercard, Visa, Switch/Delta

ROCK

Cornwall
Map ref 1B2

Small resort and boating centre beside the abundant sands of the Camel Estuary. A fine golf-course stretches northward along the shore to Brea Hill, thought to be the site of a Roman settlement. Passenger ferry service from Padstow.

The Mariners Hotel ⚠

COMMENDED

The Slipway, Rock, Wadebridge PL27 6LD
☎ (01208) 862312
Fax (01208) 863827
Email: Annette-miller@msn.co
Situated in a popular water sports area with panoramic views over the Camel Estuary to Padstow. Wrecker's Bar and Samantha's Restaurant.

Bedrooms: 1 single, 8 double, 7 twin, 2 family rooms
Bathrooms: 18 en-suite

Bed & breakfast
per night:	£min	£max
Single	30.00	40.00
Double	60.00	70.00

Half board per
person:	£min	£max
Weekly	250.00	300.00

Lunch available
Evening meal 1900 (last orders 2100)
Parking for 29
Open March–October
Cards accepted: Amex, Mastercard, Visa, Switch/Delta

Roskarnon House Hotel ⚠

APPROVED

Rock, Wadebridge PL27 6LD
☎ (01208) 862329
Fax (01208) 862785
Edwardian house in an acre of lawned gardens, facing south and overlooking Camel Estuary. 20 yards from the beach and 50 yards from the golf-course.
Bedrooms: 1 single, 4 double, 6 twin, 1 triple
Bathrooms: 8 en-suite, 2 private, 3 public

Bed & breakfast
per night:	£min	£max
Single	25.00	
Double	50.00	

Half board per
person:	£min	£max
Daily	30.00	
Weekly	200.00	

Lunch available
Evening meal 1900 (last orders 2000)
Parking for 16
Open March–October
Cards accepted: Amex

Silvermead ⚠

COMMENDED

Rock, Wadebridge PL27 6LB
☎ (01208) 862425

Off main road affording superb estuary views. Sailing club and windsurfing. 150
Continued ▶

ROCK
Continued

yards from beach and adjacent to St Enodoc 36-hole golf-course. Residential licence.
Bedrooms: 1 single, 2 double, 2 twin, 2 triple
Bathrooms: 4 en-suite, 1 public

Bed & breakfast

per night:	£min	£max
Single	17.50	46.00
Double	35.00	46.00

Half board per person:

	£min	£max
Daily	27.50	56.00
Weekly	175.00	210.00

Evening meal 1800 (last orders 2000)
Parking for 13

RUAN HIGH LANES
Cornwall
Map ref 1B3

Village at the northern end of the Roseland Peninsula.

The Hundred House Hotel ⋔
👑👑👑 HIGHLY COMMENDED
Ruan High Lanes, Near Truro TR2 5JR
☎ (01872) 501336
Fax (01872) 501151

Delightful 19th C house in 3-acre garden, near St Mawes, Fal estuary and 12 miles from Truro. Antiques, log fires, delicious dinners. Pretty en-suite bedrooms. Ideal for walking, touring, gardens and National Trust properties.
Bedrooms: 2 single, 4 double, 4 twin, 2 family rooms
Bathrooms: 12 en-suite

Bed & breakfast

per night:	£min	£max
Single	37.00	39.50
Double	74.00	79.00

Half board per person:

	£min	£max
Daily	53.00	60.00
Weekly	329.00	378.00

Evening meal 1930 (last orders 1900)
Parking for 15

Open March–October
Cards accepted: Amex, Mastercard, Visa

ST AGNES
Cornwall
Map ref 1B3

Small town in a once-rich mining area on the north coast. Terraced cottages and granite houses slope to the church. Some old mine workings remain, but the attraction must be the magnificent coastal scenery and superb walks. St Agnes Beacon offers one of Cornwall's most extensive views.

Driftwood Spars Hotel
👑👑👑 COMMENDED
Trevaunance Cove, St Agnes TR5 ORT
☎ (01872) 552428 & 553323
Fax (01872) 552428
Delightful old inn with enormous beams, stone walls and log fires. Most bedrooms have wonderful sea views. Candelit restaurant. Parking.
Bedrooms: 7 double, 1 twin, 1 family room
Bathrooms: 9 en-suite

Bed & breakfast

per night:	£min	£max
Single	30.00	
Double	60.00	

Lunch available
Evening meal 1900 (last orders 2300)
Parking for 100
Cards accepted: Amex, Diners, Mastercard, Visa, Switch/Delta

Penkerris ⋔
👑👑 APPROVED
Penwinnick Road, St Agnes TR5 0PA
☎ (01872) 552262
Enchanting Edwardian residence with own grounds in unspoilt Cornish village. Beautiful rooms, log fires in winter, good home cooking. Dramatic cliff walks and beaches nearby.
Bedrooms: 3 double, 1 twin, 3 triple
Bathrooms: 3 en-suite, 2 public

Bed & breakfast

per night:	£min	£max
Single	15.00	30.00
Double	27.00	45.00

Half board per person:

	£min	£max
Daily	22.50	

Lunch available
Evening meal from 1830

Parking for 9
Cards accepted: Amex, Diners, Mastercard, Visa

Rose-in-Vale Country House Hotel ⋔
👑👑👑 HIGHLY COMMENDED
Mithian, St Agnes TR5 0QD
☎ (01872) 552202
Fax (01872) 552700
CR Logis of GB

Secluded Georgian country house in secret wooded valley. Recently refurbished. High standards of comfort, service, cuisine. Extensive grounds. Beaches close by. Excellent touring base.
Bedrooms: 2 single, 9 double, 8 twin
Suites available
Bathrooms: 19 en-suite

Bed & breakfast

per night:	£min	£max
Single	45.00	45.00
Double	80.00	96.00

Half board per person:

	£min	£max
Daily	54.00	62.50

Lunch available
Evening meal 1900 (last orders 2030)
Parking for 40
Cards accepted: Amex, Diners, Mastercard, Visa, Switch/Delta

Sunholme Hotel ⋔
👑👑👑 COMMENDED
Goonvrea Road, St Agnes TR5 0NW
☎ (01872) 552318
Comfortable country house in extensive grounds with magnificent country and coastal views and walks. Traditional food, personal service, en-suite rooms.
Bedrooms: 1 single, 4 double, 2 twin, 2 triple, 1 family room
Bathrooms: 10 en-suite, 1 public

Bed & breakfast

per night:	£min	£max
Single	23.00	32.00
Double	46.00	64.00

Half board per person:

	£min	£max
Daily	40.00	45.00
Weekly	231.00	273.00

Evening meal 1900 (last orders 2000)
Parking for 12
Open March–October
Cards accepted: Mastercard, Visa, Switch/Delta

🏇7🛁📞🖵🕯📶🛇⌁🎀📺▭🛒✿ SP

ST AUSTELL

Cornwall
Map ref 1B3

Leading market town, the meeting point of old and new Cornwall. One mile from St Austell Bay with its sandy beaches, old fishing villages and attractive countryside. Ancient narrow streets, pedestrian shopping precincts. Fine church of Pentewan stone and Italianate Town Hall.

Alexandra Hotel

👑 APPROVED

52-54 Alexandra Road, St Austell PL25 4QN
☎ (01726) 66111
Fax (01726) 74242
In quietish position just 5 minutes from town centre. Within easy reach of St Austell Bay and very near bus and rail station.
Bedrooms: 5 single, 4 double, 3 twin
Bathrooms: 4 en-suite, 3 public

Bed & breakfast
per night:	£min	£max
Single	24.00	29.00
Double	42.00	52.00

Half board per person:
	£min	£max
Daily	33.75	38.75
Weekly	180.00	212.00

Evening meal 1830 (last orders 1700)
Parking for 16
Cards accepted: Amex, Diners, Mastercard, Visa, Switch/Delta

🏇🛁🖵🕯🛇🎀📺▭🛒✆20 SP T

White Hart Hotel 🏔

👑👑👑 COMMENDED

Church Street, St Austell PL25 4AT
☎ (01726) 72100
Fax (01726) 74705
Built in the late 16th C, became the chief coaching inn in the 17th C and is now a family-run hotel.
Bedrooms: 2 single, 13 double, 2 twin, 1 triple
Bathrooms: 17 en-suite, 1 private

Bed & breakfast
per night:	£min	£max
Single	40.00	45.00
Double	63.00	68.00

Lunch available

Evening meal 1900 (last orders 2100)
Cards accepted: Amex, Diners, Mastercard, Visa, Switch/Delta

🏇📞🖵🕯🍴🛇📶🎀▭🛒✆50▶ 🚐 SP 🅿 T

ST IVES

Cornwall
Map ref 1B3

Old fishing port, artists' colony and holiday town with good surfing beach. Fishermen's cottages, granite fish cellars, a sandy harbour and magnificent headlands typify a charm that has survived since the 19th C pilchard boom. Tate Gallery opened in 1993.
Tourist Information Centre ☎ (01736) 796297

Blue Hayes

👑👑👑 HIGHLY COMMENDED

Trelyon Avenue, St Ives TR26 2AD
☎ (01736) 797129
A country house by the sea at St Ives.
Bedrooms: 2 single, 5 double, 1 triple
Suite available
Bathrooms: 4 en-suite, 1 private, 2 public

Bed & breakfast
per night:	£min	£max
Single	30.00	37.00
Double	59.00	86.00

Half board per person:
	£min	£max
Daily	44.00	54.00
Weekly	250.00	330.00

Evening meal 1830 (last orders 1830)
Parking for 9
Open March–October
Cards accepted: Mastercard, Visa

🏇5📶🖵🕯🍴🛇⌁🎀▭🛒✆🚶 ✿🚐 SP

Chy-an-Dour Hotel 🏔

👑👑👑 COMMENDED

Trelyon Avenue, St Ives TR26 2AD
☎ (01736) 796436
Fax (01736) 795772
Former sea captain's house built of dressed granite, with superb sea views. All rooms en-suite. Chef/proprietor.
Wheelchair access category 2 ♿
Bedrooms: 13 double, 7 twin, 1 triple, 2 family rooms
Suite available
Bathrooms: 23 en-suite

Bed & breakfast
per night:	£min	£max
Single	30.00	42.00
Double	60.00	84.00

Half board per person:
	£min	£max
Daily	45.00	57.00
Weekly	260.00	350.00

Evening meal 1900 (last orders 2030)
Parking for 23
Cards accepted: Mastercard, Visa, Switch/Delta

🏇🛁📶🖵🕯🍴🛇📶⌁🎀📺▤ ▭🛒✆▶✿✈🐾🚭 SP T

Chy Harbro 🏔

👑👑 COMMENDED

16 Parc Avenue, St Ives TR26 2DN
☎ (01736) 794617

Superb sea views overlooking the harbour. Reputation for good food and hospitality. Some rooms en-suite and with sea views.
Bedrooms: 1 single, 3 double, 1 twin
Bathrooms: 4 en-suite, 1 private

Bed & breakfast
per night:	£min	£max
Single	17.00	20.00
Double	34.00	40.00

Half board per person:
	£min	£max
Daily	27.00	30.00
Weekly	171.00	191.00

Evening meal from 1900
Cards accepted: Mastercard, Visa, Switch/Delta

🏇12📶🖵🕯🍴🛇⌁🎀📺▭🛒 🚐 DAP SP

Dean Court Hotel

👑👑👑 COMMENDED

Trelyon Avenue, St Ives TR26 2AD
☎ (01736) 796023
Fax (01736) 796233
Former gentleman's residence set in own grounds. Enjoys panoramic views across St Ives Bay and overlooks Porthminster Beach and St Ives harbour. Good food, ample parking.
Bedrooms: 2 single, 8 double, 2 twin
Bathrooms: 12 en-suite

Bed & breakfast
per night:	£min	£max
Single	30.00	36.00
Double	56.00	72.00

Half board per person:
	£min	£max
Daily	37.00	43.00
Weekly	230.00	270.00

Continued ▶

ST IVES

Continued

Evening meal 1830 (last orders 1800)
Parking for 12
Open March–October
Cards accepted: Mastercard, Visa

Garrack Hotel and Restaurant

COMMENDED

Higher Ayr, Burthallan Lane, St Ives
TR26 3AA
☎ (01736) 796199
Fax (01736) 798955
Logis of GB

Delightful family-owned hotel. Quiet location. Superb coastal views. Ample parking. Heated indoor pool and leisure centre. Fabulous bargain breaks October-March.
Bedrooms: 1 single, 8 double, 5 twin, 3 triple
Bathrooms: 17 en-suite, 1 public

Bed & breakfast per night:	£min	£max
Single	65.50	85.00
Double	95.50	135.00

Half board per person:	£min	£max
Daily	66.00	90.00
Weekly	420.00	585.00

Lunch available
Evening meal 1900 (last orders 2030)
Parking for 30
Cards accepted: Amex, Diners, Mastercard, Visa, Switch/Delta

Nook Hotel

APPROVED

Ayr, St Ives TR26 1EQ
☎ (01736) 795913
Family hotel in secluded gardens, near cliff path, beaches and harbour. Children's play area and car park. Traditional home cooking.
Bedrooms: 1 single, 7 double, 2 twin, 3 family rooms
Bathrooms: 6 en-suite, 2 public

Bed & breakfast per night:	£min	£max
Single	17.00	20.00
Double	34.00	40.00

Half board per person:	£min	£max
Daily	26.00	30.00
Weekly	180.00	200.00

Parking for 13
Open March–September

Pondarosa Hotel

COMMENDED

10 Porthminster Terrace, St Ives
TR26 2DQ
☎ (01736) 795875
Private licensed hotel with en-suite rooms. Warm and friendly atmosphere. Quiet location yet convenient for town and beaches. Large private car park.
Bedrooms: 5 double, 2 triple, 2 family rooms
Bathrooms: 9 en-suite

Bed & breakfast per night:	£min	£max
Single	16.00	21.00
Double	32.00	42.00

Half board per person:	£min	£max
Daily	24.50	29.50
Weekly	168.00	203.00

Lunch available
Evening meal 1800 (last orders 1930)
Parking for 12
Cards accepted: Amex, Mastercard, Visa

Porthminster Hotel

COMMENDED

The Terrace, St Ives TR26 2BN
☎ (01736) 795221
Fax (01736) 797043
Best Western
Established family hotel overlooking Porthminster Beach, with magnificent views of bay from most bedrooms and public rooms.
Bedrooms: 5 single, 13 double, 15 twin, 1 triple, 13 family rooms
Bathrooms: 47 en-suite

Bed & breakfast per night:	£min	£max
Single	49.50	65.00
Double	99.00	130.00

Half board per person:	£min	£max
Daily	58.00	73.00

Lunch available
Evening meal 1915 (last orders 2030)
Parking for 38

Cards accepted: Amex, Diners, Mastercard, Visa, Switch/Delta

Primavera Private Hotel

COMMENDED

14 Draycott Terrace, St Ives
TR26 2EF
☎ (01736) 795595
Email: clarkprima@aol.com
Small, friendly hotel overlooking Porthminster Beach, with warm, personal and efficient service. Carefully prepared food - special dietary needs catered for. Bar meals served all day.
Bedrooms: 2 single, 1 double, 1 triple, 1 family room
Bathrooms: 2 en-suite, 1 public

Bed & breakfast per night:	£min	£max
Single	17.00	20.00
Double	34.00	40.00

Lunch available
Evening meal 1830 (last orders 2100)
Open July–August

ST JUST-IN-PENWITH

Cornwall
Map ref 1A3

Coastal parish of craggy moorland scattered with engine houses and chimney stacks of disused mines. The old mining town of St Just has handsome 19th C granite buildings. North of the town are the dramatic ruined tin mines at Botallack.

Roseudian

COMMENDED

Crippas Hill, Kelynack, St. Just, Penzance TR19 7RE
☎ (01736) 788556
Comfortable modernised cottage in rural surroundings. Friendly, relaxing atmosphere. Good home cooking based on own produce. South-facing terraced gardens. Dogs by arrangement only.
Bedrooms: 2 double, 1 twin
Bathrooms: 3 en-suite

Bed & breakfast per night:	£min	£max
Single	18.00	23.00
Double	36.00	

Half board per person:	£min	£max
Daily	28.50	33.50
Weekly	199.50	234.50

Evening meal 1900 (last orders
1600)
Parking for 4
Open March–October

🛏10 ♿🔌🍴 Ⓢ ⥽ 🎿 TV 🖼 ⊠ ❄
🚐

SALCOMBE

Devon
Map ref 1C3

Sheltered yachting resort of
whitewashed houses and narrow
streets in a balmy setting on the
Salcombe Estuary. Palm, myrtle and
other Mediterranean plants flourish.
There are sandy bays and creeks for
boating.
*Tourist Information Centre ☎ (01548)
843927*

Heron House Hotel 🔥
👑👑👑 COMMENDED

Thurlestone Sands, Salcombe
TQ7 3JY
☎ (01548) 561308 & 561600
Fax (01548) 560180
*Idyllic sea-edge location, surrounded by
National Trust countryside and
adjacent to bird reserve. Beautifully
appointed. Noted for food.*
Bedrooms: 1 single, 13 double,
2 twin, 1 triple, 1 family room
Bathrooms: 18 en-suite

Bed & breakfast

per night:	£min	£max
Single	30.00	50.00
Double	60.00	112.00

Half board per person:

	£min	£max
Daily	45.00	75.00
Weekly	210.00	462.00

Lunch available
Evening meal 1900 (last orders
2050)
Parking for 50
Cards accepted: Mastercard, Visa,
Switch/Delta

🛏 ℄ 📞 🖥 ♿🔌 🍴 Ⓢ ⥽ 🎿 🖼 ⊠ 🛢 🍽
♦ ⚲ ∪ ∱ ❄ 🚭 SP T ⊛

Torre View Hotel
👑👑👑 COMMENDED

Devon Road, Salcombe TQ8 8HJ
☎ (01548) 842633
Fax (01548) 842633
*Detached Victorian residence with
every modern comfort, commanding
extensive views of the estuary and
surrounding countryside. Congenial
atmosphere. No smoking, please.*
Bedrooms: 6 double, 2 twin
Suites available
Bathrooms: 5 en-suite, 3 private

Bed & breakfast

per night:	£min	£max
Single	25.00	29.00
Double	46.50	53.00

Half board per person:

	£min	£max
Daily	35.00	39.00
Weekly	228.00	255.00

Evening meal 1900 (last orders
1800)
Parking for 5
Open March–October
Cards accepted: Mastercard, Visa

🛏 ⥽4 🖥 ♿🍴 ⥽ 🎿 🖼 ⊠ 🛢 ⚲ ∪ ∱ ❄ ⥽
🚐 SP

SALISBURY

Wiltshire
Map ref 2B3

Beautiful city and ancient regional
capital set amid water meadows.
Buildings of all periods are
dominated by the cathedral whose
spire is the tallest in England. Built
between 1220 and 1258, it is one of
the purest examples of Early English
architecture.
*Tourist Information Centre ☎ (01722)
334956*

Byways House 🔥
👑👑 APPROVED

31 Fowlers Road, City Centre,
Salisbury SP1 2QP
☎ (01722) 328364
Fax (01722) 322146

*Attractive family-run Victorian house
close to cathedral in quiet area of city
centre. Car park. Bedrooms with private
bathrooms and colour satellite TV.
Traditional English and vegetarian
breakfasts.*
Bedrooms: 4 single, 7 double, 3 twin,
2 triple, 7 family rooms
Bathrooms: 19 en-suite, 1 public

Bed & breakfast

per night:	£min	£max
Single	24.00	
Double	39.00	

Parking for 15
Cards accepted: Mastercard, Visa

🛏 ♿🖥 ♿🔌 🍴 Ⓢ ⥽ 🎿 🖼 ⊠
🍽 43 ∪ ∱ ❄ 🚭 DAP SP 🏠 T

Cranston Guest House
👑👑 APPROVED

5 Wain-a-Long Road, Salisbury
SP1 1LJ
☎ (01722) 336776
*Large detached town house covered in
Virginia creeper. 10 minutes' walk from
town centre and cathedral.*
Bedrooms: 2 single, 1 double,
2 family rooms
Bathrooms: 3 en-suite, 1 public

Bed & breakfast

per night:	£min	£max
Single	17.00	18.00
Double	35.00	36.00

Parking for 4

🛏 ♿🖥 ♿🔌 Ⓤ 🍴 Ⓢ ⥽ 🎿 TV 🛢 ❄ 🚐
DAP SP

The Edwardian Lodge
👑👑👑 APPROVED

59 Castle Road, Salisbury SP1 3RH
☎ (01722) 413329 & 410500
Fax (01722) 503105
*Edwardian house, home-cooked evening
meals, good parking off main road,
short walk city centre, cathedral, Old
Sarum. Beautiful valley drive to
Stonehenge.*
Bedrooms: 1 single, 3 double, 2 twin,
1 family room
Bathrooms: 7 en-suite

Bed & breakfast

per night:	£min	£max
Single	25.00	30.00
Double	38.00	42.00

Half board per person:

	£min	£max
Daily	25.00	28.00

Evening meal 1800 (last orders
2030)
Parking for 8

🛏 ♿🖥 ♿🔌 Ⓤ 🍴 Ⓢ ⥽ 🎿 TV 🖼 🛢
❄ 🚭

Grasmere House 🔥
👑👑👑👑 COMMENDED

70 Harnham Road, Salisbury
SP2 8JN
☎ (01722) 338388
Fax (01722) 333710
ⓒ Minotel/The Independents
*19th C family residence delightfully
converted into a private hotel within a
setting of rural tranquillity with views of
Rivers Avon, Nadder and Salisbury
Cathedral. Access off A3094.*
Wheelchair access category 2 ♿
Bedrooms: 2 single, 7 double,
10 twin, 1 family room
Bathrooms: 20 en-suite

Bed & breakfast

per night:	£min	£max
Single	65.00	95.00
Double	85.00	125.00

Continued ▶

411

SALISBURY
Continued

Half board per person:

	£min	£max
Daily	67.50	97.50

Lunch available
Evening meal 1900 (last orders 2130)
Parking for 36
Cards accepted: Amex, Diners, Mastercard, Visa, Switch/Delta

🛏🚍🥢📞🖙🖵📺🖥⚲🌀📶⓪

🖿🖃🍽80♻♩🎵❀🌸DAP🏞 SP 🏠 T

The Milford Hall Hotel and Restaurant
🥖🥖🥖 HIGHLY COMMENDED

206 Castle Street, Salisbury SP1 3TE
☎ (01722) 417411
Fax (01722) 419444
This fine Georgian city centre mansion has been sympathetically restored to create a magnificent hotel and restaurant that is becoming a landmark in this historic cathedral city.
Bedrooms: 20 double, 15 twin
Bathrooms: 35 en-suite

Bed & breakfast per night:

	£min	£max
Single	55.00	67.00
Double	69.00	77.50

Half board per person:

	£min	£max
Daily	70.50	83.00
Weekly	444.15	522.90

Lunch available
Evening meal 1900 (last orders 2130)
Parking for 50
Cards accepted: Amex, Mastercard, Visa, Switch/Delta

🛏🚍🥢📞🖙🖵📺🖥⚲🌀📶⓪

🖿🖃🍽70♻❀ SP T

Old Mill Hotel ⚄
🥖🥖🥖 COMMENDED

Town Path, Harnham, Salisbury SP2 8EU
☎ (01722) 327517
Fax (01722) 333367
14th C former mill, peacefully located on the River Nadder. Surrounded by water meadows with views of the cathedral (a short stroll away). Well-appointed bedrooms. Restaurant specialises in traditional fare and fresh seafood. Pub offers a range of real ales and inexpensive meals.
Bedrooms: 2 single, 6 double, 2 twin
Bathrooms: 10 en-suite

Bed & breakfast per night:

	£min	£max
Single	40.00	50.00
Double	65.00	75.00

Lunch available

Evening meal 1830 (last orders 2145)
Parking for 16
Cards accepted: Amex, Mastercard, Visa

🛏🚍🥢📞🖙🖵📺🖥⚲🌀🆂🖭📺⓪🖿

🖃🍽♩🎵❀🌸✈🏞 SP 🏠 T

Red Lion Hotel
🥖🥖🥖 COMMENDED

Milford Street, Salisbury SP1 2AN
☎ (01722) 323334
Fax (01722) 325756
Ⓡ Best Western

Originally a coaching inn, now a city centre hotel with all modern facilities. Ideal for business or pleasure. Daily half-board price based on minimum 2-night stay.
Bedrooms: 11 single, 22 double, 19 twin, 2 family rooms
Suites available
Bathrooms: 54 en-suite

Bed & breakfast per night:

	£min	£max
Single	85.00	95.00
Double	115.00	125.00

Half board per person:

	£min	£max
Daily	100.00	110.00
Weekly	406.00	455.00

Lunch available
Evening meal 1900 (last orders 2100)
Parking for 10
Cards accepted: Amex, Diners, Mastercard, Visa, Switch/Delta

🛏🚍🥢📞🖙🖵📺🖥⚲🌀🆂⓪🖽🖿

🖃🍽100✈🏞 SP 🏠 T

The Rokeby Guest House
🥖🥖🥖 COMMENDED

3 Wain-a-Long Road, Salisbury SP1 1LJ
☎ (01722) 329800
Fax (01722) 329800

Beautiful, nostalgic, Edwardian house. Quietly situated, 10 minutes' stroll city centre/cathedral. Large landscaped gardens, summerhouse, fishpond,

---

2-storey conservatory. Satellite TV, licensed restaurant, gymnasium. Brochure available.
Bedrooms: 1 double, 3 twin, 1 triple, 2 family rooms
Bathrooms: 5 en-suite, 2 private, 1 public

Bed & breakfast per night:

	£min	£max
Single	30.00	32.00
Double	40.00	42.00

Evening meal 1830 (last orders 2100)
Parking for 9

🛏🥢12🖵⚲🌀🆂🖙🖭🖿🖃🌟❀✈

🚚🏞 SP 🏠

Victoria Lodge Guest House
🥖🥖 APPROVED

61 Castle Road, Salisbury SP1 3RH
☎ (01722) 320586
Fax (01722) 414507
Victorian lodge, a short walk from city centre, cathedral and Old Sarum. Home-cooked evening meals, good parking. Stonehenge 8 miles.
Bedrooms: 4 single, 2 double, 2 twin, 4 triple, 3 family rooms
Bathrooms: 15 en-suite

Bed & breakfast per night:

	£min	£max
Single	25.00	29.50
Double	35.00	42.00

Half board per person:

	£min	£max
Daily	32.00	36.50

Lunch available
Evening meal 1800 (last orders 2000)
Parking for 15

🛏🚍🖵⚲🌀🆂🖙🖭📺🖿🖃🍽♩

🌸❀ SP T

SALISBURY PLAIN
See under Amesbury, Salisbury

SAUNTON
Devon
Map ref 1C1

Houses situated on a minor road at the end of Braunton Burrows, part of which is a nature reserve, important to botanists and ornithologists. Nearby is a fine golf-course and a 3 mile beach, Saunton Sands.

Saunton Sands Hotel ⚄
🥖🥖🥖 HIGHLY COMMENDED

Saunton, Braunton EX33 1LQ
☎ (01271) 890212
Fax (01271) 890145
Ⓡ Brend
Directly overlooking 5 miles of golden sands and surrounded by unspoilt

countryside, offering a wealth of sports and leisure facilities. Seasonal break rates available.
Bedrooms: 17 single, 15 double, 28 twin, 32 family rooms
Suites available
Bathrooms: 92 en-suite, 5 public

Bed & breakfast

per night:	£min	£max
Single	65.00	87.00
Double	126.00	192.00

Half board per

person:	£min	£max
Daily	75.00	108.00
Weekly	350.00	756.00

Lunch available
Evening meal 1930 (last orders 2100)
Parking for 200
Cards accepted: Amex, Diners, Mastercard, Visa, Switch/Delta

SEATON

Devon
Map ref 1D2

Small resort lying near the mouth of the River Axe. A mile-long beach extends to the dramatic cliffs of Beer Head. Annual art exhibition in July.
Tourist Information Centre ☎ (01297) 21660

Beach End Guest House ⚠

HIGHLY COMMENDED

8 Trevelyan Road, Seaton EX12 2NL
☎ (01297) 23388

Enjoy unrivalled views of Seaton Bay. We offer fine food, friendly and attentive service in our lovely Edwardian guesthouse.
Bedrooms: 4 double, 1 twin
Bathrooms: 5 en-suite

Bed & breakfast

per night:	£min	£max
Double		43.00

Half board per

person:	£min	£max
Daily		63.00
Weekly		420.00

Evening meal 1900 (last orders 1500)
Parking for 5
Open February–October

Beaumont ⚠

COMMENDED

Castle Hill, Seaton EX12 2QW
☎ (01297) 20832
Attractive and spacious guesthouse in select seafront position, offering en-suite comfort, personal attention and traditional home cooking.
Bedrooms: 2 double, 2 triple, 1 family room
Suites available
Bathrooms: 5 en-suite

Bed & breakfast

per night:	£min	£max
Single	19.00	21.00
Double	38.00	42.00

Half board per

person:	£min	£max
Daily	31.00	33.00
Weekly	200.00	215.00

Evening meal 1900 (last orders 1700)
Parking for 6
Open January–October, December

SEAVINGTON ST MARY

Somerset
Map ref 1D2

The Pheasant

HIGHLY COMMENDED

Seavington St Mary, Ilminster TA19 0QH
☎ (01460) 240502
Fax (01460) 242388
Beautiful 17th C farmhouse converted into a sumptuously furnished old-world style hotel and restaurant. Renowned for comfort, atmosphere and food. Just off A303.
Bedrooms: 6 double, 2 twin
Suites available
Bathrooms: 8 en-suite

Bed & breakfast

per night:	£min	£max
Single	70.00	90.00
Double	90.00	120.00

Evening meal 1930 (last orders 2130)
Parking for 60
Cards accepted: Amex, Mastercard, Visa, Switch/Delta

ACCESSIBILITY

Look for the 🦽♿ symbols which indicate accessibility for wheelchair users. These are described in detail at the front of this guide.

SHALDON

Devon
Map ref 1D2

Pretty resort facing Teignmouth from the south bank of the Teign Estuary. Regency houses harmonise with others of later periods; there are old cottages and narrow lanes. On the Ness, a sandstone promontory nearby, a tunnel built in the 19th C leads to a beach revealed at low tide.

Glenside Hotel ⚠

COMMENDED

Ringmore Road, Shaldon, Teignmouth TQ14 0EP
☎ (01626) 872448
Old world cottage-style hotel by the riverside. Licensed and family-run, with home cooking. Easy walking. Car park.
Bedrooms: 1 single, 5 double, 3 twin
Bathrooms: 8 en-suite, 1 public

Bed & breakfast

per night:	£min	£max
Single	19.50	24.50
Double	38.00	49.00

Half board per

person:	£min	£max
Daily	32.50	37.50
Weekly	185.00	235.00

Evening meal 1900 (last orders 1900)
Parking for 10

Ness House Hotel

COMMENDED

Marine Parade, Shaldon, Teignmouth TQ14 0HP
☎ (01626) 873480
Fax (01626) 873486
Overlooking Teign Estuary. Elegant restaurant and comfortable bars. Most rooms have balconies overlooking the sea. En-suite facilities. Easy access to Torquay, Exeter and Dartmoor.
Bedrooms: 1 single, 9 double, 2 triple
Suite available
Bathrooms: 12 en-suite

Bed & breakfast

per night:	£min	£max
Single	39.00	60.00
Double	70.00	85.00

Half board per

person:	£min	£max
Daily	52.50	72.50
Weekly	255.00	285.00

Lunch available
Evening meal 1900 (last orders 2215)

Continued ▶

SHALDON
Continued

Parking for 20
Cards accepted: Amex, Mastercard, Visa, Switch/Delta

🐎♿📞📠🖥️🛁🎿📶♨️🛎️🍴📺 📻🏧✿🚍🚭 SP 🏤 T

SHERBORNE
Dorset
Map ref 2B3

Dorset's "Cathedral City" of medieval streets, golden hamstone buildings and great abbey church, resting place of Saxon kings. Formidable 12th C castle ruins and Sir Walter Raleigh's splendid Tudor mansion and deer park. Street markets, leisure centre, many cultural activities.
Tourist Information Centre ☎ (01935) 815341

Britannia Inn
👑 APPROVED

Westbury, Sherborne DT9 3EH
☎ (01935) 813300
Originally the Lord Digby School for Girls, built in 1743, now a listed building.
Bedrooms: 1 single, 1 double, 3 twin, 2 triple
Bathrooms: 3 public

Bed & breakfast per night:

	£min	£max
Single	18.50	22.50
Double	34.00	38.00

Evening meal 1900 (last orders 2100)
Parking for 13
Cards accepted: Amex, Mastercard, Visa

🐎🖥️🛁🎿♨️🛎️🏧 📻🍺🚍🏤

Eastbury Hotel ⚊
👑👑👑 COMMENDED

Long Street, Sherborne DT9 3BY
☎ (01935) 813131
Fax (01935) 817296
Gracious Georgian town house hotel with attractive walled garden, near town centre. Private car park.
Bedrooms: 6 single, 5 double, 4 twin
Bathrooms: 15 en-suite

Bed & breakfast per night:

	£min	£max
Single	45.00	55.00
Double	62.00	80.00

Half board per person:

	£min	£max
Daily	53.50	58.50

Lunch available
Evening meal 1930 (last orders 2130)

Parking for 27
Cards accepted: Mastercard, Visa

🐎♿📞📠🖥️🛁🎿📶♨️🛎️🍴📻🏧 🍴60🅿️✿🚍🚭 SP 🏤

SIDMOUTH
Devon
Map ref 1D2

Charming resort set amid lofty red cliffs where the River Sid meets the sea. The wealth of ornate Regency and Victorian villas recalls the time when this was one of the south coast's most exclusive resorts. Museum; August International Festival of Folk Arts.
Tourist Information Centre ☎ (01395) 516441

The Belmont Hotel ⚊
👑👑👑👑 HIGHLY COMMENDED

The Esplanade, Sidmouth EX10 8RX
☎ (01395) 512555
Fax (01395) 579101
Ⓡ Brend
Traditionally one of Sidmouth's finest seafront hotels. Leisure facilities are available at adjacent hotel, the Victoria. Seasonal break rates available.
Bedrooms: 9 single, 11 double, 28 twin, 3 family rooms
Bathrooms: 51 en-suite

Bed & breakfast per night:

	£min	£max
Single	57.00	100.00
Double	98.00	200.00

Half board per person:

	£min	£max
Daily	59.00	110.00
Weekly	350.00	665.00

Lunch available
Evening meal 1900 (last orders 2100)
Parking for 45
Cards accepted: Amex, Diners, Mastercard, Visa, Switch/Delta

🐎♿📞📠🖥️🛁🎿📶♨️🛎️🍴🚭 📻🍺🍴40✿🚍🚭 SP 🏤 T

Devoran Hotel
👑👑👑 HIGHLY COMMENDED

Esplanade, Sidmouth EX10 8AU
☎ (01395) 513151 & 0800 317171
Fax (01395) 579929
Family-run hotel overlooking beach, very close to town centre and amenities. Relaxed, happy atmosphere, with traditional home-cooked food using local produce.
Bedrooms: 5 single, 7 double, 7 twin, 4 triple
Bathrooms: 20 en-suite, 2 public

Bed & breakfast per night:

	£min	£max
Single	27.00	38.00
Double	54.00	76.00

Half board per person:

	£min	£max
Daily	32.50	49.00
Weekly	205.00	290.00

Evening meal 1845 (last orders 1930)
Parking for 4
Open March–November
Cards accepted: Mastercard, Visa, Switch/Delta

🐎🖥️🛁🎿📶♨️🛎️🍴📺📻🏧 🍴🚭 DAP SP T ♨️

Hotel Elizabeth ⚊
👑👑👑 COMMENDED

Esplanade, Sidmouth EX10 8AT
☎ (01395) 513503
Superbly positioned Victorian seafront hotel on the level esplanade. Refurbished and now totally non-smoking. Comfortable rooms, excellent food, friendly staff.
Bedrooms: 1 single, 7 double, 20 twin
Bathrooms: 28 en-suite, 1 public

Bed & breakfast per night:

	£min	£max
Single	22.00	44.00
Double	44.00	90.00

Half board per person:

	£min	£max
Daily	27.00	67.00
Weekly	191.00	403.00

Lunch available
Evening meal 1830 (last orders 1915)
Parking for 10
Open February–November
Cards accepted: Mastercard, Visa, Switch/Delta

🐎♿📠🖥️🛁🎿📶♨️🛎️🍴🛎️📻 ✈️ SP T

Kingswood Hotel ⚊
👑👑👑 HIGHLY COMMENDED

Esplanade, Sidmouth EX10 8AX
☎ (01395) 516367
Fax (01395) 513185

Delightful central location on Sidmouth's Regency seafront. Emphasis on good food. Comfortable relaxed atmosphere in former Victorian spa baths. 45 years of same family ownership.

Bedrooms: 8 single, 2 double, 9 twin,
7 triple
Bathrooms: 18 en-suite, 8 private

Bed & breakfast

per night:	£min	£max
Single	30.00	40.00
Double	60.00	80.00

Half board per

person:	£min	£max
Daily	35.50	47.00
Weekly	225.00	300.00

Lunch available
Evening meal 1845 (last orders
1930)
Parking for 17
Open March–November
Cards accepted: Mastercard, Visa,
Switch/Delta

Littlecourt Hotel ∧∧

👑👑👑 COMMENDED

Seafield Road, Sidmouth EX10 8HF
☎ (01395) 515279

*Regency country house built for the
Duke of St Albans. Tastefully
modernised yet retaining its charm and
elegance. Set in award-winning gardens.
Excellent cuisine, mainly Devon/Dorset
regional dishes. Short walk to
sea/shops.*
Bedrooms: 4 single, 5 double, 8 twin,
3 triple
Bathrooms: 19 en-suite, 1 private,
2 public

Bed & breakfast

per night:	£min	£max
Single	28.50	36.00
Double	57.00	72.00

Half board per

person:	£min	£max
Daily	37.00	51.00
Weekly	240.00	359.00

Lunch available
Evening meal 1900 (last orders
2000)
Parking for 17
Open March–October and
Christmas
Cards accepted: Amex, Diners,
Mastercard, Visa, Switch/Delta

Hotel Riviera ∧∧

👑👑👑👑 DE LUXE

The Esplanade, Sidmouth EX10 8AY
☎ (01395) 515201
Fax (01395) 577775
Email: enquiries@hotelriviera.co.uk

*Majestic Regency hotel on the
Esplanade, with panoramic sea views
and a splendid terrace overlooking
Lyme Bay.*
http://www.hotelriviera.co.uk
Bedrooms: 7 single, 6 double,
14 twin
Suites available
Bathrooms: 27 en-suite, 1 public

Bed & breakfast

per night:	£min	£max
Single	66.00	90.00
Double	114.00	162.00

Half board per

person:	£min	£max
Daily	66.00	90.00
Weekly	462.00	567.00

Lunch available
Evening meal 1900 (last orders
2100)
Parking for 24
Open February–December
Cards accepted: Amex, Diners,
Mastercard, Visa

Royal York and Faulkner Hotel ∧∧

👑👑👑 COMMENDED

Esplanade, Sidmouth EX10 8AZ
☎ (01395) 513043 & 513184
Fax (01395) 577472
*Charming Regency hotel on centre of
Sidmouth's delightful Esplanade. Long
established, family-run hotel offering all
amenities and excellent leisure
facilities.*
Bedrooms: 22 single, 9 double,
29 twin, 8 triple
Bathrooms: 66 en-suite, 2 private,
4 public

Bed & breakfast

per night:	£min	£max
Single	25.75	43.00
Double	51.50	86.00

Half board per

person:	£min	£max
Daily	28.50	51.00
Weekly	210.00	315.00

Lunch available
Evening meal 1915 (last orders
2030)

Parking for 18
Open February–December
Cards accepted: Mastercard, Visa,
Switch/Delta

Ryton Guest House

👑👑 COMMENDED

52-54 Winslade Road, Sidmouth
EX10 9EX
☎ (01395) 513981

*Quietly situated within walking distance
of town and seafront. Personal
attention, warm, friendly hospitality and
good home cooking.*
Bedrooms: 2 single, 2 double, 1 twin,
3 triple, 1 family room
Bathrooms: 7 en-suite, 2 private,
1 public

Bed & breakfast

per night:	£min	£max
Single	20.00	25.00
Double	36.00	40.00

Half board per

person:	£min	£max
Daily	26.00	30.00
Weekly	175.00	200.00

Evening meal 1830 (last orders
1600)
Parking for 8
Open February–October

Information on
accommodation listed in this
guide has been supplied by the
proprietors. As changes may
occur you are advised to check
details at the time of booking.

The symbols in each entry
give information about
services and facilities.
A key to these symbols
appears at the back
of this guide.

SIDMOUTH

Continued

The Victoria Hotel

♛♛♛♛♛ HIGHLY COMMENDED

The Esplanade, Sidmouth EX10 8RY
☎ (01395) 512651
Fax (01395) 579154
Email: 42551exoniagrefbrend2
[CR] Brend

One of England's finest hotels on Sidmouth's famous Esplanade. Guests are assured of high standards of service, comfort and cuisine. Seasonal break rates available.

Bedrooms: 14 single, 18 double, 20 twin, 9 triple
Suites available
Bathrooms: 61 en-suite

Bed & breakfast per night:	£min	£max
Single	65.00	98.00
Double	110.00	212.00

Half board per person:	£min	£max
Daily	65.00	116.00
Weekly	350.00	693.00

Lunch available
Evening meal 1915 (last orders 2100)
Parking for 54
Cards accepted: Amex, Diners, Mastercard, Visa, Switch/Delta
☎ [S] [TV] 50 [SP] [T]

Woodlands Hotel

♛♛♛ APPROVED

Cotmaton Cross, Sidmouth EX10 8HG
☎ (01395) 513120 & 513166
Fax (01395) 513292

Family-owned Regency country house, set in award-winning seaside gardens, offering complete relaxation. Near sea and shops. Traditionally high standards.

Bedrooms: 5 single, 6 double, 15 twin
Bathrooms: 21 en-suite, 3 public

Bed & breakfast per night:	£min	£max
Single	18.50	29.50
Double	37.00	59.00

Half board per person:	£min	£max
Daily	27.50	42.00
Weekly	165.00	294.00

Lunch available
Evening meal 1900 (last orders 2000)
Parking for 23
Cards accepted: Mastercard, Visa, Switch/Delta
3 [S] [TV] [SP]

SOUTH MOLTON

Devon
Map ref 1C1

Busy market town at the mouth of the Yeo Valley near southern Exmoor. Wool, mining and coaching brought prosperity between the Middle Ages and the 19th C and the fine square with Georgian buildings, a Guildhall and Assembly Rooms reflect this former affluence.

The George Hotel

♛♛♛ COMMENDED

1 Broad Street, South Molton EX36 3AB
☎ (01769) 572514 & 574816 (Guests)
Fax (01769) 572514
[CR] The Independents

17th C Grade II listed building, formerly the town's main coaching inn and known as the George Inn and Theatre.

Bedrooms: 1 single, 4 double, 3 twin, 2 triple
Bathrooms: 6 en-suite, 2 public

Bed & breakfast per night:	£min	£max
Single	25.00	30.00
Double	45.00	50.00

Lunch available
Evening meal 1900 (last orders 2100)
Parking for 12
Cards accepted: Amex, Mastercard, Visa, Switch/Delta
[S] 100

STREET

Somerset
Map ref 2A2

Busy shoe-making town set beneath the Polden Hills. A museum at the factory, which was developed with the rest of the town in the 19th C, can be visited. Just south, the National Trust has care of woodland on Ivythorn Hill which gives wide views northward. Factory shopping village.

Wessex Hotel

♛♛♛♛ COMMENDED

High Street, Street BA16 0EF
☎ (01458) 443383
Fax (01458) 446589

Modern en-suite bedrooms, situated in the heart of Somerset, legendary country of King Arthur and the Knights of the Round Table. Nearby attractions include Bath, Glastonbury Abbey, Cheddar Gorge, Wookey Hole Caves and Wells Cathedral.

Bedrooms: 7 double, 43 twin
Bathrooms: 50 en-suite

Bed & breakfast per night:	£min	£max
Single	40.00	50.00
Double	50.00	60.00

Half board per person:	£min	£max
Daily	50.00	57.50
Weekly	356.50	356.50

Lunch available
Evening meal 1900 (last orders 2130)
Parking for 85
Cards accepted: Amex, Diners, Mastercard, Visa, Switch/Delta
[S] [TV] 250 [DAP] [SP] [T]

SUTTON BENGER

Wiltshire
Map ref 2B2

Bell House Hotel

♛♛♛♛ APPROVED

High Street, Sutton Benger, Chippenham SN15 4RH
☎ (01249) 720401
Fax (01249) 720401

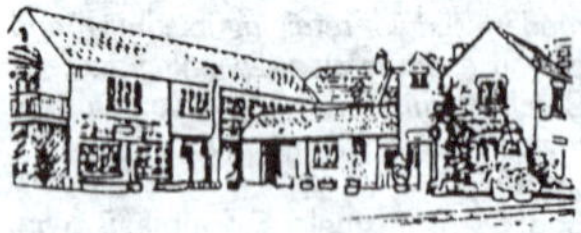

Pretty country hotel set in small quiet village. Suitable for a quiet weekend away yet near M4 and town.

Bedrooms: 3 single, 5 double, 6 twin
Bathrooms: 14 en-suite

Bed & breakfast per night:	£min	£max
Single	45.00	69.45
Double	57.50	96.40

Half board per person:	£min	£max
Daily	60.00	94.45

Lunch available
Evening meal 1830 (last orders 2230)
Parking for 35
Cards accepted: Amex, Diners, Mastercard, Visa, Switch/Delta
[S] 50 [SP]

SWINDON

Wiltshire
Map ref 2B2

Wiltshire's industrial and commercial centre, an important railway town in the 19th C, situated just north of the Marlborough Downs. The railway village created in the mid-19th C has been preserved. Railway museum, art gallery, theatre and leisure centre. Designer shopping village.
Tourist Information Centre ☎ *(01793) 530328 or 493007*

Blunsdon House Hotel and Leisure Club ♏

♛♛♛♛ HIGHLY COMMENDED

Blunsdon, Swindon SN2 4AD
☎ (01793) 721701
Fax (01793) 721056
ⓒ® Best Western
Peacefully set on the edge of the Cotswolds. Facilities include a leisure club and 9 hole par 3 golf-course. Special breaks available. Half-board price based on shared room, minimum 2-night stay.
Bedrooms: 9 single, 50 double, 18 twin, 10 triple
Suite available
Bathrooms: 87 en-suite

Bed & breakfast per night:

	£min	£max
Single	90.00	
Double	145.00	

Half board per person:

	£min	£max
Daily	68.00	

Lunch available
Evening meal 1900 (last orders 2230)
Parking for 300
Cards accepted: Amex, Diners, Mastercard, Visa, Switch/Delta

🛏🛄🚗📞🖤📺🚭🖥📺◐
✳🖥🖨🚪👤300 🐕✗🔍♨️🐾🔍♈
✳🏃 DAP 🚭 SP T

Fairview Guest House

♛♛ COMMENDED

52 Swindon Road, Wootton Bassett, Swindon SN4 8EU
☎ (01793) 852283
Fax (01793) 848076
Detached guesthouse, west of Swindon, close to M4 junction 16 (1.25 miles). Ground floor rooms available.
Bedrooms: 5 single, 3 double, 2 twin, 2 triple
Bathrooms: 6 en-suite, 2 public, 1 private shower

Bed & breakfast per night:

	£min	£max
Single	19.50	35.00
Double	30.00	40.00

Parking for 17
Cards accepted: Amex, Diners, Mastercard, Visa

🛏🛄🚪🖤 UL 🖥 S 🚭 📺 📺 ◐ 🔔
✳ DAP 🚭 SP T

Goddard Arms Hotel

♛♛ COMMENDED

High Street, Old Town, Swindon SN1 3EG
☎ (01793) 692313
Fax (01793) 512984

Old world hotel built in 1790 and named after famous local family in the old town. Short distance from M4 motorway, Cotswolds, Avebury and Wiltshire Downs. Half board prices are for a special weekend break.
Bedrooms: 12 single, 16 double, 37 twin
Suite available
Bathrooms: 65 private

Bed & breakfast per night:

	£min	£max
Single	40.00	75.00
Double	65.00	85.00

Half board per person:

	£min	£max
Daily	39.00	45.00

Lunch available
Evening meal 1830 (last orders 2130)
Parking for 115
Cards accepted: Amex, Diners, Mastercard, Visa, Switch/Delta

🛏🛄🚗📞🖤🖥S🚭🖥◐🖥🖨🚪
🍴200✳🚭 SP 🏛

The School House Hotel and Restaurant ♏

♛♛♛ COMMENDED

Hook Street, Hook, Swindon SN4 8EF
☎ (01793) 851198
Fax (01793) 851025

Charming country house hotel in a converted 1860 school house. Combining modern facilities and Victorian decor. In rural hamlet but close to M4, Swindon and Cotswolds.
Bedrooms: 9 double, 1 twin
Bathrooms: 10 en-suite

Bed & breakfast per night:

	£min	£max
Single	59.00	79.00
Double	69.00	89.00

Half board per person:

	£min	£max
Daily	79.00	99.00
Weekly	475.00	595.00

Lunch available
Evening meal 1800 (last orders 2200)
Parking for 40

Continued ▶

SWINDON

Continued

Cards accepted: Amex, Diners, Mastercard, Visa, Switch/Delta

🛏🛇🖫☎🖵🖿♨🍽🐾🖂🆂🍴📺◑
💷🍳🏧🛏60♨✿♿🚆ᴰᴬᴾ🐾🆂🅿📶Ⓣ

📖 See display advertisement on page 417

Villiers Inn ⚠

👑👑👑 COMMENDED

Moormead Road, Wroughton, Swindon SN4 9BY
☎ (01793) 814744
Fax (01793) 814119
Warm-hearted, full-service hotel with personality! An 18th C farmhouse with first class en-suite bedrooms and two popular restaurants.
Bedrooms: 9 single, 10 double, 15 twin
Bathrooms: 34 en-suite

Bed & breakfast per night:

	£min	£max
Single	50.00	70.00
Double	70.00	80.00

Half board per person:

	£min	£max
Daily	65.00	85.00

Lunch available
Evening meal 1900 (last orders 2130)
Parking for 60
Cards accepted: Amex, Diners, Mastercard, Visa

🛏🛇🖫☎🖵🖿♨🍽🐾🆂🖂◑
💷🍳🏧75✿🚆🐾🆂🅿Ⓣ

TAUNTON

Somerset
Map ref 1D1

County town, well-known for its public schools, sheltered by gentle hill-ranges on the River Tone. Medieval prosperity from wool has continued in marketing and manufacturing and the town retains many fine period buildings.
Tourist Information Centre ☎ (01823) 336344

Falcon Hotel ⚠

👑👑 COMMENDED

Henlade, Taunton TA3 5DH
☎ (01823) 442502
Fax (01823) 442670

Family-owned country house hotel in own grounds, only 1 mile east of M5 (junction 25). Informal atmosphere, comfortable and well equipped.
Bedrooms: 3 double, 5 twin, 2 family rooms
Bathrooms: 10 en-suite

Bed & breakfast per night:

	£min	£max
Single	45.00	49.50
Double	55.00	59.50

Half board per person:

	£min	£max
Daily	60.00	64.50

Evening meal 1900 (last orders 2030)
Parking for 25
Cards accepted: Amex, Diners, Mastercard, Visa

🛏🛇🖫☎🖵🖿♨🍽🐾🆂🖂🍴💷🍳
🛏40♨✿ᴰᴬᴾ🆂Ⓣ

Farthings Hotel and Restaurant ⚠

👑👑👑 HIGHLY COMMENDED

Hatch Beauchamp, Taunton TA3 6SG
☎ (01823) 480664
Fax (01823) 481118
Elegant Georgian house in lovely gardens, tastefully decorated and furnished. Friendly personal service in a comfortable and relaxed atmosphere. Only 5 minutes from junction 25 of M5 at Taunton.
Bedrooms: 4 double, 4 twin
Bathrooms: 8 en-suite

Bed & breakfast per night:

	£min	£max
Single	55.00	65.00
Double	80.00	90.00

Half board per person:

	£min	£max
Daily	47.50	58.50

Lunch available
Evening meal 1900 (last orders 2100)
Parking for 27
Cards accepted: Amex, Mastercard, Visa, Switch/Delta

🛏🛇☎🖵🖿♨🍽🐾🆂🖂🍴💷
🛏25♿♨✿🚆ᴰᴬᴾ🆂🏘

Forde House ⚠

👑👑 COMMENDED

9 Upper High Street, Taunton TA1 3PX
☎ (01823) 279042
Fax (01823) 279042
Peaceful location in the centre of town, close to all amenities, including public park and golf-course. Warm welcome guaranteed.
Bedrooms: 1 single, 2 double, 2 twin
Bathrooms: 4 en-suite, 1 private

Bed & breakfast per night:

	£min	£max
Single	26.00	30.00
Double	48.00	50.00

Parking for 5

🛏8🖿🖵♨🍽ᵁᴸ🐾🖂💷♨🍳✿🍴🚆Ⓣ

Higher Dipford Farm

Trull, Taunton TA3 7NU
☎ (01823) 275770 & 257916
120-acre dairy farm. 14th C listed Somerset longhouse with magnificent walks and views. Antique furniture, log fires and spacious en-suite rooms. Renowned for high class cuisine using fresh dairy produce.
Bedrooms: 1 double, 2 twin
Bathrooms: 3 en-suite

Bed & breakfast per night:

	£min	£max
Single	30.00	35.00
Double	46.00	54.00

Half board per person:

	£min	£max
Daily	42.00	50.00
Weekly	266.00	315.00

Lunch available
Evening meal 1900 (last orders 2130)
Parking for 6
Cards accepted: Amex

🛏🛇🖿🖵♨🍽🐾🆂🖂🍴📺◑💷🍳🍴
◑♨♿🍴✎✿🍴🚆ᴰᴾ🐾🏘Ⓣ

Orchard House ⚠

👑👑👑 HIGHLY COMMENDED

Fons George, Middleway, Taunton TA1 3JS
☎ (01823) 351783
Fax (01823) 351785

Elegant Georgian house within 5 minutes' walk of town centre and all amenities. Fine selection of pubs and restaurants nearby. Easy access from M5.
Bedrooms: 1 double, 5 twin
Bathrooms: 6 en-suite

Bed & breakfast per night:

	£min	£max
Single	35.00	40.00
Double	50.00	55.00

Lunch available
Evening meal 1900 (last orders 2130)
Parking for 8
Cards accepted: Mastercard, Visa, Switch/Delta

🖵♨🍽🐾🆂🖂🍴💷🍳🍴♨✿🍴🚆Ⓣ

RoadChef Lodge ⋀

COMMENDED

Taunton Deane Motorway Service Area, M5 Southbound, Trull, Taunton TA1 4BA
☎ (01823) 332228 & 0800 834719 (Freephone)
Fax (01823) 338131
CR RoadChef
RoadChef Lodges offer high specification rooms at affordable prices, in popular locations suited to both the business and private traveller. Prices are per room and do not include breakfast.
Bedrooms: 14 double, 14 twin, 1 family room
Bathrooms: 29 en-suite

Bed & breakfast

per night:	£min	£max
Double	43.50	

Parking for 500
Cards accepted: Amex, Diners, Mastercard, Visa, Switch/Delta

TEFFONT EVIAS

Wiltshire
Map ref 2B2

Howards House Hotel

HIGHLY COMMENDED

Teffont Evias, Salisbury SP3 5RJ
☎ (01722) 716392 & 716821
Fax (01722) 716820

17th C dower house in idyllic rural setting with high quality accommodation, award-winning restaurant and an atmosphere of tranquillity and friendliness.
Bedrooms: 8 double, 1 twin
Bathrooms: 9 en-suite

Bed & breakfast

per night:	£min	£max
Single	65.00	95.00
Double	95.00	140.00

Half board per person:

	£min	£max
Daily	90.00	120.00

Lunch available
Evening meal 1930 (last orders 2130)
Parking for 23
Cards accepted: Amex, Diners, Mastercard, Visa, Switch/Delta

TEIGNMOUTH

Devon
Map ref 1D2

Set on the north bank of the beautiful Teign Estuary, busy fishing and shipbuilding port handling timber and locally-quarried ball-clay. A bridge crosses to the pretty village of Shaldon and there are good views of the estuary from here.
Tourist Information Centre ☎ (01626) 779769

Belvedere Hotel ⋀

COMMENDED

Barnpark Road, Teignmouth TQ14 8PJ
☎ (01626) 774561
Fax (01626) 770009
Comfortable detached family-run Victorian villa with its own garden and car park. Close to beach and town centre. Many rooms with sea views.
Bedrooms: 1 single, 7 double, 2 twin, 1 triple, 2 family rooms
Bathrooms: 12 en-suite, 1 private

Bed & breakfast

per night:	£min	£max
Single	20.00	24.00
Double	40.00	48.00

Half board per person:

	£min	£max
Daily	28.00	32.00
Weekly	180.00	195.00

Lunch available
Evening meal 1830 (last orders 2000)
Parking for 10
Cards accepted: Amex, Mastercard, Visa, Switch/Delta

The Coombe Bank Hotel

COMMENDED

Landscore Road, Teignmouth TQ14 9JL
☎ (01626) 772369
Fax (01626) 774159
Spacious, detached Victorian house, quietly situated above town centre, 10 minutes' walk from shops and beach. Well-appointed bedrooms with private facilities. Private parking.
Bedrooms: 3 double, 6 twin, 1 triple
Bathrooms: 6 en-suite, 3 private

Bed & breakfast

per night:	£min	£max
Single	25.00	30.00
Double	44.00	50.00

Half board per person:

	£min	£max
Daily	29.00	38.00
Weekly	200.00	234.00

Evening meal 1900 (last orders 2030)
Parking for 12
Cards accepted: Mastercard, Visa

London Hotel ⋀

APPROVED

Bank Street, Teignmouth TQ14 8AW
☎ (01626) 776336
Fax (01626) 778457
Situated in town centre with easy access to beaches and moors. Families catered for. Leisure facilities include indoor swimming pool.
Bedrooms: 1 single, 17 double, 2 twin, 6 triple, 6 family rooms
Bathrooms: 32 en-suite

Bed & breakfast

per night:	£min	£max
Single	22.00	32.00
Double	44.00	64.00

Half board per person:

	£min	£max
Daily	32.00	40.00
Weekly	224.00	280.00

Lunch available
Evening meal 1800 (last orders 2200)
Parking for 8
Cards accepted: Amex, Diners, Mastercard, Visa, Switch/Delta

THURLESTONE

Devon
Map ref 1C3

Small resort of thatched cottages standing above coastal cliffs near the winding estuary of Devon's River Avon. The village has a fine golf-course and a good beach.

Thurlestone Hotel ⋀

HIGHLY COMMENDED

Thurlestone, Kingsbridge TQ7 3NN
☎ (01548) 560382
Fax (01548) 561069
A peaceful setting in old world village with thatched cottages. International cuisine and outstanding indoor sporting amenities.
Bedrooms: 5 single, 18 double, 26 twin, 13 triple, 3 family rooms
Suites available
Bathrooms: 65 en-suite

Bed & breakfast

per night:	£min	£max
Single	40.00	85.00
Double	80.00	160.00

Continued ▶

THURLESTONE

Continued

Half board per person:	£min	£max
Daily	45.00	104.00
Weekly	315.00	728.00

Lunch available
Evening meal 1930 (last orders 2100)
Parking for 119
Cards accepted: Amex, Mastercard, Visa

🛥🕯📬💻♿🎯🗄⚒🔓⛢☎🖥
🍳🛎100♨✕♨⚓🎯🚶🏇♿🏊⛱
🚱 SP T

TINTAGEL

Cornwall
Map ref 1B2

Coastal village near the legendary home of King Arthur. There is a lofty headland with the ruin of a Norman castle and traces of a Celtic monastery are still visible in the turf.

Bossiney House Hotel 🅰

☸☸☸ COMMENDED

Bossiney Road, Tintagel PL34 0AX
☎ (01840) 770240 & (0370) 951411
Fax (01840) 770501
Family-run hotel set in 2.5 acres of garden. Close to castle and overlooking the beautiful north Cornwall coast.
Bedrooms: 8 double, 9 twin, 2 triple, 1 family room
Bathrooms: 18 en-suite, 2 private

Bed & breakfast per night:	£min	£max
Single	28.00	40.00
Double	56.00	60.00

Half board per person:	£min	£max
Daily	40.00	42.00
Weekly	280.00	296.00

Lunch available
Evening meal 1900 (last orders 2100)
Parking for 30
Open March–October
Cards accepted: Amex, Diners, Mastercard, Visa, Switch/Delta

🛥🛎📬💻♿🎯🗄⚒📺🖥🎁
♨♨⚓🎯🚶♿ DAP SP

King Arthur's Castle Hotel

☸☸☸ APPROVED

Atlanta Road, Tintagel PL34 0DQ
☎ (01840) 770202
Fax (01840) 770978
Located in one of the most spectacular parts of Cornwall, standing on a very high and rugged coastline which

commands majestic views. Overlooks the ruins of Tintagel Castle, reputedly the home of King Arthur.
Bedrooms: 12 single, 14 double, 18 twin, 6 triple
Bathrooms: 50 en-suite, 12 public

Bed & breakfast per night:	£min	£max
Single	25.00	
Double	50.00	

Half board per person:	£min	£max
Daily	35.00	
Weekly	222.00	

Lunch available
Evening meal 1900 (last orders 2200)
Parking for 106
Open April–October
Cards accepted: Mastercard, Visa

🛥🕯💻♿🎯🗄⚒📺🔓☎🖥
🍳🍴⚓🎯🚶♿🏊✕ DAP 🏇

Polkerr Guest House 🅰

☸☸☸ HIGHLY COMMENDED

Tintagel PL34 0BY
☎ (01840) 770382
Period country house offering quality accommodation, central heating, TV and tea-making facilities in all rooms. Ideal for touring, bathing, golf and coastal walks.
Bedrooms: 1 single, 3 double, 1 twin, 1 triple, 1 family room
Bathrooms: 6 en-suite, 1 private

Bed & breakfast per night:	£min	£max
Single	17.00	22.00
Double	34.00	44.00

Half board per person:	£min	£max
Daily	26.00	31.00
Weekly	182.00	217.00

Evening meal 1830 (last orders 1200)
Parking for 9

🛥♿💻♿🎯 UL S 🖥🍳🎯✕
🏇🏇

Port William Inn 🅰

☸☸☸ COMMENDED

Trebarwith Strand, Tintagel PL34 0HB
☎ (01840) 770230
Fax (01840) 770936
Email: phale@william.zynet.co.uk

Probably the best located inn in Cornwall, overlooking sea and beach. All rooms en-suite with TV and telephone.

Extensive menu, including local seafood. Open all day, all year.
Bedrooms: 2 double, 1 twin, 1 triple, 2 family rooms
Bathrooms: 6 en-suite

Bed & breakfast per night:	£min	£max
Single	35.00	55.00
Double	50.00	90.00

Lunch available
Evening meal 1800 (last orders 2130)
Parking for 50
Cards accepted: Amex, Mastercard, Visa, Switch/Delta

🛥🕯📬💻♿🎯🗄⚒🖥🎁🛎⚓
▶🎯🚶 SP 🏇

Willapark Manor Hotel 🅰

☸☸☸ COMMENDED

Bossiney, Tintagel PL34 0BA
☎ (01840) 770782

One of the most beautifully situated hotels in England, set in 14 acres of garden and woodland, overlooking bay. Warm welcome and good cuisine ensure a memorable holiday.
Bedrooms: 3 single, 7 double, 2 twin, 1 triple, 1 family room
Bathrooms: 14 en-suite

Bed & breakfast per night:	£min	£max
Single	26.00	30.00
Double	52.00	60.00

Half board per person:	£min	£max
Daily	38.00	76.00
Weekly	230.00	265.00

Lunch available
Evening meal 1900 (last orders 2000)
Parking for 20

🛥♿🚗💻♿🎯 S 🖥📺🛎🎯🏇 SP
🏇 T

The Wootons Country Hotel 🅰

☸☸☸ COMMENDED

Fore Street, Tintagel PL34 0DD
☎ (01840) 770170
Fax (01840) 770978
Located at entrance road to Tintagel Castle, reputedly home of King Arthur, and overlooking the Vale of Avalon.
Bedrooms: 1 single, 7 double, 3 twin
Bathrooms: 11 en-suite

Bed & breakfast per night:	£min	£max
Single	20.00	
Double	40.00	

Half board per person:	£min	£max
Daily	29.50	
Weekly	206.50	

Lunch available
Evening meal 1900 (last orders 2130)
Parking for 30
Cards accepted: Mastercard, Visa

TIVERTON

Devon
Map ref 1D2

Busy market and textile town, settled since the 9th C, at the meeting of 2 rivers. Town houses, Tudor almshouses and parts of the fine church were built by wealthy cloth merchants; a medieval castle is incorporated into a private house; Blundells School.
Tourist Information Centre ☎ (01884) 255827

Bridge Guest House

COMMENDED

23 Angel Hill, Tiverton EX16 6PE
☎ (01884) 252804
Fax (01884) 253949

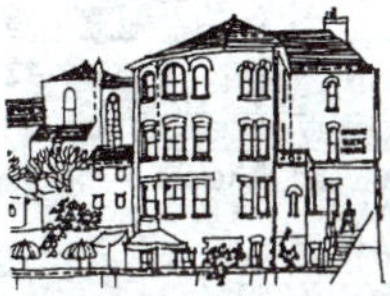

Attractive Victorian town house on a bank of the River Exe, with pretty riverside tea garden. Ideal for touring the heart of Devon.
Bedrooms: 4 single, 2 double, 1 twin, 2 triple
Bathrooms: 5 en-suite, 2 public

Bed & breakfast per night:	£min	£max
Single	18.50	25.00
Double	36.00	46.00

Half board per person:	£min	£max
Daily	29.50	34.00
Weekly	190.00	215.00

Evening meal 1830 (last orders 1930)
Parking for 7

The Tiverton Hotel

COMMENDED

Blundells Road, Tiverton EX16 4DB
☎ (01884) 256120
Fax (01884) 258101
Superbly located minutes from junction 27 M5. Modern, comfortable hotel on edge of town in heart of beautiful River Exe valley.
Bedrooms: 9 double, 63 twin, 3 triple
Bathrooms: 75 en-suite

Bed & breakfast per night:	£min	£max
Single	41.00	48.00
Double	72.00	86.00

Half board per person:	£min	£max
Daily	57.75	64.75

Lunch available
Evening meal 1900 (last orders 2115)
Parking for 130
Cards accepted: Amex, Diners, Mastercard, Visa, Switch/Delta
300

TORPOINT

Cornwall
Map ref 1C2

Town beside the part of the Tamar Estuary known as the Hamoaze, linked by car ferry to Devonport. The fine 18th C Anthony House (National Trust) is noted for its 19th C entrance portico.

Whitsand Bay Hotel

COMMENDED

Portwrinkle, Torpoint PL11 3BU
☎ (01503) 230276
Fax (01503) 230329
Spectacularly sited elegant country mansion with sea views. Own 18-hole golf-course. Indoor heated pools and leisure complex. Self-catering units also available.
Bedrooms: 5 single, 9 double, 9 twin, 2 triple, 11 family rooms
Suites available
Bathrooms: 35 en-suite, 2 public

Bed & breakfast per night:	£min	£max
Single	21.00	32.00
Double	40.00	64.00

Half board per person:	£min	£max
Daily	36.00	47.00

Lunch available
Evening meal 1930 (last orders 2030)
Parking for 60
Open March–December
Cards accepted: Mastercard, Visa, Switch/Delta
70

TORQUAY

Devon
Map ref 1D2

Devon's grandest resort, developed from a fishing village. Smart apartments and terraces rise from the seafront and Marine Drive along the headland gives views of beaches and colourful cliffs.
Tourist Information Centre ☎ (01803) 297428

Bahamas Hotel

COMMENDED

17 Avenue Road, Torquay TQ2 5LB
☎ (01803) 296005 & 0500 526022
Family hotel with emphasis on food and service. 5 minutes from the sea and English Riviera Centre. All en-suite rooms with TV, radio and central heating.
Bedrooms: 1 single, 3 double, 4 twin, 1 triple, 2 family rooms
Bathrooms: 11 en-suite

Bed & breakfast per night:	£min	£max
Single	19.00	23.00
Double	38.00	46.00

Half board per person:	£min	£max
Daily	28.50	32.50
Weekly	190.00	213.00

Evening meal 1830 (last orders 1830)
Parking for 14
Cards accepted: Amex, Diners, Mastercard, Visa

Barn Hayes Country Hotel

HIGHLY COMMENDED

Brim Hill, Maidencombe, Torquay TQ1 4TR
☎ (01803) 327980
Fax (01803) 327980

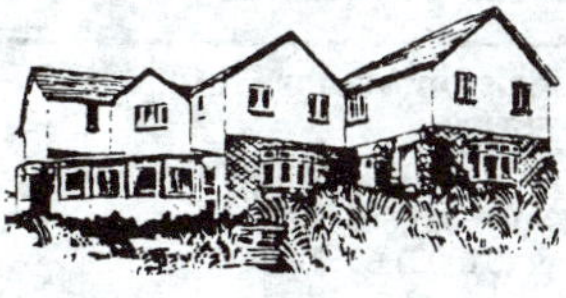

Warm, friendly and comfortable country house hotel in an Area of Outstanding Natural Beauty overlooking countryside and sea. Relaxation is guaranteed in these lovely

Continued ▶

TORQUAY

Continued

surroundings by personal service, good food and fine wines.
Bedrooms: 2 single, 4 double, 2 twin, 2 triple, 2 family rooms
Bathrooms: 10 en-suite, 2 private

Bed & breakfast

per night:	£min	£max
Single	25.00	30.00
Double	50.00	60.00

Half board per

person:	£min	£max
Daily	38.00	44.00

Lunch available
Evening meal 1830 (last orders 1900)
Parking for 16
Open February–December
Cards accepted: Mastercard, Visa

Bute Court Hotel

COMMENDED

Belgrave Road, Torquay TQ2 5HQ
☎ (01803) 213055
Fax (01803) 213429
Family-run hotel overlooking Torbay and adjoining English Riviera Centre. Large lounges and bar. 5-course choice menu.
Bedrooms: 10 single, 14 double, 11 twin, 8 triple, 2 family rooms
Bathrooms: 45 en-suite, 4 public

Bed & breakfast

per night:	£min	£max
Single	20.00	32.00
Double	40.00	64.00

Half board per

person:	£min	£max
Daily	25.00	39.00
Weekly	149.00	265.00

Lunch available
Evening meal 1830 (last orders 2000)
Parking for 38
Cards accepted: Amex, Diners, Mastercard, Visa

Chelston Manor Hotel 𝔸

Old Mill Road, Torquay TQ2 6HW
☎ (01803) 605142
Fax (01803) 605142

Old world bed and breakfast inn. Reputation for good pub food and hospitality. Sun-trap gardens with heated swimming pool.
Bedrooms: 1 single, 10 double, 3 twin, 1 triple
Bathrooms: 10 en-suite, 1 private, 1 public, 1 private shower

Bed & breakfast

per night:	£min	£max
Single	21.00	30.00
Double	42.00	60.00

Lunch available
Evening meal 1800 (last orders 2130)
Parking for 40
Open April–October

Cranborne Hotel 𝔸

COMMENDED

58 Belgrave Road, Torquay TQ2 5HY
☎ (01803) 298046
Fax (01803) 298046
Family-run hotel, close to town centre, seafront and conference centre. We take pride in our service, home cooking and friendly atmosphere.
Bedrooms: 2 single, 4 double, 1 twin, 4 triple, 2 family rooms
Bathrooms: 11 en-suite, 1 public

Bed & breakfast

per night:	£min	£max
Single	15.00	25.00
Double	30.00	50.00

Half board per

person:	£min	£max
Daily	23.00	33.00
Weekly	135.00	188.00

Evening meal 1800 (last orders 1500)
Parking for 3
Cards accepted: Mastercard, Visa

Cranmore Guest House

APPROVED

89 Avenue Road, Torquay TQ2 5LH
☎ (01803) 298488
Friendly, family-run, small hotel offering home cooking. No restrictions, close to all amenities. Level walk to seafront.
Bedrooms: 4 double, 2 twin, 2 family rooms
Bathrooms: 7 en-suite, 1 private

Bed & breakfast

per night:	£min	£max
Single	14.00	16.00
Double	28.00	32.00

Half board per

person:	£min	£max
Daily	20.50	22.50
Weekly	143.50	157.50

Lunch available
Evening meal 1800 (last orders 1830)
Parking for 4
Cards accepted: Amex, Diners, Mastercard, Visa

Elmdene Hotel

COMMENDED

Rathmore Road, Chelston, Torquay TQ2 6NZ
☎ (01803) 294940
Fax (01803) 294940
Rural setting close to seafront and amenities. Warm, friendly and welcoming. Licensed, open all year. Car park.
Bedrooms: 2 single, 5 double, 2 triple, 2 family rooms
Bathrooms: 7 en-suite, 1 public

Bed & breakfast

per night:	£min	£max
Single	17.00	19.00
Double	39.00	42.00

Half board per

person:	£min	£max
Daily	25.00	27.50
Weekly	175.00	192.50

Evening meal 1815 (last orders 1845)
Parking for 10
Cards accepted: Mastercard, Visa, Switch/Delta

Fairmount House Hotel 𝔸

HIGHLY COMMENDED

Herbert Road, Chelston, Torquay TQ2 6RW
☎ (01803) 605446
Fax (01803) 605446
Ⓒ Logis of GB
Award-winning hotel, peacefully situated in lovely gardens near Cockington village. Excellent home cooking, comfortable, spotless accommodation, great hospitality. Dogs welcome, too.
Bedrooms: 2 single, 4 double, 2 triple
Bathrooms: 8 en-suite, 2 public

Bed & breakfast

per night:	£min	£max
Single	25.50	32.00
Double	51.00	64.00

Half board per

person:	£min	£max
Daily	37.50	44.50
Weekly	243.50	291.50

Lunch available
Evening meal 1830 (last orders 1930)
Parking for 8

Open March–October
Cards accepted: Amex, Mastercard, Visa
🐴 [G] 🛏 📺 ☕ ☎ 🔒 [S] [R] [TV] ▥ 🚗 ✽
[OAP] [SP] [T] ⊛

Frognel Hall

★★★ COMMENDED

Higher Woodfield Road, Torquay TQ1 2LD
☎ (01803) 298339
Fax (01803) 215115

Warm and friendly listed mansion, set in 2 acres of peaceful gardens with beautiful views. Close to town centre and lovely Meadfoot Beach. Intimate restaurant - holder of the Bay Award for Hygiene and Healthy Eating.

Wheelchair access category 3
Bedrooms: 4 single, 8 double, 7 twin, 7 triple, 2 family rooms
Bathrooms: 27 en-suite, 1 private

Bed & breakfast per night:	£min	£max
Single	19.00	28.00
Double	38.00	56.00

Half board per person:	£min	£max
Daily	27.00	36.00
Weekly	189.00	224.00

Lunch available
Evening meal 1830 (last orders 2000)
Parking for 20
Cards accepted: Amex, Mastercard, Visa, Switch/Delta
🐴 [G] 🛏 📺 ☕ 🔒 [S] ⚡ [R] [TV] ⇕ ▥ 🚗
T50 ✽ [SP] [T]

Grosvenor House Hotel

★★★ APPROVED

Falkland Road, Torquay TQ2 5JP
☎ (01803) 294110

Comfortable, licensed hotel in quiet, central area, run by Christian family. Sea 400 metres. Excellent home-cooked food with choice of menu.

Bedrooms: 1 single, 5 double, 1 twin, 2 triple, 1 family room
Bathrooms: 10 en-suite

Bed & breakfast per night:	£min	£max
Single	18.00	22.00
Double	36.00	44.00

Half board per person:	£min	£max
Daily	26.00	30.00
Weekly	169.00	194.00

Evening meal from 1830
Parking for 7
Cards accepted: Mastercard, Visa, Switch/Delta
🐴 [G] 🛏 📺 ☕ ☎ 🔒 [S] [R] [TV] ▥ 🚗
[OAP] [SP] [T]

Millbrook House Hotel

★★★ HIGHLY COMMENDED

Old Mill Road, Chelston, Torquay TQ9 6AP
☎ (01803) 297394
Fax (01803) 297394

Small, elegant hotel noted for comfort and food. Level walk to seafront, Abbey Gardens. Cellar bar, games room, satellite TV.

Bedrooms: 6 double, 3 twin, 2 family rooms
Bathrooms: 10 en-suite, 1 private shower

Bed & breakfast per night:	£min	£max
Single	18.00	25.00
Double	36.00	44.00

Half board per person:	£min	£max
Daily	28.00	32.00
Weekly	155.00	175.00

Evening meal 1900 (last orders 2000)
Parking for 12
Cards accepted: Mastercard, Visa
🐴 [G] 🛏 📺 ☕ ☎ 🔒 [S] ⚡ [R] [TV] ▥
🚗 T ✽ [SP] [T]

Norcliffe Hotel

★★★ COMMENDED

Sea Front, Babbacombe Downs, Torquay TQ1 3LF
☎ (01803) 328456

Traditional family hotel in a seafront corner position, close to beaches, shops and golf-course. Swimming pool, sauna, keep-fit facilities.

Bedrooms: 4 single, 7 double, 6 twin, 4 triple
Bathrooms: 21 en-suite

Bed & breakfast per night:	£min	£max
Single	20.00	30.00
Double	36.00	60.00

Half board per person:	£min	£max
Daily	28.00	38.00
Weekly	196.00	266.00

Lunch available
Evening meal 1830 (last orders 1930)
Parking for 16
Cards accepted: Visa
🐴 [G] 🛏 📞 📺 ☕ ☎ 🔒 [S] ⚡ [R] ⇕
▥ 🚗 T80 ✽ [OAP] [SP]

Palace Hotel

★★★★★ COMMENDED

Babbacombe Road, Torquay TQ1 3TG
☎ (01803) 200200
Fax (01803) 299899

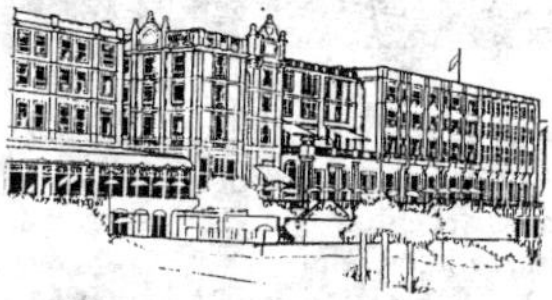

Gracious former Bishop's Palace situated in 25 acres of beautiful gardens and woodland. Extensive and unrivalled leisure facilities.

Bedrooms: 45 single, 40 double, 36 twin, 6 triple, 14 family rooms
Suites available
Bathrooms: 141 en-suite

Bed & breakfast per night:	£min	£max
Single	65.00	75.00
Double	130.00	150.00

Half board per person:	£min	£max
Daily	75.00	85.00
Weekly	450.00	595.00

Lunch available
Evening meal 1930 (last orders 2115)
Parking for 140
Cards accepted: Amex, Diners, Mastercard, Visa, Switch/Delta
🐴 📞 🛏 📺 ☕ ☎ 🔒 [S] ⚡ [R] [TV] ◐ ⇕
▥ 🚗 T1000 ✽ [SP] [T]

Palm Court Hotel

★★★ APPROVED

Sea Front, Torquay TQ2 5HD
☎ (01803) 294881 & (0468) 738070
Fax (01803) 211199

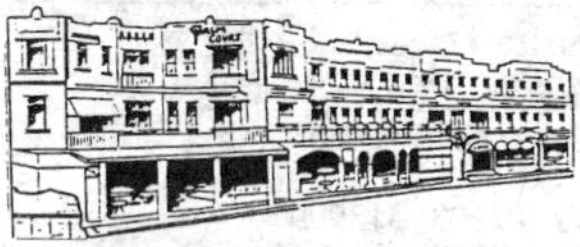

On seafront opposite sandy beach, sunny level position - short walk to harbour and shops. Four bars, restaurant. Self-catering suites available.

Bedrooms: 7 single, 14 double, 8 twin, 6 triple, 1 family room
Bathrooms: 36 en-suite

Bed & breakfast per night:	£min	£max
Single	21.00	28.00
Double	42.00	56.00

Half board per person:	£min	£max
Daily	30.00	37.00
Weekly	210.00	259.00

Lunch available
Evening meal 1800 (last orders 2130)

Continued ▶

TORQUAY
Continued

Open March–December
Cards accepted: Diners, Mastercard,
Visa, Switch/Delta

Hotel Regina 🅜
⚜⚜⚜ APPROVED
Victoria Parade, Torquay TQ1 2BE
☎ (01803) 292904
Fax (01803) 290270
*Pleasant hotel adjacent to Torquay
harbour, in level position and within
walking distance of many of the
resort's amenities.*
Bedrooms: 9 single, 21 double,
34 twin, 5 triple
Bathrooms: 69 en-suite

Bed & breakfast per night:	£min	£max
Single	23.00	36.00
Double	40.00	62.00

Half board per person:	£min	£max
Daily	31.00	40.00
Weekly	161.00	240.00

Evening meal 1800 (last orders
1900)
Parking for 12
Open March–November and
Christmas
Cards accepted: Mastercard, Visa

Suite Dreams Hotel
⚜⚜⚜ HIGHLY COMMENDED
Steep Hill, Maidencombe, Torquay
TQ1 4TS
☎ (01803) 313900
Fax (01803) 313841
CR The Independents

*In unspoilt seaside hamlet.
Pub/restaurant adjacent. About 4 miles
from Torquay centre.*
Bedrooms: 9 double, 3 twin
Bathrooms: 12 en-suite

Bed & breakfast per night:	£min	£max
Single	30.00	45.00
Double	40.00	65.00

Evening meal 1900 (last orders
2030)

Parking for 12
Cards accepted: Amex, Mastercard,
Visa

Torbay Star Guesthouse
⚜⚜ COMMENDED
73 Avenue Road, Torquay TQ2 5LL
☎ (01803) 293998
*Friendly guesthouse in level position.
Free car park, own keys,
tea/coffee-making facilities, TV. En-suite
or private facilities. Non-smoking.*
Bedrooms: 2 double, 1 triple,
2 family rooms
Bathrooms: 4 en-suite, 1 private

Bed & breakfast per night:	£min	£max
Double	26.00	36.00

Parking for 6

Wilsbrook Guest House
⚜⚜ COMMENDED
77 Avenue Road, Torquay TQ2 5LL
☎ (01803) 298413
*Attractive Victorian house, a level walk
to seafront, Torre Abbey Gardens and
Riviera Centre. En-suite non-smoking
bedrooms with tea-making and TV.
Guest lounge (smoking). Car park.*
Bedrooms: 1 single, 3 double,
1 family room
Bathrooms: 3 en-suite, 1 public,
1 private shower

Bed & breakfast per night:	£min	£max
Single	13.00	16.00
Double	28.00	36.00

Half board per person:	£min	£max
Daily	20.00	24.00
Weekly	125.00	

Evening meal 1800 (last orders
1000)
Parking for 6
Cards accepted: Mastercard, Visa

TORRINGTON
Devon
Map ref 1C1

Perched high above the River
Torridge, with a charming market
square, Georgian Town Hall and a
museum. The famous Dartington
Crystal Factory, Rosemoor Gardens
and Plough Arts Centre are all
located in the town.

Beaford House Hotel
⚜⚜⚜ APPROVED
Beaford, Winkleigh EX19 8AB
☎ (01805) 603305 & 603330

*Beautiful country hotel overlooking the
River Torridge and 5 miles south east
of Torrington, near Tarka Trail. Excellent
cuisine, friendly atmosphere. Ideal for a
peaceful break. Heated pool, tennis,
golf and riding. Near Rosemoor
Gardens.*
Bedrooms: 1 single, 1 double, 1 twin,
2 triple, 4 family rooms
Bathrooms: 7 en-suite, 2 public

Bed & breakfast per night:	£min	£max
Single	29.00	
Double	58.00	

Half board per person:	£min	£max
Daily	42.00	

Lunch available
Evening meal from 1900
Parking for 50
Open January, March–December
Cards accepted: Mastercard, Visa

TOTNES
Devon
Map ref 1D2

Old market town steeply built near
the head of the Dart Estuary.
Remains of medieval gateways, a
noble church, 16th C Guildhall and
medley of period houses recall
former wealth from cloth and
shipping, continued in rural and
water industries.
*Tourist Information Centre ☎ (01803)
863168*

Old Church House Inn 🅜
⚜⚜⚜⚜ COMMENDED
Torbryan, Newton Abbot
TQ12 5UR
☎ (01803) 812372 & 812180
Fax (01803) 812180
CR Minotel
*13th C coaching house of immense
character and old world charm with
inglenook fireplaces, stone walls and
oak beamed ceilings. Situated in a
beautiful valley between Dartmoor and
Torquay.*
Bedrooms: 5 double, 5 triple,
1 family room
Bathrooms: 11 en-suite

Bed & breakfast per night:	£min	£max
Single	40.00	50.00
Double	55.00	65.00

Half board per person:	£min	£max
Daily	40.00	47.50
Weekly	250.00	300.00

Lunch available
Evening meal 1800 (last orders
2130)

Parking for 30
Cards accepted: Mastercard, Visa

🐎♿&📞📧🖥📺♿🎱📶S✂🛏▦🗄
🍴30♾♪✈✏☀🌙DAP🔌SP🏬T

The Old Forge at Totnes ⋔

👑👑 HIGHLY COMMENDED

Seymour Place, Totnes TQ9 5AY
☎ (01803) 862174
Fax (01803) 865385
CR Distinctly Different
*Delightful 600-year-old stone building,
with walled garden and working smithy.
Cottage suite suitable for family or
disabled guests. No smoking indoors.
Extensive breakfast menu (traditional,
vegetarian, fish and continental).
Whirlpool spa. Speciality: golf breaks.*
Bedrooms: 1 single, 5 double, 2 twin,
2 family rooms
Suites available
Bathrooms: 9 en-suite, 1 private,
1 public
**Bed & breakfast
per night:**

	£min	£max
Single	40.00	50.00
Double	50.00	70.00

Parking for 10
Cards accepted: Mastercard, Visa,
Switch/Delta

🐎♿&📞📧🖥♿🎱📶S✂🛏TV▦
🗄🍴♾♪✈☀🌙🐾🔌SP🏬T

Royal Seven Stars Hotel ⋔

👑👑👑 APPROVED

The Plains, Totnes TQ9 5DD
☎ (01803) 862125 & 863241
Fax (01803) 867925
*Old coaching inn in the centre of
Totnes, near River Dart. Short drive to
coast and Dartmoor. Brochures
available on request. Weekend breaks
available.*
Bedrooms: 1 single, 11 double,
3 twin, 2 triple, 1 family room
Bathrooms: 12 en-suite, 3 public
**Bed & breakfast
per night:**

	£min	£max
Single	44.00	54.00
Double	54.00	62.00

**Half board per
person:**

	£min	£max
Daily	42.00	68.00
Weekly	250.00	395.00

Lunch available
Evening meal 1900 (last orders
2115)
Parking for 20
Cards accepted: Diners, Mastercard,
Visa

🐎♿&📞📧🖥♿🎱S✂🛏▦🗄
🍴60🔌SP🏬T

TREYARNON BAY

Cornwall
Map ref 1B2

Waterbeach Hotel ⋔

👑👑👑 COMMENDED

Treyarnon Bay, Padstow PL28 8JW
☎ (01841) 520292
Fax (01841) 521102

*Designed to take advantage of the
sunshine and views across the Atlantic.
Accommodates 30 people in comfort.*
Bedrooms: 4 single, 5 double, 5 twin,
7 triple
Bathrooms: 14 en-suite, 2 public
**Bed & breakfast
per night:**

	£min	£max
Single	25.00	41.00
Double	50.00	82.00

**Half board per
person:**

	£min	£max
Daily	34.00	48.00
Weekly	230.00	310.00

Evening meal 1930 (last orders
2015)
Parking for 25
Open March–October
Cards accepted: Mastercard, Visa,
Switch/Delta

🐎♿&📞📧🖥♿🎱S🛏TV▦🗄🔍
🎱☀🌙T

TRURO

Cornwall
Map ref 1B3

Cornwall's administrative centre
and cathedral city, set at the head of
Truro River on the Fal Estuary. A
medieval stannary town, it handled
mineral ore from west Cornwall;
fine Georgian buildings recall its
heyday as a society haunt in the
second mining boom.
*Tourist Information Centre ☎ (01872)
274555*

Bissick Old Mill ⋔

👑👑👑 HIGHLY COMMENDED

Ladock, Truro TR2 4PG
☎ (01726) 882557
Fax (01726) 884057
CR The Independents
*17th C water mill sympathetically
converted to provide well-appointed
accommodation with exceptional
standards of comfort, cuisine and*

---

*hospitality. Central rural location makes
ideal base for touring or business.*
Bedrooms: 1 single, 2 double, 1 twin
Bathrooms: 4 en-suite
**Bed & breakfast
per night:**

	£min	£max
Single	35.25	39.95
Double	54.40	62.50

**Half board per
person:**

	£min	£max
Daily	39.95	55.70
Weekly	273.00	375.00

Lunch available
Evening meal 1900 (last orders
1700)
Parking for 9
Cards accepted: Mastercard, Visa,
Switch/Delta

🐎10📧🖥♿🎱📶S✂🛏▦🗄🔌☀
🐾SP🏬

Carlton Hotel

👑👑👑 APPROVED

Falmouth Road, Truro TR1 2HL
☎ (01872) 272450
Fax (01872) 223938
*Established, family-run hotel with
friendly atmosphere. Varied choice of
menus. Sauna, spa bath and solarium
available.*
Bedrooms: 8 single, 14 double,
6 twin, 2 triple, 1 family room
Bathrooms: 27 en-suite, 1 public
**Bed & breakfast
per night:**

	£min	£max
Single	33.50	38.50
Double	45.00	45.00

**Half board per
person:**

	£min	£max
Daily	42.45	47.45
Weekly	219.00	256.00

Evening meal 1900 (last orders
2000)
Parking for 35
Cards accepted: Amex, Diners,
Mastercard, Visa, Switch/Delta

🐎♿&📞📧🖥♿S🛏▦🗄🔌🍴90
🐾✈DAP🔌SP

Marcorrie Hotel ⋔

👑👑 APPROVED

20 Falmouth Road, Truro TR1 2HX
☎ (01872) 277374
Fax (01872) 241666

*Family-run hotel 5 minutes' walk from
city centre and cathedral. Ideal for*
Continued ▶

TRURO

Continued

business or holiday, central for visiting the country houses and gardens of Cornwall.
Bedrooms: 3 single, 3 double, 2 twin, 1 triple, 3 family rooms
Bathrooms: 12 en-suite, 1 public

Bed & breakfast per night:	£min	£max
Single	33.00	35.00
Double	44.00	46.00

Half board per person:	£min	£max
Daily	42.00	
Weekly	280.00	

Evening meal 1900 (last orders 1700)
Parking for 16
Cards accepted: Amex, Diners, Mastercard, Visa, Switch/Delta
🐴 ♿ ☎ 📺 ☕ 🔒 [S] ⚡ 🍴 [TV] ▦ 🧺
🏊 20 ⛳ ✿ 🚐 [SP] 🏛 [T] ◎

TWO BRIDGES

Devon
Map ref 1C2

Dartmoor hamlet on the banks of the West Dart River, at the heart of the moor.

Prince Hall Hotel 🏔

[COMMENDED]

Two Bridges, Yelverton PL20 6SA
☎ (01822) 890403
Fax (01822) 890676
[CR] Logis of GB
Small, friendly, country house hotel set in the heart of Dartmoor. Owner/chef. Good wine list. Ideal for walking, riding and fishing.
Bedrooms: 1 single, 3 double, 3 twin, 1 triple
Bathrooms: 8 en-suite

Bed & breakfast per night:	£min	£max
Single		35.00
Double	65.00	75.00

Half board per person:	£min	£max
Daily	52.50	57.50
Weekly	332.50	367.50

Evening meal 1900 (last orders 2030)
Parking for 15
Open February–December
Cards accepted: Amex, Diners, Mastercard, Visa, Switch/Delta
🐴 8 🛏 ☎ 📺 ☕ 🔒 [S] ⚡ 🍴 [TV] ▦ 🧺
🏊 ∪ 🎣 ⛳ ✿ 🚐 ✈ [SP] 🏛

Two Bridges Hotel 🏔

[COMMENDED]

Two Bridges Dartmoor, Princetown PL20 6SW
☎ (01822) 890581
Fax (01822) 890575
[CR] Consort
18th C riverside inn, old world atmosphere, log fires, good food, wine and own real ales. Ideal for walking, riding, fishing and golf. Heart of Dartmoor. Addictive.
Bedrooms: 1 single, 16 double, 6 twin, 2 triple
Bathrooms: 25 en-suite

Bed & breakfast per night:	£min	£max
Single	38.00	
Double	69.00	

Half board per person:	£min	£max
Daily	49.50	
Weekly	297.00	

Lunch available
Evening meal 1800 (last orders 2100)
Parking for 120
Cards accepted: Amex, Diners, Mastercard, Visa, Switch/Delta
🐴 ♿ 🛏 ☎ 📺 ☕ 🔒 [S] ⚡ ▦ 🧺
🏊 120 ∪ 🎣 ⛳ ✿ ✈ [SP] 🏛 [T]

WADEBRIDGE

Cornwall
Map ref 1B2

Old market town with Cornwall's finest medieval bridge, spanning the Camel at its highest navigable point. Twice widened, the bridge is said to have been built on woolpacks sunk in the unstable sands of the river bed.
Tourist Information Centre ☎ (01208) 813725

Hendra Country House 🏔

[COMMENDED]

St Kew Highway, Wadebridge, Bodmin PL30 3EQ
☎ (01208) 841343
Fax (01208) 841343

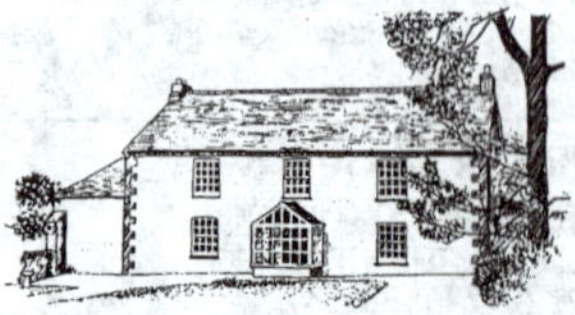

19th C manor house in quiet seclusion in rural tranquillity, 3 miles north-east of Wadebridge. Exceptional menu using home-grown produce. Warm, friendly atmosphere.
Bedrooms: 1 single, 2 double, 2 twin
Bathrooms: 4 en-suite, 1 private

Bed & breakfast per night:	£min	£max
Double	44.00	54.00

Half board per person:	£min	£max
Daily	37.00	42.00
Weekly	245.00	278.00

Evening meal 1930 (last orders 1730)
Parking for 8
Open February–November and Christmas
Cards accepted: Amex, Mastercard, Visa
🐴 📺 ☕ 🍷 🔒 [S] ⚡ 🍴 [TV] ▦ 🧺 🔍
∪ ⛳ ✿ 🚐 ✈ [SP] 🏛

WATCHET

Somerset
Map ref 1D1

Small port on Bridgwater Bay, sheltered by the Quantocks and the Brendon Hills. A thriving paper industry keeps the harbour busy; in the 19th C it handled iron from the Brendon Hills. Cleeve Abbey, a ruined Cistercian monastery, is 3 miles to the south-west.

Downfield House 🏔

[COMMENDED]

16 St Decuman's Road, Watchet TA23 0HR
☎ (01984) 631267
Fax (01984) 634369

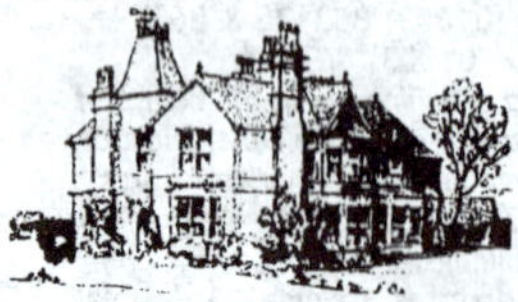

Attractive Victorian country house, set in secluded grounds with views over harbour and town. Comfortable lounge, chandeliered dining room. Close to Quantocks and Exmoor.
Bedrooms: 6 double, 2 twin
Bathrooms: 8 en-suite

Bed & breakfast per night:	£min	£max
Single	21.00	29.00
Double	42.00	58.00

Half board per person:	£min	£max
Daily	34.00	42.00
Weekly	238.00	294.00

Evening meal 1845 (last orders 1930)
Parking for 12
Open February–December
Cards accepted: Amex, Mastercard, Visa, Switch/Delta
🐴 ☎ 📺 ☕ 🍷 🔒 [S] ⚡ 🍴 ▦ 🧺
🏊 10 ⛳ ✿ 🚐 🏛 [T] ◎

WATERGATE BAY

Cornwall
Map ref 1B2

Beautiful long board-riders' beach backed by tall cliffs, north-west of Newquay. A small holiday village nestles in a steep river valley making a cleft in the cliffs.

Watergate Bay Hotel

♛♛♛♛ COMMENDED

Watergate Bay TR8 4AA
☎ (01637) 860543
Fax (01637) 860333

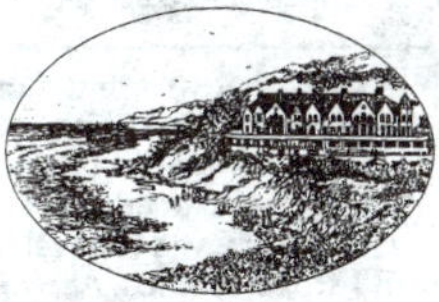

Family-run hotel beside own beach on the coastal path. Wonderful indoor/outdoor leisure facilities. Dogs welcome. Spring and autumn superbreaks.
Bedrooms: 8 single, 20 double, 4 twin, 7 triple, 18 family rooms
Bathrooms: 57 en-suite, 4 public

Bed & breakfast per night:	£min	£max
Single	25.00	40.00
Double	48.00	80.00

Half board per person:	£min	£max
Daily	29.00	54.00
Weekly	203.00	364.00

Lunch available
Evening meal 1900 (last orders 2030)
Parking for 80
Open March–November
Cards accepted: Mastercard, Visa
[S] [TV] 100 [OAP] [SP] [T]

WELCOME HOST
This is a nationally recognised customer care programme which aims to promote the highest standards of service and a warm welcome. Establishments who are taking part in this initiative are indicated by the symbol.

WELLS

Somerset
Map ref 2A2

Small city set beneath the southern slopes of the Mendips. Built between 1180 and 1424, the magnificent cathedral is preserved in much of its original glory and with its ancient precincts forms one of our loveliest and most unified groups of medieval buildings.
Tourist Information Centre ☎ (01749) 672552

Beryl

♛♛♛ HIGHLY COMMENDED

Beryl, Wells BA5 3JP
☎ (01749) 678738
Fax (01749) 670508
Bed and breakfast accommodation in 13 acres of parkland, 1 mile from Wells. Take the Radstock road from Wells, turn opposite the BP garage.
Bedrooms: 3 double, 4 twin
Bathrooms: 7 en-suite

Bed & breakfast per night:	£min	£max
Single	50.00	75.00
Double	65.00	85.00

Half board per person:	£min	£max
Daily	52.50	62.50
Weekly	367.50	437.50

Evening meal from 2000
Parking for 14
Cards accepted: Mastercard, Visa
[TV] [T]

All accommodation in this guide has been graded, or is awaiting a grading, by a trained Tourist Board inspector.

TOWN INDEX
This can be found at the back of the guide. If you know where you want to stay, the index will give you the page number listing all accommodation in your chosen town, city or village.

Burcott Mill

♛♛ COMMENDED

Burcott, Wells BA5 1NJ
☎ (01749) 673118 & (0421) 378773
Fax (01749) 673118
[CR] Distinctly Different
Restored working watermill with attached house and craft workshops. Friendly country atmosphere. Birds and animals. Home cooking. Opposite good country pub. Accommodation available for wheelchair user.
Wheelchair access category 1♿
Bedrooms: 1 single, 1 double, 3 triple, 1 family room
Suite available
Bathrooms: 5 en-suite, 1 private

Bed & breakfast per night:	£min	£max
Single	19.00	30.00
Double	33.00	50.00

Half board per person:	£min	£max
Daily	27.50	36.00
Weekly	181.00	234.00

Evening meal 1800 (last orders 2200)
Parking for 10
Cards accepted: Diners, Mastercard, Visa
[UL] [S] [TV] [SP]

Coxley Vineyard

♛♛♛ COMMENDED

Coxley, Wells BA5 1PQ
☎ (01749) 670285
Fax (01749) 679708

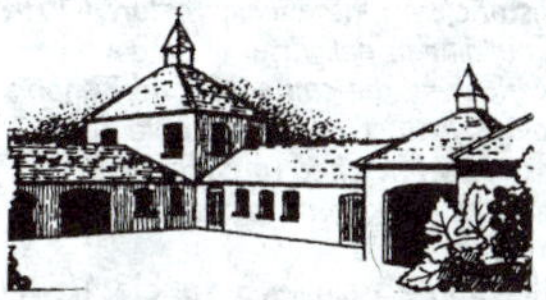

Small charming hotel with a distinctly Mediterranean feel, set in the heart of a vineyard.
Bedrooms: 3 double, 1 twin, 6 triple
Bathrooms: 10 en-suite

Bed & breakfast per night:	£min	£max
Single	40.00	50.00
Double	50.00	60.00

Half board per person:	£min	£max
Daily	45.00	55.00

Lunch available
Evening meal 1800 (last orders 2200)
Parking for 8
Cards accepted: Mastercard, Visa
[S] [SP]

WELLS

Continued

Swan Hotel ♔
【HIGHLY COMMENDED】
Sadler Street, Wells BA5 2RX
☎ (01749) 678877
Fax (01749) 677647
ⓒ Best Western
Privately-owned 15th C hotel with views of the cathedral's west front. Restaurant, saddle bar, log fires. Four-poster beds available.
Bedrooms: 9 single, 19 double, 10 twin
Bathrooms: 38 en-suite

Bed & breakfast per night:

	£min	£max
Single	69.50	75.00
Double	89.50	95.00

Half board per person:

	£min	£max
Daily	45.00	57.50

Lunch available
Evening meal 1900 (last orders 2130)
Parking for 35
Cards accepted: Amex, Diners, Mastercard, Visa, Switch/Delta

Tor House
【HIGHLY COMMENDED】
20 Tor Street, Wells BA5 2US
☎ (01749) 672322 & 672084
Fax (01749) 672322
Historic, sympathetically restored 17th C building in delightful grounds overlooking the cathedral and Bishop's Palace. Attractive, comfortable and tastefully furnished throughout. 3 minutes' walk to town centre. Ample parking.
Bedrooms: 1 single, 3 double, 1 twin, 3 family rooms
Bathrooms: 5 en-suite, 2 public

Bed & breakfast per night:

	£min	£max
Single	22.00	40.00
Double	38.00	55.00

Evening meal 1830 (last orders 1000)
Parking for 12
Cards accepted: Mastercard, Visa, Switch/Delta

WEST BAY

Dorset
Map ref 2A3

Westpoint Tavern ♔
【APPROVED】
The Esplanade, West Bay, Bridport DT6 4HG
☎ (01308) 423636
On seafront and promenade. All rooms en-suite with TV, coffee facilities and sea or harbour views. Fishing, golf, cliff walks in Thomas Hardy country. Daily half-board prices apply to 2-day breaks.
Bedrooms: 2 double, 3 twin
Bathrooms: 5 en-suite

Bed & breakfast per night:

	£min	£max
Single	23.00	25.00
Double	36.00	38.00

Half board per person:

	£min	£max
Daily	26.00	28.50
Weekly	137.00	179.00

Lunch available
Evening meal 1900 (last orders 2200)
Parking for 6
Cards accepted: Mastercard, Visa, Switch/Delta

WEST BEXINGTON

Dorset
Map ref 2A3

The Manor Hotel ♔
【COMMENDED】
West Bexington, Dorchester DT2 9DF
☎ (01308) 897616 & 897785
Fax (01308) 897035
ⓒ Logis of GB

16th C manor house, 500 yards from Chesil Beach. Panoramic views from most bedrooms. 3 real ales and character cellar bar.
Bedrooms: 1 single, 8 double, 3 twin, 1 triple
Bathrooms: 13 en-suite

Bed & breakfast per night:

	£min	£max
Single	51.00	52.00
Double	86.00	88.00

Half board per person:

	£min	£max
Daily	64.00	65.00
Weekly	375.00	385.00

Lunch available
Evening meal 1900 (last orders 2200)
Parking for 20
Cards accepted: Amex, Diners, Mastercard, Visa

WESTBURY

Wiltshire
Map ref 2B2

Wiltshire's best-known white horse looks down on the town with its Georgian houses around the Market Place. Handsome Perpendicular church with fine carved chancel screen and stone reredos. Above the white horse are the prehistoric earthworks of Bratton Castle.
Tourist Information Centre ☎ *(01373) 827158*

The Cedar Hotel ♔
【COMMENDED】
Warminster Road, Westbury BA13 3PR
☎ (01373) 822753
Fax (01373) 858423
ⓒ Logis of GB
18th C country house hotel with a friendly and relaxed atmosphere. Offering comfortable, well-appointed accommodation and good cuisine.
Bedrooms: 1 single, 12 double, 3 twin
Bathrooms: 16 en-suite

Bed & breakfast per night:

	£min	£max
Single	40.00	45.00
Double	45.00	55.00

Half board per person:

	£min	£max
Daily	55.00	65.00
Weekly	315.00	350.00

Lunch available
Evening meal 1900 (last orders 2100)
Parking for 35
Cards accepted: Amex, Mastercard, Visa, Switch/Delta

WESTON-SUPER-MARE

North Somerset
Map ref 1D1

Large, friendly resort developed in the 19th C. Traditional seaside attractions include theatres and a dance hall. The museum has a Victorian seaside gallery and Iron Age finds from a hill fort on Worlebury Hill in Weston Woods.
Tourist Information Centre ☎ (01934) 888800

Arosfa Hotel

COMMENDED

Lower Church Road,
Weston-super-Mare BS23 2AG
☎ (01934) 419523
Fax (01934) 636084
The Independents
Refurbished hotel with 3 lounges, bars, dining room and comfortable bedrooms. Situated on level ground 100 yards from the town centre and seafront.
Bedrooms: 14 single, 12 double, 15 twin, 3 triple, 2 family rooms
Bathrooms: 46 en-suite

Bed & breakfast per night:

	£min	£max
Single	38.50	40.00
Double	50.00	60.00

Half board per person:

	£min	£max
Daily	38.50	45.00
Weekly	246.00	252.00

Lunch available
Evening meal 1830 (last orders 2030)
Parking for 6
Cards accepted: Amex, Diners, Mastercard, Visa, Switch/Delta

Baymead Hotel

COMMENDED

19/23 Longton Grove Road,
Weston-super-Mare BS23 1LS
☎ (01934) 622951
Fax (01934) 628110

Central, level and quiet location, 500 yards from seafront. Privately owned by Cutler family since 1965. Comfortable en-suite rooms with TV, tea/coffee making. Lift to all levels.

Bedrooms: 11 single, 8 double, 11 twin, 3 triple
Bathrooms: 28 en-suite, 2 private, 2 public

Bed & breakfast per night:

	£min	£max
Single	15.00	22.00
Double	30.00	42.00

Half board per person:

	£min	£max
Daily	20.00	31.00
Weekly	150.00	205.00

Evening meal 1815 (last orders 1900)
Parking for 10

Braeside Hotel

COMMENDED

2 Victoria Park, Weston-super-Mare BS23 2HZ
☎ (01934) 626642
Fax (01934) 626642
Delightful, family-run hotel, ideally situated near seafront. All rooms en-suite. Single rooms always available. Unrestricted on-street parking.
Bedrooms: 1 single, 5 double, 1 twin, 2 triple
Bathrooms: 9 en-suite

Bed & breakfast per night:

	£min	£max
Single	24.00	24.00
Double	48.00	48.00

Half board per person:

	£min	£max
Daily	34.00	34.00
Weekly	196.00	196.00

Lunch available
Evening meal 1830 (last orders 1800)

Commodore Hotel

HIGHLY COMMENDED

Sand Bay, Kewstoke,
Weston-super-Mare BS22 9UZ
☎ (01934) 415778
Fax (01934) 636483
Traditional hotel facilities with popular restaurant, lounge bar and buffet services. Situated in unspoilt bay close to major resort amenities.
Bedrooms: 2 single, 10 double, 3 twin, 3 family rooms
Bathrooms: 18 en-suite

Bed & breakfast per night:

	£min	£max
Single	50.00	
Double	65.00	

Half board per person:

	£min	£max
Daily	42.50	
Weekly	275.00	

Lunch available

Evening meal 1700 (last orders 1900)
Parking for 80
Cards accepted: Mastercard, Visa

Daunceys Hotels

COMMENDED

9-14 Claremont Crescent,
Weston-super-Mare BS23 2EE
☎ (01934) 621144 & 621212
Fax (01934) 620281
Family-run hotel, directly overlooking the sea. Garden for guests' enjoyment. Lifts to all floors. Fully licensed. Open all year, special breaks available.
Bedrooms: 24 single, 20 double, 28 twin, 3 triple, 8 family rooms
Bathrooms: 73 en-suite, 5 public

Bed & breakfast per night:

	£min	£max
Single	27.50	32.00
Double	55.00	64.00

Half board per person:

	£min	£max
Daily	37.00	80.00
Weekly	225.00	260.00

Lunch available
Evening meal 1830 (last orders 1900)
Cards accepted: Mastercard, Visa, Switch/Delta

Dorville Hotel

Madeira Road, Weston-super-Mare BS23 2EX
☎ (01934) 621522 & 621139
Fax (01934) 645585
Fully licensed, friendly family hotel. Some four-poster rooms and penthouse. Two bars, lounge, terrace lounge. Quiet position overlooking sea. Established over 65 years.
Bedrooms: 10 single, 20 double, 9 twin, 1 triple, 1 family room
Bathrooms: 26 en-suite, 6 public

Bed & breakfast per night:

	£min	£max
Single	22.00	29.00
Double	40.00	56.00

Half board per person:

	£min	£max
Daily	25.00	32.00
Weekly	121.50	210.00

Lunch available
Evening meal 1800 (last orders 1930)
Parking for 14
Open March–November

WESTON-SUPER-MARE
Continued

The Grand Atlantic ⚲
👑👑👑👑 COMMENDED

Beach Road, Weston-super-Mare
BS23 1BA
☎ (01934) 626543
Fax (01934) 415048
CR Regal
Spacious hotel in a splendid position overlooking the sea and sandy beach, offering the best in service, comfort and traditional food in a friendly and relaxing atmosphere. Daily half board price below for stays of 2 nights or more.
Bedrooms: 17 single, 32 double, 23 twin, 3 triple, 1 family room
Suite available
Bathrooms: 76 en-suite
Bed & breakfast per night:

	£min	£max
Single	34.00	43.00
Double	68.00	86.00

Half board per person:

	£min	£max
Daily	37.00	53.00
Weekly	233.00	334.00

Lunch available
Evening meal 1830 (last orders 2130)
Parking for 100
Cards accepted: Amex, Diners, Mastercard, Visa, Switch/Delta

Moorlands ⚲
👑👑 COMMENDED

Hutton, Weston-super-Mare,
Somerset BS24 9QH
☎ (01934) 812283
Family-run 18th C house in mature landscaped grounds. Beach 10 minutes' drive. Good centre for many places of beauty and interest. Log fires.
Wheelchair access category 3
Bedrooms: 1 single, 2 double, 2 twin, 1 triple, 1 family room
Bathrooms: 5 en-suite, 1 public
Bed & breakfast per night:

	£min	£max
Single	18.50	28.50
Double	37.00	44.00

Parking for 8
Cards accepted: Amex, Mastercard, Visa

Queenswood Hotel
👑👑👑 COMMENDED

Victoria Park, Weston-super-Mare,
Somerset BS23 2HZ
☎ (01934) 416141
Fax (01934) 621759
CR The Independents
Friendly family hotel set off the seafront with panoramic views. Emphasis on comfort, food, wine and service.
Bedrooms: 3 single, 11 double, 2 triple, 1 family room
Bathrooms: 17 en-suite
Bed & breakfast per night:

	£min	£max
Single	30.00	42.50
Double	50.00	75.00

Half board per person:

	£min	£max
Daily	44.50	57.00
Weekly	252.00	266.00

Lunch available
Evening meal 1830 (last orders 2030)
Parking for 6
Cards accepted: Amex, Diners, Mastercard, Visa, Switch/Delta

Royal Pier Hotel
👑👑👑 APPROVED

Birnbeck Road, Weston-super-Mare
BS23 2EJ
☎ (01934) 626644
Fax (01934) 624169
Situated on the water's edge overlooking Weston Bay. Refurbished throughout to high standards, complementing food and service. Free parking.
Bedrooms: 7 single, 8 double, 21 twin, 4 triple
Bathrooms: 38 en-suite, 3 public
Bed & breakfast per night:

	£min	£max
Single	38.00	55.00
Double	70.00	80.00

Half board per person:

	£min	£max
Daily	46.00	56.00
Weekly	232.00	262.00

Lunch available
Evening meal 1900 (last orders 2115)
Parking for 70
Cards accepted: Amex, Diners, Mastercard, Visa, Switch/Delta

Saxonia
👑👑 COMMENDED

95 Locking Road,
Weston-super-Mare BS23 3EW
☎ (01934) 633856
Fax (01934) 623141
Friendly, family-run guesthouse near beach, 15 minutes from Tropicana Leisure Centre and Sea Life Centre. All rooms en-suite with shower, hairdryer, colour TV. Air conditioned dining room.
http:www.s-h-systems,co.uk/hotels/saxonia.hml.
Bedrooms: 2 single, 2 double, 3 twin, 1 triple, 1 family room
Bathrooms: 7 en-suite, 2 private showers
Bed & breakfast per night:

	£min	£max
Single	25.00	35.00
Double	36.00	50.00

Evening meal 1830 (last orders 1600)
Parking for 4
Cards accepted: Amex, Diners, Mastercard, Visa, Switch/Delta

Tralee Hotel ⚲
👑👑 APPROVED

Sea Front, Madeira Cove,
Weston-super-Mare BS23 2BX
☎ (01934) 626707
Detached, licensed, seafront hotel with views across Weston Bay. Lift. Entertainment. Easy level walk to all main amenities.
Bedrooms: 6 single, 7 double, 9 twin, 9 triple
Bathrooms: 29 en-suite, 3 public
Bed & breakfast per night:

	£min	£max
Single	17.50	22.50
Double	35.00	40.00

Half board per person:

	£min	£max
Daily	22.50	27.50
Weekly	132.00	162.00

Evening meal 1800 (last orders 1800)
Parking for 8
Open April–October

National gradings and classifications were correct at the time of going to press but are subject to change. Please check at the time of booking.

WESTWARD HO!

Devon
Map ref 1C1

Small resort, whose name comes from the title of Charles Kingsley's famous novel, on Barnstaple Bay, close to the Taw and Torridge Estuary. There are good sands and a notable golf-course - one of the oldest in Britain.

Buckleigh Lodge

⚜⚜⚜ COMMENDED

135 Bay View Road, Westward Ho!, Bideford EX39 1BJ
☎ (01237) 475988
Fine late Victorian house in own grounds, with magnificent views over the bay and close to a large, safe sandy beach. Ideal touring centre.
Bedrooms: 1 single, 3 double, 2 twin
Suites available
Bathrooms: 4 en-suite, 1 public, 1 private shower

Bed & breakfast per night:

	£min	£max
Single	18.00	19.00
Double	36.00	38.00

Half board per person:

	£min	£max
Daily	28.00	29.00
Weekly	186.00	192.00

Evening meal 1900 (last orders 1700)
Parking for 7

Culloden House Hotel

⚜⚜ COMMENDED

Fosketh Hill, Westward Ho!, Bideford EX39 1JA
☎ (01237) 479421
Carefully converted Victorian house with fabulous sea views. Family-run, good food. Ideal base for golfing, walking and family holidays.
Bedrooms: 7 twin, 2 family rooms
Suites available
Bathrooms: 7 en-suite, 1 public

Bed & breakfast per night:

	£min	£max
Single	22.50	26.50
Double	45.00	50.00

Half board per person:

	£min	£max
Daily	36.00	45.00
Weekly	230.00	280.00

Evening meal 1900 (last orders 2030)
Parking for 12

Open February–December
Cards accepted: Mastercard, Visa, Switch/Delta

WEYMOUTH

Dorset
Map ref 2B3

Ancient port and one of the south's earliest resorts. Curving beside a long, sandy beach, the elegant Georgian esplanade is graced with a statue of George III and a cheerful Victorian Jubilee clock tower.
Tourist Information Centre ☎ (01305) 785747

Bay Lodge ⚜

⚜⚜ HIGHLY COMMENDED

27 Greenhill, Weymouth DT4 7SW
☎ (01305) 782419
Fax (01305) 782828
Email: barbara@baylodge.co.uk

Once in a while, you will discover a hotel which is completely unique. Spectacular seafront setting, magnificent bedrooms (some with jacuzzi), excellent cuisine, friendly and informal. Bargain breaks available.
http://www.baylodge.co.uk.
Bedrooms: 1 single, 5 double, 4 twin, 2 triple
Bathrooms: 12 en-suite

Bed & breakfast per night:

	£min	£max
Single	29.50	
Double	50.00	

Half board per person:

	£min	£max
Daily	39.50	
Weekly	230.00	

Evening meal 1830 (last orders 1900)
Parking for 18
Cards accepted: Amex, Diners, Mastercard, Visa, Switch/Delta

Kenora Private Hotel ⚜

⚜⚜ COMMENDED

5 Stavordale Road, Weymouth DT4 0AB
☎ (01305) 771215 & 0976 826067
Email: kenora.hotel@wdi.co.uk
Family-run hotel offering good food, comfortable accommodation, easy

parking, garden and play area. 700 metres from town, harbour and sandy beach.
Bedrooms: 3 single, 7 double, 2 twin, 2 triple, 1 family room
Bathrooms: 13 en-suite, 1 public

Bed & breakfast per night:

	£min	£max
Single	24.00	33.00
Double	48.00	56.00

Half board per person:

	£min	£max
Daily	34.00	43.00
Weekly	185.00	215.00

Evening meal (last orders 1630)
Parking for 15
Open May–September
Cards accepted: Mastercard, Visa, Switch/Delta

Rembrandt Hotel ⚜

⚜⚜⚜ COMMENDED

12-16 Dorchester Road, Weymouth DT4 7JU
☎ (01305) 764000
Fax (01305) 764022

Premier hotel in Weymouth, walking distance from the seafront and town centre. Hotel has leisure club with sauna, whirlpool bath, sunbeds, toning beds, large heated indoor swimming pool.
Bedrooms: 6 single, 27 double, 12 twin, 35 triple, 8 family rooms
Suites available
Bathrooms: 88 en-suite, 3 public

Bed & breakfast per night:

	£min	£max
Single	40.00	67.00
Double	65.00	90.00

Half board per person:

	£min	£max
Daily	45.00	90.00
Weekly	230.00	600.00

Lunch available
Evening meal 1830 (last orders 2115)
Parking for 80
Cards accepted: Amex, Diners, Mastercard, Visa, Switch/Delta

WEYMOUTH

Continued

Hotel Rex ᴍ

👑👑👑👑 COMMENDED

29 The Esplanade, Weymouth
DT4 8DN
☎ (01305) 760400
Fax (01305) 760500
*Georgian town house situated on the
Esplanade overlooking Weymouth Bay,
adjacent to the harbour and town
centre and close to the Pavilion.*
Bedrooms: 13 single, 6 double,
7 twin, 5 triple
Bathrooms: 31 en-suite

Bed & breakfast per night:

	£min	£max
Single	45.00	52.00
Double	74.00	95.00

Half board per person:

	£min	£max
Daily	54.00	65.00
Weekly	234.00	280.00

Lunch available
Evening meal 1800 (last orders
2200)
Parking for 8
Cards accepted: Amex, Diners,
Mastercard, Visa

Sunningdale Hotel ᴍ

👑👑👑

52 Preston Road, Weymouth
DT3 6QD
☎ (01305) 832179
Fax (01305) 832179
*Family hotel with a relaxed and
comfortable atmosphere, set in
attractive gardens with an outdoor
swimming pool. 2 miles to the town
centre.*
Bedrooms: 1 single, 7 double, 3 twin,
3 triple, 4 family rooms
Suite available
Bathrooms: 11 en-suite, 3 public,
4 private showers

Bed & breakfast per night:

	£min	£max
Single	22.00	28.00
Double	44.00	56.00

Half board per person:

	£min	£max
Daily	29.00	35.00
Weekly	173.00	217.00

Lunch available
Evening meal 1800 (last orders
1900)
Parking for 25
Open April–October
Cards accepted: Diners, Mastercard,
Visa, Switch/Delta

WHEDDON CROSS

Somerset
Map ref 1D1

Crossroads hamlet in the heart of
Exmoor National Park.

Exmoor House ᴍ

👑👑👑 HIGHLY COMMENDED

Wheddon Cross TA24 7DU
☎ (01643) 841432
Fax (01643) 841432
*Edwardian house. Elegant spacious
accommodation. Excellent meals from
local produce. Good wines. Exclusively
for non-smokers. Perfect centre for
touring and walking in Exmoor
National Park.*
Bedrooms: 2 double, 3 twin, 1 triple
Bathrooms: 4 en-suite, 2 private,
1 public

Bed & breakfast per night:

	£min	£max
Single	31.00	32.00
Double	42.00	44.00

Half board per person:

	£min	£max
Daily	34.50	35.50
Weekly	217.00	224.00

Evening meal 1900 (last orders
1800)
Parking for 9
Open March–November
Cards accepted: Mastercard, Visa,
Switch/Delta

The Rest And Be Thankful Inn ᴍ

👑👑👑 HIGHLY COMMENDED

Wheddon Cross, Minehead
TA24 7DR
☎ (01643) 841222
Fax (01643) 841222
*Superior accommodation in the heart
of Exmoor. Beautiful walking and
touring base. Restaurant, fine wines,
real ale. Log fires in cooler months.*
Bedrooms: 1 single, 3 double, 1 twin
Bathrooms: 5 en-suite, 1 public

Bed & breakfast per night:

	£min	£max
Single	23.00	26.00
Double	46.00	52.00

Half board per person:

	£min	£max
Daily	33.00	36.00
Weekly	230.00	230.00

Lunch available
Evening meal 1900 (last orders
2200)
Parking for 35

Cards accepted: Amex, Mastercard,
Visa, Switch/Delta

WINSLEY

Wiltshire
Map ref 2B2

Nash House ᴍ

👑👑👑 COMMENDED

Ashley Lane, Winsley,
Bradford-on-Avon BA15 2HR
☎ (01225) 862855
Fax (01225) 862855

*Designer-decorated house of character,
set in tranquil location a few minutes
away from historic Bradford-on-Avon
and a wonderful 6-mile drive through
the Golden Valley to Bath.*
Bedrooms: 1 double, 2 twin
Bathrooms: 2 en-suite, 1 private

Bed & breakfast per night:

	£min	£max
Single	27.00	35.00
Double	54.00	70.00

Half board per person:

	£min	£max
Daily	37.00	45.00

Evening meal 1900 (last orders
2000)
Parking for 6

ACCESSIBILITY

Look for the 🧑‍🦽🧑‍🦽🚶 symbols
which indicate accessibility for
wheelchair users. These are
described in detail at the
front of this guide.

Information on
accommodation listed in this
guide has been supplied by the
proprietors. As changes may
occur you are advised to check
details at the time of booking.

WOOKEY

Somerset
Map ref 2A2

Small village below the southern slopes of the Mendips, near the River Axe. A mile or so north-east, the river runs through spectacular limestone caverns at Wookey Hole.

Worth House Hotel

🏚🏚 COMMENDED

Worth, Wookey, Wells BA5 1LW
☎ (01749) 672041
Fax (01749) 672041

Small country hotel, dating from the 16th C, 2 miles from Wells on the B3139. Exposed beams and log fires.
Bedrooms: 1 single, 3 double, 2 twin, 1 family room
Bathrooms: 7 en-suite

Bed & breakfast

per night:	£min	£max
Single	20.00	
Double	34.00	

Half board per

person:	£min	£max
Daily	27.50	
Weekly	160.00	

Lunch available
Evening meal 1900 (last orders 1900)
Parking for 20
Cards accepted: Mastercard, Visa, Switch/Delta

🏇🍺🖵♨🏮📷⚓🍴🕊⛱📺🖳🖴❀🐾🚐♨ SP 🗓 T

WOOKEY HOLE

Somerset
Map ref 2A2

A series of spectacular limestone caverns on the southern slopes of the Mendips, near the source of the River Axe. The river flows through elaborate formations of stalactites and stalagmites.

Glencot House 🅜

🏚🏚🏚 HIGHLY COMMENDED

Glencot Lane, Wookey Hole, Wells BA5 1BH
☎ (01749) 677160
Fax (01749) 670210

Elegant country house in idyllic setting with river frontage. Small indoor pool, sauna, snooker and table-tennis.
Bedrooms: 3 single, 8 double, 2 twin
Bathrooms: 13 en-suite

Bed & breakfast

per night:	£min	£max
Single	56.00	
Double	80.00	95.00

Half board per

person:	£min	£max
Daily	60.00	68.00

Lunch available
Evening meal 1830 (last orders 2030)
Parking for 21
Cards accepted: Amex, Mastercard, Visa

🏇🍺🍴📞📧🖵♨🏮📷⚓🍴🕊⛱📺 🖳🖴🗓35 ❀🔍❀🔔🎵🐾❀ SP 🏮

WOOLACOMBE

Devon
Map ref 1C1

Between Morte Point and Baggy Point, Woolacombe and Mortehoe offer 3 miles of the finest sand and surf on this outstanding coastline. Much of the area is owned by the National Trust.

Crossways Hotel

🏚🏚🏚 HIGHLY COMMENDED

The Esplanade, Woolacombe
EX34 7DJ
☎ (01271) 870395
Fax (01271) 870395
Friendly, family-run hotel in quiet seafront position overlooking Combesgate beach and Lundy. Personal service, menu choice. Children and pets welcome.
Bedrooms: 1 single, 3 double, 2 twin, 3 family rooms
Bathrooms: 6 en-suite, 1 public, 1 private shower

Bed & breakfast

per night:	£min	£max
Single	20.00	27.00
Double	40.00	54.00

Half board per

person:	£min	£max
Daily	25.00	32.00
Weekly	170.00	213.00

Lunch available

Evening meal 1830 (last orders 1830)
Parking for 10
Open March–October

🏇🍺🖵📷⚓🍴🕊⛱🖴🚐🐾 DAP SP

Little Beach Hotel 🅜

🏚🏚🏚 HIGHLY COMMENDED

The Esplanade, Woolacombe
EX34 7DJ
☎ (01271) 870398
Fax (01271) 870051
Elegant family-run hotel with superb seafront location. Renowned for comfort and cuisine. Ideal for the walker or just to relax.
Bedrooms: 2 single, 7 double, 1 twin
Bathrooms: 8 en-suite, 1 public

Bed & breakfast

per night:	£min	£max
Single	30.00	35.00
Double	72.00	104.00

Half board per

person:	£min	£max
Daily	40.00	45.00
Weekly	250.00	280.00

Evening meal 1915 (last orders 2000)
Parking for 5
Open March–October
Cards accepted: Mastercard, Visa

🏇🍺6🍴📧🖵♨🏮🕊⛱🖴⚓🚗U❀ 🚐🐾 SP

Narracott Grand Hotel 🅜

🏚🏚🏚🏚 APPROVED

Beach Road, Woolacombe
EX34 7BS
☎ (01271) 870418
Fax (01271) 870600
Superbly situated seafront hotel with extensive leisure facilities, ideal for family holidays, breaks and large parties.
Bedrooms: 11 single, 24 double, 6 twin, 41 triple, 18 family rooms
Bathrooms: 100 en-suite, 5 public

Bed & breakfast

per night:	£min	£max
Single	16.00	34.00
Double	32.00	68.00

Half board per

person:	£min	£max
Daily	24.00	44.00
Weekly	152.00	278.00

Evening meal 1800 (last orders 2030)
Parking for 140
Open February–December
Cards accepted: Mastercard, Visa, Switch/Delta

🏇1🍴📧🖵♨🏮📷⚓🍴📺🎯🖀🖴 🖴🗓180❀🔍🛥🎿U🏌❀🏇🐾 SP T

WOOLACOMBE

Continued

Pebbles Hotel and Restaurant 🄼

👑👑👑 APPROVED

Combesgate Beach, Mortehoe,
Woolacombe EX34 7EA
☎ (01271) 870426
Email: Keith.spears@virgin.net
*Family-run hotel with
restaurant-standard cuisine. Adjoining
National Trust land, with spectacular
views of sea and coast and direct
access to beach. Short breaks
available.*
Bedrooms: 1 single, 6 double, 1 twin,
3 family rooms
Bathrooms: 10 en-suite, 1 private

Bed & breakfast

per night:	£min	£max
Single	23.00	25.00
Double	46.00	50.00

Half board per

person:	£min	£max
Daily	33.00	35.00
Weekly	176.00	231.00

Lunch available
Evening meal 1900 (last orders
2030)
Open February–October
Cards accepted: Mastercard, Visa,
Switch/Delta

YELVERTON

Devon
Map ref 1C2

Village on the edge of Dartmoor,
where ponies wander over the flat
common. Buckland Abbey is 2 miles
south-west, while Burrator
Reservoir is 2 miles to the east.

Blowiscombe Barton 🄼

👑👑👑 COMMENDED

Milton Combe, Yelverton PL20 6HR
☎ (01822) 854853
Fax (01822) 854853
*Modernised farmhouse surrounded by
rolling farmland. Beautiful garden and
heated swimming pool. Close village
pub and Dartmoor National Park.
Plymouth/Tavistock 8 miles.*
Bedrooms: 2 double, 1 twin
Bathrooms: 3 en-suite, 1 public

Bed & breakfast

per night:	£min	£max
Single	22.00	25.00
Double	38.00	40.00

Half board per

person:	£min	£max
Daily	30.00	34.00

Evening meal 1830 (last orders
1200)
Parking for 6
Cards accepted: Mastercard, Visa

Harrabeer Country House Hotel

👑👑👑 COMMENDED

Harrowbeer Lane, Yelverton
PL20 6EA
☎ (01822) 853302
Fax (01822) 853302
*Delightful country house hotel, formerly
a Devon longhouse, set in secluded
gardens. Specialising in good food,
comfort and hospitality.*
Bedrooms: 1 single, 4 double, 2 twin
Bathrooms: 4 en-suite, 1 private,
1 public

Bed & breakfast

per night:	£min	£max
Single	19.00	24.00
Double	40.00	53.00

Half board per

person:	£min	£max
Daily	28.00	35.50
Weekly	185.50	234.50

Evening meal 1930 (last orders
2100)
Parking for 7
Cards accepted: Mastercard, Visa

CHECK THE MAPS

The colour maps at the back of this guide show

all the cities, towns and villages for which you will

find accommodation entries.

Refer to the town index to find the page

on which it is listed.

SOUTH OF ENGLAND

England's south is ideal for a coast and countryside holiday. Enjoy the lively resorts of Poole and Swanage, or visit Portsmouth, at the heart of England's ancient naval heritage. Then it's a short trip to the delightful Isle of Wight or inland to the lovely New Forest.

The region's packed with English tradition. Historic cities include magnificent Oxford, Windsor and Winchester - home of King Arthur's Round Table. The recently-restored Kennet and Avon canal and nearby waterways offer trips in a traditional horse-drawn canal boat. And attractive spots can be found all along the Thames, perfect for a picnic lunch.

Henley Regatta and the Ascot race meeting are just two of the area's famed annual events.

The counties of Berkshire, Buckinghamshire, Dorset (Eastern), Hampshire, Isle of Wight and Oxfordshire

FOR MORE INFORMATION CONTACT:
Southern Tourist Board
40 Chamberlayne Road, Eastleigh,
Hampshire SO50 5JH
Tel: (01703) 620555 **Fax:** (01703) 620010

Where to Go in the South of England –
see pages 436-439
Where to Stay in the South of England –
see pages 440-482

SOUTH OF ENGLAND

Where to Go and What to See

You will find hundreds of interesting places to visit during your stay in the South of England, just some of which are listed in these pages. The number against each name will help you locate it on the map (page 439). Contact any Tourist Information Centre in the region for more ideas on days out in the South of England.

1 Blenheim Palace
Woodstock,
Oxfordshire OX20 1PX
Tel: (01993) 811091
Home of the 11th Duke of Marlborough. Birthplace of Sir Winston Churchill. Designed by Vanbrugh in the English baroque style. Landscaped by Capability Brown.

2 Waterperry Gardens
Waterperry,
Oxford OX33 1JZ
Tel: (01844) 339254
Ornamental gardens covering six acres of the 83-acre 18thC Waterperry House estate. Saxon village church, garden shop, teashop, art and craft gallery.

3 Sheldonian Theatre
Broad Street, Oxford OX1 3AZ
Tel: (01865) 277299
One of Sir Christopher Wren's earliest works. Built in 1664-1669 it is the Ceremonial Hall of the University.

4 Didcot Railway Centre
Great Western Society,
Didcot, Oxfordshire OX11 7NJ
Tel: (01235) 817200
Living museum recreating the golden age of the Great Western Railway. Steam locomotives and trains, engine shed and small relics museum.

5 Bekonscot Model Village
Warwick Road, Beaconsfield,
Buckinghamshire HP9 2PL
Tel: (01494) 672919
A complete model village of the 1930s, with outdoor gauge 1 model railway. The world's first model village with zoo, cinema, minster, cricket match and 1,400 inhabitants.

6 Legoland Windsor
Winkfield Road, Windsor,
Berkshire SL4 4AY
Tel: (0990) 626375
A unique family park with hands-on activities, rides, themed playscapes and more Lego bricks than you ever dreamed possible.

7 The Vyne
Sherborne St John, Basingstoke,
Hampshire RG24 9HL
Tel: (01256) 881337
*Original house dating back to
Henry VIII's time, extensively
altered in the mid 17thC. Tudor
chapel, beautiful gardens and lake.*

8 Whitchurch Silk Mill
28 Winchester Street,
Whitchurch,
Hampshire RG28 7AL
Tel: (01256) 893882
*A working silk mill situated on Frog
Island on the River Test. See
historic looms weaving silk,
waterwheel powering machinery,
video on silk production.*

9 Jane Austen's House
Chawton, Alton, Hampshire
GU34 1SD Tel: (01420) 83262
*17thC house where Jane Austen
lived from 1809-1817 and wrote or
revised her six great novels. Letters,
pictures, memorabilia, garden with
old fashioned flowers.*

10 Gilbert White's House and Garden and The Oates Museum
The Wakes, High Street,
Selborne, Alton,
Hampshire GU34 3JH
Tel: (01420) 511275
*Historic house and garden, home of
Gilbert White, author of* The
Natural History of Selborne.
*Exhibition on Frank Oates, explorer,
and Captain Lawrence Oates of
Antarctic fame.*

11 The Sir Harold Hillier Gardens and Arboretum
Jermyns Lane, Ampfield, Romsey,
Hampshire SO51 0QA
Tel: (01794) 368787
*The largest collection of trees and
shrubs of its kind in the British Isles,
planted within an attractive
landscape of over 166 acres.
Rhododendrons, camellias and other
plants.*

12 Marwell Zoological Park
Colden Common,
Winchester,
Hampshire SO21 1JH
Tel: (01962) 777407
*Conservation zoo set in 100 acres
of parkland with over 150 rare
species including Siberian tiger,
jaguar, hippo and rhino. Road and
rail trains, children's amusements
and restaurant.*

13 Broadlands
Romsey,
Hampshire SO51 9ZD
Tel: (01794) 517888
*Home of late Lord Mountbatten.
Magnificent 18thC house and
contents. Superb views across the
River Test. Mountbatten exhibition
and audio-visual presentation.*

14 The Dorset Heavy Horse Centre
Grains Hill, Edmondsham,
Verwood, Wimborne
Minster,
Dorset BH21 5RJ
Tel: (01202) 824040
*Various breeds of heavy
horses plus miniature and
shetland ponies. Old farm
wagons and implements.
Demonstrations of plaiting
and harnessing. Information,
pets and aviaries.*

15 New Forest Nature Quest
Longdown,
Ashurst,
Southampton
SO4 4UH
Tel: (01703)
292166
*Situated in a beautiful
part of the New
Forest, this is your
chance to become
a nature detective
and discover
Britain's wealth of wildlife.*

16 The New Forest Owl Sanctuary
Crow Lane, Crow,
Ringwood, Hampshire BH24 1EA
Tel: (01425) 476487
*All the barn owls are destined to be
released into the wild. The
sanctuary includes an incubation
room, hospital unit and 100
aviaries of various sizes.*

17 Royal Signals Museum
Blandford Camp,
Blandford Forum,
Dorset DT11 8RH
Tel: (01258) 482248
*History of army communication
from Crimean War to Gulf War.
Vehicles, uniforms, medals and
badges on display.*

437

18 National Motor Museum
John Montagu Building,
Beaulieu, Brockenhurst,
Hampshire SO42 7ZN
Tel: (01590) 612345
*Motor museum with over 250
exhibits showing the history of
motoring from 1895. Palace House,
Wheels Experience, abbey ruins,
and a display of monastic life.*

**19 The D Day Museum and
Overlord Embroidery**
Clarence Esplanade,
Portsmouth PO5 3NT
Tel: (01705) 827261/875276
*Incorporates Overlord Embroidery
depicting allied invasion of
Normandy. Displays of D-Day
action with some of the vehicles
that took part.*

20 HMS Victory
HM Naval Base,
Portsmouth PO1 3LJ
Tel: (01705) 839766/295252
*Vice Admiral Lord Nelson's flagship
at Trafalgar. See his cabin, the
'cockpit' where he died. Memorable
tours of the sombre gun decks
where men lived.*

**21 Mary Rose Ship Hall &
Exhibition**
HM Naval Base,
Portsmouth PO1 3PZ
Tel: (01705) 812931
*See the restoration and
conservation of Henry VIII's warship
exhibition. Plus the ship's treasures
with film and slide presentation on
the sinking and raising of the Mary
Rose.*

22 Bembridge Windmill
High Street, Bembridge,
Isle of Wight PO35 5SQ
Tel: (01983) 873945
*Dating from 1700, it is the only
remaining windmill on the Island.
Last used in 1913 it contains much
of its original wooden machinery.
Delightful views from the Cap.*

**23 Butterfly World and
Fountain World**
Staplers Road, Wootton,
Isle of Wight PO33 4RW
Tel: (01983) 883430
*Tropical indoor garden with
butterflies from around the world.
Many fountains, water features and
huge fish. Italian and Japanese
garden.*

**24 Barton Manor Gardens and
Vineyards**
Whippingham, East Cowes,
Isle of Wight PO32 6LB
Tel: (01983) 292835/293923
*Vineyard, 20-acre gardens, wine
bar, shop. Island's largest rose
maze, art and music memorabilia
collection.*

25 Osborne House
East Cowes,
Isle of Wight PO32 6JY
Tel: (01983) 200022
*Queen Victoria and Prince Albert's
seaside holiday home. Swiss Cottage
where royal children learnt cooking
and gardening. Victorian carriage
service to the cottage.*

**26 Calbourne Watermill and
Rural Museum**
Newport,
Isle of Wight PO30 4JN
Tel: (01983) 531227
*Fine example of an early 17thC
watermill still in working order.
Granary, waterwheel, water and
pea fowl.*

27 The Needles Pleasure Park
Alum Bay,
Isle of Wight PO39 0JD
Tel: (01983) 752401
*Chairlift to beach. Famous coloured
sand cliffs. Glasswork studio. View
of Needles lighthouse. Adventure
playground. Super X motion
simulator and carousel. Vision 180
cinema.*

**28 The Alice in Wonderland
Family Park**
Merritown Lane,
Hurn, Christchurch,
Dorset BH23 6BA
Tel: (01202) 483444
*Hedge maze, Mad Hatter's
restaurant, Queen of Hearts
croquet lawn, Cheshire Cat's
adventure playground, Duchess'
rose and herb garden, Alice
Theatre, Alice shop, animals.*

WARWICKSHIRE

HEREFORD & WORCESTER

NORTHANTS

- Newport Pagnell
- Cropredy
- Wolverton
- Banbury
- Buckingham
- Milton Keynes
- Chipping Norton
- Bletchley

BEDS

- Bicester
- **BUCKINGHAM-SHIRE**
- **1** Woodstock
- Witney
- Waterperry **2**
- Aylesbury
- Wendover
- Oxford **3**
- Thame
- Chesham

GLOUCESTERSHIRE

OXFORDSHIRE

- Faringdon
- Abingdon
- Princes Risborough
- High Wycombe
- Wantage
- Didcot
- Wallingford
- Beaconsfield **5**
- Henley on-Thames
- Marlow
- Slough
- Maidenhead
- **6**
- Windsor

BERKSHIRE

- Twyford
- Hungerford
- Newbury
- Reading
- Wokingham
- Bracknell

WILTSHIRE

- Stratfield Saye
- Farnborough
- Sherborne St John **7**
- Fleet
- Aldershot
- Whitchurch **8**
- Basingstoke

SURREY

HAMPSHIRE

- Alton
- Chawton **9**
- **10**
- Winchester
- Selborne
- Liss
- Ampfield
- Colden Common
- Petersfield
- Romsey **13** **11** **12**
- Eastleigh
- Gillingham
- Southampton
- Shaftesbury
- Fordingbridge
- Totton
- Waterlooville

WEST SUSSEX

DORSET (eastern)

- **14**
- Verwood
- Ashurst **15**
- Locks Heath
- Ringwood **16**
- Brockenhurst
- Fawley
- Lee-on-the-Solent
- Blandford Forum **17**
- Wimborne Minster
- West Moors
- Beaulieu **18**
- Gosport
- **19** **20**
- Lymington
- East Cowes
- Ryde
- **21** Portsmouth
- Poole **30** **29**
- **28**
- Newport **25**
- **26**
- Whippingham
- Christchurch
- Yarmouth
- **24**
- **22** Bembridge
- Bournemouth
- Alum Bay **27**
- Wootton
- **23**
- Sandown
- Swanage
- **ISLE OF WIGHT**
- Shanklin
- Ventnor

0   20 Miles

---

29 Compton Acres

Canford Cliffs Road, Poole,
Dorset BH13 7ES
Tel: (01202) 700778
*Nine separate and distinct gardens
of the world. The gardens include
Italian, Japanese, sub tropical glen,
rock, water and heather garden.
Collection of statues.*

30 Poole Pottery

The Quay, Poole,
Dorset BH15 1RF
Tel: (01202) 666200
*Factory tour, self-guided commentary
includes museum, cinema, factory
and craft area where visitors can
'have a go'. Craft village, throwing,
painting, plus craft demonstrations.*

FIND OUT MORE

Further information about
holidays and attractions in the
South of England is available
from:
Southern Tourist Board,
40 Chamberlayne Road,
Eastleigh, Hampshire SO50 5JH.
Tel: (01703) 620555

WHERE TO STAY (SOUTH OF ENGLAND)

Accommodation entries in this region are listed in alphabetical order of place name, and then in alphabetical order of establishment.

Map references refer to the colour location maps at the back of this guide. The first number indicates the map to use; the letter and number which follow refer to the grid reference on the map.

At-a-glance symbols at the end of each accommodation entry give useful information about services and facilities. A key to symbols can be found inside the back cover flap. Keep this open for easy reference.

ADDERBURY

Oxfordshire
Map ref 2C1

Village with fine ironstone houses set around a green. Its Perpendicular church has a magnificent spire.

Red Lion Inn

☺☺☺☺ COMMENDED

The Green, Oxford Road, Adderbury, Banbury OX17 3LU
☎ (01295) 810269
Fax (01295) 811906
16th C coaching inn with superb rooms, restaurant and conference facility. A4260 Banbury-Oxford road. Junction 11, M40, Banbury.
Bedrooms: 2 single, 9 double, 3 twin
Bathrooms: 14 en-suite, 1 public

Bed & breakfast

per night:	£min	£max
Single	49.50	51.50
Double	67.00	69.50

Lunch available
Evening meal 1900 (last orders 2200)
Parking for 30
Cards accepted: Amex, Diners, Mastercard, Visa, Switch/Delta

⌖♿⚲ℂ⌂☐♦⬡§⚒▦▥
🚗⌘30▸✻⚘ SP ⋒ ◉

Information on accommodation listed in this guide has been supplied by the proprietors. As changes may occur you are advised to check details at the time of booking.

ALRESFORD

Hampshire
Map ref 2C2

Between Old and New Alresford lie the remains of Bishop de Lucy's splendid 12th C reservoir. New Alresford is a pleasant market town and Old Alresford a smaller village with a stream running through the green.

The Swan Hotel 🅜

☺☺☺☺ COMMENDED

11 West Street, Alresford
SO24 9AD
☎ (01962) 732302 & 734427
Fax (01962) 735274
Warm and friendly, 18th C coaching inn.
Bedrooms: 1 single, 14 double, 5 twin, 3 family rooms
Bathrooms: 23 en-suite, 1 public

Bed & breakfast

per night:	£min	£max
Single	35.00	40.00
Double	45.00	55.00

Half board per

person:	£min	£max
Daily	47.50	52.50

Lunch available
Evening meal 1830 (last orders 2130)
Parking for 70
Cards accepted: Mastercard, Visa, Switch/Delta

⌖♿⛭ℂ⌂☐♦⬡§⚒▦🚗
⛾100⋃▸✻⚘ OAP ⋒ ⋒ ⊤

ANDOVER

Hampshire
Map ref 2C2

Town that achieved importance from the wool trade and now has much modern development. A good centre for visiting places of interest. *Tourist Information Centre ☎ (01264) 324320*

Amberley Hotel 🅜

☺☺☺ APPROVED

70 Weyhill Road, Andover
SP10 3NP
☎ (01264) 352224
Fax (01264) 392555
Small, comfortably furnished hotel, with attractive restaurant open to non-residents. Private meetings, luncheons and wedding receptions can be booked.
Bedrooms: 6 single, 4 double, 5 twin, 1 triple, 1 family room
Bathrooms: 9 en-suite, 2 public

Bed & breakfast

per night:	£min	£max
Single	29.00	42.00
Double	42.00	52.00

Half board per

person:	£min	£max
Daily	30.00	
Weekly	190.00	

Lunch available
Evening meal 1845 (last orders 2115)
Parking for 16
Cards accepted: Amex, Diners, Mastercard, Visa, Switch/Delta

⌖♿⚲ℂ⌂☐♦⬡§⚒▦▥🚗⌘30
🚌

Amport Inn 🏠

⚜⚜⚜ APPROVED

Amport, Andover SP11 8AE
☎ (01264) 710371
Fax (01264) 710112
*Friendly inn in attractive Hampshire
village, with racecourses, riding and
fishing nearby. Business people
welcome weekdays. Breakaway
weekends available. Sauna and indoor
pool.*
Bedrooms: 3 double, 4 twin, 2 triple
Bathrooms: 9 en-suite, 1 public
**Bed & breakfast
per night:**

	£min	£max
Single	27.50	42.50
Double	35.00	52.50

**Half board per
person:**

	£min	£max
Daily	30.00	50.00

Lunch available
Evening meal 1930 (last orders
2130)
Parking for 54
Cards accepted: Mastercard, Visa
🖥☎🖂🖵♨🛎Ⓢ🅿📺◐🖳⛱
🍴📶14🏊🥢🔍∪🎣☼🐴🆂🅿🏤

Ashley Court Hotel 🏠

⚜⚜⚜ COMMENDED

Micheldever Road, Andover
SP11 6LA
☎ (01264) 357344
Fax (01264) 356755
*Half a mile from town centre, quietly
set in nearly 3 acres of grounds.
Friendly atmosphere, good restaurant,
conference and air conditioned
banqueting facilities.*
Bedrooms: 7 single, 16 double,
12 twin
Bathrooms: 35 en-suite
**Bed & breakfast
per night:**

	£min	£max
Single	39.50	59.50
Double	45.00	85.00

**Half board per
person:**

	£min	£max
Daily	24.50	59.50
Weekly	290.00	425.00

Lunch available
Evening meal 1900 (last orders
2130)
Parking for 80
Cards accepted: Amex, Mastercard,
Visa, Switch/Delta
🖥♨🖂🖵🍴⛱Ⓢ🅿📺🖳
◉🖳🍴📶200∪☼🥢🆂🅿🅣◉

For further information on
accommodation establishments
use the coupons at the
back of this guide.

Buckinghamshire
Map ref 2C1

*Historic county town in the Vale of
Aylesbury. The cobbled market
square has a Victorian clock tower
and the 15th C King's Head Inn
(National Trust). Interesting county
museum and 13th C parish church.
Twice-weekly livestock market.
Tourist Information Centre* ☎ *(01296)
330559*

West Lodge Hotel 🏠

⚜⚜⚜ COMMENDED

45 London Road, Aston Clinton,
Aylesbury HP22 5HL
☎ (01296) 630331 & 630362
Fax (01296) 630151
*Elegant Victorian hotel with
Montgolfier French restaurant. Indoor
swimming, sauna, hot-air balloon trips.
On A41, within 50 minutes of London,
Heathrow and Birmingham and close
to Aylesbury.*
Bedrooms: 2 single, 2 double, 2 twin
Bathrooms: 6 en-suite
**Bed & breakfast
per night:**

	£min	£max
Single	32.00	48.00
Double	60.00	60.00

**Half board per
person:**

	£min	£max
Daily	49.50	65.50
Weekly	346.50	458.50

Evening meal 1900 (last orders
2000)
Parking for 11
Cards accepted: Amex, Diners,
Mastercard, Visa, Switch/Delta
🖥♨8🖵☎🖂🖵♨🛎Ⓢ🅿📺◐🖳
🖳🍴📶12🏊🥢🔍♈☼🥢⛱🏤

Oxfordshire
Map ref 2C1

*Famous for its cattle market, cakes
and nursery rhyme Cross. Founded
in Saxon times, it has some fine
houses and interesting old inns. A
good centre for touring
Warwickshire and the Cotswolds.
Tourist Information Centre* ☎ *(01295)
259855*

Banbury House Hotel

⚜⚜⚜ COMMENDED

Oxford Road, Banbury OX16 9AH
☎ (01295) 259361
Fax (01295) 270954
Email: 100607.2057
@compuserve.com
Ⓒ Consort
Elegant Georgian building with all

*modern facilities. Ideal for touring the
Cotswolds, Stratford-upon-Avon and
Oxford.*
Bedrooms: 16 single, 28 double,
15 twin, 4 triple
Suite available
Bathrooms: 63 en-suite
**Bed & breakfast
per night:**

	£min	£max
Single	35.00	88.50
Double	70.00	107.00

**Half board per
person:**

	£min	£max
Daily	45.00	131.00
Weekly	315.00	917.00

Lunch available
Evening meal 1900 (last orders
2145)
Parking for 40
Cards accepted: Amex, Diners,
Mastercard, Visa, Switch/Delta
🖥♨📺🖵☎🖂🖵♨🛎Ⓢ🅿📺🖳
🖳🖳🍴66🥢🔍🥢⛱🆂🅿🏤🅣

Prospect House Guest House 🏠

⚜⚜ COMMENDED

70 Oxford Road, Banbury
OX16 9AN
☎ (01295) 268749 & 0468 525538
Fax (01295) 268749

*Detached house with lovely grounds, in
the most convenient area of town.*
Bedrooms: 1 single, 6 double, 2 twin,
1 triple
Bathrooms: 1 en-suite, 9 private,
1 public
**Bed & breakfast
per night:**

	£min	£max
Single	30.00	35.00
Double	40.00	45.00

Parking for 10
Cards accepted: Amex, Mastercard,
Visa
🖥♨🖂🖵☎🛎Ⓢ🔍🥢📺🖳🖳⛱
🥢🏤🆂🅣

The symbols in each entry
give information about
services and facilities.
A key to these symbols
appears at the back
of this guide.

BARTON ON SEA

Hampshire
Map ref 2B3

Seaside village with views of the Isle of Wight. Within easy driving distance of the New Forest.

The Old Coastguard Hotel ♠

👑 COMMENDED

53 Marine Drive East, Barton on Sea, New Milton BH25 7DX
☎ (01425) 612987
Fax (01425) 612987
Peaceful clifftop hotel close to the New Forest, with excellent cuisine and personal service in a friendly atmosphere. Some ground floor rooms.
Bedrooms: 1 single, 3 double, 3 twin
Bathrooms: 7 en-suite, 1 public

Bed & breakfast

per night:	£min	£max
Single	30.00	
Double	55.00	

Half board per person:

	£min	£max
Daily	41.75	
Weekly	277.00	

Evening meal 1900 (last orders 1800)
Parking for 10
Cards accepted: Mastercard, Visa, Switch/Delta

🐎 12 🔓 ♿ 🖵 👤 🗄 🟦 🔏 🛏 📺 🚗 ☀ 🐕
🐎 SP T

BASINGSTOKE

Hampshire
Map ref 2C2

Rapidly developing commercial and industrial centre. The town is surrounded by charming villages and places to visit.
Tourist Information Centre ☎ *(01256) 817618*

Cedar Court

👑👑 COMMENDED

Reading Road, Hook, Basingstoke RG27 9DB
☎ (01256) 762178
Fax (01256) 762178
Comfortable ground floor accommodation with delightful gardens. On B3349 between the M3 and M4, 6 miles east of Basingstoke, 1 hour from London and the coast.
Bedrooms: 2 single, 3 double, 1 twin
Bathrooms: 5 en-suite, 1 public

Bed & breakfast

per night:	£min	£max
Single	22.00	31.00
Double	36.00	39.50

Parking for 6
Cards accepted: Mastercard, Visa

🐎 🔓 🖵 👤 ♿ UL 🔏 📺 🛏 ☀ 🐕 🚗

The Centrecourt Hotel & Tennis & Health Club ♠

👑👑👑👑 HIGHLY COMMENDED

Centre Drive, Chineham, Basingstoke RG24 8FY
☎ (01256) 816664
Fax (01256) 816727
Hotel is complemented by a superb purpose-built tennis centre, including 5 indoor and 5 outdoor tennis courts, indoor heated pool, spa bath, steam room, sauna and gym.
Bedrooms: 24 double, 26 twin
Bathrooms: 50 en-suite

Bed & breakfast per night

	£min	£max
Single	60.00	95.00
Double	60.00	110.00

Half board per person:

	£min	£max
Daily	95.00	

Lunch available
Evening meal 1900 (last orders 2130)
Parking for 123
Cards accepted: Amex, Diners, Mastercard, Visa, Switch/Delta

🐎 ♿ 📞 🖵 👤 🟦 🔏 📺 🌐 ⊞
🛏 🖨 ♟ 100 🎱 🎯 🏹 🎣 🚶 U DAP 🏊 SP
T

Fernbank Hotel ♠

👑👑 HIGHLY COMMENDED

4 Fairfields Road, Basingstoke RG21 3DR
☎ (01256) 321191
Fax (01256) 321191
Extremely well-appointed family-run hotel, full of character. In residential area within a short walk of town's facilities. Charming conservatory/lounge. First class breakfast.
Bedrooms: 8 single, 6 double, 2 twin
Bathrooms: 16 en-suite

Bed & breakfast per night:

	£min	£max
Single	47.00	57.00
Double	54.00	62.00

Parking for 18
Cards accepted: Mastercard, Visa, Switch/Delta

🐎 ♿ 📞 🖵 👤 ♿ 🟦 S 🔏 🛏 📺 🛏
🖨 ♟ ✈ T

All accommodation in this guide has been graded, or is awaiting a grading, by a trained Tourist Board inspector.

BEACONSFIELD

Buckinghamshire
Map ref 2C2

Former coaching town with several inns still surviving. The old town has many fine houses and an interesting church. Beautiful countryside and beech woods nearby.

Highclere Farm ♠

👑 COMMENDED

Newbarn Lane, Seer Green, Beaconsfield HP9 2QZ
☎ (01494) 875665 & 874505
Fax (01494) 875238
En-suite twin-bedded rooms with views to horse paddock. Quiet location, close to M25, M40 and only half an hour by train to London (Marylebone).
Bedrooms: 1 single, 6 twin, 2 family rooms
Bathrooms: 9 en-suite

Bed & breakfast per night:

	£min	£max
Single	35.00	45.00
Double	48.00	56.00

Parking for 12
Open January, March–December
Cards accepted: Mastercard, Visa, Switch/Delta

🐎 ♿ 📞 🖵 👤 ♿ UL 🔏 🛏 🖨 U ☀
🐕 🚗 ⊚

BICESTER

Oxfordshire
Map ref 2C1

Market town with large army depot and well-known hunting centre with hunt established in the late 18th C. The ancient parish church displays work of many periods. Nearby is the Jacobean mansion of Rousham House with gardens landscaped by William Kent.
Tourist Information Centre ☎ *(01869) 369055*

Littlebury Hotel ♠

👑👑👑 COMMENDED

Kings End, Bicester OX6 7DR
☎ (01869) 252595
Fax (01869) 253225
Family-owned and run town centre hotel in quiet location with plenty of parking, offering fine food and hospitality.
Bedrooms: 5 single, 5 double, 16 twin, 2 triple, 7 family rooms
Bathrooms: 35 en-suite

Bed & breakfast per night:

	£min	£max
Single	51.50	58.50
Double	68.50	75.50

Half board per person:	£min	£max
Daily	57.50	74.50

Lunch available
Evening meal 1900 (last orders 2200)
Parking for 52
Cards accepted: Amex, Diners, Mastercard, Visa, Switch/Delta

🛏🔥🛎📧⌨♥🦢📶🛇⚡👪📺🖥 ☎👗100🅿❄🌙 DAP 🚭 SP T

BLANDFORD FORUM

Dorset
Map ref 2B3

Almost completely destroyed by fire in 1731, the town was rebuilt in a handsome Georgian style. The church is large and grand and the town is the hub of a rich farming area.
Tourist Information Centre ☎ (01258) 454770

Anvil Hotel & Restaurant ⚔

👑👑👑 COMMENDED

Salisbury Road, Pimperne, Blandford Forum DT11 8UQ
☎ (01258) 453431 & 480182
Fax (01258) 480182
Picturesque 16th C thatched, fully licensed hotel. Separate beamed a la carte restaurant with log fire. Mouth-watering menu with delicious desserts. Comprehensive tasty bar meals. Clay pigeon tuition.
Bedrooms: 2 single, 6 double, 2 twin, 1 triple
Bathrooms: 11 en-suite

Bed & breakfast per night:	£min	£max
Single	45.00	47.50
Double	70.00	75.00

Lunch available
Evening meal 1900 (last orders 2145)
Parking for 25
Cards accepted: Amex, Diners, Mastercard, Visa, Switch/Delta

🛏☎📧⌨♥🦢📶🛇⚡🌙🖥☎26 U ♫▶✓❄🌙 SP T

Please mention this guide when making your booking.

Half board prices are given per person, but in some cases these may be based on double/twin occupancy.

Crown Hotel ⚔

👑👑👑👑 COMMENDED

1 West Street, Blandford Forum DT11 7AJ
☎ (01258) 456626
Fax (01258) 451084
CR Consort

Original Georgian coaching hotel built in 1756, overlooking watermeadows on the southern edge of town. Half board prices based on minimum 2-night stay.
Bedrooms: 12 single, 7 double, 11 twin, 2 family rooms
Bathrooms: 32 en-suite

Bed & breakfast per night:	£min	£max
Single	50.00	64.00
Double	60.00	75.00

Half board per person:	£min	£max
Daily	40.00	45.00

Lunch available
Evening meal 1915 (last orders 2115)
Parking for 255
Cards accepted: Amex, Diners, Mastercard, Visa, Switch/Delta

🛏🍴☎📧⌨♥🦢📶🛇⚡🌙🖥 ☎250♪❄🌙 SP 🏛 T

BONCHURCH

Isle of Wight
Map ref 2C3

Sheltered suburb at the foot of St Boniface Down.

The Lake Hotel

👑👑👑 COMMENDED

Shore Road, Bonchurch, Ventnor PO38 1RF
☎ (01983) 852613
Fax (01983) 852613
Charming country house hotel set in 2 acres of beautiful gardens, in secluded situation 400 metres from beach. In the old world village of Bonchurch.
Bedrooms: 9 double, 4 twin, 4 triple, 3 family rooms
Bathrooms: 20 en-suite, 3 public

Bed & breakfast per night:	£min	£max
Single	22.50	30.00
Double	45.00	60.00

Half board per person:	£min	£max
Daily	30.00	35.00
Weekly	190.00	205.00

Evening meal 1830 (last orders 1900)
Parking for 20
Open March–October

🛏☎3🍴📧⌨♥🦢📶🛇⚡🌙📺🖥 ☎▶❄🚲 DAP SP 🏛 T

Leconfield Hotel

👑👑👑 COMMENDED

85 Leeson Road, Upper Bonchurch, Bonchurch, Ventnor PO38 1PU
☎ (01983) 852196
Fax (01983) 852196
Small, comfortable hotel, with heated outdoor pool, superb sea views and informal, relaxing atmosphere. Restaurant with extensive wine list and freehouse bar. All rooms en-suite and non-smoking.
Bedrooms: 6 double, 2 twin, 1 triple, 3 family rooms
Bathrooms: 12 en-suite

Bed & breakfast per night:	£min	£max
Single	23.00	35.50
Double	46.00	71.00

Half board per person:	£min	£max
Daily	30.00	42.50
Weekly	210.00	297.50

Lunch available
Evening meal 1900 (last orders 2000)
Parking for 20
Cards accepted: Mastercard, Visa, Switch/Delta

🛏🔥⌨♥🦢📶🛇⚡🌙🖥☎❄🌟✗ 🚲 DAP 🚭 SP T

BOURNEMOUTH

Dorset
Map ref 2B3

Seaside town set among the pines with a mild climate, sandy beaches and fine coastal views. The town has wide streets with excellent shops, a pier, a pavilion, museums and conference centre.
Tourist Information Centre ☎ (01202) 451700

Acorns Hotel

👑👑👑 COMMENDED

14 Southwood Avenue, Southbourne, Bournemouth BH6 3QA
☎ (01202) 422438
Family-run hotel, all rooms en-suite with TV. Good food. Only 5 minutes from sea.
Bedrooms: 1 single, 2 double, 1 twin, 2 triple
Bathrooms: 6 en-suite, 1 public

Continued ▶

BOURNEMOUTH

Continued

Bed & breakfast

per night:	£min	£max
Single	15.00	20.00
Double	30.00	40.00

Half board per

person:	£min	£max
Daily	21.00	27.00
Weekly	130.00	165.00

Evening meal 1800 (last orders 1800)
Parking for 5
Open March–October

⛵🛏6🖵💺⚒🖭📺🖵🚗✕🚚 DAP
SP

Arlington Hotel ▲▲

👑👑👑 COMMENDED

Exeter Park Road, Lower Gardens,
Bournemouth BH2 5BD
☎ (01202) 552879 & 553012
Fax (01202) 298317
*Family-run hotel overlooking
Bournemouth pine gardens. 100
metres traffic-free, level walk to square,
beach, shops and Bournemouth
International Centre.*
Bedrooms: 4 single, 11 double,
9 twin, 4 triple
Bathrooms: 27 en-suite, 1 public

Bed & breakfast

per night:	£min	£max
Single	28.00	34.00
Double	56.00	68.00

Half board per

person:	£min	£max
Daily	31.50	41.00
Weekly	208.50	260.00

Lunch available
Evening meal 1830 (last orders
2000)
Parking for 24
Cards accepted: Mastercard, Visa

⛵1🖵🌡🖵💺🛁S⚒🖭📺◐
⬚🖵🚗✕🐾 DAP 🔖 SP T

Audmore Hotel ▲▲

👑👑 COMMENDED

3 Cecil Road, Boscombe,
Bournemouth BH5 1DU
☎ (01202) 395166
*Friendly, family-run licensed hotel only a
few minutes from beach, shops and
theatres.*
Bedrooms: 2 single, 3 double, 1 twin,
2 triple, 2 family rooms
Bathrooms: 6 en-suite, 3 public

Bed & breakfast

per night:	£min	£max
Single	13.00	19.00
Double	26.00	38.00

Half board per

person:	£min	£max
Daily	19.00	25.00
Weekly	99.00	165.00

Evening meal 1800 (last orders
1600)
Parking for 4
Open March–November

⛵🖵💺🛁S⚒🖭📺🖵🚗✕🚚 DAP
SP

Babbacombe Court Hotel ▲▲

👑👑👑 COMMENDED

28 West Hill Road, West Cliff,
Bournemouth BH2 5PG
☎ (01202) 552823 & 551746
Fax (01202) 789030

*Family-run hotel, with good home
cooking. Close to shops, beach and
Bournemouth International Centre.
Ample parking.*
Bedrooms: 4 single, 6 double, 2 twin,
2 triple, 1 family room
Bathrooms: 15 en-suite

Bed & breakfast

per night:	£min	£max
Single	16.00	28.00
Double	38.00	52.00

Half board per

person:	£min	£max
Daily	23.00	35.00
Weekly	155.00	205.00

Evening meal 1800 (last orders
1800)
Parking for 24
Cards accepted: Amex, Diners,
Mastercard, Visa, Switch/Delta

⛵🛏🖵💺🖵🛁S⚒🖭📺🖵🚗
✕✕ DAP SP T

Belvedere Hotel ▲▲

👑👑👑 HIGHLY COMMENDED

Bath Road, Bournemouth BH1 2EU
☎ (01202) 297556
Fax (01202) 294699
Email: 101452.2567
@compuserve.com
*Centrally located with a large car park.
Superb food and friendly service. Ideal
for both business and holidays, offering
high standards all round. Group rates
available on request.*
Bedrooms: 11 single, 25 double,
13 twin, 11 triple, 1 family room
Bathrooms: 61 en-suite

Bed & breakfast

per night:	£min	£max
Single	35.00	52.00
Double	50.00	98.00

Half board per

person:	£min	£max
Daily	35.00	64.50
Weekly	227.50	380.00

Lunch available
Evening meal 1830 (last orders
2100)
Parking for 55
Cards accepted: Amex, Diners,
Mastercard, Visa, Switch/Delta

⛵🛏🌡🖵🚗🖵🛁S⚒◐🖭⬚🖵
🖵⬚180🖵☀✕ DAP 🔖 SP T ◎

Carisbrooke Hotel ▲▲

👑👑👑 COMMENDED

42 Tregonwell Road, Bournemouth
BH2 5NT
☎ (01202) 290432
Fax (01202) 310499
*Modernised traditional family-owned
hotel in excellent central location close
sea and International Centre. High
standards of home cooking, special
diets. Ground floor rooms. Golf holidays
arranged.*
Bedrooms: 3 single, 6 double, 6 twin,
7 triple
Bathrooms: 19 en-suite, 2 public

Bed & breakfast

per night:	£min	£max
Single	19.00	29.00
Double	36.00	56.00

Half board per

person:	£min	£max
Daily	24.00	37.00
Weekly	150.00	220.00

Evening meal 1830 (last orders
1900)
Parking for 19
Cards accepted: Amex, Diners,
Mastercard, Visa, Switch/Delta

⛵🛏🖵🌡🖵💺🛁S⚒🖭📺🖵🖵🚗 DAP
SP T ◎

Cliffeside Hotel

👑👑👑 COMMENDED

East Overcliff Drive, Bournemouth
BH1 3AQ
☎ (01202) 555724
Fax (01202) 555724
*On East Cliff with views to the Isle of
Wight and the Purbeck Hills. Within
easy reach of the town centre.*
Bedrooms: 7 single, 27 double,
23 twin, 1 triple, 3 family rooms
Bathrooms: 61 en-suite

Bed & breakfast

per night:	£min	£max
Single	35.00	49.50
Double	70.00	89.00

Half board per

person:	£min	£max
Daily	39.50	57.50
Weekly		315.00

Lunch available

Evening meal 1845 (last orders 2030)
Parking for 50
Cards accepted: Amex, Diners, Mastercard, Visa, Switch/Delta

The Cottage Hotel

COMMENDED

12 Southern Road, Southbourne, Bournemouth BH6 3SR
☎ (01202) 422764

Charming, character, family-run hotel. Restful location. Noted for home-prepared fresh cooking, cleanliness and tastefully furnished accommodation. Ample parking. Non-smoking.

Bedrooms: 1 single, 1 double, 2 twin, 1 triple, 2 family rooms
Bathrooms: 4 en-suite, 2 public, 1 private shower

Bed & breakfast per night:	£min	£max
Single	18.50	25.00
Double	37.00	46.00
Half board per person:	£min	£max
Daily	26.50	33.00
Weekly	170.00	182.00

Evening meal 1800 (last orders 1800)
Parking for 8
Open March–October

Crosbie Hall Hotel

COMMENDED

21 Florence Road, Boscombe, Bournemouth BH5 1HJ
☎ (01202) 394714
Fax (01202) 394714

Delightful character hotel offering comfort, cleanliness, fine food, friendly atmosphere and good value. Near beach, gardens, shops and transport.

Bedrooms: 3 single, 8 double, 2 twin, 4 triple
Bathrooms: 12 en-suite, 2 public

Bed & breakfast per night:	£min	£max
Single	15.00	19.50
Double	30.00	39.00
Half board per person:	£min	£max
Daily	23.50	27.50
Weekly	139.00	169.00

Evening meal 1800 (last orders 1800)
Parking for 10
Cards accepted: Mastercard, Visa

Cumberland Hotel

COMMENDED

East Overcliff Drive, Bournemouth BH1 3AF
☎ (01202) 290722
Fax (01202) 311394

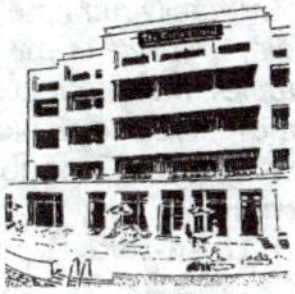

Family hotel on East Cliff overlooking the bay and offering a high standard of service and cuisine for all ages. Complimentary use of nearby indoor leisure facility.

Bedrooms: 12 single, 34 double, 44 twin, 12 triple
Suite available
Bathrooms: 102 en-suite

Bed & breakfast per night:	£min	£max
Single	39.50	51.00
Double	79.00	102.00
Half board per person:	£min	£max
Daily	45.50	58.50
Weekly	269.00	350.00

Lunch available
Evening meal 1900 (last orders 2030)
Parking for 50
Cards accepted: Amex, Diners, Mastercard, Visa, Switch/Delta

Dene Court Hotel

19 Boscombe Spa Road, Bournemouth BH5 1AR
☎ (01202) 394874

Family-run hotel 5 minutes from sandy beach. Good home cooking served in relaxed surroundings. Come as a guest, leave as a friend.

Bedrooms: 1 single, 6 double, 5 twin, 8 triple
Bathrooms: 17 en-suite, 1 public

Bed & breakfast per night:	£min	£max
Single	12.50	22.50
Double	25.00	45.00
Half board per person:	£min	£max
Daily	20.50	28.50

Evening meal 1800 (last orders 1800)
Parking for 12
Cards accepted: Visa

East Cliff Cottage Hotel

APPROVED

57 Grove Road, Bournemouth BH1 3AT
☎ (01202) 552788
Fax (01202) 556400

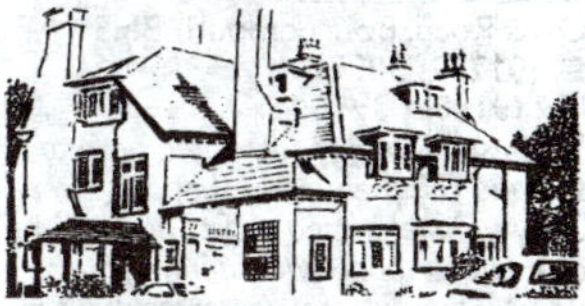

High standard old world hotel in central position. Some sea views. Large family rooms, good food, garden, car park. Long or short stays.

Bedrooms: 1 single, 3 double, 1 twin, 5 triple
Bathrooms: 5 en-suite, 2 public

Bed & breakfast per night:	£min	£max
Single	19.50	27.00
Double	39.00	54.00
Half board per person:	£min	£max
Daily	28.50	36.00
Weekly	148.00	208.00

Evening meal 1830 (last orders 1930)
Parking for 10
Cards accepted: Amex, Mastercard, Visa

Fielden Court Hotel

COMMENDED

20 Southern Road, Southbourne, Bournemouth BH6 3SR
☎ (01202) 427459
Fax (01202) 427459

Relaxing, family-run hotel. All rooms en-suite, with tea/coffee and TV. 3 minutes' walk to clifftop/lift/shops. Licensed. Evening meal optional.

Bedrooms: 1 single, 3 double, 2 twin, 1 triple, 1 family room
Bathrooms: 8 en-suite

Bed & breakfast per night:	£min	£max
Single	15.00	19.00
Double	30.00	38.00
Half board per person:	£min	£max
Daily	20.00	25.00
Weekly	128.00	155.00

Evening meal from 1800
Parking for 6

You are advised to confirm your booking in writing.

BOURNEMOUTH

Continued

Fircroft Hotel

♛♛♛ [COMMENDED]

Owls Road, Bournemouth BH5 1AE
☎ (01202) 309771
Fax (01202) 395644

Long-established family hotel, close to sea and comprehensive shopping. Free entry to hotel-owned sports and leisure club (indoor pool, gym, sauna, squash) 9am - 6pm. Licensed, entertainment in season. Large car park.

Bedrooms: 6 single, 16 double, 12 twin, 16 triple
Bathrooms: 50 en-suite

Bed & breakfast per night:	£min	£max
Single	18.00	28.00
Double	36.00	56.00

Half board per person:	£min	£max
Daily	27.00	36.00
Weekly	175.00	224.00

Lunch available
Evening meal 1830 (last orders 2000)
Parking for 50
Cards accepted: Amex, Diners, Mastercard, Visa, Switch/Delta

☎ [S] [TV] 200 [OAP] [SP] [T]

Highclere Private Hotel

♛♛♛ [COMMENDED]

15 Burnaby Road, Alum Chine, Bournemouth BH4 8JF
☎ (01202) 761350

Small family hotel with ample parking, garden, playroom. Some bedrooms with sea views. Children very welcome at reduced tariff.

Bedrooms: 3 double, 1 twin, 1 triple, 4 family rooms
Bathrooms: 9 en-suite

Bed & breakfast per night:	£min	£max
Single	19.00	24.00
Double	38.00	48.00

Half board per person:	£min	£max
Daily	25.00	30.00
Weekly	150.00	168.00

Evening meal 1800 (last orders 1630)
Parking for 7
Open April–October
Cards accepted: Amex, Diners, Mastercard, Visa, Switch/Delta

3 ☎ [S] [TV] [SP]

Holmcroft Hotel

♛♛♛ [COMMENDED]

Earle Road, Alum Chine, Bournemouth BH4 8JQ
☎ (01202) 761289 & 761395
Fax (01202) 761289

Subtly elegant family-run hotel, quietly situated. Enjoy a choice of menu, all fresh vegetables, within a relaxed, friendly atmosphere. No smoking.

Bedrooms: 2 single, 12 double, 3 twin, 2 triple
Bathrooms: 18 en-suite, 1 private, 1 public

Bed & breakfast per night:	£min	£max
Single	16.00	25.00
Double	38.00	50.00

Half board per person:	£min	£max
Daily	26.00	35.00
Weekly	168.00	210.00

Evening meal 1800 (last orders 1745)
Parking for 12
Cards accepted: Mastercard, Visa

6 ☎ [TV] [OAP] [SP]

Langdale Hotel

♛♛♛ [COMMENDED]

6 Earle Road, Alum Chine, Bournemouth BH4 8JQ
☎ (01202) 761174
Fax (01202) 761174

Quietly located in pine-clad Alum Chine, close to seafront. All rooms en-suite (bath or shower) with TV and radio alarm. Trouble free parking.

Bedrooms: 2 single, 5 double, 2 twin, 1 triple
Bathrooms: 10 en-suite

Bed & breakfast per night:	£min	£max
Single	20.00	24.00
Double	40.00	48.00

Half board per person:	£min	£max
Daily	28.00	30.00
Weekly	160.00	180.00

Evening meal from 1800
Parking for 12
Cards accepted: Mastercard, Visa

[TV] [OAP] [SP] [T]

Marsham Court Hotel

♛♛♛♛ [COMMENDED]

Russell-Cotes Road, East Cliff, Bournemouth BH1 3AB
☎ (01202) 552111
Fax (01202) 294744

Overlooking bay in quiet central situation with sun terraces, outdoor swimming pool. Edwardian bar and summer entertainment. Free accommodation for children. Snooker. Parking.

Bedrooms: 8 single, 23 double, 44 twin, 11 triple
Suites available
Bathrooms: 86 en-suite

Bed & breakfast per night:	£min	£max
Single	43.00	55.00
Double	66.00	112.00

Evening meal 1900 (last orders 2100)
Parking for 100
Cards accepted: Amex, Diners, Mastercard, Visa, Switch/Delta

☎ [S] 200 [OAP] [SP] [T]

Mayfield Private Hotel

♛♛ [COMMENDED]

46 Frances Road, Bournemouth BH1 3SA
☎ (01202) 551839

Overlooking public gardens with tennis, bowling greens, crazy-golf. Central for sea, shops and main rail/coach stations. Some rooms have shower or toilet/shower. Licensed.

Bedrooms: 1 single, 4 double, 2 twin, 1 family room
Bathrooms: 5 en-suite, 2 public, 2 private showers

Bed & breakfast per night:	£min	£max
Single	15.00	17.00
Double	30.00	34.00

Half board per person:	£min	£max
Daily	21.00	23.00
Weekly	110.00	131.00

Evening meal from 1800
Parking for 5
Open January–November

6 [S] [TV] [OAP] [SP]

New Durley Dean Hotel

♛♛♛♛ [COMMENDED]

Westcliff Road, Bournemouth BH2 5HE
☎ (01202) 557711
Fax (01202) 292815

This elegant Victorian hotel, situated on the West Cliff in close proximity to both beaches and town, offers the latest in modern amenities, whilst maintaining the charm of a bygone era.

Bedrooms: 25 single, 32 double, 25 twin, 28 triple, 3 family rooms
Suite available
Bathrooms: 113 en-suite

Bed & breakfast per night:	£min	£max
Single	49.50	59.00
Double	99.00	118.00

Half board per person:	£min	£max
Daily	59.00	69.00
Weekly	210.00	483.00

Lunch available
Evening meal 1830 (last orders 2030)
Parking for 40
Cards accepted: Amex, Mastercard, Visa, Switch/Delta

Queen's Hotel

COMMENDED

Meyrick Road, East Cliff, Bournemouth BH1 3DL
☎ (01202) 554415
Fax (01202) 294810

Modern, family-run hotel near the beach, ideal for family holidays and with facilities for business conventions. Leisure club.

Bedrooms: 12 single, 43 double, 46 twin, 8 triple
Bathrooms: 109 en-suite

Bed & breakfast per night:	£min	£max
Single	39.50	49.50
Double	69.50	89.50

Half board per person:	£min	£max
Daily	45.00	58.50
Weekly	276.50	335.00

Lunch available
Evening meal 1900 (last orders 2100)
Parking for 80
Cards accepted: Amex, Mastercard, Visa

Riviera Hotel

COMMENDED

12-16 Burnaby Road, Alum Chine, Bournemouth BH4 8JF
☎ (01202) 763653
Fax (01202) 768422

Family hotel in Alum Chine. Views of the Isle of Wight. Short walk to sandy beach. Extensive leisure facilities including indoor/outdoor pools.

Bedrooms: 6 single, 22 double, 20 twin, 17 triple, 12 family rooms
Bathrooms: 77 en-suite

Half board per person:	£min	£max
Daily	45.00	75.00
Weekly	210.00	280.00

Lunch available
Evening meal 1845 (last orders 2015)
Parking for 70
Open February–December
Cards accepted: Mastercard, Visa, Switch/Delta

Hotel Riviera

COMMENDED

Westcliff Gardens, Bournemouth BH2 5HL
☎ (01202) 552845

On the West Cliff of Bournemouth overlooking the sea, with an award-winning garden which has direct access to the clifftop.

Bedrooms: 8 single, 14 double, 8 twin, 4 triple
Bathrooms: 34 en-suite

Bed & breakfast per night:	£min	£max
Single	24.00	33.00
Double	48.00	66.00

Half board per person:	£min	£max
Daily	31.50	40.50
Weekly	190.00	240.00

Lunch available
Evening meal 1830 (last orders 1930)
Parking for 24
Open April–October and Christmas
Cards accepted: Mastercard, Visa

Rosedene Cottage Hotel

COMMENDED

St Peter's Road, Bournemouth BH1 2LA
☎ (01202) 554102
Fax (01202) 246995

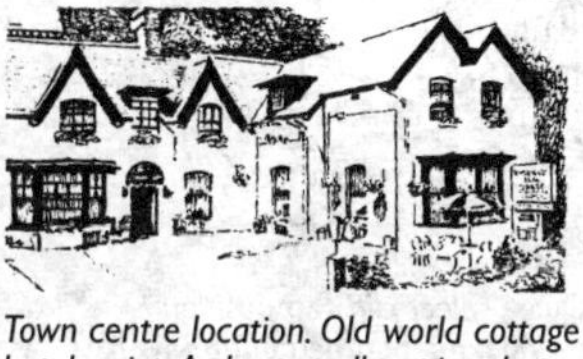

Town centre location. Old world cottage hotel, quiet. A short stroll to pier, shops, gardens, Bournemouth International Centre, theatres and beaches. 20 minutes from airport.

Bedrooms: 3 single, 5 double, 1 twin, 1 triple
Bathrooms: 7 en-suite, 1 public

Bed & breakfast per night:	£min	£max
Single	18.00	24.00
Double	32.00	48.00

Parking for 8
Cards accepted: Amex, Diners, Mastercard, Visa

Shoreline Hotel

COMMENDED

7 Pinecliffe Avenue, Southbourne, Bournemouth BH6 3PY
☎ (01202) 429654

Small, licensed hotel providing comfortable accommodation and home cooking. Close to beach and local shops, in quiet area.

Bedrooms: 2 single, 6 double, 2 triple
Bathrooms: 5 en-suite, 2 public

Bed & breakfast per night:	£min	£max
Single	14.00	20.00
Double	28.00	40.00

Half board per person:	£min	£max
Daily	19.50	26.00
Weekly	115.00	160.00

Evening meal 1800 (last orders 1900)
Parking for 5

Southernhay Hotel

COMMENDED

42 Alum Chine Road, Westbourne, Bournemouth BH4 8DX
☎ (01202) 761251
Fax (01202) 761251

Welcoming hotel, a short walk to beach and Westbourne shops and restaurants. Large car park. Full English breakfast.

Bedrooms: 1 single, 4 double, 1 twin, 1 triple
Bathrooms: 5 en-suite, 2 public

Bed & breakfast per night:	£min	£max
Single	15.00	20.00
Double	34.00	40.00

Parking for 10

Suncliff Hotel

COMMENDED

East Overcliff Drive, Bournemouth BH1 3AG
☎ (01202) 291711
Fax (01202) 293788

Clifftop location overlooking bay. Short walk to sandy beach and town centre. Extensive indoor leisure facilities including pool and evening entertainment.

Bedrooms: 12 single, 29 double, 24 twin, 18 triple, 11 family rooms
Bathrooms: 94 en-suite

Bed & breakfast per night:	£min	£max
Single	25.00	35.00
Double	50.00	86.00

Continued ▶

BOURNEMOUTH

Continued

Lunch available
Evening meal 1900 (last orders
2045)
Parking for 60
Cards accepted: Amex, Diners,
Mastercard, Visa, Switch/Delta

Sydney House Hotel ⚑

COMMENDED

6 West Cliff Road, West Cliff,
Bournemouth BH2 5EY
☎ (01202) 555536
*150 yards from seafront on West Cliff
and a few minutes from
entertainments and shops. Tea room
serving cream teas. Parking. Special
interest Dorset holidays available.*
Bedrooms: 2 single, 7 double, 2 twin,
2 triple, 2 family rooms
Bathrooms: 13 en-suite, 2 public
Bed & breakfast

per night:	£min	£max
Single	15.00	23.00
Double	30.00	46.00

Half board per

person:	£min	£max
Daily	23.00	30.00
Weekly	140.00	180.00

Evening meal 1800 (last orders
1900)
Parking for 14
Cards accepted: Mastercard, Visa

Trouville Hotel ⚑

COMMENDED

Priory Road, West Cliff,
Bournemouth BH2 5DH
☎ (01202) 552262
Fax (01202) 293324
*Centrally located close to all amenities,
the Trouville boasts a leisure centre and
has a fine reputation for friendly
service and superb food.*
Bedrooms: 9 single, 28 double,
29 twin, 13 triple
Bathrooms: 79 en-suite, 1 public
Bed & breakfast

per night:	£min	£max
Single	45.00	50.00
Double	90.00	100.00

Half board per

person:	£min	£max
Daily	55.00	60.00
Weekly	330.00	360.00

Lunch available
Evening meal 1900 (last orders
2030)
Parking for 76

Cards accepted: Amex, Diners,
Mastercard, Visa, Switch/Delta

Ullswater Hotel ⚑

COMMENDED

Westcliff Gardens, Bournemouth
BH2 5HW
☎ (01202) 555181
Fax (01202) 317896
*On the West Cliff, a few minutes from
the town centre and shops, 150 yards
from the clifftop and path to beach.*
Bedrooms: 9 single, 13 double,
13 twin, 7 triple
Bathrooms: 42 en-suite
Bed & breakfast

per night:	£min	£max
Single	25.00	30.00
Double	50.00	60.00

Half board per

person:	£min	£max
Daily	30.00	36.50
Weekly	144.00	225.00

Lunch available
Evening meal 1900 (last orders
2000)
Parking for 10
Cards accepted: Amex, Mastercard,
Visa

West Dene Hotel ⚑

COMMENDED

117 Alumhurst Road, Alum Chine,
Bournemouth BH4 8HS
☎ (01202) 764843

*Quiet, select cliff top position
overlooking Bournemouth Bay, 150
yards from sandy beach and woodland
glade of Alum Chine.*
Bedrooms: 1 single, 7 double, 4 twin,
3 triple, 2 family rooms
Bathrooms: 12 en-suite, 3 public
Bed & breakfast

per night:	£min	£max
Single	24.50	27.50
Double	49.00	55.00

Half board per

person:	£min	£max
Daily	33.50	40.50
Weekly	199.50	248.50

Evening meal 1815 (last orders
1500)
Parking for 17

Open March–October
Cards accepted: Amex, Diners,
Mastercard, Visa

Westleigh Hotel ⚑

COMMENDED

26 West Hill Road, West Cliff,
Bournemouth BH2 5PG
☎ (01202) 296989
Fax (01202) 296989
*Central location close to shops and
beaches. All rooms with colour TV,
tea/coffee facilities, hairdryer. Sauna,
spa bath, solarium, indoor pool, lift, car
park.*
Bedrooms: 3 single, 13 double,
9 twin, 1 triple, 4 family rooms
Bathrooms: 28 en-suite, 2 private,
2 public
Bed & breakfast

per night:	£min	£max
Single	40.00	45.00
Double	70.00	80.00

Half board per

person:	£min	£max
Daily	40.00	45.00
Weekly	280.00	315.00

Lunch available
Evening meal 1800 (last orders
1930)
Parking for 27
Cards accepted: Amex, Diners,
Mastercard, Visa

Winterbourne Hotel ⚑

COMMENDED

Priory Road, Bournemouth BH2 5DJ
☎ (01202) 296366
Fax (01202) 780073
ⓒ The Independents

*Enjoying a prime position with
magnificent sea views, the hotel is
within 400 metres of shops, theatres,
pier and beaches. Free golf tickets.*
Bedrooms: 6 single, 13 double,
10 twin, 8 triple, 4 family rooms
Bathrooms: 41 en-suite
Bed & breakfast

per night:	£min	£max
Single	29.00	41.00
Double	50.00	74.00

Lunch available
Evening meal 1830 (last orders
2030)
Parking for 34

Cards accepted: Amex, Mastercard, Visa, Switch/Delta

⛲🚏♿🖺🖵💷👤🛈⚿🎿🍴🎱📻🖧
🍽80🕭🎣🏴❋🌷🏕 SP T

Wrenwood Hotel M

🏰🏰🏰 APPROVED

11 Florence Road, Boscombe,
Bournemouth BH5 1HH
☎ (01202) 395086
Licensed, family hotel, 5 minutes' walk to pier, shopping centre and entertainments. Convenient for tennis, bowling, golf and New Forest area.
Bedrooms: 5 double, 3 triple, 2 family rooms
Bathrooms: 10 en-suite, 1 public

Bed & breakfast per night:

	£min	£max
Single	15.50	22.00
Double	27.00	36.00

Half board per person:

	£min	£max
Daily	22.00	24.50
Weekly	136.00	161.00

Evening meal 1900 (last orders 1700)
Parking for 7
Cards accepted: Mastercard, Visa

⛲🖺🖵💷👤🛈⚿🎿🍴TV📻🖧 DAP
🌷 SP T

Wychcote Hotel M

🏰🏰🏰 COMMENDED

2 Somerville Road, West Cliff,
Bournemouth BH2 5LH
☎ (01202) 557898
Small, well-appointed Victorian house hotel standing in its own tree-lined grounds. Quiet but near all facilities. Home cooking.
Bedrooms: 3 single, 5 double, 3 twin, 1 triple
Bathrooms: 11 en-suite, 1 private

Bed & breakfast per night:

	£min	£max
Single	20.00	29.50
Double	40.00	59.00

Half board per person:

	£min	£max
Daily	26.00	37.50
Weekly	144.00	224.00

Evening meal 1815 (last orders 2000)
Parking for 15
Open February–November and Christmas
Cards accepted: Mastercard, Visa, Switch/Delta

⛲5🖺🖵💷👤🛈S🎿🍴TV📻🖧🏕❋🍴
🏕🌷 SP

Hampshire
Map ref 2C3

Attractive village with thatched cottages and a ford in its main street. Well placed for visiting the New Forest.

The Cottage Hotel M

🏰🏰 HIGHLY COMMENDED

Sway Road, Brockenhurst SO42 7SH
☎ (01590) 622296
Fax (01590) 623014
Email: 100604.22@compuserve.com
Delightfully converted cosy oak-beamed forester's cottage, noted for comfort and service. Two minutes' walk from forest and village centre.
Bedrooms: 1 single, 5 double, 1 twin
Bathrooms: 6 en-suite, 1 private shower

Bed & breakfast per night:

	£min	£max
Single	49.00	69.00
Double	69.00	83.00

Parking for 12
Open February–November
Cards accepted: Mastercard, Visa, Switch/Delta

⛲10🚏🖺🖵👤🛈🎱S🎿🍴TV📻
🏕❋🏕 SP 🏨 T

New Park Manor Hotel M

🏰🏰🏰 HIGHLY COMMENDED

Lyndhurst Road, Brockenhurst
SO42 7QH
☎ (01590) 623467
Fax (01590) 622268

Prestigious and romantic country house hotel, dating from 16th C. Former royal hunting lodge of Charles II, set amidst New Forest parklands. Log fire ambience, Stag Head Restaurant, individually designed rooms. Horse riding, seasonal heated swimming pool, tennis court.
Bedrooms: 16 double, 5 twin
Bathrooms: 21 en-suite

Bed & breakfast per night:

	£min	£max
Single	75.00	150.00
Double	90.00	150.00

Half board per person:

	£min	£max
Daily	65.00	85.00
Weekly	455.00	595.00

Lunch available

Evening meal 1930 (last orders 2145)
Parking for 40
Cards accepted: Amex, Diners, Mastercard, Visa, Switch/Delta

⛲7🖺♿🖺🖵💷👤🎱🛈S🎿🍴📻
🏕🍽80🎣🏇U❋🏏🏕🏇🌷 SP 🏨 T

Buckinghamshire
Map ref 2C1

Interesting old market town surrounded by rich farmland. It has many Georgian buildings, including the Town Hall and Old Jail and many old almshouses and inns. Stowe School nearby has magnificent 18th C landscaped gardens. *Tourist Information Centre ☎ (01280) 823020*

Villiers Hotel M

🏰🏰🏰 HIGHLY COMMENDED

3 Castle Street, Buckingham
MK18 1BS
☎ (01280) 822444
Fax (01280) 822113
Individually designed bedrooms are set around an old coaching inn courtyard, incorporating English restaurant, Italian bistro and Jacobean pub.
Bedrooms: 3 single, 18 double, 17 twin
Suites available
Bathrooms: 38 en-suite

Bed & breakfast per night:

	£min	£max
Single	59.00	80.00
Double	60.00	95.00

Half board per person:

	£min	£max
Daily	77.75	97.75

Lunch available
Evening meal 1900 (last orders 2230)
Parking for 36
Cards accepted: Amex, Diners, Mastercard, Visa, Switch/Delta

⛲🏰♿🖺🖵💷👤🎱🛈S🍴◎🛏📻
🏕🍽300U🏇❋🏏🌷 SP 🏨 T

Please check prices and other details at the time of booking.

The National Grading and Classification Scheme is explained at the back of this guide.

BURFORD

Oxfordshire
Map ref 2B1

One of the most beautiful Cotswold wool towns with Georgian and Tudor houses, many antique shops and a picturesque High Street sloping to the River Windrush. *Tourist Information Centre* ☎ *(01993) 823558*

Elm House Hotel ⋀

👑👑👑 HIGHLY COMMENDED

Meadow Lane, Fulbrook, Burford
OX18 4BW
☎ (01993) 823611
Fax (01993) 823937
Cotswold-stone manor-style house with attractive walled gardens. Homely, welcoming atmosphere, fine home-cooked food served in comfortable surroundings. Centrally located for exploring Cotswolds and Oxfordshire.
Bedrooms: 4 double, 3 twin
Bathrooms: 6 en-suite, 1 private
Bed & breakfast

per night:	£min	£max
Single	41.00	70.00
Double	50.00	75.00

Evening meal 1900 (last orders 2030)
Parking for 10
Cards accepted: Mastercard, Visa

📞📭🖵♿🅿🔌✕📺🏧📷☼🚐
🛏 SP T

Golden Pheasant Hotel ⋀

👑👑👑 COMMENDED

High Street, Burford, Oxford
OX18 4QA
☎ (01993) 823223
Fax (01993) 822621
Beautifully restored 15th C inn with informal and friendly atmosphere. Large open fireplaces, antique furniture and individually styled rooms. Notable restaurant.
Bedrooms: 8 double, 4 twin
Bathrooms: 11 en-suite, 1 private
Bed & breakfast

per night:	£min	£max
Single	50.00	65.00
Double	80.00	110.00

Half board per person:	£min	£max
Daily	115.00	145.00

Lunch available
Evening meal 1900 (last orders 2130)
Parking for 10
Cards accepted: Amex, Mastercard, Visa, Switch/Delta

📞👿🏧📭📞📭♿🔌🅂✕🏧📷
🏳☼🚐🛏 SP T

The Highway Hotel ⋀

👑👑 COMMENDED

117 High Street, Burford, Oxford
OX18 4RG
☎ (01993) 822136
Fax (01993) 822136
Beamed medieval Cotswold guesthouse offering en-suite rooms with TV. Ideal touring base for Cotswolds. Incorporates acclaimed needlecraft centre.
Bedrooms: 9 double, 2 triple
Bathrooms: 9 en-suite, 1 public
Bed & breakfast

per night:	£min	£max
Single	30.00	50.00
Double	40.00	55.00

Cards accepted: Amex, Diners, Mastercard, Visa, Switch/Delta

📷🚗📞📭🖵♿🆄🅼🏧📞20🔱🅿☼
🏠

Romany Inn

👑👑 APPROVED

Bridge Street, Bampton, Oxford
OX18 2HA
☎ (01993) 850237

19th C listed Georgian building, recently refurbished, at nearby Bampton. Lounge bar, separate restaurant, chef/proprietor. Noted in pub and beer guides. Brochure available.
Bedrooms: 4 double, 2 twin, 3 triple
Bathrooms: 9 en-suite, 1 public
Bed & breakfast

per night:	£min	£max
Single	25.00	30.00
Double	35.00	40.00

Lunch available
Evening meal 1830 (last orders 2200)
Parking for 6
Cards accepted: Mastercard, Visa, Switch/Delta

📷🚗📭♿🔌✕📺🏧📷☼🚐✕
SP 🏠

National gradings and classifications were correct at the time of going to press but are subject to change. Please check at the time of booking.

BURLEY

Hampshire
Map ref 2B3

Attractive centre from which to explore the south-west part of the New Forest. There is an ancient earthwork on Castle Hill nearby, which also offers good views.

Moorhill House Hotel ⋀

👑👑👑👑 COMMENDED

Burley, Ringwood BH24 4AG
☎ (01425) 403285
Fax (01425) 403715
Quiet country house hotel in secluded two and a half acres, half a mile from picturesque village of Burley. Will appeal to those who love beauty, quiet surroundings and complete freedom of the New Forest. Daily half board price based on minimum 2-night stay.
Bedrooms: 2 single, 13 double, 2 twin, 7 triple
Bathrooms: 24 en-suite
Bed & breakfast

per night:	£min	£max
Single	55.00	70.00
Double	85.00	110.00

Half board per person:	£min	£max
Daily	52.50	60.00
Weekly	330.00	435.00

Evening meal 1900 (last orders 2045)
Parking for 40
Cards accepted: Amex, Diners, Mastercard, Visa

📷🚲📞📭🖵♿🔌🅂✕🏧📺🏧
🏳📞40🏊🔱♿☼🚐✕ SP 🏠 T

CHALE

Isle of Wight
Map ref 2C3

Village overlooking Chale Bay and near Blackgang Chine which has a children's maze, a water garden and a museum displaying many objects from shipwrecks.

Clarendon Hotel & Wight Mouse Inn ⋀

👑👑👑 HIGHLY COMMENDED

Nr Blackgang, Chale, Ventnor
PO38 2HA
☎ (01983) 730431
Fax (01983) 730431

17th C coaching hotel overlooking Freshwater Bay and the Needles. Children most welcome. 6 real ales, 365 whiskies and live entertainment nightly, all year round. Well-appointed bedrooms, good food, service and hospitality.
Bedrooms: 1 single, 3 double, 9 family rooms
Suites available
Bathrooms: 10 en-suite, 2 public

Bed & breakfast per night:

	£min	£max
Single	25.00	35.00
Double	50.00	70.00

Lunch available
Evening meal 1900 (last orders 2200)
Parking for 200
Cards accepted: Mastercard, Visa, Switch/Delta

CHESTERTON

Oxfordshire
Map ref 2C1

Bignell Park Hotel
Chesterton, Bicester OX6 8UE
☎ (01869) 241444 & 241192
Fax (01869) 241444
Cotswold period house circa 1740, set in 2.5 acres with mature gardens in rural Oxfordshire.
Bedrooms: 1 single, 11 double, 2 twin
Bathrooms: 2 en-suite, 12 private

Bed & breakfast per night:

	£min	£max
Single	60.00	75.00
Double	65.00	135.00

Lunch available
Evening meal 1900 (last orders 2130)
Parking for 18
Cards accepted: Amex, Mastercard, Visa

WELCOME HOST

This is a nationally recognised customer care programme which aims to promote the highest standards of service and a warm welcome. Establishments who are taking part in this initiative are indicated by the 🏵 symbol.

CHIPPING NORTON

Oxfordshire
Map ref 2C1

Old market town set high in the Cotswolds and an ideal touring centre. The wide market-place contains many 16th C and 17th C stone houses and the Town Hall and Tudor Guildhall.
Tourist Information Centre ☎ (01608) 644379

Southcombe Lodge Guest House
👑 COMMENDED
Southcombe, Chipping Norton OX7 5QH
☎ (01608) 643068
Well-decorated pebbledash guesthouse set in 3.5 acres, at the junction of the A44/A3400, close to Chipping Norton.
Bedrooms: 2 double, 3 twin, 1 triple
Bathrooms: 2 en-suite, 2 public

Bed & breakfast per night:

	£min	£max
Single	22.00	28.00
Double	38.00	46.00

Half board per person:

	£min	£max
Daily	29.00	34.00

Lunch available
Evening meal 1900 (last orders 1800)
Parking for 10

CHOLDERTON

Hampshire
Map ref 2B2

Parkhouse Motel
👑👑👑 COMMENDED
Cholderton, Salisbury, Wiltshire SP4 0EG
☎ (01980) 629256
Fax (01980) 629256
17th C former coaching inn built of brick and flint with slate roof. 5 miles east of Stonehenge, 10 miles north of Salisbury and 7 miles west of Andover.
Bedrooms: 6 single, 18 double, 6 twin, 3 triple
Suites available
Bathrooms: 23 en-suite, 10 private, 3 public

Bed & breakfast per night:

	£min	£max
Single	24.00	37.00
Double	44.00	48.00

Half board per person:

	£min	£max
Daily	30.00	43.00
Weekly	210.00	301.00

Evening meal 1900 (last orders 2030)
Parking for 30
Cards accepted: Mastercard, Visa

COLWELL BAY

Isle of Wight
Map ref 2C3

2-mile curving stretch of sand.

Ontario Private Hotel
👑👑👑 COMMENDED
Colwell Common Road, Colwell Bay, Freshwater PO39 0DD
☎ (01983) 753237
Four minutes from seaside award beach, offering accommodation of a high standard with licensed bar, choice of menu. Children and pets welcome.
Bedrooms: 1 single, 2 double, 2 triple, 1 family room
Bathrooms: 3 en-suite, 2 public, 1 private shower

Bed & breakfast per night:

	£min	£max
Single	20.00	22.00
Double	40.00	44.00

Half board per person:

	£min	£max
Daily	28.50	30.50
Weekly	195.00	205.00

Evening meal 1830 (last orders 1900)
Parking for 9
Open March–December

COOKHAM

Berkshire
Map ref 2C2

The Inn on the Green
👑👑👑 COMMENDED
The Old Cricket Common, Cookham Dean, Cookham, Maidenhead SL6 9NZ
☎ (01628) 482638
Fax (01628) 487474

An extensive restaurant menu is available, offering freshly cooked dishes for all meals. Residents' menu available from midday until midnight.

Continued ▶

COOKHAM

Continued

Bedrooms: 1 single, 3 double, 2 twin
Bathrooms: 6 en-suite

Bed & breakfast per night:

	£min	£max
Single	45.00	75.00
Double	80.00	100.00

Half board per person:

	£min	£max
Daily	60.00	90.00
Weekly	380.00	570.00

Lunch available
Evening meal 1930 (last orders 2200)
Parking for 40
Cards accepted: Amex, Mastercard, Visa, Switch/Delta

⌖⛺♿📞📺🖵🏊🐾❓🛈Ⓢ📷🚶▥🛏♉14♉
✿🚐ᴅᴀᴘ⚲ SP

CORFE CASTLE

Dorset
Map ref 2B3

One of the most spectacular ruined castles in Britain. Norman in origin, the castle was a Royalist stronghold during the Civil War and held out until 1645. The village had a considerable marble-carving industry in the Middle Ages.

Mortons House Hotel ♨

♛♛♛ HIGHLY COMMENDED

East Street, Corfe Castle, Wareham
BH20 5EE
☎ (01929) 480988
Fax (01929) 480820
Attractive Elizabethan manor house with castle views. Walled gardens, coastal and country pursuits. Suites and four-poster bed. Licensed gourmet restaurant.
Bedrooms: 13 double, 3 twin, 1 family room
Suite available
Bathrooms: 17 en-suite

Bed & breakfast per night:

	£min	£max
Single	65.00	75.00
Double	80.00	96.00

Half board per person:

	£min	£max
Daily	60.00	68.00
Weekly	320.00	375.00

Lunch available
Evening meal 1900 (last orders 2030)
Parking for 35
Cards accepted: Amex, Diners, Mastercard, Visa, Switch/Delta

⌖⛺♿📞📺🖵🏊🛈❓🗝🚶▥🛏
♉40✿🚐⚲ SP

COTSWOLDS

See under Burford, Chipping Norton, Deddington, Shipton-under-Wychwood, Witney, Woodstock
See also Cotswolds in Heart of England region

CUDDESDON

Oxfordshire
Map ref 2C1

The Bat & Ball Inn ♨

⬛

28 High Street, Cuddesdon, Oxford
OX44 9HJ
☎ (01865) 874379
Fax (01865) 873363
Old coaching inn with scenic views and interesting collection of cricket memorabilia. Cuddesdon is an attractive small village, well placed for Oxford and the M40.
Bedrooms: 2 single, 3 double, 1 twin, 1 triple
Bathrooms: 7 en-suite

Bed & breakfast per night:

	£min	£max
Single	30.00	40.00
Double	35.00	50.00

Lunch available
Evening meal 1830 (last orders 2130)
Parking for 15
Cards accepted: Mastercard, Visa, Switch/Delta

⌖⛺♿📞📺🛈❓Ⓢ🗝▥🛏♉♉✿
🗡🚐⚲ SP 🏮

DEDDINGTON

Oxfordshire
Map ref 2C1

On the edge of the Cotswolds and settled since the Stone Age, this is the only village in England to have been granted a full Coat of Arms, displayed on the 16th C Town Hall in the picturesque market square. Many places of interest include the Church of St Peter and St Paul.

The Deddington Arms ♨

♛♛♛ COMMENDED

Horsefair, Deddington, Banbury
OX15 0SH
☎ (01869) 338364
Fax (01869) 337010

16th C coaching inn, tastefully refurbishd to provide air-conditioned

restaurant and en-suite bedrooms whilst retaining the village inn atmosphere. Ideal base for Banbury, Oxford, Stratford, Warwick, Blenheim Palace and the Cotswolds.
Bedrooms: 18 double, 3 twin, 1 triple, 1 family room
Suites available
Bathrooms: 23 en-suite

Bed & breakfast per night:

	£min	£max
Single	49.50	75.00
Double	59.50	75.00'

Lunch available
Evening meal 1830 (last orders 2130)
Parking for 36
Cards accepted: Amex, Mastercard, Visa, Switch/Delta

⌖♿🍴📞📺🖵🏊🛈Ⓢ🗝🛏📺▥
Ⓢ🚗🛏40🗡♉✿🐾⚲ SP 🏮

Holcombe Hotel & Restaurant

♛♛♛♛ COMMENDED

High Street, Deddington, Banbury
OX15 0SL
☎ (01869) 338274
Fax (01869) 337167
Ⓒ Best Western/The Independents

Delightful 17th C award-winning family-run hotel in lovely village on A4260 Banbury to Oxford road, M40 exit 10. Ideal for visiting the Cotswolds, Stratford, Warwick, Woodstock and Blenheim.
Bedrooms: 2 single, 8 double, 6 twin, 1 triple
Bathrooms: 17 en-suite

Bed & breakfast per night:

	£min	£max
Single	59.50	69.50
Double	89.50	98.50

Half board per person:

	£min	£max
Daily	59.00	64.00
Weekly	315.00	350.00

Lunch available
Evening meal 1900 (last orders 2200)
Parking for 40
Cards accepted: Amex, Mastercard, Visa, Switch/Delta

⌖♿🍴📞📺🖵🏊🗝🛈Ⓢ🗝▥📺
▥🚗🛏28♉✿🐾ᴅᴀᴘ⚲ SP 🏮 Ⓣ

DROXFORD

Hampshire
Map ref 2C3

Village with numerous Georgian buildings. Izaak Walton was a frequent visitor to the 18th C rectory now owned by the National Trust.

Upland Park Hotel ♠
COMMENDED
Garrison Hill (A32), Droxford, Southampton SO32 3QL
☎ (01489) 878507
Fax (01489) 877853

Family-run hotel in picturesque country surroundings, well situated for touring Southern England. Good reputation for cuisine.
Bedrooms: 3 single, 9 double, 3 twin, 2 family rooms
Bathrooms: 17 en-suite

Bed & breakfast per night:

	£min	£max
Single	35.00	37.50
Double	46.00	52.00

Lunch available
Evening meal 1900 (last orders 2130)
Parking for 100
Cards accepted: Amex, Diners, Mastercard, Visa

♿🛏🛁📻☎🖵🖵♨🐕🛄Ⓢⓧ🅿🎾📺▥ ♣🏊40🗝↻♪🗡✿✈OAP🐾 SP T

EMSWORTH

Hampshire
Map ref 2C3

Old port, now a yachting centre, set between 2 small creeks on Chichester Harbour. Yachtbuilding is the chief industry. There are some good Georgian buildings and 2 tide-mills.

The Brookfield Hotel ♠
HIGHLY COMMENDED
Havant Road, Emsworth PO10 7LF
☎ (01243) 373363
Fax (01243) 376342
Privately owned and run country house hotel, near the old fishing village of Emsworth and close to Chichester and its festival theatre. Bargain break rates at weekends.
Bedrooms: 5 single, 23 double, 12 twin

Suite available
Bathrooms: 40 en-suite

Bed & breakfast per night:

	£min	£max
Single	54.00	60.00
Double	79.00	90.00

Half board per person:

	£min	£max
Daily	57.00	60.00

Lunch available
Evening meal 1900 (last orders 2130)
Parking for 80
Cards accepted: Amex, Diners, Mastercard, Visa, Switch/Delta

♿🛏🛁📻☎🖵🖵♨🐕🛄Ⓢⓧ🅿🎾◑ ▥♣🏊70✿✈ SP

Jingles Hotel ♠
COMMENDED
77 Horndean Road, Emsworth PO10 7PU
☎ (01243) 373755
Fax (01243) 373755
Fully modernised and comfortably furnished Victorian house located between the South Downs and Chichester harbour.
Bedrooms: 5 single, 5 double, 3 twin
Bathrooms: 6 en-suite, 2 private, 2 public

Bed & breakfast per night:

	£min	£max
Single	24.00	32.00
Double	42.00	52.00

Lunch available
Evening meal 1900 (last orders 2000)
Parking for 14
Cards accepted: Amex, Mastercard, Visa

♿🛏🛁🖵🖵♨🐕Ⓢⓧ🅿🎾 TV ▥♣🏊 ✿

FAREHAM

Hampshire
Map ref 2C3

Lies on a quiet backwater of Portsmouth Harbour. The High Street is lined with fine Georgian buildings.
Tourist Information Centre ☎ (01329) 221342

Avenue House Hotel ♠
COMMENDED
22 The Avenue, Fareham PO14 1NS
☎ (01329) 232175
Fax (01329) 232196
ⓒ Logis of GB
Comfortable, small hotel, with charm and character, set in mature gardens. 5 minutes' walk to town centre, railway station and restaurants.
Wheelchair access category 3♿

Bedrooms: 3 single, 8 double, 3 twin, 3 triple
Bathrooms: 17 en-suite

Bed & breakfast per night:

	£min	£max
Single	41.50	44.00
Double	48.00	55.00

Parking for 17
Cards accepted: Amex, Diners, Mastercard, Visa

♿🛏🛁📻☎🖵🖵♨UL🐕Ⓢⓧ🅿🎾▥ ♣🏊35✿ SP T

The Red Lion Hotel ♠
COMMENDED
East Street, Fareham PO16 0BP
☎ (01329) 822640
Fax (01329) 823579
ⓒ Countryside

Restored coaching inn, a Grade II listed building, in the heart of Fareham and convenient for Portsmouth and Southampton. Half board prices shown apply at weekends.
Bedrooms: 15 single, 18 double, 7 twin, 2 family rooms
Bathrooms: 42 en-suite

Bed & breakfast per night:

	£min	£max
Single	24.00	70.00
Double	48.00	85.00

Half board per person:

	£min	£max
Daily	28.00	36.00

Lunch available
Evening meal 1900 (last orders 2200)
Parking for 136
Cards accepted: Amex, Diners, Mastercard, Visa, Switch/Delta

♿🛏🛁📻☎🖵🖵♨🐕Ⓢⓧ🅿 TV ◑ ▥♣🏊120🗝🐾✿🐾 SP 🏨

WELCOME HOST

This is a nationally recognised customer care programme which aims to promote the highest standards of service and a warm welcome. Establishments who are taking part in this initiative are indicated by the ⚘ symbol.

FARINGDON

Oxfordshire
Map ref 2B2

Ancient stone-built market town in the Vale of the White Horse. The 17th C market hall stands on pillars and the 13th C church has some fine monuments. A great monastic tithe barn is nearby at Great Coxwell.

Faringdon Hotel M

👑 👑 👑 COMMENDED

Market Place, Faringdon SN7 7HL
☎ (01367) 240536
Fax (01367) 243250
All en-suite rooms, equipped with remote-control colour TV, direct-dial telephone, tea/coffee-making facilities, hairdryer. Open fire, lounge bar and restaurant.
Bedrooms: 3 single, 13 double, 1 twin, 3 triple
Bathrooms: 20 en-suite

Bed & breakfast

per night:	£min	£max
Single	40.00	50.00
Double	50.00	60.00

Half board per

person:	£min	£max
Daily	25.00	35.00

Lunch available
Evening meal 1900 (last orders 2100)
Parking for 5
Cards accepted: Amex, Diners, Mastercard, Visa, Switch/Delta

Portwell House Hotel M

👑 👑 👑 APPROVED

Market Place, Faringdon SN7 7HU
☎ (01367) 240197
Fax (01367) 244330
In the centre of the market-place of this country market town. Within easy reach of the Cotswolds.
Bedrooms: 1 single, 2 double, 2 twin, 3 triple
Bathrooms: 8 en-suite

Bed & breakfast

per night:	£min	£max
Single	32.00	40.00
Double	40.00	55.00

Half board per

person:	£min	£max
Daily	35.00	40.00
Weekly	180.00	250.00

Evening meal 1900 (last orders 2100)

Parking for 3
Cards accepted: Mastercard, Visa, Switch/Delta

Sudbury House Hotel M

👑 👑 👑 👑 HIGHLY COMMENDED

56 London Street, Faringdon SN7 8AA
☎ (01367) 241272
Fax (01367) 242346
CR Best Western
Peacefully situated midway between Oxford and Swindon, within an easy drive of the Cotswolds, Blenheim Palace and Warwick Castle. Special weekend rates.
Bedrooms: 39 double, 10 twin
Suite available
Bathrooms: 49 en-suite

Bed & breakfast

per night:	£min	£max
Single	45.00	80.00
Double	55.00	95.00

Half board per

person:	£min	£max
Daily	49.50	69.00
Weekly	297.00	376.00

Lunch available
Evening meal 1900 (last orders 2115)
Parking for 85
Cards accepted: Amex, Diners, Mastercard, Visa, Switch/Delta

FERNDOWN

Dorset
Map ref 2B3

Sharing the attractions of Bournemouth, of which it is now a part, and well placed for exploring the New Forest.

Coach House Inn M

👑 👑 👑 👑 APPROVED

579 Wimborne Road East, Ferndown BH22 9NW
☎ (01202) 861222
Fax (01202) 894130
CR Consort
Set in beautiful wooded surroundings, close to the New Forest and 6 miles from Bournemouth with its golden beaches. Half board daily prices based on minimum 2-night stay.
Bedrooms: 16 double, 20 twin, 3 triple, 4 family rooms
Bathrooms: 43 en-suite

Bed & breakfast

per night:	£min	£max
Single	40.00	42.00
Double	52.00	55.00

Half board per

person:	£min	£max
Daily	37.00	39.00

Lunch available
Evening meal 1900 (last orders 2130)
Parking for 118
Cards accepted: Amex, Diners, Mastercard, Visa, Switch/Delta

FRESHWATER

Isle of Wight
Map ref 2C3

This part of the island is associated with Tennyson, who lived in the village for 30 years. A monument on Tennyson's Down commemorates the poet.

Farringford Hotel M

👑 👑 👑 COMMENDED

Bedbury Lane, Freshwater PO40 9PE
☎ (01983) 752500 & 752700
Fax (01983) 756515
Set in 33-acre grounds, offering traditional hotel service and also self-catering suites, the best of both worlds. 9-hole golf-course, swimming and tennis.
Bedrooms: 3 single, 2 double, 7 twin, 7 triple
Bathrooms: 19 en-suite

Bed & breakfast

per night:	£min	£max
Single	26.00	48.00
Double	52.00	96.00

Half board per

person:	£min	£max
Daily	39.00	61.00
Weekly	234.00	366.00

Lunch available
Evening meal 1930 (last orders 2130)
Parking for 152
Cards accepted: Amex, Diners, Mastercard, Visa, Switch/Delta

The map references refer to the colour maps towards the end of the guide. The first figure is the map number; the letter and figure which follow indicate the grid reference on the map.

Royal Standard Hotel ⋒

⚜⚜⚜ **APPROVED**

School Green Road, Freshwater
PO40 9AJ
☎ (01983) 753227
*Small, family-run hotel. Freehouse with
2 bars, restaurant, function room.
En-suite rooms with TV and tea/coffee.
Groups welcome.*
Bedrooms: 4 single, 3 double, 1 twin,
2 triple, 1 family room
Bathrooms: 9 en-suite, 2 private
showers
**Bed & breakfast
per night:**

	£min	£max
Single	18.00	20.00
Double	36.00	40.00

Lunch available
Evening meal 1900 (last orders
2130)
Parking for 5
Cards accepted: Mastercard, Visa
🛏🛅♿📞▭🖥♦🅿🔒✂🖼🚲🍴50☎
🅃

GILLINGHAM

Dorset
Map ref 2B3

Stock Hill Country House Hotel ⋒

⚜⚜⚜⚜ **DE LUXE**

Stock Hill, Gillingham SP8 5NR
☎ (01747) 823626
Fax (01747) 825628
*A de luxe country house - a haven of
peace, offering personal hospitality,
service and food at its best.*
Bedrooms: 2 single, 3 double, 3 twin,
1 triple
Suite available
Bathrooms: 9 en-suite
**Half board per
person:**

	£min	£max
Daily	120.00	150.00

Lunch available
Evening meal 1930 (last orders
2045)
Parking for 40
Cards accepted: Amex, Diners,
Mastercard, Visa, Switch/Delta
🛏7🛅♿🚗📞▭🖥🔒✂
▭🚲🔍♿🌸✈🚐 🅳🅰🅿 🆂🆂🏦

Please mention this guide
when making your booking.

A key to symbols can be
found inside the back
cover flap.

GORING

Oxfordshire
Map ref 2C2

Riverside town on the
Oxfordshire/Berkshire border,
linked by an attractive bridge to
Streatley with views to the Goring
Gap.

Miller of Mansfield ⋒

⚜⚜⚜ **COMMENDED**

High Street, Goring, Reading,
Berkshire RG8 9AW
☎ (01491) 872829
Fax (01491) 874200
*Ivy-covered inn with Tudor-style exterior.
Interior has original beams, open fires
and comfortable bedrooms.*
Bedrooms: 2 single, 5 double, 3 twin
Bathrooms: 7 en-suite, 2 public
**Bed & breakfast
per night:**

	£min	£max
Single	30.00	45.00
Double	48.00	60.00

Lunch available
Evening meal 1900 (last orders
2200)
Parking for 10
Cards accepted: Mastercard, Visa,
Switch/Delta
🛏▭🖥♦🅿🔒🆂🖼🚲🚲 🆂🆂🏦🌸

GOSPORT

Hampshire
Map ref 2C3

From a tiny fishing hamlet, Gosport
has grown into an important centre
with many naval establishments,
including HMS Dolphin, the
submarine base, with the Naval
Submarine Museum which preserves
HMS Alliance and Holland I.
Tourist Information Centre ☎ (01705)
522944

Belle Vue Hotel ⋒

⚜⚜⚜ **COMMENDED**

39 Marine Parade East, Lee on the
Solent PO13 9BW
☎ (01705) 550258
Fax (01705) 552624
*Modern hotel on the seafront with
uninterrupted views across the Solent.
Lounge bar, fine restaurant and
banqueting facilities, entertainment.*
Bedrooms: 3 single, 20 double,
4 twin
Bathrooms: 27 en-suite
**Bed & breakfast
per night:**

	£min	£max
Single	49.50	68.00
Double	65.00	80.00

Lunch available

Evening meal 1900 (last orders
2145)
Parking for 55
Cards accepted: Amex, Mastercard,
Visa, Switch/Delta
🛏🛅♿📞▭🖥♦🅿🔒🆂✂🖼📺◑
🖼🚲🍴130🔍🍴 🅳🅰🅿 🆂🆂

The Manor Hotel ⋒

⚜⚜⚜ **COMMENDED**

Brewers Lane, Gosport PO13 0JY
☎ (01329) 232946
Fax (01329) 220392
*Very popular private hotel and public
house. Close to Portsmouth's naval
history. Midway between Fareham and
Gosport.*
Bedrooms: 1 single, 6 double, 1 twin,
4 triple, 2 family rooms
Bathrooms: 13 en-suite, 1 private
**Bed & breakfast
per night:**

	£min	£max
Single	35.00	42.50
Double	55.00	65.00

Lunch available
Evening meal 1800 (last orders
2200)
Parking for 46
Cards accepted: Amex, Mastercard,
Visa, Switch/Delta
🛏🛅♿📞▭🖥♦🅿🔒🆂🖼🖼🚲
🍴50🔍✈🌸 🆂🆂🅃

HAVANT

Hampshire
Map ref 2C3

Once a market town famous for
making parchment. Nearby at Leigh
Park extensive early 19th C
landscape gardens and parklands are
open to the public. Right in the
centre of the town stands the
interesting 13th C church of St
Faith.
Tourist Information Centre ☎ (01705)
480024

Bear Hotel ⋒

⚜⚜⚜ **COMMENDED**

East Street, Havant PO9 1AA
☎ (01705) 486501
Fax (01705) 470551
🅒🆁 Countryside
*Hotel in a town centre location, close to
shops, A27/M27, bus and rail station,
Chichester and Portsmouth. Half board
prices shown apply at weekends.*
Bedrooms: 10 single, 25 double,
7 twin
Bathrooms: 42 en-suite
**Bed & breakfast
per night:**

	£min	£max
Single	33.50	65.00
Double	42.00	80.00

Continued ▶

455

HAVANT

Continued

Half board per
person:	£min	£max
Daily	28.00	36.00

Lunch available
Evening meal 1900 (last orders 2200)
Parking for 150
Cards accepted: Amex, Diners, Mastercard, Visa, Switch/Delta

꒐🏠🚗📞📧⌂🖥♦🐾🍽✂🚭◐▥ 🖳🛎170🌸❄🛩⟋🌲 SP 🎬 T

The Old Mill Guest House ♏

COMMENDED

Mill Lane, Bedhampton, Havant
PO9 3JH
☎ (01705) 454948
Fax (01705) 499677
Georgian house in large grounds by a lake abundant in wildlife. Modernised, comfortable retreat. John Keats rested here.
Bedrooms: 1 double, 4 triple
Bathrooms: 5 en-suite
Bed & breakfast
per night:	£min	£max
Single	24.00	28.00
Double	38.00	42.00

Parking for 10

꒐📧🖥 UL ▣ S 🖳 TV ▥ 🛎⌖❄🌲🎬

HAYLING ISLAND

Hampshire
Map ref 2C3

Small island of historic interest, surrounded by natural harbours and with fine sandy beaches, linked to the mainland by an attractive bridge under which boats sail. Birthplace of windsurfing and home to many international sailing events.

Newtown House Hotel ♏

APPROVED

Manor Road, Hayling Island
PO11 0QR
☎ (01705) 466131
Fax (01705) 461366
Email: newton@primex.co.uk

18th C converted farmhouse, set in own grounds a quarter of a mile from seafront. Indoor leisure complex with heated pool, gym, steamroom, jacuzzi and sauna. Tennis.

Bedrooms: 9 single, 9 double, 4 twin, 3 triple
Bathrooms: 25 en-suite, 1 public
Bed & breakfast
per night:	£min	£max
Single	30.00	43.00
Double	60.00	70.00

Half board per
person:	£min	£max
Daily	45.00	51.00

Lunch available
Evening meal 1900 (last orders 2130)
Parking for 45
Cards accepted: Amex, Diners, Mastercard, Visa, Switch/Delta

꒐🏠🚗📞📧⌂🖥♦🐾▣ S ✂🖳 TV ◐▥ 🛎🍴⌖🎭🏹🎣🔭✿🚗⟋ SP 🎬 T

HECKFIELD

Hampshire
Map ref 2C2

The New Inn ♏

HIGHLY COMMENDED

Heckfield, Basingstoke RG27 0LE
☎ (0118) 932 6374
Fax (0118) 932 6550
15th C inn set in the picturesque countryside of North Hampshire, recently extended but retaining its unique character. Conference facilities and restaurant.
Bedrooms: 9 double, 7 twin
Bathrooms: 16 en-suite
Bed & breakfast
per night:	£min	£max
Single	42.50	62.00
Double	60.00	74.50

Lunch available
Evening meal 1900 (last orders 2200)
Parking for 95
Cards accepted: Amex, Mastercard, Visa, Switch/Delta

꒐5🏠🚗📞📧⌂🖥♦🐾▣ S ✂🖳▥ 🛎🍴35 U SP 🎬

WELCOME HOST

This is a nationally recognised customer care programme which aims to promote the highest standards of service and a warm welcome. Establishments who are taking part in this initiative are indicated by the 🏵 symbol.

HENLEY-ON-THAMES

Oxfordshire
Map ref 2C2

The famous Thames Regatta is held in this prosperous and attractive town at the beginning of July each year. The town has many Georgian buildings and old coaching inns and the parish church has some fine monuments.
Tourist Information Centre ☎ (01491) 578034

Henley House ♏

Listed **HIGHLY COMMENDED**

School Lane, Medmenham, Marlow, Buckinghamshire SL7 2HJ
☎ (01491) 576100
Fax (01491) 571764
Email: 100646.1676
@compuserve.com
Elegant, spacious property, set in a Victorian walled garden in an Area of Outstanding Natural Beauty. All modern home comforts, with a relaxed, friendly atmosphere. Very convenient for M4 and access to London, Oxford and Windsor.
Bedrooms: 3 double
Bathrooms: 3 en-suite
Bed & breakfast
per night:	£min	£max
Single	35.00	45.00
Double	45.00	50.00

Evening meal 1800 (last orders 2100)
Parking for 6

꒐📧⌂♦ UL S ✂🖳▥ 🛎🍴10✿🛩🚗

HIGH WYCOMBE

Buckinghamshire
Map ref 2C2

Famous for furniture-making, historic examples of which feature in the museum. The 18th C Guildhall and the octagonal market house were designed by the Adam brothers. West Wycombe Park and Hughenden Manor (National Trust) are nearby.
Tourist Information Centre ☎ (01494) 421892

Clifton Lodge Hotel

COMMENDED

210 West Wycombe Road, High Wycombe HP12 3AR
☎ (01494) 440095 & 529062
Fax (01494) 536322
Situated on the A40 approximately 1 mile from the M40 Oxford to London motorway. Ideal for touring Thames Valley and Oxford.

Bedrooms: 10 single, 13 double,
7 twin, 2 family rooms
Bathrooms: 19 en-suite, 4 public,
2 private showers
Bed & breakfast

per night:	£min	£max
Single	35.00	75.00
Double	58.00	80.00

**Half board per
person:**

	£min	£max
Daily	45.00	85.00

Lunch available
Evening meal 1900 (last orders
2100)
Parking for 30
Cards accepted: Amex, Diners,
Mastercard, Visa, Switch/Delta
🐕🕭👵📞🖭🖵💷📶🛈⟨S⟩✂🕭⟨TV⟩🖳
🛏🍴32🛋❄✈DAP🔌SP

HOOK

Hampshire
Map ref 2C2

Astride the A30 some 6 miles east
of Basingstoke.

Raven Hotel ♔

👑👑👑 COMMENDED
Station Road, Hook, Basingstoke
RG27 9HS
☎ (01256) 762541
Fax (01256) 768677
CR The Independents/Countryside
*In Hook village, convenient for
Basingstoke and Hampshire
countryside. Local attractions include
Birdworld and Stratfield Saye House.
Weekly jazz. Half board prices shown
apply at weekends.*
Bedrooms: 2 single, 21 double,
15 twin
Bathrooms: 38 en-suite
Bed & breakfast

per night:	£min	£max
Single	36.50	70.00
Double	48.00	80.00

**Half board per
person:**

	£min	£max
Daily	31.00	42.00

Lunch available
Evening meal 1900 (last orders
2200)
Parking for 100
Cards accepted: Amex, Diners,
Mastercard, Visa, Switch/Delta
🐕🕭👵📞🖭🖵💷📶🛈⟨S⟩✂●🖳
🛏100✈🔌SP

For ideas on places to visit
refer to the introduction at
the beginning of this section.

HUNGERFORD

Berkshire
Map ref 2C2

Attractive town on the Avon Canal
and the River Kennet, famous for its
fishing. It has a wide High Street and
many antique shops. Nearby is the
Tudor manor of Littlecote with its
large Roman mosaic.

The Bear at Hungerford ♔

👑👑👑 COMMENDED
Charnham Street, Hungerford
RG17 0EL
☎ (01488) 682512
Fax (01488) 684357
CR Jarvis/Utell International
*13th C coaching inn, traditionally
furnished, with timber beams and open
fires. 3 miles from junction 14 of the
M4, ideally situated for the Cotswolds,
Berkshire Downs and Newbury races. A
Jarvis hotel, refurbished in July 1997.*
Bedrooms: 3 single, 29 double,
9 twin
Suites available
Bathrooms: 41 en-suite
Bed & breakfast

per night:	£min	£max
Single	46.50	89.00
Double	93.00	98.00

**Half board per
person:**

	£min	£max
Daily	50.00	103.00
Weekly	299.00	495.00

Lunch available
Evening meal 1900 (last orders
2130)
Parking for 60
Cards accepted: Amex, Diners,
Mastercard, Visa, Switch/Delta
🐕🕭👵📞🖭🖵💷📶🛈⟨S⟩✂🕭⟨TV⟩
◑🖳🛏🍴70✈⟨U⟩▸❄DAP🔌SP🏛⟨T⟩

ISLE OF WIGHT

*See under Bonchurch, Chale, Colwell Bay,
Freshwater, Sandown, Shanklin, Totland
Bay, Ventnor*

KNOWL HILL

Berkshire
Map ref 2C2

Bird In Hand ♔

👑👑👑 COMMENDED
Bath Road, Knowl Hill, Reading
RG10 9UP
☎ (01628) 822781 & 826622
Fax (01628) 826748
*Extended 14th C coaching inn,
between London and Oxford. Close to
Henley, Maidenhead and Windsor. 25
minutes to Heathrow.*
Bedrooms: 1 single, 4 double,
10 twin

Bathrooms: 15 en-suite
Bed & breakfast

per night:	£min	£max
Single	55.00	80.00
Double	70.00	100.00

**Half board per
person:**

	£min	£max
Daily	70.00	95.00
Weekly	490.00	665.00

Lunch available
Evening meal 1900 (last orders
2200)
Parking for 80
Cards accepted: Amex, Diners,
Mastercard, Visa, Switch/Delta
🐕🕭👵📞🖭🖵💷📶🛈⟨S⟩🖳🛏🖳
🍴20▸❄🔌SP

LONGHAM

Dorset
Map ref 2B3

Astride the A348 Poole to
Ringwood road and on the north
bank of the River Stour. The river
floods its banks in this area when
the weather is severe.

Bridge House Hotel ♔

👑👑👑 COMMENDED
2 Ringwood Road, Longham,
Ferndown BH22 9AN
☎ (01202) 578828
Fax (01202) 572620

*Located between Poole and
Bournemouth, on the banks of the
beautiful River Stour. A la carte
restaurant, carvery bar. Four-poster
beds available.*
Bedrooms: 4 single, 21 double,
11 twin, 1 triple
Bathrooms: 37 en-suite
Bed & breakfast

per night:	£min	£max
Single	30.00	40.00
Double	40.00	50.00

Lunch available
Evening meal 1900 (last orders
2200)
Parking for 200
Cards accepted: Amex, Diners,
Mastercard, Visa
🐕🕭👵📞🖭🖵💷📶🛈⟨S⟩✂🕭⟨TV⟩
◑🖳🛏🍴100🎵▸❄DAP🔌SP⟨T⟩

457

LYMINGTON

Hampshire
Map ref 2C3

Small, pleasant town with bright cottages and attractive Georgian houses, lying on the edge of the New Forest with a ferry service to the Isle of Wight. A sheltered harbour makes it a busy yachting centre.

Our Bench ♠

👑 COMMENDED

9 Lodge Road, Pennington, Lymington SO41 8HH
☎ (01590) 673141
Fax (01590) 673141
Email: ourbench
@newforest.demon.co.uk
All en-suite bedrooms with TV. Indoor heated pool, jacuzzi and sauna. Non-smokers only, please. Sorry, no children. Large quiet garden. Close to forest. Nominee for Southern Tourist Board regional heat in England for Excellence awards 1997.
Wheelchair access category 3♿
Bedrooms: 2 double, 1 twin
Bathrooms: 3 en-suite

Bed & breakfast

per night:	£min	£max
Single	20.00	26.00
Double	40.00	48.00

Half board per

person:	£min	£max
Daily	27.00	36.00
Weekly	187.00	252.00

Evening meal 1800 (last orders 1800)
Parking for 5
Cards accepted: Mastercard, Visa, Switch/Delta

🛏🍴📺♿🕴📶🆙👜ⓢ🕭📺📺🏧🚗
🐕🎣♨✖🚲 ᴅᴀᴘ SP ♿

LYNDHURST

Hampshire
Map ref 2C3

The "capital" of the New Forest, surrounded by attractive woodland scenery and delightful villages. The town is dominated by the Victorian Gothic-style church where the original Alice in Wonderland is buried.
Tourist Information Centre ☎ (01703) 282269

Burwood Lodge ♠

👑 COMMENDED

Romsey Road, Lyndhurst SO43 7AA
☎ (01703) 282445
Fax (01703) 282445
Lovely house in half-acre garden, near the village centre. All rooms with en-suite shower, WC and washbasin. Parking in grounds.
Bedrooms: 1 single, 3 double, 1 triple, 1 family room
Bathrooms: 6 en-suite

Bed & breakfast

per night:	£min	£max
Single	22.00	26.00
Double	40.00	50.00

Parking for 8

🛏🍴📺♿📶🆙👜ⓢ🕭📺🏧🚲
♨✖🚲

Knightwood Lodge ♠

👑👑👑 HIGHLY COMMENDED

Southampton Road, Lyndhurst SO43 7BU
☎ (01703) 282502
Fax (01703) 283730
ⒼⓇ Minotel/The Independents

On the edge of Lyndhurst overlooking

the New Forest. Facilities include an indoor health centre with spa, sauna, swimming pool and steam room. Cosy bar. Parking.
Bedrooms: 2 single, 9 double, 1 twin, 2 triple
Bathrooms: 14 en-suite, 1 public

Bed & breakfast

per night:	£min	£max
Single	30.00	40.00
Double	60.00	75.00

Half board per

person:	£min	£max
Daily	40.50	48.50

Lunch available
Evening meal 1830 (last orders 2000)
Parking for 15
Cards accepted: Amex, Diners, Mastercard, Visa, Switch/Delta

🛏🍴📺♿🕴📶🆙👜ⓢ🕭📺🏧
🚗🎣✖♨🕴🚲 ᴅᴀᴘ SP Ⓣ

The Penny Farthing Hotel ♠

👑 COMMENDED

Romsey Road, Lyndhurst SO43 7AA
☎ (01703) 284422
Fax (01703) 284488
Perfectly situated, cheerful, small hotel, 1 minute's walk from village centre, shops, restaurants, 2 minutes from open forest. Tastefully furnished rooms ensure a comfortable stay. New cottage annexe.
Bedrooms: 3 single, 5 double, 1 twin, 1 triple, 1 family room
Bathrooms: 10 en-suite, 1 private

Bed & breakfast

per night:	£min	£max
Single	25.00	40.00
Double	49.00	75.00

Parking for 15
Cards accepted: Amex, Mastercard, Visa, Switch/Delta

🛏🍴♿🕴📶🆙👜ⓢ🕭📺📺🏧🕴
🚲 SP

ᴬᵈ See display advertisement on this page

MAIDENHEAD

Berkshire
Map ref 2C2

Attractive town on the River Thames which is crossed by an elegant 18th C bridge and by Brunel's well-known railway bridge. It is a popular place for boating with delightful riverside walks. The Courage Shire Horse Centre is nearby.
Tourist Information Centre ☎ (01628) 781110

Elva Lodge Hotel ⚠

≋≋ COMMENDED

Castle Hill, Maidenhead SL6 4AD
☎ (01628) 22948 & 34883
Fax (01628) 38855
Family-run hotel in central Maidenhead. Friendly atmosphere and personal attention. Ideal for Heathrow, Windsor, Henley and Ascot. M4 5 minutes, M40 and M25 10 minutes.
Bedrooms: 10 single, 10 double, 4 twin, 2 triple, 1 family room
Bathrooms: 14 en-suite, 6 public, 6 private showers

Bed & breakfast per night:	£min	£max
Single	36.50	67.50
Double	50.00	78.00

Half board per person:	£min	£max
Daily	49.00	87.00
Weekly	308.70	609.00

Lunch available
Evening meal 1830 (last orders 2130)
Parking for 31
Cards accepted: Amex, Diners, Mastercard, Visa, Switch/Delta

⛄🚶♿📞🍽️🖥️🛆💷⚔📺🖥️🖨️ 🍴👖50🔍❄️🔌 SP T

MARLOW

Buckinghamshire
Map ref 2C2

Attractive Georgian town on the River Thames, famous for its 19th C suspension bridge. The High Street contains many old houses and there are connections with writers including Shelley and T S Eliot.

Holly Tree House ⚠

≋≋ HIGHLY COMMENDED

Burford Close, Marlow Bottom, Marlow SL7 3NF
☎ (01628) 891110
Fax (01628) 481278
Detached house set in large gardens with fine views over the valley. Quiet yet

convenient location. All rooms fully en-suite. Outdoor heated swimming pool.
Bedrooms: 1 single, 4 double
Bathrooms: 5 en-suite

Bed & breakfast per night:	£min	£max
Single	62.50	74.50
Double	69.50	79.50

Parking for 10
Cards accepted: Amex, Mastercard, Visa

⛄🚶♿🍴📞🍽️🖥️🛆💷⚔📺🖥️ 🍴👖8🍴❄️🔌 T

The White House

≋≋ COMMENDED

194 Little Marlow Road, Marlow SL7 1HX
☎ (01628) 485765
Fax (01628) 485765
Victorian house of character, convenient for M4 and M40. Evening meal on request.
Bedrooms: 1 single, 2 twin
Bathrooms: 2 en-suite, 1 private

Bed & breakfast per night:	£min	£max
Single	30.00	35.00
Double	45.00	50.00

Parking for 2
Cards accepted: Mastercard, Visa

🖥️🛆💷⚔🖥️🖨️❄️🍴🍴

MILFORD-ON-SEA

Hampshire
Map ref 2C3

Victorian seaside resort with shingle beach and good bathing, set in pleasant countryside and looking out over the Isle of Wight. Nearby is Hurst Castle, built by Henry VIII.

Compton Hotel ⚠

≋ APPROVED

59 Keyhaven Road, Milford-on-Sea, Lymington SO41 0QX
☎ (01590) 643117
Small, private hotel with en-suite rooms and TV. Outdoor heated swimming pool. English and vegetarian cooking. Licensed.
Bedrooms: 2 single, 3 double, 1 twin, 1 family room
Bathrooms: 4 en-suite, 1 public

Bed & breakfast per night:	£min	£max
Single	26.00	40.00
Double	40.00	45.00

Half board per person:	£min	£max
Daily	30.00	50.00
Weekly	200.00	220.00

Evening meal from 1830
Parking for 7

⛄🚶♿📞🍽️🖥️🛆🅢⚔📺🖥️🖨️🍴50🔍❄️ 🍴🍴❄️🍴 DAP SP

South Lawn Hotel ⚠

≋≋≋ HIGHLY COMMENDED

Lymington Road, Milford-on-Sea, Lymington SO41 0RF
☎ (01590) 643911
Fax (01590) 644820

Attractive country house in peaceful surroundings, where chef/proprietor ensures that food, comfort and personal service predominate.
Bedrooms: 6 double, 18 twin
Bathrooms: 24 en-suite

Bed & breakfast per night:	£min	£max
Single	49.00	52.50
Double	88.00	98.00

Half board per person:	£min	£max
Daily	62.50	67.50
Weekly	385.00	420.00

Lunch available
Evening meal 1900 (last orders 2030)
Parking for 50
Cards accepted: Mastercard, Visa, Switch/Delta

⛄🚶7♿📞🍽️🖥️🛆🍴🅢⚔📺🔵🖥️ 🍴🍴❄️🍴 SP

Westover Hall Hotel ⚠

≋≋≋ COMMENDED

Park Lane, Milford-on-Sea, Lymington SO41 0PT
☎ (01590) 643044
Fax (01590) 644490
Grade II listed Victorian mansion with stunning views of Christchurch Bay and the Needles. Stylish and individual with excellent service and award-winning Italian cuisine.
Bedrooms: 1 single, 5 double, 6 twin
Bathrooms: 12 en-suite

Bed & breakfast per night:	£min	£max
Single	55.00	65.00
Double	100.00	120.00

Half board per person:	£min	£max
Daily	65.00	80.00
Weekly	400.00	450.00

Lunch available

MILFORD-ON-SEA

Continued

Evening meal 1930 (last orders 2130)
Parking for 40
Cards accepted: Amex, Diners, Mastercard, Visa, Switch/Delta

🐃🖐️🗘🖳➡️⚙️🍴📺🖿
🍽️🎱50🖐️🛰️❄️🚗🐾🚭 SP 🏬 T

MILTON ABBAS

Dorset
Map ref 2B3

Sloping village street of thatched houses. A boys' school lies in Capability Brown's landscaped gardens amid hills and woods where the town once stood. The school chapel, former abbey church, can be visited.

Dunbury Heights

👑👑 HIGHLY COMMENDED

Milton Abbas, Blandford Forum
DT11 0DH
☎ (01258) 880445
Always a friendly welcome at this brick and flint cottage. Outstanding views to Poole and Isle of Wight. 6 miles from Blandford Forum. Rural countryside, ideal for walking and touring.
Bedrooms: 1 double, 1 twin
Bathrooms: 1 en-suite, 1 public
Bed & breakfast

per night:	£min	£max
Single	17.50	20.00
Double	40.00	40.00

Parking for 10

🐃🖐️ UL S 🍴 📺 🖿 🍽️❄️🚗

MILTON COMMON

Oxfordshire
Map ref 2C1

Oxford Belfry Hotel 🗚

👑👑👑 HIGHLY COMMENDED

Milton Common, Thame OX9 2JW
☎ (01844) 279381
Fax (01844) 279624
Tudor-style country hotel, privately owned. Well-placed for touring. Indoor leisure complex with swimming pool, sauna, solarium, mini-gym. Half board daily prices based on a minimum 2-night stay.
Bedrooms: 11 single, 54 double, 32 twin
Suites available
Bathrooms: 97 en-suite
Bed & breakfast

per night:	£min	£max
Single	98.50	118.50
Double	124.00	164.00

Half board per person:	£min	£max
Daily	60.00	80.00
Weekly	360.00	480.00

Lunch available
Evening meal 1930 (last orders 2130)
Parking for 200
Cards accepted: Amex, Diners, Mastercard, Visa, Switch/Delta

🐃🖐️🗘🖳♿🛇 S 🖐️ 🍴 🌐🖿🍽️250
🏊🏋️🎣❄️🚭 SP T

MILTON KEYNES

Buckinghamshire
Map ref 2C1

Designated a New Town in 1967, Milton Keynes offers a wide range of housing and is abundantly planted with trees. It has excellent shopping facilities and 3 centres for leisure and sporting activities. The Open University is based here.
Tourist Information Centre ☎ *(01908) 232525*

The Different Drummer Hotel 🗚

👑👑👑 COMMENDED

94 High Street, Stony Stratford, Milton Keynes MK11 1AH
☎ (01908) 564733
Fax (01908) 260646
Historic oak-beamed coaching inn, circa 1470, tastefully restored and modernised throughout and incorporating a high class Italian and English restaurant. Prices shown are weekend rates.
Bedrooms: 5 single, 5 double, 1 twin, 1 triple
Bathrooms: 12 en-suite
Bed & breakfast

per night:	£min	£max
Single	45.00	70.00
Double	55.00	80.00

Lunch available
Evening meal 1900 (last orders 2200)
Cards accepted: Amex, Diners, Mastercard, Visa, Switch/Delta

🐃🖐️🗘🖳♿🛇 S 🍴 📺🌐
🖿🍽️❄️🍴🏬 T 🅿️

ACCESSIBILITY

Look for the ♿🦽🚶 symbols which indicate accessibility for wheelchair users. These are described in detail at the front of this guide.

Kingfishers

Listed COMMENDED

9 Rylstone Close, Heelands, Milton Keynes MK13 7QT
☎ (01908) 310231
Fax (01908) 310231
Large private home set in quarter of an acre of grounds, close to Milton Keynes city centre, bus and railway stations.
Bedrooms: 1 single, 1 double, 1 triple
Bathrooms: 2 en-suite, 1 public
Bed & breakfast

per night:	£min	£max
Single	20.00	25.00
Double	35.00	40.00

Half board per person:	£min	£max
Daily	24.00	32.00
Weekly	165.00	190.00

Evening meal 1800 (last orders 2000)
Parking for 6

🐃2🖐️🗘🖳♿ UL 🖐️🍴📺🖿🍽️
❄️🚗

Swan Revived Hotel 🗚

👑👑👑 HIGHLY COMMENDED

High Street, Newport Pagnell, Milton Keynes MK16 8AR
☎ (01908) 610565
Fax (01908) 210995
CR The Independents
Independently owned famous coaching inn, where guests can enjoy every modern comfort. Convenient for thriving city of Milton Keynes, Woburn, Towcester, Silverstone.
Bedrooms: 17 single, 19 double, 4 twin, 1 triple, 1 family room
Suites available
Bathrooms: 42 en-suite
Bed & breakfast

per night:	£min	£max
Single	42.50	65.00
Double	60.00	72.50

Half board per person:	£min	£max
Daily	57.50	80.00

Lunch available
Evening meal 1915 (last orders 2200)
Parking for 18
Cards accepted: Amex, Diners, Mastercard, Visa, Switch/Delta

🐃🖐️🗘🖳♿🛇 S 🍴 🌐🖿
🖿🍽️75 DAP SP 🏬 T

The 🗚 symbol after an establishment name indicates that it is a Regional Tourist Board member.

NETLEY ABBEY

Hampshire
Map ref 2C3

Romantic ruin, set in green lawns against a background of trees on the east bank of Southampton Water. The abbey was built in the 13th C by Cistercian monks from Beaulieu.

La Casa Blanca M

≝≝ COMMENDED

48 Victoria Road, Netley Abbey, Southampton SO31 5DQ
☎ (01703) 453718
Fax (01703) 453718
Small, pleasantly situated licensed hotel. Friendly welcome, well-equipped en-suite bedrooms and home cooking.
Bedrooms: 4 single, 1 double, 1 twin, 2 triple, 1 family room
Bathrooms: 9 en-suite, 1 public

Bed & breakfast per night:	£min	£max
Single	26.00	26.00
Double	48.00	48.00

Half board per person:	£min	£max
Daily	29.00	36.00

Lunch available
Evening meal 1830 (last orders 2100)
Parking for 8
Cards accepted: Mastercard, Visa, Switch/Delta

☞🖐✆🖃⌧♨🛠Ⓢ📺▥🖪
♩30❀✕🚲 SP T

NETTLEBED

Oxfordshire
Map ref 2C2

The White Hart Hotel M

≝≝≝≝ COMMENDED

High Street, Nettlebed, Henley-on-Thames RG9 5DD
☎ (01491) 641245
Fax (01491) 641423
Historic coaching inn, combining traditional architecture with modern facilities. Convenient for Henley and Oxford.
Bedrooms: 3 double, 3 twin
Bathrooms: 6 en-suite

Bed & breakfast per night:	£min	£max
Single	49.50	54.50
Double	69.50	84.50

Lunch available
Evening meal 1830 (last orders 2200)
Parking for 50
Cards accepted: Mastercard, Visa

☞🖐✆🖃⌧♨🛠Ⓢ✂▥🖪♩40
►❀✕🚲 SP ⌖

NEW FOREST

See under Barton on Sea, Brockenhurst, Burley, Lymington, Lyndhurst, Milford-on-Sea, New Milton, Sway, Woodlands

NEW MILTON

Hampshire
Map ref 2B3

New Forest residential town on the mainline railway.

Chewton Glen Hotel, Health & Country Club M

≝≝≝≝ DE LUXE

Christchurch Road, New Milton BH25 6QS
☎ (01425) 275341
Fax (01425) 272310
Email:reservations
@chewtonglen.com

House of Georgian origin with unobtrusive additions and high standard of interior decoration. Set in 70 acres of parkland.
Bedrooms: 52 double
Suites available
Bathrooms: 52 en-suite

Bed & breakfast per night:	£min	£max
Single	210.00	506.00
Double	230.00	450.00

Half board per person:	£min	£max
Daily	325.00	563.00

Lunch available
Evening meal 1930 (last orders 2130)
Parking for 125
Cards accepted: Amex, Diners, Mastercard, Visa, Switch/Delta

☞7🖐✆🖃⌧♨📶Ⓢ✂🛠◎▥
🖪♩120🏊❀✕🏹🎣♪Ⓤ⌖❀✕🚲
🐾 SP 🎿

Information on accommodation listed in this guide has been supplied by the proprietors. As changes may occur you are advised to check details at the time of booking.

NEWBURY

Berkshire
Map ref 2C2

Ancient town surrounded by the Downs and on the Kennet and Avon Canal. It has many buildings of interest, including the 17th C Cloth Hall, which is now a museum. The famous racecourse is nearby.
Tourist Information Centre ☎ (01635) 30267

Bacon Arms Hotel & Restaurant

≝≝ APPROVED

10 Oxford Street, Newbury RG14 1JB
☎ (01635) 31822
Fax (01635) 552496
Small, 16th C coaching inn, in the town centre. Oak-beamed bar and restaurant, family-run with good home-cooked food. Large car park at rear.
Bedrooms: 7 double, 7 twin
Bathrooms: 13 en-suite, 1 private, 1 public

Bed & breakfast per night:	£min	£max
Single	45.00	50.00
Double	50.00	60.00

Lunch available
Evening meal 1900 (last orders 2130)
Parking for 50
Cards accepted: Amex, Mastercard, Visa, Switch/Delta

☞🖐🖃♨Ⓢ▥🖪♩40✕⌖T

Donnington Valley Hotel & Golf Course M

≝≝≝≝≝ HIGHLY COMMENDED

Old Oxford Road, Donnington, Newbury RG14 3AG
☎ (01635) 551199
Fax (01635) 551123
Stylish country house hotel set in Berkshire countryside. 18-hole golf-course, award-winning restaurant. Excellent touring base for southern England.
Bedrooms: 43 double, 15 twin
Suites available
Bathrooms: 58 en-suite, 2 public

Bed & breakfast per night:	£min	£max
Single	65.00	124.50
Double	45.00	149.00

Lunch available
Evening meal 1900 (last orders 2200)
Parking for 150
Cards accepted: Amex, Diners, Mastercard, Visa

☞🖐✆🖃⌧♨📶Ⓢ✂◎▥
🖪♩140🎣Ⓤ⌖❀🐾 SP

NEWBURY
Continued

Jarvis Elcot Park Hotel M
⚜⚜⚜⚜ HIGHLY COMMENDED
Elcot, Newbury RG20 8NJ
☎ (01488) 658100
Fax (01488) 658288
Ⓒ Jarvis/Utell International
Elegant and peaceful 18th C mansion, in beautiful park and gardens laid out by the Royal Gardener, Sir William Paxton. Log fires, individually decorated bedrooms and Seb Coe Health Club.
Bedrooms: 2 single, 64 double, 9 twin
Bathrooms: 75 en-suite

Bed & breakfast

per night:	£min	£max
Single	47.50	52.50
Double	95.00	105.00

Half board per

person:	£min	£max
Daily	55.00	65.00
Weekly	385.00	455.00

Lunch available
Evening meal 1900 (last orders 2130)
Parking for 138
Cards accepted: Amex, Diners, Mastercard, Visa, Switch/Delta

Regency Park Hotel M
⚜⚜⚜⚜ HIGHLY COMMENDED
Bowling Green Road, Thatcham, Newbury RG18 3RP
☎ (01635) 871555
Fax (01635) 871571
Ⓒ MacDonald
Standing in 5 acres of Berkshire countryside, 7 minutes from junction 13 of M4. Renowned restaurant and bar. Ideal weekend retreat. Weekend breaks from £54 per person per night.
Bedrooms: 19 single, 15 double, 14 twin, 1 triple
Suite available
Bathrooms: 49 en-suite

Bed & breakfast

per night:	£min	£max
Single	52.50	95.00
Double	75.00	115.00

Half board per

person:	£min	£max
Daily	49.50	65.00

Lunch available
Evening meal 1830 (last orders 2230)
Parking for 125

Cards accepted: Amex, Diners, Mastercard, Visa, Switch/Delta

NORTHMOOR
Oxfordshire
Map ref 2C1

The Ferryman Inn M
Bablock Hythe, Northmoor, Oxford OX8 1BL
☎ (01865) 880028
Fax (01865) 880028

Riverside inn on site of ancient ferry crossing. Recently renovated to give two bars, restaurant and en-suite bedrooms.
Bedrooms: 3 double, 1 twin, 2 triple
Bathrooms: 6 en-suite

Bed & breakfast

per night:	£min	£max
Single	35.00	35.00
Double	40.00	40.00

Lunch available
Evening meal 1830 (last orders 2200)
Parking for 100

OXFORD
Oxfordshire
Map ref 2C1

Beautiful university town with many ancient colleges, some dating from the 13th C, and numerous buildings of historic and architectural interest. The Ashmolean Museum has outstanding collections. Lovely gardens and meadows with punting on the Cherwell.
Tourist Information Centre ☎ *(01865) 726871*

Acorn Guest House
Listed COMMENDED
260 Iffley Road, Oxford OX4 1SE
☎ (01865) 247998
Victorian house situated midway between the city centre and the ring-road. Convenient for all local amenities and more distant attractions.
Bedrooms: 4 single, 2 twin, 7 triple
Bathrooms: 4 public

Bed & breakfast

per night:	£min	£max
Single	22.00	25.00
Double	34.00	40.00

Parking for 11
Cards accepted: Diners, Mastercard, Visa

All Seasons Guest House M
⚜ COMMENDED
63 Windmill Road, Headington, Oxford OX3 7BP
☎ (01865) 742215
Victorian house with lots of character, spacious rooms, car parking, patio, 2 miles from city centre. Frequent bus service. Convenient for Cotswolds and close to M40 motorway.
Bedrooms: 1 single, 3 double, 2 twin
Bathrooms: 3 en-suite, 1 public

Bed & breakfast

per night:	£min	£max
Single	25.00	30.00
Double	45.00	55.00

Parking for 6

All Views
⚜⚜ COMMENDED
67 Old Witney Road, On main A40, Eynsham, Oxford OX8 1PU
☎ (01865) 880891
7-acre nursery. 1991-built Cotswold-stone chalet bungalow, adjacent A40 between Oxford and Witney. Designed with guests' comfort in mind. All rooms have full facilities.
Bedrooms: 1 single, 2 double, 1 twin
Bathrooms: 4 en-suite

Bed & breakfast

per night:	£min	£max
Single	39.95	39.95
Double	45.00	49.95

Parking for 10
Cards accepted: Mastercard, Visa, Switch/Delta

The Balkan Lodge Hotel
⚜⚜ COMMENDED
315 Iffley Road, Oxford OX4 4AG
☎ (01865) 244524
Delightful small hotel, recently refurbished. En-suite bedrooms with Sky TV, hairdryer, trouser press, direct-dial telephone, tea/coffee facilities. Car park at rear.
Bedrooms: 3 single, 9 double, 1 twin
Bathrooms: 13 private

Bed & breakfast

per night:	£min	£max
Single	50.00	
Double	58.50	

Evening meal 1900 (last orders 2100)
Parking for 13
Cards accepted: Mastercard, Visa, Switch/Delta

❄️🍴📞📠🗄️🕹️🎿🛗📺🛏️🖨️ ♨️✪🐾 DAP SP

Bravalla Guest House ⋀⋀
Listed COMMENDED

242 Iffley Road, Oxford OX4 1SE
☎ (01865) 241326 & 250511
Fax (01865) 250511
Small family-run guesthouse, mostly en-suite, within half a mile of Magdalen College with its famous deer park. 1 mile from city centre.
Bedrooms: 2 double, 2 twin, 1 triple, 1 family room
Bathrooms: 5 en-suite, 1 public, 1 private shower
Bed & breakfast

per night:	£min	£max
Single	25.00	35.00
Double	40.00	48.00

Parking for 4
Cards accepted: Diners, Mastercard, Visa

🐴🖵🍴 UL S 🛏️🎠 DAP SP

Casa Villa Guest House ⋀⋀
👑 COMMENDED

388 Banbury Road, Summertown, Oxford OX2 7PW
☎ (01865) 512642
Fax (01865) 512642
Detached guesthouse in north Oxford, one and three-quarter miles from city centre. Friendly and pleasant service provided. Close to all amenities and easy access to M40.
Bedrooms: 2 single, 5 double, 1 twin, 1 family room
Bathrooms: 5 en-suite, 2 public
Bed & breakfast

per night:	£min	£max
Single	29.00	45.00
Double	54.00	59.00

Evening meal 1830 (last orders 2030)
Parking for 6
Cards accepted: Amex, Mastercard, Visa

🐴📠📞🖵🕹️ UL 🎿🛗📺🛏️♨️ 🐾🚭 SP T

The symbols in each entry give information about services and facilities. A key to these symbols appears at the back of this guide.

Combermere House ⋀⋀
Listed COMMENDED

11 Polstead Road, Oxford OX2 6TW
☎ (01865) 556971
Fax (01865) 556971

Family-run Victorian house in quiet tree-lined road in residential north Oxford, 1 mile from city centre and colleges.
Bedrooms: 4 single, 1 double, 3 triple, 1 family room
Bathrooms: 9 en-suite
Bed & breakfast

per night:	£min	£max
Single	23.00	35.00
Double	38.00	56.00

Parking for 3
Cards accepted: Amex, Diners, Mastercard, Visa

🐴❄️🖵🕹️ UL 🔒S🎿🛏️🎠✿🚂🏨 T

Cotswold House
👑👑 HIGHLY COMMENDED

363 Banbury Road, Oxford OX2 7PL
☎ (01865) 310558
Fax (01865) 310558
Well-situated elegant property offering a high standard of furnishings and facilities in each of its rooms.
Bedrooms: 2 single, 2 double, 1 twin, 2 triple
Bathrooms: 7 en-suite
Bed & breakfast

per night:	£min	£max
Single	39.00	41.00
Double	58.00	62.00

Parking for 7

🐴5❄️📠🖵🕹️ UL S🎿🛏️🛗🎠 🐾🚂

Falcon Private Hotel ⋀⋀
👑👑 COMMENDED

88-90 Abingdon Road, Oxford OX1 4PX
☎ (01865) 722995
Fax (01865) 246642
Victorian building with modern facilities, overlooking Queens College playing fields. 10 minutes' walk to colleges and city centre.
Bedrooms: 2 single, 5 double, 2 twin, 1 triple, 2 family rooms
Bathrooms: 12 en-suite, 1 public

per night:	£min	£max
Single	29.00	
Double		54.00

Parking for 9
Cards accepted: Mastercard, Visa, Switch/Delta

🐴❄️📠📞🖵🕹️ UL 🔒S🎿🛏️📺🛏️♨️🎠✕

Isis Guest House ⋀⋀
Listed APPROVED

45-53 Iffley Road, Oxford OX4 1ED
☎ (01865) 248894 & 242466
Fax (01865) 243492
Modernised, Victorian, city centre guesthouse within walking distance of colleges and shops. Easy access to ring road.
Bedrooms: 12 single, 6 double, 17 twin, 2 triple
Bathrooms: 15 private, 10 public
Bed & breakfast

per night:	£min	£max
Single	21.00	25.00
Double	42.00	46.00

Parking for 18
Open June–September
Cards accepted: Mastercard, Visa

🐴❄️📞🖵🕹️ UL 🎿🛏️♨️🎠 DAP T

King's Arms Hotel ⋀⋀
👑👑👑 COMMENDED

The Old Green, Horton cum Studley, Oxford OX33 1AY
☎ (01865) 351235
Fax (01865) 351721
Charming Cotswold-stone country hotel in village location with golf course nearby. Ideal base for visiting Oxford, Blenheim Palace and the Cotswolds.
Bedrooms: 2 single, 5 double, 2 twin, 1 triple
Suites available
Bathrooms: 10 en-suite
Bed & breakfast

per night:	£min	£max
Single	30.00	39.00
Double	45.00	65.00

Half board per person:	£min	£max
Daily	32.50	49.00
Weekly	225.00	280.00

Lunch available
Evening meal 1900 (last orders 2100)
Parking for 30
Cards accepted: Amex, Mastercard, Visa, Switch/Delta

🐴📠🖵🕹️🔒S🎿🛗♨️🛏️25 U🕹️ ✕🚭 SP T

OXFORD
Continued

Marlborough House Hotel M

Listed HIGHLY COMMENDED

321 Woodstock Road, Oxford
OX2 7NY
☎ (01865) 311321
Fax (01865) 515329
Email: enquiries@marlbhouse.win-
uk.net

*1.5 miles from Oxford city centre. All
rooms en-suite with telephone, TV,
fridge, desk, armchair, tea/coffee
facilities. Continental breakfast. Parking.*
Bedrooms: 2 single, 8 double, 4 twin,
2 triple
Bathrooms: 16 en-suite, 1 public

Bed & breakfast per night:	£min	£max
Single	59.50	59.50
Double	69.50	69.50

Parking for 6
Cards accepted: Amex, Mastercard,
Visa, Switch/Delta

Milka's Guest House M

COMMENDED

379 Iffley Road, Oxford OX4 4DP
☎ (01865) 778458
Fax (01865) 776477
*Pleasant semi-detached house on main
road, 1 mile from city centre.*
Bedrooms: 2 double, 1 twin
Bathrooms: 1 en-suite, 1 public

Bed & breakfast per night:	£min	£max
Single	25.00	35.00
Double	45.00	55.00

Parking for 3

Mount Pleasant M

APPROVED

76 London Road, Headington,
Oxford OX3 9AJ
☎ (01865) 62749
Fax (01865) 62749
*Small, no smoking, family-run hotel
offering full facilities. On the A40 and
convenient for Oxford shopping,
hospitals, colleges, visiting the Chilterns
and the Cotswolds.*
Bedrooms: 2 double, 5 twin, 1 triple
Bathrooms: 8 en-suite

Bed & breakfast per night:	£min	£max
Single	37.50	45.00
Double	48.00	75.00

Half board per person:	£min	£max
Daily	37.50	45.00

Lunch available
Evening meal 1800 (last orders
2130)
Parking for 6
Cards accepted: Amex, Diners,
Mastercard, Visa

Newton House M

82-84 Abingdon Road, Oxford
OX1 4PL
☎ (01865) 240561 & 0585 485656
Fax (01865) 244647
*Centrally located Victorian town house
within walking distance of city centre,
university, meadows, River Isis and
university boat houses.*
Bedrooms: 7 double, 4 twin, 2 family
rooms
Bathrooms: 5 private, 3 public

Bed & breakfast per night:	£min	£max
Single	22.00	30.00
Double	34.00	50.00

Parking for 8
Cards accepted: Amex, Mastercard,
Visa, Switch/Delta

The Old Black Horse Hotel M

COMMENDED

102 St Clements, Oxford OX4 1AR
☎ (01865) 244691
Fax (01865) 242771
*Former coaching inn with private car
park, close to Magdalen Bridge,
colleges, riverside walks and city centre.
Easy access M40 north and south.*
Bedrooms: 1 single, 4 double, 3 twin,
2 triple
Bathrooms: 10 en-suite, 1 public

Bed & breakfast per night:	£min	£max
Single	50.00	65.00
Double	75.00	85.00

Lunch available
Evening meal 1900 (last orders
2100)
Parking for 25
Cards accepted: Amex, Mastercard,
Visa

The Old Parsonage Hotel M

HIGHLY COMMENDED

1 Banbury Road, Oxford OX2 6NN
☎ (01865) 310210
Fax (01865) 311262
Email: oldparsonage@dial.pipex.com
*Independently owned hotel in the
centre of the city. 17th C building with
an informal restaurant, open from 7am
until late.*
Bedrooms: 1 single, 19 double,
6 twin, 4 triple
Suites available
Bathrooms: 30 en-suite

Bed & breakfast per night:	£min	£max
Single	120.00	
Double	145.00	160.00

Lunch available
Evening meal 1800 (last orders
2300)
Parking for 15
Cards accepted: Amex, Diners,
Mastercard, Visa, Switch/Delta

Pine Castle Hotel M

HIGHLY COMMENDED

290 Iffley Road, Oxford OX4 4AE
☎ (01865) 241497 & 728887
Fax (01865) 727230
Email: pinebeds.oxfhotel
@pop3.hiway.co.uk
*Characterful Edwardian guesthouse
close to city centre and picturesque
River Thames. A warm welcome awaits
you from the resident proprietor.*
Bedrooms: 5 double, 2 twin, 1 family
room
Bathrooms: 8 en-suite

Bed & breakfast per night:	£min	£max
Double	55.00	65.00

Evening meal 1800 (last orders
1900)
Parking for 4
Cards accepted: Mastercard, Visa,
Switch/Delta

The Randolph M

HIGHLY COMMENDED

Beaumont Street, Oxford OX1 2LN
☎ (01865) 247481
Fax (01865) 791678
Ⓡ Forte/Utell International
*Oxford's most famous hotel, with
magnificent public rooms and
bedrooms in a traditional style. Situated
in the heart of the city.*
Bedrooms: 41 single, 41 double,
20 twin, 7 family rooms
Suites available
Bathrooms: 109 en-suite

Bed & breakfast per night:	£min	£max
Single	59.00	74.00

Half board per person:	£min	£max
Daily	74.00	89.00

Lunch available
Evening meal 1730 (last orders 2200)
Parking for 65
Cards accepted: Amex, Diners, Mastercard, Visa, Switch/Delta

🐕♿🖥📞💷🖵🚿♿🛡⚓S⚒🕅◑⊞ 🏨🅿📶300 🐾 SP 🎯 T

River Hotel 𝔐

♨♨♨ COMMENDED

17 Botley Road, Oxford OX2 0AA
☎ (01865) 243475
Fax (01865) 724306
Riverside setting within walking distance of city, colleges and bus/rail stations. Residents' bar, car park. "Large enough to be comfortable, small enough to be friendly."
Bedrooms: 6 single, 8 double, 2 twin, 5 triple
Bathrooms: 17 en-suite, 2 private, 2 private showers

Bed & breakfast per night:	£min	£max
Single	45.00	60.00
Double	67.50	75.00

Evening meal 1830 (last orders 2000)
Parking for 25
Cards accepted: Mastercard, Visa

🐕♿🖥📞💷🖵🚿🛡S⚒📺🏨🅿 🍴50 🎣🚴🎿🚗

Studley Priory Hotel 𝔐

♨♨♨♨ HIGHLY COMMENDED

Horton cum Studley, Oxford OX33 1AZ
☎ (01865) 351203 & 351254
Fax (01865) 351613
ⓒ Thames Valley
Converted Elizabethan manor house in a rural setting north east of Oxford, with a restaurant that specialises in English cooking.
Bedrooms: 6 single, 8 double, 5 twin
Suite available
Bathrooms: 19 en-suite

Bed & breakfast per night:	£min	£max
Single	100.00	130.00
Double	135.00	200.00

Lunch available
Evening meal 1930 (last orders 2130)
Parking for 101
Cards accepted: Amex, Diners, Mastercard, Visa

🐕♿🖥📞💷🖵🚿🛡S⚒🕅◑ 🏨🅿🍴35🎾🌸🚴🎿🚗 SP 🎯 T

Victoria Hotel 𝔐

♨♨♨ COMMENDED

180 Abingdon Road, Oxford OX1 4RA
☎ (01865) 724536
Fax (01865) 794909
Completely modernised Victorian hotel. En-suite rooms with direct-dial telephone, colour TV, radio, hairdryer, tea/coffee facilities. Walking distance to city centre. Competitive prices. Car park at rear.
Bedrooms: 7 single, 12 double, 1 twin, 2 triple
Bathrooms: 15 en-suite, 2 public

Bed & breakfast per night:	£min	£max
Single	37.50	55.50
Double	58.50	72.50

Lunch available
Evening meal 1900 (last orders 2100)
Parking for 20
Cards accepted: Mastercard, Visa

🐕🍴1♿🖥📞💷🖵🚿🛡🕅🏨 🅿🚗🌸 DAP SP T

Westwood Country Hotel 𝔐

♨♨♨ COMMENDED

Hinksey Hill Top, Oxford OX1 5BG
☎ (01865) 735408
Fax (01865) 736536
ⓒ Minotel/Logis of GB
In 4 acres of woodland and wildlife gardens, opened by David Bellamy. Winner of award for facilities for disabled people. High standard of cuisine. Oxford city centre 3.5 miles.
Wheelchair access category 1♿
Bedrooms: 6 single, 8 double, 3 twin, 4 triple
Bathrooms: 21 en-suite

Bed & breakfast per night:	£min	£max
Single	55.00	65.00
Double	80.00	99.00

Lunch available
Evening meal 1900 (last orders 2030)
Parking for 50
Cards accepted: Amex, Diners, Mastercard, Visa, Switch/Delta

🐕♿🖥📞💷🖵🚿🛡S⚒🕅📺 🏨🅿🍴70🎣🎾⛳🎣🌸🚴🎿🚗 DAP SP T

PANGBOURNE

Berkshire
Map ref 2C2

A pretty stretch of river where the Pang joins the Thames with views of the lock, weir and toll bridge. Once the home of Kenneth Grahame, author of "Wind in the Willows".

The Copper Inn Hotel & Restaurant 𝔐

♨♨♨♨ HIGHLY COMMENDED

Church Road, Pangbourne, Reading RG8 7AR
☎ (0118) 984 2244
Fax (0118) 984 5542
ⓒ Best Western

Elegantly restored Georgian coaching inn with a restaurant overlooking secluded gardens. Good base for exploring the beautiful Thames Valley and all its attractions. Special weekend rates.
Bedrooms: 2 single, 14 double, 5 twin, 1 triple
Bathrooms: 22 en-suite

Bed & breakfast per night:	£min	£max
Single	42.50	95.00
Double	85.00	120.00

Half board per person:	£min	£max
Daily	60.00	112.50

Lunch available
Evening meal 1900 (last orders 2200)
Parking for 20
Cards accepted: Amex, Diners, Mastercard, Visa, Switch/Delta

🐕♿🖥📞💷🖵🚿🛡S⚒🏨🅿 🍴60🎾🌸🐾 SP 🎯 T

PETERSFIELD

Hampshire
Map ref 2C3

Grew prosperous from the wool trade and was famous as a coaching centre. Its attractive market square is dominated by a statue of William III. Close by are Petersfield Heath with numerous ancient barrows and Butser Hill with magnificent views.
Tourist Information Centre ☎ (01730) 268829

Langrish House

COMMENDED

Langrish, Petersfield GU32 1RN
☎ (01730) 266941
Fax (01730) 260543

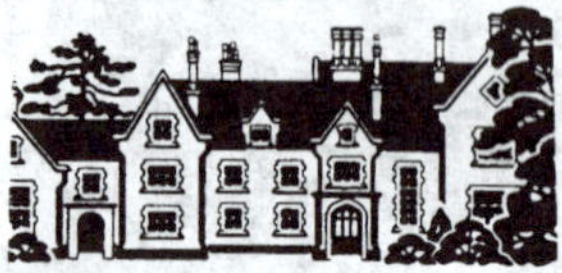

Delightful old English manor house with panoramic views set in 13 acres of beautiful countryside. Idyllic country walks and 7 golf-courses nearby.
Bedrooms: 6 single, 6 double, 6 twin
Bathrooms: 18 en-suite

Bed & breakfast per night:	£min	£max
Single	35.00	48.00
Double	75.00	85.00

Half board per person:	£min	£max
Daily	50.00	61.00

Evening meal 1930 (last orders 2130)
Parking for 50
Cards accepted: Amex, Diners, Mastercard, Visa
[S] [TV] 60 [SP] [T]

A key to symbols can be found inside the back cover flap.

ACCESSIBILITY

Look for the symbols which indicate accessibility for wheelchair users. These are described in detail at the front of this guide.

POOLE

Dorset
Map ref 2B3

Tremendous natural harbour makes Poole a superb boating centre. The harbour area is crowded with historic buildings including the 15th C Town Cellars housing a maritime museum.
Tourist Information Centre ☎ (01202) 253253

The Golden Sovereigns Hotel

COMMENDED

97 Alumhurst Road, Alum Chine, Bournemouth BH4 8HR
☎ (01202) 762088
Attractively decorated Victorian character hotel. Quiet, convenient location; beach 4 minutes' walk. Comfortable rooms, traditional home-cooking. Early booking special discounts.
Bedrooms: 2 single, 2 double, 1 twin, 2 triple, 2 family rooms
Bathrooms: 6 en-suite, 1 private, 1 public

Bed & breakfast per night:	£min	£max
Single	15.50	30.00
Double	30.00	50.00

Half board per person:	£min	£max
Daily	23.00	37.50
Weekly	140.00	190.00

Lunch available
Evening meal 1800 (last orders 1600)
Parking for 9
Cards accepted: Mastercard, Visa
[S] [TV] OAP [SP]

Harmony Hotel

APPROVED

19 St Peter's Road, Parkstone, Poole BH14 0NZ
☎ (01202) 747510
Fax (01202) 747510
Friendly service in peaceful, residential area close to all local amenities. Ideally placed as a touring centre.
Bedrooms: 5 double, 4 twin, 2 triple
Bathrooms: 8 en-suite, 1 public

Bed & breakfast per night:	£min	£max
Single	16.00	27.00
Double	26.00	44.00

Half board per person:	£min	£max
Daily	22.00	

Lunch available
Evening meal 1900 (last orders 1945)
Parking for 14
Cards accepted: Mastercard, Visa
[S] [TV] OAP [SP] [T]

PORTSMOUTH & SOUTHSEA

Hampshire
Map ref 2C3

The first dock was built in 1194. HMS Victory, Nelson's flagship, is here and Charles Dickens' former home is open to the public. Neighbouring Southsea has a promenade with magnificent views of Spithead.
Tourist Information Centre ☎ (01705) 838382 or 826722

Beaufort Hotel

HIGHLY COMMENDED

71 Festing Road, Southsea, Portsmouth, Hampshire PO4 0NQ
☎ (01705) 823707 & Freephone 0800 919237
Fax (01705) 870270
[CR] Logis of GB/The Independents
Hotel with en-suite bedrooms, standing in its own grounds, 1 minute's walk from seafront. Car park.
Bedrooms: 3 single, 11 double, 2 twin, 2 triple, 1 family room
Bathrooms: 19 en-suite

Bed & breakfast per night:	£min	£max
Single	40.00	50.00
Double	56.00	70.00

Half board per person:	£min	£max
Daily	50.00	60.00
Weekly	220.00	270.00

Lunch available
Evening meal 1830 (last orders 2030)
Parking for 10
Cards accepted: Amex, Mastercard, Visa, Switch/Delta
[S] OAP [SP] [T]

Bembell Court Hotel

COMMENDED

69 Festing Road, Southsea, Portsmouth, Hampshire PO4 0NQ
☎ (01705) 735915 & 750497
Fax (01705) 756497
Friendly, family-run, licensed hotel, ideally situated in Southsea's prime holiday area, with an excellent selection of shops, pubs and restaurants nearby.
Bedrooms: 2 single, 4 double, 4 twin, 3 triple, 1 family room
Bathrooms: 10 en-suite, 3 public

Bed & breakfast

per night:	£min	£max
Single	25.00	35.00
Double	39.00	46.00

Half board per

person:	£min	£max
Daily	35.00	45.00
Weekly	210.00	229.00

Evening meal 1800 (last orders 1900)
Parking for 12
Cards accepted: Amex, Diners, Mastercard, Visa, Switch/Delta
🛏🖨📞🖃📺👤🕮📶⚡🅂↙🖳📺▭ 🚗 OAP ⚹ SP T

The Dolphins Hotel & Snobbs Cocktail Bar & Restaurant ♠
♛♛♛ APPROVED
10-11 Western Parade, Southsea, Hampshire PO5 3JF
☎ (01705) 823823 & 820833
Fax (01705) 820833
On the seafront, overlooking the common. Attractive bar and restaurant. Near Mary Rose, HMS Victory, HMS Warrior, ferry terminals, shopping centres, museums, sport and entertainment.
Bedrooms: 10 single, 6 double, 13 twin, 4 triple
Bathrooms: 20 en-suite, 5 public, 2 private showers

Bed & breakfast

per night:	£min	£max
Single	24.00	33.00
Double	42.00	46.00

Half board per

person:	£min	£max
Daily	30.00	42.00

Evening meal 1930 (last orders 2145)
Cards accepted: Amex, Diners, Mastercard, Visa, Switch/Delta
🛏1🖨📞🖃📺👤🅂🖳📺🌙▭ 🚗🍴 OAP ⚹ SP T

Fairlea Guest House ♠
Listed COMMENDED
19 Beach Road, Southsea, Hampshire PO5 2JH
☎ (01705) 733090
Comfortable homely accommodation close to shops, seafront and museums. Own keys, access at all times.
Bedrooms: 2 double, 2 triple
Bathrooms: 2 public

Bed & breakfast

per night:	£min	£max
Single	12.00	12.50
Double	24.00	25.00

🛏🖨📞👤🖳UL📺▭ 🚗 OAP SP

Forte Posthouse Portsmouth ♠
♛♛♛♛ COMMENDED
Pembroke Road, Portsmouth, Hampshire PO1 2TA
☎ (01705) 827651
Fax (01705) 756715
©® Forte

Completely refurbished to include full leisure facilities. In a central position overlooking the seafront at Southsea. Business services available. Half board prices based on a minimum 2-night stay.
Bedrooms: 79 double, 75 twin, 9 family rooms
Bathrooms: 163 en-suite

Bed & breakfast

per night:	£min	£max
Single	68.95	
Double	78.90	

Half board per

person:	£min	£max
Daily	47.00	56.00

Lunch available
Evening meal 1730 (last orders 2230)
Parking for 70
Cards accepted: Amex, Diners, Mastercard, Visa, Switch/Delta
🛏🖨📞🖃📺👤🕮📶🅂↙🖳📺 ⬆▭🚗220⚽🍴🎾🏊⚹ SP T ⊚

Keppel's Head Hotel ♠
♛♛♛ APPROVED
The Hard, Portsmouth, Hampshire PO1 3DT
☎ (01705) 833231
Fax (01705) 838688
©® Regal
A hotel with historic naval connections, close to HMS Victory and the Continental ferries.
Bedrooms: 9 single, 10 double, 5 twin, 3 triple
Bathrooms: 27 en-suite

Bed & breakfast

per night:	£min	£max
Single	49.00	55.00
Double	59.00	69.00

Lunch available
Evening meal 1900 (last orders 2100)
Parking for 18
Cards accepted: Amex, Diners, Mastercard, Visa, Switch/Delta
🛏📞📞👤📶🅂↙🌙▭🚗
🍴60🏊 SP 🎯 T

Newleaze Guest House ♠
Listed COMMENDED
11 St Edward's Road, Southsea, Hampshire PO5 3DH
☎ (01705) 832735
Small friendly establishment with home cooking, giving good value for money. Within easy reach of continental ferry port.
Bedrooms: 1 single, 1 double, 3 twin, 1 family room
Bathrooms: 1 en-suite, 1 public, 1 private shower

Bed & breakfast

per night:	£min	£max
Single	16.00	17.00
Double	30.00	40.00

Half board per

person:	£min	£max
Daily	22.50	23.50
Weekly	90.00	120.00

Evening meal from 1800
Cards accepted: Mastercard, Visa, Switch/Delta
🛏🖨📞👤UL🅂↙🖳▭🚗🚗 OAP
SP T

Oakdale Guest House ♠
♛♛♛ COMMENDED
71 St Ronans Road, Southsea, Hampshire PO4 0PP
☎ (01705) 737358
Fax (01705) 737358
Elegant, comfortable Edwardian house, 5 minutes from flower-filled seafront and handy for historic ships, shops and restaurants.
Bedrooms: 2 single, 2 double, 2 twin
Bathrooms: 6 en-suite

Bed & breakfast

per night:	£min	£max
Single	23.00	31.00
Double	31.00	45.00

Half board per

person:	£min	£max
Daily	35.50	43.50
Weekly	237.50	304.50

Evening meal from 1800
Open February–December
Cards accepted: Mastercard, Visa
🛏🖨📞👤UL🅂↙🖳▭🚗🌸✳
🚗 OAP SP

> You are advised to confirm your booking in writing.

> For ideas on places to visit refer to the introduction at the beginning of this section.

PORTSMOUTH & SOUTHSEA
Continued

Oakleigh Guest House ⏶

Listed COMMENDED

48 Festing Grove, Southsea,
Hampshire PO4 9QD
☎ (01705) 812276
*Family-run guesthouse, 5 minutes from
seafront and ferries. All modern
amenities, colour TV, tea/coffee making
facilities.*
Bedrooms: 2 single, 2 double, 1 twin,
2 family rooms
Suites available
Bathrooms: 2 en-suite, 1 public
Bed & breakfast

per night:	£min	£max
Single	14.00	14.00
Double	28.00	32.00

Half board per person:	£min	£max
Daily	20.00	22.00
Weekly	120.00	130.00

Lunch available
Evening meal 1800 (last orders
1600)

Ocean Hotel & Apartments ⏶

👑👑👑 COMMENDED

8-10 St Helens Parade, Southsea,
Hampshire PO4 0RW
☎ (01705) 734233
Fax (01705) 297046
*Imposing building in foremost seafront
position between South Parade Pier
and Canoe Lake with magnificent sea
views. Choice of hotel rooms, suites, or
self-contained apartments. Lift to all
floors. Car park.*
Bedrooms: 1 single, 4 double,
4 triple, 7 family rooms
Suites available
Bathrooms: 15 en-suite, 4 public
Bed & breakfast

per night:	£min	£max
Single	20.00	40.00
Double	40.00	50.00

Half board per person:	£min	£max
Daily	30.00	38.00
Weekly	190.00	280.00

Evening meal 1830 (last orders
2130)
Parking for 37
Cards accepted: Mastercard, Visa

Rydeview Hotel ⏶

👑 APPROVED

9 Western Parade, Southsea,
Hampshire PO5 3JF
☎ (01705) 820865
Fax (01705) 863664
*Very friendly family hotel on the
seafront. Few minutes' walk to the
shopping centre. Most rooms with
private facilities.*
Bedrooms: 3 single, 4 double, 2 twin,
5 family rooms
Suites available
Bathrooms: 7 en-suite, 3 public,
2 private showers
Bed & breakfast

per night:	£min	£max
Single	15.00	17.50
Double	30.00	38.00

Cards accepted: Amex, Mastercard,
Visa

Salisbury Hotel

👑👑👑 COMMENDED

57-59 Festing Road, Southsea,
Hampshire PO4 0NQ
☎ (01705) 823606 & 0958 222851
Fax (01705) 820955
*Friendly family hotel with character.
Two minutes' walk from sea and other
attractions. Recently refurbished. Private
car park.*
Bedrooms: 6 single, 5 double, 3 twin,
4 triple
Suites available
Bathrooms: 9 en-suite, 3 public,
7 private showers
Bed & breakfast

per night:	£min	£max
Single	19.00	34.00
Double	38.00	48.00

Half board per person:	£min	£max
Daily	30.00	45.00
Weekly	200.00	260.00

Evening meal 1900 (last orders
2000)
Parking for 14
Cards accepted: Mastercard, Visa

> Please check prices and other
> details at the time of booking.

> Establishments should be
> open throughout the year,
> unless otherwise stated.

Sally Port Inn ⏶

👑👑 COMMENDED

57-58 High Street, Portsmouth,
Hampshire PO1 2LU
☎ (01705) 821860
Fax (01705) 821293

*16th C timber-framed inn, with a
charming atmosphere of bygone days.
Situated opposite the cathedral in the
heart of the "old" city. Nearby are
museums, promenades and historic
ships.*
Bedrooms: 4 single, 3 double, 2 twin,
1 triple
Bathrooms: 2 public, 7 private
showers
Bed & breakfast

per night:	£min	£max
Single	32.00	39.00
Double	49.00	59.00

Half board per person:	£min	£max
Weekly	199.00	229.00

Lunch available
Evening meal 1900 (last orders
2200)
Cards accepted: Amex, Diners,
Mastercard, Visa, Switch/Delta

The Sandringham Hotel ⏶

👑👑👑 COMMENDED

Osborne Road/Clarence Parade,
Southsea, Hampshire PO5 3LR
☎ (01705) 826969 & 822914
Fax (01705) 822330
*Seafront hotel with sea views from
most bedrooms. Recently refurbished to
the highest standards. 100-seat
restaurant, function/conference room,
large ballroom. Free car park opposite.
Two minutes' walk to Southsea
shopping centre.*
Bedrooms: 7 single, 14 double,
10 twin, 7 triple, 4 family rooms
Bathrooms: 42 en-suite, 2 public
Bed & breakfast

per night:	£min	£max
Single	25.00	35.00
Double	40.00	50.00

Half board per person:	£min	£max
Daily	32.00	37.00
Weekly	175.00	250.00

Lunch available
Evening meal 1900 (last orders
2130)
Parking for 5

Cards accepted: Amex, Diners, Mastercard, Visa

🐕🏠📞🖥🖳♿👤🛡S✂🍴TV◐●
⬆🛏🅿🍴200✿❀DAP🚭SP🎪T

Solent Hotel
♛♛♛ APPROVED

14-17 South Parade, Southsea, Hampshire PO5 2JB
☎ (01705) 875566
Fax (01705) 872023
Recently refurbished hotel occupying a prime position on the seafront, with magnificent views of the Solent and Isle of Wight. Lift to all floors. Restaurant and games rooms.
Bedrooms: 9 single, 21 double, 9 twin, 6 triple, 5 family rooms
Bathrooms: 50 en-suite, 4 public
Bed & breakfast

per night:	£min	£max
Single	37.50	45.00
Double	47.50	65.00

Half board per

person:	£min	£max
Daily	37.50	57.50
Weekly	215.00	275.00

Lunch available
Evening meal 1900 (last orders 2045)
Parking for 4
Cards accepted: Amex, Diners, Mastercard, Visa, Switch/Delta

🐕📞🖥🖳♿👤🛡S✂🍴TV◐●⬆
🛏🅿🍴80✿❀DAP🚭SP T

Westfield Hall Hotel M
♛♛♛ HIGHLY COMMENDED

65 Festing Road, Southsea, Hampshire PO4 0NQ
☎ (01705) 826971
Fax (01705) 870200
Small, exclusive hotel in own grounds, with large car park, 3 minutes from Southsea's seafront, promenade and canoe lake. Half board prices below are for single occupancy.
Bedrooms: 2 single, 7 double, 4 twin, 4 triple, 3 family rooms
Bathrooms: 20 en-suite
Bed & breakfast

per night:	£min	£max
Single	38.00	46.00
Double	48.00	65.00

Half board per

person:	£min	£max
Daily	52.00	60.00
Weekly	312.00	444.00

Evening meal 1830 (last orders 2030)
Parking for 18
Cards accepted: Amex, Diners, Mastercard, Visa, Switch/Delta

🐕♿📞🖥🖳♿👤🛡✂🍴TV🖳
🅿🐾DAP🚭SP T

Busy, modern county town with large shopping centre and many leisure and recreation facilities. There are several interesting museums and the Duke of Wellington's Stratfield Saye is nearby.
Tourist Information Centre ☎ (0118) 956 6226

Abbey House Private Hotel M
♛♛♛ COMMENDED

118 Connaught Road, Reading RG30 2UF
☎ (0118) 959 0549
Fax (0118) 956 9299
CR The Independents
Hotel run by the proprietors and situated close to the town centre.
Bedrooms: 6 single, 5 double, 9 twin
Bathrooms: 17 en-suite, 2 public, 1 private shower
Bed & breakfast

per night:	£min	£max
Single	30.00	49.50
Double	45.00	66.00

Evening meal 1900 (last orders 2030)
Parking for 14
Cards accepted: Amex, Diners, Mastercard, Visa, Switch/Delta

🐕♿📞🖥🖳♿👤🛡S🍴TV🖳🅿
🍴14✂SP T ◉

The Great House at Sonning M
♛♛♛ HIGHLY COMMENDED

Thames Street, Sonning-on-Thames, Reading RG4 6UT
☎ (0118) 969 2277
Fax (0118) 944 1296

Riverside hotel, dating from 16th C, in 4-acre estate. Moorings Restaurant overlooking gardens and river. Riverside terrace dining in summer. Beautiful, traditional bedrooms. All prices shown below are for weekends only and based on minimum 2-night stay.
Bedrooms: 6 single, 25 double, 8 twin, 2 triple
Bathrooms: 41 en-suite

Bed & breakfast

per night:	£min	£max
Single	52.00	62.00
Double	84.00	94.00

Half board per

person:	£min	£max
Daily	52.00	

Lunch available
Evening meal 1900 (last orders 2215)
Parking for 100
Cards accepted: Amex, Diners, Mastercard, Visa, Switch/Delta

🐕♿🏠📞🖥🖳♿👤🛡S✂🍴◐●⬆🛏
🍴80✿❀U♪✂❀SP🎪

Hanover International Hotel & Club M
♛♛♛♛ HIGHLY COMMENDED

Pingewood, Reading RG30 3UN
☎ (0118) 950 0885
Fax (0118) 939 1996
Unrivalled combination of spacious lakeside bedrooms with private balconies, choice of restaurants and extensive leisure facilities, including water-skiing, tennis and squash. Call for details.
Bedrooms: 57 double, 24 twin
Suites available
Bathrooms: 81 en-suite
Bed & breakfast

per night:	£min	£max
Single	42.00	102.00
Double	84.00	127.00

Half board per

person:	£min	£max
Daily	55.00	119.00

Lunch available
Evening meal 1900 (last orders 2130)
Parking for 250
Cards accepted: Amex, Diners, Mastercard, Visa, Switch/Delta

🐕♿📞🖥🖳♿👤🛡S✂🍴TV◐
⬆🛏🅿🍴120🐾🏊🏹🎣⛷U♪
▶🚭SP🎪T◉

Rainbow Corner Hotel M
♛♛ COMMENDED

132-138 Caversham Road, Reading RG1 8AY
☎ (0118) 958 8140
Fax (0118) 958 6500
Victorian hotel. All rooms fully en-suite, bar and restaurant. 10 minutes from station and town centre, 100 yards from River Thames. Car parking at rear.
Bedrooms: 10 single, 14 double, 7 twin, 1 triple
Bathrooms: 32 en-suite

Continued ▶

READING

Continued

Bed & breakfast per night:

	£min	£max
Single	35.00	65.00
Double	42.00	85.00

Half board per person:

	£min	£max
Daily	48.00	72.00
Weekly	302.00	540.00

Lunch available
Evening meal 1900 (last orders 2130)
Parking for 21
Cards accepted: Amex, Diners, Mastercard, Visa, Switch/Delta

🛇🖐🛆📞🖵🖵💆🕯🛈S⚲🖎📺◉🖿 🖿🛉25 DAP 🛇 SP

The Ship Hotel ♨

👑👑👑 COMMENDED

4-8 Duke Street, Reading RG1 4RY
☎ (0118) 958 3455
Fax (0118) 950 4450
ⒼⓇ Best Western
Town centre location, with easy access to M4, A4, M40. Few minutes' walk from rail station. Own free parking.
Bedrooms: 10 single, 17 double, 4 twin, 1 triple
Suite available
Bathrooms: 32 en-suite

Bed & breakfast per night:

	£min	£max
Single	40.00	86.95
Double	70.00	104.90

Half board per person:

	£min	£max
Daily	50.00	75.00

Lunch available
Evening meal 1900 (last orders 2130)
Parking for 30
Cards accepted: Amex, Diners, Mastercard, Visa, Switch/Delta

🛇📞🖵🖵💆🕯🛈S⚲🖎📺◉🖿 🖿🛉60 U🖐🛇 SP 🎦T ◉

Upcross Hotel ♨

👑👑👑 COMMENDED

68 Berkeley Avenue, Reading
RG1 6HY
☎ (0118) 959 0796
Fax (0118) 957 6517
Privately-owned country house hotel of character and warmth, featured on BBC TV. Reputed to have one of the best restaurants in Berkshire. Large garden, ample parking. Town centre/railway station 10 minutes. Easy access M4, junctions 11 and 12.
Bedrooms: 7 single, 6 double, 6 twin, 1 triple
Bathrooms: 20 en-suite

Bed & breakfast per night:

	£min	£max
Single	25.00	59.00
Double	45.00	69.00

Half board per person:

	£min	£max
Daily	40.00	74.00

Lunch available
Evening meal 1900 (last orders 2200)
Parking for 40
Cards accepted: Amex, Diners, Mastercard, Visa, Switch/Delta

🛇🖐🛆📞🖵🖵💆🕯🛈S⚲🖎🖿🖿 🖿🛉50 U🖐❅ DAP SP 🎦 T

ROMSEY

Hampshire
Map ref 2C3

Town grew up around the important abbey and lies on the banks of the River Test, famous for trout and salmon. Broadlands House, home of the late Lord Mountbatten, is open to the public.
Tourist Information Centre ☎ (01794) 512987

Country Accommodation ♨

👑 COMMENDED

The Old Post Office, New Road, Michelmersh, Romsey SO51 0NL
☎ (01794) 368739 & 0374 734478

Character rooms in ground floor independent annexe. Quiet village, 3 miles from Romsey. All en-suite, tea/coffee, TV. Good local pubs and restaurants.
Bedrooms: 2 double, 1 twin
Bathrooms: 3 en-suite

Bed & breakfast per night:

	£min	£max
Single	28.00	28.00
Double	45.00	45.00

Parking for 4
Cards accepted: Mastercard, Visa

🛇🖐🛆🖵💆UL S⚲🖿✕🎦🎦

COLOUR MAPS

Colour maps at the back of this guide pinpoint all places in which you will find accommodation listed.

Highfield House ♨

👑👑👑 HIGHLY COMMENDED

Newtown Road, Awbridge, Romsey
SO51 0GG
☎ (01794) 340727
Fax (01794) 341450

In unspoilt rural village, overlooking golf-course. Delightful setting and charming gardens. Home cooking a speciality. Close to Mottisfont Abbey National Trust and Hillier Arboretum.
Bedrooms: 1 double, 2 twin
Bathrooms: 3 en-suite, 1 public

Bed & breakfast per night:

	£min	£max
Double	45.00	50.00

Evening meal from 1900
Parking for 10

🛇🖐12🖵🖵💆🕯UL🛈S⚲📺🖿 🖿U🖐❅✕🚃

ST LEONARDS

Dorset
Map ref 2B3

The St Leonards Hotel ♨

👑👑👑 COMMENDED

185 Ringwood Road, St Leonards, Ringwood, Hampshire BH24 2NP
☎ (01425) 471220
Fax (01425) 480274
ⒼⓇ Countryside
Rural hotel set in attractive grounds, convenient for New Forest and Bournemouth. Local attractions include Beaulieu, Corfe Castle and Poole Harbour. Half board prices shown apply at weekends.
Bedrooms: 20 double, 8 twin, 6 family rooms
Suite available
Bathrooms: 34 en-suite

Bed & breakfast per night:

	£min	£max
Single	37.50	60.00
Double	48.00	75.00

Half board per person:

	£min	£max
Daily	31.00	42.00

Lunch available
Evening meal 1900 (last orders 2200)
Parking for 250
Cards accepted: Amex, Diners, Mastercard, Visa, Switch/Delta

🛇🖐🛆🚃📞🖵🖵💆🕯🛈S⚲🖎 🖿🖿🛉100 ♣U🖐❅✕🛇 SP 🎦

SANDOWN

Isle of Wight
Map ref 2C3

The 6-mile sweep of Sandown Bay is one of the island's finest stretches, with excellent sands. The pier has a pavilion and sun terrace; the esplanade has amusements, bars, eating-places and gardens.
Tourist Information Centre ☎ (01983) 403886

Culver Lodge Hotel
⚜⚜⚜ COMMENDED
Albert Road, Sandown PO36 8AW
☎ (01983) 403819 & 0500 121252
Fax (01983) 403819
Warm, comfortable hotel offering traditional English hospitality. Overlooking sun terrace, swimming pool and garden. Close to town, beach and leisure facilities.
Bedrooms: 4 single, 7 double, 4 twin, 4 triple, 1 family room
Bathrooms: 20 en-suite
Bed & breakfast per night:

	£min	£max
Single	19.00	25.00
Double	38.00	50.00

Half board per person:

	£min	£max
Daily	27.00	33.00
Weekly	176.00	216.00

Lunch available
Evening meal 1830 (last orders 1900)
Parking for 20
Open March–October
Cards accepted: Amex, Diners, Mastercard, Visa

Regina Hotel
⚜⚜⚜ APPROVED
Esplanade, Sandown PO36 8AE
☎ (01983) 403219
Small seafront hotel with all rooms en-suite, specialising in personal service, food, comfort and the desire to give value for money.
Bedrooms: 7 double, 2 twin, 4 triple
Bathrooms: 13 en-suite
Bed & breakfast per night:

	£min	£max
Single	18.00	22.00
Double	32.00	40.00

Half board per person:

	£min	£max
Daily	21.00	26.00
Weekly	135.00	180.00

Evening meal from 1830
Parking for 5

Open January–October and Christmas
Cards accepted: Mastercard, Visa

Willow Dene Guest House
Listed APPROVED
110 Station Avenue, Sandown PO36 8HD
☎ (01983) 403100
Small, friendly guesthouse, offering home cooking and a homely atmosphere. Near station and a few minutes from shops, beach and buses to all parts of the island. Pets welcome.
Bedrooms: 1 single, 1 double, 2 triple, 1 family room
Bathrooms: 1 public
Bed & breakfast per night:

	£min	£max
Single	12.00	14.00
Double	24.00	28.00

Half board per person:

	£min	£max
Daily	18.00	20.00
Weekly	110.00	120.00

Evening meal from 1930
Open January–November

Woodlynch Hall Hotel
⚜⚜⚜ COMMENDED
Broadway, Sandown PO36 9BB
☎ (01983) 403733
Ideally situated family-run hotel offering good cuisine and all-round value for money. Heated swimming pool, live entertainment, parking.
Bedrooms: 6 single, 6 double, 6 twin, 1 triple, 6 family rooms
Bathrooms: 25 en-suite, 1 public
Bed & breakfast per night:

	£min	£max
Single	20.00	28.00
Double	40.00	56.00

Half board per person:

	£min	£max
Daily	26.00	30.00
Weekly	139.00	205.00

Evening meal 1800 (last orders 1800)
Parking for 18
Open April–October
Cards accepted: Visa

A key to symbols can be found inside the back cover flap.

SAUNDERTON

Buckinghamshire
Map ref 2C1

Small village close to the Ridgeway long distance footpath. The site of a Roman villa is near the church.

The Rose & Crown Inn
⚜⚜ COMMENDED
Wycombe Road, Saunderton, Princes Risborough HP27 9NP
☎ (01844) 345299
Fax (01844) 343140
Logis of GB
Family-run, Georgian-style country inn set in Chiltern Hills. Log fires. 1 mile from the village of Saunderton, half a mile from Ridgeway Path.
Bedrooms: 6 single, 10 double, 1 twin
Bathrooms: 14 en-suite, 1 public
Bed & breakfast per night:

	£min	£max
Single	42.00	67.95
Double	74.25	78.45

Lunch available
Evening meal 1900 (last orders 2130)
Parking for 40
Cards accepted: Amex, Diners, Mastercard, Visa

SHANKLIN

Isle of Wight
Map ref 2C3

Set on a cliff with gentle slopes leading down to the beach, esplanade and marine gardens. The picturesque, old thatched village nestles at the end of the wooded chine.
Tourist Information Centre ☎ (01983) 862942

Alverstone Manor Hotel
⚜⚜⚜ HIGHLY COMMENDED
32 Luccombe Road, Shanklin PO37 6RR
☎ (01983) 862586
Fax (01983) 855127

Charming country house hotel overlooking Sandown/Shanklin Bay. Within easy reach of Old Village, town
Continued ▶

SHANKLIN

Continued

and beach. 2 acres of gardens with heated swimming pool, lawn tennis court and putting green.
Bedrooms: 1 single, 3 double, 1 twin, 7 triple
Bathrooms: 10 en-suite, 3 public

Bed & breakfast

per night:	£min	£max
Single	25.00	32.00
Double	50.00	64.00

Half board per person:

	£min	£max
Daily	33.00	42.00
Weekly	231.00	294.00

Lunch available
Evening meal 1830 (last orders 1930)
Parking for 15
Open March–October
Cards accepted: Mastercard, Visa

Chine Court Hotel

HIGHLY COMMENDED

Popham Road, Shanklin PO37 6RG
☎ (01983) 862732
Fax (01983) 862732
Elegant, lavishly decorated Victorian residence situated in large grounds and enjoying magnificent sea views from its elevated clifftop position.
Bedrooms: 3 single, 8 double, 6 twin, 5 triple, 4 family rooms
Bathrooms: 25 en-suite, 1 public

Bed & breakfast

per night:	£min	£max
Single	24.00	31.00
Double	48.00	62.00

Half board per person:

	£min	£max
Daily	33.00	40.00
Weekly	205.00	264.00

Evening meal 1830 (last orders 1915)
Parking for 24
Open April–October

Please mention this guide when making your booking.

For ideas on places to visit refer to the introduction at the beginning of this section.

Rozelle Hotel

Atherley Road, Shanklin PO37 7AT
☎ (01983) 862745
Conveniently situated, close to station and town centre and on main road to beach.
Bedrooms: 4 single, 5 double, 2 twin, 4 triple, 5 family rooms
Bathrooms: 8 en-suite, 4 public, 4 private showers

Bed & breakfast

per night:	£min	£max
Single	15.00	19.00
Double	30.00	38.00

Half board per person:

	£min	£max
Daily	18.00	22.00
Weekly	120.00	150.00

Evening meal from 1800
Open April–September

SHIPTON-UNDER-WYCHWOOD

Oxfordshire
Map ref 2B1

Situated in the ancient Forest of Wychwood with many fine old houses and an interesting parish church. Nearby is Shipton Court, a gabled Elizabethan house set in beautiful grounds that include an ornamental lake and a tree-lined avenue approach.

The Shaven Crown Hotel

COMMENDED

High Street,
Shipton-under-Wychwood, Oxford
OX7 6BA
☎ (01993) 830330
Fax (01993) 830330
Minotel
Abbey hospice, built around a courtyard garden, delightfully located in the Cotswolds. Midway between Oxford and Stratford-upon-Avon. Baronial Hall, beautiful Tudor archway.
Bedrooms: 1 single, 4 double, 3 twin, 1 family room
Bathrooms: 8 en-suite, 1 private, 1 public

Bed & breakfast

per night:	£min	£max
Single	35.00	53.00
Double	72.00	100.00

Lunch available
Evening meal 1800 (last orders 2100)
Parking for 20
Cards accepted: Amex, Mastercard, Visa, Switch/Delta

SOUTHAMPTON

Hampshire
Map ref 2C3

One of Britain's leading seaports with a long history, now a major container port. In the 18th C it became a fashionable resort with the assembly rooms and theatre. The old Guildhall and the Wool House are now museums. Sections of the medieval wall can still be seen.
Tourist Information Centre ☎ (01703) 221106

Addenro House Hotel

Listed **APPROVED**

40-42 Howard Road, Shirley, Southampton SO15 5BD
☎ (01703) 227144
Family-run small hotel, offering friendly, reliable service at a reasonable cost.
Bedrooms: 7 single, 2 double, 4 twin, 5 triple
Bathrooms: 9 en-suite, 5 public

Bed & breakfast

per night:	£min	£max
Single	15.00	16.00
Double	30.00	32.00

Parking for 18

Banister House Hotel

COMMENDED

Banister Road, Southampton SO15 2JJ
☎ (01703) 221279
Fax (01703) 221279
Friendly welcome in this family-run hotel which is central and in a residential area. Off A33 (The Avenue) into Southampton.
Bedrooms: 13 single, 4 double, 3 twin, 2 triple, 1 family room
Bathrooms: 13 en-suite, 4 public, 3 private showers

Bed & breakfast

per night:	£min	£max
Single	22.50	26.50
Double	30.50	35.00

Half board per person:

	£min	£max
Daily	21.75	35.00

Evening meal 1800 (last orders 1945)
Parking for 14
Cards accepted: Amex, Mastercard, Visa

Botley Park Hotel, Golf & Country Club ⚏

⚜⚜⚜⚜ HIGHLY COMMENDED

Winchester Road, Boorley Green, Botley, Southampton SO3 2UA
☎ (01489) 780888
Fax (01489) 789242
ⓒⓡ MacDonald/Utell International
Purpose-designed to cater for the leisure and business demands of the 1990s. Few minutes' drive from M27, 60 minutes from London, 50 minutes to Heathrow. Golf, sauna, solaria, gymnasium, jacuzzi, indoor heated pool, tennis and squash courts.
Wheelchair access category 1 ♿
Bedrooms: 44 double, 56 twin
Bathrooms: 100 private

Bed & breakfast per night:

	£min	£max
Single	70.00	110.00
Double	90.00	140.00

Half board per person:

	£min	£max
Daily	75.00	95.00

Lunch available
Evening meal 1900 (last orders 2145)
Parking for 250
Cards accepted: Amex, Diners, Mastercard, Visa, Switch/Delta

🛏📞📺▢♦🅿📶🅢✂▥◎🈂
🅿🛗240🕭🍴🥂🍸✈🔍U⏰❄ DAP
🐾 SP T

Eaton Court Hotel ⚏

⚜⚜⚜ COMMENDED

32 Hill Lane, Southampton SO15 5AY
☎ (01703) 223081
Fax (01703) 322006
Comfortable, small, owner-run hotel for business or leisure stays. Bedrooms have all amenities and the breakfasts are generous!
Bedrooms: 8 single, 3 double, 3 twin
Bathrooms: 7 en-suite, 2 public, 1 private shower

Bed & breakfast per night:

	£min	£max
Single	23.00	30.00
Double	37.00	42.00

Half board per person:

	£min	£max
Daily	28.00	39.50

Evening meal 1830 (last orders 2000)
Parking for 12
Cards accepted: Amex, Diners, Mastercard, Visa, Switch/Delta

🛏📞📺♦🅢▥📺▥🈂🅿 SP T

Hunters Lodge Hotel ⚏

⚜⚜⚜ COMMENDED

25 Landguard Road, Shirley, Southampton SO15 5DL
☎ (01703) 227919
Fax (01703) 230913

You will receive a warm welcome at this personally-run hotel. Convenient for city centre, ferry ports and motorways. Attractive en-suite bedrooms with telephone and satellite TV. Cosy lounge with well-stocked bar. Evening meals on request.
Bedrooms: 5 single, 7 double, 4 twin, 1 triple
Bathrooms: 17 en-suite, 2 public

Bed & breakfast per night:

	£min	£max
Single		29.38
Double		44.00

Half board per person:

	£min	£max
Daily		39.38
Weekly		196.90

Evening meal 1830 (last orders 1830)
Parking for 21
Cards accepted: Amex, Mastercard, Visa, Switch/Delta

🛏📞📺♦🅢✂📺▥🅿30 SP T

The Lodge

⚜⚜⚜ COMMENDED

No 1 Winn Road, The Avenue, Southampton SO12 1EH
☎ (01703) 557537
ⓒⓡ The Independents
Friendly owner-managed hotel in quiet surroundings, close to city centre and university and convenient for airport.
Bedrooms: 9 single, 2 double, 2 twin, 1 triple
Bathrooms: 8 en-suite, 2 public

Bed & breakfast per night:

	£min	£max
Single	21.50	32.50
Double	39.50	44.50

Half board per person:

	£min	£max
Daily	29.50	40.50

Lunch available
Evening meal 1900 (last orders 2100)
Parking for 10
Cards accepted: Amex, Mastercard, Visa

🛏📞📞📺♦🅢▥📺▥🅿
🐾 DAP SP T

RoadChef Lodge Rownhams ⚏

ⓒⓒⓒ COMMENDED

Motorway Service Area, M27 Southbound, Rownhams, Southampton SO51 8AW
☎ (01703) 734480
Fax (01703) 739517
ⓒⓡ RoadChef
RoadChef Lodges offer high specification rooms at affordable prices, in popular locations suited to both the business and private traveller. Prices are per room and do not include breakfast.
Bedrooms: 23 double, 15 twin, 1 family room
Bathrooms: 39 en-suite

Bed & breakfast per night:

	£min	£max
Double	43.50	

Parking for 65
Cards accepted: Amex, Diners, Mastercard, Visa, Switch/Delta

🛏🐾📞📺▢♦🥂UL✂◎▥🍴❄
🍴🦽 SP T

De Vere Grand Harbour ⚏

⚜⚜⚜⚜⚜ DE LUXE

West Quay Road, Southampton SO15 1AG
☎ (01703) 633033
Fax (01703) 633066
Magnificent granite and glass building offering luxurious yet comfortable accommodation. Conveniently situated overlooking the waterfront, adjacent to the medieval city walls.
Bedrooms: 98 double, 34 twin, 20 triple, 20 family rooms
Suites available
Bathrooms: 172 en-suite

Bed & breakfast per night:

	£min	£max
Single	125.00	325.00
Double	135.00	325.00

Lunch available
Evening meal 1900 (last orders 2145)
Parking for 190
Cards accepted: Amex, Diners, Mastercard, Visa, Switch/Delta

🛏🐾📞📺▢♦🅿🅢✂📺◎🈂
▥🈂🅿🛗500🕭🍴🥂❄🍴🐾 SP 🏧
T ◎

SOUTHSEA

Hampshire

See under Portsmouth & Southsea

You are advised to confirm your booking in writing.

STEEPLE ASTON

Oxfordshire
Map ref 2C1

Oxfordshire village whose church has one of the finest examples of church embroidery in the world. Nearby is the Jacobean Rousham House which stands in William Kent's only surviving landscaped garden.

Hopcrofts Holt Hotel M

👑👑👑 COMMENDED

Banbury Road, Steeple Aston, Oxford OX6 3QQ
☎ (01869) 340259
Fax (01869) 340865
15th C hotel with en-suite bedrooms, restaurant and extensive banqueting facilities. Located 11 miles north of Oxford.
Bedrooms: 17 single, 44 double, 25 twin, 2 triple
Suites available
Bathrooms: 88 en-suite

Bed & breakfast

per night:	£min	£max
Single	65.00	72.50
Double	75.00	85.00

Lunch available
Evening meal 1900 (last orders 2200)
Parking for 200
Cards accepted: Amex, Diners, Mastercard, Visa, Switch/Delta

Westfield Farm Motel M

👑👑👑 COMMENDED

Fenway, Steeple Aston, Bicester OX6 3SS
☎ (01869) 340591
Fax (01869) 347594
Ⓒ Logis of GB
Converted stable block with comfortable en-suite bedroom units. Combined lounge, dining room and bar. TV all rooms. Good touring centre. Fringe of Cotswolds, off A4260, 9 miles from Banbury and 5 miles from Woodstock.
Bedrooms: 1 single, 3 double, 3 twin
Suite available
Bathrooms: 7 en-suite

Bed & breakfast

per night:	£min	£max
Single	38.00	42.00
Double	50.00	65.00

Half board per person:

	£min	£max
Daily	53.00	57.00

Evening meal 1900 (last orders 2030)

Parking for 24
Cards accepted: Amex, Mastercard, Visa, Switch/Delta

STOCKBRIDGE

Hampshire
Map ref 2C2

Set in the Test Valley which has some of the best fishing in England. The wide main street has houses of all styles, mainly Tudor and Georgian.

Carbery Guest House M

👑👑 COMMENDED

Salisbury Hill, Stockbridge SO20 6EZ
☎ (01264) 810771
Fax (01264) 811022

Fine old Georgian house in an acre of landscaped gardens and lawns, overlooking the River Test. Games and swimming facilities, riding and fishing can be arranged. Ideal for touring the South Coast and the New Forest.
Bedrooms: 4 single, 3 double, 2 twin, 1 triple, 1 family room
Bathrooms: 8 en-suite, 1 public

Bed & breakfast

per night:	£min	£max
Single	25.00	32.00
Double	48.00	51.00

Half board per person:

	£min	£max
Daily	37.50	44.50
Weekly	170.00	220.00

Evening meal 1900 (last orders 1800)
Parking for 12

The symbol Ⓒ and a group name following an hotel address indicates that bookings can be made through a central reservations office. These offices are listed in the information pages at the back of this guide.

Grosvenor Hotel M

👑👑👑👑 COMMENDED

High Street, Stockbridge SO20 6EU
☎ (01264) 810606
Fax (01264) 810747
Ⓒ The Independents/Countryside
Country town hotel in Test Valley, within easy reach of Romsey, Salisbury and Winchester. Enclosed garden. Half board prices shown apply at weekends.
Bedrooms: 4 single, 14 double, 7 twin
Bathrooms: 25 en-suite

Bed & breakfast

per night	£min	£max
Single	36.50	70.00
Double	48.00	90.00

Half board per person:

	£min	£max
Daily	34.00	42.00

Lunch available
Evening meal 1930 (last orders 2145)
Parking for 35
Cards accepted: Amex, Diners, Mastercard, Visa, Switch/Delta

STRATFIELD TURGIS

Hampshire
Map ref 2C2

The Wellington Arms M

👑👑👑 HIGHLY COMMENDED

Stratfield Turgis, Hook RG27 0AS
☎ (01256) 882214
Fax (01256) 882934
Ⓒ Logis of GB
Traditional coaching inn on the Duke of Wellington's estate. Situated midway between Basingstoke and Reading on the main A33. Motorway access is from junction 6 of M3, junction 11 of M4.
Bedrooms: 7 single, 19 double, 5 twin, 2 family rooms
Bathrooms: 33 en-suite

Bed & breakfast

per night:	£min	£max
Single	50.00	90.00
Double	55.00	105.00

Lunch available
Evening meal 1900 (last orders 2200)
Parking for 75
Cards accepted: Amex, Diners, Mastercard, Visa, Switch/Delta

Establishments should be open throughout the year, unless otherwise stated.

STREATLEY

Berkshire
Map ref 2C2

Pretty village on the River Thames, linked to Goring by an attractive bridge. It has Georgian houses and cottages and beautiful views over the countryside and the Goring Gap.

The Swan Diplomat ⚠

⚜⚜⚜ HIGHLY COMMENDED

Streatley on Thames, Streatley, Reading RG8 9HR
☎ (01491) 873737
Fax (01491) 872554
Email: sales@swan_diplomat.co.uk
Beautifully situated on the banks of the River Thames, within one hour's drive of Oxford, Windsor, London and London Heathrow Airport. Special half board weekend rate £79.50 per person per night.
Bedrooms: 9 single, 27 double, 10 twin
Suite available
Bathrooms: 46 en-suite

Bed & breakfast per night:	£min	£max
Single	66.50	104.50
Double	102.00	159.00

Half board per person:	£min	£max
Daily	96.00	134.00

Lunch available
Evening meal 1930 (last orders 2130)
Parking for 145
Cards accepted: Amex, Diners, Mastercard, Visa, Switch/Delta

🛏🐕♿🦽📞🖥🖵🖵💺📶🛎Ⓢ✗📺🖬TV
⓿🕾.🖫🅿🛏80♨✗⬅ℚ∪✿⚓SP🏬
Ⓣ

STUDLAND

Dorset
Map ref 2B3

On a beautiful stretch of coast and good for walking, with a National Nature Reserve to the north. The Norman church is the finest in the country, with superb rounded arches and vaulting. Brownsea Island, where the first scout camp was held, lies in Poole Harbour.

Knoll House Hotel

⚜⚜⚜ COMMENDED

Studland, Swanage BH19 3AH
☎ (01929) 450450 & 450251
Fax (01929) 450423

Independent country hotel in National Trust reserve. Access to 3-mile beach from 100-acre grounds. Many facilities. Weekly rates below are for full board.
Bedrooms: 29 single, 20 twin, 30 triple
Bathrooms: 57 en-suite, 10 public

Half board per person:	£min	£max
Daily	64.00	105.00
Weekly	448.00	735.00

Lunch available
Evening meal 1930 (last orders 2015)
Parking for 100
Open April–October
Cards accepted: Mastercard, Visa, Switch/Delta

🛏🐕♿📞Ⓢ🖬TV⓿🖵🖫♨✗⚓ℚ⚓
ℚ∪✿🚲🎿SP🏬Ⓣ

The Manor House Hotel ⚠

⚜⚜⚜ COMMENDED

Beach Road, Studland, Swanage BH19 3AU
☎ (01929) 450288
Fax (01929) 450288

18th C manor house in secluded gardens overlooking the sea and safe, sandy beaches. Oak-panelled bar and dining room, with conservatory. Two hard tennis courts.
Bedrooms: 6 double, 6 twin, 6 triple
Suites available
Bathrooms: 18 en-suite, 1 public

Bed & breakfast per night:	£min	£max
Single	35.00	52.00
Double	70.00	104.00

Half board per person:	£min	£max
Daily	50.00	68.00
Weekly	280.00	380.00

Lunch available
Evening meal 1900 (last orders 2030)
Parking for 65
Open February–December
Cards accepted: Amex, Mastercard, Visa

🛏🐕5♿🖵📞🖵🖵💺📶🛎Ⓢ🖬🖫
🖫🅿30ℚ∪✿🚲SP🏬

STURMINSTER NEWTON

Dorset
Map ref 2B3

Every Monday this small town holds a livestock market. One of the bridges over the River Stour is a fine medieval example and bears a plaque declaring that anyone "injuring" it will be deported.

Plumber Manor ⚠

⚜⚜⚜ HIGHLY COMMENDED

Sturminster Newton DT10 2AF
☎ (01258) 472507
Fax (01258) 473370

Run as a restaurant with bedrooms and supervised by the family. Set in the middle of Hardy's Dorset and surrounded by the home farm.
Bedrooms: 10 double, 6 twin
Bathrooms: 15 en-suite, 1 private

Bed & breakfast per night:	£min	£max
Single	75.00	85.00
Double	90.00	130.00

Evening meal 1930 (last orders 2130)
Parking for 25
Open January, March–December
Cards accepted: Amex, Diners, Mastercard, Visa, Switch/Delta

🛏🐕10♿📞🖵🖵💺♨🛎Ⓢ🖬🖫
🍴25ℚ∪✿🚲SP🏬Ⓣ

Swan Inn ⚠

⚜⚜ COMMENDED

Market Place, Sturminster Newton DT10 1AR
☎ (01258) 472208
Fax (01258) 473767

Old coaching inn, located in the heart of Thomas Hardy's Blackmore Vale. All rooms en-suite with remote-control TV. Extensive a la carte menu plus bar meals.
Bedrooms: 1 single, 3 double, 1 twin
Bathrooms: 5 en-suite

Continued ▶

STURMINSTER NEWTON

Continued

Bed & breakfast

per night:	£min	£max
Single	40.00	
Double	55.00	

Half board per person:

	£min	£max
Daily	40.00	50.00

Lunch available
Evening meal 1830 (last orders 2100)
Parking for 20
Cards accepted: Amex, Diners, Mastercard, Visa, Switch/Delta

⌂📞💷🖥♿🔌🍴Ⓢ✂🎿🛏🗄
🍴30Ⓤ↑❄🚐 SP 🏮

SWANAGE

Dorset
Map ref 2B3

Began life as an Anglo-Saxon port, then a quarrying centre of Purbeck marble. Now the safe, sandy beach set in a sweeping bay and flanked by downs is good walking country, making it an ideal resort.
Tourist Information Centre ☎ (01929) 422885

Glenlee Hotel ⋒

👑
6 Cauldon Avenue, Swanage BH19 1PQ
☎ (01929) 425794
Delightful position overlooking beach gardens, bowling green and tennis courts. 150 yards to beach. All rooms en-suite, with colour TV and hot drinks facilities.
Bedrooms: 4 double, 2 twin, 1 triple
Bathrooms: 7 en-suite

Bed & breakfast

per night:	£min	£max
Double	40.00	50.00

Half board per person:

	£min	£max
Daily	28.00	33.00
Weekly	176.00	208.00

Evening meal 1830 (last orders 1700)
Parking for 8
Open March–October
Cards accepted: Mastercard, Visa

🐎♿📞💷🖥♿🔌Ⓢ♿ TV 🗄💷❄🚐 SP

All accommodation in this guide has been graded, or is awaiting a grading, by a trained Tourist Board inspector.

Havenhurst Hotel ⋒

👑👑👑 COMMENDED
3 Cranborne Road, Swanage BH19 1EA
☎ (01929) 424224
Fax (01929) 424224
Charming, detached, licensed hotel, quietly situated on level. Short walk to beach and shops. Special attention given.
Bedrooms: 3 single, 6 double, 4 twin, 2 triple, 2 family rooms
Bathrooms: 17 en-suite

Bed & breakfast

per night:	£min	£max
Single	18.00	30.00
Double	36.00	60.00

Half board per person:

	£min	£max
Daily	30.00	41.00
Weekly	180.00	245.00

Lunch available
Evening meal from 1900
Parking for 19
Cards accepted: Mastercard, Visa, Switch/Delta

🐎♿💷🖥♿🔌Ⓢ✂🎿 TV 🗄💷❄🍴
✈⚲ SP

The Pines Hotel ⋒

👑👑👑 COMMENDED
Burlington Road, Swanage BH19 1LT
☎ (01929) 425211
Fax (01929) 422075

Family-run hotel set amid the Purbeck countryside at quiet end of Swanage Bay. Own access to beach.
Wheelchair access category 3♿
Bedrooms: 4 single, 10 double, 11 twin, 24 triple
Bathrooms: 47 en-suite, 1 public

Bed & breakfast

per night:	£min	£max
Single	35.00	45.00
Double	70.00	90.00

Half board per person:

	£min	£max
Daily	49.50	62.50
Weekly	350.00	415.00

Lunch available
Evening meal 1930 (last orders 2100)
Parking for 60
Cards accepted: Mastercard, Visa

🐎♿📞💷🖥♿🔌Ⓢ✂🎿◐Ⓣ
🗄💷🍴60❄⚲ SP

Purbeck House Hotel ⋒

👑👑👑👑 HIGHLY COMMENDED
91 High Street, Swanage BH19 2LZ
☎ (01929) 422872
Fax (01929) 421194
Email: purbeckhouse
@easynet.co.uk.
Family-run hotel, set in 2 acres of gardens, 300 yards from beach. Off-street parking. Fully licensed.
Bedrooms: 2 single, 9 double, 2 twin, 1 triple, 4 family rooms
Bathrooms: 18 en-suite

Bed & breakfast

per night:	£min	£max
Single	36.00	50.00
Double	72.00	100.00

Half board per person:

	£min	£max
Daily	55.00	65.00
Weekly	350.00	420.00

Lunch available
Evening meal 1830 (last orders 2130)
Parking for 23
Cards accepted: Amex, Diners, Mastercard, Visa, Switch/Delta

🐎♿♿💷🖥♿🔌Ⓢ🗄💷🍴80❄
🚐 DAP ⚲ 🏮

SWAY

Hampshire
Map ref 2C3

Small village on the south-western edge of the New Forest. It is noted for its 220-ft tower, Peterson's Folly, built in the 1870s by a retired Indian judge to demonstrate the value of concrete as a building material.

String of Horses ⋒

👑👑👑👑 HIGHLY COMMENDED
Mead End Road, Sway, Lymington SO41 6EH
☎ (01590) 682631
Fax (01590) 682631
Unique, secluded hotel set in 4 acres in the New Forest. Individually designed bedrooms with fantasy bathrooms. Intimate candlelit restaurant.
Bedrooms: 7 double
Bathrooms: 7 en-suite

Bed & breakfast

per night:	£min	£max
Single	52.50	55.00
Double	75.00	100.00

Half board per person:

	£min	£max
Daily	57.45	69.95
Weekly	362.00	440.00

Lunch available
Evening meal 1900 (last orders 2030)
Parking for 24

Cards accepted: Amex, Diners, Mastercard, Visa, Switch/Delta

THAME

Oxfordshire
Map ref 2C1

Historic market town on the River Thame. The wide, unspoilt High Street has many styles of architecture with medieval timber-framed cottages, Georgian houses and some famous inns. *Tourist Information Centre ☎ (01844) 212834*

The Spread Eagle Hotel ♠

HIGHLY COMMENDED

Cornmarket, Thame OX9 2BW
☎ (01844) 213661
Fax (01844) 261380
Ⓒ Thames Valley
Converted 17th C coaching inn, in centre of small country market town. Fothergills Restaurant features a choice of menus. Banqueting and conference facilities. Good base for touring the Thames Valley.
Bedrooms: 5 single, 22 double, 5 twin, 1 triple
Suites available
Bathrooms: 33 en-suite

Bed & breakfast per night:

	£min	£max
Single	92.90	104.90
Double	115.95	133.95

Half board per person:

	£min	£max
Daily	114.95	126.95
Weekly	645.00	725.00

Lunch available
Evening meal 1900 (last orders 2200)
Parking for 80
Cards accepted: Amex, Diners, Mastercard, Visa

TOTLAND BAY

Isle of Wight
Map ref 2C3

On the Freshwater Peninsula. It is possible to walk from here around to Alum Bay.

Country Garden Hotel ♠

HIGHLY COMMENDED

Church Hill, Totland Bay PO39 1QE
☎ (01983) 754521
Fax (01983) 754521

Country house hotel set in lovely gardens overlooking the sea. In the words of one hotel reviewer: "Relish the superb cuisine, fantastic walks, wonderful views".
Bedrooms: 2 single, 9 double, 5 twin
Suite available
Bathrooms: 16 en-suite

Bed & breakfast per night:

	£min	£max
Single	38.00	46.00
Double	78.00	92.00

Half board per person:

	£min	£max
Daily	44.00	55.00
Weekly	295.00	340.00

Lunch available
Evening meal 1900 (last orders 2100)
Parking for 30
Open February–December
Cards accepted: Mastercard, Visa

Littledene Lodge ♠

COMMENDED

Granville Road, Totland Bay PO39 0AX
☎ (01983) 752411
Small, private hotel, situated between shops and beach at Totland Bay. Comfortable accommodation with good service and value.
Bedrooms: 2 double, 1 twin, 3 triple
Bathrooms: 6 en-suite

Bed & breakfast per night:

	£min	£max
Double	40.00	44.00

Half board per person:

	£min	£max
Daily	30.00	31.00

Evening meal 1830 (last orders 1830)
Parking for 5
Open March–October
Cards accepted: Mastercard, Visa

COLOUR MAPS

Colour maps at the back of this guide pinpoint all places in which you will find accommodation listed.

Sandford Lodge Hotel

COMMENDED

61 The Avenue, Totland Bay PO39 0DN
☎ (01983) 753478
Fax (01983) 753478
Small, family-run establishment of high standards and reputation, excellently placed for beaches and downland walks. Quality home cuisine and comfort for your enjoyment. Five minutes from Yarmouth ferry.
Bedrooms: 1 single, 2 double, 1 twin, 2 triple
Bathrooms: 6 en-suite

Bed & breakfast per night:

	£min	£max
Single	19.00	24.00
Double	38.00	44.00

Half board per person:

	£min	£max
Daily	29.00	32.00
Weekly	176.00	205.00

Evening meal 1830 (last orders 1600)
Parking for 6
Open March–October
Cards accepted: Visa

Sentry Mead Hotel

COMMENDED

Madeira Road, Totland Bay PO39 0BJ
☎ (01983) 753212
Fax (01983) 753212
Tranquil location. Ideal base for walking. Two minutes' walk to beach. Comfortable and tastefully furnished. Delicious 5-course dinner menus.
Bedrooms: 2 single, 5 double, 3 twin, 3 triple, 1 family room
Bathrooms: 14 en-suite

Bed & breakfast per night:

	£min	£max
Single	22.00	35.00
Double	44.00	70.00

Half board per person:

	£min	£max
Daily	35.00	48.00
Weekly	225.00	315.00

Lunch available
Evening meal 1900 (last orders 2000)
Parking for 10
Cards accepted: Amex, Mastercard, Visa, Switch/Delta

Please check prices and other details at the time of booking.

TWYFORD

Berkshire
Map ref 2C2

Stands on the edge of the Loddon water meadows. There is a pleasant group of almshouses built by Sir Richard Harrison in 1640. The 19th C church is notable for the coloured marble on the floor of the baptistry.

Chesham House

👑 HIGHLY COMMENDED

79 Wargrave Road, Twyford, Reading RG40 9PE
☎ (0118) 932 0428
In triangle formed by Reading, Maidenhead and Henley-on-Thames. Each room has en-suite bathroom, colour TV, refrigerator, tea and coffee facilities. Three-quarters of an acre of garden. Parking in grounds.
Bedrooms: 1 double, 1 twin
Bathrooms: 2 en-suite

Bed & breakfast

per night:	£min	£max
Single	22.00	25.00
Double	36.00	38.00

Parking for 6

VENTNOR

Isle of Wight
Map ref 2C3

Town lies at the bottom of an 800-ft hill and has a reputation as a winter holiday and health resort due to its mild climate. The mile-long esplanade reaches the shore of the delightful village of Bonchurch, and in the other direction are the 22-acre Botanical Gardens.

Burlington Hotel ₪

👑👑👑 HIGHLY COMMENDED

Bellevue Road, Ventnor PO38 1DB
☎ (01983) 852113
Fax (01983) 852113
Friendly family-run hotel with heated swimming pool, commanding wonderful sea views. Central, yet affords peace and quiet.
Bedrooms: 4 single, 5 double, 9 twin, 5 triple
Bathrooms: 23 en-suite

Bed & breakfast

per night:	£min	£max
Single	28.00	38.00
Double	56.00	76.00

Half board per

person:	£min	£max
Daily	36.00	44.00

Evening meal 1900 (last orders 2030)
Parking for 20
Open March–October
Cards accepted: Mastercard, Visa

WANTAGE

Oxfordshire
Map ref 2C2

Market town in the Vale of the White Horse where King Alfred was born. His statue stands in the town square.
Tourist Information Centre ☎ (01235) 760176

The Bear Hotel ₪

👑👑👑 COMMENDED

Market Place, Wantage OX12 8AB
☎ (01235) 766366
Fax (01235) 768826
Historic coaching inn with renowned cuisine and traditional ales. Friendly staff and comfortable accommodation. Ideal for visiting Oxford and excellent location for relaxing with the family.
Bedrooms: 9 single, 14 double, 10 twin, 3 triple
Bathrooms: 36 en-suite

Bed & breakfast

per night:	£min	£max
Single	56.00	59.00
Double	65.00	80.00

Lunch available
Evening meal 1900 (last orders 2130)
Cards accepted: Amex, Diners, Mastercard, Visa, Switch/Delta

WEST LULWORTH

Dorset
Map ref 2B3

Well-known for Lulworth Cove, the almost landlocked circular bay of chalk and limestone cliffs.

Cromwell House Hotel ₪

👑👑 COMMENDED

Lulworth Cove, West Lulworth, Wareham BH20 5RJ
☎ (01929) 400253 & 400332
Fax (01929) 400566
Family hotel on the Dorset Heritage Coast footpath. Outstanding sea views over Lulworth Cove. Secluded garden. Good walking country. Swimming pool (May-October).
Bedrooms: 1 single, 7 double, 5 twin, 1 triple
Bathrooms: 14 en-suite

Bed & breakfast

per night:	£min	£max
Single	23.00	42.00
Double	46.00	63.00

Half board per

person:	£min	£max
Daily	37.00	54.00
Weekly	259.00	287.00

Evening meal 1900 (last orders 2030)
Parking for 15
Cards accepted: Amex, Mastercard, Visa, Switch/Delta

Lulworth Cove Hotel ₪

👑 APPROVED

Main Road, West Lulworth, Wareham BH20 5RQ
☎ (01929) 400333
Fax (01929) 400534
Email: rjflulworthcove@msn.com
One hundred yards from the cove on the Dorset Coastal Path. Some sea-view balcony rooms. Wide variety of restaurant and bar meals.
Bedrooms: 1 single, 12 double, 1 triple, 1 family room
Bathrooms: 10 en-suite, 1 public, 4 private showers

Bed & breakfast

per night:	£min	£max
Single	21.00	27.00
Double	42.00	54.00

Half board per

person:	£min	£max
Daily	29.00	35.00

Lunch available
Evening meal 1900 (last orders 2150)
Cards accepted: Amex, Mastercard, Visa, Switch/Delta

Shirley Hotel ₪

👑👑👑 HIGHLY COMMENDED

West Lulworth, Wareham BH20 5RL
☎ (01929) 400358
Fax (01929) 400167

In the country by the sea. Small, friendly hotel close to Lulworth Cove. Good food and relaxed atmosphere. Indoor heated pool and jacuzzi.
Bedrooms: 3 single, 8 double, 4 twin, 1 triple, 2 family rooms
Bathrooms: 18 en-suite, 1 public

Bed & breakfast per night:	£min	£max
Single	30.00	32.50
Double	60.00	65.00

Half board per person:	£min	£max
Daily	43.50	46.00
Weekly	272.50	292.00

Evening meal 1830 (last orders 1930)
Parking for 22
Open February–November and Christmas
Cards accepted: Amex, Diners, Mastercard, Visa, Switch/Delta

WINCHESTER

Hampshire
Map ref 2C3

King Alfred the Great made Winchester the capital of Saxon England. A magnificent Norman cathedral, with one of the longest naves in Europe, dominates the city. Home of Winchester College founded in 1382.
Tourist Information Centre ☎ *(01962) 840500*

Cathedral View ⋀⋀
COMMENDED

9A Magdalen Hill, Winchester SO23 0HJ
☎ (01962) 863802
Guesthouse with views across historic city and cathedral. 5 minutes' walk from city centre. En-suite facilities, TV, parking.
Bedrooms: 4 double, 1 twin, 1 family room
Bathrooms: 3 en-suite, 3 private

Bed & breakfast per night:	£min	£max
Single	33.00	35.00
Double	42.00	48.00

Parking for 4

Harestock Lodge Hotel ⋀⋀
COMMENDED

Harestock Road, Winchester SO22 6NX
☎ (01962) 881870 & 880038
Fax (01962) 886959
Ⓖ The Independents
Privately-run country house hotel set in secluded gardens on the edge of historic Winchester. Offering a warm welcome and good food with menus to suit all tastes.
Bedrooms: 4 single, 8 double, 4 twin, 2 triple

Bathrooms: 14 en-suite, 1 public, 4 private showers

Bed & breakfast per night:	£min	£max
Single	36.00	46.00
Double	46.00	60.00

Half board per person:	£min	£max
Daily	33.00	40.00

Lunch available
Evening meal 1830 (last orders 2245)
Parking for 26
Cards accepted: Amex, Mastercard, Visa, Switch/Delta

Lainston House ⋀⋀
DE LUXE

Sparsholt, Winchester SO21 2LT
☎ (01962) 863588
Fax (01962) 776672
Ⓖ Grand Heritage

Magnificent, Georgian, listed 17th C country house set in 63 acres of parkland. Recently refurbished. Noted for food and service. Half board daily prices are based on 2-night weekend stay.
Bedrooms: 7 single, 16 double, 14 twin, 1 triple
Bathrooms: 38 en-suite

Bed & breakfast per night:	£min	£max
Single	95.00	
Double	135.00	225.00

Half board per person:	£min	£max
Daily	95.00	155.00

Lunch available
Evening meal 1900 (last orders 2200)
Parking for 96
Cards accepted: Amex, Diners, Mastercard, Visa, Switch/Delta

COLOUR MAPS

Colour maps at the back of this guide pinpoint all places in which you will find accommodation listed.

Stratton House ⋀⋀
COMMENDED

Stratton Road, St Giles Hill, Winchester SO23 0JQ
☎ (01962) 863919 & 864529
Fax (01962) 842095
Email: strattongroup @btinternet.com
Lovely old Victorian house with an acre of grounds, in an elevated position on St Giles Hill.
Bedrooms: 1 single, 3 double, 2 twin, 1 triple
Bathrooms: 6 en-suite, 1 private

Bed & breakfast per night:	£min	£max
Single	33.00	39.00
Double	48.00	59.00

Half board per person:	£min	£max
Daily	41.00	47.00
Weekly	258.00	296.00

Evening meal 1800 (last orders 1600)
Parking for 8
Cards accepted: Mastercard, Visa, Switch/Delta

WINDSOR

Berkshire
Map ref 2D2

Town dominated by the spectacular castle, home of the Royal Family for over 900 years. Parts are open to the public. There are many attractions including the Great Park, Eton and trips on the river.
Tourist Information Centre ☎ *(01753) 852010*

Alma House
Listed COMMENDED

56 Alma Road, Windsor SL4 3HA
☎ (01753) 862983 & 855620
Fax (01753) 855620
Elegant, family-run Victorian house within 5 minutes' walk of castle, town centre, river and parks. Internationally known.
Bedrooms: 1 single, 1 triple, 2 family rooms
Bathrooms: 1 en-suite, 1 public

Bed & breakfast per night:	£min	£max
Single	28.00	45.00
Double	38.00	50.00

Parking for 5

WINDSOR
Continued

Beaumont Lodge ♨
HIGHLY COMMENDED

1 Beaumont Road, Windsor
SL4 1HY
☎ (01753) 863436 & 0374 841273
Fax (01753) 863436
*Very close to town centre. All rooms
have colour TV, video, clock/radio alarm,
tea/coffee facilities and trouser press.
Double has spa bath.*
Bedrooms: 1 double, 2 twin
Bathrooms: 3 en-suite

**Bed & breakfast
per night:**

	£min	£max
Single	40.00	45.00
Double	50.00	55.00

The Christopher Hotel ♨
APPROVED

110 High Street, Eton, Windsor
SL4 6AN
☎ (01753) 852359
Fax (01753) 830914
Ⓒ Consort

*Once a coaching inn, backing on to the
playing fields of Eton College. Close to
Royal Windsor and the Thames,
offering a high level of comfort,
hospitality and food.*
Bedrooms: 8 single, 12 double,
5 twin, 5 triple, 3 family rooms
Bathrooms: 33 en-suite

**Bed & breakfast
per night:**

	£min	£max
Single	45.00	83.00
Double	102.00	112.00

**Half board per
person:**

	£min	£max
Daily	56.00	116.00

Lunch available
Evening meal 1900 (last orders
2130)
Parking for 30
Cards accepted: Amex, Diners,
Mastercard, Visa, Switch/Delta

Clarence Hotel ♨
Listed **COMMENDED**

9 Clarence Road, Windsor SL4 5AE
☎ (01753) 864436
Fax (01753) 857060
*Comfortable hotel with licensed bar
and steam room, near town centre,
castle and Eton. All rooms en-suite, TV,
hairdryer, radio and tea-maker.
Convenient for Heathrow Airport.*
Bedrooms: 4 single, 4 double, 7 twin,
4 triple, 2 family rooms
Bathrooms: 21 en-suite, 1 public

**Bed & breakfast
per night:**

	£min	£max
Single	35.00	41.00
Double	39.00	54.00

Parking for 4
Cards accepted: Amex, Diners,
Mastercard, Visa, Switch/Delta

Fairlight Lodge Royal Windsor Hotel ♨
COMMENDED

41 Frances Road, Windsor SL4 3AQ
☎ (01753) 861207
Fax (01753) 865963
*Comfortable Victorian property, once
the mayoral residence, quietly situated,
but close to River Thames, castle and
town centre. Fully licensed bar and
restaurant.*
Bedrooms: 2 single, 5 double, 2 twin,
1 family room
Bathrooms: 10 en-suite

**Bed & breakfast
per night:**

	£min	£max
Single	50.00	55.00
Double	69.00	80.00

**Half board per
person:**

	£min	£max
Daily	44.00	49.00
Weekly	280.00	310.00

Evening meal 1900 (last orders
2130)
Parking for 10
Cards accepted: Amex, Mastercard,
Visa, Switch/Delta

The Manor Hotel ♨
COMMENDED

The Village Green, Datchet, Slough
SL3 9EA
☎ (01753) 543442
Fax (01753) 545292
*Tudor period hotel overlooking village
green, within easy reach of Windsor
and Heathrow. Renowned cuisine in
Alexander's restaurant. Traditional ales
in bar.*
Bedrooms: 7 single, 14 double,
10 twin
Bathrooms: 31 en-suite

**Bed & breakfast
per night:**

	£min	£max
Single	35.00	75.00
Double	50.00	100.00

Lunch available
Evening meal 1900 (last orders
2145)
Parking for 15
Cards accepted: Amex, Diners,
Mastercard, Visa, Switch/Delta

Melrose House ♨
COMMENDED

53 Frances Road, Windsor SL4 3AQ
☎ (01753) 865328
Fax (01753) 865328
*Elegant Victorian detached residence,
in the heart of Windsor. Five minutes'
walk from the castle.*
Bedrooms: 1 single, 3 double, 2 twin,
2 triple, 1 family room
Bathrooms: 9 en-suite

**Bed & breakfast
per night:**

	£min	£max
Single	38.00	45.00
Double	50.00	60.00

Parking for 9
Cards accepted: Mastercard, Visa,
Switch/Delta

Oscar Hotel ♨
APPROVED

65 Vansittart Road, Windsor
SL4 5DB
☎ (01753) 830613
Fax (01753) 833744
*Fully licensed hotel, all rooms en-suite
with direct-dial telephone, colour TV,
tea/coffee facilities. Own car park.
Minutes' drive to Legoland.*
Bedrooms: 3 single, 4 double, 2 twin,
1 triple, 2 family rooms
Bathrooms: 12 en-suite

**Bed & breakfast
per night:**

	£min	£max
Single	45.00	55.00
Double	55.00	65.00

**Half board per
person:**

	£min	£max
Daily	37.50	40.00
Weekly	245.00	275.00

Evening meal 1800 (last orders
1930)
Parking for 10
Cards accepted: Amex, Diners,
Mastercard, Visa, Switch/Delta

Please mention this guide
when making your booking.

Stirrups Country House Hotel ♜

♛♛♛♛ HIGHLY COMMENDED

Maidens Green, Bracknell
RG42 6LD
☎ (01344) 882284
Fax (01344) 882300
CR Best Western
Privately owned hotel in Berkshire, situated between Windsor, Ascot and Bracknell and only 3 miles from the Windsor Legoland park.
Bedrooms: 19 double, 4 twin, 1 triple
Bathrooms: 24 en-suite
Bed & breakfast

per night:	£min	£max
Single	60.00	110.00
Double	80.00	120.00

Lunch available
Evening meal 1900 (last orders 2200)
Parking for 100
Cards accepted: Amex, Diners, Mastercard, Visa, Switch/Delta

WITNEY

Oxfordshire
Map ref 2C1

Town famous for its blanket-making and mentioned in the Domesday Book. The market-place contains the Butter Cross, a medieval meeting place, and there is a green with merchants' houses.
Tourist Information Centre ☎ (01993) 775802

Greystones Lodge Hotel

♛♛ HIGHLY COMMENDED

34 Tower Hill, Witney OX8 5ES
☎ (01993) 771898
Fax (01993) 771898
Quiet, comfortable private hotel set in three-quarters of an acre of pleasant garden. Conveniently located for visiting Oxford and the Cotswolds.
Bedrooms: 4 single, 4 double, 2 twin, 1 triple
Bathrooms: 6 en-suite, 1 public, 5 private showers
Bed & breakfast

per night:	£min	£max
Single	27.00	32.00
Double	42.00	48.00

Half board per

person:	£min	£max
Daily	35.50	42.50
Weekly	213.50	262.50

Evening meal 1900 (last orders 2100)

Parking for 12
Cards accepted: Amex, Diners, Mastercard, Visa

The Marlborough Hotel

♛♛♛ COMMENDED

28 Market Square, Witney OX8 7BB
☎ (01993) 776353
Fax (01993) 702152
Situated in the town centre. Ideal for touring the Cotswolds, Oxford City and Woodstock (Blenheim Palace).
Bedrooms: 6 single, 11 double, 3 twin, 2 triple
Bathrooms: 22 en-suite
Bed & breakfast

per night:	£min	£max
Single		48.00
Double		65.00

Half board per

person:	£min	£max
Daily		60.00

Lunch available
Evening meal 1800 (last orders 2130)
Parking for 18
Cards accepted: Amex, Mastercard, Visa, Switch/Delta

WOKINGHAM

Berkshire
Map ref 2C2

Pleasant town which grew up around the silk trade and has some half-timbered and Georgian houses.
Tourist Information Centre ☎ (0118) 977 4722

Cantley House Hotel ♜

♛♛♛♛ HIGHLY COMMENDED

Milton Road, Wokingham
RG41 5QG
☎ (0118) 978 9912
Fax (0118) 977 4294
Victorian country house hotel of great charm and character, set in quiet parkland just outside Wokingham. En-suite rooms, splendid restaurant and bistro. Only 5 minutes from M4, junction 10.
Bedrooms: 15 single, 12 double, 2 twin
Suite available
Bathrooms: 29 en-suite
Bed & breakfast

per night:	£min	£max
Single	45.00	85.00
Double	65.00	93.00

Lunch available
Evening meal 1900 (last orders 2200)
Parking for 70

Cards accepted: Amex, Diners, Mastercard, Visa, Switch/Delta

WOODLANDS

Hampshire
Map ref 2C3

Scattered village on the edge of the New Forest west of Southampton.

Busketts Lawn Hotel ♜

♛♛♛ COMMENDED

174 Woodlands Road, Woodlands, Southampton SO40 7GL
☎ (01703) 292272 & 292077
Fax (01703) 292487

Delightful family-run country house hotel in quiet forest surroundings, 8 miles west of Southampton. Heated swimming pool. Every amenity.
Bedrooms: 4 single, 5 double, 3 twin, 2 triple
Bathrooms: 14 en-suite
Bed & breakfast

per night:	£min	£max
Single	37.50	50.00
Double	70.00	80.00

Half board per

person:	£min	£max
Daily	49.50	54.00
Weekly	287.00	297.50

Lunch available
Evening meal 1900 (last orders 2030)
Parking for 50
Cards accepted: Amex, Diners, Mastercard, Visa

WELCOME HOST

This is a nationally recognised customer care programme which aims to promote the highest standards of service and a warm welcome. Establishments who are taking part in this initiative are indicated by the ⚙ symbol.

WOODSTOCK

Oxfordshire
Map ref 2C1

Small country town clustered around the park gates of Blenheim Palace, the superb 18th C home of the Duke of Marlborough. The town has well-known inns and an interesting museum. Sir Winston Churchill was born and buried nearby.
Tourist Information Centre ☎ *(01993) 811038*

Gorselands Farmhouse Auberge ⋔
👑👑
Boddington Lane, Long Hanborough, Witney OX8 6PU
☎ (01993) 881895
Fax (01993) 882799
Cotswold stone country farmhouse with exposed beams, snooker room, conservatory. Convenient for Blenheim Palace, Oxford, Cotswold villages. Evening meals available. Licensed for wine and beer. Grass tennis court.
Bedrooms: 1 single, 2 double, 1 twin, 2 family rooms
Suite available
Bathrooms: 6 en-suite

Bed & breakfast per night:	£min	£max
Single	30.00	35.00
Double	42.00	50.00
Half board per person:	£min	£max
Daily	44.95	49.95
Weekly	250.00	350.00

Evening meal 1900 (last orders 2100)
Parking for 7
Cards accepted: Amex, Mastercard, Visa

AT-A-GLANCE SYMBOLS

Symbols at the end of each accommodation entry
give useful information about services
and facilities. A key to symbols can be found
inside the back cover flap.

Keep this open for easy reference.

ENQUIRY COUPONS

To help you obtain further information
about advertisers and accommodation featured in
this guide you will find enquiry coupons at the back.
Send these directly to the establishments
in which you are interested.
Remember to complete both sides of the coupon.

SOUTH EAST ENGLAND

The South East is brimming with bright holiday ideas. From seaside resorts to unhurried villages, open downland, grand cathedrals and historic houses - there's lots to interest everyone.

The charm of Kent's 'Garden of England' rolls gently on to the pretty South Downs of Sussex with their majestic chalk cliffs and excellent walking country. In the heart of historic 1066 Country tour the ruins of Battle Abbey or discover some of the region's many beautiful gardens.

There's a huge variety of sports, from golf and sailing to bowls and surfing. While entertainments range from the annual Glyndebourne Opera season to the Brighton Festival and end-of-the-pier fun.

The counties of East Sussex, Kent, Surrey and West Sussex

FOR MORE INFORMATION CONTACT:
South East England Tourist Board,
The Old Brew House, Warwick Park,
Tunbridge Wells, Kent TN2 5TU
Tel: (01892) 540766 **Fax:** (01892) 511008

Where to Go in South East England –
see pages 484-487
Where to Stay in South East England –
see pages 488-521

SOUTH EAST ENGLAND

Where to Go and What to See

You will find hundreds of interesting places to visit during your stay in South East England, just some of which are listed in these pages. The number against each name will help you locate it on the map (page 487). Contact any Tourist Information Centre in the region for more ideas on days out in South East England.

1 The Dickens Centre
Eastgate House,
High Street,
Rochester,
Kent ME1 1EW
Tel: (01634) 844176/827980
Unique experience of Dickens' life and novels. Life-size models, sound and light effects. New 'Dickens Dream' tableau/audio-visual presentation on Dickens' life.

2 Great Stour Brewery
75 Stour Street,
Canterbury,
Kent CT1 2NR
Tel: (01227) 763579
An historic 250-year-old building. Members of the public can brew their own beer and visit the on-site museum of brewing. Shop and beer garden.

3 St Augustine's Abbey
Longport,
Canterbury,
Kent CT1 1TF
Tel: (01227) 767345
A World Heritage Site founded in AD598 by St Augustine, first Archbishop of Canterbury. Remains include Norman church and ruins of the 7thC church of St Pancras.

4 Yalding Organic Gardens
Benover Road,
Yalding, Maidstone,
Kent ME18 6EX
Tel: (01622) 814650
Newly created 'green' history of gardening through the ages - 11thC herb garden, Tudor knot, 19thC cottage gardens, and Victorian herbaceous border with 1950s allotment.

5 Ightham Mote
Ivy Hatch,
Sevenoaks,
Kent TN15 0NT
Tel: (01732) 810378
Medieval moated manor house remodelled in the 16thC. Great hall, two chapels and 18thC drawing room. Garden. Woodland walk. Pretty courtyard.

6 Knole
Sevenoaks,
Kent TN15 0RP
Tel: (01732) 462100
Large house dating from 1456, home of the Sackvilles. Richly panelled and furnished. 17thC silk and velvet tapestries. State rooms, Old Master paintings. Deer park.

7 Godstone Vineyards
Quarry Road,
Godstone,
Surrey RH9 8ZA
Tel: (01883) 744590
*Ten-acre vineyard with modern
winery set in 50 acres of beautiful
farmland. Vineyard shop. Coarse
fishing lake (day tickets available)
and pick-your-own crops (seasonal).*

8 Brooklands Museum
Brooklands Road,
Weybridge,
Surrey KT13 0QN
Tel: (01932) 857381
*Opened in 1991 on 30 acres of the
original 1907 motor racing circuit.
Features the most historic and
steepest section of the old banked
track and 1-in-4 Test Hill. Motoring
village.*

9 Painshill Park
Between Streets,
Cobham, Surrey KT11 1JE
Tel: (01932) 864674/868113
18thC landscape gardens with lake,

*lawns, woodland, specimen trees
and shrubberies. Gothic temple,
grotto, Chinese bridge, waterwheel,
vineyard, historic plantings and
Turkish tent.*

10 Chapel Farm Animal Trail
Chapel Farm,
Westhumble,
Dorking,
Surrey RH5 6AY
Tel: (01306) 882865
*See a full range of farm animals
and follow marked routes through
the farmyard. Rabbits, lambs, chicks
and ducklings can be touched.
Tractor trailer rides.*

11 Clandon Park
West Clandon,
Guildford,
Surrey GU4 7RQ
Tel: (01483) 222482
*Palladian-style house built for Lord
Onslow circa 1730. Marble hall,
Gubbay collection of furniture,
needlework and porcelain. Royal
Surrey Regiment Museum.*

12 Rural Life Centre
Old Kiln Museum,
Reeds Road,
Tilford, Farnham,
Surrey GU10 2DL
Tel: (01252) 792300
*Museum with farm machines,
implements and waggons.
Wheelwright's shop, working smith
and displays on past village life.
Hop press. Small arboretum and
woodland walk.*

13 Owl House Gardens
Mount Pleasant,
Lamberhurst,
Kent TN3 8LY
Tel: (01892) 890230/890963
*Over 16 acres of romantic walks
through woodland, dell and sunken
gardens. Azaleas, rhododendrons,
spring flowers and rare shrubs.
Gardens surround 16thC wood-
smuggler's cottage.*

14 Lathe Barn
Donkey Street,
Burmarsh, Romney Marsh,
Kent TN29 0JN
Tel: (01303) 873618
*Museum with collection of rural and
domestic bygones. Children's farm
with sheep, donkey, pigs, goats,
geese, rabbits, calves, chickens and
peacocks. Children's play area.*

**15 Romney, Hythe and
Dymchurch Railway**
New Romney Station,
New Romney, Kent TN28 8PL
Tel: (01797) 362353/363256
*The world's only main line in
miniature runs for 14 miles across
Romney Marsh. Steam and diesel
locomotives, yards, engine sheds,
toy and model museum at New
Romney.*

16 The High Beeches Gardens
Handcross,
Haywards Heath,
West Sussex RH17 6HQ
Tel: (01444) 400589
*Twenty acres of landscaped
woodland and water gardens with
many rare plants, a wildflower
meadow and glorious
autumn colour.*

17 Borde Hill Garden

Balcombe Road,
Haywards Heath,
West Sussex RH16 1XP
Tel: (01444) 450326
Large private collection of champion trees. Peaceful gardens with rich variety of all season colour set in 200 acres of parkland and woods. Children's trout fishing and playground.

18 Lavender Line Steam Railway Museum

Isfield Station, Near Uckfield,
East Sussex TN22 5XB
Tel: (01825) 750515/
(01825) 750515
Fully-restored station buildings. Three standard-gauge steam engines pull carriages along one mile of track. Museum and signal box.

19 Battle Abbey and Battlefield

High Street, Battle,
East Sussex TN33 0AD
Tel: (01424) 773792
Abbey founded by William the Conqueror on the Battle of Hastings site. Church alter marks the spot where Harold was killed. Gatehouse exhibition and Monk's dormitory.

20 Herstmonceux Castle Gardens

Herstmonceux,
East Sussex BN27 1RP
Tel: (01323) 834444
Elizabethan courtyard. Flower garden and nature trail surrounding castle (tours daily). Walled and herbal gardens. Visitor and Science centres.

21 Michelham Priory

Upper Dicker, Hailsham,
East Sussex BN27 3QS
Tel: (01323) 844224
A 13th-16thC priory, country house and gatehouse, working watermill, physic garden, rope museum, blacksmith's and wheelwright's museum. Gardens, grounds, moat and play area.

22 Bentley Wildfowl and Motor Museum

Halland, Near Lewes,
East Sussex BN8 5AF
Tel: (01825) 840573
Over 1,000 wildfowl in parkland with lakes. Motor museum. Antiques and wildfowl paintings in house. Indoor children's activity centre, children's playground and woodland walk.

23 Anne of Cleves House Museum

52 Southover High Street,
Lewes,
East Sussex BN7 1JA
Tel: (01273) 474610
Old timber-framed house and workshops housing folk museum. 17th-18thC Wealden ironwork, furnished rooms with domestic utensils and trade equipment. Tudor-style garden.

24 Drusillas Park

Alfriston, Polegate,
East Sussex BN26 5QS
Tel: (01323) 870234/870656
Award-winning zoo with animals in natural habitats, farmyard, miniature railway and adventure playground. Japanese and rose gardens.

25 Filching Manor Motor Museum

Wannock,
Polegate,
East Sussex BN26 5QA
Tel: (01323) 487838/487124
Wealden hall house on site of 600AD priory. Over 100 veteran, vintage, sports and racing cars, Jupiter aircraft and racing motor boats.

26 Eastbourne Miniature Steam Railway Park

Lottbridge Drove, Eastbourne,
East Sussex BN23 6NS
Tel: (01323) 520229
Miniature steam and diesel-hauled passenger trains. New railway-style buildings, engine shed and large man-made lake. Children's playground. Fishing available.

27 The Body Shop Tour

Watersmead Business Park,
Littlehampton,
West Sussex BN17 6LS
Follow the life of a product from an idea to raw ingredients, testing, manufacturing, filling and distribution. Information on the environment.

28 Pulborough Brooks RSPB Nature Reserve

Wiggonholt,
Pulborough,
West Sussex RH20 2EL
Tel: (01798) 875851
Upperton's Barn visitor centre with displays, extensive nature reserve featuring nature trail, scenic views and viewing hides.

Map Labels

BUCKS

ESSEX

GREATER LONDON

BERKS

1 Gravesend · Gillingham
Dartford · Rochester
Herne Bay · Margate
Whitstable · Broadstairs

Weybridge **8**
Chatham · Sittingbourne
Ramsgate
Cobham **9** Epsom
Sevenoaks
Faversham **2** **3**
Sandwich
Woking · Leatherhead · Godstone
5 Ivy
4 Maidstone
Canterbury · Deal

Guildford **11** · Dorking **10** · Reigate
Oxted
Paddock Wood
KENT

Farnham **12**
Horley
Royal Tunbridge Wells
Ashford · Dover

SURREY
Crawley
Tenterden
Folkestone

Cranleigh
13 Lamberhurst
Hythe **14**
Haslemere · Horsham
Crowborough
Burmarsh

WEST SUSSEX
Handcross **16**
EAST SUSSEX
Heathfield
15 New Romney

Midhurst
Haywards Heath
17 Uckfield **18**

Pulborough **28**
Cuckfield
Halland **22**
19 Battle
20 Herstmonceux

Arundel
Brighton **23** Lewes
21 Hailsham
Hastings

29 **30** **31**
Shoreham
24 **25** Pevensey
Bexhill-on-Sea

Chichester **27** · Worthing · Newhaven · Polegate
Bognor · Littlehampton · Seaford
26
Regis
Eastbourne

0 — 20 Miles
0 — 30 Kms

---

29 Chichester Harbour Water Tours
Itchenor,
Chichester,
West Sussex
Tel: (01243) 786418
Leisurely hour-and-a-half trips from Itchenor around the attractive Chichester Harbour - an Area of Outstanding Natural Beauty and wildlife reserve.

30 Fishbourne Roman Palace and Museum
Salthill Road,
Fishbourne,
Chichester,
West Sussex PO19 3QR
Tel: (01243) 785859
Remains of the largest Roman residence in Britain. Many beautiful mosaics now under cover. Hypocaust and restored

formal garden. Museum of finds. Model and audio-visual programme.

31 Sculpture at Goodwood
Hat Hill Copse,
Goodwood,
Chichester,
West Sussex PO18 0QP
Tel: (01243) 538449
A changing collection of contemporary British sculpture set in 20 acres of beautiful grounds on the South Downs overlooking Chichester.

FIND OUT MORE

Further information about holidays and attractions in South East England is available from:
South East England Tourist Board,
The Old Brew House,

Warwick Park, Tunbridge Wells, Kent TN2 5TU.
Tel: (01892) 540766

These publications are available free from the South East England Tourist Board:
■ **Great Escapes**
■ **Accommodation Guide**
■ **Bed and Breakfast Touring Map**
■ **Outstanding Churches and Cathedrals**

Also available is (price includes postage and packaging):
■ **South East England Leisure Map** £4
■ **Hundreds of Places to Visit in the South East** UK £3.15, *Overseas* £3.50
■ **Villages to Visit** UK £2.60, *Overseas* £2.95

WHERE TO STAY (SOUTH EAST ENGLAND)

Accommodation entries in this region are listed in alphabetical order of place name, and then in alphabetical order of establishment.

Map references refer to the colour location maps at the back of this guide. The first number indicates the map to use; the letter and number which follow refer to the grid reference on the map.

At-a-glance symbols at the end of each accommodation entry give useful information about services and facilities. A key to symbols can be found inside the back cover flap.

Keep this open for easy reference.

ALFRISTON

East Sussex
Map ref 2D3

Old village in the Cuckmere Valley and a former smugglers' haunt. The 14th C Clergy House was the first building to be bought by the National Trust. Spacious 14th C St Andrew's church is known as the "Cathedral of the South Downs" and the 13th C Star Inn is one of the oldest in England.

White Lodge Country House Hotel

♛♛♛♛ HIGHLY COMMENDED

Sloe Lane, Alfriston, Polegate
BN26 5UR
☎ (01323) 870265
Fax (01323) 870284

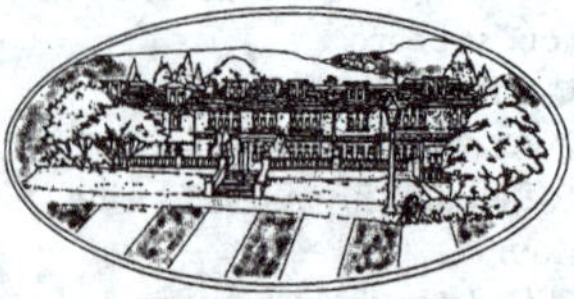

Set in 5 acres of gardens overlooking scenic Sussex downland. Tasteful and elegant furnishings, excellent cooking, large comfortable bedrooms, experienced personal attention. Maximum prices below are for single occupancy of double room.

Bedrooms: 3 single, 7 double, 6 twin, 1 triple
Suite available
Bathrooms: 16 en-suite, 1 private

Bed & breakfast per night:	£min	£max
Single	50.00	75.00
Double	90.00	125.00

Half board per person:	£min	£max
Daily	67.00	92.00
Weekly	320.00	680.00

Lunch available
Evening meal 1915 (last orders 2130)
Parking for 25
Cards accepted: Amex, Mastercard, Visa, Switch/Delta
[S] 17 [SP] [T]

ARUNDEL

West Sussex
Map ref 2D3

Picturesque, historic town on the River Arun, dominated by Arundel Castle, home of the Dukes of Norfolk. There are many 18th C houses, the Toy and Military Museum, Wildfowl and Wetlands Centre and Museum and Heritage Centre.
Tourist Information Centre ☎ (01903) 882268

Bridge House

♛♛♛ COMMENDED

18 Queen Street, Arundel
BN18 9JG
☎ (01903) 882779 & 0500 323224
Fax (01903) 883600

Family-run guesthouse, in centre of town, with views of castle, river, and Downs. Ideal centre for exploring beautiful Sussex, ancestral homes, Roman ruins and for visiting Fontwell and Goodwood racecourses.

Bedrooms: 2 single, 8 double, 2 twin, 4 triple, 3 family rooms
Bathrooms: 14 en-suite, 2 public

Bed & breakfast per night:	£min	£max
Single	20.00	28.00
Double	32.00	44.00

Lunch available
Evening meal 1800 (last orders 1930)
Parking for 12
Cards accepted: Amex, Mastercard, Visa, Switch/Delta
[S] [TV] [SP] [T]

Burpham Country House Hotel

♛♛♛ HIGHLY COMMENDED

Burpham, Arundel BN18 9RJ
☎ (01903) 882160
Fax (01903) 884627
[CR] Logis of GB

In one of the most peaceful and unspoilt villages in West Sussex, with superb downland views. Ideal for walking holidays. Perfect for a stress remedy break. Award-winning restaurant (open to non-residents).

Bedrooms: 1 single, 6 double, 3 twin
Bathrooms: 10 en-suite

Bed & breakfast per night:	£min	£max
Single	37.00	47.00
Double	76.00	83.00

Half board per person:	£min	£max
Daily	58.00	61.50
Weekly	367.50	395.50

Evening meal 1915 (last orders 2045)
Parking for 12
Cards accepted: Amex, Mastercard, Visa
10 [S] [TV] 15 [SP] [T]

Swan Hotel

👑👑👑 **HIGHLY COMMENDED**

27-29 High Street, Arundel
BN18 9AG
☎ (01903) 882314
Fax (01903) 883759

Elegant Grade II listed building situated in the heart of historic Arundel. Completely refurbished in 1994. Award-winning restaurant with traditional bar.
Bedrooms: 3 single, 10 double, 2 twin
Bathrooms: 15 en-suite

Bed & breakfast

per night:	£min	£max
Single	40.00	50.00
Double	50.00	70.00

Half board per person:

	£min	£max
Daily	50.00	60.00
Weekly	350.00	420.00

Lunch available
Evening meal 1830 (last orders 2200)
Parking for 20
Cards accepted: Amex, Diners, Mastercard, Visa, Switch/Delta

🐎🕯️📧🖵👜🍴🅂🔏🔊⏻▭🧺
🍴👟🚶🏃🚶🅰🅿️🆎🅣

ASHFORD

Kent
Map ref 3B4

Once a market centre for the farmers of the Weald of Kent and Romney Marsh. The town centre has a number of Tudor and Georgian houses and a museum. Eurostar trains stop at Ashford International station.
Tourist Information Centre ☎ (01233) 629165

Croft Hotel

👑👑 **COMMENDED**

Canterbury Road, Kennington, Ashford TN25 4DU
☎ (01233) 622140
Fax (01233) 622140
ⓒⓡ The Independents

> A key to symbols can be found inside the back cover flap.

Country house in 2 acres of gardens. Channel Tunnel 10 miles, Canterbury 12 miles, Dover 22 miles. Ideal for business people and tourists alike.
Bedrooms: 6 single, 8 double, 9 twin, 4 triple, 1 family room
Bathrooms: 28 en-suite

Bed & breakfast

per night:	£min	£max
Single	39.50	45.00
Double	50.00	60.00

Evening meal 1830 (last orders 2000)
Parking for 32
Cards accepted: Amex, Mastercard, Visa, Switch/Delta

🐎🛁🕯️📧🖵👜🍴🅂🔊⏻▭🧺
🆂🅿️

Warren Cottage Hotel

👑👑👑 **COMMENDED**

136 The Street, Willesborough, Ashford TN24 0NB
☎ (01233) 621905 & 632929
Fax (01233) 623400

17th C hotel and restaurant, set in 2.5 acres, where a cosy atmosphere awaits. All rooms en-suite with colour TV, large car park. M20 junction 10 and minutes from Ashford International Station, Channel Tunnel, Dover and Folkestone.
Bedrooms: 2 single, 2 double, 1 twin, 1 triple, 1 family room
Bathrooms: 7 en-suite, 1 public

Bed & breakfast

per night:	£min	£max
Single	34.90	39.90
Double	45.00	59.90

Half board per person:

	£min	£max
Daily	44.90	
Weekly	314.30	

Lunch available
Evening meal 1830 (last orders 2130)
Parking for 23
Cards accepted: Diners, Mastercard, Visa, Switch/Delta

🐎🛁📧🖵👜🍴🅂🔏🔊⏻▭🧺🅿
🍴👟🔄🅰️

BEXHILL-ON-SEA

East Sussex
Map ref 3B4

Popular resort with beach of shingle and firm sand at low tide. The impressive 1930s designed De la Warr Pavilion has good entertainment facilities. Costume Museum in Manor Gardens.
Tourist Information Centre ☎ (01424) 732208

Bedford Lodge Hotel

👑👑👑 **COMMENDED**

Cantelupe Road, Bexhill-on-Sea TN40 1PR
☎ (01424) 730097
Fax (01424) 217552
Comfortable, family-run, Victorian building in quiet residential area close to promenade and town. Appetising home cooking. Easy parking.
Bedrooms: 2 single, 2 double, 2 twin
Bathrooms: 3 en-suite, 3 public

Bed & breakfast

per night:	£min	£max
Single	21.00	26.00
Double	40.00	52.00

Half board per person:

	£min	£max
Daily	27.00	35.00
Weekly	150.00	210.00

Lunch available
Evening meal 1800 (last orders 1900)
Parking for 1
Cards accepted: Mastercard, Visa, Switch/Delta

🐎🛁📧🖵👜🍴🅂🔏✂️▭🧺🅿❄️🚗
🅰️🆎🆂🅣

The Northern Hotel

👑👑👑 **COMMENDED**

72-82 Sea Road, Bexhill-on-Sea TN40 1JL
☎ (01424) 212836
Fax (01424) 213036
Warm and friendly hotel comprising terrace of 6 large Edwardian town houses in quiet seaside resort. Family-managed for over 40 years. Ideal touring base for 1066 country.
Bedrooms: 12 single, 4 double, 4 twin
Bathrooms: 20 en-suite, 3 public

Bed & breakfast

per night:	£min	£max
Single	30.00	42.00
Double	47.00	72.50

Half board per person:

	£min	£max
Daily	41.00	53.50
Weekly	287.00	337.05

Continued ▶

BEXHILL-ON-SEA
Continued

Lunch available
Evening meal 1745 (last orders 2000)
Cards accepted: Amex, Mastercard, Visa

BIRLING GAP

East Sussex
Map ref 2D3

Beauty spot on the famous Seven Sisters cliffs near Beachy Head, surrounded by magnificent National Trust downland. Ancient home of the Saxon tribe, the Boerls, who inhabited a gap in the cliffs. Famous for former smuggling activities.

Birling Gap Hotel

👑👑👑 APPROVED

Birling Gap, Seven Sisters Cliffs, East Dean, Eastbourne BN20 0AB
☎ (01323) 423197
Fax (01323) 423030
Logis of GB

Magnificent Seven Sisters clifftop position, with views of country, sea, beach. Superb downland and beach walks. Old world "Thatched Bar" and "Oak Room Restaurant". Coffee shop and games room, function and conference suite. Off A259 coast road at East Dean, 1.5 miles west of Beachy Head.
Bedrooms: 1 single, 2 double, 3 twin, 3 triple
Bathrooms: 9 en-suite, 1 public

Bed & breakfast

per night:	£min	£max
Single	20.00	50.00
Double	30.00	60.00

Half board per person:

	£min	£max
Daily	29.00	38.00
Weekly	183.00	245.00

Lunch available
Evening meal 1830 (last orders 2115)
Parking for 100
Cards accepted: Amex, Diners, Mastercard, Visa, Switch/Delta

BOGNOR REGIS

West Sussex
Map ref 2D3

5 miles of firm, flat sand have made the town a popular family resort. Well supplied with gardens, children's activities in Hotham Park and the Bognor Regis Centre for entertainment.
Tourist Information Centre ☎ (01243) 823140

Beachcroft Hotel

👑👑👑 COMMENDED

Clyde Road, Felpham, Bognor Regis PO22 7AH
☎ (01243) 827142
Fax (01243) 827142
Family-run hotel in south-facing beachside village location. Garden, indoor heated pool, car park. All rooms en-suite with TV, telephone, tea and coffee. Comprehensive restaurant and bar facilities.
Bedrooms: 9 single, 6 double, 16 twin, 2 triple, 4 family rooms
Bathrooms: 37 en-suite

Bed & breakfast

per night:	£min	£max
Single	26.00	40.00
Double	44.00	62.00

Half board per person:

	£min	£max
Daily	32.00	52.00
Weekly	193.00	320.00

Evening meal 1900 (last orders 2100)
Parking for 40
Cards accepted: Amex, Mastercard, Visa

Camelot Hotel & Restaurant

👑👑👑 COMMENDED

3 Flansham Lane, Felpham, Bognor Regis PO22 6AA
☎ (01243) 585875
Fax (01243) 587500
Whilst away from home do what King Arthur did: think of Camelot. Situated on A259 Littlehampton-Bognor main road in the village of Felpham, West Sussex.
Bedrooms: 1 single, 7 double, 1 twin
Bathrooms: 9 en-suite

Bed & breakfast

per night:	£min	£max
Single	32.50	40.00
Double	48.50	52.50

Half board per person:

	£min	£max
Daily	37.00	52.50
Weekly	225.00	297.50

Lunch available
Evening meal 1910 (last orders 2145)
Parking for 25
Cards accepted: Amex, Diners, Mastercard, Visa, Switch/Delta

Jubilee Guest House

Listed COMMENDED

5 Gloucester Road, Bognor Regis PO21 1NU
☎ (01243) 863016
Fax (01243) 868016
Family-run business, 75 yards from seafront and beach. Ideally situated for visiting "South Coast World", Chichester, Goodwood, Fontwell, Arundel and the South Downs.
Bedrooms: 2 single, 1 double, 1 triple, 1 family room
Bathrooms: 1 private, 1 public, 2 private showers

Bed & breakfast

per night:	£min	£max
Single	18.00	25.00
Double	36.00	50.00

Parking for 4
Open February–December

Sea Crest Private Hotel

👑👑 COMMENDED

19 Nyewood Lane, Bognor Regis PO21 2QB
☎ (01243) 821438
Small, comfortable, private hotel near the sea with particularly attractive and modern en-suite rooms available at reasonable prices.
Bedrooms: 1 single, 3 double, 1 twin, 2 triple
Bathrooms: 5 en-suite, 1 public

Bed & breakfast

per night:	£min	£max
Single	19.00	24.00
Double	38.00	48.00

Half board per person:

	£min	£max
Daily	27.50	32.50
Weekly	185.00	225.00

Evening meal from 1745
Parking for 7

BRIGHTON & HOVE

East Sussex
Map ref 2D3

Brighton's attractions include the Royal Pavilion, Volks Electric Railway, Sea Life Centre and Marina Village, Conference Centre and "The Lanes" and several theatres. Neighbouring Hove is a resort in its own right.
Tourist Information Centre ☎ (01273) 323755; for Hove (01273) 778087

Ainsley House Hotel ⚠

👑👑👑 COMMENDED

28 New Steine, Brighton, East Sussex BN2 1PD
☎ (01273) 605310
Fax (01273) 688604
Elegant listed Regency town house overlooking a garden square and the sea. 10 minutes from conference centre, shops and theatres.
Bedrooms: 3 single, 3 double, 1 twin, 3 triple
Bathrooms: 8 en-suite, 1 public
Bed & breakfast

per night:	£min	£max
Single	24.00	30.00
Double	48.00	70.00

Cards accepted: Amex, Diners, Mastercard, Visa

Allendale Hotel ⚠

👑👑👑 COMMENDED

3 New Steine, Brighton, East Sussex BN2 1PB
☎ (01273) 675436
Fax (01273) 602603
Regency hotel, offering every facility for a comfortable, enjoyable and stress-free stay. Privately run, overlooking garden square and sea.
Bedrooms: 5 single, 3 double, 1 twin, 2 triple, 1 family room
Bathrooms: 9 en-suite, 2 public, 1 private shower
Bed & breakfast

per night:	£min	£max
Single	25.00	35.00
Double	44.00	70.00

Half board per person:

	£min	£max
Daily	37.00	47.00
Weekly	259.00	329.00

Evening meal 1800 (last orders 2000)
Cards accepted: Amex, Mastercard, Visa

Ambassador Hotel ⚠

👑👑👑 COMMENDED

22 New Steine, Marine Parade, Brighton, East Sussex BN2 1PD
☎ (01273) 676869
Fax (01273) 689988
Family-run, licensed hotel overlooking sea, near conference centres. Colour TV, telephone, radio, tea/coffee facilities.
Bedrooms: 6 single, 8 double, 6 triple, 1 family room
Bathrooms: 21 en-suite, 2 public
Bed & breakfast

per night:	£min	£max
Single	25.00	36.00
Double	45.00	60.00

Cards accepted: Amex, Diners, Mastercard, Visa, Switch/Delta

Arlanda Hotel ⚠

👑👑👑 HIGHLY COMMENDED

20 New Steine, Brighton, East Sussex BN2 1PD
☎ (01273) 699300
Fax (01273) 600930
Enjoy good food and company in a licensed, family-run hotel. Our warm rooms have full en-suite facilities. The hotel is in a quiet 200-year-old Regency square, yet close to Brighton's attractions.
Bedrooms: 4 single, 4 double, 1 twin, 3 triple
Bathrooms: 12 en-suite
Bed & breakfast

per night:	£min	£max
Single	20.00	40.00
Double	40.00	80.00

Lunch available
Evening meal 1800 (last orders 2000)
Cards accepted: Amex, Diners, Mastercard, Visa

For ideas on places to visit refer to the introduction at the beginning of this section.

The symbols in each entry give information about services and facilities. A key to these symbols appears at the back of this guide.

Ascott House Hotel

👑👑👑 HIGHLY COMMENDED

21 New Steine, Marine Parade, Brighton, East Sussex BN2 1PD
☎ (01273) 688085
Fax (01273) 623733
Well established, popular hotel with sea views, close to all amenities. Reputation for comfort, cleanliness and delicious breakfasts.
Bedrooms: 4 single, 6 triple, 2 family rooms
Bathrooms: 10 en-suite, 1 public, 1 private shower
Bed & breakfast

per night:	£min	£max
Single	20.00	40.00
Double	40.00	80.00

Evening meal from 1830
Cards accepted: Amex, Diners, Mastercard, Visa

Brighton Marina House Hotel ⚠

👑👑👑 APPROVED

8 Charlotte Street, Marine Parade, Brighton, East Sussex BN2 1AG
☎ (01273) 605349 & 679484
Fax (01273) 605349
Email: the21@pavilion.co.uk

Cosy, elegantly furnished, well-equipped, clean, comfortable, caring, family-run. Near sea, central for Palace Pier, Royal Pavilion, conference and exhibition halls, the famous Lanes, tourist attractions. Flexible breakfast, check-in/out times. Offering all facilities. Free street parking. Best in price range.
Bedrooms: 3 single, 3 double, 1 twin, 3 triple
Bathrooms: 7 en-suite, 1 public
Bed & breakfast

per night:	£min	£max
Single	15.00	39.00
Double	35.00	59.00

Half board per person:

	£min	£max
Daily	26.00	49.00
Weekly	167.00	371.00

Lunch available

Continued ▶

Please mention this guide when making your booking.

BRIGHTON & HOVE
Continued

Evening meal 1830 (last orders 1700)
Cards accepted: Amex, Diners, Mastercard, Visa

🛏🕹🖥💻🖨☎♿🖐🕽⬢S🅿💻🚗
⚔🛫 OAP 🚲 SP T

Brighton Oak Hotel 🏨
👑👑👑👑 COMMENDED

West Street, Brighton, East Sussex
BN1 2RQ
☎ (01273) 220033
Fax (01273) 778000
Elegant city centre hotel, designed in 1930s art deco style. Close to the seafront and adjacent to conference centre and the famous Lanes.
Wheelchair access category 3♿
Bedrooms: 2 single, 56 double, 80 twin
Bathrooms: 138 en-suite

Bed & breakfast per night:

	£min	£max
Single	56.00	97.50
Double	66.00	120.00

Half board per person:

	£min	£max
Daily	47.25	74.25
Weekly	283.50	445.50

Lunch available
Evening meal 1830 (last orders 2200)
Cards accepted: Amex, Diners, Mastercard, Visa, Switch/Delta

🛏☎🖥💻🖨♿🕽⬢S🗝☀💻🚗
🍴200 OAP 🚲 SP T

Brighton Twenty One Hotel 🏨
👑👑👑 COMMENDED

21 Charlotte Street, Marine Parade, Brighton, East Sussex BN2 1AG
☎ (01273) 686450 & 681617
Fax (01273) 695560
Email: the21@pavilion.co.uk

Exquisite rooms, including the Green Room, the executive Victorian Room or the Suite. Discounts: 10% 2 nights, 15% 4 nights, 20% 7 nights.
Bedrooms: 4 double, 2 twin
Suite available
Bathrooms: 6 en-suite, 1 public

Bed & breakfast per night:

	£min	£max
Single	25.00	65.00
Double	45.00	89.00

Half board per person:

	£min	£max
Daily	43.00	81.00
Weekly	240.00	498.00

Evening meal 1830 (last orders 2000)
Cards accepted: Amex, Diners, Mastercard, Visa, Switch/Delta

🛏10🖥☎💻🖨♿🕽⬢UL S🗝📺●
💻🚗🍴🛫🚲🚲 SP T ♨

Cavalaire House 🏨
👑👑👑 COMMENDED

34 Upper Rock Gardens, Brighton, East Sussex BN2 1QF
☎ (01273) 696899
Fax (01273) 600504
Victorian townhouse, close to sea and town centre. Resident proprietors offer comfortably furnished rooms with or without private facilities. Book 7 nights and get 1 night free.
Bedrooms: 1 single, 3 double, 3 twin, 2 triple
Bathrooms: 3 en-suite, 1 public, 3 private showers

Bed & breakfast per night:

	£min	£max
Single	18.00	20.00
Double	38.00	54.00

Cards accepted: Amex, Mastercard, Visa

🛏5🖥💻♿🕽⬢UL S🗝💻🚗🛫
🚲 T

Cosmopolitan Hotel 🏨
👑👑👑 APPROVED

31 New Steine, Marine Parade, Brighton, East Sussex BN2 1PD
☎ (01273) 682461
Fax (01273) 622311
In a seafront garden square with views of the beach and Palace Pier. Central for shopping, entertainments and conference centres.
Bedrooms: 12 single, 11 double, 3 twin, 10 triple, 2 family rooms
Bathrooms: 32 en-suite, 3 public, 3 private showers

Bed & breakfast per night:

	£min	£max
Single	22.00	35.00
Double	40.00	55.00

Evening meal 1800 (last orders 1900)
Cards accepted: Amex, Diners, Mastercard, Visa, Switch/Delta

🛏🕹🖥☎💻🖨♿S🗝📺●💻
💻🛫 OAP SP 🚲 T

The Dudley Hotel 🏨
👑👑👑👑 COMMENDED

Lansdowne Place, Hove, Brighton, East Sussex BN3 1HQ
☎ (01273) 736266
Fax (01273) 729802
🆑 Regal
A fine resort hotel, situated in the elegance of Regency Hove close to the seafront and all Brighton's attractions.
Bedrooms: 15 single, 22 double, 31 twin, 3 triple
Bathrooms: 71 en-suite

Bed & breakfast per night:

	£min	£max
Single	35.00	85.00
Double	64.00	115.00

Half board per person:

	£min	£max
Daily	43.00	100.00
Weekly	300.00	700.00

Lunch available
Evening meal 1900 (last orders 2145)
Parking for 39
Cards accepted: Amex, Diners, Mastercard, Visa, Switch/Delta

🛏☎💻🖨♿🕽⬢S🗝📺●🔆💻
💻🍴140 U🅿☀🚲 SP 🚲 T

Fyfield House 🏨
👑👑👑 COMMENDED

26 New Steine, Brighton, East Sussex BN2 1PD
☎ (01273) 602770
Fax (01273) 602770
Established over 25 years. Excellent home-from-home hotel, close to all attractions in and out of town. Peter and Anna ensure a nice stay.
Bedrooms: 4 single, 5 double
Bathrooms: 5 en-suite, 1 private, 1 public

Bed & breakfast per night:

	£min	£max
Single	16.00	30.00
Double	35.00	60.00

Evening meal 1800 (last orders 1900)
Cards accepted: Amex, Diners, Mastercard, Visa, Switch/Delta

🛏🖥🖨♿🕽⬢UL S🗝📺💻🚗
🚲 SP T

Kempton House Hotel
👑👑👑 COMMENDED

33-34 Marine Parade, Brighton, East Sussex BN2 1TR
☎ (01273) 570248
Fax (01273) 570248
Seafront hotel overlooking beach and Palace Pier. Central to all amenities. En-suite sea view rooms. Licensed bar and sea-facing patio garden.
Bedrooms: 7 double, 2 twin, 3 triple
Bathrooms: 12 en-suite

Bed & breakfast per night:	£min	£max
Single	32.00	45.00
Double	40.00	62.00

Evening meal from 1800
Cards accepted: Amex, Mastercard, Visa, Switch/Delta

Kimberley Hotel

APPROVED

17 Atlingworth Street, Brighton, East Sussex BN2 1PL
☎ (01273) 603504
Fax (01273) 603504
Family-run hotel, 2 minutes from seafront and central for amusements, shopping, marina and conference centre. Licensed residents' bar.
Bedrooms: 3 single, 3 double, 5 twin, 2 triple, 2 family rooms
Bathrooms: 4 en-suite, 1 public, 11 private showers

Bed & breakfast per night:	£min	£max
Single	20.00	23.00
Double	36.00	42.00

Cards accepted: Amex, Diners, Mastercard, Visa, Switch/Delta

Leona House

APPROVED

74 Middle Street, Brighton, East Sussex BN1 1AL
☎ (01273) 327309
Privately run guesthouse close to sea, conference centre and all amenities.
Bedrooms: 2 single, 3 double, 2 twin, 1 triple
Bathrooms: 3 en-suite, 1 public

Bed & breakfast per night:	£min	£max
Single	18.00	22.00
Double	28.00	34.00

Cards accepted: Amex, Mastercard, Visa

Melford Hall Hotel

APPROVED

41 Marine Parade, Brighton, East Sussex BN2 1PE
☎ (01273) 681435
Fax (01273) 624186
Listed building, well positioned on seafront and within easy walking distance of all the entertainment that Brighton has to offer. Many rooms with sea views.
Bedrooms: 4 single, 16 double, 4 twin, 1 triple
Bathrooms: 23 en-suite, 1 public, 2 private showers

Bed & breakfast per night:	£min	£max
Single	30.00	35.00
Double	46.00	60.00

Parking for 12
Cards accepted: Amex, Diners, Mastercard, Visa

New Madeira Hotel

COMMENDED

19-23 Marine Parade, Brighton, East Sussex BN2 1TL
☎ (01273) 698331
Fax (01273) 606193
Regency hotel overlooking the sea, directly opposite the famous dolphinarium and aquarium and next to Palace Pier.
Bedrooms: 10 single, 10 double, 13 twin, 4 triple
Bathrooms: 37 en-suite

Bed & breakfast per night:	£min	£max
Single	25.00	40.00
Double	50.00	80.00

Lunch available
Evening meal 1900 (last orders 2200)
Parking for 9
Cards accepted: Amex, Diners, Mastercard, Visa, Switch/Delta

Old Ship Hotel

COMMENDED

King's Road, Brighton, East Sussex BN1 1NR
☎ (01273) 329001
Fax (01273) 820718
Best Western
Refurbished old world character hotel on Brighton's seafront. Noted restaurant. Sea view and executive rooms available.
Bedrooms: 11 single, 88 double, 53 twin
Bathrooms: 152 en-suite

Bed & breakfast per night:	£min	£max
Single	60.00	80.00
Double	80.00	110.00

Half board per person:	£min	£max
Daily	78.00	98.00

Lunch available
Evening meal 1930 (last orders 2130)
Parking for 70
Cards accepted: Amex, Diners, Mastercard, Visa

St Catherines Lodge Hotel

COMMENDED

Kingsway, Hove, East Sussex BN3 2RZ
☎ (01273) 778181
Fax (01273) 774949

Well-established seafront hotel. Restaurant specialises in traditional English dishes. Four-poster honeymoon rooms. Attractive cocktail bar, games rooms, garden, and easy parking. Opposite King Alfred sports and leisure centre.
Bedrooms: 8 single, 17 double, 11 twin, 1 triple, 3 family rooms
Bathrooms: 40 en-suite, 5 public

Bed & breakfast per night:	£min	£max
Single	36.00	45.00
Double	54.00	65.00

Half board per person:	£min	£max
Daily	37.00	40.00
Weekly	190.00	240.00

Lunch available
Evening meal 1900 (last orders 2100)
Parking for 4
Cards accepted: Amex, Diners, Mastercard, Visa, Switch/Delta

Hotel Seafield

APPROVED

23 Seafield Road, Hove, East Sussex BN3 2TP
☎ (01273) 735912
Fax (01273) 323525
Family-run hotel with home-cooked food, close to the seafront and main shopping centre. Free street parking in addition to private parking. Most rooms en-suite with shower/toilet.
Bedrooms: 2 single, 5 double, 1 twin, 2 triple, 3 family rooms
Bathrooms: 12 en-suite, 3 public

Bed & breakfast per night:	£min	£max
Single	20.00	35.00
Double	45.00	55.00

Half board per person:	£min	£max
Daily	40.00	55.00
Weekly	185.00	200.00

Lunch available

Continued ▶

BRIGHTON & HOVE
Continued

Evening meal 1900 (last orders 1700)
Parking for 8
Cards accepted: Mastercard, Visa, Switch/Delta

[symbols]

CAMBERLEY
Surrey
Map ref 2C2

Well-known for the Royal Staff College and the nearby Royal Military Academy, Sandhurst.

Burwood House Hotel ⋀
COMMENDED
15 London Road, Camberley
GU15 3UQ
☎ (01276) 685686
Fax (01276) 62220
Friendly, family-run hotel where Richard and Jenny Cave enjoy looking after you. Approximately 2 miles from junctions 3 and 4 of M3.
Bedrooms: 8 single, 7 double, 2 twin, 2 triple
Bathrooms: 19 en-suite

Bed & breakfast per night:	£min	£max
Single	35.00	60.00
Double	50.00	70.00

Half board per person:	£min	£max
Daily	48.00	73.00

Evening meal 1900 (last orders 2030)
Parking for 21
Cards accepted: Amex, Diners, Mastercard, Visa, Switch/Delta

[symbols]

Establishments should be open throughout the year, unless otherwise stated.

National gradings and classifications were correct at the time of going to press but are subject to change. Please check at the time of booking.

CANTERBURY
Kent
Map ref 3B3

Place of pilgrimage since the martyrdom of Becket in 1170 and the site of Canterbury Cathedral. Visit St Augustine's Abbey, St Martin's (the oldest church in England), Royal Museum and Art Gallery and the Canterbury Tales. Nearby is Howletts Wild Animal Park. Good shopping centre.
Tourist Information Centre ☎ *(01227) 451026*

Canterbury Hotel ⋀
COMMENDED
71 New Dover Road, Canterbury
CT1 3DZ
☎ (01227) 450551
Fax (01227) 780145

Elegant Victorian hotel, 10 minutes from city centre, providing high standards of personal service and comfort. Famed for its "La Bonne Cuisine" French restaurant. Some executive rooms, one four-poster suite.
Bedrooms: 5 single, 5 double, 13 twin, 1 triple, 2 family rooms
Bathrooms: 26 en-suite

Bed & breakfast per night:	£min	£max
Single	45.00	48.00
Double	58.00	68.00

Half board per person:	£min	£max
Daily	60.50	63.50
Weekly	400.00	425.00

Lunch available
Evening meal 1900 (last orders 2200)
Parking for 40
Cards accepted: Amex, Diners, Mastercard, Visa

[symbols] 30

Cathedral Gate Hotel ⋀
APPROVED
36 Burgate, Canterbury CT1 2HA
☎ (01227) 464381
Fax (01227) 462800
Email: 101336.430
@compuserve.com
Central position at main entrance to the cathedral. Car parking nearby. Old

world charm at reasonable prices. English breakfast extra. A la carte dinner available.
Bedrooms: 4 single, 8 double, 7 twin, 3 triple, 2 family rooms
Bathrooms: 12 en-suite, 3 public

Bed & breakfast per night:	£min	£max
Single	22.00	50.00
Double	40.00	75.00

Evening meal 1900 (last orders 2100)
Cards accepted: Amex, Diners, Mastercard, Visa, Switch/Delta

[symbols]

Chaucer Lodge ⋀
HIGHLY COMMENDED
62 New Dover Road, Canterbury
CT1 3DT
☎ (01227) 459141
Fax (01227) 459141
Maria and Alistair Wilson extend a warm, friendly welcome to this comfortable family guesthouse. City 10 minutes' walk, county cricket ground 5 minutes. High standard of cleanliness and furnishings. Breakfast menu.
Bedrooms: 2 double, 2 twin, 1 triple, 1 family room
Bathrooms: 6 en-suite

Bed & breakfast per night:	£min	£max
Single	22.00	45.00
Double	40.00	50.00

Evening meal 1800 (last orders 2000)
Parking for 12
Cards accepted: Amex, Mastercard, Visa

[symbols]

Clare-Ellen Guest House ⋀
HIGHLY COMMENDED
9 Victoria Road, Wincheap, Canterbury CT1 3SG
☎ (01227) 760205
Fax (01227) 784482
Email: loraine.williams@virgin.net

Victorian house with large, elegant en-suite rooms, 6 minutes' walk to town centre. 5 minutes to Canterbury East train station. Car park and garage available.
Bedrooms: 1 single, 1 double, 1 twin, 1 triple, 1 family room
Bathrooms: 4 en-suite, 1 private, 1 public

Bed & breakfast per night:	£min	£max
Single	23.00	26.00
Double	42.00	48.00

Parking for 9
Cards accepted: Mastercard, Visa, Switch/Delta

County Hotel ⚑

HIGHLY COMMENDED

High Street, Canterbury CT1 2RX
☎ (01227) 766266
Fax (01227) 451512
Ⓡ MacDonald
Situated in the heart of the city, close to the cathedral, with gourmet restaurant and coffee shop.
Bedrooms: 15 single, 27 double, 30 twin, 1 family room
Suite available
Bathrooms: 73 en-suite

Bed & breakfast per night:	£min	£max
Single	88.95	93.50
Double	112.90	118.50

Lunch available
Evening meal 1900 (last orders 2200)
Parking for 60
Cards accepted: Amex, Diners, Mastercard, Visa, Switch/Delta

Ebury Hotel ⚑

HIGHLY COMMENDED

New Dover Road, Canterbury
CT1 3DX
☎ (01227) 768433
Fax (01227) 459187
Family-run, Victorian hotel just outside city centre. Licensed restaurant, large public rooms and bedrooms. Heated indoor pool and spa. Overnight half board prices based on minimum 2-night stay.
Bedrooms: 2 single, 7 double, 4 twin, 1 triple, 1 family room
Bathrooms: 15 en-suite

Bed & breakfast per night:	£min	£max
Single	45.00	50.00
Double	60.00	68.00

Half board per person:	£min	£max
Daily	51.00	65.00
Weekly	250.00	300.00

Evening meal 1900 (last orders 2030)
Parking for 21
Cards accepted: Amex, Mastercard, Visa, Switch/Delta

House of Agnes Hotel ⚑

APPROVED

71 St Dunstan's Street, Canterbury
CT2 8BN
☎ (01227) 464771 & 472185
Fax (01227) 471616
Email: J.Durcan@nsn.com
Home of Agnes Wickfield from Charles Dickens' novel "David Copperfield", this friendly hotel combines the atmosphere of bygone days with modern comforts.
Bedrooms: 2 single, 4 double, 1 twin, 2 family rooms
Bathrooms: 9 en-suite

Bed & breakfast per night:	£min	£max
Single	34.50	59.00
Double	49.00	59.00

Half board per person:	£min	£max
Daily	39.00	59.00

Lunch available
Evening meal 1830 (last orders 2130)
Parking for 31
Cards accepted: Amex, Diners, Mastercard, Visa, Switch/Delta

Magnolia House ⚑

HIGHLY COMMENDED

36 St Dunstans Terrace, Canterbury
CT2 8AX
☎ (01227) 765121 & 0585 595970
Fax (01227) 765121

Quiet Georgian house in attractive city street. Close to university, gardens, river and city centre. Pretty walled garden in which to relax. Winner 1995 "Welcome to Kent Hospitality Award".
Bedrooms: 1 single, 4 double, 2 twin
Bathrooms: 7 en-suite

Bed & breakfast per night:	£min	£max
Single	36.00	50.00
Double	60.00	95.00

Evening meal 1800 (last orders 1900)
Parking for 5
Cards accepted: Amex, Mastercard, Visa, Switch/Delta

The Old Coach House

COMMENDED

Dover Road (A2), Barham,
Canterbury CT4 6SA
☎ (01227) 831218
Fax (01227) 831932
Ⓡ Logis of GB/The Independents

Originally a coaching inn (c 1815), the hotel is run along the lines of a French auberge by chef/patron. Licensed restaurant specialising in local fish and game. Large car park. Ideally placed midway between Dover and Canterbury.
Bedrooms: 2 double, 2 twin, 1 family room
Bathrooms: 5 en-suite

Bed & breakfast per night:	£min	£max
Single	47.00	49.00
Double	58.00	62.00

Half board per person:	£min	£max
Daily	37.50	

Lunch available
Evening meal 1900 (last orders 2130)
Parking for 82
Cards accepted: Amex, Diners, Mastercard, Visa, Switch/Delta

Oriel Lodge ⚑

HIGHLY COMMENDED

3 Queens Avenue, Canterbury
CT2 8AY
☎ (01227) 462845
Fax (01227) 462845
In a tree-lined residential avenue, an attractive Edwardian house with private parking close to the city centre. Afternoon tea in the garden or lounge with log fire. Restricted smoking.
Bedrooms: 1 single, 3 double, 1 twin, 1 triple
Bathrooms: 2 en-suite, 2 public

Bed & breakfast per night:	£min	£max
Single	22.00	28.00
Double	38.00	58.00

Parking for 6
Cards accepted: Mastercard, Visa

CANTERBURY

Continued

Pointers Hotel ⚑

⚜⚜⚜ COMMENDED

1 London Road, Canterbury
CT2 8LR
☎ (01227) 456846
Fax (01227) 831131
Email: Pointers.Hotel
@Pop.Dial.Pipex.Com
Ⓡ Logis of GB

*Family-run Georgian hotel close to city
centre, cathedral and university.
Licensed restaurant.*
Bedrooms: 1 single, 6 double, 2 twin,
3 family rooms
Bathrooms: 11 en-suite, 1 private

**Bed & breakfast
per night:**

	£min	£max
Single	40.00	45.00
Double	50.00	60.00

**Half board per
person:**

	£min	£max
Daily	40.00	57.50
Weekly	280.00	

Evening meal 1930 (last orders
2030)
Parking for 10
Cards accepted: Amex, Diners,
Mastercard, Visa, Switch/Delta

⬧📞🖪🖵🕭🎗️🏊🚫♿⚓️🔥▦ 🛏️ SP 🏠 T

Thanington Hotel ⚑

⚜⚜ HIGHLY COMMENDED

140 Wincheap, Canterbury
CT1 3RY
☎ (01227) 453227
Fax (01227) 453225

*Beautiful, spacious Georgian bed and
breakfast hotel close to city centre.
Four poster and antique bedsteads,
indoor pool, snooker room, car park. 30
minutes' drive to Channel ports and
tunnel.*
Bedrooms: 5 double, 3 twin, 2 family
rooms
Bathrooms: 10 en-suite, 2 public

**Bed & breakfast
per night:**

	£min	£max
Single	45.00	50.00
Double	65.00	75.00

Parking for 12
Cards accepted: Amex, Diners,
Mastercard, Visa

⬧🏊🖪🖵🕭🎗️♿🚫🔥✗🗡️📺▦
⬛🔍❄️✳️🚐 SP 🏠 T ⊚

CHICHESTER

West Sussex
Map ref 2C3

The county town of West Sussex
with a beautiful Norman cathedral.
Noted for its Georgian architecture
but also has modern buildings like
the Festival Theatre. Surrounded by
places of interest, including
Fishbourne Roman Palace, Weald
and Downland Open-Air Museum
and West Dean Gardens.
*Tourist Information Centre ☎ (01243)
775888*

Riverside Lodge

⚜⚜ COMMENDED

7 Market Avenue, Chichester
PO19 1JU
☎ (01243) 783164
*City centre traditional brick and flint
house. En-suite double bedrooms.
Walled garden with river course. No
smoking, please.*
Bedrooms: 3 double
Bathrooms: 2 en-suite, 1 private

**Bed & breakfast
per night:**

	£min	£max
Single	20.00	25.00
Double	40.00	50.00

Parking for 2

🏊🖵🕭🎗️UL Ⓢ✗🗡️▦ ⬛❄️✗🚐
🏠

CLIFTONVILLE

Kent

See under Margate

WELCOME HOST

This is a nationally recognised
customer care programme
which aims to promote
the highest standards of
service and a warm welcome.
Establishments who are taking
part in this initiative are
indicated by the ⚜ symbol.

COBHAM

Surrey
Map ref 2D2

Village in 2 parts, Street Cobham on
the A3 Portsmouth Road and
Church Cobham with the restored
Norman church of St Andrew and a
19th C mill.

Cedar House Hotel and Restaurant

⚜⚜ COMMENDED

Mill Road, Cobham KT11 3AL
☎ (01932) 863424
Fax (01932) 862023
*15th C house with later additions,
popular timbered main restaurant and
garden overlooking River Mole. Close to
village. Excellent access to M25 and
London.*
Bedrooms: 4 double, 2 twin
Bathrooms: 6 en-suite, 1 public

**Bed & breakfast
per night:**

	£min	£max
Single	80.00	80.00
Double	90.00	90.00

**Half board per
person:**

	£min	£max
Daily	94.00	106.95
Weekly	658.00	748.65

Lunch available
Evening meal 1900 (last orders
2130)
Parking for 15
Cards accepted: Amex, Diners,
Mastercard, Visa, Switch/Delta

⬧📞🖪🖵🕭🎗️♿🚫✗🗡️📺▦ ⬛
🍽️30❄️✗🚐🏠

CUCKFIELD

West Sussex
Map ref 2D3

The High Street is lined with
Elizabethan and Georgian shops,
inns and houses and was once part
of the London to Brighton coach
road. Nearby Nymans (National
Trust) is a 30-acre garden with fine
topiary work.

Hilton Park Hotel ⚑

⚜⚜⚜ APPROVED

Cuckfield, Haywards Heath
RH17 5EG
☎ (01444) 454555
Fax (01444) 457222
*Victorian country house in 3 acres of
gardens, with magnificent views of
South Downs from conservatory bar
and bedrooms.*
Bedrooms: 5 double, 1 twin, 3 triple
Bathrooms: 9 en-suite, 2 public

Bed & breakfast

Bed & breakfast per night:	£min	£max
Single	55.00	60.00
Double	75.00	80.00

Lunch available
Evening meal 1900 (last orders 2030)
Parking for 52
Cards accepted: Amex, Diners, Mastercard, Visa

🛇🐴📞📠🖵🏠♿🍴♨️🛏️🅿️� 🏵️❄️ 🗗 SP T

DARTFORD

Kent
Map ref 2D2

Industrial town probably most famous for the Dartford Tunnel and the Queen Elizabeth II bridge across the Thames. Large Orchard Theatre has a fine variety of entertainment.

The Brands Hatch Thistle ▲

👑👑👑👑 COMMENDED
Brands Hatch, Dartford DA3 8PE
☎ (01474) 854900
Fax (01474) 853220
🆑 Mount Charlotte Thistle/Utell International
Set at the entrance to the world-famous motor racing circuit, the hotel offers elegance and varied cuisine. Easy access, near M20, M25 and M26.
Bedrooms: 67 double, 63 twin, 7 triple
Suites available
Bathrooms: 137 en-suite

Bed & breakfast per night:	£min	£max
Single	57.00	95.00
Double	84.00	120.00

Half board per person:	£min	£max
Daily	72.00	115.00

Lunch available
Evening meal 1900 (last orders 2230)
Parking for 180
Cards accepted: Amex, Diners, Mastercard, Visa, Switch/Delta

🛇🐴📞📠🖵🏠♿🍴🅿️♨️🛏️🍴270 ⛳⚓❄️ ⟳ SP T

ACCESSIBILITY

Look for the ♿👓🚶 symbols which indicate accessibility for wheelchair users. These are described in detail at the front of this guide.

DEAL

Kent
Map ref 3C4

Coastal town and popular holiday resort. Deal Castle was built by Henry VIII as a fort and the museum is devoted to finds excavated in the area. Also the Time-Ball Tower museum. Angling available from both beach and pier.
Tourist Information Centre ☎ (01304) 369576

Ilex Cottage ▲

👑 COMMENDED
Temple Way, Worth, Deal
CT14 0DA
☎ (01304) 617026
Renovated 1736 house with lovely conservatory and country views. Secluded yet convenient village location north of Deal. Sandwich 5 minutes, Canterbury, Dover and Ramsgate 25 minutes.
Bedrooms: 1 double, 2 twin
Bathrooms: 3 en-suite

Bed & breakfast per night:	£min	£max
Single	20.00	26.00
Double	35.00	40.00

Half board per person:	£min	£max
Daily	30.00	38.00
Weekly		190.00

Evening meal 1900 (last orders 2030)
Parking for 6

🛇🐴📠🖵🏠♿🛒♨️🍴🔌🅿️🛏️ TV🖵 🏠❄️🚐 SP 🗗 T

Royal Hotel

👑👑👑 COMMENDED
Beach Street, Deal CT14 6JD
☎ (01304) 375555
Fax (01304) 375555
Georgian town hotel, famous for hosting Lord Nelson and Lady Hamilton. Delightful rooms with sea views. Excellent restaurant specialising in fish.
Bedrooms: 1 single, 5 double, 4 twin, 2 family rooms
Bathrooms: 12 en-suite

Bed & breakfast per night:	£min	£max
Single	40.00	50.00
Double	55.00	100.00

Half board per person:	£min	£max
Daily	50.00	60.00

Lunch available
Evening meal 1800 (last orders 2200)
Open February–December

Cards accepted: Amex, Mastercard, Visa, Switch/Delta

🛇🐴📞📠🖵🏠♿🍴♨️🛏️🆂🍴♨️🛏️🚐 🍴40⛳🏵️🚐 SP 🗗 T

DORKING

Surrey
Map ref 2D2

Ancient market town and a good centre for walking, delightfully set between Box Hill and the Downs. Denbies Wine Estate - England's largest vineyard - is situated here.

Fairdene Guest House

👑 APPROVED
Moores Road, Dorking RH4 2BG
☎ (01306) 888337
Late-Victorian house in convenient location, close to town centre and Gatwick Airport. Friendly and homely atmosphere. Off-street parking.
Bedrooms: 2 double, 2 twin, 1 triple
Bathrooms: 2 public

Bed & breakfast per night:	£min	£max
Single	25.00	30.00
Double	40.00	45.00

Parking for 7

🛇🐴🖵♨️🔌⛔✂️🛏️ TV🖵🏠🚐

Gatton Manor Hotel, Golf & Country Club ▲

👑👑👑 COMMENDED
Standon Lane, Ockley, Dorking
RH5 5PQ
☎ (01306) 627555
Fax (01306) 627713

18th C manor house on 200-acre estate. Championship length golf-course, hotel, a la carte restaurants, conference suites, bowls, fishing, tennis, gym and health club. Village is 6 miles south of Dorking.
Bedrooms: 3 double, 13 twin
Bathrooms: 16 en-suite

Bed & breakfast per night:	£min	£max
Single	55.00	
Double	85.00	

Half board per person:	£min	£max
Daily	60.00	73.00
Weekly	402.50	479.50

Lunch available

Continued ▶

DORKING

Continued

Evening meal 1900 (last orders 2130)
Parking for 200
Cards accepted: Amex, Diners, Mastercard, Visa, Switch/Delta

≫⊱₵🗘◻♨🛈S🛗TV📠≞🏋60
🏇☆🔍⚲∪♪✦/❀♿SP

DOVER

Kent
Map ref 3C4

A Cinque Port and busiest passenger port in the world. Still a historic town and seaside resort beside the famous White Cliffs. The White Cliffs Experience attraction traces the town's history through the Roman, Saxon, Norman and Victorian periods.
Tourist Information Centre ☎ (01304) 205108

Blakes of Dover ▲▲

♛♛ COMMENDED

52 Castle Street, Dover CT16 1PJ
☎ (01304) 202194
Fax (01304) 202194
Family-run bistro, wine bar and restaurant, having en-suite guest suites (bed, lounge and bath). Lunch and evening meals. Special tourist and early bird menus, real ales.
Bedrooms: 3 double, 2 twin, 1 triple
Bathrooms: 6 en-suite

Bed & breakfast
per night:	£min	£max
Single	37.50	47.50
Double	47.50	55.50

Half board per
person:	£min	£max
Daily	36.50	36.50
Weekly	225.50	225.50

Lunch available
Evening meal 1800 (last orders 2150)
Parking for 3
Cards accepted: Mastercard, Visa, Switch/Delta

≫⊱&🗘◻♨S✂TV📠≞❀🚚
OAP♿SP🏛

Castle Guest House ▲▲

♛♛♛ COMMENDED

10 Castle Hill Road, Dover CT16 1QW
☎ (01304) 201656
Fax (01304) 210197
A non-smoking policy operates in this Georgian guesthouse (circa 1830), just below Dover Castle. Close to port and town centre and 10 minutes from Channel Tunnel.

Bedrooms: 1 single, 3 double, 1 twin, 1 family room
Bathrooms: 5 en-suite, 1 private

Bed & breakfast
per night:	£min	£max
Single	24.00	28.00
Double	34.00	42.00

Half board per
person:	£min	£max
Daily	25.00	30.00

Evening meal 1800 (last orders 2100)
Cards accepted: Amex, Mastercard, Visa, Switch/Delta

≫⊱□◻♨⋡✂🗡TV📠≞♨🚚
SP🏛T◉

The Churchill ▲▲

♛♛♛ HIGHLY COMMENDED

Dover Waterfront, Dover CT17 9BP
☎ (01304) 203633
Fax (01304) 216320
CR Best Western

Under the White Cliffs, between East and West Docks and only 10 minutes away from Channel Tunnel. En-suite rooms with satellite TV.
Bedrooms: 6 single, 37 double, 20 twin, 5 family rooms
Bathrooms: 68 en-suite

Bed & breakfast
per night:	£min	£max
Single	63.00	
Double	91.00	

Half board per
person:	£min	£max
Daily	72.00	

Lunch available
Evening meal 1930 (last orders 2115)
Parking for 32
Cards accepted: Amex, Diners, Mastercard, Visa, Switch/Delta

≫⊱₵🗘◻♨⋡🛈S✂🗡TV◉⊞
📠≞🏋120❀♿SP🏛T

Conifers Guest House ▲▲

♛♛ COMMENDED

241 Folkestone Road, Dover CT17 9LL
☎ (01304) 205609
Family guesthouse, 5 minutes from rail station, town centre, seafront and Channel Tunnel terminus. En-suite rooms. Early breakfast available.
Bedrooms: 1 single, 2 double, 1 twin, 2 family rooms
Bathrooms: 4 en-suite, 2 public

Bed & breakfast
per night:	£min	£max
Single	16.00	20.00
Double	30.00	42.00

Parking for 6

🏇3🗘♨UL📠✂🚚SP

Forte Posthouse Dover ▲▲

♛♛♛ COMMENDED

Singledge Lane, Whitfield, Dover CT16 3LF
☎ (01304) 821222
Fax (01304) 825576
CR Forte
Modern hotel in spacious surroundings. All rooms designed for comfort. Just outside Dover on the main A2/M2.
Bedrooms: 33 double, 6 twin, 18 triple, 10 family rooms
Bathrooms: 67 en-suite

Bed & breakfast
per night:	£min	£max
Single	79.00	
Double	88.00	

Lunch available
Evening meal 1900 (last orders 2230)
Parking for 90
Cards accepted: Amex, Diners, Mastercard, Visa, Switch/Delta

≫⊱&₵🗘◻♨⋡🛈S✂TV◉📠
≞🏋60❀♿SP🏛◉

Walletts Court Hotel & Restaurant ▲▲

♛♛♛ HIGHLY COMMENDED

West-Cliffe, St-Margarets-at-Cliffe, Dover CT15 6EW
☎ (01304) 852424
Fax (01304) 853430
Lovely 17th C manor and barns, with carved oak beams and inglenook fireplaces. Ideal for history enthusiasts. In rural setting, 3 miles from Dover Docks and Castle. Open as a full evening restaurant, Monday to Sunday.
Bedrooms: 1 single, 7 double, 2 twin, 2 triple
Bathrooms: 11 en-suite, 1 private

Bed & breakfast
per night:	£min	£max
Single	40.00	75.00
Double	65.00	90.00

Half board per
person:	£min	£max
Daily	65.00	100.00

Evening meal 1900 (last orders 2130)
Parking for 20
Cards accepted: Amex, Diners, Mastercard, Visa, Switch/Delta

≫⊱&🏛₵🗘◻♨S✂🗡📠≞
🏋🔍⚲U♪❀☆🚚SP🏛T◉

Whitmore Guest House

☒☒ APPROVED

261 Folkestone Road, Dover
CT17 9LL
☎ (01304) 203080 & 0378 958797
Fax (01304) 240110
*Friendly, family-run guesthouse where
you will be made welcome.
Conveniently situated for railway
station, town centre, docks, Hoverport
and Channel Tunnel.*
Bedrooms: 1 double, 2 twin, 1 family
room
Bathrooms: 1 en-suite, 1 public
Bed & breakfast

per night:	£min	£max
Single	13.00	18.00
Double	26.00	32.00

Parking for 4

DYMCHURCH

Kent
Map ref 3B4

For centuries the headquarters of
the Lords of the Level, the local
government of this area. Probably
best known today because of the
fame of its fictional parson, the
notorious Dr Syn, who has inspired
a regular festival.

Waterside Guest House ⋀

☒☒ COMMENDED

15 Hythe Road, Dymchurch,
Romney Marsh TN29 0LN
☎ (01303) 872253
*Ideally situated for Channel Tunnel,
ferry ports or touring the historic
countryside of Kent. Overlooking
Romney, Hythe and Dymchurch
Railway. Sandy beaches close by. Home
cooking, catering for all tastes.*
Bedrooms: 1 single, 2 double, 2 twin,
1 family room
Bathrooms: 3 en-suite, 2 public
Bed & breakfast

per night:	£min	£max
Single	16.00	20.00
Double	30.00	38.00

Half board per

person:	£min	£max
Daily	23.00	27.00
Weekly	145.00	170.00

Lunch available
Evening meal 1730 (last orders
2000)
Parking for 7

EASTBOURNE

East Sussex
Map ref 3B4

One of the finest, most elegant
resorts on the south-east coast
situated beside Beachy Head. Long
promenade, well known Carpet
Gardens on the seafront,
Devonshire Park tennis and indoor
leisure complex, theatres, Towner
Art Gallery, "How We Lived Then"
Museum of Shops and Social
History.
*Tourist Information Centre ☎ (01323)
411400*

Adrian House ⋀

☒☒ COMMENDED

24 Selwyn Road, Eastbourne
BN21 2LR
☎ (01323) 720372
*Small, family-run private hotel in quiet
area. Diets catered for. Children
welcome. Ample private parking.*
Bedrooms: 2 single, 3 double, 1 twin,
2 triple
Bathrooms: 5 en-suite, 2 public
Bed & breakfast

per night:	£min	£max
Single	18.00	18.00
Double	36.00	42.00

Half board per

person:	£min	£max
Daily	25.00	28.00
Weekly	160.00	180.00

Evening meal 1800 (last orders
1800)
Parking for 10

Bay Lodge Hotel ⋀

☒☒ COMMENDED

61-62 Royal Parade, Eastbourne
BN22 7AQ
☎ (01323) 732515
Fax (01323) 735009

*Small seafront hotel opposite Pavilion
Gardens, close to bowling greens and
marina. Large sun-lounge. All
double/twin bedrooms have en-suite or
private facilities. Non-smokers' lounge.*
Bedrooms: 3 single, 5 double, 3 twin
Bathrooms: 4 en-suite, 5 private,
2 public

Bed & breakfast

per night:	£min	£max
Single	20.00	26.00
Double	38.00	45.00

Half board per

person:	£min	£max
Daily	28.00	34.00
Weekly	165.00	225.00

Evening meal 1800 (last orders
1800)
Parking for 2
Open March–October and
Christmas
Cards accepted: Mastercard, Visa

Brayscroft Private Hotel

☒☒ HIGHLY COMMENDED

13 South Cliff Avenue, Eastbourne
BN20 7AH
☎ (01323) 647005

*Elegant Edwardian town house in quiet
Meads area. Two minutes from
seafront. Ideally situated for South
Downs, theatres and town.*
Bedrooms: 1 single, 2 double, 2 twin
Bathrooms: 5 en-suite
Bed & breakfast

per night:	£min	£max
Single	21.00	21.00
Double	42.00	42.00

Carlton Court Hotel ⋀

☒☒ COMMENDED

10 Wilmington Square, Eastbourne
BN21 4EA
☎ (01323) 430668
Fax (01323) 732787
Email: carlton@fastnet.co.uk
*Well-established family-owned hotel
overlooking beautiful lawned square.
Close to seafront, Devonshire Park and
theatres.*
Bedrooms: 4 single, 6 double,
14 twin, 3 triple
Bathrooms: 27 en-suite
Bed & breakfast

per night:	£min	£max
Single	19.50	32.00
Double	39.00	64.00

Half board per

person:	£min	£max
Daily	23.00	36.00
Weekly	135.00	215.00

Lunch available

Continued ▶

EASTBOURNE
Continued

Evening meal 1830 (last orders 1930)
Open February–December
Cards accepted: Mastercard, Visa

🛏️⛷️🖥️📞♿🛜🆂♨️🕐⬆️🖥️🚗💼OAP🚫 SP

Chatsworth Hotel ♙
👑👑👑👑 APPROVED

Grand Parade, Eastbourne
BN21 3YR
☎ (01323) 411016
Fax (01323) 643270
Elegant Victorian detached hotel in a prominent position on seafront, very close to shops and theatres.
Bedrooms: 10 single, 13 double, 22 twin, 2 family rooms
Suite available
Bathrooms: 47 en-suite

Bed & breakfast
per night:	£min	£max
Single	38.00	56.00
Double	72.00	104.00

Half board per
person:	£min	£max
Daily	48.00	66.00
Weekly	288.00	396.00

Lunch available
Evening meal 1900 (last orders 2030)
Cards accepted: Amex, Diners, Mastercard, Visa, Switch/Delta

🛏️📞🖥️📞♿🎛️🆂✂️🕐⬆️🖥️💼♙160🔍♻️OAP🚫 SP T

Cherry Tree Hotel ♙
👑👑 HIGHLY COMMENDED

15 Silverdale Road, Eastbourne
BN20 7AJ
☎ (01323) 722406
Fax (01323) 648838
Email: jclarke@pavilion.co.uk
Small hotel and restaurant. All bedrooms en-suite with colour TV, telephone, tea/coffee-making. A la carte and table d'hote restaurant.
Bedrooms: 2 single, 3 double, 3 twin, 2 triple
Bathrooms: 10 en-suite

Bed & breakfast
per night:	£min	£max
Single	23.00	29.00
Double	46.00	58.00

Half board per
person:	£min	£max
Daily	35.00	41.00
Weekly	205.00	245.00

Evening meal 1800 (last orders 2100)
Cards accepted: Amex, Mastercard, Visa

🛏️7🛏️📞🖥️♿🆂✂️🕐💼🚗♙20 ✈️🚲🚫 SP ⊛

Congress Hotel ♙
👑👑👑 COMMENDED

31-41 Carlisle Road, Eastbourne
BN21 4JS
☎ (01323) 732118 & 644605
Fax (01323) 720016
Family-run hotel in peaceful location. Close to theatres and seafront. Suitable for wheelchair users.
Wheelchair access category 3♿
Bedrooms: 14 single, 11 double, 32 twin, 5 triple
Bathrooms: 58 en-suite, 1 public

Bed & breakfast
per night:	£min	£max
Single	29.00	39.00
Double	58.00	78.00

Half board per
person:	£min	£max
Daily	33.00	42.00
Weekly	225.00	280.00

Lunch available
Evening meal 1830 (last orders 1945)
Parking for 16
Open March–November and Christmas
Cards accepted: Mastercard, Visa, Switch/Delta

🛏️⛷️🛏️🖥️📞♿🆂✂️🕐⬆️🖥️💼♙25🔍❄️🚫 SP T

Cumberland Hotel ♙
👑👑👑 COMMENDED

Grand Parade, Eastbourne
BN21 3YT
☎ (01323) 730342
Fax (01323) 646314
Beautiful hotel right on the seafront, opposite bandstand. Spacious, comfortable lounge and elegant dining room, both sea-facing. Friendly, professional service. Close to shops and theatres.
Bedrooms: 17 single, 9 double, 46 twin
Bathrooms: 72 private

Bed & breakfast
per night:	£min	£max
Single	28.00	37.00
Double	56.00	74.00

Half board per
person:	£min	£max
Daily	32.00	41.00
Weekly	224.00	287.00

Lunch available
Evening meal 1845 (last orders 2030)

Cards accepted: Amex, Mastercard, Visa, Switch/Delta

🛏️📞🖥️📞♿🛜🆂✂️🕐🖥️🕐⬆️🖥️💼♙180🔍OAP🚫 SP T

Downland Hotel ♙
👑👑👑 HIGHLY COMMENDED

37 Lewes Road, Eastbourne
BN21 2BU
☎ (01323) 732689
Fax (01323) 720321
Ⓜ Minotel
Charming small hotel in quiet yet convenient location. Warm welcome, relaxed atmosphere, personal service. Award-winning restaurant, private car park.
Bedrooms: 1 single, 8 double, 5 twin
Bathrooms: 14 en-suite

Bed & breakfast
per night:	£min	£max
Single	35.00	49.00
Double	49.00	75.00

Half board per
person:	£min	£max
Weekly	225.00	255.00

Evening meal 1830 (last orders 2030)
Parking for 10
Cards accepted: Amex, Diners, Mastercard, Visa

🛏️10🛏️📞🖥️📞♿🛜🆂🕐💼🚗❄️✈️🚲 SP T

Edelweiss Private Hotel ♙
👑👑 COMMENDED

10-12 Elms Avenue, Eastbourne
BN21 3DN
☎ (01323) 732071
Fax (01323) 732071
Small family-run hotel 50 yards from the pier. Comfortable bedrooms with TV and tea-making. En-suite rooms available. Guests' lounge and bar. Off-peak rates available.
Bedrooms: 2 single, 6 double, 5 twin, 1 family room
Bathrooms: 3 en-suite, 4 public

Bed & breakfast
per night:	£min	£max
Single	14.00	20.00
Double	28.00	40.00

Half board per
person:	£min	£max
Daily	19.00	24.00
Weekly	120.00	150.00

Evening meal 1800 (last orders 1500)
Cards accepted: Mastercard, Visa

🛏️⛷️🖥️♿🛜🆂🖥️🕐⬆️🖥️💼✈️🚫 SP 🏠

Farrar's Hotel ♏

Wilmington Gardens, Eastbourne
BN21 4JN
☎ (01323) 723737
Fax (01323) 732902
*Family-run hotel in quiet square, 200
yards from the seafront, opposite
Devonshire Park and Congress Theatre.
Send for brochure giving details of
mini-breaks.*
Bedrooms: 13 single, 7 double,
23 twin, 2 triple
Bathrooms: 45 en-suite

Bed & breakfast per night:

	£min	£max
Single	20.00	34.00
Double	40.00	64.00

Half board per person:

	£min	£max
Daily	29.00	42.00
Weekly	196.00	287.00

Lunch available
Evening meal 1845 (last orders
2030)
Parking for 26
Open February–December
Cards accepted: Amex, Mastercard,
Visa, Switch/Delta

Jenric Guest House ♏

COMMENDED
36 Ceylon Place, Eastbourne
BN21 3JF
☎ (01323) 728857
*Safe, comfortable, clean rooms with
showers, tea/coffee-making facilities, at
reasonable rates. Good breakfast.
Central location, excellent connections
for Ashford (Channel Tunnel), Hastings
and Rye.*
Bedrooms: 1 single, 1 double, 2 twin
Bathrooms: 1 public, 4 private
showers

Bed & breakfast per night:

	£min	£max
Single	13.00	15.00
Double	26.00	30.00

Half board per person:

	£min	£max
Daily	20.00	22.00
Weekly	135.00	149.00

Lansdowne Hotel ♏

COMMENDED
King Edward's Parade, Eastbourne
BN21 4EE
☎ (01323) 725174
Fax (01323) 739721
Best Western
*Privately owned and run hotel in
premier seafront position, with bar,
spacious lounges and elegant public
areas. Theatres, shops and sporting
facilities nearby. Minimum half-board
prices below are special off-season
rates.*
Bedrooms: 42 single, 18 double,
58 twin, 4 triple
Bathrooms: 122 en-suite, 2 public

Bed & breakfast per night:

	£min	£max
Single	50.00	58.00
Double	78.00	96.00

Half board per person:

	£min	£max
Daily	35.00	69.00
Weekly	245.00	462.00

Lunch available
Evening meal 1830 (last orders
2030)
Parking for 23
Cards accepted: Amex, Diners,
Mastercard, Visa, Switch/Delta

Princes Hotel ♏

COMMENDED
Lascelles Terrace, Eastbourne
BN21 4BL
☎ (01323) 722056
Fax (01323) 727469
*Friendly family hotel, ideal centre for
exploring the many historic monuments
and beauty spots of Sussex.*
Bedrooms: 13 single, 13 double,
16 twin, 2 triple
Bathrooms: 44 en-suite, 2 public

Bed & breakfast per night:

	£min	£max
Single	27.50	39.00
Double	55.00	78.00

Half board per person:

	£min	£max
Daily	37.50	42.50
Weekly	195.00	325.00

Lunch available
Evening meal 1845 (last orders
2030)
Cards accepted: Amex, Diners,
Mastercard, Visa, Switch/Delta

St Omer Hotel

COMMENDED
13 Royal Parade, Eastbourne
BN22 7AR
☎ (01323) 722152
Fax (01323) 726756
*Fine seafront, licensed, family-run hotel.
Sun lounge and terrace. Colour TV and
tea-making in all rooms. Home-cooked
meals.*
Bedrooms: 1 single, 2 double, 6 twin,
1 triple
Bathrooms: 8 en-suite, 2 public

Bed & breakfast per night:

	£min	£max
Single	19.00	25.00
Double	38.00	50.00

Half board per person:

	£min	£max
Daily	26.50	34.50
Weekly	162.00	209.00

Lunch available
Evening meal 1800 (last orders
1700)
Open April–September and
Christmas
Cards accepted: Mastercard, Visa,
Switch/Delta

Stratford Hotel & Restaurant ♏

APPROVED
59 Cavendish Place, Eastbourne
BN21 3RL
☎ (01323) 724051 & 726391
*Ideally situated near promenade,
coaches and shopping centre. Licensed,
centrally heated throughout. Ground
floor and family rooms available.
Tea-making facilities and colour TV in
all rooms. Most rooms en-suite.*
Bedrooms: 2 single, 5 double, 4 twin,
2 triple
Bathrooms: 11 en-suite, 1 public

Bed & breakfast per night:

	£min	£max
Single	18.00	20.00
Double	36.00	40.00

Half board per person:

	£min	£max
Daily	25.00	28.00
Weekly	138.00	165.00

Lunch available
Evening meal 1800 (last orders
2300)
Cards accepted: Amex, Diners,
Mastercard, Visa

EASTBOURNE
Continued

The Wish Tower Hotel ⋒

👑👑👑👑 COMMENDED

King Edward's Parade, Eastbourne
BN21 4EB
☎ (01323) 722676
Fax (01323) 721474
Ⓒ Principal/Utell International

*Elegant seaside hotel within easy reach
of all attractions. Most rooms have sea
views. Refurbished public rooms invite
total relaxation.*
Bedrooms: 25 single, 11 double,
29 twin
Bathrooms: 65 en-suite

**Bed & breakfast
per night:**

	£min	£max
Single	27.00	50.00
Double	54.00	100.00

**Half board per
person:**

	£min	£max
Daily	38.00	61.00
Weekly	228.00	366.00

Lunch available
Evening meal 1830 (last orders
2045)
Parking for 3
Cards accepted: Amex, Diners,
Mastercard, Visa, Switch/Delta

🛏🛋🕭📞🖵🖵🛅♿🕭⌂🖪🔲Ⓢ✂🕭☀🖂🖩
🖩🎧🛎60🅿🚭 SP T

York House Hotel ⋒

👑👑👑 COMMENDED

14-22 Royal Parade, Eastbourne
BN22 7AP
☎ (01323) 412918
Fax (01323) 646238
Ⓒ Consort

*Exceptional sea-views and bar lunches
on the terrace of the Verandah Bar.
5-course dinner, followed by dancing in
the Lancaster Room. An early dip in the
heated indoor pool.*
Bedrooms: 24 single, 26 double,
40 twin, 6 triple, 1 family room
Bathrooms: 97 en-suite, 2 public

**Bed & breakfast
per night:**

	£min	£max
Single	38.00	
Double	76.00	

**Half board per
person:**

	£min	£max
Daily	50.50	
Weekly	182.00	280.00

Lunch available

Evening meal 1830 (last orders
2000)
Cards accepted: Amex, Diners,
Mastercard, Visa, Switch/Delta

🛏🛋🕭📞🖵🖵🛅♿🕭Ⓢ✂🕭⌂🖪🖩
🖩🎧🛎100🕭❀🚭🖂 SP T ⌾

EGHAM
Surrey
Map ref 2D2

In attractive and historic area beside
the Thames, adjoining Runnymede
and near Windsor, Thorpe Park and
Savill Garden. Convenient for
Heathrow Airport and good base
for London, Wisley Gardens and
Hampton Court Palace.

Great Fosters ⋒

👑👑👑👑 HIGHLY COMMENDED

Stroude Road, Egham TW20 9UR
☎ (01784) 433822
Fax (01784) 472455

*16th C hunting lodge, now a
comfortable hotel, retaining decor and
atmosphere of former times. Set in 17
acres of formal grounds.*
Bedrooms: 25 single, 11 double,
9 twin
Suites available
Bathrooms: 44 en-suite, 1 private

**Bed & breakfast
per night:**

	£min	£max
Single	93.00	
Double	102.00	

Lunch available
Evening meal 1930 (last orders
2115)
Parking for 150
Cards accepted: Amex, Diners,
Mastercard, Visa, Switch/Delta

🛏🛋🏛📞🖵🖵🛅♿🕭Ⓢ🕭TV🖩
🖩🎧🛎100🕭❀🕭❀✕🐾🚭
SP 🏇

The map references refer
to the colour maps towards
the end of the guide.
The first figure is the
map number; the letter and
figure which follow indicate
the grid reference
on the map.

Runnymede Hotel ⋒

👑👑👑👑 HIGHLY COMMENDED

Windsor Road, Egham TW20 0AG
☎ (01784) 436171
Fax (01784) 436340
*Delightfully situated overlooking the
Thames at Bell-Weir Lock, a privately
owned modern hotel standing in 12
acres of landscaped gardens. On A308,
off the M25 junction 13. Prices below
are for weekends.*
Bedrooms: 80 single, 54 double,
29 twin, 7 triple
Bathrooms: 170 en-suite

**Bed & breakfast
per night:**

	£min	£max
Single	58.95	78.95
Double	117.90	137.90

**Half board per
person:**

	£min	£max
Daily	80.00	90.00

Lunch available
Evening meal 1900 (last orders
2145)
Parking for 300
Cards accepted: Amex, Diners,
Mastercard, Visa

🛏🛋🕭📞🖵🖵🛅♿🕭Ⓢ✂🕭⌂🖪🖩
Ⓢ🖩🎧🛎350🕭✕🕭🕭🅿🚭🐾 SP

EPSOM
Surrey
Map ref 2D2

Horse races have been held on the
slopes of Epsom Downs for
centuries. The racecourse is the
home of the world-famous Derby.
Many famous old homes are here,
among them the 17th C Waterloo
House.

Angleside Guest House

Listed COMMENDED

27 Ashley Road, Epsom KT18 5BD
☎ (01372) 724303
*Owner-run establishment midway
between Gatwick and Heathrow
Airports, close to the High Street,
downs and racecourse.*
Bedrooms: 1 single, 3 twin, 3 triple,
1 family room
Bathrooms: 1 public, 4 private
showers

**Bed & breakfast
per night:**

	£min	£max
Single	18.00	27.00
Double	32.00	36.00

Parking for 8

🛏🕭📞🖵UL🛅🕭🖩🖂❄✕ SP

Map references apply to
the colour maps at the
back of this guide.

White House Hotel ⚠

〰〰〰 COMMENDED

Downs Hill Road, Epsom
KT18 5HW
☎ (01372) 722472
Fax (01372) 744447

Charming, spacious, traditional mansion
converted into a modern hotel. Epsom
town and station only minutes away
with regular train services to London.
Bedrooms: 7 single, 2 double, 3 twin,
1 family room
Bathrooms: 7 en-suite, 1 public,
6 private showers
Bed & breakfast

per night:	£min	£max
Single	42.50	52.50
Double	49.50	69.50

Lunch available
Evening meal 1800 (last orders
2300)
Parking for 15
Cards accepted: Mastercard, Visa

🛇🛢🖒📞🖵👜🏕🅂📺⚏🛋
🖐🏊❄🐾 SP

FARNHAM

Surrey
Map ref 2C2

Town noted for its Georgian houses.
Willmer House (now a museum)
has a facade of cut and moulded
brick with fine carving and panelling
in the interior. The 12th C castle has
been occupied by Bishops of both
Winchester and Guildford.
*Tourist Information Centre ☎ (01252)
715109*

The Mariners Hotel ⚠

〰〰〰 APPROVED

Millbridge, Frensham, Farnham
GU10 3DJ
☎ (01252) 792050 & 794745
Fax (01252) 792649

On A287 between Farnham and
Hindhead, a traditional country inn
with spacious function room for
conferences, receptions, etc.
Comfortable bedrooms a friendly

---

atmosphere, real ales and a
reasonably-priced menu.
Bedrooms: 6 single, 4 double, 8 twin,
3 triple
Bathrooms: 21 en-suite
Bed & breakfast

per night:	£min	£max
Single	49.50	55.00
Double	60.00	65.00

Half board per

person:	£min	£max
Daily	60.00	65.00
Weekly		350.00

Lunch available
Evening meal 1800 (last orders
2200)
Parking for 100
Cards accepted: Amex, Diners,
Mastercard, Visa, Switch/Delta

🛇🛢🖒📞🖵👜🏕🅂⚏🛋🅃80
🖐🅿 OAP SP T

FOLKESTONE

Kent
Map ref 3C4

Popular resort and important
cross-channel port. The town has a
fine promenade, the Leas, from
where orchestral concerts and
other entertainments are presented.
Horse-racing at Westenhanger
Racecourse nearby.
*Tourist Information Centre ☎ (01303)
258594*

Augusta Hotel ⚠

〰〰 APPROVED

4 Augusta Gardens, Folkestone
CT20 2RR
☎ (01303) 850952
Fax (01303) 240282
*Small, licensed hotel in central position,
close to sea and Leas and with easy
access to ferries and Eurotunnel.
Spacious patio with access to private
gardens. An elegant Victorian building
with style (but no lift).*
Bedrooms: 3 single, 8 double, 1 twin
Bathrooms: 12 en-suite, 1 public
Bed & breakfast

per night:	£min	£max
Single	15.00	25.00
Double	30.00	50.00

Lunch available
Evening meal 1830 (last orders
2030)
Cards accepted: Amex, Diners,
Mastercard, Visa, Switch/Delta

🛇🛢📞🖵👜🏕🅂✂🅙📺⚏🛋
🅃20❄🐾 OAP SP

You are advised to confirm
your booking in writing.

Banque Hotel ⚠

〰〰 COMMENDED

4 Castle Hill Avenue, Folkestone
CT20 2QT
☎ (01303) 253797
Fax (01303) 253797
*Hotel near seafront and shops. All
rooms en-suite with colour TV,
telephone, radio, tea/coffee facilities.
Exercise room with sauna and solarium.
Car park.*
Bedrooms: 3 single, 5 double, 4 twin
Bathrooms: 12 en-suite
Bed & breakfast

per night:	£min	£max
Single	20.00	25.00
Double	40.00	50.00

Parking for 4
Cards accepted: Amex, Diners,
Mastercard, Visa

🛇📞🖵👜🏕🅄🅛🛋🏕🖐🎿🐾
🚑 SP T

Clifton Hotel ⚠

〰〰〰 COMMENDED

The Leas, Clifton Gardens,
Folkestone CT20 2EB
☎ (01303) 851231
Fax (01303) 851231
Ⓒ Consort
*Regency-style house in centre of the
Leas, minutes from town centre, ferry
and Channel Tunnel and with views of
the English Channel. Good base for
Canterbury, Weald of Kent and France.*
Bedrooms: 20 single, 25 double,
29 twin, 5 triple
Suite available
Bathrooms: 79 en-suite
Bed & breakfast

per night:	£min	£max
Single	56.00	73.00
Double	65.00	96.00

Half board per

person:	£min	£max
Daily	55.00	75.00
Weekly	318.50	490.00

Lunch available
Evening meal 1900 (last orders
2115)
Cards accepted: Amex, Diners,
Mastercard, Visa, Switch/Delta

🛇📞🖵👜🏕🅂✂🅙◑⬡🛋
⚏🅃80🍷❄🐾 SP 🛏 T

Harbourside Bed and
Breakfast Hotel ⚠

〰〰 HIGHLY COMMENDED

14 Wear Bay Road, Folkestone
CT19 6AT
☎ (01303) 256528 & 0468 123884
Fax (01303) 241299
Email: r.j.pye@dial.pipex.com
Victorian houses, superior en-suite
Continued ▶

FOLKESTONE

Continued

rooms. The service, hospitality and views are truly unique. Adult. Licensed. No smoking. See our web site: http://www.s-h-systems.co.uk/hotels/harbour.html
Bedrooms: 4 double, 2 twin
Bathrooms: 5 en-suite, 1 private

Bed & breakfast

per night:	£min	£max
Single	35.00	60.00
Double	50.00	70.00

Parking for 1
Cards accepted: Amex, Mastercard, Visa, Switch/Delta

☐☐12☐☐☐☐♦☐☐S☐☐TV☐
☐☐☐☐☐☐☐☐☐SP☐T

Normandie Guest House

Listed APPROVED
39 Cheriton Road, Folkestone
CT20 1DD
☎ (01303) 256233
Central, near all local amenities, with parking nearby. Early breakfast served. Convenient for the harbour and trips to the continent.
Bedrooms: 1 single, 1 double, 2 twin, 1 triple, 1 family room
Bathrooms: 1 public

Bed & breakfast

per night:	£min	£max
Single	14.00	16.00
Double	28.00	32.00

☐☐4☐☐UL☐☐☐☐

Sunny Lodge Guest House ♏

COMMENDED
85 Cheriton Road, Folkestone
CT20 2QL
☎ (01303) 251498
Long established guesthouse noted for its high standard, surrounded by lovely garden. Walking distance town centre, railway station, seafront, minutes Seacat, Channel Tunnel. M20 junction 12. Private car park.
Bedrooms: 2 single, 2 double, 2 twin, 2 family rooms
Bathrooms: 2 public

Bed & breakfast

per night:	£min	£max
Single	16.00	17.50
Double	32.00	35.00

Parking for 5

☐☐6☐☐UL☐S☐☐☐☐☐DAP SP
⊚

A key to symbols can be found inside the back cover flap.

FRIMLEY GREEN

Surrey
Map ref 2C2

Lakeside International Hotel ♏

COMMENDED
Wharf Road, Frimley Green, Camberley GU16 6JR
☎ (01252) 838000
Fax (01252) 837857
Hotel with fine restaurant, seminar and conference facilities. Just 5 minutes from M3 junction 4. Easy access for rail and air.
Bedrooms: 55 double, 43 twin
Bathrooms: 98 en-suite

Bed & breakfast

per night:	£min	£max
Single	95.00	
Double	108.00	

Lunch available
Evening meal 1800 (last orders 2230)
Parking for 100
Cards accepted: Amex, Diners, Mastercard, Visa, Switch/Delta

☐☐☐☐☐♦☐☐S☐☐TV☐
☐☐☐☐100☐☐☐☐☐☐☐SP
T

GATWICK AIRPORT

West Sussex

See under Horley, Redhill, Reigate

GILLINGHAM

Kent
Map ref 3B3

The largest Medway Town merging into its neighbour Chatham. The Royal Engineers Museum is an interesting attraction.

King Charles Hotel ♏

COMMENDED APPROVED
Brompton Road, Gillingham
ME7 5QT
☎ (01634) 830303
Fax (01634) 829430

Friendly, modern hotel run by family, catering for all requirements at very reasonable rates in comfortable accommodation.
Bedrooms: 1 single, 30 double, 21 twin, 21 triple, 5 family rooms
Bathrooms: 78 en-suite

Bed & breakfast

per night:	£min	£max
Single	25.00	25.00
Double	34.00	34.00

Half board per person:

	£min	£max
Daily	30.00	40.00

Lunch available
Evening meal 1900 (last orders 2230)
Parking for 201
Cards accepted: Amex, Diners, Mastercard, Visa, Switch/Delta

☐☐☐☐☐♦☐S☐☐TV☐☐☐
☐150☐☐☐☐T

GUILDFORD

Surrey
Map ref 2D2

Bustling town with many historic monuments, one of which is the Guildhall clock jutting out over the old High Street. The modern cathedral occupies a commanding position on Stag Hill.
Tourist Information Centre ☎ *(01483) 444333*

Stream Cottage ♏

COMMENDED
The Street, Albury, Guildford
GU5 9AG
☎ (01483) 202228 & 0860 726090
Fax (01483) 202793
Picturesque village location in beautiful countryside. Charming period beamed cottage with lounge, dining room, sauna, spa bath. Pub food locally. Courtesy transport to and from Gatwick/Heathrow.
Bedrooms: 1 double, 2 twin
Suites available
Bathrooms: 1 en-suite, 2 private

Bed & breakfast

per night:	£min	£max
Single	25.00	35.00
Double	45.00	55.00

Parking for 3
Open February–December
Cards accepted: Amex, Mastercard, Visa, Switch/Delta

☐☐☐☐☐UL☐☐☐TV☐☐☐
U☐☐SP☐T

HAILSHAM

East Sussex
Map ref 2D3

An important market town since Norman times and still one of the largest markets in Sussex. Two miles west, at Upper Dicker, is Michelham Priory, an Augustinian house founded in 1229.
Tourist Information Centre ☎ (01323) 844426

Olde Forge Hotel and Restaurant ᴍ

👑👑👑 COMMENDED

Magham Down, Hailsham
BN27 1PN
☎ (01323) 842893
Fax (01323) 842893
Pretty, beamed 16th C building on A271. Comfortable bedrooms, log fires and candlelit dining room. Traditional and reasonably priced menu.
Bedrooms: 2 single, 4 double, 2 twin
Bathrooms: 6 en-suite, 2 private
Bed & breakfast

per night:	£min	£max
Single	39.50	
Double	46.00	65.00

Evening meal 1900 (last orders 2130)
Parking for 11
Cards accepted: Amex, Diners, Mastercard, Visa, Switch/Delta

🐴🏛📞🚭💧🍴⌚📶Ⓢ🍽⏰🛏🏧❄🚐 SP 🎪

HASLEMERE

Surrey
Map ref 2C2

Town set in hilly, wooded countryside, much of it in the care of the National Trust. Its attractions include the educational museum and the annual music festival.

Lythe Hill Hotel ᴍ

👑👑👑👑 HIGHLY COMMENDED

Petworth Road, Haslemere
GU27 3BQ
☎ (01428) 651251
Fax (01428) 644131
Email: lythehill@grayswood.co.uk
Ⓒ Grand Heritage

Hotel forms a hamlet of beautifully restored historic buildings in 14 acres

of parkland in the Surrey hills. French and English restaurant, tennis, croquet. One hour from London.
Bedrooms: 4 single, 20 double, 8 twin, 8 family rooms
Suites available
Bathrooms: 40 en-suite
Bed & breakfast

per night:	£min	£max
Single	103.00	143.00
Double	123.00	

Half board per person:

	£min	£max
Daily	122.50	162.50
Weekly	469.00	724.00

Lunch available
Evening meal 1915 (last orders 2115)
Parking for 150
Cards accepted: Amex, Diners, Mastercard, Visa, Switch/Delta

🐴♿👣🚭📞🍴⌚🅿Ⓢ🚭🍴Ⓜ💻◻
🏊🛥60⛳❄🏹⛵♪✈❄🏞 SP 🎪Ⓣ⊚

HASTINGS

East Sussex
Map ref 3B4

Ancient town which became famous as the base from which William the Conqueror set out to fight the Battle of Hastings. Later became one of the Cinque Ports, now a leading resort. Castle, Hastings Embroidery inspired by the Bayeux Tapestry and Sea Life Centre.
Tourist Information Centre ☎ (01424) 781111

Beechwood Hotel

👑👑 APPROVED

59 Baldslow Road, Hastings
TN34 2EY
☎ (01424) 420078
Late Victorian building with panoramic views of sea, castle and park, in quiet residential area. 1 mile from station and beach.
Bedrooms: 4 double, 2 twin, 1 triple, 2 family rooms
Bathrooms: 4 en-suite, 1 public
Bed & breakfast

per night:	£min	£max
Single	15.00	27.00
Double	28.00	45.00

Half board per person:

	£min	£max
Daily	24.00	36.00
Weekly	153.00	225.00

Lunch available
Evening meal 1800 (last orders 2200)
Parking for 6

🐴🏛♿Ⓢ🍴🚭 TV 🛏🖥🛏🍴❄ OAP ⌀
SP 🎪Ⓣ⊚

Eagle House Hotel ᴍ

👑👑👑 COMMENDED

12 Pevensey Road, St Leonards-on-Sea, Hastings
TN38 0JZ
☎ (01424) 430535 & 441273
Fax (01424) 437771

Large Victorian residence in its own grounds. Well placed for most local amenities and for visiting "1066" country.
Bedrooms: 14 double, 4 twin
Bathrooms: 18 en-suite, 2 public
Bed & breakfast

per night:	£min	£max
Single	29.00	32.00
Double	44.50	49.00

Lunch available
Evening meal 1830 (last orders 2030)
Parking for 14
Cards accepted: Amex, Diners, Mastercard, Visa

🐴🚭5♿📞🍴◻💧🅿Ⓜ🖥🛏🍴
❄🐕🚐

Lionsdown House

👑👑 COMMENDED

116 High Street, Old Town, Hastings
TN34 3ET
☎ (01424) 420802
Fax (01424) 420802

Medieval 15th C hall house. Historic character with exposed timbers, Tudor fireplaces and en-suite rooms with antique furnishings. In picturesque old town, 5 minutes from beach.
Bedrooms: 2 double, 1 twin
Bathrooms: 2 en-suite, 1 private
Bed & breakfast

per night:	£min	£max
Single	20.00	22.00
Double	40.00	44.00

🐴📞◻💧🚭Ⓤ🅿Ⓢ TV 🛏🍴❄
🚐🎪

Please check prices and other details at the time of booking.

505

HASTINGS

Continued

Mayfair Hotel

⚜⚜⚜ APPROVED

9 Eversfield Place, St
Leonards-on-Sea, Hastings
TN37 6BY
☎ (01424) 434061
*Family-owned and run hotel on the
seafront. Several rooms are en-suite
and face the sea. Close to town centre.*
Bedrooms: 3 single, 2 double, 3 twin,
3 triple
Bathrooms: 6 en-suite, 1 public,
2 private showers
**Bed & breakfast
per night:**

	£min	£max
Single	16.00	25.00
Double	32.00	50.00

**Half board per
person:**

	£min	£max
Daily	21.00	32.00
Weekly	125.00	200.00

Evening meal 1800 (last orders
1900)
Cards accepted: Mastercard, Visa

Royal Victoria Hotel ⋒

⚜⚜⚜⚜ COMMENDED

Marina, St Leonards-on-Sea, Hastings
TN38 OBD
☎ (01424) 445544
Fax (01424) 721995
ⓒⓡ Consort

*Elegant Victorian building on the
seafront, within walking distance of
Hastings. Tastefully furnished,
individually styled bedrooms. Renowned
sea terrace restaurant, piano bar and 6
conference rooms. The perfect location
for every occasion: business or
pleasure.*
Bedrooms: 34 double, 11 twin,
5 triple
Bathrooms: 50 en-suite
**Bed & breakfast
per night:**

	£min	£max
Single	65.00	
Double	85.00	

**Half board per
person:**

	£min	£max
Daily	70.00	80.00
Weekly	400.00	550.00

Evening meal 1900 (last orders
2130)

Parking for 6
Cards accepted: Amex, Diners,
Mastercard, Visa, Switch/Delta

Tower House ⋒

⚜⚜ HIGHLY COMMENDED

26-28 Tower Road West, St
Leonards-on-Sea, Hastings
TN38 0RG
☎ (01424) 427217
Fax (01424) 427217
*Elegant Victorian house situated half a
mile from seafront. Pleasant gardens.
Separate licensed bar leading to
garden patio. Freshly-cooked meals
including vegetarian. Ample parking.*
Bedrooms: 1 single, 7 double, 2 twin
Bathrooms: 10 en-suite
**Bed & breakfast
per night:**

	£min	£max
Single	31.00	34.50
Double	45.00	58.00

**Half board per
person:**

	£min	£max
Daily	44.00	47.50
Weekly	207.00	279.00

Evening meal 1900 (last orders
1900)
Cards accepted: Amex, Diners,
Mastercard, Visa, Switch/Delta

HAWKHURST

Kent
Map ref 3B4

*Village in 3 parts: Gill's Green,
Highgate and the Moor. There is a
colonnaded shopping centre, large
village green, church and inn which
is associated with the Hawkhurst
smuggling gang.*

Woodham Hall Hotel

⚜⚜ COMMENDED

Rye Road, Hawkhurst TN18 5DA
☎ (01580) 753428
Fax (01580) 753428
*Country house on the edge of the
village, in interesting, historic
surroundings. Personal, friendly service.
Tennis, snooker and horse-riding
available. Ideal for holidays or business.*
Bedrooms: 3 double, 2 family rooms
Bathrooms: 5 en-suite
**Bed & breakfast
per night:**

	£min	£max
Single	35.00	45.00
Double	45.00	55.00

Parking for 30
Cards accepted: Amex, Mastercard,
Visa

HERSTMONCEUX

East Sussex
Map ref 3B4

*Pleasant village noted for its
woodcrafts and the beautiful 15th C
moated Herstmonceux Castle with
its Science Centre and gardens open
to the public.*

White Friars Hotel

⚜⚜⚜⚜ COMMENDED

Boreham Street Village, Boreham
Street, Herstmonceux BN27 4SE
☎ (01323) 832355
Fax (01323) 833882
ⓒⓡ Best Western
*16th C country house, with cheerful
and friendly atmosphere. Log fire, some
rooms with four-poster beds, excellent
food. Two acres of beautiful gardens.
On the A271.*
Bedrooms: 2 single, 10 double,
5 twin, 3 triple
Bathrooms: 20 en-suite
**Bed & breakfast
per night:**

	£min	£max
Single	55.00	65.00
Double	75.00	90.00

**Half board per
person:**

	£min	£max
Daily	50.00	60.00
Weekly	300.00	360.00

Lunch available
Evening meal 1900 (last orders
2100)
Parking for 50
Cards accepted: Amex, Diners,
Mastercard, Visa, Switch/Delta

HORLEY

Surrey
Map ref 2D2

*Town on the London to Brighton
road, just north of Gatwick Airport,
with an ancient parish church and
15th C inn.*

Aintree & Gables Guest House ⋒

Listed COMMENDED

50 Bonehurst Road, Horley
RH6 8QG
☎ (01293) 774553
Approximately 2 miles from Gatwick

and the railway station. Long term parking. Transport to the airport available.

Bedrooms: 3 single, 7 double, 9 twin, 5 triple
Bathrooms: 9 en-suite, 4 public

Bed & breakfast

per night:	£min	£max
Single	25.00	25.00
Double	32.00	39.00

Parking for 25

Felcourt Guest House ♈

Listed APPROVED

79 Massetts Road, Horley RH6 7EB
☎ (01293) 782651 & 776255
Fax (01293) 782651
Friendly Victorian house, close to pubs, restaurants, shopping centre and railway station. One mile from motorway and Gatwick Airport. Long-term parking available at £10 per week.
Bedrooms: 2 single, 3 triple
Bathrooms: 3 en-suite, 1 public

Bed & breakfast

per night:	£min	£max
Single	20.00	28.00
Double	30.00	38.00

Half board per

person:	£min	£max
Daily	25.00	35.00
Weekly	175.00	245.00

Evening meal 1800 (last orders 2000)
Parking for 12
Cards accepted: Amex, Diners, Mastercard, Visa

Gainsborough Lodge ♈

≝≝ COMMENDED

39 Massetts Road, Gatwick, West Sussex RH6 7DT
☎ (01293) 783982
Fax (01293) 785365
Extended Edwardian house set in attractive garden. Five minutes' walk from Horley station and town centre. Five minutes' drive from Gatwick Airport.
Bedrooms: 5 single, 4 double, 6 twin, 1 triple, 2 family rooms
Bathrooms: 16 en-suite, 1 public

Bed & breakfast

per night:	£min	£max
Single	34.00	38.00
Double	45.00	50.00

Parking for 16
Cards accepted: Amex, Diners, Mastercard, Visa, Switch/Delta

The Lawn Guest House ♈

≝≝ HIGHLY COMMENDED

30 Massetts Road, Horley RH6 7DE
☎ (01293) 775751
Fax (01293) 821803
Classic Victorian house with mature garden, 2 minutes from Horley centre, restaurants, pubs and main rail station to London/Brighton. 5 minutes' drive to Gatwick, long-term parking. Non-smoking.
Bedrooms: 1 double, 2 twin, 4 triple
Bathrooms: 7 en-suite

Bed & breakfast

per night:	£min	£max
Double	45.00	47.00

Parking for 10
Cards accepted: Amex, Mastercard, Visa

Masslink House ♈

Listed COMMENDED

70 Massetts Road, Horley RH6 7ED
☎ (01293) 785798
Comfortable, well-maintained Victorian house with full range of rooms, including downstairs en-suite. TV and tea/coffee facilities. Near Gatwick Airport.
Bedrooms: 2 single, 2 double, 2 twin, 1 family room
Bathrooms: 1 en-suite, 2 public

Bed & breakfast

per night:	£min	£max
Single	20.00	25.00
Double	36.00	44.00

Parking for 13
Cards accepted: Amex, Mastercard, Visa, Switch/Delta

Oakdene Guest House ♈

Listed APPROVED

32 Massetts Road, Horley RH6 7DS
☎ (01293) 772047
Family-run guesthouse, 5 minutes from Gatwick Airport and 30 minutes by train from London or the coast. Long-term car parking available.
Bedrooms: 3 single, 3 twin, 2 triple, 1 family room
Bathrooms: 3 en-suite, 1 private, 2 public

Bed & breakfast

per night:	£min	£max
Single	20.00	24.00
Double	32.00	34.00

Parking for 10
Cards accepted: Amex, Mastercard, Visa

Rosemead Guest House ♈

Listed COMMENDED

19 Church Road, Horley RH6 7EY
☎ (01293) 430546 & 784965
Fax (01293) 430547
Small guesthouse (non-smoking) 5 minutes from Gatwick Airport, providing English breakfast after 7.30 am, Continental before. Car parking. French spoken.
Bedrooms: 2 single, 2 double, 1 twin, 1 family room
Bathrooms: 3 en-suite, 2 public

Bed & breakfast

per night:	£min	£max
Single	25.00	
Double	38.00	45.00

Parking for 8
Cards accepted: Diners, Mastercard, Visa

Stanhill Court Hotel ♈

≝≝≝ HIGHLY COMMENDED

Stanhill, Charlwood, Horley RH6 0EP
☎ (01293) 862166
Fax (01293) 862773
Award-winning Victorian country house hotel. 4 miles from Gatwick Airport and station, but quiet. Magnificent architecture set in 35 acres of ancient woodland. Fully licensed restaurant.
Bedrooms: 12 double, 2 twin, 3 triple
Bathrooms: 17 en-suite

Bed & breakfast

per night:	£min	£max
Single	85.00	
Double	99.00	

Lunch available
Evening meal 1900 (last orders 2130)
Parking for 150
Cards accepted: Amex, Diners, Mastercard, Visa, Switch/Delta

For ideas on places to visit refer to the introduction at the beginning of this section.

The symbols in each entry give information about services and facilities. A key to these symbols appears at the back of this guide.

HORLEY

Continued

Woodlands Guest House ▲▲
👑👑 COMMENDED

42 Massetts Road, Horley RH6 7DS
☎ (01293) 782994
Fax (01293) 776358
1 mile from Gatwick airport. All rooms en-suite with colour TV, tea/coffee facilities. Residents' lounge. Car parking. Courtesy car by arrangement. Non-smoking.
Bedrooms: 1 single, 2 double, 2 twin
Bathrooms: 5 en-suite, 1 public
Bed & breakfast per night:

	£min	£max
Single	28.00	30.00
Double	38.00	42.00

Parking for 32

Yew Tree ▲▲
Listed APPROVED

31 Massetts Road, Horley RH6 7DQ
☎ (01293) 785855
Fax (01293) 785855
Tudor-style house with half an acre of garden. 3 minutes by taxi from Gatwick Airport and 3 minutes' walk from town centre.
Bedrooms: 1 single, 2 double, 1 twin, 1 triple
Bathrooms: 1 public
Bed & breakfast per night:

	£min	£max
Single	15.00	20.00
Double	30.00	35.00

Parking for 10
Cards accepted: Diners, Mastercard, Visa

HOVE

East Sussex

See under Brighton & Hove

WELCOME HOST

This is a nationally recognised customer care programme which aims to promote the highest standards of service and a warm welcome. Establishments who are taking part in this initiative are indicated by the 🌸 symbol.

HYTHE

Kent
Map ref 3B4

Once one of the Cinque Ports, the town today stands back from the sea. The Royal Military Canal is the scene of a summer pageant, the Romney, Hythe and Dymchurch Railway terminates here and Port Lympne Wild Animal Park, Mansion and Gardens is nearby.

Stade Court Hotel ▲▲
👑👑👑 HIGHLY COMMENDED

West Parade, Hythe CT21 6DT
☎ (01303) 268263
Fax (01303) 261803
CR Best Western
Seafront hotel, with well-appointed family suites. Indoor heated pool, golf, squash, sauna, solarium and so much more, 600 metres away at our sister hotel. Daily half board price based on minimum 2-night stay.
Bedrooms: 10 single, 11 double, 16 twin, 5 triple
Suites available
Bathrooms: 42 en-suite
Bed & breakfast per night:

	£min	£max
Single	67.50	77.50
Double	95.00	105.00

Half board per person:

	£min	£max
Daily	52.50	
Weekly	367.00	

Lunch available
Evening meal 1900 (last orders 2100)
Parking for 12
Cards accepted: Amex, Diners, Mastercard, Visa, Switch/Delta

KINGSDOWN

Kent
Map ref 3C4

Quaint, tranquil, historic fishing village surrounded by castles, first-class golf courses and scenic cliff and country walks. Overlooking the Goodwin Sands towards the French coast.

Kingsdown Country Hotel & Captains Table ▲▲
👑👑 COMMENDED

Cliffe Road, Kingsdown, Deal CT14 8AJ
☎ (01304) 373755
Fax (01304) 373755
Family-run village hotel with full en-suite bedrooms, bar, comfortable dining room, secluded rear car park and gardens with a gate to the beach.
Bedrooms: 1 single, 2 double, 1 twin
Bathrooms: 4 en-suite
Bed & breakfast per night:

	£min	£max
Single	22.00	35.00
Double	44.00	60.00

Half board per person:

	£min	£max
Daily	34.00	47.00

Evening meal 1830 (last orders 2130)
Parking for 6
Cards accepted: Mastercard, Visa

LEATHERHEAD

Surrey
Map ref 2D2

Old county town in the Green Belt, with the modern Thorndike Theatre.

Bookham Grange Hotel ▲▲
👑👑 COMMENDED

Little Bookham Common, Bookham, Leatherhead KT23 3HS
☎ (01372) 452742
Fax (01372) 450080
CR Minotel/The Independents/Logis of GB

Country house hotel in ideal location for M25, A3, Gatwick, Heathrow and central London. Good food and friendly service.
Bedrooms: 3 single, 8 double, 5 twin, 2 triple
Bathrooms: 18 en-suite
Bed & breakfast per night:

	£min	£max
Single	59.00	65.00
Double	75.00	80.00

Half board per person:

	£min	£max
Daily	50.00	75.00
Weekly	350.00	500.00

Lunch available
Evening meal 1900 (last orders 2200)
Parking for 100
Cards accepted: Amex, Diners, Mastercard, Visa, Switch/Delta

LEWES

East Sussex
Map ref 2D3

Historic county town with Norman castle. The steep High Street has mainly Georgian buildings. There is a folk museum at Anne of Cleves House and the archaeological museum is in Barbican House.
Tourist Information Centre ☎ (01273) 483448

Shelleys Hotel ♨

👑👑👑 HIGHLY COMMENDED

High Street, Lewes BN7 1XS
☎ (01273) 472361
Fax (01273) 483152
ⓒⓡ Mount Charlotte Thistle/Utell International

16th C manor house in 1 acre of garden. Convenient for the South Downs and Glyndebourne.
Bedrooms: 1 single, 9 double, 9 twin
Suite available
Bathrooms: 19 en-suite
Bed & breakfast

per night:	£min	£max
Single	53.00	117.50
Double	106.00	160.00

Half board per person:

	£min	£max
Daily	73.00	144.00

Lunch available
Evening meal 1900 (last orders 2115)
Parking for 25
Cards accepted: Amex, Diners, Mastercard, Visa, Switch/Delta
🛇🛆🕭🕻📞🖵📺🌙📶🆔Ⓢ🅿️🎦🌃◐🔟
🛋🍴150🏌️❄🐾💢SP🏤Ⓣ

MAIDSTONE

Kent
Map ref 3B3

Busy county town of Kent on the River Medway has many interesting features and is an excellent centre for excursions. Museum of Carriages, Museum and Art Gallery, Mote Park.
Tourist Information Centre ☎ (01622) 602169

Grangemoor Hotel ♨

👑👑👑 COMMENDED

St Michael's Road, Maidstone
ME16 8BS
☎ (01622) 677623
Fax (01622) 678246
One hour from London and the Kent coast, in a quiet position on the edge of town. The hotel has rear gardens, restaurant and bar.
Bedrooms: 10 single, 15 double, 15 twin, 5 triple, 2 family rooms
Bathrooms: 46 en-suite, 2 public
Bed & breakfast

per night:	£min	£max
Single	35.00	48.00
Double	45.00	56.00

Lunch available
Evening meal 1830 (last orders 2200)
Parking for 79
Cards accepted: Mastercard, Visa
🛇🛆🕭🕻🖵📶🆔Ⓢ🎦◐🌙▥⊜🛋
🍴150❄SPⓉ

Russell Hotel ♨

👑👑 COMMENDED

136 Boxley Road, Maidstone
ME14 2AH
☎ (01622) 692221
Fax (01622) 762084
ⓒⓡ Consort
Converted convent school a few minutes from Maidstone and 1.5 miles from the M20. Set in secluded grounds with ample parking.
Bedrooms: 14 single, 16 double, 7 twin, 2 triple, 2 family rooms
Bathrooms: 41 en-suite
Bed & breakfast

per night:	£min	£max
Single	45.00	60.00
Double	60.00	95.00

Half board per person:

	£min	£max
Daily	55.00	65.00

Lunch available
Evening meal 1900 (last orders 2130)
Parking for 100

Cards accepted: Amex, Diners, Mastercard, Visa, Switch/Delta
🛇🛆🕭🕻📞🖵📺🌙📶🆔Ⓢ🖊🎦📺
◐▥🛋🍴300🏌️❄🐾OAP🈁SP🏤Ⓣ
♨

Willington Court ♨

👑👑👑 HIGHLY COMMENDED

Willington Street, Maidstone
ME15 8JW
☎ (01622) 738885
Fax (01622) 631790
Charming Grade II listed building. Antiques, four-poster bed. Friendly and relaxed atmosphere. Adjacent to Mote Park and near Leeds Castle.
Bedrooms: 2 double, 1 twin
Bathrooms: 2 en-suite, 1 private
Bed & breakfast

per night:	£min	£max
Single	26.00	36.00
Double	40.00	50.00

Parking for 6
Cards accepted: Amex, Diners, Mastercard, Visa
🏠🕻🖵🌙📺🆔UL🆔🖊🎦📺🛋💠🔌☀
🐾💢SP🏤Ⓣ◎

MARGATE

Kent
Map ref 3C3

Oldest and most famous resort in Kent. Many Regency and Victorian buildings survive from the town's early days. There are 9 miles of sandy beach. "Dreamland" is a 20-acre amusement park and the Winter Gardens offers concert hall entertainment.
Tourist Information Centre ☎ (01843) 220241

Clintons

👑👑👑 COMMENDED

9 Dalby Square, Cliftonville, Margate
CT9 2ER
☎ (01843) 290598 & 299550
Set in illuminated garden square, this elegant hotel offers comfortable en-suite bedrooms, spacious lounge, licensed restaurant, saunas, jacuzzi, gymnasium and solarium.
Bedrooms: 5 double, 5 twin, 3 triple
Bathrooms: 13 en-suite, 4 public
Bed & breakfast

per night:	£min	£max
Single	28.00	32.00
Double	42.00	45.00

Half board per person:

	£min	£max
Daily	34.00	38.00
Weekly	165.00	185.00

Continued ▶

MARGATE

Continued

Evening meal 1800 (last orders 1930)
Parking for 4
Cards accepted: Diners, Mastercard, Visa

🛎☎💻📺♿📶S♨📺🖥️💼🚭♻️✕⚡
✈ DAP 🚭 SP T

Lonsdale Court Hotel ♈

👑👑👑 APPROVED

51-61 Norfolk Road, Cliftonville, Margate CT9 2HX
☎ (01843) 221053
Fax (01843) 299993
Family-run hotel near sea and shops. En-suite bedrooms, TV, telephone, tea-making. Entertainment, bars, coffee shop. Sports hall for badminton, indoor bowls, etc, sauna, solarium, heated indoor pool.
Wheelchair access category 3♿
Bedrooms: 11 single, 17 double, 15 twin, 18 triple, 2 family rooms
Suites available
Bathrooms: 61 en-suite, 2 private, 3 public

Bed & breakfast per night:

	£min	£max
Single	29.00	37.00
Double	53.00	63.00

Half board per person:

	£min	£max
Daily	35.00	46.00
Weekly	245.00	322.00

Lunch available
Evening meal 1830 (last orders 2100)
Cards accepted: Amex, Diners, Mastercard, Visa, Switch/Delta

🛎☺🏨☎💻📶♿📶S♨📺⦿
🖥️💼🏋150♻️⚡🎾❄️✕✈ DAP 🚭 SP T
⊚

> All accommodation in this guide has been graded, or is awaiting a grading, by a trained Tourist Board inspector.

> National gradings and classifications were correct at the time of going to press but are subject to change. Please check at the time of booking.

MIDHURST

West Sussex
Map ref 2C3

Historic, picturesque town just north of the South Downs, with the ruins of Cowdray House, medieval castle and 15th C parish church. Polo at Cowdray Park. Excellent base for Chichester, Petworth, Glorious Goodwood and the South Downs Way.
Tourist Information Centre ☎ (01730) 817322

Park House Hotel ♈

👑👑👑 HIGHLY COMMENDED

Bepton, Midhurst GU29 0JB
☎ (01730) 812880
Fax (01730) 815643
Beautifully situated country house hotel, equipped to give maximum comfort, with the atmosphere and amenities of an English country home. Outdoor pool, pitch and putt course, tennis courts, conference facilities.
Bedrooms: 2 single, 5 double, 6 twin, 1 triple
Bathrooms: 14 en-suite, 1 public

Bed & breakfast per night:

	£min	£max
Single	49.00	70.00
Double	90.00	120.00

Half board per person:

	£min	£max
Daily	66.50	87.50
Weekly	420.00	540.00

Lunch available
Evening meal from 2000
Parking for 40
Cards accepted: Amex, Mastercard, Visa, Switch/Delta

🛎☺🏨☎💻📶♿♨📶S♨📺🖥️💼
🏋80♻️⚡🎾U❄️🚲🚭 SP

Southdown's Country Hotel & Restaurant

👑👑👑 COMMENDED

Trotton, Rogate, Petersfield, Hampshire GU31 5JN
☎ (01730) 821521
Fax (01730) 821790
CR Best Western

Country hotel set in its own gardens with full leisure facilities. Ideal for a peaceful rest away from it all. 3 miles west of Midhurst.
Bedrooms: 9 double, 9 twin, 2 triple
Bathrooms: 20 en-suite

Bed & breakfast per night:

	£min	£max
Single	60.00	85.00
Double	90.00	120.00

Half board per person:

	£min	£max
Daily	60.00	70.00

Lunch available
Evening meal 1900 (last orders 2130)
Parking for 70
Cards accepted: Amex, Diners, Mastercard, Visa, Switch/Delta

🛎☺🏨☎💻📶♿♨📶S✕🍴🖥️
🚪♻️120✕❄️🎾🍴U❄️✿✕🚭 SP
🏧T

NEW ROMNEY

Kent
Map ref 3B4

Capital of Romney Marsh. Now a mile from the sea, it was one of the original Cinque Ports. Romney, Hythe and Dymchurch Railway's main station is here.

Broadacre Hotel ♈

👑👑👑 COMMENDED

North Street, New Romney TN28 8DR
☎ (01797) 362381
Fax (01797) 362381
Small 16th C family-run hotel offering a warm, friendly welcome and personal attention. Intimate restaurants, lounge bar, garden. Weekend breaks.
Bedrooms: 3 single, 4 double, 2 twin, 1 family room
Bathrooms: 10 en-suite

Bed & breakfast per night:

	£min	£max
Single	35.00	42.00
Double	45.00	60.00

Half board per person:

	£min	£max
Daily	34.00	50.00
Weekly	210.00	

Lunch available
Evening meal 1900 (last orders 2100)
Parking for 9
Cards accepted: Mastercard, Visa, Switch/Delta

🛎☺🏨💻📶♿♨📶S✕🍴🖥️🚪🏋
❄️🚲🚭 SP 🏧

> Half board prices are given per person, but in some cases these may be based on double/twin occupancy.

PENSHURST

Kent
Map ref 2D2

Pretty village in a hilly wooded setting with Penshurst Place, the ancestral home of the Sidney family since 1552, standing in delightful grounds with a formal Tudor garden.

Swale Cottage ⚊

Listed HIGHLY COMMENDED

Off Poundsbridge Lane, Penshurst, Tonbridge TN11 8AH
☎ (01892) 870738
CR Distinctly Different

Charmingly converted Grade II* listed barn overlooking medieval manor house and gardens. Idyllic and tranquil. Delightful bedrooms (1 with four-poster). Close to Penshurst Place, Hever and Chartwell. Near A26 off B2176.
Bedrooms: 2 double, 1 twin
Bathrooms: 2 en-suite, 1 private
**Bed & breakfast
per night:**

	£min	£max
Single	36.00	45.00
Double	52.00	63.00

Parking for 7

PETWORTH

West Sussex
Map ref 2D3

Town dominated by Petworth House (National Trust), the great 17th C mansion, set in 2000 acres of parkland laid out by Capability Brown. The house contains wood-carvings by Grinling Gibbons.
Tourist Information Centre ☎ (01798) 343523

White Horse Inn ⚊

♛♛♛ HIGHLY COMMENDED

The Street, Sutton, Pulborough
RH20 1PS
☎ (01798) 869221
Fax (01798) 869291
CR Logis of GB

Pretty Georgian village inn close to South Downs Way. Roman villa 1 mile. Garden, log fires. 4 miles Petworth, 5 miles Pulborough.
Bedrooms: 4 double, 2 twin
Bathrooms: 5 en-suite, 1 private shower
**Bed & breakfast
per night:**

	£min	£max
Single	48.00	48.00
Double	58.00	68.00

Lunch available
Evening meal 1900 (last orders 2145)
Parking for 10
Cards accepted: Amex, Diners, Mastercard, Visa

PULBOROUGH

West Sussex
Map ref 2D3

Here is Parham, an Elizabethan mansion with unusually tall, mullioned windows and a long gallery measuring 158 ft. The house and the surrounding park and garden can be visited. In the grounds stands the church of St Peter.

Chequers Hotel ⚊

♛♛♛ HIGHLY COMMENDED

Church Place, Pulborough
RH20 1AD
☎ (01798) 872486
Fax (01798) 872715
CR Minotel/Logis of GB
Country hotel, dating from 1548, in picturesque village, overlooking the South Downs. Licensed restaurant, coffee shop. Bedrooms with all facilities, some on ground floor and some with four-posters. Lovely walks in private 9-acre meadow.
Bedrooms: 1 single, 5 double, 2 twin, 3 triple
Bathrooms: 10 en-suite, 1 private
**Bed & breakfast
per night:**

	£min	£max
Single	49.50	59.50
Double	79.00	89.00

**Half board per
person:**

	£min	£max
Daily	48.00	53.00
Weekly	309.00	344.00

Lunch available
Evening meal 1930 (last orders 2045)

Parking for 16
Cards accepted: Amex, Diners, Mastercard, Visa

RAMSGATE

Kent
Map ref 3C3

Popular holiday resort with good sandy beaches. At Pegwell Bay is replica of a Viking longship. Terminal for car-ferry service to Dunkirk and Ostend.
Tourist Information Centre ☎ (01843) 583333

Eastwood Guest House ⚊

Listed COMMENDED

28 Augusta Road, Ramsgate
CT11 8JS
☎ (01843) 591505
Fax (01843) 591505

Pretty Victorian villa, close to ferry port and amenities. Comfortable rooms, mostly en-suite. Lock-up garages available. Breakfast served from 6.45 am, dinner available.
Bedrooms: 1 single, 4 double, 4 twin, 6 family rooms
Bathrooms: 10 en-suite, 3 public
**Bed & breakfast
per night:**

	£min	£max
Single	20.00	30.00
Double	40.00	50.00

**Half board per
person:**

	£min	£max
Daily	25.00	35.00
Weekly	165.00	220.00

Evening meal 1830 (last orders 1930)
Parking for 20

Please mention this guide when making your booking.

Map references apply to the colour maps at the back of this guide.

511

RAMSGATE

Continued

Goodwin View Hotel ⋔

👑 APPROVED

19 Wellington Crescent, Ramsgate
CT11 8JD
☎ (01843) 591419
Seafront licensed hotel in Grade II listed historic building overlooking harbour and beach. Terminal and town within walking distance. Ideal base for touring Kent. Ferry travellers welcome.
Bedrooms: 4 single, 3 double, 2 twin, 2 triple, 2 family rooms
Bathrooms: 4 en-suite, 3 public

Bed & breakfast

per night:	£min	£max
Single	19.00	27.00
Double	32.00	44.00

Cards accepted: Amex, Diners, Mastercard, Visa, Switch/Delta

🛏🏠🕯⭐🅢🖿📺📠💻🖭🚗♿30☀ ✈ DAP SP 🅣

San Clu Hotel ⋔

👑👑👑 COMMENDED

Victoria Parade, East Cliff, Ramsgate
CT11 8DT
☎ (01843) 592345
Fax (01843) 580157
Grade II listed Victorian cliff top hotel, recently refurbished. Overlooking sea and sands and near cross-Channel ferry terminals and harbour. Quiet location out of town centre, but within easy reach of ample parking.
Bedrooms: 7 single, 18 double, 5 twin, 12 triple, 2 family rooms
Suites available
Bathrooms: 44 en-suite

Bed & breakfast

per night:	£min	£max
Single	45.00	75.00
Double	65.00	140.00

Half board per person:

	£min	£max
Daily	55.00	85.00
Weekly	310.00	460.00

Lunch available
Evening meal 1900 (last orders 2130)
Parking for 22
Cards accepted: Amex, Diners, Mastercard, Visa, Switch/Delta

🛏🏨📞🖿📠💻🕯✏🅢✂🖿📺◐ 🖭💻🚗180▶☀✈🚭 SP 🏮🅣

Shirley's Hotel ⋔

👑👑 APPROVED

8 Nelson Crescent, Ramsgate
CT11 9JF
☎ (01843) 584198
Fax (01843) 586759
Overlooking Ramsgate harbour and

Sally Line ferry terminal. 2 minutes from town centre. All rooms have colour TV and tea-making facilities and some rooms are en-suite.
Bedrooms: 2 single, 2 double, 2 twin, 3 triple, 2 family rooms
Bathrooms: 5 en-suite, 2 public

Bed & breakfast

per night:	£min	£max
Single	15.00	18.00
Double	30.00	35.00

🛏🖵🕯🅢📺💻🚗✈ DAP SP 🏮

REDHILL

Surrey
Map ref 2D2

Part of the borough of Reigate and now the commercial centre with good shopping facilities. Gatwick Airport is 3 miles to the south.

Ashleigh House Hotel

Listed HIGHLY COMMENDED

39 Redstone Hill, Redhill RH1 4BG
☎ (01737) 764763
Fax (01737) 780308
Friendly, family-run early Edwardian house with most rooms en-suite. 500 yards from railway station, London 30 minutes, Gatwick Airport 15 minutes.
Bedrooms: 1 single, 2 double, 3 twin, 1 triple, 1 family room
Bathrooms: 6 en-suite, 1 public

Bed & breakfast

per night:	£min	£max
Single	30.00	42.00
Double	42.00	48.00

Parking for 9
Cards accepted: Mastercard, Visa

🛏🏠🖿🖵🕯✏ UL 💻🕭☀✈🚗🏮

REIGATE

Surrey
Map ref 2D2

Old town with modern developments, on the edge of the North Downs. Just outside the town on Reigate Heath stands an old windmill, which has been converted into a church.

Bridge House Hotel & Restaurant

👑👑👑 HIGHLY COMMENDED

Reigate Hill, Reigate RH2 9RP
☎ (01737) 246801
Fax (01737) 223756
Most rooms have own balcony with views over South Downs. 2 minutes from junction 8 of M25, 15 minutes from Gatwick and 35 minutes from Heathrow.
Bedrooms: 8 single, 20 double, 8 twin, 3 family rooms
Bathrooms: 39 en-suite

Bed & breakfast

per night:	£min	£max
Single	55.00	80.00
Double	83.50	96.50

Half board per person:

	£min	£max
Daily	82.50	91.00

Lunch available
Evening meal 1930 (last orders 2200)
Parking for 110
Cards accepted: Amex, Diners, Mastercard, Visa

🛏🏠📞🖿🖵🕯✏🅢🖿◐💻🚗 🍽100✈🚭 SP

Cranleigh Hotel ⋔

👑👑👑 COMMENDED

41 West Street, Reigate RH2 9BL
☎ (01737) 223417
Fax (01737) 223734
Ⓡ Minotel/Logis of GB
Close to town centre and railway station, on main road to the south-west a short distance from Gatwick Airport and within easy reach of central London. 1 mile from M25.
Bedrooms: 2 single, 3 double, 2 twin, 1 triple, 1 family room
Bathrooms: 8 en-suite, 1 private, 1 public

Bed & breakfast

per night:	£min	£max
Single	55.00	66.00
Double	75.00	86.00

Evening meal 1900 (last orders 2100)
Parking for 6
Open February–November
Cards accepted: Amex, Diners, Mastercard, Visa

🛏📞🖿🖵🕯✏🅢🖿📺💻🚗🍽20 🕭🅤▶☀✈ DAP SP 🅣

ROCHESTER

Kent
Map ref 3B3

Ancient cathedral city on the River Medway. Has many places of interest connected with Charles Dickens (who lived nearby) including the fascinating Dickens Centre. Also massive castle overlooking the river and Guildhall Museum.
Tourist Information Centre ☎ (01634) 843666

Bridgewood Manor Hotel ⋔

👑👑👑👑 HIGHLY COMMENDED

Bridgewood Roundabout, Maidstone Road, Rochester ME5 9AX
☎ (01634) 201333
Fax (01634) 201330
Ⓡ Best Western
Modern manor built around a classical

courtyard. Superb leisure facilities make it an ideal choice for exploring Kent's many attractions. Daily half board price based on minimum 2-night stay.
Bedrooms: 57 double, 43 twin
Suites available
Bathrooms: 100 en-suite

Bed & breakfast per night:	£min	£max
Single	73.50	93.50
Double	97.00	117.00

Half board per person:	£min	£max
Daily	62.50	
Weekly	375.00	

Lunch available
Evening meal 1900 (last orders 2200)
Parking for 175
Cards accepted: Amex, Diners, Mastercard, Visa, Switch/Delta
[S] 200 [SP] [T]

ROYAL TUNBRIDGE WELLS

Kent
Map ref 2D2

This "Royal" town became famous as a spa in the 17th C and much of its charm is retained, as in the Pantiles, a shaded walk lined with elegant shops. Heritage attraction "A Day at the Wells". Excellent shopping centre.
Tourist Information Centre ☎ (01892) 515675

Danehurst

HIGHLY COMMENDED

41 Lower Green Road, Rusthall, Royal Tunbridge Wells TN4 8TW
☎ (01892) 527739
Fax (01892) 514804

Charming gabled house in village setting in the heart of Kent. Bedrooms afford excellent accommodation. Breakfast is served in Victorian conservatory. From October to May you can enjoy a candlelit dinner in the elegant dining room. We would be delighted to welcome you to our home.
Bedrooms: 3 double, 2 twin
Bathrooms: 4 en-suite, 1 private

Bed & breakfast per night:	£min	£max
Single	30.00	45.00
Double	45.00	65.00

Half board per person:	£min	£max
Daily	58.45	67.95
Weekly	409.15	475.65

Parking for 5
Cards accepted: Amex, Mastercard, Visa
8 [TV] [SP] [T]

Four Keys

APPROVED

Station Road, Wadhurst, East Sussex TN5 6RZ
☎ (01892) 782252 & 784113
Public house with separate accommodation built on both sides.
Bedrooms: 3 double, 3 twin, 1 triple
Bathrooms: 7 en-suite

Bed & breakfast per night:	£min	£max
Single	18.50	22.50
Double	37.00	45.00

Half board per person:	£min	£max
Daily	23.50	27.50

Lunch available
Evening meal 1900 (last orders 2200)
Parking for 30
Cards accepted: Amex, Mastercard, Visa
[S]

The Old Parsonage

DE LUXE

Church Lane, Frant, Royal Tunbridge Wells TN3 9DX
☎ (01892) 750773
Fax (01892) 750773

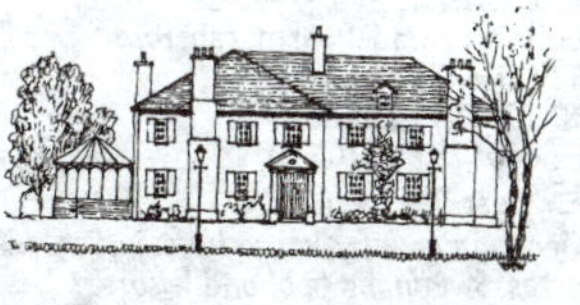

Peacefully situated by the village church (2 pubs and restaurant nearby), this classic Georgian country house provides superior accommodation: en-suite bedrooms, antique-furnished reception rooms, spacious conservatory and ballustraded terrace overlooking the secluded walled garden. SEETB 1995 "Bed and Breakfast of the Year" Award winner.
Bedrooms: 2 double, 1 twin
Bathrooms: 3 en-suite

Bed & breakfast per night:	£min	£max
Single	42.00	52.00
Double	59.00	69.00

Parking for 12
Cards accepted: Mastercard, Visa
[UL] [S] [TV] [T]

Russell Hotel

COMMENDED

80 London Road, Royal Tunbridge Wells TN1 1DZ
☎ (01892) 544833
Fax (01892) 515846
Email: russell_hotel@globalnet.co.uk
[CR] Logis of GB

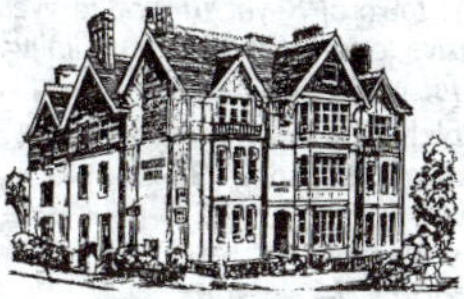

Large Victorian house facing common, only minutes from town centre. Totally refurbished to highest modern standards.
Bedrooms: 11 double, 10 twin, 3 triple
Suites available
Bathrooms: 24 en-suite

Bed & breakfast per night:	£min	£max
Single	40.00	68.00
Double	55.00	99.00

Half board per person:	£min	£max
Daily	47.00	59.00
Weekly	280.00	350.00

Lunch available
Evening meal 1900 (last orders 2200)
Parking for 20
Cards accepted: Amex, Diners, Mastercard, Visa, Switch/Delta
[S] 40 [DAP] [SP] [T]

The National Grading and Classification Scheme is explained at the back of this guide.

ACCESSIBILITY

Look for the symbols which indicate accessibility for wheelchair users. These are described in detail at the front of this guide.

ROYAL TUNBRIDGE WELLS

Continued

The Spa Hotel ⚐

👑👑👑👑 **COMMENDED**

Mount Ephraim, Royal Tunbridge
Wells TN4 8XJ
☎ (01892) 520331
Fax (01892) 510575
Email: info@spahotel.co.uk
Ⓒ Best Western
*Elegant mansion overlooking the
historic town of Royal Tunbridge
Wells. Extensive leisure facilities, fine dining.
Ideal for weekend breaks.*
Wheelchair access category 3 ⚐
Bedrooms: 16 single, 32 double,
22 twin, 4 triple
Suites available
Bathrooms: 74 en-suite
Bed & breakfast

per night:	£min	£max
Single	88.00	93.00
Double	112.00	133.00

Half board per person:	£min	£max
Daily	70.00	75.00
Weekly	490.00	525.00

Lunch available
Evening meal 1930 (last orders
2130)
Parking for 150
Cards accepted: Amex, Diners,
Mastercard, Visa, Switch/Delta

🛏♿🏩℡📞📺🖥♿🎇🍴🌺☉🍽☀🗑
🖥🍷300🐎🧩✕🔍🔍∪♪▶✿🗑 SP
🏠 T

RUSTINGTON

West Sussex
Map ref 2D3

Village with thatched cottages and a
medieval church.

Kenmore ⚐

👑👑👑 **HIGHLY COMMENDED**

Claigmar Road, Rustington
BN16 2NL
☎ (01903) 784634
Fax (01903) 784634
*Secluded Edwardian house in the heart
of village close to sea. Ideal for historic
towns, castles, cathedrals and stately
homes.*
Bedrooms: 1 single, 1 double, 1 twin,
3 triple, 1 family room
Bathrooms: 7 en-suite, 1 public
Bed & breakfast

per night:	£min	£max
Single	22.50	25.00
Double	45.00	50.00

Parking for 7
Cards accepted: Amex, Mastercard,
Visa, Switch/Delta

🛏♿🏩📺🖥♿🎇UL🍴🖥🛏🌺🚗
T

RYE

East Sussex
Map ref 3B4

Cobbled, hilly streets and fine old
buildings make Rye, once a Cinque
Port, a most picturesque town.
Noted for its church with ancient
clock, potteries and antique shops.
Town Model Sound and Light Show
gives a good introduction to the
town.
*Tourist Information Centre ☎ (01797)
226696*

Arndale Cottage ⚐

Listed **COMMENDED**

Northiam Road, Broad Oak, Brede,
Rye TN31 6EP
☎ (01424) 882813 & 0585 790451
Fax (01424) 882813
*Period style country cottage set in 1.5
acres, ideally situated as a base for
exploring Kent and East Sussex.*
Bedrooms: 2 double, 1 twin
Bathrooms: 3 en-suite
Bed & breakfast

per night:	£min	£max
Single	25.00	30.00
Double	36.00	48.00

Parking for 8

🛏♿🏩📺♿🎇UL🖥🛏✕🚗 SP

Flackley Ash Hotel & Restaurant ⚐

👑👑👑👑 **HIGHLY COMMENDED**

London Road, Peasmarsh, Rye
TN31 6YH
☎ (01797) 230651
Fax (01797) 230510
Ⓒ Best Western
*Georgian country house hotel in 5
acres. Swimming pool and leisure
centre. Fresh fish, well-stocked cellar.
Half board daily prices based on
minimum 2-night stay.*
Bedrooms: 21 double, 9 twin,
1 triple, 1 family room
Bathrooms: 32 en-suite
Bed & breakfast

per night:	£min	£max
Single	69.00	79.00
Double	108.00	128.00

Half board per person:	£min	£max
Daily	49.50	69.00
Weekly	325.00	415.00

Lunch available
Evening meal 1900 (last orders
2130)
Parking for 60

Cards accepted: Amex, Diners,
Mastercard, Visa, Switch/Delta

🛏♿🏩℡📞📺🖥♿🎇S🍴🖥🛏🌺🚗
🖥🍷100🐎✕🔍☀🌺 DAF 🗑 SP 🏠 T

Jeake's House ⚐

👑👑 **HIGHLY COMMENDED**

Mermaid Street, Rye TN31 7ET
☎ (01797) 222828
Fax (01797) 222623
Email: jeakeshouse@btinternet.com
Ⓒ Distinctly Different

*Recapture the past in this historic
building, in a cobblestoned street at the
heart of the old town. Honeymoon
suite available.*
Bedrooms: 1 single, 7 double, 1 twin,
2 triple, 1 family room
Bathrooms: 9 en-suite, 1 private,
2 public
Bed & breakfast

per night:	£min	£max
Single	24.50	56.50
Double	45.00	63.00

Cards accepted: Amex, Mastercard,
Visa

🛏♿℡📞📺♿🎇S🍴🖥🛏🚗
SP 🏠 T ◎

Little Orchard House ⚐

👑👑 **HIGHLY COMMENDED**

West Street, Rye TN31 7ES
☎ (01797) 223831
*Georgian town house in centre of Rye.
Antique furnishings and large walled
garden give country house atmosphere.*
Bedrooms: 2 double, 1 twin
Bathrooms: 3 en-suite
Bed & breakfast

per night:	£min	£max
Single	45.00	65.00
Double	60.00	84.00

Cards accepted: Mastercard, Visa

🛏12🏩📞📺♿🎇UL S🖥🛏🚗🌺
✕🚗 SP 🏠

The Old Vicarage Hotel ⚐

👑👑👑 **HIGHLY COMMENDED**

15 East Street, Rye TN31 7JY
☎ (01797) 225131
Fax (01797) 225131
Ⓒ Logis of GB
*Family-run Queen Anne hotel and
restaurant in conservation area.
Spacious rooms and elegant restaurant
with panoramic views over Romney
Marsh.*
Bedrooms: 2 double, 2 triple
Bathrooms: 4 en-suite

Bed & breakfast per night:	£min	£max
Double	70.00	88.00

Half board per person:	£min	£max
Daily	50.00	59.00

Evening meal 1900 (last orders 2100)
Open February–December
Cards accepted: Amex, Mastercard, Visa, Switch/Delta

🛏🚗🕾📞💷🖵👜🅿🛎Ⓢ🛏🖵🛄🔌☎
❀🚲🛇 SP 🏮

Rye Lodge Hotel 🗚

⚜⚜⚜ HIGHLY COMMENDED

Hilders Cliff, Rye TN31 7LD
☎ (01797) 223838
Fax (01797) 223585
Stunning estuary views. Close to town centre. Elegant rooms all en-suite. Candlelit dinners, delicious food and wine. Room service (breakfast in bed!). Attentive service. Car park.
Bedrooms: 2 single, 11 double, 7 twin
Bathrooms: 20 en-suite

Bed & breakfast per night:	£min	£max
Single	47.50	65.00
Double	65.00	105.00

Half board per person:	£min	£max
Daily	52.50	62.50
Weekly	350.00	425.00

Evening meal 1930 (last orders 2130)
Parking for 20
Cards accepted: Amex, Diners, Mastercard, Visa, Switch/Delta

🛏🚗♿🕾💷🖵👜🅿🛎Ⓢ🛏🖵🛄❀
🚲🛇 SP T

Ship Inn 🗚

⚜⚜⚜ APPROVED

The Strand, Rye TN31 7DS
☎ (01797) 222233
Fax (01580) 881545

Situated at the foot of Mermaid Street and in the oldest part of town. Wide selection of bar snacks served all day. Seafood bar. Dinner served in our panelled restaurant.
Bedrooms: 6 double, 2 twin, 1 triple
Bathrooms: 9 en-suite

Bed & breakfast per night:	£min	£max
Single	20.00	35.00
Double	50.00	60.00

Half board per person:	£min	£max
Daily	32.50	47.50

Lunch available
Evening meal 1900 (last orders 2200)
Parking for 6
Cards accepted: Mastercard, Visa, Switch/Delta

🛏🚗5🕾💷📞💷👜Ⓢ🍴🛄📇🛎🅿50🔫
🛇 SP 🏮 T

Strand House 🗚

⚜⚜⚜ COMMENDED

Winchelsea TN36 4JT
☎ (01797) 226276
Fax (01797) 224806

The old-world charm of one of Winchelsea's oldest houses, dating from the 15th C, with oak beams and inglenooks. Overlooking National Trust pastureland. Four-poster bedroom. Residents' licence.
Bedrooms: 8 double, 1 twin, 1 triple
Bathrooms: 9 en-suite, 1 private, 1 public

Bed & breakfast per night:	£min	£max
Single	28.00	34.00
Double	45.00	58.00

Evening meal 1800 (last orders 1900)
Parking for 12
Cards accepted: Mastercard, Visa, Switch/Delta

🛏🚗5🖵🚲💷🖵👜📞💷Ⓢ🍴🛄🔌TV
🛄📇🅿❀🚲🛇 SP 🏮

SANDWICH

Kent
Map ref 3C3

Delightful old market town, once a Cinque Port, now 2 miles from the sea. Many interesting old buildings including the 16th C Barbican and the Guildhall which contains the town's treasures. Several excellent golf-courses.

Bell Hotel 🗚

⚜⚜⚜ COMMENDED

The Quay, Sandwich CT13 9EF
☎ (01304) 613388
Fax (01304) 615308

17th C riverside inn extended during Victorian times, recently refurbished in traditional manner to provide individual and comfortable accommodation with quality restaurant and cellar. Own golf club, Princes, just a short drive away.
Bedrooms: 7 single, 6 double, 19 twin, 1 family room
Bathrooms: 33 en-suite

Bed & breakfast per night:	£min	£max
Single	70.00	75.00
Double	90.00	140.00

Half board per person:	£min	£max
Daily	55.00	

Lunch available
Evening meal 1900 (last orders 2145)
Parking for 10
Cards accepted: Amex, Diners, Mastercard, Visa, Switch/Delta

🛏🚗♿🕾💷🖵👜📞💷Ⓢ🍴🛄🔌⊙🛄
🅿🍴150♿Ⓤ🅿🛇 SP 🏮

The Blazing Donkey Country Hotel & Inn 🗚

⚜⚜ COMMENDED

Hay Hill, Ham, Sandwich CT13 0HU
☎ (01304) 617362
Fax (01304) 615264
One of East Kent's most atmospheric country inns. Situated in the heart of the countryside, between the coastal towns of Sandwich and Deal. Specialises in golf packages.
Bedrooms: 7 single, 6 double, 6 triple
Bathrooms: 19 en-suite

Bed & breakfast per night:	£min	£max
Single	35.00	49.00
Double	49.00	59.00

Lunch available
Evening meal 1800 (last orders 2200)
Parking for 95
Cards accepted: Amex, Diners, Mastercard, Visa, Switch/Delta

🛏🚗♿🖵💷🖵👜📞💷Ⓢ🍴🛄TV⊙
🛄⊙🅿🍴45Ⓤ🅿❀🔫🚲🛇 SP 🏮
T⊚

SEAFORD

East Sussex
Map ref 2D3

The town was a bustling port until 1579 when the course of the River Ouse was diverted. The downlands around the town make good walking country, with fine views of the Seven Sisters cliffs.
Tourist Information Centre ☎ (01323) 897426

The Silverdale 🅰

👑 👑 👑 COMMENDED

21 Sutton Park Road, Seaford BN25 1RH
☎ (01323) 491849
Fax (01323) 891131
Email: silverdale@mistral.co.uk
Traditional spacious Edwardian house in this historic town. Very warm welcome. Within an easy walk of antique shops and seafronts.
Bedrooms: 2 single, 3 double, 1 triple, 2 family rooms
Bathrooms: 5 en-suite, 1 public

Bed & breakfast per night:

	£min	£max
Single	15.00	28.00
Double	28.00	45.00

Half board per person:

	£min	£max
Daily	22.50	35.50

Lunch available
Evening meal 1800 (last orders 2030)
Parking for 6
Cards accepted: Amex, Mastercard, Visa, Switch/Delta

🛇 👤 📞 📨 🖥 👤 🦮 🛈 S ✂ 🧍 TV ◑
🖩 🚗 🅿 🚲 DAP 🐾 SP ◉

SEALE

Surrey
Map ref 2C2

Village 4 miles east of Farnham.

Jarvis Hogs Back Hotel 🅰

👑 👑 👑 COMMENDED

Hog's Back, Seale, Farnham GU10 1EX
☎ (01252) 782345
Fax (01252) 783113
CR Jarvis/Utell International
Extensively refurbished country house style hotel offering modern facilities. Magnificent views over Surrey countryside.
Bedrooms: 6 single, 41 double, 26 twin, 6 triple
Bathrooms: 79 en-suite

Bed & breakfast per night:

	£min	£max
Single	42.50	118.50
Double	85.00	138.00

Lunch available
Evening meal 1900 (last orders 2130)
Parking for 150
Cards accepted: Amex, Diners, Mastercard, Visa, Switch/Delta

🛇 👤 📞 📨 🖥 👤 🦮 🛈 S ✂ 🧍 ◑ 🖩
◉ 🚗 🍽 140 🚲 🗙 🦮 🌸 🐾 SP 🏠

SELSEY

West Sussex
Map ref 2C3

Almost surrounded by water, with the English Channel on two sides and an inland lake, once Pagham Harbour, and the Brook on the other two. Ideal for yachting, swimming, fishing and wildlife.

St Andrews Lodge 🅰

👑 👑 👑 COMMENDED

Chichester Road, Selsey, Chichester PO20 0LX
☎ (01243) 606899
Fax (01243) 607826
CR Logis of GB

Family-run, friendly relaxed atmosphere, licensed. En-suite bedrooms, cosy lounge, log fire, peaceful sun trap garden. Close to natural beaches and countryside, south of Chichester.
Wheelchair access category 1 ♿
Bedrooms: 1 single, 3 double, 3 twin, 2 family rooms
Bathrooms: 9 en-suite

Bed & breakfast per night:

	£min	£max
Single	25.00	40.00
Double	45.00	60.00

Half board per person:

	£min	£max
Daily	37.50	44.95

Evening meal 1800 (last orders 1930)
Parking for 15
Cards accepted: Amex, Mastercard, Visa, Switch/Delta

🛇 👤 📨 🖥 👤 🦮 🛈 S ✂ 🧍 TV 🖩 🚗
🍽 👤 🌸 🚲 SP ◉

SEVENOAKS

Kent
Map ref 2D2

Set in pleasant wooded country, with a distinctive character and charm. Nearby is Knole (National Trust), home of the Sackville family and one of the largest houses in England, set in a vast deer park.
Tourist Information Centre ☎ (01732) 450305

The Bull Hotel 🅰

👑 👑 APPROVED

Wrotham, Sevenoaks TN15 7RF
☎ (01732) 885522 & 883092
Fax (01732) 886288
CR The Independents

Privately-run 14th C coaching inn, in secluded historic village 15 minutes from Sevenoaks. Just off M20 and M25/26, 30 minutes from Gatwick and London, 1 hour from Dover. Oak beams and inglenook fireplaces. Ideal for local places of interest.
Bedrooms: 1 single, 3 double, 6 twin
Bathrooms: 6 en-suite, 1 public

Bed & breakfast per night:

	£min	£max
Single	37.00	42.00
Double	47.00	52.00

Lunch available
Evening meal 1900 (last orders 2200)
Parking for 50
Cards accepted: Amex, Diners, Mastercard, Visa

🛇 🐎 📞 📨 🖥 👤 🛈 S 🧍 🖩 🚗 🍽 50 🌸
🚲 🐾 SP 🏠 T

Donnington Manor Hotel 🅰

👑 👑 👑 APPROVED

London Road, Dunton Green, Sevenoaks TN13 2TD
☎ (01732) 462681
Fax (01732) 458116
Hotel with full leisure facilities, in delightful countryside of Kent. Close to M25 and M26. Good base for many places of interest.
Bedrooms: 34 double, 27 twin, 2 family rooms
Bathrooms: 63 en-suite, 1 public

Bed & breakfast per night:

	£min	£max
Single	55.00	85.00
Double	60.00	90.00

Half board per person:	£min	£max
Daily	70.00	100.00
Weekly	420.00	600.00

Lunch available
Evening meal 1900 (last orders 2130)
Parking for 120
Cards accepted: Amex, Diners, Mastercard, Visa, Switch/Delta

🐕♿📞💶🖥🗐🕭❓Ⓢ✂🅿📺①
🏨🖨🍴150 ⚡🎯☂🏊♀🚲🏧 SP 🏮 T

The Moorings Hotel ▲▲

🏵🏵🏵 APPROVED

97 Hitchen Hatch Lane, Sevenoaks
TN13 3BE
☎ (01732) 452589 & 742323
Fax (01732) 456462
Email: theryans
@mooringshotel.demon.co.uk
Friendly family hotel offering high standard accommodation for tourists and business travellers. 30 minutes from London. Close to BR station.
Bedrooms: 5 single, 5 double, 9 twin, 2 triple
Bathrooms: 21 en-suite, 1 public

Bed & breakfast per night:	£min	£max
Single	34.00	42.00
Double	49.00	59.00

Half board per person:	£min	£max
Daily	44.00	52.00
Weekly	308.00	364.00

Lunch available
Evening meal 1900 (last orders 2100)
Parking for 24
Cards accepted: Amex, Mastercard, Visa, Switch/Delta

🐕♿📞🖥Ⓢ✂🅿📺🏨🖨
🍴45 ∪🏇❄✈ DAP SP T ◎

SHIPBOURNE

Kent
Map ref 2D2

Due north of Tonbridge and halfway to Ightham, Shipbourne is sandwiched between acres of Forestry Commission conifers and the park of Fairbourne.

The Chaser Inn ▲▲

🏵🏵🏵 COMMENDED

Stumble Hill, Shipbourne, Tonbridge
TN11 9PE
☎ (01732) 810360
Fax (01732) 810941
Ⓖ Logis of GB
Recently refurbished village inn next to Shipbourne Church and set around an attractive courtyard. Imaginative bar

and restaurant food served. All rooms with private facilities.
Bedrooms: 5 single, 6 double, 4 twin
Bathrooms: 15 en-suite

Bed & breakfast per night:	£min	£max
Single	50.00	
Double	65.00	

Lunch available
Evening meal 1900 (last orders 2130)
Parking for 40
Cards accepted: Amex, Mastercard, Visa, Switch/Delta

🐕♿📞🖥💶❓🗐Ⓢ✂🅿🏨🖨
▶🚗🏊 SP

SITTINGBOURNE

Kent
Map ref 3B3

The town's position and its ample supply of water make it an ideal site for the paper-making industry. Delightful villages and orchards lie round about.

The Beaumont

🏵🏵 COMMENDED

74 London Road, Sittingbourne
ME10 1NS
☎ (01795) 472536
Fax (01795) 425921
Email: beaumont74@aol.com
Comfortable, friendly 17th C former farmhouse, conveniently located for historic Canterbury, Rochester and Leeds Castle. Superb prize-winning breakfast menu and private car park.
Bedrooms: 3 single, 4 double, 1 twin, 1 family room
Bathrooms: 5 en-suite, 1 private, 1 public, 2 private showers

Bed & breakfast per night:	£min	£max
Single	26.00	47.00
Double	40.00	52.00

Half board per person:	£min	£max
Daily	36.00	57.00
Weekly	225.00	350.00

Evening meal 1830 (last orders 2000)
Parking for 9
Cards accepted: Amex, Diners, Mastercard, Visa, Switch/Delta

🐕♿📞🖥💶Ⓤ🗐Ⓢ✂🅿📺🏨
🖨🍴12 ❄🚗 DAP SP 🏮 T

Hempstead House ▲▲

🏵🏵🏵 HIGHLY COMMENDED

London Road, Bapchild,
Sittingbourne ME9 9PP
☎ (01795) 428020
Fax (01795) 428020
Ⓖ Logis of GB

Exclusive private Victorian country house hotel on main A2 between Canterbury and Sittingbourne, offering quality accommodation, fine cuisine and friendly hospitality.
Bedrooms: 11 double, 2 twin
Bathrooms: 13 en-suite

Bed & breakfast per night:	£min	£max
Single	62.00	62.00
Double	72.00	72.00

Half board per person:	£min	£max
Daily	55.50	81.50
Weekly	350.00	550.00

Lunch available
Evening meal 1800 (last orders 2200)
Parking for 22
Cards accepted: Amex, Diners, Mastercard, Visa, Switch/Delta

🐕♿📞🖥💶❓🗐Ⓢ✂🅿📺
①🏨🖨🍴18 ❄🌸🚗 DAP SP

STEYNING

West Sussex
Map ref 2D3

An important market town and thriving port before the Norman Conquest, lying at the foot of the South Downs. Retains a picturesque charm with fascinating timber-framed and stone buildings.

The Old Tollgate Restaurant & Hotel ▲▲

🏵🏵🏵 HIGHLY COMMENDED

The Street, Bramber, Steyning
BN44 3WE
☎ (01903) 879494
Fax (01903) 813399
Ⓖ Best Western

Beautifully appointed hotel at the foot of South Downs, opposite Bramber Castle ruins. Stunning, award-winning carvery - better described as "visual a la carte".
Bedrooms: 21 double, 10 twin
Suites available

Continued ▶

STEYNING

Continued

Bathrooms: 31 en-suite

Bed & breakfast per night:

	£min	£max
Single	67.95	89.95
Double	74.90	96.90

Half board per person:

	£min	£max
Daily	55.95	66.95

Lunch available
Evening meal 1900 (last orders 2130)
Parking for 60
Cards accepted: Amex, Diners, Mastercard, Visa, Switch/Delta

🏃👓🏛🛏✆🖃🖵🌙🎱💺🚭🍴⛵☀

🎿🖳🚗✝60⛵☀✿🐎🛒🎣📺 SP T

TENTERDEN

Kent
Map ref 3B4

Most attractive market town with a broad main street full of 16th C houses and shops. The tower of the 15th C parish church is the finest in Kent. Fine antiques centre.

Collina House Hotel

🏰🏰 COMMENDED

East Hill, Tenterden TN30 6RL
☎ (01580) 764852 & 764004
Fax (01580) 762224
Edwardian house overlooking orchards and garden, within walking distance of picturesque town. Swiss-trained proprietors offering both English and continental cooking.
Bedrooms: 1 single, 5 double, 1 twin, 4 triple, 3 family rooms
Bathrooms: 14 en-suite

Bed & breakfast per night:

	£min	£max
Single	28.00	38.00
Double	40.00	55.00

Half board per person:

	£min	£max
Daily	43.00	55.00
Weekly	280.00	300.00

Lunch available
Evening meal 1900 (last orders 2130)
Parking for 16
Cards accepted: Amex, Mastercard, Visa

🏃👓✆🖵💺📺📺🖳🚗✝24 SP
T

You are advised to confirm your booking in writing.

Little Silver Country Hotel ⚑

🏰🏰🏰🏰 HIGHLY COMMENDED

Ashford Road, St Michaels,
Tenterden TN30 6SP
☎ (01233) 850321
Fax (01233) 850647

Quality accommodation in Tudor-style country house hotel. Four-poster, brass bedded, family, disabled facilities (all en-suite). A la carte menu. Personal service in a truly delightful and unique atmosphere. Landscaped gardens.
Wheelchair access category 3♿
Bedrooms: 5 double, 3 twin, 1 triple, 1 family room
Bathrooms: 10 en-suite

Bed & breakfast per night:

	£min	£max
Single	60.00	85.00
Double	85.00	110.00

Half board per person:

	£min	£max
Daily	60.00	75.00
Weekly	400.00	500.00

Lunch available
Evening meal 1830 (last orders 2200)
Parking for 50
Cards accepted: Amex, Mastercard, Visa, Switch/Delta

🏃👓🏛✆🖃🖵🌙🎱💺🚭🍴🖳
🚗✝150⛵☀✿DAP🐎 SP 🏧T◉

TICEHURST

East Sussex
Map ref 3B4

Dale Hill Hotel & Golf Club ⚑

🏰🏰🏰🏰 HIGHLY COMMENDED

Ticehurst, Wadhurst TN5 7DQ
☎ (01580) 200112
Fax (01580) 201249
Set in over 300 acres, high on the Kentish Weald, a quality hotel with 2 golf-courses and swimming pool.
Bedrooms: 6 double, 20 twin
Suite available
Bathrooms: 26 en-suite

Bed & breakfast per night:

	£min	£max
Single	58.00	68.00
Double	96.00	136.00

Half board per person:

	£min	£max
Daily	71.00	76.00

Lunch available

Evening meal 1900 (last orders 2130)
Parking for 220
Cards accepted: Amex, Mastercard, Visa, Switch/Delta

🏃👓✆🖃🖵🌙🎱💺🍴📺◉🏊
🖳🚗✝32☀🍴🎱🎣⛵☀🐎🛒🛟
SP T

TUNBRIDGE WELLS

Kent

See under Royal Tunbridge Wells

UCKFIELD

East Sussex
Map ref 2D3

Once a medieval market town and centre of the iron industry, Uckfield is now a busy country town on the edge of the Ashdown Forest.

Buxted Park Country House Hotel ⚑

🏰🏰🏰🏰 HIGHLY COMMENDED

Buxted, Uckfield TN22 4AY
☎ (01825) 732711
Fax (01825) 732770
Email: buxtedpark
@cnc.compulink.co.uk
Beautiful Georgian mansion set in 312 acres of gardens, lakes and parkland, near Ashdown Forest. Excellent cuisine, comfortable accommodation, well-equipped health club and impeccable service.
Bedrooms: 3 single, 34 double, 7 twin
Suites available
Bathrooms: 44 en-suite

Bed & breakfast per night:

	£min	£max
Single	85.00	100.00
Double	120.00	190.00

Half board per person:

	£min	£max
Daily	113.00	123.00

Lunch available
Evening meal 1900 (last orders 2130)
Parking for 150
Cards accepted: Amex, Mastercard, Visa, Switch/Delta

🏃👓🏛✆🖃🖵🌙🎱💺🍴🖳◉🖳
🚗✝150🏊☀🍴🎱⛵♪🎣✿🐎🛟 SP 🏧

Halland Forge Hotel & Restaurant ⚑

🏰🏰 COMMENDED

Halland, Lewes BN8 6PW
☎ (01825) 840456
Fax (01825) 840773
Ⓖ Logis of GB/The Independents

Attractive hotel with fully licensed restaurant and coffee shop. Facilities for meetings and functions. Garden and woodland walks. Ideal touring centre, 4 miles from Uckfield, 15 miles from Brighton and Eastbourne.
Bedrooms: 11 double, 7 twin, 2 triple
Bathrooms: 20 en-suite

Bed & breakfast

per night:	£min	£max
Single	44.00	56.00
Double	52.00	77.00

Half board per person:

	£min	£max
Daily	61.00	73.00
Weekly	250.00	286.00

Lunch available
Evening meal 1900 (last orders 2130)
Parking for 70
Cards accepted: Amex, Diners, Mastercard, Visa, Switch/Delta

Hooke Hall ⚑

HIGHLY COMMENDED

250 High Street, Uckfield
TN22 1EN
☎ (01825) 761578
Fax (01825) 768025

Elegant Queen Anne town house, recently completely refurbished, with individual comfortably designed rooms equipped to a high standard. Friendly and informal atmosphere.
Bedrooms: 5 double, 4 twin
Bathrooms: 9 en-suite

Bed & breakfast

per night:	£min	£max
Single	45.00	80.00
Double	75.00	130.00

Lunch available
Evening meal 1930 (last orders 2100)
Parking for 7
Cards accepted: Amex, Mastercard, Visa

Horsted Place Sporting Estate & Hotel ⚑

DE LUXE

Little Horsted, Uckfield TN22 5TS
☎ (01825) 750581
Fax (01825) 750459
Grand Heritage

Victorian mansion off A26 south of Uckfield, set in 23 acres of Sussex countryside. Part of 1,100-acre estate of East Sussex National Golf Club. Heated indoor swimming pool, tennis and croquet. All rooms individually decorated.
Bedrooms: 9 double, 8 twin
Suites available
Bathrooms: 17 en-suite

Bed & breakfast

per night:	£min	£max
Single	120.00	250.00
Double	120.00	250.00

Lunch available
Evening meal 1930 (last orders 2130)
Parking for 100
Cards accepted: Amex, Diners, Mastercard, Visa, Switch/Delta

WEST CHILTINGTON

West Sussex
Map ref 2D3

Well-kept village caught in the maze of lanes leading to and from the South Downs.

Roundabout Hotel ⚑

COMMENDED

Monkmead Lane, West Chiltington, Pulborough RH20 2PF
☎ (01798) 813838
Fax (01798) 812962
Best Western

Tudor-style hotel in the countryside. Nowhere near a roundabout - in fact, a haven of tranquillity. Plenty of historic castles to see in the immediate area.
Bedrooms: 3 single, 7 double, 9 twin, 4 triple
Bathrooms: 23 en-suite

Bed & breakfast

per night:	£min	£max
Single	65.95	72.95
Double	89.95	96.45

Half board per person:

	£min	£max
Daily	84.45	89.45
Weekly	375.15	431.00

Lunch available
Evening meal 1930 (last orders 2100)
Parking for 40

Cards accepted: Amex, Diners, Mastercard, Visa, Switch/Delta

WESTERHAM

Kent
Map ref 2D2

This small country town near the Kent/Surrey border sits in the wooded slopes of the glorious North Downs. Famous as the birthplace of General Wolfe and close to Churchill's house at Chartwell (National Trust).
Tourist Information Centre ☎ (01959) 565063

RoadChef Lodge ⚑

COMMENDED

Clacket Lane Motorway Service Area, M25 Westbound, Westerham TN16 2ER
☎ (01959) 565789
RoadChef

RoadChef Lodges offer high specification rooms at affordable prices, in popular locations suited to both the business and private traveller. Price below is per room and does not include breakfast.
Bedrooms: 35 double, 22 twin, 1 family room
Bathrooms: 58 en-suite

Bed & breakfast

per night:	£min	£max
Double	47.50	

Lunch available
Cards accepted: Amex, Diners, Mastercard, Visa, Switch/Delta

Information on accommodation listed in this guide has been supplied by the proprietors. As changes may occur you are advised to check details at the time of booking.

The symbols in each entry give information about services and facilities. A key to these symbols appears at the back of this guide.

WHITSTABLE

Kent
Map ref 3B3

Seaside resort and yachting centre on Kent's north shore. The beach is shingle and there are the usual seaside amenities and entertainments and a museum. *Tourist Information Centre ☎ (01227) 275482*

Marine ⚓

👑👑👑 COMMENDED

Marine Parade, Tankerton, Whitstable CT5 2BE
☎ (01227) 272672
Fax (01227) 264721

A hotel of original character recently refurbished with every modern facility. Good food, Kentish beers, comfortable en-suite accommodation, sea-facing bedrooms. Half board daily prices are based on a minimum 2-night stay.
Bedrooms: 4 double, 6 twin, 1 triple
Bathrooms: 11 en-suite
Bed & breakfast per night:

	£min	£max
Single	35.00	37.50
Double	49.50	52.00

Half board per person:

	£min	£max
Daily	37.50	40.00

Lunch available
Evening meal 1900 (last orders 2100)
Parking for 20
Cards accepted: Mastercard, Visa, Switch/Delta
🛇🕭🕿📪🖵🐾🦮🍴🛋️🅂🏥📺🔲💼
🍽️200❄️🆂🅿️

WELCOME HOST

This is a nationally recognised customer care programme which aims to promote the highest standards of service and a warm welcome. Establishments who are taking part in this initiative are indicated by the 🏵️ symbol.

WOKING

Surrey
Map ref 2D2

One of the largest towns in Surrey, which developed with the coming of the railway in the 1830s. Old Woking was a market town in the 17th C and still retains several interesting buildings. Large arts and entertainment centre.

The Dutch

👑👑 COMMENDED

Woodham Road, Woking
GU21 4EQ
☎ (01483) 724255
Fax (01483) 724255
Small, peaceful, private hotel, ideally situated for touring Surrey and for business visits to Woking. 27 minutes from London.
Bedrooms: 2 double, 2 twin
Bathrooms: 4 en-suite, 1 public
Bed & breakfast per night:

	£min	£max
Single	40.00	50.00
Double	54.00	64.00

Half board per person:

	£min	£max
Daily	54.00	64.00
Weekly	350.00	350.00

Evening meal 1900 (last orders 2000)
Parking for 6
Cards accepted: Mastercard, Visa
🛇1🕿📪🖵🐾🦮🆄🅻🆂🏥📺💼🖐️
❄️🚐🆂🅿️🏠🔲

WORTHING

West Sussex
Map ref 2D3

Town in the West Sussex countryside and by the South Coast, with excellent shopping and many pavement cafes and restaurants. Attractions include the award-winning Museum and Art Gallery, beautiful gardens, pier, elegant town houses, Cissbury Ring hill fort and the South Downs. *Tourist Information Centre ☎ (01903) 210022*

Ardington Hotel ⚓

👑👑👑👑 HIGHLY COMMENDED

Steyne Gardens, Worthing
BN11 3DZ
☎ (01903) 230451
Fax (01903) 526526
Privately-owned and managed hotel overlooking Steyne Gardens adjacent to seafront. Town centre, national bowling

greens 5 minutes' walk. Conference facilities. All bedrooms have "work stations".
Bedrooms: 20 single, 17 double, 8 twin, 3 triple
Bathrooms: 48 en-suite, 1 public
Bed & breakfast per night:

	£min	£max
Single	45.00	74.00
Double	70.00	95.00

Half board per person:

	£min	£max
Daily	47.50	90.00
Weekly	304.50	420.00

Lunch available
Evening meal 1900 (last orders 2030)
Parking for 20
Cards accepted: Amex, Diners, Mastercard, Visa, Switch/Delta
🛇🦽🕭🕿📪🖵🐾🦮🍴🅂🏥📺🔲💼
🍽️🍽️120❄️🆂🅿️🔲

Cavendish Hotel ⚓

👑👑👑 COMMENDED

115-116 Marine Parade, Worthing
BN11 3QG
☎ (01903) 236767
Fax (01903) 823840
Ⓒ Minotel

Fully licensed seafront hotel with en-suite rooms. A la carte and extensive bar snack menus. Open to non-residents.
Bedrooms: 4 single, 4 double, 3 twin, 4 triple
Bathrooms: 15 en-suite, 1 public
Bed & breakfast per night:

	£min	£max
Single	42.50	47.00
Double	60.00	80.00

Half board per person:

	£min	£max
Daily	50.00	60.00
Weekly	325.00	395.00

Lunch available
Evening meal 1900 (last orders 2100)
Parking for 4
Cards accepted: Amex, Diners, Mastercard, Visa
🛇🦽🕭🕿📪🖵🐾🦮🍴🅂🏥📺🍴
🔲💼🍽️36🛥️🚐🆂🅿️🔲

Please check prices and other details at the time of booking.

Chatsworth Hotel ᴀ

🛏🛏🛏🛏 COMMENDED

Steyne, Worthing BN11 3DU
☎ (01903) 236103
Fax (01903) 823726

Situated in the town centre overlooking gardens and sea. Modernised Georgian terrace. Lift, bars, games room. Secure ground-level NCP parking opposite the hotel.

Bedrooms: 30 single, 24 double, 52 twin, 1 triple
Bathrooms: 107 en-suite

Bed & breakfast per night:

	£min	£max
Single	29.50	66.00
Double	59.00	90.00

Half board per person:

	£min	£max
Daily	39.50	60.95
Weekly	276.50	315.00

Lunch available
Evening meal 1830 (last orders 2030)
Cards accepted: Amex, Diners, Mastercard, Visa, Switch/Delta

🛋📞💻🖥👤🍴⑤🌙🅜◉⚓📺♨
🛏🍴150🏮 ᴼᴬᴾ 🚭 SP 🎹 Ⓣ ◎

Delmar Hotel ᴀ

🛏🛏🛏 COMMENDED

1-2 New Parade, Worthing
BN11 2BQ
☎ (01903) 211834 & 0589 890393
Fax (01903) 219052

Family-run licensed hotel, extensively refurbished, overlooking sea and gardens. In quiet situation, convenient for all local amenities and town.

Bedrooms: 5 single, 2 double, 1 twin, 4 triple
Bathrooms: 12 en-suite

Bed & breakfast per night:

	£min	£max
Single	28.50	29.50
Double	55.00	75.00

Half board per person:

	£min	£max
Daily	45.00	55.00
Weekly	383.50	346.50

Evening meal 1830 (last orders 1630)
Parking for 5
Cards accepted: Amex, Diners, Mastercard, Visa, Switch/Delta

🛋🐾🅟⚓📞💻🖥👤🍴🌙🅜📺🅘
🛏♨ SP Ⓣ

For ideas on places to visit refer to the introduction at the beginning of this section.

Tudor Guest House ᴀ

🛏 COMMENDED

5 Windsor Road, Worthing
BN11 2LU
☎ (01903) 210265 & 202042

Ideally situated! 1 minute from seafront, restaurants, pubs, entertainment, etc. Very friendly atmosphere, top class service. Comfortable bedrooms with free trays tea/coffee/chocolate. 3 satellite channels in all rooms. Parking on premises. En-suite rooms available. English or continental breakfast.

Bedrooms: 5 single, 3 double, 1 twin
Bathrooms: 3 en-suite, 1 public, 1 private shower

Bed & breakfast per night:

	£min	£max
Single	15.00	17.50
Double	30.00	49.00

Parking for 5

🐾1🅟🅐📞💻🖥👤⑤🌙🅜📺🅘🛏
♨ 🚐 ᴼᴬᴾ SP

Woodlands Guest House ᴀ

🛏 COMMENDED

20-22 Warwick Gardens, Worthing
BN11 1PF
☎ (01903) 233557 & 231957
Fax (01903) 233557

Family-run guesthouse providing home-cooked food and friendly service. All bedrooms are well-appointed and comfortably furnished.

Bedrooms: 3 single, 3 double, 3 twin, 2 triple
Bathrooms: 6 en-suite, 2 public

Bed & breakfast per night:

	£min	£max
Single	18.00	25.00
Double	34.00	48.00

Half board per person:

	£min	£max
Daily	26.00	33.00
Weekly	165.00	220.00

Evening meal 1800 (last orders 1700)
Parking for 8
Cards accepted: Mastercard, Visa, Switch/Delta

🐾🅟🖥👤🍴⑤🌙🅜📺🅘🛏♨🚐
ᴼᴬᴾ 🚭 SP

Ashdown Park Hotel ᴀ

🛏🛏🛏🛏🛏 DE LUXE

Wych Cross, Forest Row RH18 5JR
☎ (01342) 824988
Fax (01342) 826206

Built in the 1860s, sympathetically restored for luxury in the 1990s. Relaxation is guaranteed, with 187 acres of landscaped grounds, lake and parkland, a superb restaurant and wine cellar, large elegant rooms and suites and impressive leisure facilities. Just off the A22. Half board prices based on minimum 2-night stay.

Bedrooms: 6 single, 42 double, 47 twin
Suites available
Bathrooms: 95 en-suite

Bed & breakfast per night:

	£min	£max
Single	105.00	260.00
Double	130.00	285.00

Half board per person:

	£min	£max
Daily	84.50	162.00

Lunch available
Evening meal 1930 (last orders 2200)
Parking for 120
Cards accepted: Amex, Diners, Mastercard, Visa, Switch/Delta

🛋🐾🅟📞💻🖥👤🍴⑤◉🌙🅜🛏
🛏180🏊🍴🏮🎣🎾⛳👟🚶♨🐕🐾🚭
SP 🎹 Ⓣ

TOWN INDEX

This can be found at the back of the guide. If you know where you want to stay, the index will give you the page number listing all accommodation in your chosen town, city or village.

USE YOUR *i*'s

There are more than 550 Tourist Information Centres throughout England offering friendly help with accommodation and holiday ideas as well as suggestions of places to visit and things to do. There may well be a centre in your home town which can help you before you set out.

You'll find addresses in the local Phone Book or simply call Freepages 0800 192 192.

COUNTRY CODE

Always follow the Country Code 🌳 Enjoy the countryside and respect its life and work 🌳 Guard against all risk of fire 🌳 Fasten all gates 🌳 Keep your dogs under close control 🌳 Keep to public paths across farmland 🌳 Use gates and stiles to cross fences, hedges and walls 🌳 Leave livestock, crops and machinery alone 🌳 Take your litter home 🌳 Help to keep all water clean 🌳 Protect wildlife, plants and trees 🌳 Take special care on country roads 🌳 Make no unnecessary noise

*i*NFORMATION
PAGES

National Grading and Classification Scheme

Sure Signs

The Tourist Boards in Britain operate a National Quality Grading and Classification Scheme for all types of accommodation. The purpose of the scheme is to identify and promote those establishments that the public can use with confidence. The system of facility classification and quality grading also acknowledges those that provide a wider range of facilities and services and higher quality standards. Over 30,000 places to stay are inspected under the scheme and offer the reassurance of a national grading and classification.

For 'serviced' accommodation (which includes hotels, motels, guesthouses, inns, B&Bs and farmhouses) there are six classification bands, starting with LISTED and then from ONE to FIVE CROWN. For the new generation of 'lodges', offering budget accommodation along major roads and motorways, there are three classification bands, from ONE to THREE MOON.

Quite simply, the more Crowns or Moons, the wider the range of facilities and services offered.

Quality Grading

To help you find accommodation that offers even higher standards than those required for a Crown or Moon rating, there are four levels of quality grading, using the terms DE LUXE, HIGHLY COMMENDED, COMMENDED

and APPROVED. Wherever you see a national grading and classification sign, you can be sure that a Tourist Board inspector has been there before you, checking the place on your behalf - and will be there again, because every place with a national rating is inspected annually.

Establishments are subject to a detailed inspection that assesses the quality standard of the facilities and services provided. The initial inspection invariably involves the Tourist Board inspector staying overnight, as a normal guest, until the bill is paid the following morning. This quality assessment includes such aspects as warmth of welcome and efficiency of service, as well as the standard of furnishing, fittings and decor. The standard of meals and their presentation is also taken into account. Everything that impinges on the experience of a guest is included in the assessment. Tourist Board inspectors receive careful training to enable them to apply the quality standards consistently and fairly. Only those facilities and services provided are assessed, and due consideration is given to the style and nature of the establishment. B&Bs, farmhouses and guesthouses are not expected to operate in the style of large city centre hotels, and vice versa. This means that all types of establishment, whatever their Crown or Moon classification, can achieve a high quality grade if the facilities and services they provide, however

limited in range, are to a high quality standard.

The quality grade that is awarded to an establishment is a reflection of the overall standard, taking everything into account. It is a balanced view of what is provided and, as such, cannot acknowledge individual areas of excellence. Quality grades are not intended to indicate value for money. A high quality product can be over-priced; a product of modest quality, if offered at a low price, can represent good value. The information provided by the combination of the classification and quality grade will enable you to determine for yourself what represents good value for money.

All Inspected

All establishments listed in this guide have been inspected or are awaiting inspection under the National Grading and Classification Scheme. The ratings that appear in the accommodation entries were correct at the time of going to press but are subject to change. If no rating appears in that entry it means that the inspection had not been carried out by the time of going to press. An information leaflet giving full details of the National Grading and Classification Scheme - which also covers self-catering holiday homes and caravan, chalet and camping parks - is available from any Tourist Information Centre.

GENERAL ADVICE AND INFORMATION

Making a Booking

When enquiring about accommodation, make sure you check prices and other important details. You will also need to state your requirements, clearly and precisely - for example:

- **Arrival and departure dates**, with acceptable alternatives if appropriate.
- **The type of accommodation** you need; for example, room with twin beds, private bathroom.
- **The terms** you want; for example, room only, bed and breakfast, half board, full board.
- **If you have children** with you; their ages, whether you want them to share your room or be next door, any other special requirements, such as a cot.
- **Particular requirements** you may have, such as a special diet.

Booking by letter

Misunderstandings can easily happen over the telephone, so we strongly advise you to confirm your booking in writing if there is time.

If you decide to enquire in writing in the first place, you might find it helpful to use the Accommodation Coupons on pages 539-546, which can be cut out and posted to the places of your choice.

Remember to include your name and address, and a stamped self-addressed envelope, or an international reply coupon if you are writing from outside Britain.

Please note that the English Tourist Board does not make reservations - you should write direct to the accommodation.

Deposits

If you make your reservation weeks or months in advance, you will probably be asked for a deposit. The amount will vary according to the time of year, the number of people in your party and how long you plan to stay. The deposit will then be deducted from the final bill when you leave.

Payment on Arrival

Some establishments, especially large hotels in big towns, ask you to pay for your room on arrival if you have not booked it in advance. This is especially likely to happen if you arrive late and have little or no luggage.

If you are asked to pay on arrival, it is a good idea to see your room first, to make sure it meets your requirements.

Cancellations

Legal contract

When you accept accommodation that is offered to you, by telephone or in writing, you enter a legally binding contract with the proprietor.

This means that if you cancel your booking, fail to take up the accommodation or leave early, the proprietor may be entitled to compensation if he cannot re-let for all or a good part of the booked period. You will probably forfeit any deposit you have paid, and may well be asked for an additional payment.

The proprietor cannot make a claim until after the booked period, however, and during that time every effort should be made by the proprietor to re-let the accommodation.

If there is a dispute it is sensible for both sides to seek legal advice on the matter.

If you do have to change your travel plans, it is in your own interests to let the proprietors know in writing as soon as possible, to give them a chance to re-let your accommodation.

And remember, if you book by telephone and are asked for your credit card number, you should check whether the proprietor intends charging your credit card account should you later cancel your reservation. A proprietor should not be able to charge your credit card account with a cancellation unless he or she has made this clear at the time of your booking and you have agreed. However, to avoid later disputes, we suggest you check with the proprietor whether he or she intends to charge you credit card account if you cancel.

Insurance

A travel or holiday insurance policy will safeguard you if you have to cancel or change your holiday plans. You can arrange a policy quite cheaply through your insurance company or travel agent. Some hotels also offer their own insurance schemes.

Arriving Late

If you know you will be arriving late in the evening, it is a good idea to say so when you book. If you are delayed on your way, a telephone call to say that you will be late will help prevent any problems when you arrive.

Service Charges and Tipping

These days many places levy service charges automatically. If they do, they must clearly say so in their offer of accommodation, at the time of booking. Then the service charge becomes part of the legal contract when you accept the offer of accommodation.

If a service charge is levied automatically, there is no need to tip the staff, unless they provide some exceptional service. The usual tip for meals is ten per cent of the total bill.

Telephone Charges

Hotels can set their own charges for telephone calls made through their switchboard or from direct-dial telephones in bedrooms. These charges are often much higher than telephone companies' standard charges (to defray the cost of providing the service).

Comparing costs

It is a condition of the National Grading and Classification Scheme, that a hotel's unit charges are on display, by the telephones or with the room information. But in practice it is not always easy to compare these charges with standard telephone rates. Before using a hotel telephone for long-distance calls, you may decide to ask how the charges compare.

Security of Valuables

You can deposit your valuables with the proprietor or manager during your stay, and we recommend you do this as a sensible precaution. Make sure you obtain a receipt for them.

Some places do not accept articles for safe custody, and in that case it is wisest to keep your valuables with you.

Disclaimer

Some proprietors put up a notice which disclaims liability for property brought on to their premises by a guest. In fact, they can only restrict their liability to a minimum laid down by law (The Hotel Proprietors Act 1956).

Under that Act, a proprietor is liable for the value of the loss or damage to any property (except a motor car or its contents) of a guest who has engaged overnight accommodation, but if the proprietor has the notice on display as prescribed under that Act, liability is limited to £50 for one article and a total of £100 for any one guest. The notice must be prominently displayed in the reception area or main entrance. These limits do not

apply to valuables you have deposited with the proprietor for safe-keeping, or to property lost through the default, neglect of wilful act of the proprietor or his staff.

Code of Conduct

All the places featured in this guide have agreed to observe the following Codes of Conduct:

1 To ensure high standards of courtesy and cleanliness, catering and service appropriate to the type of establishment.

2 To describe fairly to all visitors and prospective visitors the amenities, facilities and services provided by the establishment, whether by advertisement, brochure, word of mouth or any other means. To allow visitors to see accommodation, if requested, before booking.

3 To make clear to visitors exactly what is included in all prices quoted for accommodation, meals and refreshments, including service charges, taxes and other surcharges. Details of charges, if any, for heating or additional service of facilities should also be made clear.

4 To adhere to, and not to exceed, prices current at time of occupation for accommodation or other services.

5 To advise visitors at the time of booking, and subsequently of any change, if the accommodation offered is in an unconnected annexe, or similar, or by boarding out; and to indicate the location of such accommodation and any difference in comfort or amenities from accommodation in the main establishment.

6 To give each visitor, on request, details of payments due and a

receipt if required.

7 To deal promptly and courteously with all enquiries, requests, reservations, correspondence and complaints from visitors.

8 To allow an English Tourist Board representative reasonable access to the establishment, on request, to confirm that the Code of Conduct is being observed.

Comments and Complaints

Hotels and the law

Places that offer accommodation have legal and statutory responsibilities to their customers, such as providing information about prices, providing adequate fire precautions and safeguarding valuables. Like other businesses, they must also abide by the Trades Description Acts 1968 and 1972 when they describe their accommodation and facilities.

All the places featured in this guide have declared that they do fulfil all applicable statutory obligations.

Information

The proprietors themselves supply the descriptions of their establishments and other information for the listings, and they pay to have their entries included in the guide. All the places featured in the guide have also been inspected or have applied for inspection under the National Grading and Classification Scheme.

The English Tourist Board cannot guarantee accuracy of information in this guide, and accepts no responsibility for any error or misrepresentation. All liability for loss, disappointment, negligence or other damage caused by reliance on the information contained in this guide, or in the event of bankruptcy or liquidation or cessation of trade of any company, individual or firm mentioned, is hereby excluded.

We strongly recommend that you carefully check prices and other details when you book your accommodation.

Problems

Of course, we hope you will not have cause for complaint, but problems do occur from time to time.

If you are dissatisfied with anything, make your complaint to the management immediately. Then the management can take action at once to investigate the matter and put things right. The longer you leave a complaint, the harder it is to deal with it effectively.

In certain circumstances, the English Tourist Board may look into complaints. However, the Board has no statutory control over establishments or their methods of operating. The Board cannot become involved in legal or contractual matters.

Feedback Questionnaire

We find it very helpful to receive your comments about the places featured in *Where to Stay* and your suggestions on how to improve the guide. Please send us your views using the Customer Feedback Questionnaire on pages 559-560 - we would like to hear from you.

Return it to:
Department AS,
English Tourist Board,
Thames Tower,
Black's Road,
Hammersmith,
London W6 9EL.

ENQUIRY COUPONS

To help you obtain further information
about advertisers and accommodation featured in
this guide you will find enquiry coupons at the back.
Send these directly to the establishments
in which you are interested.
Remember to complete both sides of the coupon.

 *a BOUT THE GUIDE*
ENTRIES

Locations

Places to stay are listed under the town, city or village where they are located. If a place is out in the countryside, you will find it listed under the nearest village or town.

Town names are listed alphabetically within each regional section of the guide, along with the name of the county they fall under, and their map reference.

Map references

These refer to the colour location maps at the back of the guide. The first figure shown is the map number, the following letter and figure indicate the grid reference on the map.

Some entries were included just before the guide went to press, so they do not appear on the maps.

Addresses

County names, which appear in the town headings, are not repeated in the entries. When you are writing, you should of course make sure you use the full address and postcode.

Telephone numbers

Telephone numbers are listed below the accommodation address for each entry. Area codes are shown in brackets, and the exchange name is also included (before the code) if it differs from that of the town under which a place is listed.

Price

The prices shown in *Where to Stay 1998* are only a general guide; they were supplied to us by proprietors in summer 1997. Remember, changes may occur after the guide goes to press, so we strongly advise you to check prices when you book your accommodation.

Prices are shown in pounds sterling and include VAT where applicable. Some places also include a service charge in their standard tariff so check this when you book.

Standardised method

There are many different ways of quoting prices for accommodation. We use a standardised method in the guide to allow you to compare prices. For example when we show:

Bed and breakfast, the prices shown are for overnight accommodation with breakfast, for single and double rooms. **The double-room price** is for two people. If a double room is occupied by one person there is sometimes a reduction in price.

Halfboard, the prices shown are for room, breakfast and evening meal, per person per day and per person per week.

Some places provide only a continental breakfast in the set price, and you may have to pay extra if you want a full English breakfast.

Checking prices

According to the law, hotels with at least four bedrooms or eight beds must display their overnight accommodation charges in the reception area or entrance. In your own interests, do make sure you check prices and what they include.

Children's rates

You will find that many places charge a reduced rate for children especially if they share a room with their parents. Some places charge the full rate, however, when a child occupies a room which might otherwise have been let to an adult.

The upper age limit for reductions for children varies from one hotel to another, so check this when you book.

Seasonal packages

Prices often vary through the year, and may be significantly lower outside peak holiday weeks. Many places offer special package rates - fully inclusive weekend breaks, for example - in the autumn, winter and spring.

You can get details of bargain packages from the establishment themselves, the Regional Tourist Boards or your local Tourist Information Centre (TIC). Your local travel agent may also have information, and can help you make bookings.

Bathrooms

Each accommodation entry shows you the number of en-suite and private bathrooms available, the number of private showers and the number of public bathrooms.

'En-suite bathroom' means the bath or shower and WC are contained behind the main door of the bedroom. 'Private bathroom' means a bath or shower and WC solely for the occupants of one bedroom, on the same floor, reasonably close and with a key provided. 'Private shower' means a shower en-suite with the bedroom but no WC.

Public bathrooms normally have a bath, sometimes with a shower attachment. If the availability of a bath is important to you, remember to check when you book.

Meals

If an establishment serves evening meals, you will find the starting time and the last order times shown in the listing; some smaller places may ask you at breakfast or at midday whether you want an evening meal.

The prices shown in each entry are for bed and breakfast or half board, but many places also offer lunch, as you will see indicated on the listing.

Opening Period

All places are open all year, except where a specific opening period is indicated.

Symbols

The at-a-glance symbols included at the end of each entry show many of the services and facilities available at each place.
You will find the key to these symbols on the back cover flap. Open out the flap and you can check the meanings of the symbols as you go.

Alcoholic Drinks

All the places listed in the guide are licensed to serve alcohol, unless the symbol ⓤ appears. The license may be restricted - to diners only, for example - so you may want to check this when you book.

Smoking

Many places provide non-smoking areas - from no-smoking bedrooms and lounges to no-smoking sections of the restaurant. Some places prefer not to accommodate smokers, and in such cases the listing information makes this clear.

Pets

Many places accept guests with pets, but we do advise you to check this when you book, and ask about any extra charges or any rules about exactly where your pet is allowed.

Some establishments do not accept dogs at all, and these places are marked with the symbol 🐕.

Visitors from overseas must not bring pets of any kind into Britain, unless they are prepared for the animals to go into lengthy quarantine. Because of the continuing threat of rabies, the penalties for ignoring these regulations are extremely severe.

Credit and Charge Cards

The credit and charge cards accepted by a place are listed immediately above the line of symbols at the end of each entry. The abbreviations used are:
Amex - American Express
Diners - Diners
Mastercard - Mastercard/ Eurocard
Visa - Visa/Barclaycard
Switch/Delta - Direct debit cards

If you do plan to pay by card, check that the establishment will take your card before you book.

Some proprietors will charge you a higher rate if you pay by credit card rather than cash or cheque. The difference is to cover the percentage paid by the proprietor to the credit card company.

If you are planning to pay by credit card, you may want to ask whether it would, in fact, be cheaper to pay by cheque or cash. When you book by telephone, you may be asked for your credit card number as 'confirmation'. But remember, the proprietor may then charge your credit card account if you cancel your booking. See under Cancellations on page 525.

Conferences and Groups

Places which cater for conferences and meetings are marked with the symbol ♟ (the number that follows the symbol shows the capacity). Rates are often negotiable, depending on the time of year, numbers of people involved and any special requirements you may have.

CENTRAL RESERVATIONS
OFFICES

Some of the accommodation establishments in this guide are members of hotel groups or consortia which maintain a central reservations office. These entries are identified with the symbol (CR), and the name of the group or consortium, appearing after the establishment's address and telephone number. Bookings or enquiries can be made direct to the establishment or to the central reservations office.

Best Western
Best Western Hotels,
Vine House, 143 London Road,
Kingston upon Thames,
Surrey KT2 6NA
Tel: (0181) 541 0033
Fax: (0181) 547 3941

Brend Hotels
Brend Hotels Travel Centre,
(Central Reservations &
Information), 1 Park Villas,
Taw Vale, Barnstaple,
Devon EX32 8NJ
Tel: (01271) 344496
Fax: (01271) 378558

Consort
Consort Hotels Group,
Consort House,
Amy Johnson Way,
Clifton Moor,
York YO3 4XT
Reservations: (01904) 695495
Information: (01904) 695400
Fax: (01904) 695401

Countryside Inns and Hotels
Consort House,
Amy Johnson Way,
Clifton Moor,
York YO3 4XT
Tel: 0345 998800
(calls charged at local rate)
Fax: (01904) 695401

Distinctly Different
Masons Lane,
Bradford on Avon,
Wiltshire BA15 1QN
Tel: (01225) 866842
Fax: (01225) 866648

Forte
Forte Hotels,
Oak Court,
Dudley Road,
Brierley Hill,
West Midlands DY5 1LG
Tel: 0345 40 40 40

Grand Heritage Hotels
First Floor,
Warwick House,
Warwick Road,
London W14 8PU
Tel: (0171) 244 6699
Fax: (0171) 244 7799
0800 28 28 11 (toll free)

The Independents
The Independents Hotel
Consortium,
Beambridge,
Sampford,
Arundel,
Wellington,
Somerset TA21 0HB
Information line: (01823) 672100
Bookings: 0800 885544
Fax: (01823) 673100

Inter Europe Hotels (IEH)
(Reservations by phone)
c/o HPS Hotels,
Archgate,
823-825 High Road, Finchley,
London N12 8UB
Reservations: 0800 136 234
Admin: (0181) 446 1306
Internet:
http://www.hpshotels.demon.co.uk
http://www.iehotels.com

Jarvis
Jarvis Reservations Centre,
PO Box 671,
London SW7 5JQ
Tel: 0345 303040
(calls charged at local rate)
Fax: (0171) 589 8193

Logis of Great Britain
Logis of Great Britain,
20 Church Road, Horspath,
Oxford OX9 1RU
Tel: (01865) 875888
Fax: (01865) 875777

Lyric
Lyric Hotels,
Bredbury Business Park,
Bredbury Parkway,
Stockport SK6 2TN
Tel: 0345 626633
(calls charged at local rate)
Fax: (0161) 406 8784

McDonald Hotels
Whiteside House, Bathgate,
West Lothian EH48 2RX
Tel: (01506) 815215

Minotel
Minotel, 37 Springfield Road,
Blackpool FY1 1PZ
Tel: (01253) 292000
Fax: (01253) 291191
E-mail: admin@minotel.com

Novotel
Central Reservation Office,
112-114 Bath Road, Hayes,
Middlesex UB3 5AL
Tel: (0181) 283 4500
Fax: (0181) 283 4650

Principal
Principal Hotels Group,
Principal House,
11 Ripon Road, Harrogate,
North Yorkshire HG1 2JA
Tel: 0800 454454 (calls are free)
Fax: (01423) 500086

Moat House Hotels
QUEENS-*LINE* UK Reservations,
Queens Court, 9-17 Eastern
Road, Romford, Essex RM1 3NG
Tel: (01708) 766677
Fax: (01708) 761033
E-mail: sales@hotelsqmh.com.uk

Regal Hotels Group
Regal Reservations,
5th Floor,
Elgar House,
Shrub Hill Road,
Worcester WR4 9EE
Tel: 0345 33 44 00
Fax: (01905) 730 311

RoadChef Lodges
Freephone: 0800 834719
Fax: (01823) 338131

**Stagecoach Hotels and
Inns plc**
Hotel Management
International Ltd,
86 East Lane, Wembley,
Middlesex HA0 3NJ
Tel: (0181) 908 3348
Fax: (0181) 904 0094

Swallow Hotels
Central Reservation Office,
PO Box 30,
Washington,
Tyne & Wear NE37 1QS
Tel: 0645 404 404 (local call)
Fax: (0191) 415 1777
E-mail: info@swallowhotels.com

Thames Valley
Thames Valley Hotels,
Northway House,
1379 High Road,
London N20 9LP
Tel: (0181) 446 6633

**Thistle and Mount Charlotte
Hotels**
2 The Calls,
Leeds LS2 7JU
Tel: 0800 18 17 16
Fax: (0113) 246 1357

Utell International
Quadrant House,
The Quadrant, Sutton,
Surrey SM2 5AR
Tel: 0990 300200
Northern Ireland: 0800 660066

Wayfarer Inns
Wayfarer Inns,
16 Little London,
Chichester,
West Sussex PO19 1PA
Tel: (01243) 528733
Fax: (01243) 531331

AT-A-GLANCE SYMBOLS

Symbols at the end of each accommodation entry
give useful information about services
and facilities. A key to symbols can be found
inside the back cover flap.

Keep this open for easy reference.

*e*VENTS FOR 1998

This is a selection of the many cultural, sporting and other events that will be taking place throughout England during 1998. Dates marked with an asterisk* were provisional at the time of going to press.

January 1998

1-6 January
(began 4 December 1997)
Christmas Tree
Trafalgar Square, London WC2
Contact: (0171) 211 6393

6 January
Old Custom: Haxey Hood Game
The Village, Haxey,
North Lincolnshire
Contact: (01427) 752845

9-18 January
44th London International Boat Show
Earls Court Exhibition Centre,
Warwick Road, London SW5
Contact: (01784) 473377

23-25 January*
Weekend Book Festival
Dove Cottage and Wordsworth Museum, Town End, Grasmere, Cumbria
Contact: (015394) 35544

February 1998

1 February
Chinese New Year Celebrations 1998: Year Of The Tiger
Centered on Gerrard Street and Leicester Square, London WC2
Contact: (0171) 734 5161

8-13 February
The Wordsworth Winter School
Dove Cottage and Wordsworth Museum, Town End, Grasmere, Cumbria
Contact: (015394) 35544

11-15 February
Tomorrow's World Exhibition
National Exhibition Centre,
Birmingham, West Midlands
Contact: (0181) 948 1666

14-22 February
National Boat, Caravan and Leisure Show
National Exhibition Centre,
Birmingham, West Midlands
Contact: (0121) 7804141

March 1998

5-8 March
Crufts Dog Show
National Exhibition Centre,
Birmingham, West Midlands
Contact: (0171) 493 7838

14-15 March
Ambleside Daffodil and Spring Flower Show
The Old Junior School,
Compston Road, Ambleside,
Cumbria
Contact: (015394) 32252

17-19 March*
Cheltenham Gold Cup National Hunt Racing Festival
Cheltenham Racecourse,
Prestbury Park, Cheltenham,
Gloucestershire
Contact: (01242) 513014

19 March-13 April
Ideal Home Exhibition
Earls Court Exhibition Centre,
Warwick Road, London SW5
Contact: (0121) 767 4114

28 March
Oxford and Cambridge Boat Race
River Thames, London

April 1998

2-4 April
Grand National Meeting
Aintree Racecourse, Ormskirk Road, Aintree, Merseyside
Contact: (0151) 523 2600

10 April
Grand Steam Rally
Wetheriggs Country Pottery, Clifton Dykes, Penrith, Cumbria
Contact: (01768) 892733

11-12 April
Gateshead Spring Flower Show
Gateshead Central Nurseries, Whickham Highway, Lobley Hill, Gateshead, Tyne and Wear
Contact: (0191) 477 1011

13 April
Old Custom: World Coal Carrying Championship
Start: Royal Oak Public House, Owl Lane, Ossett, West Yorkshire

17-19 April
Morpeth Northumbrian Gathering
Morpeth Town Hall, Town Hall, Market Place, Morpeth, Northumberland
Contact: (01670) 519466

26 April
London Marathon 1998
Greenwich Park, London SE10
Contact: (0171) 620 4117

May 1998

1-31 May
Daventry and District Arts Festival 98
Various venues, Daventry, Northamptonshire
Contact: (01327) 302418

2-3 May
Wallingford Regatta
River Thames Wallingford, Oxfordshire
Contact: (01491) 836517

2-4 May*
Rochester Sweeps Festival
Various venues, Rochester, Kent
Contact: (01634) 843666

2-4 May
Spalding Flower Festival and Springfields Country Fair
Springfields Show Gardens, Camelgate, Spalding, Lincolnshire
Contact: (01775) 724843

2-24 May
Brighton International Festival
Various venues, Brighton, East Sussex
Contact: (01273) 709709

7-10 May
The Badminton Horse Trials
Badminton House, Badminton, South Gloucestershire
Contact: (01454) 218375

8-17 May*
Lewis Carroll Centenary Celebration
Various venues, Guildford, Surrey
Contact: (01483) 444333

9-10 May
Fighter Meet 98
North Weald Airfield, Epping, Essex
Contact: (0181) 866 9993

9-23 May
International Newbury Spring Festival
Various venues, Newbury, Berkshire
Contact: (01635) 522733

13-17 May
Royal Windsor Horse Show
Windsor Home Park, Datchet Road, Windsor, Berkshire
Contact: (0171) 341 9341

15-31 May
Bath International Music Festival
Various venues in and around Bath and North East Somerset
Contact: (01225) 463362

16 May
Football: F.A. Challenge Cup Final
Wembley Stadium, London
Contact: (0171) 402 7151

19-22 May
Chelsea Flower Show
Royal Hospital Chelsea, Royal Hospital Road, London SW3

22 May-6 June
English Riviera Dance Festival
Victoria Hotel Ballroom and Town Hall, Torquay, Devon
Contact: (01895) 632143

23-24 May
Air Fete 98
RAF Mildenhall, Suffolk

25 May
Northumberland County Show
Tynedale Park, Corbridge,
Northumberland
Contact: (01434) 344443

25 May
Surrey County Show
Stoke Park, Guildford, Surrey
Contact: (01483) 414651

27-28 May
Suffolk Show
Suffolk Showground, Bucklesham
Road, Ipswich, Suffolk
Contact: (01473) 726847

June 1998

1 June-29 August
Stamford Shakespeare Company: 1998 Open Air Season
Rutland Open Air Theatre,
Tolethorpe Hall, Little
Casterton, Leicestershire
Contact: (01780) 756133

12-28 June
51st Aldeburgh Foundation of Music and the Arts
Snape Maltings Concert Hall,
Snape, Suffolk
Contact: (01728) 453543

13 June
Trooping the Colour - The Queen's Birthday Parade
Horse Guards Parade,
London SW1
Contact: (0171) 414 2479

13-14 June
Northamptonshire Motorshow
Wicksteed Park, Kettering,
Northamptonshire
Contact: (01536) 81111

13-20 June
International Ladies Tennis Tournament
Devonshire Park, College Road,
Eastbourne, East Sussex
Contact: (01323) 412000

19-27 June
Newcastle Hoppings
Town Moor, Grandstand Road,
Newcastle upon Tyne,
Tyne and Wear
Contact: (0191) 454 6239

20-27 June
Broadstairs Dickens Festival
Various venues, Broadstairs,
Kent
Contact: (01843) 861045

20 June-5 July
Ludlow Festival
Ludlow Castle (ruin), Castle
Square, Ludlow, Shropshire
Contact: (01584) 872150

22 June-5 July
Wimbledon Lawn Tennis Championships
All England Lawn Tennis and
Croquet Club, Church Road,
London SW19
Contact: (0181) 946 2244

23-24 June
Cheshire Show
The Showground, Tabley,
Cheshire
Contact: (01829) 760020

27-28 June
Meols Hall Annual Vintage Vehicle Rally
Meols Hall, Churchtown,
Southport, Merseyside
Contact: (01704) 28326

28 June-13 July*
Chichester Festivities
Various venues, Chichester,
West Sussex
Contact: (01243) 780192

July 1998

1-4 July
Wisbech Rose Fair
Saint Peters Parish Church,
Church Terrace, Wisbech,
Cambridgeshire
Contact: (01945) 583086

1-5 July
Henley Royal Regatta
Henley Reach, Henley-on-
Thames, Oxfordshire
Contact: (01491) 572153/4

1-31 July*
Hull International Festival
Various venues, Hull, Kingston
upon Hull
Contact: (01482) 223559

4-5 July*
International Kite Festival
Northern Area Playing Fields,
District 12, Washington,
Tyne and Wear
Contact: (0191) 514 1235

4-5 July*
Preston Maritime Festival
Preston Dock Marina, Riversway,
Ashton-on-Ribble, Lancashire
Contact: (01772) 558111

4-5 July
Southampton Balloon and Flower Festival
Southampton Common,
The Avenue, Southampton,
Hampshire
Contact: (01703) 832755

8-11 July
Henley Festival
Henley-on-Thames, Oxfordshire
Contact: (01491) 411353

9-12 July
British Grand Prix 98
Silverstone, Northamptonshire
Contact: (01327) 857273

10-26 July
Buxton Festival
Various venues, Buxton,
Derbyshire
Contact: (01298) 72190

12 July
Whalley Abbey Open Day
Whalley Abbey, Whalley,
Lancashire
Contact: (01254) 822268

13 July
**Yeovilton International
Air Day**
RNAS Yeovilton, Ilchester,
Somerset
Contact: (01935) 456752

14-16 July
Great Yorkshire Show
Great Yorkshire Showground,
Wetherby Road, Harrogate,
North Yorkshire
Contact: (01423) 561536

16-18 July*
**Reading Real Ale and Jazz
Festival**
Christchurch Meadow, George
Street, Caversham, Reading,
Berkshire
Contact: (0118) 956 6226

17-19 July
Weeting Steam Engine Rally
Fengate Farm, Weeting, Brandon,
Suffolk
Contact: (01842) 810317

18 July
Cumberland County Show
Rickerby Park, Carlisle, Cumbria
Contact: (01228) 560364

19 July
Cutty Sark Tall Ships' Race
The Harbour, Falmouth,
Cornwall
Contact: (01872) 223527

21 July-2 August
Royal Tournament
Earls Court Exhibition Centre,
Warwick Road, London SW5
Contact: (0171) 370 8202

23 July
**Horse Racing: Glorious
Goodwood**
Goodwood Racecourse,
Goodwood, West Sussex
Contact: (01243) 779922

25-26 July
Family Fun Weekend
The Lawn, Union Road, Lincoln,
Lincolnshire
Contact: (01522) 511411

25-26 July
**Gateshead Summer Flower
Show**
Gateshead Central Nurseries,
Whickham Highway, Gateshead,
Tyne and Wear
Contact: (0191) 477 1011

25-26 July
**'Heart Link' Steam and
Vintage Festival**
Hillside Farm, Rempstone Road,
Wymeswold, Leicestershire
Contact: (01509) 880803

26-28 July
Royal Lancashire Show 98
Astley Hall, Astley Park, Chorley,
Lancashire
Contact: (01254) 813769

28-30 July
**New Forest and Hampshire
County Show**
New Park, Brockenhurst,
Hampshire
Contact: (01590) 622400

29 July
Sandringham Flower Show
Sandringham Park, Sandringham,
Norfolk
Contact: (01485) 540860

31 July-7 August
**Sidmouth International
Festival of Folk Arts**
Various venues, Sidmouth,
Devon
Contact: (01296) 393293

August 1998

1-2 August
**Wigan Pier Cross Country
Boat and Steam Rally**
Wigan Pier, Greater Manchester
Contact: (01942) 323666

2-3 August
**Woodvale International
Rally**
RAF Woodvale, Southport,
Merseyside
Contact: (01704) 578816

5-6 August
168th Bakewell Show
The Showground, Coombs Road,
Bakewell, Derbyshire
Contact: (01629) 812736

*5-9 August**
**Jazz on the Waterfront -
Hull Jazz Festival**
Various venues, Hull,
Kingston upon Hull
Contact: (01482) 223559

7-9 August
**Ambleside Great Summer
Flower Show and Craft Fair**
Ambleside Rugby Field, Borrans
Road, Ambleside, Cumbria
Contact: (015394) 32252

7-9 August
**Bristol International Balloon
Fiesta**
Ashton Court Estate, Long
Ashton, Bristol
Contact: (0117) 953 5884

7-9 August
**Lowther Horse Driving
Trials and Country Fair**
Lowther Castle, Lowther,
Cumbria
Contact: (01931) 712378

7-9 August
**Portsmouth and Southsea
Show**
Southsea Common, Portsmouth,
Hampshire
Contact: (01705) 824355

13-16 August
**Guild of Sussex Craftsmen in
Action**
Michelham Priory, Upper Dicker,
East Sussex
Contact: (01273) 890088

14-16 August
**Northampton Hot-Air
Balloon Festival**
Northampton Racecourse, St
George's Avenue, Northampton,
Northamptonshire
Contact: (01604) 238791

15-16 August
**Morecambe Festival of
Light and Water**
Morecambe Bay, Morecambe,
Lancashire
Contact: (01254) 582828

16 August
**Lincolnshire Steam and
Vintage Rally**
Lincolnshire Showground,
Grange-de-Lings, Lincoln,
Lincolnshire
Contact: (01507) 605937

20-23 August
Southport Flower Show
Victoria Park, Southport,
Merseyside
Contact: (01704) 547147

*21 August**
**Southwood Pro-Am
Tournament**
Southwood Golf Club, Ively
Road, Farnborough, Hampshire
Contact: (01252) 548700

26 August-1 September
International Beatles Week
Cavern Club, 8-10 Mathew
Street, City Centre, Liverpool,
Merseyside
Contact: (0151) 236 9091

27-29 August
**Port of Dartmouth Royal
Regatta**
Various venues, Dartmouth,
Devon
Contact: (01803) 832435

28-31 August
**34th Towersey Village
Festival**
Towersey Village, Towersey,
Oxfordshire
Contact: (01296) 394411

29-30 August
Southport Airshow
Southport Beach, Merseyside
Contact: (01704) 533333

29-31 August
**The Diamond Fuchsia
Festival**
Harlow Carr Botanical Gardens,
Crag Lane, Harrogate,
North Yorkshire
Contact: (01423) 565418

30-31 August
Notting Hill Carnival
Streets around Ladbroke Grove,
London W11
Contact: (0181) 964 0544

31 August
Silloth Carnival
Silloth, Cumbria
Contact: (016973) 31257

September 1998

2-6 September
Great Dorset Steam Fair
South Down, Tarrant Hinton,
Dorset
Contact: (01258) 860361

3 September
**Buckinghamshire County
Show**
Weedon Park, Weedon,
Aylesbury, Buckinghamshire
Contact: (01296) 83734

4 September-8 November
Blackpool Illuminations
Blackpool Promenade, Blackpool,
Lancashire
Contact: (01253) 25212

5-6 September*
Berwick Military Tattoo
Berwick Barracks, Berwick-upon-
Tweed, Northumberland
Contact: (01289) 307113

5-6 September
Chatsworth Country Fair
Chatsworth House and Garden,
Bakewell, Derbyshire
Contact: (01263) 711736

5-6 September
Kirkby Lonsdale Victorian Fair
Kirkby Lonsdale, Cumbria
Contact: (015242) 71237

8 September
Widecombe Fair
Old Field, Widecombe-in-the-
Moor, Devon

10-13 September*
**International Sea Shanty
Festival**
Hull Marina and various venues,
Hull, Kingston upon Hull
Contact: (01482) 223559

12 September
Romsey Show
Broadlands Park, Romsey,
Hampshire
Contact: (01794) 517521

12-13 September
**Essex Steam Rally and
Country Fair**
Barleylands Farm Museum and
Visitor Centre, Barleylands Road,
Billericay, Essex
Contact: (01268) 532253

12-13 September
**Farnborough International
Airshow**
Farnborough Airfield,

Farnborough, Hampshire
Contact: (0171) 227 100

17 September
Thame Agricultural Show
The Showground, Kingsey Road,
Thame, Oxfordshire
Contact: (01844) 212737

19-26 September
Scarborough Angling Festival
Scarborough
Contact: (01723) 859480

October 1998

9-17 October*
Hull Fair
Walton Street Fairground, Hull,
Kingston-upon-Hull
Contact: (01482) 223559

9-18 October
**Cheltenham Festival of
Literature**
Town Hall, Imperial Square,
Cheltenham, Gloucestershire
Contact: (01242) 22979

11 October
World Conker Championships
The Village Green, Ashton,
Northamptonshire

19-20 October
**Northampton St Crispin
Street Fair**
Main Streets of Northampton,
Northamptonshire
Contact: (01604) 233500

19-23 October*
**Windermere Powerboat
Record Attempts**
Low Wood Watersports Centre,
Low Wood, Windermere,
Cumbria
Contact: (015394) 42595

20 October-1 November
**British International Motor
Show**
National Exhibition Centre,

Birmingham, West Midlands
Contact: (0121) 7804141

31 October*
Grand Firework Spectacular
Leeds Castle, Leeds, Kent
Contact: (01622) 880008

November 1998

5 November
**Bridgwater Guy Fawkes
Carnival**
Town Centre, Bridgwater,
Somerset
Contact: (01278) 429288

14 November
Lord Mayor's Show
City of London, London

19 November
**Biggest Liar in the World
Competition**
Bridge Inn, Wasdale, Santon
Bridge, Cumbria
Contact: (01946) 67575

28-29 November
National Classic Motor Show
National Exhibition Centre,
Birmingham, West Midlands
Contact: (0121) 767 2770

December 1998

4-9 December*
BBC Clothes Show Live
National Exhibition Centre,
Birmingham, West Midlands
Contact: (0121) 780 4133

5-6 December
**Festive Food and Drink
Fayre**
South of England Showground,
Ardingly, West Sussex
Contact: (01444) 892048

31 December
Allendale Baal Festival
Market Square, Allendale,
Northumberland
Contact: (01434) 683763

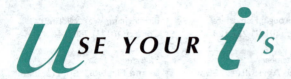 # USE YOUR i's

Tourist Information

When it comes to your next England break, the first stage of your journey could be closer than you think. You've probably got a Tourist Information Centre nearby which is there to serve the local community - as well as visitors.

So make us your first stop. We'll be happy to help you, wherever you're heading.

Many Tourist Information Centres can provide you with maps and guides, helping you plan well in advance. And sometimes it's even possible for us to book your accommodation, too.

A visit to your nearest Tourist Information Centre can pay off in other ways as well. We can point you in the right direction when it comes to finding out about all the special events which are happening in the local region.

In fact, we can give you details of places to visit within easy reach... and perhaps tempt you to plan a day trip or weekend away.

Across the country, there are more than 550 Tourist Information Centres so you're never far away. You'll find the address of your nearest Tourist Information Centre in your local Phone Book or call Freepages on 0800 192 192.

IS IT ACCESSIBLE?

If you are a wheelchair user or someone who has difficulty walking, look for the national 'Accessible' symbol when choosing where to stay.

All the places that display a symbol have been checked by a Tourist Board inspector against standard criteria that reflect the practical needs of wheelchair users.

There are three categories of accessibility:

Category 1 Accessible to all wheelchair users including those travelling independently

Category 2 Accessible to a wheelchair user with assistance

Category 3 Accessible to a wheelchair user able to walk short distances and up at least three steps

Establishments in this guide which have a wheelchair access category are listed on pages 10 and 11.

ACCOMMODATION COUPONS

▶ **Complete this coupon and mail it direct to the establishment in which you are interested. Do not send it to the English Tourist Board.** Remember to enclose a stamped addressed envelope (or international reply coupon).

▶ **Tick as appropriate and complete the reverse side if you are interested in making a booking.**

❑ Please send me a brochure or further information, and details of prices charged.
❑ Please advise me, as soon as possible, if accommodation is available as detailed overleaf.

Name: (BLOCK CAPITALS)

Address:

                                                    Postcode:

Telephone number: Date:

Where to Stay 1998
Hotels & Guesthouses

ENGLISH
TOURIST BOARD

▶ **Complete this coupon and mail it direct to the establishment in which you are interested. Do not send it to the English Tourist Board.** Remember to enclose a stamped addressed envelope (or international reply coupon).

▶ **Tick as appropriate and complete the reverse side if you are interested in making a booking.**

❑ Please send me a brochure or further information, and details of prices charged.
❑ Please advise me, as soon as possible, if accommodation is available as detailed overleaf.

Name: (BLOCK CAPITALS)

Address:

                                                    Postcode:

Telephone number: Date:

Where to Stay 1998
Hotels & Guesthouses

ENGLISH
TOURIST BOARD

ACCOMMODATION COUPONS

► **Complete this side if you are interested in making a booking.**

► **Please read the information on pages 525-529 before confirming any booking.**

Please advise me if accommodation is available as detailed below.

From (date of arrival): _____ To (date of departure): _____

or alternatively from: _____ To: _____

Adults _____ Children _____ (ages _____)
Please give the number of people and ages of children

Accommodation required: _____

_____

Meals required: _____

Other/special requirements: _____

► **Please enclose a stamped addressed envelope (or international reply coupon).**

► **Complete this side if you are interested in making a booking.**

► **Please read the information on pages 525-529 before confirming any booking.**

Please advise me if accommodation is available as detailed below.

From (date of arrival): _____ To (date of departure): _____

or alternatively from: _____ To: _____

Adults _____ Children _____ (ages _____)
Please give the number of people and ages of children

Accommodation required: _____

_____

Meals required: _____

Other/special requirements: _____

► **Please enclose a stamped addressed envelope (or international reply coupon).**

ACCOMMODATION COUPONS

▶ **Complete this coupon and mail it direct to the establishment in which you are interested. Do not send it to the English Tourist Board. Remember to enclose a stamped addressed envelope (or international reply coupon).**

▶ **Tick as appropriate and complete the reverse side if you are interested in making a booking.**

❏ Please send me a brochure or further information, and details of prices charged.
❏ Please advise me, as soon as possible, if accommodation is available as detailed overleaf.

Name: _____ (BLOCK CAPITALS)

Address: _____

_____

_____ Postcode: _____

Telephone number: _____ Date: _____

Where to Stay 1998
Hotels & Guesthouses

ENGLISH
TOURIST BOARD

▶ **Complete this coupon and mail it direct to the establishment in which you are interested. Do not send it to the English Tourist Board. Remember to enclose a stamped addressed envelope (or international reply coupon).**

▶ **Tick as appropriate and complete the reverse side if you are interested in making a booking.**

❏ Please send me a brochure or further information, and details of prices charged.
❏ Please advise me, as soon as possible, if accommodation is available as detailed overleaf.

Name: _____ (BLOCK CAPITALS)

Address: _____

_____

_____ Postcode: _____

Telephone number: _____ Date: _____

Where to Stay 1998
Hotels & Guesthouses

ENGLISH
TOURIST BOARD

ACCOMMODATION COUPONS

► *Complete this side if you are interested in making a booking.*

► *Please read the information on pages 525-529 before confirming any booking.*

Please advise me if accommodation is available as detailed below.

From (date of arrival): _____ To (date of departure): _____

or alternatively from: _____ To: _____

Adults _____ Children _____ (ages _____)
Please give the number of people and ages of children

Accommodation required: _____

_____

Meals required: _____

Other/special requirements: _____

► *Please enclose a stamped addressed envelope (or international reply coupon).*

► *Complete this side if you are interested in making a booking.*

► *Please read the information on pages 525-529 before confirming any booking.*

Please advise me if accommodation is available as detailed below.

From (date of arrival): _____ To (date of departure): _____

or alternatively from: _____ To: _____

Adults _____ Children _____ (ages _____)
Please give the number of people and ages of children

Accommodation required: _____

_____

Meals required: _____

Other/special requirements: _____

► *Please enclose a stamped addressed envelope (or international reply coupon).*

ACCOMMODATION COUPONS

▶ *Complete this coupon and mail it direct to the establishment in which you are interested. Do not send it to the English Tourist Board. Remember to enclose a stamped addressed envelope (or international reply coupon).*

▶ *Tick as appropriate and complete the reverse side if you are interested in making a booking.*

❏ *Please send me a brochure or further information, and details of prices charged.*
❏ *Please advise me, as soon as possible, if accommodation is available as detailed overleaf.*

Name: _____ (BLOCK CAPITALS)

Address: _____

_____

_____

Postcode: _____

Telephone number: _____ Date: _____

Where to Stay 1998
Hotels & Guesthouses

ENGLISH
TOURIST BOARD

▶ *Complete this coupon and mail it direct to the establishment in which you are interested. Do not send it to the English Tourist Board. Remember to enclose a stamped addressed envelope (or international reply coupon).*

▶ *Tick as appropriate and complete the reverse side if you are interested in making a booking.*

❏ *Please send me a brochure or further information, and details of prices charged.*
❏ *Please advise me, as soon as possible, if accommodation is available as detailed overleaf.*

Name: _____ (BLOCK CAPITALS)

Address: _____

_____

_____

Postcode: _____

Telephone number: _____ Date: _____

Where to Stay 1998
Hotels & Guesthouses

ENGLISH
TOURIST BOARD

ACCOMMODATION COUPONS

▶ Complete this side if you are interested in making a booking.

▶ Please read the information on pages 525–529 before confirming any booking.

Please advise me if accommodation is available as detailed below.

From (date of arrival): _____   To (date of departure): _____

or alternatively from: _____   To: _____

Adults _____ Children _____   (ages _____)
Please give the number of people and ages of children

Accommodation required: _____

_____

Meals required: _____

Other/special requirements: _____

▶ Please enclose a stamped addressed envelope (or international reply coupon).

▶ Complete this side if you are interested in making a booking.

▶ Please read the information on pages 525–529 before confirming any booking.

Please advise me if accommodation is available as detailed below.

From (date of arrival): _____   To (date of departure): _____

or alternatively from: _____   To: _____

Adults _____ Children _____   (ages _____)
Please give the number of people and ages of children

Accommodation required: _____

_____

Meals required: _____

Other/special requirements: _____

▶ Please enclose a stamped addressed envelope (or international reply coupon).

ACCOMMODATION COUPONS

▶ *Complete this coupon and mail it direct to the establishment in which you are interested. Do not send it to the English Tourist Board. Remember to enclose a stamped addressed envelope (or international reply coupon).*

▶ *Tick as appropriate and complete the reverse side if you are interested in making a booking.*

❏ *Please send me a brochure or further information, and details of prices charged.*
❏ *Please advise me, as soon as possible, if accommodation is available as detailed overleaf.*

Name: _____ (BLOCK CAPITALS)

Address: _____

_____

_____ Postcode: _____

Telephone number: _____ Date: _____

Where to Stay 1998
Hotels & Guesthouses

▶ *Complete this coupon and mail it direct to the establishment in which you are interested. Do not send it to the English Tourist Board. Remember to enclose a stamped addressed envelope (or international reply coupon).*

▶ *Tick as appropriate and complete the reverse side if you are interested in making a booking.*

❏ *Please send me a brochure or further information, and details of prices charged.*
❏ *Please advise me, as soon as possible, if accommodation is available as detailed overleaf.*

Name: _____ (BLOCK CAPITALS)

Address: _____

_____

_____ Postcode: _____

Telephone number: _____ Date: _____

Where to Stay 1998
Hotels & Guesthouses

ACCOMMODATION COUPONS

▶ *Complete this side if you are interested in making a booking.*

▶ *Please read the information on pages 525-529 before confirming any booking.*

Please advise me if accommodation is available as detailed below.

From (date of arrival): _____   To (date of departure): _____

or alternatively from: _____   To: _____

Adults _____ Children _____ (ages _____)
Please give the number of people and ages of children

Accommodation required: _____

_____

_____

Meals required: _____

Other/special requirements: _____

▶ *Please enclose a stamped addressed envelope (or international reply coupon).*

▶ *Complete this side if you are interested in making a booking.*

▶ *Please read the information on pages 525-529 before confirming any booking.*

Please advise me if accommodation is available as detailed below.

From (date of arrival): _____   To (date of departure): _____

or alternatively from: _____   To: _____

Adults _____ Children _____ (ages _____)
Please give the number of people and ages of children

Accommodation required: _____

_____

_____

Meals required: _____

Other/special requirements: _____

▶ *Please enclose a stamped addressed envelope (or international reply coupon).*

ADVERTISEMENT COUPONS

▶ **Complete this coupon and mail it direct to the advertiser from whom you would like to receive further information. Do not send it to the English Tourist Board.**

To (advertiser's name): _____

Please send me a brochure or further information on the following, as advertised by you in the English Tourist Board's **Where to Stay** 1998 Guide:

_____

_____

My name and address are on the reverse.

▶ **Complete this coupon and mail it direct to the advertiser from whom you would like to receive further information. Do not send it to the English Tourist Board.**

To (advertiser's name): _____

Please send me a brochure or further information on the following, as advertised by you in the English Tourist Board's **Where to Stay** 1998 Guide:

_____

_____

My name and address are on the reverse.

▶ **Complete this coupon and mail it direct to the advertiser from whom you would like to receive further information. Do not send it to the English Tourist Board.**

To (advertiser's name): _____

Please send me a brochure or further information on the following, as advertised by you in the English Tourist Board's **Where to Stay** 1998 Guide:

_____

_____

My name and address are on the reverse.

ADVERTISEMENT COUPONS

Name: _____ (BLOCK CAPITALS)

Address: _____

_____

_____ Postcode: _____

Telephone Number: _____ Date: _____

Where to Stay 1998
Hotels & Guesthouses

ENGLISH
TOURIST BOARD

Name: _____ (BLOCK CAPITALS)

Address: _____

_____

_____ Postcode: _____

Telephone Number: _____ Date: _____

Where to Stay 1998
Hotels & Guesthouses

ENGLISH
TOURIST BOARD

Name: _____ (BLOCK CAPITALS)

Address: _____

_____

_____ Postcode: _____

Telephone Number: _____ Date: _____

Where to Stay 1998
Hotels & Guesthouses

ENGLISH
TOURIST BOARD

ADVERTISEMENT COUPONS

► **Complete this coupon and mail it direct to the advertiser from whom you would like to receive further information. Do not send it to the English Tourist Board.**

To (advertiser's name): _____

Please send me a brochure or further information on the following, as advertised by you in the English Tourist Board's Where to Stay 1998 *Guide:*

_____

_____

My name and address are on the reverse.

► **Complete this coupon and mail it direct to the advertiser from whom you would like to receive further information. Do not send it to the English Tourist Board.**

To (advertiser's name): _____

Please send me a brochure or further information on the following, as advertised by you in the English Tourist Board's Where to Stay 1998 *Guide:*

_____

_____

My name and address are on the reverse.

► **Complete this coupon and mail it direct to the advertiser from whom you would like to receive further information. Do not send it to the English Tourist Board.**

To (advertiser's name): _____

Please send me a brochure or further information on the following, as advertised by you in the English Tourist Board's Where to Stay 1998 *Guide:*

_____

_____

My name and address are on the reverse.

ADVERTISEMENT COUPONS

Name: _____ (BLOCK CAPITALS)

Address: _____

_____

_____ Postcode: _____

Telephone Number: _____ Date: _____

Where to Stay 1998
Hotels & Guesthouses

ENGLISH
TOURIST BOARD

Name: _____ (BLOCK CAPITALS)

Address: _____

_____

_____ Postcode: _____

Telephone Number: _____ Date: _____

Where to Stay 1998
Hotels & Guesthouses

ENGLISH
TOURIST BOARD

Name: _____ (BLOCK CAPITALS)

Address: _____

_____

_____ Postcode: _____

Telephone Number: _____ Date: _____

Where to Stay 1998
Hotels & Guesthouses

ENGLISH
TOURIST BOARD

TOWN INDEX

The following cities, towns and villages all have accommodation listed in this guide.

If the place where you wish to stay is not shown, the location maps (starting on page 561)

will help you to find somewhere suitable in the same area.

USE YOUR *i*'s

There are more than 550 Tourist Information Centres throughout England offering friendly help with accommodation and holiday ideas as well as suggestions of places to visit and things to do. You'll find TIC addresses in the local Phone Book or simply call Freepages on 0800 192 192.

AT-A-GLANCE SYMBOLS

Symbols at the end of each accommodation entry give useful information about services and facilities. A key to symbols can be found inside the back cover flap.

Keep this open for easy reference.

COUNTRY CODE

Always follow the Country Code ✿ Enjoy the countryside and respect its life and work ✿ Guard against all risk of fire ✿ Fasten all gates ✿ Keep your dogs under close control ✿ Keep to public paths across farmland ✿ Use gates and stiles to cross fences, hedges and walls ✿ Leave livestock, crops and machinery alone ✿ Take your litter home ✿ Help to keep all water clean ✿ Protect wildlife, plants and trees ✿ Take special care on country roads ✿ Make no unnecessary noise

CHECK THE MAPS

The colour maps at the back of this guide show

all the cities, towns and villages for which you will

find accommodation entries.

Refer to the town index to find the page

on which it is listed.

AT-A-GLANCE SYMBOLS

Symbols at the end of each accommodation entry
give useful information about services
and facilities. A key to symbols can be found
inside the back cover flap.

Keep this open for easy reference.

INDEX TO ADVERTISERS

You can obtain further information from any display advertiser in this guide by completing an advertisement enquiry coupon. You will find these coupons on pages 547-550.

MILEAGE CHART

The distances between towns on the mileage chart are given to the nearest mile, and are measured along routes based on the quickest travelling time, making maximum use of motorways or dual-carriageway roads. The chart is based upon information supplied by the Automobile Association.

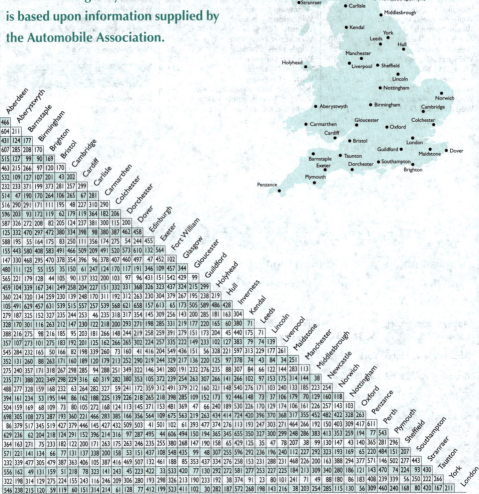

Map of Great Britain showing: Inverness, Fort William, Aberdeen, Perth, Glasgow, Edinburgh, Stranraer, Carlisle, Newcastle upon Tyne, Middlesbrough, Kendal, Leeds, York, Hull, Manchester, Liverpool, Sheffield, Holyhead, Lincoln, Nottingham, Norwich, Aberystwyth, Birmingham, Cambridge, Gloucester, Colchester, Carmarthen, Cardiff, Oxford, London, Bristol, Guildford, Maidstone, Dover, Barnstaple, Taunton, Southampton, Exeter, Dorchester, Brighton, Plymouth, Penzance.

Mileage chart (distances in miles). Column/row town labels in order:
Aberdeen, Aberystwyth, Barnstaple, Birmingham, Brighton, Bristol, Cambridge, Cardiff, Carlisle, Carmarthen, Colchester, Dorchester, Dover, Edinburgh, Exeter, Fort William, Glasgow, Gloucester, Guildford, Holyhead, Hull, Inverness, Kendal, Leeds, Lincoln, Liverpool, Maidstone, Manchester, Middlesbrough, Newcastle, Norwich, Nottingham, Oxford, Penzance, Perth, Plymouth, Sheffield, Southampton, Stranraer, Taunton, York, London.

```
Aberystwyth   466
Barnstaple    604 211
Birmingham    431 124 177
Brighton      607 285 208 170
Bristol       515 127 99 90 169
Cambridge     463 215 266 97 120 170
Cardiff       532 109 127 107 201 43 202
Carlisle      232 233 371 199 373 281 257 299
Carmarthen    514 47 190 170 264 106 265 67 281
Colchester    516 290 291 171 111 195 48 227 310 290
Dorchester    596 203 93 172 119 62 179 119 364 182 206
Dover         587 326 272 208 82 205 124 237 381 300 115 200
Edinburgh     125 332 470 297 472 380 334 398 98 380 387 462 458
Exeter        588 195 55 164 175 83 250 111 356 174 275 54 244 455
Fort William  155 443 580 408 583 491 466 509 209 491 520 573 610 132 564
Glasgow       147 330 468 295 470 378 354 396 96 378 407 460 497 47 452 102
Gloucester    480 111 125 55 155 35 150 61 247 124 170 117 191 346 109 457 344
Guildford     565 221 179 128 44 105 90 137 332 200 103 97 96 431 151 542 429 99
Holyhead      459 104 339 167 341 249 258 204 227 151 332 331 368 326 323 437 324 215 299
Hull          360 224 320 134 259 230 139 248 170 311 192 312 263 230 304 379 267 195 238 219
Inverness     105 491 629 457 631 539 515 557 257 539 568 621 658 157 613 65 173 505 589 486 428
Kendal        279 187 325 152 327 235 244 253 46 235 318 317 354 145 309 256 143 200 285 181 163 304
Leeds         328 170 301 116 263 212 147 230 122 218 200 293 271 198 285 331 219 177 220 165 60 380 71
Lincoln       388 216 275 98 216 185 95 203 181 266 148 244 219 258 259 391 151 173 204 45 440 175 71
Liverpool     357 107 273 101 275 183 192 201 125 162 266 265 302 224 257 335 222 149 233 102 127 383 79 74 139
Maidstone     545 284 232 165 50 166 82 198 339 260 73 160 41 416 204 549 436 151 56 328 221 597 313 229 177 261
Manchester    352 131 260 88 263 171 160 189 120 179 213 252 290 219 244 329 217 136 220 177 213 160 41 84 34 251
Middlesbrough 275 240 357 171 318 267 298 285 94 288 251 349 322 146 341 280 191 232 276 235 88 307 84 66 122 144 283 113
Newcastle     235 271 388 202 349 298 229 316 60 319 282 380 353 105 372 239 254 263 307 266 141 266 102 97 153 175 314 144 38
Norwich       488 277 328 159 168 93 264 282 171 288 148 291 379 212 160 321 148 306 276 171 103 240 133 185 223 254
Nottingham    394 161 234 53 195 144 86 162 188 225 139 226 218 265 218 398 285 109 152 173 92 446 148 73 37 106 179 70 129 160 118
Oxford        504 159 169 68 109 73 80 105 272 168 124 113 145 371 153 481 369 47 66 240 189 226 170 129 257 143 103
Penzance      698 305 108 273 287 193 360 221 466 186 356 564 109 675 563 219 263 434 414 724 420 396 370 368 317 355 452 482 422 328 263
Perth         86 379 517 345 519 427 379 446 145 427 432 509 503 41 501 102 61 393 477 374 276 113 193 247 303 271 464 266 192 150 403 309 417 611
Plymouth      629 236 62 204 218 124 291 152 396 214 316 97 287 495 44 606 494 150 194 365 345 655 350 327 299 248 388 413 353 295 194 77 543
Sheffield     364 163 271 75 233 182 122 200 171 263 147 248 316 196 ... 190 158 65 429 125 35 47 78 207 38 99 130 147 43 140 365 281 296
Southampton   571 121 141 134 66 77 131 137 338 200 158 53 151 437 108 548 435 99 48 307 215 596 292 236 196 240 112 227 292 323 193 169 65 220 484 151 207
Stranraer     232 339 477 305 479 387 363 406 105 387 416 469 507 132 461 188 85 353 437 374 258 153 231 288 231 468 226 200 163 388 294 277 571 146 502 277 443
Taunton       556 162 49 131 159 52 276 126 341 141 243 45 223 422 33 533 420 77 130 292 272 581 277 253 227 225 184 213 309 340 280 186 121 143 470 74 224 93 430
York          322 198 314 129 275 224 155 243 116 246 209 306 280 193 298 326 213 190 233 192 38 374 91 23 80 101 241 71 49 88 180 86 183 408 239 339 56 250 222 266
London        546 238 215 120 59 119 60 151 314 214 61 128 77 412 199 523 411 102 30 282 187 572 268 198 143 216 38 203 254 285 115 130 56 309 460 240 168 80 420 167 211
```

CUSTOMER FEEDBACK
QUESTIONNAIRE

We hope you have found this guide useful in selecting accommodation in England which suits your needs.

It is very helpful to the English Tourist Board to receive comments about establishments in *Where to Stay* and suggestions on how to improve the guide, and also on the National Grading and Classification Schemes.

We would like to hear from you. If you wish to do so, you can send us your views using this questionnaire. You need not name the establishment concerned.

Q1 Did you use the *Where to Stay* guide to find:

Holiday accommodation ☐

Business accommodation ☐

Both ☐

Q2 Did you use the establishment's Quality Grading/Crown or Key Classification to help you in making your choice?

Yes ☐

No ☐

Q3 If you did, was it the Quality Grading (Approved, Commended, Highly Commended or De Luxe) or the number of Crowns or Keys for facilities that influenced you most?

The Quality Grading ☐

The number of Crowns/Keys ☐

Both ☐

Q4 What was the Quality Grading and Crown or Key Classification of the establishment you chose?

....

Q5 Do you find the National Grades and Classifications:

Very easy to understand ☐

Fairly easy to understand ☐

Difficult to understand ☐

If you found them difficult to understand, please specify why:

....

....

Q6 Was the accommodation you used:

Hotel ☐

Guesthouse ☐

Farmhouse ☐

Bed & Breakfast ☐

Self-Catering Holiday Home ☐

Q7 Did the establishment chosen:

Exceed your expectations ☐

Meet your expectations ☐

Fail to meet your expectations ☐

If it failed to meet your expectations, please specify how:

....

....

Q8 Would you say the establishment offered good value for money?

Yes ☐

No ☐

Q9 Was there any feature of your stay that you would particularly praise or criticise (please specify):

....
....
....

Q10 Have you bought a *Where to Stay* guide before?

Yes ☐
No ☐

If yes, how long ago:

Last year ☐
2 years ago ☐
More than 2 years ago ☐

Q11 Did you find the *Where to Stay* guide:

Very easy to use ☐
Fairly easy to use ☐
Difficult to use ☐

Q12 Are there any aspects of the *Where to Stay* guide that you would particularly praise or criticise (please specify):

....
....
....

Q13 Is there any additional information not already featured in this guide that you would find helpful (please specify):

....
....
....

Please would you give us a few details about yourself:

Q14 Are you:

Married ☐
Single ☐

Q15 Do you have dependent children?

Yes ☐
No ☐
If yes, how many ☐

Q16 Into which age group do you fall?

17-24 ☐
25-34 ☐
35-44 ☐
45-54 ☐
55+ ☐

Q17 Are you an overseas visitor (i.e. from outside the UK visiting this country)?

Yes ☐
No ☐

Q18 Did you travel alone or with a party?

Alone ☐
Party of people ☐
of which   were adults
and   children

Q19 How long did you stay in the establishment?
                                         nights

Q20 Do you plan to use the guide to book any further stays this year?

Yes ☐
No ☐
If yes, how many ☐

Q21 What other sources of information did you use in selecting your accommodation (please specify):

....
....
....

Q22 Did you obtain your copy of *Where to Stay* from

Bookshop ☐
Tourist Information Centre ☐
Other (please specify) ☐

Thank you for giving us your views. Please return this questionnaire to: Department AS, English Tourist Board, Thames Tower, Black's Road, Hammersmith, London W6 9EL.

*L*OCATION
MAPS

Every place name featured in the accommodation listings pages of this Where to Stay *guide has a map reference to help you locate it on the maps which follow. For example, to find Colchester, Essex, which has 'Map ref 3B2', turn to Map 3 and refer to grid square B2.*

All place names in the listings pages are shown in black type on the maps. This enables you to find other places in your chosen area which may have suitable accommodation - the Town Index (preceding pages) gives page numbers.

MAP 5
Newcastle upon Tyne
Carlisle

MAP 4
York
Manchester
Lincoln

Birmingham

Ipswich

MAP 2
Oxford
Bristol
Southampton

MAPS 6&7
London

MAP 1

Dover

Exeter

MAP 3

MAP 1

Boscastle
Tintagel
Port Isaac
Port Gaverne
Polzeath
Rock
Padstow
Treyarnon Bay
Wadebridge
A39
A39
Mawgan Porth
Bodmin
Watergate Bay
Newquay
Newquay
Lostwithiel
Crantock
A392
A30
A30
A391
A390
Perranporth
Carlyon Bay
St Agnes
A39
St Austell
Fowey
Illogan
Truro
Mevagissey
St Ives
Redruth
A390
Carbis Bay
Hayle
Camborne
A39
Ruan High Lanes
Portloe
St Just-in-Penwith
A30
Portscatho
Penzance
A394
Falmouth
Lands End
Mousehole
Helston
Mawnan Smith
Porthleven
Mullion
Isles of Scilly
Isles of Scilly (St. Mary's)
The Lizard

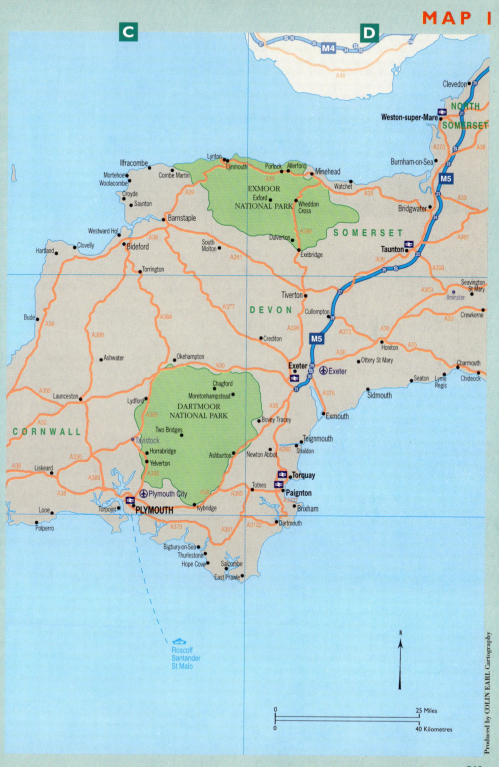

MAP I

C   D

NORTH SOMERSET

Clevedon
Weston-super-Mare
Burnham-on-Sea
M5
Bridgwater

SOMERSET

Ilfracombe
Lynton
Lynmouth
Porlock
Allerford
Minehead
Watchet
Mortehoe
Woolacombe
Combe Martin
EXMOOR NATIONAL PARK
Exford
Wheddon Cross
Croyde
Saunton
Barnstaple
South Molton
Dulverton
Exebridge
Taunton
Seavington St Mary
Ilminster
Westward Ho!
Hartland
Clovelly
Bideford
Torrington
Tiverton
Crewkerne
DEVON
Cullompton
Bude
Crediton
Honiton
Charmouth
Ashwater
Okehampton
Ottery St Mary
Seaton
Lyme Regis
Chideock
Launceston
Lydford
Chagford
Moretonhampstead
DARTMOOR NATIONAL PARK
Exeter
Exeter
Sidmouth
CORNWALL
Two Bridges
Tavistock
Horrabridge
Yelverton
Bovey Tracey
Ashburton
Newton Abbot
Staldon
Teignmouth
Exmouth
Liskeard
Plymouth City
Torpoint
PLYMOUTH
Ivybridge
Totnes
Torquay
Paignton
Brixham
Dartmouth
Looe
Polperro
Bigbury-on-Sea
Thurlestone
Hope Cove
Salcombe
East Prawle

Roscoff
Santander
St Malo

N

0   25 Miles
0   40 Kilometres

Produced by COLIN EARL Cartography

563

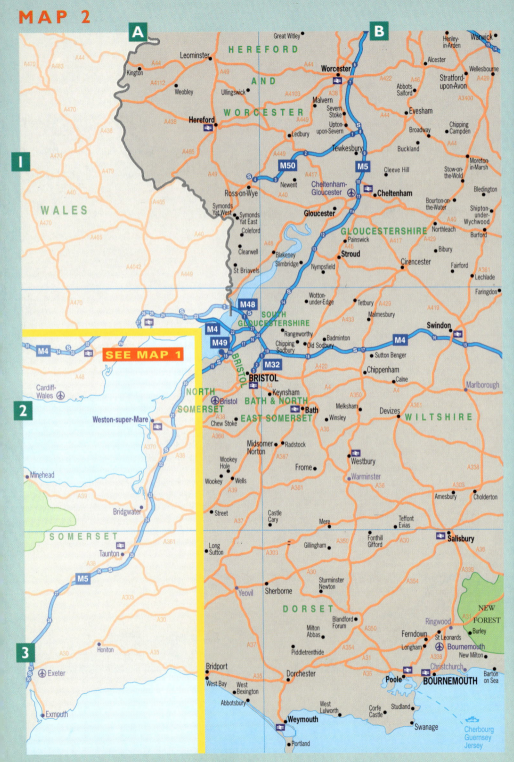

MAP 2

A   **B**

HEREFORD

AND

WORCESTER

Great Witley   Henley-in-Arden   Warwick

Leominster   Worcester   Alcester   Wellesbourne

Kington   Malvern   Abbots Salford   Stratford-upon-Avon

Weobley   Ullingswick   Severn Stoke   Evesham

Hereford   Ledbury   Upton-upon-Severn   Broadway   Chipping Campden

Buckland   Moreton-in-Marsh

M50   Tewkesbury   **M5**   Cleeve Hill   Stow-on-the-Wold

Ross-on-Wye   Newent   Cheltenham-Gloucester   Cheltenham   Bourton-on-the-Water   Bledington

WALES

Symonds Yat West   Gloucester   Shipton-under-Wychwood

Symonds Yat East   Coleford   **GLOUCESTERSHIRE**   Northleach   Burford

Clearwell   Painswick   Bibury

St Briavels   Blakeney   Slimbridge   **Stroud**   Cirencester   Fairford   Lechlade

Nympsfield   Faringdon

M48   Wotton-under-Edge   Tetbury   Swindon

SOUTH GLOUCESTERSHIRE   Malmesbury

M4   Rangeworthy   Badminton

M49   Chipping Sodbury   Old Sodbury   **M4**

M32   Sutton Benger

BRISTOL   Chippenham   Marlborough

SEE MAP 1

M4   Keynsham

Cardiff-Wales   Bristol   **NORTH SOMERSET**   **BATH & NORTH EAST SOMERSET**   Bath   Melksham   Devizes   **WILTSHIRE**

Weston-super-Mare   Chew Stoke   Winsley

Minehead   Midsomer Norton   Radstock   Frome   Westbury   Amesbury   Cholderton

Wookey Hole   Warminster

Wookey   Wells

Bridgwater   A39   Street   Castle Cary   Mere   Teffont Evias   Salisbury

SOMERSET   Long Sutton   Gillingham   Fonthill Gifford

Taunton   Sturminster Newton

M5   Yeovil   Sherborne   **DORSET**

Honiton   Blandford Forum   **NEW FOREST**

Exeter   Milton Abbas   Ferndown   Burley

Piddletrenthide   Longham   St Leonards   **Bournemouth**   New Milton

Exmouth   Bridport   Dorchester   Poole   Christchurch   Barton on Sea

West Bay   West Bexington   **BOURNEMOUTH**

Abbotsbury   West Lulworth   Corfe Castle   Studland

Weymouth   Swanage   Cherbourg Guernsey Jersey

Portland

I

2

3

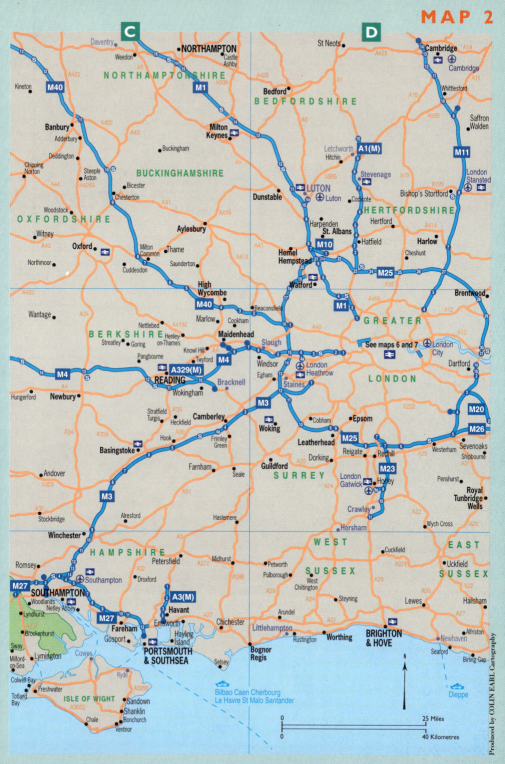

MAP 2

565

MAP 3

566

MAP 3

3

4

25 Miles
40 Kilometres

Dunkirk
Ostend

Calais

Channel Tunnel

Boulogne

Margate
Ramsgate
Sandwich
Deal
Kingsdown
Dover
Folkestone
Hythe
Whitstable
Canterbury
Dymchurch
New Romney

Clacton-on-Sea

West Mersea

K E N T

Sheerness
Sittingbourne
Faversham
Gillingham
Chatham
Rochester
Gravesend
Maidstone
Ashford
Tenterden
Rye
Hastings
Bexhill-on-Sea

E S S E X

SOUTHEND-ON-SEA
Southend
Battlesbridge
Margaretting
Basildon
Chelmsford

Hawkhurst

Ticehurst
Herstmonceux
Eastbourne

M2
M20

M26

See maps 6 and 7

H E R T F O R D S H I R E
Harlow
Hatfield
M11
M25
A1(M)
M1
Watford
M40
M4
M3
Woking
Guildford

G R E A T E R   L O N D O N

London City

London Heathrow

M25
Reigate
M23
London Gatwick
Crawley

S U R R E Y

W E S T   S U S S E X

Chichester
Worthing

E A S T   S U S S E X

Brighton

Dieppe

Produced by COLIN EARL Cartography

567

MAP 4

MAP 4

C

D

25 Miles
40 Kilometres

N

A19
A64
York
YORK
A166
Driffield
A59
EAST RIDING
OF
YORKSHIRE
A614
Brandesburton
Hornsea
A1079
Beverley
A54
A1079
A19
A614
A165
A63
Selby
Monk Fryston
A1041
Howden
M62
KINGSTON
UPON HULL
A63
HULL
A1
A845
Pontefract
Goole
A15
A180
NORTH
LINCOLNSHIRE
Scunthorpe
A1173
Grimsby
Humberside
NORTH EAST
LINCOLNSHIRE
A46
Doncaster
M180
A614
Rotterdam
Zeebrugge
A159
YORKSHIRE
A630
A15
A18
A1(M)
A631
A631
Gainsborough
Louth
Blyth
A57
A156
A46
Worksop
A1
A155
A60
A614
Horncastle
A57
Lincoln
A158
Skegness
LINCOLNSHIRE
M1
Mansfield
A16
A52
NOTTINGHAMSHIRE
A617
A46
Woodhall Spa
A16
A1
South Normanton
A60
Newark
A6097
A60
A46

SEE MAP 3
A16
A52
Boston
A17
NOTTINGHAM
Redmile
Grantham
A149
Beeston
Langar
A52
A453
Castle Donington
A606
A15
Kegworth
East Midlands
A6
Melton
Mowbray
A607
A1
A16
A17
King's Lynn
A46
Loughborough
A1101
A47
Quorn
A6
RUTLAND
A10
LEICESTERSHIRE
Stamford
A47
Markfield
Oakham
A47
A134
LEICESTER
A47
M69
Uppingham
A43
Peterborough
A6
Medbourne
CAMBRIDGESHIRE
M1
A141
Ely
Theddingworth
A6
A1065
A4304
Kettering
A6116
A605
A1(M)
Ely
M6
A5
A1
A142
Rugby
M45
NORTHAMPTONSHIRE
A508
A14
Huntingdon
A10

Produced by COLIN EARL Cartography

MAP 5

MAP 5

0   25 Miles
0   40 Kilometres

N

Amsterdam
Bergen
Esbjerg
Gothenburg
Hamburg
Haugesund
Stavanger

Bamburgh
Seahouses
A1
Embleton
Alnwick
Alnmouth
A1068
A697
Morpeth
A1
A189
A696
Whitley Bay
NEWCASTLE UPON TYNE
Newcastle
Tynemouth
A19
South Shields
Gateshead
A7
TYNE AND WEAR
A19
A692
SUNDERLAND
Stanley
A691
63
64
65
A690
Durham
62
A19
A167
A88
S 61
Fir Tree
A698
A1(M)
Bishop Auckland
Rushyford 60
A689
West Auckland
Newton Aycliffe 59
A68
58
Darlington
A66
57
Tees-side
A66
56
Richmond
A13
Eaglescliffe
Stockton-on-Tees
TEES VALLEY
Brotton
MIDDLESBROUGH
A171
Ellerby
Runswick
Whitby
Castleton
NORTH YORK MOORS
NATIONAL PARK
Goathland
Ravenscar
A172
A170
A171
Hartlepool
Redcar
Catterick
A1
A684
Northallerton
Leeming Bar
Rosedale Abbey
A169
Scarborough
Middleham
Bedale
A684
Thornton Watlass
Newby Wiske
Kirkbymoorside
Appleton-le-Moors
Thirsk
Helmsley
Pickering
Filey
A170
Kilburn
A170
NORTH YORKSHIRE
A168
Hovingham
A64
Flamborough
Ripon
A61
A19
Easingwold
Malton
A165
A1(M)
Boroughbridge
Bridlington
Pateley Bridge
A614

Produced by COLIN EARL Cartography

571

MAP 6

LONGDON *See also Map 7*

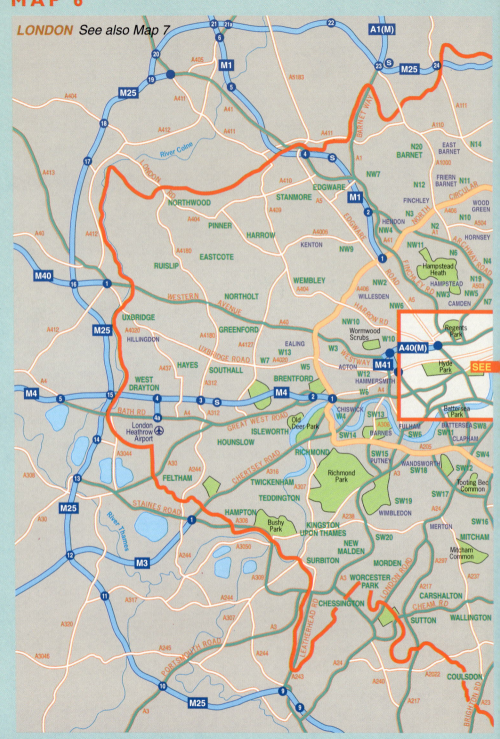

MAP 6

Produced by COLIN EARL Cartography

MAP 7

LONDON *See also Map 6*

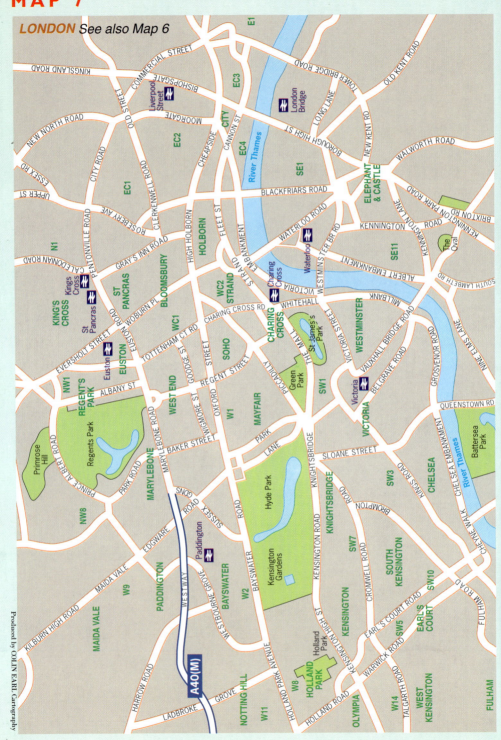

Produced by COLIN EARL Cartography

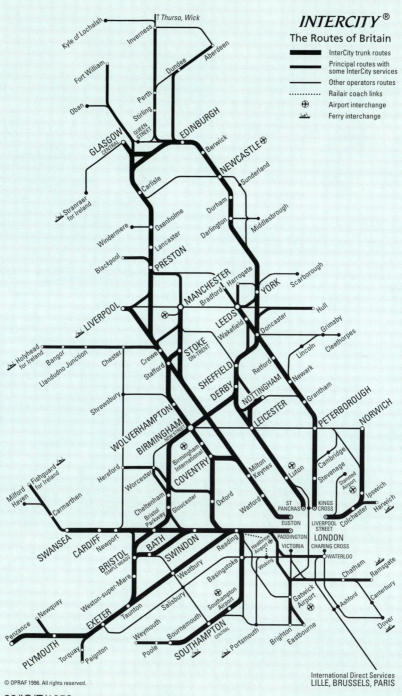

INTERCITY ®
The Routes of Britain

▬▬▬	InterCity trunk routes
▬▬	Principal routes with some InterCity services
──	Other operators routes
·········	Railair coach links
✈	Airport interchange
⚓	Ferry interchange

↑ Thurso, Wick

Kyle of Lochalsh
Inverness
Fort William
Aberdeen
Dundee
Oban
Perth
Stirling
GLASGOW CENTRAL
QUEEN STREET
EDINBURGH
Berwick
NEWCASTLE ✈
Stranraer for Ireland
Carlisle
Sunderland
Durham
Middlesbrough
Oxenholme
Darlington
Windermere
Lancaster
Blackpool
PRESTON
MANCHESTER
Bradford Harrogate
YORK
Scarborough
LIVERPOOL
Hull
LEEDS
Wakefield
Doncaster
Grimsby
Holyhead for Ireland
Bangor
Llandudno Junction
Chester
Crewe
STOKE ON-TRENT
SHEFFIELD
Lincoln
Cleethorpes
Stafford
DERBY
Retford
Newark
Shrewsbury
NOTTINGHAM
Grantham
PETERBOROUGH
NORWICH
WOLVERHAMPTON
BIRMINGHAM NEW STREET
LEICESTER
Hereford
Birmingham International
COVENTRY
Milton Keynes
Luton
Cambridge
Stevenage
Stansted Airport
Ipswich
Worcester
Oxford
Watford
Harwich
Milford Haven
Fishguard for Ireland
Carmarthen
Cheltenham
Bristol Parkway
Gloucester
ST PANCRAS
KINGS CROSS
Colchester
EUSTON
LIVERPOOL STREET
SWANSEA
CARDIFF
Newport
BATH
SWINDON
Reading
PADDINGTON
VICTORIA
LONDON
CHARING CROSS
Heathrow Airport ✈
WATERLOO
Chatham
Ramsgate
BRISTOL TEMPLE MEADS
Westbury
Basingstoke
Woking
Canterbury
Weston-super-Mare
Salisbury
Southampton Airport
Gatwick Airport ✈
Ashford
Dover
Newquay
Taunton
Penzance
EXETER
Weymouth
Bournemouth
SOUTHAMPTON CENTRAL
Portsmouth
Brighton
Eastbourne
PLYMOUTH
Torquay
Paignton
Poole

98/IC/E/1053

International Direct Services
LILLE, BRUSSELS, PARIS

*Y*OUR QUICK GUIDE

Where to Stay *makes it quick and easy to find a place to stay that offers the standard of quality and facilities you're looking for.*

The TOWN INDEX (starting on page 551) and the LOCATION MAPS (starting on page 561) show all cities, towns and villages with accommodation listings in this guide.

1 Town Index

If the place you plan to visit is included in the town index, turn to the page number given to find accommodation available there. Also check that location on the colour maps to find other places nearby which also have accommodation listings in this guide.

1	
Batley West Yorkshire	158
Battlesbridge Essex	317
Beadnell Northumberland	100
Bedale North Yorkshire	158
Bedford Bedfordshire	317
Belford Northumberland	100
Bellingham Northumberland	100
Belper Derbyshire	285
Belton Leicestershire	286
Berkhamsted Hertfordshire	318
Berrynarbor Devon	372
Berwick-upon-Tweed Northumberland	100
Bexhill-on-Sea East Sussex	509
Bexleyheath Greater London	43
Bibury Gloucestershire	217

2 Location Maps

If the place you want is not in the town index - or you only have a general idea of the area in which you wish to stay - use the colour location maps to find places in the area which have accommodation listings in this guide.

When you have found suitable accommodation, check its availability with the establishment and also confirm any other information in the published entry which may be important to you (price, whether bath and/or shower available, children/dogs/credit cards welcome, months open, etc).

If you are happy with everything, make your booking and, if time permits, confirm it in writing.